MODERN MILITARY JUSTICE

CASES AND MATERIALS

■ ■ ■

By

Gregory E. Maggs

Professor of Law
George Washington University Law School

Lisa M. Schenck

Associate Dean for Academic Affairs
George Washington University Law School

AMERICAN CASEBOOK SERIES®

WEST®

A Thomson Reuters business

Mat #41064545

© 2012 Thomson Reuters
    610 Opperman Drive
    St. Paul, MN 55123
    1–800–313–9378
Printed in the United States of America

ISBN: 978–0–314–26803–7

With great admiration and many thanks to members of the U.S. Army Judge Advocate General's Corps who have devoted countless hours to teaching me about Military Justice. —GEM

To my family and my students for their consistent support, encouragement, and inspiration.—LMS

PREFACE

This textbook is about the modern military justice system of the United States. It covers court-martial procedures, substantive criminal law, and nonjudicial punishment under the Uniform Code of Military Justice, in addition to other administrative and disciplinary measures. The book also addresses both the Military Extraterritorial Jurisdiction Act, which gives the federal courts jurisdiction over certain acts committed abroad, and the Military Commissions Acts of 2006 and 2009, which created military tribunals for trying enemy belligerents.

The military justice system serves the nation as a whole by helping to establish and maintain good order and discipline in the Armed Forces, making our military power more reliable and effective. The system also strives to treat fairly and appropriately the millions of American service members who are subject to it. For these reasons, we have sought to make the textbook accessible to a wide audience. We believe that it is suitable for all law students, whether or not they hope to pursue military careers, and also for non-law students such as cadets, midshipmen, officer candidates, and others who have an interest in the subject of military justice. The book focuses on what is common to all of the Armed Forces—the Air Force, the Army, the Coast Guard, the Marine Corps, and the Navy—while noting certain differences among them. To make this book especially relevant to cadets and midshipmen, we have addressed a number of cases arising out of the U.S. Air Force Academy, U.S. Coast Guard Academy, U.S. Military Academy, and U.S. Naval Academy.[1] No prior knowledge of military matters, however, is necessary for using this book.

Each of the authors has extensive practical experience with the military justice system. Dean Lisa Schenck served on active duty in the U.S. Army Judge Advocate General's Corps for more than 25 years, retiring with the rank of Colonel. Following various assignments as a military lawyer and professor at the U.S. Military Academy, she was appointed an appellate military judge on the U.S. Army Court of Criminal Appeals and, in 2005, she became the first female Senior Judge on that court. In 2007, the Secretary of Defense appointed her to serve concurrently as an Associate Judge on the U.S. Court of Military Commission Review. After retiring from the military, Dean Schenck served as Senior Advisor to the Defense Task Force on Sexual

---

[1] The cases involving cadets and midshipmen are *United States v. Perry*, 48 M.J. 197 (C.A.A.F. 1998) [p. 340]; *United States v. Van Vliet*, 64 M.J. 539 (A.F. Ct. Crim. App. 2006) [p. 358]; *United States v. Smith*, 68 M.J. 445 (C.A.A.F. 2010) [p. 425]; *United States v. Gibson*, 39 M.J. 319 (C.M.A. 1994) [p. 435]; *United States v. Green*, 58 M.J. 855 (Army Ct. Crim. App. 2003) [p. 452]; *United States v. Conliffe*, 67 M.J. 127 (C.A.A.F. 2009) [p. 511]; and *United States v. Powell*, 55 M.J. 633 (A.F. Ct. Crim. App. 2001) [p. 538].

Assault in the Military Services. She now teaches Military Justice at the George Washington University Law School, where she is also a senior administrator. Professor Gregory E. Maggs is a lieutenant colonel in the U.S. Army Reserve, Judge Advocate General's Corps, and is currently assigned as a reserve military appellate judge on the U.S. Army Court of Criminal Appeals. In previous reserve assignments, he has served as a prosecutor, as an appellate attorney for both the government and the defense, and as an adviser on policies concerning the military justice system and military commissions. In addition, the Secretary of Defense appointed Professor Maggs to serve as a civilian member of the Military Justice Code Committee, a body established by Congress to oversee the military justice system. *See* Article 146, UCMJ, 10 U.S.C. § 946.

The views expressed in this book are the personal views of the authors, and are not intended to represent the views of the U.S. Army, the Department of Defense, or the U.S. government. The textbook contains several cases in which we have had personal involvement as military judges. We find that these cases are of particular interest to our students. But by including them, we do not mean to suggest that they are the definitive words on the subjects that they address.

Throughout this book we have used the following editorial conventions. When editing cases, we have used three asterisks (* * *) to indicate an omitted paragraph or paragraphs. We have used ellipses (. . .) to indicate omitted words or sentences within a paragraph. We also have slightly changed the format of certain citations within quoted materials to promote uniformity throughout the textbook. We recommend that anyone citing the materials included in this book consult the original sources.

The book cites the Manual for Courts-Martial (MCM) in numerous places. The MCM contains the Rules for Courts-Martial, the Military Rules of Evidence, the Uniform Code of Military Justice, and many other relevant materials. While this book is available for purchase in printed form, we recommend that students download it for free (as most military attorneys do). It is available at http://armypubs.army.mil/epubs/pdf/mcm.pdf.

Finally, we are extremely grateful for the assistance of Colonel (ret.) Mark Harvey, formerly a senior judge on the U.S. Army Court of Criminal Appeals and mentor to both of us, for carefully reading the entire manuscript and making invaluable suggestions. We thank Alexis McClellan and Erica Geiser of the George Washington University Law School staff for help in preparing this manuscript. We also heartily thank George Washington Law School students and recent graduates Elizabeth Barnes, Captain Brandon W. Barnett, Karl Brozyna, Tal Castro, Aditya Luthra, and Kenneth Rotter for their extremely helpful research assistance. Finally, we express our great appreciation to Louis Higgins of West Academic Publishing for his support and encouragement throughout the process.

We hope that you will find this book both useful and interesting. We would be happy to hear your reactions so that we may make improvements to future editions.

Gregory E. Maggs
Lisa M. Schenck

Washington, D.C.
February 2012

SUMMARY OF CONTENTS

TABLE OF CONTENTS

Part V. Substantive Military Criminal Law

TABLE OF CASES AND OTHER AUTHORITIES

The principal cases are in bold type. Cases cited or discussed in the text are in Roman type. References are to pages. Cases cited in principal cases and within other quoted materials are not included. Cases in which the United States is a party are included alphabetically by the other party's name.

OTHER AUTHORITIES

MODERN
MILITARY JUSTICE
CASES AND MATERIALS

CHAPTER 1

OVERVIEW OF THE MILITARY
JUSTICE SYSTEM

1-1. History of the Military Justice System and Sources of Law

In the 1770s, acrimonious disputes arose between the United Kingdom of Great Britain and the inhabitants of some of its colonies in North America. The disagreements concerned taxation, self-governance, individual rights, and western expansion. Harsh measures by the Crown and Parliament prompted rebellious actions by the colonists. Armed conflict erupted on April 18-19, 1775, when British troops garrisoned in Boston unsuccessfully attempted to seize colonial weapons at nearby Lexington and Concord. The British Army was forced to retreat to Boston, where it was besieged by volunteer New England militiamen. Shortly afterward, representatives from the various colonies met in Philadelphia to address the crisis. The gathering of these representatives became known as the Second Continental Congress.

On June 14, 1775, the Second Continental Congress voted to create the Continental Army, a military force that has existed continuously for more than two centuries and that is now known as the United States Army. The Second Continental Congress resolved that ten "companies of expert riflemen be immediately raised" and that "each company, as soon as compleated, shall march and join the army near Boston, to be there employed as light infantry, under the command of the chief Officer in that army." 2 Journals of the Continental Congress 90 (1775). The same day that Congress created the Army, Congress also formed a committee to prepare "a dra't of Rules and regulations for the government of the army." *Id.* This committee, whose members included George Washington and four others, soon afterward proposed sixty-nine "Articles of War" based on British and colonial military law. *Id.* at 112-123.

These Articles of War, which Congress approved on June 30, 1775, specified offenses that could be tried by a court-martial. Here are two typical examples:

> Art. VII. Any officer or soldier, who shall strike his superior officer, or draw, or offer to draw, or shall lift up any weapon, or offer any violence

1

against him, being in the execution of his office, on any pretence whatsoever, or shall disobey any lawful commands of his superior officer, shall
suffer such punishment as shall, according to the nature of his offence, be
ordered by the sentence of a general court-martial.

Art. VIII. Any non-commissioned officer, or soldier, who shall desert, or
without leave of his commanding officer, absent himself from the troop or
company to which he belongs, or from any detachment of the same, shall,
upon being convicted thereof, be punished according to the nature of his
offence, at the discretion of a general court-martial.

Id. at 113.

On June 20, 1775, the Second Continental Congress appointed George
Washington to be the "General and Commander in chief, of the army of the
United Colonies, and of all the forces now raised, and to be raised, by them."
Id. at 100-101. Just a few days later, on June 29, 1775, Washington asked
Congress to appoint a Harvard-educated and successful Boston lawyer, Wil-
liam Tudor, to be the Judge Advocate of the Continental Army, the army's top
legal officer. John Marshall, who later would become Chief Justice of the
United States, served as the Deputy Judge Advocate of the Army. Among the
15 or so other judge advocates in the Army during the Revolution, several
subsequently became members of the House of Representatives or Senate
and one became a governor. *See The Army Lawyer: The History of the
Judge Advocate General's Corps 1775-1975* 10-12, 23-24 (1975).

Why was it immediately necessary for the Second Continental Congress to
create a military justice system for the new Army? Why did the Army immediately need extremely capable lawyers among its officers? These questions
traditionally have yielded two standard answers.

One answer concerns the need for military discipline. As the Supreme
Court has explained, a separate military law is needed because the military is

"... a specialized society separate from civilian society" with "laws and
traditions of its own [developed] during its long history." *Parker v. Levy*,
417 U.S. [733, 743 (1973)]. ... To prepare for and perform its vital role, the
military must insist upon a respect for duty and a discipline without counterpart in civilian life. The laws and traditions governing that discipline
have a long history; but they are founded on unique military exigencies as
powerful now as in the past.

Schlesinger v. Councilman, 420 U.S. 738, 757 (1975).

The second answer concerns mobility. The military often operates where
civil authority does not exist. When deployed against enemies, whether in the
Middle East, Asia, Europe, or elsewhere, U.S. Armed Forces must carry their
justice system with them. They cannot postpone addressing disciplinary
problems until the fighting stops and all can go home. The Supreme Court
has explained: "Court-martial jurisdiction sprang from the belief that within
the military ranks there is need for a prompt, ready-at-hand means of com-

pelling obedience and order." *United States ex rel. Toth v. Quarles*, 350 U.S. 11 (1955).

Points for Discussion

1. How do the offenses stated in Articles VII and VIII of the 1775 Articles of War illustrate the idea that a separate military law is required because of the unique need for order and discipline in the military?

2. During the Revolutionary War, who would have tried soldiers for offenses if not courts-martial? Who would have assisted with the legal issues presented if not military lawyers? Are courts-martial still needed to provide "ready-at-hand" justice?

More than two hundred years have passed since 1775, but much of the original military justice system remains the same. Service members are still tried by court-martial. Most of the original military offenses in the Articles of War approved by the Continental Congress remain offenses today. The Armed Forces still use military lawyers called judge advocates to implement the military justice system. Military proceedings are still mobile, with courts-martial being held around the world wherever U.S. Armed Forces are located.

But there have been several important developments and improvements in military law. The military law governing the Army, Navy, Marines, Coast Guard, and Air Force has been largely unified since 1950. This unification brought about a modern appellate system for review of court-martial decisions. Military judges have presided over general courts-martial and nearly all special courts-martial since 1969. The rules of evidence applicable to courts-martial have been codified since 1984.

The aim of this casebook is to outline and explain the modern military justice system. The first subject addressed is the basic sources of military law, which you will see throughout this text.

The Constitution

The Constitution addresses military justice in several provisions. Article I, § 8, clause 14 gives Congress the power to "make Rules for the Government and Regulation of the land and naval Forces." Pursuant to this power, Congress has established offenses that may be tried by court-martial and procedures for conducting these trials. Two cases in this chapter consider the scope of this power in some depth.

In addition, Article II, § 2, clause 1 makes the President the "Commander in Chief of the Army and Navy of the United States, and of the Militia of the several States, when called into the actual Service of the United States." Pursuant to this provision the President has the power, even without a specific legislative grant of authority, to exercise all of the powers military commanders have traditionally enjoyed. These powers include convening courts-martial for trying service members and military commissions for trying war criminals. *See Swaim v. United States*, 165 U.S. 553, 558 (1897) ("[I]t is within the power of the president of the United States, as commander in chief, to validly convene a general court-martial" even in circumstances not authorized by Congress); *Hamdan v. Rumsfeld*, 548 U.S. 557, 595 (2006) (recognizing a "general Presidential authority to convene military commissions" even in the absence of Congressional authorization, in circumstances justified under the Constitution and law of war").

The Constitution addresses the rights of the accused in a number of provisions in the Bill of Rights. An important question has been the extent to which the Bill of Rights protects service members. The Fifth Amendment to the Constitution expressly does not require a grand jury indictment "in cases arising in the land or naval forces, or in the Militia, when in actual service in time of War or public danger." But the courts have held that most other provisions of the Bill of Rights do apply to service members. *United States v. Jacoby*, 29 C.M.R. 244, 246-47 (C.M.A. 1960) ("the protections in the Bill of Rights, except those which are expressly or by necessary implication inapplicable, are available to the members of our armed forces"). Further discussion of these matters appears in later chapters.

The Uniform Code of Military Justice

Prior to 1950, military justice varied from service to service. The Army and Navy, in particular, had separate laws, customs, and practices. In 1950, however, Congress enacted the Uniform Code of Military Justice for the purpose of creating a single, comprehensive military justice system for all service members. The UCMJ is divided into "articles" and codified at 10 U.S.C. § 801 to § 809.

Articles 77-134, UCMJ, 10 U.S.C. §§ 877-934, closely resemble the original articles of war adopted by the Second Continental Congress. They contain the so-called "punitive articles," the provisions that define the various crimes that courts-martial may try. For example, just as article VII from the 1775 Articles of War (quoted above) made it a crime to strike or disobey a superior officer, article 90, 10 U.S.C. § 890, now says:

Any person subject to this chapter who—

(1) strikes his superior commissioned officer or draws or lifts up any weapon or offers any violence against him while he is in the execution of his office; or

(2) willfully disobeys a lawful command of his superior commissioned officer;

shall be punished, if the offense is committed in time of war, by death or such other punishment as a court-martial may direct, and if the offense is committed at any other time, by such punishment, other than death, as a court-martial may direct.

Similarly, Articles 85 and 86, UCMJ, 10 U.S.C. §§ 885-886, like article VIII of the original Articles of War (quoted above), address the subjects of desertion and being absent without leave.

One can see in these and other provisions that most of the disciplinary problems facing the military two hundred years ago remain issues today. But the UCMJ also contains new provisions aimed at modern forms of misconduct, like drunk driving, *see id.* § 911, or wrongful drug use, *see id.* § 912a, that were not known in 1775. We will consider the punitive articles in later chapters of this book.

Articles 30-76, UCMJ, 10 U.S.C. §§ 830-876, address pre-trial, trial, post-trial, and appellate procedures. These sections, however, contain only the broad outlines of how the military justice system is to work. The UCMJ leaves it to the President to specify the details by promulgating rules of evidence and procedure. Article 36, UCMJ, 10 U.S.C. § 836, one of the most important provisions in the UCMJ, says in part:

> Pretrial, trial, and post-trial procedures, including modes of proof, for cases arising under this chapter triable in courts-martial, military commissions and other military tribunals, and procedures for courts of inquiry, may be prescribed by the President by regulations which shall, so far as he considers practicable, apply the principles of law and the rules of evidence generally recognized in the trial of criminal cases in the United States district courts, but which may not, except as provided in chapter 47A of this title, be contrary to or inconsistent with this chapter.

Pursuant to this provision, the President has issued executive orders establishing the Rules for Court-Martial and the Military Rules of Evidence. These rules appear in a very important government publication called the *Manual for Courts-Martial*, which is discussed below. The President also has authority under Article 56, UCMJ, 10 U.S.C. § 856, to establish the maximum limits for punishment for various offenses.

Other articles of the UCMJ address apprehension and restraint, 10 U.S.C. §§ 807-814, nonjudicial punishment, *id.* § 815, the composition of courts-martial, *id.* §§ 822-29, and general and miscellaneous other matters, *id.* §§ 801-805, 835-841. Article 146, UCMJ, 10 U.S.C. § 946, creates a "Code Committee" consisting of the judges of the Court of Appeals for the Armed Forces, the senior military attorneys for each service, and two civilians. Its purpose is to study the functioning of the military justice system and submit a report to Congress each year. The reports contain useful statistics, which are cited in various places in this book.

The Manual for Courts-Martial

The *Manual for Courts-Martial* (MCM) has been called the military lawyer's Bible. It includes five Parts plus numerous appendices. Part I is a short explanatory preamble. Parts II and III contain the Rules of Court-Martial Procedure (RCM) and Military Rules of Evidence (MRE). These rules resemble the Federal Rules of Criminal Procedure and the Federal Rules of Evidence, and largely serve the same function. Interspersed among these rules are helpful but non-binding "discussions" of the rules. Court-martial procedures are different in many ways from those in civilian courts, but the rules of evidence are largely the same. Accordingly, once a trial by court-martial gets underway, it has much the same feel as a civilian criminal trial.

Part IV of the MCM contains what amounts to a guide to the UCMJ's punitive articles. It quotes the text of each offense, identifies the elements of the offense, explains the offense, lists lesser included offenses, and provides sample specifications to be used for charging an accused service member. Military lawyers and judges rely very heavily on Part IV to determine exactly what the evidence must show for a court-martial to find someone guilty.

Part V concerns nonjudicial punishment, a subject that is addressed in Chapter 3 of this casebook. The rest of the MCM contains various important appendices, including copies of the Constitution and UCMJ, a table of maximum penalties, and helpful analyses of the procedural and evidentiary rules.

Service Regulations

Each service also has promulgated regulations that address various aspects of the military justice system. Army Regulation 27-10, *Military Justice*, for example, states numerous policies concerning subjects such as the assignment of defense counsel, military justice within the reserve components, and so forth. Although these service regulations do not directly control the conduct of a court-martial trial, they do affect many important aspects of the military justice system. We will see several examples in subsequent chapters.

Reported Judicial Decisions

The Chart below illustrates the structure of the military justice court system. Courts-martials—the trial courts of the Armed Forces—prepare complete records of trial, including a complete verbatim transcript of the entire proceeding from start to finish. But courts-martial rarely issue published opinions. Published opinions, however, are prepared by the three levels of appellate courts that may review the results of a court-martial.

Secondary Sources

Many excellent secondary sources cover the military justice system. Two publications are especially helpful. The *Military Judges' Benchbook*, Department of Army Pamphlet 27-9, is an instructional guide for the conduct of trials. This book is available online at the U.S. Army Publishing Directorate <www.apd.army.mil>. It contains model "scripts" for most parts of a court-martial, panel instructions, and many other materials. The best historical source is William Winthrop, *Military Law and Precedents* (2d ed. 1896, 1920 reprint), which courts often consult when deciding constitutional issues. It is available at the Library of Congress's website <www.loc.gov/rr/frd/Military_Law/military-legal-resources-home.html>.

THE MILITARY JUSTICE COURT SYSTEM

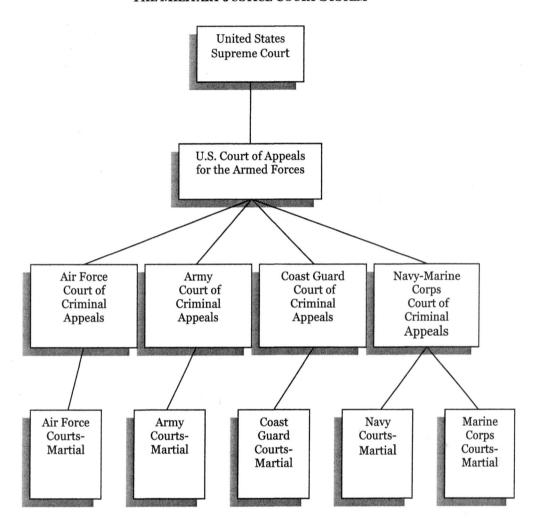

As discussed more fully in subsequent chapters, an appeal from a court-martial goes first to one of the four Service Courts of Criminal Appeals—the Air Force Court of Criminal Appeals, the Army Court of Criminal Appeals, the Coast Guard Court of Criminal Appeals, or the Navy-Marine Corps Court of Criminal Appeals. All of the decisions they designate as publishable are included in West's *Military Justice Reporter*. Military lawyers constantly look to and cite these decisions because they often answer issues arising under the UCMJ, the Rules for Court-Martial and Military Rules of Evidence.

Decisions of the Service Courts of Criminal Appeals are subject to discretionary review by the United States Court of Appeals for the Armed Forces. Decisions of the Court of Appeals for the Armed Forces (or C.A.A.F.) are also published in West's *Military Justice Reporter*. From the Court of Appeals for the Armed Forces, litigants may petition the U.S. Supreme Court for review by writ of certiorari. The Supreme Court's decisions appear in the *United States Reports.*

The military judges and members of the courts-martial for all Services are uniformed service members. The judges of the Air Force, Army, and Navy-Marine Corps Courts of Criminal Appeals are JAG officers, but the Coast Guard Court of Criminal Appeals includes civilians. The Supreme Court has upheld the constitutionality of this arrangement. *See Edmond v. United States*, 520 U.S. 651 (1997).

One initially challenging aspect of researching military justice cases is that the names of the military courts have changed over time. Prior to 1994, the U.S. Court of Appeals for the Armed Forces was called the Court of Military Appeals. The Courts of Criminal Appeals for the various Services have undergone two name changes. Prior to 1994, they were called Courts of Military Review, and prior to 1968, they were called Boards of Review (i.e., the Army Board of Review became the Army Court of Military Review, and then later became the Army Court of Criminal Appeals). Prior to 1951, there was no court equivalent to the Court of Appeals for the Armed Forces and the precursors to the Boards of Review were considerably different in structure and function.

The following case illustrates how parties and judges sometimes may dispute what is and is not a binding source of military law.

UNITED STATES v. LAZAUSKAS
U.S. Court of Appeals for the Armed Forces
62 M.J. 39 (C.A.A.F. 2005)

Judge CRAWFORD delivered the opinion of the Court.

In March 2001, a confidential informant reported to the law enforcement officials at Lackland Air Force Base that Appellant was selling and using ecstasy. After the controlled purchase of ecstasy by the confidential informer, follow-up inquiries led to the discovery of a number of witnesses who stated that Appellant [Stephen J. Lazauskas, Airman Basic, U.S. Air Force] used drugs in February, March, April, and May 2001, at various times both on and off the installation.

At his arraignment, Appellant made a motion to dismiss the charges against him based on a violation of his right to speedy trial under Rule for Courts–Martial (R.C.M.) 707, Article 10, UCMJ, 10 U.S.C. § 810 (2000), and the Sixth Amendment. The military judge denied his motion on all grounds.... [T]he military judge determined that the Government was excluded from accountability for a total of seventy-two days out of the 189–day delay and was therefore left accountable for a total delay of 117 days, which was within the R.C.M. 707 allowable limit of 120 days....

* * *

[One] period of time in dispute is a six-day continuance allowed during an Article 32 hearing [from August 8-13]. The convening authority appointed an investigating officer for the Article 32 hearing, and in the Appointment Memorandum stated the officer was "delegated the authority to grant any reasonably requested delays of the Article 32 investigation." . . . Two days prior to the date originally scheduled for the Article 32 hearing, the Government representative provided the military defense counsel with a list of eight witnesses the Government expected to testify at the Article 32 hearing. . . . At the Article 32 hearing, six of these witnesses testified; however, two witnesses were on leave. The defense then requested the witnesses and objected to taking their testimony over the telephone. Based on the defense objection, the Article 32 investigating officer delayed the hearing until August 13, 2001, to procure their live testimony. . . .

* * *

. . . Under R.C.M. 707(c), all pretrial delays approved by the convening authority are excludable so long as approving them was not an abuse of the convening authority's discretion. It does not matter which party is responsible.

The discussion pertaining to this rule provides: "Prior to referral, the convening authority may delegate the authority to grant continuances to an Article 32 investigating officer." R.C.M. 707(a)(1) discussion.

Additionally, where, as here, the convening authority has delegated to an investigating officer the "authority to grant any reasonably requested delays of the Article 32 investigation," then any delays approved by the Article 32 investigating officer also are excludable.

Thus, when an investigating officer has been delegated authority to grant delays, the period covered by the delay is excludable from the 120–day period under R.C.M. 707. If the issue of speedy trial under R.C.M. 707 is raised before the military judge at trial, the issue is not which party is responsible for the delay but whether the decision of the officer granting the delay was an abuse of discretion. . . .

. . . R.C.M. 405(g)(1)(A) provides that the parties are entitled to the presence of witnesses who have relevant testimony and the evidence is "not cumulative." However, R.C.M. 405(g)(4)(B) provides that the investigating officer may take sworn statements of unavailable witnesses over the telephone. The first period of time involved the delay to obtain the personal testimony of two witnesses who were on leave. The investigating officer, under the authority delegated to him by the convening authority, granted the delay. As to this period, the military judge found that:

[A]t some point during the Article 32 hearing, the defense learned that several witnesses it believed the government would be calling live were actually going to be called telephonically. The defense objected to their being called telephonically and the Article 32 hearing was delayed so that the defense could question them when they were personally available which was on 13 August 2001.

We hold that the military judge did not abuse his discretion in excluding this delay.

* * *

GIERKE, Chief Judge (concurring in the result):

The discussion to R.C.M. 707(c)(1) states that "[p]rior to referral, the convening authority may delegate the authority to grant continuances to an Article 32 investigating officer." [Although the court relies on this statement, the] . . . discussion does not definitively resolve this issue for two reasons. First, the authority to grant a continuance is not necessarily the same as the authority to exclude the resulting delay from Government accountability. A rational military justice system could give the investigating officer the power to grant delays but reserve for other officials the power to exclude such delay from Government accountability. . . .

Second, the discussion accompanying the Rules for Courts–Martial, while in the *Manual for Courts–Martial, United States* (2002 ed.) (*MCM*), is not part of the presidentially-prescribed portion of the *MCM*. The *MCM* expressly states that it consists of its "Preamble, the Rules for Courts-Martial, the Military Rules of Evidence, the Punitive Articles, and Nonjudicial Punishment Procedures." Absent from this list are the discussion accompanying the Preamble, the Rules for Courts-Martial, and the Punitive Articles, as well as the MCM's appendices, including the MCM's drafters' analysis. As Professor Gregory E. Maggs helpfully explains, "The President played no role in preparing these supplementary materials, and he did not promulgate them by executive order; on the contrary, these materials represent only the beliefs of staff personnel who worked on the Manual."[5] So, as Professor Maggs concludes, the courts "do not violate the principle of deference to the President when they disagree with them."[6]

Nevertheless, I agree with the majority opinion that the time was properly excluded. . . .

* * *

. . . I would recognize that after charges have been referred, the Government may seek a ruling from the military judge retroactively excluding pre-referral delay from Government accountability. To rule otherwise would elevate form over substance. If the time should be excluded from Government accountability, a different result should not arise merely because a specific official did not bless the delay when it occurred. And allowing a military judge to retroactively exclude pre-referral delay from Government accountability is

---

[5] Gregory E. Maggs, *Judicial Review of the Manual for Courts-Martial*, 160 Mil. L. Rev. 96, 115 (1999).

[6] *Id.*

consistent with R.C.M. 707(c) because the pretrial delay would be "approved by a military judge."

In this case, the military judge's ruling approved the pretrial delay. That ruling was neither unreasonable nor an abuse of discretion. Therefore, the time was properly excluded from Government accountability.

* * *

Points for Discussion

1. How many different sources of military law are cited in this short opinion?

2. Is the majority opinion's reliance on the "discussion" of RCM 707, which is included in the MCM improper if the discussion is not binding as Judge Gierke says?

1-2. Overview of the System from Start to End

With this background, consider now how the modern military justice system might handle a violation of the UCMJ. The "Court-Martial Process" chart (on the following page) shows the many steps in the process from start to finish. Perhaps the best way to understand this chart is by considering a hypothetical.

The following imaginary facts draw in part upon sample forms in an appendix to the MCM: Suppose that at 0630 on 15 July 2007, Company A of the 61st Infantry Brigade, garrisoned at Fort Blank in Missouri, called roll. All were present or accounted for except Private First Class (PFC) Reuben J. James, who was absent without leave. PFC James's squad leader immediately asked other members of the squad if they knew where he was. No one knew, but one soldier said, "I bet PFC James is off post buying drugs." When the sergeant asked why he thought so, the soldier replied: "Three days ago, PFC James showed me 10 grams of marijuana that he had bought. I imagine he is out looking for some more."

The squad leader informed the platoon sergeant and platoon leader, who told the company commander, Captain (CPT) Jonathan E. Richards. Richards relayed the information to the Military Police, who immediately began looking for PFC James. They apprehended him a few hours later as he tried to reenter Fort Blank through the main gate. When the MPs searched his person, they found 10 grams of vegetable matter which a screening test subsequently determined to be marijuana. The processes of the military justice system had begun.

The Court-Martial Process

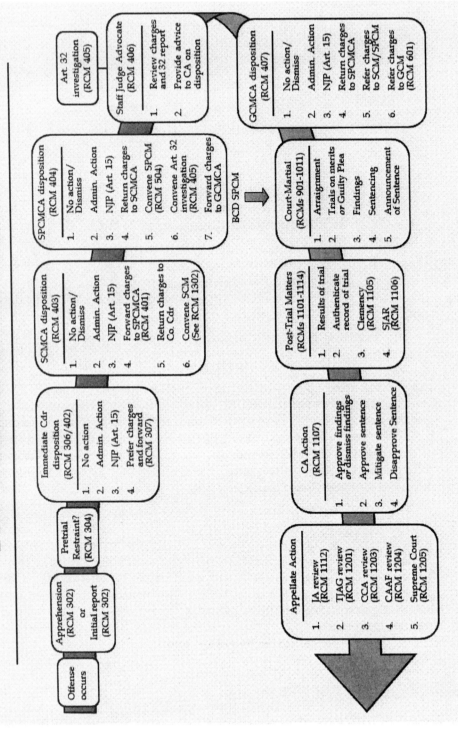

Following the Court-Martial Process Chart, you can see that once PFC James has been apprehended, CPT Richards had a few important decisions to make. The first decision was whether to impose "pretrial restraint." Under RCM 304, pretrial restraint "may consist of conditions on liberty, restriction in lieu of arrest, arrest, or confinement." After consulting with a military attorney, CPT Richards decided to order PFC James not to leave the confines of the post, a typical restriction imposed on soldiers who have gone absent without leave for a brief time.

As PFC James's immediate commander, CPT Richards also had to decide how to dispose of the apparent AWOL and marijuana offenses. Military commanders have considerable discretion in such questions because upon them falls the responsibility of deciding what is necessary for discipline within their units. According to RCM 306, Captain Richards had several options. One option would have been to take no action. That choice might be appropriate for a trivial or technical violation of the UCMJ, or where the commander feels the evidence is too lacking to proceed. But CPT Richards felt that drug use leading a soldier to miss duty required a more forceful response.

A second option under RCM 306 would have been to address the misconduct with "administrative corrective measures," such as counseling, admonitions, reprimands, exhortations, disapprovals, criticisms, censures, reproaches, rebukes, or extra military instruction. While more than nothing, CPT Richards decided that administrative corrective measures were still not enough of a response to the alleged misconduct.

A third option would have been to address the misconduct with "nonjudicial punishment." Also as described in Chapter 3, Article 15, UCMJ, 10 U.S.C. § 815, empowers the commander to impose minor punishments on soldiers for violations of the UCMJ, without trying them by court-martial unless the accused insists on a court-martial. While offenses disposed of under Article 15 are "criminal" offenses, their level of disposition does not result in a criminal conviction, and the permissible punishments are limited. For example, CPT Richards might have ordered a forfeiture of pay or a period of additional duty as a punishment for the misconduct. But again, CPT Richards thought the apparent offenses called for something more.

Accordingly, CPT Richards chose a fourth option, namely, "preferring" charges against PFC James so that he could be tried by a court-martial. Under RCM 307, a person prefers charges by putting them in writing, stating that he or she has personal knowledge of or has investigated the matters set forth in the charges and specifications, and by signing them under oath. The following sample form from the MCM, called a "Charge Sheet," illustrates CPT Richards's action in this hypothetical story.

CHARGE SHEET				
I. PERSONAL DATA				
1. NAME OF ACCUSED *(Last, First, Middle Initial)* James, Reuben J.		**2. SSN** 111-11-1111	**3. GRADE OR RANK** PFC	**4. PAY GRADE** E-3
5. UNIT OR ORGANIZATION Co A, 1st Battalion, 61st Inf. Bde., Fort Blank, MO		**6. CURRENT SERVICE**		

7. PAY PER MONTH

a. BASIC	b. SEA/FOREIGN DUTY	c. TOTAL	**8. NATURE OF RESTRAINT OF ACCUSED** Restriction	**9. DATE(S) IMPOSED** 1 August 2007
1,534.00	0.00	1,534.00		

(6. CURRENT SERVICE — **a. INITIAL DATE** 1 April 2006, **b. TERM** 3 years)

II. CHARGES AND SPECIFICATIONS

10. CHARGE:
I

VIOLATION OF THE UCMJ, ARTICLE 86

SPECIFICATION:

In that Private First Class Reuben J. James, U.S. Army, Company A, 1st Battalion, 61st Infantry Brigade, Fort Blank, Missouri, did, on or about 15 July 2007, without authority, absent himself from his unit, to wit: Company A, 1st Battalion, 61st Infantry Brigade, located at Fort Blank, Missouri, and did remain so absent until on or about 30 July 2007.

Charge II: Violation of the UCMJ, Article 112a

In that Private First Class Reuben J. James, U.S. Army, Company A, 1st Battalion, 61st Infantry Brigade, Fort Blank, Missouri, did, on or about 12 July 2007, wrongfully possess 10 grams of marijuana.

III. PREFERRAL

11a. NAME OF ACCUSER *(Last, First, Middle Initial)* Richards, Jonathan E.	**b. GRADE** CPT	**c. ORGANIZATION OF ACCUSER** Co A, 1st Bn, 61st Inf Bde
d. SIGNATURE OF ACCUSER *Jonathan E. Richards*		**e. DATE** *(YYYYMMDD)* 1 AUG 07

AFFIDAVIT: Before me, the undersigned, authorized by law to administer oath in cases of this character, personally appeared the above named accuser this **1st** day of **August**, **2007**, and signed the foregoing charges and specifications under oath that he/she is a person subject to the Uniform Code of Military Justice and that he/she either haspersonal knowledge of or has investigated the matters set forth therein and that the same are true to the best of his/her knowledge and belief.

Will M. Wilson	1st Bn, 61st Inf Bde
Typed Name of Officer	*Organization of Officer*
CPT	Adjutant
Grade	*Official Capacity to Administer Oath (See R.C.M. 307(b)_ must be commissioned officer)*
Will M Wilson	
Signature	

DD FORM 458, MAY 2000   PREVIOUS EDITION IS OBSOLETE.

12.

On _____ 2 August _____ , _____ 2007 _____ , the accused was informed of the charges against him/her and of the name(s) of the accuser(s) known to me *(See R.C.M. 308(a)).* *(See R.C.M. 308 if notification cannot be made.)*

Jonathan E. Richards
_____
Typed Name of Immediate Commander

Co A, 1st Bn, 61st Inf Bde
_____
Organization of Immediate Commander

O-3/CPT
_____
Grade

[signature]
_____
Signature

IV. RECEIPT BY SUMMARY COURT-MARTIAL CONVENING AUTHORITY

13.

The sworn charges were received at _____ 1100 _____ hours, _____ 2 August _____ , _____ 2007 _____ at _____ 1st Bn, 61st Inf Bde _____
_____
Designation of Command or

Officer Exercising Summary Court-Martial Jurisdiction (See R.C.M. 403)

FOR THE ' _____ COMMANDER _____

Will M. Wilson
_____
Typed Name of Officer

Adjutant
_____
Official Capacity of Officer Signing

CPT
_____
Grade

[signature] Will M Wilson
_____
Signature

V. REFERRAL; SERVICE OF CHARGES

14a. DESIGNATION OF COMMAND OF CONVENING AUTHORITY	b. PLACE	c. DATE *(YYYYMMDD)*
61st Infantry Brigade	Fort Blank, Missouri	2 August 2007

Referred for trial to the _____ special _____ court-martial convened by _____ CMCO number 12 dated _____

_____

_____ 1 August _____ , _____ 2007 _____ , subject to the following instructions: 2

None.

By _____
Command or Order

Carl E. Nevens
_____
Typed Name of Officer

Commander, 61st Infantry Brigade
_____
Official Capacity of Officer Signing

O-6/COL
_____
Grade

[signature] Carl E Nevens
_____
Signature

15.

On _____ 8 August _____ , _____ 2007 _____ , I (caused to be) served a copy hereof on (each of) the above named accused.

Hamilton Burger
_____
Typed Name of Trial Counsel

CPT, JAGC
_____
Grade or Rank of Trial Counsel

[signature] Hamilton Burger
_____
Signature

FOOTNOTES: 1 - When an appropriate commander signs personally, inapplicable words are stricken.
2 - See R.C.M. 601(e) concerning instructions. If none, so state.

DD FORM 458 (BACK), MAY 2000

Box 10 of the Charge Sheet shows that CPT Richards formally accused PFC Williams of one specification of being absent without leave in violation of Article 86, UCMJ, 10 U.S.C. § 886, and one specification of possessing marijuana in violation of Article 112a, UCMJ, 10 U.S.C. § 912a. In box 11, CPT Richards signed the charges under oath. The reverse side of the form shows what happened next.

As indicated in box 12, CPT Richards informed PFC Williams of the charges against him. Box 13 shows that the form was forwarded to CPT Will M. Wilson, an officer who was designated as the "Summary Court-Martial Convening Authority" for the 1st Battalion of the 61st Infantry Brigade.

As shown on the Court-Martial Process Chart, CPT Wilson, like CPT Richards, also had several choices. Under RCM 403, he could dismiss the charges or forward the charges to a subordinate or superior commander for disposition. Alternatively, he could refer the charges to a "summary court-martial."

As discussed at considerable length later in this book, there are three types of courts-martial: a summary court-martial, a special court-martial, or a general court-martial. *See* R.C.M. 201(f). These three types of courts-martial differ in the formality of their procedures and the range of penalties that they may impose.

A summary court-martial is a very informal proceeding that takes place without a military judge or a prosecutor. Instead, a junior officer typically serves alone and hears the evidence. Findings of guilt are not considered criminal convictions. The sentences that can be imposed are modest, and vary according to the rank of the accused. Chapter 3 considers summary courts-martial in more depth.

A special court-martial is an adversary criminal trial, almost always presided over by a military judge, with both the government and the accused represented by counsel. Witnesses testify according to regular rules of evidence, and the trial follows very formal procedural rules—much like any state or federal criminal trial. The maximum penalties that a special court-martial may impose are a bad-conduct discharge, one year of confinement, and forfeiture of two-thirds pay and benefits for one year.[1] A rough analogy in civilian practice is that a special court-martial is typically used for misdemeanors.[2]

---

[1] Article 19, UCMJ, does not require pre-trial advice from the staff judge advocate prior to the convening of a special court-martial empowered to impose a bad-conduct discharge. Under stricter Army Regulations, however, an Army Special Court-Martial Convening Authority has the power to convene a special court-martial with the power to adjudge a bad-conduct discharge only if he receives pretrial advice from the staff judge advocate.

[2] The following table illustrates approximate analogues among the Federal, State, and military court systems:

A general court-martial, like a special court-martial, is also an adversary criminal trial conducted according to formal evidentiary and procedural rules. One major difference is that a general court-martial is typically used for more serious crimes. A general court-martial can impose any lawful sentence authorized for the offense of which the accused is convicted, including life imprisonment or even death for serious crimes.

In this case, box 14 of the Charge Sheet indicates that CPT Wilson did not refer the charges to a summary court-martial, but instead forwarded them to Colonel (COL) Carl E. Nevin, an officer designated as the Special Courts-Martial Convening Authority. Under RCM 404, COL Nevin also had several choices. He could take no action and dismiss the charges. He could employ administrative corrective measures or possibly nonjudicial punishment to address the situation. He could return the charges to CPT James. He could convene a special court-martial. He could order a "pretrial investigation" for the purpose of securing more information about the best disposition of the

	Federal Civil & Criminal	Typical State Civil & Criminal	Military Criminal Only
Appeals	U.S. Supreme Court	U.S. Supreme Court	U.S. Supreme Court
Appeals		State Supreme Court	U.S. Court of Appeals for the Armed Forces
Appeals	U.S. Circuit Courts of Appeals	State Appellate Courts	U.S. Army Court of Criminal Appeals U.S. Navy-Marine Court of Criminal Appeals U.S. Air Force Court of Criminal Appeals U.S. Coast Guard Court of Criminal Appeals
Trials	U.S. District Court	Court of General Jurisdiction (e.g., County Court)	General Court-Martial
Trials	U.S. Magistrate	Misdemeanor Court Juvenile Court Traffic Court Probate Court Family Court	Special Court-Martial Summary Court-Martial

charges. (Unless waived, a pre-trial investigation is necessary before referral of charges to a general court-martial.) Finally, COL Nevin could forward the charges to the officer designated as the General Courts-Martial Convening Authority, who might be a Major General or Lieutenant General commanding the division at Fort Blank or the corps of which the division is a part.

The reverse side of the Charge Sheet shows that COL Nevin chose to refer the case to a Special Court-Martial. Accordingly, there was no pre-trial investigation and the case was not referred to the general court-martial convening authority.

When PFC Wilson is tried by a special court-martial, the trial will resemble a civilian criminal trial in most respects. As the Court-Martial Process Chart indicates, under RCMs 901-1011, there will be an arraignment, and unless he pleads guilty, a trial on the merits in which rules of evidence are used, followed by a finding of guilty or not guilty. If he is found guilty, each side will produce evidence relevant to sentencing, and a decision on the sentence will follow. PFC James can request a trial either by a judge or a panel. The panel, however, is not exactly like a civilian jury. Its members will consist of officers or enlisted members chosen by the convening authority to hear the case. PFC James may request that the panel include at least one-third enlisted members. And unlike a civilian jury, the panel's finding does not have to be unanimous. It could find him guilty by a two-thirds vote.

If the special court-martial finds PFC James guilty, he will have two chances for review of his conviction. First, the results of the trial will be forwarded to COL Nevin. Under RCMs 1105 and 1106, PFC James will have the opportunity to submit documents and arguments to COL Nevin. COL Nevin will have the power to approve the findings or dismiss them, or to approve the sentence, mitigate the sentence, or disapprove the sentence. He can base a decision not to approve the findings or sentence as adjudged either on grounds that errors occurred at the trial or that PFC Wilson deserves clemency.

If PFC Wilson is sentenced to one year of confinement or given a punitive discharge, he will also have a right to have his case reviewed by the Army Court of Criminal Appeals. *See* RCM 1201(a)(2). He then may seek discretionary review by the U.S. Court of Appeals and then review by the Supreme Court. *See* RCM 1204. If he receives a lesser sentence, he may still seek review by the Judge Advocate General. *See* RCM 1201(b).

Points for Discussion

1. Is the military justice system necessary or could civilian courts handle the trials of service members accused of committing crimes? The answer perhaps depends on how frequently the military justice system is invoked. This figure varies over time, depending on what the military is doing and how many service members are on duty. During World War II, there were 1.7 million courts-martial in the Armed Forces, the equivalent of one-third of all the civilian criminal cases tried in the United States during the War. *See The Army Lawyer: A History of the Judge Advocate General's Corps, 1775-1975* 192 (1975). Most of the World War II-era courts-martial, however, were summary courts-martial, as commanders at the time could not impose punishment for minor offenses as is now permitted using Article 15, UCMJ. In recent years, with an all-volunteer force, the number of courts-martial has declined substantially. To look at just one service, in fiscal year 2010, there were 566,045 soldiers on active duty in the Army. Of these soldiers, 610 were tried by general court-martial, 454 by special court-martial, and 819 by summary court-martial. In addition, 36,624 received nonjudicial punishment. *See* Uniform Code of Military Justice Committee, Annual Report for the period October 1, 2009 to September 30, 2010, http://www.armfor. U.S.C.ourts.gov/newcaaf/annual/FY10AnnualReport.pdf. Although the number of prosecutions has declined, what might still be some of the practical difficulties of turning all of these matters over to civilian courts?

2. Who provides legal advice to commanders and the accused as cases proceed through the military justice system? Could civilian lawyers operate as effectively as military lawyers in this role?

The following two cases are included for different reasons. The first one illustrates how cases sometimes encounter difficulties as they move through the complex path of military justice. The second case illustrates the seriousness of some of the cases that the military justice system must address.

UNITED STATES v. TITTEL
U.S. Court of Appeals for the Armed Forces
53 M.J. 313 (C.A.A.F. 2000)

Senior Judge COX delivered opinion of the Court.

Prior to the case at hand, in June of 1996, a general court-martial convicted appellant [Specialist Third Class Todd A. Tittel, U.S. Navy] of a number of charges, one of which was shoplifting from the Navy Exchange in Sasebo, Japan. He was sentenced to be confined for 90 days and reduced to paygrade E-4. In September of 1996, appellant was processed at an administrative separation board because of his earlier court-martial conviction; the board recommended a General Discharge.

The case at hand begins in October of 1996, one day before the execution date of appellant's discharge, when he was caught shoplifting from the Navy Exchange, Yokosuka, Japan. While being filmed by a video surveillance camera, appellant stole 44 items with the total value of about $366.33. After this incident, Captain William D. Lynch, Commanding Officer Fleet Activities, Yokosuka, Japan, ordered appellant not to enter any Navy Exchange facility. Appellant disobeyed that order by entering a Navy Exchange.

Appellant was apprehended and charged with several offenses. He was tried by a special court-martial, and pursuant to his pleas was convicted of willful disobedience of a superior officer, Captain Lynch, in violation of Article 90, Uniform Code of Military Justice, 10 U.S.C. § 890 and larceny, in violation of Article 121, UCMJ, 10 U.S.C. § 921. The court-martial sentenced appellant to be confined for 103 days, to forfeit $578 pay per month for 1 month, to be reduced to the paygrade of E–1, and to be discharged from the Navy with a bad-conduct discharge. The convening authority, also Captain Lynch, approved the sentence.

In an unpublished opinion the Court of Criminal Appeals affirmed the conviction. However, the Court reduced the sentenced confinement period from 103 days to 73 in order to comply with the pretrial agreement.

We granted review of the following issue:

WHETHER THE NAVY–MARINE CORPS COURT OF CRIMINAL APPEALS ERRED BY AFFIRMING APPELLANT'S CONVICTION, WHERE THE CONVENING AUTHORITY WAS AN ACCUSER AND THUS COULD NOT CONVENE APPELLANT'S COURT–MARTIAL.

For the first time on appeal, appellant seeks relief. Appellant contends that where an officer's order is willfully disobeyed, the officer is the victim of that crime. As such, the officer has a personal interest in the disposition of the offense and becomes an "accuser." An "accuser" is disqualified from convening a special court-martial. RCM 504(c)(1), Manual for Courts–Martial, United States (1955 ed.).

Appellant's argument is facially appealing. Convening authorities must be neutral. His rationale is that where an officer is the victim of willful disobedience, he cannot be neutral. Therefore, he cannot be the convening authority for that same case of willful disobedience.

When addressing the question, the Court of Criminal Appeals stated the following:

[T]he appellant contends that the convening authority was an accuser and prohibited from convening his court-martial. Based on the record before us, we find no evidence that Captain Lynch became personally involved with the appellant to the extent that he became an accuser. Assuming arguendo that he did become an accuser, which we do not, his failure to forward the charges to the next higher level of command for disposition was a nonjurisdictional error, which was waived by the appellant's failure to raise it at his court-martial. RULE FOR COURTS–MARTIAL 904(e), MANUAL FOR COURTS–MARTIAL, UNITED STATES (1998 ed.); [United States v.] Shiner, 40 M.J. [155, 157 (C.M.A. 1994)]. We find no plain error. See United States v. Fisher, 21 M.J. 327, 328 (C.M.A. 1986); United States v. Powell, [49 M.J. 460 (1998)]. In light of the serious nature of the charges facing the appellant, we find it unlikely that any competent authority would not have referred this case to a special court-martial. Consequently, we find no fair risk that the appellant was prejudiced by the error. See Art. 59(a), UCMJ, 10 U.S.C. § 859(a).

Having reviewed the record, we agree with the analysis of the Court of Criminal Appeals. Accordingly, we find that the Navy–Marine Corps Court of Criminal Appeals did not err by affirming appellant's conviction.

The decision of the United States Navy–Marine Corps Court of Criminal Appeals is affirmed.

EFFRON, Judge, with whom SULLIVAN, Judge, joins (concurring in part and in the result):

I agree with the majority opinion, except to the extent that it may be read to suggest that this case provides an appropriate vehicle for deciding whether the status of a convening authority as an accuser can be passively waived, as opposed to being the subject of a knowing and intelligent waiver. I note that the decision in this case is not based upon waiver, but rests instead upon the conclusion that the convening authority was not an accuser. The majority opinion appropriately endorses the holding of the lower court that "[b]ased on the record before us, we find no evidence that Captain Lynch became personally involved with the appellant to the extent that he became an accuser."

A personal order does not necessarily implicate a commander's personal interest such that he becomes an "accuser" and is disqualified as a convening authority. *See United States v. Voorhees*, 50 M.J. 494 (1999). The order that appellant disobeyed was a routine, administrative type of order that virtually automatically flowed from the fact of appellant's arrest for shoplifting. No reasonable person would conclude that it represented any personal, versus official, interest of Captain Lynch or that its violation was an act that a commander would take personally. *See* Art. 1(9) and 23(b), UCMJ, 10 U.S.C. §§ 801(9) and 823(b), respectively; *United States v. Gordon*, 1 U.S.C.MA 255, 261, 2 CMR 161, 167(1952). Under these circumstances, the issue of waiver does not arise because the record does not support appellant's contention that the convening authority had become an accuser.

Points for Discussion

1. How would you trace the path of this case on the Court-Martial Process chart included on page 12?

2. In how many ways did the Navy respond to Tittel's various acts of misconduct? Which officers and courts reviewed the finding of guilt and the sentence in this case?

3. Why shouldn't the convening authority—the officer who convenes the court-martial—be a person who has an interest in any of the charges? Is it appropriate to describe Captain Lynch, the officer who convened the court-martial, as the victim of one of the crimes?

UNITED STATES v. SCHAP
Army Court of Criminal Appeals
44 M.J. 512 (Army Ct. Crim. App. 1996)

JOHNSTON, Judge:

Contrary to his plea, the appellant [Stephen J. Schap, Sergeant, U.S. Army] was found guilty by a general court-martial composed of officer and enlisted members of premeditated murder in violation of Article 118, Uniform Code of Military Justice, 10 U.S.C. § 918 (1988) [hereinafter UCMJ]. Although the appellant was sentenced by the members to a dishonorable discharge, confinement for life, forfeiture of all pay and allowances, and reduction to Private E1, they recommended that the confinement be reduced as a matter of clemency. The convening authority approved only so much of the sentence as provided for a dishonorable discharge, confinement for forty-five years, forfeiture of all pay and allowances and reduction to Private E1.

The appellant contends, inter alia, that the evidence is legally and factually insufficient to support a conviction for any offense greater than voluntary manslaughter, that the military judge made numerous errors in regard to instructions to the members, and that the military judge abused his discretion in improperly limiting the testimony of a defense expert and in admitting evidence that was unduly prejudicial. We disagree and affirm.

Facts

This case involves a sordid tale of infidelity and murder by decapitation.

The appellant and his wife were married in 1989 after a six-month courtship. The appellant took his marriage seriously and wanted it to be a permanent commitment. Because his wife had suffered through three miscarriages during the marriage, the appellant obtained a vasectomy to preclude further suffering on her part.

By December 1991, the wife felt that her feelings for her husband "had pretty much died" and she decided that she could not continue with the marriage. Nevertheless, in December, 1992, she followed her husband to Fulda, Germany, where he was assigned after joining the Army in January, 1992. During 1993, she took advantage of the assignment to Germany and often traveled throughout Europe without him.

The appellant and the victim, Specialist (SPC) Glover, became friends in early 1993. On two or three occasions, SPC Glover visited the appellant and his wife in their quarters. In the summer of 1993, the appellant was required to attend a military leadership training course. While the appellant was away from home, SPC Glover went to the appellant's quarters at least six times and had sexual intercourse with the appellant's wife. The appellant wrote love letters to his wife while attending the course. Although by her own account she no longer loved the appellant at the time and she was having an affair with SPC Glover, she responded with equally passionate correspondence.

By October, 1993, the appellant's wife learned that she was pregnant as a result of her sexual liaisons with SPC Glover. She did not tell the appellant about the pregnancy. She and her husband stopped having sexual relations that same month. In mid-November, 1993, she told the appellant that she no longer loved him and wanted a divorce. Over the Thanksgiving weekend, the couple talked about the details of a separation and divorce. Ultimately they agreed to a separation and her early return to the United States.

Although the appellant's wife assured him that there was no other man in her life, the appellant was suspicious. He intercepted a letter to her postmarked 29 November 1993, that suggested that she was pregnant. On 5 December 1993, the appellant found his wife's secret diary that indicated she may have had many other lovers during their marriage. When the appellant confronted her, she tried to explain the journal entries as fantasies or innocent relationships. On 6 December 1993, they met with a chaplain as a prelude to the pending separation, and both claimed to have been faithful during the marriage.

On 7 December 1993, the appellant went to work as normal while his wife intended to go to the bank. On the way, she experienced very heavy vaginal bleeding. Because she was afraid she was having another miscarriage, she asked an acquaintance to take her to the local German hospital. After she arrived at the hospital, she was told she would be there for at least a week. She attempted to contact SPC Glover through a legal clerk at the legal assistance office where she had worked as a volunteer. Later in the morning, when the appellant coincidentally stopped by the legal assistance office to obtain some papers in connection with the pending marital separation, that same legal clerk told the appellant that his wife was in the hospital. The appellant was concerned and went to the hospital at approximately 1420 while dressed in his battle dress uniform.

When the appellant arrived at the hospital, his wife informed him that she was pregnant because of an extramarital affair with a person she did not identify. He remained calm and appeared to be concerned about her condition. The appellant left the hospital around 1500 and returned to his quarters to retrieve items his wife had requested for her stay at the hospital. When he had not returned by 1530, she called the quarters twice, but received no answer.

The appellant arrived back at the hospital at approximately 1610 wearing jeans and a jeans jacket. He appeared agitated and questioned his wife about the identity of her lover and the circumstances of the relationship. She told him that the child was conceived while she made love on a quilt in the appellant's living room. The appellant and his wife agreed that the lover should come to the hospital where she was undergoing treatment for the possible miscarriage. She also informed him that she had made arrangements for a message to be delivered to her lover so he could come to her side. While the appellant was in the room with her, she called the legal clerk to see if the message had been delivered. Although the appellant did not learn of SPC Glover's identity at that time, he learned that the lover held the rank of specialist.

Approximately ten minutes later, the appellant called the legal clerk and asked, "did you deliver the message to the specialist?" The legal clerk said he was going to do so, but did not reveal the identity of the intended recipient. He then asked the appellant if he knew where a particular barracks was located.

The appellant immediately drove to the location of the barracks, approached the staff duty noncommissioned officer (NCO), and explained that he needed to find the legal clerk who was looking for a room and that he also needed to find that same room. When the staff duty NCO asked the appellant which soldier he was looking for, the appellant said, "forget it" and departed. At approximately the same time, the legal clerk found the correct room and placed a message under SPC Glover's door. He also had SPC Glover paged to ensure that he was notified that the appellant's wife wanted him to join her at the hospital.

The appellant, who by this time was aware that SPC Glover was the paramour, began looking for him. At some point the appellant had obtained a fighting knife with an eight-inch double-edged blade that he brought with him in his car. The appellant, acting normal, asked a soldier near the barracks dining facility if he had seen SPC Glover. The soldier informed the appellant that SPC Glover was in the telephone booth adjacent to the dining facility. The appellant replied, "[w]ell, I guess he got the message."

Specialist Glover had answered the page and had spoken with the legal clerk. He also had retrieved the message from under his door. At approximately 1715 he called the appellant's wife at the hospital. While SPC Glover was talking on the telephone with the appellant's wife, the appellant approached the telephone booth. Without confronting SPC Glover or giving him any chance to explain what had happened, the appellant stabbed and slashed his intended victim in the back of the neck. Specialist Glover attempted to flee but slipped to the ground. The appellant pursued, ran past his fallen victim, turned and knelt over him and stabbed and cut him ten to twenty times in the throat, practically severing his head. A witness described some of the motions involved in the attack as if the appellant was "cutting meat or skinning a deer." Another witness described it as "slow" and "rhythmic," "sort of like a sawing motion."

After stabbing the victim, the appellant stood up and kicked SPC Glover in the head several times. The head separated from the body and rolled several feet away. The onlookers were stunned at the severity of the attack and sickened with the results. One soldier, who observed the attack, vomited at the sight. The appellant, on the other hand, walked over to the head, picked it up by the hair, held it aloft and announced in a loud clear voice, "[t]his is what happens when you commit adultery." He also stated in a sarcastic tone, "[a]nd he said he was sorry." The appellant then turned and walked at a brisk pace to his car, carrying the head under his arm "like a football."

A short time later the appellant was observed near his car that was stopped on a bridge over a stream. When another car approached, he quickly departed from the area. The appellant continued on his way and parked several hundred yards from the hospital. He removed his blood-stained jacket and shirt, put on an olive-colored jacket, and entered the hospital while carrying an athletic bag. He entered his wife's small hospital room and removed SPC Glover's head from the athletic bag. He appeared agitated and very upset. He held the head in both hands and thrust it toward his wife's face and chest. She screamed and cowered while the appellant set the head facing his wife on an adjacent night stand. He sat down on the bed and said, "Glover's here, he'll sleep with you every night now, only you won't sleep, because all you'll see is this."

As startled medical personnel rushed to the room, the appellant remained seated on the bed, with his legs extended over his wife's legs, his hand on her chest trying to make her look at the head. He said to the German doctors "[g]ood, you stay here, and listen to everything that I have to say, remember as much as you can." He also stated, "I'm her husband, and she's an adulteress, not just with that man, . . . but many times over." His wife described his statements as follows:

> He turned to me, he said, "you know," he said, "you gave me enough clues. It was easy enough to figure out who it was. It was easy enough to do this." And he told the doctors, "I'm not normally a violent man. This is my only violent act, but don't underestimate me, I'm very skilled at what I do. I studied this, I planned this, I calculated this." And he turned to me and he said, "I did this for you, because I love you."

When she asked him what he did with the body and the knife the appellant replied:

> I'm not that stupid . . . . I don't care if they put me in jail for the rest of my life, because I'll just think about you. And I don't care if they put me to sleep, if they kill me, because I'll just think about you while they do it.

One of the German doctors testified that the appellant "behaved in a calm way" in the midst of the extraordinary situation at the hospital. The appellant asked for a bucket of water to wash his hands. He told the doctor that he "felt mistreated, humiliated, cheated on." He took off his identification tags and threw them at the German police who arrived on the scene and said, "[t]here's my name, I'm Stephen Schap." He also said they should stay and listen to everything he had to say and be witnesses, but he'd go peacefully only when the military police arrived. Ultimately, the German police on the scene dragged the appellant from the room.

Shortly after he was apprehended, the appellant stated that his wife "shouldn't have done what she'd done," and that he "shouldn't have done what he'd done either," but he "realized what he did" and he would just have to "pay for it." He was described by one witness as being "mighty calm about it." The witness testified that the appellant "didn't appear upset at all."

The appellant's car was located several hundred yards from the hospital. The gas tank was full. Inside, authorities found a change of clothing, food, shaving items, closed-out bank account records, appellant's passport, small amounts of six types of foreign currency, telephone records, diplomas, and tax records. Although prior to the incident, the appellant had received permission to travel to the Netherlands for the weekend of 11–13 December 1993, some of the items found in the car normally were stored in boxes at the appellant's quarters.

At his court-martial the appellant, who did not testify on the merits, never contested the fact that he had brutally attacked SPC Glover and taken the severed head to the hospital. His entire defense was that he acted in the sudden heat of passion in committing the crime of voluntary manslaughter.

Assigned Errors

The appellant contends, *inter alia*, that the evidence at trial was legally and factually insufficient to sustain any offense other than voluntary manslaughter. Although the law recognizes that a "person may be provoked to such an extent" that "a fatal blow may be struck before self-control has returned," there are very specific requirements for a finding of voluntary manslaughter. *See* Manual for Courts–Martial (1995 Edition) [hereinafter MCM], Part IV, para. 44c(1)(a); *see also United States v. Maxie*, 25 C.M.R. 418 (C.M.A. 1958). . . .

In order for an unlawful killing to be reduced from murder to voluntary manslaughter the homicide must be committed in the "heat of sudden passion" which is "caused by adequate provocation." MCM, Part IV, para. 44c(1)(a). For the provocation to be "adequate," however, the provocation must be of a nature to "excite uncontrollable passion in a reasonable person, and the act of killing must be committed under and because of the passion." *Id*. Although the "passion may result from fear or rage," the provocation can not be "sought or induced" by the killer. *Id*. Furthermore, "[i]f, judged by the standard of a reasonable person, sufficient cooling time elapses between the provocation and the killing, the offense is murder, even if the accused's passion persists." *Id*.

The test for legal sufficiency is whether, considering the evidence in the light most favorable to the prosecution, a reasonable fact finder could have found all the essential elements of the offense beyond a reasonable doubt. *Jackson v. Virginia*, 443 U.S. 307 (1979); *accord United States v. Turner*, 25 M.J. 324 (C.M.A. 1987). We are satisfied that the evidence of record more than meets this standard as to premeditated murder.

The test for factual sufficiency is whether, after weighing the evidence in the record of trial and making allowances for not having personally observed the witnesses, we are convinced of the appellant's guilt beyond a reasonable doubt. *Turner*, 25 M.J. at 325. In applying this test, we make the following findings.

First, we find that upon his wife's verification of his suspicions that she was unfaithful, the appellant set about to identify and track down the paramour. This was to be accomplished through his questioning of his wife, his contact with the legal clerk who was to deliver the message to the paramour, and his questions to the staff duty NCO.

Next, and most importantly, we find that the appellant intended to murder his wife's paramour, regardless of who it was. He planned to accomplish this objective by using the large fighting knife he brought along for that very purpose. We reject the suggestion that the appellant only intended to confront the paramour and brought along the knife in case matters became unmanageable.

We also find that the nature and severity of the attack, coupled with the appellant's vigorously kicking SPC Glover's head, led to the head being severed from the body. Once the head was severed the appellant picked it up and made his coldly calculated comment about the deadly price of adultery.

We further find that the appellant carefully prepared for his escape and intended to flee from the scene of the crime. Once he held the severed head aloft, however, he realized that his identity would become known. Consequently, he determined to inflict the maximum emotional suffering upon his wife before he was apprehended. All of his conduct prior to the attack, along with his comments at the scene, at the hospital to his wife and the doctors, and to the police, convinces us that the murder was a premeditated act rather than a crime committed in the heat of passion.

In order to prevail on his contention that his crime was voluntary manslaughter, we would have to be persuaded that the evidence presented by the government was insufficient to prove premeditated murder or unpremeditated murder. We find, however, that the murder was consummated in a cold and calculating manner. We further find that the appellant had not lost self-control at the time he killed SPC Glover. We specifically reject the defense contention that the learning of the paramour's identity triggered an uncontrollable rage. The evidence shows that the intent to kill was present before the identity of the paramour was known.

We also specifically find the appellant did not kill SPC Glover while under the influence of uncontrolled passion and because of that passion. Our conclusion is that once the appellant learned of the lover's identity, he specifically intended to kill SPC Glover, that he contemplated and planned SPC Glover's murder, and that he had adequate "cooling off" time to reflect upon the consequences before he acted.

We have carefully evaluated the entire record of trial, and conclude, applying our fact-finding powers of Article 66, UCMJ, that the appellant methodically planned the murder. In short, this was a premeditated murder in violation of Article 118(1), UCMJ, rather than voluntary manslaughter under Article 119, UCMJ.

The appellant has assigned three errors in regard to instructions or lack thereof from the military judge. In this case the military judge gave the standard instructions for premeditated murder, unpremeditated murder, and voluntary manslaughter. See Dep't of the Army, Pam. 27–9, Military Judges' Benchbook, para 3–86; 3–87. At various points in the instructions he correctly discussed heat of passion. At no time did the defense object to or request additional instructions. The trial defense counsel's failure to object to an instruction or omission of an instruction constitutes waiver of the objection in the absence of plain error. Rule for Courts–Martial 920(f). *See United States v. Morgan*, 37 M.J. 407 (C.M.A. 1993); *see also United States v. Olano*, 507 U.S. 725 (1993). We are satisfied that the instructional errors, if any, did not rise to the level of plain error. The instructions, when taken as a whole, were appropriate and complete. We hold that the assignments of error concerning the military judge's instructions or lack of instructions are without merit.

* * *

The appellant next contends that the military judge abused his discretion in limiting the testimony of the defense expert about rage and premeditation. The military judge permitted the defense expert to testify over government objection. The expert's testimony was directed at states of mind in general. The military judge permitted the witness to testify about how long an individual could remain in a state of rage. He also correctly allowed the expert to discuss a person's ability to reflect on their actions. The military judge properly limited the expert discussion to prevent confusion between the concept of reflection and the legal standard of premeditation. Thus, the assigned error is without merit.

The appellant also contends that the military judge abused his discretion in refusing to allow the defense psychiatrist to testify that at the time of the offense the appellant was in a rage. To the contrary, the military judge allowed the expert to testify about these matters. He properly would not allow the expert to bring before the members those comments made by the appellant during his clinical interviews. The expert was allowed to testify about the basis of his conclusions, but he was not allowed to place the appellant's version of events before the members without the benefit of cross-examination of the appellant himself. The assigned error is without merit.

The appellant further contends that the military judge abused his discretion in admitting several books and catalogs concerning knives into evidence. Apparently government investigators searched through the appellant's bookshelves in an effort to find any link to the use of knives as weapons. This issue was fully litigated at an Article 39(a), UCMJ, session prior to trial on the merits. Government counsel offered the books on the theory that they provided corroboration of the appellant's admissions or confession. See Military Rule of Evidence. 304(g). The trial defense counsel contended that the books would be taken out of context and would prove to be more prejudicial than probative. In his view, it would not be unusual or probative of anything to find that a soldier in the United States Army possessed books or catalogs that had pictures or articles about knives and self-defense. The military judge made specific findings that the items were probative and that no unfair prejudice would result to the appellant if the books were admitted into evidence. In addition, he offered the trial defense counsel the opportunity to put the books into their proper context by use of testimony and photographs. The defense presented evidence, and directed its cross-examination to highlight that the appellant merely possessed the books and that the government presented no proof that he relied upon them in executing his alleged crime.

We are satisfied that the military judge did not abuse his discretion regarding this issue. In addition, even if the military judge erred in allowing the materials into evidence, we hold that the appellant suffered no unfair prejudice, as we are confident that the members gave the books little weight. The members certainly recognized that many soldiers, including the appellant, possess books and catalogs that featured military equipment, including knives. We also are confident that the members recognized that many soldiers were likely to have materials about knives and guns in their personal libraries.

This murder case is unusual only in regard to the decapitation and display of the head. There was little if any dispute as to the acts involved. Our review of the record convinces us that the government carried the burden to prove premeditated murder beyond a reasonable doubt. Our review also convinces us that the alleged errors are without merit.

The findings of guilty and the sentence are affirmed.

Senior Judge GRAVELLE and Judge ECKER concur.

[The Court of Appeals for the Armed Forces granted review of several issues but affirmed the judgment of the Army Court of Criminal Appeals. *See* 49 M.J. 317 (C.A.A.F. 1998). The Supreme Court denied certiorari. *See* 525 U.S. 1179 (1999).—Eds.]

Points for Discussion

1. Are the military courts capable of handling crimes of this magnitude? Should the military courts have jurisdiction over cases that have little to do with military discipline? Would the outcome of the case likely have been the same or different if the case had been tried in a civilian court?

2. Pursuant to a "Status of Forces Agreement" with Germany, most crimes by U.S. service members in Germany are tried by courts-martial rather than German courts. Why might both Germany and the United States favor this arrangement?

1-3. Jurisdiction Over Military Persons and Offenses

Nearly everyone tried by court-martial is a service member accused of committing a crime while on active duty. This includes both regular service members (i.e., those who are always on active duty) and reservists and national guardsmen who have been mobilized or placed on active duty for train-training. Article 2(a)(1), UCMJ, 10 U.S.C. § 802(a)(1), unambiguously gives courts-martial jurisdiction over these service members by saying: "The following persons are subject to this chapter . . . [m]embers of a regular component of the armed force . . . and other persons lawfully called or ordered into, or to duty in or for training in, the armed forces, from the dates when they are required by the terms of the call or order to obey it."

This observation raises two questions. The first is whether a court-martial has jurisdiction to try anyone other than a service member on active duty. The second is whether the offense for which a person is tried by court-martial must be connected to the person's service. These questions are considered in turn.

Persons Subject to Court-Martial

Although most of the accused who are tried by court-martial are service members on active duty, Article 2(a)(2)-(13), UCMJ, 10 U.S.C. § 802(a)(2)-(13), reprinted in the margin,* lists twelve additional categories of persons

---

* 10 U.S.C . § 802. Art. 2. Persons subject to this chapter

(a) The following persons are subject to this chapter:

(1) Members of a regular component of the armed forces, including those awaiting discharge after expiration of their terms of enlistment; volunteers from the time of their muster or acceptance into the armed forces; inductees from the time of their actual induction into the armed forces; and other persons lawfully called or ordered into, or to duty in or for training in, the armed forces, from the dates when they are required by the terms of the call or order to obey it.

(2) Cadets, aviation cadets, and midshipmen.

(3) Members of a reserve component while on inactive-duty training, but in the case of members of the Army National Guard of the United States or the Air National Guard of the United States only when in Federal service.

(4) Retired members of a regular component of the armed forces who are entitled to pay.

(5) Retired members of a reserve component who are receiving hospitalization from an armed force.

(6) Members of the Fleet Reserve and Fleet Marine Corps Reserve.

(7) Persons in custody of the armed forces serving a sentence imposed by a court-martial.

(8) Members of the National Oceanic and Atmospheric Administration, Public Health Service, and other organizations, when assigned to and serving with the armed forces.

(9) Prisoners of war in custody of the armed forces.

(10) In time of declared war or a contingency operation, persons serving with or accompanying an armed force in the field.

(11) Subject to any treaty or agreement to which the United States is or may be a party or to any accepted rule of international law, persons serving with, employed by, or

subject to trial by court-martial. Some of these additional categories are well-accepted. For example, it is perhaps not surprising that Military Academy cadets and Naval Academy midshipmen are subject to court-martial jurisdiction, under Article 2(a)(2), UCMJ, 10 U.S.C. § 802(a)(2), because they live according to very strict military discipline. But other categories are more controversial. Few military retirees who are receiving retired pay probably realize that retirees can be and occasionally are tried by court-martial. Indeed, in recent years a retired Army major general was convicted of a fraternization-type offense, *see* Robert Burns, *Retired General Demoted*, Wash. Post, Sept. 3, 1999, at A25, and a retired Army master sergeant was sentenced to death for committing three murders, *see Hennis v. Hemlick*, 2012 WL 120054 (4th Cir. 2012). Similarly, during the United States' military engagements in Iraq and Afghanistan, it has relied on private companies (typically called "contractors") to carry out tasks such as driving trucks, running dining facilities, translating foreign languages, and so forth. The employees for these contractors are all subject to trial by court-martial because they are, in the words of Article 2(a)(11), UCMJ, 10 U.S.C. § 802(a)(11), "[i]n time of declared war or a contingency operation, persons serving with or accompanying an armed force in the field." In reality, however, only a few have faced a court-martial to date.

An interesting though mostly theoretical question is whether the Constitution places any limits on the power of courts-martial to try civilians. The Supreme Court addressed this issue most notably in the following landmark decision. In reading the decision, note that it lacks a majority opinion: Justice Black wrote a plurality opinion for four justices and Justice Frankfurter and Justice Harlan wrote separate concurrences in the judgment, while Justice Clark wrote a dissent which Justice Burton joined. Justice Whitaker did not participate. Thus, there were seven Justices on one side, and two on the other, but no opinion received five votes.

---

accompanying the armed forces outside the United States and outside the Commonwealth of Puerto Rico, Guam, and the Virgin Islands.

(12) Subject to any treaty or agreement to which the United States is or may be a party or to any accepted rule of international law, persons within an area leased by or otherwise reserved or acquired for the use of the United States which is under the control of the Secretary concerned and which is outside the United States and outside the Commonwealth of Puerto Rico, Guam, and the Virgin Islands.

(13) Individuals belonging to one of the eight categories enumerated in Article 4 of the Convention Relative to the Treatment of Prisoners of War, done at Geneva August 12, 1949 (6 UST 3316), who violate the law of war.

REID v. COVERT
U.S. Supreme Court
354 U.S. 1 (1957)

Mr. Justice BLACK announced the judgment of the Court and delivered an opinion, in which The CHIEF JUSTICE, Mr. Justice DOUGLAS, and Mr. Justice BRENNAN join.

These cases raise basic constitutional issues of the utmost concern. They call into question the role of the military under our system of government. They involve the power of Congress to expose civilians to trial by military tribunals, under military regulations and procedures, for offenses against the United States thereby depriving them of trial in civilian courts, under civilian laws and procedures and with all the safeguards of the Bill of Rights. These cases are particularly significant because for the first time since the adoption of the Constitution wives of soldiers have been denied trial by jury in a court of law and forced to trial before courts-martial.

In No. 701 Mrs. Clarice Covert killed her husband, a sergeant in the United States Air Force, at an airbase in England. Mrs. Covert, who was not a member of the armed services, was residing on the base with her husband at the time. She was tried by a court-martial for murder under Article 118 of the Uniform Code of Military Justice (UCMJ). The trial was on charges preferred by Air Force personnel and the court-martial was composed of Air Force officers. The court-martial asserted jurisdiction over Mrs. Covert under Article 2(11) of the UCMJ, which provides:

The following persons are subject to this code:

(11) Subject to the provisions of any treaty or agreement to which the United States is or may be a party or to any accepted rule of international law, all persons serving with, employed by, or accompanying the armed forces without the continental limits of the United States * * *.

Counsel for Mrs. Covert contended that she was insane at the time she killed her husband, but the military tribunal found her guilty of murder and sentenced her to life imprisonment. The judgment was affirmed by the Air Force Board of Review, but was reversed by the Court of Military Appeals, because of prejudicial errors concerning the defense of insanity. While Mrs. Covert was being held in this country pending a proposed retrial by court-martial in the District of Columbia, her counsel petitioned the District Court for a writ of habeas corpus to set her free on the ground that the Constitution forbade her trial by military authorities. Construing this Court's decision in *United States ex rel. Toth v. Quarles*, 350 U.S. 11 (1955) as holding that 'a civilian is entitled to a civilian trial' the District Court held that Mrs. Covert could not be tried by courtmartial and ordered her released from custody. The Government appealed directly to this Court under 28 U.S.C. § 1252.

In No. 713 Mrs. Dorothy Smith killed her husband, an Army officer, at a post in Japan where she was living with him. She was tried for murder by a court-martial and despite considerable evidence that she was insane was found guilty and sentenced to life imprisonment. The judgment was approved by the Army Board of Review, and the Court of Military Appeals. Mrs. Smith was then confined in a federal penitentiary in West Virginia. Her father, respondent here, filed a petition for habeas corpus in a District Court for West Virginia. The petition charged that the court-martial was without jurisdiction because Article 2(11) of the UCMJ was unconstitutional insofar as it authorized the trial of civilian dependents accompanying servicemen overseas. The District Court refused to issue the writ, and while an appeal was pending in the Court of Appeals for the Fourth Circuit we granted certiorari at the request of the Government.

The two cases were consolidated and argued last Term and a majority of the Court, with three Justices dissenting and one reserving opinion, held that military trial of Mrs. Smith and Mrs. Covert for their alleged offenses was constitutional. 351 U.S. 470 (1956). The majority held that the provisions of Article III and the Fifth and Sixth Amendments which require that crimes be tried by a jury after indictment by a grand jury did not protect an American citizen when he was tried by the American Government in foreign lands for offenses committed there and that Congress could provide for the trial of such offenses in any manner it saw fit so long as the procedures established were reasonable and consonant with due process. The opinion then went on to express the view that military trials, as now practiced, were not unreasonable or arbitrary when applied to dependents accompanying members of the armed forces overseas. In reaching their conclusion the majority found it unnecessary to consider the power of Congress "To make Rules for the Government and Regulation of the land and naval Forces" under Article I, § 8, cl. 14 of the Constitution.

Subsequently, the Court granted a petition for rehearing. Now, after further argument and consideration, we conclude that the previous decisions cannot be permitted to stand. We hold that Mrs. Smith and Mrs. Covert could not constitutionally be tried by military authorities.

I.

At the beginning we reject the idea that when the United States acts against citizens abroad it can do so free of the Bill of Rights. The United States is entirely a creature of the Constitution. Its power and authority have no other source. It can only act in accordance with all the limitations imposed by the Constitution. When the Government reaches out to punish a citizen who is abroad, the shield which the Bill of Rights and other parts of the Constitution provide to protect his life and liberty should not be stripped away just because he happens to be in another land. . . .

The rights and liberties which citizens of our country enjoy are not protected by custom and tradition alone, they have been jealously preserved from the encroachments of Government by express provisions of our written Constitution.

Among those provisions, Art. III, § 2 and the Fifth and Sixth Amendments are directly relevant to these cases. Article III, § 2 lays down the rule that:

> The Trial of all Crimes, except in Cases of Impeachment, shall be by Jury; and such Trial shall be held in the State where the said Crimes shall have been committed; but when not committed within any State, the Trial shall be at such Place or Places as the Congress may by Law have directed.

The Fifth Amendment declares:

> No person shall be held to answer for a capital, or otherwise infamous crime, unless on a presentment or indictment of a Grand Jury, except in cases arising in the land or naval forces, or in the Militia, when in actual service in time of War or public danger; * * *.

And the Sixth Amendment provides:

> In all criminal prosecutions, the accused shall enjoy the right to a speedy and public trial, by an impartial jury of the State and district wherein the crime shall have been committed * * *.

The language of Art. III, § 2 manifests that constitutional protections for the individual were designed to restrict the United States Government when it acts outside of this country, as well as here at home. After declaring that all criminal trials must be by jury, the section states that when a crime is "not committed within any State, the Trial shall be at such Place or Places as the Congress may by Law have directed." If this language is permitted to have its obvious meaning, § 2 is applicable to criminal trials outside of the States as a group without regard to where the offense is committed or the trial held. From the very first Congress, federal statutes have implemented the provisions of § 2 by providing for trial of murder and other crimes committed outside the jurisdiction of any State "in the district where the offender is apprehended, or into which he may first be brought." The Fifth and Sixth Amendments, like Art. III, § 2, are also all inclusive with their sweeping references to "no person" and to "all criminal prosecutions."

* * *

II.

At the time of Mrs. Covert's alleged offense, an executive agreement was in effect between the United States and Great Britain which permitted United States' military courts to exercise exclusive jurisdiction over offenses committed in Great Britain by American servicemen or their dependents. For its part, the United States agreed that these military courts would be willing and able to try and to punish all offenses against the laws of Great Britain by such persons. In all material respects, the same situation existed in Japan when Mrs. Smith killed her husband. Even though a court-martial does not give an accused trial by jury and other Bill of Rights protections, the Government contends that article 2(11) of UCMJ, insofar as it provides for the military trial of dependents accompanying the armed forces in Great Britain and Japan, can be sustained as legislation which is necessary and proper to carry out the

United States' obligations under the international agreements made with those countries. The obvious and decisive answer to this, of course, is that no agreement with a foreign nation can confer power on the Congress, or on any other branch of Government, which is free from the restraints of the Constitution.

* * *

In summary, we conclude that the Constitution in its entirety applied to the trials of Mrs. Smith and Mrs. Covert. Since their court-martial did not meet the requirements of Art. III, § 2, or the Fifth and Sixth Amendments we are compelled to determine if there is anything within the Constitution which authorizes the military trial of dependents accompanying the armed forces overseas.

III.

Article I, § 8, cl. 14, empowers Congress "To make Rules for the Government and Regulation of the land and naval Forces." It has been held that this creates an exception to the normal method of trial in civilian courts as provided by the Constitution and permits Congress to authorize military trial of members of the armed services without all the safeguards given an accused by Article III and the Bill of Rights. But if the language of Clause 14 is given its natural meaning, the power granted does not extend to civilians—even though they may be dependents living with servicemen on a military base. The term "land and naval Forces" refers to persons who are members of the armed services and not to their civilian wives, children and other dependents. It seems inconceivable that Mrs. Covert or Mrs. Smith could have been tried by military authorities as members of the "land and naval Forces" had they been living on a military post in this country. Yet this constitutional term surely has the same meaning everywhere. The wives of servicemen are no more members of the "land and naval Forces" when living at a military post in England or Japan than when living at a base in this country or in Hawaii or Alaska.

* * *

The tradition of keeping the military subordinate to civilian authority may not be so strong in the minds of this generation as it was in the minds of those who wrote the Constitution. The idea that the relatives of soldiers could be denied a jury trial in a court of law and instead be tried by court-martial under the guise of regulating the armed forces would have seemed incredible to those men, in whose lifetime the right of the military to try soldiers for any offenses in time of peace had only been grudgingly conceded. The Founders envisioned the army as a necessary institution, but one dangerous to liberty if not confined within its essential bounds. Their fears were rooted in history. They knew that ancient republics had been overthrown by their military leaders. They were familiar with the history of Seventeenth Century England, where Charles I tried to govern through the army and without Parliament. During this attempt, contrary to the Common Law, he used courts-martial to try soldiers for certain non-military offenses. This court-martialing of soldiers in peacetime evoked strong protests from Parliament. . . .

* * *

The generation that adopted the Constitution did not distrust the military because of past history alone. Within their own lives they had seen royal governors sometimes resort to military rule. British troops were quartered in Boston at various times from 1768 until the outbreak of the Revolutionary War to support unpopular royal governors and to intimidate the local populace. The trial of soldiers by courts-martial and the interference of the military with the civil courts aroused great anxiety and antagonism not only in Massachusetts but throughout the colonies. . . .

In light of this history, it seems clear that the Founders had no intention to permit the trial of civilians in military courts, where they would be denied jury trials and other constitutional protections, merely by giving Congress the power to make rules which were "necessary and proper" for the regulation of the "land and naval Forces." Such a latitudinarian interpretation of these clauses would be at war with the well-established purpose of the Founders to keep the military strictly within its proper sphere, subordinate to civil authority. The Constitution does not say that Congress can regulate "the land and naval Forces and all other persons whose regulation might have some relationship to maintenance of the land and naval Forces." There is no indication that the Founders contemplated setting up a rival system of military courts to compete with civilian courts for jurisdiction over civilians who might have some contact or relationship with the armed forces. Courts-martial were not to have concurrent jurisdiction with courts of law over non-military America.

In No. 701, Reid v. Covert, the judgment of the District Court directing the Mrs. Covert be released from custody is affirmed.

In No. 713, Kinsella v. Krueger, the judgment of the District Court is reversed and the case is remanded with instructions to order Mrs. Smith released from custody.

Mr. Justice WHITTAKER took no part in the consideration or decision of these cases.

Mr. Justice FRANKFURTER,* concurring in the result.

---

* Justice Felix Frankfurter was a major in the U.S. Army Reserve, Judge Advocate General's Corps, while serving on the U.S. Supreme Court. By his own admission, he avoided wearing his uniform whenever possible. He explained: "The reason I didn't want to go into uniform was because I knew enough about the doings in the War Department to know that every pipsqueak Colonel would feel that he was more important than a Major . . . . As a civilian I could get into the presence of a General without saluting, clicking my heels, and having the Colonel outside say, 'You wait. He's got a Colonel in there.' " *The Army Lawyer: A History of the Judge Advocate General's Corps, 1775-1975* 118 (1975).—Eds.

* * *

Trial by court-martial is constitutionally permissible only for persons who can, on a fair appraisal, be regarded as falling within the authority given to Congress under Article I to regulate the "land and naval Forces," and who therefore are not protected by specific provisions of Article III and the Fifth and Sixth Amendments. . . .

* * *

The prosecution by court-martial for capital crimes committed by civilian dependents of members of the armed forces abroad is hardly to be deemed, under modern conditions, obviously appropriate to the effective exercise of the power to "make Rules for the Government and Regulation of the land and naval Forces" when it is a question of deciding what power is granted under Article I and therefore what restriction is made on Article III and the Fifth and Sixth Amendments. I do not think that the proximity, physical and social, of these women to the 'land and naval Forces' is, with due regard to all that has been put before us, so clearly demanded by the effective "Government and Regulation" of those forces as reasonably to demonstrate a justification for court-martial jurisdiction over capital offenses.

The Government speaks of the "great potential impact on military discipline" of these accompanying civilian dependents. This cannot be denied, nor should its implications be minimized. But the notion that discipline over military personnel is to be furthered by subjecting their civilian dependents to the threat of capital punishment imposed by court-martial is too hostile to the reasons that underlie the procedural safeguards of the Bill of Rights for those safeguards to be displaced. It is true that military discipline might be affected seriously if civilian dependents could commit murders and other capital crimes with impunity. No one, however, challenges the availability to Congress of a power to provide for trial and punishment of these dependents for such crimes. The method of trial alone is in issue. . . .

* * *

I therefore conclude that, in capital cases, the exercise of court-martial jurisdiction over civilian dependents in time of peace cannot be justified by Article I, considered in connection with the specific protections of Article III and the Fifth and Sixth Amendments.

* * *

Mr. Justice HARLAN, concurring in the result.

I concur in the result, on the narrow ground that where the offense is capital, Article 2(11) cannot constitutionally be applied to the trial of civilian dependents of members of the armed forces over-seas in times of peace.

* * *

For analytical purposes, I think it useful to break down the issue before us into two questions: First, is there a rational connection between the trial of these army wives by court-martial and the power of Congress to make rules for the governance of the land and naval forces; in other words, is there any initial power here at all? Second, if there is such a rational connection, to what extent does this statute, though reasonably calculated to subserve an enumerated power, collide with other express limitations on congressional power; in other words, can this statute, however appropriate to the Article I power looked at in isolation, survive against the requirements of Article III and the Fifth and Sixth Amendments? I recognize that these two questions are ultimately one and the same, since the scope of the Article I power is not separable from the limitations imposed by Article III and the Fifth and Sixth Amendments. Nevertheless I think it will make for clarity of analysis to consider them separately.

* * *

. . . I cannot say that the court-martial jurisdiction here involved has no rational connection with the stated power. The Government, it seems to me, has made a strong showing that the court-martial of civilian dependents abroad has a close connection to the proper and effective functioning of our overseas military contingents. There is no need to detail here the various aspects of this connection, which have been well dealt with in the dissenting opinion of my brother CLARK. Suffice it to say that to all intents and purposes these civilian dependents are part of the military community overseas, are so regarded by the host country, and must be subjected to the same discipline if the military commander is to have the power to prevent activities which would jeopardize the security and effectiveness of his command. . . .

It seems to me clear on such a basis that these dependents, when sent overseas by the Government, become pro tanto a part of the military community. I cannot say, therefore, that it is irrational or arbitrary for Congress to subject them to military discipline. I do not deal now, of course, with the problem of alternatives to court-martial jurisdiction; all that needs to be established at this stage is that, viewing Art. I, § 8, cl. 14 in isolation, subjection of civilian dependents overseas to court-martial jurisdiction can in no wise be deemed unrelated to the power of Congress to make all necessary and proper laws to insure the effective governance of our overseas land and naval forces.

I turn now to the other side of the coin. For no matter how practical and how reasonable this jurisdiction might be, it still cannot be sustained if the Constitution guarantees to these army wives a trial in an Article III court, with indictment by grand jury and jury trial as provided by the Fifth and Sixth Amendments.

* * *

. . . I cannot agree with the sweeping proposition that a full Article III trial, with indictment and trial by jury, is required in every case for the trial of a civilian dependent of a serviceman overseas. The Government, it seems to me, has made an impressive showing that at least for the run-of-the-mill offenses committed by dependents overseas, such a requirement would be as impractical and anomalous as it would have been to require jury trial for Balzac in Porto Rico. Again, I need not go into details, beyond stating that except for capital offenses, such as we have here, to which, in my opinion, special considerations apply, I am by no means ready to say that Congress' power to provide for trial by court-martial of civilian dependents overseas is limited by Article III and the Fifth and Sixth Amendments. Where, if at all, the dividing line should be drawn among cases not capital, need not now be decided. We are confronted here with capital offenses alone; and it seems to me particularly unwise now to decide more than we have to. Our far-flung foreign military establishments are a new phenomenon in our national life, and I think it would be unfortunate were we unnecessarily to foreclose, as my four brothers would do, our future consideration of the broad questions involved in maintaining the effectiveness of these national outposts, in the light of continuing experience with these problems.

So far as capital cases are concerned, I think they stand on quite a different footing than other offenses. In such cases the law is especially sensitive to demands for that procedural fairness which inheres in a civilian trial where the judge and trier of fact are not responsive to the command of the convening authority. I do not concede that whatever process is "due" an offender faced with a fine or a prison sentence necessarily satisfies the requirements of the Constitution in a capital case. . . . In fact, the Government itself has conceded that one grave offense, treason, presents a special case: 'The gravity of this offense is such that we can well assume that, whatever difficulties may be involved in trial far from the scene of the offense . . . the trial should be in our courts." I see no reason for not applying the same principle to any case where a civilian dependent stands trial on pain of life itself. The number of such cases would appear to be so negligible that the practical problems of affording the defendant a civilian trial would not present insuperable problems.

On this narrow ground I concur in the result in these cases.

Mr. Justice CLARK, with whom Mr. Justice BURTON joins, dissenting.

The Court today releases two women from prosecution though the evidence shows that they brutally killed their husbands, both American soldiers, while stationed with them in quarters furnished by our armed forces on its military installations in foreign lands. . . .

Mr. Justice BURTON and I remain convinced that the former opinions of the Court are correct and that they set forth valid constitutional doctrine under the long-recognized cases of this Court. The opinions were neither written nor agreed to in haste and they reflect the consensus of the majority reached after thorough discussion at many conferences. In fact, the cases were here longer both before and after argument than many of the cases we decide. We adhere to the views there expressed since we are convinced that through them we were neither "mortgaging the future," as is claimed, nor foreclosing the present, as does the judgment today. We do not include a discussion of the theory upon which those former judgments were entered because we are satisfied with its handling in the earlier opinions.

Points for Discussion

1. How did the plurality opinion and the two concurrences in judgment differ from each other?

2. Does *Reid v. Covert* prevent a court-martial from trying a civilian accompanying the force in the field, such as a cafeteria worker or truck mechanic who commits murder?

3. Clarice Covert killed her husband, a master sergeant in the Air Force, by striking him with an ax as he lay sleeping. Dorothy Smith, who happened to be the daughter of an Army General, killed her husband, an Army Colonel, by stabbing him with a knife while he slept. Both wives appeared to have psychiatric problems and the murders had nothing directly to do with their husband's military service. Imagine, however, that the facts were different and that the wives had committed crimes such as espionage on the military or murder for the purpose of sabotaging a military mission. Could a court-martial try them in such circumstances?

4. This case is said to be the only case in which the Supreme Court overruled its previous judgment on rehearing. It was successfully litigated by Frederick Bernays Wiener, a retired Army judge advocate and distinguished legal scholar at George Washington University, who gained considerable renown for this accomplishment.

In *Reid v. Covert,* the plurality opinion observes that people of England were outraged that Charles I had used courts-martial to try soldiers for non-military offenses during peacetime. This practice, however, occurs constantly in the United States. The military prosecutes soldiers for crimes that have no military connection and that take place not on any military premises. For example, if a soldier left the garrison, went into town in civilian clothes and used illegal drugs in a private home, he could be tried by a court-martial. Is this constitutional? In *O'Callahan v. Parker,* 395 U.S. 258 (1969), the Supreme Court said that service members could be tried by court-martial only for service-related crimes. But *O'Callahan* was overruled in the following case:

SOLORIO v. UNITED STATES
U.S. Supreme Court
483 U.S. 435 (1987)

Chief Justice REHNQUIST delivered the opinion of the Court.

This case presents the question whether the jurisdiction of a court-martial convened pursuant to the Uniform Code of Military Justice (U.C.M.J.) to try a member of the Armed Forces depends on the "service connection" of the offense charged. We hold that it does not, and overrule our earlier decision in *O'Callahan v. Parker*, 395 U.S. 258 (1969).

While petitioner Richard Solorio was on active duty in the Seventeenth Coast Guard District in Juneau, Alaska, he sexually abused two young daughters of fellow coastguardsmen. Petitioner engaged in this abuse over a 2-year period until he was transferred by the Coast Guard to Governors Island, New York. Coast Guard authorities learned of the Alaska crimes only after petitioner's transfer, and investigation revealed that he had later committed similar sexual abuse offenses while stationed in New York. The Governors Island commander convened a general court-martial to try petitioner for crimes alleged to have occurred in Alaska and New York.

There is no "base" or "post" where Coast Guard personnel live and work in Juneau. Consequently, nearly all Coast Guard military personnel reside in the civilian community. Petitioner's Alaska offenses were committed in his privately owned home, and the fathers of the 10- to 12-year-old victims in Alaska were active duty members of the Coast Guard assigned to the same command as petitioner. Petitioner's New York offenses also involved daughters of fellow coastguardsmen, but were committed in Government quarters on the Governors Island base.

After the general court-martial was convened in New York, petitioner moved to dismiss the charges for crimes committed in Alaska on the ground that the court lacked jurisdiction under this Court's decisions in *O'Callahan v. Parker* and *Relford v. Commandant, U.S. Disciplinary Barracks*, 401 U.S. 355 (1971). Ruling that the Alaska offenses were not sufficiently "service connected" to be tried in the military criminal justice system, the court-martial judge granted the motion to dismiss. The Government appealed the dismissal of the charges to the United States Coast Guard Court of Military Review, which reversed the trial judge's order and reinstated the charges.

The United States Court of Military Appeals affirmed the Court of Military Review, concluding that the Alaska offenses were service connected within the meaning of *O'Callahan* and *Relford*. 21 M.J. 251 (1986). Stating that "not every off-base offense against a servicemember's dependent is service-connected," the court reasoned that "sex offenses against young children . . . have a continuing effect on the victims and their families and ultimately on the morale of any military unit or organization to which the family member is assigned." . . . We now affirm.

The Constitution grants to Congress the power "[t]o make Rules for the Government and Regulation of the land and naval Forces." U.S. Const., Art. I, § 8, cl. 14. Exercising this authority, Congress has empowered courts-martial to try servicemen for the crimes proscribed by the U.C.M.J., Arts. 2, 17, 10 U.S.C. §§ 802, 817. The Alaska offenses with which petitioner was charged are each described in the U.C.M.J. Thus it is not disputed that the court-martial convened in New York possessed the statutory authority to try petitioner on the Alaska child abuse specifications.

In an unbroken line of decisions from 1866 to 1960, this Court interpreted the Constitution as conditioning the proper exercise of court-martial jurisdiction over an offense on one factor: the military status of the accused. *Gosa v. Mayden*, 413 U.S. 665, 673 (1973) (plurality opinion); *see Kinsella v. United States ex rel. Singleton*, 361 U.S. 234, 240-241, 243 (1960); *Reid v. Covert*, 354 U.S. 1, 22-23 (1957) (plurality opinion) . . . ; *cf. United States ex rel. Toth v. Quarles*, 350 U.S. 11, 15 (1955) . . . . This view was premised on what the Court described as the "natural meaning" of Art. I, § 8, cl. 14, as well as the Fifth Amendment's exception for "cases arising in the land or naval forces." *Reid v. Covert*, *supra*, 354 U.S., at 19; *United States ex rel. Toth v. Quarles*, *supra*, 350 U.S., at 15. As explained in *Kinsella v. Singleton, supra*:

> "The test for jurisdiction . . . is one of status, namely, whether the accused in the court-martial proceeding is a person who can be regarded as falling within the term 'land and naval Forces.'. . ." *Id.*, 361 U.S., at 240-241.

> "Without contradiction, the materials . . . show that military jurisdiction has always been based on the 'status' of the accused, rather than on the nature of the offense. To say that military jurisdiction 'defies definition in terms of military "status" ' is to defy the unambiguous language of Art. I, § 8, cl. 14, as well as the historical background thereof and the precedents with reference thereto." Id., at 243.

Implicit in the military status test was the principle that determinations concerning the scope of court-martial jurisdiction over offenses committed by servicemen was a matter reserved for Congress:

> "[T]he rights of men in the armed forces must perforce be conditioned to meet certain overriding demands of discipline and duty, and the civil courts are not the agencies which must determine the precise balance to be struck in this adjustment. The Framers expressly entrusted that task to Congress." *Burns v. Wilson*, 346 U.S. 137, 140 (1953) (plurality opinion) (footnote omitted).

In 1969, the Court in *O'Callahan v. Parker* departed from the military status test and announced the "new constitutional principle" that a military tribunal may not try a serviceman charged with a crime that has no service connection. *See Gosa v. Mayden*, *supra*, 361 U.S., at 673. Applying this principle, the *O'Callahan* Court held that a serviceman's off-base sexual assault on a civilian with no connection with the military could not be tried by court-martial. On reexamination of *O'Callahan*, we have decided that the service connection test announced in that decision should be abandoned.

The constitutional grant of power to Congress to regulate the Armed Forces, Art. I, § 8, cl. 14, appears in the same section as do the provisions granting Congress authority, inter alia, to regulate commerce among the several States, to coin money, and to declare war. On its face there is no indication that the grant of power in Clause 14 was any less plenary than the grants of other authority to Congress in the same section. Whatever doubts there might be about the extent of Congress' power under Clause 14 to make rules for the "Government and Regulation of the land and naval Forces," that power surely embraces the authority to regulate the conduct of persons who are actually members of the Armed Services. As noted by Justice Harlan in his *O'Callahan* dissent, there is no evidence in the debates over the adoption of the Constitution that the Framers intended the language of Clause 14 to be accorded anything other than its plain meaning. Alexander Hamilton described these powers of Congress "essential to the common defense" as follows:

> "These powers ought to exist without limitation, because it is impossible to foresee or define the extent and variety of national exigencies, or the correspondent extent and variety of the means which may be necessary to satisfy them. . . .

> * * *

> ". . . Are fleets and armies and revenues necessary for this purpose [common safety]? The government of the Union must be empowered to pass all laws, and to make all regulations which have relation to them." *The Federalist* No. 23, pp. 152-154 (E. Bourne ed. 1947).

The O'Callahan Court's historical foundation for its holding rests on the view that "[b]oth in England prior to the American Revolution and in our own national history military trial of soldiers committing civilian offenses has been viewed with suspicion." 395 U.S., at 268. According to the Court, the historical evidence demonstrates that, during the late 17th and 18th centuries in England as well as the early years of this country, courts-martial did not have authority to try soldiers for civilian offenses. . . .

The *O'Callahan* Court's representation of English history following the Mutiny Act of 1689, however, is less than accurate. In particular, the Court posited that "[i]t was . . . the rule in Britain at the time of the American Revolution that a soldier could not be tried for a civilian offense committed in Britain; instead military officers were required to use their energies and office to insure that the accused soldier would be tried before a civil court." 395 U.S., at 269. In making this statement, the Court was apparently referring to Section XI, Article I, of the British Articles of War in effect at the time of the Revolution. This Article provided:

> "Whenever any Officer or Soldier shall be accused of a Capital Crime, or of having used Violence, or committed any Offence against the Persons or Property of Our Subjects, . . . the Commanding Officer, and Officers of every Regiment, Troop, or Party to which the . . . accused shall belong, are hereby required, upon Application duly made by, or in behalf of the Party or Parties injured, to use . . . utmost Endeavors to deliver over such accused . . . to the Civil Magistrate." British Articles of War of 1774, reprinted in G. Davis, *Military Law of the United States* 581, 589 (3d rev. ed. 1915).

This provision, however, is not the sole statement in the Articles bearing on court-martial jurisdiction over civilian offenses. Specifically, Section XIV, Article XVI, provided that all officers and soldiers who

"shall maliciously destroy any Property whatsoever belonging to any of Our Subjects, unless by Order of the then Commander in Chief of Our Forces, to annoy Rebels or other Enemies in Arms against Us, he or they that shall be found guilty of offending herein shall (besides such Penalties as they are liable to by law) be punished according to the Nature and Degree of the Offence, by the Judgment of a Regimental or General Court Martial." *Id.*, at 593.

Under this provision, military tribunals had jurisdiction over offenses punishable under civil law. Accordingly, the O'Callahan Court erred in suggesting that, at the time of the American Revolution, military tribunals in England were available "only where ordinary civil courts were unavailable." 395 U.S., at 269, and n. 11.

The history of early American practice furnishes even less support to *O'Callahan's* historical thesis. The American Articles of War of 1776, which were based on the British Articles, contained a provision similar to Section XI, Article I, of the British Articles, requiring commanding officers to deliver over to civil magistrates any officer or soldier accused of "a capital crime, . . . having used violence, or . . . any offence against the persons or property of the good people of any of the United American States" upon application by or on behalf of an injured party. It has been postulated that American courts-martial had jurisdiction over the crimes described in this provision where no application for a civilian trial was made by or on behalf of the injured civilian. Indeed, American military records reflect trials by court-martial during the late 18th century for offenses against civilians and punishable under civil law, such as theft and assault.

The authority to try soldiers for civilian crimes may be found in the much-disputed "general article" of the 1776 Articles of War, which allowed court-martial jurisdiction over "[a]ll crimes not capital, and all disorders and neglects which officers and soldiers may be guilty of, to the prejudice of good order and military discipline." American Articles of War of 1776, Section XVIII, Article 5. Some authorities, such as those cited by the *O'Callahan* Court, interpreted this language as limiting court-martial jurisdiction to crimes that had a direct impact on military discipline. Several others, however, have interpreted the language as encompassing all noncapital crimes proscribed by the civil law. . . .

George Washington also seems to have held this view. When informed of the decision of a military court that a complaint by a civilian against a member of the military should be redressed only in a civilian court, he stated in a General Order dated February 24, 1779:

"All improper treatment of an inhabitant by an officer or soldier being destructive of good order and discipline as well as subversive of the rights of society is as much a breach of military, as civil law and as punishable by the one as the other." 14 *Writings of George Washington* 140-141 (J. Fitzpatrick ed. 1936).

We think the history of court-martial jurisdiction in England and in this country during the 17th and 18th centuries is far too ambiguous to justify the restriction on the plain language of Clause 14 which *O'Callahan* imported into it. There is no doubt that the English practice during this period shows a strong desire in that country to transfer from the Crown to Parliament the control of the scope of court-martial jurisdiction. And it is equally true that Parliament was chary in granting jurisdiction to courts-martial, although not as chary as the *O'Callahan* opinion suggests. But reading Clause 14 consistently with its plain language does not disserve that concern; Congress, and not the Executive, was given the authority to make rules for the regulation of the Armed Forces.

* * *

When considered together with the doubtful foundations of *O'Callahan*, the confusion wrought by the decision leads us to conclude that we should read Clause 14 in accord with the plain meaning of its language as we did in the many years before *O'Callahan* was decided. That case's novel approach to court-martial jurisdiction must bow "to the lessons of experience and the force of better reasoning." *Burnet v. Coronado Oil & Gas Co.*, 285 U.S. 393, 406-408 (1932) (Brandeis, J., dissenting). We therefore hold that the requirements of the Constitution are not violated where, as here, a court-martial* is convened to try a serviceman who was a member of the Armed Services at the time of the offense charged. The judgment of the Court of Military Appeals is

Affirmed.

Justice STEVENS, concurring in the judgment.

Today's unnecessary overruling of precedent is most unwise. The opinion of the United States Court of Military Appeals demonstrates that petitioner's offenses were sufficiently "service connected" to confer jurisdiction on the military tribunal. . . .

Justice MARSHALL, with whom Justice BRENNAN joins, and with whom Justice BLACKMUN joins . . . .

* * *

The requirement of service connection recognized in *O'Callahan* has a legitimate basis in constitutional language and a solid historical foundation. It should be applied in this case.

* * *

Points for Discussion

1. If a court-martial could not try soldiers for crimes that are not service-related, could they still be tried by some other court?

2. What advantages and disadvantages did the *O'Callahan* decision have for soldiers and the Armed Forces?

3. Could Congress by statute strip courts-martial of jurisdiction to try service members for crimes that are not service related? If so, why might Congress not have done so?

Overlapping Jurisdiction

Service members who commit crimes in the United States potentially could face prosecution in any of three different court systems. For example, suppose that Army Private Pogie sells marijuana in Virginia. He could be prosecuted in a court-martial for violating Article 112a, UCMJ. Alternatively, he could be prosecuted in federal court for violating federal anti-narcotics laws applicable to all persons within the United States. In addition, he could be prosecuted in Virginia state court for violating a Virginia state anti-narcotics law. Private Pogie's status as a service member does not exempt him from the application of any federal or state laws.

That said, it is most likely that Private Pogie would be tried in a court-martial. The Department of Justice and the Department of Defense have entered into a memorandum of understanding, reprinted in Appendix 3 of the *Manual for Courts-Martial*, that establishes a presumption that service members will be tried in courts-martial rather than federal district court for crimes usually prosecuted under the UCMJ. The Fifth Amendment's prohibition against Double Jeopardy prevents a service member from being tried by both a federal district court and a court-martial.

Most state prosecutors are eager to allow military prosecutors to bring cases against service members. But nothing prevents state prosecution of a service member for violating state law. Indeed, because the states and federal government are separate sovereigns, a service member could be tried in both a state court and court-martial for the same offense without violating the prohibition against double-jeopardy. Although dual prosecutions are rare, they do happen. Consider the following case:

UNITED STATES v. SCHNEIDER
U.S. Army Court of Military Review
34 M.J. 639 (A.C.M.R. 1992)

De GIULIO, Senior Judge:

Appellant [Major David P. Schneider, U.S. Army] was tried by general court-martial for attempted murder of his wife and two specifications of conduct unbecoming an officer and a gentleman by committing perjury and by having sexual intercourse with and otherwise engaging in a sexual or other improper affair with a woman not his wife in violation of Articles 80 and 133, Uniform Code of Military Justice, 10 U.S.C. §§ 880 and 933 (1982) [hereinafter UCMJ]. Contrary to his pleas, a court consisting of officer members found him guilty and sentenced him to dismissal, confinement for twenty-three years, and total forfeitures. The convening authority approved the sentence except that he conditionally suspended the forfeiture in excess of $400.00 pay per month until execution of the dismissal.

Appellant asserts several errors which we find to be without merit. We affirm the findings of guilty and the sentence.

This is a case where the offenses were motivated by love and money. In 1987, appellant was assigned to the Lawrence Livermore National Laboratory in California. He moved to the area with his wife and two children. While working at the laboratory, he met Paula, with whom he worked for a time on a daily basis. In August 1987, Paula's friends asked Paula, the appellant, and appellant's family to accompany them on a boat trip. Appellant indicated that his wife and children would not go because his wife feared for the safety of the children but, if permitted, he would go. During the boat trip which lasted overnight, appellant and Paula shared adjoining quarters at the opposite end of the boat from where the other passengers were quartered. In April of 1989, according to Paula, her relationship with appellant became sexual and intimate. [2]

In July 1989, appellant told his wife that he had to go on a mission for the laboratory; but, due to its classified nature, he could not tell her of its location, other details, or point of contact for emergencies. In fact, appellant and Paula traveled to Hawaii where they stayed together in the King Kamehameha Hotel, Kailua, Hawaii.

In 1989, appellant was assigned to attend the U.S. Army Command and General Staff College, Fort Leavenworth, Kansas. At Fort Leavenworth, he moved his family into government quarters. In August 1989, he met with an insurance agent. Although the agent recommended appellant increase insurance coverage on himself, appellant declined to do so but stated he wanted an additional $150,000 coverage on his wife, Debbie. This policy, with appellant as the beneficiary, was effective 1 October 1989.

In the fall of 1989, appellant purchased a home in Tracey, California. He convinced Debbie that her name should not be on the title. He used the proceeds from the sale of the family home near his prior assignment for the purchase of this house. He told her that he had to go to California to take care of details of this purchase over Labor Day weekend of 1989. He spent that weekend with Paula. Paula told a friend that it was the best weekend of her life.

---

[2] Paula did not testify at the court-martial because she could not be found. Her prior testimony at appellant's state criminal trial was admitted into evidence. It is evident from that testimony that she was re-luctant to testify and had refused to talk to prosecutors before she testified.

Numerous telephone calls were made between appellant at Fort Leavenworth and Paula in California.

After returning home from a party on the evening of 20 October 1989,
Debbie went to bed and fell asleep. She awoke with intense pain in her head
and was pulled up to a sitting position on the bed. She saw appellant standing
next to the bed. The toilet tank lid from the bathroom was on the floor near
his feet. The toilet tank lid was broken. She felt a baseball-sized lump on her
head. The lump was "oozing."

She brushed small pieces of porcelain from her hair. She described appellant, who was normally calm and cool in time of crisis, as visibly shaken. He
stated repeatedly, "you must have hit your head." Appellant assisted her to
the bathroom where she sat on the toilet. When she began shaking, he helped
her to the bathroom floor and covered her with a quilt. He wanted to take her
for medical attention but she wanted only to go back to bed. He assisted her
to the bed. The next morning, he took her to the medical facility. When asked
what had happened to her head, appellant stated to medical personnel that
Debbie was sleepwalking, picked up the toilet tank lid, tripped, and hit her
head. The statement that she was injured while sleepwalking was recorded on
medical documents. Evidence of record indicates appellant's wife had never
walked in her sleep. When she returned home, Debbie found small pieces of
the toilet tank lid on her pillow. This incident was the subject of the specification alleging attempted murder.

On 28 October 1989, appellant took his wife for a "romantic" overnight
stay in a local downtown hotel. The room was on the top floor. After dinner
he tried to get her to drink more champagne than she normally consumed.
After they went to their room, appellant tried to get her out on the balcony.
She refused because it was too cold and because she was afraid of heights.

On 4 November 1989, appellant and his wife were to attend the Armor
Ball. Without her knowledge, appellant made arrangements for another "romantic" night at Embassy Suites Hotel. She discovered his plans when the
babysitter told him she could not stay overnight. Appellant decided to go to
the hotel after the ball anyway but to return home early. At the ball Debbie
enjoyed the dancing and only left early to go to the hotel at appellant's insist-
ence. Although ap-pellant had asked for an eighth floor room when making
reservations, he was given a room on the seventh floor.

Two sixteen-year-old girls, Chantel and Brandi, who were on the eighth
floor, observed appellant and his wife when they entered the hotel. They were
attracted to the couple because of their "extravagant attire." They watched
appellant and his wife ride the glass elevator to the eighth floor and watched
them walk side by side down the hallway. Brandi looked away. Chantel saw
appellant make vigorous hand movements in front of his wife as she faced
him with her back to the rail. She observed appellant put his left arm around
Debbie where the rail met her back, put his right hand on her chest, and flip
her over the rail. Chantel watched Debbie plunge 70-80 feet and hit a table on

the atrium floor.[3] Chantel watched appellant look over the railing, walk toward the elevator, walk back to the railing and call for someone to call an ambulance. He then walked back to the elevator and proceeded down. Testimony indicates that appellant's conduct when he reached the atrium floor can be described as cool and collected. Debbie's pelvis was fractured in thirteen places. Both left and right femurs were broken in several places, with one bone penetrating her abdominal cavity, damaging her colon. She also had a fractured ankle and a fractured rib. Her colon injury required a temporary colostomy. While his wife was being wheeled into the operating room, he asked the doctor to give her a "tummy tuck." Debbie's roommate at the hospital and the roommate's mother described appellant's attitude toward his wife while she was hospitalized as cool and distant. He was also described as a "jerk" in his attitude toward his wife.

On 2 December 1989, Debbie returned home from the hospital confined to a wheelchair. On 4 December, appellant told her that he didn't love her anymore and was getting a divorce. On 5 December, in an interview with local police, appellant admitted having an affair with Paula, stated he loved her and hoped to marry her when his divorce was final. On 6 December, appellant filed for divorce. Later, appellant was charged by local authorities with first degree assault for the incident at the Embassy Suites Hotel on 4 November. On 18 December, appellant moved to have his petition for divorce dismissed.

At his trial for attempted murder in state court, appellant testified that, at the Embassy Suites Hotel, they mistakenly went to the eighth floor. He told his wife that he wanted to carry her across the threshold. He picked her up and was carrying her at high port when she told him they were in the wrong place. He turned and in doing so tripped. His wife slipped from his grasp, causing her to fall over the balcony railing to the atrium floor. He testified that he did not intend to injure his wife. Appellant was acquitted of this offense in the state court.

At the state trial, appellant also testified regarding the October toilet tank lid incident. He stated that his wife went to bed, and he stayed up to do his school homework. Before he went to bed, he noted the toilet was running. He removed the tank lid and set it down against the cabinet. He fixed the toilet but decided to leave the tank lid off. He then went to bed and to sleep. He was awakened by a motion on the bed or noise. His wife was sitting on the bed, moaning, with her hand to her head. He got up to go to her but stepped on something. When he turned on the light, he discovered it to be "shards of obviously pieces of the toilet tank lid." She complained her head hurt, but upon his inquiry stated she didn't know what had happened. He stated that it was clear to him that she had hurt herself somehow. He helped her to the bathroom where she started to go into shock. He sat her on the toilet and turned on the faucet in the tub, in case he needed water. He then wrapped her in a blanket and checked to see if she could discern the number of fingers he held

---

[3] Debbie has no memory of this event from the time she entered the hotel.

before her. He wanted to take her to the hospital but she refused. He concluded she did not have a fracture, gave her aspirin, and took her to bed. He testified at his state trial that he told personnel at the hospital that, "She was probably sleepwalking. I don't know or words to that effect." He testified, "I don't believe I would have told them she was sleepwalking, 'cause Debbie has never sleptwalked, and so I wouldn't say that."

* * *

. . . [A]ppellant contends that the military judge erred by denying a motion to dismiss the specification of perjury because it violated appellant's right against double jeopardy. Appellant's argument is that his testimony in his state court trial went to the heart of the issue of the offense for which he was tried and was determined favorable to him. Thus, he argues, the government is collaterally estopped from charging appellant with perjury for his testimony. We do not agree with appellant that double jeopardy applies here.

The doctrine of collateral estoppel has not been applied in military criminal law. *United States v. Cuellar*, 27 M.J. 50 (C.M.A. 1988), *cert. denied*, 493 U.S. 811 (1989). We see no reason to apply it here. Additionally, prosecution of an offense in state court does not normally bar a federal prosecution of the same criminal matter. *Heath v. Alabama*, 474 U.S. 82 (1985); *Bartkus v. Illinois*, 359 U.S. 121 (1959); *United States v. Lanza*, 260 U.S. 377 (1922). We find no merit in this assertion of error.

* * *

The findings of guilty and the sentence are affirmed.

Judge HAESSIG and Judge ARKOW concur.

[The Court of Military Appeals affirmed this decision, 38 M.J. 387 (C.M.A. 1993), and the Supreme Court denied certiorari, 511 U.S. 1106 (1994).—Eds.]

Points for Discussion

1. Why do you think both state and military authorities wanted to prosecute Major Schneider? Is it unfair that he must face two prosecutions?

2. Could the court-martial have tried appellant for attempted murder even though he was acquitted of this offense in state court? If so, why was he not charged with this offense?

3. Would it make any difference if the accused was acquitted of capital murder in state court and then was recalled from retirement to face capital charges at a court-martial? *See Hennis v. Hemlick,* 2012 WL 120054 (4th Cir. 2012).

1-4. Role of the Commander and Unlawful Command Influence

The Military Justice system rests on two key postulates that are not inherently in conflict, but that may collide in some instances. The first postulate, clearly and concisely articulated by the President in the *Manual for Courts-*

Martial, is: "Commanders are responsible for good order and discipline in their commands." MCM, pt. V, ¶1.d.(1). The second postulate, expressed by Congress directly in the UCMJ, is: "No person subject to [the UCMJ] may attempt to coerce or, by any unauthorized means, influence the action of a court-martial or any other military tribunal or any member thereof . . . ." Article 37, UCMJ, 10 U.S.C. § 837(a).

① By Pres.

② Congress in UCMJ

The first postulate rests on the idea that a fighting force will be ineffective and perhaps dangerous unless it obeys orders and deports itself in a controlled manner. The only person who can achieve good order and discipline is the unit's commander. The commander accomplishes this difficult task primarily through strong leadership and effective drills and training. But these measures are not always enough. When service members commit serious misconduct, the commander may decide that it is necessary to invoke the military justice system. Crimes that go unprosecuted may lead to other wrongdoing, and the breakdown of all order in the unit.

① Analysis

The second postulate rests on the idea that the military justice system must be just. A court-martial must be a real court, where guilt or innocence is determined by disinterested judges and panel members based solely on the facts and the law. Nothing could harm morale more, and in turn frustrate the mission of a military unit, than a belief among service members that they may be punished for acts they did not commit or that they may be treated overly harshly for crimes they did commit.

② Analysis

A potential conflict may arise because of the hierarchical nature of military life. It is not difficult to imagine that, without constant vigilance, subordinate participants in the military justice system could be influenced by their superiors, resulting in unfairness to the accused. The general or admiral who convenes a court-martial in the belief that a prosecution is necessary typically is senior in rank to the military judge and the military lawyers involved in the trial, is senior in rank to all of the witnesses who are to testify, and is senior in rank to all of the officers and enlisted members who sit in judgment of the accused. The system must provide protections so that everyone involved is not improperly influenced from those above.

The military justice system attempts to prevent this conflict in several ways. It makes improper command influence a crime. It pushes the initial decisions on how to address misconduct to the lowest level. As described above, the service member's immediate commander decides in the first instance how to address alleged misconduct. The immediate commander can forward the matter to a superior commander, or the superior commander can take the case from the immediate commander, but the superior commander cannot tell the immediate commander what to do. There also can be no service-wide or unit-wide prosecutorial policies.

How well do these measures work? In general, most observers consider the military justice system to be fair. Occasionally, however, allegations of misconduct arise. The following cases clarify the standards and provide modern illustrations.

UNITED STATES v. BIAGASE
U.S. Court of Appeals for the Armed Forces
50 M.J. 143 (C.A.A.F. 1999)

Judge GIERKE delivered the opinion of the Court.

A general court-martial composed of officer and enlisted members convicted appellant [Keith J. Bagase, Lance Corporal, U.S. Marine Corps], contrary to his pleas, of attempted robbery (2 specifications), conspiracy to commit robbery (2 specifications), robbery (3 specifications), and assault consummated by a battery, in violation of Articles 80, 81, 122, and 128, Uniform Code of Military Justice, 10 U.S.C. §§ 880, 881, 922, and 928, respectively. The court-martial sentenced appellant to a bad-conduct discharge, confinement for 15 years, total forfeitures, and reduction to the lowest enlisted grade. The convening authority approved the sentence but suspended confinement in excess of 7 years for 4 years from the date of his action. The Court of Criminal Appeals affirmed the findings and sentence in an unpublished opinion.

Factual Background

Appellant was apprehended as one of several suspects in a series of beatings and robberies. He was interviewed by agents of the Naval Criminal Investigative Service (NCIS), and he gave them a detailed confession admitting his involvement in one of the incidents. In his confession, he admitted conspiring with a group of fellow Marines to "jack people . . . because it sounded fun." He defined the term "jack" as follows:

> When I say "jack people" I mean that we beat them up, kick them or whatever we have to do until they are hurt pretty bad and do not resist us any more. After the people are down, laying on the ground and cannot resist because we hurt them, we take their money or whatever else we want to take.

Appellant admitted being one of a group of seven black Marines who surrounded four "white guys" and "jacked" them.

At his court-martial, appellant made a timely motion to dismiss all charges and specifications on the grounds of unlawful command influence. His defense counsel asserted that, shortly after appellant confessed, copies of his confession were circulated within his unit, and references were made to his confession in unit formations. The defense asserted that the actions by appellant's command had a chilling effect on potential defense witnesses that made a fair trial impossible. The defense further asserted that the potential witnesses could testify to appellant's good military character. The defense did not assert that any substantive witnesses, i.e., eyewitnesses to the incident, were deterred from testifying.

In support of the motion to dismiss, two witnesses were called by the defense. Staff Sergeant (SSgt) Lawson, the noncommissioned officer-in-charge (NCOIC) of appellant's duty section, testified that he learned about the "jacking" incident on the Monday after it happened. He was "pretty distraught-overwhelmed," and "couldn't really believe that it happened." He felt that it was his fault that one of his Marines was in trouble. He visited the senior NCO in the company, First Sergeant (1stSgt) Bressler, who "consoled" him and "tried to convey to [him] that it wasn't really [his] fault." The first sergeant told SSgt Lawson that he wanted him to hold a formation and "let the Marines know that Marines don't do these types of things." The first sergeant gave him a copy of appellant's confession.

SSgt Lawson testified that his section, the bulk storage section, had a formation every Tuesday. As platoon sergeant, he ordinarily held the formation. Because of "the magnitude of this incident," he asked Master Sergeant (MSgt) Stanton, the senior staff NCOIC, to discuss the incident. SSgt Lawson was not present when MSgt Stanton talked about it.

SSgt Lawson testified that no one tried to intimidate him or prevent him from testifying for appellant. He testified:

> I never thought that it would affect my career-in any way, shape, or form affect my career. But perhaps it would affect the way people—some people thought of me as a person and as a staff NCO. Even though they would have never said it or would have affected my career on paper, but just the way people thought of me.

SSgt Lawson was asked if his officer-in-charge (OIC), Chief Warrant Officer (CWO) Harris, had made any comments about appellant. He testified that CWO Harris did not know appellant, but based solely on the statement, he thought that she would consider him a "thug or a punk."

LCpl Calloway testified that he worked with appellant, and that appellant had taught him how to do his job in the hazardous materials section. LCpl Calloway testified that, immediately after appellant was placed in pretrial confinement, "people from privates all the way up to staff NCOs" began to talk about what had happened. LCpl Calloway testified that 1stSgt Bressler talked about appellant's confession at a unit formation, quoting from the statement with words like "jack," "beat down," and "robbed," and telling the Marines, "I'm not going to tolerate this kind of stuff."

LCpl Calloway testified that he was reluctant to testify when first approached by defense counsel, because he thought that if he helped appellant, "it might be harder for me here." During direct examination, he did not elaborate on the basis for his reluctance.

On cross-examination, LCpl Calloway testified that he already knew appellant was "in trouble" when he attended the formation at which the "jacking" incident was discussed. He testified that no one threatened any repercussions if he testified. When asked to explain why he was initially reluctant to testify, he testified that he thought "maybe [his] leave might be cancelled or, you know, someone might say, well, he did that so, you know-and something of that matter." He testified that some members of the section read appellant's statement and decided not to help him, believing that "he gets what he deserves." He testified that most of the Marines in his section "don't want to have anything with it just because of the way the statement was read out and the things they read." He testified, "[H]alf the people that work in my section, they wouldn't have anything to do with it."

LCpl Calloway testified that someone in his shop had a copy of appellant's statement, and it was discussed by most of the 90 people in the shop. He described their reaction to appellant's statement as follows:

> And it was like they were upset because they knew that he couldn't say anything, you know—he wouldn't say anything like that. And even if he did, it was so dismal for him just to turn himself in and then say what he said, you know. It made them upset. And then you had other people who don't know him who really believe he did all that stuff, and it's weird. It's messed up.

On examination by the military judge, LCpl Calloway testified that those who did not know appellant before the incident did not want anything to do with him, but those who knew appellant and had favorable opinions were willing to come forward. LCpl Calloway testified that, when the statement was disclosed, he felt that "the command" would look unfavorably on those who were trying to help appellant. He explained that, when he said "the command," he meant "Top Stanton, maybe the First Sergeant, the Captain, Chief Warrant Officer Harris." He explained further that he thought the command might disapprove of testifying for appellant because the command had talked about "how stupid it was and how racial and violent it was," causing LCpl Calloway to think that, if he tried to help appellant, the command might think that he "just want[s] to be like him." Notwithstanding his initial reluctance, LCpl Calloway told the military judge that, if he testified for appellant, he was not concerned that his command would rate him less favorably or make it hard on him.

After LCpl Calloway and SSgt Lawson testified, the military judge sua sponte directed that Captain (Capt) Fuhs, 1stSgt Bressler, MSgt Stanton, and CWO Harris be produced to testify.

Capt Fuhs, appellant's company commander, testified that the incident to which appellant confessed occurred on a weekend. The NCIS delivered a copy of the confession to the Battalion Officer of the Day (OOD), who called Capt Fuhs at his quarters. Capt Fuhs took a copy of the confession home, notified his executive officer of the incident, and on Monday, he made a copy of the statement and gave it to 1stSgt Bressler. He told 1stSgt Bressler that he could use the statement, with the name and social security number blacked out, "to teach the staff NCOs about what's going on with our Marines." He told 1stSgt Bressler to "get the word out . . . that this type of behavior will not be tolerated within this command." Capt Fuhs testified that, at the weekly company formation, he told his Marines that "we had a Marine that did something that Marines do not do, and we will not tolerate this type of behavior." He quoted the portion of the statement reciting that "they thought it would be fun to go out and jack somebody up," and told his Marines that he "was appalled and disgusted . . . by just that type of an attitude of a U.S. Marine." Capt Fuhs testified that, in a discussion with his noncommissioned officers (NCOs) and section heads, he told them that "any Marine that would portray this type of behavior does not deserve to wear the uniform."

Capt Fuhs testified that he had "no personal dealings" with appellant and had "no personal opinion as to his military character," but that he formed an opinion after reading appellant's confession. He testified that, after reading the confession, he "was disgusted by the behavior."

1stSgt Bressler testified that, after his discussion with Capt Fuhs, he talked with two of the senior enlisted Marines in the unit, Master Gunnery Sergeant (MGSgt) Wright and MGSgt Truelove. He told them that he "felt there was a void in some type of leadership." He testified that he "was concerned that maybe something went wrong, and it was leadership." He made "a couple copies" of the statement, one for CWO Harris, the OIC of appellant's duty section, and one for "the master gunny."

At a regularly scheduled formation, 1stSgt Bressler had "a school circle," at which he addressed "a number of things," including the "jacking" incident. 1stSgt Bressler described the formation as follows:

> And basically at the formation I said that people hearing that type of terminology [referring to "jacking"] as good sorts or good Marines are more-have a responsibility to talk to their fellow neighbors about that type of behavior or that type of language, number one; and number two, that I was available to help anybody with problems or-someone that thought that they might have to conduct this type of behavior or this type of language-and that we need to get in touch as Marines with each other and the environment we live in because I felt a void.

> I was astonished that-how could a Marine that-I mean, I had never heard [appellant's] name before in our company be allegedly involved in something like this, and no one can tell me or give me any information on it. I mean, how can we let that happen? So, I felt that I needed to tell everybody you're not in touch. I mean, we need to get-be more aware of what's happening around us and with each other, and that was basically the point of it, sir.

Although 1stSgt Bressler did not mention appellant by name, he testified that he thought "a few people there probably knew who I was talking about," particularly those Marines from appellant's section. By this time, appellant was not present for duty, having been placed in pretrial confinement.

1stSgt Bressler testified that he did not "personally know" appellant before the incident. He testified that, after reading appellant's confession, he "was a little embarrassed." He reacted to the confession by thinking, "I guess we have a problem. Let's see how we can set out to fix it." Asked about the impact of the confession on his opinion of appellant, the first sergeant testified that he did not think any more or less of appellant, because he "didn't even recognize the name."

CWO Harris testified that she was uncertain how she learned about the incident involving appellant, but she thought it might have been from one of her senior staff NCOs, "because usually that's how they come in." She never received a copy of appellant's statement, but saw a copy with appellant's name blacked out. She admitted that she probably had told SSgt Lawson that she thought appellant was a thug. CWO Harris was asked if she thought her comment might have intimidated SSgt Lawson from testifying. She responded as follows:

> In the case of Staff Sergeant Lawson, no, sir, because the only reason I said what I said was because of what Staff Sergeant Lawson said first. Staff Sergeant Lawson, as I said, thinks Lance Corporal Biagase's impeccable . . . .

Asked if she might have indirectly intimidated SSgt Lawson, she responded in the negative, "because I know Staff Sergeant Lawson." She explained that, if she had been speaking to a Marine who "was a little weak," her comment may have been intimidating, but she did not think she swayed SSgt Lawson.

CWO Harris testified that her evaluation of any Marines whom she rated would not be affected by the fact that they testified on appellant's behalf. She testified that her opinion of appellant, based on the information in his confession, "[was] totally irrelevant to what anybody else above me or below me thinks." She testified that she did not know appellant "whatsoever."

MSgt Stanton testified that, when he learned about the incident and saw appellant's confession, he did not believe it, because "until the incident, he was one of the best Marines I had." At the regularly scheduled formation, he told his Marines "that the military really couldn't tolerate situations like that because it was unbecoming." He told them that "when they go out in town, they got to conduct themselves as Marines." MSgt Stanton did not have a copy of appellant's confession at the formation, but "just went off the top of [his] head." He did not mention appellant, but he believed that the Marines knew he was talking about appellant, because "everybody already knew he was in the brig." MSgt Stanton testified that he did not feel "in any way reluctant" to express his favorable opinion of appellant. He did not believe that any of his superiors would affect his fitness reports if he testified favorably for appellant.

After the witnesses on the motion to dismiss had testified, the military judge asked defense counsel if any witnesses had refused to testify. Defense counsel responded that no witnesses had refused, but that the dissemination of appellant's statement by the command "definitely had an impact on them" by painting appellant as a "bad character," even before the trial began.

The military judge denied the motion to dismiss. His explanation of the basis for his ruling included the following comments:

> Certainly I do not deem it appropriate that a statement of an accused be Xeroxed, somehow reproduced, and provided to various members of the command even though it may have been with good intentions; that is, even though it may have been for the purpose, as has been expressed here, to teach others of the kind of conduct that should not be tolerated. . . . However, after having heard all of the evidence to include that by the potential witnesses on behalf of the defense and the questioning by both counsel as well as that by myself, I believe the government has likewise sustained its burden by clear and convincing evidence that unlawful command influence did not, in fact, exist.

> I am satisfied beyond a reasonable doubt that there has been no unlawful command influence in this case based on everything that I have heard.

The military judge then directed that Capt Fuhs, 1stSgt Bressler, CWO Harris, MSgt Stanton, and SSgt Lawson be brought into the courtroom, where he chastised them for distributing and commenting on appellant's statement in unit formations. The military judge's comments included the following:

> Ladies and gentlemen, I have, after a lot of searching, denied a defense motion for unlawful command influence. I do not believe that there has been unlawful command influence. That is not to say that I do believe things were done properly. I believe that you have come carelessly close to compromising the judicial integrity of these proceedings, and I want to make sure that all of you understand that this is a Federal Court of the United States, and I will not under any circumstances tolerate anybody that even remotely attempts to compromise the integrity of these proceedings . . . .

> [A]nd although I have denied the motion, I am going to take some remedial action. I am directing and ordering at this time that with regard to anyone who testified on behalf of Lance Corporal Biagase that First Sergeant Bressler be removed from their reporting chain, that he have no influence whatsoever over the fitness reports or pro/con marks or any evaluation of anybody that testifies in these proceedings. Second of all, anyone who testifies in these proceedings on behalf of Lance Corporal Biagase, if their pro/con marks or fitness report or evaluation of any sort is lower than it was on their last reporting period, I am directing that written justification be attached to that.

The military judge further announced that he would allow the defense "a great deal of latitude" during voir dire of prospective court members, and would liberally grant challenges for cause. Finally, he told the assembled members of appellant's command:

Additionally, if there are witnesses which the defense desires be called on behalf of Lance Corporal Biagase that you are aware of that have otherwise been reluctant to testify out of fear or concern for their professional well being, I will issue a blanket order to produce any such witness.

The Court of Criminal Appeals came to the same conclusion as the military judge, stating that it was "convinced beyond a reasonable doubt that unlawful command influence, actual or apparent, did not exist," and concluding further that, "[e]ven assuming, arguendo, that unlawful command influence existed, we are convinced beyond a reasonable doubt that neither the findings nor the sentence were affected." Unpub. op. at 4-5.

Discussion

* * *

... [O]nce the issue of unlawful command influence is raised, the Government must prove beyond a reasonable doubt: (1) that the predicate facts do not exist; or (2) that the facts do not constitute unlawful command influence; or (3) that the unlawful command influence will not prejudice the proceedings or did not affect the findings and sentence. Accordingly, we hold that the military judge erred by applying the wrong legal test when he concluded that the prosecution had "sustained its burden by clear and convincing evidence that unlawful command influence did not, in fact, exist."

Notwithstanding the military judge's use of the wrong legal test, appellant is not entitled to relief. The prosecution did not dispute the predicate facts, i.e., that various members of the chain of command disclosed the details of appellant's confession to members of the unit at regularly scheduled formations, and expressed strong disapproval of the conduct described in appellant's confession. The prosecution did not dispute that, even though appellant's name was not disclosed, appellant's co-workers knew he was the person whose confession was being discussed. The military judge recognized that the command's pretrial condemnation of appellant's conduct had the potential to deter members of the command from coming forward and supporting appellant. He concluded that the defense had produced "some evidence," but expressed doubt whether it was sufficient to raise the issue of unlawful command influence.

SSgt Lawson testified that his concern about his credibility as a noncommissioned officer was based on his feeling of guilt about the adequacy of his leadership, and not as a result of command pressure. He testified unequivocally that no one tried to intimidate him or dissuade him from testifying.

On the other hand, LCpl Calloway was initially reluctant to testify, because he did not want his command to think that he wanted "to be like [appellant]." In short, he was afraid of guilt by association. His fear arose from the command's improper exploitation of appellant's confession. However, at the court-martial, he also testified that he was not concerned about any adverse action if he testified for appellant. He further testified that those Marines who did not know appellant before the incident did not want anything to do with him, but those Marines who had a favorable opinion of his conduct and performance before the incident were willing to come forward and testify.

The military judge ultimately concluded that the issue of unlawful command influence had been raised by the defense. Because we are satisfied beyond a reasonable doubt that the findings and sentence were unaffected, we need not review or disturb his ruling that the issue wasraised; nor do we find prejudice from his use of the wrong legal test.

* * *

The best indicator of the lack of prejudice is the fact that all the members of appellant's chain of command who knew him testified favorably. Four non-commissioned officers, MSgt Stanton, SSgt Lawson, Sgt Thomas, and Cpl Gibbs, all gave strong and favorable testimony on findings as well as sentence. The three members of his chain of command who did not testify for appellant (Capt Fuhs, 1stSgt Bressler, and CWO Harris) testified during the motion hearing that they had no personal knowledge of appellant's military qualities. LCpl Calloway, who testified on the motion to dismiss, expressed his willingness to testify during the motion hearing, but was not called as a character witness, for reasons not disclosed by the record. Defense counsel stated on the record that no witnesses had refused to testify. To date, appellant has proffered no evidence that any witnesses were deterred from testifying. Accordingly, we are satisfied beyond a reasonable doubt that the findings and sentence were untainted by unlawful command influence.

* * *

The decision of the United States Navy-Marine Corps Court of Criminal Appeals is affirmed.

SULLIVAN, Judge (concurring in the result):

* * *

. . . I agree with the result of the majority opinion. Its prejudice analysis shows beyond a reasonable doubt that appellant was not harmed by the misguided actions of his military superiors. The real hero in this case is the military judge, who took strong steps to insure (1) that the jury and witness pools were not poisoned; and (2) that appellant received a fair trial.

Points for Discussion

1. Commanders cannot be indifferent to crimes committed by members of their units. But they must be very careful about what they say. Commenting on the *Biagase* decision, then-Lieutenant Colonel Mark Johnson wrote: "If commanders must address [crime within a unit] they are reminded to talk about the offense, rather than the offender, and the process, rather than the result." Mark L. Johnson, *Unlawful Command Influence—Still with Us; Perspectives of the Chair in the Continuing Struggle against the "Mortal En-*

emy" of Military Justice, Army Lawyer, Jun. 2008, at 104, 111. What are examples of what commanders can say and cannot say?

2. Is there anything analogous to unlawful command influence in the civilian context? Could the mayor of a city urge citizens to be "tough on crime" when sitting on juries? How is the military different?

UNITED STATES v. BALDWIN
U.S. Court of Appeals for the Armed Forces
54 M.J. 308 (C.A.A.F. 2001)

Judge SULLIVAN delivered the opinion of the Court.

[handwritten: Cpt. Baldwin Δ]

During the fall of 1997 and in February of 1998, appellant [Captain Holly Baldwin, U.S. Army] was tried by a general court-martial composed of officer members at Fort Bliss, Texas. Contrary to her pleas, she was found guilty of two specifications of larceny, conduct unbecoming an officer, and two specifications of service-discrediting conduct (mail tampering and obstruction of justice), in violation of Articles 121, 133, and 134, Uniform Code of Military Justice, 10 U.S.C. §§ 921, 933, and 934, respectively. The military judge then dismissed the two larceny specifications as multiplicious with the remaining offenses, and the members sentenced appellant to a dismissal, 1 year's confinement, and total forfeitures on February 6, 1998. The convening authority on May 19, 1998, approved this sentence, and the Court of Criminal Appeals affirmed on October 1, 1999.

[handwritten left margin: Found guilty of conduct unbecoming officer & mail tampering & obstruction of justice.]

On May 19, 2000, this Court granted review on the following [issue] of law:

[handwritten: (I)]

I. WHETHER THE CONVENING AUTHORITY EXERCISED UNLAWFUL COMMAND INFLUENCE OVER THE PROCEEDINGS BY REQUIRING THE COURT MEMBERS, IN THE MIDDLE OF THE TRIAL, TO ATTEND AN OFFICER PROFESSIONAL DEVELOPMENT PROGRAM WHERE "APPROPRIATE" PUNISHMENTS FOR OFFICER COURT–MARTIAL DEFENDANTS WAS DISCUSSED.

* * *

Nine months after her court-martial, appellant signed a statement and later filed it with the Court of Criminal Appeals. *See United States v. Grostefon*, 12 M.J. 431 (C.M.A. 1982). It said:

[handwritten: Grostefon — an issue a military lawyer deems ineffective the client can still raise it.]

AFFADAVIT [sic]

November 20, 1998

I, Holly M. Baldwin, would like to make the following statement. Shortly after I was transferred from Fort Lewis to Fort Bliss (fall 1997), Ft. Bliss was having a Family Values Week. One of the Officer Professional Development programs mandated by Commanding General Costello was one directed at Ethics. At that particular OPD, one of the topics discussed was

[handwritten top margin: Mid - C.M. Court members were req. to attend an OPD program that insisted punishment for officers was to lenient.]

an incident that happened with three of the Officers in the 31st ADA BDE that were being court-martialed. The address included comments that the court-martial sentences were too lenient and that the minimum sentence should be at least one year and that Officers should be punished harsher than enlisted soldiers because Officers should always set the example and be above reproach. The day after this OPD one of the officers from the 31st was set to be sentenced. I believe his name was Major Brennan. I attended this OPD, but didn't learn of the sentencing until a discussion I had with his attorney, Mr. Jim Maus. He is an attorney in my civilian attorney's (Jim Darnell) law office in El Paso, TX. Mr. Maus was Major Brennan's civilian counsel. Mr. Maus also informed me that this type of OPD was inappropriate and that it could be considered jury tampering and he was filing an appeal on Major Brennan's behalf stating such.

[handwritten right margin: This OPD could be considered jury tamp.]

On the day of my conviction and sentencing, the final part of the trial was delayed for another OPD that was mandatory for all Officers on post. This OPD dealt with the situation Lt. Kelly Flynn was embroiled [sic].[*] The theme about this OPD was that she was not punished as she should have been and that she had basically gotten over. It was then stated she should not have been allowed to resign, but should have been court-martialed. I would also like to note here that I submitted a Resignation for Good of Service [sic] on or about 1 May 97 and it was held and never sent up as the regulation states. That afternoon after the officers on my panel went to the OPD, I was convicted and sentenced to 1 year at Ft. Leavenworth. It should also be noted that 4 of the officers on my panel were in the same rating chain. They included the Brigade Commander, Brigade Deputy Commander, the HHC Company Commander and another BDE Primary Officer.

[handwritten right margin: — Q punished how she should have been Resigned.]

[handwritten right margin: Δ submitted resignation & passed on]

I swear the above mentioned statement is true to the best of knowledge.

Signed Holly Morris Baldwin

Date November 20, 1998

(Emphasis added).

Appellant argued that "her sentence to one year in confinement and the rejection of her request for Resignation for the Good of the Service was the result of these actions, which clearly constitute unlawful command influence in this case." The Government did not oppose this motion to file, but in its final brief it simply asserted that "it [appellant's claim] lacks merit." The Court of Criminal Appeals summarily affirmed this case.

[handwritten right margin: Ap. Ct. Δs claim lacked merit Affirmed CM]

* * *

---

[*] Air Force First Lieutenant Kelly Flinn was the first female assigned to pilot a B-52 aircraft. She was allowed to resign from the Air Force after being charged with making a false official statement, committing adultery with a subordinate's spouse, and disobeying an order. Her case received national media attention in 1997.—Eds.

The Government argues that appellant's post-trial claim of unlawful command influence should be denied because she "has failed to meet her threshold burden of production in this case." Final Brief at 7. It further contends that "[a]ppellant's own ambiguous, self-serving, and unsubstantiated declaration does not establish a viable claim of unlawful command influence." Moreover, it notes that "appellant never raised this issue at trial" nor made any "effort to bring this allegation to the military judge's attention and conduct some minimal voir dire before findings and sentence deliberations." Id. We conclude that none of these reasons legally justifies the lower appellate court's summary denial of appellant's post-trial claim of unlawful command influence.

Article 37, UCMJ, 10 U.S.C. § 837, states:

§ 837. Art. 37. Unlawfully influencing action of court

(a) No authority convening a general, special, or summary court-martial, nor any other commanding officer, may censure, reprimand, or admonish the court or any member, military judge, or counsel thereof, with respect to the findings or sentence adjudged by the court, or with respect to any other exercises of its or his functions in the conduct of the proceedings. No person subject to this chapter may attempt to coerce or, by any unauthorized means, influence the action of a court-martial or any other military tribunal or any member thereof, in reaching the findings or sentence in any case, or the action of any convening, approving, or reviewing authority with respect to his judicial acts. The foregoing provisions of the subsection shall not apply with respect to (1) general instructional or informational courses in military justice if such courses are designed solely for the purpose of instructing members of a command in the substantive and procedural aspects of courts-martial, or (2) to statements and instructions given in open court by the military judge, president of a special court-martial, or counsel.

(Emphasis added.)

We have long held that the use of command meetings to purposefully influence the members in determining a court-martial sentence violates Article 37, UCMJ. *United States v. Levite*, 25 M.J. 334, 339 (C.M.A. 1987); *United States v. Cruz*, 25 M.J. 326, 329 (C.M.A. 1987); *United States v. Thomas*, 22 M.J. 388, 393 (C.M.A. 1986); *United States v. McCann*, 8 U.S.C.MA 675, 676, 25 CMR 179, 180 (1958). Moreover, we have also held that the mere "confluence" of the timing of such meetings with members during ongoing courts-martials and their subject matter dealing with court-martial sentences can require a sentence rehearing. *See United States v. Brice*, 19 M.J. 170, 172 n. 3 (C.M.A. 1985).

Here, appellant avers that there were two command officer meetings before and during her court-martial, which she and the officers of her panel attended. She also avers that various court-martial situations on base and in the Air Force at large were discussed. Furthermore, she asserts that comments were made that court-martial sentences were too lenient; that officers should always be punished more harshly than enlisted persons; and that the minimum sentences should be 1 year. Finally, appellant points out that she, an officer, subsequently received a 1–year sentence at her court-martial. If appellant's averments are true, then as in Brice, a confluence of timing and subject matter would exist.

If Δ's statement is true then unlawful command inflt.may exist

The Government contends, however, that appellant's self-serving averments are not legally sufficient (or competent) to raise her post-trial claim. We disagree. In *United States v. Ayala*, 43 M.J. 296, 300 (1995), this Court held that "[t]he quantum of evidence necessary to raise unlawful command influence is the same as that required to submit a factual issue to the trier of fact." While not particularly delineating the proof required, we have generally held that it must be more than "mere speculation." *See United States v. Biagase*, 50 M.J. 143, 150 (1999). Here, appellant's post-trial statement was based on her own observations (*cf. United States v. Ruiz*, 49 M.J. 340, 348 (1998) (no abuse of discretion for convening authority to refuse to order post-trial hearing on basis of unsubstantiated assertions of unlawful command influence by counsel)), and it was detailed in nature. *Cf. United States v. Johnston*, 39 M.J. 242, 244 (C.M.A. 1994) (must be more than a bare allegation). Moreover, the record of trial, which contains an unexplained decision to delay any sessions on the date in question until the early afternoon, may be viewed as tending to corroborate appellant's allegation that there was a command meeting at that time. In the absence of any post-trial submission from the Government, we conclude appellant's allegations in this context are sufficient to raise a post-trial complaint of unlawful command influence. *See United States v. Ayala*, supra (some evidence to which a member might reasonably attach credit); *see generally United States v. Ginn*, 47 M.J. 236, 248 (1997) (third principle: "if the affidavit is factually adequate on its face to state a claim of legal error . . . .").

Gov. arg. Δ statement legally insufficient to raise claim post trial.

Ct. Disagreed

Δ needs more than mere speculat

Δ had her 1st hand Observations

Trial rec corroborate delay

Although we reject the Government's legal insufficiency claim, we are reluctant to order relief without a complete record concerning appellant's claim. A full development of the material facts surrounding these command meetings and their effect on appellant's court-martial is required. *See United States v. Dykes*, 38 M.J. 270; *see also United States v. Fricke*, 53 M.J. 149, 155 (2000). Accordingly, [an evidentiary] hearing should be ordered.

Δ Relief until Δ's claim is supported by evidence of material facts.

* * *

The decision of the United States Army Court of Criminal Appeals is set aside. The record of trial is returned to the Judge Advocate General of the Army for submission to a convening authority for a limited hearing on the issue of command influence. At the conclusion of the hearing, the judge will make specific findings of fact on that issue. A verbatim record of the proceedings will be submitted after authentication to the Court of Criminal Appeals for further review. Thereafter, Article 67(a)(3), UCMJ, 10 U.S.C. § 867(a)(3), shall apply.

Points for Discussion

1. If General Costello is responsible for maintaining good order and discipline, what is wrong with expressing his opinion on minimum sentences and whether soldiers accused of wrongdoing should be allowed to resign? Suppose a civilian mayor of a town gave a speech urging prosecutors, judges, and juries to get tough on crime. Would that prevent fair trials in the town? Would criminal convictions have to be reversed?

2. What is the remedy for General Costello's action? Can there be no more trials at Fort Bliss after his speech?

①
There is a difference between outlining what is wrong, the channels of discipline, and reaching into the court room during a CM. Better policy would be to enact stronger command discipline, more training, drills.

Ironically mayors do this.

There's a diference, the mayor has much less influence

The equivalent would be the mayor speaking to court house staff and current juries.

CHAPTER 2

JUDGE ADVOCATE PROFESSIONAL RESPONSIBILITY

The Services provide rules regarding ethical conduct for attorneys by promulgating Rules of Professional Conduct.[1] These rules provide requirements and guidance that pertain to many areas where ethical issues arise including advocacy standards and Sixth Amendment right to effective counsel, supervisory responsibility, and restrictions in communications to the media and other third parties. Each of these issues is addressed in the cases and discussion that follow.

2-1. Separate Military Lawyers for the Prosecution and the Accused

In the military justice system, the military Services have separate, designated counsel representing the government and the accused. When engaging in official duties, both are bound by the ethical code of conduct of their Service and by state bar rules (to the extent they do not conflict with the Service requirements).[2]

Throughout the military justice process, government prosecutors (trial counsel) represent the United States government (and their particular Service) and are ethically bound to serve the best interests of the government, not the commanders or persons to whom they advise. If a commander relies and confides in an attorney (e.g., trial counsel or chief of military justice), those conversations are not protected pursuant to an attorney-client privilege. When an official (e.g., the commander) acts illegally or intends to act

---

[1] *See* U.S. Dep't of Army, Reg. 27-26, *Rules of Professional Conduct for Lawyers* (May 1, 1992); U.S. Dep't of Air Force, TJS-2, *Rules of Professional Conduct* (Aug. 17, 2005) (also known as *Rules of Profressional Conduct and Standards for Civility*); U.S. Dep't of the Navy, JAGINST5803.1C, *Professional Conduct of Attorneys Practicing Under the Cognizance and Supervision of the Judge Advocate General* (November 9, 2004); U.S. Dep't of Coast Guard, Commandant Instr. M5800.1, *Coast Guard Legal Rules of Professional Conduct* (June 1, 2005).

[2] Military attorneys who see a potential conflict between the Service ethical code and their state bar rules should seek assistance from their supervisors and Service ethics offices.

illegally, the military attorney should ask the official to reconsider or to get another legal opinion.

Before a general or special court-martial, UCMJ, Article 27 authorizes representation by a detailed military defense counsel with no cost to the accused. Unlike trial counsel and commanders they advise, defense counsel and their clients communications are protected by an attorney-client privilege. (Generally, confidentiality includes information from all sources, even if obtained prior to the establishment of the attorney-client relationship and the privilege continues after the relationship is terminated. Military Rule of Evidence 502 indicates that an attorney-client privilege prevents disclosure unless the source is not the client.) Like defense counsel representing defendants in civilian criminal trials, military defense counsel retain the authority to determine motions, select witnesses, and develop trial strategy, while their clients make the final decision regarding plea, forum, pretrial agreements, and whether to testify.

Article 27(b), UCMJ, requires that trial and defense counsel detailed to serve at a general court-martial be graduates of an accredited law school or be members "of the bar of a Federal court or of the highest court of a State." The Service Judge Advocate General must also certify them as competent. *Id.* The Services have expanded individual requirements for counsel. For example, the Army now requires attorneys to certify annually that they are members of a bar in good standing.

United States v. Steele, which follows, illustrates that having an *inactive* bar status (while still a bar member) does not disqualify military attorneys (or civilian counsel representing an accused) from serving at a court-martial, and does not necessarily render counsel ineffective or reflect a denial of the accused's Sixth Amendment right to counsel.

UNITED STATES v. STEELE
U.S. Court of Appeals for the Armed Forces
53 M.J. 274 (C.A.A.F. 2000)

EFFRON, Judge:

A general court-martial composed of a military judge sitting alone convicted appellant [Lance Corporal Milton D. Steele, U.S. Marine Corps], pursuant to mixed pleas, of conspiracy to distribute cocaine and wrongful distribution of cocaine, in violation of Articles 81 and 112a, Uniform Code of Military Justice, 10 U.S.C. §§ 881 and 912a, respectively. He was sentenced to a dishonorable discharge, confinement for 8 years, total forfeitures, and reduction to the lowest enlisted grade. The convening authority approved the sentence, and the Court of Criminal Appeals affirmed in an unpublished opinion.

On appellant's petition, we granted review of the following issue:

WHETHER APPELLANT WAS DENIED HIS SIXTH AMENDMENT RIGHT TO COUNSEL WHERE HIS CIVILIAN DEFENSE COUNSEL WAS

UNAUTHORIZED TO PRACTICE LAW IN ALL JURISDICTIONS WHERE HE HAD BEEN ADMITTED TO PRACTICE LAW.

We also specified the following issue:

WHETHER A CIVILIAN COUNSEL WHO IS IN INACTIVE OR RETIRED STATUS IN HIS BAR MEMBERSHIP(S) REMAINS AUTHORIZED TO PRACTICE BEFORE A GENERAL COURT-MARTIAL IN TERMS OF UCMJ, ARTICLES 27 AND 38(b)(2) AND RCM 502.

For the reasons set forth below, we affirm the decision of the Court of Criminal Appeals.

I. BACKGROUND

Appellant was represented at trial by detailed military counsel, Captain T, and by a civilian defense counsel, Mr. C. Detailed defense counsel announced that he was "qualified and certified in accordance with Article 27(b) and sworn in accordance with Article 42(a) of the Uniform Code of Military Justice." Similarly, civilian defense counsel announced, "I am licensed to practice law by the highest courts of the States of Iowa, Hawaii, and Texas; and I am previously qualified and certified and sworn in accordance with Articles 27(b) and 42(a) of the Uniform Code of Military Justice." The military judge then advised appellant of his rights to counsel, and appellant stated that he wished to be represented by Captain T and Mr. C.

Throughout trial and post-trial proceedings, and before the Court of Criminal Appeals, appellant made no claim challenging the qualifications, bar status, or effectiveness of either his detailed or civilian counsel. However, in his Supplement to Petition for Grant of Review filed in this Court, appellant asserted the foregoing Issue and moved to attach documents relating to Mr. C's professional status as a member of the Iowa, Hawaii, and Texas bar associations. We granted appellant's motion to attach those documents on March 2, 2000. Because the facts in those documents are not contested, we accept them as true for purposes of this appeal.

These documents reveal that Mr. C was a member of the bar in three states, Iowa, Hawaii, and Texas, as he had stated on the record. He was admitted to the bar of Iowa in 1982, but his status was later changed to "retired and inactive." According to a letter from the Board of Professional Ethics and Conduct of the Iowa Supreme Court, "[a] person who has been admitted to practice law in Iowa and has had their license to practice law suspended or is on inactive status, cannot practice law under the authority of the Iowa license outside of Iowa." Mr. C was admitted to bar membership in Hawaii in 1989, but he later entered inactive status. According to Hawaii Supreme Court Rule 17(d)(7), an attorney may "desire to assume inactive status and discontinue the practice of law in Hawaii." The rule notes that an attorney on inactive status "shall no longer be eligible to practice law." Mr. C became a member of the bar of the State of Texas in 1992. Shortly thereafter, at his request, he was placed on inactive status. The result of that action was that civilian counsel was "not authorized to practice as an attorney and counselor at law in the STATE of TEXAS."

II. QUALIFICATIONS OF COUNSEL

Article 27, UCMJ, 10 U.S.C. § 827, entitles an accused before a general or special court-martial to representation by detailed military defense counsel without regard to his ability to pay. Under Article 27(b):

> (b) Trial counsel or defense counsel detailed for a general court-martial—

> (1) must be a judge advocate who is a graduate of an accredited law school or is a member of the bar of a Federal court or of the highest court of a State; or must be a member of the bar of a Federal court or of the highest court of a State; and

> (2) must be certified as competent to perform such duties by the Judge Advocate General of the armed force of which he is a member.

Article 27 is silent with respect to the right to be represented by civilian counsel and with respect to any qualifications imposed upon civilian defense counsel.

Article 38(b), UCMJ, 10 U.S.C. § 838(b), sets forth the full penumbra of an accused's options with respect to representation before general and special courts-martial: detailed military counsel, individually requested military counsel, or civilian counsel. Under Article 38(b)(2), "The accused may be represented by civilian counsel if provided by him." Neither Article 38 nor any other provision of the Code establishes any qualifications or requisites-other than the oath-for a civilian counsel to practice before a court-martial. *See* Art. 42, UCMJ, 10 U.S.C. § 842; *see also Soriano v. Hosken*, 9 M.J. 221 (C.M.A. 1980), and *United States v. Kraskouskas*, 9 U.S.C.MA 607, 26 CMR 387, 1958 WL 3387 (1958).

The President has established basic qualifications for civilian counsel in RCM 502, Manual for Courts-Martial, United States (1995 ed.). Civilian counsel representing an accused before a court-martial must be "[a] member of the bar of a Federal court or of the bar of the highest court of a State." RCM 502(d)(3)(A). If that civilian lawyer is "not a member of such a bar," then he or she must be "a lawyer who is authorized by a recognized licensing authority to practice law and is found by the military judge to be qualified to represent the accused upon a showing to the satisfaction of the military judge that the counsel has appropriate training and familiarity with the general principles of criminal law which apply in a court-martial." RCM 502(d)(3)(B). Neither the Code nor the Manual expressly disqualifies a civilian attorney on the grounds that his or her bar status is designated as "inactive."

Federal courts in the civilian sector have dealt with the question of an attorney's bar status vis-a-vis an accused's Sixth Amendment right to counsel. In general, they hold that once an attorney is found competent and admitted to practice law in a licensing jurisdiction, subsequent changes to his or her bar membership status do not render that counsel incompetent or disqualified. "Though admission to practice before a federal court is derivative from membership in a state bar, disbarment by the State does not result in automatic disbarment by the federal court. Though that state action is entitled to respect, it is not conclusively binding on the federal courts."

* * *

Our Court has addressed the significance of a licensing authority's decision to admit a person to the bar. In *Soriano v. Hosken, supra,* we noted that a civilian counsel must be "qualified" in order to make the right to civilian counsel "meaningful as intended by the Code." 9 M.J. at 221. Civilian counsel must also be "authorized by some recognized licensing authority to engage in the practice of law." *Kraskouskas,* 9 U.S.C.MA at 609, 26 CMR at 389. There are no other restrictions on an accused's right to counsel under Article 38(b). Once licensed, "such lawyers are presumed competent for the professional undertaking of the defense of a military accused at a court-martial." *Soriano,* 9 M.J. at 222.

The decisions of our Court and other federal courts reflect that admission to practice is the necessary indicia that a level of competence has been achieved and reviewed by a competent licensing authority. This determination of competence is not necessarily eviscerated when sanctions are imposed by a state bar or by changes in counsel's status where those matters do not demonstrate a negative determination of counsel's competence.

* * *

III. DISCUSSION

In light of the foregoing considerations, we hold that Mr. C was not disqualified by virtue of his status as an "inactive" member of the bars of Iowa, Hawaii, and Texas. Contrary to appellant's assertions in his brief, there is no evidence that Mr. C was suspended from practicing in any of the states in which he held bar membership. Rather, Mr. C merely assumed an inactive status in each of those jurisdictions. This status does not reflect adversely upon his competence; nor does it reflect any change in the determination of his competence to practice law by any of these state bar associations. It follows that the mere fact that appellant's counsel did not maintain an active status in his licensing states is not a *per se* disqualifying factor.

We also note that Rule 8-6e, Comment, Department of the Navy JAGINST 5803.1A (Ch. 3, 30 May 1996), states that "an individual may be considered 'inactive' as to the practice of law within a particular jurisdiction and still be considered 'in good standing[.]'" Under this rule, therefore, inactive status does not bar military counsel from being certified as competent under Article 27(b)(2) to practice before Navy and Marine Corps courts-martial. We decline to adopt a more stringent rule for civilian counsel practicing before courts-martial. Unless an accused can demonstrate that civilian counsel had never attained any bar membership and could not be certified, we shall not deny or limit a military accused's right under Article 38 to elect civilian representation and pick his own civilian counsel. Once counsel is licensed to practice law by a state or competent licensing authority, we shall presume that civilian counsel are competent to appear as defense counsel at courts-martial.

We agree with the federal cases cited above that once a state licensing authority has reviewed the qualifications and admitted an attorney to practice, a subsequent change in bar status alone does not necessarily result in a determination that there has been a denial of the Sixth Amendment right to counsel. We conclude that appellant's civilian counsel was not disqualified to practice before courts-martial by virtue of the fact that he was "inactive" in the three states within which he was licensed.

In any case, in at least one state, Texas, Mr. C's inactive status prohibited practice of law only within the state. Texas bar membership was adequate, therefore, to support counsel's appearance before a court-martial regardless of any limitations imposed by Hawaii or Iowa.

Because appellant has presented no issue of competence arising from civilian counsel's bar status and because appellant has not shown that civilian counsel's performance was otherwise deficient, appellant has failed to meet his heavy burden of showing that he was denied the effective assistance of counsel. *Strickland v. Washington,* 466 U.S. 668, 687; *United States v. Brownfield,* 52 M.J. 40, 42 (1999); *United States v. Scott,* 24 M.J. 186, 188 (C.M.A. 1987).

IV. CONCLUSION

The decision of the United States Navy-Marine Corps Court of Criminal Appeals is affirmed.

[Senior Judge Cox's separate concurring opinion is omitted.—Eds.]

Points for Discussion

1. If the appellant's civilian counsel had been disbarred in Hawaii, Iowa, and Texas, would the *Steele* court's opinion have been different? If so, how?

2. Should bar status be a relevant factor in determining whether an accused has received effective assistance of counsel as required by the Sixth Amendment?

2-2. Standards Regarding Advocacy and Sixth Amendment Right to Effective Counsel

Standards regarding advocacy for military attorneys are comparable in most regards to the ABA Model Rules. When counsel represent the accused or the government before a judicial tribunal they must disclose adverse legal authority, represent no personal opinions at trial, and refrain from engaging in any *ex parte* discussions with the military judge or panel members. Trial counsel must disclose to the defense all evidence or matters that tend to negate the accused's guilt or mitigate the offense.

Defense counsel encounter typical issues faced by all attorneys regarding evidence or contraband and should not accept those items or if possession cannot be avoided, should turn them over without disclosing the client's identification.

Whether to assist a client in testifying to matters that may result in perjury is also a common conundrum defense counsel face. This raises a conflict for the defense counsel who must ensure he maintains confidentiality (i.e., protects information) with his client but must also ensure candor to the tribunal (i.e., candid with the court).

If counsel is faced with a client who insists upon testifying and who potentially may assert falsehoods, defense counsel should investigate before deciding that the client's testimony will result in perjury. Counsel must have a "firm factual basis" before limiting representation for the accused. Counsel should attempt to dissuade the client from testifying and discuss this issue with the client, reviewing the facts, informing the client about the consequences for lying under oath (including criminal sanctions) and about the obligation to tell the truth. Counsel should also tell the client that if he insists on testifying falsely, he will have to do so in a narrative format (without assistance of counsel) which may not be as affective with the trier of fact. Counsel should attempt to structure the client's testimony so that the client avoids areas where he might perjure himself. If the client insists upon testifying, defense counsel should request an *ex parte* hearing with the military judge on the record, without the client present. During that hearing, counsel should inform the judge that the accused will testify in a narrative format without the assistance of counsel. Of course, counsel should not inform the military judge that the client's testimony may consist of perjury. If the client proceeds to testify and engage in perjury, counsel should attempt to persuade the client to rectify the matter. Nevertheless, counsel should refrain from using the accused's perjured testimony.

When counsel face the issue of assisting a client in testimony resulting in perjury, the question of the right to effective counsel also is raised. The Army Court of Criminal Appeals (with the assistance of the Court of Appeals for the Armed Forces from a previous review of the case) in *United States v. Baker*, which follows later in this section, provides the standard for ineffective assistance of counsel and discusses the ethical conundrum counsel face. Essentially, an ethical violation does not always mean counsel was ineffective. The accused who asserts that counsel was or is ineffective, must show both deficiency of counsel and that the accused was prejudiced. To find counsel ineffective, the appellate courts must review the first prong: whether 1) the accused's allegations are true; 2) whether there is a reasonable explanation for counsel's actions; and 3) if there is such an explanation, whether the defense counsel's advocacy fell measurably below the performance expected of "fallible lawyers." If the accused meets the first prong of the so-called

"*Strickland* test," appellant must meet the second prong, measuring prejudice: Is there a reasonable probability that, but for the defense counsel's "unprofessional errors" the trial result would have been different? *United States v. Strickland*, 466 U.S. 668, 694 (1984).

UNITED STATES v. QUINTANILLA
U.S. Navy-Marine Court of Criminal Appeals
60 M.J. 852 (N.M. Ct. Crim. App. 2005)

PRICE, Senior Judge:

This is a case about a sergeant of Marines who shot his commanding officer (CO) and executive officer (XO) while they were in their command office suite, killing the XO and seriously wounding the CO. The appellant's [Sergeant Jesse A. Quintanilla, U.S. Marine Corps], sentence included the death penalty. Because the military judge committed an error that materially prejudiced a substantial right of the appellant by granting a prosecution challenge for cause, we must set aside the findings and the sentence and order a rehearing.

Contrary to his pleas, the appellant was convicted of attempted unpremeditated murder (two specifications), violation of a general order by carrying and concealing a .45 caliber pistol, premeditated murder, aggravated assault by pointing a dangerous weapon (two specifications), carrying a concealed weapon, communicating a threat, and obstructing justice. The appellant's offenses violated Articles 80, 92, 118, 128, and 134, Uniform Code of Military Justice, 10 U.S.C. §§ 880, 892, 918, 928, and 934. A general court-martial comprised of 12 members unanimously sentenced the appellant to death, reduction to pay grade E-1, and total forfeiture of pay and allowances. The convening authority approved the sentence as adjudged.

. . . While our decision as to a challenge for cause renders moot all other assignments of error, four of the additional issues warrant discussion.

I. Background

In March of 1996, the appellant was assigned to Marine Aviation Logistics Squadron 39 at Camp Pendleton, California. He worked on the night crew at the squadron, meaning that he routinely reported for work in mid-afternoon. The squadron CO was Lieutenant Colonel (LtCol) Thomas A. Heffner, United States Marine Corps (USMC). The XO was LtCol Daniel W. Kidd, USMC.

On the morning of 5 March 1996, the appellant consumed an undetermined quantity of alcohol, then left his home to drive to work. When he left his car parked in the squadron parking lot, he had a .45 caliber pistol tucked into his clothing. The appellant entered the squadron spaces, walked upstairs to the command office suite, then waited outside the XO's office until other Marines left.

A uniform inspection was scheduled for the night crew at 1500. In preparation for the inspection, LtCol Heffner was changing into his dress uniform, in a changing room located next to LtCol Kidd's office, where LtCol Kidd was working at his desk.

The appellant walked into LtCol Kidd's office, pulled out his pistol, asked him, "Remember me, f---er?" and then shot the XO as he tried to exit the office through the door into the changing room. The bullet entered the right side of his lower back, exited the right front side of his abdomen, and then amputated his right ring finger. LtCol Kidd managed to stagger into the changing room, with the appellant close behind him.

LtCol Heffner was changing uniforms when the door to the changing room burst open and LtCol Kidd rushed in. LtCol Heffner first glanced at his XO, and then noticed the appellant in the doorway. The appellant raised his pistol and shot LtCol Heffner in the chest, at which point LtCol Heffner ran out of the office suite. The appellant then shot LtCol Kidd again, the bullet entering his upper back. LtCol Kidd collapsed to the floor and bled to death within a matter of minutes.

After the third and fatal shot was fired, the appellant left the office suite and followed the bloody trail left by LtCol Heffner. As he moved down the passageway, he confronted Gunnery Sergeant (GySgt) W.J. Till and Staff Sergeant (SSgt) A.L. Karr. The appellant pointed the pistol at both Marines but did not fire.

By this time, LtCol Heffner was lying just outside one of the ground floor entrances to the building. Various Marines were providing first aid to their CO. GySgt W.E. Tiller was there and heard someone ask where the XO was. He then went up to the second floor to find the XO. As he proceeded down the passageway toward the command office suite, he saw the appellant a few feet away. GySgt Tiller stepped toward the appellant and reached for the gun. The appellant raised the gun toward GySgt Tiller and fired. GySgt Tiller avoided the shot and struggled with the appellant, eventually disarming him.

The appellant broke away from GySgt Tiller and went down the stairs to the ground floor to the Production Control Office. A number of senior enlisted Marines were in the office at the time. When the appellant entered the office, none of them knew what had just happened. The appellant said, "Gunnery Sergeant, apprehend me, I just shot the CO and XO," or words to that effect. GySgt P.T. Sullivan asked the appellant to sit down, and he did so.

Soon other Marines entered the office. The appellant talked about why he shot the CO and XO, complaining that he wasn't treated well in the squadron and that he did it for his "brown brothers," or words to that effect. At one point, the appellant stood up, pulled down his coveralls, took off his undershirt, and displayed the tattoos that covered his upper body. One of the large tattoos read "Sureno," which the Government argued was a reference to Southern California gangs. Shortly thereafter, a military policeman arrived and took the appellant into custody.

    * * *

IV. Prosecutorial Misconduct

In two assignments of error and the supplemental assignment of error, the appellant asserts that, because of prosecutorial misconduct, the findings and sentence must be set aside. While we strongly disapprove of the actions of the trial counsel and assistant trial counsel, we conclude that the appellant was not prejudiced. Even though we set aside the findings and sentence on another ground, we discuss prosecutorial misconduct to discourage any repetition of these actions in a rehearing.

The first incident occurred before the trial commenced and involved an *ex parte* communication. Following the Article 32, UCMJ, investigation, the assistant trial counsel, Major (Maj) G.P. Glazier, USMC, had a brief conversation about the case with the Article 32 Investigation Officer (IO) outside the presence of any defense counsel in this case.

Prosecutorial misconduct consists of " 'action or inaction by a prosecutor in violation of some legal norm or standard, e.g., a constitutional provision, a statute, a Manual rule, or an applicable professional ethics canon.' " . . . In evaluating an assertion of prosecutorial misconduct, we focus on the "overall effect of counsel's conduct on the trial, and not counsel's personal blameworthiness." . . . If the prosecutor violated some legal norm, and if that violation impacted on some substantial right of the appellant, we must still consider the record as a whole to determine whether the violation was harmless under all the circumstances of a particular case. *Meek,* 44 M.J. at 5.

This incident comes to our attention as an *ex parte* communication by a prosecutor. An *ex parte* communication is one "[d]one or made at the instance and for the benefit of one party only, and without notice to, or argument by, any person adversely interested." BLACK'S LAW DICTIONARY 597 (7th ed.1999). As set forth by the Judge Advocate General of the Navy, the rule against *ex parte* communications prohibits Navy and Marine Corps judge advocates serving as trial counsel (prosecutors) and defense counsel from taking the following actions:

(1) seek to influence a judge, court member, member of a tribunal, prospective court member or member of a tribunal, or other official by means prohibited by law or regulation; [or]

(2) communicate ex parte with such a person except as permitted by law or regulation;

* * *

Judge Advocate General Instruction 5803.1A, Rule 3.5a (13 Jul 1992). Thus, the general rule is that an advocate cannot communicate with a judge or "other official," such as an IO, in a court-martial about a particular case in the absence of opposing counsel or without advance notice to, and consent of, that opposing counsel. Even when opposing counsel has been notified, such communications should be restricted to administrative matters that have no bearing on the substantive issues of the case.

. . . Based on our review of the record, we concur with the military judge's conclusion that Maj Glazier's brief conversation with the IO was "ill advised" and certainly gave rise to an "appearance of impropriety." Record at 869-70. However, we also conclude that this conversation did not just *appear* to be improper, it was improper. There was no lawful reason for Maj Glazier to communicate with the IO about the investigation, particularly when all the evidence had been taken and the IO would next be considering the evidence and making his recommendations. Nonetheless, we hold that the conversation had no impact on the IO's report or recommendations or on the eventual trial in this case. Based on our review of the record, we are confident that the appellant was no worse off because of Maj Glazier's behavior than if Maj Glazier had conducted himself in accordance with the law and applicable ethical canons. Accordingly, the appellant is not entitled to relief on this ground.

Unfortunately, this was not the only prosecution misstep in this capital case. Because of the nature and number of such missteps, some of which are detailed in the Supplemental Assignment of Error and the Petition for New Trial, we feel compelled to discuss some of them.

The first is the trial counsel's argument on a motion as to which he also offered testimony. The trial counsel in this case was Captain (Capt) C.E. Feldman, USMC. To understand the issue, we first summarize the background. Hours after the shootings, the appellant was detained in the brig in pretrial confinement. A hearing was held to determine whether legal grounds existed to continue that pretrial confinement or whether the appellant should be released from that status. Capt Feldman represented the Government and the unit at this hearing. Capt D.G. Bellon, USMC, represented the appellant. Those in attendance included five or six representatives from the media, including at least one local television station. The prosecution team had no prior knowledge that media representatives would be present for the hearing. During the hearing, Capt Feldman presented witness statements to justify continued pretrial confinement. He did so by delivering copies to the Initial Review Officer (IRO) and to Capt Bellon, then reading aloud from the statements. The defense objected to the reading from the documents in front of the media, fearing that the media would publish the substance of the statements and potentially taint the pool of potential members in the Camp Pendleton area. The hearing officer asked Capt Feldman to stop reading, which he did. Nevertheless, as the defense feared, media representatives did publish the substance of the statements. Later, during voir dire, every member revealed that he/she had been exposed to media accounts of the shootings and investigation, although it was not clear whether the members had read or seen media accounts of this particular hearing.

Based on this and other actions by the prosecution team, the defense filed a pretrial motion to dismiss all charges based on prosecutorial misconduct. Among other evidence, Capt Feldman testified for the Government regarding his participation in the pretrial magistrate's hearing. Following direct examination, he was cross-examined on that issue. He later presented argument on the same motion addressing, in part, his own testimony. Thus, Capt Feldman both testified and argued on a contested issue. We note that in making that argument, he specifically addressed his own testimony and the propriety of his own actions.

In doing so, Capt Feldman violated the ethical rule against attorneys acting as an advocate and witness in the same matter. JAGINST 5803.1A, Rule 3.7(a) (13 Jul 1992).[5] The only arguable exception to that rule in this case applies for testimony regarding "the nature and quality of legal services rendered in the case." *Id.* However, although his testimony on the issue was certainly appropriate, there was no need for him to make argument on that testimony, particularly where two other prosecutors were available to present the argument. We note that the defense team did not object to this ethical violation, apparently concluding that no prejudice occurred. Based on our review of the record, we concur that no prejudice occurred, but do not condone yet another example where a prosecutor ran out of his lane.

The next, and most egregious, incident that merits discussion is Maj Glazier's unauthorized withholding of evidence from the evidence custodian. Without exploring all the details, suffice it to say that a Naval Criminal Investigative Service (NCIS) report attached to the Petition for New Trial demonstrates to our satisfaction that:

1. Following the adjournment of this court-martial, Maj Glazier and Capt Feldman gave the bullet that pierced LtCol Heffner's chest to him. This was done at the request of LtCol Heffner.

2. Maj Glazier gave the ring LtCol Kidd was wearing at the time of his murder to his widow, Mrs. Kidd.

3. Maj Glazier kept a knife seized from the appellant for himself.

4. Maj Glazier withheld the pistol used by the appellant in the shootings. Capt Feldman later received the pistol, mounted it on a plaque, and hung it in his office, where he served as a Deputy District Attorney in Steamboat Springs, Colorado. The plaque was engraved as follows: Capt Charles Feldman and Maj Guy Glazier, Sureno Busters.

5. Neither Maj Glazier nor Capt Feldman had any permission or authority for their actions.

6. During the investigation, each of the items were returned to the Naval Criminal Investigative Service.

---

[5] As noted above, our judicial duties require us to determine if a prosecutor's conduct violates any ethical canon. Our judicial determination does not usurp the province of the Judge Advocate General under the Instruction to decide whether sanctions would be appropriate for the same conduct. See JAGINST 5803.1A, Encl.2 (13 Jul 1992).

It goes without saying that it is highly unethical, if not illegal, for prosecutors to take or withhold evidence, without authority, in a court-martial, and convert it to their personal use or that of others. *See* JAGINST 5803.1A at Rule 8.4. This is particularly true in the military justice system where a conviction is inchoate until the convening authority takes his action on the case, and not final until this court completes its review under Articles 59(a) and 66(c), UCMJ. Moreover, in a capital case such as this, review by our superior court is mandatory. Art. 67(a), UCMJ, 10 U.S.C. § 867(a). Thus, evidence admitted at trial must be preserved under established evidence custody rules until such time that appellate review is final.

We rebuke Maj Glazier and Capt Feldman for their actions and trust that no Navy or Marine Corps prosecutor will follow their bad example. Testing for prejudice, we conclude that the prosecutors' post-trial actions had no impact on the findings and sentence.

We cite one last example of questionable prosecutorial conduct that occurred during Maj Glazier's sentencing argument. Maj Glazier described the incident at a presentation he made to the Government Capital Litigation Course at the Naval Justice School in March and May of 1997:

> And I'm getting louder and louder and louder and the members who are starting to go to sleep on me are saying, "Boy, this is really building. What is he getting to?" And then I get down to my objectionable stuff, you know, you're getting louder and I'm moving and I'm moving around the court-room too. I'm up in front of the members when I'm starting my closing argument and I'm loud and I'm in their face but I'm not near the accused, I'm up with the members. And then I'm backing off, I'm softer and I'm softer and I'm talking about the victims and the impact on them and I'm getting further away from the jury. It's hard for them to hear me. They're straining to listen. *I get over, I actually take a seat on the witness stand, which is highly objectionable, and I start talking about what Colonel Kidd would have testified to if I could have called him as a witness.* And then, as I'm building this crescendo, I get off the witness stand and I go over to the accused ... and I start talking about, you know, "We do re-member you. Gentlem[e]n, answer that question." And by the time I get down to the bottom, *I'm screaming, I'm right in the accused'[s] face and I'm pointing at him,* "You're that gang banging, murdering animal who literally tore the heart out of a man. Tore the heart out of a family. Tore the heart out of the squadron. Tore the heart out of the eagle on that flag over there. We remember you, by God, we remember you."

Appellant's Motion to Attach of 19 Apr 2001, Glazier Transcript IV of 29 May 1997 at 45-46 (emphasis added). Maj Glazier's description is corroborated by the record and by a post-trial clemency request. Record at 3032-33; LtCol G.S. Barthel ltr of 10 Feb 98 at ¶ 14.

As Maj Glazier observed, his sentencing argument was highly objectionable, violating various ethical canons. The American Bar Association

Standards for Criminal Justice state that "the prosecutor should support the authority of the court and the dignity of the trial courtroom by strict adherence to codes of professionalism and by manifesting a professional attitude toward the judge, opposing counsel, witnesses, defendants, jurors, and others in the courtroom." Prosecution Function Standard 3-5.2(a). In other words, Maj Glazier's overbearing, intemperate, and deliberate conduct and language improperly tended to inflame the passions and possible prejudices of the members and placed the fairness of the sentencing proceedings in jeopardy. *See United States v. Barrazamartinez,* 58 M.J. 173, 176 (C.A.A.F. 2003); Prosecution Function Standard 3-5.8(c).

The [Assistant Defense Counsel] made a timely objection to Maj Glazier's entire sentencing argument, focusing on the words used, namely "bad hombre," "animal" (three times), "gang-banging" (twice) and drive-by shooting (twice). The military judge sustained the objection and gave a curative instruction. The members stated they understood the instruction and agreed to follow it. Presuming that the members did indeed follow the instruction in their deliberations, we conclude that these references had no impact on the sentence. *See United States v. Garrett,* 24 M.J. 413, 418 (C.M.A. 1987). Nonetheless, Maj Glazier's argument was an affront to principles of justice and fair play.

We do not begrudge an advocate's effort to influence the members and the military judge to accept his/her arguments on the facts and the law. That is what advocates are expected to do.... counsel should be zealous in their advocacy. But, such zealous advocacy must be kept within the bounds of law, military regulation and ethical rules....

> A sensitiveness to fair play and sportsmanship is perhaps the best protection against the abuse of power, and the citizen's safety lies in the prosecutor who tempers zeal with human kindness, who seeks truth and not victims, who serves the law and not factional purposes, and who approaches his task with humility.

United States Att'y Gen. Robert H. Jackson, Address at the Second Annual Conference of United States Attorneys at 4-5 (Apr. 1, 1940).

We understand that the facts of this case cry out for justice for the appellant's heinous crimes, particularly as to LtCol Kidd and LtCol Heffner. We also understand the zeal displayed by Maj Glazier and Capt Feldman throughout this court-martial. But there is a line between zealous prosecution infused with righteous indignation, on the one hand, and unethical conduct, on the other. These two judge advocates crossed that line on several occasions in this capital court-martial. In so doing, they jeopardized the integrity of the trial proceedings and besmirched the military justice system in the United States Marine Corps.

    * * *

VII. Conclusion

Based on our decision on the challenge for cause, the remaining assignments of error are moot. The findings and sentence are set aside. The record is returned to the Judge Advocate General for remand to an appropriate convening authority. A rehearing may be ordered. If a rehearing is not ordered, the charges and specifications shall be dismissed.

Senior Judge CARVER concurs.

[Senior Judge Ritter's separate opinion concurring in part and dissenting in part is omitted.—Eds.]

Points for Discussion

1. How did the conduct of Maj Glazier and Capt Feldman cross the line from zealous advocacy to unethical conduct?

2. What prosecutorial misconduct did you find the most offensive? Most unethical? Why?

UNITED STATES v. BAKER
Army Court of Criminal Appeals
65 M.J. 691 (Army Ct. Crim. App. 2007)

MAHER, Senior Judge:

A special court-martial composed of officers convicted appellant [Staff Sergeant Michael L. Baker, U.S. Army], contrary to his pleas, of attempted larceny, absence from his appointed place of duty on divers occasions, and willful disobedience of a superior commissioned officer (two specifications), in violation of Articles 80, 86, and 90, Uniform Code of Military Justice, 10 U.S.C. §§ 880, 886, and 890 [hereinafter UCMJ]. The convening authority approved the adjudged sentence to a bad-conduct discharge and reduction to Private E1.

PROCEDURAL HISTORY

In our initial review of appellant's case under Article 66, UCMJ, this court affirmed the findings and the sentence. *United States v. Baker*, ARMY 9800743 (Army Ct. Crim. App. 18 Jan. 2002) (unpub.). The United States Court of Appeals for the Armed Forces (C.A.A.F.) granted review as to whether appellant received effective assistance of counsel. On 1 July 2003, our superior court stated it could not "determine whether the actions of trial defense counsel resulted in a denial of Appellant's Sixth Amendment right to the effective assistance of counsel" given the record's posture. *United States v. Baker*, 58 M.J. 380, 387 (C.A.A.F. 2003). The C.A.A.F. set aside our decision and remanded the case for a hearing pursuant to *United States v. DuBay*, 37 C.M.R. 411 (C.M.A. 1967), to address the following questions:

(1) What information, if any, led defense counsel to perceive that testimony by appellant would present an ethical problem? (2) What

inquiry, if any, did defense counsel make? (3) What facts were revealed by the inquiry? (4) What standard, if any, did defense counsel apply in evaluating those facts? (5) What determination, if any, did defense counsel make with respect to prospective testimony by appellant in light of those facts? (6) After making any such determination, what information and advice, if any, did counsel provide to the appellant? (7) What response, if any, did appellant make? (8) What information was disclosed by the two defense counsel during their off-the-record conversation with the military judge?

Baker, 58 M.J. at 387. On 15 October 2003, a convening authority ordered a *DuBay* hearing to address the issues our superior court identified. A military judge held the hearing on 9 January 2004, entered his findings on 20 February 2004, and returned the record to this court for further review. We determined *en banc* that the military judge, by allowing counsel to testify in a conclusory fashion and expressly declining to delve into specific facts, failed to provide a record on which we could reach a decision on the merits of appellant's claims. *United States v. Baker,* ARMY 9800743 (Army Ct. Crim. App. 11 May 2005) (order) (unpub.).

Accordingly, we returned the record for another *DuBay* hearing. *Id.* On 23 September 2005, the convening authority ordered a second hearing which a different military judge conducted on 5 December 2005. The military judge entered his findings on 6 January 2006.

The record is again before us for further review. Appellant asserts: (1) the military judges at the *DuBay* hearings erred in finding that trial defense counsel acted in accordance with their legal and ethical obligations and (2) appellant received ineffective assistance of counsel when his two trial defense counsel provided no assistance during his testimony. After reviewing the entire record, to include both *DuBay* hearings, both military judges' findings, appellate counsels' supplemental briefs, and oral arguments, we find appellant's trial defense counsel provided appellant with effective assistance at trial.

BACKGROUND

Captain (CPT) B and CPT M represented appellant at his court-martial. Captain B had served on active duty for approximately four years prior to appellant's court-martial and as a defense counsel on fifteen to twenty courts-martial before appellant's trial. She did not practice law prior to entering active military service. Captain M, a reservist on active duty, began practicing law in 1982 in Utah and had previously tried thirty-five jury trials in federal court and two capital cases in state court as a defense attorney.

During trial on the merits, the defense presented testimony of two witnesses, stipulated to the testimony of four other witnesses, and offered eight exhibits into evidence. Before the close of the defense case, the military judge granted a defense request for "a short recess." During the recess, appellant consulted with his counsel; appellant's counsel then engaged in *ex parte* communications with the military judge without appellant present. Defense counsel told the military judge they could no longer ethically represent appellant and requested permission to withdraw from the case. The military judge assumed counsel were talking about perjured testimony; however, she did not ask counsel for specifics and counsel did not proffer any specifics regarding appellant's prospective testimony.

The proceedings resumed in an Article 39(a) session without the members present. The military judge informed appellant his counsel wished to withdraw because his counsel expected him to testify inconsistently with prior statements he made to them. Responding to questions from the military judge, both counsel stated they could not ethically call appellant to the stand to testify.   The military judge explained the narrative procedure through which appellant would testify and informed appellant he would testify without the benefit of counsel.   She further explained that trial counsel, members, and the military judge could examine appellant, but that his trial defense counsel could not argue to the members anything appellant said during his narrative. Appellant said he understood the military judge's explanation and accepted her offer to discuss the matter further with his counsel. After another recess, the military judge confirmed appellant wanted to testify, called the members to the courtroom, and called appellant to the stand. Appellant testified in narrative form for approximately two hours without the assistance of counsel. He responded to the prosecution's detailed cross-examination and answered a series of questions from the members asked by the military judge. The defense rested its case at the conclusion of his testimony. The government offered brief testimony in rebuttal, calling appellant's first sergeant who testified that, in his opinion, appellant was untruthful.

First DuBay Hearing

At the first *DuBay* hearing, both CPT B and CPT M refused to specify why they concluded appellant would testify falsely. Captain B said she still had an attorney-client relationship with appellant, while CPT M said he "believed he still had an obligation to [appellant]."   Both counsel said the Rules of Professional Conduct of their respective bars prohibited them from disclosing any confidential communications,[3] even though CPT B acknowledged appellant had executed a limited waiver, consenting to a "limited disclosure of confidential communication . . . reasonably necessary for CPT [B] to respond to allegations concerning her representation of [appellant]."

---

[3] At the time of trial, CPT B was a member of the Texas Bar, while CPT M was a member of the Utah and District of Columbia (D.C.) Bars. In accordance with the applicable Rules of Professional Conduct, counsel were required to try to persuade an accused to refrain from perjurious testimony.   If counsel could not dissuade an accused, withdrawal may have been an acceptable resolution. *See* Army Reg. 27-26, Legal Services: Rules of Professional Conduct for Lawyers [hereinafter AR 27-26], 3.3 cmt (1 May 1992); Utah Code Jud. Admin. Rule 3.3 cmt; D.C. Bar Appx. A, Rule 3.3 cmt; Tex. R. Prof. Conduct 3.03 cmt.

Although appellant's *DuBay* defense counsel repeatedly asked the military judge to direct CPT B and CPT M to provide specific responses, the military judge failed to order specific responses, stating he was unsure whether he had the authority to do so.

The military judge found "the information that led counsel to conclude that there was an ethical problem is mostly conceptual, although there are some specific facts that support counsel's decision." He explained "conceptual" to mean: "I do not have specific instances or matters other than [appellant's] inconsistencies in describing the conviction." Although counsel failed to provide any specific details, the military judge found "counsel determined that they could not ethically call [appellant] to the stand."

Second DuBay Hearing

At the second *DuBay* hearing, CPT B and CPT M testified with greater specificity. The *DuBay* judge made extensive findings of fact, which we summarize as follows:

(1) Both of appellant's trial defense counsel thoroughly investigated appellant's case and were well prepared to represent him at trial;

(2) While trial defense counsel requested appellant provide details and specific information to prepare his defense, he did not do so until the day of trial, and then provided a binder of documents and proposed areas of inquiry that were either cumulative or tangential;

(3) Trial defense counsel believed appellant would perjure himself by claiming he left his place of duty to get a haircut; claiming his unit used the particular type of color printer cartridges that appellant allegedly stole; lying about his 1985 federal convictions for making false, fictitious, and fraudulent statements, and possessing a falsified document to aid someone to obtain money from the federal government;

(4) Trial defense counsel based their conclusion regarding the haircut on appellant's admission to them on one occasion that he failed to get a haircut; his subsequent retraction of that admission; and his failure to provide any corroborating information for his retraction;

(5) Trial defense counsel based their conclusion that appellant was untruthful regarding the stolen printer cartridges on: supply room logs revealing the unit never stocked the printer cartridges in question; information from the supply room noncommissioned officers (NCOs) that none of the unit's computers used those printer cartridges; CPT B's observation that appellant had hundreds of color copy resumes and a personal computer printer that used that type of cartridge in his barracks room; the discovery of a bag full of printer cartridges for appellant's personal printer that had been paid for with a government credit card; and the bag containing the cartridges was found in a military vehicle operated

by appellant. After investigating, CPT M independently reached the same conclusion as CPT B;[4]

(6) Trial defense counsel based their conclusion on appellant's veracity regarding his prior federal conviction on his varied accounts of the facts underlying his conviction which conflicted with CPT B's electronic research regarding the conviction and documentation the prosecution provided the defense team;

(7) Captain B's standard for concluding appellant would testify falsely was whether she *knew* her client would lie, which she saw as a high standard of proof. She did not believe her client had to admit guilt to an underlying offense before she refused to present his testimony;

(8) Captain M's standard was likewise very high, akin to beyond a reasonable doubt, and he also did not believe the analysis depended on whether his client admitted guilt;

(9) Trial defense counsel and appellant originally agreed, as a tactical decision, appellant would not testify because of appellant's "very desultory thought process," poor character for truthfulness which CPT B uncovered in her investigation, and prior federal conviction. At the last moment, appellant changed his mind and decided to testify. Given appellant's unpredictable nature, it was not possible for counsel to have appellant tailor his testimony;

(10) Both counsel were confident they confronted appellant about his falsehoods prior to trial; and

(11) Consistent with their "fiduciary obligations" [sic], both counsel refrained from divulging specifics to the military judge at trial. They exercised the best option they saw available to protect themselves and appellant.

Summary

We adopt the second *DuBay* judge's findings of fact. In addition, based on the entire record before us, we conclude: prior to trial, CPT B and CPT M together confronted appellant about his perceived falsehoods and could not obtain explanations from him; during the court-martial, appellant notified his defense counsel of his intent to testify; CPT B specifically informed appellant during recess she could not call him to testify because she believed he would lie; and both counsel possessed an objective, firm, factual basis to conclude appellant would perjure himself.

We also find appellant was untruthful regarding the haircut offenses at trial when he testified he got a haircut every time he was ordered to get one. We further find appellant was untruthful when he testified he regularly

---

[4] The *DuBay* judge found that CPT B and CPT M accounted for the supply NCOs' own credibility issues, and relied heavily on the documented fact that appellant's unit supply room never stocked those particular cartridges.

placed the printer cartridges on the shelves in the supply room and they regularly disappeared over the course of the following month.

DISCUSSION

A determination regarding the effectiveness of counsel is a mixed question of law and fact. . . . We review findings of fact under a clearly erroneous standard, but the question of ineffective assistance of counsel flowing from those facts is a question of law we review de novo. *United States v. McClain,* 50 M.J. 483, 487 (C.A.A.F. 1999).

> Under the first prong of *Strickland,* which examines the issue of deficiency in performance, we ask: (A) Are appellant's allegations true? (B) If so, is there a reasonable explanation for counsel's actions? (C) If there is not a reasonable explanation, did defense counsel's level of advocacy fall measurably below the performance ordinarily expected of fallible lawyers?

* * *

"Even if counsel's performance was deficient, the defense must ordinarily surmount the second prong of *Strickland,* which measures prejudice. The defense bears the burden of demonstrating that 'there is a reasonable probability that, but for counsel's unprofessional errors, the result of the proceeding would have been different.' " 63 M.J. at 10 (quoting *Strickland,* 466 U.S. at 694). In most cases, the prejudice prong is the most critical, for " 'if we conclude that any error would not have been prejudicial under the second prong of *Strickland,* we need not ascertain the validity of the allegations or grade the quality of counsel's performance under the first prong.' " *Id.* (quoting *United States v. Saintaude,* 61 M.J. 175, 179-80 (C.A.A.F. 2005)).

* * *

I. *The Legal Standard*

An attorney must have a firm factual basis to believe the client intends to commit perjury before acting in a manner limiting representation of a client and must first attempt to dissuade the client from committing perjury. *See Baker,* 58 M.J. at 387-88.[6] Should counsel's efforts to dissuade the client fail, counsel must take appropriate, remedial measures. First, the attorney should try to structure the client's testimony to avoid areas where the client will

---

[6] The CAAF also provided guidance for counsel confronting a problem with potential client perjury. The court suggested counsel first investigate the validity of the evidence to be offered at trial; if such an investigation provides a firm factual basis to anticipate perjury, counsel should discuss the issue with the client and review the facts, the basis for the attorney's concern, and potential consequences for the client, such as the obligation to tell the truth, possible criminal sanctions, trial tactics, and the effect of narrative testimony; should the client persist in testifying, the attorney should request an *ex parte* proceeding on the record with the accused in attendance. *Baker,* 58 M.J. at 387. The CAAF also noted it was not establishing mandatory practices. *Id.* at 388.

commit perjury. Should this prove impossible, the next step is to provide the court nonspecific notice the client will testify in the free narrative form. *See id.* at 386. Finally, only in situations where the attorney-client relationship is irreparably damaged should counsel seek to withdraw. *See id.* at 387.

Not only have we found trial defense counsel possessed a firm factual basis to conclude appellant would commit perjury if he testified, we also hold counsel did not deprive appellant of the effective assistance of counsel during his court-martial. Prior to analyzing appellant's assignments of error, however, we need to address several procedural aspects of the trial proceedings.

II. *Trial Practice*

Counsel who are convinced a client intends to commit perjury are caught between two conflicting obligations: confidentiality of information and candor toward the tribunal. *See* AR 27-26, Rule 1.6 (confidentiality of information); Rule 3.3 (candor toward the tribunal). A lawyer's duty to maintain a client's confidences and secrets is a cornerstone of building trust and communication. *See United States ex rel, Wilcox v. Johnson,* 555 F.2d 115, 122 (3d Cir. 1977) (keeping inviolate client's ability to communicate confidentially with counsel essential to adversary system). If an accused cannot trust his counsel to keep information confidential, the accused will not disclose confidences, limiting counsel's ability to render effective assistance. Military Rule of Evidence 502(a); *see generally United States v. Marrelli,* 15 C.M.R. 276, 281-82 (C.M.A. 1954).

As officers of the court, counsel also have a duty not to offer false testimony. *Baker,* 58 M.J. at 385 (citing AR 27-26, Rule 3.3, Rule 3.4(a) (obligation of fairness to opposing party and counsel)). If an attorney says nothing to the court and offers perjured testimony in the usual manner, counsel will have participated in a fraud upon the court. *See Nix v. Whiteside,* 475 U.S. 157, 169, 173 (1986) (lawyer complicit in client perjury faces prosecution or disciplinary action). In the course of attempting to prevent perjury, an attorney might disclose a client's confidential communications to the court either directly or indirectly, depending on the tactical approach counsel takes to the problem. *See United States v. Long,* 857 F.2d 436, 447 (8th Cir. 1988) (moving to withdraw or having client testify in narrative form discloses suspicion of perjury). Counsel should refrain from directly disclosing specific confidences if at all possible. *See Baker,* 58 M.J. at 386 (counsel made nonspecific disclosure to court that client will testify in free narrative form); *Johnson,* 555 F.2d at 122 (counsel should not disclose private conjectures about client to the court); *cf. United States v. Midgett,* 342 F.3d 321, 326 (4th Cir. 2003) (not lawyer's place to decide client was lying and to disclose that belief to the court based on suspicion of perjury).

An example of an indirect disclosure occurred in the present case. Counsel's motion to withdraw led the military judge to suspect potential perjury, which constitutes at least an implied revelation of client confidences.

Notification of the accused's intent to testify in the narrative form would also have led the military judge to suspect potential perjury.

At trial, the military judge instructed CPT B and CPT M to prepare memoranda for record outlining circumstances before and after appellant's testimony to assist evaluating potential claims regarding ineffective assistance of counsel. At the first *DuBay* hearing, both counsel testified they prepared a memorandum in accordance with the judge's instructions. Due to the passage of time and subsequent events, neither counsel could produce their respective memoranda. Although we commend the military judge's foresight, in the future military judges should obtain, seal, and attach such memoranda as appellate exhibits. *Baker*, 58 M.J. at 388. Where a military judge is not the trier of fact, an *ex parte* proceeding to ensure counsel has a firm factual basis for believing the client will commit perjury may be appropriate. *United States v. Roberts*, 20 M.J. 689, 691-92 (A.C.M.R. 1985); *see United States v. Elzy*, 25 M.J. 416 (C.M.A. 1988); *Lowery v. Cardwell*, 575 F.2d 727 (9th Cir. 1978).[7] Only with the accused's express and informed consent should such a proceeding address areas within the scope of the attorney-client privilege and work product doctrine.

III. *Sixth Amendment Right to Effective Assistance of Counsel*

The Sixth Amendment guarantees a criminal appellant the right to the assistance of counsel at trial. U.S. Const. amend. VI. To satisfy the guarantee of the Sixth Amendment, counsel must provide effective assistance. *Strickland*, 466 U.S. at 686. An accused also has a Constitutional right to testify. *Harris v. New York*, 401 U.S. 222, 225 (1971). Notwithstanding its Constitutional stature, however, an accused's right to testify has its limits. In *Whiteside*, 475 U.S. at 173, the Supreme Court made clear an appellant has no Sixth Amendment right to a counsel willing to participate in presenting perjured testimony. Accordingly, the right to testify includes neither the right to commit perjury nor the right to the assistance of counsel in doing so. *Harris*, 401 U.S. at 225; *Whiteside*, 475 U.S. at 173.

IV. *Suspicions of Perjury*

Courts employ a variety of standards to determine whether an attorney justifiably believed a client intended to commit perjury.... In previously reviewing this case, the C.A.A.F. announced it "shall not require a higher standard than [the] firm factual basis" standard discussed in *Johnson. Baker*, 58 M.J. at 386.

> When the question of perjured testimony by a defendant arises, we require that the lawyer act in good faith and have a firm basis in objective fact. Conjecture or speculation that the defendant intends to testify falsely are not enough. Inconsistencies in the evidence or in the defendant's version

---

[7] In civilian proceedings, the recommended practice is to have an *ex parte* proceeding before a judge who is not presiding over the trial.... At courts-martial, another military judge could be detailed for such hearings.

of events are also not enough to trigger the lawyer's obligation not to elicit false testimony, even though the inconsistencies, considered in light of the Commonwealth's proof, raise concerns in counsel's mind that the defendant is equivocating and is not an honest person. Similarly, the existence of strong physical and forensic evidence implicating the defendant would not be sufficient. Counsel can rely on facts made known to him, and is under no duty to conduct an independent investigation.

Calhoun, 287 Ill.Dec. 89, 815 N.E.2d at 503 (quoting *Mitchell,* 781 N.E.2d at 1250-51) (calling for Illinois Supreme Court to adopt firm factual basis test).

V. *Counsel's Firm Factual Basis*

In appellant's case, CPT B and CPT M obtained proof of appellant's falsehoods through their investigations which were further complicated by appellant's constantly changing version of the facts. The varying accounts were more than merely inconsistent; they were directly contradictory. As defense counsel observed, the contradictions rendered appellant's story "physically impossible." Further, appellant confessed to an instance of failing to obtain a haircut and, despite his subsequent recantation, never provided any evidence to support his retraction.

While inconsistencies alone are insufficient to justify a motion to withdraw, appellant's inconsistencies included an admission of guilt. Captain B and CPT M were entitled to rely on appellant's admission that he failed to obtain a haircut. *See Mitchell,* 781 N.E.2d at 1247 (investigation unnecessary where accused admits guilt). Appellant's failure to explain his confession and its subsequent retraction further solidified his counsel's basis to conclude he would lie.

We reach the same conclusion as to appellant's explanation of the larceny offenses. Unlike the haircut question, appellant did not admit to stealing the cartridges. His lie, however, involves the reason he obtained the cartridges from the Self-Service Supply Center. Appellant's claim he needed to restock the unit's supply room since the cartridges were "flying off the shelves" is patently untrue. First, the unit records establish it never stocked that brand of printer cartridges, and the supply sergeants told the defense team none of the unit's computers used those cartridges. Second, defense counsel knew appellant used a large number of cartridges of the same type as the stolen ones.

Appellant's case closely resembles *Commonwealth v. Mitchell.* Like Mitchell, appellant confessed to one of his offenses to his counsel, then denied it. The *Mitchell* court determined "[t]he defendant's admission was different in kind from inconsistencies in details." 781 N.E.2d at 1247. Such is the case here; appellant's admission that he did not get a haircut when ordered to do so is not the same as giving varying accounts of the same denial of wrongdoing.

VI. *Counsel's Actions Based on the Firm Factual Basis*

A. Attempt to Dissuade

During the recess, when appellant told his counsel he changed his mind and wanted to testify, CPT B attempted to dissuade appellant from testifying. CPT B advised him he was not permitted to lie on the stand and explained the tactical reasons why he should not testify, to include his prior conviction and the evidence of his poor character for truthfulness. She warned appellant of the repercussions should he insist on testifying falsely, specifically counsel's inability to assist him in presenting perjured testimony and losing the assistance of counsel if he testified falsely. Counsel did not clearly explain to appellant which portions of his prospective testimony they believed to be perjurious. Neither CPT B nor CPT M testified they advised appellant of the potential criminal sanctions he might face if he committed perjury. While this failure to advise appellant more fully of the ramifications of presenting perjured testimony might under other circumstances constitute error, under the specific circumstances of this case we find defense counsel adequately discharged their duties under *Strickland*.

Both defense counsel repeatedly confronted appellant with their concerns about his proposed testimony prior to his decision to testify. In the second *DuBay* hearing, CPT B told the military judge that appellant would shrug his shoulders, "would shut down," or would change the subject when counsel confronted him before trial about his lies.[8] Captain B spent several months with appellant preparing his case and clearly relayed her concerns to him; CPT M had a less-involved history with appellant, but was no less clear in expressing his concerns. Counsel tailored the confrontational aspects of their conversations with appellant to convey their message without causing him to "shut down" completely. Appellant's initial agreement with counsel's recommendation not to testify understandably forestalled further efforts to extract a true account of events from him. When appellant changed his mind mid-trial, counsel had less of an opportunity to address his new decision. Counsel's initial confrontations with appellant, however, suffice to satisfy their duty to address their concerns about his testimony with him.

The second *DuBay* judge, having had the benefit of observing appellant's testimony and demeanor under both direct and cross examinations, concluded:

> Appellant's personality and nature, and his inability to follow a narrow, focused train of thought[,] made it virtually impossible for [CPT M] and

---

[8] Notably, appellant's reticence in the face of a challenge to his veracity prompted CPT M to have appellant psychiatrically evaluated. According to the testimony at the *DuBay* proceedings, the evaluation did not indicate appellant suffered from any mental disease or defect impairing his ability to communicate with counsel or to understand their communications. While counsel's descriptions of appellant's actions may indicate appellant did not communicate with them, any inability to do so was not due to appellant's lacking the capacity to communicate.

CPT [B] to limit direct examination . . . to avoid potential areas of false testimony, especially given the last minute reversal of the mutual decision that . . . appellant would not testify.

Based upon our review of the record, we agree. Appellant was unmanageable. Had defense counsel attempted to present his testimony in a controlled manner designed to avoid perjury, they most likely would have failed.

We also note that in the course of receiving advice on the initial offer of nonjudicial punishment, appellant spoke with every defense counsel in the local Trial Defense Service office, meaning he spoke with at least two other attorneys before returning to CPT B. After initially demanding his right to trial by court-martial when offered nonjudicial punishment for the haircut offenses, appellant twice agreed with defense counsel to accept nonjudicial punishment proceedings in lieu of the court-martial. Each time defense counsel persuaded appellant's command to re-offer nonjudicial punishment proceedings, appellant rejected those proceedings.

Both defense counsel had extensive experience and characterized appellant as unique based on his unpredictable and difficult nature. . . .

Regarding counsel's duty to advise appellant of potential criminal sanctions, it is important to note appellant was familiar with the legal consequences for making false statements. He defended himself in his prior federal prosecution, presented his own appeal after his conviction, and sought a writ of certiorari from the United States Supreme Court after the appellate court affirmed his case. Appellant, therefore, was on actual notice that making false statements in an official federal government matter could result in criminal liability. Failure to reiterate that point to appellant when he decided to disregard counsel's advice in the middle of his court-martial and testify does not constitute a professional deficiency on these facts.

Counsel also did not advise appellant of the risks of testifying in the free narrative form. While counsel's advice to appellant could have been more complete under the *Baker* standard, we find they adequately discharged their duties. The military judge explained the free narrative form to appellant before obtaining his decision to testify. While neither counsel nor the military judge specifically advised appellant of the tactical problems inherent in free narrative form testimony, we find the absence of such advice in this case does not render counsel professionally deficient. In any event, counsel advised appellant he would have to testify without their assistance and he chose to testify.

Indeed, in the beginning of his testimony, appellant gave a facially plausible reason for his testifying in the free narrative form: "I chose to give a category [sic] explanation to you gentleman [sic] for each individual charge because you're here to judge me as a soldier and an individual. So you get to hear from me." Even if we were to characterize counsel's performance as deficient, we cannot say there is a reasonable probability of a different result based on their advice to appellant. . . . Ironically, therefore, appellant's perjured testimony resulted in no prejudice to him-it actually inured to his benefit.

Appellant also wanted to testify in part so he could explain his belief that his unit discriminated against activated Reserve Component Soldiers, despite counsel's warnings of the problems he would create by doing so. Even after counsels' efforts and attempt to withdraw, appellant did not heed this advice. It is clear appellant intended to testify and perjure himself no matter what his counsel said. While a difficult and unpredictable client does not forfeit his right to effective assistance of counsel, we are satisfied there is nothing CPT B or CPT M could have done to prevent appellant from committing perjury. Under these facts, counsel acted properly in accordance with their duty of candor to the tribunal.

B. *The Motion to Withdraw*

The next question is whether counsel acted appropriately in moving to withdraw. Withdrawal is a more drastic remedy than the use of the free narrative form, and has the potential effect of depriving the client of the assistance of counsel for the remainder of the trial. *Cf. Baker,* 58 M.J. at 386 (noting some authorities see withdrawal as too disruptive "and simply foists the issue on the next attorney"). Our superior court would limit motions to withdraw to situations where the attorney-client relationship has deteriorated to the point where effective representation is no longer possible. *Id.* at 387. Nothing indicates such was the case here. Counsels' decision to withdraw was premature.

Nevertheless, counsel moved to withdraw in a manner that preserved appellant's confidences as much as possible. The military judge denied the motion to withdraw, leaving appellant in the same position he would have occupied had counsel initially chosen the free narrative form. We do not fault counsel for their no-notice decision in the middle of this hotly contested trial. . . .

While counsel should not have sought to withdraw and only should have notified the military judge their client would testify in the free narrative form, the end result was the same: appellant testified, and his counsel did not aid in the presentation of perjured testimony. There is no reasonable probability of a different result if counsel had made the ideal motion. In the future, however, counsel should not seek to withdraw "unless the circumstances as a whole have produced such an irreconcilable conflict between counsel and the accused that effective representation no longer is possible." *Baker,* 58 M.J. at 387.

CONCLUSION

Prior to trial, appellant told his defense counsel he failed to comply with an order to get a haircut. The unit's supply records and MSG Hyde's information established the printer cartridges in question never entered the supply room. Appellant clearly informed his counsel he intended to testify to the contrary on these matters and changed his mind in the middle of the trial to reverse his decision not to testify and drastically altered the defense trial strategy. Under these circumstances, his counsel could not participate in appellant's testimony. Defense counsel's decision did not deprive appellant of effective assistance of counsel, and his claims to that effect are without merit.

We have reviewed the matters personally raised by appellant under *United States v. Grostefon,* 12 M.J. 431 (C.M.A. 1982), and find them to be without merit.

DECISION

The findings of guilty and the sentence are affirmed.

Judge SULLIVAN and Judge HOLDEN concur.

Points for Discussion

1. Assessing this case, one expert has written: "Counsel in the *Baker* case failed to submit the memorandum suggested by the court explaining their reasons for suspecting perjury. That failure led to two *DuBay* hearings and a decade of litigation in lieu of summary affirmance. The lesson is there is value in complying with the court's request to document your reasons, because your client could put you on the edge despite your best efforts. If that happens savvy counsel will document how they got there in line with C.A.A.F.'s guidance." Kwasi L. Hawks, *Professional Responsibility on the Edge*, Army Law., Jun. 2008, at 93, 103. What risks might counsel have faced if they had provided the memorandum?

2. Should the appellant in this case face any sanction for his plan to testify falsely and for imposing great burdens on the military justice system and his counsel by alleging without merit and as a result of his conduct that he had received ineffective assistance?

UNITED STATES v. CAIN
U.S. Court Appeals for the Armed Forces
59 M.J. 285 (C.A.A.F. 2004)

EFFRON, Judge:

At a general court-martial composed of a military judge sitting alone, Appellant [Sergeant Billy E. Cain, U.S. Army] was convicted, pursuant to his pleas, of indecent assault (two specifications), in violation of Article 134, Uniform Code of Military Justice [hereinafter UCMJ], 10 U.S.C. § 934 (2000). He was sentenced to a dishonorable discharge, confinement for five years, forfeiture of all pay and allowances, and reduction to Private E-1. Pursuant to a pretrial agreement, the convening authority approved a sentence providing for a dishonorable discharge, 24 months' confinement, forfeiture of all pay and allowances, and reduction to Private E-1. The Court of Criminal Appeals affirmed. *United States v. Cain,* 57 M.J. 733 (A.Ct. Crim. App. 2002).

On Appellant's petition, we granted review of the following issues:

I. WHETHER APPELLANT WAS DENIED THE FUNDAMENTAL RIGHT TO CONFLICT FREE AND EFFECTIVE ASSISTANCE OF COUNSEL WHEN THE LEAD DEFENSE COUNSEL AND APPELLANT ENGAGED IN A SECRETIVE HOMOSEXUAL RELATIONSHIP.

II. WHETHER THE ARMY COURT OF CRIMINAL APPEALS ERRED WHEN IT DETERMINED THAT APPELLANT'S SEXUAL RELATIONSHIP WITH HIS LEAD DEFENSE COUNSEL DID NOT CREATE A CONFLICT OF INTEREST DENYING APPELLANT EFFECTIVE ASSISTANCE OF COUNSEL.

For the reasons set forth below, we conclude that Appellant did not receive effective assistance of counsel and reverse.

I. BACKGROUND
A. COURT-MARTIAL PROCEEDINGS

1. *Assignment of defense counsel to represent Appellant*

In October 1997, Appellant was charged with three specifications of forcible sodomy under Article 125, UCMJ, 10 U.S.C. § 925 (2000). The charges alleged that the offenses occurred between 1993 and 1995.

At the time of the first charged offense, Appellant was assigned to the Reserve Officer Training Corps (ROTC) Department at Norwich University in Vermont. The alleged victim was a male non-ROTC student at Norwich University. At the time of the second and third charged offenses, Appellant was serving at ROTC 1st Brigade Headquarters at Fort Devens, Massachusetts. The alleged victims were male civilians unconnected with Norwich University or the Army.

The military justice chain of command over Appellant included his brigade commander at Fort Devens, the summary court-martial convening authority; the Commander of the 1st Region (ROTC) at Fort Bragg, North Carolina, the special court-martial convening authority; and the Commander of the XVIII Airborne Corps at Fort Bragg, the general court-martial convening authority.

Civilian authorities began an investigation into similar charges in 1995. The brigade commander at Fort Devens, who informed his superiors at Fort Bragg of these matters, decided to let civilian authorities take the lead. The civilian authorities dismissed the charges in the spring of 1996, and the Army permitted Appellant to reenlist shortly thereafter.

Subsequent to Appellant's reenlistment, a new brigade commander was assigned to Fort Devens. The ensuing year was marked by growing tension between Appellant and the command, exacerbated by Appellant's allegations that the brigade commander and his executive officer were involved in sexual improprieties.

After Appellant submitted his allegations against the commander and executive officer, military authorities decided to reopen the investigation into the charges against Appellant that had been dismissed by civilian authorities. In the meantime, the brigade commander was relieved, but the renewed investigation into Appellant's activities continued apace. Charges were preferred against Appellant on October 15, 1997, and forwarded to the special court-martial convening authority at Fort Bragg.

The special court-martial convening authority appointed an investigating officer under Article 32, UCMJ, 10 U.S.C. § 832 (2000), to look into the allegations. The Article 32 hearing was conducted at Fort Devens. Because Fort Devens did not have a trial defense office, the responsibility for detailing counsel to represent Appellant at the Article 32 hearing was exercised by Major S, the senior defense counsel at Fort Bragg. Major S assigned himself to represent Appellant during the Article 32 proceedings. The Article 32 proceedings and subsequent review by the chain of command resulted in referral of the charges on December 18, 1997, for trial by a general court-martial.

In January 1998, Appellant was assigned temporarily to Fort Bragg for the duration of the trial. During pretrial sessions in January, Appellant agreed to be represented at trial by Major S, adding that he was pursuing the possibility of representation by civilian counsel. He expressed concern with the large caseload facing defense counsel at Fort Bragg and the impact that it might have on his representation. He requested assignment of an additional counsel to assist Major S, noting that the prosecution already had two attorneys assigned to the case. In February, Major S detailed Captain L as assistant defense counsel and informed the military judge that Appellant would not be represented by civilian defense counsel. Appellant confirmed these arrangements on the record.

2. Pretrial motions

In February and March, the defense filed two motions to dismiss the case on procedural grounds. The first challenged the delay in bringing the case to trial. *See* U.S. Const. amend. V (due process) and Rule for Courts-Martial 907 [hereinafter R.C.M.] (speedy trial). The military judge denied the motion. . . .

The second motion alleged selective prosecution in violation of Appellant's due process and equal protection rights. *See* U.S. Const. amend. V. The motion noted that civilian authorities had dismissed the underlying charges against Appellant; that military officials knew of the charges when Appellant was permitted to reenlist in April 1996; that the charges were resurrected because the command believed that Appellant was homosexual; and that the charges were filed in retaliation for Appellant's "whistleblower" complaint against the command. The military judge denied the motion.

3. The plea agreement

In mid-May, the defense entered into negotiations with the Government, which resulted in a pretrial agreement. Appellant agreed to plead guilty to two specifications of indecent assault in lieu of two of the forcible sodomy specifications. The convening authority agreed to direct the trial counsel to dismiss the remaining forcible sodomy specification and to disapprove any sentence greater than a dishonorable discharge, 24 months' confinement, forfeiture of all pay and allowances, and reduction to Private E-1.

At a court-martial session on June 2, Appellant entered pleas consistent with the pretrial agreement.... After concluding that the pleas were provident, the military judge entered findings consistent with those pleas, and sentenced him to a dishonorable discharge, confinement for five years, forfeiture of all pay and allowances, and reduction to Private E-1.

B. POST-TRIAL DEVELOPMENTS

1. Defense counsel's suicide

Two weeks after trial, a senior officer in the Army Trial Defense Service (TDS) visited Fort Bragg to investigate a professional conduct complaint that had been lodged against Major S. The complaint involved a matter distinct from his representation of Appellant. Major S, who was on leave in Chicago with his wife and son in preparation for an expected reassignment to Germany, returned to Fort Bragg alone to address the allegations. His reassignment had been tentatively placed on hold pending the results of the investigation.

Prior to meeting with Major S, the senior TDS officer visited the Staff Judge Advocate (SJA) of the XVIII Airborne Corps. The SJA showed the senior TDS officer a letter that had been sent to the convening authority by Appellant's parents. The letter, dated four days after the conclusion of trial, alleged that Major S had pressured the Appellant for sexual favors.

During a June 18 meeting with the senior TDS officer, Major S asked if there were potential delays that might affect his reassignment. In response, the senior TDS officer informed Major S of the allegations made by Appellant's parents. Major S, who was upset, denied the allegations. He expressed concern that a long delay could cause the cancellation of his reassignment to Germany, but he appeared to be resigned to the fact that the matter could not be resolved on the spot by the senior TDS officer.

Early the next morning, Major S took his own life. In a package of materials prepared for his personal attorney, Major S left a tape recording made shortly before his death. Although the recording did not provide detailed information about his relationship with Appellant or his conduct as lead defense counsel, it contained the following statements:

I fully deny that I ever forcibly had sex with [Appellant]. . . .

. . . .

My suicide is not an admission of guilt. . . .

. . . .

I want you to know that my death is not an admission of any of the charges against me . . .

. . . .

Concerning [Appellant's] parents' allegation, that I forced their son to have sex with me, the allegation is preposterous. . . .

2. *Assignment of a new defense counsel and the request for a post-trial inquiry*

In July, the assistant defense counsel, Captain L, determined that he should disqualify himself from further representation of Appellant so that counsel not connected with Fort Bragg could represent Appellant during post-trial proceedings. On July 23, Captain H was detailed as Appellant's new defense counsel. On July 29, Captain L, although no longer representing the Appellant, signed the record of trial, which was authenticated on the same day by the military judge.

On July 30, the acting SJA prepared the post-trial recommendation to the convening authority required by R.C.M. 1106. The recommendation proposed approval of the adjudged sentence as modified by the pretrial agreement. The recommendation did not discuss the allegations made by Appellant's parents, the suicide of Major S, or any other intervening events. Pursuant to R.C.M. 1106(f), the recommendation was served on Appellant and Captain H. The defense then requested, and was granted, an extension of time to file post-trial matters.

On September 11, 1998, Captain H submitted a discovery request for information concerning the representation of Appellant by Major S and his subsequent suicide. In the alternative, defense counsel requested an in camera inspection of evidence pertaining to that information by the military judge. The request was denied on September 16 on the grounds that Appellant was not entitled to post-trial discovery and that the military judge's authority to act on the case ended upon authentication of the record of trial.

Defense counsel filed another request on September 28, asking the convening authority to refer the matter to the military judge for a post-trial session under Article 39(a), UCMJ, 10 U.S.C. § 839(a)(2000). *See* R.C.M. 1102(d). The defense asserted that an inquiry by the military judge on the record was necessary to determine whether Appellant had been denied his right to effective assistance of counsel in light of alleged improper activities by Major S. In an analysis prepared for the convening authority, the SJA noted that the defense team had secured a favorable outcome for Appellant, that the asserted improper relationship had not created an actual conflict of interest, and that a post-trial hearing would not serve any useful purpose in the absence of specific allegations by the defense of ineffective representation. In accordance with his SJA's recommendation, the convening authority rejected the request for further proceedings before the military judge on November 2.

On December 8, the defense submitted a post-trial memorandum under R.C.M. 1105 and 1106(f) for consideration by the convening authority. The memorandum emphasized the defense's continuing objection to the Government's refusal to release information regarding the events surrounding Major S's suicide. In addition, the defense contended that Appellant had not received effective assistance of counsel and that the deficiencies in representation rendered his guilty pleas improvident. The defense asked the convening authority to order a new trial. In addition, the defense proposed three alternative remedies: (1) issuance of an administrative discharge of Appellant in lieu of approval of the court-martial proceedings; (2) referral of the matter for review by the military judge in a post-trial session under Article 39(a); or (3) clemency through a reduction in sentence to time served, emphasizing a post-trial diagnosis of Appellant as HIV-positive.

The SJA advised the convening authority that the allegations of legal error were without merit and that the case did not warrant either corrective action or clemency. On December 11, the convening authority adopted the SJA's recommendations and approved the sentence as modified by the pretrial agreement.

3. *The order for an evidentiary hearing*

Over the next two years, Appellant continued to challenge the representation he had received at trial. On October 26, 2000, the Army Court of Criminal Appeals ordered an evidentiary hearing pursuant to *United States v. DuBay,* 37 C.M.R. 411 (C.M.A. 1967). The *DuBay* hearing was held on May 14, 2001. The following section summarizes information from the *DuBay* proceedings and from the record of trial concerning the relationship between Major S and Appellant.

C. THE PERSONAL AND PROFESSIONAL RELATIONSHIP BETWEEN MAJOR S AND APPELLANT

1. *The sexual relationship*

Before he assigned himself to represent Appellant, Major S was aware of Appellant's homosexuality. According to Appellant, Major S had assisted him on another matter six years earlier. The assistant defense counsel at trial, Captain L, testified at the *DuBay* hearing that it was not unusual for Major S to involve himself in a case of this type because Major S was very interested in cases involving sexual misconduct or sex of any kind.

Major S initiated a sexual relationship with Appellant at the very outset of their attorney-client relationship in the present case. In the fall of 1998, Appellant traveled to Fort Bragg for their initial meeting. On the evening that Appellant arrived at Fort Bragg, Major S made sexual advances, which Appellant regarded as unwelcome and inappropriate. In December, when Major S came to Fort Devens for Appellant's Article 32 hearing, he made further sexual advances, which led to acts of oral and anal sodomy between Major S and Appellant.

Subsequent to referral of charges for trial by general court-martial, Appellant learned that he was being transferred temporarily to Fort Bragg in January 1998 at the behest of Major S. While at Fort Bragg, Appellant worked as an enlisted clerk-typist at the TDS office under the supervision of Major S. He worked on the cases of other servicemembers, as well as on his own, and also provided assistance to the ROTC program office.

In addition to his official duties, Appellant performed errands for Major S and frequently drove him to and from his home. On more than one occasion, they engaged in sexual activity during these drives. Another sexual encounter occurred in the TDS office. Although the military judge presiding at the *DuBay* hearing expressed skepticism as to some of Appellant's testimony, he nonetheless concluded that Major S engaged in six or seven acts of sodomy with Appellant during the period in which he served as counsel in the present case.

Major S did not manifest his homosexual activity to his colleagues. At the *DuBay* hearing, the judge advocate who served as trial counsel at Appellant's court-martial characterized Major S as "one of the last people I would think" was a homosexual. The assistant trial counsel at Appellant's court-martial described Major S as "a man's man" who "during the course of plea negotiations, . . . described . . . homosexual behavior in a less than favorable light. . . ." The assistant trial counsel added that "if you were to have asked that question at any point during the course of this, or any other case, . . . I probably would've laughed you out of the room."

2. *The professional relationship*

The *DuBay* record and the record of trial reflect various statements made by Appellant prior to adjudication of findings and sentence in which he expressed satisfaction with Major S as his attorney, often speaking in highly complimentary terms. When he approached Captain L in January to request his assistance with the case, Appellant said that Major S was doing a "great job." Later, Captain L recalled that Appellant had stated "that he was very grateful for the work [Major S] and I were doing and that he was very happy with us." When asked by the military judge during the providence inquiry whether he was satisfied with his attorneys, he responded in the affirmative.

The information developed in the *DuBay* proceeding, however, indicates that Appellant had significant misgivings about Major S throughout the court-martial process. Early in December 1997, Appellant contacted Mr. C, who worked on the staff of an organization providing assistance to servicemembers affected by military policies related to homosexuality. Because the organization did not directly represent persons before courts-martial, Mr. C referred Appellant to a civilian lawyer, Attorney W. Mr. C also contacted Attorney W directly and advised her that Appellant appeared to be "distraught about the nature of his relationship" with Major S. Mr. C also told

Attorney W that when he suggested to Appellant that he report his concerns about Major S to the appropriate authorities, Appellant "expressed great fear of potential consequences should he expose Major [S's] misconduct."

Appellant contacted Attorney W per Mr. C's recommendation. Attorney W did not discuss the underlying court-martial charges with Appellant, confining the conversation to "the problem in his relationship with defense counsel, Major [S]." According to Attorney W, Appellant "was extremely tentative in tone, his voice quavered, and he rambled. He described himself as frightened and depressed."

Appellant told Attorney W that Major S had a reputation as "an extremely talented defense attorney." Appellant "believed that no one but Major [S] could help him be exonerated by the court." Appellant added that Major S had told him that he "would receive a very long prison sentence if he, Major [S], were not his defense counsel."

According to Attorney W, Appellant was torn by conflicting emotions. On the one hand, the sexual relationship initiated by Major S, who was married and had a son, "caused him a great deal of distress, anxiety, and fear." On the other hand, "he was fearful of discontinuing the sexual relationship or reporting it because of his entrenched belief that he would spend a lengthy time in prison without Major [S] as his defense attorney."

Attorney W informed Appellant that Major S's actions were "unethical and illegal" and that the sexual contact "was potentially criminal under Articles 125 or 134 . . ., whether related to sodomy or indecent acts." She expressed concern "that this improper relationship could impair [Major S's] objectivity with regard to his representation" of Appellant.

Appellant "continued to plead that he believed that he would be unable to 'survive' this court without the assistance of Major [S] and that he would simply find himself with inferior counsel were he to report Major [S]." Attorney W attempted to convince Appellant that he should seek new counsel, even if he did not report the misconduct of Major S to the authorities, but Appellant declined this advice. Appellant "reiterat[ed] his complete trust and dependence on [Major S's] legal skills, [and] he informed [Attorney W] that he did not believe he could take the risk of abandoning his [defense] counsel." According to Attorney W, "[i]t was apparent to me from my own experience as counsel and my conversation with him that he was incapable of rejecting [Major S's] professional services or his inappropriate advances because of the deep need of [Appellant] to believe his defense counsel could 'save' him."

Subsequent to his contact with Attorney W in December, Appellant expressed concern about his representation during the initial pretrial sessions of his court-martial. At the first pretrial session on January 15-well after Major S initiated sexual activity with Appellant-the military judge provided Appellant with the standard advice as to his counsel rights, and inquired as to who would represent him. Appellant responded:

> I would like to retain Major [S]; but, due to the serious[ness] of the
> charges, I also-I am new to the area, like I said. I just-I just got here
> basically-here this morning; and, if I had the means-that I'd also like to
> pursue a civilian counsel and have that right to look for that civilian
> counsel. Like I said, I am not from here. I am not familiar with the area or
> the legal people who are out there. So, I would like to retain, at the time
> being, Major [S], but I want the election to seek out legal, civilian counsel.

He then focused on the fact that the prosecution had assigned two judge
advocates to the case:

> If-if-if the government also has two-two prosecutors, I would ask that-I've
> seen the case load, sir. I have some concerns that the defense counsel here
> on-on Bragg-being short the assigned attorneys that they have present-I
> would-I do not feel that I would get the full benefit of a-of a government
> defense, with this case load. This is a[sic] serious charges; and if this is
> being the case, Major [S]-I know he is overloaded. I-like I said, I may be
> from Massachusetts, but I've seen the case load that this office has. I don't
> think that, at this time, that with Major [S's] case load or the trial defense,
> with the shortage of attorneys they do have present to help with my
> defense, that I would get that full benefit of the government providing that
> defense.

> * * *

The military judge then directed Major S to assist Appellant in finding a
civilian counsel.

Shortly thereafter, Major S met with a civilian lawyer, Attorney T, to
discuss an unrelated case. Major S asked Attorney T if he would consider
talking to Appellant. According to Attorney T, Major S stated that the case
was "enormously complicated," adding that he needed "extra help,"
particularly in terms of investigating events in New England, as well as with
negotiations with the convening authority aimed at having the charges
dropped based upon unlawful command influence.

Attorney T met with Appellant on the evening of January 21 to discuss
representation of Appellant at his court-martial. After obtaining assurances
from Attorney T that any discussions preliminary to forming such an
attorney-client relationship would be confidential, Appellant told the attorney
that Major S had initiated a homosexual relationship with him shortly after
Major S became his defense counsel. Attorney T told Appellant that the
relationship was unethical, and that he would insist that the relationship
cease if he became Appellant's counsel. Appellant responded that Major S
was working hard and doing well with the case, and that although Major S
was not his "type," the homosexual relationship had not become so
burdensome that Appellant felt the need to terminate it.

Attorney T raised the possibility of disclosing the details of the illegal
relationship to military officials with a view towards obtaining a dismissal of

the case. Appellant responded that he did not want to anger Major S or affect his career, and emphasized the confidential nature of the information.

During further discussions the next day, Attorney T reiterated his view that the actions of Major S were unethical. He added that he could take the case only if Major S was removed from the defense team. According to the attorney, Appellant was anxious to ensure that he not tell anyone, including Major S, that Appellant had divulged the homosexual nature of the relationship. Attorney T maintained the confidence of their preliminary discussions, and did not represent Appellant at his court-martial.

As the case moved towards trial on the merits in the spring of 1998, Appellant told a fellow soldier that "he was upset over the way his case was being handled" and revealed that Major S had required sexual favors of him. When asked why he did not get another attorney, he replied that "he was between a rock and hard place . . . [He] was not happy with [Major S], but he had gone so far with [Major S] that he could not turn back." His former roommate, in whom he also confided, described him as "distraught" and fearful of retaliation or additional charges if he revealed that he had been pressured into a sexual relationship. Appellant's mother gave a similar account.

Appellant consistently maintained to his defense team that he would not plead guilty to forcible sodomy. He asserted that he had not engaged in any non-consensual sexual activity with the alleged victims. Major S believed that the allegations of forcible sodomy were false and also was inclined to view the case as a matter of consensual sodomy. His investigation of the case led him to conclude that there were substantial grounds for contesting the charges, taking the position that the evidence was stale, the victims had credibility problems, and there was evidence of improper bias by the command in terms of retaliation against Appellant for whistleblower activities. Until shortly before the case was resolved, he appeared intent on contesting all charges. As noted in Section I.A.2, *supra,* the defense twice sought dismissal of the charges on procedural grounds, which were rejected by the military judge.

In May of 1998, Captain L told Major S and Appellant that he viewed the prosecution as having a strong case, and he recommended that the defense initiate discussions with a view towards obtaining a pretrial agreement. Major S by then had alienated the prosecution to the point that he was not in a position to conduct such negotiations, so he delegated the task to Captain L. After a week of negotiations, the parties reached an agreement, and Appellant entered his guilty pleas to two specifications of indecent assault.

The military judge presiding over the *DuBay* proceedings found that there had been a sexual relationship between Major S and Appellant throughout the period of representation. The military judge concluded that the relationship was not coerced, that it played no role in Appellant's decision to enter guilty pleas, and that it did not create a conflict of interest. The military judge also concluded that the defense team provided Appellant with effective counsel in terms of filing motions that challenged the government's case, advising the Appellant about the state of the evidence, and negotiating a favorable pretrial agreement. The Court of Criminal Appeals, which agreed with these conclusions, also concluded that Appellant waived any conflict of interest when he declined to follow the recommendation of two separate civilian attorneys to sever his relationship with Major S.

II. DISCUSSION

A. POTENTIAL CRIMINAL AND ADMINISTRATIVE ACTIONS RESULTING FROM THE CONDUCT BETWEEN THE ATTORNEY AND HIS CLIENT

Major S, the attorney, engaged in a course of conduct with Appellant, his client, which exposed both of them to the possibility of prosecution, conviction, and substantial confinement for the military crimes of fraternization and sodomy. An officer who violates the custom of the armed forces against fraternization with an enlisted person may receive a sentence that includes confinement for two years, a punitive separation, and forfeiture of all pay and allowances. *See* Article 134; *Manual for Courts-Martial, United States* (2002 ed.) [hereinafter *MCM*], Part IV, para. 83.(e). Officers and enlisted members who engage in sodomy, even if not forcible, may receive a sentence for each offense that includes five years confinement, a punitive separation, and forfeiture of all pay and allowances. Article 125; *MCM*, Part IV, para. 51.e.

Fraternization and sodomy are not minor or obscure matters. . . . As a result, even if not prosecuted for sodomy in a court-martial, the conduct initiated by Major S exposed him and Appellant to administrative proceedings that could have resulted in involuntary termination for homosexuality. Moreover, Major S would have faced the possibility of a discharge for soliciting and committing homosexual acts "with a subordinate in circumstances that violate customary military superior-subordinate relationship." Dep't of the Army Regulation (AR) 600-8-24, Officer Transfers and Discharges (Feb. 3, 2003) para. 4-22h(3)(current version substantively identical to the version in effect at trial).

B. ETHICAL CONSIDERATIONS

In addition to potential criminal or administrative action for misconduct as an Army officer, Major S engaged in conduct that subjected him to the possibility of additional disciplinary action for violation of the ethical rules applicable to attorneys in the Army. Rule 1.7(b) of the Army Rules of Professional Conduct for Lawyers prohibits representational conflicts of interest, specifying that "[a] lawyer shall not represent a client if the representation of that client may be materially limited . . . by the lawyer's own interests. . . ." AR 27-26, Army Rules of Professional Conduct, Appendix B (May 1, 1992). Rule 1.2(d) states that "[a] lawyer shall not counsel a client to engage, or assist a client, in conduct that the lawyer knows is criminal or fraudulent." *Id.*

With respect to sexual activity between attorneys and clients, civilian jurisdictions have taken a variety of positions on whether there should be a complete prohibition during an ongoing attorney-client relationship, or whether sexual activity should be prohibited only in specified circumstances. *See, e.g.,* Abed Awad, *Attorney-Client Sexual Relations,* 22 J. Legal Prof. 131 (1998). The Army has endorsed the views of the American Bar Association Standing Committee on Ethics and Professional Responsibility, as expressed in Formal Opinion 92-364 (1992) [hereinafter ABA Formal Op. 92-364]. *See* Army Office of the Judge Advocate General Standards of Conduct Office, *Professional Responsibility Notes,* 1993 Army Law. 48 (August 1993) (quoting ABA Formal Op. 92-364 in full). The ABA opinion observed that sexual relations between an attorney and client-

> may involve unfair exploitation of the lawyer's fiduciary position and presents a significant danger that the lawyer's ability to represent the client adequately may be impaired.... The roles of lover and lawyer are potentially conflicting ones as the emotional involvement that is fostered by a sexual relationship has the potential to undercut the objective detachment that is often demanded for adequate representation.

Id. at 49. The ABA opinion also observed that-

> the client may not feel free to rebuff unwanted sexual advances because of fear that such a rejection will either reduce the lawyer's ardor for the client's cause or, worse yet, require finding a new lawyer, causing the client to lose the time and money that has already been invested in the present representation and possibly damaging the client's legal position.

Id. at 51. *See Colorado v. Good,* 893 P.2d 101, 104 (Colo.1995) (quoting ABA Formal Op. 92-364); *see also* Restatement (Third) of Law Governing Lawyers, § 16, Comment e (2000)("A lawyer may not ... enter a sexual relationship with a client when that would undermine the client's case, abuse the client's dependence on the lawyer, or create risk to the lawyer's independent judgment. . . .")

C. THE IMPACT OF CRIMINAL CONDUCT AND ETHICAL VIOLATIONS ON THE CONSTITUTIONAL RIGHT TO EFFECTIVE ASSISTANCE OF COUNSEL

Members of the armed forces facing criminal charges, like their civilian counterparts, have a constitutional right to effective assistance of counsel. U.S. Const. amend VI. Our Court reviews claims of ineffective assistance of counsel de novo. *United States v. Key,* 57 M.J. 246, 249 (C.A.A.F. 2002)(applying the two-prong test established by the Supreme Court in *Strickland v. Washington,* 466 U.S. 668, 687 (1984): "First, the defendant must show that counsel's performance was deficient.... Second, the defendant must show that the deficient performance prejudiced the defense.").

An attorney's violation of the canons of legal ethics does not necessarily render the attorney's assistance ineffective. . . . .

When an attorney has engaged in criminal misconduct similar to the conduct at issue in Appellant's trial, the federal courts have taken different approaches on the question of whether there is inherent prejudice or whether prejudice must be specifically demonstrated. . . . .

In *United States v. Babbitt*, 26 M.J. 157 (C.M.A. 1988), our Court considered the impact on the effective assistance of counsel in a case where a male civilian defense attorney engaged in a consensual sexual act with his female military client during the evening before the final day of her trial. In those circumstances, our Court declined to hold that every sexual relationship between an attorney and client necessarily creates a conflict of interest that violates a client's Sixth Amendment right to the effective assistance of counsel. *Id.* at 158-59.

D. THE COMBINATION OF POTENTIAL CRIMINAL LIABILITY AND ETHICAL MISCONDUCT

The appeal before us presents a case of first impression, with no direct counterpart in civilian law. The case involves a volatile mixture of sex and crime in the context of the military's treatment of fraternization and sodomy as criminal offenses.

Defense counsel's conduct with his client placed both the attorney and client at the risk of criminal prosecution for violating the very article of the UCMJ, Article 125, that was the subject of the present case. Well before the onset of trial, Major S repeatedly placed himself at risk of severe personal and professional consequences, including the possibility of confinement by court-martial, administrative termination of his military career, and professional discipline. The extraordinary pressure under which he labored during his representation of Appellant is underscored tragically by the fact that he took his own life less than a day after he was informed that his superiors had learned of his personal relationship with Appellant.

Because of counsel's suicide, we do not have the benefit of any testimony that he might have provided as to what consideration he gave potential defense strategies in this case. In the absence of such testimony, we consider the case from the perspective of a military defense counsel caught between the conflicting pressures generated by his own sexual misconduct and his professional responsibilities. By his actions, counsel placed himself and his client in a position where testimony by the client entailed significant risks. Any exploration into Appellant's conduct would have raised the possibility that the prosecution would have endeavored through cross-examination or rebuttal to elicit evidence of similar sexual misconduct. This would have created the potential for exposing counsel's sexual misconduct with Appellant.

In those circumstances, defense counsel faced a conflict between his personal interests and his responsibility to give thoughtful, dispassionate consideration and advice concerning the range of options facing the defense. We do not know whether the defense counsel in this case rejected any specific option on the grounds that it was not in his client's best interest, or because it was not in his own best interest. We do know that when confronted about the sexual misconduct with his client, it was only a matter of hours before he took his own life.

The uniquely proscribed relationship before us was inherently prejudicial and created a per se conflict of interest in counsel's representation of the Appellant. The facts of this case are distinguishable from the limited, consensual relationship between a civilian counsel and his client that we considered in *Babbitt,* where we declined to find such a per se conflict. 26 M.J. at 158-59. Here, we confront a course of conduct involving an attorney's abuse of a military office, a violation of the duty of loyalty, fraternization, and repeated commission of the same criminal offense for which the attorney's client was on trial. . . .

The problems flowing from the conduct of Major S are not overcome in this case by actions of the assistant defense counsel, Captain L, who negotiated the pretrial agreement. Major S was the experienced, lead counsel in the case. Appellant relied on Major S and was entitled to the benefit of conflict-free advice from Major S about the range of alternatives before him. He did not receive that advice.

With respect to waiver, we note that the court below relied on Appellant's discussions with two civilian lawyers, Attorney W and Attorney T, in concluding that he waived any objection to Major S as his counsel. Both attorneys advised him to sever the relationship because the behavior of Major S was unethical. Neither attorney, however, provided him with a detailed explanation of the relationship between the merits of the case and the attorney's ethical obligations. Both focused on the matter from the attorney's perspective, not the client's perspective. Attorney W declined to discuss the substance of the charges with Appellant, and Attorney T focused primarily on the fact that he would not take the case if Major S remained on it. We do not fault either attorney for not engaging in a detailed discussion with Appellant of the impact of any unethical behavior by Appellant on the merits of his case. In both cases, the discussions between the apparently distraught Appellant and the cautious lawyers simply did not advance to the point of forming an attorney-client relationship with respect to the charged offenses. . . .

DECISION

The decision of the United States Army Court of Criminal Appeals is reversed. The findings of guilty and sentence are set aside. The record of trial is returned to the Judge Advocate General of the Army. A rehearing may be ordered.

[Chief Judge Crawford's dissenting opinion is omitted.—Eds.]

Points for Discussion

1. How would the court's opinion have changed if sodomy and fraternization were not criminal offenses? How would your opinion change if at all?

2. Why is this case, which involves a consensual homosexual relationship between an officer and an enlisted soldier, as the court describes it, "inherently prejudicial, and why does it create "a per se conflict of interest"? How is it different from a brief consensual heterosexual relationship between a civilian counsel and his client as in the *Babbitt* case the court mentions?

2-3. Supervisory Responsibility

Military attorneys who supervise subordinate attorneys must take reasonable efforts to ensure their subordinates comply with the Service ethics rules. U.S. Dep't of the Army, Reg. 27-26, *Rules of Professional Conduct for Lawyers*, Rule 5.1 at App. B (May 1, 1992); U.S. Dep't of the Navy, JAGINST 5803.1c, *Professional Conduct of Attorneys Practicing Under the Cognizance and Supervision of the Judge Advocate General*, Rule 5.1(b) at Encl. 1 (Nov. 9, 2004); U.S. Dep't of the Air Force, TJS-2, *Rules of Professional Conduct*, Rule 5.1(b), at Att. 1 (Aug. 17, 2005); U.S. Dep't of the Coast Guard, Commandant Instr. M5800.1., *Coast Guard Legal Rules of Professional Conduct*, Rule 5.2, at Encl. 1 (June 1, 2005). A senior military attorney is responsible for conduct of a subordinate attorney if the superior attorney orders or ratifies the conduct or if the superior knows of the conduct but fails to take remedial action. If a senior military attorney orders conduct amounting to ethical violations, the subordinate is still bound by the rules even when acting at the supervisor's direction. *Id.*

2-4. RESTRICTIONS IN COMMUNICATIONS TO THE MEDIA AND OTHER THIRD PARTIES

In the scope of trial publicity, counsel cannot knowingly tell a falsity and cannot affirm another's false statement or make public statements that will have a substantial likelihood of prejudicing the judicial proceeding. *See* U.S. Dep't of the Army, Reg. 27-26, *Rules of Professional Conduct for Lawyers*, Rule 3.6 (May 1, 1992); U.S. Dep't of the Navy, JAGINST 5803.1c, *Professional Conduct of Attorneys Practicing Under the Cognizance and Supervision of the Judge Advocate General*, Rule 3.6, at Encl. 1 (Nov. 9, 2004); U.S. Dep't of the Air Force, AFI 51-201, Administration of Military Justice, Rule 13.6, (Dec. 21, 2007); U.S. Dep't of Coast Guard, Commandant Instr. M5800.1., *Coast Guard Legal Rules of Professional Conduct*, Rule 3.6, at Encl. 1 (June 1, 2005). Counsel must be candid, truthful to, and respectful of third parties. Counsel cannot discuss the case with another person who is represented by counsel, but can talk to that person's commander. Trial counsel may advise the witness of penalties for testifying falsely, but cannot use threats of prosecution to intimidate the witness.

Point for Discussion

In *United States v. Edmond*, 63 M.J. 343 (C.A.A.F. 2006), trial counsel spoke to a civilian who planned to testify for the accused. After hearing what the civilian proposed saying, trial counsel told the witness, "I know that that is a lie. . . . I am going to make sure that the S.A.U.S.A. [Special Assistant United States Attorney] sits in and listens to you testify to that and then basically admonish you—not admonish you, but let [you] know what the potential repercussions would be for committing perjury." *Id.* at 349. After this reproach by trial counsel, the witness did not testify. Under what circumstances would the trial counsel's statement be misconduct?

Restriction of communication to 3rd Parties & treats of prosecution.

CHAPTER 3

ALTERNATIVES TO ADVERSARY CRIMINAL TRIALS BY COURT-MARTIAL

3-1. Administrative Corrective Measures

Experience of military forces throughout history instructs that commanders cannot effectively conduct their missions unless they take steps to ensure that their subordinates obey orders and deport themselves in a lawful manner, even with respect to minor matters. On this point, General George S. Patton, one of America's greatest leaders during World War II, intoned: "It is absurd to believe that soldiers who cannot be made to wear the proper uniform can be induced to move forward in battle. Officers who fail to perform their duty by correcting small violations and in enforcing proper conduct are incapable of leading." Martin Blumenson, The Patton Papers 1940-1945 at 225 (1974).

But how do commanders correct small violations and enforce proper conduct? Is it always by bringing criminal charges against service members who misbehave? For example, should a company commander seek to try a new private by court-martial the first time the private shows up late for a formation and then speaks insubordinately to a superior—forms of misconduct that Articles 89 (disrespect), 86 (unauthorized absence), 91 (insubordination), UCMJ, make criminal offenses? The answer is clearly no. A court-martial for such minor offenses by someone new to military life would be both unjust and wasteful. The new private needs correction, not a criminal conviction.

The military justice system and related regulations wisely provide several other alternatives to an adversarial criminal trial by court-martial that are more appropriate responses to minor forms of misconduct. This chapter addresses four of these alternatives: administrative corrective measures, non-judicial punishment, administrative separation, and trial by summary court-martial. In reading the chapter, consider how these options strive to make the military justice system both more efficient and fairer to service members. Consider also whether these measures have any civilian analogues.

We begin with "administrative corrective measures." Administrative corrective measures (verbal or written) are non-punitive methods of inducing compliance with military laws, regulations, and customs. The Rules for

Court-Martial gives these examples of administrative corrective procedures: "counseling, admonitions, reprimands, exhortations, disapprovals, criticisms, censures, reproofs, rebukes, extra military instruction, and administrative withholding of privileges." R.C.M. 306(c)(2). These instructional and disciplinary tools are not unique to the military. Coaches, employers, teachers, scout leaders, and others in charge of civilian groups use similar methods to maintain order. But they are very important in the military context, where discipline and good order are paramount, and where the alternative of trial by court-martial looms in the background.

To return to the example of the tardy and insolent new private, the company commander does not need to resort to criminal charges to correct the problem. Instead, to impress upon the private the wrongfulness of being late and speaking insubordinately, the commander might direct a non-commissioned officer within the company to upbraid the private for being late and speaking inappropriately, to tell the private in no uncertain terms that excuses are not acceptable in the Army, and perhaps to direct the private to stay after the rest of the formation has been dismissed for additional instruction and training. (The additional instruction and training may very well include push-ups, which time has shown are remarkably effective in aiding privates to remember what sergeants say). These kinds of corrective measures address countless disciplinary problems on a daily basis, with no need for legal intervention.

When should a commander use administrative corrective measures instead of alternatives that impose actual punishment for wrongdoing? The *Manual for Courts-Martial* instructs: "Nonpunitive measures usually deal with misconduct resulting from simple neglect, forgetfulness, laziness, inattention to instructions, sloppy habits, immaturity, difficulty in adjusting to disciplined military life, and similar deficiencies." MCM, pt. V, ¶ 3-3. It furthers says that "punishment is ordinarily appropriate when administrative corrective measures are inadequate due to the nature of the . . . offense."MCM pt. V, ¶ 1.d.(1). Reprimands, criticisms, and extra instruction might be appropriate choices for correcting soldiers who wear their uniforms incorrectly or fail to salute, but these administrative measures would not be proper for addressing crimes like murder or robbery.

In the end, the choice of how to respond to misconduct does not fall on police officers or professional prosecutors. A fundamental principle, passed down from centuries of military tradition and stated clearly in the *Manual for Courts-Martial*, is that "[c]ommanders are responsible for good order and discipline in their commands."MCM pt. V, ¶ 1.d.(1). Sometimes the choice is not clear. The Rules for Court-Martial offers these important words of guidance:

> The [decision of how to handle an accusation of misconduct] is one of the most important and difficult decisions facing a commander. Many factors must be taken into consideration and balanced, including, to the extent practicable, the nature of the offenses, any mitigating or extenuating

circumstances, the character and military service of the accused, any recommendations made by subordinate commanders, the interest of justice, military exigencies, and the effect of the decision on the accused and the command. The goal should be a disposition that is warranted, appropriate, and fair.

R.C.M. 306(b) Discussion.

Points for Discussion

1. The discussion to the Rules for Court-Martial suggests that commanders consider these factors in deciding how to respond to misconduct:

(A) the character and military service of the accused;

(B) the nature of and circumstances surrounding the offense and the extent of the harm caused by the offense, including the offense's effect on morale, health, safety, welfare, and discipline;

(C) appropriateness of the authorized punishment to the particular accused or offense;

(D) possible improper motives of the accuser;

(E) reluctance of the victim or others to testify;

(F) cooperation of the accused in the apprehension or conviction of others;

(G) availability and likelihood of prosecution of the same or similar and related charges against the accused by another jurisdiction;

(H) availability and admissibility of evidence;

(I) existence of jurisdiction over the accused and the offense; and

(J) likely issues.

R.C.M. 306(b) discussion. Can you think of examples of how each of these factors might weigh in favor either of mere administrative corrective measures or of something more severe?

2. If a commander chooses to address minor misconduct in the first instance with administrative corrective measures—like criticism and additional training—should the commander be precluded from later resorting to more punitive measures? Does your answer suggest anything about how a commander might wish to exercise his or her discretion?

3. Why are commanders given so much discretion in deciding how to respond to misconduct? Should it really be up to a commander to decide whether a soldier who refuses to obey an order should receive anything from an oral reprimand to trial by a court-martial empowered to impose a prison sentence and dishonorable discharge? What harm might arise from limiting a commander's discretion?

Are there ever times when a commander might be tempted to refer charges to a court-martial that would be more appropriately handled by administrative corrective measures, such as rebukes, withholding of privileges, and additional instruction? How should the military justice system react in such cases? Consider the following decision.

UNITED STATES v. WOLFSON
U.S. Army Board of Review
36 C.M.R. 722 (A.B.R. 1966)

BARON, Judge Advocate.

The accused [Captain Sanford Wolfson, U.S. Army] was tried by general court-martial for dereliction of duty, feigning illness to avoid duty, and for conduct unbecoming an officer and a gentleman, in violation of Articles 92, 115 and 133, respectively, of the Uniform Code of Military Justice. He pleaded not guilty to all charges and specifications. The law officer granted a motion for a finding of not guilty of the specification [feigning illness to avoid duty] and Charge II, in violation of Article 115. The court found him guilty of the remaining specifications, with certain exceptions, in violation of Articles 92 and 133, and sentenced him to be dismissed from the service. The convening authority approved the adjudged sentence.

The accused is a medical doctor and general surgeon with particular interest in thorax and vascular surgery. He graduated from Williams College, Williamstown, Massachusetts with a Bachelor of Arts degree in 1954 and attended the Harvard Medical School for four years, graduating in 1958. He was a surgical intern at the University of Minnesota Hospital for one year and completed a four and one-half year residency in general surgery at Washington University Medical School in St. Louis, Missouri. . . .

Captain Wolfson entered on active duty in the Army on 4 January 1964 with a two-year obligatory active duty commitment . . .

* * *

Captain Wolfson was ordered on temporary duty to Vietnam on 22 December 1964 and assigned as the general surgeon to the 2nd Medical Dispensary, located at SocTrang, in the Mekong Delta. The mission of this dispensary was to render emergency and surgical treatment to seriously wounded casualties who needed immediate care and who would present a hazard if evacuated directly to the more distant medical facilities in Saigon. Normally, patients would be held at the dispensary not more than 72 hours and then be transported to a larger medical facility.

The alleged offenses that led to the filing of charges against Captain Wolfson occurred in Vietnam; however, they had their inception in Okinawa. Basic to some of the incidents was his dissatisfaction with his orders to Vietnam. He was of the opinion that his temporary duty tour there was punitive because he had complained that doctors in the grade of Major at the Okinawa Army Hospital were not required to perform OD duties thus throwing an additional burden on Captains of which he was one. Further, he did not want to be separated from his family. He frequently expressed the attitude that it was unfair "that two year physicians are assigned to every position which smacks of danger, while the career Army Surgeons remain safely at home."After his arrival in Vietnam his discontent continued. He believed that his surgical talents were not adequately utilized because of a lack of surgical patients at the dispensary. He was unable to obtain certain items of supply that he believed were essential to perform good surgery. His final complaint, if we have not overlooked any, was that he, a Captain was sent to a position that called for a Major.

Events came to a head when General Westmoreland* arrived at the SocTrang dispensary on a tour of inspection. Captain Wolfsonseized this opportunity to express his dissatisfactions to the General. This embarrassed the local commander who immediately after the General's departure secured the doctor's forthwith return to Okinawa. Thereafter a report on Captain Wolfson's actions was forwarded to the Commanding General in Okinawa which resulted in this general court-martial. With this background we may proceed to a consideration of the offenses of which the accused was found guilty.

Dereliction of Duty

The accused was found guilty of the specification, Charge I, in that he,

> * * * at SocTrang, Vietnam from 22 December 1964 to about 22 January 1965, was derelict in the performance of his duties * * * to shave, and to present a disciplined appearance in that he * * * negligently failed to shave, thereby presenting an undisciplined appearance, as it was his duty to do. [sic]

The testimony as to the accused's failure to shave is not conflicting. Some witnesses said that he presented an unshaved appearance. A Captain, Army Nurse Corps, called as a witness by the prosecution was more specific in describing the unshaved appearance. She testified that except while he was in quarters, the accused did not have more than a one day's growth. "It was like leaping out of bed and coming to work and not shaving."We find from the record of trial that the accused did not shave in the morning upon arising. He explained that he preferred to shave in the afternoon when he "stood a better chance of getting hot water" or be shaved at the barber shop which did not open for business until afternoon. . . .

---

* General William C. Westmoreland commanded all U.S. military operations in the Vietnam War from 1964-1968 and served as Army Chief of Staff from 1968 to 1972. He graduated from West Point as first captain of cadets, served with great distinction in World War II, attended Harvard Business School, and became the youngest major general in the Army at age 42. He was a strict disciplinarian. His record in Vietnam is controversial, with critics charging that he gave overly optimistic advice about the prospects of success in the war and recklessly increased U.S. involvement in a losing cause.—Eds.

* * *

We must first determine the "duty" the accused was charged with neglecting. (The language used in the specification would suggest that the duty was to present an undisciplined appearance. Obviously this was inept drafting of the specification.) We do not interpret the pleading to allege a separate duty to "present a disciplined appearance." This allegation standing alone is too indefinite, uncertain and ambiguous to be made the basis of a charge. We agree with one of the witnesses who testified "well, quite frankly, I have seen the charge sheet and I'm not quibbling, but I really don't know what you mean by 'undisciplined,' * * *." We read this allegation together with and as referring to the negligent failure to shave.

Paragraph 171c, Manual for Courts-Martial, United States, 1951 provides that "a duty may be imposed by regulation, lawful order or custom of the service."

The evidence established that there was no local regulation on the subject of shaving or otherwise proscribing the growing of a mustache or beard. Other than being told to shave his beard as set forth above, the accused received no order from his superiors to shave.

We have searched the Army Regulations on the subject. We have not found nor have we been directed to any regulation that would be helpful.

AR 600-20, paragraph 31a, dated 3 July 1962, provides:

Appearance and conduct. a. Discipline is a function of command; hence, it is the responsibility of all leaders in the Army, whether they are on duty or in a leave status, to see that all military personnel present a neat and soldierly appearance, and to take action in cases of conduct prejudicial to good order and military discipline by any military personnel which may take place with their knowledge."

Field Manual 21-10, May 1957, provides at paragraph 129c: "The Hair, * * * The soldier should be clean shaven. * * *" Field Manual 21-10 is entitled "Military Sanitation" and paragraph 4 thereof makes "the commanding officer of a military organization [is] responsible for the health of his command."

It is stated in JAGJ 1960/8230:

Although the provisions of field manuals merely provide guidance and do not have the force and effect of departmental regulations and directives, it is readily apparent that the above cited excerpt [the cited excerpt includes the statement from FM 21-10 quoted above] pertaining to personal cleanliness certainly complements Regulations making it a command function to require a neat and soldierly appearance. In view of the above directions to commanders, an order to shave and thereby present a neat personal appearance takes on considerable military significance, and, it is deemed to be a lawful command. * * *

The statement in Field Manual 21-10 that "The soldier should be clean shaven," is used in JAGJ 1960/8230 above to support the legality of an order to shave. Army Regulations 600-20 set forth above, as we read it does not fix a duty on the individual, rather it places the responsibility on the commander to require military personnel to "present a neat and soldierly appearance."

We are also unable to find a usage or custom that places a duty on a soldier or officer to shave, let alone the hour or manner of shaving.

In the absence of an order, or at least local regulations that military personnel will shave, we fail to see how the accused herein can be charged with offense of negligently failing to shave.

Consequently, it is our opinion, based on the foregoing, that the findings of guilty of the specification and Charge I must be disapproved and set aside.

Conduct Unbecoming an Officer and Gentleman

The accused was found guilty of conduct unbecoming an officer and a gentleman, in violation of Article 133, Uniform Code of Military Justice, in that he:

> * * * did, at SocTrang, Vietnam from 22 December 1964 to 22 January 1965, so grossly fail to comport himself as a medical officer and a gentleman by * * * his negligent failure to shave; his presentation of an undisciplined appearance; * * * by constantly complaining about his temporary assignment to Vietnam in the presence of superior and subordinate officer and enlisted men; * * * by announcing in a public place to his commanding officer that the surgical capabilities of the dispensary to which he was temporarily assigned were terminated effective immediately, or words to that effect; by presenting erroneous factual data to General Westmoreland, while in a friendly foreign country, in the presence of superior officers, subordinate officers, enlisted personnel, civilian personnel and foreign nationals, as to require his removal from the unit to which he was temporarily assigned; such conduct constituting conduct unbecoming of an officer and a gentleman.

The specification of which the accused was found guilty alleges five ways in which the accused "grossly failed to comport himself as a medical officer and a gentleman."We shall take each allegation and discuss it separately, but before we do we will dispose of that portion of the specification that sets forth the above quoted statement and "such conduct constituting conduct unbecoming an officer and a gentleman."

* * *

Negligent Failure to Shave.—The facts giving rise to this allegation have already been discussed. . . .

In discussing the misconduct contemplated by Article 133, Colonel Winthrop in his Military Law and Precedents (2d Ed., 1920 reprint), at page 711, states, "Though it need not amount to a crime, it must offend so seriously against law, justice, morality or decorum as to expose to disgrace, socially or as a man, the offender, and at the same time must be of such a nature or committed under such circumstances as to bring dishonor or disrepute upon the military profession which he represents."

It is quite evident that the accused's practice of shaving in the afternoon rather than the morning falls far short of misconduct unbecoming an officer and a gentleman.

His presentation of an undisciplined appearance.—Reference to this allegation has already been mentioned. We find it too indefinite to set forth an offense. We do not know to what evidence in the record of trial it refers. Does the allegation refer to the appearance of his uniform, condition of his clothes, his shaving, his stance, table manners, his bearing or the way he combed or failed to comb his hair? We have no way of knowing if all the members who voted to find him guilty of presenting an "undisciplined appearance" found him guilty of even the same specific "undisciplined appearance."

It is hornbook law that a specification should set forth in simple and concise language just what the accused did or failed to do in violation of the Code. A crime must be charged with precision and certainty. No specification may be averred in such general indefinite and meaningless terms, as we have here.

Constantly complaining about his temporary assignment in Vietnam in the presence of superior and subordinate officers and enlisted men.—The evidence amply supports this allegation. He "griped" that he was misassigned, grumbled that he shouldn't be in Vietnam and carped that a regular Army officer should fill his assignment in Vietnam rather than he a reservist. His opinions on this subject were made to all and sundry, to enlisted men up to and including a four star General.

The dispensary commander summed up Captain Wolfson's offense when he testified, "Yes, everybody complained to a certain extent. Well, when I say everybody, I mean a lot of the people did; a lot of the personnel did. * * * I think possibly that Dr. Wolfson didn't use as much discretion as the rest of us when we were bitching, as he should have."

That military personnel complain is not a classified matter. Complaining is indulged in by enlisted men and officers of all grades and rank. Complaints may be registered on any topic and frequently are. "Bitching," to use the vernacular, may be expressed in gutter talk or in well articulated phrases and has frequently been developed into a fine art. Nevertheless it sometimes serves a useful purpose. It provides an outlet for pent-up emotions, therapy for frustrations and a palliative for rebuffs and rejections. A noticeable failure to complain in a military organization is considered by some commanders as an indication of approaching morale problems.

The right to complain is undoubtedly within the protection of the first amendment of the Constitution of the United States guaranteeing freedom of speech. Congress has recognized this right by enacting Article 138 of the Uniform Code of Military Justice which provides a procedure whereby "Any member of the armed forces who believes himself wronged by his commanding officer, and, upon due application to such commander, is refused redress, may complain to any superior officer who shall forward the complaint to the officer exercising general court-martial jurisdiction over the officer against whom it is made. * * *"

Army Regulation 20-1 further guarantees to all military personnel the right to present to military authorities "orally or in writing their individual complaints or grievances of any nature," and insures that "any type of disciplinary or other type of adverse action against an individual for registering a complaint is prohibited; * * * ."

Dr. Wolfson's complaints to General Westmoreland are not actionable, irrespective of whether the complaint was justified or not. It, of course, would be an empty right if military personnel had to gamble whether the complaint was proper under the circumstances and subject themselves to punitive action should the complaint be ultimately considered unjustified.

Dr. Wolfson's complaints to his juniors may be classified as inappropriate and improper and his whining exhibited bad taste and poor judgment. In our opinion, however, it did not reach the level of conduct unbecoming an officer and gentleman.

[The Board of Review's discussion of the other specifications of conduct unbecoming an officer and gentleman are omitted.]

* * *

A few general concepts relating to Article 133 might be in order. In discussing Article 133 the Manual provides:

There are certain moral attributes common to the ideal officer and the perfect gentleman, a lack of which is indicated by acts of dishonesty or unfair dealing, of indecency or indecorum, or of lawlessness, injustice, or cruelty. Not everyone is or can be expected to meet ideal moral standards, but there is a limit of tolerance below which the individual standards of an officer, cadet, or midshipman cannot fall without seriously compromising his standing as an officer, cadet, or midshipman or his character as a gentleman. This article contemplates conduct by an officer, cadet, or midshipman which, taking all the circumstances into consideration, is thus compromising.

This article includes acts made punishable by any other article, provided such acts amount to conduct unbecoming an officer and a gentleman; thus an officer who steals property violates both this and Article 121.

Instances of violation of this article are: "Knowingly making a false official statement; dishonorable failure to pay debts; opening and reading the letters of another without authority; using insulting or defamatory language to another officer in his presence or about him to other military persons; being grossly drunk and conspicuously disorderly in a public place; public association with notorious prostitutes; committing or attempting to commit a crime involving moral turpitude; failing without a good cause to support his family."

Colonel Winthrop in his Treatise, Military Law and Precedents, (2d Ed, 1920 reprint), page 711, stated: "* * * to become the subject of a charge, the unbecoming conduct should not be slight but of a material and pronounced character." Further, " 'Unbecoming' as here employed, is understood to mean not merely inappropriate or unsuitable, as being opposed to good taste or propriety or not consonant with usage, but morally unbefitting and unworthy."

* * *

Article 133 is to be reserved for serious delicts of officers. The article should not be demeaned by using it to charge minor delinquencies that can be more appropriately handled by instruction, counselling or other types of administrative corrective action.

The reaction of the accused to his assignment to Vietnam could be characterized as emotional and immature, his announcement of the termination of surgical capability may have been ill advised and his complaints to General Westmoreland were ill-timed, indiscreet and impolitic but certainly his behavior cannot be stigmatized as conduct unbecoming an officer and gentleman.

The findings of guilty and sentence are found incorrect in law and are hereby set a side. The Charges and Specifications are ordered dismissed.

GUIMOND, and BARON, Judge Advocates.

PETKOFF, Judge Advocate (dissenting and concurring in part):

* * *

For a commissioned officer of the United States Army to complain of his assignment to a hazardous duty area, under the circumstances of this case, is conduct beyond the level of tolerance below which the individual standards of an officer cannot fall without seriously compromising his standing as an officer and bringing disrepute upon the military and medical professions which he represents.

* * *

Points for Discussion

1. The Board of Review concludes that Captain Wolfson's misconduct could have been "more appropriately handled by instruction, counseling or other types of administrative corrective action." What specific administrative corrective actions would you have recommended his commander take?

2. Why do you think the commander did not take non-punitive actions but instead referred this case to a court-martial? Note that *Time* magazine reported that General Westmoreland was personally "irked" by Captain Wolfson, called him a "crybaby," and wanted him to stand trial by a general court-martial. *See Criminal Justice: The Serviceman's Rights*, Time, Aug. 13, 1965, at 41. Does this case show the importance of appellate review in the military justice system? Should the case perhaps have been reversed on grounds of unlawful command influence?

3. Why would Captain Wolfson want to appeal his conviction of the charged offenses and his dismissal from the Army when he apparently was so unhappy about being in the Army?

3-2. Nonjudicial Punishment

In considering methods of dealing with misconduct other than through an adversary criminal trial by court-martial, one of the most important alternatives is found in article 15 of the UCMJ, 10 U.S.C. § 815. Article 15 is a long and complex provision that grants commanders the authority to impose "nonjudicial punishment" on subordinates. In the Army and the Air Force, a nonjudicial punishment is called simply an "Article 15," as in "Private Smedlock got an Article 15 for cheating on his PT test and was given extra duties for two weeks." In the Navy and the Coast Guard, nonjudicial punishment—and the process of receiving it—is called "Captain's Mast" or "Mast." In the Marine Corps, the same is known as "Office Hours."

Part V of the *Manual for Courts-Martial* treats nonjudicial punishment in great depth, as do separate regulations promulgated by each of the services. While the parameters of nonjudicial punishment differ from one service to another, this form of punishment has several salient features that are uniform. Perhaps most significantly, nonjudicial punishment is a means of responding to misconduct that lies somewhere between administrative corrective measures on one hand and an adversarial criminal trial by court-martial on the other.

Unlike administrative corrective measures, nonjudicial punishment is punitive in nature and can only be imposed for a violation of the UCMJ. When a commander imposes nonjudicial punishment, the goal is to punish a service member for committing an offense, not merely to steer the service member toward behaving correctly in the future. But even though the punishment is imposed for a violation of the UCMJ, and even though documentation of the punishment is kept in the service member's record, no court is involved and the punishment is not treated as a criminal conviction and does not carry nearly as much stigma.

While nonjudicial punishment has no exact civilian analogue, it is somewhat similar to what occurs when a police officer issues a ticket to a driver for speeding. The fine is a kind of civil punishment for an offense, imposed by the officer rather than a court. And similar to the way a driver may challenge a speeding ticket in court, a service member may have a right to refuse the imposition of nonjudicial punishment and have the offense tried by court-martial. Finally, like speeding tickets, non-judicial punishment is also common. For example, in fiscal year 2010, there were 36,624 instances of non-judicial punishment in the Army alone—a rate of 64 for every 1000 soldiers. *See* Annual Report of the Code Committee on Military Justice for the Period October 1, 2009 to September 30, 2010 at 23.

The analogy to a speeding ticket ends, however, when the potential severity of nonjudicial punishment under Article 15 is considered. As discussed in detail below, the punishment may include a reduction in rank, loss of pay, imposition of extra duties, restrictions to the barracks or post, correctional custody, and so forth. Receiving an Article 15 generally will end the career of an officer, but will not necessarily prevent the subsequent promotion of junior enlisted members.

The *Manual for Courts-Martial* gives the following reasons for using nonjudicial punishment instead of a court-martial: "Nonjudicial punishment may be imposed to—a. Correct, educate, and reform offenders who the imposing commander determines cannot benefit from less stringent measures. b. Preserve a Soldier's record of service from unnecessary stigma by record of court-martial conviction. c. Further military efficiency by disposing of minor offenses in a manner requiring less time and personnel than trial by court-martial." MCM, pt. V, ¶3-2.

According to Article 15, nonjudicial punishment is to be used only for "minor offenses." Although the UCMJ does not define this term, offenses for which commanders commonly impose nonjudicial punishment include misuse of government property, fraternization, unprofessional relationships, driving while intoxicated, underage drinking, cheating on tests, disobeying orders, and so forth. More serious offenses, like thefts or using illegal drugs, could be the basis for nonjudicial punishment, but more commonly are addressed in a different manner.

There are two procedures for imposing nonjudicial punishment under Article 15: summarized and formal. Under the summarized Article 15 procedure, the accused does not have a right to counsel and does not have a right to demand trial by court-martial. The summarized procedure generally is used only to impose punishment on junior enlisted service members and the maximum punishments are much more limited than those available under the formal procedure. Under the formal Article 15 procedure, the accused has a right to consult with counsel before his or her Article 15 hearing and can demand to have a trial by court-martial.[1]

Perhaps the best way to acquire an understanding of nonjudicial punishment is to study the types of punishment that are authorized and then to see a sample record of Article 15 that has been imposed.

Nonjudicial Punishments Authorized

Subject to important additional restrictions that may be imposed by the different services, the *Manual for Courts-Martial* authorizes the following types of nonjudicial punishment, which are described roughly in order from the most common to the least common.

Extra duties. The punishment of "extra duties" typically involves working for additional hours after the normal duty day for others in the unit is over. A soldier in garrison, for example, might be assigned to work in the evenings or on weekends checking basketballs in and out at the gym, cleaning equipment, maintaining the barracks, sorting papers, or doing anything else that needs to be done. These obligations may not sound like much, but they are punishment for a soldier who is tired from other duties and who would rather spend the limited available free time doing something else. Past abuses in the imposition of "extra duties" have led the Army to prohibit additional tasks that are "required to be performed in a ridiculous or unnecessarily degrading manner; for example, an order to clean a barracks floor with a toothbrush." AR 27-10, para. 3-19b(5)(c) (Oct. 3, 2011). The punishment of extra duties may only be imposed on enlisted members; officers below the rank of major or lieutenant commander may impose 14 days of extra duties, while other officers may impose up to 45 days. *See* MCM pt. V, ¶5.b.(2)(A)(ii) & (B)(ii).

Restriction to specified limits. The punishment of restriction to specified limits is a restraint on a service member's movement. For example, an Army commander might punish a soldier by restricting the soldier to the barracks, the dining facility, the soldier's duty station, the gym, the post exchange, and the chapel. The soldier under these restrictions could not go to other places on or off post, severely limiting recreational activities and making life less pleasant. Excessive restrictions may be viewed as custodial confinement, a separate type of punishment described below. Enlisted members may be restricted for 14 days by officers below the grade of major or lieutenant colonel, and 30 days by other officers. Officers may be restricted for 30 days

---

[1] Service members might demand a trial by court-martial because they believe that they will be treated more fairly by a military judge or panel than by their commander, but there are serious risks in making such a demand. For example, in *United States v. Bass*, 11 M.J. 545 (A.C.M.R. 1981), the accused refused to accept nonjudicial punishment and demanded a court-martial. He was found guilty at the court-martial and sentenced to 8 years of confinement and a dishonorable discharge. This punishment is far more severe than any Article 15 punishment could have been.

by other officers, or 45 days by general officers or general court-martial convening authorities, but this is very uncommon. *See* MCM pt. V, ¶5.b.(1)(A), (1)(B)(iii), (2)(A)(vi) & (B)(vi).

Reduction in grade. Reduction in grade is a demotion in rank. This punishment is commonly called "being busted." *See, e.g., United States v. Czerwonky*, 32 C.M.R. 353, 354 (C.M.A. 1962) ("[H]e's a private. He was busted at office hours."). Being reduced in grade is a more serious punishment than extra duties or restriction to limits because it results in a reduction in salary and sometimes a less desirable duty assignment. Enlisted members in the grade of E-6 and below may be reduced by one grade; junior enlisted members may receive further reductions in grade in certain instances. *See* MCM pt. V, ¶5.b.(2)(A)(iv) & (B)(iv).

Forfeiture of pay. Another common form of punishment is forfeiture of pay. In punishing enlisted members, officers below the grade of major or lieutenant commander may order the forfeiture of up to 7 days' pay, while other officers may also order the forfeiture of not more than one-half of 1 month's pay per month for 2 months. Only general officers and officers exercising general court-martial convening authority may order the forfeiture of an officer's pay, and not more than one-half of 1 month's pay per month for 2 months. *See* MCM pt. V, ¶5.b(1)(B)(ii), (2)(A)(iii), (2)(B)(iii).

Correctional custody. Correctional custody, as its name suggests, is a form of imprisonment. But generally the custody is not served in a traditional prison or jail, and it is not served with service members convicted of crimes or awaiting trial for crimes. In the Army, the custody occurs in a "Correctional Custody Facility," which is usually a fenced-in barracks building specifically established for nonjudicial punishment. *See* AR 190-47, para. 2-3a. The theory is that nonjudicial punishment should not be equated with judicial punishment, for which imprisonment is common. In each Service, the Secretary concerned may limit the categories of enlisted members upon whom correctional custody may be imposed. Officers below the rank of major or lieutenant commander may impose up to 7 days of custody, while higher ranking officers may impose up to 30 days custody. *See* MCM pt. V, ¶5.b.(2)(A)(ii) & (B)(ii).

Confinement on bread and water or diminished rations. This restriction may be imposed only on junior enlisted members (E1-E3) who are attached to or embarked on a vessel. The idea is that all sailors, in effect, have restricted liberty while on a ship, so some greater punishment beyond a restriction on movement is necessary for punishment. A threat often made in jest in the Navy—funny only to those who do not face this punishment—is that "nothing in the UCMJ says you can't put the bread and water in a blender first." In practice, this punishment is rare, and sailors typically are restricted to something a little more appealing than just bread and water. Officers below the rank of major or lieutenant commander may impose up to 3 days of confinement on bread and water, while in custody, while higher ranking officers may impose up to 4 days. *See* MCM pt. V, ¶5.b.(2)(A)(i) & (B)(i).

Arrest in quarters. While officers cannot be confined, a general officer or general courts-martial convening authority may order an officer arrested in quarters for up to 30 days. *See* MCM pt. V, ¶5.b.(1)(B)(i). This form of nonjudicial punishment is extremely rare.

Points for Discussion

1. Although Article 15 punishments are not published like judicial decisions, the commander typically announces them at formation or posts them on a bulletin board for others to see. Do such announcements increase the punishment by humiliating the punished soldier? If so, is that proper? On this point, see AR 27-10, para. 3-22 (Oct. 3, 2011) ("The purpose of announcing the results of punishments is to preclude perceptions of unfairness of punishment and to deter similar misconduct by other soldiers.").

2. Why should commanders have the authority to impose nonjudicial punishment that includes correctional custody, a form of imprisonment? Would anything similar be tolerated in civilian society?

3. Generally, records of nonjudicial punishment are considered private personal records and release outside the military is prohibited by federal privacy laws. If a high-ranking officer received nonjudicial punishment, should the Department of Defense have authority to release the record? *See Cochran v. United States*, 770 F.2d 949 (11th Cir. 1985) (discussing the release of a nonjudicial punishment record for a major general who used government aircraft to fly to West Point for his son's graduation).

Sample Completed DA Form 2627

RECORD OF PROCEEDINGS UNDER ARTICLE 15, UCMJ
For use of this form, see AR 27-10; the proponent agency is TJAG.
See Notes on Reverse Before Completing Form

NAME	GRADE	SSN	UNIT	PAY (Basic & Sea/Foreign)
AGER, Robert L.	E4	000-10-0000	D Co, 1/5 Inf, Ft Blank, VA 00000	1,695.60

1. I am considering whether you should be punished under Article 15, UCMJ, for the following misconduct: 1/
In that you did, on or about 0600 hours, 21 Sep 05, without authority, fail to go at the time prescribed to your appointed place of duty, to wit: Formation, D Co, 1/5 Inf, in front of building 15. This is in violation of Article 86, UCMJ.

2. You are not required to make any statements, but if you do, they may be used against you in this proceeding or at a trial by court-martial. You have several rights under this Article 15 proceeding. First I want you to understand I have not yet made a decision whether or not you will be punished. I will not impose any punishment unless I am convinced beyond a reasonable doubt that you committed the offense(s). You may ordinarily have an open hearing before me. You may request a person to speak on your behalf. You may present witnesses or other evidence to show why you shouldn't be punished at all *(matters of defense)* or why punishment should be very light *(matters of extenuation and mitigation)*. I will consider everything you present before deciding whether I will impose punishment or the type and amount of punishment I will impose. 2/ If you do not want me to dispose of this report of misconduct under Article 15, you have the right to demand trial by court-martial instead. 3/ In deciding what you want to do you have the right to consult with legal counsel located at   Room 7, Building 10, Fort Blank, VA . You now have 48 hours to decide what you want to do. 4/

DATE 21 Sep 05	NAME, GRADE, AND ORGANIZATION OF COMMANDER	SIGNATURE
TIME 0800	JAMES A. SMITH, CPT, D Co, 1/5 Inf	*James A. Smith*

3. Having been afforded the opportunity to consult with counsel, my decisions are as follow: *(initial appropriate blocks, date, and sign)*
a. [ ]   I demand trial by court-martial.
b. [RLA]   I do not demand trial by court-martial and in the Article 15 proceedings:
(1) I request the hearing be [RLA] Open [ ] Closed. (2) A person to speak in my behalf [ ] Is [RLA] Is not requested.
(3) Matters in defense, mitigation, and/or extenuation: [ ] Are not presented [RLA] Will be presented in person [ ] Are attached.

DATE 23 Sep 05	NAME AND GRADE OF SERVICE MEMBER	SIGNATURE
	ROBERT L. AGER, SPC	*Robert L. Ager*

4. In a(n) [X] Open [ ] Closed hearing 5/ all matters presented in defense, mitigation, and/or extenuation, having been considered, the following punishment is imposed: 5/ 6/
Reduction to the grade of Private First Class, (E3), suspended, to be automatically remitted if not vacated before 23 Jan 06; and forfeiture of $100.00 pay.

[NOTE: Refer to Para 3-37b(1) prior to completing item 5]

5. [crossed out text] 7/
6. You are advised of your right to appeal to the _____ within 5 calendar days. An appeal made after that time may be rejected as untimely. Punishment is effective immediately unless otherwise stated above.

DATE 23 Sep 05	NAME, GRADE, AND ORGANIZATION OF COMMANDER	SIGNATURE
	JAMES A. SMITH, CPT, D Co, 1/5 Inf	*James A. Smith*

7. *(Initial appropriate block, date, and sign)*
a. [ ] I do not appeal   b. [RLA] I appeal and do not submit additional matters 8/ 9/   c. [ ] I appeal and submit additional matters 8/ 9/

DATE 23 Sep 05	NAME AND GRADE OF SERVICE MEMBER	SIGNATURE
	ROBERT L. AGER, SPC	*Robert L. Ager*

8. I have considered the appeal and it is my opinion that: The proceedings were conducted in accordance with law and regulation and the punishments imposed were not unjust nor disproportionate to the offense committed.

DATE 27 Sep 05	NAME AND GRADE OF JUDGE ADVOCATE	SIGNATURE
	LEWIS H. RANE, MAJ	*Lewis H. Rane*

9. After consideration of all matters presented in appeal, the appeal is:
[X] Denied   [ ] Granted as follows: 10/

DATE 30 SEP 05	NAME, GRADE, AND ORGANIZATION OF COMMANDER	SIGNATURE
	LYMAN Z. LIPE, LTC, 1/5 INF	*Lyman Z. Lipe*

10. I have seen the action taken on my appeal.

DATE 30 Sep 05	SIGNATURE OF SERVICE MEMBER *Robert L. Ager*

11. ALLIED DOCUMENTS AND/OR COMMENTS 11/ 12/ 13/
"Paragraph 3-18(f)(1), AR 27-10 complied with."
statement by SFC Jones, dated 22 Sep 05

DA FORM 2627, AUG 84   EDITION OF NOV 82 IS OBSOLETE   ORIGINAL
USAPPC V1.00

In the Army, DA Form 2627 is used for recording the imposition of nonjudicial punishment. Above is a sample completed version of this form taken from Army Regulation 27-10, *Military Justice*. Although the information on the form is fictional, the completed form provides a practical illustration of how nonjudicial punishment works. (The sample is used because actual Article 15 records are generally not matters of public record.)

This form records the hypothetical imposition of nonjudicial punishment on a hypothetical soldier, Specialist Robert L. Ager, for failing to go to formation at 6:00 a.m. on September 21, 2005.

In the first large box, Specialist Ager's company commander, Captain James A. Smith, states the charged offense ("you did, on or about 0600 hours, 21 Sep 05, without authority, fail to go at the time prescribed to your appointed place of duty, to wit: Formation, D Co, 1/5 Inf, in front of building 15"), which is a violation of UCMJ art. 86. In the second paragraph, Captain Smith advises Special Ager of his rights:

> You are not required to make any statements, but if you do, they may be used against you in this proceeding or at a trial by court-martial. You have several rights under this Article 15 proceeding. First, I want you to understand I have not yet made a decision whether or not you will be punished. I will not impose any punishment unless I am convinced beyond a reasonable doubt that you committed the offense(s). You may ordinarily have an open hearing before me. You may request a person to speak on your behalf. You may present witnesses or other evidence to show why you shouldn't be punished at all (matters of defense) or why punishment should be very light (matters of extenuation and mitigation). I will consider everything you present before deciding whether I will impose punishment or the type and amount of punishment I will impose. If you do not want me to dispose of this report of misconduct under Article 15, you have the right to demand trial by court-martial instead. In deciding what you want to do you have the right to consult with legal counsel located at Room 7, Building 10, Port Blank, VA. You now have 48 hours to decide what you want to do.

The sample form then contains a second box asking Specialist Ager three questions: (1) whether he demands trial by court-martial; (2) whether he wants the hearing to be open or closed; and (3) whether he intends to present matters "in defense, mitigation, and/or extenuation," and if so, whether these matters are to be presented in person or will be attached to the form. On the sample form, Specialist Ager asked for an open hearing and indicated that he did not want to present any materials to Captain Smith.

The third box, evidently completed by Captain Smith after he heard from Specialist Ager, states the nonjudicial punishment imposed. In the form, specialist Ager is reduced to the grade of Private First Class and ordered to forfeit $100 pay. In the next set of boxes, Specialist Ager exercises his right to appeal to a superior officer. In this case, the superior officer is Major Lewis Rane. The boxes indicate that Major Rane denied the appeal.

Points for Discussion

1. What are the advantages of nonjudicial punishment in comparison to an adversarial criminal trial? What are the disadvantages? (Hint for both questions: Looking at the form, how long did it take from the time the offense was committed until the appeals were finished?)

2. Why would someone refuse nonjudicial punishment and seek trial by court-martial?

3. A soldier who receives a nonjudicial punishment for committing a serious offense in theory could complain that the punishment is improper because Article 15 is only for "minor offenses." But such complaints are rare in practice. Why is this? Colonel Lawrence J. Morris writes "the soldier receiving the NJP is not likely to insist that it is not minor when the alternative would be trying [the offense] at a court-martial rather than NJP, where the sanction and the consequences are lower." Lawrence J. Morris, Military Justice a Guide to the Issues 150 (2010). Can you think of another reason that such disputes would be rare?

———————

A significant question regarding non-judicial punishment is whether it precludes subsequent punishment by a court-martial for the same offense. For instance, in the example above, could Specialist Ager be tried by court-martial for being absent without leave after receiving nonjudicial punishment for the same instance of misconduct? Consider the following case.

UNITED STATES v. PIERCE
Court of Military Appeals
27 M.J. 367 (C.M.A. 1989)

COX, Judge:

Appellant [Private James A. Pierce, U.S. Army] was convicted by general court-martial, military judge alone, at Fort Bragg, North Carolina, of absence without leave, larceny, wrongful appropriation, assault and battery on two servicemembers, and being drunk and disorderly, in violation of Articles 86, 121, 128, and 134 of the Uniform Code of Military Justice, 10 U.S.C. §§ 886, 921, 928, and 934, respectively. He was sentenced to a bad-conduct discharge, confinement for 13 months, total forfeitures, and reduction to E-1. The convening authority approved the sentence except for confinement exceeding 10 months and forfeiture exceeding one-half month's pay per month for 10 months.

This appeal arises out of the larceny specification. We granted review of the following issue:

WHETHER REFERRAL TO A COURT-MARTIAL OF AN OFFENSE FOR WHICH APPELLANT HAD BEEN PREVIOUSLY PUNISHED CONSTITUTED A DENIAL OF MILITARY DUE PROCESS AND A VIOLATION OF ARTICLE 13, UCMJ [10 U.S.C. § 813].

On or about July 5, 1986, appellant stole an aviator kit bag containing a parachute and personal items belonging to post personnel. Shortly thereafter, on July 11, in keeping with the 82d Airborne Division policy of prompt discipline, appellant was given nonjudicial punishment (Art. 15, UCMJ, 10 U.S.C. § 815) by his battalion commander. His punishment included restriction for 45 days, extra duty for 45 days, reduction from pay grade E-4 to E-2, and forfeiture of $358 pay per month for 2 months.

On August 25, 1986, the same battalion commander forwarded this charge and the others for which appellant now stands convicted to the regimental commander, who recommended that appellant be tried by general court-martial.[2] Appellant pleaded guilty pursuant to a pretrial agreement.

On appeal, appellant now contests his plea of guilty to the larceny specification, claiming that his prior punishment under Article 15 barred a subsequent trial on the same charge. We disagree.

Article 15(f) provides:

The imposition and enforcement of disciplinary punishment under this article for any act or omission *is not a bar to trial by court-martial for a serious crime or offense growing out of the same act or omission*, and not properly punishable under this article; but the fact that a disciplinary punishment has been enforced may be shown by the accused upon trial, and when so shown shall be considered in determining the measure of punishment to be adjudged in the event of a finding of guilty.

(Emphasis added.)

It is clear from the language of this provision that Congress did not intend for imposition of nonjudicial punishment to preclude the subsequent court-martial of a servicemember accused of a serious offense. *See also* RCM 907(b)(2)(D)(iv), Manual for Courts-Martial, United States, 1984. Article 44, UCMJ, 10 U.S.C. § 844 (Former jeopardy), does not, by its terms, apply to nonjudicial punishments. *See United States v. Fretwell*, 11 U.S.C.MA 377, 29 CMR 193 (1960). Likewise, Article 13 (Punishment prohibited before trial) is inapplicable as appellant was not punished "while [he was] being held for trial." Absent some sinister design, evil motive, bad faith, etc., on the part of military authorities, it is not a violation of military due process to court-martial a servicemember for a serious offense, even though he has already been punished nonjudicially. That, however, is all Article 15(f) implies.

It does not follow that a servicemember can be twice punished for the same offense or that the fact of a prior nonjudicial punishment can be exploited by the prosecution at a court-martial for the same conduct. Either consequence would violate the most obvious, fundamental notions of due process of law. Thus, in these rare cases, an accused must be given complete

---

[2] It appears that, at the time the nonjudicial punishment was administered, the full magnitude of appellant's pattern of misconduct was only just beginning to be discerned.

credit for any and all nonjudicial punishment suffered: day-for-day, dollar-for-dollar, stripe-for-stripe. Furthermore, the nonjudicial punishment may not be used for any purpose at trial, such as impeachment (even of an accused who asserts he had no prior misconduct); to show that an accused has a bad service record; or any other evidentiary purpose, *e.g.*, Mil. R. Evid. 404(b), Manual, *supra*. Under these circumstances, the nonjudicial punishment simply has no legal relevance to the court-martial.

***

In the instant case, the convening authority reduced appellant's adjudged punishment to conform with the terms of the pretrial agreement. The sentence as approved is the maximum allowed by the agreement. Thus, it is clear that the convening authority did not credit the nonjudicial punishment against the sentence. *See United States v. Larner*, 1 M.J. 371 (C.M.A. 1976). The military judge, in assessing the sentence, did indicate that he would "consider[]" the previous punishment. However, we do not know what he meant by that pronouncement. We conclude that it is appropriate for the court below to either (1) ascertain from the judge an explanation of what his consideration of the nonjudicial punishment implied; or (2) adjust appellant's sentence to assure that he was not twice punished.

The decision of the United States Army Court of Military Review is set aside as to sentence. The record of trial is returned to the Judge Advocate General of the Army for resubmission to that court for further review.

Points for Discussion

1. How could the punishment be adjusted to make sure that Private Pierce is not punished twice? Why does the court have to return the case? Could the court adjust the sentence itself?

2. The court explains in footnote 2 that "at the time the nonjudicial punishment was administered, the full magnitude of appellant's pattern of misconduct was only just beginning to be discerned." Should commanders impose nonjudicial punishment before they have the opportunity to determine the full extent of a service member's wrongdoing? Does this case discourage acting too hastily or does it have no real impact?

3-3. Administrative Separation   *equivalent = being fired*

Private employers have a simple and effective method of dealing with employees who engage in improper behavior—they simply fire the employees from their jobs. The Armed Forces have an analogue to this civilian remedy. If commanders follow certain procedures, they can "administratively separate" service members for misconduct. Many of the details concerning military separations are beyond the scope of this textbook. But there are four very important points to understand.

First, administrative separation can be a means of addressing misconduct. *Prefered over NJP & C-m sent.* Many more enlisted service members are administratively removed for misconduct than are discharged as a result of a court-martial sentence. Commanders generally can seek administrative separation either in addition to or instead of nonjudicial punishment or trial by court-martial.

Second, when a service member is administratively separated from one of the Armed Forces, the service member receives one of three kinds of *& Punitive* administrative discharges: an "honorable discharge," a "general discharge under honorable conditions," or an "other than honorable discharge." (These three kinds of administrative discharges are not to be confused with the two *Affects rights to benefits* kinds of punitive discharges that can be ordered only by a court-martial for enlisted personnel: a "dishonorable discharge" and "bad-conduct discharge.") The type of discharge that a service member receives affects the service member's right to benefits. Accordingly, as we will see below in *Clifford v. United States,* 120 Fed. Appx. 355 (Fed. Cir. 2005), within certain limits, *Separation & type may be contested.* service members may contest both their separation and their type of discharge.

Third, the Fifth Amendment of the U.S. Constitution prohibits the federal government from depriving any person of liberty without due process of law. Federal courts have assumed that service members have a "liberty interest" in not being discharged from the service with a stigmatizing discharge, such as a discharge under other than honorable conditions or even possibly a general discharge under honorable conditions.[1] *See Holley v. United States,* 124 F.3d 1462, 1469 (Fed. Cir. 1997). Therefore, service members cannot be discharged without being afforded due process. Due process generally means *Due Process* that the government must give the service member notice of the grounds for *Fed gov req. a hearing* discharge and an opportunity to be heard before the discharge occurs. *See Canonica v. United States,* 41 Fed. Cl. 516, 524 (1998). The federal *before a* government has attempted to provide this due process by requiring a hearing *Sep. Board (enlisted) &* before a "separation board" prior to separating enlisted members from *Investigation* service and an investigation by a "board of inquiry" before officers are *by Board of* separated. *Inquiry (Officers)*

A report of the Congressional Research Service, "Administrative Separations for Misconduct: An Alternative or Companion to Military Courts-Martial," written by Estela I. Velez Pollack, describes the process for administrative separation of enlisted soldiers:

> *Process of Separating →* When separation is contemplated the servicemember is afforded certain rights. At the outset of the process servicemembers are notified of these rights in writing. This notification includes the factual basis of the proposed separation, the least favorable discharge being considered, the right to obtain copies of the documents being forwarded in support of the proposed separation, the right to submit statements, the right to counsel,

and, if he or she qualifies for one,[13] the right to an Administrative Board, a hearing to contest the separation or the type of discharge sought. If a servicemember is not entitled to an administrative separation board, the member may still submit letters and evidence on his or her behalf to prove suitability for continued service.

Admin. Sep. Board
Ø Punitive

... Administrative Separation Boards (hereinafter "Boards"), although not punitive in nature, are similar to trials in that they are adjudicatory in nature. They are intended to determine the servicemember's suitability for continued service in the military and, if not, how their past service should be characterized. The Boards are composed of at least three officers, the "judge" and "jury," who both decide on procedural issues and vote on whether the evidence supports separation and if so, the character of the separation. An enlisted servicemember in the rank of at least E-7 and senior to the servicemember may also be appointed. A non-voting legal advisor, the "prosecutor," may be appointed to assist the Board. Much like at a trial, the servicemember has the right to testify on his or her own behalf, be represented by counsel, call witnesses on his or her behalf, question witnesses testifying against him or her, and present arguments on his or her behalf. However, rules of evidence applicable during a criminal trial do not apply at a Board. The standard of proof is "preponderance of the evidence," rather than the "beyond a reasonable doubt" standard of criminal trials, and the recommendation of the Board need not be unanimous.

Operates Similarly to a trial.

Ø Rules of Evidence

Standard of Proof Prep. of the Evid.

Once the Board makes its recommendation, the record of the proceedings is forwarded to the "separation authority" for an independent review. In case of a recommendation of an other than honorable discharge, the proceedings are also reviewed by an attorney. If the Board recommends retention and the "separation authority" believes separation is warranted, the separation authority will forward his or her recommendation and the Board's recommendation to the Secretary of the servicemember's military branch for final review and decision. Additional challenges to the service's decision may be brought by the servicemember in the Court of Federal Claims and the respective board of correction of military records.

Post Admin Sep Board→ Sep. Autho → Possibly an Attny → Sec. of the Mil. Branch (final review)

For Officers: CM is more common than Admin. Sep

Finally, administrative separations of officers are much less common. Usually an officer who engages in misconduct severe enough to warrant an administrative discharge will face trial by court-martial instead. If administrative separation of an officer is sought, the secretary of the officer's service (e.g., the Secretary of the Army) will convene a Board of Inquiry composed of three officers to conduct a hearing to see if separation is

---

[13] Only servicemembers who have served for at least six years of combined active and reserve duty are entitled to an administrative board unless they are facing the possibility of an other-than-honorable discharge. DoD Dir. 1332.14, E3.A3.1.2., E3.A3.1.3.1.

warranted. The officer will have rights similar to those available if the officer were facing a court-martial, but the Board of Inquiry is not criminal in nature and the burden of proof is a preponderance of the evidence rather than the criminal standard of beyond a reasonable doubt. If the Board of Inquiry recommends to the Secretary that the officer should be separated, the officer may appeal to a Board of Review.

Sample Record of Administrative Separation

Army Regulation 635-200, Active Duty Enlisted Administrative Separations (Jun. 6, 2005) (Figure B-1) contains the following sample record of a separation proceeding:

HEADQUARTERS
118th INFANTRY DIVISION
FORT JACKSON, SC 29207

28 March 2000

SUBJECT: Notification to Appear Before the Board of Officers

TO: Private John A. Doe, 000-00-0000
     Company A. 4th Battalion, 96th Infantry
     Fort Jackson, SC 29207

1. Under the provisions of Army Regulation 15-6, paragraph 5-5, and Army Regulation 635-200 notice is hereby given that a Board of Officers appointed by memorandum of appointment, this Headquarters, dated 1 February2000, will hold a hearing at Building T-4321 at 0900 hours on 15 June 2000, to determine whether you should be discharged because of misconduct before the expiration of your terra of service. If you fail to appear before the board due to being absent without leave, you may be discharged from or retained in the service by the discharge authority without personal appearance before the board.

2. The following witnesses are expected to be called:

Captain Winfield M. Elrod
Company C, 4th Battalion, 96th Infantry
Fort Jackson, SC 29207

1LT Titus L. Moody
Company B, 4th Battalion, 96th Infantry
Fort Jackson, SC 29207

Sergeant Robert H. Brown
Company C. 4th Battalion, 96th infantry
Fort Jackson, SC 29207

Captain William P. Peters
Company A, 4th Battalion, 96th infantry
Fort Jackson, SC 29207

3. The recorder will endeavor to arrange for the presence of any reasonably available and necessary witnesses whom you may desire to call, upon written request from you for such action.

4. Attached is a copy of a deposition from Captain Duane Evans, who will be unable to appear in person at the board hearings.

1 Encl.   ALBERT A. FAKIAN
                   2LT, Artillery
                   Recorder

* * *

SUMMARY OF PROCEEDINGS

The board was appointed by letters of appointment. Headquarters, 118th Infantry Division and Fort Jackson, SC, dated 1 February 2000, a copy of which is attached.

The respondent was referred to this board for a hearing by letter, Headquarters, 118th infantry Division and Fort Jackson, SC, dated 28 March 2000.

The board convened at Fort Jackson, SC, on IS June 2000. The board met pursuant to the foregoing letter of appointment at 09Co hours on (date).

PERSONS PRESENT:

Major Walter C. Brown, 000-00-0000, Infantry, President

Major Robert Johnson, 000-00-0000, Infantry. Member

Captain Lewis B. Johnson, 000-00-0000, Infantry, Member

Second Lieutenant Albert A. Fakian, 000-00-0000, Infantry (Recorder)

First Lieutenant George P. Huffnagle, 000-00-0000, JAGC (Counsel for Respondent)

Captain James R. Cronkhite, 000-00-0000, Infantry (Counsel for Respondent)

PERSONS ABSENT:

None.

Private John A. Doe, 000-00-0000, Company A, 4th Battalion, 96th Infantry, appeared before the board with his counsel (1LT George P. Huffnagel) (Captain James R. Cronkhite).

The memorandum appointing the board and the applicable substance of the regulations under which it was convened was read aloud by the recorder.

Private John A. Doe was asked if he desired to challenge any member of the board for cause; he replied he did not.

A true copy of written advance notification to Private John A. Doe, dated 28 March 2000, was received and read and is hereto appended.

Private John A. Doe was present during all open sessions of the board with his counsel and was afforded full opportunity to cross-examine adverse witnesses to present evidence in his own behalf, and to testify in person orsubmit a written statement.

[handwritten margin note: Doe had the op to cross, present evid, testify]

A memorandum, subject: Discharge for Misconduct Under AR 635-200, Company A, 4th Battalion, 96th Infantry, with two endorsements (enclosures withdrawn), was offered in evidence by the recorder. There being no objection,the memorandum was admitted in evidence.

A certificate of 1LT Paul O. May, dated 10 January 2000, was offered in evidence by the recorder. There being no objection, the certificate was admitted in evidence.

A duly authenticated extract copy of the respondent's service record containing record of convictions by court-martial was offered in evidence by the recorder. There being no objections the document was admitted in evidence.

[handwritten margin note: C-M Record Admitted]

True copies of summarized records of proceedings under Article 15, UCMJ (DA Form 2627) pertaining to nonjudicial punishment imposed upon the respondent on (date(s)), were offered into evidence by the recorder, and admitted into evidence.

[handwritten margin note: NJP Rec. Admitted.]

The following witnesses called by the board were sworn and testified in substance as follows:

Captain Winfield K. Elrod, Company C, 4th Battalion, 96th Infantry.

I am the company commander of Company C, 4th Battalion, 96th Infantry. Private Doe was assigned to my company from 10 December 1998 until 05 December 1999. Before his assignment to my company, he had been in basic training. I initially assigned Doe to a squad in the company, and apparently he performed satisfactorily for the first month. About that time, he went AWOL for 7 days. Thereafter, Doe developed a bad attitude toward his job and the Army. I assigned Doe to another platoon as assistant supply clerk, and then as assistant to the company clerk where the first sergeant could keep an eye on him, but he performed unsatisfactorily in all of them. I then assigned Doe as an armorer-artificer's helper under the direct supervision of Sergeant Brown, and that is where Doe remained until his transfer out of my company. I gave him nonjudicial punishment under Article 15 2 times, once for being late to formation, and once for insubordination to a non-commissioned officer. As time passed, he became more sullen and uncooperative.

[handwritten margin notes: Basic Training / Assigned to Comp. C / 1st month ✓ / 7 days AWOL / Bad Attitude / Assigned to dif platoon then another / Bad perf.]

CROSS-EXAMINATION

I counseled Doe several times, but he refused to say what was bothering him. I counseled this soldier the' first time when he was punished for being AWOL. About a month later, I counseled him again and explained to him that some changes would have to be made for his own good and for the good of the Army. I counseled him in those instances then I imposed nonjudicial punishment. I told Doe that his prior record indicated that he could perform the duties required and that his tour would be much better if he did his job. He did not respond to my counseling.

Note. All subsequent testimony should be recorded similarly. After all testimony has been recorded, continue as shown below.

A statement signed by the respondent, dated 25 May 2000, to the effect that he had been advised of the basis of this action, desired to have a board hearing, and desired counsel, was offered in evidence by the recorder. There being no objections, the document was admitted in evidence.

The recorder stated that he had nothing further to offer. The rights of the respondent were explained to him by the president of the board. The respondent elected to take the stand as a witness. He was sworn and testified in substance as follows.

DIRECT EXAMINATION

I have been in the Army since 04 December 1998, I am 20 years old, I lived in Jersey City, NJ, and went to school there up to the 9th grade. Before I finished the 9th grade, I was 16 years old, so I quit. I got mixed up with a bad crowd. So to improve my chance in life, I enlisted in the Army in December 1998. At first, I liked the Army, but then I got tired of being bossed around all the time. The sergeants gave me a bad time. Everything was jump, jump, jump. At first I did my work, but I didn't make PPC, so I figured it was no use and wanted out. I guess I don't want a bad discharge, but I don't want all those rotten details either.

CROSS- EXAMINATION

I have heard what the officers and sergeants have said about me. The only way I can explain it is that they don't understand me. They were always pushing me around.

The recorder made on argument.

Counsel for the respondent made an argument. Then the recorder made a closing statement.

Neither the recorder nor the respondent having anything further to offer, the board was closed.

Attached is the verbatim record of the findings and recommendations of the board.

The board adjourned at 1400 hours on 15 June 2000,

VERBATIM FINDINGS AND RECOMMENDATIONS

FINDINGS: In the board proceedings concerning Private (B2) John A. Doe, 000-00-0000, the board carefully considered the evidence before it and finds:

1. Private Doe is undesirable for further retention in the military service because of the following misconduct:

a. Frequent incidents of a discreditable nature with military authorities.

b. Habitual shirking.

2. His rehabilitation is not deemed possible.

RECOMMENDATIONS:

In view of the findings, the board recommends that Private Doe be discharged from the Service because of misconduct under other than honorable conditions.

(President)
(Member)
(Recorder)

Points for Discussion

1. How would you compare Private Doe's discharge from the Army to the discharge of an employee from a private employer? Did Doe have greater procedural protections? Does his discharge have a greater stigma?

Absolutely more procedure

2. How had Doe's misconduct previously been addressed? Why would Doe's commander want to separate him from the service rather than seek further punishment?

1. NJP & C-M
2. It is evident he does not want to save his military career.

It depends on the employer & their opinion of the military

Service members who are separated have a right to challenge their separation, first to a higher level commander, then to the Court of Federal Claims, then to the U.S. Court of Appeals for the Federal Circuit, and finally to the Supreme Court. They may contend that the Service that separated them violated the Constitution or statutes or regulations. Challenges, however, generally can only address the procedures followed by the separation board. On the substantive question of whether a soldier should be separated, the courts generally defer to the Services. *See Adkins v. United States*, 68 F.3d 1317, 1322 (Fed.Cir. 1995).

CLIFFORD v. UNITED STATES

U.S. Court of Appeals for the Federal Circuit
120 Fed.Appx. 355 (Fed. Cir. 2005)

PER CURIAM.

Mark A. Clifford appeals an order from the United States Court of Federal Claims in case No. 02-982C, in which the court denied Mr. Clifford's request to set aside his discharge characterization of other than honorable, to set aside his demotion, and to award him back pay and allowances. We affirm.

1. Admin Sep.
2. Sep. Authorities
3. Sec. of Army
4. Higher level commander appeal
5. Ct. of Fed Claims

BACKGROUND

[margin note: Served 1984-1999]

Mr. Clifford served as a recruiter for the United States Army from February 24, 1984, until May 12, 1999, when he was discharged under other than honorable conditions. On December 31, 1997, the Sheriff's Office in Kanawha County, West Virginia, commenced a criminal investigation of Mr. Clifford regarding an alleged sexual assault on a prospective Army recruit. As a result of the investigation, the state charged Mr. Clifford with second degree sexual assault. On January 8, 1998, the Army's Criminal Investigation Division ("CID") began its own investigation of the same incident and subsequently issued a Report of Investigation finding probable cause to believe that Mr. Clifford committed the offenses of second degree sexual assault in violation of the West Virginia Code and adultery in violation of United States Code of Military Justice ("UCMJ").

[margin note: 1997 Prospective recruit was sexually assaulted "by Δ"]

[margin note: Army then investigate & found probable cause]

A military attorney, Capt. Scharfenberger, was appointed to represent Mr. Clifford in the military criminal proceedings arising out of the CID investigation. In addition, in January 1998, Mr. Clifford hired a civilian attorney to assist him with all legal matters arising out of the criminal allegations against him. Based on advice from Capt. Scharfenberger, Mr. Clifford waived his right to a court-martial trial for the alleged offenses and opted to proceed instead with a hearing under Article 15 of the UCMJ. Following the Article 15 hearing, his commanding officer found that Mr. Clifford had committed the charged offenses of absence without leave, failure to obey an order regarding personal contact with a recruit, and making a false official statement. He imposed nonjudicial punishment of forfeiture of half pay for two months.

[margin note: Cpt. advised him to waive Cm & take Art XV]

Mr. Clifford's commanding officer also initiated an administrative action to separate Mr. Clifford from the Army. He recommended that Mr. Clifford be discharged under other than honorable conditions. Mr. Clifford appealed his commanding officer's recommendation and sought a personal appearance before an administrative separation board.

[margin note: Commander Initiated Admin Sep.]

On January 7, 1999, the administrative separation board notified Mr. Clifford that the board was scheduled to convene for a hearing on January 22, 1999. On January 15, 1999, Capt. Scharfenberger submitted a request on Mr. Clifford's behalf for a six-week delay of the board hearing until March 2, 1999. The board denied that request, but agreed to delay the board proceeding for two weeks, until February 3, 1999. During the two week delay, Mr. Clifford had the option of making a request for the appointment of military counsel or retaining civilian counsel to represent him at the proceedings. As stated in a memorandum from the president of the separation board and a letter from Capt. Scharfenberger, Mr. Clifford did not make a request for the appointment of military counsel for the board proceedings but instead intended to proceed with his retained civilian counsel. Mr. Clifford's civilian counsel contacted the board to request that the hearing be delayed until after June 1, 1999, because of his own scheduling conflicts. The board denied that request based on an Army regulation that

[margin note: Date for personal appearance set.]

[margin note: Δ req. 6 week ext]

[margin note: Denied 2 week grant]

[margin note: Civilian counsel req. ext. Denied.]

provides that board proceedings should not be delayed unduly to permit a respondent to obtain a particular counsel or to accommodate counsel's schedule.

In response, Capt. Scharfenberger sent a letter to the Office of the Staff Judge Advocate, noting that he had not been detailed to represent Mr. Clifford before the board, but urging the Office to delay the board proceedings further in order to accommodate Mr. Clifford and his civilian attorney. A deputy staff judge advocate responded that the board had made reasonable attempts to accommodate Mr. Clifford and could not postpone the hearing until after June 1, 1999, as Mr. Clifford's civilian attorney had requested, because that date would be after Mr. Clifford's expiration of time of service ("ETS"), which was on May 26, 1999. The ETS establishes a deadline beyond which the board is not permitted to meet.

The board convened on February 3, 1999. Before the members of the board were sworn in, Mr. Clifford addressed the issue of the requested delays. He stated that he had sought a delay in the board proceedings to accommodate his civilian attorney. The board president concluded that Mr. Clifford had "had the opportunity to get military counsel," but instead "elected to go with civilian counsel who could not be here today." The board then went ahead with the proceeding.

Following the hearing, the board decided unanimously that Mr. Clifford should "be separated from the military service because of commission of [two] serious offense[s]." The board also decided that Mr. Clifford receive an other than honorable discharge, although one of the three board members disagreed with that aspect of the decision, finding that while Mr. Clifford had committed serious offenses, his service record justified a general discharge rather than an "other than honorable" discharge.

Mr. Clifford appealed the board's decision to the Commander of the Army Recruiting Command. Mr. Clifford did not challenge the factual findings of the board nor its recommendation that he be separated from the army, but asserted that he "merit[s] an upgrade to an honorable discharge." The Commander of the Army Recruiting Command accepted the board's findings and recommendations, and on March 31, 1999, ordered that Mr. Clifford be separated from the Army, discharged under other than honorable conditions, and immediately reduced in rank to the lowest enlisted grade. Accordingly, Mr. Clifford was immediately reduced from his rank of Sergeant First Class (E-7) to the lowest enlisted grade of Private (E-1) as of March 31, 1999, was separated from the Army on May 15, 1999, and was discharged on May 19, 1999, under other than honorable circumstances.

On August 16, 2002, Mr. Clifford filed suit in the United States Court of Federal Claims, asserting that the administrative separation board's actions violated his right to due process. As a remedy, he sought to set aside his other than honorable discharge and his demotion, and to have his discharge upgraded to "honorable." He also sought monetary relief, including back pay and allowances from March 31 to May 26, 1999, at the E-7 level, back pay and allowances for the 14-day involuntary separation preceding his ETS, and compensation for the separation and severance pay that he would have received if he had been awarded an honorable discharge.

Ct. of Fed
Claims
SJ for US
& Dismissed

The Court of Federal Claims granted summary judgment in favor of the United States and dismissed Mr. Clifford's complaint. The court found that the board did not abuse its discretion by rejecting Mr. Clifford's attorneys' requests for delays, as "[t]he board president was constrained by two imperatives: the requirement that proceedings not be unduly delayed and the immutable ETS date." The court also stated that "[b]ecause the Army followed its regulations permitting representation by counsel, but within the confines of directives disallowing counsel from disrupting the schedule of the board, plaintiff received the process to which he was due." The court further found that while neither of Mr. Clifford's lawyers appeared at the hearing before the administrative separation board, he was not without representation. As a result, the court held that he was not proceeding pro se and therefore was not entitled to certain rights, such as counseling by the president of the board during the hearing.

US Ct. of Ap
for Fed.
Cir

DISCUSSION

3 (I)

Mr. Clifford asserts that his right to due process was violated for three reasons: (1) he was denied his right to legal representation; (2) the president of the board did not counsel him during the board's hearing pursuant to Army Regulation 635-200, ¶ 2-10b; and (3) his Non-Commissioned Officer Evaluation Reports were not in evidence before the board.

Mr. Clifford asserts that he was denied legal representation because the board proceeded with its hearing in the absence of his lawyer. In support of his argument, Mr. Clifford cites Army Regulation 3.7, stating that "[n]o soldier will be discharged per this regulation under other than honorable conditions unless he or she is afforded the right to present his or her case before an administrative discharge board" and that "[each] soldier will be offered the advice and assistance of counsel." However, Mr. Clifford was afforded the right to present his case before an administrative separation board, and he had the advice and assistance of his chosen counsel. The fact that his attorney did not appear at the hearing does not mean that his right to counsel was violated. See Ponce-Leiva v. Ashcroft, 331 F.3d 369 (3d Cir. 2003). As the trial court stated, "[a]lthough counsel was absent, [Mr. Clifford] acted pursuant to the advice of his counsel at the board proceedings."

The board was not required to delay its hearing until March or June of 1999 in order to accommodate Mr. Clifford's civilian counsel. While the Army Regulations provide that "a respondent is entitled . . . to be present with counsel at all open sessions of the board," AR 15-6, ¶ 5-6a, that entitlement is not absolute. Army Regulation 15-6, ¶ 5-6c provides that:

Whenever practicable, the board proceedings will be held in abeyance pending respondent's reasonable and diligent efforts to obtain civilian counsel. However, the proceedings should not be delayed unduly to permit a respondent to obtain a particular counsel or to accommodate the schedule of such counsel.

We agree with the trial court that the record demonstrates that the board provided Mr. Clifford with an opportunity to find counsel by granting him a delay of two weeks and that the board permissibly decided, within its discretion, that any additional time would cause undue delay.*See Ungar v. Sarafite*, 376 U.S. 575, 589 (1964) ("The matter of continuance is traditionally within the discretion of the trial judge, and it is not every denial of a request for more time that violates due process"). Rather than obtaining an attorney who would be able to accompany him to the hearing, Mr. Clifford chose to retain an attorney who would not be available until June 1, 1999, which fell after Mr. Clifford's ETS date of May 26, 1999. The fact that he appeared without counsel at the hearing was thus the product of his choice, not the product of unreasonable haste on the part of the board.

Mr. Clifford states that his military attorney abandoned him, leaving him without counsel at the hearing. The record reflects, however, that Mr. Clifford did not request that he be represented by a military attorney at the board hearing and that, accordingly, a military lawyer was not appointed for him in connection with that hearing. Instead, as the board president explained to him during the board proceedings, "You have had the opportunity to get military counsel and you have elected to go with civilian counsel." The inability of his chosen lawyer to be present at the board hearing, despite a reasonable delay granted by the board to accommodate his civilian counsel, did not result in the violation of any of Mr. Clifford's rights.

Mr. Clifford next argues that he was denied due process because the president of the board did not counsel him during the board's hearing pursuant to Army Regulation 635-200, ¶ 2-10b. However, in order to be entitled to counseling by the board president under that regulation, Mr. Clifford needed to be pro se. As the trial court determined, Mr. Clifford was not proceeding pro se. While he did not have counsel with him at the hearing, he nevertheless was represented throughout the board proceedings. As the trial court explained, he was "not in the same position as a pro se servicemember who lacks counsel" and who needs the guidance offered by counseling from the board president.

Finally, Mr. Clifford argues that he was denied due process because the board failed to admit into evidence his Non-Commissioned Officer Evaluation Reports. Citing Army Regulation 635-200, Mr. Clifford argues that a soldier's entire military record must be considered in a case pertaining to separation. However, Mr. Clifford did not attempt to introduce the reports into evidence, and the board never rejected them. Mr. Clifford notes that the board president acknowledged the absence of the reports, but he does not assert that the board president prevented him from introducing them into evidence.

Aside from his three main arguments, Mr. Clifford also appears to argue that we should consider the report of the dissenting board member who favored awarding him a general discharge. That board member found that "although [Mr. Clifford] has committed an offense that is very serious in nature, the soldier's record and the whole soldier concept was not taken into account . . . a general discharge will in every way make him realize the gravity of what he has done and at the same time give him a fair chance to provide adequately for his family." To the extent that Mr. Clifford asks us to change his discharge characterization based on a dissenting board member's opinion, his argument fails. Neither the trial court nor this court can simply choose to adopt the opinion of a dissenting board member, particularly on a matter such as military discharge decisions. *See Heisig v. United States*, 719 F.2d 1153, 1156 (Fed.Cir. 1983) ("responsibility for determining who is fit or unfit to serve in the armed services is not a judicial province"). The board speaks through its decisions, and if those decisions are not legally flawed in a manner that is subject to judicial correction, the courts must defer to the decisions made by the board on behalf of the military.

Points for Discussion

1. Although the court examines the procedures used to separate Clifford, it does not consider whether the substance of his offense warrants a discharge under other than honorable conditions. The court says that it "must defer to the decisions made by the board on behalf of the military," but it does not explain the reason for this deference. What reasons can you think of?

2. Is it appropriate to separate a soldier from the Army on the basis of conduct for which he has already received nonjudicial punishment?

3-4. Summary Courts-Martial

In addition to administrative corrective measures, nonjudicial punishment, and administrative corrective measures, a fourth option for dealing with misconduct short of a full adversarial criminal trial is the summary court-martial. One enthusiast of this procedure writes:

> Speedier than a special court-martial and more deadly than nonjudicial punishment under Article 15 of the Uniform Code of Military Justice, a summary court-martial is a great option for a commander who is looking at an offense that is in the gray area between an Article 15 and a special court-martial. The summary court-martial also is valuable when a military member needs to be taught a swift lesson that will serve as a message to others about to fall off the precipice of good order and discipline.

Michael H. Gilbert, *Summary Courts-Martial: Rediscovering the Spumoni of Military Justice*, 39 Air Force L. Rev. 119, 119 (1996).

A summary court-martial is a tribunal, authorized by Article 20 of the UCMJ, that consists of just one officer. According to R.C.M. 1301, which specifies the procedures, the purpose of a summary court-martial is "to promptly adjudicate minor offenses under a simple procedure." The officer who serves as the summary court-martial is usually not a judge advocate, but may seek advice from a judge advocate on questions of law. Summary courts-martial may only try enlisted members who are accused of non-capital offenses. The accused may refuse trial by summary court-martial and demand trial by a special or general court-martial.

A summary court-martial cannot discharge a service member or impose a punishment greater than 45 days' confinement or 1 month of hard labor, restriction to specified limits for more than 2 months, or forfeiture of more than two-thirds of 1 month's pay. It may reduce enlisted members to the lowest pay grade if they are grade E4 or below. Special rules apply to grades above E4.

The accused does not have a right to appointed counsel. The accused, however, may retain civilian counsel. This is usually a good idea. A defense attorney writes:

> More than [in] any other military proceeding the civilian defense counsel has the biggest overall effect on a Summary Court Martial [(SCM)]. This is because at a [SCM] the person that is most confused and feeling like a fish out of water is the SCM Officer. As military officers, they have probably never been around a trial or administrative hearing. They do not understand the law. They do not understand the introduction of evidence and they do not understand the proper way to question a witness on the stand. All of these things . . . allow the civilian defense counsel to help guide both the SCM Officer and the outcome. The civilian defense counsel in subtle ways can both befriend and harass the SCM Officer into making a favorable decision for the accused soldier.

James Phillips, Summary Court-Martial: A Fair Process? Or a Foregone Conclusion?, <http://jaglaw.wordpress.com/2009/02/22/summary-court-martial-a-fair-process/>.

Summary courts-martial are less common than non-judicial punishments, but they are not uncommon. In the Army, there were 819 summary courts-martial in 2009, compared to 36,624 instances of non-judicial punishment. *See* Annual Report of the Code Committee on Military Justice for the Period October 1, 2009 to September 30, 2010 at 23.

The Supreme Court addressed the constitutionality of denying the accused a right to appointed counsel by summary court-martial in the following case. The Court, additionally, compared the summary courts-martial to nonjudicial punishment.

MIDDENDORF v. HENRY
U.S. Supreme Court
425 U.S. 25 (1973)

Mr. Justice REHNQUIST delivered the opinion of the Court.

Marine Corps

Class Action

In February 1973 plaintiffs then enlisted members of the United States Marine Corps brought this class action in the United States District Court for the Central District of California challenging the authority of the military to try them at summary courts-martial without providing them with counsel.

5 π

20-30 days
confinement
hard labor

Five plaintiffs had been charged with "unauthorized absences" in violation of Art. 86 UCMJ, 10 U.S.C. § 886, convicted at summary courts-martial, and sentenced, *inter alia*, to periods of confinement ranging from 20 to 30 days at hard labor. The other three plaintiffs, two of whom were charged, *inter alia*, with unauthorized absence and one with assault, Art. 128, UCMJ, 10 U.S.C.

3 π
Ordered SCM
& convened

§ 928, had been ordered to stand trial at summary courts-martial which had not been convened. Those who were convicted had not been provided counsel those who were awaiting trial had been informed that counsel would not be provided. All convicted plaintiffs were informed prior to trial that they would not be afforded counsel and that they could refuse trial by summary

If refuse
Sum CM
then Spec.
CM

court-martial if they so desired. In the event of such refusal their cases would be referred to special courts-martial at which counsel would be provided. All plaintiffs consented in writing to proceed to trial by summary court-martial, without counsel. Plaintiffs' court-martial records were reviewed and approved by the Staff Judge Advocate pursuant to Art. 65(c), UCMJ, 10 U.S.C. § 865(c). . . .

I

The UCMJ provides four methods for disposing of cases involving offenses committed by servicemen: the general, special, and summary courts-martial, and disciplinary punishment administered by the commanding officer pursuant to Art. 15 UCMJ, 10 U.S.C. § 815. General and special courts-martial resemble judicial proceedings, nearly always presided over by lawyer judges with lawyer counsel for both the prosecution and the defense. General courts-martial are authorized to award any lawful sentence, including death. Art. 18 UCMJ, 10 U.S.C. § 818. Special courts-martial may award a bad-conduct discharge, up to six months' confinement at hard labor, forfeiture of two-thirds pay per month for six months, and in the case of an enlisted member, reduction to the lowest pay grade, Art. 19, UCMJ, 10 U.S.C. § 819. Article 15 punishment, conducted personally by the accused's commanding officer, is an administrative method of dealing with the most minor offenses. *Parker v. Levy*, 417 U.S. 733 (1974).

The summary court-martial occupies a position between informal nonjudicial disposition under Art. 15 and the courtroom-type procedure of the general and special courts-martial. Its purpose, "is to exercise justice promptly for relatively minor offenses under a simple form of procedure." Manual for Courts-Martial ¶ 79A (1969) (MCM). It is an informal proceeding conducted by a single commissioned officer with jurisdiction only over noncommissioned officers and other enlisted personnel. Art. 20, UCMJ, 10 U.S.C. § 820. The presiding officer acts as judge, factfinder, prosecutor, and defense counsel. The presiding officer must inform the accused of the charges and the name of the accuser and call all witnesses whom he or the accused desires to call.[10] MCM ¶79D. The accused must consent to trial by summary court-martial; if he does not do so trial may be ordered by special or general court-martial, or the case will be either dismissed or referred to a special or general court-martial.

The maximum sentence elements which may be imposed by summary courts-martial are: one month's confinement at hard labor; 45 days' hard labor without confinement; two months' restriction to specified limits; reduction to the lowest enlisted pay grade; and forfeiture of two-thirds pay for one month. Art. 20, UCMJ, 10 U.S.C. § 820.

[handwritten margin note: Possible Punishments.]

II

The question of <u>whether an accused in a court-martial has a constitutional right to counsel has been much debated and never squarely resolved.</u> *See Reid v. Covert*, 354 U.S. 1, 37 (1957). Dicta in *Ex parte Milligan*, 4 Wall. 2, 123 (1866), said that "the framers of the Constitution, doubtless, meant to limit the right of trial by jury, in the sixth amendment, to those persons who were subject to indictment or presentment in the fifth." In *Ex parte Quirin*, 317 U.S. 1, 40 (1942), it was said that " 'cases arising in the land or naval forces' . . . are expressly excepted from the Fifth Amendment, and are deemed excepted by implication from the Sixth."

We find it unnecessary in this case to finally resolve the broader aspects of this question, since we conclude that even were the Sixth Amendment to be held applicable to court-martial proceedings, the summary court-martial provided for in these cases was not a "criminal prosecution" within the meaning of that Amendment.

[handwritten margin note: Sum CM & crim prosec. within 6th Am.]

***

Argersinger v. Hamlin, 407 U.S. 25 (1972), held that the Sixth Amendment's provision for the assistance of counsel extended to misdemeanor prosecutions in civilian courts if conviction would result in imprisonment. A summary court-martial may impose 30 days' confinement at hard labor, which is doubtless the military equivalent of imprisonment. Yet the fact that the outcome of a proceeding may result in loss of liberty does

---

[10] Additionally, the officer must inform the accused of his right to remain silent and allow him to cross-examine witnesses or have the summary court officer cross-examine them for him. The accused may testify and present evidence in his own behalf. If the accused is found guilty he may make a statement, sworn or unsworn, in extenuation or mitigation. MCM ¶ 79D. The record of the trial is then reviewed by the convening officer, Art. 60, UCMJ, 10 U.S.C. § 860, and thereafter by a judge advocate. Art. 65(c), UCMJ, 10 U.S.C. § 865(c).

not by itself, even in civilian life, mean that the Sixth Amendment's guarantee of counsel is applicable. In *Gagnon v. Scarpelli*, 411 U.S. 778 (1973), the respondent faced the prospect of being sent to prison as a result of the revocation of his probation, but we held that the revocation proceeding was nonetheless not a "criminal proceeding." We took pains in that case to observe:

> "[T]here are critical differences between criminal trials and probation or parole revocation hearings, and both society and the probationer or parolee have stakes in preserving these differences.
>
> "In a criminal trial, the State is represented by a prosecutor; formal rules of evidence are in force; a defendant enjoys a number of procedural rights which may be lost if not timely raised; and, in a jury trial, a defendant must make a presentation understandable to untrained jurors. In short, a criminal trial under our system is an adversary proceeding with its own unique characteristics. In a revocation hearing, on the other hand, the State is represented, not by a prosecutor, but by a parole officer with the orientation described above; formal procedures and rules of evidence are not employed; and the members of the hearing body are familiar with the problems and practice of probation or parole." *Id.*, at 788-789.

In re Gault, 387 U.S. 1 (1967), involved a proceeding in which a juvenile was threatened with confinement. The Court, although holding counsel was required, went on to say:

> " 'We do not mean . . . to indicate that the hearing to be held must conform with all of the requirements of a criminal trial or even of the usual administrative hearing; but we do hold that the hearing must measure up to the essentials of due process and fair treatment.' "*Id.*, at 30.

The Court's distinction between various civilian proceedings, and its conclusion that, notwithstanding the potential loss of liberty, neither juvenile hearings nor probation revocation hearings are "criminal proceedings," are equally relevant in assessing the role of the summary court-martial in the military.

The summary court-martial is, as noted above, one of four types of proceedings by which the military imposes discipline or punishment. If we were to remove the holding of *Argersinger* from its civilian context and apply it to require counsel before a summary court-martial proceeding simply because loss of liberty may result from such a proceeding, it would seem all but inescapable that counsel would likewise be required for the lowest level of military proceeding for dealing with the most minor offenses. For even the so-called Art. 15 "nonjudicial punishment," which may be imposed administratively by the commanding officer, may result in the imposition upon an enlisted man of "correctional custody" with hard labor for not more than 30 consecutive days. 10 U.S.C. § 815(b). But we think that the analysis made in cases such as *Gagnon* and *Gault*, as well as considerations peculiar to the military, counsel against such a mechanical application of *Argersinger*.

We have only recently noted the difference between the diverse civilian community and the much more tightly regimented military community in *Parker v. Levy*, 417 U.S. 733, 749 (1974). We said there that the UCMJ "cannot be equated to a civilian criminal code. It, and the various versions of the Articles of War which have preceded it, regulate aspects of the conduct of members of the military which in the civilian sphere are left unregulated. While a civilian criminal code carves out a relatively small segment of potential conduct and declares it criminal, the Uniform Code of Military Justice essays more varied regulation of a much larger segment of the activities of the more tightly knit military community."*Ibid.* Much of the conduct proscribed by the military is not "criminal" conduct in the civilian sense of the word.*Id.*, at 749-751.

Here for example, most of the plaintiffs were charged solely with "unauthorized absence," an offense which has no common-law counterpart and which carries little popular opprobrium. Conviction of such an offense would likely have no consequences for the accused beyond the immediate punishment meted out by the military, unlike conviction for such civilian misdemeanors as vagrancy or larceny which could carry a stamp of "bad character" with conviction.

By the same token, the penalties which may be meted out in summary courts-martial are limited to one month's confinement at hard labor, 45 days' hard labor without confinement, or two months' restriction to a specified limits. Sanctions which may be imposed affecting a property interest are limited to reduction in grade with attendant loss of pay, or forfeiture or detention of a portion of one month's pay.

Finally, a summary court-martial is procedurally quite different from a criminal trial. In the first place, it is not an adversary proceeding. . . .   *Adversarial*

The function of the presiding officer is quite different from that of any participant in a civilian trial. He is guided by the admonition in ¶ 79A of the MCM: "The function of a summary court-martial is to exercise justice promptly for relatively minor offenses under a simple form of procedure. The summary court will thoroughly and impartially inquire into both sides of the matter and will assure that the interests of both the Government and the accused are safeguarded." The presiding officer is more specifically enjoined to attend to the interests of the accused by these provisions of the same paragraph:

"The accused will be extended the right to cross-examine these witnesses. The summary court will aid the accused in the cross-examination, and, if the accused desires, will ask questions suggested by the accused. On behalf of the accused, the court will obtain the attendance of witnesses, administer the oath and examine them, and obtain such other evidence as may tend to disprove or negative guilt of the charges, explain the acts or omissions charged, show extenuating circumstances, or establish grounds for mitigation. Before determining the findings, he will explain to the

The presiding officer must coach to some extent

accused his right to testify on the merits or to remain silent and will give the accused full opportunity to exercise his election."MCM ¶79D (3).

We believe there are significant parallels between the Court's description of probation and parole revocation proceedings in *Gagnon* and the summary court-martial, which parallels tend to distinguish both of these proceedings from the civilian misdemeanor prosecution upon which *Argersinger* focused. When we consider in addition that the court-martial proceeding takes place not in civilian society, as does the parole revocation proceeding, but in the military community with all of its distinctive qualities, we conclude that a summary court-martial is not a "criminal prosecution" for purposes of the Sixth Amendment.

III

The Court of Appeals likewise concluded that there was no Sixth Amendment right to counsel in summary court-martial proceedings such as this, but applying the due process standards of the Fifth Amendment adopted a standard from *Gagnon v. Scarpelli*, 411 U.S. 778 (1973), which would have made the right to counsel depend upon the nature of the serviceman's defense. We are unable to agree that the Court of Appeals property applied *Gagnon* in this military context.

We recognize that plaintiffs, who have either been convicted or are due to appear before a summary court-martial, may be subjected to loss of liberty or property, and consequently are entitled to the due process of law guaranteed by the Fifth Amendment.

However, whether this process embodies a right to counsel depends upon an analysis of the interests of the individual and those of the regime to which he is subject. *Wolff v. McDonnell*, 418 U.S. 539, 556 (1974).

We first consider the effect of providing counsel at summary courts-martial. As we observed in *Gagnon v. Scarpelli*, *supra*, 411 U.S. at 787:

> "The introduction of counsel into a . . . proceeding will alter significantly the nature of the proceeding. If counsel is provided for the (accused), the State in turn will normally provide its own counsel; lawyers, by training and disposition, are advocates and bound by professional duty to present all available evidence and arguments in support of their clients' positions and to contest with vigor all adverse evidence and views."

In short, presence of counsel will turn a brief, informal hearing which may be quickly convened and rapidly concluded into an attenuated proceeding which consumes the resources of the military to a degree which Congress could properly have felt to be beyond what is warranted by the relative insignificance of the offenses being tried. Such a lengthy proceeding is a particular burden to the Armed Forces because virtually all the participants, including the defendant and his counsel, are members of the military whose time may be better spent than in possibly protracted disputes over the imposition of discipline.

As we observed in *U. S. ex rel. Toth v. Quarles*, 350 U.S. 11, 17 (1955):

> "[I]t is the primary business of armies and navies to fight or be ready to fight wars should the occasion arise. But trial of soldiers to maintain discipline is merely incidental to an army's primary fighting function. To the extent that those responsible for performance of this primary function are diverted from it by the necessity of trying cases, the basic fighting purpose of armies is not served. . . . [M]ilitary tribunals have not been and probably never can be constituted in such way that they can have the same kind of qualifications that the Constitution has deemed essential to fair trials of civilians in federal courts."

However, the Court of Appeals did not find counsel necessary in all proceedings but only, pursuant to *Daigle v. Warner*, where the accused makes

> "a timely and colorable claim (1) that he has a defense, or (2) that there are mitigating circumstances, and the assistance of counsel is necessary in order adequately to present the defense or mitigating circumstances." 490 F.2d at 365.

But if the accused has such a claim, if he feels that in order to properly air his views and vindicate his rights, a formal, counseled proceeding is necessary he may simply refuse trial by summary court-martial and proceed to trial by special court-martial at which may have counsel. Thus, he stands in a considerably more favorable position than the probationer in *Gagnon* who, though subject to the possibility of longer periods of incarceration, had no such absolute right to counsel.

It is true that by exercising this option the accused subjects himself to greater possible penalties imposed in the special court-martial proceeding. However, we do not find that possible detriment to be constitutionally decisive. We have frequently approved the much more difficult decision, daily faced by civilian criminal defendants, to plead guilty to a lesser included offense. *E.g., Brady v. United States*, 397 U.S. 742, 749-750 (1970). In such a case the defendant gives up not only his right to counsel but his right to any trial at all. Furthermore, if he elects to exercise his right to trial he stands to be convicted of a more serious offense which will likely bear increased penalties.

Such choices are a necessary part of the criminal justice system:

> "The criminal process, like the rest of the legal system, is replete with situations requiring 'the making of difficult judgments' as to which course to follow.*McMann v. Richardson*, 397 U.S. 759, 769 (1970). Although a defendant may have a right, even of constitutional dimensions, to follow whichever course he chooses, the Constitution does not by that token always forbid requiring him to choose."*McGautha v. California*, 402 U.S. 183, 213 (1971).

We therefore agree with the defendants that neither the Sixth nor the Fifth Amendment to the United States Constitution empowers us to overturn the congressional determination that counsel is not required in summary courts-martial. The judgment of the Court of Appeals is therefore reversed.

Reversed.

Mr. Justice MARSHALL, with whom Mr. Justice BRENNAN joins, dissenting.

***

The substance of the asserted justification [for denying appointed counsel] here is that discipline, efficiency, and morale demand the utilization of an expeditious disciplinary procedure for relatively minor offenses. It would seem, however, that Art. 15 nonjudicial punishment which can be speedily imposed by a commander, but which does not carry with it the stigma of a criminal conviction provides just such a procedure. Indeed, the 1962 amendments to Art. 15, 10 U.S.C. § 815, greatly expanded the availability of nonjudicial punishment and resulted in a sharp decrease in the utilization of the summary court-martial. There is, therefore no pressing need to have a streamlined summary court-martial proceeding in order to supply an expeditious disciplinary procedure. Moreover, it is by no means clear that guaranteeing counsel to summary court-martial defendants would result in significantly longer time periods from preferral of charges to punishment than fairly conducted proceedings in the absence of counsel; any timesaving that is now enjoyed might well result from the presiding officer's being something less than an adequate substitute for independent defense counsel.

***

Points for Discussion

1. Although the Supreme Court concluded in 1973 that a summary court-martial is not an adversary criminal proceeding, is that the popular perception either in the military or outside the military?

2. The Court justifies its conclusion in part on grounds that a service member can refuse a summary court-martial and demand a trial by either special or general court-martial. Could the summary court-martial follow any procedure, no matter how unfair, merely because the service member is given a choice?

3. Is Justice Marshall correct that there is no pressing need for the summary court-martial procedure given the alternative of nonjudicial punishment?

CHAPTER 4

PRETRIAL ISSUES

4-1. Self-Incrimination and UCMJ, Article 31(b) Rights

In many instances, when commanders are conducting inquiries pursuant to Rule for Courts-Martial 303 or military police, security forces, or other investigators are reviewing a matter, persons subject to the UCMJ may be questioned. Service members are afforded the Constitutional protection of the Fifth Amendment right against self-incrimination. Members of the Armed Forces have been provided this protection since 1951 when Congress established Article 31(b) of the UCMJ, predating the *Miranda* warnings developed as a result of *Miranda v. Arizona*, 384 U.S. 436 (1966).[1] Originally designed as a prophylactic procedural measure to eliminate inherent military coercion due to the rank structure, UCMJ, Article 31(b) prohibits persons subject to the Code from compelling "any person to incriminate himself or to answer any question the answer to which may tend to incriminate him." Essentially, persons subject to the Code (when questioning persons subject to the Code who are suspected of UCMJ violations) must inform the person being questioned of the nature of the accusation and the right to remain silent, and must warn that any statement made may be used as evidence against

---

[1] The *Miranda* warnings (which are directed at limiting police coercion and inappropriate pressure during questioning) encompass the Fifth Amendment protection against self-incrimination as well as the right to the presence of counsel. *Miranda v. Arizona*, 384 U.S. 436, 467-68, 473 (1966). Law enforcement officers must provide *Miranda* warnings if questioning a subject (or making comments to elicit a response) during a custodial interrogation. *Id.* Subjects must be warned that they have a right to remain silent, any statement may be used as evidence against them, and they have the right to the presence of an attorney, either retained or appointed. *Id.* In *United States v. Tempia*, 37 C.M.R. 249 (C.M.A. 1967), the Court of Military Appeals applied the *Miranda* warnings procedural requirement to military interrogations. In some circumstances, such warnings may be required when a commander questions a servicemember suspected of UCMJ violations, if the servicemember is not free to leave. *See United States v. Jordan*, 44 C.M.R. 44 (C.M.A. 1971) (discussing questioning by a superior as potentially "custodial"). Section III of the Military Rules of Evidence provides an excellent summary of exclusionary rules and related matters concerning self-incrimination. Also, Military Rule of Evidence 305(d)(1)(B) indicates that the Sixth Amendment right to counsel warning is triggered when persons subject to the Code acting in a law enforcement capacity interrogate persons subject to the Code who have charges preferred against them and the questions pertain to the offenses preferred.

them. Unlike the *Miranda* warnings, Article 31(b) warnings do not include notice of the right to counsel.

The literal language of Article 31(b) could lead to an overly broad interpretation, requiring Article 31(b) rights advisement for many conversations with persons subject to UCMJ violations. Military courts through case law have limited circumstances in which Article 31(b) rights advisements are required. In the case that follows, the Court of Military Appeals limits the Article 31(b) rights advisement to situations where military rank, duty, or similar circumstances may result in pressure on a military suspect to respond to questioning.

In 1981, the Court of Military Appeals in *United States v. Duga*, 10 M.J. 206 (C.M.A. 1981), established a two-pronged test to determine whether Article 31(b) rights advisements are required. Specifically, the person subject to the Code questioning the military suspect must be acting in an "official capacity" not for personal motives, and the person questioned must perceive the questioning or conversation as more than a "casual conversation." *Id.* Subsequently, in *United States v. Loukas*, 29 M.J. 385 (C.M.A. 1990), the case that follows *Duga* below, the court further clarified the circumstances when warnings would be required, limiting the requirement of a rights advisement to questioning during "an official law-enforcement investigation or disciplinary inquiry."

Inculpatory statements made following a proper Article 31(b) rights advisement may still be found inadmissible if the statements were not made voluntarily. *See* Articles 31(a) & 31(d). Underlining voluntariness depends on whether the subject's free will was overborne (reviewing the totality of the circumstances of the interview) and whether the subject knowingly and voluntarily waived his rights.

UNITED STATES v. DUGA
U.S. Court of Military Appeals
10 M.J. 206 (C.M.A. 1981)

EVERETT, Chief Judge:

Appellant [Airman First Class Dennis J. Duga, U.S. Air Force] was tried by a special court-martial with members on November 20-22, 1978, at Lowry Air Force Base, Colorado, and was convicted of larceny of a canoe which he stole from the recreational vehicle storage area on base. He was sentenced to a bad-conduct discharge, confinement at hard labor for 3 months, forfeiture of $279.00 pay per month for 3 months, and reduction to the grade of Airman Basic. The convening authority approved the sentence. Thereafter, the United States Air Force Court of Military Review affirmed the appellant's conviction after it concluded that certain pretrial admissions made by the appellant to a policeman-friend had not been obtained in violation of Article 31(b). . . . We subsequently granted review on this same question of law.

I

On the morning of August 7, 1978, Mr. Bruce, a special agent of the Office of Special Investigations (OSI), questioned Airman Byers, who was a security policeman, about anything he knew which connected the appellant to certain thefts the OSI was investigating. After Byers gave him a "statement ... of everything (he) knew," Bruce told him that "if (he) could give him any more information, it would be of help to him." Byers replied, "If anything comes up, I'll see what I can do."

On the evening of August 7, Byers was posted on security police duty at one of the base gates when the appellant rode up to the gate on a bicycle. He began to chat with the appellant-first asking him "How's it going?"-and then they "just talked a little bit about various things." As Byers explained how this conversation commenced, "he was the only one there and it was kind of a long night. It was kind of nice to have somebody around to talk to." He had known the appellant for approximately a year and a half, and the two of them had lived and consorted in the same military dormitory and had "go(ne) out socially ... together" during the evenings. Moreover, both of them were Airmen First Class, and were assigned to the same security police squadron.[3] And since he was curious about rumors he had heard concerning "things that had been happening and (because) he just kind of wondered whether he had been (left) in the dark about it," he asked the appellant "what he was up to." Duga responded that he was looking for a place to hide his van because the OSI was looking for it and that he still had something in it. Byers then asked the appellant "what was the deal that was going on back when he was on leave?" The appellant stated he had been caught with a canoe and chain saw, which he later admitted had been stolen from the base. No Article 31(b) warning had preceded any of the questions asked by Byers.

On the night of August 8, Byers "had another conversation with Duga and some other people in the room." This conversation apparently occurred in the dormitory, where the appellant further discussed his criminal involvement.

On August 10, Byers "voluntarily" went back to OSI and reported the substance of the conversations he had had with the appellant at the gate and "in the room." Charges were eventually preferred against the appellant for larceny of a canoe and chain saw.

At the appellant's court-martial, defense counsel moved to prevent Byers from testifying to any inculpatory statements that Duga had made to him. He argued that Byers should have warned the appellant of his Article 31(b) rights before questioning him about the canoe.

During the evidentiary hearing held on this objection, only Byers testified. He denied that he questioned the appellant while acting officially as a security

---

[3] Even though the appellant and Byers were assigned to the same security police squadron, the appellant had not worked as a security policeman for several months due to his involvement in the offenses charged.

policeman and insisted that their conversation was only "more or less buddy-to-buddy talk you might say[ ]" ... Byers repudiated that "OSI had asked (him) to go ahead and find out anything (he) could"; he said that OSI merely stated "that if (he) could find anything out for them, it would be helpful and to give the man (he) talked to a call." He then maintained that his purpose in questioning the appellant was not to find out information for the OSI. Again, he averred that he was "speaking more or less like a friend to a friend" and "(j)ust out of my own curiosity." Finally, he told the military judge that at the time the conversation took place, "(he) never really thought about" what he would do with the information he learned from the appellant.

After listening to Byers' testimony, the military judge denied the defense motion ... The appellant also contended before the United States Air Force Court of Military Review that his pretrial admissions were inadmissible because Byers had not prefaced his questions with Article 31(b) advice. However, as stated earlier, that Court held against the appellant [finding] that Byers was not an OSI informant and that the OSI had not asked him to question the appellant [and] "that Byers' conversation with the accused was solely personal and that the questions asked were prompted only by his desire to satisfy his own curiosity." *United States v. Duga, supra* at 895. Therefore, Byers had not acted officially in obtaining his information and, thus, the military judge had properly received the incriminating statements as evidence.

Before us the appellant makes the same appeal. He contends that, since at the time of questioning Byers was performing law enforcement duties, which required him to interview witnesses and obtain statements from those suspected of having committed crimes against the Uniform Code of Military Justice, and since Byers had been specifically requested by military authorities to provide information relevant to the investigation of the appellant, he was acting in an official capacity, which required the prefatory warnings. We still disagree.

II

Article 31(b) provides in pertinent part:

No person subject to this chapter may interrogate, or request any statement from, an accused or a person suspected of an offense without first informing him of the nature of the accusation and advising him that he does not have to make any statement regarding the offense of which he is accused or suspected and that any statement made by him may be used as evidence against him in a trial by court-martial.

Of course, if this codal provision is applied literally, we would have to hold that the questioning of the appellant by Byers came within the interdiction of the Article, since it is clear that he was a "person subject to this chapter" interrogating someone whom he "suspected of an offense." However, long ago in *United States v. Gibson,* 14 C.M.R. 164 (C.M.A. 1954), this Court concluded, after a careful study of the Article's purpose and legislative history, that Congress did not intend a literal application of that provision:

> Taken literally, this Article is applicable to interrogation by all persons included within the term "persons subject to the code" as defined by Article 2 of the Code, supra, 50 U.S.C. § 552, or any other who is suspected or accused of an offense. However, this phrase was used in a limited sense. In our opinion, in addition to the limitation referred to in the legislative history of the requirement, there is a definitely restrictive element of officiality in the choice of the language "interrogate, or request any statement," wholly absent from the relatively loose phrase "person subject to this code," for military persons not assigned to investigate offenses, do not ordinarily interrogate nor do they request statements from others accused or suspected of crime. *See United States v. Wilson and Harvey*, 2 U.S.C.MA 248, 8 CMR 48. This is not the sole limitation upon the Article's applicability, however. Judicial discretion indicates a necessity for denying its application to a situation not considered by its framers, and wholly unrelated to the reasons for its creation.

> Careful consideration of the history of the requirement of warning, compels a conclusion that its purpose is to avoid impairment of the constitutional guarantee against compulsory self incrimination. Because of the effect of superior rank or official position upon one subject to military law, the mere asking of a question under certain circumstances is the equivalent of a command. A person subjected to these pressures may rightly be regarded as deprived of his freedom to answer or to remain silent. Under such circumstances, we do not hesitate to reverse convictions whenever the accused has been deprived of the full benefit of the rights granted him by Congress. *See United States v. Wilson and Harvey, supra; United States v. Rosato*, 3 U.S.C.MA 143, 11 CMR 143. By the same token, however, it is our duty to see to it that such rights are not extended beyond the reasonable intendment of the Code at the expense of substantial justice and on grounds that are fanciful or unsubstantial.

* * *

Conditioned to obey, a serviceperson asked for a statement about an offense may feel himself to be under a special obligation to make such a statement. Moreover, he may be especially amenable to saying what he thinks his military superior wants him to say-whether it is true or not. Thus, the serviceperson needs the reminder required under Article 31 to the effect that he need not be a witness against himself. . . . To paraphrase a remark by Mr. Justice Stewart in *Rhode Island v. Innis*, 446 U.S. 291 (1980), "(t)he concern of the (Congress) in (enacting Article 31(b)) was that the 'interrogation environment' created by the interplay of interrogation and (military relationships) would 'subjugate the individual to the will of his examiner' and thereby undermine the privilege against compulsory incrimination" contained in Article 31(a) of the Uniform Code of Military Justice.

Therefore, in light of Article 31(b)'s purpose and its legislative history, the Article applies only to situations in which, because of military rank, duty, or other similar relationship, there might be subtle pressure on a suspect to respond to an inquiry.... Accordingly, in each case it is necessary to determine whether (1) a questioner subject to the Code was acting in an official capacity in his inquiry or only had a personal motivation; and (2) whether the person questioned perceived that the inquiry involved more than a casual conversation.... Unless both prerequisites are met, Article 31(b) does not apply.

* * *

Not every inculpatory statement made by an accused in conversation with another is inadmissible because of a failure to warn him of his rights under Article 31. The prohibition of the Article extends only to statements elicited in the course of official interrogation.

* * *

III

In the case at hand, the evidence only permits the conclusion reached by the Air Force Court of Military Review that the questioning of appellant by Byers did not fall within the purview of Article 31(b). The two prerequisites which determine whether Article 31(b) warnings were required are not met in this case. As found by the Court of Military Review, the record reveals that the questioning was not done in an official capacity-that is, Byers was not acting on behalf of the Air Force-either as a security policeman or as an agent of the OSI. Since the appellant declined to present any evidence on the issue, cf. United States v. Beck, supra at 339, 35 C.M.R. at 311, Byers' testimony is completely uncontroverted as to their camaraderie and affiliation in the same security police squadron, and his statement that when the appellant rode up to the gate on his bike, he was only "speaking (to him) more or less like a friend to a friend," or, as elsewhere described by him-it was "more or less like-buddy-to-buddy talk you might say." No evidence contradicts the inference that the questioning by Byers was solely motivated by his own personal curiosity and was entirely unconnected with his previous contact with the OSI. In any case, in what the OSI told Byers, it neither directed nor advised him to question the appellant. In view of the uncontradicted nature of the testimony, we have no choice but to uphold the lower court's finding of a lack of the officiality which is essential to requiring the Article 31(b) warning.

Even if the officiality prerequisite had been met, the evidence is undisputed that the appellant could not possibly have perceived his interrogation as being official in nature. The evidence portrays a casual conversation between comrades, in which the appellant voluntarily discussed with Byers his general involvement in crime, as well as his current plight. Apparently boasting, the appellant was telling his friend that "(h)e knew how to get into most buildings on the base"; among other things, he had stolen from the base a canoe, trailer and chain saw. He even felt comfortable enough to tell Byers that he was looking for a place to hide his van because he had something in it and the OSI was looking for it. Certainly, had he perceived that Byers was questioning him as a security policeman, or had he known that Byers had spoken to the OSI, he would not have told Byers that he was looking for a place to hide his van, because he had contraband in it and the OSI was looking for the van. Equally significant, on the following day the appellant even had another conversation with Byers and "other people in the room," where again Duga apparently incriminated himself. Thus, the appellant could not have envisioned that Byers was acting in an official capacity. Moreover, there was no subtle coercion of any sort which could have impelled the appellant to answer Byers' questions. Here, the appellant was himself a security policeman; and, as Byers stated, the appellant even "outranked" him. Therefore, there is nothing in this case which calls for the application of Article 31(b). It follows that the appellant's incriminating statements were properly before the court despite the absence of a preliminary warning.

IV

The decision of the United States Air Force Court of Military Review is affirmed.

Judge FLETCHER concurs.

COOK, Judge (concurring in the result).

I concur in the result. See my separate opinion in *United States v. Kirby*, 8 M.J. 8, 11 (C.M.A. 1979).

Point for Discussion

Consider these facts: Sergeant First Class McClelland sought help from Major Niemeyer, an Army social worker, after SFC McClelland's stepdaughter raised allegations of sex abuse. MAJ Niemeyer at the time had reason to suspect SFC McClelland of an offense, but did not give him an Article 31 rights advisement. SFC McClelland admitted misconduct to MAJ Niemeyer. MAJ Niemeyer then told SFC McClelland to seek the assistance of an attorney. MAJ Niemayer gave information about the misconduct to the Army's Criminal Investigation Division. Is SFC McClelland's admission to MAJ Niemeyer admissible under the *Duga* test? *See United States v. McClelland*, 26 M.J. 504 (A.C.M.R. 1988).

UNITED STATES v. LOUKAS
U.S. Court of Military Appeals
29 M.J. 385 (C.M.A. 1990)

SULLIVAN, Judge:

During August 1987, the accused [Airman John G. Loukas, U.S. Air Force,] was tried by a general court-martial composed of a military judge sitting alone at Pope Air Force Base, North Carolina. Contrary to his pleas, he was found guilty of wrongfully using cocaine and being incapacitated for duty, in violation of Articles 112a and 134, Uniform Code of Military Justice, 10 U.S.C. §§ 912a and 934, respectively. He was sentenced to a dishonorable discharge, confinement for 8 months, total forfeitures, and reduction to the lowest enlisted grade. On December 7, 1987, the convening authority approved the findings and sentence as adjudged.

On December 16, 1988, a panel of the Court of Military Review set aside the findings of guilty and the sentence because evidence was admitted in violation of Article 31(d), UCMJ, 10 U.S.C. § 831(d). 27 M.J. 788. On January 5, 1989, the Government moved for en banc reconsideration of part of that decision. This motion was granted but the en banc court affirmed the previous action of its panel on March 16, 1989. 28 M.J. 620.

The Judge Advocate General of the Air Force, pursuant to Article 67(b)(2), UCMJ, 10 U.S.C. § 867(b)(2), certified the following question to this Court on April 12, 1989:

> WHETHER THE AIR FORCE COURT OF MILITARY REVIEW ERRED AS A MATTER OF LAW IN HOLDING THAT THE *NEW YORK V. QUARLES,* 467 U.S. 649 (1984), "PUBLIC SAFETY EXCEPTION" DID NOT APPLY TO THE FACTS OF THIS CASE.

We hold that the Court of Military Review need not have made such a legal holding because admission of the challenged testimony was not barred in the first instance by the Fifth Amendment or by Article 31.

In its initial decision, the Court of Military Review panel stated the facts pertinent to admission of Sergeant Dryer's testimony concerning the accused's first pretrial admission of cocaine use, as follows:

> [Loukas'] admissions were made during the course of a C-130 aircraft mission in support of drug suppression efforts in South America.

The evidence developed during the suppression hearing was that [Loukas] was on temporary duty from Pope Air Force Base, North Carolina, along with other crew members. [Loukas] was the loadmaster. Following an overnight stay at Panama City, Panama, [Loukas'] crew was scheduled to depart Howard Air Force Base for an early morning flight to Trinidad, Bolivia, where they were to receive a load of unspecified cargo. [Loukas] was not present at the scheduled crew show time. When he finally arrived at the aircraft he was two hours late. The record, surprisingly, does not reflect that he received a particularly unfriendly or otherwise negative greeting from his fellow crew members, all of whom were senior in grade to him. The co-pilot kidded him about the number of ladies he had been with the evening before. SSgt Dryer recalled in his testimony that he teased [Loukas] about his lateness. Apparently none of the crew members, at that point, noted anything in [Loukas'] appearance or demeanor that was alarming.

After the aircraft had been in flight for four or more hours the assistant crew chief, an Airman First Class Taranto, stepped into the cargo section. [Loukas] was the only other person present in that portion of the plane. There was no cargo or equipment on board at that time. *Airman Taranto testified that he observed that [Loukas] was acting in an irrational manner. He pointed in the direction of the flight deck and inquired of Airman Taranto, "Do you see them?" and, "Do you see her?" Airman Taranto did not see anyone. It was apparent to him that [Loukas] was experiencing a hallucination. [Loukas] handed Airman Taranto his survival vest and .38 calibre pistol and told him to take it (apparently referring to the firearm) and that he didn't want it.* The witness reported the incident to his immediate superior, SSgt Dryer, the crew chief.

SSgt Dryer went to the back of the aircraft and confronted [Loukas]. He testified during the hearing on the motion to suppress that he noted he *[Loukas] appeared to be nervous and that he was perspiring profusely even though it was cool in that portion of the plane. [Loukas] continued to hallucinate. Gesturing in the direction of the flight deck, he inquired why "those people" were there and wondered why "they" didn't just come down and get him. The witness stated that he asked [Loukas] if he had taken any drugs. [Loukas] responded that he had not. SSgt Dryer leaned over close to where [Loukas] was sitting so that he could observe his eyes and asked in a more insistent manner, "Come on, what have you taken?" or, "What are you on?" or words to that effect. [Loukas] replied that he had taken some cocaine the night before. SSgt Dryer asked, "Is that all?" He received an affirmative answer.* SSgt Dryer advised [Loukas] to secure his seatbelt and relax. According to his testimony he was somewhat concerned for the safety of the aircraft and its flight crew, particularly if [Loukas] started "freaking out."

SSgt Dryer reported his observations of [Loukas] to the flight engineer, a Technical Sergeant Drummond. The latter went to the back of the aircraft and observed [Loukas]. He retrieved bullets that [Loukas] had on his person. He returned to the flight deck area and consulted with SSgt Dryer. They concluded that the situation was under control and that it would not be necessary to alert the aircraft commander, Captain Cottam. It was agreed that someone would maintain direct observation of [Loukas] during the remainder of the flight.

27 M.J. at 790-91 (emphasis added).

The stated premise of the Court of Military Review majority opinions, both panel and en banc, (6-3), was that Sergeant Dryer was obligated by Article 31(b) to warn the accused of his rights before questioning him about possible drug use. This legal conclusion was drawn on the basis of the decision of this Court in *United States v. Duga,* 10 M.J. 206 (C.M.A. 1981), and a finding of fact that Sergeant Dryer was acting officially and not simply out of "idle curiosity." 27 M.J. at 792. We disagree as a matter of law because the crew chief's inquiry was not a *law-enforcement or disciplinary* investigation which is also required before Article 31(b) becomes applicable. . . .

In reaching this conclusion we first note the statutory language of Article 31, which states:

* * *

(b) No person subject to this chapter *may interrogate, or request any statement from an accused or a person suspected of an offense* without first informing him of the nature of the accusation and advising him that he does not have to make any statement regarding the offense of which he is accused or suspected and that any statement made by him may be used as evidence against him in a trial by court-martial.

* * *

(Emphasis added.)

This Court has long intimated that this statute requires warnings only when questioning is done during an official law-enforcement investigation or disciplinary inquiry. . . . Chief Judge Quinn has articulated the following rationale for our construction of this important codal provision:

Article 31(b), *supra,* extends the provisions of its predecessor, Article of War 24, . . . to persons "suspected" as well as "accused," but no intention to extend the requirement to other than "official investigation" is found in the legislative history of the Uniform Code.

Taken literally, this Article is applicable to interrogation by all persons included within the term "persons subject to the code" as defined by Article 2 of the Code, *supra,* 50 U.S.C. § 552, or any other who is suspected or accused of an offense. However, this phrase was used in a limited sense. *In our opinion, in addition to the limitation referred to in the legislative history of the requirement, there is a definitely restrictive element of officiality in the choice of the language "interrogate or request any statement," wholly absent from the relatively loose phrase "person subject to this code," for military persons not assigned to investigate offenses, do not ordinarily interrogate nor do they request statements from others accused or suspected of crime. See United States v. Wilson and Harvey,* 2 U.S.C.MA 248, 8 CMR 48. This is not the sole limitation upon the Article's applicability, however. Judicial discretion indicates a necessity for denying its application to a situation not considered by its framers, and wholly unrelated to the reasons for its creation.

United States v. Gibson, supra at 752, 14 CMR at 170 (emphasis added).

Judge Latimer opined similarly in his opinion concurring in the result in the same case:

I would affirm the conviction on the basis of the test laid down by me in my dissent in *United States v. Wilson and Harvey, supra.* In that case I stated:

"... Accordingly, I believe before the advice required by the Article need be given, three conditions should be fulfilled: *first, the party asking the question should occupy some official position in connection with law enforcement or crime detection;* second, that the inquiry be in furtherance of some official investigation; and third, the facts be developed far enough that the party conducting the investigation has reasonable grounds to suspect the person interrogated has committed an offense."

Collectively, all three conditions suggest that the interrogation be surrounded with an air of some officiality and I believe the Manual for Courts-Martial, United States, 1951, ... , and the hearings before the Committees of Congress support that proposition (see Comments, pages 990-991, Hearings Before the House Committee on Armed Services, 81st Congress, 1st Session, on H.R. 2498, Uniform Code of Military Justice). Moreover, a reading of the Article is convincing that Congress could not have intended Article 31(b) to cover casual conversations, because the language used compels the conclusion that the interrogator is pursuing some official inquiry as he must know that the person to whom he is talking is suspected of a crime; he must inform him of the nature of the accusation; and he must explain to him that what he says may be used against him in a court-martial.

3 U.S.C.MA at 763, 14 CMR at 181 (emphasis added).

* * *

Accordingly, we conclude that the Court of Military Review in both its panel and its en banc decisions too broadly construed and applied this codal provision. 10 M.J. at 210 n.6, citing *United States v. Dohle,* 1 M.J. 223 (C.M.A. 1975).

An example of official, but not law-enforcement or disciplinary, questioning which is permitted without warnings under Article 31 is found in *United States v. Fisher,* 21 U.S.C.MA 223, 44 CMR 277 (1972). . . . In that case, we held that a military doctor, not performing an investigative or disciplinary function or engaged in perfecting a criminal case, was not required to preface his medical diagnostic questions to a military subordinate with Article 31 warnings. *See United States v. Malumphy,* 13 U.S.C.MA 60, 61-62, 32 CMR 60, 61-62 (1962); *United States v. Malumphy,* 12 U.S.C.MA 639, 640, 31 CMR 225, 226 (1962); *United States v. Baker,* 11 U.S.C.MA 313, 29 CMR 129 (1960).

In the case before us, Sergeant Dryer was the crew chief of an operational military aircraft who was similarly responsible for the plane's safety and that of its crew, including the accused, his military subordinate. In addition, his questioning of the accused was limited to that required to fulfill his operational responsibilities, and there was no evidence suggesting his inquiries were designed to evade constitutional or codal rights. *United States v. Cross,* 14 U.S.C.MA 660, 662-63, 34 CMR 440, 442-43 (1964). *See United*

States v. Malumphy, 13 U.S.C.MA at 62, 32 CMR at 62. *Cf. United States v. Lee,* 25 M.J. 457 (C.M.A. 1988). Finally, the unquestionable urgency of the threat and the immediacy of the crew chief's response underscore the legitimate operational nature of his queries.* *See United States v. Hessler,* 7 M.J. 9 (C.M.A. 1979). *See also United States v. Henry,* 21 U.S.C.MA 98, 44 CMR 152 (1971). Under our precedents, the prosecution satisfactorily showed that Article 31 warnings were not required in this operational context. *United States v. Beck,* 15 U.S.C.MA 333, 35 CMR 305 (1965); *see* Mil. R. Evid. 304(e), Manual for Courts-Martial, United States, 1984. *See generally United States v. Battles,* 25 M.J. 58, 60 (C.M.A. 1987).

As far as the so-called "public safety exception" referenced in the certified issue is concerned, we note that, strictly speaking, this is an exception to the *Miranda* warning requirements established by the Supreme Court to preserve Fifth-Amendment rights. *New York v. Quarles,* 467 U.S. 649, 655-56 (1984). These warnings apply to a suspect in custody and his interrogation by law-enforcement officials. There is no contention in this case that the accused was a suspect in custody or that Sergeant Dryer was a law-enforcement official, so *New York v. Quarles, supra,* is not readily applicable. *Cf. United States v. Morris,* 28 M.J. 8, 13 (C.M.A. 1989); *United States v. Jones,* 26 M.J. 353, 355 (C.M.A. 1988). Whether a similar exception to Article 31 exists for military superiors acting in a command disciplinary function when questioning a suspect who is not in custody is an issue beyond the facts of this case. *See generally United States v. Beck, supra* at 339, 35 CMR at 311; *see United States v. Ricks,* 2 M.J. 99, 101 (C.M.A. 1977); *United States v. Vail,* 11 U.S.C.MA 134, 28 CMR 358 (1960).

Finally, we agree with the court below that Captain Cottam's subsequent questioning of the accused without warnings violated Article 31(b) of the Code. *See United States v. Loukas,* 27 M.J. at 791-92. However, his testimony was cumulative of Sergeant Dryer's testimony and, accordingly, we hold that its admission under the circumstances of this case was harmless error. Art. 59(a), UCMJ, 10 U.S.C. § 859(a). . . .

The decision of the United States Air Force Court of Military Review setting aside the findings of guilty and the sentence is reversed. The record of trial is returned to the Judge Advocate General of the Air Force for resubmission to that court for further review under Article 66, UCMJ, 10 U.S.C. § 866.

---

* This Court has implicitly held that a superior in the immediate chain of command of the suspect subordinate will normally be presumed to be acting in a command disciplinary function. *United States v. Seay,* 1 M.J. 201 (C.M.A. 1975). *See United States v. Doyle,* 9 U.S.C.MA 302, 310, 26 CMR 82, 90 (1958); *cf. United States v. Hopkins,* 7 U.S.C.MA 519, 521-22, 22 CMR 309, 311-12 (1957). However, this presumption is not so broad or inflexible as to preclude a limited exception where clearly justified. *See United States v. Beck,* 15 U.S.C.MA 333, 338-39, 35 CMR 305, 310-11 (1965).

Points for Discussion

1. Do you agree with the *Loukas* Court that *Miranda* warnings were not required when the commander questioned the accused? Why or why not?

2. Why does the *Loukas* Court "agree with the court below that Captain Cottam's subsequent questioning of the accused without warnings violated Article 31(b) of the Code"?

4-2. Apprehension and Pretrial Confinement in the Military

Another pretrial issue that occurs in the military is the issue of apprehension as described in UCMJ, Article 7. Any commissioned officer, warrant officer, petty officer, noncommissioned, member of the military police, and others performing police or guard duties, may apprehend service members (i.e., place a person in custody). (Noncommissioned and petty officers should not apprehend an officer unless another commissioned officer directs them to do so.) Apprehension in the military context is the same as a civilian "arrest." In the military services, "arrest" signifies a form of restraint as described below. To apprehend a person in the military requires probable cause, which is a "reasonable belief that an offense was committed and the person to be apprehended committed the offense" *Id*.

Unlike their civilian counterparts, military service members may lose their liberty rights and become subject to lesser forms of pretrial restraint (moral or physical restraint on a person's liberty) besides pretrial confinement. Commanders may order pretrial restraint for officers over whom they have authority. This authority may not be delegated. Any commissioned officer may order pretrial restraint for any enlisted personnel. This authority, in contrast, may be delegated to warrant, petty, or noncommissioned officers within the officer's command.

Guidelines for pretrial restraint and pretrial confinement for service members are described in UCMJ Articles 9-13 and Rule for Courts-Martial (R.C.M.) 304-305. Pretrial restraint may be imposed if there is a reasonable belief the service member to be restrained committed an offense triable by court-martial and the restraint ordered is "required by the circumstances" (i.e., the person will not appear at trial, prehearing, or investigation, or the person will engage in serious criminal conduct, and lesser forms of restraint are inadequate). In the military, the types of pretrial restraint are conditions on liberty (ordering a person to do certain acts or refrain from doing specific acts); restriction in lieu of arrest (ordering a person to remain within certain limits, but still performing military duties); arrest (ordering a person to remain within specific limits without requiring the person to perform full military duties); and pretrial confinement.

Before and during disposition of offenses, the commander or person authorizing pretrial restraint must notify the service member orally or in writing of the terms and limits of the restraint. None of the forms of restraint can be used as punishment for offenses serving as the basis for restraint. If this rule is violated, at trial, the service member may request, and is likely to receive, Article 13 credit (days credited to the sentence of confinement). Article 13 credit may be awarded for unduly harsh arrest or pretrial confinement conditions (illegal pretrial confinement) or unlawful pretrial punishment before a finding of guilt at trial (illegal pretrial punishment). The cases that follow represent examples where the court awarded credit to an accused at trial.

UNITED STATES v. GILCHRIST
Army Court of Criminal Appeals
61 M.J. 785 (Army Ct. Crim. App. 2005)

SCHENCK, Senior Judge:

A military judge sitting as a general court-martial convicted appellant [Private First Class Aaron P. Gilchrist, U.S. Army], pursuant to his pleas, of going from his appointed place of duty, disrespect toward a superior noncommissioned officer, failure to obey a lawful order (three specifications), wrongful use of marijuana, Xanax, and cocaine (one specification each), wrongful distribution of Xanax (two specifications), and larceny of other than military property (two specifications), in violation of Articles 86, 91, 92, 112a, and 121, Uniform Code of Military Justice, 10 U.S.C. §§ 886, 891, 892, 912a, and 921 [hereinafter UCMJ]. The military judge convicted appellant, contrary to his plea, of failure to obey a lawful order, in violation of Article 92, UCMJ. The convening authority approved the adjudged sentence to a bad-conduct discharge, confinement for fifteen months, forfeiture of all pay and allowances, and reduction to Private E1. The convening authority ordered 176 days of confinement credit. This case is before the court for review under Article 66, UCMJ.

Appellant's record of trial is fraught with issues; several merit discussion and relief. First, we agree with appellate government counsel that appellant's court-martial had jurisdiction. Second, we agree with appellate defense counsel that Specifications 1 and 2 of Charge III, both alleging larceny on 21 July 2001, should be merged because appellant stole the property listed in these specifications at substantially the same place and time. Third, we hold that the record of trial raises a substantial, unresolved question of law and fact as to the providence of appellant's guilty plea to the Specification of Additional Charge I and Additional Charge I (going from his appointed place of duty). Fourth, we find the record of trial lacks sufficient evidence to convict appellant of Specification 3 of Additional Charge III (failure to obey a lawful order). Finally, we agree, in part, with appellant's personal averment that shackling him to a barracks room cot-when he was a pretrial prisoner and the detention cell was unavailable-was more rigorous than required and constituted a violation of Article 13, UCMJ. Based on the errors noted, we will grant appropriate relief and reassess the sentence in our decretal paragraph.

* * *

III. Improvident Plea

Facts

Appellant pleaded guilty to, and was found guilty of, the Specification of Additional Charge I, going from his appointed place of duty, "a doctor's appointment at William Beaumont Army Medical Center [WBAMC]," on or about 3 October 2001, in violation of Article 86(2), UCMJ. Appellant now asserts his plea to this specification was improvident. We agree.

The stipulation of fact states appellant informed his chain of command he had a doctor's appointment at WBAMC at 0900 on 3 October 2001. Drill Sergeant Yates drove appellant to the hospital for this appointment, but subsequently "spotted [appellant] running . . . to a convenience store located across the street" from the hospital.

During the *Care* inquiry, the military judge described the elements for leaving a place of duty, Article 86(2), UCMJ, as follows:

> One, that a medical authority appointed a certain time and place of duty for you, that is, a 0900 hours doctor's appointment at [WBMAC];
>
> Two, that you knew you were required to be present at this appointed time and place of duty; and
>
> Three, that on or about 3 October 2001, you, without proper authority, went from the appointed place of duty after having reported at such place.

Appellant agreed that the elements correctly described what he did. He further told the military judge:

> I had an appointment with physical therapy after lunch at the hospital, but the drill sergeants were going to be running around all day, so they'd have to bring me to the hospital early. So they brought me to the hospital around 0900. I would've had to wait around, so myself and [PVT] Kelso walked across the street to the store. As we were walking out, Drill Sergeant Yates told us to get back in the van and he brought us back to post and I missed my appointment.

The following colloquy then ensued:

> MJ: When they dropped you off, what did the drill sergeants tell you, if anything?
>
> ACC: "Call me when you get done with your appointment," Your Honor.
>
> MJ: Did they tell you you couldn't leave the hospital?
>
> ACC: No, Your Honor.
>
> MJ: You're certain that the time of the appointment was 1300, not 0900?
>
> ACC: I'm positive, Your Honor.

The military judge, without objection from the parties, amended the time of appellant's doctor's appointment in the stipulation of fact from "0900" to "1300." However, he changed only one of the two references to "0900." Appellant also told the military judge that after Drill Sergeant Yates dropped them off at "around 0845," he and PVT Kelso left the hospital to go to the 7-Eleven convenience store across the street. Appellant indicated that food or other items were not available in the hospital "for another hour or so." When the military judge asked appellant if he thought he was to remain in the hospital until his appointment, appellant said, "I suppose, Your Honor-I wasn't real sure." The military judge then asked appellant, "Is it fair to say that your place of duty was the hospital until your appointment?" and "You were just trying to kill some time, is that right?" Appellant affirmatively answered, "Yes," and subsequently agreed that no one gave him permission to leave the hospital.

At the end of the plea inquiry, appellant again agreed with the military judge that "a medical authority appointed a certain time and place of duty for [appellant], that is, [a] 1300 hours doctor's appointment at [WBAMC]," that he knew he was required to be at "[that] appointed time and place of duty," and on 3 October 2001, he, "without proper authority, went from the appointed place of duty after having reported to such place."

Discussion

We review a military judge's acceptance of a guilty plea for an abuse of discretion. *United States v. Eberle*, 44 M.J. 374, 375 (C.A.A.F. 1996) (citations omitted). We will not overturn a military judge's acceptance of a guilty plea unless the record of trial shows a substantial basis in law and fact for questioning it. *United States v. Prater*, 32 M.J. 433, 436 (C.M.A. 1991).

A providence inquiry into a guilty plea must establish that the accused believes and admits he is guilty of the offense and that the factual circumstances admitted by the accused objectively support the guilty plea. *United States v. Garcia*, 44 M.J. 496, 497-98 (C.A.A.F. 1996) (citing *United States v. Higgins*, 40 M.J. 67, 68 (C.M.A. 1994); *United States v. Davenport*, 9 M.J. 364, 367 (C.M.A. 1980); and R.C.M. 910(e)). Should the accused set up a matter inconsistent with the plea at any time during the proceeding, "the military judge must either resolve the apparent inconsistency or reject the guilty plea." *Garcia*, 44 M.J. at 498 (citing UCMJ art. 45(a) and R.C.M. 910(h)(2)); *see also Davenport*, 9 M.J. at 367 (stating same). Furthermore, when such inconsistent matters "reasonably raise[] the question of a defense . . . it [is] incumbent upon the military judge to make a more searching inquiry to determine the accused's position on the apparent inconsistency with his plea of guilty." *United States v. Timmins*, 45 C.M.R. 249, 253 (C.M.A. 1972).

"Mere conclusions of law recited by an accused are insufficient to provide a factual basis for a guilty plea." *United States v. Outhier*, 45 M.J. 326, 331 (C.A.A.F. 1996) (citing *United States v. Terry*, 45 C.M.R. 216). In determining whether the providence inquiry provides facts inconsistent with the guilty plea, we take the accused's version of the facts "at face value." *United States v. Jemmings,* 1 M.J. 414, 418 (C.M.A. 1976).

Appellant's providence inquiry does not provide an adequate factual basis to meet the requirements of *Care,* Article 45(a), UCMJ, and R.C.M. 910(e). *See United States v. Jordan,* 57 M.J. 236, 238-39 (C.A.A.F. 2002). Unlike Article 86(1), UCMJ, (failure to go to an appointed place of duty), Article 86(2), UCMJ, (going from an appointed place of duty), requires a soldier *to report* at the "certain time and place," then depart from that place of duty. The Specification of Additional Charge I, as alleged on the charge sheet, does not reflect a specific time, but only states "a doctor's appointment at [WBAMC]." Based upon appellant's assertions during the plea inquiry, the military judge twice advised, and appellant agreed, that his time and place of duty was a 1300 doctor's appointment at the hospital. Therefore, the time agreed to by the parties and reinforced by the military judge's description of the elements, established appellant's "certain time" of duty as 1300.

Appellant did not admit he was required to be at the hospital at 0845 when he was dropped off. Appellant merely agreed that a "medical authority" required him to be present for his 1300 doctor's appointment at WBAMC. Appellant's statements during the providence inquiry indicate he did not understand he was reporting to his place of duty, a 1300 doctor's appointment at WBAMC, when he arrived over four hours early. Furthermore, appellant's responses to the military judge's questions regarding his departure from the hospital set up matters inconsistent with his guilty plea. Therefore, we hold that the record of trial raises a substantial, unresolved question of law and fact as to the providence of appellant's guilty plea to a violation of Article 86(2), UCMJ. *See Jordan,* 57 M.J. at 238; *Prater,* 32 M.J. at 436. We will set aside and dismiss this specification in our decretal paragraph.

* * *

V. Article 13, UCMJ

Facts

Pursuant to *United States v. Grostefon,* 12 M.J. 431 (C.M.A. 1982), appellant asserts that "he should have received Article 13 credit for being shackled to a cot [for eight hours] in 'The Ice House.'" Appellate government counsel respond without elaboration that the issues submitted under *Grostefon, supra,* lack merit.

Trial defense counsel made a motion for appropriate relief requesting credit for violations of Article 13, UCMJ. He requested credit for incidents involving the first sergeant calling appellant names, transporting appellant while shackled and in an improperly adorned uniform (without name tag and rank), and for appellant's "left arm and right leg [being] shackled to a cot" while being held overnight in the barracks as a pretrial confinement prisoner.

We adopt the following findings of fact made by the military judge:

> On or about 16 January 2002, the accused was transported back to Fort Bliss from Fort Knox for the Article 32 investigation relating to the additional charges in this case. Because the Provost Marshal [detention] cell was full, the accused was placed in a utility room on the first floor of his barracks. The room was called the Ice House because an ice-making machine was housed inside the room. It was well known to those in the unit. The room also contained a metal cot, several tables, as well as barracks maintenance equipment. There is no latrine in the room. The [charge of quarters (CQ)] desk was located 10-20 feet away from the door to the room. The duty drill sergeant's office was located another 10 feet from the CQ desk.

The military judge also found that appellant arrived between 2200 and 2300, was "secured with leg irons to one of the legs of the cot,"[18] and that SFC Wyatt "had to wake [appellant] in the morning at approximately 0630." Sergeant First Class Wyatt, PVT MacMahan, and two CQ runners were in "close proximity to the room [appellant] was billeted in throughout the evening." Sergeant First Class Wyatt and PVT MacMahan also checked on appellant on several occasions "during the course of the evening."[19] The utility room door remained "open throughout the night" except between 0430 and 0730 on 17 January when soldiers were performing physical training. During that time, appellant testified that no one could hear him call out for assistance. Prior to appellant's placement in the "Ice House," PVT Rasch, another soldier in the unit, was placed there when the detention cell was full. The military judge found that "[PVT] Rasch, who had been ordered into pretrial confinement by his battery commander, was not placed in hand irons while he was billeted in the room, and escaped out of one of the room's windows, which did not have any security bars." We also adopt these findings of fact.

Applying these facts, the military judge made the following legal conclusions:

> The conditions surrounding [appellant's] shackling to the cot were not unduly harsh and were reasonably related to military command and

---

[18] According to appellant's testimony, at 1SG Thompson's direction, Sergeant First Class (SFC) Wyatt (a drill sergeant) chained appellant's right leg and left arm to the cot. In response to questions from the military judge, appellant stated that he was "secured to the cot" with "one shackle-leg iron-and one handcuff." First Sergeant Thompson testified that he told SFC Wyatt "to shackle one arm, at least, to the cot," but could not recall if he told him "to shackle a leg as well." Sergeant First Class Wyatt testified he only shackled appellant's leg to the cot using a leg iron with a chain two to three feet in length and weighing approximately one to two pounds.

[19] Sergeant First Class Wyatt testified he saw appellant "throughout the night," and "no one ever left [appellant's] area unoccupied with just [appellant] staying in that room."

control needs, particularly in light of the fact that the [Provost Marshal detention cell] was not available to billet [appellant] for the evening in question ... [and] the conditions were not implemented with intent to punish or stigmatize [appellant] while he was facing disciplinary action.

The military judge granted five days of credit for the name calling and "public denunciation" in violation of Article 13, UCMJ, but no credit for having been shackled to the cot.

Discussion

Unlawful pretrial punishment or confinement issues involve mixed questions of law and fact. *United States v. Smith,* 53 M.J. 168, 170 (C.A.A.F. 2000); *United States v. McCarthy,* 47 M.J. 162, 164-65 (C.A.A.F. 1997). Our court conducts a de novo review of conclusions of law. *See Smith,* 53 M.J. at 170; *McCarthy,* 47 M.J. at 167. We will defer to the military judge's findings of fact that are not clearly erroneous and apply those facts in our review. *See United States v. King,* 61 M.J. 225, 227 (C.A.A.F. 2005).

Article 13, UCMJ, states:

No person, while being held for trial, may be subjected to punishment or penalty other than arrest or confinement upon the charges pending against him, nor shall the arrest or confinement imposed upon him be any more rigorous than the circumstances required to insure his presence, but he may be subjected to minor punishment during that period for infractions of discipline.

Thus, Article 13, UCMJ, prohibits: (1) purposefully imposing punishment or penalty on an accused before guilt is established at trial, that is, illegal pretrial punishment, and (2) arrest or pretrial confinement conditions more rigorous than circumstances require to ensure an accused's presence at trial, that is, illegal pretrial confinement. *See United States v. Fischer,* 61 M.J. 415, 418 (C.A.A.F. 2005); *United States v. Inong,* 58 M.J. 460, 463 (C.A.A.F. 2003) (citing *United States v. Fricke,* 53 M.J. 149, 154 (C.A.A.F. 2000)). If an appellant can establish that either prohibition was violated, he is entitled to sentence relief. *Inong,* 58 M.J. at 463 (citing *United States v. Mosby,* 56 M.J. 309, 310 (C.A.A.F. 2000)); *see* R.C.M. 905(c)(2). We will address appellant's pretrial confinement conditions under both prongs. *See McCarthy,* 47 M.J. at 165.

First, we must decide whether appellant's pretrial confinement conditions constitute illegal pretrial punishment or constitute legally permissible restraint. In doing so, we must determine whether the conditions are imposed " 'for the purpose of punishment or whether it is but an incident of some other legitimate governmental purpose.' " *United States v. Palmiter,* 20 M.J. 90, 99 (C.M.A. 1985) (Everett, C.J., concurring in the result) (quoting *Bell v. Wolfish,* 441 U.S. 520, 538 (1979)). Moreover, "[o]ne significant factor, but not the only one, in determining whether the conditions or terms of confinement violate Article 13 is the intent of the detention officials." *United*

States v. James, 28 M.J. 214, 216 (C.M.A. 1989). Additionally, if the particular condition of pretrial confinement is reasonably related to a legitimate government objective, and is reasonable under the circumstances, without more, it does not amount to punishment. *See United States v. Cruz,* 25 M.J. 326, 331 n. 4 (C.M.A. 1987); *Palmiter,* 20 M.J. at 99. Imposing "unduly rigorous circumstances during pretrial detention [may,] in sufficiently egregious circumstances, . . . give rise to a permissible inference that an accused is being punished, or may be so excessive as to constitute punishment." *McCarthy,* 47 M.J. at 165; *see also* R.C.M. 304(f); *James,* 28 M.J. at 216; *Palmiter,* 20 M.J. at 95.

We do not find that appellant's pretrial confinement conditions—being temporarily housed and shackled in a barracks utility room—constitute illegal pretrial punishment. We agree with the military judge's finding that appellant's pretrial confinement "conditions were not implemented with intent to punish or stigmatize" appellant. Our review of the record indicates that unit officials did not place appellant in the "Ice House" to punish or inflict any penalty upon him. The record establishes appellant was a pretrial prisoner who could not be secured in the detention cell overnight. Furthermore, unit officials did not want appellant to escape from the same room from which an unshackled pretrial prisoner previously escaped.[20]

Thus, we find no clear abuse of the military judge's discretion in his conclusion that appellant's [pretrial confinement conditions were] not done with any intent to punish appellant or inflict any penalty upon him for his alleged underlying misconduct, and that no impermissible 'punishment or penalty' actually occurred as a result. *McCarthy,* 47 M.J. at 167.

We must next determine if appellant's shackling to a barracks room cot was "more rigorous" confinement "than . . . required to insure" appellant's presence. *See* UCMJ art. 13. Army Reg. 190-47, Military Police: The Army Corrections System, para. 3-1c (15 Aug. 1996), requires a pretrial prisoner be housed in a detention cell or in a local civilian facility with which the installation has an agreement. According to the regulation, leg and hand irons are appropriate for pretrial prisoners in transit. *See id.* at paras. 11-3b(2), 11-3b(6), and 11-9. Appellant was not in transit; the barracks room provided temporary housing for a pretrial prisoner. *See id.* at para. 15-5 (defining temporary confinement); *see also id.* at para. 9-7e (prohibiting "securing a prisoner to a fixed object" while in a confinement facility except in emergency situations) and para. 11-9 ("Guards will not secure prisoners to any portion of an aircraft. . . .").

The record contains no evidence indicating appellant was a flight risk or posed a risk to others. Moreover, the record does not reflect any violent,

---

[20] First Sergeant Thompson testified PVT Rasch's escape from the same room, while awaiting pretrial confinement, was "a major factor" leading him to make the decision "directing . . . Sergeant Wyatt [to] shackle [appellant] to the cot."

predatory, or excessively dangerous criminal behavior by appellant.[21] Furthermore, if unit officials believed appellant was a flight risk, other methods of restraint were available. The military judge found that at least four soldiers were on duty in the barracks building the entire night, and were within ten to twenty feet from appellant while he slept shackled to the cot.[22] Placing one of these soldiers-or any other properly supervised soldier in the same barracks-in the room with appellant overnight could have easily served the purpose of securing appellant's presence at his Article 32, UCMJ, hearing the following morning. Despite the apparent availability of unit personnel to provide for this lesser form of restraint, appellant was severely restrained without an individualized showing of cause that he would flee or otherwise fail to present himself the following day.

While we do not find that shackling a pretrial prisoner to a cot is per se unduly harsh, we are not persuaded that appellant's shackling was required to ensure he did not escape through an unsecured window as did an unshackled PVT Rasch awaiting pretrial confinement at a regular facility. Such restraint was, therefore, not required to ensure appellant's presence at

---

[21] The record of trial does not contain any documentation reflecting the decision to place appellant into pretrial confinement. See R.C.M. 405 (referring to a "24-hour" commander's report, a "72-hour memorandum," a "48-hour probable cause determination," and a "7-day review of pretrial confinement"). During his opening statement on the motion for Article 13 credit, and again in his written R.C.M. 1105 submission, trial defense counsel stated that appellant waived his pretrial confinement hearing. We need not decide whether ordering appellant into pretrial confinement was appropriate. On his original charge sheet, dated 14 September 2001, appellant was charged with several offenses: violating the unit "no alcohol policy;" using, possessing, and distributing controlled substances (five specifications); larceny (two specifications); and false swearing. These offenses occurred between 14 July 2001 and 2 August 2001. On an additional charge sheet, dated 28 November 2001, appellant was charged with additional offenses: wrongfully going from his appointed place of duty (see Section III, supra); disrespect toward the first sergeant and a unit noncommissioned officer (three specifications); violating the unit "no alcohol policy" (three specifications); violating various orders from the first sergeant (four specifications), e.g., "at ease" and "get your hair cut;" using and distributing controlled substances (two specifications); and extortion. These offenses occurred between 14 July 2001 and 13 October 2001. On 14 October 2001, appellant was placed in pretrial confinement, after the original charges were preferred and prior to preferral of the additional charges.

[22] Private MacMahan testified that he was "the cadre monitor that night," and that appellant's door "was open . . . with two CQ's watching him . . . [who were] seated directly across from the door." Sergeant First Class Wyatt testified that he saw appellant "all throughout the night," that the cadre monitor was present, and that he "briefed the fireguards . . . to watch [appellant], and if he needed anything, to let the cadre monitor or [himself] know." First Sergeant Thompson testified that "there's two CQ runners on duty[, and] also a drill sergeant[; they are] there 24 hours a day, 7 days a week."

his pretrial Article 32, UCMJ, hearing scheduled the next day. *See generally Smith,* 53 M.J. at 172.

Based on the totality of the circumstances, we find that shackling appellant to the cot was a confinement condition "more rigorous than the circumstances required to insure his presence." UCMJ art. 13. Although appellant does not request a specific remedy, we will award ten days of confinement credit for the unusually harsh circumstances of appellant's pretrial confinement while awaiting his Article 32, UCMJ, investigative hearing. *See United States v. Spaustat,* 57 M.J. 256, 261-62 (C.A.A.F. 2002) (stating R.C.M. 305(k) "specifically authorizes more than day-for-day credit" for unduly harsh conditions of pretrial confinement); *see also United States v. Rendon,* 58 M.J. 221, 224-25 (C.A.A.F. 2003) (finding R.C.M. 305(k) credit appropriate remedy for physical restraint).

VI. Conclusion

* * *

Reassessing the sentence on the basis of the errors noted, the entire record, and applying the principles of *United States v. Sales,* 22 M.J. 305 (C.M.A. 1986), the court affirms only so much of the sentence as provides for a bad-conduct discharge, confinement for twelve months and twenty days, and reduction to Private E1. Appellant will also be credited with 177 days of confinement credit. All rights, privileges, and property, of which appellant has been deprived by virtue of that portion of his sentence set aside by this decision, are ordered restored, as mandated by Articles 58b(c) and 75(a), UCMJ.

Judge ZOLPER and Judge WALBURN concur.

Points for Discussion

1. Would Private First Class Gilchrist have been entitled to article 13 credit if he had been a flight risk? What sort of evidence would be necessary to show that he was a flight risk?

2. The court recognizes that Private First Class Gilchrist needed to be held in the Ice House because he could not be secured in a detention cell. The court further recognizes that another soldier kept in confinement in the Ice House without being shackled had escaped. And yet the court still concludes that it was improper to have shackled Gilchrist. What would the reaction have been if Gilchrist had not been shackled and he had escaped? Can you think of an alternative way that his escape might be prevented?

———————————

UNITED STATES v. CRUZ
U.S. Court of Military Appeals
25 M.J. 326 (C.M.A. 1987)

SULLIVAN, Judge:

On June 9, 1983, appellant [Juan C. Cruz, Sergeant, U.S. Army] was tried by a military judge sitting alone as a general court-martial at Fuerth, Federal Republic of Germany. Pursuant to his pleas, he was found guilty of one specification of possession of marijuana in the hashish form and two specifications of distribution of the same substance, in violation of Article 134, Uniform Code of Military Justice, 10 U.S.C. § 934. He was sentenced to a dishonorable discharge, confinement for 16 months, total forfeitures, and reduction to the lowest enlisted grade. The convening authority approved the sentence as adjudged. On appeal, the Court of Military Review dismissed the possession charge and affirmed the remaining findings of guilty and the sentence. 20 M.J. 873 (1985).

* * *

We hold that appellant was punished prior to trial in violation of Article 13, UCMJ, 10 U.S.C. § 813, and a rehearing on sentence is required.

The facts surrounding the granted issues are fully reported in the decision below, 20 M.J. at 875-78. They are based on extra-record sworn statements offered by both parties on appeal, id. at 875 n.1, and an administrative investigation conducted pursuant to Army Regulation (AR) 15-6 (C 1, June 15, 1981). A brief summary follows.

Early in 1983, the Army Criminal Investigation Command (CID) uncovered the presence of "large-scale drug abuse" at Pinder Barracks, Federal Republic of Germany. Approximately one quarter of the soldiers of the 6th Battalion, 14th Field Artillery (6/14th FA) of the Division Artillery (DIVARTY), 1st Armored Division, had positive urinalysis test results. The DIVARTY commander, Colonel Leslie E. Beavers, who also was the installation commander for Pinder Barracks, was notified of the large number of positive test results for his unit.

On March 24, 1983, Colonel Beavers held a meeting with Lieutenant Colonel (LTC) Glen D. Skirvin, Jr., battalion commander of the 6/14th FA, and LTC John Dubia, battalion commander of the 1/22d FA. He informed them of his planned mass apprehension of suspected drug abusers within DIVARTY. LTC Dubia initiated a discussion regarding removal of unit crests from the uniforms; Colonel Beavers assented to this action.

At 0630 on March 25, 1983, the battalion commanders informed their battery commanders that a mass formation was to be held that same day. Major Richard H. Witherspoon, battalion executive officer of the 6/14th FA, later stated that LTC Skirvin ordered his battery commanders and senior non-commissioned officers to remove the unit crests from the arrestees identified at the formation. Moreover, the procedure to be used at the formation was also established at this time. When a soldier's name was called, he would be escorted by his battery commander and first sergeant to the platform situated at the front of the formation. Once in front of the platform, the soldier's unit crests would be removed from his uniform by his escorts. He would then salute Colonel Beavers and await further instructions.

At 0800 on March 25, 1983, the formation was held. Approximately 1,200 soldiers were present. (*See* Appendix 1.) Colonel Beavers began speaking about trust and how that trust had been betrayed by members of the assembled unit. As he spoke, German Polizei and Army military police entered the base and took stations around the formation. Then, Colonel Beavers began calling the names of the suspected drug abusers. Approximately 40 soldiers, including appellant, were called out of the formation. As previously arranged, the soldiers were escorted to the platform, whereupon the majority of the soldiers had their unit crests removed. They saluted, but Colonel Beavers failed to return the salutes. The Court of Military Review assumed for purposes of its decision that, severally or jointly, the assembled collection of soldiers were called "bastards" or "criminals" or both by Colonel Beavers. This assembled collection was then marched to an adjacent site where the soldiers were individually searched and handcuffed by CID agents, in full view of the soldiers remaining in the formation. (*See* Appendix 2.)

These soldiers were then transported to the CID office for questioning. After being questioned by the CID, the soldiers were returned to their units. Thirty-five arrestees were members of the 6/14th FA. These soldiers, including appellant, were then billeted separately from their unit. After preferral of charges, they were given the opportunity to return to their individual barracks, but twenty-seven elected to remain separate. They were given or adopted the name "Peyote Platoon." This "unit" assembled separately from the battalion in subsequent formations and allegedly marched to the cadence of "peyote, peyote, peyote." Of these soldiers, fourteen were tried by general court-martial and one by a BCD special court-martial; eleven were tried by summary court-martial; five were given nonjudicial punishment; and four received administrative discharges in lieu of trial.

No assertion of command influence or prior punishment was made by appellant at his court-martial. However, 4 months after his trial, he complained that the activities described above induced him to accept a pretrial agreement for 16 months' confinement. On December 12, 1983, Brigadier General H.L. Olson was appointed to investigate the circumstances surrounding appellant's complaint. In his report dated December 20, 1983, General Olson concluded that Colonel Beavers' actions "cast a taint over some levels of subsequent legal proceedings" and recommended rehearings in the summary courts-martial and the nonjudicial- punishment cases. The Commanding General, VII Corps, substantially agreed but ordered review of these proceedings on a case-by-case basis. This investigation was later released to the Court of Military Review. Finally, on February 7, 1984, Major General Crosbie E. Saint, Commander of the 1st Armored Division, issued a directive which prohibited the above-noted conduct and strictly limited use of mass apprehensions.

* * *

The second question raised on this appeal is whether the treatment afforded appellant prior to his court-martial amounted to unlawful punishment prohibited by Article 13. The Court of Military Review held that appellant waived this issue by failing to raise it at his court-martial. 20 M.J. at 892-93. Compare United States v. Palmiter, 20 M.J. 90, 96 (Cox, J., lead opinion) with 100 (Everett, C.J., concurring in the result). We note, however, that the post-trial materials which first raised this issue also suggest that there may have been a subrosa agreement between the staff judge advocate and defense counsel to prevent its litigation. *Cf. United States v. Jones*, 23 M.J. 305 (C.M.A. 1987). Moreover, a *DuBay* hearing was not ordered in this case by military authorities to resolve these post-trial questions. *See United States v. Levite, supra.* Finally, the failure to raise the issue of pretrial punishment at the court-martial, absent some properly disclosed sentence consideration, comes perilously close to inadequate representation by counsel. *See generally United States v. Scott*, 24 M.J. 186 (C.M.A. 1987). Accordingly, a finding of a valid waiver in these circumstances is unwarranted.

Turning to the pretrial punishment issue in this case, we are convinced that appellant's treatment on the parade ground and as a member of the so-called "Peyote Platoon" violated Article 13. *See generally United States v. Bayhand*, 21 C.M.R. 84, 92 (C.M.A. 1956). This codal provision states:

§ 813. Art. 13. Punishment prohibited before trial

No person, while being held for trial, may be subjected to punishment or penalty other than arrest or confinement upon the charges pending against him, nor shall the arrest or confinement imposed upon him be any more rigorous than the circumstances require to insure his presence, but he may be subjected to minor punishment during that period for infractions of discipline.

In determining whether the treatment afforded appellant was a punishment or penalty for purposes of this provision, recourse to the military experience is particularly helpful.

Colonel Winthrop, in his work Military Law and Precedents 434 (2d ed. 1920 Reprint), stated the following in this regard:

Discharge with ignominy. A mode of dishonorable discharge, sanctioned by usage for time of war, is drumming, (or bugling,) *out of the service,* with the "Rogue's March," *in the presence of the command.* This ignominious form is sometimes conjoined with circumstances of special ignominy. *Thus soldiers have been sentenced to be drummed out after having their clothing stripped of all military insignia,* or after being tarred and feathered, or with their heads shaved or half-shaved, or with straw halters around their necks, or bearing placards inscribed with the names of their offences.

(Some emphasis added; footnotes omitted.) He also described the disused punishment of placarding as follows:

> *Standing or marching for a certain time bearing a placard or label inscribed with the name of the offence*—as "Deserter," "Coward," "Mutineer," "Marauder," "Pillager," "Thief," "Habitual Drunkard" was at one time a not uncommon punishment. In some cases the inscriptions were more extended—as "Deserter: Skulked through the war;" "A chicken-thief;" "For selling liquor to recruits;" "I forged liquor orders;" "I presented a forged order for liquor and got caught at it;" "I struck a noncommissioned officer;" "I robbed the mail—I am sent to the penitentiary for 5 years;" "The man who took the bribe from deserters and assisted in their escape."

Id. at 441-42 (emphasis added; footnotes omitted).

An historic example of this type of military punishment, although from another country, was the public ignominy or ceremony of degradation imposed on Captain Dreyfus. See J. Bredin, The Affair: The Case of Alfred Dreyfus 3-8 (J. Mehlman trans.) (George Braziller Inc., New York, 1986). Of course, even the alleged traitor Dreyfus was not subjected to this treatment until after he had undergone a trial by court-martial, albeit a highly irregular one. Clearly, public denunciation by the commander and subsequent military degradation before the troops prior to courts-martial constitute unlawful pretrial punishment prohibited by Article 13. *See* paras. 18b (3) and 125, Manual for Courts-Martial, United States, 1969 (Revised edition); Winthrop, supra at 124-25. The treatment appellant suffered was substantially the same.

Military authorities subsequent to appellant's court-martial frankly recognized that his pretrial treatment violated Article 13. Brigadier General Olsen, the AR 15-6 investigating officer, and Lieutenant General Galvin, Commander of VII Corps, who ordered the investigation of appellant's post-trial complaint, had no difficulty in finding that the conduct of the Brigade Commander violated or probably violated this codal provision. Moreover, a directive was issued shortly thereafter advising commanders that mass apprehensions conducted under these circumstances were unlawful and prohibited.

We agree and hold that a new sentence hearing must be ordered so appellant can bring this prior punishment to the attention of his court-martial. *See* para. 75 c(1)(b), Manual, supra; *see also United States v. Suzuki*, 14 M.J. 491, 493 (C.M.A. 1983).

* * *

The decision of the United States Army Court of Military Review is reversed as to sentence, and the sentence is set aside. The record of trial is returned to the Judge Advocate General of the Army. A rehearing on sentence based on the approved findings may be ordered.

Chief Judge EVERETT and Judge COX concur.

APPENDIX 1

APPENDIX 2

4-3. Searches Versus Inspections

Service members also enjoy the protection of the Fourth Amendment which grants all persons the right "to be secure in their persons, houses, papers, and effects, against unreasonable searches and seizures shall not be violated . . . . [and] no Warrants shall issue, but upon probable cause, supported by oath or affirmation, and particularly describing the place to be searched, and the persons or things to be seized . . . ."

Designed to protect citizens from law enforcement excesses, evidence obtained in violation of the Fourth Amendment is not admissible in either civilian criminal trials or military courts-martial. When the defense objects at trial, Military Rule of Evidence 311 prohibits the government from admitting evidence obtained as a result of an unlawful search or seizure, (i.e., the exclusionary rule) unless the prosecution can prove by a preponderance that the evidence was not obtained from an unlawful search or seizure or obtained as a result of an exception to the exclusionary rule.

Specifically, evidence obtained from an unlawful search or seizure may be used if the evidence would have been inevitably obtained even if such unlawful search or seizure had not been made ("inevitable discovery") or if the officials who obtained the evidence reasonably and in good faith relied on a warrant or authorization to search, seize, apprehend, or arrest ("good faith" exception). *Id.* (Military Rule of Evidence 311 also authorizes the prosecutor to use evidence obtained as a result of an unlawful search or seizure "to impeach by contradiction the in-court testimony of the accused.") The "good faith" exception requires that the authorizing official who issued the warrant or authorization to have been neutral and detached and to have had a substantial basis for believing probable cause existed when issuing the warrant or authorization and the law enforcement personnel relied on that document in good faith.

The exclusionary rule also requires that evidence directly derived from an unlawful search or seizure ("derivative evidence" or "fruit of the poisonous tree") be excluded from trial. The military judge must determine by a preponderance of the evidence that the government official did not obtain the evidence as a result of the unlawful search or seizure that the evidence obtained would have been found as a result of "inevitable discovery" or was obtained as a result of the "good faith" exception. *Id.*

As in the civilian sector, Fourth Amendment protection is triggered when there is a government intrusion (i.e., a search or seizure conducted, instigated, or participated in by military members, their agents, or other government officials) and the person has a reasonable expectation of privacy. The U.S. Supreme Court in the *Katz* case that follows describes the Fourth Amendment as protecting people and not places and Justice Harlan describes a two-part test to determine whether a reasonable expectation of privacy exists, stating that a reasonable expectation of privacy requires "first that a person have exhibited an actual (subjective) expectation of privacy and, second, that the expectation be one that society is prepared to recognize as 'reasonable.' " *United States v. Katz*, 389 U.S. 347 (1967). Military Rule of Evidence 311 is consistent with the Court's opinion in *Katz*, indicating that military members are protected when there is a "reasonable expectation of privacy in the person, place or property searched [or the service member has] a legitimate interest in the property or evidence seized when challenging a seizure; or the [service member] would otherwise have grounds to object to the search or seizure under the Constitution of the United States as applied to members of the armed forces."

KATZ v. UNITED STATES
U.S. Supreme Court
389 U.S. 347 (1967)

MR. JUSTICE STEWART delivered the opinion of the Court.

The petitioner was convicted in the District Court for the Southern District of California under an eight-count indictment charging him with transmitting wagering information by telephone from Los Angeles to Miami and Boston in violation of a federal statute. At trial the Government was permitted, over the petitioner's objection, to introduce evidence of the petitioner's end of telephone conversations, overheard by FBI agents who had attached an electronic listening and recording device to the outside of the public telephone booth from which he had placed his calls. In affirming his conviction, the Court of Appeals rejected the contention that the recordings had been obtained in violation of the Fourth Amendment, because '(t)here was no physical entrance into the area occupied by, (the petitioner).' We granted certiorari in order to consider the constitutional questions thus presented.

The petitioner had phrased those questions as follows:

A. Whether a public telephone booth is a constitutionally protected area so that evidence obtained by attaching an electronic listening recording device to the top of such a booth is obtained in violation of the right to privacy of the user of the booth.

B. Whether physical penetration of a constitutionally protected area is necessary before a search and seizure can be said to be violative of the Fourth Amendment to the United States Constitution.

We decline to adopt this formulation of the issues. In the first place the correct solution of Fourth Amendment problems is not necessarily promoted by incantation of the phrase 'constitutionally protected area.' Secondly, the Fourth Amendment cannot be translated into a general constitutional 'right to privacy.' That Amendment protects individual privacy against certain kinds of governmental intrusion, but its protections go further, and often have nothing to do with privacy at all. Other provisions of the Constitution protect personal privacy from other forms of governmental invasion. But the protection of a person's general right to privacy-his right to be let alone by other people-is, like the protection of his property and of his very life, left largely to the law of the individual States.

Because of the misleading way the issues have been formulated, the parties have attached great significance to the characterization of the telephone booth from which the petitioner placed his calls. The petitioner has strenuously argued that the booth was a "constitutionally protected area." The Government has maintained with equal vigor that it was not. But this effort to decide whether or not a given "area," viewed in the abstract, is 'constitutionally protected' deflects attention from the problem presented by this case. For the Fourth Amendment protects people, not places. What a person knowingly exposes to the public, even in his own home or office, is not a subject of Fourth Amendment protection. *See Lewis v. United States*, 385 U.S. 206, 210; *United States v. Lee*, 274 U.S. 559, 563. But what he seeks to preserve as private, even in an area accessible to the public, may be constitutionally protected. *See Rios v. United States*, 364 U.S. 253 *Ex parte Jackson*, 96 U.S. 727, 733.

The Government stresses the fact that the telephone booth from which the petitioner made his calls was constructed partly of glass, so that he was as visible after he entered it as he would have been if he had remained outside. But what he sought to exclude when he entered the booth was not the intruding eye-it was the uninvited ear. He did not shed his right to do so simply because he made his calls from a place where he might be seen. No less than an individual in a business office, in a friend's apartment, or in a taxicab, a person in a telephone booth may rely upon the protection of the Fourth Amendment. One who occupies it, shuts the door behind him, and pays the toll that permits him to place a call is surely entitled to assume that the words he utters into the mouthpiece will not be broadcast to the world. To read the Constitution more narrowly is to ignore the vital role that the public telephone has come to play in private communication.

The Government contends, however, that the activities of its agents in this case should not be tested by Fourth Amendment requirements, for the surveillance technique they employed involved no physical penetration of the telephone booth from which the petitioner placed his calls. It is true that the absence of such penetration was at one time thought to foreclose further Fourth Amendment inquiry.... Once this much is acknowledged, and once it is recognized that the Fourth Amendment protects people-and not simply "areas"-against unreasonable searches and seizures it becomes clear that the reach of that Amendment cannot turn upon the presence or absence of a physical intrusion into any given enclosure.... The Government's activities in electronically listening to and recording the petitioner's words violated the privacy upon which he justifiably relied while using the telephone booth and thus constituted a "search and seizure" within the meaning of the Fourth Amendment. The fact that the electronic device employed to achieve that end did not happen to penetrate the wall of the booth can have no constitutional significance.

The question remaining for decision, then, is whether the search and seizure conducted in this case complied with constitutional standards. In that regard, the Government's position is that its agents acted in an entirely defensible manner: They did not begin their electronic surveillance until investigation of the petitioner's activities had established a strong probability that he was using the telephone in question to transmit gambling information to persons in other States, in violation of federal law. Moreover, the surveillance was limited, both in scope and in duration, to the specific purpose of establishing the contents of the petitioner's unlawful telephonic communications. The agents confined their surveillance to the brief periods during which he used the telephone booth, and they took great care to overhear only the conversations of the petitioner himself.

Accepting this account of the Government's actions as accurate, it is clear that this surveillance was so narrowly circumscribed that a duly authorized magistrate, properly notified of the need for such investigation, specifically informed of the basis on which it was to proceed, and clearly apprised of the precise intrusion it would entail, could constitutionally have authorized, with appropriate safeguards, the very limited search and seizure that the Government asserts in fact took place. . . .

The Government urges that, because its agents relied upon the decisions in Olmstead and Goldman, and because they did no more here than they might properly have done with prior judicial sanction, we should retroactively validate their conduct. That we cannot do. It is apparent that the agents in this case acted with restraint. Yet the inescapable fact is that this restraint was imposed by the agents themselves, not by a judicial officer. They were not required, before commencing the search, to present their estimate of probable cause for detached scrutiny by a neutral magistrate. They were not compelled, during the conduct of the search itself, to observe precise limits established in advance by a specific court order. Nor were they directed, after the search had been completed, to notify the authorizing magistrate in detail of all that had been seized. In the absence of such safeguards, this Court has never sustained a search upon the sole ground that officers reasonably expected to find evidence of a particular crime and voluntarily confined their activities to the least intrusive means consistent with that end. Searches conducted without warrants have been held unlawful "notwithstanding facts unquestionably showing probable cause, *Agnello v. United States*, 269 U.S. 20, 33, for the Constitution requires 'that the deliberate, impartial judgment of a judicial officer * * * be interposed between the citizen and the police * * *.' *Wong Sun v. United States*, 371 U.S. 471, 481-482. 'Over and again this Court has emphasized that the mandate of the (Fourth) Amendment requires adherence to judicial processes,' *United States v. Jeffers*, 342 U.S. 48, 51, and that searches conducted outside the judicial process, without prior approval by judge or magistrate, are per se unreasonable under the Fourth

Amendment—subject only to a few specifically established and well-delineated exceptions.

It is difficult to imagine how any of those exceptions could ever apply to the sort of search and seizure involved in this case. Even electronic surveillance substantially contemporaneous with an individual"s arrest could hardly be deemed an "incident" of that arrest. Nor could the use of electronic surveillance without prior authorization be justified on grounds of "hot pursuit." And, of course, the very nature of electronic surveillance precludes its use pursuant to the suspect's consent.

The Government does not question these basic principles. Rather, it urges the creation of a new exception to cover this case. It argues that surveillance of a telephone booth should be exempted from the usual requirement of advance authorization by a magistrate upon a showing of probable cause. We cannot agree. Omission of such authorization "bypasses the safeguards provided by an objective predetermination of probable cause, and substitutes instead the far less reliable procedure of an after-the-event justification for the * * * search, too likely to be subtly influenced by the familiar shortcomings of hindsight judgment." *Beck v. State of Ohio*, 379 U.S. 89, 96.

And bypassing a neutral predetermination of the scope of a search leaves individuals secure from Fourth Amendment violations "only in the discretion of the police." *Id.*, at 97.

These considerations do not vanish when the search in question is transferred from the setting of a home, an office, or a hotel room to that of a telephone booth. Wherever a man may be, he is entitled to know that he will remain free from unreasonable searches and seizures. The government agents here ignored "the procedure of antecedent justification * * * that is central to the Fourth Amendment," a procedure that we hold to be a constitutional precondition of the kind of electronic surveillance involved in this case. Because the surveillance here failed to meet that condition, and because it led to the petitioner's conviction, the judgment must be reversed.

It is so ordered.

Judgment reversed.

Mr. Justice MARSHALL took no part in the consideration or decision of this case.   Mr. Justice DOUGLAS, with whom Mr. Justice BRENNAN joins, concurring.

Mr. Justice HARLAN, concurring.

I join the opinion of the Court, which I read to hold only (a) that an enclosed telephone booth is an area where, like a home . . . and unlike a field . . . a person has a constitutionally protected reasonable expectation of privacy; (b) that electronic as well as physical intrusion into a place that is in this sense private may constitute a violation of the Fourth Amendment; and (c) that the invasion of a constitutionally protected area by federal authorities is, as the Court has long held, presumptively unreasonable in the absence of a search warrant.

As the Court's opinion states, "the Fourth Amendment protects people, not places." The question, however, is what protection it affords to those people. Generally, as here, the answer to that question requires reference to a "place." My understanding of the rule that has emerged from prior decisions is that there is a twofold requirement, first that a person have exhibited an actual (subjective) expectation of privacy and, second, that the expectation be one that society is prepared to recognize as "reasonable." Thus a man's home is, for most purposes, a place where he expects privacy, but objects, activities, or statements that he exposes to the "plain view" of outsiders are not "protected" because no intention to keep them to himself has been exhibited. On the other hand, conversations in the open would not be protected against being overheard, for the expectation of privacy under the circumstances would be unreasonable. *Cf. Hester v. United States, supra.*

The critical fact in this case is that "[o]ne who occupies it, (a telephone booth) shuts the door behind him, and pays the toll that permits him to place a call is surely entitled to assume" that his conversation is not being intercepted. Ante, at 511. The point is not that the booth is "accessible to the public" at other times, ante, at 511, but that it is a temporarily private place whose momentary occupants" expectations of freedom from intrusion are recognized as reasonable. *Cf. Rios v. United States*, 364 U.S. 253.

* * *

Finally, I do not read the Court's opinion to declare that no interception of a conversation one-half of which occurs in a public telephone booth can be reasonable in the absence of a warrant. As elsewhere under the Fourth Amendment, warrants are the general rule, to which the legitimate needs of law enforcement may demand specific exceptions. It will be time enough to consider any such exceptions when an appropriate occasion presents itself, and I agree with the Court that this is not one.

Point for Discussion

What is the consequence of *Katz*'s emphasis on the "expectation of privacy" in the military context? Two leading scholars have argued that it generally makes the protections of the Fourth Amendment largely inapplicable to service members. They write:

> The often smaller, if not sometimes *de minimis*, expectation of privacy held by military personnel, coupled with the substantial social policy justification for privacy intrusions in the military framework, would at least justify a sharply different manner of fourth amendment application to the military when compared to its civilian application.

Fredric I. Lederer & Frederic L. Borch, *Does The Fourth Amendment Apply To The Armed Forces?*, 3 Wm. & Mary Bill Rts. J. 219, 227 (1994). Do you agree?

Government Searches in the Military Context

Military Rules of Evidence 313 (inspections and inventories), 314 (searches not requiring probable cause), and 315 (probable cause searches) lay out the foundational rules for Fourth Amendment protections in the military context and the admission of evidence obtained from a search and seizure. Once a reasonable expectation of privacy exists, law enforcement must obtain a search warrant based on probable cause or an exception must exist or the intrusion must be outside the scope of the warrant requirement.

In the military, magistrates, military judges, or commanders have the power to issue search *authorizations* based on probable cause. Civilian authorities issue search *warrants* based on probable cause. Neutral and detached military commanders may issue search authorizations for areas over which they have control. Military judges or magistrates (who are appointed pursuant to regulation) may also issue search authorizations based on probable cause. Search authorizations may be oral or written and need not be under oath. But probable cause must exist—that is, reasonable grounds to believe items connected with criminal activity will be located in the specific place or person to be searched. M.R.E. 315(f)(2). Similarly, Military Rule of Evidence 316(b) indicates that probable cause to seize an item exists "when there is a reasonable belief that the property or evidence is an unlawful weapon, contraband, evidence of crime, or might be used to resist apprehension or to escape." (Note, if probable cause exists and exigent circumstances arise such as insufficient time (i.e., delay would result in removal, destruction, or concealment of the evidence), operational necessity prevents communication with a person authorized to issue a search warrant or authorization, or the place to be searched is an operable vehicle, no warrant or authorization is required). M.R.E. 315(g).

In determining whether probable cause exists, issuing authorities must look at the totality of the circumstances and ensure sufficient information exists that connects the suspected criminal offense to a specific person or place to be searched. The facts from trustworthy sources should be based on direct witness observations, admissions of an accused or co-accused, or provide detailed descriptions or specific facts such as location that are easily verified or corroborated.

Military Rules of Evidence 314 (Searches not requiring probable cause) and 315 (Probable cause searches) reflect rules applicable in the civilian sector. Military Rule of Evidence 314 describes certain government intrusions (i.e., searches) that may take place regardless of whether the government personnel performing the search have probable cause. For example, customs or immigration border searches, or searches during entrance to or exit from a military installation, aircraft, or vessel (which are generally to ensure security, military fitness, or good order and discipline of the command) may take place without probable cause.

Searches incident to a lawful law enforcement stop do not require probable cause. In addition, persons with authority to apprehend and members of law enforcement may conduct brief investigative "*Terry*" stops based on information or observation that in their experience leads them to have a reasonable suspicion that "criminal activity may be afoot." M.R.E. 314(f)(1); *Terry v. Ohio*, 392 U.S. 1 (1968); *see* R.C.M. 302(b) and chapter 4-2 of this text, discussing military apprehension. Similarly, when there is a lawful stop of a driver or passenger in a vehicle and the official conducting the stop "has a reasonable belief that the person stopped is dangerous and that the person stopped may gain immediate control of a weapon" the passenger compartment may be searched for weapons. M.R.E. 314(f)(3). Other searches not requiring probable cause include searches incident to apprehension (i.e., wing span search), searches within jails or confinement facilities, emergency searches to render immediate medical aid, and searches of open fields or woodlands. M.R.E. 314(g)-(k).

Military Rule of Evidence 314 also indicates that searches of government property may occur without probable cause "unless the person to whom the property is issued or assigned has a reasonable expectation of privacy therein at the time of the search." M.R.E. 314(d). Generally, service members do not have a reasonable expectation of privacy over government property unless items are issued for personal use only and even those cases involving wall lockers, for example, require a determination based on specific facts and circumstances at the time of the search. In *United States v. Larson*, 66 M.J. 212 (C.A.A.F. 2008), a case that appears later in this chapter, the Court of Appeals for the Armed Forces analyzes whether appellant had a reasonable expectation of privacy in his government laptop. As the *Larson* case illustrates, searches of government property such as desks or laptops require a fact-specific analysis.

Searches pursuant to voluntary consent from a person who has control over the property may occur without probable cause and evidence that is obtained within the scope of the consent will be admissible. The Court of Appeals for the Armed Forces in the *Weston* case explains the reasonableness of a consent search when consent to search is not provided by the accused.

UNITED STATES v. WESTON
U.S. Court of Appeals for the Armed Forces
67 M.J. 390 (C.A.A.F. 2009)

STUCKY, Judge:

There was something odd about the electric razor in the bathroom. Staff Sergeant (SSgt) ME, a female Marine court reporter, noticed it sitting on the wall locker shelf in the bathroom she shared with Appellant [Staff Sergeant Daniel A. Weston, U.S. Marine Corps], the senior court reporter, whom she knew to be experienced with computers and surveillance equipment. SSgt ME typically changed clothes in the bathroom and for the past year had felt that she was being watched, a feeling that she attributed to paranoia. But this time the circumstances were simply too odd and her suspicions too strong. SSgt ME took the razor with her when she left work that day. Her attempt to open the razor's casing ended at Sears with a "Torque" T7 screwdriver. Inside the razor she found a camera.

We granted review in this case to determine two issues. First, whether the search of Appellant's house was reasonable where Appellant objected to the search, but was not physically present when the search was conducted pursuant to his wife's consent. Second, if, as Appellant argues, the search was unreasonable under *Georgia v. Randolph*, 547 U.S. 103 (2006), whether the inevitable discovery exception would allow admission of the seized evidence. As we find that the search was reasonable under these circumstances, we do not reach the second issue.

I. Background

Following her discovery of the hidden camera, SSgt ME contacted both the Provost Marshal's Office (PMO) and Appellant's wife to report the discovery. When Appellant and his wife arrived at their home that evening, they were met by military police who, after granting the wife permission to accompany Appellant, followed them to the PMO where they were placed in separate rooms.

Once in the room, agents of the Criminal Investigative Division informed Appellant of his rights under Article 31, Uniform Code of Military Justice (UCMJ), 10 U.S.C. § 831 (2000), and Military Rule of Evidence (M.R.E.) 305. Appellant promptly invoked his right to remain silent and to consult with an attorney. When the agent questioning Appellant asked for consent to search Appellant's home, Appellant unequivocally objected. The agent then left Appellant alone in the room. Appellant used the time to call a friend, Robert Fricke, who was a former military judge and Marine Corps judge advocate. That conversation was interrupted when the agents took Appellant's cellular phone away and placed him incommunicado in a holding cell.

Following Appellant's refusal to consent to a search of the home, the same agent who asked Appellant for consent asked Mrs. Weston, who was sitting in a different room, the same question. Mrs. Weston consented to the search. She did not ask whether the investigators had asked her husband to consent, and the investigators did not inform her that he had refused consent.

The search of the house Appellant and his wife lived in proceeded with Mrs. Weston present. During the search Mr. Fricke telephoned Mrs. Weston twice. The first call was to inquire as to the family's welfare; the second was to inform Mrs. Weston that she could, and in Mr. Fricke's opinion should, withdraw her consent to the search. Mrs. Weston did so immediately. The agents searching the home gathered up the materials they had already seized and left the home. Among those items was Appellant's computer. A subsequent search of the computer revealed nonconsensual images of SSgt

ME changing her clothes and using the bathroom. The computer also contained photos of the interior of SSgt ME's house.

II. Procedural Posture

Appellant was charged with three violations of the Uniform Code of Military Justice (UCMJ). The first two charges were for assault and housebreaking, under Articles 128 and 130, UCMJ, 10 U.S.C. §§ 928, 930 (2000). The third charge involved two specifications of invasion of privacy and one specification of wrongfully impeding an investigation. Article 134, UCMJ, 10 U.S.C. § 934 (2000). A general court-martial with members found Appellant guilty of housebreaking and of the two specifications of invasion of privacy.

Prior to trial, Appellant moved to suppress the evidence that was seized from his home. The military judge denied this motion. On appeal, a panel of the United States Navy-Marine Corps Court of Criminal Appeals (CCA) held that the search of Appellant's home was unreasonable and violated Appellant's Fourth Amendment rights. *United States v. Weston*, 65 M.J. 774, 785 (N.M. Ct. Crim. App. 2007). The Government moved for a rehearing en banc. On rehearing, the CCA reversed the panel, holding that the military judge did not abuse his discretion in denying the defense motion to suppress. *United States v. Weston*, 66 M.J. 544, 546-47 (N.M. Ct. Crim. App. 2008).

III. Discussion

Appellant argues that the search of his home was unreasonable under *Georgia v. Randolph*, and, therefore, the en banc CCA opinion must be overturned. We disagree. The facts of this case are distinguishable from those of Randolph, and are more like those of the cases *Randolph* specifically preserved.

We review a military judge's decision to admit evidence for an abuse of discretion. *United States v. Gallagher*, 66 M.J. 250, 253 (C.A.A.F. 2008). We review findings of fact for clear error and conclusions of law de novo. Id. at 253 (citing *United States v. Flores*, 64 M.J. 451, 454 (C.A.A.F. 2007)).

* * *

Ordinarily, warrantless entry into a person's house is unreasonable per se. *Randolph*, 547 U.S. at 109. While the rule against warrantless entry is vigilantly guarded, the voluntary consent of an individual possessing authority is one "carefully drawn" exception. *Jones v. United States*, 357 U.S. 493, 499 (1958); *see Illinois v. Rodriguez*, 497 U.S. 177, 181 (1990). Voluntary consent to search may be obtained from the person whose property is to be searched or from a fellow occupant who shares common authority over the property. *United States v. Matlock*, 415 U.S. 164, 171 (1974); *United States v. Gallagher*, 66 M.J. 250, 253 (C.A.A.F. 2008).

In *Matlock*, consent to search was granted by the co-occupant, who was on the premises while the defendant was detained in a police car nearby. *Matlock*, 415 U.S. at 166; *Randolph*, 547 U.S. at 109-10. Ultimately, the Court determined that "the consent of one who possesses common authority [or other sufficient relationship] over premises or effects is valid as against the absent, nonconsenting person with whom that authority is shared." *Matlock*, 415 U.S. at 170-71; *see Gallagher*, 66 M.J. at 253; *United States v. Rader*, 65 M.J. 30, 30-31 (C.A.A.F. 2007). . . .

Appellant wishes us to find that the search of his home was unreasonable in light of *Randolph*. In *Randolph*, the Supreme Court addressed the application of the *Matlock* rule where the nonconsenting occupant was "physically present" when he refused permission to search. *Randolph*, 547 U.S. at 109. The Supreme Court held that express refusal by a physically present co-occupant renders a warrantless search unreasonable and invalid as to him. *Id.* at 106. The specific combination of the physical presence of the cotenant at the scene, plus the cotenant's "immediate challenge" renders the warrantless search unreasonable and invalid. *Randolph*, 547 U.S. at 111, 113.

The distinction between an objection to a search lodged by a cotenant who is physically present and one who is not is a formal one, but it is the one explicitly drawn by the Supreme Court in *Randolph*:

> If those cases [*Matlock* and *Rodriguez*] are not to be undercut by today's holding, we have to admit that we are drawing a fine line; if a potential defendant with self-interest in objecting is in fact at the door and objects, the co-tenant's permission does not suffice for a reasonable search, whereas the potential objector, nearby but not invited to take part in the threshold colloquy, loses out.

> This is the line we draw, and we think the formalism is justified.

Randolph, 547 U.S. at 121.

In his separate opinion, Judge Erdmann distinguishes a "nonconsenting" cotenant, such as Matlock (sitting in the squad car) and Rodriguez (asleep in another room), from an "objecting" one. *United States v. Weston*, 67 M.J. at 398 (C.A.A.F. 2008) (Erdmann, J., concurring in the result). This distinction is not compelled by Supreme Court precedent, and we are unwilling to draw it. The term "nonconsenting" is general and inclusive. It encompasses all who do not expressly consent, including those who refuse, those who remain silent, and those who are not asked. Reasonableness of a warrantless search due to voluntary consent is a simple binary proposition; either there is consent or there is not. *Matlock* determined that a cotenant can provide consent to search, and *Randolph* merely laid out the limited circumstances under which a cotenant's objection can overrule that consent.

Appellant urges us to extend the holding of *Randolph* and adopt the reasoning of the United States Court of Appeals for the Ninth Circuit in *United States v. Murphy*, where the court discounted the significance of the physical presence and immediate challenge of the party not consenting to the search. 516 F.3d 1117, 1123-24 (9th Cir. 2008). Appellant further argues that we should look more generally to society's widely shared social expectations in determining the reasonableness of consent searches. We decline to do so.

While "widely shared social expectations" underlie the reasoning in Randolph, 547 U.S. at 111 ("The constant element in assessing Fourth Amendment reasonableness in the consent cases, then, is the great significance given to widely shared social expectations . . ."), the Supreme Court specifically declined to overrule Matlock and drew the line with the physical presence at the threshold. *See id.* at 120-22 We decline to adopt the Ninth Circuit's reasoning and thus do not expand the holding of *Randolph* at the expense of *Matlock*.

Where one party has joint access and control to a property and voluntarily consents to a search, the warrantless search is reasonable. Rather than *Murphy*, we find more persuasive the approach adopted by the United States Courts of Appeals for the Seventh and Eighth Circuits, which held that *Randolph* did not "permanently disabl[e] [a cotenant's] shared authority to consent to an evidentiary search of her home." *United States v. Henderson*, 536 F.3d 776, 777 (7th Cir. 2008); *see United States v. Hudspeth*, 518 F.3d 954, 960-61 (8th Cir. 2008).

Appellant also argues that the Criminal Investigative Division (CID) agents removed him from his home in order to prevent him from voicing an effective objection to the search. *Randolph* recognizes an exception to its holding in cases where there is evidence "that the police have removed the potentially objecting tenant from the entrance for the sake of avoiding a possible objection." *Randolph*, 547 U.S. at 121. In such cases, a search consented to by the remaining tenant may not be reasonable. *Id.* In this case, however, there is no evidence that the agents removed Appellant from his home so that he could not effectively object to its search; the objection was not lodged until Appellant was at the PMO and there were no circumstances that should have led the police to anticipate it.

Here, the search was reasonable; the CID obtained consent from Appellant's wife who possessed common authority over the premises. As in Matlock, Appellant was a nonconsenting party who shared authority over the premises, but was not present to provide immediate challenge to his wife's consent to search. The "fine line" drawn by the Supreme Court in *Randolph* indicates that physical presence and immediate challenge is required for the nonconsenting tenant's objection to nullify the reasonableness of the search. That was not the case here, thus the holding of *Randolph* does not apply and the search was reasonable.

IV. Decision

The decision of the United States Navy-Marine Corps Court of Criminal Appeals is affirmed.

[The separate opinions of Chief Judge Efron and Judge Erdmann concurring in the result omitted.—Eds.]

Point for Discussion

Does the military context affect the outcome of this case in any way? Or would the case be analyzed exactly the same way if all of the parties had been civilians?

UNITED STATES v. LARSON
U.S. Court of Appeals for the Armed Forces
66 M.J. 212 (C.A.A.F. 2008)

RYAN, Judge:

A general court-martial composed of officer members convicted Appellant [Major John R. Larson, U.S. Air Force], contrary to his pleas, of one specification each of attempted carnal knowledge and attempted indecent acts with a minor, violations of Article 80, Uniform Code of Military Justice (UCMJ), 10 U.S.C. § 880 (2000); one specification of violating a lawful general regulation, a violation of Article 92, UCMJ, 10 U.S.C. § 892 (2000); and one specification each of communicating indecent language and using a facility or means of interstate commerce to attempt to entice a minor to engage in sexual activity, violations of Article 134, UCMJ, 10 U.S.C. § 934 (2000).

The members sentenced Appellant to dismissal from the service, confinement for nine years, and forfeiture of all pay and allowances. The convening authority approved the dismissal and forfeitures, but reduced Appellant's confinement to six years. The United States Air Force Court of Criminal Appeals affirmed. *United States v. Larson*, 64 M.J. 559 (A.F. Ct. Crim. App. 2006).

We granted review of the following issues:

I.

WHETHER THE AIR FORCE COURT OF CRIMINAL APPEALS ERRED IN HOLDING THAT APPELLANT HAD NO REASONABLE EXPECTATION OF PRIVACY IN HIS GOVERNMENT COMPUTER DESPITE THIS COURT'S RULING IN UNITED STATES v. LONG, 64 M.J. 57 (C.A.A.F. 2006).

* * *

For the reasons stated below, we affirm the decision of the lower court.

I. Appellant's Motion to Suppress

A. Factual Background

Appellant used the government computer in his military office to obtain sexually explicit material, to include pornographic images and video, from the Internet and to initiate instant message conversations with "Kristin," someone he believed to be a fourteen-year-old girl. "Kristin" was actually a civilian police detective working to catch online sexual predators.

Civilian police and the Air Force Office of Special Investigations (AFOSI) cooperated in the investigation of Appellant. The police used a proposed meeting between Appellant and "Kristin" at a local mall as a sting operation. When Appellant arrived at the mall at the time he had arranged with "Kristin," the police arrested Appellant. While conducting a search incident to arrest the police discovered a receipt for a package of condoms purchased just fifteen minutes earlier in Appellant's pocket. During a consensual search of Appellant's car, police found a package of condoms and a book entitled Sexaholics Anonymous.

After Appellant's arrest, AFOSI continued to pursue its own investigation. Appellant's commander, using a master key to the government office occupied by Appellant, allowed AFOSI agents to enter and to seize the government computer in the office. A search of the computer's hard drive revealed stored pornographic material, a web browser history that showed Appellant visited pornographic websites and engaged in sexually explicit chat sessions in his office on his government computer, and other electronic data implicating Appellant in the charged offenses.

At trial, Appellant asserted that the warrantless search of his government computer violated the Fourth Amendment and that the evidence obtained from it should be suppressed. The military judge held an Article 39(a), UCMJ, 10 U.S.C. § 839(a) (2000), session to determine the admissibility of the evidence. Based on the testimony elicited at the Article 39(a), UCMJ, session the military judge made initial findings of fact on the record and later made detailed supplemental findings of fact.

The military judge found that Appellant was assigned to a private office and had a key to lock the office, but other Air Force personnel, including the fire department and the command's facility manager also had keys to his office. The office contained a government computer that was provided to Appellant to accomplish official business. The military judge found that Appellant could secure the computer with a personal password, but a system administrator could still access the computer. When Appellant logged on to the computer, he was required to click a button accepting conditions listed in a banner, which stated that the computer was Department of Defense property, was for official use, and that he consented to monitoring. The military judge found that, while Appellant "reasonably understood that he was allowed to send personal e-mail or visit the internet as long as it didn't interfere with [his] duties," this did not change the fact that the government owned the computer and had a right to access it. This finding was largely based on the testimony of Appellant's commander, who testified that he could log onto Appellant's computer with his own password and access all portions of the hard drive unless Appellant had protected something with his own password. Although the military judge did not specifically reference the commander's access in his findings, this testimony adds further support to the military judge's ultimate ruling. Moreover, no evidence was presented that any of the evidence recovered from the hard drive was password protected.

In light of these facts, the military judge ruled that the Government had established by a preponderance of the evidence that Appellant had no reasonable expectation of privacy in the government computer because the computer had a "consent to monitoring" banner that had to be acknowledged with each log on, the system administrator had access to every part of the computer, including the hard drive, and the computer was government property.

B. Fourth Amendment Analysis

We review the denial of a motion to suppress for an abuse of discretion. *United States v. Khamsouk*, 57 M.J. 282, 286 (C.A.A.F. 2002). Findings of fact are affirmed unless they are clearly erroneous; conclusions of law are reviewed de novo. *United States v. Flores*, 64 M.J. 451, 454 (C.A.A.F. 2007) (citing *Khamsouk*, 57 M.J. at 286). We consider the evidence in the light most favorable to the prevailing party. *United States v. Reister*, 44 M.J. 409, 413 (C.A.A.F. 1996).

The military judge concluded that the Government had carried its burden of establishing that Appellant had no reasonable expectation of privacy in the government computer. The lower court agreed, and held that the military judge did not abuse his discretion. *Larson*, 64 M.J. at 563. We agree.

The Fourth Amendment of the Constitution generally requires probable cause for searches of places and things in which people have a reasonable expectation of privacy. U.S. Const. amend. IV. In addressing Fourth Amendment privacy claims, the threshold issue is whether the person has a legitimate expectation of privacy in the invaded place. *Rakas v. Illinois*, 439 U.S. 128, 143 (1978). This inquiry invites a court to address whether the individual had a subjective expectation of privacy, and if so whether the subjective expectation of privacy is one that society is prepared to accept as reasonable. *Smith v. Maryland*, 442 U.S. 735, 740 (1979), *superseded by statute*, Electronic Communications Privacy Act of 1986, 18 U.S.C. § 3121(a) (2000) (prohibiting installation of a pen register without a court order).

As the property searched here was a government computer, Military Rule of Evidence (M.R.E.) 314(d), which addresses the search of government property, pertains.

* * *

The discussion to this rule recognizes that the presumption that there is no reasonable expectation of privacy in government property is rebuttable. Manual for Courts-Martial, United States, Analysis of the Military Rules of Evidence app. 22 at A22-26 (2005 ed.). Whether there is a reasonable expectation of privacy in government property is determined under that totality of the circumstances, which includes the rebuttable presumption. *See, e.g., Samson v. California*, 547 U.S. 843, 848 (2006); M.R.E. 314(d).

In this case, based on the totality of circumstances presented including the factors identified below, Appellant fails to rebut and overcome the presumption that he had no reasonable expectation of privacy in the government computer provided to him for official use. M.R.E. 314(d). There is no evidence Appellant had a subjective expectation of privacy in the government computer, and he did not testify that he did. *See Flores*, 64 M.J. at 454 (factoring into the reasonable expectation of privacy analysis the fact that the accused did not testify on the motion to suppress). Moreover the access to this computer by both Appellant's commander and the system administrator supports the validity of the presumption that he had no reasonable expectation of privacy in the government computer.

Finally, the military judge found as fact that when Appellant used the computer "a banner appeared that state[d] that it was a DOD computer, it [was] for official use, not to be used for illegal activity. [And that] [i]t also had a statement that users of the computer consent to monitoring." This factual finding is supported by the record, is not clearly erroneous and, taking the facts in the light most favorable to the prevailing party, establishes both that Appellant was put on notice that the computer was not to be used for illegal activity and that there could be third-party monitoring.

Appellant argues that this case is controlled by this Court's decision in *United States v. Long*, 64 M.J. 57 (C.A.A.F. 2006), which he claims establishes that he had a reasonable expectation of privacy in his government computer. That reliance is misplaced. We made clear in Long that our decision was rooted in the "particular facts of that case, [and] we conclude[d] that the lower court was not clearly erroneous in its determination that Appellee had a subjective expectation of privacy in the e-mails she sent from her office computer and in the e-mails that were stored on the government server." *Id.* at 63.

The present case is factually distinguishable from *Long*. *Long* rested in large part on the testimony of the command's network administrator: "the testimony of the network administrator [as to the agency practice of recognizing the privacy interests of users in their e-mail] is the most compelling evidence supporting the notion that Appellee had a subjective expectation of privacy." *Id.*

Here, unlike in *Long*, Appellant presented no evidence that he enjoyed an expectation of privacy in materials on his government computer. And, unlike in Long, the testimony of Appellant's commander and the military judge's findings of fact established both monitoring of and command access to the government computer.

Long does not control the decision here, and we agree with the CCA that the military judge did not abuse his discretion in concluding that Appellant had no expectation of privacy in the government computer. *Larson*, 64 M.J. at 563.

II. Appellant's Ineffective Assistance of Counsel Claim

* * *

First, the evidence supporting the charged offenses was overwhelming. The prosecution presented pornographic material taken from Appellant's computer, sexually explicit chat sessions between Appellant and an individual who said she was underage, Appellant's online profile, which included his picture, testimony that showed Appellant was apprehended at a rendezvous based on a meeting set up in the aforementioned chat sessions, and evidence that Appellant had purchased a package of condoms only fifteen minutes before the meeting. Second, no plausible defense to the Article 92, UCMJ, offense of wrongful use of a computer or other offense has been raised by Appellant. Relatedly, Appellant fails to tell us what he would have testified to absent his counsel's comments. Third, Appellant does not argue that his defense at trial to the remaining charges-that he believed he was actually talking to someone of a more appropriate age-was in any way undercut by counsel's strategic choice. And finally, the military judge instructed the members three times that the arguments of counsel were not evidence.

While, post hoc, Appellant may wish that his attorney had engaged in a "useless charade," *United States v. Cronic*, 466 U.S. 648, 656 n. 19 (1984), given the facts of this case we conclude that there was no prejudice stemming from the fact that he did not.

III. Decision

The decision of the United States Air Force Court of Criminal Appeals is affirmed.

[The separate opinion of Chief Judge Effron concurring in the result is omitted.—Eds.]

Points for Discussion

1. What distinction does the *Weston* court make based on the U.S. Supreme Court's decision in *Georgia v. Randolph*, 547 U.S. 103 (2006)? Do you agree with the *Weston* court? Why or why not?

2. In the *Weston* case, if the criminal investigators did not obtain consent from the accused's wife, how else could they have lawfully searched the Westons' on-post house?

3. In *United States v. Long*, 64 M.J. 57 (C.A.A.F. 2006), unlike in *Larson*, the Court of Appeals determined that the appellant established that he had a reasonable expectation of privacy in his government computer. What facts could help prove that an accused had a subjective expectation of privacy in the emails sent from a government office computer?

Military Inspections

Military service members have a different expectation of privacy when commanders perform inspections or inventories. Unlike a search which is designed to obtain evidence for use at trial, the primary purpose of a military inspection is to ensure a unit and its members are fit for duty. Administrative inspections are not based on probable cause and no warrants or authorizations are required because they are not part of a criminal investigative process. Rather, inspections are regulatory and are performed to protect a government interest. The Military Rules of Evidence provide strict guidelines for inspections and illegal items found during a *valid* inspection are admissible evidence at a court-martial or criminal trial.

Similar to other administrative inspections such as those to verify that restaurant owners are complying with fire or health safety codes, military commanders order administrative inspections to fulfill a valid government interest. Commanders have authority to order inspections to ensure military readiness and effectiveness, security, health, welfare, fitness, or good order and discipline.

Military commanders may only order inspections of areas or persons within their command and the inspections cannot be targeted at specific individuals, but should be random. Commanders need not provide notice to the service members prior to the inspection. For example, many Army commanders will order a unit urinalysis inspection following a long weekend or order randomly selected individuals to participate in a urinalysis inspection to ensure the health and safety of unit members. An inspection may also include the purpose of locating weapons and contraband, as this is to ensure unit health and safety as well.

Military Rule of Evidence 313 describes military inventories and inspections as follows.

Military Rule of Evidence 313
Inspections and Inventories in the Armed Forces

(b) *Inspections.* An "inspection" is an examination of the whole or part of a unit, organization, installation, vessel, aircraft, or vehicle . . . conducted as an incident of command the *primary purpose of which is to determine and to ensure the security, military fitness, or good order and discipline of the unit*, organization, installation, vessel, aircraft, or vehicle. An inspection *may include but is not limited to an examination to determine and to ensure that any or all of the following requirements are met: that the command is properly equipped, functioning properly, maintaining proper standards of readiness, sea or air worthiness, sanitation and cleanliness, and that personnel are present, fit, and ready for duty. An inspection also includes an examination to locate and confiscate unlawful weapons and other contraband.* An order to produce body fluids, such as urine, is permissible in accordance with this rule. *An examination made for the primary purpose of obtaining evidence for use in a trial by court-martial or in other disciplinary proceedings is not an inspection within the meaning of this rule. If a purpose of an examination is to locate weapons or contraband, and if: (1) the examination was directed immediately following a report of a specific offense in the unit, organization, installation, vessel, aircraft, or vehicle and was not previously scheduled;*

(2) specific individuals are selected for examination; or (3) persons examined are subjected to substantially different intrusions during the same examination, the prosecution must prove by clear and convincing evidence that the examination was an inspection within the meaning of this rule. [Emphasis added.]

Essentially, if a commander orders an inspection with the primary purpose of establishing and ensuring the unit's security, military fitness, or good order and discipline and evidence is obtained, that evidence may be entered at trial if relevant and otherwise admissible. *Id.*

At trial, the government has an elevated burden of proof for admissibility if a commander uses an inspection as a *subterfuge* to obtain evidence of a criminal offense. As Military Rule of Evidence 313 states, if the purpose of the inspection includes locating weapons or contraband and if: (1) the inspection was not previously scheduled but was ordered immediately after report of an offense in the unit; (2) specific individuals are identified to be included in the inspection; or (3) during the inspection service members are subject to "substantially different intrusions," the government must prove by clear and convincing evidence that it was a *valid* inspection.

UNITED STATES v. CAMPBELL
U.S. Court of Military Appeals
41 M.J. 177 (C.M.A. 1994)

SULLIVAN, Chief Judge:

In October of 1991, appellant [Staff Sergeant Keith W. Campbell, U.S. Army] was tried by a military judge sitting alone as a general court-martial at Fort Bragg, North Carolina. Pursuant to his pleas, he was found guilty of absence without leave (6 days), violating a lawful general regulation (3 specifications), and dishonorable failure to maintain sufficient funds (18 specifications), in violation of Articles 86, 92, and 134, Uniform Code of Military Justice, 10 U.S.C. §§ 886, 892, and 934, respectively. Contrary to his pleas, he was found guilty of wrongful use of cocaine, in violation of Article 112a, UCMJ, 10 U.S.C. § 912a. He was sentenced to a bad-conduct discharge, confinement for 18 months, total forfeitures, and reduction to Private E1. On February 24, 1992, the convening authority approved the sentence as adjudged. On September 30, 1992, the Court of Military Review affirmed these findings of guilty and the sentence.

* * *

We hold that appellant's positive urinalysis test results and his subsequent confessions were improperly admitted in evidence at his court-martial. Mil. R. Evid. 311(a) and (e)(2), Manual for Courts-Martial, United States (1984); *United States v. Johnston,* 24 M.J. 271 (C.M.A. 1987); *United States v. Kaliski,* 37 M.J. 105 (C.M.A. 1993). Furthermore, we hold that appellant was prejudiced by admission of this evidence with respect to his conviction for wrongful use of cocaine. Mil. R. Evid. 103(a). *See generally Arizona v. Fulminante,* 499 U.S. 279 (1991).

The military judge in this case held an evidentiary hearing on a defense motion to suppress government evidence of appellant's positive urinalysis test and his subsequent confessions. Art. 39(a), UCMJ, 10 U.S.C. § 839(a). Defense counsel made the following argument:

> The urinalysis in question, sir, was ordered on the 15th. The primary factor behind this urinalysis was the first sergeant, First Sergeant Sharp of Alpha Company.

> First Sergeant Sharp hears rumors of suspected drug use in the company. He has no other concrete facts, but he does hear rumors. He eventually boils it down to that it is someone or some people in either Headquarters Platoon or 1st Platoon. The first [s]ergeant then takes a look at both platoons, hand-picks those people who he wants to be tested. He does this partially based upon who somebody would have associated with. For instance, somebody in Headquarters Platoon who hangs out with somebody in 1st Platoon would then become, in the first sergeant's eyes, a suspect. He then compiles this list of twelve, fifteen suspects, gives it to the Company Commander, Captain Bangs, and then the test is ordered.

> *There's no independent basis for probable cause.* My interviews with the first sergeant reveal that he did not suspect Sergeant Campbell at all of being involved in drugs. *But still, the way he selected this list is a subterfuge. It certainly was an invalid inspection.* On the fact that it's coming on the heel of rumors makes it highly suspect, Your Honor, and I think it should be suppressed.

(Emphasis added.)

The military judge then prompted defense counsel to state the specific grounds for the defense motion to suppress:

MJ: So, based upon your motion to suppress, your written motion to suppress, and what you've represented here in court today, the basis of your motion is-am I correct-that the urinalysis test that the accused was subjected to on the 15th of May, was not a valid military inspection?

DC: Yes, sir.

MJ: Under M.R.E. [Mil. R. Evid.] 313?

DC: Yes, sir.

MJ: And it was not because it was just a subterfuge for an illegal search.

DC: Yes, sir.

MJ: And it was just a subterfuge because the first sergeant just heard these generalized rumors.

DC: Yes, sir, involving unknown members of certain platoons. Rather than testing Headquarters Platoon entirely or 1st Platoon entirely, he subjectively starts to compile a list of those people who he feels should be tested.

MJ: And it's your further contention then that but for the positive urinalysis test, the accused would never have landed in the CID [Criminal Investigation Command] office on the 5th and 6th of June and would never have rendered statements which were incriminating.

DC: Yes, sir.

MJ: All right, Captain Didier, that's the ground upon which you have to- that's the field of battle, if you will. So, it's now your ball game.

Trial counsel then offered an opening statement:

TC: Your Honor, before I call my first witness, if I may just make a few points on the record.

MJ: Sure.

TC: And that is, yes, we are dealing with a 4th Amendment search here. However, we are also dealing with not magistrates nor law enforcement agencies nor lawyers, we're talking about a command that was trying to be responsive to what was perceived to be a realistic and on going drug problem within the unit. Therefore, we're talking about a more reasonable standard under the 4th Amendment. We're talking about, good faith when *the first sergeant submitted his list to his company commander based on what he thought was probable cause. That, I hope to elicit through the testimony of the company's first sergeant, First Sergeant Sharp. However, be that as it may, if the court finds that there was not probable cause for that particular urinalysis, there are other doctrines which would make the subsequent confessions to CID by the accused admissible. Those are the inevitable discovery rule, and again, the good faith exception.*

The Government's burden of proving the evidence was not obtained- excuse me, that these confessions were not obtained as the result of an unlawful search, is a mere preponderance of the evidence. For that, the government cites [Mil. R. Evid.] 311(e)(1) and (2).

(Emphasis added.) Later he impliedly suggested that the challenged urinalysis might be upheld as a valid inspection under Mil. R. Evid. 313(b).

As its first witness, and the only witness to testify to the circumstances leading to the command-directed urinalysis, the prosecution called appellant's first sergeant, First Sergeant (1SG) Sharp. 1SG Sharp testified that "there were rumors that there were drugs being used, consumed and distributed within the barracks." He further testified that he had been specifically informed by one soldier in his command, Sergeant (SGT) Rouse, that the drug problem was in the Headquarters and 1st Platoons. 1SG Sharp testified, "I was looking at every soldier in the headquarters element and trying to figure out who was actually dealing with guys in the 1st Platoon or what guys in the 1st Platoon were interacting with guys in Headquarters Platoon." 1SG Sharp stated that appellant associated with a soldier, SGT Anderson, who "had previously come up hot" on a urinalysis. Prior to appellant's urinalysis, 1SG Sharp observed appellant in the presence of SGT Anderson, and he characterized their presence in the barracks area as "suspicious." Finally, when asked by trial counsel if he had "probable cause to conduct the urinalysis," 1SG Sharp responded, "Yes, sir. The indication was that we already had a guy that came up positive on a urinalysis and that my concern was the health and welfare of the soldiers that are in the unit."

During questioning by the military judge, 1SG Sharp testified that he had specifically asked SGT Rouse to identify those soldiers who SGT Rouse knew were using drugs. 1SG Sharp told the military judge that when SGT Rouse declined to provide that information, 1SG Sharp stated to SGT Rouse, "Just kind of give me an idea of which platoon I should be looking at." Prior to questioning SGT Rouse, 1SG Sharp "read him his rights so there wouldn't be any violation of his rights, and began to ask him questions." The first sergeant also questioned another soldier, Private First Class (PFC) Gochenaur, after reading him his rights. The first sergeant decided to take PFC Gochenaur's name off the list because he was personally "satisfied" with PFC Gochenaur's answers during the interview. Finally, when asked by the military judge who ordered the urinalysis, 1SG Sharp responded, "The company commander, sir. I advised him. He directed it."

The military judge denied the defense motion to suppress the results of the urinalysis and any evidence derived from that scientific test. He made the following findings regarding the command-directed urinalysis:

> First, that one of the purposes of the first sergeant and the CO [commanding officer] in conducting a urinalysis in this case, was to locate and detect contraband in the form of illegal drugs in the unit.

> Secondly, that in the process of conducting this urinalysis, there were two elements in the unit in which illegal drug activity was reasonably suspected to be occurring and these two elements, Headquarters and 1st Platoon, consisted of about 52 soldiers, and of these 52 soldiers, about 20 or 38 percent were selected to undergo urinalysis. Though this is a substantial portion of those unit elements, nevertheless, specific individuals were selected for urinalysis, and thus, I believe the standard of proof that the Government must meet in this case of clear and convincing evidence is triggered, as opposed to preponderance of the evidence.

> I further find that First Sergeant Sharp and the unit CO had a reasonable basis for believing that there was contraband in the form of illegal drugs in the unit. I find that on the date of the urinalysis in question, the CO and the first sergeant had no suspicion whatsoever that the accused was in any way involved with illegal drugs.

> I also find that on the date of the urinalysis in question, neither the first sergeant or [sic] the CO were looking for any particular individual in

the unit whom they suspected of involvement with illegal drugs, and I further find that they did not, in fact, suspect any particular individual, including the accused, as being involved with illegal drugs.

I also find that the accused was not selected out to be subjected to any increased examination or any closer scrutiny than anyone else required to undergo urinalysis.

I also find that the sole basis of the first sergeant for recommending and of the CO for directing that a health and welfare inspection urinalysis be conducted, was to ensure the unit was free of illegal contraband and to ensure that the unit was prepared to perform its mission.

Based on those findings-I also find that the urinalysis in question was not conducted following any report of any specific offense.

Therefore, *I find by clear and convincing evidence, that the urinalysis in question, the inspection in question in the form of a urinalysis was not a subterfuge for a search for criminal evidence, but rather was a valid health and welfare inspection to ensure that the unit was prepared to perform its mission by being free of illegal drugs.* Therefore, I deny the defense motion.

(Emphasis added.)

The Court of Military Review affirmed the decision of the judge below. It said:

The determination whether an inspection is for legitimate administrative decisions versus a search to discover evidence to be used in disciplinary proceedings is a factual question to be resolved by the military judge. *United States v. Barnett,* 18 M.J. 166 (C.M.A. 1984); *United States v. Austin,* 21 M.J. 592 (ACMR 1985). Reviewing the military judge's findings of fact with our "awesome, plenary, de novo power of review" pursuant to Article 66, UCMJ, we find that the military judge correctly found that the government established by clear and convincing evidence that the urinalysis was an inspection and not a subterfuge for a search. Accordingly, we hold that the results of the urinalysis was [sic] properly admitted at trial.

Unpub. op. at 3.

I
INVALID INSPECTION

Mil. R. Evid. 313(b) provides, in pertinent part, that "an 'inspection' is an examination of the whole or part of a unit, . . . conducted as an incident of command *the primary purpose of which* is to determine and to ensure the security, military fitness, or good order and discipline of the unit. . . ." (Emphasis added.) It also states that "an order to produce body fluids, such as urine, is permissible in accordance with this rule." . . . In accord, Mil. R. Evid. 313(b) provides that a urinalysis conducted "for the primary purpose of obtaining evidence for use in a trial by court-martial" or in an "[un]reasonable fashion," is "not an inspection within the meaning of this rule." *See also New York v. Burger,* 482 U.S. 691, 716 n. 27 (1987).

Mil. R. Evid. 313(b) expressly permits inspections to "locate . . . unlawful weapons and other contraband." However, if "specific individuals are selected for examination," Mil. R. Evid. 313(b) requires a showing "by clear and convincing evidence that the examination was an inspection" and not conducted for the primary purpose of "obtain[ing] a criminal conviction." *United States v. Bickel,* 30 M.J. 277, 286 (C.M.A. 1990). In *Bickel* this Court also stated

> that neither Mil. R. Evid. 313 nor the Fourth Amendment permits a military commander to pick and choose the members of his unit who will be tested for drugs and then to use the resulting evidence to obtain a criminal conviction. Instead, *the testing must be performed on a nondiscriminatory basis* pursuant to an established policy or guideline that will eliminate the opportunity for arbitrariness by the person performing the tests. *Cf. Florida v. Wells,* 495 U.S. 1 (1990).

30 M.J. at 286 (emphasis added). Proof of selection based on standard criteria or routine practice is well recognized as clear and convincing evidence that the persons inspected were not principally chosen on the basis of suspicion of criminal activity amounting to less than probable cause. *See United States v. Konieczka,* 31 M.J. 289, 291 (C.M.A. 1990); *United States v. Johnston, supra* at 275; *cf. United States v. Flowers,* 26 M.J. 463 (C.M.A. 1988). *See generally Florida v. Wells,* 495 U.S. at 3-4; *Colorado v. Bertine,* 479 U.S. 367, 373, 375-76 (1987).

In the case *sub judice,* trial counsel conceded the weakness of his valid inspection argument, and we agree. There was no evidence whatsoever that 1SG Sharp used anything but his suspicion of criminal activity to select appellant for this urinalysis test. *See Florida v. Wells, supra.* As noted above, 1SG Sharp testified that he began compiling a list of soldiers to be tested after SGT Rouse informed him of a "drug problem" in the Headquarters and 1st Platoons. Appellant was assigned to 1st Platoon. 1SG Sharp also had information that SGT Anderson, a soldier in Headquarters Platoon, had recently tested positive on a urinalysis. Furthermore, he testified that on one occasion he observed appellant "associat[ing]" with SGT Anderson in the vicinity of the barracks and opined that it "looked suspicious." Finally, while he was compiling the list of names to present to the unit commander for urinalysis, 1SG Sharp found it necessary to advise two soldiers, SGT Rouse and PFC Gochenaur, of their "rights, and began to ask [them] questions." In such circumstances, we conclude that the military judge legally erred in holding the challenged urinalysis was shown by clear and convincing evidence to be a valid "inspection" within the meaning of Mil. R. Evid. 313(b). *See United States v. Thatcher,* 28 M.J. 20, 25 (C.M.A. 1989); *see also United States v. Konieczka, supra* at 297; *cf. United States v. Barnett,* 18 M.J. 166, 171 (C.M.A. 1984); *United States v. Johnston, supra.*

II
INSUFFICIENT PROBABLE CAUSE SEARCH

Trial counsel somewhat more enthusiastically argued that 1SG Sharp had probable cause to advise the company commander to direct the challenged urinalysis of appellant. *See* Mil. R. Evid. 315; *Murray v. Haldeman,* 16 M.J. 74 (C.M.A. 1983), *cited in* Drafters' Analysis of Mil. R. Evid. 312(d), Manual, *supra* at A22-19. In this regard, he elicited testimony from 1SG Sharp that he believed that he had probable cause to conduct the urinalysis or more accurately to advise the commander to direct the urinalysis.

The military judge did not make a finding on probable cause, and the Court of Military Review did not address this issue in its opinion. Moreover, before this Court, the Government has not taken the position that the challenged urinalysis could be lawfully justified on this basis. Nevertheless, our conclusion that the command-directed urinalysis was not shown to be a Mil. R. Evid. 313(b) inspection requires a brief comment on whether it could lawfully be justified as a search based on probable cause. . . .

This Court recently set forth the framework in which to review a search authorization based on probable cause. *United States v. Figueroa,* 35 M.J. 54 (C.M.A. 1992), *cert. denied,* 507 U.S. 910 (1993). In the context of a search of an accused's quarters, Judge Gierke wrote:

> Mil. R. Evid. 315(f)(2), Manual for Courts-Martial, United States, 1984, provides, "Probable cause to search exists when there is a reasonable belief that the person, property, or evidence sought is located in the place [or on the person] to be searched." In determining whether the base commander had probable cause to authorize the search of appellant's quarters, the question is "whether, given all the circumstances set forth in the affidavit before him, . . . a fair probability" exists that the weapons would be found in appellant's quarters. . . .

35 M.J. at 55-56 (footnote omitted).

Examination of the record in this case fails to meet the above standard. A bald assertion of probable cause, of course, is not sufficient to meet this test. Moreover, a general suspicion of criminal activity based on an unspecific hearsay report coupled with speculation based on association with known criminal offenders is also an insufficient basis to establish probable cause. . . . Therefore, the urinalysis test in this case and evidence of its results should not have been admitted at appellant's court-martial. Mil. R. Evid. 315(a), and 311(a) and (b)(3).[2]

---

[2] The challenged urinalysis in this case was ordered by appellant's company commander on the advice of 1SG Sharp. Our conclusion that 1SG Sharp had no substantial basis for finding probable cause applies as well to the commander he advised. Accordingly, the good-faith exception did not apply, *see* Mil.R.Evid. 311(b)(3)(B).

III
ILLEGALLY-DERIVED CONFESSION

The next question we must address is whether the illegality of the urinalysis under Mil. R. Evid. 313(b) also precludes admission of appellant's statements to CID on June 5 and 6, 1991. Mil. R. Evid. 311(a) generally prohibits admission of "evidence obtained as a result of an unlawful search and seizure. . . ." Mil. R. Evid. 311(e)(2) further makes clear that this prohibition also applies to evidence derived from an unlawful search.

* * *

Trial counsel and appellate government counsel both argued that any possible taint from the urinalysis in this case was attenuated by the time appellant made his pretrial confessions. Trial counsel articulated his reasoning as follows:

> The long and short of it, Your Honor, is that when the accused came in for his interview some approximately twenty days after the urinalysis, he had the opportunity to decline to be interviewed. Nonetheless, he gave intelligent, knowing and free waiver and confessed to CID. In addition, this accused, this Sergeant, E-5, with a GT score of 118, he had approximately twenty days to figure out some way of reducing his potential liability or criminal culpability. He could have conferred with counsel, he could have taken the time to reflect on the possible legal consequences of the test or to take any other steps necessary to protect his interests. He did not. Any possible taint is therefore attenuated.

Government appellate counsel echoed this argument as follows:

> Appellant's confession took place during a routine interview by law enforcement agents following up his positive urinalysis (R. 48-49, 62). Appellant cooperated with law enforcement agents, and returned the next day to execute another statement (P.E. 4). Appellant's confession was preceded by a complete rights warning, and took place 20 days after the urinalysis (*id.*). This voluntary confession was sufficiently attenuated from the urinalysis such that it was not the product of any alleged illegal government conduct. . . .

Answer to Final Brief at 10.

The military judge issued no ruling on this government argument since he denied the defense suppression motion on other grounds. The Court of Military Review likewise eschewed a decision on this question. For ourselves, we are not persuaded by it. In this regard, we note that the urinalysis results were delivered to appellant on June 5, 1991, the day he made his initial confession. In addition, we note that he was directed to bring the form notifying him of the positive results to the CID office on June 5, 1991. Finally, it was uncontroverted that the positive results of the challenged urinalysis were the sole basis for appellant's questioning by the military police investigator on June 5, 1991. In these circumstances, the prosecution has not shown by a preponderance of evidence that appellant's confessions were not obtained as a result of the challenged urinalysis. Mil. R. Evid. 311(e)(2). *Cf. United States v. Marquardt,* 39 M.J. 239 (C.M.A. 1994); *United States v. Phillips,* 32 M.J. 76, 80-82 (C.M.A. 1991). *See also* Mil. R. Evid. 311(e)(1).

IV
INEVITABLE DISCOVERY

Trial counsel next argued that appellant's confessions, even if derived from the positive urinalysis test, were admissible under the inevitable discovery rule. *See* Mil. R. Evid. 311(b)(2) and (e)(2); *Nix v. Williams,* 467 U.S. 431 (1984); *United States v. Kozak,* 12 M.J. 389 (C.M.A. 1982). Trial counsel presented one witness, Military Police Investigator Leiser, to offer testimonial evidence in support of this government theory. In addition, both parties stipulated to the expected testimony of Investigator Broker, the military police investigator who interviewed appellant about the wrongful-use-of-cocaine charge.

Investigator Leiser testified during direct examination that he interrogated Specialist (SPC) McGee who also had tested positive on the urinalysis earlier discussed in this case. SPC McGee informed Investigator Leiser that he had smoked crack cocaine with appellant three or four times at SPC McGee's home. In response to questioning by the military judge, Investigator Leiser testified that he reviewed SPC McGee's statement "two or three times until we get it straight" and then he informed Investigator Broker of SPC McGee's accusations about appellant.

In the stipulation of expected testimony, then-Investigator Broker states that "[o]ur office had not previously suspected SGT Campbell of being involved with cocaine or any other type of drug. I interviewed him solely because he was reported to have come up positive in an urinalysis." Broker states that, after "explain[ing] his rights to" appellant, he used a "question and answer" format during the interrogation. The questions and answers were typed on Department of the Army Form 2823, Sworn Statement, and signed by appellant. After asking appellant if he understood his "legal rights," the very first question appears to be "[h]ave you ever used controlled substances while in the military?" Appellant responded, "Yes." There was no evidence that suggests appellant knew of SPC McGee's implicating statements about alleged communal use or distribution of cocaine.

The military judge made the following findings regarding the inevitable discovery of appellant's statements based on SPC McGee's statements to Investigator Leiser:

> *I also find that the Government would have inevitably focused upon the accused as a suspect as a result of the statement given by a Specialist McGee to CID.* And I find that as a result of that statement, the Government would have clearly had probable cause to direct this specific accused undergo a urinalysis and would have clearly had reasonable basis for bringing the accused in for questioning. *Whether or not the accused*

would have made a statement or not, that's a bit of speculation, but I do find by clear and convincing evidence that the statement by Specialist McGee would have inevitably lead the Government to focus on Sergeant Campbell as a suspect in a criminal investigation.

(Emphasis added.)

This Court reviews the military judge's determination of inevitable discovery for abuse of discretion. *United States v. Kaliski,* 37 M.J. 105, 109 (C.M.A. 1993). An abuse of discretion occurs

if the findings of fact upon which he predicates his ruling are not supported by evidence of record; *if incorrect legal principles were used by him in deciding this motion;* or if his application of the correct legal principles to the facts of a particular case is clearly unreasonable. . . .

Here, the judge's ruling was premised on an incorrect legal principle. . .

In the case *sub judice,* the military judge stated that, based on the evidence presented, it would have been "a bit of speculation" to find that appellant would have made a statement to CID solely because of the statement given by SPC McGee and in the absence of positive results on the urinalysis. Instead, he found only that appellant's identity as a suspect would inevitably have been discovered. This, alone, is not enough to lawfully conclude that appellant's confession would inevitably have been procured. *Cf. United States v. Kaliski,* 37 M.J. at 109.

V

HARMLESS ERROR

Appellant's conviction for using cocaine was based on evidence of a positive urinalysis, his own subsequent confessions, and testimony of an accomplice, SPC McGee. This Court has previously concluded that the urinalysis evidence and appellant's confessions were improperly admitted at his court-martial.[3] A remaining question is whether the findings of guilty to cocaine use can still be affirmed on the basis of harmless error. Mil. R. Evid. 103(a). *See Arizona v. Fulminante,* 499 U.S. 279 (1991). We think not.

The testimony of SPC McGee was offered for the purpose of proving that appellant both distributed cocaine to him in March 1991 and wrongfully used cocaine with him sometime in May 1991. The distribution of cocaine in March 1991 was the basis for specification 2 of Charge III, and SPC McGee's testimony was the only evidence offered by the prosecution against appellant for that specification. SPC McGee testified on direct examination that he and

---

[3] The challenged confessions in this case were taken by military police agents as a result of the inadmissible urinalysis results. Trial counsel, relying on Mil.R.Evid. 311(e)(2), also argued that the "good faith" exception applied to the interrogation leading to appellant's confession. However, the military police investigator did not rely on issuance of a search authorization to interrogate appellant. Mil.R.Evid. 311(b)(3)(A).

appellant smoked what SPC McGee believed was crack cocaine. During examination by defense counsel, SPC McGee testified that he had never "actually done crack cocaine" before, never held or touched cocaine before, "never smelled crack cocaine before," never saw "anyone high on cocaine before," and never saw it smoked from a beer can as he testified that he and appellant had smoked it. SPC McGee also testified that the smoked substance did not have any effect on him either in March or May; he never discussed drugs with appellant before, during, or after the March and May incidents; and appellant appeared and acted "the way he was acting before he inhaled this from the can." *The military judge entered a finding of not guilty to the distribution charge.*

This Court has previously upheld use of lay-witness testimony to express an opinion about the identity of a particular substance alleged to be a controlled substance. *United States v. Day,* 20 M.J. 213 (C.M.A. 1985). However, unlike the lay witness who testified to the identity of hashish in *Day,* SPC McGee had practically no experience with use or distribution of cocaine. We have doubts whether such uninformed lay testimony by itself is "legal and competent evidence from which a court-martial may find or infer beyond a reasonable doubt . . ." that appellant used cocaine in May of 1991. *United States v. Harper,* 22 M.J. 157, 161 (C.M.A. 1986); *cf. United States v. Tyler,* 17 M.J. 381 (C.M.A. 1984). In any event, it surely is not the type of evidence to persuade us that erroneous admission of the positive urinalysis evidence and appellant's confession on this charge was harmless error.

VI
DECISION

The decision of the United States Army Court of Military Review is reversed as to specification 1 of Charge III. The findings of guilty thereon are set aside and that specification and Charge are dismissed. The record of trial is returned to the Judge Advocate General of the Army for remand to that court for reassessment of the sentence based on the remaining findings of guilty.

Judges WISS and GIERKE concurring. Judge CRAWFORD concurring in the result. Judge COX dissenting.

Points for Discussion

1. Why does it matter that a commander uses an "inspection" as a subterfuge to obtain evidence of a criminal offense? What if a commander orders a valid health and welfare inspection of his unit and then discovers evidence of a crime, why should that evidence be admissible at trial? Should the same subterfuge rule apply to urinalysis testing as inspections?

2. In the *Campbell* case, what is the prosecutor's best argument for admissibility of the evidence?

4-4. Immunity: Testimonial, Transactional, *De Facto*

In many cases, successful prosecution depends on the testimony of service members who may also be possible subjects of criminal prosecution. The general court-martial convening authority may grant immunity to those possible subjects to secure their testimony at trial. Pursuant to R.C.M. 704, a general court-martial convening authority may grant *transactional immunity* from trial by court-martial for UCMJ offenses or may grant *testimonial immunity* ("use immunity") which ensures the witness that his or her testimony, statements, or other information derived there from, will not be used at trial by court-martial. The latter is more beneficial to the government because the person may still be prosecuted for the underlying offenses for which his or her testimony or information is provided under the grant of immunity. In any case, the R.C.M. 704 discussion points out immunity should only be granted "when testimony or other information from the person is necessary to the public interest, including the needs of good order and discipline, and when the person has refused or is likely to refuse to testify or provide other information on the basis of the privilege against self-incrimination."

Persons who testify under grants of testimonial immunity may still be prosecuted for the underlying offense, or for perjury, false swearing, making a false official statement, or failing to comply with the order to provide immunized testimony. If the government prosecutes a person who was promised testimonial immunity after that person testifies or provides information, the government must show that it has not used any of the person's testimony, statements or any information derived there from. This high burden on the government may make subsequent prosecution difficult. To protect government records and ensure the government can meet its burden, the government may try the person promised testimonial immunity first or may just screen the information from the trial team, seal the information, and ensure the record indicates that the prosecution did not have access to the immunized testimony. The government should decide to prosecute before the person provides the immunized testimony or show by a preponderance of the evidence that the immunized testimony did not influence the government's decision to prosecute. *Kastigar v. United States*, 406 U.S. 441 (1972).

The general court-martial convening authority is the only person authorized to grant immunity* but in some cases persons subject to the Code may appear to have apparent authority. Consequently, although not

___

* A general court-martial convening authority may grant immunity to persons subject to the Code, but must obtain approval from the attorney general to obtain immunity for other persons who may be prosecuted in U.S. District Court. R.C.M. 704(c)(1). If a general court-martial convening authority denies a defense request for witness immunity, the defense may make a motion to the military judge for appropriate relief and the military judge may either direct the convening authority to grant immunity or may grant testimonial immunity to the defense witness as to certain charges and specifications. R.C.M. 704(e).

authorized to grant immunity, such conduct may result in providing "de facto immunity." Persons such as investigators or prosecutors may inadvertently grant *de facto* immunity when their conduct provides the impression that they have apparent authority to grant immunity, manifested by making representations to subjects who may honestly and reasonably believe they will not be prosecuted if they do what is requested of them. It is especially problematic for the government if a subject detrimentally relies on representations prosecutors or investigators make. *See Cooke v. Orson*, 12 M.J. 335 (C.M.A. 1982) (court-martial of accused not allowed after staff judge advocate created a reasonable expectation that if accused satisfactorily cooperated with command in matters concerning national security, there would be no prosecution).

UNITED STATES v. OLIVERO
U.S. Court of Military Appeals
39 M.J. 246 (C.M.A. 1994)

GIERKE, Judge:

A military judge sitting as a special court-martial convicted appellant [Staff Sergeant Robert D. Olivero, U.S. Air Force] contrary to his pleas, of using marijuana and committing perjury, in violation of Articles 112a and 131, Uniform Code of Military Justice, 10 U.S.C. §§ 912a and 931, respectively. The approved sentence provides for a bad-conduct discharge, confinement for 4 months, reduction to the lowest enlisted grade, and a reprimand. The Court of Military Review affirmed the findings and sentence in an unpublished opinion.

* * *

Factual Background

The charges in this case arose out of a drug investigation in which Technical Sergeant (TSgt) Terry Stuart was a subject. As a part of that investigation, Captain Humphrey, Chief of Military Justice at March Air Force Base, California, interviewed TSgt Stuart's wife in June 1990. Mrs. Stuart told Capt. Humphrey that she had "used marijuana with" appellant. Because Mrs. Stuart also said that appellant was "a possible person using marijuana with her husband," Capt. Humphrey requested immunity for appellant as "a potential witness against" TSgt Stuart. Capt. Humphrey made no notes of this interview with Mrs. Stuart, and Mrs. Stuart's statement was never reduced to writing.

On August 1, 1990, the general court-martial convening authority gave appellant testimonial immunity regarding his knowledge of TSgt Stuart's use of controlled substances. The Government did not certify, seal, or memorialize any evidence of appellant's drug use prior to this grant.

On August 2, 1990, Capt. Humphrey gave appellant a copy of the written grant of immunity and order to testify, told him to read it carefully and then left him alone in the room so that he could consult with his lawyer by telephone. After "quite a long time," appellant informed Capt. Humphrey that he had consulted with his lawyer and asked if he could have a few minutes alone, and Capt. Humphrey agreed. After a 5-10 minute break, she met again with him and asked if he understood the grant of immunity. While he said he did, she explained what immunity meant and informed appellant that he could be prosecuted for perjury if he lied.

Capt. Humphrey then proceeded to interview appellant, who described two specific instances in which he had used marijuana with TSgt Stuart, one in March 1990 and a second at the end of May or beginning of June 1990. Appellant said that in both instances he and TSgt Stuart smoked the marijuana while riding off-base in TSgt Stuart's car. At Capt. Humphrey's request, Capt. Hamstra-Havermann of the base legal office witnessed the interview. At the end of the interview, appellant asked Capt. Humphrey what was going to happen to him, and she responded that she could not "make any promises."

The investigation under Article 32, UCMJ, 10 U.S.C. § 832, into the charges against TSgt Stuart convened on August 3, with Capt. Humphrey as the government representative. Contrary to his oral, unsworn statement on the previous day, appellant testified under oath at the Article 32 investigation that he had never used marijuana with TSgt Stuart.

The formal charges against appellant were not preferred until August 16, 1990. On that date appellant was charged with use of marijuana, apparently on the basis of Mrs. Stuart's statement to Capt. Humphrey that she had used marijuana with appellant on one occasion. The perjury charge was based on appellant's testimony at TSgt Stuart's Article 32 investigation, in which he denied ever using marijuana with TSgt Stuart.

At a conference pursuant to RCM 802, Manual for Courts-Martial, United States, 1984, on the day before appellant's court-martial convened, defense counsel presented the military judge with a motion to dismiss Charge I and its specification (use of marijuana), based on the Government's improper use of immunized testimony, and citing *Kastigar v. United States*, 406 U.S. 441 (1972). In his written motion to dismiss, defense counsel's offer of proof included the following assertions:

> Prior to the accused's testimony at the Article 32 in the Stuart case, *a decision to prosecute the accused had not been made*. No evidence was cataloged or sealed in preparation for the accused's prosecution prior to his immunized statements. Capt. Humphries [sic] did not make any notes, nor a memo of record of her interview with Deidre Stuart. Miss Regina Taylor [a potential witness to appellant's use of marijuana with Mrs. Stuart] had not been located and contacted by the Government until after the accused's immunized statements. . . .

(Emphasis added.)

When the court-martial convened, the military judge announced that he "would reserve ruling on the motion" to dismiss until after presentation of the prosecution case on the merits.

During the trial on the merits, Capt. Humphrey testified that she "didn't catalog any evidence or certify any evidence in preparation for the prosecution of" appellant. Mrs. Stuart's oral statement to Capt. Humphrey was not reduced to writing prior to her testimony at the Article 32 investigation. When appellant's defense counsel asked Capt. Humphrey if, prior to the Article 32 investigation in TSgt Stuart's case, there had been a decision whether to prosecute appellant, she responded, "I guess, I don't understand your question." No other evidence regarding the timing of the decision to prosecute appellant was presented by either side. Appellant's offer of proof in support of his motion to dismiss was unchallenged by the prosecution.

Mrs. Stuart testified that appellant used marijuana with her and another woman on one occasion in August or September 1989. She also testified that, on another occasion, she came to her house, smelled marijuana smoke, and saw the remains of a marijuana cigarette. TSgt Stuart was in the house with appellant at the time. When Mrs. Stuart asked, " 'Where is mine?,' " TSgt Stuart said, "[T]hat's all we had." Mrs. Stuart did not actually see either appellant or TSgt Stuart smoking marijuana.

At the close of the prosecution case, defense counsel renewed the motion to dismiss Charge I and its specification, specifically arguing that prosecutorial misuse of immunized testimony "could include assistance in focusing the investigation, deciding to prosecute, refusing to plea bargain, interpreting the evidence, planning cross-examination, and planning trial strategy." (Emphasis added.) This language was taken almost verbatim from *United States v. McDaniel*, 482 F.2d 305, 311 (8th Cir. 1973).

The military judge denied the motion, finding "that the sole evidence" of appellant's use of marijuana was the testimony of Mrs. Stuart, who had provided evidence of appellant's marijuana use "well before the issuance of the grant of immunity." Although the issue was squarely raised by defense counsel, neither the military judge nor the Court of Military Review ruled specifically on the failure of the Government to show that the decision to prosecute was unaffected by appellant's immunized testimony at the Article 32 investigation.

Use of Immunized Testimony (Issue I)

In *Kastigar v. United States*, 406 U.S. 441 (1972), the Supreme Court held that prosecutorial authorities are prohibited from using testimony which is compelled by grants of immunity. In *United States v. Kimble*, 33 M.J. 284 (1991), this Court held that immunity protection extends to nonevidentiary uses of immunized statements such as the decision to initiate prosecution. *Id.* at 291. In such cases, prosecution may only proceed "if the Government shows, by a preponderance of the evidence, that the . . . decision to prosecute was untainted by" the immunized witness' testimony. *See Cunningham v. Gilevich*, 36 M.J. 94, 102 (C.M.A. 1992); *United States v. North*, 910 F.2d 843, 856-60 (D.C. Cir.) (discussion of nonevidentiary use of immunized testimony), modified in part, 920 F.2d 940 (1990), cert. denied, 500 U.S. 941 (1991); *see also United States v. Harris*, 973 F.2d 333, 336 (4th Cir. 1992) (Government may not alter investigative strategy as result of immunized statement).[1]

We recognize that the federal circuits are divided on the question "whether *Kastigar* permits . . . 'nonevidentiary use of immunized testimony.'" *See United States v. Harris*, 973 F.2d at 337 n. 2; *United States v. North*, 910 F.2d at 856-60. Nevertheless, after Cunningham and Kimble, military law is clear: the Government may not prosecute unless it can show, by a preponderance of the evidence, that the prosecutorial decision was untainted by the immunized testimony.

The record in appellant's case is devoid of any evidence that there was a decision to prosecute appellant before his compelled and allegedly perjured testimony on August 3. The Government concedes that "[i]t is unclear from the record when the decision to prosecute appellant was made." Answer to Final Brief at 3. Had the Government decided to prosecute appellant prior to his immunized testimony, it would be obvious that the prosecutorial decision was independent of his testimony.

Because the Government was unable to show that the prosecutorial decision was made before the immunized testimony, it had the burden of showing by a preponderance of the evidence that the prosecutorial decision was untainted by the immunized testimony. . . . Accordingly, appellant's conviction of wrongful use of marijuana cannot stand unless the Government established, by a preponderance of the evidence, that the decision to prosecute appellant was independent of his compelled testimony at the Stuart Article 32 investigation. *Cunningham v. Gilevich* and *United States v. Kimble*, both *supra*.

In this case the issue was squarely raised by defense counsel. The Government introduced evidence that Mrs. Stuart's testimony against appellant was obtained prior to and independent of appellant's compelled testimony, but they failed to show that the decision to prosecute was untainted by appellant's compelled testimony at the Stuart Article 32 hearing. In fact, all the evidence indicates the contrary: appellant was prosecuted because of what he said at the Article 32 hearing.

In *Cunningham v. Gilevich, supra*, we remanded the case to the convening authority and authorized a *Kastigar* hearing on the specific issue whether the decision to prosecute was tainted by compelled testimony. In appellant's case,

---

[1] Judge Crawford correctly observes in her dissent (39 M.J. at 251) that appellant was not charged with using marijuana with TSgt Stuart in 1990, but with using marijuana with Mrs. Stuart in 1989.

the military judge has already held the required trial-level *Kastigar* hearing. The issue of a tainted prosecutorial decision was squarely raised by defense counsel, but the Government did not carry its burden of proof. *See United States v. Kimble, 33 M.J. at 291* (Government did not demonstrate that decision to prosecute was not based on compelled testimony); *United States v. Poindexter*, 951 F.2d 369, 375 (DC Cir. 1991) (Remand for further hearing "would be pointless" where Government "neither met [its] burden of proof nor indicated that there might be any additional evidence ... to meet that burden."), cert. denied, 506 U.S. 1021 (1992). Accordingly, we must reverse the decision below as to appellant's conviction of Charge I and its specification. [5]

* * *

The decision of the United States Air Force Court of Military Review is reversed. The findings of guilty and the sentence are set aside. The charges and specifications are dismissed.

Chief Judge SULLIVAN and Judges COX and WISS concur.

Judge CRAWFORD dissenting.

Points for Discussion

1. Why should the general court-martial convening authority be the only one authorized to grant immunity? Shouldn't the criminal investigators have that authority as well?

2. Why do we need testimonial and transactional immunity?

---

[5] Our decision does not disturb the military judge's ruling with respect to evidentiary use of the immunized testimony. Our decision turns on the non-evidentiary use, which was expressly raised by defense counsel's motion but not expressly ruled on by the military judge.

CHAPTER 5

PRETRIAL PROCEDURAL REQUIREMENTS

5-1. Preferral and Forwarding of Charges

If an immediate commander (i.e., company commander) decides to initiate the court-martial process in lieu of taking administrative action or some lesser form of disposition, the commander may prefer charges against a military accused and forward the case with a recommendation as to disposition to a superior commander. (In some cases, a superior commander may withhold disposition authority over certain types of offenses or cases involving offenses allegedly committed by individuals of certain ranks, or specific cases as they occur.) Any person subject to the UCMJ may prefer charges and initiate the court-martial process. Preferral entails merely signing the charge sheet under oath. The person signing swears that he has personal knowledge of or that he has investigated the matters in the charges and that he believes that the matters set forth therein are true to the best of his knowledge or belief.

Once preferral occurs, the accused's immediate commander (who is unlikely to be authorized to convene a court-martial) may choose to dismiss the charges. But in a typical case, the immediate commander will forward the case to a commander who is authorized to convene a court-martial. This "convening authority" is in a position to refer a case to trial by virtue of his position and rank. Commanders, depending on their rank and position, are empowered to convene or refer a case to trial by summary court-martial, special court-martial, or general court-martial. If a convening authority receives a charge sheet, he or she may dismiss the charges, forward the case to a higher commander, appoint an Article 32 Investigating Officer (required prior to a general court-martial) or refer the case to a court-martial at the level of court-martial to which that convening authority has the power to convene. *See* R.C.M. 401 and 404(d).

As the case that follows illustrates, the convening authority must act without bias or prejudice. Acting as an accuser by preferring charges reflects partiality. A convening authority who is an accuser must not refer the case to trial. Art. 22 and 23, UCMJ; R.C.M. 601(c). Participating in the case as an accuser causes the convening authority to be disqualified from referring the case to a court-martial, but the convening authority is not disqualified from administratively disposing of the case. If the convening authority is partial or has a personal interest in the case, he should not participate in processing the case by providing a recommendation or perform functions as a convening authority. The *Nix* case which follows involves a special court-martial convening authority who did not disqualify himself from acting on a case. Rather, the commander obtained the report of investigation from the Article 32 investigating officer and then forwarded the case with a recommendation as to disposition, thereby performing his responsibilities as the special court-martial convening authority.

The *Manual for Courts-Martial* prohibits a convening authority who acts as accuser from referring the case, but not from forwarding the case with a recommendation as to disposition. A convening authority who merely signs the charge sheet and is "technically" an accuser may forward the case with a recommendation as to disposition only if the convening authority has remained impartial.* The key to determining "impartiality" rests with whether the convening authority maintains an official interest in the case.

UNITED STATES v. NIX
U.S. Court of Military Appeals
40 M.J. 6 (C.M.A. 1994)

COX, Judge:

Appellant [Aviation Fire Control Technician Second Class William E. Nix, U.S. Navy] stands convicted of wrongfully socializing with students while he was an instructor, maltreating a subordinate, wrongfully using marijuana, and committing consensual sodomy.[1]

On appeal, appellant complains that referral of the charges against him was tainted by the vindictive motives of his commanding officer, who was the special court-martial (SPCM) convening authority. We granted review of the following issue:

WHETHER AN OFFICER WITH AN OTHER-THAN-OFFICIAL INTEREST IN A CASE MAY MAKE THE DISCRETIONARY DECISION TO ORDER A PRETRIAL INVESTIGATION OF THE CHARGES AND THEN OFFICIALLY RECOMMEND THAT THE CHARGES BE REFERRED TO A GENERAL COURT-MARTIAL.

---

* This is the conclusion the Army Court of Criminal Appeals draws in *McKinney v. Jarvis*, 46 M.J. 870 (A.C.C.A. 1997), which appears in Chapter 7, Pretrial Motions and Interlocutory Appeals.

[1] On July 8-9, 1991, appellant was tried by general court-martial before a military judge alone. Following mixed pleas, he was convicted of one specification which consolidated the 7 specifications referred to trial of wrongfully socializing with students while he was an instructor; 2 specifications of maltreating a subordinate consolidated into one; wrongfully using marijuana and sodomy (2 specifications each), in violation of Articles 92, 112a, 125, and 128, Uniform Code of Military Justice, 10 U.S.C. §§ 892, 912a, 925, and 928, respectively. He was sentenced to confinement for 8 months, total forfeitures, reduction to the lowest enlisted grade, and a bad-conduct discharge. The convening authority approved the sentence, and the Court of Military Review affirmed the findings and sentence. 36 M.J. 660 (1992).

An Article 32, Uniform Code of Military Justice, 10 U.S.C. § 832, pretrial investigation into appellant's misconduct was ordered by Commander J.C. Van Dyke, USN, the acting Commanding Officer of the Naval Air Technical Training Center, Naval Air Station Memphis, Millington, Tennessee. Captain T.W. Finta, USN, the Commanding Officer, was absent. The investigating officer filed a report and recommended that appellant be tried by general court-martial. Captain Finta, a SPCM convening authority, forwarded the charges to the general court-martial (GCM) convening authority, Rear Admiral R.L. Rich, Jr., USN, Chief of Naval Technical Training, with a recommendation for a general court-martial. The staff judge advocate also recommended trial by general court-martial in his Article 34, UCMJ, 10 U.S.C. § 834, advice.

At trial, appellant made a "Motion to Dismiss All Charges and Specifications by Reason of Selective and Vindictive Prosecution." He made the following offers of proof, according to the court below:

> Ms. Sherry Clay, now Mrs. Finta, was formerly employed as a bartender at the station golf course. The appellant, an avid golfer, was acquainted with Ms. Clay. The appellant and Ms. Clay were friends and bantered frequently. The content of the bantering was often sexual in nature by way of innuendo and double entendre. The appellant and Ms. Clay were not having an affair although people at the golf course might have held the opinion that they were. Captain Finta was aware of this opinion. On one occasion in the presence of witnesses, Captain Finta ordered the appellant to cease the bantering with Ms. Clay and to stay away from her. After the charges in this case were preferred, but before the pretrial investigation, Ms. Clay telephoned Captain Finta to intercede on the appellant's behalf. She was rebuffed by Captain Finta. Shortly prior to trial, Ms. Clay and Captain Finta married.

36 M.J. at 662. Appellant argued Captain Finta was biased against him because of appellant's friendship with the former Ms. Clay, and Captain Finta, therefore, was disqualified to act on appellant's case. The military judge denied appellant's motion to dismiss.

On appeal, the Court of Military Review construed appellant's motion to dismiss to include a request to present witnesses. The court held that, if the military judge erred in not allowing appellant to call Captain and Mrs. Finta, appellant suffered no substantial prejudice. 36 M.J. at 663.

We hold that the Court of Military Review erred. Appellant reasonably raised the issue of Captain Finta's possible bias against him. Thus, appellant was entitled to present evidence on the issue or have the military judge presume the correctness of his proffer. See 75 AmJur2d Trial § 436 (1991); see generally Art. 46, UCMJ, 10 U.S.C. § 846; RCM 703(b), Manual for Courts-Martial, United States 1984. Because the record has not been developed on the issue and presuming the truth of appellant's assertions of

Captain Finta's bias, we cannot say appellant suffered no prejudice. Art. 59(a), UCMJ, 10 U.S.C. § 859(a).

Captain Finta occupied an essential position in the court-martial process, one that requires exercise of discretion, without bias, prejudice or disqualification. Upon receiving the investigating officer's recommendation, Captain Finta had the option of dismissing the charges against appellant; disposing of the charges through nonjudicial punishment, a summary court-martial, or a SPCM; or forwarding the charges to the GCM convening authority. RCM 404. Captain Finta chose to forward the charges to a higher authority. RCM 401(c)(2)(A)2 requires commanders who forward charges, unless disqualified from acting on the case, to submit a recommendation to the higher convening authority. If the SPCM convening authority is disqualified, he should advise the GCM convening authority of that fact. RCM 401(c)(2)(A). Captain Finta apparently did not consider himself to be disqualified from acting on appellant's case, and he forwarded the charges with a recommendation for a general court-martial.

Captain Finta's recommendation is not binding on the GCM convening authority. Nevertheless, we cannot assume Captain Finta's recommendation had no bearing on the ultimate decision to refer the charges against appellant to general court-martial. To do so would render the RCM 401(c)(2)(A) requirement that Captain Finta make a recommendation regarding disposition without tenor. Accordingly, we must assume the recommendation influenced the GCM convening authority's decision to refer the charges to a general court-martial.

Captain Finta's qualification to act on appellant's case was called into question, and the record fails to establish that Finta acted without improper motives. We cannot divine how a neutral SPCM convening authority would have acted under the same circumstances. The cloud of the alleged conflict of interest has not been removed. *See United States v. Gordon*, 1 U.S.C.MA 255, 262, 2 CMR 161, 168 (1952) (anyone with other than an official interest in a case prohibited from making decisions regarding that case).

The decision of the United States Navy-Marine Corps Court of Military Review is reversed. The findings and sentence are set aside. The record of trial is returned to the Judge Advocate General of the Navy. A rehearing may be ordered.

Chief Judge SULLIVAN and Judges CRAWFORD and WISS concur.

[Judge Gierke's dissenting opinion is omitted.—Eds.]

Points for Discussion

1. In the *Nix* case, how was the commander (Captain Finta) biased, prejudiced, or disqualified from making a recommendation to the general court-martial convening authority?

2. Is it relevant that the general court-martial convening authority is not bound by the recommendation of Captain Finta (the special court-martial convening authority) in appellant's case? Why or why not?

5-2. UCMJ, Article 32, Pretrial Investigations

Before a convening authority can refer a case to a general court-martial, the highest level of court-martial, an independent investigating officer must conduct an Article 32, UCMJ, investigative pretrial hearing or the accused must waive that hearing. Usually apppointed by the special court-martial convening authority, the investigating officer (one commissioned officer) conducts a fact-finding investigation, hearing witnesses and reviewing evidence. The investigating officer will weigh the facts and provide a report with conclusions and recommendations to the appointing authority. These recommendations are advisory only. An Article 32, UCMJ, hearing serves as an opportunity for discovery and is designed to "inquire into the truth of the matters set forth in the charges, the form of the charges, and to secure information on which to determine what disposition should be made of the case." R.C.M. 405 discussion.

The Article 32 hearing serves many of the pretrial procedural functions of a grand jury, but a military accused is provided more rights. Unlike a grand jury hearing which is held in secrecy, in an Article 32 pretrial hearing, the accused has the right to be present and represented by counsel (military defense counsel at no cost to the accused or civilian counsel at his own expense). Generally, Article 32 pretrial hearings should be open to the public and closed only during portions when classified information is presented. Rule for Court-Martial 405(h)(3). *See MacDonald v. Hodgson*, 42 C.M.R. 184 (C.M.A. 1970) (petition for writ of injunction and temporary restraining order to open hearing). The accused has the opportunity to review all non-testimonial evidence (documentary or real evidence), and to call and examine witnesses who testify under oath. The defense has an opportunity to request available witnesses and present evidence including matters in extenuation and mitigation. The accused has the right to remain silent or may present a statement (sworn or unsworn, written or oral) or the defense counsel's statement on behalf of the accused. The Military Rules of Evidence do not apply with the exception of privileges, the rape shield rule, along with other limited evidentiary requirements. The investigating officer will, however, comment on evidentiary issues.

[handwritten marginal note: Generally open to public]

Rule for Court-Martial 405 describes what the Article 32 investigating officer's report must include. Among other requirements, the report must include summarized witness testimony, a determination whether reasonable grounds exist to believe the accused is not mentally responsible for offense, was not competent to participate in the defense, or whether a question of accused's competency to stand trial exists. The report must also include a conclusion whether charges and specifications are in the proper form, a conclusion whether reasonable grounds exist to believe accused committed the alleged offense, and a recommendation regarding appropriate disposition of the charges.

UNITED STATES v. PAYNE
U.S. Court of Military Appeals
3 M.J. 354 (C.M.A. 1977)

FLETCHER, Chief Judge:

The appellant [Specialist Five Leslie J. Payne, U.S. Army] was convicted of failure to safeguard classified material, wrongful appropriation of government documents, and furnishing classified materials to an unauthorized person in violation of Articles 92, 121 and 134, Uniform Code of Military Justice, 10 U.S.C. §§ 892, 921, and 934, respectively. He was sentenced to a dishonorable discharge, total forfeitures, and confinement at hard labor for 4 years. The convening authority and the U. S. Army Court of Military Review approved the findings and sentence without modification. We granted review to determine whether the appellant was denied his pretrial rights under Article 32, UCMJ, 10 U.S.C. § 832. Counsel for the appellant argue that the actions of the investigating officer in consulting with the trial counsel were so substantial as to constitute an abandonment of the required impartiality, and resulted in a derogation of the judicial functions inherent in that office. Upon examination of the record, we conclude that the appropriate standards were not observed.

The investigating officer, Major Payne, was appointed on October 30, 1974. After his appointment he testified that he reported to the trial counsel, Captain Gravelle, for a "briefing on the facts and evidence that was available at that time." The matter of his role and responsibilities as an investigating officer were discussed, and Major Payne was subsequently informed that a Major Runke from the office of the staff judge advocate would be available to advise him on the various questions which might develop during the course of the investigation. Despite the availability of Major Runke, Major Payne instead chose to confer with Captain Gravelle on seven additional occasions concerning various facets of the investigation. Although Major Payne characterized the matters discussed as "procedural" rather than "legal" in nature, our examination of the matters discussed and his testimony explaining these discussions lead us to a different conclusion.[4] However laudable his desires to confer with someone more "familiar" with the case may have been, we find

---

[4] Many of the items on the list (and Major Payne's further explanation of the notations at trial) did concern procedural aspects of an Article 32 investigation; however, several related to questions of the applicable burden of proof, evidentiary standards, and, most critically, the legality of the search which produced the incriminating evidence against the appellant. Although Major Payne may have felt these matters were also "procedural" in nature, we conclude otherwise; nor can we accept the proposition that any judge, especially the lay judge, should be soliciting or accepting ex parte advice on such matters from counsel from either side.

that these ex parte discussions with the prosecuting attorney were violative of his role as a judicial officer.

We believe that much of the difficulty encountered in resolving this issue has resulted from a misperception of the proper focus of analysis. Since correct examination of this question must involve a recognition that the Article 32 investigating officer performs a judicial function, the pertinent determination for a court must be whether the judicial nature of that office has been maintained. We are not unmindful of the problems inherent with the use of "lay judges," yet we cannot agree with any suggestion that one serving in this capacity need not conduct himself in accordance with proper judicial standards. The Supreme Court has sanctioned the use of lay judges only upon satisfaction that the officeholder is neutral and independent, and is able to render a detached judgment on the given question or controversy. *Shadwick v. City of Tampa*, 407 U.S. 345 (1972). . . .

Application of these concepts to the question presented in the instant case demonstrates the defect in this Article 32 investigation, as well as the underlying weakness of our previous method of analysis. This investigating officer, despite the ready availability of an impartial legal advisor, chose to conduct ex parte communications with the man he knew would ultimately prosecute the case. We believe that in view of the contents of the matters discussed and the ex parte nature of these conversations, the standards of neutrality, detachment, and independence demanded by Article 32, and required by the Supreme Court, have been violated. Further, they directly conflict with the provisions of the ABA Standards Relating to the Administration of Criminal Justice, which we consider applicable to the pretrial investigation. Those standards specifically provide:

> The trial judge should insist that neither the prosecutor nor the defense counsel nor any other person discuss a pending case with him ex parte, except after adequate notice to all other parties and when authorized by law or in accordance with approved practice.

We, therefore, conclude that this Article 32 investigation was defective under these standards.

We cannot complete our discussion of this issue without examination of our holding in *United States v. Young*, 32 C.M.R. 134 (C.M.A. 1962), which counsel for the government have argued is dispositive. In *Young*, a majority of this Court held it was permissible for one attorney to serve the dual functions of legal advisor to the Article 32 investigating officer and prosecutor. The majority chose to focus its inquiry on whether that attorney participated in the actual investigation to such an extent as to either usurp the duties of the investigating officer, or to become an associate investigator, and hence be statutorily disqualified under the provisions of Article 27(a). Although such an inquiry may be useful in resolution of certain aspects of the statutory qualifications of the prosecutor, it has created a cumbersome and unsatisfactory method of analysis which consistently fails to evaluate whether the Congressional intent underlying Article 32 of providing an impartial pretrial investigation has been met. We believe that Judge Ferguson, in his dissent in *Young*, correctly observed that although a counsel can appear in his role as prosecutor to help establish the validity of the charges and to develop the case for the government, he cannot assume the function of assistant to or counsel for the investigating officer. . . .

* * *

Although we determine that the Article 32 investigating officer was acting in violation of the applicable standards of conduct for the judicial office he served, it is nonetheless incumbent upon us to examine the record for a determination of whether this impropriety prejudiced the appellant. We are not unmindful of the inherent difficulties presented by requiring a defendant to demonstrate the prejudice resulting from improper actions by a judicial officer, the full extent or text of which he may be unaware in part or whole. We, conclude that this is a matter requiring a presumption of prejudice. Absent clear and convincing evidence to the contrary, we will be obliged to reverse the case. Upon examination of this record under this presumption, we determine that this Article 32 investigating officer's actions, although improper, do not require reversal, as the presumption was overcome through the testimony of Major Payne at trial and other matters presented by the government. That we do not now choose to view this matter as one within the narrow category of error per se should not be interpreted as any indication of approval or sanction of the practice found in this case. In future cases when testing for prejudice, we will resolve doubts against the judicial officer who participates in such a practice.

The decision of the United States Army Court of Military Review is affirmed.

Judge PERRY concurs.

[APPENDIX I omitted]

[Judge Cook's separate opinion concurring in part and dissenting in part is omitted.—Eds.]

Points for Discussion

1. On what kinds of legal issues might an investigating officer need legal advice from an independent legal adviser (like Major Runke)? To eliminate the need for an independent legal advisor, would it be preferable just to appoint a military attorney or judge to serve as the investigating officer (something that is occasionally done)?

2. Would the communications between the Major Payne and Captain Gravelle have been less problematic if the counsel for the accused had been present?

5-3. Staff Judge Advocate Pretrial Advice to the Convening Authority

The accused is afforded protections through the Article 32 pretrial hearing. The Staff Judge Advocate's pretrial review of the charges and specifications also protects the accused from trial based on trumped up allegations or disposition of the case at an inappropriately high level of court-martial. Once the Article 32 pretrial hearing is completed, the convening authority cannot refer the case to a general court-martial without the Staff Judge Advocate reviewing the case and providing written Article 34 pretrial advice.[1]

The Staff Judge Advocate's written advice must include: (1) a determination whether each specification alleges an offense (2) a conclusion regarding whether each alleged offense is warranted by the evidence (3) a determination whether a court-martial would have jurisdiction over the accused, and (4) a recommendation regarding the appropriate level of disposition for the case (i.e., the level court-martial to which to refer the case). UCMJ, Article 34, Rule for Court-Martial 406. The Staff Judge Advocate may recommend that the convening authority dismiss any specification, or refer the case to a lower-level commander for disposition, to a court-martial level lower than a general court-martial, or to trial by general court-martial. The Staff Judge Advocate's pretrial advice need not include any analysis or justification for the conclusions in the Article 34 pretrial advice. The Staff Judge Advocate must personally sign this formal document before submitting it to the general court-martial convening authority.

UNITED STATES v. PLUMB
Air Force Court of Criminal Appeals
47 M.J. 771 (A.F. Ct. Crim. App. 1997)

SPISAK, Judge:

What should have been a straight-forward case of fraternization, adultery, and conduct unbecoming an officer, became a complex, lengthy, and often confusing testament to how not to conduct criminal investigations and prepare courts-martial for trial. Numerous allegations of unlawful command influence and interference with defense witnesses resulted in extensive judicial hearings, over 1700 pages of transcript and 30 volumes in the record of trial (17 dedicated to exhibits alone), and a total of four investigations under Article 32, UCMJ, 10 U.S.C. § 832.

---

[1] The Rule for Court-Martial 406(a) discussion indicates that pretrial advice from the Staff Judge Advocate is not required before referring a case to a summary or special court-martial. The Army, however, has promulgated a regulatory provision requiring pretrial advice from the Staff Judge Advocate before a case may be referred to a special court-martial with the power to adjudge confinement exceeding 6 months, forfeiture of pay for more than 6 months, or a bad-conduct discharge. *See* Army Regulation 27-10, "Military Justice," para. 5-28(b) (Oct. 3, 2011).

The appellant [Captain John D. Plumb, Jr., U.S. Air Force], a special agent for the Air Force Office of Special Investigations (AFOSI), was tried by general court-martial on charges of conduct unbecoming an officer,[1] indecent assault, adultery, fraternization, violating a lawful general order, sodomy, impeding an Article 32 investigation, and attempting to influence the testimony of a witness. He pled not guilty to all charges. After convicting him of one specification each of adultery and fraternization with Airman A, the court sentenced the appellant to a dismissal and 30 days confinement.

The appellant contends that the evidence is factually insufficient to support the findings of guilty; that the military judge erred in refusing to grant an evidentiary hearing on the admissibility of an exculpatory polygraph; that court members may have improperly considered extraneous information; that the sentence is inappropriate; and, that the case was so permeated with unlawful command influence that the findings and sentence should be set aside. We agree with the appellant's contentions on the polygraph and unlawful command influence and set aside the findings and sentence.

* * *

III. DISQUALIFICATION OF THE STAFF JUDGE ADVOCATE

While not raised on appeal, we note that Major F, the same judge advocate who authored the defective April 19, 1995, Article 34, UCMJ, pretrial advice, also authored and signed the post-trial staff judge advocate's recommendation. Preparation of the pretrial advice does not ordinarily disqualify a SJA from participation in the post-trial review, at least if his pretrial advice was "proper in all material respects." *United States v. Collins*, 6 M.J. 256, 257 (C.M.A. 1979). *See also United States v. Lynch*, 39 M.J. 223, 228 (C.M.A. 1994); *United States v. Engle*, 1 M.J. 387 (C.M.A. 1976). However, R.C.M. 1106 contemplates that the SJA who authors the post-trial recommendation will be sufficiently impartial as to provide the convening authority with a balanced and objective evaluation of the evidence. *United States v. Crunk*, 15 C.M.R. 290, 293 (1954). Where the pretrial advice misstates a material fact or arrives at an erroneous factual conclusion, the staff judge advocate is disqualified from the post-trial review. *Collins*, 6 M.J. at 257. Here, the convening authority's SJA did recuse himself and his staff, including Major F, from writing the third pretrial advice after the military judge declared the April 19, 1995, advice to be defective. We commend him for doing so. However, Major F then signed the post-trial recommendation as Acting Staff Judge Advocate, totally negating the SJA's earlier cleansing acts. While Major F's recommendation did not discuss the prior pretrial advice or argue that it was not defective as had occurred in Engle, or enter into a factual

---

[1] Two specifications of engaging in an unprofessional relationships with two female airmen; one specification of having sexual intercourse with an airman while on duty; and, one specification of making a "wrongful and dishonorable" statement to a non-commissioned officer.

dispute with defense counsel as occurred in Lynch, the blatant inaccuracies of the April 19, 1995, recommendation disqualified Major F from authoring the post-trial recommendation. *Id.*

Here, however, there is more to disqualify Major F than a defective pretrial advice. Major F also authored the first pretrial advice which characterized the appellant as being "like a shark in the waters, [who] goes after the weak and leaves the strong alone." Some pre-trial acts or comments by a SJA may be so antithetical to the integrity of the military justice system as to disqualify the SJA from further participation. *Engle*, 1 M.J. at 389. We believe this language is so contrary to the integrity and fairness of the military justice system that it has no place in a pretrial advice. Having the author of those hostile words and of the defective pretrial advice sign the staff judge advocate's post-trial recommendation to the convening authority had the effect of causing this simmering pot of unlawful command influence to boil over and extinguish the fire of fairness altogether.

IV. CONCLUSIONS

The appellant's trial was so permeated with unlawful command influence that we are unable to say beyond a reasonable doubt that neither the findings nor sentence were tainted. Additionally, the appellant was entitled to an evidentiary hearing to determine whether or not the polygraph evidence was relevant, material, and sufficiently reliable to warrant presentation to the court members. For these reasons, the findings and sentence are set aside and the case is returned to The Judge Advocate General for referral to a new convening authority who may authorize a rehearing. Should a rehearing be ordered, we expect the military judge to take appropriate measures to purge the proceedings of any residual taint.

Chief Judge ROTHENBURG, Senior Judge PEARSON, and Judge MORGAN concur.

Point for Discussion

Why exactly was Major F's "shark in the waters" comment "contrary to the integrity and fairness of the military justice system"? Could Major F have rephrased the comment to convey essentially the same message without being improper? Would it have been better for the SJA to withhold all comment and instead simply advise the convening authority in a yes-or-no manner whether to refer the charges and specifications to trial by court-martial?

5-4. Referral of Case to Court-Martial

As convening authorities, commanders may possess the power to send or "refer" a case to trial by summary court-martial, special court-martial, or general court-martial. When the commander "refers" a case to court-martial, he orders that an accused be tried at a particular court-martial level and the charge sheet is annotated with the court-martial convening order number and that convening order reflects a list of service members (selected by the convening authority) who are to sit as the panel if the accused decides that he wants a panel to hear his case.

Consequently, commanders play a critical and extensive role in disposing of military criminal cases, from preferral through referral and post-trial processing (i.e., acting on the findings and sentence of the court-martial). Critics of a separate military justice system assert that the system provides convening authorities with too much control over the disposition of criminal offenses in violation of the Fifth Amendment Due Process Clause. Nevertheless, federal courts have upheld the essential and multifaceted role of the convening authority in the military justice system, as reflected in the court's holding in the *Curry* case below.

SECRETARY OF THE ARMY. v. CURRY
U.S. Court of Appeals for District of Columbia Circuit
595 F.2d. 873 (D.C. Cir. 1979)

TAMM, Circuit Judge:

We review in this appeal a due process attack on provisions of the Uniform Code of Military Justice (UCMJ) which assign multiple roles to the convening authority in court-martial proceedings. The district court (Gesell, J.) upheld the constitutionality of these provisions, and we affirm.

I

The facts of this case are not in dispute. [Robert E.] Curry was an enlisted man, stationed in Germany, in the United States Army. On March 8, 1975, he was convicted of two homicides by a general court-martial. The sentence imposed by the court-martial included hard labor for twelve years, reduction to the lowest enlisted grade, and dishonorable discharge. The convening authority approved Curry's conviction and sentence. The Army Court of Military Review affirmed his conviction, but reduced his sentence to eight years. The United States Court of Military Appeals declined review. Curry later requested relief from the Board for Correction of Military Records, which was denied.

Curry then brought suit in the United States District Court for the District of Columbia against appellees, the Secretary of the Army, Et al. (Army), seeking injunctive and monetary relief. Curry collaterally attacked the validity of his conviction on the ground that provisions of the UCMJ assigning multiple roles to the convening authority in the initiation, prosecution, and review of courts-martial deprive military defendants of a fair and impartial trial in violation of the due process clause of the fifth amendment. Both parties filed motions for summary judgment. Judge Gerhard Gesell heard arguments on the cross-motions and, in a memorandum opinion and order, granted the Army's motion. *See Curry v. Secretary of Army*, 439 F.Supp. 261, 262 (D.D.C.1977). This appeal ensued.

II

General courts-martial are judicial tribunals that try members of the Armed Forces who are charged with violations of the UCMJ. They can consist of either a military judge and not less than five members who are military personnel, or, at the request of the accused, a military judge alone. The members of a court-martial decide whether the accused is guilty and, if so, what sentence should be imposed. The military judge rules on questions of law and instructs the members on what they must find to convict the accused. If the court-martial is composed only of a military judge, the judge rules on all matters.

The convening authority, who is generally the commanding officer, ... participates in various levels of the court-martial process. He determines whether charges should be referred to the court-martial, selects the members of the court-martial, details the military judge, and details the prosecuting and defense counsel. The convening authority also reviews the court-martial record. He can approve the findings and sentence, return for reconsideration and appropriate action specifications dismissed without a finding of not guilty, or disapprove findings of guilty and the sentence imposed.

Curry maintains this system places the convening authority in the position of grand jury, selector of the trial judge, jury, and counsel, and appellate court. Brief for the Appellant at 8-9. He submits that the convening authority, having initiated the prosecution, has an interest in the result of the case and is therefore constitutionally incapable of insuring that the accused receives a fair and impartial trial. *See generally In re Murchinson*, 349 U.S. 133, 136-37 (1955). Curry suggests that the convening authority, because of his prior interest, is likely to appoint individuals to serve as counsel and court members who generally are more inclined to find an accused guilty than would a random sampling of military personnel. The accused could thus be denied vigorous representation as well as the wide spectrum of attitudes basic to the American idea of trial by jury.

Moreover, Curry asserts that the possibility for unfairness persists, even if the individuals selected by the convening authority are not predisposed toward conviction. The court members and the counsel, usually under the command of the appointing officer, may be particularly sU.S.C.eptible to his influence. They are dependent upon him for their promotions, their efficiency ratings, their assignments of duty, and their furloughs. Curry argues that because the court members and counsel know they are subject to the convening authority, who has ample opportunity to manifest his displeasure with the manner in which those under his command have handled a case, the likelihood is increased that the court-martial will return a guilty verdict.

Curry alleges, and it is undisputed, that the convening authority referred the charges against him to the court-martial for trial. The convening authority detailed the military judge who presided at the court-martial, and he selected the members of the court and the counsel. The convening authority reviewed the record on both the facts and the law. Curry therefore claims his conviction is invalid.

III

A person convicted by a court-martial is entitled to due process of law under the fifth amendment. What process is due, however, depends upon "an analysis of the interest of the individual and those of the regime to which he is subject." *Middendorf v. Henry*, 425 U.S. 25, 43 (1976); *See Burns v. Wilson*, 346 U.S. 137, 140 (1943) ("(T)he rights of men in the Armed Forces must perforce be conditioned to meet certain overriding demands of discipline and duty."). At the outset, we note the difficult burden a litigant shoulders when he challenges congressional decisions governing military practices. Article I, section 8 of the Constitution empowers Congress to "make Rules for the Government and Regulation of the land and naval Forces." The importance of maintaining an effective military to insure national security renders this power especially broad. Consequently, a court reviewing legislatively approved military procedure "must give particular deference to the determination(s) of Congress." *Middendorf v. Henry*, 425 U.S. at 43; *See Schlesinger v. Councilman*, 420 U.S. 738, 757-58 (1975).

Curry premises his challenge on two points. First, he contends that the present structure of the court-martial system is fundamentally incompatible with the fifth amendment guarantee of due process and clearly would be prohibited in a civilian context. Next, he argues that the military has failed to produce any justification for the system. Absent compelling military exigencies, Curry submits, departure from the traditional structure of the civilian system of criminal justice is unwarranted. Brief for Appellant at 6, 15, 34. We agree that the system established in the UCMJ would be inconsistent with due process if instituted in the context of a civilian criminal trial. We do not agree, however, with Curry's second contention.

We begin with the unassailable principle that the fundamental function of the armed forces is "to fight or be ready to fight wars." *Toth v. Quarles*, 350 U.S. 11, 17 (1955). Obedience, discipline, and centralized leadership and control, including the ability to mobilize forces rapidly, are all essential if the military is to perform effectively. The system of military justice must respond to these needs for all branches of the service, at home and abroad, in time of peace, and in time of war. It must be practical, efficient, and flexible.

The Supreme Court has recognized that the military is "a specialized society separate from civilian society," and its unique circumstances and needs justify a departure from civilian legal standards. *See Parker v. Levy*, 417 U.S. 733, 743-44 (1974) ("fundamental necessity for obedience, and the consequent necessity for imposition of discipline, may render permissible within the military that which would be constitutionally impermissible outside it"); *See also Middendorf v. Henry*, 425 U.S. at 38-39; *Schlesinger v. Councilman*, 420 U.S. at 757; *Burns v. Wilson*, 346 U.S. at 140. The Court specifically stated that the peculiar nature of military service is such that courts-martial "probably never can be constituted in such way that they can have the same kind of qualifications that the Constitution has deemed essential to fair trials of civilians in federal courts." *Toth v. Quarles*, 350 U.S. at 17. This court, too, has noted the differences between military life and civilian life and the concomitant need for different procedures and rules. . . .

Curry primarily attacks the power of the convening authority to refer charges to the court-martial and then to select its members. Contrary to his assertions, however, we find these provisions sufficiently responsive to the unique needs of the military to withstand constitutional challenge. In reviewing the proffered rationale, we are reminded that the administration of justice on the battlefield involves consideration of factors far removed from day-to-day civilian life. We again emphasize that the standards of military justice in peacetime must be equally applicable in time of war and national emergency. . . .

[handwritten margin note: Unique char. of military allows for this.]

The power of the convening authority to refer charges to the court-martial is justifiable on two grounds. First, prosecutorial discretion may be essential to efficient use of limited supplies and manpower. The decision to employ resources in a court-martial proceeding is one particularly within the expertise of the convening authority who, as chief administrator as well as troop commander, can best weigh the benefits to be gained from such a proceeding against those that would accrue if men and supplies were used elsewhere. The balance struck is crucial in times of crisis when prudent management of scarce resources is at a premium. Second, as we previously have stated, maintenance of discipline and order is imperative to the successful functioning of the military. The commanding officer's power to refer charges may be necessary to establish and to preserve both.

Provisions of the UCMJ authorizing the convening authority to select the members of the court-martial also respond to unique military needs. In order for the command to function effectively, the officer in charge must be assured that he has capable personnel available to perform various tasks. The duties his troops will be called upon to carry out may be difficult, if not impossible, to predict in advance. *See* UCMJ: Hearings on H.R. 2498 Before Subcomm. of House Comm. on Armed Services, 81st Cong., 1st Sess. 1114 (1949) ("absolutely impossible in wartime for a commander to determine in advance what men he could spare for a panel") (statement of Prof. Edmund M. Morgan, Harvard Law School). The commanding officer is well situated to determine whether the various needs of the service will be best served by the selection and participation of particular individuals in a court-martial proceeding. If, on the other hand, court-martial members were required to be chosen from a broad panel of military personnel, a large number of men would be immobilized and effectively removed from the direct control of the commanding officer pending completion of the selection process. Strategic success and human safety could be jeopardized by so impeding the commanding officer's ability to deploy troops. In addition, assembling a panel is frequently a logistic impossibility in combat situations, *See* 92 Cong.Rec.

1444 (1950) (remarks of Sen. Kefauver), or if the jury is chosen from troops dispersed over a widespread geographic area.

Proponents of the present system also assert that selection of court members by the commanding officer is the most expeditious way to convene a military jury. Assurance of a prompt and speedy trial, a desirable feature in any system of criminal justice, is especially important in the armed services. The very nature of military life requires prompt judicial action. Tactical and training situations necessitate movement of units; witnesses may be transferred or move into combat. If a case is not tried quickly, evidence or testimony may be irretrievably lost. Further, the deterrent effect of immediate punishment may be crucial to the maintenance of discipline in crisis situations.

Congress, in drafting the UCMJ, was aware of the potential for unfairness in the system created to respond to the needs of military justice. Indeed, the problem of unlawful "command influence" was a major point in dispute in the discussions that preceded enactment of the UCMJ, as well as in subsequent legislative hearings. Congress responded by taking specific precautions to protect against its improper exercise. For example, before ordering a trial, the convening authority must consult his staff judge advocate concerning the sufficiency of the charges and the availability of the evidence. Upon review of a conviction, the staff judge advocate must submit to the convening authority an opinion which becomes part of the record. If the convening authority approves a sentence that extends to death, dismissal of a commissioned officer, cadet, or midshipman, dishonorable discharge, or confinement for one year or more, a Court of Military Review must review the record. The United States Court of Military Appeals, a court composed of civilian judges " 'completely removed from all military influence or persuasion,' " *Schlesinger v. Councilman*, 420 U.S. at 758 (quoting H.R.Rep.No.491, 81st Cong., 1st Sess. 7 (1949)), may review legal challenges raised by the defendant. Congress further provided the accused with a wide range of procedural rights to guard against command influence. A defendant is guaranteed legal representation at both trial and appellate levels. He may select his own military counsel, so long as the counsel is "reasonably available," or he may provide his own civilian counsel. He may request that the general court-martial include at least one-third enlisted members. He may challenge any member for cause, and he has one preemptory challenge. The accused may also elect to be tried by a military judge alone, who is designated by the Judge Advocate General and well insulated from command influence.

Finally, and most importantly, Article 37 of the UCMJ broadly prohibits the improper use of command influence. Article 98 makes a violation of Article 37 a military offense.

We find the justifications offered in support of the provisions now under review, coupled with the safeguards specifically provided by Congress to protect against improper command influence, *See Committee for G.I. Rights v. Callaway*, 518 F.2d at 480, sufficient to withstand Curry's challenge. We do not imply, however, that the system of military justice, as presently constructed, is the sole means capable of satisfying the unique needs of the armed services. We hold only that, given our substantial deference to Congress in military matters, the balance struck is constitutionally permissible.

IV

We conclude by again recognizing that establishing the proper relationship "between the legitimate needs of the military and the rights of the individual soldier presents a complex problem which lends itself to no easy solution." *Id.* The inquiry involves reconciliation of the conflicting social values inherent in the maintenance of a standing army in a democratic nation. The need for national defense mandates an armed force whose discipline and readiness is not unnecessarily undermined by the often deliberately cumbersome concepts of civilian jurisprudence. Yet, the dictates of individual liberty clearly require some check on military authority in the conduct of courts-martial. The provisions of the UCMJ with respect to court-martial proceedings represent a congressional attempt to accommodate the interests of justice, on the one hand, with the demands for an efficient, well-disciplined military, on the other.

For the foregoing reasons, we find the balance struck by Congress constitutionally permissible, and the judgment of the district court is

Affirmed.

Points for Discussion

1. What "unique needs of the military" justifies the convening authority's multiple roles in the court-martial process? Do those unique military needs override the rights of individual service members? Why or why not?

2. How does the court in the *Curry* case apply deference to Congress? Why do they defer to Congress on this matter?

CHAPTER 6

PRETRIAL DECISIONS

6-1. The Accused's Plea

Like a commander who faces many difficult decisions before referring a case to trial,[1] an accused also has difficult decisions. An accused must decide whether to accept an Article 15, nonjudicial punishment or trial by summary court-martial, or demand trial at a higher level. An accused must also decide whether to plead guilty or not guilty to each specification and charge and must select the type of forum in which to be tried (e.g., trial by military judge alone, trial with officer members, or trial with at least one-third enlisted members). These weighty decisions must be made prior to trial by court-martial and some restrictions exist in the military justice system.

6-2. Forum Options

The military court-martial is a bifurcated process with a hearing dedicated to findings, and if any findings of guilt are made, a hearing to determine the sentence follows. At the start of the trial, the accused is arraigned and must plead guilty or not guilty to each specification and charge, including a "mixed plea"—guilty to some and not guilty to others. (An accused has the opportunity to make motions and conduct a voir dire of the panel members if a court-martial panel sits for any portion of the case.)

For charges to which the accused pleads not guilty, the accused may be tried by military judge alone (findings and sentence) or panel (findings and sentence). Enlisted members may request that the panel be at least one-third enlisted members.

If the accused pleads guilty, the military judge will conduct a providence inquiry (usually with a stipulation of fact) to ensure that the accused can admit guilt to all elements of the offenses and is knowingly and voluntarily pleading guilty. There are no *Alford* or nolo contendere pleas in the military

---

[1] As described in previous chapters, commanders may take other adverse actions besides sending a case to a court-martial (e.g., administrative separation from the service or UCMJ Article 15, nonjudicial punishment). In lieu of lesser administrative actions, commanders may send a case to the lowest level of court-martial, a summary court-martial. The immediate commander decides whether to take lesser action, or forward the case to the commander authorized to convene summary courts-martial.

justice system.[2] For a military accused to please guilty, the military judge must explain the offenses and ensure the accused understands the rights he has waived.

If an accused pleads not guilty to any charge, he may decide to have a panel or judge alone sit as the trier of fact. During trial on the merits, similar to the civilian criminal trial process, the government presents its case in chief, followed by the defense case. Once trial on the merits is completed, the trier of fact must deliberate, determine findings, and announce the findings. Prior to a panel deliberating on findings, the military Judge provides instructions on deliberation, voting, and findings.

The accused waives trial on the merits (or findings) if he enters a guilty plea. If the accused pleads guilty to all charges and specifications, the case moves directly to the sentencing phase.

During the sentencing phase of the court-martial, a separate hearing occurs, in which witnesses are called and evidence is admitted. If the accused is tried by a panel, the same panel will also sentence the accused. If the accused is tied by a military judge alone, the accused may request sentencing by judge alone or a panel. The government presents matters in aggravation, while the defense presents matters in extenuation and mitigation. The accused has an opportunity to provide a written sworn or unsworn statement or testify under oath subject to cross examination, or present an unsworn statement, not subject to cross examination. The sentencing authority (either military judge or panel) will then deliberate, vote on the sentence, and announce the sentence. Prior to deliberations, the military judge provides the panel instructions on sentencing.

Point for Discussion

Should an enlisted service member always exercise the right to request a panel that includes at least one-third enlisted members? One author writes: "When an accused selects an enlisted panel, conventional wisdom is that he does so because he wants their viewpoints and collective life-experiences, which may be different from those of officers." Robert Best, *Peremptory Challenges in Military Criminal Justice Practice: It is Time to Challenge Them Off*, 183 Mil. L. Rev. 1, 53-54 (2005). But another author cautions: "Officers, better educated and more broadly exposed to the social sciences, may be more lenient sentencers than NCOs, who may in other instances be

---

[2] An *Alford* pleading occurs when a defendant in a civilian criminal trial admits that sufficient evidence exists that the prosecutor could use to convince a judge or jury to find the defendant guilty beyond a reasonable doubt. *See North Carolina v. Alford*, 400 U.S. 25 (1970). In the Armed Forces, prior to the military judge accepting a guilty plea, an accused must admit to all the elements of the offenses during the providence inquiry. *See United States v. Care*, 40 C.M.R. 247 (C.M.A. 1969), and Chapter 8-1 *infra* describing the providence inquiry process in detail.

Nolo contendere is a plea of no contest (rather than entering a plea of guilty or not guilty) in criminal trials, whereby the defendant neither admits or denies the charge.

sympathetic to an accused. The idea that either type of panel generally issues harsher sentences is one of the trite shortcuts that substitutes for serious thought." Lawrence J. Morris, *Keystones of the Military Justice System: A Primer for Chiefs of Justice*, Army Law., Oct. 1994, at 15, 38 (footnote omitted).

6-3. Pretrial Agreements

The accused and convening authority may negotiate a pretrial agreement which will limit the sentence if the accused pleads guilty. Pursuant to Rule for Courts-Martial 705, Pretrial Agreements, the convening authority may agree to limit the sentence to the sentence set forth in the quantum portion of the agreement. The convening authority may also promise to refer the accused's case to a certain level of court-martial or refer what could be a capital case (i.e., a case in which the death penalty is the maximum sentence possible) as a noncapital case (i.e., case in which the death penalty is not a punishment option). The convening authority may promise to withdraw one or more charges or specifications from the court-martial, or have trial counsel present no evidence as to one or more specifications.

During trial, the military judge reviews the pretrial agreement with the accused on the record and ensures that the accused understands the terms of the agreement and that no ambiguities exist. The sentencing authority at trial (judge or panel) does not know the quantum portion or sentence limitation and the accused receives the sentence of whichever is lesser, either the adjudged sentence or the maximum provided by the pretrial agreement. If it is the latter, the convening authority fulfills the agreement by approving only so much of the findings and sentence as the agreement reflects. Essentially, if the accused fulfills his obligations set forth in the pretrial agreement, when the case comes before the convening authority for post-trial action on the findings and sentence, the convening authority must limit the approved sentence to the agreed upon sentence cap (i.e., the maximum reflected in the pretrial agreement).

UNITED STATES v. DUNBAR
Army Court of Criminal Appeals
60 M.J. 748 (Army Ct. Crim. App. 2004)

SCHENCK, Judge:

A military judge sitting as a special court-martial convicted appellant [Staff Sergeant James L. Dunbar, U.S. Army], consistent with his pleas, of larceny (three specifications), and making false and fraudulent claims against the United States (two specifications), in violation of Articles 121 and 132, Uniform Code of Military Justice, 10 U.S.C. §§ 921 and 932 [hereinafter UCMJ]. The military judge sentenced appellant to a bad-conduct discharge, confinement for two months, and reduction to Private First Class E3. The convening authority approved only so much of the sentence as provides for a bad-conduct discharge, and reduction to Private First Class E3. This case is before the court for review under Article 66, UCMJ, 10 U.S.C. § 866.

Appellate government and defense counsel agree that the military judge failed to resolve a mutual misunderstanding between the parties regarding a material term in appellant's pretrial agreement with the convening authority. Appellate counsel urge us to set aside the findings and sentence. We will grant this request in our decretal paragraph, and authorize a rehearing.

Facts

Appellant's pretrial agreement states:

Any adjudged confinement of three (3) months or more shall be converted into a [bad-conduct discharge], which may be approved; any adjudged confinement of less than three (3) months shall be disapproved upon submission by the accused of an administrative separation in lieu of court-martial IAW AR 635-200, Chapter 10. The convening authority may approve all other lawful punishments adjudged by the court-martial. Any pretrial confinement credit shall be applied to the sentence finally approved by the convening authority.

A handwritten annotation stating "with an Other Than Honorable discharge" follows the words "Chapter 10." Appellant, as well as what appears to be trial defense counsel's initials, are written next to this note. Trial counsel, defense counsel, and appellant agreed on the record that the notation was part of the agreement.

Prior to findings, the military judge reviewed provisions in the pretrial agreement with counsel and appellant. *See* Rule for Courts-Martial [hereinafter R.C.M.] 910(f)(4). In accordance with the Military Judges' Benchbook, the military judge asked trial defense counsel whether the quantum portion of the pretrial agreement contained any conditions or terms other than a sentence limitation. Trial defense counsel replied that it did, but informed the military judge that he could not disclose those conditions "without violating the rules." The military judge then completed the standard inquiry regarding the agreement. *Id.*

After a brief recess, the military judge again questioned counsel regarding the conditions in the quantum portion. Trial defense counsel responded that the quantum portion "could be considered to be something other than a . . . mere limitation on sentence." Trial counsel told the military judge that the only conditions in the quantum portion were sentence limitations. The military judge then questioned appellant who affirmed that the agreement did not contain anything other than a sentence limitation. After confirming that appellant still wanted to plead guilty, the military judge accepted the plea as provident.

After announcing the sentence, the military judge stated that the pretrial agreement allowed the convening authority to approve the reduction to the grade of E3 and the bad-conduct discharge. The military judge asked counsel about their understanding of the pretrial agreement's limitations on appellant's sentence. Trial defense counsel disagreed as to approval of the discharge, asked to submit the request for administrative separation in lieu of court-martial, and requested an opportunity to seek a deferral of confinement. Trial counsel told the military judge that the convening authority could not approve confinement, but could approve the discharge and reduction. Trial defense counsel posed the question, "How could we have an other than honorable discharge at the same time we have a bad[-]conduct discharge?" The military judge responded that the pretrial agreement did not expressly require the convening authority to disapprove the bad-conduct discharge. He then told the parties that "the next sentence [of the agreement] says, 'The [c]onvening [a]uthority may approve all other lawful punishments adjudged by the court-martial.' "

The military judge informed counsel that the agreement "doesn't indicate anything about the [c]onvening [a]uthority's action on the Chapter 10." Trial defense counsel told the military judge, "We can agree to disagree on that point . . . and I would respectfully request the opportunity to submit the request for Chapter 10 along with a request for deferment of confinement . . . ." The military judge never asked appellant about his understanding of the effect of the pretrial agreement on the adjudged sentence.

The staff judge advocate's (SJA) memorandum advising the convening authority regarding appellant's request to defer execution of the reduction in rank, forfeitures, and confinement states, "Due to SSG Dunbar's pretrial agreement, the convening authority agreed to disapprove any confinement by converting any adjudged confinement of three months or more into a bad-conduct discharge. SSG Dunbar was sentenced to 2 months confinement, therefore, SSG Dunbar has not and will not serve any confinement." The SJA's memorandum did not: (1) state whether the adjudged bad-conduct discharge could be approved; (2) explain whether the pretrial agreement required deferment or disapproval of two months of confinement; or (3) elucidate what the government was receiving in return for disapproving appellant's adjudged confinement.

The SJA's post-trial recommendation quoted the sentence limitations from the pretrial agreement and recommended that the convening authority approve "only so much of the sentence as provides for reduction to the grade of E3 and bad-conduct discharge." Trial defense counsel's R.C.M. 1105 submission included an unsigned request on behalf of appellant for a Chapter 10 discharge in lieu of trial and made no reference to the "agreement to disagree" made at trial by court-martial. *See* R.C.M. 1105 and 1106(f)(4).

In his post-trial affidavit submitted with appellate counsel's brief, appellant states "my trial defense counsel . . . assured me that he would raise the issue of the misunderstanding regarding the quantum portion of my pretrial agreement to the convening authority. I do not know whether [he] was referring to the [R.C.M. 1105 submission] or through some other approach . . . ." Appellant's affidavit does not discuss his understanding of the quantum portion, assert that he was misled by the pretrial agreement, or indicate any expectation that the convening authority would implement the Chapter 10 discharge provision in exchange for his plea.

Law

The military judge is required to ensure that the accused understands the pretrial agreement and the parties agree to its terms. R.C.M. 910(f)(4); *see also United States v. King*, 3 M.J. 458 (C.M.A. 1977); *United States v. Green*, 1 M.J. 453, 456 (C.M.A. 1976). "The accused must know and understand not only the agreement's impact on the charges and specifications which bear on the plea, the limitation on the sentence, but also other terms of the agreement, including consequences of future misconduct or waiver of various rights." *United States v. Felder*, 59 M.J. 444, 445 (C.A.A.F. 2004).

Once the sentence is announced, "[i]f the military judge determines that the accused does not understand the material terms of the agreement, or that the parties disagree as to such terms, the military judge shall conform, with the consent of the [g]overnment, the agreement to the accused's understanding or permit the accused to withdraw the plea." R.C.M. 910(h)(3).

Discussion

As reflected in basic principles of contract law, we accept the government's concession that "no meeting of the minds" occurred in this case. The terms on the face of the agreement are ambiguous because the pretrial agreement does not specifically provide for whether the Chapter 10 request for discharge would be approved in lieu of the bad-conduct discharge if appellant was sentenced to less than three months of confinement and submitted a Chapter 10 request for discharge. The annotation on the pretrial agreement (written next to the Chapter 10 provision and indicating "other than honorable discharge") and trial defense counsel's statements at trial reflect a rational interpretation of the pretrial agreement. While the agreement did not specifically bind the convening authority to approval of a request for Chapter 10 discharge, there is a strong inference that if appellant received less than three months confinement the convening authority would approve a Chapter 10 discharge in lieu of the bad-conduct discharge. Appellant and trial defense counsel may have detrimentally relied on such an interpretation.

Additionally, despite the apparent "misunderstanding" of a "material term" of the pretrial agreement at trial, the military judge failed to remedy the conflict by either ordering specific performance of the agreement or offering appellant the opportunity to withdraw from the plea. *See United States v. Smith*, 56 M.J. 271, 273 (C.A.A.F. 2002) (citing *Santobello v. New York*, 404 U.S. 257, 263 (1971)); R.C.M. 910(h)(3). Instead, the parties left the courtroom "agreeing to disagree," with no discussion between appellant and the military judge about the issue.

Further, trial defense counsel did not raise the issue in the R.C.M. 1105 submission. As our superior court has stated, the convening authority and an accused may,

> avail[] themselves post-trial of the opportunity to renegotiate a new plea agreement to avoid a contest to the providence of the plea.... "Where there has been a mutual misunderstanding as to a material term, the convening authority and an accused may enter into a written post-trial agreement under which the accused, with the assistance of counsel, makes a knowing, voluntary, and intelligent waiver of his right to contest the providence of his pleas in exchange for an alternative form of relief."

United States v. Perron, 58 M.J. 78, 86 n. 7 (C.A.A.F. 2003) (quoting Smith, 56 M.J. at 279).

We agree with appellate defense counsel that the military judge should have personally discussed this provision with appellant to determine appellant's understanding on the record. *See generally United States v. Reedy*, 4 M.J. 505, 506 (A.C.M.R. 1977); Benchbook at para. 2-4-1. We also note that appellant's affidavit filed with our court does not explicitly assert that he believed the convening authority could not approve a bad-conduct discharge or was required to approve a Chapter 10 discharge. In any case,

> [i]t is fundamental to a knowing and intelligent plea that where an accused pleads guilty in reliance on promises made by the [g]overnment in a pretrial agreement, the voluntariness of that plea depends on the fulfillment of those promises by the [g]overnment.... [and] where there is a mutual misunderstanding regarding a material term of a pretrial agreement, resulting in an accused not receiving the benefit of his bargain, the accused's pleas are improvident.... In such instances ... remedial action, in the form of specific performance, withdrawal of the plea, or alternative relief, is required.

Perron, 58 M.J. at 82 (citations omitted).

The parties' statements at trial and the agreement's ambiguity establish that "a meeting of the minds never occurred with respect to the [discharge] provision in the pretrial agreement. On that premise, appellant is entitled to have his pleas of guilty withdrawn or to have the agreement conformed, with the [g]overnment's consent, to appellant's understanding." *See United States v. Olson*, 25 M.J. 293, 298 (C.M.A. 1987). Because of the government's request that we set aside the findings and sentence, we decline to take remedial action "in the form of specific performance ... or alternative relief." *See United States v. Lundy*, 60 M.J. 52, 60 (C.A.A.F. 2004).[7] We choose to "nul-

---

[7] We reiterate that appellant failed to submit a signed request for a Chapter 10 discharge. We conclude that appellant has not complied with a critical term of his pretrial agreement. In light of the government's concession, however, we elect not to pursue fact finding to clarify this ambiguous situation.

lify the original pretrial agreement, returning the parties to status quo ante." *See Perron*, 58 M.J. at 86.

The findings of guilty and the sentence are set aside. A rehearing may be ordered by the same or a different convening authority.

Chief Judge CAREY and Senior Judge HARVEY concur.

Points for Discussion

1. If the government and the accused ever entered into a pretrial agreement in which the accused agrees to plead guilty and the government agrees to a maximum, the agreement typically provides that the military judge is not allowed to see the quantum portion of the agreement before determining the sentence. In that way, the accused receives the lesser of whatever the agreement provides or what the judge determines. What if by accident the accused blurts out the agreement in court during the plea inquiry, do you think the military judge should be precluded from determining the sentence? Why or why not?

2. Do you think the pretrial agreement in the *Dunbar* case was ambiguous? If so, what provisions were unclear? Could the military judge have resolved the ambiguities on the record? If so, how?

6-4. Military Panel (Jury) Requirements and Selection

Convening authorities convene courts-martial by publishing courts-martial convening orders. Those orders appoint specified service members to serve as panel members in these courts-martial. The orders direct the appointed service members to serve at a particular level of court-martial (e.g., general court-martial) and may direct hem to "sit" for a specific case or for a temporary specified period of time (e.g., one year) as an additional duty.

The convening authority may select persons for panels who meet the criteria listed in Article 25, UCMJ. In the military, there is no right to a jury of your peers. *See e.g., United States v. Smith*, 27 M.J. 242 (C.M.A. 1988); *United States v. Kemp*, 46 C.M.R. 152, 154 (C.M.A. 1973). Rather, the convening authority picks or "details" the "best qualified," to serve on the court-martial panel based on their age, education, experience, training, length of service, and judicial temperament. *See* UCMJ, Art. 25(d)(2). Whenever the convening authority can avoid it, panel members who are junior in rank to the accused or a member of the accused's unit cannot be detailed to the panel. An enlisted accused may request a panel comprised of at least one-third enlisted members.

Convening authorities and those who participate in the court-martial panel member selection process must insure that Article 25 criteria are followed and no improper motive exists in creating the panels.[1] Article 25, UCMJ provides as follows:

UCMJ, Article 25. Who may serve on courts-martial

(a) Any commissioned officer on active duty is eligible to serve on all courts-martial for the trial of any person . . .

(b) Any warrant officer on active duty is eligible to serve on general and special courts-martial for the trial of any person, other than a commissioned officer . . .

(c)(1) Any enlisted member of an armed force on active duty who is not a member of the same unit as the accused is eligible to serve on general and special courts-martial for the trial of any enlisted member . . . only if, prior to trial or . . . before the court is assembled for the trial of the accused, the accused personally has requested orally on the record or in writing that enlisted members serve on it. . . .

* * *

(d)(1) When it can be avoided, no member of an armed force may be tried by a court-martial any member of which is junior to him in rank or grade.

(2) When convening a court-martial, the convening authority shall detail as members thereof such members of the armed forces as, in his opinion, are best qualified for the duty by reason of age, education, training, experience, length of service, and judicial temperament. . . .

(e) Before a court-martial is assembled for the trial of a case, the convening authority may excuse a member of the court from participating in the case.

In *United States v. Bartlett*, 66 M.J. 426 (C.A.A.F. 2008), the case that follows, the Court of Appeals for the Armed Forces critically reviews the Army's restrictions (promulgated in an Army regulation) on court-martial panel member selection. As the court notes, Article 25, UCMJ, includes specific prohibitions on panel membership including disqualifying panel members who are junior in rank to the accused or who are accusers, witnesses, or investigating officers in the case. These Article 25 standards for disqualification of certain military members are based on involvement with the case, the accused unit, or on distinctions in grade or rank. The Army regulation applied during the process of establishing the court-martial panel in the *Bartlett* murder case, however, excluded chaplains, inspectors general, veterinarians, and medical personnel. The Court of Appeals for the Armed Forces finds the Army's regulatory restrictions improper.

---

[1] Allegations of unlawful command influence may arise if a convening authority or other person involved in the selection process attempts to include panel members based on an improper motive. *See* chapter 1-4 of this text.

UNITED STATES v. BARTLETT
U.S. Court of Appeals for the Armed Forces
66 M.J. 426 (C.A.A.F. 2008)

STUCKY, Judge:

A military judge sitting as a general court-martial convicted Appellant, Lieutenant Colonel David P. Bartlett Jr., [U.S. Army] pursuant to his pleas, of unpremeditated murder, in violation of Article 118, Uniform Code of Military Justice (UCMJ), 10 U.S.C. § 918 (2000). A panel of members sentenced him to a dismissal and confinement for twenty-five years. In accordance with a pretrial agreement, the convening authority deferred automatic forfeitures until his action, waived them thereafter for six months, and otherwise approved the findings and sentence. The United States Army Court of Criminal Appeals affirmed the findings and sentence. *United States v. Bartlett,* 64 M.J. 641, 649 (Army Ct. Crim. App. 2007).

We granted review of the following issue:

WHETHER THE SECRETARY OF THE ARMY'S DECISION TO EXEMPT FROM COURT-MARTIAL SERVICE OFFICERS OF THE SPECIAL BRANCHES NAMED IN AR 27-10 CONTRADICTS ARTICLE 25(d)(2), UCMJ, WHICH REQUIRES A CONVENING AUTHORITY TO SELECT COURT-MARTIAL MEMBERS BASED UPON AGE, EDUCATION, TRAINING, EXPERIENCE, LENGTH OF SERVICE, AND JUDICIAL TEMPERAMENT.

We hold that the Secretary of the Army impermissibly contravened the provisions of Article 25, UCMJ, 10 U.S.C. § 825 (2000). However, we conclude that on these facts, the error was harmless. We therefore affirm.

I.

Prior to trial, on July 18, 2002, the garrison staff judge advocate for Fort Meade, Maryland, sent a memorandum to the garrison commander, who was the general court-martial convening authority (GCMCA) for the present case. The memorandum dealt with the selection of court members for Appellant's trial. It recited, inter alia, that the GCMCA could not "detail officers assigned to the Medical Corps, Medical Specialist Corps, Army Nurse Corps, Dental Corps, Chaplain Corps, Veterinary Corps, nor those detailed to Inspector General duties as courts-martial panel members." The authority for this statement was given as "AR 27-10, Chapter 7." The parties stipulated that the GCMCA acted in accordance with this advice and did not detail any officer to the court-martial who fell within one of the prohibited classes. The parties further stipulated that the GCMCA had, at the time of selecting the panel, eleven officers within his general court-martial convening authority who were senior in grade or rank to Appellant but who fell within one of the prohibited classes.

At trial, the defense moved for a new court-martial panel, arguing that the Secretary of the Army exceeded his authority in exempting officers of the branches, set out in Dep't of the Army Reg. (AR) 27-10, Military Justice (Aug. 20, 1999), from service on courts-martial. The military judge made extensive findings of fact and law and denied the motion. The Army Court of Criminal Appeals affirmed, citing *Chevron U.S.A., Inc. v. Natural Resources Defense Council, Inc.*, 467 U.S. 837 (1984), and the analysis therein. *Bartlett*, 64 M.J. at 645-49.

II.

We review claims of error in the selection of members of courts-martial de novo as questions of law. *United States v. Dowty*, 60 M.J. 163, 171 (C.A.A.F. 2004); *United States v. Kirkland*, 53 M.J. 22, 24 (C.A.A.F. 2000).

At the outset, we are constrained to point out that although relied on by both sides, *Chevron* is in-apposite to this case. *Chevron* deals with the deference given to an administrative agency's interpretation of a regulatory statute, the administration of which has been committed to it by Congress. 467 U.S. at 839. That is not this case. Instead, here Congress has enacted a detailed statute-Article 25, UCMJ-which deals explicitly with the question of who may serve on courts-martial. Congress has further, in Article 36, UCMJ, 10 U.S.C. § 836 (2000), delegated to the President the authority to prescribe by regulation procedures for the trial of courts-martial, insofar as such regulations are not inconsistent with the UCMJ. *United States v. Jenkins*, 262-63, 22 C.M.R. 51, 52-53 (C.M.A. 1956). Such regulations are also to be "uniform insofar as practica-ble." Article 36(b), UCMJ.

A general and wholly separate statute, 10 U.S.C. § 3013 (2000), establishes the position of Secretary of the Army and grants the Secretary broad general powers over the Department of the Army. Subsection (g), in pertinent part, states:

(g) The Secretary of the Army may-

(1) assign, detail, and prescribe the duties of members of the Army and civilian personnel of the Department of the Army;

. . . .

(3) prescribe regulations to carry out his functions, powers, and duties under this title.

It appears clear that the Secretary issued the underlying personnel management regulations collected in AR 27-10 pursuant to his authority to "prescribe the duties of members of the Army." *Id.* We, therefore, are faced with a situation in which Congress has enacted detailed and specific legislation dealing with a subject common to all the armed forces, while a service secretary, pursuant to a separate general statute, has issued regulations[2] dealing with the same subject.

---

[2] It appears that only the Army exempts medical and related personnel and inspectors general from court-martial duty by regulation. The services appear to have a uniform policy of exempting chaplains. . . . . Navy chaplains serve the needs of the

In addressing the apparent tension between Article 25, UCMJ, and the Secretary's implementation of his enabling authority, we apply standard principles of statutory construction. *See United States v. Lopez*, 35 M.J. 35, 39 (C.M.A. 1992); *United States v. Baker*, 507, 40 C.M.R. 216, 219 (C.M.A. 1969). While statutes covering the same subject matter should be construed to harmonize them if possible, this does not empower courts to undercut the clearly expressed intent of Congress in enacting a particular statute. *United States v. Johnson*, 3 M.J. 361, 363 (C.M.A. 1977); *United States v. Walker*, 23 C.M.R. 133, 138 (C.MA. 1957); *United States v. Lucas*, 1 C.M.R. 19, 22 (C.M.A. 1951).

Congress did not see fit to include in Article 25, UCMJ, any limitations on court-martial service by any branch, corps, or occupational specialty among commissioned officers of the armed forces. Rather, it cast the eligibility of such officers to serve in broad and inclusive terms in Article 25(a), UCMJ (emphasis added): "*Any* commissioned officer on active duty is eligible to serve on *all* courts-martial for the trial of *any* person who may lawfully be brought before such courts for trial." Within that broad class, the convening authority of a court-martial is to detail those members who, "in his opinion, are best qualified for the duty by reason of age, education, training, experience, length of service, and judicial temperament." Article 25(d)(2), UCMJ.

Equally as important, Congress limited the broad and inclusive terms of Article 25, UCMJ, by prohibiting only certain members of the armed forces from acting as members of courts-martial. For example, a member who is the accuser or a witness for the prosecution, or who has acted as investigating officer or counsel in a case, may not sit on that case. Article 25(d)(2), UCMJ. Nor may a warrant officer or enlisted person sit as a member in a case involving a commissioned officer, like this one. Article 25(b), 25(c)(1), UCMJ. Unless it is unavoidable, no member of the armed forces junior in rank or grade to the accused member may sit on that member's court-martial. Article 25(d)(1), UCMJ.

The President, to whom regulatory authority is committed by Article 36, UCMJ, has similarly seen fit to take a nonrestrictive view of court-martial service. Rule for Courts-Martial (R.C.M.) 502(a), which sets out the basic qualifications of members of courts-martial, adds nothing to the statutory language. R.C.M. 912(f), which does deal with disqualification for service, is cast not in terms of prohibition from detail to court-martial service, but in terms of allowable challenges for cause. The disqualifying factors in the Rules for Courts-Martial, as in Article 25, UCMJ, are limited to two: (1) actual involvement in the case (as, for example, an investigating officer); and (2) formal distinctions of grade or rank (as in, for example, the prohibition of a warrant officer's sitting on a commissioned officer's court-martial). The implication is clear: Congress and the President crafted few prohibitions on

---

Coast Guard and are not to be assigned collateral duties which involve serving as a member of a court-martial. . . .

court-martial service to ensure maximum discretion to the convening authority in the selection process, while maintaining the basic fairness of the military justice system.

It is inescapable, then, that the Army regulations limiting detail of commissioned officers to court-martial duty, collected in AR 27-10, directly conflict with the provisions of Article 25, UCMJ, on the same subject. Congress did not simply set out broad criteria in that article and leave it to administrative implementation; rather, it set out detailed requirements, disqualifications, and prohibitions for courts-martial of varying classes of members of the armed forces. As such, the Army regulations must yield to the clear language of Article 25, UCMJ. *See, e.g., United States v. Simpson*, 27 C.M.R. 303, 306 (C.M.A. 1959).

Moreover, the Secretary's application of 10 U.S.C. § 3013(g) (2000) runs afoul of the accepted principle of statutory construction that in cases of direct conflict, a specific statute overrides a general one, regardless of their dates of enactment. 2B Norman J. Singer, Statutes and Statutory Con-struction § 51.02, at 187 (7th ed.2000); *Morton v. Mancari*, 417 U.S. 535, 550-51 (1974); *Bulova Watch Co. v. United States*, 365 U.S. 753, 758 (1961); *United States v. Mitchell*, 44 C.M.R. 649, 651 (A.C.M.R. 1971). The general grant of authority to the Secretary to run the Army, broad and necessary as it is, cannot trump Article 25, UCMJ, which is narrowly tailored legislation dealing with the precise question in issue. We are left, then, with a clear explication of the convening authority's broad power to detail any officer to a panel as long as the requirements of Article 25, UCMJ, are met.

III.

This does not, however, end our inquiry. Having found error, we must determine what, if any, relief to grant Appellant. As Appellant pled guilty before the military judge, he has asked only for a new sentencing hearing. We may not find the sentence incorrect in law "unless the error materially pre-judice[d] the substantial rights to the accused." Article 59(a), UCMJ, 10 U.S.C. § 859(a) (2000).

Citing *Arizona v. Fulminante*, 499 U.S. 279, 310 (1991), and *United States v. Greene*, 43 C.M.R. 72, 79 (C.M.A. 1970), Appellant asserts that the error was structural, thus obviating the need to show prejudice. Alternatively, he argues that he was prejudiced because his panel lacked the benefit of the special skills and education of the special branch officers. Both arguments fail.

A.

There is a strong presumption that an error is not structural. *Rose v. Clark*, 478 U.S. 570, 579 (1986), overruled on other grounds by *Brecht v. Abrahamson*, 507 U.S. 619, 637 (1993). In *Fulminante*, the Supreme Court noted that certain constitutional errors, such as "the unlawful exclusion of members of the defendant's race from a grand jury," were structural defects in the trial mechanism which defied analysis for harmless error. 499 U.S. at

309-10 (citing *Vasquez v. Hillery*, 474 U.S. 254 (1986)). Appellant's case, however, deals with a statutory rather than constitutional error.

Both before and after the Supreme Court's decision in *Fulminante*, this Court has employed a case-specific rather than a structural-error analysis in deciding issues of improper court member selection. . . . Appellant has not shown that a structural error approach is warranted under the circumstances of this case.

The burden of demonstrating prejudice, or the lack thereof, from nonconstitutional error in the detailing of court members depends on the manner in which the error occurred. In those cases where we have concluded that the error resulted from unlawful command influence-attempts to affect the outcome of the trial through the selection of particular members-we have not affirmed unless the government established beyond a reasonable doubt that the error was harmless. *See Hilow*, 32 M.J. at 442; *McClain*, 22 M.J. at 132. Where a convening authority has intentionally included or ex-cluded certain classes of individuals from membership, in an attempt to comply with the requirements of Article 25, UCMJ-such as exclusion of junior officers and enlisted members because senior officers possess better maturity and judgment-we have placed the burden on the government to demonstrate lack of harm. . . . On the other hand, when there is a simple administrative error, the burden is on the appellant to show prejudice. . . .

B.

This case represents a novel question in that the source of the error is the Army regulation that required the convening authority to exclude certain classes of officers from consideration. Nevertheless, as this error was not a simple administrative mistake, we conclude the Government has the burden of showing the error was harmless.[4]

In Appellant's case (1) there is no evidence that the Secretary of the Army enacted the regulation with an improper motive; (2) there is no evidence that the convening authority's motivation in detailing the members he assigned to Appellant's court-martial was anything but benign-the desire to comply with a facially valid Army regulation; (3) the convening authority who referred Appellant's case to trial was a person authorized to convene a general court-martial; (4) Appellant was sentenced by court members personally chosen by the convening authority from a pool of eligible officers; (5) the court members all met the criteria in Article 25, UCMJ; and, (6) as the military judge

---

[4] Although the burden is on the Government to show there was no prejudice, Appellant has alleged that he was prejudiced because his panel lacked the benefit of the special skills and education of the special branch officers. Appellant offers nothing more than supposition that the special branch officers would bring skills unique to their occupations—"critical thinking" (doctors and nurses), "compassion" (chaplains), and "neutrality" (inspectors general). While such prejudice is speculative at best, we considered this allegation of prejudice in determining whether the Government had met its burden.

found, the panel was "well-balanced across gender, racial, staff, command, and branch lines." Under these circumstances, we are convinced the error in this case was harmless.

IV.

The decision of the United States Army Court of Criminal Appeals is affirmed.

[Judge Erdmann's separate concurring opinion is omitted – Eds.]

Points for Discussion

1. Do you agree with the *Bartlett* court's determination that "Congress and the President crafted few prohibitions on court-martial service to ensure maximum discretion to the convening authority in the selection process, while maintaining the basic fairness of the military justice system"?

2. Why did the court in *Bartlett* decide that Article 36, UCMJ, which delegates "to the President the authority to prescribe by regulation procedures for the trial of courts-martial, insofar as such regulations are not inconsistent with the UCMJ" and 10 U.S.C. § 3013 (2000), which "establishes the position of Secretary of the Army and grants the Secretary broad general powers over the Department of the Army" did not allow for the expansion of the prohibitions in Article 25, UCMJ?

CHAPTER 7

PRETRIAL MOTIONS AND INTERLOCUTORY APPEALS

7-1. Pretrial Motions in General

The *Art of War,* an ancient Chinese military treatise, proclaims a truth still evident today: "the general who wins a battle makes many calculations . . . ere the battle is fought." Sun Tzu, The Art of War 4 (Lionel Giles, trans., 2009). Although the context is different, the same principle holds in courts-martial. Successful military prosecutors and defense attorneys undertake important strategic preparations before the actual trial begins. These preparations often include filing pretrial motions requesting rulings from the military judge that effectively may determine the outcome of the trial before it occurs.

A "motion," in the words of R.C.M. 905(a), is "an application to the military judge for particular relief." Through motions made before trial, the accused may seek the dismissal of some or all of the charges or specifications, and either side may seek favorable rulings on witnesses, evidence, and other matters that ultimately may determine the outcome of the trial if the case is not dismissed. For these reasons, the filing of pretrial motions is one of the most important parts of court-martial practice.

The military justice system encourages parties to make pretrial motions. Under R.C.M. 905(b), the parties may raise "any defense, request, or objection" in a pretrial motion that is "capable of determination without the trial of the general issue of guilt." The same rule requires the following types of motions to be raised "before a plea is entered":

(1) Defenses or objections based on defects (other than jurisdictional defects) in the preferral forwarding, investigation, or referral of charges:

(2) Defenses or objections based on defects in the charges and specifications (other than any failure to show jurisdiction or to charge an offense, which objections shall be resolved by the military judge at any time during the pendency of the proceedings);

(3) Motions to suppress evidence:

(4) Motions for discovery under R.C.M. 701 or for production of witnesses or evidence;

(5) Motions for severance of charges or accused:

(6) Objections based on denial of request for individual military counsel or for retention of detailed defense counsel when individual military counsel has been granted.

A party's failure to raise a defense or objection that must be raised in a pretrial motion under R.C.M. 905(b) is a waiver of the defense or objection. *See* R.C.M. 905(e). Even if a party raises an issue in a pretrial motion, appellate review may be waived by a subsequent guilty plea. For example, subject to an exception discussed below in *United States v. Mizgala*, 61 M.J. 122 (C.A.A.F. 2005), an unconditional guilty plea ordinarily waives any complaint concerning violation of the right to a speedy trial. *See* R.C.M. 707(e) ("[A] plea of guilty which results in a finding of guilty waives any speedy trial issue as to that offense.); *see also* R.C.M. 910(j) (providing that an unconditional "plea of guilty which results in a finding of guilty waives any objection, whether or not previously raised, insofar as the objection relates to the factual issue of guilt of the offense(s) to which the plea was made.") Once an issue is waived, appellant authorities may review the issue only for "plain error." To constitute "plain error," the defense must show that there was error, that the error was plain or obvious, and that the error materially prejudiced a substantial right. *See United States v. Powell*, 49 M.J. 460, 464 (1998).

Points for Discussion

1. Why would the Rules for Courts-Martial require the six types of motions, defenses, and objections listed in R.C.M. 905(b), to be raised before trial? Why can objections to the jurisdiction of the court-martial be raised at any time?

2. Although most pretrial motions are filed with the military judge, R.C.M. 905(j) also permits parties to submit pretrial motions to the convening authority. Are there types of motions that convening authorities are likely to grant which military judges are not, or vice versa?

7-2. Examples of Common Pretrial Motions

While the parties can file motions on many subjects before trial, three very common pretrial requests for relief concern speedy trials, sanity boards, and the admissibility of evidence. Examples of each are considered below.

Motion for a Speedy Trial

Service members, like civilians, enjoy a right to a speedy trial. Protection of this right comes from the Sixth Amendment, Article 10, UCMJ, and R.C.M. 707, all of which are discussed in the following case. The consequences of denying the accused of a speedy trial may be dismissal of the charges. The following case controversially interprets the provision in R.C.M. 707(e) which—as quoted above—provides that an unconditional guilty plea waives an accused's right to complain of a speedy trial violation.

UNITED STATES v. MIZGALA
U.S. Court of Appeals for the Armed Forces
61 M.J. 122 (C.A.A.F. 2005)

Judge ERDMANN delivered the opinion of the court.

Airman First Class Patrick A. Mizgala entered guilty pleas to numerous offenses[1] and was sentenced to a bad-conduct discharge, confinement for nine months, forfeiture of all pay and allowances, and reduction to the grade of E–1. The convening authority reduced the amount of forfeitures but approved the balance of the sentence. The United States Air Force Court of Criminal Appeals affirmed the findings and sentence. . . .

Article 10, Uniform Code of Military Justice (UCMJ), 10 U.S.C. § 810 (2000), assures the right of a speedy trial to military members by providing that "[w]hen any person subject to this chapter is placed in arrest or confinement prior to trial, immediate steps shall be taken to inform him of the specific wrong of which he is accused and to try him or to dismiss the charges and release him."

Mizgala was initially held in pretrial confinement for 117 days. His timely motion to dismiss for lack of a speedy trial under Article 10 was denied by the military judge and Mizgala entered unconditional guilty pleas to all of the charges. We granted review to determine whether Mizgala's unconditional guilty pleas waived appellate review of the speedy trial motion and, if not, whether Mizgala was denied his Article 10 right to a speedy trial. We find that Mizgala's unconditional guilty plea did not waive his right to appellate review of his litigated speedy trial motion, but find that his Article 10 right to speedy trial was not violated.

WAIVER

The Air Force Court of Criminal Appeals found that Mizgala waived consideration of his Article 10 claim by his unconditional guilty plea. In addition, that court held that even if the speedy trial issue had not been waived, there was no violation of Mizgala's Article 10 rights. After noting that the military judge incorrectly used a "gross negligence" standard, the court concluded that the military judge's error was not prejudicial, citing *Barker v. Wingo*, 407 U.S. 514 (1972).

---

[1] Mizgala entered guilty pleas to attempted larceny, unauthorized absence, unauthorized absence terminated by apprehension, two specifications of wrongfully using cocaine, wrongfully using marijuana, larceny of a motor vehicle, and larceny of personal property in violation of Articles 80, 86, 112a, and 121, Uniform Code of Military Justice (UCMJ), 10 U.S.C. §§ 880, 886, 912a, 921 (2000), respectively.

Speedy Trial under the UCMJ

Congress enacted various speedy trial provisions in the UCMJ to address concerns about "the length of time that a man will be placed in confinement and held there pending his trial"; to prevent an accused from "languish[ing] in a jail somewhere for a considerable length of time" awaiting trial or disposition of charges; to protect the accused's rights to a speedy trial without sacrificing the ability to defend himself; to provide responsibility in the event that someone unnecessarily delays a trial; and to establish speedy trial protections under the UCMJ "consistent with good procedure and justice." Uniform Code of Military Justice: Hearings on H.R. 2498 Before a Subcomm. of the House Comm. on Armed Services, 81st Cong. 905–12, 980–983, 1005 (1949). *See United States v. Tibbs*, 35 C.M.R. 322, 331 (C.M.A. 1965) (Ferguson, J., dissenting); *United States v. Hounshell*, 21 C.M.R. 129, 133–34 (C.M.A. 1956).

Where an accused is incarcerated pending disposition of charges under the UCMJ, Congress has placed the onus on the Government to take "immediate steps" to move that case to trial. Article 10, UCMJ. "Particularly, [Congress] indicated that delay cannot be condoned if the accused is in arrest or confinement." *United States v. Wilson*, 27 C.M.R. 411, 414 (C.M.A. 1959).

While our cases have sometimes adopted different approaches to Article 10 speedy trial issues, they have consistently stressed the significant role Article 10 plays when servicemembers are confined prior to trial. We have referred to the right to a speedy trial as a "fundamental right" of the accused, *United States v. Parish*, 38 C.M.R. 209, 214 (C.M.A. 1968), and as "[u]nquestionably . . . a substantial right," *Hounshell*, 21 C.M.R. at 132. A number of our earlier cases included speedy disposition of charges under the concept of "military due process." *United States v. Prater*, 43 C.M.R. 179, 182 (C.M.A. 1971) (citing *United States v. Schlack*, 34 C.M.R. 151 (C.M.A. 1964)). *See also United States v. Williams*, 37 C.M.R. 209 (C.M.A. 1967).

The Government urges us to find that an unconditional guilty plea effectively waives a servicemember's Article 10 speedy trial rights in all instances. In support of their argument the Government directs our attention to Sixth Amendment jurisprudence, Rule for Courts-Martial (R.C.M.) 707(e), and the Speedy Trial Act of 1974, Pub.L. No. 93–619, 88 Stat. 2070, and points out that the speedy trial protection under each of those provisions is waived by an unconditional guilty plea. We will examine each of these areas in turn.

Sixth Amendment

The Sixth Amendment to the United States Constitution contains the constitutional guarantee to a speedy trial.[3]   Although the text of the amendment does not address waiver, courts have held that the Sixth

---

[3] The Sixth Amendment provides, in pertinent part: In all criminal prosecutions, the accused shall enjoy the right to a speedy and public trial . . . .

Amendment right is waived by a voluntary guilty plea. *See Cox v. Lockhart*, 970 F.2d 448, 453 (8th Cir. 1992) . . . .

We have consistently noted that Article 10 creates a more exacting speedy trial demand than does the Sixth Amendment. *United States v. Cooper*, 58 M.J. 54, 60 (C.A.A.F. 2003); *United States v. King*, 30 M.J. 59, 62 (C.M.A. 1990) (citing *United States v. Powell*, 2 M.J. 6 (C.M.A. 1976); *United States v. Marshall*, 47 C.M.R. 409 (C.M.A. 1973)). Not only is the demand for a speedy trial under the UCMJ more exacting, by virtue of Article 98, UCMJ, 10 U.S.C. § 898 (2000), unreasonable delay in disposing of criminal charges in the military is unlawful.[4] *See Powell*, 2 M.J. at 8; *United States v. Mason*, 45 C.M.R. 163, 167 (C.M.A. 1972). While the full scope of this "more exacting" Article 10 right has not been precisely defined by this court, it cannot be "more exacting" and at the same time be "consistent" with Sixth Amendment protections.

Rule for Courts-Martial 707

Rule for Courts-Martial 707 contains the speedy trial provision in the Rules for Courts-Martial. Rule for Courts-Martial 707(e) provides that "a plea of guilty which results in a finding of guilty waives any speedy trial issue as to that offense." We have found, however, that the language of Article 10 is "clearly different" from R.C.M. 707 and have held that Article 10 is not restricted by R.C.M. 707. *Cooper*, 58 M.J. at 58–60 (holding that the protections of Article 10 extend beyond arraignment); *Kossman*, 38 M.J. at 261 ("[I]n the area of subconstitutional speedy trial, Article 10 reigns preeminent over anything propounded by the President.").

The protections afforded confined or arrested servicemembers under Article 10 are distinct and greater given the nature of other speedy trial protections. *See United States v. Reed*, 41 M.J. 449, 451 (C.A.A.F. 1995) (listing sources for the right to a speedy trial in the military); *United States v. Vogan*, 35 M.J. 32, 33 (C.M.A. 1992) (also listing military speedy trial right sources). *Rule for Courts-Martial* 707(e) therefore does not act as a limitation on the rights afforded under Article 10.

Speedy Trial Act

Courts have uniformly held that a guilty plea "constitutes a waiver of [an accused's] rights under the [Speedy Trial] Act." *United States v. Morgan*, 384 F.3d 439, 442 (7th Cir. 2004). While the Speedy Trial Act does not apply to

---

[4] Article 98, UCMJ, 10 U.S.C. § 898 (2000), provides: "Any person subject to this chapter, who (1) is responsible for unnecessary delay in the disposition of any case of a person accused of an offense under this chapter; or (2) knowingly and intentionally fails to enforce or comply with any provision of this chapter regulating the proceedings before, during, or after trial of an accused; shall be punished as a court-martial may direct."

offenses under the UCMJ,[5] there is a further distinction in the allocation of burdens under the two statutes. The Speedy Trial Act imposes the burden of proof upon an accused to support a motion to dismiss. 18 U.S.C. § 3162(a)(2)(2000). Under Article 10, the Government has the burden to show that the prosecution moved forward with reasonable diligence in response to a motion to dismiss. *United States v. Brown*, 28 C.M.R. 64, 69 (C.M.A. 1959). This distinction is additional proof of the importance of Article 10 to the incarcerated servicemember.

We therefore find nothing in the comparisons to the Sixth Amendment, R.C.M. 707 or the Speedy Trial Act that would compel our application of their speedy trial waiver rules to Article 10. It falls to this court then to determine whether an unconditional guilty plea waives a litigated Article 10 speedy trial motion.

Article 10 Waiver Precedent

Over the years our cases have taken different views as to how or whether the right to a speedy trial under Article 10 could be waived. These divergent views have manifested themselves in cases involving forfeiture for failure to raise the issue at trial and as well as in cases considering waiver of the right due to an unconditional guilty plea. In an early case that considered Article 10 speedy trial rights, the court adopted the view that the right to a speedy trial could be forfeited for failing to raise the issue at trial:

> The right to a speedy trial is a personal right which can be waived. If the accused does not demand a trial or does not object to the continuance of a case at the prosecution's request or if he goes to trial without making any objection to the lapse of time between the initiation of the charges and the trial, he cannot complain of the delay after he has been convicted.

Hounshell, 21 C.M.R. at 133 (citation omitted). A short time later, however, Judge Quinn, the author judge in *Hounshell*, wrote with regard to speedy trial in another contested case that "[i]n the military, application of the rule of waiver, where the accused is confined, has little to recommend it." *Wilson*, 27 C.M.R. at 415.

Similarly, our cases involving waiver and unconditional guilty pleas have vacillated. In *United States v. Rehorn*, 26 C.M.R. 267, 268–69 (C.M.A. 1958), the court stated, "It is a fundamental principle of Federal criminal law that a plea of guilty waives all defects which are neither jurisdictional nor a deprivation of due process of law." Subsequently in *United States v. Schalck* the court held "that delay in preferring charges against the accused was not waived by his failure to raise the issue at trial and by his plea of guilty." 34 C.M.R. at 155. *See also United States v. Goode*, 38 C.M.R. 382, 385 (C.M.A. 1968) (finding that guilty plea does not deprive accused of protection afforded by Article 10); *United States v. Cummings*, 38 C.M.R. 174, 179

---

[5] 18 U.S.C. § 3172(2)(2000) (stating that offense as used in the Speedy Trial Act specifically excludes an offense triable by court-martial).

(C.M.A. 1968) (finding that a waiver of the right to a speedy trial as part of a pretrial agreement is contrary to public policy); *Tibbs*, 35 C.M.R. at 325 (reiterating that accused who pleads guilty does not lose protection accorded by Article 10).

A short time later, the court again changed direction on waiver in another case involving a guilty plea: "We answer in the affirmative the certified question . . . which asks whether '. . . an accused who does not object at the time of trial to a delay in excess of three months in bringing him to trial will be precluded from raising the issue at the appellate level. . . .' " *United States v. Sloan*, 48 C.M.R. 211, 214 (C.M.A. 1974) (citation omitted). Recently, in *United States v. Birge*, this court acknowledged the rule of waiver from Sloan but declined to address whether an Article 10 speedy trial claim was waived by a guilty plea under R.C.M. 707(e). 52 M.J. 209, 211–12 (C.A.A.F. 1999).

We take this opportunity to revisit our examination of whether an Article 10 claim is waived by an unconditional guilty plea or whether it may be reviewed by an appellate court in cases where the accused unsuccessfully raises an Article 10 issue at trial and then enters an unconditional guilty plea. In view of the legislative importance given to a speedy trial under the UCMJ and the unique nature of the protections of Article 10 discussed above, we believe that where an accused unsuccessfully raises an Article 10 issue and thereafter pleads guilty, waiver does not apply. Such a rule for Article 10 rights properly reflects the importance of a servicemember's right to a speedy trial under Article 10. Preservation of the right to appeal adverse Article 10 rulings is not only supported by the congressional intent behind Article 10, it also maintains the high standards of speedy disposition of charges against members of the armed forces and recognizes "military procedure as the exemplar of prompt action in bringing to trial those members of the armed forces charged with offenses." *United States v. Pierce*, 41 C.M.R. 225, 227 (C.M.A. 1970). *See also United States v. Hatfield*, 44 M.J. 22, 24 (C.A.A.F. 1996) ("[T]he mandate that the Government take immediate steps to try arrested or confined accused must ever be borne in mind."). A fundamental, substantial, personal right—a right that dates from our earlier cases—should not be diminished by applying ordinary rules of waiver and forfeiture associated with guilty pleas.

We therefore hold that a litigated speedy trial motion under Article 10 is not waived by a subsequent unconditional guilty plea. Thus, Mizgala's unconditional guilty plea did not waive his right to contest the military judge's denial of his Article 10 motion on appeal.

Having concluded that Mizgala did not waive review of his Article 10 claim by entering an unconditional guilty plea, we proceed to the merits of that claim.

ARTICLE 10 SPEEDY TRIAL

The standard of diligence under which we review claims of a denial of speedy trial under Article 10 "is not constant motion, but reasonable diligence in bringing the charges to trial." *Tibbs*, 35 C.M.R. at 325. *See also Kossman*, 38 M.J. at 262; *United States v. Johnson*, 1 M.J. 101 (C.M.A. 1975). Short periods of inactivity are not fatal to an otherwise active prosecution. *Tibbs*, 35 C.M.R. at 325 (citing *United States v. Williams*, 30 C.M.R. 81, 83 (C.M.A. 1961)). Further, although Sixth Amendment speedy trial standards cannot dictate whether there has been an Article 10 violation, the factors from *Barker v. Wingo* are an apt structure for examining the facts and circumstances surrounding an alleged Article 10 violation. *Cooper*, 58 M.J. at 61; *Birge*, 52 M.J. at 212.

We review the decision of whether an accused has received a speedy trial de novo as a legal question, giving substantial deference to a military judge's findings of fact that will be reversed only if they are clearly erroneous. *Cooper*, 58 M.J. at 57–59; *United States v. Doty*, 51 M.J. 464, 465 (C.A.A.F. 1999).

Facts Relevant to the Speedy Trial Determination

The parties stipulated at trial to a chronology of events relating to the pretrial processing of this case. Additional information was provided by testimony from the deputy staff judge advocate and the former chief of military justice at Sheppard Air Force Base (AFB). Ultimately, the military judge made findings of fact in support of his ruling on the speedy trial motion.

Mizgala was absent without leave (AWOL) on January 18 and 19, 2001. Upon his return to military control, he confessed to using cocaine while absent. He went AWOL again on February 5, and remained absent until February 28. This second absence ended because Mizgala became involved in an off-base incident concerning an attempt to steal beer. Upon his return, he confessed that he used both cocaine and marijuana during this absence.

Mizgala was placed in pretrial confinement on February 28 and a pretrial confinement hearing was conducted three days later on March 3. The hearing officer determined that continued pretrial confinement was warranted because Mizgala was a flight risk and likely to engage in additional misconduct.

On March 12, 2001, the Government received the results of a urinalysis on a sample given when Mizgala entered pretrial confinement. Those results indicated the presence of both cocaine and marijuana in Mizgala's urine sample. At the end of March or early in April, the trial counsel prepared draft charges and forwarded them to the staff judge advocate. The draft charge sheet was returned to add a charge for the attempt to steal beer in the civilian community. Trial counsel then requested Security Forces to obtain the Wichita Falls Police Department report pertaining to this incident.

Of importance in this case is that during the time that this case was processed, the legal office at Sheppard AFB was operating out of a temporary facility because a fire had destroyed their facility. On April 13, 2001, the office moved to a semipermanent facility. On April 16, 2001, Mizgala made a request for a speedy trial. The deputy staff judge advocate testified that because Mizgala was in pretrial confinement when he made his demand for speedy trial, his case was already in a priority status.

The trial counsel requested the litigation packet pertaining to the pretrial confinement urinalysis from the laboratory at Brooks AFB, Texas, on April 23. On May 10, a police report pertaining to the attempted larceny of beer was received from the Wichita Falls Police Department. On May 14, seventy-five days after the initiation of pretrial confinement, charges were preferred against Mizgala.

An investigating officer was appointed under Article 32, UCMJ, 10 U.S.C. § 832 (2000), on May 22. He conducted the investigation on May 24 and completed the report of investigation the following day. The completed Article 32 investigation was forwarded to the defense on May 29. The record contains no indication that the defense made any objections or filed any comments on the report of investigation. In the interim, a memorandum indicating that Wichita Falls would not prosecute the attempted larceny of beer was received by the legal office.

On June 5, the referral package and a related request for immunity were forwarded by the Sheppard AFB legal office to the staff judge advocate for the convening authority. The R.C.M. 406 pretrial advice was completed on June 20, and the case was referred to trial the following day. However, Mizgala was rapidly approaching the 120–day limit contained in R.C.M. 707 and because the Government did not believe that he could be tried before then, they released him from pretrial confinement on June 21, 2001. The following day, Mizgala once again went AWOL.

After considering the stipulated chronology of events, two witnesses, and arguments, the military judge denied the motion to dismiss for violation of Article 10. Although the military judge found "inefficiencies throughout this process," he ultimately held:

As such, at least as it applies to this case, I find that the government has exercised reasonable diligence insofar as it has complied with R.C.M. 707 and as that equates to Article 10 in this particular circumstance. I do not believe that the inefficiencies mentioned equate to negligence that's outlined in Kossman, and I believe that is a standard that effectively would have to amount to gross negligence. And I find that by a preponderance of the evidence.

When he later announced additional findings, the military judge adhered to his speedy trial ruling and reiterated that "I must essentially equate the R.C.M. standard with an Article 10 violation." He further stated that gross negligence was required to support an Article 10 violation. Also, while the military judge's ruling did reflect some consideration of the Barker factors, it did so in a manner that indicated that the military judge limited his consideration to a Sixth Amendment speedy trial analysis.

DISCUSSION

We agree with the Court of Criminal Appeals that the military judge plainly erred in the manner in which he reviewed Mizgala's Article 10 motion. His ruling was erroneous as a matter of law in three regards. First, Article 10 and R.C.M. 707 are distinct, each providing its own speedy trial protection. The fact that a prosecution meets the 120–day rule of R.C.M. 707 does not directly "or indirectly" demonstrate that the Government moved to trial with reasonable diligence as required by Article 10. *See United States v. Edmond*, 41 M.J. 419, 421 (C.A.A.F. 1995); *Kossman*, 38 M.J. at 260–61.

Second, the military judge erred in determining that he was required to find gross negligence to support an Article 10 violation in the absence of Government spite or bad faith. An Article 10 violation rests in the failure of the Government to proceed with reasonable diligence. A conclusion of unreasonable diligence may arise from a number of different causes and need not rise to the level of gross neglect to support a violation. *Kossman*, 38 M.J. at 261. Finally, the military judge erred by limiting his consideration of the *Barker v. Wingo* factors to a Sixth Amendment speedy trial analysis. We have held that "it is 'appropriate' to consider those factors 'in determining whether a particular set of circumstances violates a servicemember's speedy trial rights under Article 10.'" *Cooper*, 58 M.J. at 61 (quoting *Birge*, 52 M.J. at 212).

Turning to the substance of Mizgala's claim, our framework to determine whether the Government proceeded with reasonable diligence includes balancing the following four factors: (1) the length of the delay; (2) the reasons for the delay; (3) whether the appellant made a demand for a speedy trial; and (4) prejudice to the appellant. *See Barker*, 407 U.S. at 530. *See also Birge*, 52 M.J. at 212. Applying those factors to Mizgala's case, we remain mindful that we are looking at the proceeding as a whole and not mere speed: "[T]he essential ingredient is orderly expedition and not mere speed." *United States v. Mason*, 45 C.M.R. 163, 167 (C.M.A. 1972) (quoting *Smith v. United States*, 360 U.S. 1, 10 (1959)).

The processing of this case is not stellar. We share the military judge's concern with several periods during which the Government seems to have been in a waiting posture: waiting for formal evidence prior to preferring charges and waiting for a release of jurisdiction for an offense that occurred in the civilian community. There are periods evidencing delay in seeking evidence of the off-post offense and seeking litigation packages to support prosecution of the drug offenses. Nevertheless, constant motion is not the standard so long as the processing reflects reasonable diligence under all the circumstances. Our evaluation must balance the delay against the reasons for these periods of delay (such as the need to investigate offenses and obtain evidence), with the need to coordinate investigation and jurisdiction with civilian authorities. Once these necessary steps were completed, the Government moved expeditiously to refer the charges.

As to the consideration of possible prejudice, we find no material prejudice to Mizgala's substantial rights. In this regard, we note the test for prejudice set forth by the Supreme Court:

> Prejudice, of course, should be assessed in the light of the interests of defendants which the speedy trial right was designed to protect. This Court has identified three such interests: (i) to prevent oppressive pretrial incarceration; (ii) to minimize anxiety and concern of the accused; and (iii) to limit the possibility that the defense will be impaired. Of these, the most serious is the last, because the inability of a defendant adequately to prepare his case skews the fairness of the entire system.

Barker, 407 U.S. at 532 (footnote omitted). Mizgala experienced 117 days of pretrial confinement, which necessarily involves some anxiety and stress, but there is no evidence in the record that the conditions of that confinement were harsh or oppressive. Finally, there is no indication that his preparation for trial, defense evidence, trial strategy, or ability to present witnesses, on both the merits and sentencing, were compromised by the processing time in this case. Balancing those factors identified by the Supreme Court, we find that prejudice, if any, was minimal.

We hold that Mizgala was not denied his Article 10 right to a speedy trial and, after our de novo review of the speedy trial issue, we find there was no prejudice from the military judge's application of an erroneous standard of law.

DECISION

The decision of the United States Air Force Court of Criminal Appeals is affirmed.

CRAWFORD, Judge (dissenting in part and concurring in the result):

While the majority notes that Article 10, Uniform Code of Military Justice (UCMJ), 10 U.S.C. § 810 (2000), is a "more exacting" right, it overlooks the history behind the UCMJ provisions of the Manual for Courts-Martial, United States (2002 ed.)(MCM), and mainstream jurisprudence in this area. Thus, I respectfully dissent from the majority opinion that an unconditional plea of guilty does not waive Appellant's rights to a speedy trial whether asserted under the Sixth Amendment, the UCMJ, or the MCM. The congressional history underlying Article 10 has not altered what a majority of the courts have held concerning unconditional guilty pleas.

History Behind the UCMJ. When Congress passed the UCMJ in 1950, there was some question as to the applicability of the Bill of Rights to members of the Armed Forces. Fifty-five years later, the Supreme Court still has never expressly held that the Bill of Rights applies to servicemembers. In *United States ex rel. Innes v. Crystal*, 131 F.2d 576, 577 n. 2 (2d Cir. 1943) (citing *Ex parte Quirin*, 317 U.S. 1 (1942)), the court stated, "The Fifth and Sixth Amendments are, of course, inapplicable to courts-martial." This question about the application of the Bill of Rights to the military resulted in Congress passing Articles 10, 27, 31, 44, 46, and 63.

Early in the Court's history, when examining the question of speedy trial, it "bottom[ed] those [constitutional] rights and privileges" on the Due Process Clause of the Fourteenth Amendment rather than on the specific provisions in the Bill of Rights. *United States v. Clay*, , 1 C.M.R. 74, 77 (C.M.A. 1951). In one of our earlier cases, *United States v. Hounshell*, this Court stated, "[t]he United States Constitution guarantees to a person protected under federal law 'the right to speedy and public trial.' Article 10 of the Uniform Code . . . reiterates that guarantee . . . ." 21 C.M.R. 129, 132 (C.M.A. 1956) (quoting U.S. Const. amend. VI). Indeed, the legislative history behind Article 10 strongly suggests it was intended only to remedy delays concerning pretrial restraint. See Uniform Code of Military Justice: Hearings on H.R. 2498 Before a Subcomm. of the House Comm. on Armed Services, 81st Cong. 905–12 (1949)[hereinafter UCMJ Hearings]. That subcommittee viewed Article 10 solely as a tool to terminate lengthy pretrial confinement. *Id.*

The right to counsel guaranteed under Article 27 was not applicable through the Bill of Rights to state proceedings until 1963. It was not until that year, in *Gideon v. Wainwright*, 372 U.S. 335 (1963), that the Supreme Court extended the right to appointment of counsel in state cases to all indigent felony defendants. Prior to that, Congress had ensured some right to counsel for military members by passing Article 27, but that right was limited to general courts-martial. Congress extended this right to special courts-martial in 1968. Of course, it is not enough to have counsel; counsel must zealously represent the accused, starting with a full investigation of the case. *See, e.g., House v. Balkcom*, 725 F.2d 608 (11th Cir. 1984). The right to counsel is one of the most valuable rights that a defendant possesses, but certain decisions are for the defendant to control while the remainder are left with counsel. The Supreme Court has recognized that counsel has the authority to manage most aspects of the defense without obtaining the defendant's approval. *See, e.g., Florida v. Nixon*, 543 U.S. 175 (2004). In New York v. Hill, the Supreme Court stated: "[D]efense counsel's agreement to a trial date outside the time period required by [the Interstate Agreement on Detainers] bars the defendant from seeking dismissal because trial did not occur within that period." 528 U.S. 110, 111 (2000). Moreover, the Hill Court said, "only counsel is in a position to assess the benefit or detriment of the delay to the defendant's case," *Id.* at 115, and "only counsel is in a position to assess whether the defense would even be prepared to proceed any earlier." *Id.*

Feeling that the self-incrimination clause did not apply to military members, Congress enacted Article 31 to protect the right against self-incrimination in the military setting. Additionally, in enacting Article 31(b), Congress was concerned that the interrogation environment in the military and the interplay between military relationships and following orders deserved protection. See UCMJ Hearings at 984–85. As this Court stated, "[u]ndoubtedly it was the intent of Congress in this division of the Article to secure to persons subject to the Code the same rights secured to those of the civilian community under the Fifth Amendment to the Constitution of the United States—no more and no less." *United States v. Eggers*, 11 C.M.R. 191, 195 (C.M.A. 1953). In his testimony on the UCMJ, Mr. Felix Larkin, Assistant General Counsel in the Office of the Secretary of Defense, expressed the desire to "retain the constitutional protections against self-incrimination." UCMJ Hearings at 988. The UCMJ was enacted to ensure those constitutional rights because of the deep division as to the applicability of those rights in different factual scenarios. The commentary to Article 31(a) also underscores the intent to "extend [the] privilege against self-incrimination to all persons under all circumstances." H.R. Rep. 81–491 at 19 (1949).

Likewise, Congress enacted Article 44 because "the application of [the Fifth Amendment] is in doubt. . . .The matter could be clarified by extending the protection of the fifth amendment rather than granting protection by means of different or new statutory enactment." Uniform Code of Military Justice: Hearings on § 857 and H.R. 4080 Before a Subcomm. of the Senate Comm. on Armed Services, 81st Cong. 111 (1949) (statement of Sen. Pat McCarran, Chairman, Senate Judiciary Comm.). House commentary on the UCMJ observed: "The question is whether the constitutional provision of jeopardy follows a person who enters military service." H.R. Rep. 81–491 at 23.

As to the double jeopardy provision, this Court reiterated the theme that the Constitution did not apply, stating, "The constitutional privilege against former jeopardy, applicable to the civilian community, is granted to offenders against military law by Article 44. . . ." *United States v. Ivory*, 26 C.M.R. 296, 299–300 (C.M.A. 1958).

In the past, this Court applied a due process examination before it had announced that the Bill of Rights applies "except those [rights] which are expressly or by necessary implication inapplicable." *United States v. Jacoby*, 29 C.M.R. 244, 246–47 (C.M.A. 1960). Because the Supreme Court has not held that the Bill of Rights applies to servicemembers, our Court, in its early years, did not rely upon speedy trial rights.

The question of the application of the Fourth Amendment as to the right to privacy,[6] the self-incrimination clause of the Fifth Amendment,[7] speedy trial,[8] or the right of confrontation cross-examination under the Sixth Amendment[9] is moot based on congressional and presidential actions.

MCM Provision. The majority also overlooks R.C.M. 707(e), which states that: "Except as provided in R.C.M. 910(a)(2) [conditional pleas], a plea of

---

[6] Military Rule of Evidence (M.R.E.) 311–317.

[7] Article 31, UCMJ; M.R.E. 301–306.

[8] Article 10, 33; R.C.M. 707.

[9] Article 46, UCMJ; R.C.M. 702, 703; M.R.E. 611.

guilty which results in a finding of guilty waives any speedy trial issue as to that offense." (Emphasis added.) This provision by the President does not violate any constitutional provision—there is certainly none prohibiting this waiver, and many federal courts provide for such a waiver.

Because the majority overlooks mainstream jurisprudence and the MCM provisions, I respectfully dissent.

Points for Discussion

1. The court in this case holds that an Article 10 objection that is litigated in a pretrial motion is not waived by a subsequent unconditional guilty plea. In *United States v. Tippit*, 65 M.J. 69 (2007), however, the court subsequently held that an accused who makes an unconditional guilty plea without first raising an Article 10 objection does waive the issue. What is the logic for distinguishing the two cases?

2. What is the general theory for holding that an unconditional guilty plea may constitute a waiver of certain pretrial matters?

Motion for a Sanity Board

The military justice system takes the mental health of an accused service member into account in several ways. First, the accused must be mentally competent to stand trial. R.C.M. 909(a) provides that "[n]o person may be brought to trial by court-martial if that person is presently suffering from a mental disease or defect rendering him or her mentally incompetent to the extent that he or she is unable to understand the nature of the proceedings against them [sic] or to conduct or cooperate intelligently in the defense of the case." Second, the accused may raise lack of mental responsibility as an affirmative defense to criminal charges. UCMJ Article 50a(a) provides: "It is an affirmative defense in a trial by court-martial that at the time of the commission of the acts constituting the offense, the accused, as a result of a severe mental disease or defect was unable to appreciate the nature and quality or the wrongfulness of the acts." 10 U.S.C. § 850a(a). *See also* R.C.M. 916(k) (implementing this statutory standard). Third, the mental health of the accused may be a mitigating or extenuating circumstance to be considered during sentencing. R.C.M. 1001(f)(2)(B) provides that the "court-martial may consider— . . . [e]vidence relating to any mental impairment or deficiency of the accused." The Discussion accompanying this rule explains that the "fact that the accused is of low intelligence or that, because of a mental or neurological condition the accused's ability to adhere to the right is diminished may be extenuating." R.C.M. 1002(f)(B)(2) Discussion.

The *Manual for Courts-Martial* provides that the convening authority or military judge may order a formal inquiry into the mental condition of the accused. *See* R.C.M. 707(b). The inquiry is conducted by a board, colloquially known as a "sanity board," which consists of one or more members who are physicians or clinical psychologists. The board is directed to consider the accused's mental condition and specifically to answer the following questions:

(A) At the time of the alleged criminal conduct, did the accused have a severe mental disease or defect? . . .

(B) What is the clinical psychiatric diagnosis?

(C) Was the accused, at the time of the alleged criminal conduct and as a result of such severe mental disease or defect, unable to appreciate the nature and quality or wrongfulness of his or her conduct?

(D) Is the accused presently suffering from a mental disease or defect rendering the accused unable to understand the nature of the proceedings against the accused or to conduct or cooperate intelligently in the defense?

R.C.M. 707(c)(2).

Suppose that defense counsel suspects that the accused has a mental disease or defect and makes a pretrial motion requesting the military judge to order a sanity board. Should the military judge automatically grant the request? Must the military judge undertake a preliminary inquiry to determine whether there is sufficient justification for an insanity board? Does the military judge need expert assistance? What happens if the military judge reasonably should have ordered an inquiry by a sanity board but fails to do so? The following case considers these issues.

UNITED STATES v. JAMES
Army Court of Criminal Appeals
47 M.J. 641 (Army Ct. Crim. App. 1997)

KAPLAN, Judge:

A military judge sitting alone as a general court-martial found the appellant [Private E2 Angela L. James, U.S. Army] guilty, in accordance with her pleas, of willfully disobeying the lawful command of a superior commissioned officer, making false official statements to U.S. Army Criminal Investigation Command agents (two specifications), and making and uttering numerous checks without sufficient funds (five specifications), in violation of Articles 90, 107, and 123a, Uniform Code of Military Justice, 10 U.S.C. §§ 890, 907, and 923a (1988) [hereinafter UCMJ]. The military judge sentenced the appellant to a bad-conduct discharge, confinement for sixty days, forfeiture of all pay and allowances, reduction to Private E1, and a $1000.00 fine. The convening authority, on the advice of his staff judge advocate, reduced the forfeitures to $577.00 pay per month for six months and otherwise approved the sentence as adjudged.

* * *

Appellant alleges that the military judge committed prejudicial error when he denied a defense motion for appointment of a formal sanity board pursuant to the provisions of R.C.M. 706. Prior to trial, the defense counsel submitted a motion for a sanity board and detailed the rationale for such request. He indicated the apparently abnormal behavior of the appellant that he had personally observed, including the inability to respond coherently to his questions and to make necessary decisions regarding the defense of her case. Upon receipt of the defense motion, the trial counsel arranged for the appellant to be given a "mental status evaluation." This evaluation was performed by a mental health counselor who was not a physician, psychiatrist, or clinical psychologist. The evaluation consisted of a one-half hour interview; no psychological testing was performed. The evaluation report consisted of a one-page "check-the-blocks" form.[3] The counselor was not provided with a copy of the defense counsel's motion, and thus, was not made aware of the defense counsel's specific concerns prompting the mental status evaluation; he was told only that the appellant was pending court-martial proceedings and had begun to neglect her personal hygiene and military duties. Nor was the counselor provided with the list of required findings set forth in R.C.M. 706(c)(2). Finally, the counselor had never previously assisted in the proceedings of a sanity board ordered pursuant to R.C.M. 706.

In *United States v. Collins*, 41 M.J. 610, 612 (Army Ct. Crim. App.1994), a case legally indistinguishable from appellant's, this court held that:

> When a defense counsel requests a sanity board based on a non-frivolous, good-faith claim that an accused lacks mental capacity to stand trial, the military judge cannot rule finally on that issue pursuant to R.C.M. 909 without first considering the report of a sanity board conducted in accordance with R.C.M. 706 or *an equivalent forensic mental evaluation*. *United States v. Jancarek*, 22 M.J. 600 (A.C.M.R. 1986), *pet. Denied*, 24 M.J. 42 (C.M.A. 1987) (*citing United States v. Nix*, 36 C.M.R. 76 (C.M.A. 1965)); *United States v. Kish*, 20 M.J. 652 (A.C.M.R. 1985) (also citing *Nix*).

(Emphasis added and footnote omitted).

The *Collins* decision, relying on *Jancarek*, went on to identify four conditions which, if met, would establish that a mental status evaluation was the equivalent of a R.C.M. 706 sanity board. These conditions are:

> [1] specific psychiatric testimony concerning the appellant's capacity to understand the nature of criminal proceedings and to cooperate in her defense at a court-martial; [2] a description of the examiner's familiarity

---

[3] The form did not include separate and distinct findings as to the four questions specified in R.C.M. 706(c)(2), to wit: (1) Did the accused, at the time of the alleged offenses, have a severe mental disease or defect? (2) What is the clinical psychiatric diagnosis? (3) Was the accused, at the time of the alleged offenses and as a result of such severe mental disease or defect, unable to appreciate the nature and quality or wrongfulness of her conduct? (4) Does the accused have sufficient mental capacity to understand the nature of the proceedings and to conduct or cooperate intelligently in the defense? At most, the form attempted to answer the fourth question in summary fashion.

with forensic evaluation or participation in previous sanity boards; [3] other evidence that the examiner attempted to perform an in-depth forensic evaluation of the sort contemplated by R.C.M. 706; and [4] indication that the examiner was informed of the reasons for doubting the mental capacity of the accused as called for by R.C.M. 706(c).

Collins, 41 M.J. at 613. Additionally, in establishing equivalency, we note that R.C.M. 706(c)(1) requires that all members of a sanity board be either physicians or clinical psychologists. Thus, a mental status evaluation, if it is to qualify as a forensic evaluation having the equivalency of a sanity board for court-martial purposes, must be conducted by a person possessing the mandated professional qualifications.

Applying the analytical framework of *Collins* to the case at bar, we first find that the defense request for a sanity board was not frivolous and was made in good faith. Second, we find that the mental status evaluation that was done was not the equivalent of a sanity board. Concerning this second line of inquiry, we note that even a cursory review of the circumstances attendant to appellant's evaluation leads unavoidably to the conclusion that the mental status evaluation performed in appellant's case fell far short of meeting the *Jancarek/Collins* sanity board equivalency requirements. In addition, the R.C.M. 706(c)(1) requirement that all members of the sanity board be either physicians or clinical psychologists was not met in this case. Accordingly, we conclude, as did the *Collins* court, that a hearing pursuant to *United States v. DuBay*, 37 C.M.R. 411 (C.M.A. 1967), is necessary to resolve the issue of the appellant's mental competency at the time of her court-martial.

The record of trial is returned to The Judge Advocate General for transmittal to an appropriate convening authority who shall order an evidentiary hearing before a military judge. The military judge will order a sanity board pursuant to R.C.M. 706 to determine the appellant's mental capacity at the present time and, if possible, at the time of trial. After consideration of the full report of the sanity board, the military judge will hear the contentions of the parties and enter findings of fact and conclusions of law.

If the military judge finds that the appellant possessed appropriate mental capacity at the time of trial, the convening authority will return the record to this court for further review. If the military judge finds that the appellant is presently mentally competent, but either (1) the appellant lacked mental capacity at the time of trial, or (2) that the sanity board is unable to determine the appellant's mental capacity at that former time, then the convening authority may order a full rehearing on the charges.

If the military judge finds that the appellant currently lacks mental competence and was also lacking in mental capacity at the time of trial, then the convening authority may: (1) suspend the proceedings, (2) disapprove the findings and sentence and dismiss the charges and specifications, or (3) take any administrative action determined to be appropriate. Thereafter, the record shall be returned to this court for further review. *See* R.C.M. 909(c)(2) discussion. If an evidentiary hearing or, if required, a rehearing on the charges and sentence, is determined by the convening authority to be impracticable, then the convening authority shall return the record to this court with an explanation as to that determination.

Chief Judge COOKE and Judge GONZALES concur.

Points for Discussion

1. Why don't military judges always grant defense requests for a sanity board? Is there any cost or risk in granting requests when they are not required?

2. Is it potentially risky for defense counsel to seek an informal mental evaluation of the accused by someone other than an actual sanity board? *See* Donna M. Wright, *"Though this be Madness, Yet there is Method in it": A Practitioner's Guide to Mental Responsibility and Competency to Stand Trial*, Army Lawyer, Sep. 1997, at 18 (noting that Military Rule of Evidence 302 provides that the accused "has a privilege to prevent any statement made by the accused at a mental examination *ordered under R.C.M. 706*" (emphasis added), but not for other types of examinations).

Motion in Limine

A motion in limine is a "pretrial request that certain inadmissible evidence not be referred to or offered at trial." Black's Law Dictionary (9th ed. 2009). The evidence that the movant seeks to exclude could be anything that the Military Rules of Evidence would make inadmissible: a statement made to an investigator in violation of the privilege against self-incrimination, a statement protected by the attorney-client privilege, hearsay, and so forth. Failing to seek exclusion of evidence before trial through a motion in limine does not prevent raising an objection later during trial if the evidence is mentioned by the other side. Consider this point in reading the following case:

UNITED STATES v. SPATA
U.S. Court of Military Appeals
34 M.J. 284 (C.M.A. 1992)

GIERKE, Judge:

A special court-martial composed of officer members convicted appellant [Patrick F. Spata, Staff Sergeant, U.S. Air Force], contrary to his pleas, of wrongful use of cocaine, in violation of Article 112a, Uniform Code of Military Justice, 10 U.S.C. § 912a. The court-martial sentenced appellant to a bad-conduct discharge, confinement for 3 months, and reduction to E–1. The convening authority approved the sentence, and the Court of Military Review affirmed the findings and sentence in an unpublished opinion dated July 24,

1990.

We granted review to consider the following issue:

WHETHER THE MILITARY JUDGE ERRED BY DENYING A DEFENSE MOTION IN LIMINE TO PRECLUDE THE PROSECUTION FROM CROSS–EXAMINING APPELLANT ABOUT UNCHARGED MISCONDUCT OCCURRING THE WEEKEND PRIOR TO HIS SUBMITTING A URINE SPECIMEN.

We hold that the military judge did not abuse his discretion.

On July 31, 1989, appellant provided a urine specimen during a surprise sweep of his unit. On August 17, 1989, appellant's unit received a laboratory report reflecting that appellant's urine sample contained in excess of 11,000 nanograms of benzoylecgonine, a metabolite of cocaine.

Four days later appellant provided the local Office of Special Investigations (OSI) a statement detailing his activities during the weekend preceding the surprise urinalysis. Included in that statement was an account of an altercation in a local bar on the Friday preceding the urinalysis. According to the statement, appellant brought several miniature bottles of rum to the bar, and an unknown Hispanic woman stole one of the bottles. Appellant asked her to return it; she refused; they argued; appellant poured a mug of beer in her lap; and she poured the miniature bottle of rum on appellant. The bouncer then ejected the Hispanic woman from the bar. Appellant's statement to the OSI was not offered in evidence or disclosed to the court members.

Appellant first suggested the possibility that he had unknowingly ingested cocaine when, on August 25, he told a doctor in the local medical clinic that he believed someone might have "spiked" his drink with cocaine during the weekend before the urinalysis. Appellant's statement to the doctor was not offered in evidence or disclosed to the members.

The prosecution's case focused primarily on the laboratory report. A forensic chemist testified that the level of benzoylecgonine in appellant's urine indicated that the cocaine had been ingested "within 3 days" of the urinalysis.

After the Government rested, the defense moved in limine to prevent the prosecution from cross-examining appellant about his statement to the OSI. The military judge ruled that appellant's activities during the period preceding his urinalysis would be a permissible area of cross-examination, depending on the substance of appellant's testimony.

The defense opening statement did not suggest innocent ingestion but, rather, focused on the trustworthiness of the urinalysis system. The possibility of innocent ingestion was first suggested during cross-examination of the Government's toxicology expert, Dr. Jain. After establishing that at one time (around 1914) Coca–Cola contained cocaine and, more recently, "Health Inca Tea" was found to contain cocaine in amounts small enough to be virtually unnoticed by the user, trial defense counsel observed that the term "used" should be in quotation marks because, "One thing is clear, and I'm sure you'll agree with me: none of these tests can show anything about a person's intent or knowledge of whether they used[.]" Dr. Jain agreed: "Absolutely right. The lab test also does not tell the intention of the person." After exploring other areas, the defense concluded its cross-examination of Dr. Jain by asking, "You can't say, to any degree of certainty, that you know whether or not Sergeant Spata intentionally ingested any cocaine, can you?" Dr. Jain responded, "No, nobody can tell."

Appellant testified and denied using cocaine on or about the date charged but did not suggest innocent ingestion. The prosecution cross-examined him at length about his activities during the weekend preceding the urinalysis. The prosecutor asked appellant if he had consumed any substance which might have contained cocaine and if he noticed any effect which he might have attributed to cocaine, and appellant responded that he had not.

The prosecutor then questioned appellant about the statement he had given the OSI describing the altercation with the unknown Hispanic woman. In response to leading questions, appellant ratified his statement to the OSI describing the altercation. During closing arguments on findings, defense counsel attacked the trustworthiness of the urinalysis and suggested the possibility of innocent ingestion. At defense request, the military judge instructed the members on innocent ingestion. The military judge offered to give a cautionary instruction on uncharged misconduct, but defense counsel affirmatively waived it.

Mil. R. Evid. 404(b), Manual for Courts-Martial, United States, 1984, specifically prohibits use of "[e]vidence of other crimes, wrongs or acts . . . to prove the character of a person in order to show that the person acted in conformity therewith." This rule prohibits the prosecution from presenting uncharged acts of misconduct simply to show that the accused is a bad person and therefore more likely to have committed the offenses charged. *United States v. Brannan*, 18 M.J. 181 (C.M.A. 1984). Evidence of uncharged misconduct may be admitted to rebut an assertion of innocence based on lack of criminal intent or other affirmative defense. *See United States v. Brooks*, 22 M.J. 441, 444 (C.M.A. 1986) (evidence of prior drug sales admitted to rebut claim that accused was innocent bystander during drug sale); United States v. Brannan, supra (evidence of prior drug offenses admitted to rebut claim that drugs were planted without accused's knowledge). *See* Mil. R. Evid. 608(c) Analysis (impeachment by contradiction), Manual, *supra* at A22–42 (Change 2). Admissibility of such evidence is subject to the requirement that "its probative value" outweigh "the danger of unfair prejudice." Mil. R. Evid. 403.

The test for compliance with that rule is whether the military judge abused his discretion in admitting the evidence of the barroom altercation. *United States v. Mukes*, 18 M.J. 358 (C.M.A. 1984). We hold that he did not. In this case the evidence of the barroom altercation had some probative value in that it negated the possibility, suggested by the defense, of innocent ingestion. Appellant could not have unknowingly ingested cocaine in a drink "spiked" by the unknown Hispanic woman if he poured the drink in her lap without consuming it. Although the evidence arguably showed uncharged misconduct, it was minor and minimally prejudicial, especially since the unknown Hispanic woman, not appellant, was ejected from the bar as the party at fault.

The decision of the United States Air Force Court of Military Review is affirmed.

Chief Judge SULLIVAN and Judges COX and CRAWFORD concur.

WISS, Judge (concurring in the result):

I believe the critical issue here is the proper scope of cross-examination and of rebuttal. Because I believe that trial counsel's cross-examination of appellant exceeded that scope, I cannot agree that it was proper. I do agree, however, that the error was not prejudicial, so I concur in the result reached by the majority.

As the majority acknowledges, the only evidence arguably relating to unknowing ingestion during the prosecution's case arose incident to the defense cross-examination of Dr. Jain. As the summary of that questioning in the majority opinion, 34 M.J. at 284–85, capably demonstrates, however, the suggestion there was only a conceptual or theoretical one that possibly, through some means that we are completely unaware of today, cocaine might have been introduced into appellant's body—thus, his references to the old Coca–Cola recipe and to "Health Inca Tea." There was no suggestion at all that cocaine might have been surreptitiously delivered to appellant through tampered drink or food.

Moreover, again as the majority forthrightly recognizes, *id.* at 285, appellant "did not suggest innocent ingestion" at any time during his direct testimony—and, in fact, he did not suggest unknowing ingestion through tampered food or drink in any other way during the defense case.

It was under these circumstances that the military judge, over defense objection, permitted trial counsel to cross-examine appellant concerning the absence of opportunities for him to have ingested a "mickey" during the time period preceding his urinalysis. However, under these circumstances, it is clear to me that such questioning was outside the proper scope of cross-examination. *See* Mil. R. Evid. 611(b), Manual for Courts-Martial, United States, 1984. It "rebutted" nothing that had been testified to by appellant or offered in the defense case. Moreover, it did not rebut the "theoretical" concept of unknowing ingestion which arose in the cross-examination of Dr. Jain in the prosecution case.

If this questioning had revealed acts more detrimental to appellant's general character, I would have some difficulty concluding that this error was not prejudicial. I concur with the majority, though, that the facts of this case amply demonstrate that evidence of such relatively inconsequential misconduct did not harm appellant's defense.

Points for Discussion

1. Why would a party see an advantage to having a ruling on the admissibility of evidence before trial, rather than merely raising an objection at trial if the other side seeks to admit the evidence? Military Judge Gregg A. Marchessault explains:

> A motion in limine has several benefits to include enabling the military judge to rule on the admissibility of prejudicial evidence outside the presence of a panel. Allowing the military judge to address the admissibility of evidence at a motions hearing also affords the judge adequate time to consider and fully research evidentiary issues. Lastly, a ruling on a motion in limine provides guidance to counsel for their case preparation and presentation.

Gregg A. Marchessault, *A View from the Bench: A Military Judge's Perspective on Objections*, Army Lawyer, Sep. 2010, at 58, 59. Can you think of examples of a situation in which each of these advantages would be present?

2. Why might a military judge hesitate to grant a motion in limine? Did the military judge have the information before trial that would be necessary to resolve the issue of admissibility in this case?

7-3. Article 62 Interlocutory Appeals by the United States

The double jeopardy clause of the Fifth Amendment prevents the United States from appealing after a court-martial has found an accused not guilty. *See United States v. Rowel*, 1 M.J. 289, 289 & n.2 (C.M.A. 1976) (Fletcher, J., concurring). UCMJ Article 62(a), however, affords the United States a limited ability to pursue interlocutory appeals of an adverse ruling by a military judge. Article 62(a)(1) says:

> In a trial by court-martial in which a military judge presides and in which a punitive discharge may be adjudged, the United States may appeal the following (other than an order or ruling that is, or that amounts to, a finding of not guilty with respect to the charge or specification):

> (A) An order or ruling of the military judge which terminates the proceedings with respect to a charge or specification.

> (B) An order or ruling which excludes evidence that is substantial proof of a fact material m the proceeding.

> (C) An order or ruling which directs the disclosure of classified information.

> (D) An order or ruling which imposes sanctions for nondisclosure of classified information.

(E) A refusal of the military' judge to issue a protective order sought by the United States to prevent the disclosure of classified information.

(F) A refusal by the military judge to enforce an order described m subparagraph (E) that has previously been issued by appropriate authority.

Article 62(a)(2) provides that an "appeal of an order or ruling may not be taken unless the trial counsel provides the military judge with written notice of appeal from the order or ruling within 72 hours of the order or ruling." Article 62(a)(3) further says that an "appeal under this section shall be diligently prosecuted by appellate Government counsel." R.C.M. 908, which implements Article 62, says that an "appeal under Article 62 shall, whenever practicable, have priority over all other proceedings before the Court of Criminal Appeals." R.C.M. 908(c)(2).

UNITED STATES v. DALY
U.S. Court of Appeals for the Armed Forces
69 M.J. 485 (C.A.A.F. 2011)

PER CURIAM:

Appellee was originally charged with engaging in romantic relationships with four subordinates contrary to a Coast Guard regulation, in violation of Article 134, Uniform Code of Military Justice (UCMJ), 10 U.S.C. § 934 (2006). Before trial, the four specifications were amended by deleting references to the regulation. On motion by the defense, the military judge dismissed the charge and specifications on March 5, 2010, concluding that Appellee did not have "due process 'fair notice' that [his] conduct was . . . subject to criminal sanction" because the relevant Coast Guard regulation—viz., the Coast Guard Personnel Manual (COMDTINST M1000.6A)—"[is] clear that such conduct subjects a member to administrative—but not criminal—resolution."

Twelve days later, on March 17, 2010, the Government moved for reconsideration. The military judge denied the request on March 26, 2010, and the Government filed its notice of appeal, pursuant to Article 62, UCMJ, 10 U.S.C. § 862 (2006), on March 29, 2010. The United States Coast Guard Court of Criminal Appeals (CCA) denied the Government's appeal on the merits. *United States v. Daly*, 69 M.J. 549, 553 (C.G. Ct. Crim. App. 2010). Pursuant to Article 67(a)(2), UCMJ, 10 U.S.C. § 867(a)(2) (2006), the Acting Judge Advocate General of the Coast Guard certified three issues to this Court.

Before this Court, for the first time, Appellee asserted that this Court was without jurisdiction to hear the appeal because Appellant failed to file notice of the Article 62 appeal within seventy-two hours of the original decision of the military judge. On November 18, 2010, this Court ordered the Government to show cause why the "appeal should not be dismissed for lack of jurisdiction as untimely filed in view of the date trial counsel provided written notice of appeal."

Jurisdiction is a question of law that we review de novo. *United States v. Davis*, 63 M.J. 171, 173 (C.A.A.F. 2006). A question of jurisdiction is not subject to waiver and may be raised at any time. Rule for Courts-Martial 905(e); *United States v. Long*, 18 C.M.R. 196, 198 (C.M.A. 1955). "Federal courts are courts of limited jurisdiction. They possess only that power authorized by Constitution and statute . . . ." *Kokkonen v. Guardian Life Ins. Co. of Am.*, 511 U.S. 375, 377 (1994).

The United States may appeal "[a]n order or ruling of the military judge which terminates the proceedings with respect to a charge or specification." Article 62(a)(1)(A), UCMJ. "An appeal of an order or ruling may not be taken unless the trial counsel provides the military judge with written notice of appeal from the order or ruling within 72 hours of the order or ruling." Article 62(a)(2), UCMJ.

The Government argues that the appeal was timely because it was filed within seventy-two hours after the military judge denied the motion for reconsideration. We disagree.

The Government failed to file either a motion for reconsideration of the order to dismiss or a notice of appeal within the seventy-two-hour period for government appeals authorized in Article 62(a)(2). Instead, the Government took twelve days to finalize and submit a brief to the military judge asking for reconsideration of the order to dismiss. The Government's action was untimely under the explicit limitation of Article 62.

Because the Government's notice of appeal was not timely filed, the CCA was without jurisdiction to consider the Government's appeal. Accordingly, the judgment of the United States Coast Guard Court of Criminal Appeals is set aside, and the appeal is, hereby, dismissed.

Points for Discussion

1. Why do UCMJ Articles 62(a)(2) and 62(a)(3) and R.C.M. 908(c) require interlocutory appeals to be pursued with such speed and diligence?

2. Can you think of policy arguments for and against the court's conclusion that the 72-hour clock in UCMJ Article 62(a)(2) should run from the time of the military judge's initial order and not from the military judge's subsequent decision on a motion for rehearing?

3. Article 62(a) and (b) provide for an interlocutory appeal to the service Courts of Criminal Appeals. Does the Court of Appeals for the Armed Forces cite any statutory provision in this case that expressly gives it jurisdiction to hear interlocutory appeals? Is there such a provision? *See United States v. Lopez de Victoria*, 66 M.J. 67 (2008) (holding that cases appealed to the Service Courts of Criminal Appeals under Article 62 may be reviewed by the Court of Appeals for the Armed Forces under Article 67(a)).

UNITED STATES v. RITTENHOUSE
Army Court of Criminal Appeals
62 M.J. 509 (Army Ct. Crim. App. 2005)

JOHNSON, Judge:

The government's timely appeal under Article 62, Uniform Code of Military Justice 10 U.S.C. § 862 [hereinafter UCMJ], is granted. The military judge's decision to suppress evidence seized from [U.S. Army] Sergeant [Josh R.] Rittenhouse's (appellee's) barracks room and to suppress oral statements and a portion of the written statement made by appellee to law enforcement officials is vacated.

BACKGROUND

Appellee was charged with three violations of Article 134, UCMJ, 10 U.S.C. § 934. The allegations included two specifications asserting a violation of the Child Pornography Prevention Act, 18 U.S.C. § 2252A, and one specification alleging that appellee engaged in conduct that was prejudicial to good order and discipline or service discrediting by possessing, in the barracks, "visual depictions of minors engaging in sexually explicit conduct." At arraignment, appellee's trial defense counsel moved to suppress evidence found during a search of appellee's computer and computer disks that were seized from his barracks room. The defense argued that the seizure and removal of these items was outside the scope of appellee's consent to search. Appellee's defense counsel also moved to suppress appellee's oral and written statements made in response to questioning by agents from the Criminal Investigation Division (CID) after he allegedly invoked his right to silence.

During the Article 39a, UCMJ, 10 U.S.C. § 839a, hearing on the suppression motions, the government presented the testimony of two CID agents. Special Agent (SA) Kristie Cathers testified that the investigation of appellee began when another soldier, Private First Class (PFC) Galemore, reported that he had witnessed sexually explicit pictures of children on appellee's computer. Special Agent Cathers testified that she contacted appellee's unit and had him report to the local CID office. Special Agent Cathers said that appellee was ordered to report to the CID office and that he was not free to leave. She informed appellee that he was suspected of possession, distribution, and/or production of material constituting or containing child pornography and he was further advised of his rights under Article 31(b), UCMJ, 10 U.S.C. § 831(b), and [*Miranda v. Arizona*, 384 U.S. 436 (1966)]. Appellee acknowledged that he understood his rights and was willing to make a statement without the presence of a lawyer.

Special Agent Cathers said that she presented appellee with CID Form 87–R–E, Consent to Search. Appellee signed the form, granting his consent to search his barracks room and "computers, hard disk drives, removable data storage media, portable data storage devices, cameras, photographs, movies, manuals, notebooks, papers, and computer input and output devices." His computer was described on the consent form as a custom built desktop computer.[2]

* * *

While appellee's barracks room was being searched, SA Cathers continued to interview appellee. After they talked for approximately an hour and a half, the CID agent provided appellee with a blank sworn statement form and told appellee to write down what they had discussed using "baby steps." She told him not to "close out" the statement "since they would have to do a question and answer session after he wrote out his narrative." The agent then left the room, checking on him periodically.

She returned later and asked appellee if he was done and he stated that he was. Special Agent Cathers then read his statement and saw that he had written "End of Statement" at the end of his narrative. The agent did not ask appellee what he meant by "End of Statement," but assumed that he wrote it because "he was a squared-away NCO" and that he automatically included this language at the end of all sworn statements. The words "End of Statement" were lined through and appellee initialed next to it as SA Cathers directed. Special Agent Cathers then began asking appellee questions about the crimes of which he was suspected. She recorded her questions and appellee's answers on the remainder of the sworn statementform on which appellee wrote his narrative.

Special Agent John Lemke, the Special Agent in Charge of the Fort Wainwright CID office, also testified for the government. Special Agent Lemke was one of the agents who conducted the search of appellee's room. In accordance with standard forensic practice, the agents did not view any files or data contained on the computer or disks while they were in the room. Instead, the agents seized a computer and approximately three hundred computer disks that appeared to have something written on them so they could be searched later. The agents also seized some papers from appellee's room that contained "explicit language."

After the search was concluded, SA Lemke joined the interview of appellee. Appellee told SA Lemke that he had downloaded some child pornography and saved it to disks. Special Agent Lemke did not testify to any other oral

---

[2] The Consent to Search form also contained an unnumbered subsection under the specifically delineated places to be searched which stated:

I am authorizing the above search(s) for the following general types of property which may be removed by the authorized law enforcement personnel and retained as evidence under the provisions of Army Regulation 195–5, or other applicable laws or regulations: Text, graphics, electronic mail message, and other data including deleted files and folders, containing material related to the sexual exploitation of minors; and/or material depicting apparent or purported minors engaged in sexually explicit conduct; and data and/or information used to facilitate access to, possession, distribution, and/or production of such materials.

statements made by appellee and appellee's written statement does not indicate at which point SA Lemke joined the interview.

The military judge found by clear and convincing evidence that appellee "voluntarily consented to a search of any computers, hard disks drives, removable data storage media, portable data storage media, portable data storage devices, cameras, photographs, movies, manuals, notebooks, papers, and computer input and output devices which were located in [appellee's] room on 14 April 2004." The military judge further found by clear and convincing evidence that appellee consented to removal from his barracks room of only those items listed in the unnumbered section between sections 5 and 6 of the Consent to Search form (Appendix). The military judge found that the consent form did not authorize the seizure and removal of the items listed above that appellee allowed to be searched. The military judge also found that the evidence was not admissible pursuant to inevitable discovery because the government had no probable cause to search for or seize the items, no search authorization was sought, and there was no evidence the property would have been seized, absent the consent to search. The military judge further found that the government did not offer specific information as to what PFC Galemore had seen or where and when he had seen it.

The military judge held that so much of appellee's statement that preceded the words "End of Statement" was admissible. However, she further held "that writing 'End of Statement' was an ambiguous or equivocal invocation of the right to remain silent." The military judge ruled that this required SA Cathers to immediately cease questioning or to clarify what appellee meant by "End of Statement." Special Agent Cathers did neither. Therefore, the military judge held that any statements by appellee after he wrote "End of Statement" were inadmissible, including the oral admission to SA Lemke.

ANALYSIS

* * *

APPELLEE'S STATEMENT

We agree with the military judge's finding that appellee's writing "End of Statement" after he finished the narrative portion was an equivocal invocation of his right to remain silent. The term "equivocal" means "[h]aving different significations equally appropriate or plausible; capable of double interpretation; ambiguous." *Coleman v. Singletary*, 30 F.3d 1420, 1425 (11th Cir. 1994) (quoting 5 Oxford English Dictionary 359 (2d ed., J.A. Simpson & E.S.C. Weiner, eds., 1989)); see also Black's Law Dictionary 561 (7th ed.). That is exactly the scenario presented by this case. One interpretation of the inclusion of the phrase is that appellee did not wish to provide any further information to law enforcement and this was the end of his overall "statement" to CID on the issue. However, an equally plausible interpretation is the one given to it by SA Cathers—that it simply signaled the end of appellee's narrative statement, not his intent to avoid answering any additional questions or making any further written or oral statements in the case.

We disagree with the military judge, however, on the legal question of whether this equivocal invocation imposed a duty on the agent to ask clarifying questions regarding appellee's intent. In a similar context, the Supreme Court has held that, after a knowing and voluntary waiver of the right to counsel, law enforcement officers may continue questioning until and unless the suspect clearly requests an attorney. *Davis v. United States*, 512 U.S. 452, 462 (1994). "If the suspect's statement is not an unambiguous or unequivocal request for counsel, the officers have no obligation to stop questioning him." *Id.* at 461–62. The Eleventh Circuit Court of Appeals extended this rule to the invocation of the right to remain silent. *Coleman*, 30 F.3d at 1426; *see also United States v. Johnson*, 56 F.3d 947, 955 (8th Cir. 1995). Our superior court has also cited the holding in Coleman approvingly, stating, "[O]nce a suspect waives the right to silence, interrogators may continue questioning unless and until the suspect unequivocally invokes the right to silence." *Lincoln*, 42 M.J. at 320.

Accordingly, we likewise hold that, after a suspect has waived his right to remain silent, if he subsequently makes an ambiguous or equivocal invocation of his right to remain silent, law enforcement agents have no duty to clarify the suspect's intent and may continue with questioning. Thus, the agents had no duty to clarify appellee's equivocal statement and the subsequent questioning of him did not violate his right against self-incrimination. As such, the military judge's decision to suppress part of appellee's statement because CID agents did not either cease questioning or ask clarifying questions after appellee made an equivocal invocation of his right to remain silent is vacated.

THE COMPUTER AND DISKS

Law

The Fourth Amendment to the United States Constitution mandates that, "[t]he right of the people to be secure . . . against unreasonable searches and seizures, shall not be violated." The "touchstone of the Fourth Amendment is reasonableness." *Florida v. Jimeno*, 500 U.S. 248, 250 (1991). A search conducted pursuant to a valid consent to search is constitutionally reasonable. *United States v. Roa*, 24 M.J. 297, 298 (C.M.A. 1987). "The standard for measuring the scope of a suspect's consent under the Fourth Amendment is that of 'objective' reasonableness—what would the typical reasonable person have understood by the exchange between the officer and the suspect?" *Jimeno*, 500 U.S. at 251.

If evidence is obtained in violation of the Fourth Amendment, it may still be introduced at trial "[i]f the prosecution can establish by a preponderance of the evidence that the information ultimately or inevitably would have been discovered by the lawful means." *Nix v. Williams*, 467 U.S. 431, 444 (1984); see also Military Rule of Evidence [hereinafter Mil. R. Evid.] 311(b)(2). Where the government establishes that "the routine procedures of a law enforcement agency would inevitably [have found] the same evidence, the rule of inevitable discovery applies even in the absence of a prior or parallel investigation." *United States v. Owens*, 51 M.J. 204, 210–11 (C.A.A.F. 1999).

Discussion

We agree with the military judge's finding that appellee voluntarily consented to the search at issue in this case. See Mil. R. Evid. 314(e). Accordingly, there is no issue as to the validity of the consent to search. The issue is whether appellee gave consent to seize his computer and the computer disks discovered in his barracks room. In this regard, the military judge read the Consent to Search form too narrowly.

The consent form appellee signed specifically stated that appellee was consenting to a search of the property and places specified on the consent form. Appellee voluntarily consented to a search of his quarters, his computers, hard disk drives, removable data storage media, and portable data storage devices for material related to the sexual exploitation of minors. The Consent to Search form advised appellee that agents would be searching the above places for "text, graphics, electronic mail messages, and other data including deleted files and folders, containing material related to the sexual exploitation of minors." The bottom portion of block 5 of the form specifically stated that the "types of property" that were the subject of the search "may be removed by authorized law enforcement personnel and retained as evidence." Under these circumstances, we find that, because a reasonable person reading the consent form would have understood that the computer and disks could be seized, the military judge's finding that the appellee only consented to the removal of the items specifically listed in the unnumbered section between blocks 5 and 6 was clearly erroneous. Instead, appellee's consent to search his computers and data storage media and devices necessarily included inherent authorization for agents to remove those items from his room to conduct a search in accordance with standard forensic practices. *See United States v. Hephner*, 260 F. Supp.2d 763 (N.D. Iowa 2003), *aff'd on other grounds*, 103 Fed.Appx. 41, 46–47, 2004 U.S.App. LEXIS 10957, at **14–15 (8th Cir. June 4, 2004) (per curiam).

However, even if the seizure of the computer and the computer disks exceeded the scope of appellee's consent to search, we find that the evidence would have been inevitably discovered by the routine practices of law enforcement. The government possessed the following additional information:

(1) Appellee made an oral statement to SA Lemke that he had viewed and downloaded child pornography on his computer and saved it to disks.

(2) In her findings of fact, the military judge found that, after appellee finished writing his narrative, SA Cathers continued the interview, "using the question and answer format depicted on the remainder of Pros. Ex. 3 for identification. She wrote down a question she asked and then wrote the

accused's response." Appellee's responses recorded on Prosecution Exhibit 3 for identification contain the following admissions:

a. He had looked at pictures of naked children under the age of eighteen on his computer.

b. To find these pictures on the internet, he had typed in search words like "sex."

c. He looked at these pictures for sexual gratification, although the children were not doing "anything sexual besides being nude."

d. He saved these photos onto "DVDs" rather than his computer and that he had saved roughly 1,000 nude pictures.

e. He visited internet forums to view pictures of children and in the "thirteen to eighteen category" there were nude photos of children.

f. He believed the pictures were of real children and they were not altered pictures.

Considering the totality of this evidence, we find that the government had sufficient information to establish probable cause to obtain authorization to seize the computer and any DVD disks found in his barracks room. The government could then have conducted a forensic search of these items. As such, to paraphrase our superior court, we find "no reasonable likelihood" that the CID agents would have abandoned their efforts to conduct a forensic search of appellee's computer and related disks if they had not obtained appellee's consent to seize these items. *See Owens*, 51 M.J. at 210. The routine procedures of law enforcement would have led to them seeking and obtaining a search authorization and retrieving the same information they obtained through the consensual seizure and subsequent search. See id. at 210–11.

CONCLUSION

Based upon our review of the record, we hold that the military judge erred in applying the law. Accordingly, the military judge's rulings as to the seizure of the computer and DVD disks and the admissibility of appellee's statements are vacated. The appellee's court-martial may proceed to trial in accordance with Rule for Courts-Martial 908(c)(3).

Senior Judge SCHENCK and Judge CLEVENGER concur.

Points for Discussion

1. Why was it important to the government to take an interlocutory appeal of the Military Judge's decision to suppress the statement? If the government did not take an immediate appeal, would there be any other opportunity for review of the military judge's decision?

2. Commenting on the *Rittenhouse* decision, Lieutenant Colonel M.K. Jamison writes: "Despite this holding, practitioners and law enforcement officials should pay close and careful attention to any consent form so that the verbiage in the consent form makes it explicitly clear that the computer and associated data storage media and devices may be seized for follow-on forensic analysis." M.K. Jamison, *New Developments in Search & Seizure Law*, Army Lawyer, Apr. 2006, at 9, 19.

7-4. Petitions for Extraordinary Writs

The All Writs Act, 28 U.S.C. § 1651(a) provides that the "Supreme Court and all courts established by Act of Congress may issue all writs necessary or appropriate in aid of their respective jurisdictions and agreeable to the usages and principles of law." For many years, the Court of Appeals for the Armed Forces, the Service Courts of Criminal Appeals, and their predecessor courts viewed this statute not only as allowing them to issue writs in cases in which they had appellate jurisdiction under UCMJ Articles 62, 66, and 67, 10 U.S.C. §§ 862, 866, 867, but also as conferring upon them jurisdiction to act in other cases in which a writ might be requested. The Supreme Court rejected this view in *Clinton v. Goldsmith*, 526 U.S. 529 (1999), and *United States v. Denedo*, 129 S. Ct. 2213 (2009), concluding that the All Writs Act does not confer jurisdiction. At the same time, however, the Court in *Denedo* interpreted the jurisdiction conferred by the UCMJ very broadly.

UNITED STATES v. DENEDO
U.S. Supreme Court
129 S. Ct. 2213 (2009)

Justice KENNEDY delivered the opinion of the Court.

The case before us presents a single issue: whether an Article I military appellate court has jurisdiction to entertain a petition for a writ of error *coram nobis* to challenge its earlier, and final, decision affirming a criminal conviction. The military court which had affirmed the conviction and where the writ of *coram nobis* was sought is the Navy-Marine Corps Court of Criminal Appeals (NMCCA). Its ruling that it had jurisdiction to grant the writ, but then denying its issuance for lack of merit, was appealed to the United States Court of Appeals for the Armed Forces (C.A.A.F.). After the C.A.A.F. agreed that the NMCCA has jurisdiction to issue the writ, it remanded for further proceedings on the merits. The Government of the United States, contending that a writ of *coram nobis* directed to a final judgment of conviction is beyond the jurisdiction of the military courts, now brings the case to us.

    * * *

Respondent Jacob Denedo came to the United States in 1984 from his native Nigeria. He enlisted in the Navy in 1989 and became a lawful permanent resident in 1990. In 1998, military authorities charged him with conspiracy, larceny, and forgery-in contravention of Articles 81, 121, and 123 of the Uniform Code of Military Justice (UCMJ), 10 U.S.C. §§ 881, 921, 923-all for his role in a scheme to defraud a community college. With the assistance of both military and civilian counsel, respondent made a plea bargain to plead guilty to reduced charges. In exchange for his plea the convening authority referred respondent's case to a special court-martial, § 819, which, at that time, could not impose a sentence greater than six months' confinement.

The special court-martial, consisting of a single military judge, accepted respondent's guilty plea after determining that it was both knowing and voluntary. The court convicted respondent of conspiracy and larceny. It sentenced him to three months' confinement, a bad-conduct discharge, and a reduction to the lowest enlisted pay grade. Respondent appealed on the ground that his sentence was unduly severe. The NMCCA affirmed. App. to Pet. for Cert. 64a-67a. Respondent did not seek further review in the C.A.A.F., and he was discharged from the Navy on May 30, 2000.

In 2006, the Department of Homeland Security commenced removal proceedings against respondent based upon his special court-martial conviction. To avoid deportation, respondent decided to challenge his conviction once more, though at this point it had been final for eight years. He maintained, in a petition for a writ of *coram nobis* filed with the NMCCA, that the conviction it had earlier affirmed must be deemed void because his guilty plea was the result of ineffective assistance of counsel. Respondent alleged that he informed his civilian attorney during plea negotiations that " 'his primary concern and objective' " was to avoid deportation and that he was willing to " 'risk . . . going to jail' " to avert separation from his family. 66 M.J. 114, 118 (C.A.A.F. 2008). On respondent's account, his attorney—an alcoholic who was not sober during the course of the special court-martial proceeding—erroneously assured him that " 'if he agreed to plead guilty at a special-court-martial   he   would   avoid   any   risk   of deportation.' " *Ibid.* Petitioner argued that the NMCCA could set aside its earlier decision by issuing a writ of *coram nobis* under the authority of the All Writs Act, 28 U.S.C. § 1651(a).

The Government filed a motion to dismiss for want of jurisdiction. It contended that the NMCCA had no authority to conduct post-conviction proceedings. . . .

* * *

The writ of *coram nobis* is an ancient common-law remedy designed "to correct errors of fact." *United States v. Morgan*, 346 U.S. 502, 507 (1954). In American jurisprudence the precise contours of *coram nobis* have not been "well defined," *Bronson v. Schulten*, 104 U.S. 410, 416, 26 L.Ed. 797 (1882), but the writ traces its origins to the King's Bench and the Court of Common Pleas. *United States v. Plumer*, 27 F. Cas. 561, 573 (No. 16,056) (CC Mass. 1859) (opinion for the court by Clifford, Circuit Justice); see also *Morgan, supra*, at 507, n. 9 (citing 2 W. Tidd, Practice of Courts of King's Bench and Common Pleas *1136-*1137). In English practice the office of the writ was to foster respect for judicial rulings by enabling the same court "where the action was commenced and where the judgment was rendered" to avoid the rigid strictures of judgment finality by correcting technical errors "such as happened through the fault of the clerk in the record of the proceedings prior to the judgment." *Plumer, supra,* at 572-573.

Any rationale confining the writ to technical errors, however, has been superseded; for in its modern iteration *coram nobis* is broader than its common-law predecessor. This is confirmed by our opinion in *Morgan.* In that case we found that a writ of *coram nobis* can issue to redress a fundamental error, there a deprivation of counsel in violation of the Sixth Amendment, as opposed to mere technical errors. 346 U.S., at 513. The potential universe of cases that range from technical errors to fundamental ones perhaps illustrates, in the case of *coram nobis,* the "tendency of a principle to expand itself to the limit of its logic." B. Cardozo, The Nature of the Judicial Process 51 (1921). To confine the use of *coram nobis* so that finality is not at risk in a great number of cases, we were careful in *Morgan* to limit the availability of the writ to "extraordinary" cases presenting circumstances compelling its use "to achieve justice." 346 U.S., at 511. Another limit, of course, is that an extraordinary remedy may not issue when alternative remedies, such as habeas corpus, are available. See *id.,* at 510-511.

In federal courts the authority to grant a writ of *coram nobis* is conferred by the All Writs Act, which permits "courts established by Act of Congress" to issue "all writs necessary or appropriate in aid of their respective jurisdictions." 28 U.S.C. § 1651(a). Though military courts, like Article III tribunals, are empowered to issue extraordinary writs under the All Writs Act, *Noyd v. Bond,* 395 U.S. 683, 695, n. 7 (1969), that authority does not determine the anterior question whether military courts have jurisdiction to entertain a petition for *coram nobis.* As the text of the All Writs Act recognizes, a court's power to issue any form of relief-extraordinary or otherwise-is contingent on that court's subject-matter jurisdiction over the case or controversy.

Assuming no constraints or limitations grounded in the Constitution are implicated, it is for Congress to determine the subject-matter jurisdiction of federal courts. *Bowles v. Russell,* 551 U.S. 205, 212 (2007) ("Within constitutional bounds, Congress decides what cases the federal courts have jurisdiction to consider"). This rule applies with added force to Article I tribunals, such as the NMCCA and C.A.A.F., which owe their existence to Congress' authority to enact legislation pursuant to Art. I, § 8 of the Constitution. *Clinton v. Goldsmith,* 526 U.S 529, 533-534 (1999).

Our decision in *Goldsmith* demonstrates these teachings. There an Air Force officer, James Goldsmith, was convicted of various crimes by general court-martial and sentenced to six years' confinement. *Id.,* at 531. Following his conviction, Congress enacted a statute authorizing the President to drop convicted officers from the rolls of the Armed Forces. When the Air Force notified Goldsmith that he would be dropped from the rolls, he lodged a petition before the Air Force Court of Criminal Appeals (AFCCA) claiming that the proposed action contravened the *Ex Post Facto* Clause of the Constitution. *Id.,* at 532-533. Goldsmith sought extraordinary relief as authorized by the All Writs Act to enjoin the President from removing him from the rolls. The AFCCA denied relief, but the C.A.A.F. granted it.

Concluding that the UCMJ does not authorize military courts to review executive action—including a decision to drop an officer from the rolls—we held that the AFCCA and the C.A.A.F. lacked jurisdiction over Goldsmith's case. *Id.,* at 535. This was so, we unequivocally found, irrespective of the military court's authority to issue extraordinary relief pursuant to the All Writs Act and its previous jurisdiction over Goldsmith's criminal proceeding. The power to issue relief depends upon, rather than enlarges, a court's jurisdiction. *Id.,* at 536-537.

That principle does not control the question before us. Because *coram nobis* is but an extraordinary tool to correct a legal or factual error, an application for the writ is properly viewed as a belated extension of the original proceeding during which the error allegedly transpired. See *Morgan, supra,* at 505, n. 4 (*coram nobis* is "a step in the criminal case and not, like habeas corpus where relief is sought in a separate case and record, the beginning of a separate civil proceeding"); see also *United States v. Beggerly,* 524 U.S. 38, 46 (1998) (citing *Pacific R. Co. of Mo. v. Missouri Pacific R. Co.,* 111 U.S. 505, 522 (1884)) (noting that an "independent action"—which, like *coram nobis,* is an equitable means to obtain relief from a judgment—" 'may be regarded as ancillary to the prior suit, so that the relief asked may be granted by the court which made the decree in that suit .... The bill, though an original bill in the chancery sense of the word, is a continuation of the former suit, on the question of the jurisdiction of the [court]' "). It follows that to issue respondent a writ of *coram nobis* on remand, the NMCCA must have had statutory subject-matter jurisdiction over respondent's original judgment of conviction.

* * *

In the critical part of its opinion discussing the jurisdiction and authority of the NMCCA to issue a writ of *coram nobis* in an appropriate case, the C.A.A.F. describes respondent's request for review as one "under the All Writs Act." 66 M.J., at 119. This is correct, of course, if it simply confirms that the Act authorizes federal courts to issue writs "in aid of" their jurisdiction; but it does not advance the inquiry into whether jurisdiction exists.

And there are limits to the use of *coram nobis* to alter or interpret earlier judgments. As *Goldsmith* makes plain, the All Writs Act and the extraordinary relief the statute authorizes are not a source of subject-matter jurisdiction. 526 U.S., at 534-535. Statutes which address the power of a court to use certain writs or remedies or to decree certain forms of relief, for instance to award damages in some specified measure, in some circumstances might be construed also as a grant of jurisdiction to hear and determine the underlying cause of action. *Cf. Marbury v. Madison*, 1 Cranch 137 (1803). We have long held, however, that the All Writs Act should not be interpreted in this way. *Goldsmith, supra*, at 536; *Plumer*, 27 F. Cas., at 574 (jurisdiction cannot be acquired "by means of the writ to be issued"). The authority to issue a writ under the All Writs Act is not a fount of jurisdiction. *See Syngenta Crop Protection, Inc. v. Henson*, 537 U.S. 28, 31 (2002).

Quite apart from the All Writs Act, we conclude that the NMCCA has jurisdiction to entertain respondent's request for a writ of *coram nobis*. Article 66 of the UCMJ provides: "For the purpose of reviewing court-martial cases, the [Court of Criminal Appeals] may sit ...." 10 U.S.C. § 866(a). Because respondent's request for *coram nobis* is simply a further "step in [his] criminal" appeal, *Morgan*, 346 U.S., at 505, n. 4, the NMCCA's jurisdiction to issue the writ derives from the earlier jurisdiction it exercised to hear and determine the validity of the conviction on direct review. As even the Government concedes, the textual authority under the UCMJ to " 'revie[w] court-martial cases' " provided the NMCCA with jurisdiction to hear an appeal of respondent's judgment of conviction. See Brief for United States 17-18. That jurisdiction is sufficient to permit the NMCCA to entertain respondent's petition for *coram nobis*. *See also* Courts of Criminal Appeals Rule of Practice and Procedure 2(b) (recognizing NMCCA discretionary authority to entertain petitions for extraordinary writs).

It is true that when exercising its jurisdiction under § 866(a), the NMCCA "may act only with respect to the findings and sentence as approved by the convening authority." § 866(c). That limitation does not bar respondent's request for a writ of *coram nobis*. An alleged error in the original judgment predicated on ineffective-assistance-of-counsel challenges the validity of a conviction, see *Knowles v. Mirzayance*, 129 S. Ct. 1411, 1415-1416, so respondent's Sixth Amendment claim is "with respect to" the special-court-martial's "findings of guilty," 10 U.S.C. § 866(c). Pursuant to the UCMJ, the NMCCA has subject-matter jurisdiction to hear respondent's request for extraordinary relief.

Because the NMCCA had jurisdiction over respondent's petition for *coram nobis*, the C.A.A.F. had jurisdiction to entertain respondent's appeal from the NMCCA's judgment. When exercising its jurisdiction, the C.A.A.F.'s authority is confined "to matters of law" connected to "the findings and sentence as approved by the convening authority and as affirmed or set aside ... by the Court of Criminal Appeals," § 867(c), but these limitations pose no obstacle to respondent's requested review of the NMCCA's decision. Respondent's Sixth Amendment claim presents a "matte[r] of law" "with respect to the [guilty] findings ... as approved by the [special court-martial] and as affirmed ... by the Court of Criminal Appeals." *Ibid*. The C.A.A.F. had subject-matter jurisdiction to review the NMCCA's denial of respondent's petition challenging the validity of his original conviction.

* * *

We hold that Article I military courts have jurisdiction to entertain *coram nobis* petitions to consider allegations that an earlier judgment of conviction was flawed in a fundamental respect. That conclusion is consistent with our holding that Article III courts have a like authority. *Morgan,* 346 U.S., at 508. The result we reach today is of central importance for military courts. The military justice system relies upon courts that must take all appropriate means, consistent with their statutory jurisdiction, to ensure the neutrality and integrity of their judgments. Under the premises and statutes we have relied upon here, the jurisdiction and the responsibility of military courts to reexamine judgments in rare cases where a fundamental flaw is alleged and other judicial processes for correction are unavailable are consistent with the powers Congress has granted those courts under Article I and with the system Congress has designed.

* * *

It is so ordered.

Chief Justice ROBERTS, with whom Justice SCALIA, Justice THOMAS, and Justice ALITO join, concurring in part and dissenting in part.

The Court's approach is simple: Jurisdiction to issue writs of *coram nobis* is a "belated extension" of a court's original, statutory jurisdiction. *Ante,* at 2221. The military courts here had original jurisdiction over Denedo's case. Those courts therefore have implicit "extended" jurisdiction to consider Denedo's *coram nobis* petition.

The flaw in this syllogism is at the first step: The only arguable authority for the proposition that *coram nobis* jurisdiction marches hand in hand with original jurisdiction is a footnote in *United States v. Morgan,* 346 U.S. 502 (1954), and that case concerned Article III courts. The military courts are markedly different. They are Article I courts whose jurisdiction is precisely limited at every turn. Those careful limits cannot be overridden by judicial "extension" of statutory jurisdiction, or the addition of a "further step" to the ones marked out by Congress. *Ante,* at 2222 (internal quotation marks omitted).

I agree with the majority that this Court has jurisdiction to review the decision below, but respectfully dissent from its holding that military courts have jurisdiction to issue writs of *coram nobis.*

* * *

Point for Discussion

Why does the Supreme Court conclude that the military courts had jurisdiction in this case? Did the All Writs Act contribute to that jurisdiction?

The following decision addressed a very high-profile court-martial of the Sergeant Major of the Army, the highest ranking enlisted soldier in the Army. The decision predates the *Denedo* case. In reading it, consider whether the

U.S. Army Court of Criminal Appeals would have jurisdiction to act under *Denedo*'s interpretation of the UCMJ and the All Writs Act.

McKINNEY v. JARVIS
Army Court of Criminal Appeals
46 M.J. 870 (Army Ct. Crim. App. 1997)

CARTER, Judge.

In a PETITION FOR EXTRAORDINARY RELIEF IN THE NATURE OF A WRIT OF PROHIBITION, petitioner asks this court to disqualify Colonel (COL) Owen C. Powell, Jr., from further action in respect to petitioner's pretrial hearing because he is both the accuser and the appointing authority for the pretrial investigating officer. For the reasons indicated below, petitioner's request for a writ of prohibition is denied. We hold that a convening authority who becomes an accuser by virtue of preferring charges in his official capacity as a commander is not, per se, disqualified from appointing a pretrial investigating officer to conduct a thorough and impartial investigation of those charges.

I. HISTORY OF THE CASE

1. Colonel Powell, as the Commander of United States Army Garrison, Fort Myer, Virginia, is both the summary and special court-martial convening authority [hereinafter SPCMCA] over the petitioner. Articles 23(a) and 24(a), Uniform Code of Military Justice, 10 U.S.C. §§ 823(a) and 824(a) (1988) [hereinafter UCMJ]. On 24 February 1997, COL Powell withheld authority from two subordinate commanders to dispose of matters concerning the criminal investigation of petitioner. See Rule for Courts-Martial 306(a)[hereinafter R.C.M.] and Army Reg. 27–10, Legal Services: Military Justice, para. 3–7d (24 June 1996).

2. On 7 May 1997, COL Powell "preferred" charges against petitioner and thereby became the accuser in this case.[1] See R.C.M. 307(b) and UCMJ art. 1(9). On the same day, COL Powell appointed COL Robert L. Jarvis as the pretrial investigating officer pursuant to Article 32, UCMJ, and R.C.M. 405. Colonel Powell directed the investigating officer to close the pretrial hearing to spectators. See R.C.M. 405(h)(3).

3. On 9 May 1997, the investigating officer scheduled the Article 32, UCMJ, hearing for 14 May 1997. On 13 May 1997, petitioner requested, and COL Powell granted, a delay in the Article 32, UCMJ, hearing until 23 June 1997. Petitioner also requested access by spectators at the pretrial hearing.

4. On 16 May 1997, COL Powell denied petitioner's request for an "open pretrial hearing" and again directed that the Article 32, UCMJ, hearing be

---

[1] The military justice system, which requires that a person subject to the UCMJ prefer all charges against an accused and that a commander individually "convene" each trial, has no parallel in the civilian criminal justice system.

closed to spectators. Colonel Powell also ordered the preparation of a verbatim transcript of the pretrial hearing.

5. On 19 May 1997, petitioner joined a petition for a writ of mandamus filed by several news organizations with the United States Court of Appeals for the Armed Forces seeking a reversal of COL Powell's decision to keep the Article 32, UCMJ, hearing closed to spectators. See R.C.M. 1204(a) discussion. On 20 June 1997, the Court of Appeals for the Armed Forces issued a stay in the Article 32, UCMJ, proceedings.

6. On 23 June 1997, the Court of Appeals for the Armed Forces heard oral arguments and ordered the Article 32, UCMJ, hearing opened to the public. The court lifted the stay of the Article 32, UCMJ, proceedings. That same day, the Article 32, UCMJ, hearing was rescheduled for 25 June 1997.

7. On 24 June 1997, petitioner again requested that COL Powell delay the Article 32, UCMJ, investigation and recuse himself as the SPCMCA in this case because he was the accuser. Petitioner also requested that all further discretionary decisions concerning the Article 32, UCMJ, proceedings be forwarded to the general court-martial convening authority (GCMCA). Petitioner's request noted that during oral argument before the Court of Appeals for the Armed Forces, two judges questioned the propriety of COL Powell acting in discretionary matters concerning the Article 32, UCMJ, investigation because he was the accuser. Colonel Powell denied petitioner's request that same day.

8. On 25 June 1997, the Article 32, UCMJ, investigation began. Petitioner requested that the investigating officer delay the investigation until COL Powell's status could be appealed to this court. The investigating officer denied the requested delay, but granted petitioner a recess to file an appeal with this court.

9. Later, on 25 June 1997, petitioner filed a petition with this court for a writ of prohibition disqualifying COL Powell from further action in petitioner's Article 32, UCMJ, investigation. Alternatively, petitioner requested that this court issue a temporary restraining order staying all proceedings until the issue could be fully briefed and argued before this court. The petition did not cite any irreparable harm that would result to petitioner if this court failed to grant an immediate stay in the Article 32, UCMJ, proceedings.

10. On 26 June 1997, this court issued an order denying petitioner's request to stay the Article 32, UCMJ, hearing. The order also directed that the government respond to petitioner's request, and that the government's response, along with any supplemental brief by petitioner, be filed by 30 June 1997. Oral arguments were heard on 1 July 1997.

II. JURISDICTION

To exercise jurisdiction in this case, this court must find that the issues are matters within the scope of its statutory authority; that a writ of prohibition may be issued against the officer who appointed the Article 32, UCMJ, investigating officer; and, most importantly, that this case presents matters of such truly extraordinary circumstances that we should exercise our discretion and consider the merits of petitioner's claims. *See generally, Evans v. Kilroy*, 33 M.J. 730 (A.F.C.M.R. 1991) and *Pearson v. Bloss*, 28 M.J. 764 (A.F.C.M.R. 1989).

Congress directed the creation of the military courts of criminal appeals. UCMJ art. 66. Another statute, commonly referred to as the All Writs Act, provides that "all courts established by Act of Congress may issue all writs necessary or appropriate in aid of their respective jurisdictions and agreeable to the usages and principles of law." 28 U.S.C. § 1651(a) (1992). Accordingly, this court has statutory jurisdiction to determine issues in aid of its jurisdiction under the All Writs Act and to ensure the integrity of the judicial system in Army courts-martial. R.C.M. 1203 discussion; *United States v. Curtin*, 44 M.J. 439, 440 (1996); United States v. Boudreaux, 35 M.J. 291, 294 (C.M.A. 1992); *Dettinger v. United States*, 7 M.J. 216 (C.M.A. 1979); *Brookins v. Cullins*, 49 C.M.R. 5, 6–7 (C.M.A. 1974); *Hobdy v. United States*, 46 M.J. 653, 654 (N.M. Ct. Crim. App. 1997); *United States v. Miller*, 44 M.J. 582, 583 (A.F. Ct. Crim. App.1996); Ross v. United States, 43 M.J. 770, 771–72 (N.M. Ct. Crim. App. 1995); *United States v. Lewis*, 38 M.J. 501, 512–13 (A.C.M.R. 1993), aff'd, 42 M.J. 1 (1995); *United States v. Gray*, 32 M.J. 730, 732 (A.C.M.R.), *pet. denied*, 34 M.J. 164 (1991).

A writ of prohibition is the "process by which a superior court prevents an inferior court or *tribunal possessing judicial or quasi-judicial powers* from exceeding its jurisdiction. . . ." BLACK'S LAW DICTIONARY 1212 (6th ed.1990) (emphasis added). For purposes of this court exercising supervisory review in aid of its jurisdiction under the All Writs Act, an Article 32, UCMJ, pretrial investigation is a "judicial proceeding." *San Antonio Express–News v. Morrow*, 44 M.J. 706, 708–09 (A.F. Ct. Crim. App.1996). It is judicial in nature. *United States v. Samuels*, 216, 27 C.M.R. 280, 286 (C.M.A. 1959). The Article 32, UCMJ, investigation is a judicial proceeding and plays a necessary role in military due process of law. Dep't of Army, Pam. 27–17, Legal Services: Procedural Guide for Article 32(b) Investigating Officer, para. 2–1(b) (16 Sep. 1990). Discretionary decisions by officers who appoint Article 32, UCMJ, investigations are also subject to review under the All Writs Act. *McKinney v. Jarvis*, —M.J.—, U.S.C.A Misc. Dkt. No. 97–8023/8024 AR (23 June 1997) (Order) (Court of Appeals for the Armed Forces reviewed and reversed investigating officer appointing authority's decision to close Article 32, UCMJ, hearing). Therefore, this court, in aid of its supervisory jurisdiction over Army courts-martial, has jurisdiction to issue a writ of prohibition against an officer who appointed the Article 32, UCMJ, investigating officer.

The most important question is why this court should exercise its authority to grant extraordinary relief in this particular case. The issuance of a writ under the All Writs Act is a "drastic remedy which should only be invoked in those situations which are truly extraordinary." *Aviz v. Carver*, 36 M.J. 1026, 1028 (N.M.C.M.R. 1993); *Pearson*, 28 M.J. at 766. Historically, this court has sparingly issued writs of prohibition because they are an "extraordinary" form of relief that is not appropriate in most cases.

The petition before this court challenges the same person (COL Powell) serving as accuser and appointing authority for the Article 32, UCMJ, pretrial investigating officer in the same case. Having found no reported cases directly on point, we believe this to be a question of first impression. Additionally, during an earlier oral argument before our superior court, two judges questioned, sua sponte, COL Powell's continued participation in any discretionary capacity in the Article 32, UCMJ, proceedings because of his status as the accuser. Accordingly, we will entertain the merits of petitioner's request for a writ of prohibition.

III. STANDARD OF REVIEW

The "extraordinary" nature of relief under the All Writs Acts places an "extremely heavy burden" upon the party seeking relief. *United States v. Mahoney*, 36 M.J. 679, 685 (A.F.C.M.R.1992). The issuance of such writs is generally not favored as they disrupt the orderly judicial process of trial on the merits and then appeal. The petitioning party's right to relief must be "clear and indisputable." *Will v. Calvert Fire Insurance Co.*, 437 U.S. 655, 662 (1978); *Kerr v. United States District Court for the Northern District of California*, 426 U.S. 394, 403 (1976); *Ross*, 43 M.J. at 771; *Gray*, 32 M.J. at 732. Petitioner must show that the complained of actions were more than "gross error" and constitute a *"judicial usurpation of power."* *San Antonio Express–News*, 44 M.J. at 709 (emphasis added). The ruling or action being challenged must be "contrary to statute, settled case law, or valid regulation." *Evans*, 33 M.J. at 733.

IV. DISCUSSION

Commanders perform many different roles in the daily administration of military justice. For example, a commander may be an accuser, an investigator, an appointing authority, a convening authority, a reviewing authority, an appeal authority, an approving authority, or a superior authority. Depending on the facts, statutes, and regulations involved, a commander may legally perform more than one of these duties in the same case. In this case, petitioner challenges COL Powell's dual roles as accuser and appointing authority for the Article 32, UCMJ, investigating officer, and his discretionary actions thereunder.

Article 1(9), UCMJ, defines an "accuser" to include one who "signs and swears to charges, . . . and any other person who has an interest other than an official interest in the prosecution of the accused." A person "prefers" charges as the accuser by signing a charge sheet and swearing that he either "has personal knowledge of, or has investigated, the matters set forth therein" and that the same are true to the best of his knowledge and belief. UCMJ art.

30(a); R.C.M. 307. It is uncontested that COL Powell is the accuser in this case because he preferred the charges against the petitioner.

The Congress and the President have disqualified the accuser from performing certain other responsibilities in the same case. An accuser may not convene, or serve as a member of, a general or special court-martial to try the charges that he preferred. UCMJ arts. 22(b), 23(b), and 25(d)(2). An accuser may not refer charges to a general or special court-martial. R.C.M. 601(c). An accuser may not act as a military judge in the same case. UCMJ art. 26(d). An accuser is disqualified from performing duties as trial counsel or as an Article 32, UCMJ, investigating officer. R.C.M.s 502(d)(4)(A) and 405(d)(1). An accuser may serve as defense counsel only "when expressly requested by the accused." R.C.M. 502(d)(4). An accuser may not serve in a court-martial as an interpreter, reporter, escort, bailiff, clerk, or orderly. R.C.M. 502(e)(2)(A). An accuser may not perform the judge advocate review required by R.C.M. 1112. R.C.M. 1112(c). With the exception of the disqualification of being the actual investigating officer, the duties foreclosed to the accuser by statute and the Rules for Court–Martial involve referral and post-referral functions in the court-martial process.[3]

Likewise, the Congress and the President have agreed that there are instances when an accuser may continue to perform military justice duties in the same case. A commander may prefer charges as the accuser and then forward those charges to his superior commander for disposition. The decision to forward to a superior commander requires that "a personal recommendation as to disposition" shall accompany the transmittal of those charges. R.C.M.s 307 and 401(c)(2)(A). Additionally, an accuser is not disqualified from convening a summary court-martial to try those same charges, and may even detail himself as the summary court-martial. UCMJ art. 24; R.C.M. 307(a) discussion; R.C.M. 401 discussion; R.C.M. 504(c)(1) discussion; R.C.M. 1302(b); R.C.M. 1302 discussion; and *United States v. Kajander*, 31 C.M.R. 479, 480, 1962 WL 4424 (C.G.B.R.1962).

Any court-martial convening authority (summary, special, or general) may direct a pretrial investigation under Article 32, UCMJ. R.C.M.s 403(b)(5), 404(e), 405(c), and 407(a)(5). The Congress expressly disqualified an accuser from convening a special or general court-martial. UCMJ arts. 22(b) and 23(b). The President expressly disqualified an accuser from serving as investigating officer. R.C.M. 405(d)(1). Neither the President nor the Congress expressly disqualified an accuser from appointing the investigating officer. Accordingly, we answer the court specified issue in the negative: Colonel Powell was not disqualified by statute or regulation from appointing the Article 32, UCMJ, investigating officer solely because he preferred the charges.

---

[3] "Referral" is the order by a non-disqualified convening authority that charges against a particular accused will be tried by a specified court-martial. See R.C.M. 601(a) discussion.

However, when COL Powell became the accuser in this case, he lost his authority to convene a special court-martial to try these charges. UCMJ art. 23(b); R.C.M. 601(c); *United States v. Crews*, 49 C.M.R. 502, 1974 WL 14111 (C.G.C.M.R.1974). In addition, if he decides to forward the charges to a higher convening authority, he must note his disqualification. R.C.M. 401(c)(2)(A).   Colonel Powell may still offer petitioner nonjudicial punishment under Article 15, UCMJ, or refer the charges to a summary court-martial. However, each of these last two options requires petitioner's consent, and neither can result in petitioner's confinement or discharge from the Army. In fact, the only final disposition of these charges, other than administrative actions, that COL Powell can make without the consent of petitioner is to dismiss them.

Additionally, every commander has an obligation to dispose of charges at the lowest possible appropriate level. R.C.M. 306(b). A responsible appointing authority does not appoint an Article 32, UCMJ, investigating officer without first determining that the charges might warrant a general court-martial. R.C.M. 303; R.C.M. 306(c)(4). One of the purposes of the Article 32, UCMJ, investigation is to assist the appointing authority in making an appropriate disposition of the charges. R.C.M. 405(a) discussion. "[A] subordinate convening authority who directs an Article 32 investigation is not required to be absolutely neutral and detached. By ordering such an investigation, he has already determined that the offenses possibly merit a general court-martial. It is the investigating officer who must remain impartial." *United States v. Wojciechowski*, 19 M.J. 577, 579 (N.M.C.M.R.1984). Accordingly, COL Powell's preliminary review of the evidence as the accuser is not inconsistent with his responsibility to determine the appropriate disposition of the charges, nor is it inconsistent with his recognition, prior to appointing an Article 32, UCMJ, investigating officer, that the appropriate disposition might include a general court-martial.

One can become an accuser, even though he didn't prefer the charges, if he has an "interest other than an official interest" in the case. UCMJ art. 1(9). Petitioner argues, conversely, that because COL Powell is the accuser, he now has an "other than official interest" in the case's outcome. We reject petitioner's reverse logic.

The historical basis for this "other than an official interest" disqualification dates back to the eighteenth century and is well documented in *United States v. Gordon*, 2 C.M.R. 161, 163–66 (C.M.A. 1952). In that case, our superior court stated that the test for determining if an "other than official interest" exists in a case is "whether, under the particular facts and circumstances . . . a reasonable person would impute to [the accuser] a personal feeling or interest in the outcome of the litigation." *Gordon*, 2 C.M.R. at 166. *See also United States v. Nix*, 40 M.J. 6, 8 (C.M.A. 1994); *United States v. Jeter*, 35 M.J. 442, 445 (C.M.A. 1992); and *United States v. Conn*, 6 M.J. 351, 354 (C.M.A. 1979) where this test was cited with approval.

In an affidavit admitted as part of these proceedings, COL Powell disavows any such personal interest in the outcome of this case [in an affidavit submitted to this court]. Petitioner offers no evidence that COL Powell has an "other than official interest" in the case except for the fact that he preferred the charges. Pretrial actions performed as "command functions embraced or reasonably anticipated" under the UCMJ do not as a matter of law constitute a personal interest requiring disqualification from further participation. *Conn*, 6 M.J. at 354. Accordingly, based on the record before us, we specifically hold that COL Powell has nothing but an official interest in the outcome of these charges.

[Petitioner also asserts that COL Powell abused his discretion by making discretionary decisions concerning the conduct of the Article 32, UCMJ, investigation. The President has given a convening authority who appoints a pretrial investigating officer the expressed authority to "give procedural instructions not inconsistent with these rules." R.C.M. 405(c). Petitioner alleges that COL Powell "continues to exercise discretion for which he is not vested by virtue of his role as accuser." Petitioner does not allege, or attempt to prove, that the investigation or the investigating officer are not fair and impartial. Such generic allegations do not come close to satisfying petitioner's heavy burden to prove by "clear and indisputable" evidence that he is entitled to a writ of prohibition in this case.

V. DECISION

This court therefore holds:

1. Colonel Powell was not disqualified from appointing an Article 32, UCMJ, investigating officer because of his status as the accuser.

2. Petitioner has failed to produce "clear and indisputable" evidence that COL Powell's exercise of discretionary authority has denied petitioner a fair and impartial pretrial investigation or in any manner prejudiced the investigation.

Accordingly, petitioner's request for a writ of prohibition disqualifying COL Powell from further participation as the Article 32, UCMJ, appointing authority is DENIED.

Senior Judge TOOMEY and Judge GONZALES concur.

Points for Discussion

1. Why was immediate judicial review important to Sergeant Major McKinney in this case? Why did he need to rely on the All Writs Act in claiming that the Army Court of Criminal Appeals had jurisdiction? Note that UCMJ Article 62(a) affords only the United States a right to interlocutory appeals, and not the accused. Why is that?

2. After *Denado*, could the Army Court of Criminal Appeals exercise jurisdiction in a similar case? If not, should Congress amend the UCMJ to provide for review in cases such as this one?

CHAPTER 8

FINDINGS

8-1. Providence Inquiry for Guilty Pleas

In general and special courts-martial, about 60% of the accused plead guilty to all of the charges and specifications against them, and an even higher percentage plead guilty to some of the charges and specifications. *See Clerk of Court Note: A Closer Look at Army Court-Martial Conviction Rates*, Army Lawyer, Mar. 1993, at 26 (1993). For this reason, understanding guilty pleas and how military judges handle them is very important.

A service member charged with offenses under the UCMJ has two incentives to plead guilty rather than to put the government to the burden of proving its case at trial. First, in many cases, the accused will make the guilty plea as part of a plea bargain with the government. In military parlance, a plea bargain is called a "pretrial agreement." In exchange for the accused's plea, the government may agree to reduce the seriousness of the offenses charged, to dismiss certain charges or specifications, or to limit the maximum punishment that may be imposed on the accused. Second, in other cases the accused may enter a "naked plea"—a plea for nothing in exchange—because accepting responsibility and cooperating with the government may result in quicker resolution of the case and a lesser sentence.

When the accused pleads guilty, the military judge must conduct a "providence inquiry" to ensure that the accused has not made an improvident plea. In the providence inquiry, the military judge has a number of duties which are set out in RCM 910. The military judge must inform the accused of the nature of the offense and the maximum penalties that the accused faces if convicted. *See* RCM 910(c)(1). The military judge also must ensure that the accused's plea is both voluntary and accurate. *See* RCM 910(d), (e). Finally, the military judge must ensure that the accused understands and agrees to any pretrial agreement. *See* RCM 910(f).

Military judges take their duties in the providence inquiry very seriously. The inquiry may take several hours even if the offenses are few and minor in scope. The military judge reads the elements of the offenses to the accused as well as the definition of any difficult terms. To determine the facts, the military judge reviews the precise language of the charged specifications with the accused. The military judge asks the accused, who is put under oath, whether each and every part of the specification is true. The military judge also usually asks the accused to describe in his or her own words exactly what happened. The accused in many cases signs a sworn "stipulation of fact" as part of any pretrial agreement with the government, which the military judge will review. The military judge additionally will go over any pretrial agreement paragraph by paragraph to make sure the accused knows what the plea bargain entails. If the military judge accepts the guilty plea, a trial will proceed on the issue of sentencing. Note that the government and accused cannot agree to a specific sentence in a pretrial agreement, although they can agree on a maximum punishment. In a case with a pretrial agreement, the accused receives the lesser punishment—the punishment adjudged by the court or punishment contained in the pretrial agreement.

Acceptance of guilty pleas is not automatic. If the accused testifies or otherwise sets up facts that appear to be inconsistent with the accused's guilty plea the military judge either must resolve the apparent inconsistency or reject the plea. *See United States v. Garcia*, 44 M.J. 496, 498 (C.A.A.F. 1996); RCM 910(h)(2). If an inconsistency appears after the military judge has completed the providence inquiry—such as at sentencing—the military judge must reopen the providence inquiry. *See Garcia*, 44 M.J. at 498. When the military judge rejects a guilty plea, the government either must ask the court to dismiss or amend the charge or specification to which the accused cannot plead guilty, or the government must proceed to trial to prove the offense. Having the military judge reject a guilty plea is not usually advantageous to the accused. Most pretrial agreements contain a clause providing that the deal is terminated if the providence inquiry fails.

If the military judge accepts the guilty plea, and finds the accused guilty, the accused may challenge his conviction on appeal if the providence inquiry was insufficient. The following case describes the constitutional basis for the providence inquiry, which is now codified in R.C.M. 910 as described above.

UNITED STATES v. CARE
U.S. Court of Military Appeals
40 C.M.R. 247 (C.M.A. 1969)

DARDEN, Judge:

The Court selected this case for a grant of review to consider again the extent to which a law officer or a president of a special court-martial must question an accused about the latter's actions and his understanding of the law applicable to these actions before accepting a guilty plea.

[David E. Care, Private, U. S. Marine Corps, Appellant] pleaded guilty to desertion, in violation of Article 85, Uniform Code of Military Justice, 10 U.S.C. § 885. Under the terms of a pretrial agreement, the convening authority would approve no sentence in excess of a bad-conduct discharge, total forfeitures, and confinement at hard labor for two years, compared with the maximum sentence of a dishonorable discharge, total forfeitures, and confinement at hard labor for three years. Because of the guilty plea no evidence was presented; an absence of almost fifteen months terminated by apprehension was alleged. After the findings of guilty and the sentence were approved by the board of review, this Court granted a petition for review on the issue of whether the plea of the accused was provident in view of the law officer's failure to delineate the essential elements of the offense and to determine the factual basis of the plea.

After our grant of review, the accused submitted an affidavit asserting that his counsel did not specifically explain the elements of the offense to him; that he had denied any intent to remain away permanently; that his counsel had told him a plea of not guilty would delay his trial for four months; that inevitably he would be convicted and receive the maximum sentence, but that a negotiated pretrial agreement could limit his confinement sentence to two years; that this advice resulted in his pleading guilty; and that if he were tried again he would plead not guilty.

In a reply affidavit, Care's trial defense counsel insists that although he does not recall the specific words used in the first of at least six conferences with the accused before trial, he is certain that he followed a written guide or checklist he had prepared earlier to assure that his clients were fully informed of their rights. The items on his checklist included the lawyer-client privilege; the elements of the offense; the proof needed to convict; the maximum punishment; the effect of pleas of guilty and not guilty; pretrial agreement; and related subjects. The counsel's affidavit also indicates that he informs each client of his absolute right to plead not guilty and that he should plead guilty only if he is, in fact, guilty and "did everything the Government is charging him with." The counsel denies that he told Care there was no possibility of an acquittal or that "a guilty plea would take four months longer than a not guilty." Near the end of the affidavit he affirms that Private Care informed him that Care was guilty of desertion and that he knew the elements of the offense before he signed the pretrial agreement.

Article 45 of the Uniform Code of Military Justice, 10 U.S.C. § 845, provides, in pertinent part, that "[i]f an accused . . . after a plea of guilty sets up matter inconsistent with the plea, . . . a plea of not guilty shall be entered in the record, and the court shall proceed as though he had pleaded not guilty." The implementing regulation in effect at the time of the plea, paragraph 70, Manual for Courts-Martial, United States, 1951, directs that a court should not accept a plea of guilty "without first determining that it is made voluntarily with understanding of the nature of the charge."

Paragraph 70b, Manual, *supra*, prescribes procedure for all cases in which a plea of guilty is entered. Among the requirements here are that (1) the plea will be received and will be treated as an interlocutory one; (2) the court may entertain such a plea only after the accused has had an opportunity to consult with the counsel he selects or the one appointed for him; and (3) the law officer must explain the meaning and effect of a plea of guilty unless it otherwise affirmatively appears that the accused understands such meaning and effect. This explanation must include (a) that the plea admits every act or omission alleged and every element of the offense and authorizes conviction without further proof; (b) that the maximum sentence may be adjudged; and

(c) that unless the accused understands the explanation the plea will not be received. The explanation and reply will be set forth verbatim in the record.

Several rights, including that to knowledge of the meaning and effect of a plea of guilty, must be explained in open court "unless it otherwise affirmatively appears of record that the accused is aware of his rights in the premises." Paragraph 53h, Manual, supra.

Whether, in the absence of the law officer's open court explanation of the elements, these provisions for explanation of the meaning and effect of a guilty plea are complied with when the accused responds that he knows the elements of the offense with which he is charged is essentially the object of our examination.

In *United States v. Chancelor*, 36 C.M.R. 453 (C.M.A. 1966), this Court exhaustively considered the legislative background of Article 45 relating to guilty pleas and pointed out the congressional intent that the acceptance of a guilty plea be accompanied by certain safeguards to insure the providence of the plea, including a delineation of the elements of the offense charged and an admission of factual guilt on the record. The Court strongly recommended that the armed forces require a form of inquiry that would satisfy this congressional intent.

Three decisions by the Supreme Court of the United States in this term bear importantly on our decision. *McCarthy v. United States*, 394 U.S. 459 (1969), held that a defendant is entitled to plead anew if a United States District Court accepts a guilty plea without personally inquiring whether the defendant understood the nature of the charge. In *McCarthy*, the accused was asked only if it were true that he wished to plead guilty, if he understood that he was waiving his right to a jury trial, and if he understood the maximum punishment. During sentencing proceedings McCarthy's counsel suggested that McCarthy's failure to pay his taxes was not willful but had resulted from neglect and inadvertence traceable to his serious drinking problem. The court based its decision not on constitutional requirements but on its construction of Rule 11 of the Federal Rules of Criminal Procedure and the court's supervisory power over the lower Federal courts. Of a guilty plea, the court said in *McCarthy*:

> ". . . A defendant who enters such a plea simultaneously waives several constitutional rights, including his privilege against compulsory self-incrimination, his right to trial by jury, and his right to confront his accusers. For this waiver to be valid under the Due Process Clause, it must be 'an intentional relinquishment or abandonment of a known right or privilege.' *Johnson v. Zerbst*, 304 US 458, 464 (1938). Consequently, if a defendant's guilty plea is not equally voluntary and knowing, it has been obtained in violation of due process and is therefore void. Moreover, because a guilty plea is an admission of all the elements of a formal criminal charge, it cannot be truly voluntary unless the defendant

possesses an understanding of the law in relation to the facts." [394 US, at page 466.]

From a constitutional standpoint, the *McCarthy* opinion reiterates that the objective of Rule 11 is to assure a defendant's guilty plea is truly voluntary. *See also Machibroda v. United States*, 368 U.S. 487 (1962); *Von Moltke v. Gillies*, 332 U.S. 708 (1948); *Waley v. Johnston*, 316 U.S. 101 (1942).

In a later case, *Halliday v. United States*, 394 US 831, 833, 23 L Ed 2d 16, 89 S Ct 1498 (1969), the court declined to apply McCarthy retroactively "in view of the large number of constitutionally valid convictions that may have been obtained without full compliance with Rule 11."

The third of the three recent Supreme Court cases in this area is *Boykin v. Alabama*, 395 U.S. 238, 239 (1969). There, the court held that the Due Process Clause of the Fourteenth Amendment required the reversal of a State conviction involving a guilty plea during which "[s]o far as the record shows, the judge asked no questions of petitioner concerning his plea, and petitioner did not address the court."

Despite some difficulties in reconciling the constitutional aspects involved in *Boykin* and *Halliday*, we think that a plea of guilty may meet required standards if on the basis of the whole record the showing is clear that the plea was truly voluntary, even if the trial judge has not personally addressed the accused and determined that the defendant possesses an understanding of the law in relation to the facts. This is such a case.

The opinion of the Supreme Court in *Halliday* concludes significantly:

"... In *McCarthy* we noted that the practice we were requiring had been previously followed by only one Circuit; that over 80% of all verdicts in the federal courts are obtained after guilty pleas; and that prior to Rule 11's recent amendment, not all district judges personally questioned defendants before accepting their guilty pleas. Thus, in view of the general application of Rule 11 in a manner inconsistent with our holding in *McCarthy*, and in view of the large number of constitutionally valid convictions that may have been obtained without full compliance with Rule 11, we decline to apply *McCarthy* retroactively." [Emphasis supplied.] [394 US 831, 833.]

One might argue that the decision of the Supreme Court in *Boykin* overrules the language of *Halliday* that there are a "large number of constitutionally valid convictions that may have been obtained without full compliance with Rule 11." But we think that if on June 2 the Supreme Court were reversing its *Halliday* holding of May 5, 1969, it would have stated so forthrightly.

Appendix A is a verbatim record of the examination of Care by the law officer. It will be seen that the law officer explained that he had to determine voluntariness and providency personally and asked the accused (1) if he knew his plea subjected him to a finding of guilty without further proof; (2) if he knew he could be sentenced to the maximum sentence; (3) if he understood the meaning and effect of his plea; (4) if he knew that the burden was on the Government to prove his guilt beyond a reasonable doubt; (5) if he knew he was entitled to plead not guilty; (6) if he knew the elements of the offense; (7) if he had adequate opportunity to consult with counsel on any matters he felt necessary; (8) if he was satisfied with his counsel; (9) whether counsel advised him of the maximum punishment; (10) if the decision to negotiate a plea originated with him; (11) if his plea was given voluntarily; (12) if anyone used force or coercion to get him to enter a guilty plea; (13) if he believed it was in his best interest to plead guilty; (14) if his plea was the product of free will and a desire to confess his guilt; and (15) if he knew he could withdraw his plea. In each instance, the answer was "yes."

The procedure that was followed here fell short of the one recommended in *United States v. Chancelor, supra*, because the law officer did not personally inform the accused of the elements constituting the offense and he did not establish the factual components of the guilty plea. That the *Chancelor* recommendation was not an inflexible requirement is shown by this Court's having denied, after *Chancelor* and before *Care*, many petitions for review of cases involving guilty plea where delineation of the elements was lacking. Taken as a whole, the evidence in this record satisfies us the accused knew what he was pleading guilty to, what he must have done for his acts to constitute desertion, and that he did, in essence, know the elements of the offense just as his acknowledgment to the law officer indicates.

The specification itself, furthermore, sets forth in simple comprehensible terms all the elements of the relatively uncomplicated offense of desertion:

> "In that Private David E. CARE, U. S. Marine Corps, Support Company, Headquarters Battalion, Headquarters Regiment, Marine Corps Base, Camp Pendleton, California did, on or about 18 May 1967, without proper authority and with intent to remain away therefrom permanently, absent himself from his unit, to wit: Headquarters & Service Company, 2d Battalion, 6th Marines, 2d Marine Division, Fleet Marine Force, Camp Lejeune, North Carolina, and did remain so absent in desertion until apprehended on or about 13 August 1968." [Emphasis supplied.]

This specification appears on the charge sheet, a copy of which was served on the accused. Moreover, a copy of the charge and specification was handed to the accused at the trial.

Beyond this, the elements of desertion are (1) unauthorized absence and (2) an intent to remain away permanently. Unauthorized absence is probably one of the simplest of all military offenses. It consists of being away from duty without permission. After arguing that members of the armed forces have common knowledge that they may not leave their duty without permission, the Government points out that Care "has a special claim to expertise, in that he is one of the Marine Corp's [sic] more experienced absentees. Two of Appellant's three prior convictions by courts-martial were for three separate unauthorized absences." With this history, we find it difficult to believe that Care did not know he needed permission to be away from his duty.

The second element of desertion is an intent to remain away permanently. Care was absent for about fourteen months. Extraordinary duration of absence, standing alone, will not establish the intent required for a finding of desertion. *United States v. Cothern*, 23 C.M.R. 382 (C.M.A. 1957). But when an unauthorized absence of extended duration is combined with apprehension 3,000 miles from the last duty station, an inference of an intent to remain away permanently may be drawn. *United States v. Montoya*, 35 C.M.R. 182 (C.M.A. 1965); *United States v. Bonds*, 19 C.M.R. 357 (C.M.A. 1955).

The affidavit of the appellant concedes that his defense counsel asked him if he intended to remain away permanently. He states further that he did not intend to remain away permanently. But in the interrogation by the law officer he responded to a question that he knew the elements of the offense with which he was charged. At which point are we to believe him? *United States v. Boberg*, 38 C.M.R. 199 (C.M.A. 1968). The affidavit of the trial counsel states his certainty that he explained the elements of the offense to the appellant. Hence, again this Court must determine controverted issues on the basis of the "blizzard of . . . affidavits" that the opinion in *Chancelor* decried.

We are satisfied that at the time of his guilty plea Private Care knew the acts and intent necessary to prove desertion and consequently that his plea was voluntary. We believe, however, that further action is required toward the objective of having court-martial records reflect fully an awareness by an accused pleading guilty of what he is admitting that he did and intended and of the law that applies to his acts and intentions.

The Court noted earlier in the opinion that its recommendation in *Chancelor* that the armed forces take remedial action to assure compliance with the requirement for inquiry into guilt-in-fact. This recommendation has received less than satisfactory implementation as is evidenced by review of many records of trial in which the law officer or the president fails to explain personally the elements of an offense and to establish factual guilt directly. Although the Manual for Courts-Martial, United States, 1969, which became effective January 1, 1969, adds the elements of the offense as one of the subjects that should be included in the explanation prescribed by paragraph 70b when a guilty plea is entered, we note also that the language applicable to the explanation by a law officer or a president of a court-martial of the meaning and effect of a guilty plea has been changed from "will explain" to "should explain." Perhaps this is only a stylistic change that is not intended to convert the explanation into a discretionary procedure. But we are concerned that the new Manual's Trial Procedure Guide (Appendix 8a), Manual for Courts-Martial, supra, still contains no suggestion for an explanation of the elements of offenses and no suggestions for questions eliciting the facts leading to a guilty plea.

In any event, the record of trial for those courts-martial convened more than thirty days after the date of this opinion must reflect not only that the elements of each offense charged have been explained to the accused but also that the military trial judge or the president has questioned the accused about what he did or did not do, and what he intended (where this is pertinent), to make clear the basis for a determination by the military trial judge or president whether the acts or the omissions of the accused constitute the offense or offenses to which he is pleading guilty. *United States v. Rinehart*, 24 C.M.R. 212 (C.M.A. 1957); *United States v. Donohew*, 39 C.M.R. 149 (C.M.A. 1969). This requirement will not be satisfied by questions such as whether the accused realizes that a guilty plea admits "every element charged and every act or omission alleged and authorizes conviction of the offense without further proof." A military trial judge or a president personally addressing the accused to explain the elements of the offense with which he is charged and to question him about his actions and omissions should feel no obligation to apologize or to disclaim any intent that his actions reflect on the competence of the accused's counsel. We believe the counsel, too, should explain the elements and determine that there is a factual basis for the plea but his having done so earlier will not relieve the military trial judge or the president of his responsibility to do so on the record.

Further, the record must also demonstrate the military trial judge or president personally addressed the accused, advised him that his plea waives his right against self-incrimination, his right to a trial of the facts by a court-martial, and his right to be confronted by the witnesses against him; and that he waives such rights by his plea. *Boykin v. Alabama, supra*. Based upon the foregoing inquiries and such additional interrogation as he deems necessary, the military trial judge or president must make a finding that there is a knowing, intelligent, and conscious waiver in order to accept the plea.

The decision of the board of review is affirmed.

Chief Judge QUINN concurs.

FERGUSON, Judge (dissenting):

* * *

... [I]t is apparent the law officer's perfunctory inquiries do not make out a conscious and knowing waiver of the accused's constitutional rights or an understanding of the meaning and effect of his plea. The questions posed to the accused elicited no factual basis for understanding, and, at best, established accused freely made the plea, without at the time understanding the nature of the charges, the punishment to which he subjected himself, or the fact that he thereby waived his rights against self-incrimination, to a trial by the military counterpart of a jury, or to confront his accusers.

* * *

Points for Discussion

1. If the accused is represented by counsel, why is a providence inquiry by the military judge necessary? Does requiring a providence inquiry suggest that defense counsel are not competent to explain the elements of offenses to their clients and to investigate the facts sufficient to know whether their clients are guilty?

2. In U.S. District Courts, a defendant can plead no contest or nolo contendere and admit that there is sufficient evidence to prove guilt without actually admitting guilt. *See North Carolina v. Alford*, 400 U.S. 25 (1970). Why might a defendant want to make such a plea? Why are such pleas not permitted in a court-martial?

3. Can you think of other areas in which the Rules of Courts-Martial should impose duties on military judges to make inquiries of the accused and the accused's understanding of the proceedings?

———————————

As noted above, a military judge's decision to reject a guilty plea is not always advantageous to the accused. The government can proceed to trial and, if the accused is found guilty, may face a more severe penalty than the accused would have received if the guilty plea had been accepted. Defense counsel, perhaps ironically, therefore sometimes must strive to ensure that the military judge finds the accused guilty.

UNITED STATES v. ENGLAND
Army Court of Criminal Appeals
2009 WL 6842645 (Army Ct. Crim. App.) (ARMY 20051170)

TOZZI, Senior Judge:

An officer panel sitting as a general court-martial convicted appellant [Private First Class Lynndie R. ENGLAND United States Army], contrary to her pleas, of one specification of conspiracy to commit maltreatment, four specifications of maltreatment, and one specification of indecent acts with another, in violation of Articles 81, 93, and 134, Uniform Code of Military Justice, 10 U.S.C. §§ 881, 893, and 934 [hereinafter UCMJ]. The convening authority approved the adjudged sentence of a dishonorable discharge, three years confinement, and reduction to Private E1. The convening authority also waived automatic forfeitures and credited appellant with ten days of confinement credit against the approved sentence to confinement.

On appeal, appellant claims, inter alia, that (1) the military judge abused his discretion when he rejected her guilty plea; (2) appellant's trial defense counsel were ineffective for calling Private (PVT) Charles Graner as a presentencing witness, in the alternative; and (3) information about an Article 15, UCMJ, was erroneously included in the staff judge advocate's recommendation (SJAR). This case is before the court for review pursuant to Article 66, UCMJ. We have considered the record of trial, appellant's assignments of error, the matters personally raised by appellant pursuant to

United States v. Grostefon, 12 M.J. 431 (C .M.A.1982), and the government's response. We find the first two assignments of error merit discussion but no relief. In addition, we find appellant's third assignment of error is meritorious and will grant relief in our decretal paragraph. The remaining assignments of error are without merit.

FACTS

At the time of the offenses for which appellant was court-martialed, she was assigned to the 372d Military Police Company, a reserve unit headquartered in Maryland. In May 2003, appellant deployed with the 372d to Iraq. By the fall of that year, her unit assumed duties at the Baghdad Central Confinement Facility at Abu Ghraib, Iraq, where appellant served as a personnel administrative clerk.

Several months before the contested trial in this case, and pursuant to a pretrial agreement, appellant attempted to plead guilty to a majority of the charges against her. In the agreement, the convening authority agreed to disapprove any confinement in excess of thirty months.

Two of the specifications involved an incident where then-Corporal (CPL) Charles Graner[2] testified that he placed a "strap tied as a leash" around a nude detainee, removed the detainee from his holding cell, handed the leash to appellant, and then took photographs of appellant holding the leash. Specification 1 of Charge I alleged a conspiracy to maltreat the detainee, while Specification 1 of Charge II alleged the maltreatment itself. During the *Care*[3]i inquiry, the military judge conducted an extensive examination of appellant to establish her understanding as to why her actions were unlawful. After satisfying himself that appellant was provident to the offenses, the military judge accepted her pleas and found her guilty.

During the presentencing case before members, the defense called PVT Graner to testify. Civilian defense counsel limited their questioning of PVT Graner to his personal background—age, prior service as a Marine, and fifteen years of work experience as a civilian corrections officer; his responsibilities at the Abu Ghraib prison; and his intimate relationship with appellant at the time of the offenses. Civilian defense counsel also used PVT Graner to develop the factual backdrop for the leashed detainee incident and the pictures PVT Graner took of appellant holding the leash.

Regarding the leased detainee incident, PVT Graner stated he needed to move the detainee from an isolation cell to an assigned cell, but he wanted to conduct the movement without having to actually enter the detainee's cell. Specifically, PVT Graner testified that:

---

[2] At the time of appellant's attempted guilty plea, CPL Graner had been convicted at a court-martial for his role in crimes committed at the Abu Ghraib prison. Part of his sentence included a reduction to the grade of E1 and he testified at appellant's court-martial as a Private. We refer to him in this opinion as PVT Graner.

[3] *United States v. Care*, 40 C.M.R. 247 (C.M.A. 1969).

WIT: I had wrapped what I called the tether around his shoulders and began to pull him out of the cell, at which point it slid down around his neck. [The detainee] began to crawl out of the cell on his own . . . I asked [appellant] to hold the tether, or the lead, as the [detainee] crawled out of the cell. I took three quick pictures of the [detainee]. And then once he was fully out of the cell, I took the tether off his neck, snatched him up, I grabbed him by his neck and his arm and I escorted him to his cell on the B side.

Civilian defense counsel elicited additional details from PVT Graner about the planning and execution of the removal of the detainee from his cell.

CDC: When you handed the tether to Private England, did you tell her why you were handing it to her?

WIT: No, sir, I just asked her to hold it.

CDC: Were you asking her as the NCO [noncommissioned officer] in charge of that tier, or were you asking her as a friend or as a fellow soldier?

WIT: I was asking her as the senior person of that extraction team, I guess you would say, as the NCO.

Finally, civilian defense counsel asked PVT Graner a very specific question about an alteration he made to the photograph he took of the detainee with appellant holding the leash.

CDC: Now, you took three pictures. In one of the pictures, you seemed to have taken out Specialist Ambuhl . . . Was that done intentionally?

WIT: Yes, sir.

CDC: Why was that?

WIT: I believe that was—someone—where Specialist England had worked in the—I believe it was the processing area for the prisoners, and someone over there had wanted a picture, and I had not asked Specialist Ambuhl if she, you know, wanted to be in this picture that I was giving away, blacked her out.

After hearing PVT Graner's confusing and nonresponsive answer, the military judge asked several clarifying questions.

MJ: Private Graner, why did you take the pictures?

WIT: The three pictures I took that night, sir, was—this was going to be a planned use of force, which anything that we did at the prison, since we had no other rules besides from the 800th MP's ROE [Military Police Rules of Engagement], I tried to bring what we would have done at Pennsylvania there, and since it was a planned use of force, you document it. We didn't have a video camera. This was the closest way I could document it. Apparently, since we had a lot of information during our case, that's the Army policy for their corrections, that you document planned use of force.

MJ: So what you're saying is this cell extraction picture was part of a legitimate cell extraction technique with pictures to document what you were doing?

WIT: I can't say it that it was a legitimate . . .

MJ: Legitimate in the sense that you were doing it to extract him.

WIT: Yes, sir, it was to me the safest way to get this prisoner out of his cell.

The military judge then excused the members and voiced his concern that PVT Graner's testimony contradicted appellant's guilty pleas and the stipulation of fact, since the pictures of appellant holding the detainee on a leash could have been part of a legitimate cell extraction in the mind of one of the alleged co-conspirators. After giving both sides the opportunity to resolve the inconsistency, the government and the defense agreed, based on PVT Graner's testimony, appellant was not provident to the conspiracy to commit maltreatment charge. The military judge then entered a plea of "not guilty" for appellant as to that offense and determined there was no longer a valid stipulation of fact and appellant was no longer in compliance with the pretrial agreement. The rejected guilty plea led to appellant's contested court-martial, where she was acquitted of the conspiracy to commit maltreatment offense involving the leashed detainee.

LAW AND DISCUSSION

Military Judge's Rejection of Appellant's Guilty Plea

We review a military judge's decision to accept or reject a guilty plea for an abuse of discretion and questions of law arising from the guilty plea de novo. *United States v. Inabinette*, 66 M .J. 320, 322 (C.A.A.F. 2008); *United States v. Shaw*, 64 M.J. 460, 462 (C.A.A.F. 2007). If appellant sets up a matter inconsistent with the plea, the military judge must either resolve the inconsistency or reject the plea. UCMJ art. 45(a).

Appellant asserts the military judge erred by concluding that PVT Graner's testimony that the photograph documented a legitimate cell extraction necessarily undermined appellant's plea of guilty, because PVT Graner's "understanding, belief, or interpretation" of the incident was irrelevant to appellant's belief that she conspired with PVT Graner to commit maltreatment. Appellant further asserts that PVT Graner's testimony was simply his attempt to rationalize his behavior. See *United States v. Penister*, 25 M.J. 148, 153 (C.M.A. 1987) (Judge Cox, concurring).

Contrary to appellant's assertions, there was a direct contradiction between the evidence presented to the military judge during the Care inquiry (i.e., appellant's testimony and the stipulation of fact) and PVT Graner's testimony. During the Care inquiry, appellant admitted that she and PVT

Graner had no lawful purpose in taking the photograph of the detainee with the leash around his neck. She described the event as orchestrated to be "degrading and humiliating" for the detainee and that PVT Graner took the photographs "for his personal use and amusement." However, PVT Graner's testimony at trial pointed in a different direction and thus, "set up a matter inconsistent" with appellant's plea. He testified that his purpose in taking the photograph was to document a valid, lawful "planned use of force." He testified further that he was required under the 800th Military Police Rules of Engagement to document this "planned use of force" and he did so by taking the photograph. Private Graner's wholly inconsistent testimony casts doubt as to whether the picture was taken for a lawful or unlawful purpose, thereby affecting any common understanding or agreement between them.

As such, we find that the military judge did not abuse his discretion in rejecting appellant's plea of guilty to the conspiracy offense because the conflicting testimony of the alleged conspirators at trial showed there was no "meeting of the minds" between them at the time of the incident. *United States v. Valigura*, 54 M.J. 187, 188 (C.A.A.F. 2000).[6] Our superior court, citing the Supreme Court, has said that "agreement is the essential evil at which the crime of conspiracy is directed and it remains the essential element of the crime. If there is no actual agreement or meeting of the minds there is no conspiracy." *Id.* (citing *Iannelli v. United States*, 420 U.S. 770, 777 n. 10 (1975)) (internal citations and punctuation omitted).

Ineffective Assistance of Counsel

Appellant's second assignment of error raises an argument in the alternative to the issue discussed above. Appellant claims she was denied effective assistance of counsel when her defense counsel called PVT Graner as a presentencing witness and his testimony so contradicted her plea that the military judge rejected it.

In order to show ineffective assistance of counsel, an appellant must demonstrate that her counsel's performance was so deficient that (1) the counsel was not functioning as counsel within the meaning of the Sixth Amendment, and (2) that her counsel's deficient performance rendered the results of the trial unreliable or fundamentally unfair. *Strickland v. Washington*, 466 U.S. 668 (1984). Appellant has not met that very high burden.

---

[6] At the time of appellant's first trial, PVT Graner had been court-martialed and convicted for his role in the Abu Ghraib crimes. When he testified, he stood convicted of conspiracy to maltreat a detainee for the same incident for which appellant was charged and is the subject of this assignment of error. His conviction for the same offense for which the military judge found appellant improvident bears no relevance to our decision in this case because it is well-established that totally inconsistent results may be reached in different trials. *See Valigura*, 54 M.J. at 190 (citing *Dunn v. United States*, 284 U.S. 390, 393 (1932), and *United States v. Powell*, 469 U.S. 57 (1984); *United States v. Garcia*, 16 M.J. 52 (C.M.A. 1983).

We disagree with appellant that defense counsel was ineffective because there was no reasonable basis to call PVT Graner during sentencing. Clearly, the defense strategy at sentencing was to paint appellant as submissive and compliant in structured situations and vulnerable to strong personalities, like PVT Graner, with whom she also had an intimate relationship.

We also discern from the record strategic reasons for calling PVT Graner as a witness. *See United States v. Lewis*, 42 M.J. 1, 3 (C.A.A.F. 1995) ("in many cases review of the record itself is sufficient" to resolve claims of ineffectiveness). As part of its presentation of extenuation and mitigation evidence, appellant's defense team called three witnesses before the military judge declared a mistrial. First, Dr. Denne testified about appellant's social compliance, academic learning disabilities, and deficits in language-based reasoning and processing while attending school. Second, Major David DiNenna, the 320th Military Police Battalion S–3 officer from June 2003 to February 2004, testified about the physical conditions at Abu Ghraib prison, the personnel shortages, and the lack of training where "non-MP [military police] MOS [military operational specialty] soldiers" were involved in guarding prisoners. Finally, the defense called PVT Graner.

The defense used PVT Graner to develop the facts for the leashed detainee incident, to showcase his domineering personality, and to establish that he was clearly in charge of the entire incident from its inception. Private Graner testified that he developed the plan for removing the detainee from the cell using a leash, he brought appellant into the incident, and it was his plan-not appellant's—to extract the detainee from his cell using a leash and take photographs with appellant featured in them.

The record also shows that appellant's defense counsel attempted to limit PVT Graner's testimony. Civilian defense counsel never asked PVT Graner whether he believed pulling the detainee out of the cell on the leash was a legitimate use of force. He simply asked PVT Graner to testify how it happened—the acts that led up to him taking the photographs, that it was his idea to take the photographs, that he altered one of the photographs, and that he did not explain the "cell extraction" to appellant. While there may have been other ways to put this information before the panel, we find calling PVT Graner in person to testify a reasonable tactic by the defense. Presenting these details through PVT Graner is consistent with the overall defense sentencing strategy.

In assessing a claim of ineffective assistance, we "do not scrutinize each and every movement . . . of counsel. Rather, we satisfy ourselves that an accused has had counsel who, by his or her representation, made the adversarial process work." *United States v. Murphy*, 50 M.J. 4, 8 (C.A.A.F. 1998). In this case, we find the full scope of appellant's representation was effective. Her defense team negotiated a favorable pretrial agreement, adequately prepared appellant such that she could articulate to the military judge why she believed she was guilty in accordance with Care, and developed and presented a cogent sentencing strategy. We find the spectrum of appellant's defense counsel representation to be reasonable and certainly within the consideration of "sound trial strategy." *See Strickland*, 466 U.S. at 689.

The affidavits submitted by appellant in her post-trial submission do not reveal ineffective assistance of counsel, but they do reveal the risk inherent in calling any witness, particularly, a co-conspirator who was previously found guilty and continues to profess his innocence. But, after some investigation, appellant's defense team determined that the possible benefit to appellant outweighed that risk.

Though no counsel can know for certain how a particular witness will actually testify, due diligence requires that he or she must do a reasonable job of investigating to determine that the witness testimony is relevant. See R.C.M. 1001. We are satisfied appellant's defense counsel exercised due diligence in investigating and determining the relevancy of PVT Graner's testimony. Civilian defense counsel met with PVT Graner at least two times, discussed his expected testimony, and intentionally limited the scope of his questions. Civilian defense counsel stated that he "never would have asked [PVT] Graner the questions posed by the court during the sentencing phase" because he knew despite PVT Graner's convictions, he persisted with the notion that the photographs depicted a lawful cell extraction.

The decision by appellant's defense counsel to use PVT Graner to minimize appellant's culpability and gain sympathy from the panel posed some risk, but was well within the realm of a reasonable defense strategy. The fact that ultimately PVT Graner's testimony set up a matter inconsistent with appellant's plea does not render her counsel's assistance ineffective. *See Strickland*, 466 U.S. at 689. ("Judicial scrutiny of counsel's performance must be highly deferential" because "it is all too tempting . . . to second-guess counsel's assistance . . . after it has proved unsuccessful.")

* * *

CONCLUSION

The findings of guilty are approved. Reassessing the sentence on the basis of the error, in accordance with the principles of *United States v. Sales*, 22 M.J. 305 (C.M.A. 1986), and *United States v. Moffeit*, 63 M.J. 40 (C.A.A.F. 2006), to include the factors identified by Judge Baker in his concurring opinion, the court affirms only so much of the sentence as provides for a dishonorable discharge, confinement for thirty-five (35) months, and reduction to Private E1.

Judges COOK and MAGGS concur.

Points for Discussion

1. Because of the great interest in the charged abuse at Abu Ghraib prison, this case made front-page national news when the military judge rejected PFC England's guilty plea. One article said that PFC England "looked bewildered" by the military judge's decision and that the military judge had difficulty making her understand why he could not accept her plea. *See* Ralph Blumenthal, *Judge Tosses Out Iraq Abuse Plea*, N.Y. Times, May 5, 2005, at A1. How would you have explained the military judge's action to PFC England if you were her defense counsel?

2. Major Terry L. Elling argues that the *Care* inquiry, as subsequently interpreted by the courts, focuses too much on technical matters and not enough on the fundamental question of whether the accused who wants to plead guilty is in fact guilty: "courts-martial focus on the antiquated ... concern that no inconsistencies appear on the record as much, if not more, than on the more fundamental constitutional requisites for a legitimate waiver of the right to a trial." Terry L. Elling, *Guilty Plea Inquiries: Do We Care Too Much*, 134 Mil. L. Rev. 195 (1991). Was the trial judge's refusal to accept PFC Lynndie England's guilty plea an example of this criticism?

8-2. Instructions on Findings

If the accused does not plead guilty, the case will proceed to trial. The government first will present its evidence, and the accused then will have the opportunity to present contrary evidence. Unless the trial is by military judge alone, the military judge will then instruct them members on exactly what they must conclude the evidence shows in order to find the accused guilty of each specification and charge. The military judge typically will rely on standard instructions, most of which have previously been upheld in prior cases. The military judge also will consider the parties' requests for special or different instructions.

The Army's Military Judges' Benchbook, for example, provides the following model instruction for the offense of cruelty, oppression, or maltreatment of subordinates in violation of UCMJ article 93:

In (The) Specification (__) of (The) (Additional) Charge (__), the accused is charged with the offense of (specify the offense). To find the accused guilty of this offense, you must be convinced by legal and competent evidence beyond a reasonable doubt of the following elements:

(1) That (state the name (and rank) of the alleged victim) was subject to the orders of (state the name of the accused), the accused; and

(2) That (state the time and place alleged), the accused (was cruel toward) (oppressed) (maltreated) (state the name of the alleged victim) by (state the manner alleged).

("Subject to the orders of" includes persons under the direct or immediate command of the accused and all persons who by reason of some duty are required to obey the lawful orders of the accused, even if those persons are not in the accused's direct chain of command.)

The (cruelty) (oppression) (or) (maltreatment) must be real, although it does not have to be physical. The imposition of necessary or proper duties on a service member and the requirement that those duties be performed does not establish this offense even though the duties are hard, difficult, or hazardous.

("Cruel") ("oppressed") (and) ("maltreated") refer(s) to treatment, that, when viewed objectively under all the circumstances, is abusive or otherwise unwarranted, unjustified, and unnecessary for any lawful purpose and that results in physical or mental harm or suffering, or reasonably could have caused, physical or mental harm or suffering.

* * *

Department of the Army Pamphlet 27-9, Military Judges' Benchbook 48, 249 (Jan. 1, 2010).

Points for Discussion

1. Are instructions like this comprehensible to members of the court-martial who are not lawyers? Does it help that almost all members of a court-martial are officers or senior enlisted personnel, who with very few exceptions have college degrees?

2. What are the benefits and risks of using standard instructions?

In some cases, convicted service members will challenge on appeal the instructions given by the military judge. They may contend that the instructions fail to comport with the articles of the UCMJ or the Constitution or they may argue that the instructions do not match the specification. The following case provides an example:

UNITED STATES v. UPHAM
U.S. Court of Appeals for the Armed Forces
66 M.J. 83 (C.A.A.F. 2008)

Chief Judge EFFRON delivered the opinion of the Court.

Appellant [Christopher M. Upham, Lieutenant, U.S. Coast Guard] was charged with two offenses based on engaging in unprotected sexual intercourse with a fellow officer without informing her that he was infected with the Human Immunodeficiency Virus (HIV): aggravated assault, in violation of Article 128, Uniform Code of Military Justice (UCMJ), 10 U.S.C. § 928 (2000), and conduct unbecoming an officer and a gentleman, in violation of Article 133, UCMJ, 10 U.S.C. § 933 (2000). At a general court-martial composed of officer members, Appellant entered a plea of guilty to the conduct unbecoming an officer and a gentleman charge and contested the aggravated assault charge. He was convicted of both charges. The sentence adjudged by the court-martial and approved by the convening authority included dismissal, confinement for nine months, and forfeiture of all pay and allowances.

The United States Coast Guard Court of Criminal Appeals affirmed the conviction for conduct unbecoming an officer and a gentleman, disapproved the conviction for aggravated assault, affirmed a conviction for the lesser included offense of assault consummated by a battery, reduced the period of confinement to four months, and affirmed the balance of the sentence. *United States v. Upham*, 64 M.J. 547, 551–52 (C.G.Ct. Crim. App. 2006).

* * *

I. BACKGROUND

A. TRIAL PROCEEDINGS

The contested aggravated assault charge alleged that Appellant committed "an assault upon a female by wrongfully having unprotected vaginal intercourse with a means likely to produce death or grievous bodily harm, to wit: unprotected vaginal intercourse while knowing he was infected with the Human Immunodeficiency Virus." At trial, the prosecution introduced evidence that Appellant was HIV-positive, that military physicians informed him in writing that he could transmit the virus through sexual contact, and that he had sexual intercourse with CPT B on two occasions without informing her of his HIV-positive status. Medical testimony at trial established the effects of HIV infection on the body and various negative side effects of treatment, as well as the long-term prognosis for those infected with HIV.

Appellant testified in his own defense. He stated that he had been diagnosed with HIV several years earlier, that he had been counseled in writing about the general risks of unprotected sexual intercourse, that he twice engaged in unprotected sex with CPT B, and that he did not inform CPT B of his HIV-positive status. He acknowledged that he did not have a justification or excuse for engaging in sexual intercourse with CPT B without informing her of his medical status. He further acknowledged that his actions had caused CPT B great mental anguish, stating, "[s]he went through the entire ordeal of going to an emergency room and getting a test and talking with an HIV doctor . . . she had to go through that and it's a terrible thing."

In the course of his testimony, Appellant denied that he had committed an assault with a "means likely to produce death or grievous bodily harm." He testified that his "viral load," which refers to the number of virions per cubic milliliter in his blood, was so low as to be "undetectable." He testified that he experienced no symptoms or limitations as a result of his HIV infection. Appellant admitted that "there was not a zero risk of transmission," but testified that he did not believe that he had exposed CPT B to a fatal disease: "I do not believe that she was going to be infected."

At the close of the evidence, the military judge discussed proposed instructions on findings with the parties. The military judge asked the parties whether they wanted him to instruct the members on the lesser included offense of assault consummated by a battery. Both parties agreed to waive instruction on the lesser included offense and proceed with instructions only on the charged offense, aggravated assault.

The military judge instructed the members on the elements of aggravated assault, including the two elements at issue in the present appeal—"offensive touching" and use of a means "likely to produce death or grievous bodily harm." *See* Manual for Courts–Martial, United States pt. IV, para. 54.c. (1)(a), (4)(a) (2005 ed.) (MCM). The military judge's instruction included the following:

> You are advised that a person who engages in unprotected sexual intercourse with another person, knowing that he is HIV positive, without informing his sexual partner that [he has] HIV and without using a condom has committed an offensive touching of that person. Also a person who willfully and deliberately exposes a person to seminal fluid containing HIV without informing that person of his HIV positive status and without using a condom has acted in a manner likely to produce death or grievous bodily harm.

Defense counsel objected on the grounds that "these instructions say that [Appellant] is per se guilty of aggravated assault." The military judge overruled the objection, and said that the instruction "accurately state[s] the law that exist[s] today."

B. APPELLATE CONSIDERATION

On appeal, the Court of Criminal Appeals concluded that the military judge erred in instructing the members on the aggravated assault charge, holding that the instructions quoted above on the elements of "offensive touching" and "means likely to result in death or grievous bodily harm" improperly removed these issues from consideration by the panel members. *Upham*, 64 M.J. at 550. The court tested these errors for prejudice, and concluded that the error was prejudicial as to the aggravated assault charge: "Given the medical evidence, it is not inconceivable that the court could have had a reasonable doubt on whether the means employed was likely to produce death or grievous bodily harm." *Id.*

The court next considered whether a conviction could be affirmed for the lesser included offense of assault consummated by a battery. *Id.* The court first observed that the absence of instructions on the lesser included offense at trial did not preclude the court from considering whether a lesser included offense could be approved on appeal. *Id.*; *see* MCM pt. IV, para. 54.c.(1)(a), (4)(a) (setting forth "offensive touching" as an element common to both aggravated assault and assault consummated by a battery). Next, the court concluded that the erroneous instruction on "offensive touching" was not prejudicial as to the lesser included offense on the theory that it was "clear beyond a reasonable doubt that a rational court would have found that Appellant committed an offensive touching absent the [erroneous] instruction." *Id.* at 550–51. Based on the conclusion that the erroneous instruction was not prejudicial as to the element of offensive touching, the court affirmed a conviction for the lesser offense of assault consummated by a battery. Id. at 551.

II. DISCUSSION

On appeal to this Court, neither party has questioned the rulings of the court below with respect to the conclusion that the military judge provided erroneous instructions as to the elements of "offensive touching" and "means likely to result in death or grievous bodily harm"; nor do the parties question the decision of the court below to disapprove the conviction for the offense of aggravated assault. The granted issues concern whether the court below, in the context of those rulings and the circumstances of this case, could approve a conviction for the lesser included offense of assault consummated by a battery. In the first granted issue, Appellant contends that the lower court erred because the military judge's erroneous instructions constituted a structural error requiring reversal without testing for harmlessness. In the second granted issue, Appellant contends that even if the error was not structural, the court below was precluded from affirming a conviction for a lesser included offense where both parties expressly waived an instruction as to that lesser offense at trial.

A. EVALUATION OF CONSTITUTIONAL ERROR IN INSTRUCTIONS

Article 59(a), UCMJ, 10 U.S.C. § 859(a) (2000), states: "A finding or sentence of a court-martial may not be held incorrect on the ground of an error of law unless the error materially prejudices the substantial rights of the accused." For most constitutional errors at trial, we apply the harmless error test set forth in *Chapman v. California*, 386 U.S. 18 (1967), to determine whether the error is harmless beyond a reasonable doubt. *See United States v. Moran*, 65 M.J. 178, 187 (C.A.A.F. 2007). We apply the Supreme Court's structural error analysis, requiring mandatory reversal, when the error affects "the framework within which the trial proceeds, rather than simply an error in the trial process itself." *Arizona v. Fulminante*, 499 U.S. 279, 310 (1991); *see generally United States v. Meek*, 44 M.J. 1, 6 (C.A.A.F. 1996) (discussing per se reversal rule).

The Supreme Court has held that an instructional error as to the elements of an offense should be tested for harmlessness, and should not be treated as a structural error. *Neder v. United States*, 527 U.S. 1, 13–15 (1999). In Neder, the trial court did not instruct on materiality, an element of the charged offense. *Id.* at 6. In the course of concluding that the instructional error could. be tested for harmlessness, the Court observed that harmless error analysis can be applied not only to omitted instructions, but also to instructions that are defective because they incorrectly describe elements or presume elements. *Id.* at 9–10; *see also Carella v. California*, 491 U.S. 263, 266–67 (1989) (per curiam) (applying harmless error analysis to mandatory conclusive presumption).

In the application of the harmlessness standard in *Neder*, the Supreme Court relied on two factors in concluding that the error was harmless beyond a reasonable doubt under Chapman: (1) the element was uncontested; and (2) the element was supported by overwhelming evidence. *Neder*, 527 U.S. at 17. The Court held, "where a reviewing court concludes beyond a reasonable doubt that the omitted element was uncontested and supported by overwhelming evidence, such that the jury verdict would have been the same absent the error, the erroneous instruction is properly found to be harmless." *Id.*

With respect to the offense of assault consummated by battery, the instructional error in this case, like the error in *Neder*, involves one element of the offense. The military judge's instruction improperly directed the members to presume the element of "offensive touching" if they found proof of certain predicate facts. *See id.* at 10. The instruction did not remove the burden on the Government to prove the predicate facts beyond a reasonable doubt. In that context, the presumption was not so intrinsically harmful as to require automatic reversal. *See Carella*, 491 U.S. at 266; *Rose v. Clark*, 478 U.S. 570, 580 (1986). As such, the erroneous instruction was subject to a harmlessness test under *Neder*.

When an erroneous instruction raises constitutional error, *Neder* requires a reviewing court to assess two factors: whether the matter was contested, and whether the element at issue was established by overwhelming evidence. In the present case, the Court of Criminal Appeals weighed the evidence regarding the "offensive touching" element, but did not expressly address whether Appellant contested that element at trial. Under the circumstances of the present case, this is a question of law that may be resolved by this Court. At trial, Appellant did not contest the element of offensive touching. On the contrary, he acknowledged that he had no justification for engaging in unprotected sex with CPT B without informing her of his HIV status, and that his actions caused her great mental anguish. The defense contested the issues pertinent to aggravated assault, not the offensive touching aspects of assault consummated by a battery. Accordingly, we may affirm the conviction of the lesser included offense under *Neder*.

B. APPROVAL OF A LESSER INCLUDED OFFENSE WHEN AN INSTRUCTION HAS BEEN WAIVED AT TRIAL

Appellant contends in granted Issue II that an appellate court cannot approve a conviction for a lesser included offense when both parties waived an instruction on the lesser offense and the military judge did not instruct the court-martial panel on the lesser offense. Under Appellant's theory, the Government should be bound by its waiver of the trial court's consideration of a lesser included offense.

A military judge has a *sua sponte* duty to instruct the members on lesser included offenses reasonably raised by the evidence. *United States v. Miergrimado*, 66 M.J. 34, 36 (C.A.A.F. 2008); *United States v. Bean*, 62 M.J. 264, 266 (C.A.A.F .2005) (citing *United States v. Griffin*, 50 M.J. 480, 481 (C.A.A.F. 1999)); Rule for Courts–Martial (R.C.M.) 920(e)(2). An accused may seek to waive an instruction on lesser included offenses and present an "all or nothing" defense as a matter of trial tactics. *United States v. Pasha*, 24 M.J. 87 (C.M.A. 1987); *see also* R.C.M. 920(f). No rule prevents the Government from acquiescing in the defense "all or nothing" strategy.

On appeal, the Court of Criminal Appeals reviews the record of trial under Article 66(c), UCMJ, 10 U.S.C. § 866(c) (2000), which provides in pertinent part:

> In a case referred to it, the Court of Criminal Appeals may act only with respect to the findings and sentence as approved by the convening authority. It may affirm only such findings of guilty, and the sentence or such part or amount of the sentence, as it finds correct in law and fact and determines, on the basis of the entire record, should be approved.

When the Court of Criminal Appeals identifies error in the findings, the court, like other reviewing authorities under the UCMJ, "may approve or affirm . . . so much of the finding as includes a lesser included offense." Article 59(b), UCMJ. As this Court has observed:

> Generally, in military jurisprudence, we have long recognized that an appellate court may disapprove a finding because proof of an essential element is lacking or, as a result of instructional errors concerning lesser-included offenses, may substitute a lesser-included offense for the disapproved findings. This is true even if the lesser-included offense was neither considered nor instructed upon at the trial of the case.

United States v. McKinley, 27 M.J. 78, 79 (C.M.A. 1988) (citations omitted); *see also United States v. Wells*, 52 M.J. 126, 131–32 (C.A.A.F. 1999) (recognizing that the lower court, on remand, may affirm a lesser offense and reassess the sentence).

Appellant has not identified a case that would preclude the Court of Criminal Appeals from exercising its statutory authority to approve a lesser included offense under the circumstances of this case where evidence was presented and evaluated on the greater offense. To the extent that any instructions as to the elements of the lesser offense were omitted or misstated, such errors may be evaluated for harmlessness. See Section II.A. *supra*. Accordingly, an erroneous instruction on the lesser included offense in the present case does not preclude the court below from approving a conviction for the lesser included offense if otherwise warranted under the framework set forth in Section II.A. *supra*.

III. DECISION

The decision of the United States Coast Guard Court of Criminal Appeals is affirmed.

Point for Discussion

Of this decision, two commentators have written:

Military justice practitioners can learn lessons for both the appellate level and the trial level from *Upham*. On the appellate level, determining the standard to be applied could be critical in deciding whether instructional error requires reversal of the conviction. Also, an appellate court can approve a conviction for a lesser included offense, even if both parties at trial waived an instruction on it and the members never considered it. On the trial level, practitioners need to read appellate opinions in context, and not propose instructions that improperly remove consideration of issues from the court members.

Edward J. O'Brien & Timothy Grammel, *Annual Review of Developments in Instructions—2008*, Army Lawyer, Mar. 2009, at 1, 10. When does an instructional error require reversal of the conviction and when does it not? How do you think the erroneous instruction at issue in the case came about?

8-3. Findings with Exceptions and Substitutions

A court-martial, like any criminal court, may find the accused to be either guilty or not guilty of an offense alleged in a specification. But a court-martial also has a special power not available in most civilian criminal trials: rather than finding the accused guilty or not guilty, it may find the accused "guilty with exceptions, with or without substitutions" or "not guilty of the exceptions, but guilty of the substitutions." R.C.M. 918(a). For example, if the specification alleges that the accused smoked marijuana on June 1, July 1, and August 1, the court-martial might find the accused guilty of the specification except for the word and figure "July 1." Or the court-martial might find the accused guilty of the specification, substituting the words and figures "June 2, July 2, and August 2" for "June 1, July 1, and August 1."

While exceptions and substitutions are possible, RCM 918(a) states this limitation: "Exceptions and substitutions may not be used to substantially change the nature of the offense or to increase the seriousness of the offense or the maximum punishment for it." The Discussion to RCM 918(a) explains: "One or more words or figures may be excepted from a specification and, when necessary, others substituted, if the remaining language of the specification, with or without substitutions, states an offense by the accused which is punishable by court-martial. Changing the date or place of the offense may, but does not necessarily, change the nature or identity of an offense." In many cases, substitutions are trivial. But when does a substitution change the nature of an offense? Consider the following case.

UNITED STATES v. MARSHALL
U.S. Court of Appeals for the Armed Forces
67 M.J. 418 (C.A.A.F. 2009)

Judge STUCKY delivered the opinion of the Court.

Appellant [Bradley W. MARSHALL, Private, U.S. Army] pled not guilty to escaping from the custody of Captain (CPT) Kreitman but was convicted, by exceptions and substitutions, of escaping from the custody of Staff Sergeant

(SSG) Fleming. We granted review to consider whether the military judge's findings created a fatal variance. We hold that it did. We reverse the decision of the United States Army Court of Criminal Appeals and remand for sentence reassessment.

I. Background

A military judge sitting as a special court-martial convicted Appellant, in accordance with his pleas, of one specification of failing to go to his appointed place of duty at the time prescribed and two specifications of absenting himself from his unit; wrongfully using marijuana; and disobeying the order of a superior commissioned officer. Articles 86, 112a, and 90, Uniform Code of Military Justice (UCMJ), 10 U.S.C. §§ 886, 912a, and 890 (2000). The military judge also convicted Appellant, contrary to his pleas, of escaping from custody. The convening authority approved the adjudged sentence of a bad-conduct discharge, confinement for six months, and forfeiture of $500 pay per month for six months. The United States Army Court of Criminal Appeals (CCA) affirmed in a summary disposition over the dissent of Judge Chiarella. *United States v. Marshall*, No. ARMY 20060229 (A. Ct. Crim. App. June 30, 2008).[*]

II. Facts

The Government alleged that Appellant "did, at Fort Polk, Louisiana, on or about 19 December 2005, escape from the custody of CPT Kelvin K. Kreitman, a person authorized to apprehend the accused." The evidence established that CPT Kreitman directed one SSG Fleming to go to the local police department and assume custody of Appellant from the police. SSG Fleming did so, assuming custody of Appellant and returning him to the company offices. Appellant was told that pretrial confinement orders were being prepared and that, in the meantime, he was to sit down and not leave his seat without an escort. Appellant was permitted to step outside the building to smoke. During one of his smoke breaks, Appellant walked away.

At the conclusion of the Government's case, the defense counsel moved for a finding of not guilty under Rule for Courts–Martial (R.C.M.) 917, asserting that the Government had failed to establish that Appellant escaped from the custody of CPT Kreitman. The military judge denied the motion.

In his closing argument, the defense counsel stated the following concerning the escape from custody allegation:

> Escape from custody. The defense would reiterate that the person he is charged with violating custody from is Captain Kreitman. We have no testimony regarding the actions of Captain Kreitman as it relates to the accused, as it relates to Staff Sergeant Fleming, yes, we do.

---

[*] The other two judges on the panel of the Army Court of Criminal Appeals—who were reversed here by the Court of Appeals for the Armed Forces—were Senior Judge Gallup and Judge Maggs.—Eds.

As far as Captain Kreitman giving the order saying, "You are confined to the limits of this area. You are in custody." We have nothing.

We have the previous counseling statement he got a few days before, which, I guess, would be breaking restriction because he violated that. It's not the same thing as custody. We don't have any testimony whatsoever as to what additional restrictions Captain Kreitman placed upon Private Marshall. In the absence of that, we don't have escape from custody.

The military judge thereafter convicted Appellant, by exceptions and substitutions, of escaping from the custody of SSG Fleming.

III. Analysis

The Government argues that by failing to object to the finding of guilty by exceptions and substitutions at the time it was announced, Appellant forfeited the issue in the absence of plain error. We do not agree. The purpose of the forfeiture rule is to ensure that the trial judge has the opportunity to rule on issues arising at trial, and to prevent the raising of such issues for the first time on appeal, after any chance to correct them has vanished. *United States v. Frady*, 456 U.S. 152, 163, 1 (1982); *United States v. Reist*, 50 M.J. 108, 110 (C.A.A.F. 1999); *United States v. Causey*, 37 M.J. 308, 311 (C.M.A. 1993). The motion to dismiss under R.C.M. 917 placed the fundamental issue—whether there was any evidence that the accused escaped from the custody of CPT Kreitman rather than SSG Fleming—squarely before the military judge as trier of fact. Once that motion was denied, Appellant had no duty to engage in the empty exercise of repeating the objection after the military judge announced his findings. *United States v. Richardson*, 4 C.M.R. 150, 159–60 (C.M.A. 1952). The issue was preserved.

From the earliest days of this Court, we have held that to prevail on a fatal variance claim, an appellant must show both that the variance was material and that he was substantially prejudiced thereby. *United States v. Finch*, 64 M.J. 118, 121 (C.A.A.F. 2006); *United States v. Hunt*, 37 M.J. 344, 347 (C.M.A. 1993); *United States v. Lee*, 1 M.J. 15, 16 (C.M.A. 1975); *United States v. Hopf*, 5 C.M.R. 12, 14–15 (C.M.A. 1952). "A variance that is 'material' is one that, for instance, substantially changes the nature of the offense, increases the seriousness of the offense, or increases the punishment of the offense." *Finch*, 64 M.J. at 121 (citing *United States v. Teffeau*, 58 M.J. 62, 66 (C.A.A.F. 2003)). A variance can prejudice an appellant by (1) putting "him at risk of another prosecution for the same conduct," (2) misleading him "to the extent that he has been unable adequately to prepare for trial," or (3) denying him "the opportunity to defend against the charge." *Teffeau*, 58 M.J. at 67.

The elements of escape from custody under Article 95, UCMJ, 10 U.S.C. § 895 (2000), are as follows:

(a) That a certain person apprehended the accused;

(b) That said person was authorized to apprehend the accused; and

(c) That the accused freed himself or herself from custody before being released by proper authority.

Manual for Courts–Martial, United States pt. IV, para. 19.b(4) (2005 ed.) (MCM).

Here, Appellant was charged with escaping from the custody of CPT Kreitman. Assuming, *arguendo*, that CPT Kreitman was in fact authorized to apprehend Appellant, no evidence was presented that Appellant was in his custody at any time. In response to the R.C.M. 917 motion, the Government attempted to argue an agency theory that SSG Fleming was ordered by the captain to place Appellant in custody. The military judge denied the motion, and later found that Appellant had escaped from SSG Fleming.

At trial and on appeal, the Government has argued that the substitution of SSG Fleming for CPT Kreitman created only a minor variance, similar to the changes in *Hopf* and *Finch*. Appellant's case is different and requires a different result.

In *Hopf*, the appellant was convicted of aggravated assault on a named Korean male, but the court substituted for the victim's name the term "unknown Korean male," when the victim was unable to testify due to his injuries and the two American soldiers who witnessed the assault did not know the victim's name. 5 C.M.R. at 14. This Court concluded the variance was not fatal because neither the nature nor identity of the offense was changed. *Id.* The appellant was convicted of the same assault for which he was charged, and the defense preparations to meet the charge were unaffected. *Id.*

The appellant in *Finch* was charged with conspiracy to commit the offense of providing alcoholic beverages to a person enrolled in the delayed-entry program, in violation of a general order. *Id.* at 119–20. The military judge found the appellant guilty of the offense but substituted a different location for the place at which the overt act in furtherance of the conspiracy was alleged to have occurred. *Id.* at 120–21. We held this change did not result in a major variance. "Although an overt act is an element of the offense of conspiracy, it is not the core of the offense" and did not "substantially change the nature or seriousness of the offense or increase the punishment to which Appellant was subject." *Id.* at 122 (citations omitted).

On the facts in this case, we are convinced the substitution was material. The military judge convicted Appellant by exceptions and substitutions of an offense that was substantially different from that described in the specification upon which he was arraigned. *See Teffeau*, 58 M.J. at 67. Although the nature of the offense remained the same—escape from custody—by substituting SSG Fleming for CPT Kreitman as the custodian from whom Appellant escaped, the military judge changed the identity of the offense against which the accused had to defend. This denied him the "opportunity to defend against the charge." *Id.*

Having found the variance to be material, we must test for prejudice. Appellant argues that the military judge's findings by exceptions and substitutions "gave the appellant no chance to defend himself against this new charge." The Government argues that there is no prejudice, because regardless of whose custody he escaped from, there was only one event, Appellant knew the nature of the offense, and was able to defend against it. We disagree. Appellant was charged with escaping from CPT Kreitman's custody; the Government presented no evidence that he was in the captain's custody, but attempted to prove that SSG Fleming was acting as CPT Kreitman's agent; the military judge found Appellant guilty by exceptions and substitutions of escaping from SSG Fleming's custody. Had he known that he would be called upon to refute an agency theory or to defend against a charge that he escaped from SSG Fleming, Appellant is unlikely to have focused his defense and his closing argument on the lack of evidence that CPT Kreitman placed him in custody or that he escaped from the custody of CPT Kreitman. "Fundamental due process demands that an accused be afforded the opportunity to defend against a charge before a conviction on the basis of that charge can be sustained." Teffeau, 58 M.J. at 67; accord Dunn v. United States, 442 U.S. 100, 106–07 (1979). Under these circumstances, we do not believe that Appellant could have anticipated being forced to defend against the charge of which he was ultimately convicted. Accordingly, we find the material variance prejudiced Appellant such that the military judge's finding by exceptions and substitutions cannot stand.[3]

IV. Decision

The decision of the United States Army Court of Criminal Appeals is set aside as to the findings of guilty to Charge III and its specification and the sentence. Charge III and its specification are dismissed. The remaining findings of guilty are affirmed. The case is returned to the Judge Advocate General of the Army for remand to the CCA for sentence reassessment.

[Judge Ryan's separate opinion concurring in the judgment is omitted.]

Points for Discussion

1. How does the court distinguish *United States v. Hopf*? Do you agree that this case is distinguishable from *Hopf*?

2. What could the government have done once it learned that the accused escaped custody from a person different from the person identified in the specification? *See* Timothy Grammel & Kwasi L. Hawks, *Annual Review of Developments in Instructions*, Army Lawyer, Feb. 2010, at 52, 56 (advising

---

[3] The Government also argues that it is immaterial from whom Appellant escaped, because the escape was wrongful in any event. The fact that two alternative theories of a case may both involve criminal conduct does not relieve the government of its due process obligations of notice to the accused and proof beyond a reasonable doubt of the offense alleged. *See United States v. Ellsey*, 37 C.M.R. 75, 78–79 (C.M.A. 1966).

that "attempts to change the identity of such a person are best treated as major changes requiring the consent of the accused or re-preferral").

8-4. Military Judge's Special Findings

When a court-martial is not by a military judge alone, the members may find the appellant guilty or not guilty but apart from the use of exceptions and substitutions, the members do not have any way to explain their decisions. They cannot, for example, indicate that they found certain facts to be true and other facts to be untrue. Instead, they make their findings with respect to each specification as a whole. The same is not true for the military judge in trials by military judge alone. RCM 918(b) empowers the military judge to make "special findings" of fact. The Rule says:

> (b) Special findings. In a trial by court-martial composed of military judge alone, the military judge shall make special findings upon request by any party. Special findings may be requested only as to matters of fact reasonably in issue as to an offense and need be made only as to offenses of [which] the accused was found guilty. Special findings may be requested at any time before general findings are announced."

RCM 918(b). Special findings can be advantageous to the accused if the accused wishes to appeal following a conviction. The accused may be able to convince the appellate court that the military judge erred based on the military judge's special findings. The following case provides an example:

UNITED STATES v. RODERICK
U.S. Court of Appeals for the Armed Forces
62 M.J. 425 (C.A.A.F. 2006)

Judge ERDMANN delivered the opinion of the court.

Staff Sergeant Casey Roderick pled guilty to receiving and possessing child pornography in violation of 18 U.S.C. § 2252A (2000), of the Child Pornography Prevention Act of 1996 (CPPA), as well as one specification of using a minor to create depictions of sexually explicit conduct in violation of 18 U.S.C. § 2251(a) (2000), of the CPPA, and one specification of committing indecent acts upon the body of a child, all charged under Article 134, Uniform Code of Military Justice (UCMJ), 10 U.S.C. § 934 (2000). Roderick pled not guilty to two specifications of using a minor to create depictions of sexually explicit conduct in violation of 18 U.S.C. § 2251(a), one specification of committing indecent acts upon the body of a child, three specifications of taking indecent liberties with a child and one specification of wrongfully endeavoring to influence a witness, all charged under Article 134, UCMJ, as well. Roderick was convicted by a military judge sitting alone as a general court-martial of all charges except endeavoring to influence a witness and one specification of committing indecent acts upon a child. Roderick was sentenced to a dishonorable discharge, seven years of confinement and reduction to lowest enlisted grade.

The convening authority approved the sentence. The United States Air Force Court of Criminal Appeals modified the findings with regard to the CPPA charges in light of the Supreme Court's ruling in *Ashcroft v. Free Speech Coalition*, 535 U.S. 234 (2002), and this court's decision in *United States v. O'Connor*, 58 M.J. 450 (C.A.A.F. 2003).... The Air Force court affirmed Roderick's conviction on the child pornography charges as convictions of the lesser included offense of engaging in conduct that is of a nature to bring discredit upon the armed forces under clause 2 of Article 134, UCMJ. The court affirmed the remaining charges and Roderick's sentence....

* * *

BACKGROUND

Roderick is a single father of two young girls, CMR and LMR. While living on Andersen Air Force Base in Guam, Roderick agreed to watch a friend's two children for the weekend. The next week, one of the visiting children—eight-year-old SKA—had a regularly scheduled meeting with a psychologist. During the meeting, SKA told the psychologist that Roderick had sexually abused her and taken inappropriate photographs of her.

Based on SKA's report the Air Force Office of Special Investigation (AFOSI) launched an investigation. Agents searched Roderick's house and found computer disks, photographs, undeveloped film and negatives all depicting suspected child pornography, some of which Roderick had created and some of which he had downloaded from the Internet. Many of the photographs showed Roderick's own two daughters in various states of undress. Over one hundred of the photographs depicted SKA. In addition, AFOSI found three stories on Roderick's computer that described in graphic detail instances of sexual relations between fathers and their daughters.

DISCUSSION

* * *

When testing for legal sufficiency, we look at "whether, considering the evidence in the light most favorable to the prosecution, a reasonable factfinder could have found all the essential elements beyond a reasonable doubt." *United States v. Turner*, 25 M.J. 324, 324 (C.M.A. 1987) (citing *Jackson v. Virginia*, 443 U.S. 307, 319 (1979)). Legal sufficiency is a question of law that we review de novo....

Roderick argues that the photographs of his daughters did not depict "sexually explicit conduct" as is required for a conviction under 18 U.S.C. § 2251(a) and are therefore legally insufficient. Roderick further argues that since the evidence was legally insufficient to support the charge of "sexually explicit conduct" under 18 U.S.C. § 2251(a), it was also legally insufficient to support the specifications of taking indecent liberties with a child because the same photographs served as the basis for both charges.

Section 2251(a) prohibits any person from "us[ing], persuad[ing], induc [ing], entic[ing], or coerc[ing] any minor to engage in . . . any sexually explicit conduct for the purpose of producing any visual depiction of such conduct . . . using materials that have been mailed, shipped, or transported in interstate or foreign commerce by any means." 18 U.S.C. 2251(a). The term "sexually explicit conduct" as defined by 18 U.S.C. § 2256(2) includes five different categories of conduct: sexual intercourse, bestiality, masturbation, sadistic or masochistic abuse, or "lascivious exhibition of the genitals or pubic area of any person." Congress has not defined what constitutes a "lascivious exhibition."

Although this court has not had occasion to adopt a test for determining what constitutes a "lascivious exhibition," this issue has been considered by several federal circuit courts. All of the federal courts to address this question have relied, at least in part, on a set of six factors developed by the United States District Court for the Southern District of California in *United States v. Dost*, 636 F.Supp. 828, 832 (S.D. Cal. 1986), *aff'd sub nom. United States v. Wiegand*, 812 F.2d 1239 (9th Cir. 1987). The so-called "*Dost* factors" are:

(1) whether the focal point of the visual depiction is on the child's genitalia or pubic area;

(2) whether the setting of the visual depiction is sexually suggestive, i.e. in a place or pose generally associated with sexual activity;

(3) whether the child is depicted in an unnatural pose, or in inappropriate attire, considering the age of the child;

(4) whether the child is fully or partially clothed, or nude;

(5) whether the visual depiction suggests sexual coyness or a willingness to engage in sexual activity;

(6) whether the visual depiction is intended or designed to elicit a sexual response in the viewer.

Id. at 832. In addition to these six factors, several of the federal circuit courts have recognized that "[a]lthough *Dost* provides some specific, workable criteria, there may be other factors that are equally if not more important in determining whether a photograph contains a lascivious exhibition." *United States v. Amirault*, 173 F.3d 28, 32 (1st Cir. 1999); *see also United States v. Campbell*, 81 Fed.Appx. 532, 536 (6th Cir. 2003); *United States v. Knox*, 32 F.3d 733, 747 (3d Cir. 1994). These courts determine whether a particular photograph contains a "lascivious exhibition" by combining a review of the *Dost* factors with an overall consideration of the totality of the circumstances. We adopt this approach.

* * *

At trial the military judge admitted nearly two dozen photos of CMR into evidence. In his general verdict he announced that Roderick was guilty of Specification 1—using CMR to create sexually explicit photographs. At the request of trial defense counsel, the military judge then entered special findings. In his special findings, the military judge identified three of the photos of CMR that fell within the definition of "sexually explicit."

While CMR is fully or partially nude in each of the pictures cited by the military judge, none of the three photos specified by the military judge depicts her genitals or pubic area, a requirement of § 2256(2) and prerequisite to any analysis under Dost. Thus, the military judge's finding on Specification 1 was not supported by legally sufficient evidence. Accordingly, we are compelled to set aside the military judge's findings with regard to Specification 1 and dismiss the specification.

* * *

[The remainder of the court's decision and Judge Crawford's opinion concurring in part and dissenting in part is omitted.]

Points for Discussion

1. How was it advantageous for defense counsel to ask the military judge to make special findings of fact with respect to specification 1 instead of just finding appellant guilty?

2. Can you think of situations in which it might be disadvantageous for defense counsel to ask the military judge to make special findings of fact?

CHAPTER 9

MILITARY SENTENCING

9-1. Introduction and Purposes

Whenever an accused is found guilty of one or more offenses, the court-martial proceedings will include a sentencing phase at which the accused's sentence is adjudged. In many cases, the sentencing phase is the most important part of the trial. Depending on the evidence and the accused's pleas, the government and the accused may have little doubt before trial that the accused will be found guilty of most or all of the charges and specifications. But the government and the accused often can only estimate roughly what punishment the court-martial will impose. For this reason, trial counsel and defense counsel must work assiduously in preparing for sentencing.

If the accused is tried by a military judge alone, the military judge alone will decide the sentence. But if the accused is tried by members, then the same members will determine the sentence. The only exception is that the accused may plead guilty before a military judge, but then elect to have the members sentence him or her. *See* R.C.M. 903, 910. The accused, however, cannot request that the military judge determine the sentence if members find the accused guilty.

During the sentencing phase of the trial, the prosecution first will present evidence for the court-martial to use in determining the sentence. As discussed in more detail later in this chapter, the Rules for Court-Martial allow the prosecution to present the following matters for this purpose:

(i) service data relating to the accused taken from the charge sheet;

(ii) personal data relating to the accused and of the character of the accused's prior service as reflected in the personnel records of the accused;

(iii) evidence of prior convictions, military or civilian;

(iv) evidence of aggravation; and

(v) evidence of rehabilitative potential.

R.C.M. 1001(a)(1). The accused then has the opportunity to present matters "in extenuation" and "in mitigation." R.C.M. 1001(c)(1)(A) & (B). In addition, the accused may testify or present an unsworn statement about which the accused will not be cross-examined. *See* R.C.M. 1001(c)(1)(C). In the unsworn statement, the accused generally will apologize and make a personal plea to the court-martial for a more lenient sentence. For example, in one case, a senior airman who had pleaded guilty to misusing a government credit card made the following typical unsworn statement:

> Your Honor, I'm ashamed to be standing before you today. I knew better than to use my American Express card, but I used it anyway, and for that, I am sorry. Despite financial counseling and assistance offered to me by the Air Force, I never seemed to be able to get control of my finances. I made bad purchasing decisions and put myself and my family in debt. Before I realized it, I was in over my head again. I knew that I was not supposed to use my American Express card but I thought that somehow I could work out my financial problems by using the card. My decision to use the card turned out to be a very bad and costly one.

United States v. Girardin, 50 M.J. 185 (C.A.A.F. 1998) (Sullivan, J., concurring in the denial of the grant of review). After defense counsel has had the opportunity to present evidence and the accused has had the opportunity to make an unsworn statement, the prosecution may present matters in rebuttal. *See id.*

Once all of the sentencing evidence is in, trial counsel and defense counsel next present argument regarding what sentence the court-martial should impose. If the trial is by members, the military judge will instruct the members on what penalties are lawful, and the members will then deliberate and announce a sentence. Otherwise, the military judge will deliberate and announce a sentence.

Points for Discussion

1. The rule that the accused cannot request to be tried by members but then request to be sentenced by the military judge is controversial because, in most civilian jurisdictions, juries determine guilt or innocence but the judge determines the sentence. *See* Kevin Lovejoy, *Abolition of Court Member Sentencing in the Military*, 142 Mil. L. Rev. 1, 3 (1993). Why might the accused prefer to be tried by members and sentenced by the military judge if such an option were available?

2. What is the purpose of allowing the accused to make an unsworn statement? If the accused wishes to provide evidence, why shouldn't the accused have to testify under oath and be subject to cross examination? Note that civilian defendants in federal criminal trials also have a right to make unsworn statements during sentencing. *See* Federal Rule of Criminal Procedure 32(i)(4)(a)(ii).

––––––––––––––––––

Subsequent sections of this chapter concern the legal limitations on punishments, the proper scope of matters in aggravation and in extenuation and mitigation, and the death penalty in the military. Before addressing these topics, however, a preliminary question concerns the purposes of punishment: What is the military justice system attempting to accomplish when it sentences a service member for an offense?

Perhaps the best way to address this question is to consider certain limitations placed on trial counsel's argument on sentencing. Rule 1001(g) provides in part:

> Trial counsel may not in argument purport to speak for the convening authority or any higher authority, or refer to the views of such authorities or any policy directive relative to punishment or to any punishment or quantum of punishment greater than that court-martial may adjudge. Trial counsel may, however, recommend a specific lawful sentence and may also refer to generally accepted sentencing philosophies, including rehabilitation of the accused, general deterrence, specific deterrence of misconduct by the accused, and social retribution.

The first sentence of this quotation makes clear that commanders cannot develop, and through trial counsel, implement general policies regarding sentencing (e.g., "All drug users should be given a bad-conduct discharge"). Instead, all sentencing should focus on the individual circumstances of the accused's case. The second sentence of the quotation then indicates the permissible purposes of sentencing by spelling out what factors the government may ask the court-martial to consider. Rehabilitation is about making the accused a law-abiding person in the future. General deterrence is about setting an example so that others who are similarly situated and learn about the accused's sentence will not commit similar crimes, while specific deterrence is about imposing a punishment that will discourage the accused from personally committing offenses in the future. Social retribution is about imposing punishment for punishment's sake, based on a sense of moral outrage.

During the 1970s a substantial controversy arose over whether "general deterrence" was a proper factor for courts-martial to consider. In *United States v. Mosely*, 1 M.J. 350 (C.M.A. 1976), and *United States v. Miller*, 1 M.J. 357 (C.M.A. 1976), the Court of Military Appeals for a brief period held that it was not. In *Mosely*, the court reasoned:

> Deterrence is an important function of the criminal justice system. It has a double aspect. One aspect is focused on the individual accused; the other is oriented toward the general public. As to the first, a particular sentence may affect one accused in one way and another accused in a different way. Thus, to one accused a sentence of confinement for 1 month may be so awesome as to leave little doubt that its impact is likely to deter him from recidivism. To another accused convicted of the same offense, the stated punishment may be so disproportionate to his gain from the crime that he is more likely to repeat the offense than to be deterred by the punishment; in this situation, the deterrence factor would justify a more severe sentence. As applied to the accused, therefore, consideration of deterrence in assessment of a just sentence is consistent with the concept

that the sentence should be "individualized," that is, predicated on factors relevant to the accused. *United States v. Mamaluy*, 27 C.M.R. 176, 180 (C.M.A. 1959).

The aspect of deterrence oriented to the general public appears in the maximum punishment prescribed for the offense. That punishment represents the maximum deterrent effect upon the general populace. Once the accused has committed the crime, the general deterrence aspect of the prescribed punishment is not relevant to him as he has not been deterred. Further, his commission of the offense does not delete or diminish the general deterrent effect intended by the prescribed penalty. The sentence imposed on the accused may have an impact on the general public, but the impact is not deterrence from the same crime; that deterrence is still provided by the maximum punishment allowed by law. The impact of a particular sentence, assuming it learns of the punishment, is whether the public perceives the sentence as just or unjust. That impact is different in character and consequence from adding punishment in order to deter others.

Mosely, 1 M.J. at 351.

The *Mosely* decision was highly controversial and surprising because it conflicted with longstanding military and civilian practice. The lower courts in the military justice system had no choice but to follow their superior court, but some of their judges respectfully expressed the need for the Court of Military Appeals to reconsider its decision. Perhaps the best example of a subordinate judge's dissatisfaction with *Mosely* appears in *United States v. Lucas*, 2 M.J. 834 (A.C.M.R. 1976). In that case, the Army Court of Military Review, following *Mosely*, concluded that the prosecution had made improper comments regarding general deterrence during the sentencing phase of an accused convicted of attempted murder. Senior Judge Claus, however, wrote in a concurrence:

> I offer the following comments on the holding in *Mosely* to encourage the Court of Military Appeals to reconsider its decision. Whereas the court in *Mosely* indicated that their decision was in accordance with former practice and precedent, I do not agree with their analysis of the former cases and consider the present holding as establishing a new military rule.

> Historically, military jurisprudence has recognized general deterrence as a valid consideration in sentencing. An early military justice text states that the "court should always take into account the fact that the object of punishment is not to take vengeance for the deed but to prevent crime and the repetition of the offense by the offender and to deter others from similar acts." (Emphasis supplied.)[1] Courts were considered bound "to award a punishment in every respect proportioned to the offense found

---

[1] Dudley, Military Law and the Procedure of Courts-Martial (1907) p. 155.

and calculated for the due maintenance of military discipline."[2] Colonel Winthrop noted that a proper consideration in punishment is its effect upon military discipline.[3] Modern military legal writers have also recognized the proper consideration of general deterrence in sentencing.[4] The Court of Military Appeals in *United States v. Barrow*, 26 C.M.R. 123 (C.M.A. 1958) recognized the traditional basis for punishment and added the military consideration of retention in the service. Although discussed in the context of a convening authority's action, the court stated:

> "In civilian courts, a judge is primarily concerned with the protection of society, the discipline of the wrongdoer, the reformation and rehabilitation potential of the defendant, and the deterrent effect on others who are apt to offend against society. Those are all essential matters to be considered by a convening authority but, in addition, he must consider the accused's value to the service if he is retained and the impact on discipline if he permits an incorrigible to remain in close association with other members of the armed services."

　　　* * *

There is a distinction between the concept of general deterrence, which has as its purpose the deterrence of others, and the imposing of a stiffer sentence on one offender for the crimes of others. The latter concerns itself with fairness while the former is a traditional factor in sentencing.

It is my conclusion that the rule of *Mosely* that in the military general deterrence is a factor included within the maximum punishment prescribed by law for an offense and not a separate factor for consideration in adjudging an appropriate sentence is a new rule and a significant departure from traditional military jurisprudence. I believe that general deterrence should remain one of the several factors to be considered in military sentencing and that it is not inconsistent with the requirement that the accused's sentence be individualized. The needs of military discipline provide as much, if not more, justification for retention of general deterrence as a sentencing factor than the needs of the civilian community.

2 M.J. at 835 & 837 (Cass, S.J., concurring).

The Court of Military Appeals apparently listened thoughtfully to criticisms of this sort and, although not entirely eagerly, it changed course in

---

[2] O'Brien, A Treatise on American Military Law and the Practice of Courts-Martial (1846) p. 270.

[3] Winthrop, Military Law and O'Brien, A Treatise on American Military Law and the Practice of Courts-Martial (1846) p. 270. Precedents (2nd Ed. 1920), p. 397.

[4] J. Snedeker, Military Justice Under the Uniform Code, 1953 at 402; Morrison, *The Role of Trial Counsel in Sentencing Proceedings*, 13 A.F. JAG L.Rev. 30 (1971); Moyer, Justice and the Military, s 2-661 (1972).

the case that follows and returned to recognizing generally deterrence as an appropriate purpose of sentencing.

UNITED STATES v. VARACALLE
U.S. Court of Military Appeals
4 M.J. 181 (C.M.A. 1978)

FLETCHER, Chief Judge:

The appellant [Louis V. Varacalle, Staff Sergeant, U. S. Army] was convicted of sodomy with a child under 16 years of age, lewd and lascivious acts, solicitation of sodomy, indecent liberties with children under 16 years of age, and assault and battery on a child under 16 years of age in violation of Articles 125, 134 and 128, respectively, Uniform Code of Military Justice, 10 U.S.C. §§ 925, 934, and 928. He was sentenced by the military judge to a bad-conduct discharge, confinement at hard labor for 4 years and 3 months, forfeiture of all pay and allowances, and reduction to the lowest enlisted grade. Both the convening authority and the United States Army Court of Military Review approved the findings and sentence. We granted review to determine whether the appellant was prejudiced when the military judge considered the deterrence of others as a factor in imposing sentence. Examination of the record and the applicable legal standards leads to the conclusion that the trial judge acted properly in his sentencing deliberations.

We have been criticized for establishing a new rule in *United States v. Mosely*, 1 M.J. 350 (C.M.A. 1976), which resulted in the discarding of the time-honored concept for proper sentencing common in both military and civilian jurisprudence of utilization of the factor of general deterrence in sentence deliberations. An unfortunate result of our desire to insure strict compliance with the worthy goal of "individualized sentencing" developed in *United States v. Mamaluy*, 27 C.M.R. 176 (C.M.A. 1959), has been an improper restriction on the sentencing authorities from properly performing their function.

Numerous reasons or philosophies have been advanced for the imposition of punishment.[6] Despite the variety of methods of expressing these societal needs,[7] general deterrence is virtually universally accepted. There are three

---

[6] Mr. Justice Black, in writing for a unanimous Court in *Williams v. New York*, 337 U.S. 241, 248 n.13 (1949), after a discussion of the modern philosophy of penology of having the punishment fit the offender, and not merely the crime, noted with approval the following formulation by Judge Ulman of the purposes of punishment found in Glueck, Probation and Criminal Justice, 113 (1933): 1st. The protection of society against wrong-doers. 2nd. The punishment or much better the discipline of the wrong-doer. 3rd. The reformation and rehabilitation of the wrong-doer. 4th. The deterrence of others from the commission of like offenses. It should be obvious that a proper dealing with these factors involves a study of each case upon an individual basis.

[7] The ABA Standards Relating to Appellate Review of Sentences (Approved Draft 1968) at page 126, provides the following ethical bases for the state's punitive

reasons for prescribing punishment for those acts declared to be criminal by society. These are the protection of society, the rehabilitation of the offender, and example. The concepts of deterrence and example are not synonymous; instead deterrence comes about because of example. It should be evident that any criminal statute whose violation provides for punishment in any form is enacted with a purpose of making an example of the violator. A deterrence not only to the accused, but to all who are cognizant of the commission of the crime and of the punishment ordered, is the logical consequence of the imposition of a sentence. The punishment serves as notice that the society will not condone the act in question.

An accused properly sentenced is not being made example of for crimes committed by others. The sentence and the resultant punishment are individualized to the particular accused, but will vary as to the crime and the mores of that society at any certain time. Any sentencing authority, to be significant, must correlate its sentence with the present acceptance or nonacceptance of the given act. It must act as the community conscience within the prescribed limits at that point in time. To do otherwise, where a maximum and minimum sentence are set forth, vitiates society's mandate to that authority to individually prescribe a punishment to meet the needs of that particular offender, and to protect society from future violations of that sort.

A sentencing authority would be remiss in imposing punishment if it did not consider both the effect it will have on the individual accused, and on the community, for society is protected through a proper sentencing process not only in an immediate sense from the criminal in the dock, but in a greater sense through the announcement that at this time and place, the given crime will be punished. This is general deterrence which is a valid and necessary facet of appropriate sentencing. To conclude that sentence authorities do not, or should not, do what this trial judge verbalized is a fiction, and ignores what is inherent in the decision-making process whereby the appropriate sentence is determined.

There is a critical distinction between an enlargement of a sentence for the purpose of general deterrence only without consideration for the particular accused, and the sentencing authority saying as to this individual with all the matters peculiar to him, we make an example of him and all others like him so disposed. The latter is necessary and proper to meet the needs of society, and to comply with the goal of individualized sentencing.

The decision of the United States Army Court of Military Review is affirmed.

---

intrusion upon personal liberty: (1) retributive, (2) general deterrence, (3) specific deterrence, (4) preventive, and (5) rehabilitative. *See also* Coffee, *The Future of Sentencing Reform*, 73 Mich. L. Rev. 1361 (1975); Bailey and Smith, *Punishment: Its Severity and Certainty*, 63 J. Cr. L. & Criminology 530 (1972).

PERRY, Judge (concurring in the result):

I agree with the conclusion reached in the principal opinion that the comment made by the trial judge after announcing the sentence in this case warrants no action by us. I, therefore, join with the Chief Judge in affirming the decision of the United States Army Court of Military Review. However, I write separately to set forth the following reasons for my view concerning the issue on review.

I

The record before us indicates that, pursuant to a pretrial agreement, the appellant pleaded guilty before a military judge, sitting alone, to the following offenses with a female child under the age of 16: two charges of sodomy; assault and battery; a lewd and lascivious act; solicitation of sodomy; and indecent liberties in violation of Articles 125, 128 and 134, Uniform Code of Military Justice, 10 U.S.C. ss 925, 928, and 934, respectively.[1] Upon conviction of all offenses to which he pleaded guilty, the appellant could have received a sentence in the aggregate of 54 years' imprisonment and a dishonorable discharge, absent the pretrial agreement, which provided, inter alia, that the appellant's sentence would include 7 years' imprisonment and a dishonorable discharge. The record displays a painstaking inquiry by the judge into the appellant's involvement in the offenses to which he had pleaded guilty as well as presentation of matters in mitigation by the appellant, including favorable evidence concerning the appellant's military record. During the arguments concerning sentence, the prosecutor carefully adhered to this Court's decision in *United States v. Mosely*, 1 M.J. 350 (C.M.A. 1976), and *United States v. Miller*, 1 M.J. 357 (C.M.A. 1976), and indeed urged the Court not to consider deterrence of others in determining an appropriate sentence. After considering all relevant matters pertaining to sentencing, the judge proceeded to sentence the appellant to a bad-conduct discharge, confinement at hard labor for 4 years and 3 months, total forfeitures, and reduction in rank to the grade of Private E-1. Following the announcement of the sentence, the judge then made the following statement:

> Now, Sergeant Varacalle, I want to assure you that I gave very weighty consideration to the evidence concerning your many years of outstanding

---

[1] The gravity of these charges can readily be seen when the appellant's stipulation of fact is read. On January 4, 1975, the appellant required a 7-year-old girl, who had been entrusted to his care, to perform fellatio upon him. On that same date, he also attempted, but failed to consummate a rectal as well as vaginal intercourse upon her person. He also displayed to her a picture of a woman engaged in an act of fellatio. On February 15, 1975, when the same child was again entrusted to his care, she was made to engage in similar acts of sodomy. He also again attempted to penetrate her rectum and her vagina but was unsuccessful. The appellant admitted that in January 1974 and on June 15, 1974, he fondled the body of another thirteen year old girl. Finally, the appellant acknowledged that he attempted to induce his fifteen year old babysitter to permit him to perform cunnilingus on her.

faithful service to your country and to the military. I also, of course, considered all the arguments by counsel for both sides. Now, Sergeant Varacalle, based on the evidence before me, I do believe that you are suffering from some emotional and mental handicaps. Apparently you are somewhat emotionally immature. In normal terms you don't have a well-developed conscience, and apparently you're sexually attracted by to children. Based on what I've seen, I'm not convinced that there's any strong, almost overriding compulsion on your part to give in to that attraction you apparently feel toward children. In essence, that makes your acts all the more not only reprehensible, but lessens the danger you impose (sic) to society. Now, perhaps I'm oversimplifying the situation, but it seems to me that your sexual attraction to children is not normal, but on the other hand, it doesn't have to govern your life. I'm sure it's a very difficult problem to live with, and whether or not you'll ever mature in the sense that you won't have that attraction, I don't know. But, that certainly does not mean you have to act in accordance with your desires. Now, counsel argued that I shouldn't think of the deterrence of others. Very frankly I did, because I am convinced there are probably a good many people who are sexually attracted by children and tempted to engage in acts similar to yours, and I hope the sentence in this case will have some tendency to help them resist the temptation. I would certainly hope that what has happened to you today and during the past few months will result in your never giving in to your temptations along the lines of engaging in sexual activities with children again. You probably will be undoubtedly will be sent to Fort Leavenworth, Kansas, and there are, to my understanding, psychiatrists and psychologists available there to help you, and I hope you have the good sense to take full advantage of the assistance that will be offered to you there. And, as you stated in your statement through counsel, you will never, never, ever engage in this sort of conduct in the future.

The foregoing comments of the judge led to the grant of review in this case. The appellant contends that this Court's opinion in *United States v. Mosely*, supra, and its progeny, rendered the entire sentencing process void, thus requiring reversal as to the sentence. In his dissent, Judge Cook expresses agreement with that argument and reminds us that Mosely reviewed the special emphasis military law places upon the individualization of the sentence. He adds that Mosely concluded that it was "improper to adjudge a more severe sentence than might otherwise be imposed because of a purpose to deter others in the general population."

II

In my view, the trial judge conscientiously applied all relevant criteria and gave weighty consideration thereto in arriving at the sentence he finally imposed. During the presentence proceedings, considerable effort was expended in determining whether the mother of one of the victims should be allowed to testify on the question of aggravation. Having determined the irrelevancy of the proffered testimony, the judge finally denied the prosecution's request that she testify. The judge considered the testimony of the appellant's former commanding officer, Colonel Sherman, who testified that during the time he served with the appellant from January 1973 to July 1974, he found the appellant to be a good worker, a very good supervisor, and dedicated to his job. He stated, "I classed him as a go-getter and I have no complaints about his work at all. I thought he did a very good job." He also testified, "In today's vernacular, Sergeant Varacalle would be considered very sharp. I have never seen him in a poor uniform. His shoes and boots were always shined and I felt he always kept himself in a high state of military bearing." Additionally, he stated, "I would say Sergeant Varacalle was extremely loyal and very obedient." The judge also considered the testimony of three other officers with whom the appellant served. All of these officers testified concerning the appellant's good character and his record of outstanding military service. The appellant's counsel made a statement on his behalf and called to the attention of the judge the appellant's DA Form 20 which included two good conduct medals and the Vietnamese Campaign Medal. The judge not only considered a statement of a psychiatrist who had examined the appellant, but also satisfied himself concerning the meaning of certain words contained in the report, including "pedophilia," which the parties finally agreed meant having a sexual attraction for children. During his sentencing argument, the defense attorney emphasized the appellant's excellent military service. After the arguments were concluded, the judge sought the assistance of the attorneys in clarifying some pencil notations on prosecution exhibit 2 indicating that the appellant may have been wounded in the right leg in 1967 and in the right hand in 1970. There was no mention in the exhibit of the appellant's having received a Purple Heart, but the judge satisfied himself that the wounds were received in battle in both instances.

Throughout the record of trial there is abundant evidence that the judge gave careful, individualized attention to the formulation of an appropriate sentence. I am convinced that the sentence he finally announced was the product of individualization. In that regard, it is noted that the sentence which the judge finally imposed was considerably less than the maximum imposable sentence for the offenses to which the appellant pleaded guilty, namely imprisonment for 54 years and a dishonorable discharge. It was also considerably less than the sentence which the appellant would have received under the pretrial agreement to which he had committed himself. The dissent does not suggest what would have been a proper sentence in this case. Instead, the sentence is condemned on the "special emphasis military law places upon the individualization of sentence," which Mosely is said to express, and for the further reason that the judge admittedly took into consideration the possible deterrent effect which the sentence might have upon others.

But the concept of individualization only means that in formulating a sentence the judge must utilize sentencing discretion. *Dorszynski v. United*

States, 418 U.S. 424 (1974). In order to do this the judge should refrain from imposing "[s]entences dictated by a 'mechanistic' concept of what a particular type of crime invariably deserves." *United States v. Foss*, 501 F.2d 522, 527 (1st Cir. 1974). . . .

* * *

My review of the record reveals no evidence that the judge imposed a greater sentence than he would otherwise have imposed absent consideration of the concept of deterrence. The dissent mentions no such evidence. *Mosely* recognizes the importance of deterrence as a "function of the criminal justice system," but for the reasons stated therein, condemned the argument of the prosecutor at *Mosely*'s trial. The dissent illuminates paragraphs 75 and 76 of the Manual for Court-Martial, United States, 1969 (Revised edition), which I submit do not prohibit the action of the judge in this case. Nor is there any support in this Court's precedents for condemnation of the trial judge's approach to formulation of the sentence here. I do not find that the judge harbored any preconceived notions concerning the sentence. Nor did he approach the formulation of the sentence mechanistically.

I am convinced that the trial judge formulated a sentence after careful consideration of the past life and habits of the appellant. He gave consideration not only to the appellant's "many years of outstanding faithful service," but also to the evidence that the appellant was apparently "suffering from some emotional and mental handicaps . . ." The judge was "not convinced that there's any strong, almost overriding compulsion on your part to give in to that attraction you apparently feel toward children" and stated that in his view that lessened the danger which the appellant poses to society. If anything, that statement indicated that the judge gave a less severe sentence than he might otherwise have imposed.

I therefore vote to affirm the decision of the Court of Military Review.

COOK, Judge (dissenting):

In *United States v. Mosely*, [1 M.J. 350 (C.M.A. 1976),] we reviewed the special emphasis military law places upon the individualization of sentence, and concluded that it was improper to adjudge a more severe sentence than might otherwise be imposed because of a purpose to deter others in the general population from committing the same offense, notwithstanding such practice is commonplace in the civilian courts. The decision has been strongly criticized in some commentaries and in decisions by Courts of Military Review, but I am still persuaded that it is justified, indeed required, by the authorities upon which we relied, and should not be overruled.

* * *

Early in its history, this Court condemned the intrusion into the sentence proceedings of service policies calculated to produce a more severe sentence than might otherwise have been imposed on the basis of the evidence before the court. *United States v. Davis*, 24 C.M.R. 235 (C.M.A. 1957). The rationale of those cases finds expression in the current Manual's prohibition of reference by trial counsel to "any policy directive relative to punishment." Paragraph 75f, Manual, *supra*. It seems to me that to increase an accused's punishment out of a desire to have that sentence act as a possible deterrent to prevent others from engaging in similar conduct reflects a policy basis of aggravation of punishment so similar to that excluded by the Manual as to be condemned by our earlier cases. Scrutinizing the record of the present case, I cannot conclude that the error was purged of its adverse effects. I would, therefore, reverse the decision of the Court of Military Review as to the sentence.

Points for Discussion

1. The Court of Military Appeals completed its abandonment of *Mosely* in *United States v. Lania*, 9 M.J. 100 (C.M.A. 1980). Current law says that general deterrence is a relevant factor so long as the military judge instructs the court members that there are other factors (such as rehabilitation of the accused, etc.) and that they must take into account the circumstances of the case and the character and propensities of the accused. *See United States v. Loving*, 34 M.J. 956, 965 (A.C.M.R. 1992). Was it appropriate for a judge on the Court of Military Review to request that the Court of Appeals for the Armed Forces reconsider its position?

2. In what ways might the purposes of sentencing in the military justice system be different from the purposes of sentencing in a civilian context?

9-2. Lawful Punishments

As explained above, after trial counsel and defense counsel make their arguments on sentencing, the members or the military judge will deliberate and then announce a sentence. The Rules for Court-Martial currently list ten different kinds of punishment that a court-martial can impose, depending on the circumstances:

- No punishment
- Reprimand
- Forfeiture of pay and allowances
- Fine
- Reduction in pay grade
- Hard labor without confinement
- Confinement
- Punitive separation (a "dismissal" for officers, or a "dishonorable discharge" or "bad-conduct discharge" for enlisted members)
- Death
- Punishments under the law of war (which theoretically could be imposed if enemy soldiers were tried for violating the laws of war)

See R.C.M. 1003(b).

Whether and to what extent these punishments are available in a particular case depends principally on three factors: the jurisdiction of the court-martial, the identity of the offense, and the rank and reserve status of the accused. A general court-martial may impose any of these punishments in an appropriate case. *See* R.C.M. 201(f)(1)(A)(ii). A special court-martial, however, may impose a maximum sentence of 12 months of confinement, a forfeiture of 2/3rds pay and allowances for 12 months, a fine, a reduction to pay grade E1 (the lowest pay grade), and a bad-conduct discharge. *See* R.C.M. 201(f)(2)(b)(i). But a special court-martial cannot order the confinement or dismissal of an officer and can only impose a bad-conduct discharge on an enlisted member if the special court-martial was specifically empowered to impose such an offense when the charges were referred. *See* R.C.M. 201(f)(2)(b)(ii). As described in chapter 3, a summary court-martial's sentencing powers are even more restricted.

Most of the punitive articles do not state specific limitations on the penalties that may be imposed for their violation, but Article 56, UCMJ, authorizes the President to prescribe limitations on penalties for each offense. The President has identified these limits in Part IV of the Manual for Courts-Martial. For example, Article 87, UCMJ, makes it a crime to miss a movement by saying: "Any person subject to this chapter who through neglect or design misses the movement of a ship, aircraft, or unit with which he is required in the course of duty to move *shall be punished as a court-martial may direct*" (emphasis added). The President, however, has limited the maximum punishment for this offense by including the following provision in Part IV of the Manual for Court-Martial:

e. *Maximum punishment.*

(1) *Design.* Dishonorable discharge, forfeiture of all pay and allowances, and confinement for 2 years.

(2) *Neglect.* Bad-conduct discharge, forfeiture of all pay and allowances, and confinement for 1 year.

MCM pt. IV, ¶11.e. The Manual for Courts-Martial includes similar restrictions for other offenses.

Various other limitations also flow from the rank of the accused and the accused's reserve status. For example, officers and cadets cannot be reduced in rank by a court-martial. *See* R.C.M. 1003(c)(2). In addition, members of a reserve component who are ordered to active duty under certain circumstances can be deprived of their liberty only for the period of their active duty. *See* R.C.M. 1003(c)(3). These are just a few examples. No attorney can effectively practice military law without carefully studying all of the complicated limitations, and their exceptions, found in R.C.M. 1003 and other rules.

After the military judge instructs the panel with respect to the maximum sentence, the panel will deliberate and return the sentence. A sentence of death requires all members to vote for that sentence. *See* R.C.M. 1004(b)(7) & 1006(d)(4)(A). A sentence of imprisonment for life or confinement for more than 10 years requires at least three-fourths of the members present to vote for that sentence. *See* R.C.M. 1006(d)(4)(B). Any other sentence requires two-thirds of the panel to agree. *See* R.C.M. 1006(d)(4)(B).

In terms of confinement, the military justice system differs from the federal criminal system in several key respects. The military justice system has no sentencing guidelines and, in general, no mandatory minimum penalties (other than for murder in violation of article 118). The accused also receives just one sentence that covers all offenses, instead of receiving separate sentences for each offense that are to be served either consecutively or concurrently. In addition, detainees may be released on parole in the military justice system, but not the federal civilian system. Thus it is not unusual for a servicemember to serve much less than the full period of confinement adjudged by the court-martial.

When the convening authority receives the record of trial, the convening authority may approve the sentence as adjudged or may reduce the sentence based on perceived legal error or as a matter of clemency. R.C.M. 1107(d). The Service Courts of Criminal Appeals can reassess the sentence and reduce it if it is legally excessive or if they reverse the findings of guilty to any offense. *See* R.C.M. 1203(b) discussion. The following important case addresses the choice between reassessing a sentence on appeal and remanding the case for new sentencing.

UNITED STATES v. SALES
U.S. Court of Military Appeals
22 M.J. 305 (C.M.A. 1986)

EVERETT, Chief Judge:

A general court-martial at Keesler Air Force Base, Mississippi, tried appellant [Pervin R. Sales, Jr., Airman First Class, U.S. Air Force] on charges that he had raped a female airman and had forced her to commit sodomy with him, in violation of Articles 120 and 125, Uniform Code of Military Justice, 10 U.S.C. §§ 920 and 925, respectively. Sales pleaded not-guilty; but, by exceptions and substitutions, he was convicted of committing lewd and lascivious acts and of consensual sodomy. The court members sentenced appellant to a bad-conduct discharge, confinement for 6 months, total forfeitures, and reduction to airman basic; and the convening authority approved the findings and sentence.

The Court of Military Review concluded that appellant's conviction for committing lewd and lascivious acts by having "(1) exposed himself by removing his pants; [and] (2) voluntarily participated in a group sexual encounter" was multiplicious with the finding that he had engaged in consensual sodomy. As that court reasoned:

Indecent acts with another is a lesser included offense of sodomy. *United States v. Cheatham*, 18 M.J. 721 (A.F.C.M.R. 1984), and cases cited therein. In our view the language of this finding "fairly embraced" the conduct that resulted in a conviction of consensual sodomy. *See United States v. Baker*, 14 M.J. 361 (C.M.A. 1983). The evidence before the trial court permits no other conclusion. In *United States v. Doss*, 15 M.J. 409 (C.M.A. 1983), the Court of Military Appeals held that multiplicity for findings is apparent where one of the offenses is lesser included of the other.

Unpublished opinion at 3.

Having decided that only the conviction for consensual sodomy could be affirmed, the Court of Military Review proceeded to "reassess the sentence in light of the error discussed, the offense affirmed and the record before us." To a request by appellate defense counsel that the punitive discharge be set aside, the court replied that "[g]ood as the accused's record may be to this point, our reading of the transcript convinces us that the adjudged sentence is clearly appropriate and it is AFFIRMED." Id. at 3–4.

We granted review of the sole issue presented by appellant's petition:

WHETHER THE EFFECT OF THE AIR FORCE COURT OF MILITARY REVIEW'S REASSESSMENT OF SENTENCE DEPRIVED APPELLANT OF HIS STATUTORY RIGHT TO HAVE HIS SENTENCE ADJUDGED BY THE COURT MEMBERS.

I

At the trial level, the military judge treated the court-martial's findings as separate not only for the purpose of conviction but also in computing the maximum punishment imposable. Accordingly, the judge concluded that 10 years was the maximum confinement that could be adjudged, rather than the 5 years' confinement that would have been the maximum for committing either lewd acts or consensual sodomy with an adult. *See* Table of Maximum Punishment, para. 127 c, Manual for Courts-Martial, United States, 1969 (Revised edition).

The Government has not proceeded under Article 67(b)(2), UCMJ, 10 U.S.C. § 867(b)(2), to certify for our review the holding of the Court of Military Review that the findings of guilty were multiplicious; so this ruling constitutes the law of the case and binds the parties. *Cf. United States v. Bell*, 23 C.M.R. 208 (C.M.A. 1957); *United States v. Morris*, 13 M.J. 297, 299 (C.M.A. 1982) (Everett, C.J., concurring in the result). If, therefore, the findings must be considered multiplicious, obviously the military judge erred at trial in computing the maximum sentence imposable and instructing the members accordingly. Now, the question is whether that error obligated the Court of Military Review to give appellant relief by granting a rehearing on sentence or by reducing the sentence pursuant to its own reassessment thereof.

In some cases, the Court of Military Review may conclude that it cannot reliably determine what sentence would have been imposed at the trial level if the error had not occurred. Under these circumstances, a rehearing on sentence is in order. *Cf. United States v. Gibson*, 11 M.J. 435 (C.M.A. 1981); *United States v. Voorhees*, 16 C.M.R. 83 (C.M.A. 1954). At this rehearing, the accused would be present; and, just as if he had not previously been sentenced, both the accused and the Government could offer evidence as to what sentence would be appropriate.

The sentence originally adjudged would be relevant only in setting a ceiling on the maximum punishment imposable. *See* Art. 63, UCMJ, 10 U.S.C. § 863.

On other occasions, the Court of Military Review may be convinced that even if no error had occurred at trial, the accused's sentence would have been at least of a certain magnitude. Under those circumstances the Court of Military Review need not order a rehearing on sentence, but instead may itself reassess the sentence.[3] *United States v. Bullington*, 13 M.J. 184 (C.M.A. 1982). Although reassessment does not provide the accused an opportunity to be present or to offer new evidence in mitigation and extenuation, this procedure complies with constitutional requirements, see *Jackson v. Taylor*, 353 U.S. 569 (1957); and it has often been employed by Courts of Military Review without criticism from this Court. Of course, if the error at trial was one of constitutional magnitude, then it would seem necessary that the Court of Military Review should be persuaded beyond a reasonable doubt that its reassessment has rendered harmless any error affecting the sentence adjudged at trial. *Cf. United States v. Remai*, 19 M.J. 229 (C.M.A. 1985); *see Chapman v. California*, 386 U.S. 18 (1967).

In connection with reassessment, we have emphasized

that, when a Court of Military Review reassesses a sentence because of prejudicial error, its task differs from that which it performs in the ordinary review of a case. Under Article 66, Uniform Code of Military Justice, 10 U.S.C. § 866, the Court of Military Review must assure that the sentence adjudged is appropriate for the offenses of which the accused has been convicted; and, if the sentence is excessive, it must reduce the sentence to make it appropriate. However, when prejudicial error has occurred in a trial, not only must the Court of Military Review assure that the sentence is appropriate in relation to the affirmed findings of guilty, but also it must assure that the sentence is no greater than that which would have been imposed if the prejudicial error had not been committed. Only in this way can the requirements of Article 59(a), UCMJ, 10 U.S.C. § 859(a), be reconciled with the Code provisions that findings and

---

[3] If it cannot be reasonably certain as to the severity of the sentence that would have resulted in the absence of the error at trial, then the Court of Military Review should not reassess the sentence but should order resentencing at the trial level. *Cf. United States v. Dukes*, 5 M.J. 71 (C.M.A. 1978).

sentence be rendered by the court-martial, see Articles 51 and 52, UCMJ, 10 U.S.C. §§ 851 and 852, respectively.

United States v. Suzuki, 20 M.J. 248, 249 (C.M.A. 1985). Thus, if the court can determine to its satisfaction that, absent any error, the sentence adjudged would have been of at least a certain severity, then a sentence of that severity or less will be free of the prejudicial effects of error; and the demands of Article 59(a) will be met. Of course, even within this limit, the Court of Military Review will determine that a sentence it proposes to affirm will be "appropriate," as required by Article 66(c). In short, a reassessed sentence must be purged of prejudicial error and also must be "appropriate" for the offense involved.

Thus, in appellant's case the Court of Military Review had to consider what sentence would have been adjudged at trial if the military judge had recognized that the findings were multiplicious, had dismissed one of the guilty findings, and then had given correct instructions as to the maximum sentence. After making this determination—which is required by Article 59(a) of the Code—the court would decide what sentence would be "appropriate" for the accused in light of the entire record of trial.

II

Appellate defense counsel contend that, in this case, the Court of Military Review must have performed the reassessment improperly because it affirmed the sentence adjudged by the court-martial. This contention is in error to whatever extent it relies on a premise that reduction in sentence must be granted whenever reassessment occurs after a finding of guilty has been set aside. Not only has this Court affirmed Court of Military Review decisions which have denied such relief, but also we occasionally have set aside some findings of guilty rendered in a trial on several charges, upheld the remaining findings, and affirmed the original sentence.

In some of these cases, the findings were set aside as to charges that had been treated at trial as multiplicious with the remaining charges for sentencing purposes; and so the risk was minimal that a higher sentence had been adjudged because of the trial judge's failure to recognize multiplicious findings of guilty. *See United States v. Zubko*, 18 M.J. 378 (C.M.A. 1984). However, in other instances, this Court has affirmed the original sentence even though some of the offenses were multiplicious for findings purposes and no instruction had been given at trial as to multiplicity for sentencing purposes. *See United States v. Zupancic*, 18 M.J. 387 (C.M.A. 1984).

In this case, the presence of the multiplicious findings could not have led to the reception of evidence that otherwise would have been inadmissible. *Cf. United States v. Vickers*, 13 M.J. 403 (C.M.A. 1982). Moreover, the sentence adjudged by the court-martial was lenient in relation to the 5 years' confinement imposable for committing either lewd acts or consensual sodomy. On this record, we are convinced that a rehearing on sentence was unnecessary and that a reassessment of sentence will suffice.

Although we recognize that in some instances an error at trial will compel the grant of a reduction in sentence upon reassessment, *cf. United States v. Dukes*, 5 M.J. 71 (C.M.A. 1978), we are unpersuaded that, as a matter of law, appellant was entitled to a reduction of sentence upon reassessment. However, if the Court of Military Review chose to affirm the original sentence, he was entitled to a conscientious determination by that court that the sentence originally adjudged had not been affected by the military judge's error at trial.

Unfortunately, it is not clear that the Court of Military Review proceeded in the manner required by Article 59(a) in considering what sentence relief, if any, it should grant Sales. *See United States v. Suzuki, supra* at 249. The court below stated that the sentence adjudged was "appropriate." This term usually is associated with performance of the court's responsibility under Article 66 to assure that only an appropriate sentence is affirmed. However, it does not pertain to the court's Article 59(a) duty to determine that all prejudice caused by trial error has been removed. In short, the Court of Military Review may have considered from all the evidence that the sentence adjudged was "appropriate"—even lenient—in light of the evidence revealed by the record. Nonetheless, it was not free to affirm that sentence unless it was also convinced that—even in the absence of the multiplicity error—the court-martial would have adjudged the same sentence.

Rather than allow any uncertainty to remain as to the mental process by which the reassessment was accomplished, we believe that a remand to the Court of Military Review is in order. Thereafter, Article 67(c) will apply.

III

The decision of the United States Air Force Court of Military Review is set aside. The record of trial is returned to the Judge Advocate General of the Air Force for remand to that court for further proceedings in which it will determine explicitly whether any sentence relief is required in order to purge the effects of the judge's multiplicity error.

Points for Discussion

1. One commentator has observed that it is much more common for a court of criminal appeals to reassess the sentence than to return the case for a rehearing. *See* Grace M.W. Gallagher, *Don't Panic! Rehearings and DuBays are Not the End of the World*, Army Lawyer, Jun. 2009, at 1, 7. Why would the service courts of criminal appeals generally prefer to reassess the sentence instead of returning the case for resentencing?

2. Why are there so many different kinds of penalties in the military justice system? Are the rules and limitations on sentencing too complicated?

3. Should the military justice system have sentencing guidelines like the federal system? If not, what makes the military justice system different?

9-3. Matters in Aggravation and In Extenuation and Mitigation

At the sentencing phase of the trial, as noted above, the government first presents "evidence in aggravation." R.C.M. 1001(b)(4). This evidence may include evidence of the impact of the crime on the victim, evidence of "significant adverse impact on the mission, discipline, or efficiency of the command directly and immediately resulting from the accused's offense," and evidence that the accused selected the victim based on the victim's "race, color, religion, national origin, ethnicity, gender, disability, or sexual orientation." *Id.* For example, suppose that the accused is a soldier who has been convicted of assault and battery of another soldier in the same unit. The prosecution might present evidence regarding the impact of the injuries on the victim, evidence of how the unit was short-handed while the victim recovered, and evidence that the offense was racially motivated. All of these factors would aggravate the offense and potentially persuade the court-martial to impose greater punishment.

After the government presents its evidence during sentencing, the accused may present "matters in rebuttal of any material presented by the prosecution" and "matters in extenuation and mitigation." R.C.M. 1001(c)(1). Evidence in extenuation relates to the circumstances surrounding the accused's commission of the offense. R.C.M. 1001(c)(1)(A). Evidence in mitigation may include evidence of "acts of good conduct or bravery and evidence of the reputation or record of the accused in the service for efficiency, fidelity, subordination, temperance, courage, or any other trait that is desirable in a servicemember." R.C.M. 1001(c)(1)(B). For example, the accused could present evidence that the offense represented a momentary lapse of judgment out-of-character for someone who otherwise has a strong record. In addition, as explained above, the accused may make an "unsworn statement"—a statement not under oath that the prosecution cannot cross-examine. R.C.M. 1001(c)(2)(C). The accused often uses the unsworn statement to apologize to the victim and to ask the court-martial for leniency. The right to make an unsworn statement is generally considered very important. The following case provides an illustration.

UNITED STATES v. ROSATO
U.S. Court of Military Appeals
32 M.J. 93 (C.M.A. 1991)

SULLIVAN, Chief Judge:

On May 13, 1989, appellant [Christopher L. Rosato, Airman Basic U.S. Air Force] was tried by a general court-martial composed of officer members at Lowry Air Force Base, Colorado. Pursuant to his pleas, he was found guilty of wrongful distribution of lysergic acid diethylamide (LSD), wrongful possession of LSD, attempted wrongful use of the same drug, failure to obey a lawful order, willful disobedience of a lawful order, and disrespect to a noncommissioned officer, in violation of Articles 112a, 80, 92, 90, and 91, Uniform Code of Military Justice, 10 U.S.C. §§ 912a, 880, 892, 890, and 891, respectively. The members sentenced appellant to a bad-conduct discharge, confinement for 2 years, and total forfeitures. In accordance with a pretrial agreement the convening authority approved the sentence and suspended confinement in excess of 12 months. On January 31, 1990, the Court of Military Review affirmed the findings of guilty and the sentence. 29 M.J. 1052.

This Court granted the following issue for review:

WHETHER THE MILITARY JUDGE ERRED TO THE SUBSTANTIAL PREJUDICE OF APPELLANT BY LIMITING THE CONTENT OF APPELLANT'S UNSWORN STATEMENT AND EXCLUDING OTHER EVIDENCE RELATING TO THE 3320TH CORRECTION AND REHABILITATION SQUADRON REHABILITATION PROGRAM.

We hold that, under the circumstances of this case, the military judge did prejudicially err in limiting the contents of appellant's unsworn statement. See generally *United States v. Partyka*, 30 M.J. 242, 246 (C.M.A. 1990). *Cf. United States v. Breese*, 11 M.J. 17, 24 (C.M.A. 1981).

After appellant was found guilty, the sentence portion of his court-martial commenced. The prosecution called appellant's company commander, who testified that appellant had no rehabilitation potential. The defense called the noncommissioned officer-in-charge of the administrative section of the confinement center. He testified that, based on his daily observations in confinement, appellant did have rehabilitation potential. Another defense witness, Major Parker, was a clinical social worker in the Air Force, chief of a mental health center, and friend of appellant's father. He also testified in substance that appellant did have rehabilitation potential. Finally, appellant's father, a senior Air Force officer and clinical scientist department head, testified for the defense at this court-martial. He testified that there had been a tremendous change in his son's attitude, "a growth, maturity, an acceptance of responsibility, an acknowledgement of what he's done, of wanting to pay . . . the price."

Prior to this testimony, the defense also sought to introduce a letter from the Judge Advocate General of the Air Force recommending the 3320th Correction and Rehabilitation Squadron (CRS) Rehabilitation Program and a newspaper article describing this program. The prosecution objected on the basis that the exhibits were irrelevant and improper. The military judge sustained trial counsel's objections to these defense exhibits.

The judge also held that certain limitations needed to be placed on appellant's unsworn statement to the members. He said:

M.J.: Also, defense counsel, did you want to make an offer of proof about what your client was going to say?

DC: Yes, Your Honor.

This is not entirely what he was going to say, but this relates to what he planned to say in regards to the 3320th Rehabilitation Squadron.

I am going to read it for him.

I have been seeing a counselor at the rehabilitative squadron of the 332oth for once a week for about two months. He has been counseling me about my drug problem. I have come to realize that drugs are 95 percent of my problem.

He mentioned the rehabilitative program to me. It sounds like something that would be very helpful to me. I would like to do this program.

I have talked with prisoners who came from the rehabilitative program and were unable to complete it. Only about two or three people out of 12 people who were in the program last year completed it. The prisoners I talked to who have been in the program said it was very difficult and a good program. The prisoners who have not been in the program constantly say it is a waste of time and a waste of eight months of your life and then you'll just get discharged. I do not agree with them. I think the program will be tough, but I know I can do it and I will be better off for it.

I ask you to consider my attitude about rehabilitation training in determining my rehabilitative potential as a factor in your sentencing me.

M.J.: I don't have any problem with him testifying about his desire to go into the 3320th as I said before. But I think whatever he has to say about what other people told him about the 3320th falls within trial counsel's motion in limine which I granted.

DC: So, Your Honor, specifically could I get some guidance from you about what parts of what I just read off—?

M.J.: Well, the first couple of sentences of what you read talked about his desires to remain in the Air Force.

DC: The part about the counselor talking to him that there is a program?

M.J.: Well, read it to me again . . . the first couple of sentences.

DC: Okay.

I have been seeing a counselor at the rehabilitative squadron of the 3320th once a week for about two months. He has been counseling me about my drug problem. I've come to realize that drugs are 95 percent of my problem.

He mentioned the rehab program to me. It sounds like something that would be helpful to me. I'd like to do this program.

I have talked with prisoners—

M.J.: No. I think up to that point it's fine.

DC: Up to that point.

M.J.: But after that it gets into details about what other people said about the program which I think is not appropriate for the court's consideration.

DC: Okay.

How about the statement where he says—after he gets through the part about what people say about the program—where he asks them to consider his attitude about rehabilitation training in determining his rehabilitative potential as a factor in their sentencing?

M.J.: Certainly they can consider his attitude.

DC: Thank you, Your Honor.

Your Honor, and just for the record, of course, the defense would object to him not being able to talk about what he's heard about the program.

(Emphasis added.)

The military judge clearly restricted appellant in the exercise of his right to make an unsworn statement to the members on sentencing. See R.C.M. 1001(c)(2)(C), Manual for Courts–Martial, United States, 1984. He did so on the basis of his prior evidentiary ruling that the defense could not present evidence of the details of a particular service rehabilitation program. This ruling in turn was grounded, inter alia, on the judge's conclusion that this program was an irrelevant collateral consequence of a prison sentence. *See generally United States v. Murphy*, 26 M.J. 454, 457 (C.M.A. 1988). Consequently, the judge also concluded that appellant could not make an unsworn statement generally referring to what other persons told him about this same rehabilitative program. Accordingly, we must decide whether the rule prohibiting consideration by members of evidence of collateral administrative consequences of court-martial sentences applies to this post-sentence program and whether it extends to appellant's unsworn statement. We think not, at least in the circumstances presented in this case.

First of all, the limited references to the nature of this program in appellant's unsworn statement were not nearly so extensive as the excluded defense exhibits. Neither *United States v. Murphy*, supra, nor *United States v. Lapeer*, 28 M.J. 189 (C.M.A. 1989), holds that all evidence of service-rehabilitation programs is per se inadmissible at courts-martial. *See United States v. Flynn*, 28 M.J. 218, 221–22 (C.M.A. 1989). They do stand for the proposition that evidence concerning the details of these programs need not be generally admitted as a sentence concern. See *United States v. Griffin*, 25 M.J. 423, 425 (C.M.A.), *cert. denied*, 487 U.S. 1206 (1988). The rationale for this so-called "collateral-consequences" rule is to prevent "the waters of the military sentencing process" from being "muddied" by "an unending catalogue of administrative information." *United States v. Quesinberry*, 31 C.M.R. 195, 198 (C.M.A. 1962). *See generally* Mil. R. Evid. 403, Manual, *supra*. We see no basis for finding that such confusion would arise in this case from the deleted portions of appellant's unsworn statement.

Second, the military judge prevented appellant from presenting this rehabilitation information through his unsworn statement. The servicemember's right to make such a statement to the members on sentencing is presently found in R.C.M. 1001(c)(2). It states:

(2) Statement by the accused.

(A) In general. The accused may testify, make an unsworn statement, or both in extenuation, in mitigation, or to rebut matters presented by the prosecution, or for all three purposes whether or not the accused testified prior to findings. The accused may limit such testimony or statement to any one or more of the specifications of which the accused has been found guilty. This subsection does not permit the filing of an affidavit of the accused.

* * *

(C) Unsworn statement. The accused may make an unsworn statement and may not be cross-examined by the trial counsel upon it or examined upon it by the court-martial. The prosecution may, however, rebut any statements of facts therein. The unsworn statement may be oral, written, or both, and may be made by the accused, by counsel, or both.

Discussion

An unsworn statement ordinarily should not include what is properly argument, but inclusion of such matter by the accused when personally making an oral statement normally should not be grounds for stopping the statement.

This is a valuable right. *See United States v. Partyka*, 30 M.J. at 246. It has long been recognized by military custom. *See* G. Davis, A Treatise on the Military Law of the United States 132–33 (3d ed. rev. 1913). Moreover, it has been one generally considered unrestricted. *Id.*; W. Winthrop, Military Law and Precedents 299 (2d ed. 1920 Revision). *Cf. United States v. Harris*, 13 M.J. 653, 654 (NMCMR 1982) (Byrne, J., concurring in the result). The evidentiary policy concerns of United *States v. Quisenberry, supra*, which have been noted above, do not readily apply in this situation. *See generally United States v. Breese, supra*, 11 M.J. 17.

Finally, the military judge specifically prevented appellant from describing to the members his understanding of the demanding nature of this program and his willingness to undergo such a program as part of his rehabilitation. These statements were neither gratuitously disrespectful toward superiors or the court nor a form of insubordination or defiance of authority. *See* Davis and Winthrop, both supra. In fact, they were exceedingly respectful. Moreover, in view of the military judge's prior ruling barring evidentiary exhibits concerning this program, appellant was effectively precluded from communicating to the members the full depth of his commitment to "soldier his way back" to productive service. Finally, any concern of the military judge with muddying the sentencing waters could have been adequately addressed in his instructions. *See United States v. Breese, supra.* Accordingly, in view of the legal standards governing unsworn statements, we hold that the military judge improperly restricted appellant in his sentencing rights provided in R.C.M. 1001(c)(2).

We have examined the record of trial in this case to assess whether prejudice may have inured to appellant as a result of the judge's error. Art. 59(a), UCMJ, 10 U.S.C. § 859(a). *See generally United States v. Weeks*, 20 M.J. 22 (C.M.A. 1985). We note that appellant presented a substantial case in extenuation and mitigation on other grounds. We also note that he was permitted to make a vague reference to this service rehabilitation program in the unsworn statement which he did present to the members. Nevertheless, his commander's testimony denying his rehabilitation potential was significant contrary evidence to which he could not fully and adequately respond. *See United States v. Kirk*, 31 M.J. 84, 89 (C.M.A. 1990). Reassessment by the Court of Military Review of appellant's sentence is most appropriate in such circumstances.

The decision of the United States Air Force Court of Military Review is reversed as to sentence. The record of trial is returned to the Judge Advocate General of the Air Force for remand to that court for reassessment of the sentence.

Judge COX and Senior Judge EVERETT concur.

Points for Discussion

1. One commentator has cited the *Rosato* decision favorably as an example of the generally "paternalistic nature of military criminal procedure." Colin A. Kisor, *The Need for Sentencing Reform in Military Courts-Martial*, 58 Nav. L. Rev. 39 & n. 45 (2009). In what way is *Rosato* paternalistic? Is the court attempting to protect the accused from making a poor decision or just aiding the accused in obtaining leniency?

2. The 1951 version of the Manual for Courts-Martial, the first manual promulgated after adoption of the UCMJ in 1950, provided the following guidance on sentences: "Among other factors which may properly be considered are the penalties adjudged in other cases for similar offenses. With due regard for the nature and seriousness of the circumstances attending each particular case, sentences should be relatively uniform throughout the armed forces." *See id.* ¶76a(4). Is uniformity in sentences a worthy goal? Is it still a goal under the current Manual for Courts-Martial? If not, what is wrong or potentially wrong with uniformity?

———————————

Many criminal convictions have "collateral consequences" apart from the sentences imposed. For example, in many states, convicted sex offenders must register their place of residence with the state government. Is it ever appropriate for a court-martial to consider collateral consequences when imposing a sentence?

UNITED STATES v. PERRY
Court of Appeals for the Armed Forces
48 M.J. 197 (C.A.A.F. 1998)

GIERKE, Judge:

A general court-martial composed of officer members convicted appellant [Brian R. PERRY, Ensign, U.S. Navy], on mixed pleas, of attempted sodomy, conduct unbecoming an officer (4 specifications), and committing indecent acts (6 specifications), in violation of Articles 80, 133, and 134, Uniform Code of Military Justice, 10 USC §§ 880, 933, and 934, respectively. The court-martial sentenced appellant to a dismissal, confinement for 5 years, loss of lineal numbers, and total forfeitures. The convening authority approved the adjudged sentence but suspended confinement in excess of 4 years for 12 months from the date of trial. The Court of Criminal Appeals set aside the conviction of attempted sodomy but affirmed the remaining findings of guilty and the sentence.

Our Court granted review of the following issue:

WHETHER THE MILITARY JUDGE ERRED TO THE SUBSTANTIAL PREJUDICE OF APPELLANT WHEN HE FAILED TO GIVE A PROPOSED INSTRUCTION REGARDING RECOUPMENT OF EXPENDITURES FOR APPELLANT'S EDUCATION AT THE U.S. NAVAL ACADEMY.

Appellant graduated from the U.S. Naval Academy in May 1993. He was convicted and sentenced in July 1994. Appellant had incurred a 5–year military service commitment in return for his education at the Naval Academy. During a discussion on sentencing instructions, appellant proposed the following instruction:

A dismissal may cause Ensign Perry to be liable to reimburse the U.S. Government for all or a portion of the costs associated with his education at the U.S. Naval Academy. As computed by the U.S. Naval Academy, the total cost of education for the past four years is approximately $80,000.

Defense counsel supported this request with a memorandum from the Naval Academy Comptroller that computed the cost of education and recited,

In accordance with PL 96–357, and effective with the Class of 1985, if any individual fails to fulfill their commitment, they may be liable to reimburse the U.S. Government for all or a portion of the costs associated with their education at the Academy.

The military judge denied the request for an instruction on the possibility of reimbursement. He explained, "I don't see anything here that makes this a matter that I should instruct them [on] as a matter of law as to the potential consequences of dismissal." He offered appellant an opportunity to present additional evidence but declined to give the requested instruction because "[i]t's not evidence before the court."

Defense counsel responded that he was "puzzled by the judge's ruling" because "it's a strong probability" that an Academy graduate who fails to fulfill the service requirement "may be liable to reimburse the Government." The military judge responded again:

[I]t's not evidence before the court. You're asking me to instruct them on law. If I'm going to instruct them on this law, as you're asking me to do, then I will want to see some regulation, some implementing feature—I'd like to know a history of do they do it in a case such as this, is there any reason to believe that will happen here, other than this general assessment of 1 March '94 to the midshipmen.

The military judge concluded by explaining:

There are a lot of public laws that never come into play in terms of regulations that implement them and collections that would be applicable specifically to a case such as this one. I doubt you could make a showing necessary to get me to give that instruction, but you certainly can try.

Defense counsel concluded his argument by saying, "I've tried. The objection, obviously, is noted for the record."

During sentencing argument, defense counsel told the members: "Now, right up front I'm going to tell you what I think is an appropriate sentence in this case. We think a dismissal, total forfeitures of pay and allowances, and we think confinement not to exceed one year would be appropriate."

Appellant now contends that the military judge abused his discretion by refusing to instruct the members on the possibility of government recoupment of the cost of his education. The Government responds that the military judge did not abuse his discretion because the claimed collateral consequence was too remote. The Government points out that appellant failed to avail himself of the opportunity to present evidence on the recoupment issue. Finally, the Government argues that any error in refusing to instruct on the issue was harmless because the defense conceded that dismissal and total forfeitures were appropriate punishments.

Public Law No. 96–357, on which the defense relied at trial, is codified in 10 USC § 2005. Under § 2005(f) of this statute, cadets and midshipmen must execute agreements to serve on active duty for specific periods. Cadets and midshipmen must also agree to reimburse the United States for their educational expenses if they, "voluntarily or because of misconduct," fail to serve for "the period of active duty specified in the agreement." Under § 2005(g)(2), a cadet or midshipmen "who may be subject to a reimbursement requirement" is entitled to notice of the requirement "before (1) submitting a request for voluntary separation, or (2) making a decision on a course of action regarding personal involvement in administrative, nonjudicial, and judicial action resulting from alleged misconduct." Under § 2005(g)(1), before collection action is initiated, a factfinding hearing must be conducted "in order to determine the validity of the debt." Finally, under § 2005(h), the

Secretary of the military department concerned may modify a service agreement to reduce the active-duty obligation "if the Secretary determines that it is in the best interests of the United States to do so."

An accused has a broad right to present mitigation evidence. *United States v. Becker*, 46 MJ 141, 143 (1997). This Court has recognized that the financial impact of a punitive discharge may be relevant on sentencing, provided that it is a direct and proximate consequence of the punitive discharge and not merely a potential collateral consequence. *Id.* (error to exclude evidence of retirement benefits of accused only 3 1/2 months from retirement without reenlisting); *United States v. Greaves*, 46 MJ 133 (1997) (generic instruction on collateral consequences of punitive discharge inadequate where accused was 2 months from retirement without reenlisting); *United States v. Griffin*, 25 MJ 423 (CMA 1988) (no error to instruct on impact of punitive discharge on retirement where accused was retirement eligible).

We review a military judge's decision whether and how to instruct on the consequences of a sentence for abuse of discretion. *Greaves*, 46 MJ at 139. We hold that the military judge did not abuse his discretion in this case.

The military judge's refusal to give the requested instruction was founded on a lack of evidence. Defense counsel proffered only a memorandum based on an enabling statute that authorizes the Secretary of the Navy to recoup educational costs but also gives the Secretary broad authority to waive the service requirement. The internal publication from the Naval Academy reflects the discretionary nature of the Secretary's authority by announcing that individuals who fail to fulfill the service requirement "may be liable" to reimburse the United States. Although given ample opportunity, the defense offered no evidence that the Secretary of the Navy routinely initiated collection action or that such action was contemplated in this case. The defense offered no evidence that appellant had received the statutory notice required by § 2005(g)(2). In short, there was no evidentiary predicate for the requested instruction. See *United States v. Van Syoc*, 36 MJ 461, 464 (CMA 1993) (duty to instruct arises when "some evidence" is presented raising the issue). Accordingly, we hold that the military judge did not abuse his discretion.

The decision of the United States Navy–Marine Corps Court of Criminal Appeals is affirmed.

Chief Judge COX and Judge CRAWFORD concur.

[The separate opinion of Judge Effron is omitted.—Eds.]

Point for Discussion

How, if at all, could defense counsel ever provide sufficient proof of a collateral consequence, such as having to repay the Naval Academy for the cost of an officer's education?

9-4. The Death Penalty in the Military

The death penalty has long been a part of the American military disciplinary tradition. In 1755, after Major General Edward Braddock's death in the French and Indian War, Virginia Governor Robert Dinwiddie appointed Colonel George Washington to command the Virginia Regiment of provincial forces. Washington had to raise his soldiers through conscription, and many of them were unruly or prone to desert. Washington adopted the policy that "Any soldier who shall desert, though he return again, shall be hanged without mercy." 1 The Writings of George Washington 214 n. 1 (Worthington C. Ford, ed., 1889). Military correspondence by Washington indicates that, as the court-martial convening authority for his regiment, he approved the hanging of two draftees in July 1757 after they had deserted. *Id.* at 457. During the Civil War, President Lincoln had authority to review all court-martial sentences. Although Lincoln commuted many death sentences, he approved the execution of 267 soldiers sentenced to death by court-martial, including 141 for desertion. *See* Ida Tarbell, 2 The Life of Abraham Lincoln 168-169 (1896). In World War II, the Army executed 142 soldiers. *See* Frederick Benays Wiener, *Are the General Military Articles Unconstitutionally Vague?*, 54 ABA J. 357, 362 n.44 (1968). General Eisenhower personally approved the death sentence of Private Eddie Slovik, the only soldier executed for desertion. *See* Carlo D'Este, Eisenhower: A Soldier's Life 795-796 (2002). When Congress enacted the UCMJ in 1950, Congress retained the death penalty as a permissible penalty. Indeed, the UCMJ authorizes the death penalty for fourteen offenses: desertion (art. 85), assaulting or willfully disobeying superior commissioned officer (art. 90), mutiny or sedition (art. 94), misbehavior before the enemy (art. 99), subordinate compelling surrender (art. 100), improper use of countersign (art. 101), forcing a safeguard (art. 102), aiding the enemy (art. 104), spying (art. 106), espionage (art. 106a), improper hazarding of vessel (art. 110), misbehavior of sentinel (art. 113), murder (art. 118), and rape (art. 120). For four of these offenses—violations of arts. 85, 90, 106, and 113—the penalty is authorized only if the offense is committed during wartime.

Yet despite this tradition, the last military execution took place on April 13, 1961, when the Army hanged Private John A. Bennett. PVT Bennet, who was stationed in Siezenheim, Austria, abducted an 11-year-old Austrian girl who was returning from shopping in Austria a few days before Christmas. After raping the girl repeatedly, Bennet threw her into a nearby millstream to drown. He was convicted of rape and attempted murder and sentenced to death. *See United States v. Bennett*, 21 C.M.R. 223, 225 (C.M.A. 1956). The Court of Military Appeals wrote in its opinion affirming the sentence, "Seldom, if ever, have we been faced with a record which revealed a more vicious offense, or an accused who had less to entitle him to any consideration by the fact finders." *Id.* President Eisenhower signed the warrant for his execution before leaving office, and President Kennedy declined to intercede in the execution. *See* Tim Reid, *Private Was Hanged in 1961 for Raping Girl*, The Sunday Times, Apr. 30, 2005.

What accounts for the absence of executions for four decades? Part of the answer is that the Supreme Court held in *Furman v. Georgia*, 408 U.S. 238 (1972) (per curiam), that the death penalty was unconstitutional absent special safeguards to limit discretion and prevent the death penalty from being imposed in a ".wanton" or "freakish" manner, and it took considerable time for Congress and the President to fashion a lawful response. Colonel Dwight H. Sullivan, a leading expert on the military death penalty explains the complicated history of the post-*Furman* epoch in his influential law review article, *Killing Time: Two Decades of Military Capital Litigation*, 189 Mil. L. Rev. 1 (2006):

> In the four years that followed *Furman*, thirty-five states and the federal government revised their capital punishment systems. In 1976, the Supreme Court held that the new Georgia, Florida, and Texas death penalty systems were constitutionally permissible. The "modern era of capital punishment" in the United States had begun. But neither Congress nor the President reformed the military death penalty system. Instead, just as before *Furman*, in any case that resulted in a finding of guilty under Article 118(1) (premeditated murder) or 118(4) (felony murder), the members exercised unfettered discretion to choose between the only two congressionally authorized sentences: confinement for life and death.

> Between 1979 and 1983, courts-martial sentenced seven servicemembers to death. Each had been convicted of premeditated murder or both premeditated murder and felony murder. In June of 1983, the Air Force Court of Military Review reversed the death sentence of Airman Robert M. Gay . . . . The Air Force Court based this result on its conclusion that *Furman* invalidated the military capital punishment system. Four months later, the Court of Military Appeals (COMA) reached a similar conclusion in the landmark case of *United States v. Matthews*, [16 M.J. 354 (C.M.A. 1983)]. *Matthews* was a bold opinion. It invalidated the existing military death penalty system, ultimately leading to the reversal of the death sentences of every inmate on military death row at the time. . . .

> On 24 January 1984, President Ronald Reagan signed Executive Order 12,460. That Executive Order amended the 1969 (Revised) Manual for Courts-Martial (MCM) by establishing a new military death penalty system. With only minor modifications in wording, this new system would become Rule for Courts-Martial (R.C.M.) 1004 when the 1984 MCM went into effcct on 1 August 1984.

> The system that Executive Order 12,460 established, as codified by the 1984 MCM, allowed the members to adjudge a death sentence if three conditions were satisfied: (1) the accused was found guilty of an offense for which death was an authorized punishment; (2) the members

unanimously found beyond a reasonable doubt that one of the "aggravating circumstances" (later renamed "aggravating factors") set out in R.C.M. 1004(c) existed; and (3) the members unanimously found that any extenuating and mitigating circumstances were "substantially outweighed by any aggravating circumstances," including the "aggravating circumstances" (later renamed "aggravating factors") listed in R.C.M. 1004(c).

Dwight H. Sullivan, *Killing Time: Two Decades of Military Capital Litigation*, 189 Mil. L. Rev. 1, 3-9 (2006) (footnotes omitted).

The Rules for Courts-Martial set forth the requirements for imposition of the death penalty in RCM 1004 and 1006. As Judge Gierke explained in *Loving v. Hart*, 47 M.J. 438 (C.A.A.F. 1998), these rules set up several requirements that must be met if the accused is to be sentenced to death:

> The military capital sentencing procedure set out in RCM 1004 and 1006 establishes four "gates" to narrow the class of death-eligible offenders. The first two gates parallel nonweighing jurisdictions in that the members must convict by unanimous vote (RCM 1004(a)(2)) and then find at least one aggravating factor by unanimous vote (RCM 1004(b)(4)(A)). Only after these two gates are passed does the weighing process begin. The third gate is a "weighing" gate, where the members must all "concur" that extenuating and "mitigating circumstances are substantially outweighed by any aggravating circumstances," including the aggravating factors under RCM 1004(c). See RCM 1004(b)(4)(C). Only after these three gates are passed does an accused become "death eligible."
>
> The fourth and final gate is the sentencing decision itself under RCM 1006. Even if all members concur that extenuating and mitigating circumstances are substantially outweighed by aggravating circumstances, they must separately consider whether to impose the death sentence. A death sentence requires the unanimous vote of all members. RCM 1006(d)(4)(A)....

Id. at 442. The "aggravating factors" to which Judge Gierke refers are listed in RCM 1004(c).[1]

---

[1] RCM 1004(c) identifies the aggravating factors as follows:

(c) Aggravating factors. Death may be adjudged only if the members find, beyond a reasonable doubt, one or more of the following aggravating factors:

(1) That the offense was committed before or in the presence of the enemy, except that this factor shall not apply in the case of a violation of Article 118 or 120:

(2) That in committing the offense the accused—

(A) The accused was serving a sentence of confinement for 30 years or more or for life at the time of the murder;

(B) The murder was committed; while the accused wTas engaged in the commission or attempted commission of any robbery, rape, rape of a child,

The Supreme Court unanimously upheld the newly revised military death penalty in 1996, at least as against certain constitutional challenges, in the landmark case that follows:

---

aggravated sexual assault, aggravated sexual assault of a child, aggravated sexual contact, aggravated sexual abuse of a child, aggravated sexual contact with a child, aggravated arson, sodomy, burglary, kidnapping, mutiny, sedition, or piracy of an aircraft or vessel; or while the accused was engaged in the commission or attempted commission of any offense involving the wrongful distribution, manufacture, or introduction or possession, with intent to distribute, of a controlled substance; or. while the accused was engaged in flight or attempted flight after the commission or attempted commission of any such offense;

(C) The murder was committed for the purpose of receiving money or a thing of value;

(D) The accused procured another by means of compulsion, coercion, or a promise of an advantage, a service, or a thing of value to commit the murder;

(E) The murder was committed with the intent to avoid or to prevent lawful apprehension or effect an escape from custody or confinement;

(F) The victim was the President of the United States, the President-elect, the Vice President, or. if there was no Vice President, the officer in the order of succession to the office of President of the United States, the Vice-President-elect, or any individual who is acting as President under the Constitution and laws of the United States, any Member of Congress (including a Delegate to. or Resident Commissioner in. the Congress) or Meniber-of-Congress elect, justice or judge of the United States, a chief of state or head of government (or the political equivalent) of a foreign nation, or a foreign official (as such term is defined in section 1116(b)(3)(A) of title 18. United States Code), if the official was on official business at the time of the offense and was in the United States or hi a place described hi Mil. R. Evid.315(c)(2). 315(c)(3);

(G) The accused then knew that the victim was any of the following persons in the execution of office; a commissioned, warrant, noncommissioned, or petty officer of the armed services of the United States; a member of any law enforcement or security activity or agency, military or civilian, including correctional custody personnel; or any firefighter;

(H) The murder was committed with intent to obstruct justice;

(I) The murder was preceded by the intentional infliction of substantial physical harm or prolonged, substantial mental or physical pain and suffering to the victim. For purposes of this section, "substantial physical harm" means fractures or dislocated bones, deep cuts, torn members of the body, serious damage to internal organs, or other serious bodily injuries. The term "substantial physical harm" does not mean minor injuries, such as a black eye or bloody nose. The term "substantial mental or physical pain or suffering" is accorded its common meaning and includes torture;

(J) The accused has been found guilty in the same case of another violation of Article 118;

(K) The victim of the murder was under 15 years of age.

LOVING v. UNITED STATES
U.S. Supreme Court
517 U.S. 748 (1996)

Justice KENNEDY delivered the opinion of the Court.

The case before us concerns the authority of the President, in our system of separated powers, to prescribe aggravating factors that permit a court-martial to impose the death penalty upon a member of the Armed Forces convicted of murder.

I

On December 12, 1988, petitioner Dwight Loving, an Army private stationed at Fort Hood, Texas, murdered two taxicab drivers from the nearby town of Killeen. He attempted to murder a third, but the driver disarmed him and escaped. Civilian and Army authorities arrested Loving the next afternoon. He confessed.

After a trial, an eight-member general court-martial found Loving guilty of, among other offenses, premeditated murder and felony murder under Article 118 of the Uniform Code of Military Justice (UCMJ), 10 U.S.C. §§ 918(1), (4). In the sentencing phase of the trial, the court-martial found three aggravating factors: (1) that the premeditated murder of the second driver was committed during the course of a robbery, Rule for Courts–Martial (R.C.M.) 1004(c)(7)(B); (2) that Loving acted as the triggerman in the felony murder of the first driver, R.C.M. 1004(c)(8); and (3) that Loving, having been found guilty of the premeditated murder, had committed a second murder, also proved at the single trial, R.C.M. 1004(c)(7)(J). The court-martial sentenced Loving to death. The commander who convened the court-martial approved the findings and sentence. Cf. 10 U.S.C. § 860. The United States Army Court of Military Review and the United States Court of Appeals for the Armed Forces (formerly the United States Court of Military Appeals (CMA)) affirmed, 41 M.J. 213 (1994), relying on *United States v. Curtis*, 32 M.J. 252 (CMA), *cert. denied*, 502 U.S. 952 (1991), to reject Loving's claims that the President lacked authority to promulgate the aggravating factors that enabled the court-martial to sentence him to death. We granted certiorari. . . .

II

Although American courts-martial from their inception have had the power to decree capital punishment, they have not long had the authority to try and to sentence members of the Armed Forces for capital murder committed in the United States in peacetime. In the early days of the Republic the powers of courts-martial were fixed in the Articles of War. Congress enacted the first Articles in 1789 by adopting in full the Articles promulgated in 1775 (and revised in 1776) by the Continental Congress. Act of Sept. 29, 1789, ch. 25, § 4, 1 Stat. 96. (Congress reenacted the Articles in 1790 "as far as the same may be applicable to the constitution of the United

States," Act of Apr. 30, 1790, ch. 10, § 13, 1 Stat. 121.) The Articles adopted by the First Congress placed significant restrictions on court-martial jurisdiction over capital offenses. Although the death penalty was authorized for 14 military offenses, American Articles of War of 1776, reprinted in W. Winthrop, Military Law and Precedents 961 (reprint 2d ed.1920) (hereinafter Winthrop); Comment, Rocks and Shoals in a Sea of Otherwise Deep Commitment: General Court–Martial Size and Voting Requirements, 35 Nav. L.Rev. 153, 156–158 (1986), the Articles followed the British example of ensuring the supremacy of civil court jurisdiction over ordinary capital crimes that were punishable by the law of the land and were not special military offenses. 1776 Articles, § 10, Art. 1, reprinted in Winthrop 964 (requiring commanders, upon application, to exert utmost effort to turn offender over to civil authorities). *Cf.* British Articles of War of 1765, § 11, Art. 1, reprinted in Winthrop 937 (same). That provision was deemed protection enough for soldiers, and in 1806 Congress debated and rejected a proposal to remove the death penalty from court-martial jurisdiction. Wiener, *Courts–Martial and the Bill of Rights: The Original Practice I*, 72 Harv. L.Rev. 1, 20–21 (1958).

Over the next two centuries, Congress expanded court-martial jurisdiction. In 1863, concerned that civil courts could not function in all places during hostilities, Congress granted courts-martial jurisdiction of common-law capital crimes and the authority to impose the death penalty in wartime. Act of Mar. 3, 1863, § 30, 12 Stat. 736, Rev. Stat. § 1342, Art. 58 (1875); *Coleman v. Tennessee*, 97 U.S. 509, 514, 24 L.Ed. 1118 (1879). In 1916, Congress granted to the military courts a general jurisdiction over common-law felonies committed by service members, except for murder and rape committed within the continental United States during peacetime. Articles of War of 1916, ch. 418, § 3, Arts. 92–93, 39 Stat. 664. Persons accused of the latter two crimes were to be turned over to the civilian authorities. Art. 74, 39 Stat. 662. In 1950, with the passage of the UCMJ, Congress lifted even this restriction. Article 118 of the UCMJ describes four types of murder subject to court-martial jurisdiction, two of which are punishable by death:

> "Any person subject to this chapter who, without justification or excuse, unlawfully kills a human being, when he—
>
> "(1) has a premeditated design to kill;
>
> "(2) intends to kill or inflict great bodily harm;
>
> "(3) is engaged in an act which is inherently dangerous to another and evinces a wanton disregard of human life; or
>
> "(4) is engaged in the perpetration or attempted perpetration of burglary, sodomy, rape, robbery, or aggravated arson;
>
> "is guilty of murder, and shall suffer such punishment as a court-martial may direct, except that if found guilty under clause (1) or (4), he shall suffer death or imprisonment for life as a court-martial may direct."
> 10 U.S.C. § 918.

So matters stood until 1983, when the CMA confronted a challenge to the constitutionality of the military capital punishment scheme in light of *Furman v. Georgia*, 408 U.S. 238 (1972), and our ensuing death penalty jurisprudence. Although it held valid most of the death penalty procedures followed in courts-martial, the court found one fundamental defect: the failure of either the UCMJ or the R.C.M. to require that court-martial members "specifically identify the aggravating factors upon which they have relied in choosing to impose the death penalty." *United States v. Matthews*, 16 M.J. 354, 379. The court reversed Matthews' death sentence, but ruled that either Congress or the President could remedy the defect and that the new procedures could be applied retroactively. *Id.*, at 380–382.

The President responded to *Matthews* in 1984 with an Executive Order promulgating R.C.M. 1004. In conformity with 10 U.S.C. § 852(a)(1), the Rule, as amended, requires a unanimous finding that the accused was guilty of a capital offense before a death sentence may be imposed, R.C.M. 1004(a)(2). The Rule also requires unanimous findings (1) that at least one aggravating factor is present and (2) that any extenuating or mitigating circumstances are substantially outweighed by any admissible aggravating circumstances, 1004(b). R.C.M. 1004(c) enumerates 11 categories of aggravating factors sufficient for imposition of the death penalty. The Rule also provides that the accused is to have "broad latitude to present evidence in extenuation and mitigation," 1004(b)(3), and is entitled to have the members of the court-martial instructed to consider all such evidence before deciding upon a death sentence, 1004(b)(6).

This is the scheme Loving attacks as unconstitutional. He contends that the Eighth Amendment and the doctrine of separation of powers require that Congress, and not the President, make the fundamental policy determination respecting the factors that warrant the death penalty.

III

A preliminary question in this case is whether the Constitution requires the aggravating factors that Loving challenges. The Government does not contest the application of our death penalty jurisprudence to courts-martial, at least in the context of a conviction under Article 118 for murder committed in peacetime within the United States, and we shall assume that Furman and the case law resulting from it are applicable to the crime and sentence in question. *Cf. Trop v. Dulles*, 356 U.S. 86 (1958) (analyzing court-martial punishments under the Eighth Amendment). The Eighth Amendment requires, among other things, that "a capital sentencing scheme must 'genuinely narrow the class of persons eligible for the death penalty and must reasonably justify the imposition of a more severe sentence on the defendant compared to others found guilty of murder.' " *Lowenfield v. Phelps*, 484 U.S. 231, 244 (1988) (quoting *Zant v. Stephens*, 462 U.S. 862, 877 (1983)). Some schemes accomplish that narrowing by requiring that the sentencer find at least one aggravating circumstance. 484 U.S., at 244. The narrowing may also be achieved, however, in the definition of the capital offense, in which circumstance the requirement that the sentencer "find the existence of an aggravating circumstance in addition is no part of the constitutionally required narrowing process." *Id.*, at 246.

Although the Government suggests the contrary, Brief for United States 11, n. 6, we agree with Loving, on the assumption that Furman applies to this case, that aggravating factors are necessary to the constitutional validity of the military capital punishment scheme as now enacted. Article 118 authorizes the death penalty for but two of the four types of murder specified: premeditated and felony murder are punishable by death, 10 U.S.C. §§ 918(1), (4), whereas intentional murder without premeditation and murder resulting from wanton and dangerous conduct are not, §§ 918(2), (3). The statute's selection of the two types of murder for the death penalty, however, does not narrow the death-eligible class in a way consistent with our cases. Article 118(4) by its terms permits death to be imposed for felony murder even if the accused had no intent to kill and even if he did not do the killing himself. The Eighth Amendment does not permit the death penalty to be imposed in those circumstances. *Enmund v. Florida*, 458 U.S. 782, 801 (1982). As a result, additional aggravating factors establishing a higher culpability are necessary to save Article 118. We turn to the question whether it violated the principle of separation of powers for the President to prescribe the aggravating factors required by the Eighth Amendment.

IV

* * *

[A] strand of our separation-of-powers jurisprudence, the delegation doctrine, has developed to prevent Congress from forsaking its duties. Loving invokes this doctrine to question the authority of the President to promulgate R.C.M. 1004. The fundamental precept of the delegation doctrine is that the lawmaking function belongs to Congress, U.S. Const., Art. I, § 1, and may not be conveyed to another branch or entity. *Field v. Clark*, 143 U.S. 649, 692 (1892). . . .

Loving contends that the military death penalty scheme of Article 118 and R.C.M. 1004 does not observe the limits of the delegation doctrine. He presses his constitutional challenge on three fronts. First, he argues that Congress cannot delegate to the President the authority to prescribe aggravating factors in capital murder cases. Second, he contends that, even if it can, Congress did not delegate the authority by implicit or explicit action. Third, Loving believes that even if certain statutory provisions can be construed as delegations, they lack an intelligible principle to guide the President's discretion. Were Loving's premises to be accepted, the President would lack authority to prescribe aggravating factors in R.C.M. 1004, and the death sentence imposed upon him would be unconstitutional.

A

Loving's first argument is that Congress lacks power to allow the President to prescribe aggravating factors in military capital cases because any delegation would be inconsistent with the Framers' decision to vest in Congress the power "To make Rules for the Government and Regulation of the land and naval Forces." U.S. Const., Art. I, § 8, cl. 14. At least in the context of capital punishment for peacetime crimes, which implicates the Eighth Amendment, this power must be deemed exclusive, Loving contends. In his view, not only is the determination of aggravating factors a quintessential policy judgment for the Legislature, but the history of military capital punishment in England and America refutes a contrary interpretation. He asserts that his offense was not tried in a military court throughout most of English and American history. It is this historical exclusion of common-law capital crimes from military jurisdiction, he urges, that must inform our understanding of whether Clause 14 reserves to Congress the power to prescribe what conduct warrants a death sentence, even if it permits Congress to authorize courts-martial to try such crimes. See Brief for Petitioner 42–43; Brief for United States Navy–Marine Corps Appellate Defense Division as Amicus Curiae 7–12, 19–26. Mindful of the historical dangers of autocratic military justice and of the limits Parliament set on the peacetime jurisdiction of courts-martial over capital crimes in the first Mutiny Act, 1 Wm. & Mary, ch. 5 (1689), and having experienced the military excesses of the Crown in colonial America, the Framers harbored a deep distrust of executive military power and military tribunals. *See Reid v. Covert*, 354 U.S. 1, 23–24 (1957) (plurality); *Lee v. Madigan*, 358 U.S. 228, 232 (1959). It follows, Loving says, that the Framers intended that Congress alone should possess the power to decide what aggravating factors justify sentencing a member of the Armed Forces to death.

* * *

Under Clause 14, Congress, like Parliament, exercises a power of precedence over, not exclusion of, Executive authority. *Cf. United States v. Eliason*, 16 Pet. 291, 301, 10 L.Ed. 968 (1842) ("The power of the executive to establish rules and regulations for the government of the army, is undoubted"). This power is no less plenary than other Article I powers, . . ., and we discern no reasons why Congress should have less capacity to make measured and appropriate delegations of this power than of any other, *see Skinner v. Mid–America Pipeline Co.*, 490 U.S. 212, 220–221 (1989) (Congress may delegate authority under the taxing power); . . . . Indeed, it would be contrary to precedent and tradition for us to impose a special limitation on this particular Article I power, for we give Congress the highest deference in ordering military affairs. *Rostker v. Goldberg*, 453 U.S. 57, 64–65 (1981). And it would be contrary to the respect owed the President as Commander in Chief to hold that he may not be given wide discretion and authority. We decline to import into Clause 14 a restrictive nondelegation principle that the Framers left out.

There is no absolute rule, furthermore, against Congress' delegation of authority to define criminal punishments. We have upheld delegations whereby the Executive or an independent agency defines by regulation what conduct will be criminal, so long as Congress makes the violation of regulations a criminal offense and fixes the punishment, and the regulations "confin[e] themselves within the field covered by the statute." United States v. Grimaud, 220 U.S. 506, 518 (1911). See also Touby v. United States, 500 U.S. 160 (1991). The exercise of a delegated authority to define crimes may be sufficient in certain circumstances to supply the notice to defendants the Constitution requires. *See M. Kraus & Bros., Inc. v. United States*, 327 U.S. 614, 622 (1946). In the circumstances presented here, so too may Congress delegate authority to the President to define the aggravating factors that permit imposition of a statutory penalty, with the regulations providing the narrowing of the death-eligible class that the Eighth Amendment requires.

＊ ＊ ＊

B

Having held that Congress has the power of delegation, we further hold that it exercised the power in Articles 18 and 56 of the UCMJ. Article 56 specifies that "[t]he punishment which a court-martial may direct for an offense may not exceed such limits as the President may prescribe for that offense." 10 U.S.C. § 856. Article 18 states that a court-martial "may, under such limitations as the President may prescribe, adjudge any punishment not forbidden by [the UCMJ], including the penalty of death when specifically authorized by" the Code, § 818. As the Court of Military Appeals pointed out in Curtis, for some decades the President has used his authority under these Articles to increase the penalties for certain noncapital offenses if aggravating circumstances are present. For example, by regulation, deserters who are apprehended are punished more severely than those who surrender; drunken drivers suffer a harsher fate if they cause an accident resulting in the death of a victim; and the punishment of thieves is graded by the value of the stolen goods. *See Curtis*, 32 M.J., at 261. The President has thus provided more precision in sentencing than is provided by the statute, while remaining within statutory bounds. This past practice suggests that Articles 18 and 56 support as well an authority in the President to restrict the death sentence to murders in which certain aggravating circumstances have been established.

There is yet a third provision of the UCMJ indicative of congressional intent to delegate this authority to the President. Article 36 of the UCMJ, which gives the President the power to make procedural rules for courts-martial, provides:

"Pretrial, trial, and post-trial procedures, including modes of proof, for [courts martial] ... may be prescribed by the President by regulations which shall, so far as he considers practicable, apply the principles of law and the rules of evidence generally recognized in the trial of criminal cases in the United States district courts, but which may not be contrary to or inconsistent with this chapter." 10 U.S.C. § 836(a).

Although the language of Article 36 seems further afield from capital aggravating factors than that of Article 18 or 56, it is the provision that a later Congress identified as the source of Presidential authority to prescribe these factors. In 1985, Congress enacted Article 106a of the UCMJ, 10 U.S.C. § 906a, which authorized the death penalty for espionage. The Article requires a finding of an aggravating factor if the accused is to be sentenced to death; it enumerates three such factors, but allows death to be decreed on "[a]ny other factor that may be prescribed by the President by regulations under section 836 of this title (article 36)." § 906a(c)(4). Article 106a itself, then, is premised on the President's having authority under Article 36 to prescribe capital aggravating factors, and " '[s]ubsequent legislation declaring the intent of an earlier statute is entitled to great weight in statutory construction.' " *Consumer Product Safety Comm'n v. GTE Sylvania, Inc.*, 447 U.S. 102, 118, n. 13 (1980) (quoting *Red Lion Broadcasting Co. v. FCC*, 395 U.S. 367, 380–381 (1969)). Whether or not Article 36 would stand on its own as the source of the delegated power, we hold that Articles 18, 36, and 56 together give clear authority to the President for the promulgation of R.C.M. 1004.

Loving points out that the three Articles were enacted as part of the UCMJ in 1950, well before the need for eliminating absolute discretion in capital sentencing was established in *Furman v. Georgia*, 408 U.S. 238 (1972), and the cases that followed. (Slight amendments to the Articles have been made since but are not relevant here.) In 1950, he argues, Congress could not have understood that it was giving the President the authority to bring an otherwise invalid capital murder statute in line with Eighth Amendment strictures. Perhaps so, but *Furman* did not somehow undo the prior delegation. What would have been an act of leniency by the President prior to *Furman* may have become a constitutional necessity thereafter, . . ., but the fact remains the power to prescribe aggravating circumstances has resided with the President since 1950.

C

* * *

... From the early days of the Republic, the President has had congressional authorization to intervene in cases where courts-martial decreed death. American Articles of War of 1806, Art. 65, reprinted in Winthrop 976, 982. It would be contradictory to say that Congress cannot further empower him to limit by prospective regulation the circumstances in which [courts-martial] can impose a death sentence. Specific authority to make rules for the limitation of capital punishment contributes more toward principled and uniform military sentencing regimes than does case-by-case intervention, and it provides greater opportunity for congressional oversight and revision.

Separation-of-powers principles are vindicated, not disserved, by measured cooperation between the two political branches of the Government, each contributing to a lawful objective through its own processes. The delegation to the President as Commander in Chief of the authority to prescribe aggravating factors was in all respects consistent with these precepts, and the promulgation of R.C.M. 1004 was well within the delegated authority. Loving's sentence was lawful, and the judgment of the Court of Appeals for the Armed Forces is affirmed.

It is so ordered.

[Justice Stevens filed a concurring opinion in which Justices Souter, Ginsburg, and Breyer joined. Justice Scalia filed an opinion concurring in part and concurring in the judgment, in which Justice O'Connor joined. Justice Thomas filed an opinion concurring in the judgment.]

Points for Discussion

1. The *Loving* decision, although it upheld the death penalty procedures adopted in the Manual for Courts-Martial, has not yet led to any executions. [1] Colonel Sullivan, in his article *Killing Time*, quoted above, writes that the death penalty is rarely sought, that the death penalty is rarely imposed by a court-martial when it is sought, and that death sentences are reversed in over three quarters of the cases. *See* Sullivan, *supra*, at 2-3. In light of these factors, should military prosecutors continue to seek the death penalty? Are some crimes so heinous that the death penalty should be sought despite the expense and procedural difficulty associated with all capital cases?

2. The Supreme Court committed a rare gaff in *Kennedy v. Louisiana*, 554 U.S. 407 (2008), a case considering the constitutionality of a state law imposing the death penalty for rape of a child. The Court held that the Eighth Amendment prohibits the death penalty for the rape of a child if the perpetrator does not kill or intend to kill the child. *See id.* at 413. In its original opinion, the Court erroneously asserted that no federal law authorizes death as a penalty for rape, failing to recognize that UCMJ article 120 does authorize this punishment. *See* 554 U.S. at 425. Following a petition for rehearing, the Supreme Court subsequently amended its opinion to correct its error without commenting on whether UCMJ article 120 is constitutional. *See Kennedy v. Louisiana*, 129 S. Ct. 1 (2008). Is there an argument that the death penalty might be unconstitutional in a civilian context but not in the military for the crime of rape? For all of the other offenses in the UCMJ for which death is listed as a possible punishment?

---

[1] On April 12, 1988, Army Private Ronald A. Gray was sentenced to death. On July 29, 2008, President George W. Bush approved his execution. The case is now in habeas corpus litigation.

CHAPTER 10

POST-TRIAL REVIEW PROCEDURES

One of the unique aspects of military justice is the detailed post-trial processing procedures which provide convicted military criminal offenders with various opportunities to overturn their convictions in whole or in part and/or lessen their sentences. Opportunities for clemency or relief exist throughout the process from either the convening authority, appellate courts, confinement facility administrative regulations, or military service boards of parole, pardons, or correction of military records.

As the chart below depicts, the detailed post-trial processing procedural requirements are provided in the *Manual for Courts-Martial* and *Rules for Courts-Martial.*

Once the trial is complete, the trial counsel prepares the results of trial and confinement order, and the convening authority acts on any request from the accused. The accused can request that the convening authority defer the confinement, reduction, or forfeitures after the sentence is adjudged. An accused may also request waiver of forfeitures.

The government must then prepare the verbatim or summarized record of trial (depending on the sentence). *See* R.C.M. 1103(b)(2)(B) & (C). After counsel review the record and complete an errata sheet listing errors in the record, and after the military judge authenticates the record of trial, a copy of the authenticated record is served on the accused (and defense counsel if requested). *See* R.C.M. 1104-1106. A copy of the Staff Judge Advocate's post-trial recommendation (SJAR) as described below is delivered to the accused and defense counsel as well. At that point, the accused has an opportunity to submit clemency matters for the convening authority to consider prior to taking action.

GENERAL/SPECIAL COURT-MARTIAL POST-TRIAL PROCESSING

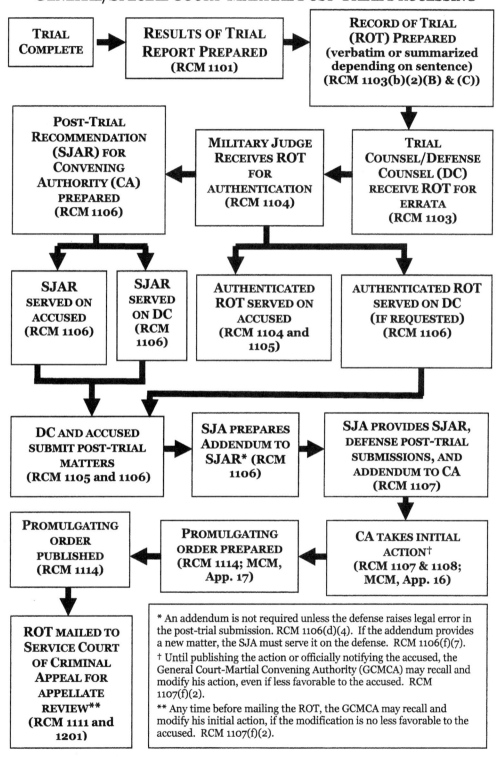

10-1. Staff Judge Advocate Recommendation

The first opportunity for clemency lies with the convening authority who takes action on the court-martial findings and sentence. Before taking action, the convening authority must consider the report of the results of trial, the written post-trial recommendation (SJAR) from his legal adviser, i.e., Staff Judge Advocate (if required), any clemency matters the accused submits (pursuant to R.C.M. 1105 or 1106(f)). The convening authority may also consider the record of trial, accused's personnel records, and "such other matters" deemed appropriate. However, if those matters are adverse to the accused from outside the record and without the accused's knowledge, the accused must be notified and provided an opportunity to rebut.

Before the convening authority takes action on a record of trial by general court-martial or special court-martial resulting in a sentence that includes a bad-conduct discharge or confinement or forfeitures of six months or more, the convening authority must receive an SJAR. Prior to 2010, much appellate litigation involved errors in the SJAR. In 2010, the President amended R.C.M. 1106(d) by executive order substantially reducing the required content of the SJAR. The SJAR now must include a concise recommendation and any clemency recommendation made by the sentencing authority when sentence was announced, a copy of the the report of results of trial (which must include the findings, sentence, and confinement credit), and a copy or summary of any pretrial agreement. R.C.M. 1106(d). The Staff Judge Advocate need not review the record of trial for legal errors, but must include an opinion whether the convening authority should take corrective action on the findings or sentence when appropriate or if the accused alleges a legal error in the post-trial matters provided to the convening authority. *Id.* The Staff Judge Advocate need not include his rationale or analysis concerning the legal error. *Id.* If an SJAR includes an error, Rule for Courts-Martial 1106(d) now grants the appellate court the authority to take corrective action without returning the case to the convening authority.

Points for Discussion

1. Why must the convening authority review the SJAR and matters submitted by the accused but not the record of trial? How will the convening authority understand what evidence was presented at the court-martial if he does not review the record of trial prior to taking initial action?

2. In determining the sentence, the military judge or panel do not have authority to grant clemency to the accused, but they do have authority to recommend that the convening authority suspend any or all of the sentence. The SJAR must include any such recommendation. Should the convening authority be bound by the sentencing authority's recommendation for clemency? For example, if a panel recommends that the convening authority suspend the bad-conduct discharge adjudged as part of the court-martial sentence, shouldn't the convening authority include that as part of the approved sentence? If not, why not?

Problem

In *United States v. Van Vliet*, 64 M.J. 539 (A.F. Ct. Crim. App. 2006), a cadet at the Air Force Academy was convicted by a general court-martial of making a false official statement, larceny, and housebreaking. The military judge sentenced him to a dismissal and confinement for 19 months. The cadet at that point informed the convening authority that he wished to request the Secretary of the Air Force to allow him resign in lieu of court-martial. The staff judge advocate advised the convening authority that a post-trial request to resign in lieu of trial by court-martial would not be processed by the Secretary because it was untimely. The convening authority then approved the findings and sentence as adjudged. The Air Force Court of Criminal Appeals determined that the staff judge advocate's advice was incorrect and that the cadet could have filed a timely request with the Secretary under Air Force regulations. What remedy is appropriate to redress the incorrect advice by the staff judge advocate?

10-2. Clemency Matters

After trial, the accused may submit matters for the convening authority to consider prior to taking action on the findings and sentence. Defense counsel have the responsibility to select and compile post-trial defense submissions. For general and special courts-martial, the defense must submit matters within ten days after the following events (whichever occurs last): 1) the authenticated record of trial is served on the accused; 2) the SJAR is served on the accused; or 3) the SJAR addendum with new matter is served on the accused. If within the ten-day period the accused shows that he requires additional time, the convening authority's SJA may for good cause extend the 10-day period for not more than 20 additional days, but only the convening authority may deny an extension request. R.C.M. 1105. (For summary courts-martial, the defense must submit matters within seven days of sentencing.) If the accused fails to submit clemency matters in a timely fashion, he waives the right to submit matters. The convening authority is required to consider only written submissions. *See id.*

In the case that follows, the defense received two short extensions to the prescribed deadlines to obtain a letter from a three-star general. This case illustrates how important it is for the SJA to ensure that the convening authority considers all clemency matters prior to taking action on a case.

UNITED STATES v. TRAVIS
Court of Appeals for the Armed Forces
66 M.J. 301 (C.A.A.F. 2008)

Judge ERDMANN delivered the opinion of the court.

Sergeant Matthew K. Travis was a Marine guard and supervisor at a detention facility in Iraq. In conjunction with other guards, Travis devised a scheme to deal with an unruly Iraqi detainee by attaching electrical wires to the detainee's cage to prevent the detainee from grabbing the cage. When this failed to electrify the cage, other guards attached the wires directly to the detainee's body. Pursuant to his pleas, Travis was found guilty of willful dereliction of duty, attempted cruelty and maltreatment of an Iraqi national detainee, conspiracy to commit cruelty and maltreatment of an Iraqi national detainee, and false official statement.

He was sentenced to a bad-conduct discharge, confinement for fifteen months, and reduction to the lowest enlisted grade. The United States Navy–Marine Corps Court of Criminal Appeals affirmed the findings but granted sentence relief under Article 66(c), Uniform Code of Military Justice (UCMJ), 10 U.S.C. § 866(c) (2000), by reducing the confinement to twelve months. *United States v. Travis*, No. NMCCA 200600519, 2007 CCA LEXIS 68, 2007 WL 1701351 (N.M. Ct. Crim. App. Feb. 27, 2007).

We granted review to determine whether the lower court erred in finding that Travis was not prejudiced when the staff judge advocate (SJA) failed to submit clemency matters to the convening authority prior to action and when the SJA subsequently did not forward those clemency materials to the convening authority for over a year. Because there was a second action taken by the same convening authority after consideration of Travis's clemency submission, we conclude that Travis suffered no material prejudice.

Background

Post-trial processing of this case involved back and forth electronic communication between Travis and his defense counsel who were located at Camp Pendleton, California, and the SJA and convening authority who were deployed in Iraq. The SJA recommendation was completed on September 29, 2004. On November 8, the recommendation was served on the defense counsel for comment pursuant to Rule for Courts–Martial (R.C.M.) 1106(f)(1). On November 17, defense counsel requested an additional twenty-four hours within which to submit clemency matters because he had not received a letter from Lieutenant General (LTG) Mattis. The request was granted.

On November 22, 2004, defense counsel noted that he was still waiting on the clemency letter from LTG Mattis. In an addendum to the SJA recommendation dated December 1, 2004, the SJA noted that the defense had been given two extensions of time up to November 29 to submit clemency matters and no clemency matters had been received. Action was taken on December 4, and no clemency matters were considered by the convening authority.

Upon reviewing the action on December 9, 2004, defense counsel noted that there was no reference to consideration of clemency materials. In acknowledging receipt of the convening authority's action, defense counsel inquired about the clemency materials. The SJA responded that no clemency matters had been received. In response, on December 13, 2004, the defense was able to retrieve a copy of an electronic message purporting to show that Travis's clemency request and supporting materials had been sent to the SJA on November 29th. A copy of this clemency package was subsequently provided to the SJA. Upon receipt of these materials, the SJA notified defense counsel that the matters were late and that they would not be forwarded to the convening authority.

On January 10, 2005, Travis filed a petition for extraordinary relief in the form of a writ of mandamus with the Court of Criminal Appeals. He requested that the Navy–Marine Corps court order the convening authority to withdraw the action dated December 4, 2004, and take new action after considering his clemency submissions. Travis's request for extraordinary relief was denied by the Navy–Marine Corps court on January 13, 2005.

On November 30, 2005, a second addendum to the SJA recommendation was prepared. This addendum recommended that the convening authority withdraw the prior action because "the previous Convening Authority's Action did not note a companion case" and also recommended that the convening authority consider the clemency matters that were "submitted by the defense after the time for submission had expired." Pursuant to this addendum, the same officer who took the initial action on the case withdrew his previous action and on December 2, 2005, took a new action approving the sentence as adjudged. The new action specifically acknowledged consideration of the defense clemency submissions.

When Travis's case was reviewed by the Court of Criminal Appeals, that court considered issues of post-trial delay and the impact of the SJA's failure to forward clemency matters to the convening authority. *Travis,* 2007 CCA LEXIS 68, at *3, 2007 WL 1701351, at *1. Concerning the clemency issue, the court stated, "Based on the record before us we are unable to determine whether these [clemency] matters were submitted before or after [the convening authority's December 4, 2004 action]." *Id.* at *5–*6, 2007 WL 1701351, at *2. The Navy–Marine Corps court went on to hold that if the clemency matters were received prior to the December 4, 2004, action there was error, but that error was cured when the December 2, 2005, action was taken after consideration of the clemency submissions. *Id.* at *6, 2007 WL 1701351, at *2. Alternatively, the lower court indicated that if the clemency matters were received after the December 4, 2004, action, there was no error. *Id.* In either event, the lower court held that there was no material prejudice to Travis's substantial rights. *Id.* at *5, 2007 WL 1701351, at *2.

Discussion

A convicted servicemember has the right to submit matters to the convening authority that reasonably tend to affect the decision whether to approve or disapprove any findings of guilt or to approve, reduce, or disapprove the adjudged sentence. Article 60(b)(1), UCMJ, 10 U.S.C. § 860(b)(1) (2000); R.C.M. 1105(a), (b). These matters may be submitted within ten days after the authenticated record of trial and SJA recommendation are served on the accused, and additional time may be requested for good cause shown. Article 60(b)(1), UCMJ; R.C.M. 1105(c)(1). "Failure to submit matters within the time prescribed by this rule shall be deemed a waiver of the right to submit such matters." R.C.M. 1105(d)(1). A convening authority must consider matters submitted by the accused. Article 60(c)(2), UCMJ; R.C.M. 1107(b)(3).

Under these rules, the threshold determination in this case is when Travis's clemency matters were submitted. However, on this record the lower court could not determine when the clemency matters were submitted. 2007 CCA LEXIS 68, at *5–*6, 2007 WL 1701351, at *2. As a court of law, we lack the authority to make factual determinations. *See United States v. Wise,* 64 M.J. 468, 470 (C.A.A.F. 2007); *United States v. Ginn,* 47 M.J. 236, 244–45 (C.A.A.F. 1997); *see also United States v. DuBay,* 37 C.M.R. 411 (C.M.A. 1967).

In terms of when clemency matters are "submitted", we agree that "submission" of clemency matters is less formal than "service" required by other rules in the *Manual for Courts-Martial.* However, in this case it is not necessary to define the qualitative subtleties that may or may not distinguish completed "submission" from completed "service." Regardless of when the defense "submitted" the clemency matters or how long it took the SJA to forward the clemency package to the convening authority, if Travis would not be entitled to relief under any construction of the facts, any alleged error would be harmless. " 'Whether an error, constitutional or otherwise, was harmless, is a question of law that we review de novo.' " *United States v. Hall,* 66 M.J. 53, 54 (C.A.A.F. 2008) (quoting *United States v. McCollum,* 58 M.J. 323, 342 (C.A.A.F. 2003)).

We conclude, as did the court below, that Travis has not suffered any material prejudice to a substantial right. Article 59(a), UCMJ, 10 U.S.C. § 859(a) (2000). We cannot and do not substitute our judgment about the merit of a request for clemency or the weight to be given any specific clemency recommendation by a convening authority. Clemency is a " 'highly discretionary' " command function of a convening authority. *United States v. Rosenthal,* 62 M.J. 261, 263 (C.A.A.F. 2005) (per curiam) (quoting *United States v. Wheelus,* 49 M.J. 283, 289 (C.A.A.F. 1998)). Where a servicemember has been deprived of full and fair clemency consideration by a convening authority, we are not reluctant to return a case for an otherwise proper review and action. *See, e.g., id.* In this case, however, we have the benefit of knowing what the results of a proper clemency consideration would have yielded, and a remand for a new action is not required.

Major General (MG) Natonski took action on both December 4, 2004, and December 2, 2005. The offenses in this case are serious. Travis's conduct reflects disdain for the human dignity of detainees under American control and custody, as well as an abandonment of his supervisory role as a noncommissioned officer. The record reflects that at the time of the second action, MG Natonski had before him all the required documents and submissions, including Travis's complete clemency package with LTG Mattis's clemency letter. In taking this action, MG Natonski stated that he "considered the results of trial, the clemency submitted by the defense counsel on behalf of the accused in accordance with Rule for Courts–Martial 1105, MCM, (2002 Ed.), the Staff Judge Advocate's Recommendation and the entire record of trial." With all that in mind, MG Natonski approved the sentence as adjudged.

There is nothing to suggest that in taking the second action MG Natonski did not perform his duty as convening authority fully, fairly, and in accordance with law. This action demonstrates clearly and convincingly that even if Travis's clemency materials had been considered at the time of the initial action, he would have been afforded no clemency. In assessing prejudice, we also take into account that the Court of Criminal Appeals reduced the period of confinement when it granted sentence relief under Article 66(c), UCMJ, to address post-trial delay. *Travis*, 2007 CCA LEXIS 68, at *8, 2007 WL 1701351, at *3. We conclude, therefore, that any possible error relating to the post-trial processing of clemency materials in this case was harmless.

We note that although the defense counsel and the SJA were acting in good faith, simple steps could have been taken to prevent this situation from arising in the first place. We recognize that the distance between Camp Pendleton, California, and Iraq is substantial, and that both distance and combat operations compound the usual difficulties of communication and post-trial processing. So too should the parties recognize that they are functioning in a more complex environment and, as a result, devote more attention to detail.

Defense counsel should take reasonable steps to guarantee that clemency submissions have in fact been received under any circumstances but particularly where communications are problematic. An SJA should be attentive to whether the defense intends to submit clemency matters and, where there are clear indications that the defense intends to submit matters, the SJA need not rush to action in the absence of the anticipated clemency material—particularly where communications are problematic. We urge a commonsense approach to guarantee a convicted servicemember gets full and fair clemency consideration and that convening authorities have everything they need to prudently exercise their unique clemency function at action.

Decision

The decision of the United States Navy–Marine Corps Court of Criminal Appeals is affirmed.

BAKER, Judge (dissenting):

Although Appellant's conduct was egregious, I do not share the majority's confidence that the second convening authority's action remedied any error or potential prejudice resulting from the convening authority's failure, during his first review, to consider the letter from Lieutenant General (LtG) J.N. Mattis.

First, the letter in question did not recommend clemency generally, or negate the seriousness of the offenses at issue. Rather, the recommendation was limited to a recommendation for confinement relief on behalf of a member of his command during combat operations in Iraq.

Second, the letter was from LtG Mattis. While the text of the letter is relatively perfunctory, its recommendation is not. Moreover, the letter is from the Marine ground combat commander who led the 1st Marine Division's push to Baghdad, and thus is a member of the Marine Corps' "warrior elite." (His successor in command at the First Marine Division would, of course, know this, as would any other Marine). During my tenure on the Court, I have not seen a clemency letter from a general, let alone one from a general with the combat stature of LtG Mattis. In the context of the Marine Corps, a letter from a warrior general to a subordinate commander might well have resulted in some measure of confinement clemency, at least on the order of symbolic relief.

Third, the second convening authority's action could not have addressed any potential prejudice resulting from the delay in submitting the Mattis letter because at the time of the second action Appellant had already served the duration of his confinement. Also, LtG Mattis's recommendation for clemency addressed confinement relief alone. Thus, we do not "have the benefit of knowing what the results of a proper clemency consideration would have yielded." *United States v. Travis*, 66 M.J. at 304 (C.A.A.F. 2008).

Nor is it possible in such a context to conclude, as does the majority, that Appellant's clemency request received *full* and *fair* consideration. The majority's analysis might ordinarily work as a matter of legal logic, that is, a second action might normally cure the error in the first action in which no relief was given. However, it falls short when considered in the actual military context presented. LtG Mattis recommended confinement clemency for a combat veteran of battles the general himself directed. A convening authority who acts without benefit of such a recommendation cannot be said to have acted on the "full" package. Neither is the review "fair," if the letter is subsequently considered after its recommendation is moot.

As a result, I would grant meaningful confinement relief and respectfully dissent.

Points for Discussion

1. The Court of Appeals for the Armed Forces urges "a commonsense approach to guarantee a convicted servicemember gets full and fair clemency consideration and that convening authorities have everything they need to prudently exercise their unique clemency function at action." What responsibility, if any, does this place on defense counsel? On the SJA? If you were the SJA, what precautions would you take prior to submitting a case to the convening authority for action?

2. Judge Baker in his dissent points out that the convening authority's second action "could not have addressed any potential prejudice resulting from the delay in submitting the Mattis letter because at the time of the second action Appellant had already served the duration of his confinement" and "LtG Mattis's recommendation for clemency addressed confinement relief alone." Do you agree with this observation? If not, why not?

10-3. Convening Authority Action

The convening authority who convened the court or his successor in command must take initial action on the finding and sentence unless it is impractical to do so. *See* R.C.M. 1107. In those circumstances the case will be transferred to another convening authority for action. As the following case depicts, a convening authority may be disqualified from taking action on a case if he was an accuser, has a personal interest in the case outcome, or has a personal bias toward the accused. The convening authority also may be disqualified if he displays or exhibits an inelastic attitude toward his post-trial responsibilities.

If the convening authority does not specifically act on the findings, there is implicit approval of the findings as reflected in the report of the results of trial. The convening authority's action on the sentence cannot increase the sentence. Unlike the sentencing authority at trial, the convening authority may suspend a punishment or reduce a mandatory sentence adjudged. Of course, the action must conform to the terms of any valid pretrial agreement with the accused.

UNITED STATES v. DAVIS
Court of Appeals for the Armed Forces
58 M.J. 100 (C.A.A.F. 2003)

Judge ERDMANN delivered the opinion of the Court.

Appellant, Airman Basic (AB) Daniel D. Davis, United States Air Force, was tried by special court-martial at Lackland Air Force Base, Texas. Pursuant to his pleas, he was convicted of unauthorized absence and one specification each of wrongful use of cocaine and wrongful use of marijuana, violations of Articles 86 and 112a, Uniform Code of Military Justice [hereinafter UCMJ], 10 U.S.C. §§ 886, 912a (2002), respectively. A court of officer members sentenced him to a bad-conduct discharge and confinement for three months. The convening authority approved the sentence as adjudged. On March 7, 2002, the Air Force Court of Criminal Appeals affirmed the findings and sentence in an unpublished opinion.

We granted review of the following issue:

WHETHER IT WAS ERROR FOR THE CONVENING AUTHORITY TO PERFORM THE POST–TRIAL REVIEW OF APPELLANT'S CASE WHEN THE CONVENING AUTHORITY MADE STATEMENTS THAT DEMONSTRATED AN INELASTIC ATTITUDE TOWARD CLEMENCY.

For the reasons set forth herein, we answer the granted issue in the affirmative and return Appellant's case for a new action by a different convening authority.

Facts

Pursuant to a pretrial agreement with the convening authority, Appellant providently pleaded guilty to using both cocaine and marijuana and to being absent without authority from December 21, 2000 until he was apprehended on February, 16, 2001.

After trial, Appellant's defense counsel submitted a "memorandum for all reviewing authorities" entitled "*Goode* Response and Clemency Petition—*US v. Davis*." The memorandum indicated that Appellant had petitioned the convening authority for clemency and stated the following:

> We object to MajGen [F], 37th TRW/CC, being the convening authority for purposes of taking action on the sentence in this case. During the early part of this year, MajGen [F] gave several briefings at Lackland Air Force Base, Texas where he discussed illicit drug use by military members as being on the rise. During the briefings, MajGen [F] also publicly commented that people caught using illegal drugs would be prosecuted to the fullest extent, and if they were convicted, they should not come crying to him about their situations or their families['], or words to that effect (Affidavit Attached). MajGen [F]'s comments seriously question his ability to act neutrally and impartially when determining whether AB Davis should receive any clemency on his case as AB Davis was indeed prosecuted and convicted of illegal drug use.

A convening authority should be able to objectively and impartially weigh all the evidence in the Record of Trial and clemency matters submitted by the accused (*United States v. Newman*, 14 M.J. 474 (C.M.A. 1983)). Based on his comments, specifically those regarding " 'don't come crying to me about your situation or your families[']," we do not believe MajGen [F] can be fair and impartial in this capacity. In our opinion, these comments illustrate MajGen [F]'s unwillingness to impartially listen to clemency petitions by those convicted of illegal drug use.

Appellant's defense counsel executed the affidavit referenced in the foregoing. In the affidavit defense counsel indicated that several individuals had told him about briefings in which Major General (MG) F stated that " 'individuals under his command who were caught using illegal drugs would be prosecuted to the fullest extent, and if they were convicted, they should not come crying to him about their situation or their families['],' or words to that effect."

An addendum to the staff judge advocate's post-trial recommendation, dated September 14, 2001, was silent about the convening authority's alleged comments. Despite Appellant's objections, MG F took action approving Appellant's sentence as adjudged.

Background

A convening authority is vested with substantial discretion when he or she takes action on the sentence of a court-martial. Article 60(c)(2)-(3), UCMJ, 10 U.S.C. § 860(c)(2)-(3) (2002); Rule for Courts-Martial 1107 [hereinafter R.C.M.]. As a matter of "command prerogative" a convening authority "in his sole discretion, may approve, disapprove, commute, or suspend the sentence in whole or in part." Article 60(c)(1)-(2). The convening authority's broad authority is a significant reason that we have noted that the convening authority is an accused's best hope for sentence relief. *United States v. Lee*, 50 M.J. 296, 297 (C.A.A.F. 1999); *United States v. Howard*, 48 C.M.R. 939, 944 (C.M.A. 1974).

Action on the sentence is not a legal review. Rather, a convening authority considers numerous factors and reasons in determining a sentence that is "warranted by the circumstances of the offense and appropriate for the accused." R.C.M. 1107(d)(2). The convening authority must consider any matters submitted by the accused pursuant to Article 60(b). Article 60(c)(2), UCMJ; *see also* R.C.M. 1105, 1106(f), 1107(b)(3)(A)(iii).

In the performance of post-trial duties, a convening authority acts in a "role ... similar to that of a judicial officer." *United States v. Fernandez*, 24 M.J. 77, 78 (C.M.A. 1987)(citing *United States v. Boatner*, 43 C.M.R. 216 (C.M.A. 1971)). The requirement for impartiality assures that the convening authority gives full and fair consideration to matters submitted by the accused and determines appropriate action on the sentence. "As a matter of right, each accused is entitled to an individualized, legally appropriate, and careful review of his sentence by the convening authority." *Fernandez*, 24 M.J. at 78. This right is violated where a convening authority cannot or will not approach post-trial responsibility with the requisite impartiality. Under such circumstances, a convening authority must be disqualified from taking action on a record of court-martial. *See Fernandez*, 24 M.J. at 79; *Howard*, 48 C.M.R. at 944.

Our decisions disqualifying convening authorities from taking post-trial action have fallen into two categories. In the first category, a convening authority will be disqualified if he or she is an accuser, has a personal interest in the outcome of the case, or has a personal bias toward the accused. ... In the second category, we have found convening authorities to be disqualified if they display an inelastic attitude toward the performance of their post-trial responsibility. *See, e.g., Fernandez*, 24 M.J. at 79; *Howard*, 48 C.M.R. at 944. We review de novo claims that a convening authority was disqualified from taking action on a court-martial sentence. See *Conn*, 6 M.J. at 353.

Discussion

Appellant has not argued that MG F was an accuser or possessed a personal, unofficial interest in Appellant's case. Rather, Appellant claims that the convening authority's comments "reflected his animosity toward drug users and his inelastic attitude about the clemency process as a whole." The Government responds that "[w]hile Major General [F's] statements were strong, they do not demonstrate a fixed and inelastic attitude toward dealing with clemency petitions." The Government has not disputed the fact that MG F made the comments attributed to him. Thus, for purposes of this appeal, we will assume that MG F made comments substantially as reported by trial defense counsel. We proceed to review those comments to determine whether MG F possessed an inflexible, disqualifying attitude toward his post-trial responsibilities.

It is not disqualifying for a convening authority to express disdain for illegal drugs and their adverse effect upon good order and discipline in the command. A commanding officer or convening authority fulfilling his or her responsibility to maintain good order and discipline in a military organization need not appear indifferent to crime. Adopting a strong anti-crime position, manifesting an awareness of criminal issues within a command, and taking active steps to deter crime are consonant with the oath to support the Constitution; they do not per se disqualify a convening authority. . . .

    * * *

In the instant case, MG F made direct reference to his post-trial role, asserting that those convicted of using drugs "should not come crying to him about their situations or their families[']." We believe that these words reflect an inflexible attitude toward the proper fulfillment of post-trial responsibilities in cases involving convictions for wrongful use of controlled substances. . . . MG F's comments lacked balance and transcended a legitimate command concern for crime or unlawful drugs.

Regardless of the nature of the offense, a convicted servicemember is entitled to individualized consideration of his case post-trial. That individualized consideration must be by a neutral convening authority capable of fulfilling his or her statutory responsibilities. Statements reflecting an unwillingness to consider each case fully and individually create a perception that a convicted servicemember will be denied the material right to individualized post-trial consideration and action. Where a convening authority reveals that the door to a full and fair post-trial review process is closed, we have held that the convening authority must be disqualified.

In *Howard*, the convening authority issued a letter communicating his views to convicted drug dealers. In that letter, he informed them that their pleas for clemency would be answered in the following manner: " 'No, you are going to the Disciplinary Barracks at Fort Leavenworth for the full term of your sentence and your punitive discharge will stand.' Drug peddlers, is that clear?", 48 C.M.R. at 943. Our Court held that the convening authority was disqualified from taking action on those cases because his statement demonstrated an inelastic attitude toward their clemency requests. *Id.* at 192, 48 C.M.R. at 944.

In *United States v. Wise*, 20 C.M.R. 188 (C.M.A. 1955), we found that a convening authority's policy that "he would not consider the retention in the military service of any individual who had been sentenced to a punitive discharge," to be "contrary to the intent and spirit of the Uniform Code of Military Justice and the provisions of the Manual[.]" *Id.* at 474, 476, 20 C.M.R. at 190, 192. In both cases, the convening authority "set [ ] forth in unmistakable terms" an unwillingness to apply required standards and give individualized consideration during the post-trial review process. *Howard*, 48 C.M.R. at 943. *See also United States v. Walker*, 56 M.J. 617 (A.F. Ct. Crim. App. 2001).

The plain meaning of MG F's words is equally as "unmistakable." He erected a barrier to clemency appeals by convicted drug users who wished to have "their situation or families[']" considered; he said, "Don't come." He revealed his attitude toward the clemency process under such circumstances; he considered pleas for sentence relief as "crying." Finally, his words reflected that the barrier and attitude related directly to his post-trial role as a convening authority: "Don't come crying *to me*." These words unmistakably reflect an inelastic attitude and predisposition to approve certain adjudged sentences. This attitude is the antithesis of the neutrality required of a "commander's prerogative that is taken in the interests of justice, discipline, mission requirements, clemency, or other appropriate reasons." *Id.* at 618 (citations omitted).

The Government has called to our attention a court-martial order reflecting that MG F provided relief in the form of reducing forfeitures for another Airman convicted, pursuant to his pleas, of using and distributing ecstasy. We need not decide whether the convening authority's action in a separate case would be sufficient to dispel evidence of an inelastic attitude. The bare order in that case does not provide information about the facts and circumstances of that case, including the timing of the convening authority's action in relation to the command briefings at issue here, nor are we privy to any circumstances surrounding the clemency or plea bargaining process in that case. Therefore, we are not persuaded that MG F in fact possessed the required impartiality with regard to his post-trial responsibilities.

Decision

The decision of the United States Air Force Court of Criminal Appeals is reversed, and the action of the convening authority is set aside. The case is returned to the Judge Advocate General of the Air Force for a new review and action before a different convening authority.

Point for Discussion

In the *Davis* case, the court finds that MG F's words reflect an "inelastic attitude and predisposition to approve certain adjudged sentences" and the government argues that the convening authority's action in another case is evidence that MG F did not have an inelastic attitude. Why is this not sufficient? Could MG F have taken corrective action prior to taking action in this case? What are some examples of corrective action the convening authority could have taken, if any?

10-4. Post-Trial Processing Time

In addition to the previously described military justice post-trial procedural requirements, the Due Process clause of the Fifth Amendment to the Constitution also requires that an accused's court-martial receive timely post-trial processing and appellate review. Service courts can ensure timeliness by granting relief for post-trial delay by using their UCMJ, Article 66(c) authority to review cases for sentence appropriateness. As the following cases depict, Service courts may grant relief pursuant to Article 66(c), if an accused's case is not expeditiously processed from sentence to action.

The Court of Appeals for the Armed Forces in *United States v. Tardif*, 57 M.J. 219 (C.A.A.F. 2002), indicated that prejudice is not required if the post-trial delay is unreasonable and unexplained, because Article 66(c) does not require that Service courts find that an error occurred that materially prejudiced the accused's substantial rights (material prejudice is the standard required pursuant to the Service courts' Article 59(a) authority). The C.A.A.F. in *United States v. Moreno*, 63 M.J. 129 (C.A.A.F. 2006), subsequently provided specific guidance on post-trial processing time requirements. The *Moreno* Court announced that there would be a presumption of unreasonable delay for cases completed after June 11, 2006 that either: 1) did not have initial action taken within 120 days of trial completion; 2) were not docketed within 30 days of the convening authority's action; or 3) were not reviewed by the Service court of appeals within 18 months of docketing. *Id.* Once this presumption of unreasonable post-trial delay is met, the Service courts must balance the following factors: "1) length of the delay; 2) the reasons for the delay; 3) the appellant's assertion of the right to timely review and appeal; and 4) prejudice." *Id.* at 135. Subsequent to the *Moreno* case, the C.A.A.F. determined that appellate courts need not conduct this balancing analysis even when the post-trial delay is unreasonable, if the court decides that any error was harmless beyond a reasonable doubt. *See United States v. Harrow*, 65 M.J. 190 (C.A.A.F. 2007).

UNITED STATES v. TARDIF
Court of Appeals for the Armed Forces
57 M.J. 219 (C.A.A.F. 2002)

Judge GIERKE delivered the opinion of the Court.

A general court-martial composed of officer and enlisted members convicted appellant [Food Service Specialist Third Class Sean M. Tardif, U.S. Coast Guard], contrary to his pleas, of a 12–day unauthorized absence and assault on a child under the age of sixteen years (two specifications), in violation of Articles 86 and 128, Uniform Code of Military Justice (UCMJ), 10 U.S.C. §§ 886 and 928, respectively. The adjudged sentence provides for a dishonorable discharge, confinement for three years, total forfeitures, and reduction to the lowest enlisted grade. The convening authority reduced the confinement to 24 months but otherwise approved the sentence.

The Court of Criminal Appeals set aside the conviction of unauthorized absence and reassessed and affirmed the sentence. 55 M.J. 666 (2001). On reconsideration, the court below granted appellant 12 days of confinement credit under *United States v. Allen,* 17 M.J. 126 (C.M.A. 1984). 54 M.J. 954 and 55 M.J. 670 (2001).

This Court granted review of the following issue:

WHETHER THE COAST GUARD COURT OF CRIMINAL APPEALS ERRED IN CONCLUDING THAT APPELLANT HAD NOT BEEN PREJUDICED BY EXCESSIVE POST–TRIAL DELAY WHERE THE COURT BELOW CONCLUDED THAT THE DELAY WAS BOTH "UNEXPLAINED AND UNREASONABLE" AND "CASTS A SHADOW OF UNFAIRNESS OVER OUR MILITARY JUSTICE SYSTEM."

For the reasons set out below, we hold that a Court of Criminal Appeals has authority under Article 66(c), UCMJ, 10 U.S.C. § 866(c), to grant appropriate relief for unreasonable and unexplained post-trial delays. We further hold that this authority under Article 66(c) is distinct from the court's authority under Article 59(a), UCMJ, 10 U.S.C. § 859(a), to overturn a finding or sentence "on the ground of an error of law[.]" Finally, we hold that the court's authority to grant relief under Article 66(c) does not require a predicate holding under Article 59(a) that "the error materially prejudices the substantial rights of the accused." Because the court below considered itself constrained from granting relief by Article 59(a) and did not consider the impact of the post-trial delays in its review under Article 66(c), we remand the case for further consideration.

Appellate History

The chronology of post-trial events in appellant's case is as follows:

DATE	ACTION	DAYS ELAPSED
October 29, 1999	Appellant sentenced	0
October 29, 1999	Confinement deferred	0
November 5, 1999	Deferment ends	7 days
December 21, 1999	Military Judge receives record of trial	53 days
February 7, 2000	Record authenticated	101 days
March 23, 2000	Record served on Defense Counsel (DC)	145 Days
April 10, 2000	Recommendation of Staff Judge Advocate (SJA) prepared	163 days
May 15, 2000	DC responds to SJA recommendation	198 days
June 9, 2000	Convening Authority's action	223 days
Oct 2, 2000	Record forwarded to Headquarters, U.S. Coast Guard	338 days
November 1, 2000	Record received at Coast Guard Headquarters	368 days
November 17, 2000	Record referred to Coast Guard Court of Criminal Appeals	384 days

The court below focused on the 115 days that elapsed after the convening authority's action and before the record was forwarded to Coast Guard Headquarters. Concluding that the delay was "unexplained and unreasonable," and that it "casts a shadow of unfairness over our military justice system," the court nevertheless held that it was without authority to grant relief. Citing this Court's decisions in *United States v. Hudson,* 46 M.J. 226 (1997), *United States v. Jenkins,* 38 M.J. 287 (C.M.A. 1993), and *United States v. Banks,* 7 M.J. 92 (C.M.A. 1979), the court below concluded that "an appellant must show that the delay, no matter how extensive or unreasonable, prejudiced his substantial rights." 55 M.J. at 668. Chief Judge Baum dissented from the decision to not grant relief for the excessive delay in forwarding the case to the Court of Criminal Appeals. In Chief Judge Baum's view, no more than 21 months of confinement should have been approved. *Id.* at 669.

Before this Court, appellant argued that the court below applied the wrong standard of review by focusing on Article 59(a) instead of Article 66(c). Appellant requested that his case be remanded to the court below for consideration under Article 66(c), with instructions that unexplained and unreasonable post-trial delay is an appropriate factor for that court to consider in determining what sentence "should be approved," regardless of whether appellant has established legal prejudice.

The Government asserted that appellant was not harmed by the delay, and that it would be a windfall for appellant if he were granted sentence relief without showing that he has been harmed. The Government conceded, however, that if an appellant has suffered "harm" falling short of "prejudice" within the meaning of Article 59(a), a Court of Criminal Appeals may grant appropriate relief through its review of sentence appropriateness under Article 66(c).

The U.S. Army Government Appellate Division, as *amicus curiae,* urged this Court to hold that a Court of Criminal Appeals must be convinced that there was material prejudice to a substantial right under Article 59(a) before it grants relief for unreasonable post-trial delay. It further urged this Court to hold that, if a Court of Criminal Appeals concludes there has been material prejudice to an appellant's substantial rights, it may fashion appropriate relief under Article 66(c), without setting aside the findings and sentence.

In contrast to the Coast Guard court's decision in this case, the Army Court of Criminal Appeals has held that its "broad power to moot claims of prejudice" under Article 66(c) empowers it to grant relief for excessive delays in the absence of a showing of "actual prejudice." *United States v. Collazo,* 53 M.J. 721, 727 (Army Ct. Crim. App. 2000), quoting *United States v. Wheelus,* 49 M.J. 283, 288 (1998). The Army court noted:

> [F]undamental fairness dictates that the government proceed with due diligence to execute a soldier's regulatory and statutory post-trial processing rights and to secure the convening authority's action as expeditiously as possible, given the totality of the circumstances in that soldier's case.

* * *

Discussion

1. *Legal Context*

A brief legal history is necessary to place the granted issue in context. This Court has long recognized that an accused has a right to timely review of the findings and sentence. . . .

In *United States v. Burton,* 21 U.S.C.MA 112, 44 CMR 166 (1971), ... This Court established a presumption of an Article 10 [speedy trial] violation whenever an accused is held in pretrial confinement for more than three months. Under the *Burton* rule, there was a "heavy burden on the Government to show diligence, and in the absence of such a showing the charges [would] be dismissed." *Id.* at 118, 44 CMR at 172.

In *Dunlap v. Convening Authority,* 23 U.S.C.MA 135, 48 CMR 751 (1974), . . . this Court concluded that the same considerations underlying the *Burton* rule for pretrial delays should be applied to post-trial delays. Thus, this Court held that "a presumption of a denial of speedy disposition of the case will arise when the accused is continuously under restraint after trial and the convening authority does not promulgate his formal and final action within 90 days of the date of such restraint after completion of trial." *Id.* at 138, 48 CMR at 754. . . . .

In *Banks, supra,* the Judge Advocate General of the Army certified an issue challenging the correctness of the lower court's decision to set aside a conviction and sentence for violation of the *Dunlap* rule by one day. This Court upheld the lower court's decision but announced a prospective abandonment of the *Dunlap* rule and a return to the rule requiring a showing of prejudice. 7 M.J. at 93–94.

     * * *

The pleadings in this case present two issues:

(1) Whether a Court of Criminal Appeals has authority under Article 66(c) to grant relief for excessive post-trial delay, whether or not the delay has "materially prejudiced [the appellant's] substantial rights"; and

(2) Whether a Court of Criminal Appeals has authority to grant relief short of dismissal of the charges if it concludes that there has been excessive post-trial delay.

These issues involve interpretation of Articles 59(a) and 66(c), and thus they present issues of law, which we review *de novo.*

2. *Authority of Courts of Criminal Appeals*

Unlike our Court's limited authority to review sentences under Article 67, a Court of Criminal Appeals has broad authority under Article 66(c) to review and modify sentences. Article 66(c) provides in pertinent part as follows:

> [The Court of Criminal Appeals] may affirm only such findings of guilty and the sentence or such part or amount of the sentence, as it finds correct in law and fact and determines, on the basis of the entire record, should be approved.

     * * *

Our Court has consistently recognized the broad power of the Courts of Criminal Appeals to protect an accused. . . . we have consistently recognized the "broad power" of a Court of Criminal Appeals "to moot claims of prejudice by 'affirm [ing] only such findings of guilty and the sentence or such part or amount of the sentence, as it finds correct in law and fact and determines, on the basis of the entire record, should be approved.' " *Wheelus,* 49 M.J. at 288, quoting Art. 66(c); *see also United States v. Higbie,* 12 U.S.C.MA 298, 30 CMR 298 (1961) (recognizing power of Board of Review to reduce sentence in order to moot issue whether convening authority considered a dismissed charge and specification in his review of the adjudged sentence).

However, the power of the Courts of Criminal Appeals is not without limits. Article 59(a) provides: "A finding or sentence of court-martial may not be held incorrect on the ground of an error of law unless the error materially prejudices the substantial rights of the accused." Article 59(a) was intended by Congress to preclude reversals for minor technical errors. *See United States v. Powell,* 49 M.J. 460, 462 (1998). In accordance with Article 67, this Court reviews the sentencing decisions of the Courts of Criminal Appeals for "obvious miscarriages of justice or abuses of discretion." *See United States v. Jones,* 39 M.J. 315, 317 (C.M.A. 1994).

Based on the legislative and judicial history of Articles 59(a) and 66(c), we conclude that the power and duty of a Court of Criminal Appeals to review sentence appropriateness under Article 66(c) is separate and distinct from its power and duty to review a sentence for legality under Article 59(a). Considered together, Articles 59(a) and 66(c) "bracket" the authority of a Court of Criminal Appeals. Article 59(a) constrains the authority to reverse "on the ground of an error of law." Article 66(c) is a broader, three-pronged constraint on the court's authority to affirm. Before it may affirm, the court must be satisfied that the findings and sentence are (1) "correct in law," and (2) "correct in fact." Even if these first two prongs are satisfied, the court may affirm only so much of the findings and sentence as it "determines, on the basis of the entire record, should be approved." *See Powell, supra* at 464–65. The first prong pertains to errors of law and, as such, it also implicates Article 59(a). The second and third prongs do not involve errors of law and, thus, do not implicate Article 59(a). Based on this statutory analysis, we agree with the Army court's conclusion in *Collazo* that a Court of Criminal Appeals has authority under Article 66(c) to grant relief for excessive post-trial delay without a showing of "actual prejudice" within the meaning of Article 59(a), if it deems relief appropriate under the circumstances. 53 M.J. at 727.

Thus, we hold that, in addition to its determination that no legal error occurred within the meaning of Article 59(a), the court below was required to determine what findings and sentence "should be approved," based on all the facts and circumstances reflected in the record, including the unexplained and unreasonable post-trial delay. Accordingly, we conclude that a remand is necessary so that the court below can exercise its broad authority under Article 66(c) to determine whether relief is warranted and, if so, what relief should be granted.

3. *Remedies for Excessive Post–Trial Delay*

The argument of *amicus curiae* raises the additional issue whether a Court of Criminal Appeals has authority to grant relief short of dismissal of the charges if it finds excessive post-trial delay. This argument reflects the longstanding concern of our Court and the Courts of Criminal Appeals about the draconian remedy required by *Dunlap* and its progeny for excessive post-trial delay.

* * *

Before this Court decided *Dunlap,* denial of the right to speedy trial resulted in dismissal of the charges only if reversible trial errors occurred and it was impossible to cure those errors at a rehearing because of the excessive post-trial delay. . . . . In *United States v. Gray,* 22 U.S.C.MA 443, 445, 47 CMR 484, 486 (1973), this Court repeated this principle:

> [B]efore ordering a dismissal of the charges because of post-trial delay there must be some error in the proceedings which requires that a rehearing be held and that because of the delay appellant would be either prejudiced in the presentation of his case at a rehearing or that no useful purpose would otherwise be served by continuing the proceedings.
>
> * * *

We conclude that the *Dunlap* "all-or-nothing" remedy for post-trial delays was laid to rest in *Banks.* We further conclude that appellate courts are not limited to either tolerating the intolerable or giving an appellant a windfall. The Courts of Criminal Appeals have authority under Article 66(c) to . . . an appropriate remedy, if any is warranted, to the circumstances of the case.

Finally, we note that counsel at the trial level are particularly well-situated to protect the interests of their clients by addressing post-trial delay issues before action by the convening authority. Trial counsel can ensure that the record contains an explanation for what otherwise might appear to be an unreasonable delay. Defense counsel can protect the interests of the accused through complaints to the military judge before authentication or to the convening authority after authentication and before action. After the convening authority's action, extraordinary writs may be appropriate in some circumstances. Appellate relief under Article 66(c) should be viewed as the last recourse to vindicate, where appropriate, an appellant's right to timely post-trial processing and appellate review.

Decision

The decision of the United States Coast Guard Court of Criminal Appeals is set aside. The record of trial is returned to the General Counsel of the Department of Transportation for remand to the Court of Criminal Appeals for reconsideration in light of this opinion. Thereafter, Article 67 will apply.

CRAWFORD, Chief Judge (dissenting):

The majority interprets Articles 66(c) and 59(a) in a manner that is contrary to the principles of statutory construction and legislative intent, as well as inconsistent with 50 years of established practice and case law. In so doing, the majority offers an incomplete recitation of the legislative history of Articles 66(c) and 59(a) and ignores the practical effects of its decision. The majority's misreading of Article 59 should not be further exacerbated. Unless there has been a substantial violation of an appellant's rights, the Courts of Criminal Appeals may not use their supervisory authority to grant further relief to the appellant. *United States v. Hasting,* 461 U.S. 499, 505 (1983). Instead, this Court should encourage corrective action by those responsible for post-trial delays. *Id.* at 506 n. 5. Because the majority is engaging in broad judicial rulemaking by amending the Code to expand Article 66(c) and contract Article 59(a), and thereby essentially creating a power of equity in the court below, I must respectfully dissent.

* * *

The starting point for interpreting a statute is, of course, the plain meaning of that statute. In addition, there are a number of factors that provide a framework for engaging in statutory interpretation. These include the contemporaneous history of the statute; the contemporaneous interpretation of the statute; and subsequent legislative action or inaction regarding the statute. These factors provide a background of the existing customs, practices, and rights and obligations against which to read the statute. Applying these principles of statutory interpretation to Articles 66(c) and 59(a) yields a different result from that reached by the majority.

Article 66(c) provides as follows:

In a case referred to it, the Court of Criminal Appeals may act only with respect to the findings and sentence as approved by the convening authority. It may affirm only such findings of guilty and the sentence or such part or amount of the sentence, as it finds correct in law and fact and determines, on the basis of the entire record, should be approved. In considering the record, it may weigh the evidence, judge the credibility of witnesses, and determine controverted questions of fact, recognizing that the trial court saw and heard the witnesses.

Additionally, Article 59(a) provides:

A finding or sentence of court-martial may not be held incorrect on the ground of an error of law unless the error materially prejudices the substantial rights of the accused.

* * *

The plain meaning of Article 66 is that the Court of Criminal Appeals may "affirm only ... findings and sentences" based on the "entire record." We have interpreted this statute to allow Courts of Criminal Appeals, based on the entire record of trial, to modify or dismiss charges based on a lack of factual sufficiency, as well as reassess sentences found to be inappropriate. But we have not allowed these courts to go outside the record, for example, by considering two nonjudicial punishments that were inadmissible at trial. *See United States v. Redhouse,* 53 M.J. 246 (2000)(summary disposition). Nor have we allowed the Courts of Criminal Appeals to grant suspension of the punishment. *See, e.g., United States v. Darville,* 5 M.J. 1 (C.M.A. 1978).

Additionally, the plain meaning of the statute in the context of its enactment in 1950 does not support the majority's position. When Congress wanted to grant discretionary power unrelated to Article 59, it knew how to do so. . . .

Authority was not granted to the Courts of Criminal Appeals to grant windfalls unrelated to Article 59 or act in their "sole discretion." ... Based upon the plain language of the statute and the legislative history, it is improbable that if Congress was asked, it would grant the authority to the Courts of Criminal Appeals to reduce sentences because of post-trial delay, even though an appellant was not prejudiced.

Contemporaneous Interpretation. In interpreting Articles 66(c) and 59(a), we should examine their construction for the last 50 years by this Court and intermediate service appellate courts. None has reached the conclusion reached by the Army court in *Collazo.* Additionally, there has been no change to the statutes that might precipitate a statutory reinterpretation. The fact that this remedy has not been previously proposed is good evidence that such was not the intent of Congress.

Legislative Action or Inaction. If Congress wanted to establish the remedy which the majority sanctions, it would have done so at the time of the UCMJ's enactment, or at any subsequent time that it became dissatisfied with decisions from the courts concerning post-trial delays. Numerous changes to the UCMJ have been enacted by Congress over the last 50 years, many in response to various judicial decisions. No changes have been forthcoming regarding the impact of post-trial delays. The majority's interpretation simply does not relate to the statutory objectives sought by Congress.

Practical Effects. There are practical reasons for not giving this authority to the lower courts. Contrary to the majority's assertion, final authority will not rest with the Courts of Criminal Appeals. Final review by this Court will be required to determine whether the lower courts abused their discretion. Neither the courts below nor this Court should be placed in the position of determining what constitutes a request for a delay, what circumstances justify delay, what constitutes extraordinary circumstances, and so forth. We do not have the flexibility or ability to gather facts that the President and his advisors have in exercising their rulemaking authority. Article 36, UCMJ, 10 U.S.C. § 836, is a clear grant of authority to the President to formulate these procedural rules. We should not be flirting with amending a statute or the Manual. That role should be left for Congress and the Executive Branch.

* * *

For all of the foregoing reasons, I would affirm the court below.

[Judge Sullivan's dissenting opinion is omitted.—Eds.]

Point for Discussion

One author criticizes the reasoning of *Tardif* and an Army Court of Criminal Appeal decision, *United States v. Bauerbach,* 55 M.J. 501 (Army Ct. Crim. App. 2001), which reached the same conclusion, as follows:

Both CAAF in *Tardif* and the Army court in *Bauerbach* acknowledged that the authority of the service courts to grant relief due to an error of law is separate and distinct from their authority to determine an appropriate sentence. Yet, inexplicably, neither court explains how you can merge these two separate and distinct authorities or how stating that a court may grant relief by finding a sentence inappropriate due to a legal error rather than granting relief for the legal error itself is anything other than a purely semantic difference. If a court reduces a sentence because it is inappropriate due to a legal error (i.e., unreasonable post-trial delay), then it is granting sentence relief on the ground of an error of law, regardless of how one chooses to characterize it.

William J. Nelson, *A Right Way and a Wrong Way: Remedying Excessive Post-Trial Delay in Light of* Tardif, Moreno, *and* Toohey, 198 Mil. L. Rev. 1, 23-24 (2008). Is this argument correct? If not, what is a court doing when it grants relief for post-trial processing delay when it reduces a sentence, correcting legal errors or adjusting an inappropriate sentence?

UNITED STATES v. MORENO
Court of Appeals for the Armed Forces
63 M.J. 129 (C.A.A.F. 2006)

Judge ERDMANN delivered the opinion of the court.

Corporal Javier A. Moreno Jr. [U.S. Marine Corps] was tried by general court-martial for the offense of rape in violation of Article 120, Uniform Code of Military Justice (UCMJ), 10 U.S.C. § 920 (2000). Moreno entered a plea of not guilty but was convicted by members who subsequently sentenced him to a dishonorable discharge, confinement for six years, forfeiture of all pay and allowances, and reduction to the lowest enlisted grade. The convening authority approved the sentence and the United States Navy–Marine Corps Court of Criminal Appeals affirmed the findings and sentence in an unpublished decision. *United States v. Moreno*, No. NMCCA 200100715, 2004 CCA LEXIS 118 (N.M. Ct. Crim. App. May 13, 2004). We granted review of three issues.

* * *

III.

WHETHER APPELLANT'S DUE PROCESS RIGHT TO TIMELY REVIEW OF HIS APPEAL HAS BEEN DENIED.

* * *

Due process entitles convicted servicemembers to a timely review and appeal of court-martial convictions. *Toohey v. United States*, 60 M.J. 100, 101 (C.A.A.F. 2004). Moreno asserts that he was denied due process because there was unreasonable delay in the 1,688 days between the end of his trial and the date upon which the United States Navy–Marine Corps Court of Criminal Appeals rendered its decision in his case. We conclude that Moreno was denied his due process right to speedy appellate review and we find that under the circumstances of this case relief is warranted.

BACKGROUND

Moreno worked in the comptroller's disbursing office. Among the members detailed to Moreno's court-martial was LtCol F, the deputy comptroller. Lieutenant Colonel F was advised of the incident that gave rise to the rape charge by Moreno's officer-in-charge. Lieutenant Colonel F decided to look into the incident further so that he could brief the comptroller. In the course of his inquiry into the incident, LtCol F became aware of information that had been entered into various logbooks. He spoke to some of the duty officers who had knowledge of the incident and he read various articles that were published in *Stars and Stripes*. Lieutenant Colonel F described his efforts to gather this information as "simply fact finding. You know, I wanted to be able to get all the—find out what was being reported in the logbook and just so I had a complete picture before I talked to my boss on what he would be hearing Monday morning."

In addition to his personal inquiries into the incident, LtCol F became aware of Moreno's co-accused's case based on what he read in *Stars and Stripes*. Lieutenant Colonel F's pretrial knowledge of the incident and the subsequent criminal cases included: (1) that the incident involved drinking at the club; (2) that the victim may have been drugged; (3) that there had been sexual contact; (4) that both Moreno and his co-accused were placed in pretrial confinement; (5) that the co-accused could be a witness at Moreno's trial; and (6) that there were delays in Moreno's trial relating to obtaining the co-accused's presence at Moreno's trial.

* * *

Moreno was sentenced on September 29, 1999. Two hundred eight days later, the 746–page record of trial was authenticated by the military judge. On January 31, 2001, 490 days after completion of the trial, the convening authority took action. Seventy-six days later, the case was docketed at the Navy–Marine Corps Court of Criminal Appeals.

The Navy–Marine Corps Court of Criminal Appeals granted eighteen motions for enlargement of time to Moreno's appellate defense attorney before the defense brief was filed on March 20, 2003 (702 days from docketing). The Government filed an answer brief on October 29, 2003 (223 days from submission of Moreno's brief). The Court of Criminal Appeals issued its unpublished decision on May 13, 2004 (197 days from the completion of briefing). Four years, seven months and fourteen days (1,688 days) elapsed between the completion of trial and the completion of Moreno's appeal of right under Article 66, UCMJ, 10 U.S.C. § 866 (2000).

DISCUSSION

Implied Bias

Moreno asserts that LtCol F's presence on his court-martial panel undermined public confidence in military justice and that, under the liberal grant mandate, the military judge should have granted the challenge for cause.

* * *

From the outset, LtCol F took an active interest in this case. He took it upon himself to seek out information so that he could get a "complete picture" to brief his boss, the comptroller. His preparations for the briefing included conducting personal interviews of duty officers and reading entries in various log books. Once he had gathered the information to brief the comptroller, his interest in Moreno's case did not wane. He read about the charges against Moreno in newspapers and also read about the court-martial of Moreno's co-accused, who was acquitted of wrongdoing for the same incident. [5]

We believe that an objective observer would perceive that LtCol F possessed an excessive level of pretrial knowledge about the incident to sit as an impartial panel member. . . .

Under these circumstances—where LtCol F had investigated the incident, weighed facts, made recommendations based on his conclusions and continued to follow both this case and the case of Moreno's co-accused in the press—an objective observer could reasonably question whether LtCol F could come to any different conclusions based solely on evidence presented in court. An observer could also reasonably question whether LtCol F would contradict his initial conclusions and recommendations to the comptroller if warranted by the evidence.

An objective observer could harbor a reasonable concern that as president of the court-martial, LtCol F would exert influence over other court-martial members arising from his in-depth personal knowledge of the facts rather than from the evidence presented in court. . . .

Thus, we hold that there is a substantial doubt that this trial was by a panel of members who were fair and impartial and the military judge therefore erred by denying the challenge for cause against LtCol F.

Speedy Post–Trial and Appellate Review

Moreno contends that the 1,688 days that elapsed between the completion of his court-martial and the decision of the Court of Criminal Appeals was unreasonable and denied him due process. Moreno argues that he had legitimate claims of error in his case and that the delay has denied him the opportunity for meaningful relief. The Government counters that the time involved in Moreno's post-trial processing and appeal was not unreasonable. Alternatively, the Government asserts that even if the delay is unreasonable,

---

[5] Moreno's co-actor was acquitted of rape on August 19, 1999. The following day, an article appeared in *Stars and Stripes* captioned "Okinawa Marine innocent of rape." On August 27, 1999, *Stars and Stripes* reported that Moreno's trial would proceed despite the co-actor's acquittal.

Moreno's due process rights have not been violated. The Supreme Court has recognized "the procedures used in deciding appeals must comport with the demands of the Due Process and Equal Protection Clauses of the Constitution." . . .

This court has recognized that convicted servicemembers have a due process right to timely review and appeal of courts-martial convictions. . . .

In conducting this review we have adopted the four factors set forth in *Barker v. Wingo,* 407 U.S. 514, 530 (1972):(1) the length of the delay; (2) the reasons for the delay; (3) the appellant's assertion of the right to timely review and appeal; and (4) prejudice. *United States v. Jones,* 61 M.J. 80, 83 (C.A.A.F. 2005); *Toohey,* 60 M.J. at 102. While *Barker* addressed speedy trial issues in a pretrial, Sixth Amendment context, its four-factor analysis has been broadly adopted for reviewing post-trial delay due process claims.

Once this due process analysis is triggered by a facially unreasonable delay, the four factors are balanced, with no single factor being required to find that post-trial delay constitutes a due process violation.

* * *

1. *Length of the delay*

Initially, unless the delay is facially unreasonable, the full due process analysis will not be triggered. . . . In this case we conclude that the overall period of post-trial review and appeal, 1,688 days, is facially unreasonable and thus we will proceed to the remaining *Barker* factors.

2. *Reasons for the delay*

Under this factor we look at the Government's responsibility for any delay, as well as any legitimate reasons for the delay, including those attributable to an appellant. In assessing the reasons for any particular delay, we examine each stage of the post-trial period because the reasons for the delay may be different at each stage and different parties are responsible for the timely completion of each segment.

The 490 days between the end of trial and the convening authority's action is excessive for the post-trial processing of this case. The processing in this segment is completely within the control of the Government and no exceptional circumstances have been offered to explain this delay. *See United States v. Bigelow,* 57 M.J. 64, 68–69 (C.A.A.F. 2002). It is striking that this period is over five times longer than that deemed reasonable by this court when we established the ninety-day rule in *Dunlap v. Convening Authority,* 48 C.M.R. 751 (C.M.A. 1974). The seventy-six days between action and docketing the case before the Court of Criminal Appeals is also unexplained. Delays involving this essentially clerical task have been categorized as "the least defensible of all" post-trial delays. *United States v. Dunbar,* 31 M.J. 70, 73 (C.M.A. 1990).

The longest delay in this case—925 days—involves the period from which the case was docketed at the Court of Criminal Appeals until briefing was complete. The Government claims that Moreno is directly responsible for the almost two years it took to file his brief at the Court of Criminal Appeals. The record reflects that appellate defense counsel sought and was granted eighteen enlargements of time within which to file a brief. Enlargement numbers four through eighteen each contained the same reason for the request: "other case load commitments."

While the Government argued that this period of delay was in Moreno's interest, there was no evidence demonstrating that the enlargements were directly attributable to Moreno or that the need for additional time arose from other factors such as the complexity of Moreno's case. The Government further argued that we should presume the delays were for Moreno's benefit, but did not provide any legal authority to support such a presumption. There is no evidence in this case that the numerous requests for delay filed by appellate defense counsel benefited Moreno or that Moreno was consulted about and agreed to these delays. "Other case load commitments" logically reflects that Moreno's case was not getting counsel's professional attention, a fact that is the very antithesis of any benefit to Moreno. We therefore decline to hold Moreno accountable for this period of delay. As we said in *Diaz*, 59 M.J. at 38:

> Appellate counsel caseloads are a result of management and administrative priorities and as such are subject to the administrative control of the Government. To allow caseloads to become a factor in determining whether appellate delay is excessive would allow administrative factors to trump the Article 66 and due process rights of appellants. To the contrary, the Government has a statutory responsibility to establish a system of appellate review under Article 66 that preserves rather than diminishes the rights of convicted servicemembers. In connection with that responsibility, the Government has a statutory duty under Article 70 to provide Petitioner with appellate defense counsel who is able to represent him in both a competent and timely manner before the Court of Criminal Appeals.

Internal footnote omitted. *See also Barker,* 407 U.S. at 531 (noting that ultimate responsibility of delay caused by negligence or overcrowded courts rests with the Government).

While appellate defense counsel's caseload is the underlying cause of much of this period of delay, responsibility for this portion of the delay and the burden placed upon appellate defense counsel initially rests with the Government. The Government must provide adequate staffing within the Appellate Defense Division to fulfill its responsibility under the UCMJ to provide competent and timely representation. *See* Article 70, UCMJ, 10 U.S.C. § 870 (2000). Ultimately the timely management and disposition of cases docketed at the Courts of Criminal Appeals is a responsibility of the Courts of Criminal Appeals. Therefore, we decline to hold Moreno responsible for the lack of "institutional vigilance" which should have been exercised in this case. *See Diaz,* 59 M.J. at 39–40.

The final period of delay is the 197 days from submission of the final briefs to the Court of Criminal Appeals' decision. We will apply a more flexible review of this period, recognizing that it involves the exercise of the Court of Criminal Appeals' judicial decision-making authority. We find that a period of slightly over six months is not an unreasonable time for review by the Court of Criminal Appeals. Thus, under *Barker's* second factor—reasons for the delay—the unreasonable delays in this case are either unexplained or the responsibility of the Government. There is no reason given for the unreasonable delays in getting this case from trial to the convening authority for action and in docketing the case before the Court of Criminal Appeals after action. The Government bears responsibility for unreasonable delay during appeal occasioned by the workload of appellate defense counsel. We conclude that this second *Barker* factor weighs heavily in favor of Moreno.

3. *Assertion of the right to a timely review and appeal*

This factor calls upon us to examine an aspect of Moreno's role in this delay. Moreno did not object to any delay or assert his right to timely review and appeal prior to his arrival at this court. . . .

We do not believe this factor weighs heavily against Moreno under the circumstances of this case. The obligation to ensure a timely review and action by the convening authority rests upon the Government and Moreno is not required to complain in order to receive timely convening authority action. *United States v. Bodkins,* 60 M.J. 322, 323–24 (C.A.A.F. 2004). Similarly, Moreno bears no responsibility for transmitting the record of trial to the Court of Criminal Appeals after action. Nor is it unreasonable to assume, as Moreno argues, that a convicted person wants anything other than a prompt resolution of his appeal. *See Harris II,* 15 F.3d at 1563.

We also recognize the paradox of requiring Moreno to complain about appellate delay either to his appellate counsel who sought multiple enlargements of time because of other case commitments or to the appellate court that granted the enlargements on a routine basis. While this factor weighs against Moreno, the weight against him is slight given that the primary responsibility for speedy processing rests with the Government and those to whom he could complain were the ones responsible for the delay.

4. *Prejudice*

In *Barker,* 407 U.S. at 532, the Supreme Court recognized a framework to analyze the "prejudice" factor in a speedy trial context. We agree with the Fifth Circuit's modification of that framework for analyzing prejudice in a due process post-trial delay analysis:

> In the case of appellate delay, prejudice should be assessed in light of the interests of those convicted of crimes to an appeal of their convictions unencumbered by excessive delay. We identify three similar interests for

prompt appeals: (1) prevention of oppressive incarceration pending appeal; (2) minimization of anxiety and concern of those convicted awaiting the outcome of their appeals; and (3) limitation of the possibility that a convicted person's grounds for appeal, and his or her defenses in case of reversal and retrial, might be impaired.

Rheuark, 628 F.2d at 303 n. 8; *see also United States v. Hawkins,* 78 F.3d 348, 351 (8th Cir. 1996); *Coe v. Thurman,* 922 F.2d 528, 532 (9th Cir. 1990); *Harris II,* 15 F.3d at 1547.

a. *Oppressive Incarceration Pending Appeal*

This sub-factor is directly related to the success or failure of an appellant's substantive appeal. If the substantive grounds for the appeal are not meritorious, an appellant is in no worse position due to the delay, even though it may have been excessive. *Cody v. Henderson,* 936 F.2d 715, 720 (2d Cir. 1991). Under these circumstances, an appellant would have served the same period of incarceration regardless of the delay. *United States v. Antoine,* 906 F.2d 1379, 1382 (9th Cir. 1990). However, if an appellant's substantive appeal is meritorious and the appellant has been incarcerated during the appeal period, the incarceration may have been oppressive. *Coe,* 922 F.2d at 532.

Moreno served his full term of confinement before his appeal of right was resolved by the Court of Criminal Appeals. Before this court he has prevailed on a substantive appellate issue, his conviction will be set aside and he is entitled to a retrial. . . .

Moreno was sentenced to six years of incarceration. Although the record does not provide us with a precise release date, we can be reasonably certain that Moreno was released from confinement prior to the Court of Criminal Appeals' decision. Based on the 150 days of pretrial confinement credit and the duration of the adjudged confinement, we estimate that Moreno's minimum release date was about April, 2003. Thus, he had served at least four years in confinement, under a conviction that has now been set aside, prior to his appeal of right being decided. We therefore find that he has suffered some degree of prejudice as the result of oppressive incarceration.

b. *Anxiety and Concern*

This sub-factor involves constitutionally cognizable anxiety that arises from excessive delay. Federal courts have adopted different approaches to this "prejudice" sub-factor.

* * *

We believe that the appropriate test for the military justice system is to require an appellant to show particularized anxiety or concern that is distinguishable from the normal anxiety experienced by prisoners awaiting an appellate decision. This particularized anxiety or concern is thus related to the timeliness of the appeal, requires an appellant to demonstrate a nexus to the processing of his appellate review, and ultimately assists this court to "fashion relief in such a way as to compensate [an appellant] for the particular harm." *Burkett*, 951 F.2d at 1447. We do not believe that the anxiety that an appellant may experience is dependent upon whether his substantive appeal is ultimately successful. An appellant may suffer constitutionally cognizable anxiety regardless of the outcome of his appeal.

Moreno argues that he suffered prejudice because he was required to register as a sex offender upon his release from incarceration without the opportunity of having his appeal of right heard and decided. *See* 42 U.S.C. § 14071(a)(1)(A), (b)(6)(A) (2000). Moreno essentially argues that had his appeal been processed in a timely manner, it would have been resolved before his release from incarceration. Had Moreno's conviction been affirmed prior to his release, registration as a sex offender would have been a proper consequence of his conviction. However, Moreno argues that he has been "living under the opprobrium of guilt when he . . . has not been properly proven guilty and may indeed be innocent under the law." *Rheuark*, 628 F.2d at 304. The excessive delay in this case and our disposition of the implied bias issue lend credence to Moreno's claim that he was prejudiced by the requirement to register as a sex offender. We find that this circumstance constitutes constitutional anxiety that is distinguishable from the normal anxiety experienced by prisoners awaiting appeal and that as a result Moreno has suffered some degree of prejudice.

c. *Impairment of Ability to Present a Defense at a Rehearing*

This final sub-factor is directly related to whether an appellant has been successful on a substantive issue of the appeal and whether a rehearing has been authorized. If an appellant does not have a meritorious appeal, there obviously will be no prejudice arising from a rehearing. If, however, a conviction has been set aside and a rehearing authorized, the appellate delay encountered by the appellant may have a negative impact on his ability to prepare and present his defense at the rehearing. Due to the passage of time, witnesses may be unavailable, memories may have faded and records of trial may have been misplaced or lost.

In order to prevail on this factor an appellant must be able to specifically identify how he would be prejudiced at rehearing due to the delay. Mere speculation is not enough. *United States v. Mohawk*, 20 F.3d 1480, 1487 (9th Cir. 1994). Moreno claims that prejudice exists under this factor because of the potential harm he would suffer in the event he is successful on appeal and a rehearing is authorized. He does not, however, identify any specific harm that he would encounter at a rehearing and he has therefore failed to establish prejudice under this sub-factor.

Conclusion—Barker Factors

Because of the unreasonably lengthy delay, the lack of any constitutionally justifiable reasons for the delay, and the prejudice suffered by Moreno as a result of oppressive incarceration and anxiety, our balancing of the four *Barker* factors leads us to conclude that Moreno was denied his due process right to speedy review and appeal. Because we have found legal error and substantial prejudice to a material right, as well as a deprivation of due process, we need to consider appropriate relief. *See Jones*, 61 M.J. at 86.

Before we turn to that consideration, we address post-trial processing standards in the military justice system. Our concern for post-trial timeliness has been heightened by the number of appellate delay cases that have come before this court and cases that are pending elsewhere in the military justice system. In recognition of the due process issues involved in timely post-trial review and appeal and in response to the cases giving rise to our concerns, we will establish post-trial processing standards to be applied to cases yet to enter the post-trial and appellate processes.

Post–Trial Processing Standards

In 1974 this court adopted a "presumption of a denial of speedy disposition of the case" if a convening authority failed to take action within ninety days of trial. *Dunlap,* 48 C.M.R. at 754. Five years later this court abandoned that rule and expressed confidence that military justice had overcome the numerous circumstances giving rise to that rule

* * *

Unfortunately, our confidence that procedural protections would suffice to ensure the speedy post-trial and appellate rights of servicemembers has been eroded. It is of some concern that the Government brief asserts that the 1,688 day delay in this case was reasonable. We reject that contention and note that Moreno's case is not an isolated case that involves excessive post-trial delay issues.

This increase in processing time stands in contrast to the lower number of cases tried in the military justice system in recent years.

* * *

Nonetheless, some action is necessary to deter excessive delay in the appellate process and remedy those instances in which there is unreasonable delay and due process violations. For courts-martial completed thirty days after the date of this opinion, we will apply a presumption of unreasonable delay that will serve to trigger the *Barker* four-factor analysis where the action of the convening authority is not taken within 120 days of the completion of trial. We will apply a similar presumption of unreasonable delay for courts-martial completed thirty days after the date of this opinion where the record of trial is not docketed by the service Court of Criminal Appeals within thirty days of the convening authority's action.

For those cases arriving at the service Courts of Criminal Appeals thirty days after the date of this decision, we will apply a presumption of unreasonable delay where appellate review is not completed and a decision is not rendered within eighteen months of docketing the case before the Court of Criminal Appeals. These presumptions of unreasonable delay will be viewed as satisfying the first *Barker* factor and they will apply whether or not the appellant was sentenced to or serving confinement. It is important to note that the presumptions serve to trigger the four-part *Barker* analysis—not resolve it. The Government can rebut the presumption by showing the delay was not unreasonable. By using these presumptions we trigger an appellate analysis and allocate the burden; we do not legislate or undermine the President's rulemaking authority under Article 36, UCMJ, 10 U.S.C. § 836 (2000).

Some cases will present specific circumstances warranting additional time, thus making those periods reasonable upon assessment of the *Barker* factors. But these must be justifiable, case-specific delays supported by the circumstances of that case and not delays based upon administrative matters, manpower constraints or the press of other cases. We expect convening authorities, reviewing authorities and the Courts of Criminal Appeals to document reasons for delay and to exercise the institutional vigilance that was absent in Moreno's case.

Once the four-factor analysis is completed and those factors balanced, reviewing authorities that find a denial of speedy post-trial or appeal "should 'tailor an appropriate remedy, if any is warranted, to the circumstances of the case.' " *Jones,* 61 M.J. at 86 (quoting *United States v. Tardif,* 57 M.J. 219, 225 (C.A.A.F. 2002)). The nature of that relief will depend on the circumstances of the case, the relief requested, and may include, but is not limited to: (a) day-for-day reduction in confinement or confinement credit; (b) reduction of forfeitures; (c) set aside of portions of an approved sentence including punitive discharges; (d) set aside of the entire sentence, leaving a sentence of no punishment; (e) a limitation upon the sentence that may be approved by a convening authority following a rehearing; and (f) dismissal of the charges and specifications with or without prejudice. Clearly this range of meaningful options to remedy the denial of speedy post-trial processing provides reviewing authorities and courts with the flexibility necessary to appropriately address these situations on a case-by-case basis.

Those cases tried or received at a Court of Criminal Appeals prior to the date of this opinion and therefore not encompassed by the foregoing presumptions of unreasonable delay will continue to be reviewed on a case-by-case basis under the *Barker* due process analysis. Delays have been tolerated at all levels in the military justice system so much so that in many instances they are now considered the norm. The effect of this opinion is to provide notice that unreasonable delays that adversely impact an appellant's due process rights will no longer be tolerated.

Relief in Moreno's Case

In Moreno's case, a rehearing is the appropriate remedy for the military judge's erroneous denial of the challenge for cause against LtCol F. In considering the range of options to address the denial of Moreno's due process right to speedy review and appeal, we considered directing a day-for-day credit for each day of unreasonable and unexplained delay. Such a credit would have no meaningful effect, however, as Moreno served the full term of adjudged confinement after his initial trial.

We have also considered dismissing the charge and specification with prejudice. Dismissal would be a consideration if the delay either impaired Moreno's ability to defend against the charge at a rehearing or resulted in some other evidentiary prejudice. *See Tardif,* 57 M.J. at 224 (citing *United States v. Timmons,* 46 C.M.R. 226, 227 (C.M.A. 1973); *United States v. Gray,* 47 C.M.R. 484, 486 (C.M.A. 1973)). We find no such evidence before us. Finally, because we must set aside the sentence in order to permit a rehearing, there is no direct sentence relief that we can afford to Moreno. *Compare Jones,* 61 M.J. at 86 (this court formulated a remedy for prejudicial denial of speedy appellate review where neither the adjudged sentence nor the convening authority's action were to be set aside).

We are not, however, without power to effect appropriate relief in this case. Should there be a rehearing resulting in a conviction and new sentencing, we believe that limiting the sentence that may be approved by the convening authority will adequately afford Moreno relief for the deprivation of his speedy appellate review due process rights.

DECISION

The decision of the United States Navy–Marine Corps Court of Criminal Appeals is reversed. The findings and sentence are set aside and a rehearing may be ordered. In the event that a rehearing is held resulting in a conviction and sentence, the convening authority may approve no portion of the sentence exceeding a punitive discharge.

CRAWFORD, Judge (concurring in part and dissenting in part):

I respectfully dissent because the majority: (1) usurps the role of Congress and the President, as delegated by Congress to the executive branch by Article 36, Uniform Code of Military Justice (UCMJ), 10 U.S.C. § 836 (2000), by establishing prospective rules setting forth timelines for the post-trial processing of cases in the military justice system; and (2) misapplies the speedy trial balancing factors of *Barker v. Wingo,* 407 U.S. 514, 529–33 (1972).

I agree with the majority that the military judge should have granted the challenge for cause, and thus concur in the result.

I. Separation of Powers

     * * *

B. *Congressional Delegation*

Under Article 36, UCMJ, Congress has delegated to the President the power to prescribe rules for post-trial procedures. By establishing prospective rules setting forth timelines for post-trial processing, the majority assumes the role delegated to the President by Congress in Article 36, UCMJ, in contravention of the constitutional separation of powers doctrine.

* * *

II. Post–Trial Delay

A. *General*

While the Supreme Court has not addressed the issue of whether the Constitution guarantees a right to a speedy appeal, the lower federal courts and this Court have. "The speedy trial guarantee of the Sixth Amendment applies only to proceedings in the trial court. Our sister circuits have held, however, that a similar guarantee applies to criminal appeals via the Due Process Clause." *United States v. Smith,* 94 F.3d 204, 206 (6th Cir. 1996) (citations omitted). . . . When examining these constitutional rights, we must look at the text, the history, the tradition behind the constitutional amendments, prior precedent, and practical consequences.

* * *

B. *Applying the Barker Analysis to This Case*

1. *Length of the Delay*

In this case, there has been delay of nearly 1,700 days between the completion of Appellant's court-martial and the Court of Criminal Appeals' decision. On its face, this delay is sufficient to trigger an inquiry using the *Barker* analysis.

2. *Reasons for the Delay*

Although there were significant delays at all phases of the post-trial process in this case, the greatest portion of that delay involves the period from when the case was docketed at the Court of Criminal Appeals until the briefing was complete. It is the majority's conclusion regarding this period of delay with which I have the greatest disagreement. The appellate defense counsel requested and was granted eighteen enlargements of time in which to file a brief. The reason stated for enlargements four through eighteen was "other case load commitments." The majority refuses to hold Appellant accountable for any portion of this delay even though neither Appellant nor his defense counsel requested assistance within the appellate division or outside the appellate division from outside contractors or other services' appellate divisions to process this appeal. Despite the lack of a request for assistance because of "case load commitments," incredibly, the majority concludes "there was no evidence demonstrating that the enlargements were directly attributable to Moreno."

In my view, unless the appellate defense counsel was ineffective or was acting unethically or outside the scope of his authority, the actions he took to obtain additional delays in the filing of the appellate briefs were performed for and on behalf of Appellant. . . .

This case reinforces the wisdom of the federal and state courts placing the burden on Appellant to show prejudice. There are a number of questions to be asked of defense counsel—What other cases did you have? How did you

CH. 10 POST-TRIAL REVIEW PROCEDURES 389

stagger them? Did you prioritize the cases? What issues were present? What were the difficulties in contacting Appellant? Was there a conflict in Appellant's wishes and your desires? Did you request assistance from your supervisor?

The Government is simply not in a position to answer questions as to why the defense counsel asked for extended delays. *See United States v. Lewis*, 42 M.J. 1 (C.A.A.F. 1995). Nor can the Government answer questions regarding the impact of the requested delays on the strategy, theories, or theme of the defense. Yet, contrary to the prevailing jurisprudence of federal and state courts, the majority relieves Appellant from his burden of demonstrating actual prejudice and incredibly shifts the responsibility for the delay to the Government. Thus, the majority has created an incentive for the defense to request enlargements knowing they will not be asked these questions absent a court order.

Delay must be examined on the basis of the facts in a specific case and not based on the length of delay alone. In fact, merely asking for numerous delays has ended up benefiting Appellant. Based on the majority decision, I predict that appellate courts will receive many more requests for enlargements from appellate defense counsels in order to get the benefit of the presumption of unreasonable delay in a speedy appellate review scenario. It is incredible that while recognizing this lengthy period of time is attributable to the appellate defense counsel's requests for delay, the majority declines to hold Appellant accountable for any of it.

3. *Appellant's Assertion of His Right to a Timely Appeal*

Appellant never asserted a post-trial speedy review right or protested the length of delay in his case. While the demand rule is not conclusive in the speedy trial or appellate review context, it is extremely important in evaluating the length and reason for the delay as well as whether there is any personal prejudice. *Barker v. Wingo*, 407 U.S. 514, 531 (1972). A complaint or protest would have at least indicated to the appellate court that Appellant was dissatisfied with the pace of his appeal.

* * *

What is the Government to do? Oppose defense requests for delay because the delay will be attributed to it? Should the Courts of Criminal Appeals deny defense requests for delays for fear the delays will be attributed to it or the Government? What is next? Will we begin to see appellate defense counsel raise the issue that an appellant was denied an opportunity to present his case on appeal because his reasonable request for a delay for filing his brief was denied?

* * *

4. *Prejudice to Appellant*

With respect to assessing the fourth factor—prejudice—the Supreme Court provided further guidance. Prejudice should be evaluated "in the light of the

interests of defendants which the speedy trial right was designed to protect."
Barker, 407 U.S. at 532. The interests are:

> (i) to prevent oppressive pretrial incarceration; (ii) to minimize anxiety
> and concern of the accused; and (iii) to limit the possibility that the
> defense will be impaired. Of these, the most serious is the last, because the
> inability of a defendant adequately to prepare his case skews the fairness
> of the entire system.

Id.

* * *

a. *Prevention of Oppressive Incarceration Pending Appeal*

Generally, incarceration will be considered "oppressive" if an appellant is
confined while the appeal is pending and the substantive appeal is
meritorious. *See Cody v. Henderson,* 936 F.2d 715, 719–21 (2d Cir. 1991). In
this case, the meritorious issue addressed by the Court concerns the denial of
a challenge for cause against a court member. There were no successful issues
regarding the sufficiency of evidence or the admissibility of evidence.
Theoretically, the Government will be able to use the same evidence used at
the original trial to retry Appellant. There is no way, based on the facts and
evidence in this case, to conclude that Appellant's incarceration was
oppressive or out of the ordinary for a person convicted of an offense and
sentenced to confinement.

Furthermore, Appellant was sentenced to six years of confinement. The
majority, without any documentary evidence on which to rely, theorizes that
Appellant was released from confinement after about four years of
confinement. Assuming the majority is correct, apparently the delay in the
appeal of Appellant's case did not affect his ability to obtain a minimum
release date and to be released from confinement when that date was
reached. Without knowing the outcome of the retrial, it is only supposition as
to whether Appellant's incarceration was excessive or oppressive.

b. *Minimization of Anxiety and Concern While Awaiting Outcome of Appeal*

I agree with the majority that "the appropriate test for the military justice
system is to require an appellant to show particularized anxiety or concern
that is distinguishable from the normal anxiety experienced by prisoners
awaiting an appellate decision" and that the anxiety is not "dependent upon
whether his substantive appeal is ultimately successful." I disagree with the
majority's conclusion that Appellant's anxiety was "distinguishable" because
he had to register as a sex offender upon his early release from confinement.
This consequence of Appellant's conviction has been deemed a collateral
consequence of a conviction by numerous courts and will not generally merit
relief in those situations where an appellant proceeds to trial without
knowledge of such a consequence. . . .

c. *Limitation of Appellant's Grounds for Appeal or Defenses at Retrial*

The most serious factor in analyzing the prejudice factor is evaluating the ability of an appellant to assert: (i) his or her arguments on appeal; and (ii) his or her defense in the event of retrial or resentencing. *See Barker,* 407 U.S. at 532; *Harris,* 15 F.3d at 1563. . . .

In this case, Appellant failed to establish any harm to his ability to present a defense or retry his case. The substantive issue raised by Appellant related to the military judge's denial of a challenge for cause against a panel member. It was a technical issue and did not relate to the presentation of the facts, the evidence, or defenses at trial. There is no danger to any of his potential arguments or ability to present a defense. At a retrial, the court member issue in this case will be cured.

As to prejudice generally, one must recognize the difference between pretrial delay prejudice and post-trial delay prejudice. Pretrial delay prejudice involves planning a defense at trial with live witnesses who may not have committed their testimony either to an oral or written form. . . . Thus, the same anxiety that might occur in a pretrial scenario does not occur to the same extent in the post-trial scenario because the defendant is no longer cloaked with the presumption of innocence. Likewise, the concern that pretrial delay may affect the defendant's ability to mount a defense because memories will dim or witnesses will become unavailable is not a concern with post-trial delay.

In the post-trial scenario, the defendant has been convicted after a full-fledged adversary proceeding and is given a complete verbatim copy of the record, together with appointed counsel and a right to appeal the case when the sentence extends to one year of confinement and/or a punitive discharge. Appellate review of military cases is much broader than in the civilian sector because the intermediate civilian appellate court has no factfinding capability. This procedure is essential because it allows defendants to have a fair chance to present persuasive arguments during the appellate process.

* * *

The most problematic aspect of the majority's opinion is its application of the *Barker* prejudice factor. Appellant and the majority in this case merely speculate as to the potential harm. Rather than placing the burden on Appellant to show prejudice, the majority is intent on placing the responsibility for the delay on the Courts of Criminal Appeals. According to the holding of the majority, the Courts of Criminal Appeals have the responsibility for "the timely management and disposition of cases" regardless of whether an appellant in fact suffers prejudice as a result of post-trial delay, whether an appellant makes efforts to foster the delay, or does nothing to assert his right to a speedy review. . . . I would conclude that Appellant has not met his burden to demonstrate actual prejudice by this post-trial delay.

III. The Reality of the Application of the Majority's Specified Time Period

The majority does not adopt a "presumption of prejudice" but a prospective "presumption of unreasonable delay" if certain timelines are not met. The majority sets forth a "presumption of unreasonable delay" to be triggered by the following events:

(1) No action by convening authority within "120 days of the completion of trial";

(2) Case not docketed with the service Court of Criminal Appeals within "thirty days" of convening authority's action; and

(3) No decision by the service Court of Criminal Appeals rendered within "eighteen months of docketing the case."

Once the timeline is violated, the "presumption of unreasonable delay" will exist, which will satisfy the first *Barker* factor regardless of whether an appellant is sentenced to or serving confinement. The timeline violation will then trigger the *Barker* four-factor analysis. Any delay beyond the time periods established must be "justifiable, case-specific delays supported by the circumstances of that case and not delays based upon administrative matters, manpower constraints or the press of other cases."

The majority stands presumptions on their heads, failing to appreciate which party has the privileged information. By shifting the responsibility to the Government rather than requiring an appellant to demonstrate actual prejudice, the Court overlooks that the evidence of prejudice is peculiarly within an appellant's control. . . . This is why federal and state courts have placed the burden on the appellant to show actual prejudice.

* * *

The majority, who does not suffer the same complications and complexities of those in the field, and who receives the benefit of receiving a completed, typed record to review, has provided that those individuals in the field should have essentially five months to get a completed record to the service courts for docketing. Then, the majority provides the Courts of Criminal Appeals with eighteen months from docketing to completion of review. This Court has not always followed its own standard of completing review within eighteen months. I suggest that if we are going to set up rules, the rules might apply to ourselves as well.

The Court's master docket reveals that as of February 7, 2006, there were three cases over 1,000 days old, which is more than the eighteen-month standard set out by the majority for the Courts of Criminal Appeals to issue opinions. There were also more than thirty cases in which the petition had been granted and no action had been taken for over 400 days. Additionally, there were more than twenty-four cases where petitions had been pending for over eighteen months in which no action had been taken on the petition.

My purpose in mentioning these delays is not to be critical of this Court, but rather to underscore that there are valid reasons for the length of time it takes to conduct a thorough appellate review of a case whether it be before this Court or a Court of Criminal Appeals. Many cases are very complex and case load commitments of counsel are often legitimate reasons to seek enlargements of time in order to represent one's client adequately and ethically. Let me be very clear that I do not condone many of the delays we have encountered in the military justice system, including the delay in this case. I share the concerns of the majority and urge the appropriate legislative and executive branch officials to take all necessary steps to address resource and other issues that impact on the efficient and timely processing of cases for appellate review. I do not, however, believe justice is served by overstepping our judicial role and establishing timeline rules, albeit cloaked in the guise of presumptions, for the post-trial processing of cases.

* * *

In evaluating what remedy it should grant in regard to the lengthy post-trial delay in this case, the majority looks at potential remedies without considering the seriousness or the nature of the offenses involved. I respectfully dissent from the majority's conclusion of a violation of Appellant's right to a speedy post-trial review absent a showing of actual prejudice to the findings or sentence by Appellant. It is not enough for an appellant to claim anxiety as to the outcome of the appeal. . . .

IV. Conclusion

This Court is not a rulemaking body. Attempts at rulemaking in the past have proven to be unworkable, and we should not venture into that area again. The Court should leave the rulemaking function where it belongs—to the executive and legislative branches. If the facts of this case establish a violation of the Appellant's right to a speedy post-trial review upon applying the *Barker* test, then so be it. But, this Court should not create rules that exceed the bounds of the separation of powers doctrine, and that will not accomplish the desired result.

Points for Discussion

1. In *United States v. Moreno*, the court notes that "the longest delay in this case—925 days—involves the period from which the case was docketed at the Court of Criminal Appeals until briefing was complete. . . . [and] appellate defense counsel sought and was granted eighteen enlargements of time within which to file a brief. Enlargement numbers four through eighteen each contained the same reason for the request: 'other case load commitments.' " The court then holds the government accountable for the two years it took for defense counsel to file an appellate brief even though defense counsel requested and was granted eighteen extensions. Why does the court do this? Do you agree with the court's rationale? Why or why not? What does Judge Crawford say in her dissent regarding this issue?

2. What are the "three presumptions of unreasonable delay" that the court establishes for action by the convening authority, for docketing in the service Court of Criminal Appeals, and for appellate review by the Service Courts of Criminal Appeals? How did the Court determine that these periods—rather than longer or shorter periods—are the correct length for presuming unreasonable delay? Is setting periods of this type a legislative, executive, or judicial function?

3. The court sets a rigid timeline for post-trial processing in the *Moreno* case. Why do you think the court did not include its own case processing in the timeline? Do you think the court should have done so?

UNITED STATES v. HARROW
Court of Appeals for the Armed Forces
65 M.J. 190 (C.A.A.F. 2007)

Judge RYAN delivered the opinion of the Court.

Appellant [Airman Basic Ashontia K. Harrow, U.S. Air Force], argues that three evidentiary errors during her trial require this Court to overturn her conviction for the unpremeditated murder of her infant daughter. She also alleges errors arising from her guilty plea to larceny, the United States Air Force Court of Criminal Appeals' sentence reassessment, as well as from post-trial and appellate delay. We address each of these six issues. Although we conclude that this case is not without error, we hold that the errors did not prejudice Appellant. Therefore, for the reasons stated below, we affirm the decision of the lower court.

I. BACKGROUND

A general court-martial composed of officer and enlisted members convicted Appellant, contrary to her plea, of the unpremeditated murder of her infant daughter, in violation of Article 118, Uniform Code of Military Justice (UCMJ), 10 U.S.C. § 918 (2000). Appellant pled guilty to violations of Articles 86, 107, 121 and 134, UCMJ, 10 U.S.C. §§ 886, 907, 921, 934 (2000), and thirteen specifications thereunder, to include: multiple failures to go, absence without leave, making a false official statement, theft of insurance proceeds, fraud in obtaining phone services, dishonorable failure to pay just debts, and making false claims to secure the approval of a loan. The sentence adjudged by the court-martial and approved by the convening authority included a dishonorable discharge, confinement for twenty-five years, and forfeiture of all pay and allowances.

The Court of Criminal Appeals affirmed all charges except one specification of absence without leave. *United States v. Harrow*, 62 M.J. 649, 661–62 (A.F. Ct. Crim. App. 2006). The Court of Criminal Appeals found that Appellant's plea of guilty to the absence without leave charge was improvident and reassessed her sentence to a dishonorable discharge, twenty-four years and six months of confinement, forfeiture of all pay and allowances, and reduction to the grade of E–1.

We granted review on the following issues:

* * *

II.

WHETHER APPELLANT'S DUE PROCESS RIGHTS WERE VIOLATED WHEN IT TOOK OVER FOUR YEARS FOR THE ARTICLE 66 REVIEW BY THE COURT BELOW TO BE COMPLETED.

* * *

II. FACTS

A. OVERVIEW

We focus first on the general background facts relevant to Appellant's conviction for the unpremeditated murder of her infant daughter, Destiny. Destiny was taken to the hospital after suffering severe brain trauma from blunt force injury on June 23, 2000. At the hospital doctors determined that Destiny had suffered serious brain damage consistent with shaken baby syndrome and blunt force trauma. Five months later Destiny died from injuries inflicted that day. She was eleven months old.

In the course of the ensuing investigation, Appellant made contradictory and incriminating statements to investigators and others. These admissions and inconsistencies implicated her in the murder of Destiny. Direct and circumstantial evidence regarding the timing of Destiny's injury and Appellant's consciousness of guilt, as well as expert testimony, corroborated Appellant's admissions and bolstered the prosecution's case against her.

The defense attempted to deflect culpability away from Appellant, arguing Antonio Jackson, Destiny's father, was the perpetrator. Some evidence showed that Appellant told investigators that Destiny's death may have been an accident. Appellant did not testify and the defense called no witnesses on the merits. All defense evidence was developed through cross-examination of the prosecution's witnesses.

* * *

B. Physical Injuries to Destiny

On June 23, 2000, Destiny lived in government housing at Eglin Air Force Base, Florida, with Appellant. Jackson, the natural father of Destiny, lived out of state, but was visiting Appellant and staying at her apartment for several days.

On the day of the incident Appellant went to work and left Destiny with Jackson. Jackson was home with Destiny throughout the morning and she slept for most of that time. Appellant returned to her base apartment at midday.

Shortly after she arrived home, Appellant took off her uniform and lay on the couch. Sometime thereafter Appellant became angry with Jackson. Appellant began arguing with Jackson. The fighting escalated into Appellant screaming, yelling, and cursing.

At some point during the argument, Appellant picked Destiny up off the couch by one arm. Appellant held Destiny by one arm, allowing her to flail about, throughout her tirade. Jackson told her to be careful with the baby and not to take her anger out on Destiny. Appellant only became angrier. Appellant picked up a broom and pointed it at Jackson. She approached him, spit in his face, and continued to yell at him.

Eventually, Jackson walked away from Appellant and went into the bathroom in order to avoid the confrontation. Appellant followed him to the bathroom and continued screaming at him. Jackson left the bathroom and returned to the living room to avoid her. She followed him and began to throw things at him, including Destiny's walker.

Appellant continued to scream at Jackson, and he returned to the bathroom and locked the door. After Jackson locked himself in the bathroom, he could hear Appellant still screaming and things hitting the wall. He turned up the radio and tried to ignore her.

At 2:50 p.m. that day, after Jackson locked himself in the bathroom, and before Appellant left the apartment, Security Forces Senior Airman (SrA) Jason Warren, a patrolman assigned to Security Forces, knocked on the front door of Appellant's apartment. SrA Warren had been dispatched to Appellant's apartment to tell her to contact the first sergeant at work. This was a common occurrence, as Appellant did not have a phone.

Appellant had the baby on her hip and the baby appeared to make eye contact with SrA Warren. During the two minutes he was at the residence, SrA Warren did not hear any yelling and nothing appeared to be out of the ordinary. SrA Warren did not see Jackson. SrA Warren delivered the message and departed. Appellant left shortly thereafter, slamming the door.

After Jackson heard the door slam, he left the bathroom and found Destiny on the couch, lying on her side. He tried to give her a bottle, but she was unresponsive and would not take it. Jackson heard gargling noises coming from Destiny and other sounds. He picked her up and observed vomit where she had been laying. He held Destiny against his body and patted her on the back in an attempt to clear out any remaining emesis. As he was holding her, she began to shake, her back arched, and her eyes rolled back in her head. She then went limp.

Jackson immediately carried Destiny next door to the apartment of Mr. and Mrs. Harris to call 911 because there was no telephone in Appellant's apartment. Only a few minutes elapsed between the time Appellant sped off and the time Jackson sought assistance from Mr. and Mrs. Harris.

Mr. and Mrs. Harris, Appellant's neighbors, both testified about what happened before Jackson arrived at their door. Mr. Harris was seated in the computer room of their apartment, and Mrs. Harris was in their living room, which directly abutted Appellant's living room. As the Harris' apartment shared a common but very thin wall with Appellant's apartment, they clearly heard the disturbance in Appellant's apartment.

Mr. and Mrs. Harris both heard Appellant, and only Appellant, yelling next door. Mrs. Harris heard Destiny crying loudly for about ten minutes during the middle of the yelling. Mrs. Harris also heard a loud bang against the shared living room wall, knocking off a picture in her apartment, and then she no longer heard Destiny crying. After the thump she heard Destiny emit one or two whimpers before going silent. Five minutes after she heard the loud bang against the wall, Mrs. Harris heard Appellant's front door slam so hard that it set off Mrs. Harris' door bell. She saw Appellant get into her car to leave, spinning her tires as she exited the parking lot. Appellant looked "very angry and very raged" as she left the apartment.

Mr. Harris also heard "thumps" and Appellant "yelling" in Appellant's apartment. Mr. Harris looked out the window and saw Appellant spin her tires as she exited the parking lot. According to both Mr. and Mrs. Harris, Jackson arrived at their door with Destiny asking them to dial 911 only a minute or two after Appellant left. Responding to Jackson's plea, Mrs. Harris called 911 and requested emergency assistance for Destiny.

Police and ambulance dispatch records, and the testimony of Jackson, SrA Warren, and Mr. and Mrs. Harris, establish the following sequence of events in a thirteen-minute period from 2:45 p.m. to 2:58 p.m.: SrA Warren was dispatched to Appellant's apartment to deliver a message to her; SrA Warren arrived at Appellant's apartment and departed shortly thereafter; Appellant left the apartment; and, almost immediately thereafter, the Harrises called 911.

C. The Death of Destiny

Destiny was hospitalized as doctors attempted to save her. She had sustained serious blunt force trauma to her brain and the left side of her face and suffered significant hemorrhaging of the brain and eyes. Notwithstanding two operations and extraordinary care, Destiny died five months later.

An autopsy confirmed significant injuries to Destiny's brain. Dr. Gary D. Cumberland, a forensic pathologist and the chief medical examiner in the local Florida coroner's office, conducted an autopsy and found: bruising on the surface of the brain, tearing of the brain tissue, swelling of the brain, and several subdural and subarachnoid hemorrhages. The autopsy also revealed hemorrhages in the eyes. The autopsy did not reveal injuries associated with external trauma (e.g., skin bruises) because the injuries occurred five months before Destiny died and had already healed.

Dr. Cumberland concluded that Destiny "died as a result of blunt force injuries to the head in the situation of the shaken baby syndrome." A complete autopsy revealed no other possible cause of death. In Dr. Cumberland's opinion, after speaking with an eye specialist and a neuropathologist, the only possible cause of death was shaken baby syndrome. Dr. Cumberland found the manner of death to be homicide, as the injuries were too severe to have happened accidentally.

D. AFOSI Investigation

Special Agent (SA) Liesl D. Davenport, an Air Force Office of Special Investigations (AFOSI) investigator, participated in four interviews with Appellant. The first interview was conducted on the 28th of June by a Federal Bureau of Investigation (FBI) agent with SA Davenport sitting in.

Initially, Appellant was not a suspect because the investigators had been told that Appellant was not home at all that day. Appellant told the investigators during the first interview that she went home at lunch because she had not been feeling well. She told the investigators that she had taken some medication once she arrived at home, placed Destiny in her crib, and that she remained on the couch napping until SrA Warren came to her door. Appellant stated that Jackson was either in the kitchen or bathroom the entire time; she did not recount any fight or argument.

During this first interview Appellant stated that she had never seen Jackson handle the baby improperly. But she told the agents that she believed Jackson had accidentally shaken Destiny when she was unresponsive after he asked the Harrises to call 911. Appellant said that Mrs. Harris told her that Jackson was shaking the baby so much that Mrs. Harris had to tell Jackson to put the baby down.

When the agents attempted to verify this point in an interview with Mrs. Harris, she denied that Jackson had shaken the baby or that she had told Appellant that version of the events. Upon finding inconsistencies in Appellant's story, the agents began to view Appellant as a possible suspect.

SA Davenport conducted a second interview with Appellant with another AFOSI agent, SA Carver, on the 15th of August. SA Davenport led the interview. Because Appellant was a suspect at this point, SA Davenport advised Appellant of her Article 31(b), UCMJ, 10 U.S.C. § 831(b) (2000) rights, which she waived.

At this interview Appellant changed her story and stated that Destiny had not been in her crib. Instead, Appellant stated that she held Destiny the entire time she was home. There was no mention of Appellant taking a nap on the couch in the second interview. Appellant stated that she may have caused Destiny's injuries accidentally when she went to the door to speak with SrA Warren. She thought she might have swung around quickly when she turned away from the door, causing Destiny's head to snap back.

At this point, the investigators knew that Jackson and Appellant had been arguing. But when SA Davenport asked Appellant about the argument she initially denied it. Eventually, Appellant admitted that she and Jackson had argued for twenty to thirty minutes during the time period in question. However, Appellant remained adamant that she had not been angry or frustrated when she left the apartment. Appellant maintained that Mrs. Harris had told her that Jackson had possibly accidentally injured the baby.

A third interview was conducted two days later. Appellant was again read her Article 31(b), UCMJ, rights, which she waived. During this interview Appellant admitted that she might have accidentally caused Destiny's injuries when she was playing with her. She described how she would regularly throw Destiny in the air and catch her, and how she thought that perhaps this caused the injuries. She again stated that the accident also might have happened when she was turning away from the door after speaking with SrA Warren. Appellant told the investigators that she tossed "it," meaning Destiny, in the air twice on that day.

Upon further questioning, Appellant asserted that only Appellant or Jackson could have injured Destiny. When asked if Jackson had injured Destiny, Appellant responded "no." According to SA Davenport, there was no additional pertinent information gleaned from the fourth interview.

E. Trial Testimony

In addition to introducing Appellant's statements to investigators, the prosecution introduced other statements made by Appellant to establish her consciousness of guilt. Jackson testified that, after the injuries to Destiny, Appellant, while crying, told him that she might be responsible. Appellant also told Jackson that they should not talk to AFOSI or the FBI and that she thought Jackson was on "their" side and not hers.

The prosecution introduced evidence to establish Appellant's possible motives to injure Destiny. Stephanie Lewis, who was a friend of Appellant's sister, testified that Appellant had asked her, prior to Destiny's injury, if Lewis, who was separated from the father of her children, thought her "man" might come back if something happened to her children.

Appellant complained to Staff Sergeant (SSgt) Tynisha Quick, a coworker, that because of money she spent on diapers and formula for Destiny, Appellant did not have a phone, cable television, or a social life. At one point, SSgt Quick observed Appellant speak directly to Destiny, blaming her for all the things she could no longer do.

SSgt Quick further testified that Appellant had told her that Destiny was more responsive to Jackson than to her. Appellant told SSgt Quick that Destiny would tremble and cry every time Appellant went near her, but would stop when Jackson was near. SSgt Quick testified that Appellant told her that she thought Jackson was trying to turn Destiny against her.

400 MODERN MILITARY JUSTICE

. . . the prosecution presented several instances of Appellant's uncharged misconduct relating to Destiny. Airman First Class (A1C) Crystal E. Mills testified to an earlier incident where she saw Appellant bite Destiny after the baby had bitten her. Destiny began crying after Appellant bit her. According to A1C Mills, Appellant ignored the cries. A1C also recounted instances where Appellant would "flick" the hand of Destiny to get her to stop doing things. SSgt Quick also recounted an incident where Appellant "thumped" or "flicked" Destiny on the thigh when she was misbehaving in a restaurant.

Finally, the Government called two expert witnesses who established the cause of Destiny's death. As previously discussed, Dr. Cumberland, a forensic pathologist from the coroner's office, explained his medical findings from the autopsy. Dr. Sharon Cooper testified as an expert witness in the field of developmental and forensic pediatrics. . . .

* * *

The Government rested at the conclusion of Dr. Cooper's testimony. After the presentation of the prosecution's case, Appellant rested. In closing, the prosecution argued that the evidence rebutted Appellant's prior claim of an accidental injury to Destiny and identified Appellant as the perpetrator of the murder of Destiny. Appellant's argument revolved around a single point—that the members could not "exclude Mr. Jackson as a potential perpetrator of the offense." After three hours of deliberations, the panel returned a verdict finding Appellant guilty of the unpremeditated murder of Destiny.

III. DISCUSSION

* * *

F. Post-trial and Appellate Delay

The final issue is whether Appellant was deprived of her right to due process by the 1,467 days that elapsed between her trial and completion of appellate review. Of that delay, 826 days was time between when the final briefs were submitted to the Court of Criminal Appeals and the issuance of its decision. Appellant contends she was prejudiced because, due to the appellate delay, her lead appellate counsel was unable to argue her case.

In this case, the overall delay of 1,467 days between the trial and completion of review at the Court of Criminal Appeals is facially unreasonable. Because we conclude that the delay is facially unreasonable, we examine the four factors set forth in *Barker v. Wingo,* 407 U.S. 514, 530 (1972): (1) the length of the delay; (2) the reasons for the delay; (3) the appellant's assertion of the right to timely review and appeal; and (4) prejudice. *United States v. Moreno,* 63 M.J. 129, 135–36 (C.A.A.F. 2006). We need not engage in a separate analysis of each factor where we can assume error and proceed directly to the conclusion that any error was harmless beyond a reasonable doubt. *See United States v. Allison,* 63 M.J. 365, 370 (C.A.A.F. 2006). This approach is appropriate in Appellant's case.

Having considered the totality of the circumstances and entire record, we conclude that any denial of Appellant's right to speedy post-trial review and appeal was harmless beyond a reasonable doubt and that no relief is warranted.

IV. CONCLUSION

In evaluating Appellant's assignments of error we have considered not only the impact of each individual error, but also any cumulative prejudice that could have arisen from a combination or errors. *See Banks,* 36 M.J. at 170–71. We conclude that neither individually nor in combination was Appellant prejudiced by the errors in this case. The decision of the United States Air Force Court of Criminal Appeals, except for that portion purporting to affirm a reduction to E–1, is affirmed.

[Chief Judge Effron's opinion concurring in part and in the result is omitted.—Eds.]

Point for Discussion

After the *Moreno* decision, many government appellate attorneys became concerned that the Court of Appeals for the Armed Forces would apply the new timelines in a way that automatically required relief in scores of cases. This concern proved unfounded. As one commentator wrote in the year following the *Moreno* decision:

> During the past court term, the CAAF published eight opinions analyzing post-trial delay in cases tried after the implementation of the *Moreno* timelines. Of those eight decisions, three resulted in the CAAF granting relief directly to the appellant and two resulted in the CAAF returning the case to the service court for favorable action. . . . As will be seen, the worst fears imagined by government post-trial practitioners in the summer of 2006 do not appear to be coming to fruition. *Moreno* is not being interpreted in a way that grants wholesale relief to appellants whose cases have taken longer to process than the timelines set out in the *Moreno* decision.

James L. Varley, *The Lion Who Squeaked: How the Moreno Decision Hasn't Changed the World and Other Post-Trial News*, Army Lawyer, Jun. 2008, at 80, 82 (footnotes omitted). How is *Harrow* a possible example of the commentator's thesis?

UNITED STATES v. ALLENDE
Court of Appeals for the Armed Forces
66 M.J. 142 (C.A.A.F. 2008)

Chief Judge EFFRON delivered the opinion of the Court.

A general court-martial composed of officer and enlisted members, convicted Appellant [Mess Management Specialist Second Class Gilbert T. Allende, U.S. Navy], contrary to his pleas, of violating a lawful order, larceny (four specifications), and obtaining services by false pretenses, in violation of

Articles 92, 121, and 134, Uniform Code of Military Justice (UCMJ), 10 U.S.C. §§ 892, 921, 934 (2000). The sentence adjudged by the court-martial and approved by the convening authority included a bad-conduct discharge, confinement for one year, forfeiture of all pay and allowances, and reduction to the lowest enlisted grade. The United States Navy–Marine Corps Court of Criminal Appeals affirmed the findings. In light of the post-trial delay, the court reduced the sentence as a matter of sentence appropriateness, approving only that portion providing for a bad-conduct discharge, confinement for nine months, and reduction to the lowest enlisted grade. *United States v. Allende*, No. 200001872, 2006 CCA LEXIS 167, 2006 WL 4572995 (N.M. Ct. Crim. App. July 11, 2006) (unpublished).

On Appellant's petition, we granted review of the following issues:

* * *

II. WHETHER THE LOWER COURT ERRED IN FINDING NO DUE PROCESS VIOLATION WHERE 2,484 DAYS ELAPSED BETWEEN THE ADJOURNMENT OF APPELLANT'S TRIAL AND COMPLETION OF ARTICLE 66, UCMJ, REVIEW, INCLUDING 734 DAYS IN PANEL.

For the reasons set forth below, we affirm.

* * *

II. APPELLATE DELAY

In the second granted issue, Appellant asserts that he was denied his due process right to speedy review and appeal. . . . The present case involves a seven-year delay between adjournment of Appellant's court-martial and resolution of his Article 66, UCMJ, appellate review. In light of the lengthy delay, and the focus of the parties on prejudice, we shall assume error and proceed directly to the question of whether any error was harmless beyond a reasonable doubt. *See United States v. Allison*, 63 M.J. 365, 370–71 (C.A.A.F. 2006).

Appellant has not suffered ongoing prejudice in the form of oppressive incarceration, undue anxiety, or the impairment of the ability to prevail in a retrial. Moreover, because we do not find the substantive grounds of Appellant's appeal as to the first granted issue meritorious, Appellant has not suffered detriment to his legal position in the appeal as a result of the delay. *See Moreno*, 63 M.J. at 139.

Appellant asserts prejudice on the grounds that his ability to obtain employment has been impaired because he has not been able to show employers a Department of Defense Form 214 (DD–214), the certificate of release from active duty. The appellate delay has delayed completion of appellate review, thereby precluding issuance of a DD–214. According to Appellant, a number of potential civilian employers were unwilling to consider him because he could not provide them with a DD–214.

Appellant's affidavit asserts that four employers declined to consider him for employment in the period of August–October 2000, approximately a year after his trial was completed, and that two employers declined to consider him for employment for that reason in 2007. Appellant has not provided documentation from potential employers regarding their employment practices, nor has he otherwise demonstrated a valid reason for failing to do so. *Compare United States v. Jones*, 61 M.J. 80, 84–85 (C.A.A.F. 2005) (relying upon affidavits from a prospective employer to confirm that the lack of a DD–214 caused the employer to deny his application for employment.) In that context, we conclude that the assumed error was harmless beyond a reasonable doubt and note that Appellant has failed to present any substantiated evidence to the contrary.

III. DECISION

For the forgoing reasons, the decision of the United States Navy–Marine Corps Court of Criminal Appeals is affirmed.

Points for Discussion

1. How does the court modify the *Moreno* analysis in *Harrow* and the *Allende* cases? Do you agree with their decisions in *Harrow* and *Allende*? Why or why not?

2. Although the court expresses consternation at the delay and backlog in post-trial processing, the court says little about the causes of delay or the reforms that might reduce delay. What are the causes and the solutions? One author attributes a large part of the delay problem to multiple levels of mandatory post-trial review. He writes:

> [T]he military justice system requires full-blown appellate review in virtually all courts-martial in which the approved sentence exceeds a relatively modest threshold, even in cases where the accused pleads guilty and receives exactly the sentence he requests. Remarkably, this appellate review system allows—indeed, encourages—accuseds pleading guilty as part of a plea bargain to turn around on appeal and argue that their convictions should be overturned.

>   * * *

> The crushing caseload caused by the mandatory appellate review of guilty-plea cases necessarily creates delays at every level of appellate review. It is hardly surprising, then, that the United States Court of Appeals for the Armed Forces ("CAAF")—the civilian court sitting atop the military justice appellate structure—has encountered a number of cases involving post-trial and appellate delays of embarrassing durations. The only durable solutions to this problem appear to be either throwing additional resources at the problem at every stage without changing the system itself, or taking a hard look at the military appellate caseload with an eye toward reducing the number of cases reviewed on appeal. Any such effort to narrow the class of courts-martial subject to mandatory appellate review

should focus on eliminating appeals where the accused has no moral right to appellate review—such as where the accused essentially raised no appealable issues at trial—while not being so overly broad as to capture cases where an accused may have legitimate issues to raise on appeal.

John F. O'Connor, *Foolish Consistencies and the Appellate Review of Courts-Martial*, 41 Akron L. Rev. 175, 178-179 (2008) (footnotes omitted). What are the strengths and weaknesses of the proposal to narrow the class of courts-martial subject to mandatory appellate review? Where would you begin to implement this proposal?

CHAPTER 11

APPELLATE REVIEW PROCEDURES

Appellate review is available for general and special courts-martial depending on the sentence approved by the convening authority. As described in previous chapters, military and civilian courts conduct appellate review (i.e., the Service Courts of Criminal Appeals, Court of Appeals for the Armed Forces, and U.S. Supreme Court). Some cases receive appellate review by the Service Judge Advocate General. The UCMJ sets forth the jurisdiction for each level of appellate review and provides for either an automatic appeal or discretionary appeal process. An accused is provided defense appellate counsel free of charge to assist him with the appellate process. *See* Art. 70, UCMJ.

11-1. Review by the Judge Advocate General

Article 69(a), UCMJ, grants the Judge Advocate General authority to review general court-martial cases with approved sentences that do not include a dismissal, dishonorable discharge or bad-conduct discharge, or confinement for a year or more. The Judge Advocate General also reviews cases where, pursuant to R.C.M. 1112,[1] a judge advocate has determined that as a matter of law the General Court-Martial Convening Authority (GCMCA) should take corrective action, but the GCMCA does not take action at least as favorable to the accused as the judge advocate recommended. *See* R.C.M. 1112(g)(1). Also, after final review if the case has not been reviewed by the Service Court of Criminal Appeals or the Judge Advocate General, the Judge Advocate General may decide to review a case or an accused may petition the Judge Advocate General for review on the grounds of newly discovered evidence, fraud on the court, lack of jurisdiction, an error prejudicial to the substantial rights of the accused, or sentence appropriateness. The Judge Advocate General has broad reviewing authority and may modify or set aside the court-martial findings or sentence, may consider the appropriateness of the sentence, or may authorize a rehearing.

---

[1] Rule for Court-Martial 1112 requires that a judge advocate review courts-martial which will not receive appellate review because the accused waived or withdrew his right to appellate review under R.C.M. 1110.

11-2. Appeal to the Service Courts of Criminal Appeals

As UCMJ, Article 66 provides, Service Courts of Criminal Appeals (previously named Courts of Military Review until 1994) each have jurisdiction to automatically review cases (from within the corresponding Service) with approved sentences which include death, a punitive discharge or confinement for a year or more, unless the accused waives appellate review or withdraws his case from review. [1] Originally Boards of Review, the Military Justice Act of 1968 converted the Boards into appellate courts. Each Service Judge Advocate General must appoint at least three military appellate judges including one chief judge to serve on the appellate court consisting of one or more panels of three judges. UCMJ, Art. 66. The judges (who are usually senior Judge Advocates) may be commissioned officers or civilians who are members of a Federal court or state bar. *Id.*

Unlike their civilian counterparts that can only review cases for legal error, Service Courts of Criminal Appeals have authority to review courts-martial for both legal error and factual sufficiency (i.e., the record includes sufficient evidence to support the findings of guilty). In reviewing the approved findings and sentence, the Service Court "may affirm only such findings of guilty and the sentence or such part or amount of the sentence, as it finds correct in law and fact and determines, on the basis of the entire record, should be approved. In considering the record, it may weigh the evidence, judge the credibility of witnesses, and determine controverted questions of fact, recognizing that the trial court saw and heard the witnesses." UCMJ, Art. 66(c). The Court of Criminal Appeals may affirm or set aside the findings and sentence or part thereof, or may remand the case and order a rehearing, ("except where the setting aside is based on lack of sufficient evidence in the record to support the findings"). *Id.*

Points for Discussion

1. Why should the Judge Advocate General have review authority over some court-martial cases when he is not a judicial body?

2. Why should the Service Courts of Criminal Appeal have the broad authority to review cases for factual sufficiency when civilian courts do not?

3. An accused who receives a sentence which includes death cannot waive appellate review or withdraw the case from appellate review. Should such an accused have a right to do so? Why or why not?

---

[1] An accused who receives a sentence of death cannot waive or withdraw the case from appellate review. As discussed in previous chapters, the UCMJ affords Service Courts the opportunity to review certain kinds of interlocutory government appeals and extraordinary writs. *See* Art. 62, UCMJ. Article 69, UCMJ, also gives Service Courts of Criminal Appeals jurisdiction to review cases in which the Judge Advocate General has taken certain actions. Article 73, UCMJ, also provides the Service Criminal Courts of Appeal with authority to review petitions for a new trial based on newly discovered evidence or fraud on the court.

11-3. The U.S. Court of Appeals for the Armed Forces Review and Supreme Court

The U.S. Court of Appeals for the Armed Forces (known as the Court of Military Appeals from 1951 to 1994) is comprised of five civilian judges appointed by the President. Except for capital cases with a sentence of death, this court's appellate review authority is discretionary. The C.A.A.F. reviews all cases in which the sentence as approved by a Court of Criminal Appeals includes death, cases reviewed by a Court of Criminal Appeals that the Judge Advocate General submits to the C.A.A.F. for review of certified issues, and cases the Service Court of Criminal Appeals reviewed and the accused petitions the C.A.A.F. "on good cause shown"[1] and the C.A.A.F. grants a review.[2] UCMJ, Art. 67.

The C.A.A.F. "may act only with respect to the findings and sentence as approved by the convening authority and as affirmed or set aside as incorrect in law by the Court of Criminal Appeals." The C.A.A.F. need only review the certified issues for cases that the court receives from the Judge Advocates General. *Id.* For cases reviewed upon the accused's petition, the court will only review issues specified in the grant of review. *Id.*

The C.A.A.F. may only take action regarding matters of law. *Id.* The C.A.A.F., unlike the Service Courts of Criminal Appeals, does not usually review cases for sentence appropriateness. *See United States v. Jones,* 39 M.J. 315 (C.M.A. 1994). Similar to the Service Courts of Criminal Appeal, the C.A.A.F. may affirm the lower court's ruling or set aside the findings and sentence or part thereof, or may remand the case and order a rehearing, ("except where the setting aside is based on lack of sufficient evidence in the record to support the findings"). *Id.*

Court of Appeals for the Armed Forces decisions may be reviewed by the Supreme Court by writ of certiorari, but the Supreme Court cannot review by writ of certiorari the C.A.A.F.'s denial of an accused's petition for review. The Supreme Court typically reviews only one or two C.A.A.F. cases per decade.

---

[1] The accused has sixty days from either: 1) notice of the Service Court of Criminal Appeals decision; or 2) from the date the Court of Criminal Appeals decision (after service on the accused's appellate defense counsel) is mailed by first class certified U.S mail to the accused (whichever is earlier) to petition the CAAF for review. UCMJ, Art. 67(b). This sets forth the CAAF's jurisdictional authority. *United States v. Rodriguez,* 67 M.J. 110 (C.A.A.F. 2009).

[2] As discussed in Chapter 7, the CAAF has jurisdiction to hear petitions for extraordinary writs.

CLINTON v. GOLDSMITH
United States Supreme Court
526 U.S. 529 (1999)

Justice SOUTER delivered the opinion of the Court.

The challenge here is to the use of the All Writs Act, 28 U.S.C. § 1651(a), by the Court of Appeals for the Armed Forces, to enjoin the President and various military officials from dropping respondent [Major James Goldsmith, U.S. Air Force] from the rolls of the Air Force. Because that court's process was neither "in aid of" its strictly circumscribed jurisdiction to review court-martial findings and sentences under 10 U.S.C. § 867 nor "necessary or appropriate" in light of a servicemember's alternative opportunities to seek relief, we hold that the Court of Appeals for the Armed Forces lacked jurisdiction to issue the injunction.

I

Respondent James Goldsmith, a major in the United States Air Force, was ordered by a superior officer to inform his sex partners that he was HIV-positive and to take measures to block any transfer of bodily fluids during sexual relations. Contrary to this order, on two occasions Goldsmith had unprotected intercourse, once with a fellow officer and once with a civilian, without informing either that he was carrying HIV.

As a consequence of his defiance, Goldsmith was convicted by general court-martial of willful disobedience of an order from a superior commissioned officer, aggravated assault with means likely to produce death or grievous bodily harm, and assault consummated by battery, in violation of Articles 90 and 128 of the Uniform Code of Military Justice (UCMJ), 10 U.S.C. §§ 890, 928(b)(1), (a). In 1994, he was sentenced to six years' confinement and forfeiture of $2,500 of his pay each month for six years. The Air Force Court of Criminal Appeals affirmed his conviction and sentence in 1995, and when he sought no review of that decision in the United States Court of Appeals for the Armed Forces (C.A.A.F.), his conviction became final, *see* § 871(c)(1)(A).

In 1996, Congress expanded the President's authority by empowering him to drop from the rolls of the Armed Forces any officer who had both been sentenced by a court-martial to more than six months' confinement and served at least six months.[1] *See* National Defense Authorization Act for Fiscal

---

[1] When a servicemember is dropped from the rolls, he forfeits his military pay. *See* 37 U.S.C. § 803. The drop-from-the-rolls remedy targets a narrow category of servicemembers who are absent without leave (AWOL) or else have been convicted of serious crimes. Since 1870, the President has had authority to drop from the rolls of the Army any officer who has been AWOL for at least three months. *See* Act of July 15, 1870, § 17, 16 Stat. 319. The power was subsequently extended to officers confined in prison after final conviction by a civil court, *see* Act of Jan. 19, 1911, ch. 22, 36 Stat. 894, and then to "any armed force" officer AWOL for at least three months or else finally sentenced to confinement in a federal or state penitentiary or correctional

Year 1996, 110 Stat. 325, 10 U.S.C. §§ 1161(b)(2), 1167 (1994 ed., Supp. III).[2] In reliance on this statutory authorization, the Air Force notified Goldsmith in 1996 that it was taking action to drop him from the rolls.

Goldsmith did not immediately contest the proposal to drop him, but rather petitioned the Air Force Court of Criminal Appeals for extraordinary relief under the All Writs Act, 28 U.S.C. § 1651(a), to redress the unrelated alleged interruption of his HIV medication during his incarceration. The Court of Criminal Appeals ruled that it lacked jurisdiction to act, and it was in Goldsmith's appeal from that determination that he took the first steps to raise the issue now before us, an entirely new claim that the Air Force's action to drop him from the rolls was unconstitutional. He did not challenge his underlying court-martial conviction (the appeal period for which had expired, *see* Rule 19(a)(1), C.A.A.F. Rules of Practice and Procedure). But he charged that the proposed action violated the *Ex Post Facto* Clause, U.S. Const., Art. I, § 9, cl. 3 (arguing that the statute authorizing it had been enacted after the date of his conviction), and the Double Jeopardy Clause, U.S. Const., Amdt. 5 (arguing that the action would inflict successive punishment based on the same conduct underlying his first conviction). 48 M.J. 84, 89-90 (1998). The C.A.A.F., on a division of 3 to 2, granted the petition for extraordinary relief and relied on the All Writs Act, 28 U.S.C. § 1651(a), in enjoining the President and various other Executive Branch officials from dropping respondent from the rolls of the Air Force. We granted certiorari, 525 U.S. 961 (1998), and now reverse.

II

When Congress exercised its power to govern and regulate the Armed Forces by establishing the C.A.A.F., *see* U.S. Const., Art. I, § 8, cl. 14; 10 U.S.C. § 941; *see generally Weiss v. United States,* 510 U.S. 163, 166-169 (1994), it confined the court's jurisdiction to the review of specified sentences imposed by courts-martial: the C.A.A.F. has the power to act "only with respect to the findings and sentence as approved by the [court-martial's] convening authority and as affirmed or set aside as incorrect in law by the Court of Criminal Appeals." 10 U.S.C. § 867(c). Cf. *Parisi v. Davidson,* 405 U.S. 34, 44 (1972) (Court of Military Appeals lacked express authority over claim for discharge based on conscientious objector status). Despite these limitations, the C.A.A.F. asserted jurisdiction and purported to justify reliance on the All Writs Act in this case on the view that "Congress intended

---

institution, *see* Act of May 5, 1950, § 10, 64 Stat. 146.

[2] Section 1161(b)(2) authorizes the President to "drop from the rolls of any armed force any commissioned officer . . . who may be separated under Section 1167 of this title by reason of a sentence to confinement adjudged by a court-martial." Section 1167 provides that "a member sentenced by a court-martial to a period of confinement for more than six months may be separated from the member's armed force at any time after the sentence to confinement has become final . . . and the member has served in confinement for a period of six months."

[it] to have broad responsibility with respect to administration of military justice," 48 M.J., at 86-87,[6] a position that Goldsmith urges us to adopt. This we cannot do.

While the All Writs Act authorizes employment of extraordinary writs, it confines the authority to the issuance of process "in aid of" the issuing court's jurisdiction. 28 U.S.C. § 1651(a) ("[A]ll courts established by Act of Congress may issue all writs necessary or appropriate in aid of their respective jurisdictions and agreeable to the usages and principles of law"). Thus, although military appellate courts are among those empowered to issue extraordinary writs under the Act, see *Noyd v. Bond*, 395 U.S. 683, 695, n. 7 (1969), the express terms of the Act confine the power of the C.A.A.F. to issuing process "in aid of" its existing statutory jurisdiction; the Act does not enlarge that jurisdiction, see, *e.g.*, *Pennsylvania Bureau of Correction v. United States Marshals Service*, 474 U.S. 34, 41 (1985). *See also* 16 Charles Alan Wright, Arthur R. Miller, & Edward H. Cooper, Federal Practice and Procedure § 3932, p. 470 (2d ed. 1996) ("The All Writs Act ... is not an independent grant of appellate jurisdiction"); 19 J. Moore & G. Pratt, Moore's Federal Practice § 204.02[4] (3d ed. 1998) ("The All Writs Act cannot enlarge a court's jurisdiction").

We have already seen that the C.A.A.F.'s independent statutory jurisdiction is narrowly circumscribed. To be more specific, the C.A.A.F. is accorded jurisdiction by statute (so far as it concerns us here) to "review the record in [specified] cases reviewed by" the service courts of criminal appeals, 10 U.S.C. §§ 867(a)(2), (3), which in turn have jurisdiction to "revie[w] court-martial cases," § 866(a). Since the Air Force's action to drop respondent from the rolls was an executive action, not a "findin[g]" or "sentence," § 867(c), that was (or could have been) imposed in a court-martial proceeding, [7] the elimination of Goldsmith from the rolls appears straightforwardly to have been beyond the C.A.A.F.'s jurisdiction to review and hence beyond the "aid" of the All Writs Act in reviewing it.

Goldsmith nonetheless claims that the C.A.A.F. has satisfied the "aid" requirement of the Act because it protected and effectuated the sentence meted out by the court-martial. Goldsmith emphasizes that the court-martial could have dismissed him from service, but instead chose to impose only

---

[6] One judge was even more emphatic: "We should use our broad jurisdiction under the [UCMJ] to correct injustices like this and we need not wait for another court to perhaps act.... Our Court has the responsibility of protecting the rights of all servicemembers in court-martial matters." 48 M.J., at 91 (Sullivan, J., concurring).

[7] A court-martial is specifically barred from dismissing or discharging an officer except as in accordance with the UCMJ, which gives it no authority to drop a servicemember from the rolls. *See* Rules for Courts-Martial 1003(b)(9)(A)-(C); Rule 1003(b)(9) ("A court-martial may not adjudge an administrative separation from the service"). Moreover, respondent brought the petition against the President, the Secretary of Defense, and military officials who were not even parties to the court-martial.

confinement and fines.[8] Hence, he says the C.A.A.F. merely preserved that sentence as the court-martial imposed it, by precluding additional punishment, which would incidentally violate the *Ex Post Facto* and Double Jeopardy Clauses. But this is beside the point, for two related reasons. First, Goldsmith's court-martial sentence has not been changed; another military agency has simply taken independent action.[9] It would presumably be an entirely different matter if a military authority attempted to alter a judgment by revising a court-martial finding and sentence to increase the punishment, contrary to the specific provisions of the UCMJ, and it certainly would be a different matter when such a judgment had been affirmed by an appellate court. In such a case, as the Government concedes, *see* Tr. of Oral Arg. 15, 19, 52, the All Writs power would allow the appellate court to compel adherence to its own judgment. *See, e.g., United States v. United States Dist. Court for Southern Dist. of N.Y.,* 334 U.S. 258, 263-264 (1948). Second, the C.A.A.F. is not given authority, by the All Writs Act or otherwise, to oversee all matters arguably related to military justice, or to act as a plenary administrator even of criminal judgments it has affirmed. Simply stated, there is no source of continuing jurisdiction for the C.A.A.F. over all actions administering sentences that the C.A.A.F. at one time had the power to review. Thus the C.A.A.F. spoke too expansively when it held itself to be "empowered by the All Writs Act to grant extraordinary relief in a case in which the court-martial rendered a sentence that constituted an adequate basis for direct review in [the C.A.A.F.] after review in the intermediate court," 48 M.J., at 87.[10]

III

Even if the C.A.A.F. had some seriously arguable basis for jurisdiction in these circumstances, resort to the All Writs Act would still be out of bounds, being unjustifiable either as "necessary" or as "appropriate" in light of alternative remedies available to a servicemember demanding to be kept on the rolls.- The All Writs Act invests a court with a power essentially equitable and, as such, not generally available to provide alternatives to other, adequate remedies at law. . . . This limitation operates here, since other administrative bodies in the military, and the federal courts, have authority to provide administrative or judicial review of the action challenged by respondent.

In response to the notice Goldsmith received that action was being considered to drop him from the rolls, he presented his claim to the Secretary of the Air Force. *See* Tr. of Oral Arg. 4-5. If the Secretary takes final action to drop him from the rolls (as he has not yet done), Goldsmith will (as the Government concedes) be entitled to present his claim to the Air Force Board

---

[8] At the court-martial, respondent faced a maximum punishment of dismissal, confinement for 10 years, forfeiture of all pay and allowances, and a fine.

[9] Indeed, the approved findings and sentence in Goldsmith's case had become final over one year before the Air Force initiated its action to drop him from the rolls.

[10] The court, moreover, was simply wrong when it treated itself as a court of original jurisdiction, see *supra,* at 1542.

of Correction for Military Records (BCMR). This is a civilian body within the military service, with broad-ranging authority to review a servicemember's "discharge or dismissal (other than a discharge or dismissal by sentence of a general court-martial)," 10 U.S.C. § 1553(a), or "to correct an error or remove an injustice" in a military record, § 1552(a)(1).

Respondent may also have recourse to the federal trial courts. We have previously held, for example, that "[BCMR] decisions are subject to judicial review [by federal courts] and can be set aside if they are arbitrary, capricious, or not based on substantial evidence." *Chappell v. Wallace*, 462 U.S. 296, 303 (1983). A servicemember claiming something other than monetary relief may challenge a BCMR's decision to sustain a decision to drop him from the rolls (or otherwise dismissing him) as final agency action under the Administrative Procedure Act (APA), 5 U.S.C. § 551 *et seq.* . . .

In sum, executive action to drop respondent from the rolls falls outside of the C.A.A.F.'s express statutory jurisdiction, and alternative statutory avenues of relief are available. The C.A.A.F.'s injunction against dropping respondent from the rolls of the Air Force was neither "in aid of [its] jurisdictio[n]" nor "necessary or appropriate." Accordingly, we reverse the court's judgment.

It is so ordered.

Points for Discussion

1. If the Service Courts of Appeals have the power to review cases for factual sufficiency, why shouldn't the Court of Appeals for the Armed Forces have that same authority?

2. Why did the Supreme Court find that review of the Air Force's decision to drop Major Goldsmith from the rolls fell outside the scope of "C.A.A.F.'s independent statutory jurisdiction"?

11-4. Parole, Boards for Correction of Military Records, and Pardons

After a conviction, while an accused's case moves through the appellate review process, the servicemember who is confined enters the corrections programs of the military Services. *See* DoD Instruction 1325.7, *Administration of Military Correctional Facilities and Clemency and Parole* (July 17, 2001, C1 June 10, 2003), *Army Reg. 15-130, Army Clemency and Parole Board* (Oct. 23, 1998), SECNAVINST 1640.9C, *Dep't of the Navy Corrections Manual*, Jan. 3, 2006), SECNAVINST 5815.3J, *Dep't of the Navy Clemency and Parole Systems* (June 12, 2003), AFI 31-205, *The Air Force Corrections System* (April 7, 2004). These corrections programs are designed to ensure convicted service members are held in a safe and secure environment away from society while preparing those convicted for release back either into the Service or into the civilian community.

While incarcerated, an accused's minimum release date from confinement may be abated (lessened) through good conduct and observance of confinement facility rules and regulations (good conduct time), and through work performance, program participation, or extraordinary achievements (earned abatement credit). *See* DoD Instruction 1325.7, *Administration of Military Correctional Facilities and Clemency and Parole* (July 17, 2001, C1 June 10, 2003).

Each Service has a parole and clemency board comprised of senior civilian employees and field grade military officers who advise the Service Secretaries. These boards have approval authority for clemency, parole (i.e, conditional release), restoration to duty, and reenlistment actions, unless the Secretary has withheld approval authority. DoD Instruction 1325.7, *Administration of Military Correctional Facilities and Clemency and Parole* (July 17, 2001, C1 June 10, 2003). In making its determinations, the board will consider the nature and circumstances of the offense, the prisoner's military and civilian history, confinement record, personal characteristics (i.e., age, education, marital and family status, and psychological profile), victim impact and prisoner's attempts at restitution, protection of society, good order and discipline in the Service, and other appropriate matters. *Id.* at ¶ 6.16.5. Within 9 months from the start of confinement or within 30 days of the convening authority's action whichever is later, the board reviews cases for prisoners whose approved unsuspended sentence to confinement is 12 months or more. *Id.* at ¶ 6.16.6.2. For prisoners with an unsuspended sentence of 12 months and less than 20 years, the board will consider their case annually. *Id.* at ¶ 6.16.6.3.1. For prisoners with an unsuspended sentence of 20 years or more, but less than 30 years, the board will consider their cases annually beginning three years from the start of confinement. *Id.* at ¶ 6.16.6.3.2. Prisoners may waive consideration. Prisoners are not eligible for parole if they are serving a sentence of death or life imprisonment without the possibility of parole. *Id.* at ¶ 6.16.6. However, a prisoner sentenced to confinement for life without the possibility of parole may receive clemency after serving 20 years of confinement and then may be paroled. *Id.* at ¶ 6.16.1.1.

The Department of Defense requires that prisoners not granted parole prior to their minimum release date be ordered into supervised release except in cases when the Service Clemency and Parole Board determines that supervised release would be inappropriate. *Id.* ¶ 6.20. The case that follows reflects an example of the implications of such a program.

If an accused exhausts all other administrative remedies, he may petition the Service Board for the Correction of Military Records, to modify or reduce his sentence or upgrade the characterization of his discharge. The board may not set aside the court-martial conviction or change the findings but will review and correct military records and take appropriate action to correct an error or injustice. 10 U.S.C. § 1552. The board may consider granting clemency on the court-martial sentence if the evidence presented warrants consideration. *See id.* These boards cannot set aside a court-martial conviction, but may reduce or modify a sentence as a matter of clemency, even if the sentence has already been executed.

Five years after release from confinement or the date of sentencing if no confinement was adjudged, convicted servicemembers, similar to others who have federal convictions, may apply through the Service Secretary to the Department of Justice Pardon Attorney to obtain a presidential pardon. *See* 28 C.F.R §§ 1.1 *et seq.* The presidential pardon may restore some rights, but will not upgrade the type of military discharge the accused received and will not expunge the conviction record.

UNITED STATES v. PENA
U.S. Court of Appeals for the Armed Forces
64 M.J. 259 (2007)

Chief Judge EFFRON delivered the opinion of the Court.

A general court-martial composed of a military judge sitting alone convicted Appellant [Timothy J. PENA, Senior Airman, U.S. Air Force], pursuant to his pleas, of attempted indecent assault, indecent assault, indecent exposure, indecent language, and adultery, in violation of Articles 80 and 134, Uniform Code of Military Justice (UCMJ), 10 U.S.C. §§ 880, 934 (2000), respectively. The sentence adjudged by the court-martial and approved by the convening authority included a dishonorable discharge, confinement for one year, and reduction to the lowest enlisted grade. The convening authority deferred mandatory forfeitures until the date of the action, and waived automatic forfeitures for a period of six months, directing payment of the mandatory forfeitures to Appellant's spouse for the benefit of his children. The United States Air Force Court of Criminal Appeals affirmed. *United States v. Pena,* 61 M.J. 776 (A.F. Ct. Crim. App. 2005).

On Appellant's petition, we granted review of the following issues:

I. WHETHER THE APPELLANT WAS IMPROPERLY PLACED ON EXCESS APPELLATE LEAVE AND DENIED PAY AND ALLOWANCES IN VIOLATION OF ARTICLE 76a, UCMJ, WHEN HIS SENTENCE TO CONFINEMENT WAS NOT COMPLETED OR REMITTED AND HE WAS FORCED TO FULFILL CONDITIONS OF MANDATORY SUPERVISION UPON HIS RELEASE FROM CONFINEMENT.

II. WHETHER THE AIR FORCE CLEMENCY AND PAROLE BOARD INCREASED THE SEVERITY OF APPELLANT'S SENTENCE IN VIOLATION OF ARTICLE 55, UCMJ, AND THE EIGHTH AMENDMENT WHEN IT FORCED APPELLANT TO FULFILL CONDITIONS OF MANDATORY SUPERVISION THAT ARE NOT AUTHORIZED BY THE UCMJ.

III. WHETHER THE IMPOSITION OF CONDITIONS OF MANDATORY SUPERVISION ON APPELLANT VIOLATES THE DUE PROCESS CLAUSE BECAUSE THE MILITARY JUDGE DID NOT ANNOUNCE A

PERIOD OF MANDATORY SUPERVISED RELEASE OR ANY OF ITS CONDITIONS AS PART OF THE SENTENCE.

* * *

Appellant, who was sentenced to confinement for one year, served all but seventy-two days of that period in confinement at the Naval Consolidated Brig Miramar, in San Diego, California. During the remaining seventy-two days, the Government placed Appellant in the Department of Defense (DoD) Mandatory Supervised Release program against his wishes.

The granted issues concern Appellant's early release from his sentence to confinement. Part I of this opinion summarizes the relationship between the DoD Mandatory Supervised Release program and other confinement and release programs in the military justice system. Part II describes the sentencing proceedings at Appellant's trial and the terms and conditions applied to Appellant through the Mandatory Supervised Release program. Part III considers whether those terms or conditions provide a basis for relief under applicable standards of review. For the reasons set forth below, we affirm.

I. THE DoD MANDATORY SUPERVISED RELEASE PROGRAM

Persons sentenced to confinement by a court-martial serve their period of imprisonment in facilities administered by the DoD, subject to exceptions not pertinent to the present appeal. Dep't of Defense Dir. 1325.4, Confinement of Military Prisoners and Administration of Military Correctional Programs and Facilities (Aug. 17, 2001) [hereinafter DoD Dir. 1325.4]. The DoD traditionally has administered a variety of early release procedures for persons in confinement, such as good time and earned credits, return to duty programs, and parole. *See* Dep't of Defense, Instr. 1325.7, Administration of Military Correctional Facilities and Clemency and Parole Authority, enclosure 26, para. E26.1–E26.5. (July 17, 2001, incorporating Change 1, June 10, 2003) [hereinafter DoD Instr. 1325.7].

Parole is a form of conditional release from confinement under the guidance and supervision of a United States probation officer. *Id.* at enclosure 2, para. E2.1.11. In addition, parole is a voluntary program, in which the inmate applies to participate during the balance of his or her period of approved confinement. *Id.* at para. 6.17; Dep't of Defense, Sentence Computation Manual 1325.7–M, at AP1.1.12 (July 27, 2004, Administrative Reissuance, incorporating Change 1, Aug. 30, 2006) [hereinafter DoD Manual 1325.7–M]. The decision as to whether parole should be granted is vested in the Clemency and Parole Boards of the military departments. The decision is highly discretionary. *See* DoD Instr. 1325.7, at para. 6.16. Prior to release on parole, the inmate must have an approved parole supervision plan, and agree in writing to abide by the plan and conditions of supervision. *Id.* at para. 6.17.9.1. Violation of the terms and conditions may result in revocation of parole. *Id.* at para. 6.17.10. In general, the supervision of persons on parole is designed to enhance the person's reintegration into civilian society. *See id.* at para. 6.17.9.2.

In 2001, the DoD introduced an additional early release mechanism, the Mandatory Supervised Release program. Mandatory Supervised Release covers specified classes of prisoners who have served sufficient time in confinement to be considered for parole, but who are not granted parole. *Id.* at para. 6.20.1. As with parole, Mandatory Supervised Release applies from the time of release from prison until the end of the prisoner's approved sentence, and it may be revoked for violation of the terms and conditions of the program. *Id.* at paras. 6.17.9.4, 6.17.9.6, 6.20.6.; DoD Manual 1325.7–M, at AP1.1.12.

In contrast to parole, which is a voluntary program, a prisoner may be placed involuntarily on Mandatory Supervised Release. *See generally* Policy Letter, Clemency and Parole Boards Mandatory Supervised Release Policy (May 23, 2003) (in Brief of Appellant at app. E). In addition to the conditions that may be imposed during parole, the Clemency and Parole Board may use the Mandatory Supervised Release program to impose "any additional reasonable supervision conditions . . . that would . . . further an orderly and successful transition to civilian life for released prisoners, and which would better protect the communities into which prisoners are released." DoD Instr. 1325.7, at para. 6.20.2. A prisoner who refuses to accept Mandatory Supervised Release or the conditions imposed by the Clemency and Parole Board is subject to discipline, including trial by court-martial. Clemency and Parole Boards Mandatory Supervised Release Policy Letter (May 23, 2003). *See* Policy Letter at ¶ E.5.

Mandatory Supervised Release differs in significant respects from the authority of the federal civilian courts to include in a sentence "a term of supervised release after imprisonment." 18 U.S.C. § 3583(a) (2000). Unlike the federal civilian program, which is based on express statutory authority and involves terms that are adjudged as part of the sentence, the military's Mandatory Supervised Release program is based on executive authority, and involves terms that are imposed by executive branch officials well after completion of trial.

II. THE ADJUDICATION AND ADMINISTRATION OF APPELLANT'S SENTENCE

A. THE PROCEEDINGS AT TRIAL

After Appellant entered a plea of guilty to various charged offenses, the military judge conducted an inquiry into the providency of the plea. *See* Rule for Courts–Martial (R.C.M.) 910. As part of the inquiry, the military judge explained the maximum punishment Appellant faced, based solely on the offenses to which he pled guilty. Appellant agreed with the military judge that he faced a dishonorable discharge from the service, forfeiture of all pay and allowances, forty-nine years of confinement, reduction to the grade of E–1, and a fine. The military judge asked Appellant if he had any questions about the specific punishments he faced, and Appellant responded in the negative. In addition, the military judge asked defense counsel whether he and Appellant had discussed the administrative ramifications of the punishments. Defense counsel responded in the affirmative. Neither the military judge nor defense counsel mentioned any specific administrative consequence.

Subsequently, during the sentencing proceeding the military judge reminded Appellant that he was facing a lengthy amount of confinement and asked him whether he had any additional questions. Appellant responded in the negative. The military judge sentenced Appellant to a dishonorable discharge, one year of confinement, and reduction to the grade of E–1.

B. PLACEMENT OF APPELLANT IN THE MANDATORY SUPERVISED RELEASE PROGRAM

The Air Force assigned Appellant to serve his period of confinement at the Naval Consolidated Brig Miramar. During that period, the Air Force Clemency and Parole Board determined that he would not be granted parole. The Board ordered him to participate in the Mandatory Supervised Release program for a seventy-two day period, terminating on his maximum release date at the end of the adjudged period of confinement.

The Certificate of Mandatory Supervised Release (certificate) issued to Appellant by the Board set forth sixteen conditions generally applicable to persons in the program, along with an attachment containing nine additional conditions tailored to Appellant's circumstances. The additional conditions required Appellant to: (1) participate in a community-based sex offender treatment program with a duration of at least twenty-four months, at his own expense; (2) have no contact with the victims without the prior approval of his probation officer; (3) abstain from the use and possession of pornography or sexually stimulating materials; (4) consent to periodic examinations of his computer, to include retrieval and copying of all data from his computer and/or removal of his computer equipment for the purpose of conducting a more thorough inspection; and consent to having installed on his computer, at his expense, any hardware or software monitoring systems; (5) abstain from adult book stores, sex shops, topless bars, or other locations that act as a sexual stimulus; (6) register as a sex offender in accordance with state law; (7) attend and participate in three meetings weekly concerning alcohol and narcotics abstention; (8) waive confidentiality in his relations with the sponsor of the treatment program so that his probation officer may monitor his progress in the program; and (9) abstain from consuming alcohol. The certificate provided that the term of mandatory supervision would expire on Appellant's maximum release date. The confinement officials at Miramar advised Appellant that he was required to accept the conditions in the certificate. If Appellant refused to do so, he could be prosecuted in a court-martial for failure to obey an order or dereliction of duty, and he could be sent before a disciplinary board with the potential of losing good time credits and confinement privileges.

A month prior to his proposed release under the Mandatory Supervised Release program, Appellant submitted a letter to the Commander of the confinement facility at Miramar requesting permission to decline participation in the program without losing his good time credits. Appellant stated that he could adhere to all of the conditions in the attachment except for participation in the sex offender treatment program. He noted that while the state of Illinois would pay for his participation in a treatment program in Chicago, he would have to make a six-hour round trip from his expected place of residence. He added that he had not yet obtained a job, his wife was unable to work due to the imminent birth of a child, and his family would have no income. He also noted that his mother would provide his family with room, board, and incidentals, but that the burden would stretch "her financial situation beyond its limits." He stated that "the bottom line is we cannot pay for transportation [to the treatment program] until I have secured a job and financially reestablished [my] family."

Appellant did not receive a response. When he reached his minimum release date with seventy-two days left in his period of confinement, he was released into the Mandatory Supervised Release program on June 22, 2003. The post-trial record contains a declaration signed by Appellant on July 10, 2003, in which he noted a number of problems created by his participation in the Mandatory Supervised Release program. The declaration notes that he was unable to stop in Colorado to ship his household goods to Illinois, that he incurred a ten dollar per week expenditure for transportation to the sex offender treatment program, that he was required to attend Alcoholics Anonymous classes three times a week at night and sex offender treatment classes once a week during the day, that he had various other appointments and a requirement to give a urine sample on short notice every two weeks, and that the conditions of mandatory supervision left him unable to find work to support his family. The declaration was submitted when Appellant had completed eighteen out of the seventy-two days of his period of mandatory supervised release. Although the declaration noted that he was not employed, it did not describe his living circumstances, sources of support, or overall financial condition. The record contains no further information documenting the impact of the Mandatory Supervised Release program on Appellant during the remaining fifty-four days that he was in the program. In addition, the record contains no indication that he was subjected to any of the conditions of the Mandatory Supervised Release program after the end of the seventy-two day period.

III. DISCUSSION

A. THE TERMS AND CONDITIONS OF APPELLANT'S MANDATORY SUPERVISED RELEASE (ISSUES II, III, AND IV)

At the outset, we note that Appellant has challenged the authority of the DoD to establish the Mandatory Supervised Release program in the absence of express statutory authority. Appellant asks us to invalidate a program under which the DoD releases individuals from prison prior to the completion of their adjudged sentence to confinement. On direct appeal, the scope of our review does not extend to supervision of all aspects of the confinement and release process. *United States v. Towns*, 52 M.J. 830, 833 (A.F. Ct. Crim. App. 2000), *aff'd*, 55 M.J. 361 (C.A.A.F. 2001). Our review of post-trial confinement and release conditions on direct appeal is limited to the impact of such conditions on the findings and the sentence. *See* Article 67(c), UCMJ, 10 U.S.C. § 867(c) (2000); *United States v. Spaustat*, 57 M.J. 256, 263 (C.A.A.F. 2002) (responsibility for determining how much good time credit, if any, will be awarded is an administrative responsibility, vested in the commander of the confinement facility). Accordingly, our review in the present appeal focuses on whether the post-trial conditions at issue: (1) constituted cruel or unusual punishment or otherwise violated an express prohibition in the UCMJ; (2) unlawfully increased Appellant's punishment; or (3) rendered his guilty plea improvident. To the extent that the issues raised by Appellant otherwise challenge the administration of the Mandatory Supervised Release program, those matters—including questions regarding the underlying legal authority for the program—are not before us on direct review.

1. *Cruel or Unusual Punishment*

The Eighth Amendment prohibits "cruel and unusual punishments." U.S. Const. amend. VIII. Similarly, Article 55, UCMJ, 10 U.S.C. § 855 (2000), prohibits "cruel or unusual punishment." Article 55, UCMJ, also prohibits specified punishments, such as use of irons except for the purpose of safe custody, which are not at issue in the present appeal. *See also* Article 12, UCMJ, 10 U.S.C. § 812 (2000) (prohibition on confinement in immediate association with enemy prisoners).

We review allegations of cruel or unusual punishment under a de novo standard. *United States v. White*, 54 M.J. 469, 471 (C.A.A.F. 2001). In our evaluation of both constitutional and statutory allegations of cruel or unusual punishment, we apply the Supreme Court's Eighth Amendment jurisprudence "in the absence of legislative intent to create greater protections in the UCMJ." *United States v. Lovett*, 63 M.J. 211, 215 (C.A.A.F. 2006).

The Eighth Amendment prohibits punishments that are " 'incompatible with the evolving standards of decency that mark the progress of a maturing society, or which involve the unnecessary and wanton infliction of pain.' " *Id.* at 214 (quoting *Estelle v. Gamble*, 429 U.S. 97, 102–03 (1976)). Although the conditions at issue in the present appeal implicate other legal issues, as discussed below, none of these conditions constitute cruel or unusual punishment within the Eighth Amendment standards articulated by the Supreme Court. *E.g.*, 18 U.S.C. § 3583 (2000) (describing the conditions of mandatory release that may be imposed in criminal trials in the federal district courts).

2. *Impact on the adjudged sentence*

Appellant contends that his punishment was increased without providing the requisite constitutional, statutory, and regulatory components of notice and an opportunity to respond. We review such claims de novo. *United States v. Rollins*, 61 M.J. 338, 343 (C.A.A.F. 2005).

The military sentencing process provides notice of the punishments at issue, an adversarial proceeding, and formal announcement of the sentence. *See* U.S. Const. amend. V; Articles 53, 56, and 60, UCMJ, 10 U.S.C. §§ 853, 856, 860 (2000); R.C.M. 1001–1007. A servicemember "cannot be subjected to a sentence greater than that adjudged" by the court-martial. *United States v. Stewart*, 62 M.J. 291, 294 (C.A.A.F. 2006) (citing *Waller v. Swift*, 30 M.J. 139, 143 (C.M.A. 1990)). *Cf. White*, 54 M.J. at 472 (noting our Court's "authority to ensure that the severity of the adjudged and approved sentence has not been unlawfully increased by prison officials"). Although reviewing authorities have the power to commute a sentence to a different form of punishment, *see* Article 60(c)(2), UCMJ; Article 71, UCMJ, 10 U.S.C. §§ 871 (2000), this authority may not be exercised in a manner that increases the severity of the punishment. *United States v. Carter*, 45 M.J. 168, 170 (C.A.A.F. 1996); *Waller*, 30 M.J. at 143; *see* R.C.M. 1107(d)(1), 1107(f)(2). The question of whether a change in the form of punishment increases the severity of the punishment is contextual, requiring consideration of "all the circumstances in a particular case." *Carter*, 45 M.J. at 170.

The foregoing considerations apply only to matters that constitute "punishment" within the meaning of the criminal law. As a general matter, the collateral administrative consequences of a sentence, such as early release programs, do not constitute punishment for purposes of the criminal law. *See, e.g., United States v. Griffin*, 25 M.J. 423, 424 (C.M.A. 1988) (impact of conviction on retirement benefits is a collateral administrative consequence, inappropriate for consideration at sentencing); *United States v. Murphy*, 26 M.J. 454, 457 (C.M.A. 1988) (classifying eligibility for a particular squadron as a collateral administrative consequence not to be considered in sentencing); *United States v. Hannan*, 17 M.J. 115, 123 (C.M.A. 1984) (recognizing parole eligibility as a collateral administrative consequence of sentence). Whether a particular aspect of an early release program is administered in a manner that constitutes punishment requires a case-specific inquiry. *Compare California Dep't of Corrections v. Morales*, 514 U.S. 499 (1995), *with Lynce v. Mathis*, 519 U.S. 433 (1997). *Cf. United States v. Fischer*, 61 M.J. 415, 420 (C.A.A.F. 2005) (setting forth factors to be considered in determining whether governmental actions are regulatory or punitive in nature) (citing *Kennedy v. Mendoza–Martinez*, 372 U.S. 144, 168 (1963)).

The terms and conditions of Appellant's Mandatory Supervised Release, as initially conveyed to him, potentially raised serious questions as to whether Appellant's sentence had been increased. On its face, the attachment accompanying the Certificate of Mandatory Release suggested that Appellant was required to subject himself involuntarily to a sex offender treatment program for twenty-four months, a period extending well beyond his maximum release date. In addition, the attachment suggested that Appellant was required to expend a substantial amount of his own funds to pay for the treatment program and computer software. As the record indicates, however, and as defense counsel confirmed during oral argument, none of the conditions were imposed upon Appellant after his maximum release date, and he was not required to pay for his treatment program or any computer software.

Although the defense brief sets forth a facial challenge to the Mandatory Supervised Release program and the conditions communicated to Appellant prior to his release, the defense has provided few details as to any actual impact on Appellant. On May 17, 2003, prior to his release, Appellant submitted a request for exemption from one of the conditions, participation in a treatment program, based upon concern as to what might occur upon release. That statement provides no information as to what actually happened to Appellant after he was released. On July 10, 2003, eighteen days after he was released under the Mandatory Supervised Release program, Appellant signed a declaration describing various difficulties that he had encountered in moving his household goods and obtaining employment as result of the requirements imposed by the Mandatory Supervised Release program. He also noted that he was required to expend ten dollars a week for transportation to a treatment program. The declaration, however, does not indicate what impact, if any, the Mandatory Supervised Release program had on Appellant's sentence during the remaining fifty-four days prior to his maximum release date.

In the context of an issue that requires a showing of increased punishment, it is not sufficient to show that the conditions of mandatory release imposed some burdens on a released prisoner. All conditions of release impose burdens to some degree. Those burdens, however, must be assessed in the context of release from a sentence to confinement. The question in each case is whether the burdens are such that they result in an increase in the punishment of confinement adjudged by the court-martial. *Carter*, 45 M.J. at 170. Such an assessment requires a case-specific analysis. *See id.*

We do not take lightly the impact of the Mandatory Supervised Release program on Appellant during the initial eighteen day period or during the subsequent fifty-four days. Likewise, we do not disregard the possibility that the Mandatory Supervised Release program could be imposed in a manner that increases the punishment above the punishment adjudged by a court-martial. The burden, however, is on the party challenging the conditions to demonstrate that there has been an increase above the punishment of confinement imposed at trial.

When an appellant asks us to review the post-trial administration of a sentence, we are typically confronted by issues in which the pertinent facts are not in the record of trial. In such a case, it is particularly important that the appellant provide us with a "clear record" of the facts and circumstances relevant to the claim of legal error. *See United States v. Miller*, 46 M.J. 248, 250 (C.A.A.F. 1997). The information about the personal, psychological, economic, and family impact of such measures is primarily in the control of the party appealing the sentence, and that party bears the responsibility of submitting detailed documentation. The generalized statements in Appellant's July 10, 2003, declaration, which cover only a portion of the time Appellant was in the Mandatory Supervised Release program, do not provide the clear record upon which we could evaluate whether the conditions of mandatory supervised release in this case produced an increase in Appellant's sentence. Accordingly, Appellant has not demonstrated that his participation in the Mandatory Supervised Release program produced an impermissible increase in the punishment adjudged by the court-martial.

3. *Effect on the providency of the guilty plea*

We review claims as to the providency of a plea under a de novo standard. *United States v. Harris*, 61 M.J. 391, 398 (C.A.A.F. 2005). An appellant who challenges the providency of a guilty plea must demonstrate "a substantial basis in law and fact for questioning the guilty plea." *United States v. Prater*, 32 M.J. 433, 436 (C.M.A. 1991) (quotation marks omitted). As a general matter, the military judge does not have an affirmative obligation to initiate an inquiry into early release programs as part of the plea inquiry. *See Hannan*, 17 M.J. at 123. When the challenge concerns an appellant's claimed misunderstanding of the collateral consequences of a court-martial, such as an early release program, an appellant must demonstrate that:

> the collateral consequences are major and the appellant's misunderstanding of the consequences (a) results foreseeably and almost inexorably from the language of a pretrial agreement; (b) is induced by the trial judge's comments during the providence inquiry; or (c) is made readily apparent to the judge, who nonetheless fails to correct that misunderstanding. In short, chief reliance must be placed on defense counsel to inform an accused about the collateral consequences of a court-martial conviction and to ascertain his willingness to accept those consequences.

United States v. Bedania, 12 M.J. 373, 376 (C.M.A. 1982). In the present case, Appellant has not demonstrated that the collateral consequences actually imposed increased his punishment. *See supra* Part III.A.2. Moreover, neither the text of the plea agreement nor the record of the military judge's plea inquiry contains any language that would have placed an obligation on the military judge to address the Mandatory Supervised Release program at that time. *See United States v. Miller*, 63 M.J. 452, 457 (C.A.A.F. 2006). We also note that Appellant has not claimed that his counsel was ineffective with respect to explaining collateral consequences, so we need not address whether counsel was under any obligation to do so. *See id.* at 458. Under the circumstances of this case, Appellant has not demonstrated that his plea was improvident.

B. APPELLATE LEAVE (ISSUE I)

* * *

Appellant contends that he should not have been placed on involuntary appellate leave for two reasons. First, he contends that as a practical matter he remained on active duty because the conditions imposed upon him by the Mandatory Supervised Release program constituted military duties for which he should have been paid. We need not decide whether such a claim is within the scope of our review under Article 67, UCMJ, because Appellant has not demonstrated that the conditions of his supervised release were so restrictive in nature or duration that they had the claimed effect of retaining him on active duty without pay. *See supra* Part III.A.2. Second, he contends that he did not "complete" his period of confinement under the Air Force Regulation because he was under a continuing threat of return to prison if he violated the terms of his release. The relationship between completion of confinement and commencement of leave is a matter governed by administrative regulations and service practices. Appellant has not demonstrated that the applicable regulations, either on their face or as applied, violated Article 76a, UCMJ, or any other provision of the UCMJ. Under these circumstances, Appellant has not demonstrated that this claim falls within the scope of our review under Article 67, UCMJ.

IV. DECISION

The decision of the United States Air Force Court of Criminal Appeals is affirmed.

Points for Discussion

1. Do you agree with the appellant that, "his punishment was increased without providing the requisite constitutional, statutory, and regulatory components of notice and an opportunity to respond"? Why or why not?

2. Should the military judge have responsibility to review early release programs with the accused as part of the plea inquiry prior to accepting a guilty plea? Wouldn't this ensure that misunderstandings of this kind are avoided in the future?

CHAPTER 12

MILITARY CRIMES IN GENERAL

12-1. Overview of the Punitive Articles

In order to further the goal of maintaining good order and discipline, the Armed Forces must have a criminal code that includes acts or omissions that may not be prohibited in the civilian community. Military commanders, unlike civilian employers, are thought to need the authority to seek criminal punishments for subordinates who fail to show up for work on time or fail to follow their instructions or commands. The punitive articles in the UCMJ, Articles 77 to 134, provide substantive criminal offenses for persons tried in the military justice system. Many of those articles mirror common law crimes and crimes in the civilian sector (including principals (Art. 77, UCMJ) and accessories (Art, 78, UCMJ) and inchoate offenses such as attempts (Art. 80, UCMJ), conspiracy (Art. 81, UCMJ), and solicitation (Art. 81, UCMJ)). Others criminalize conduct particularly important to the military. Each criminal offense includes elements of the offenses and, like their civilian counterparts, military prosecutors must prove each of those elements beyond a reasonable doubt. This chapter and Chapter 13 will provide a description of peculiarly military offenses such as absence offenses, duties and orders offenses, and relationship offenses.

Points for Discussion

1. Why should military crimes include conduct that is not criminalized in the civilian sector such as dereliction of duty or maltreatment of subordinates?

2. Can you think of examples of how military-type offenses such as dereliction of duty, absence without leave, conduct unbecoming of an officer and gentleman might be prosecuted in federal court if a military justice system and these military specific criminal offenses did not exist?

Problem

The following facts come from *United States v. Smith*, 68 M.J. 445 (C.A.A.F. 2010):

Appellant and Cadet SR were cadets at the United States Coast Guard Academy. During the summer of 2005, Cadet SR and Appellant were assigned to neighboring Coast Guard cutters in Norfolk, Virginia. While there, Cadet SR committed an indiscretion that could have jeopardized her ranking as a cadet and threatened her Coast Guard career. Shortly thereafter, Appellant sent her a text message saying that he hoped the rumors he was hearing were not true. Cadet SR discussed the situation with Appellant but lied about some of the details. Appellant "said he'd try to squash rumors, and that it would be okay."

In October of that year, after both had returned to the Academy, Appellant notified Cadet SR that the rumors were persisting. She then truthfully disclosed the details of her indiscretion. Appellant said he would continue to try to suppress the rumors, but that he needed motivation to do so. Appellant denied he was seeking sexual favors but suggested the couple take a photograph of themselves naked together to build "trust in one another." [Cadet S.R. subsequently submitted to be photographed with Appellant.]

Review the list of punitive articles. With which offense or offenses might Appellant be charged based on these facts?

12-2. The General Article—Article 134 and The Federal Assimilative Crimes Act

When Congress passed the UCMJ, that statute included The General Article, 134, which allows military prosecutors the unique ability to craft criminal specifications describing misconduct which is not described in other enumerated offenses in the Code. The UCMJ contains the following provision:

Art. 134. General article

Though not specifically mentioned in this chapter, all disorders and neglects to the prejudice of good order and discipline in the armed forces, all conduct of a nature to bring discredit upon the armed forces, and crimes and offenses not capital, of which persons subject to this chapter may be guilty, shall be taken cognizance of by a general, special, or summary court-martial, according to the nature and degree of the offense, and shall be punished at the discretion of that court.

10 U.S.C. § 934.

The Manual for Courts-Martial provides the following additional clarification regarding this offense:

(1) *In general.* Article 134 makes punishable acts in three categories of offenses not specifically covered in any other article of the code. These are referred to as "clauses 1, 2, and 3" of Article 134. Clause 1 offenses involve disorders and neglects to the prejudice of good order and discipline in the armed forces. Clause 2 offenses involve conduct of a nature to bring discredit upon the armed forces. Clause 3 offenses involve noncapital crimes or offenses which violate Federal law including law made applicable through the Federal Assimilative Crimes Act, *see* subsection (4) below. . . .

(2) *Disorders and neglects to the prejudice of good order and discipline in the armed forces (clause 1).*

    (a) *To the prejudice of good order and discipline.* "To the prejudice of good order and discipline" refers only to acts directly prejudicial to good order and discipline and not to acts which are prejudicial only in a remote or indirect sense. Almost any irregular or improper act on the part of a member of the military service could be regarded as prejudicial in some indirect or remote sense; however, this article does not include these distant effects. It is confined to cases in which the prejudice is reasonably direct and palpable. . . .

    (b) *Breach of custom of the service.* A breach of a custom of the service may result in a violation of clause 1 of Article 134. In its legal sense, "custom" means more than a method of procedure or a mode of conduct or behavior which is merely of frequent or usual occurrence. Custom arises out of long established practices which by common usage have attained the force of law in the military or other community affected by them. No custom may be contrary to existing law or regulation. . . . Violations of the customs should be charged under Article 92 as violations of the regulations in which they appear if the regulation is punitive. *See* paragraph 16c.

(3) *Conduct of a nature to bring discredit upon the armed forces (clause 2).* "Discredit" means to injure the reputation of. This clause of Article 134 makes punishable conduct which has a tendency to bring the service into disrepute or which tends to lower it in public esteem. . . .

MCM, pt. IV, ¶60.a.

The preemption doctrine prohibits military prosecutors from charging servicemembers with Article 134 violations for conduct that is covered in the other enumerated articles 80 through 132. *Id.*

In the Manual for Courts-Martial, the President defines elements for the General Article 134 as follows:

> If the conduct is punished as a crime or offense not capital, the proof must establish every element of the crime or offense as required by the applicable law. If the conduct is punished as a disorder or neglect to the prejudice of good order and discipline in the armed forces, or of a nature to bring discredit upon the armed forces, then the following proof is required: (1) That the accused did or failed to do certain acts; and (2) That, under the circumstances, the accused's conduct was to the prejudice of good order and discipline in the armed forces or was of a nature to bring discredit upon the armed forces.

Id.

    Pursuant to his Article 36, UCMJ rulemaking authority, the President, through executive order, has added specific listed criminal offenses under Article 134, UCMJ, such as adultery, bigamy, impersonating an officer, indecent language, pandering, and prostitution, which are prejudicial to good order and discipline of the Armed Forces or are of a nature to bring discredit upon the Armed Forces. The President also provided the following: "A specification alleging a violation of Article 134 need not expressly allege that the conduct was 'a disorder or neglect,' [or] that it was 'of a nature to bring discredit upon the armed forces,' . . . . The same conduct may constitute a disorder or neglect to the prejudice of good order and discipline in the armed forces and at the same time be of a nature to bring discredit upon the armed forces." *Id.*

Clauses 1 & 2 of Article 134

The U.S. Court of Appeals for the Armed Forces decision in *United States v. Fosler* below overturns the *Manual for Courts-Martial* regarding drafting specifications and inclusion of the element regarding good order and discipline or service discrediting.

UNITED STATES v. FOSLER
Court of Appeals for the Armed Forces
70 M.J. 225 (C.A.A.F. 2011)

STUCKY, Judge:

To establish a violation of Article 134, Uniform Code of Military Justice (UCMJ), 10 U.S.C. § 934 (2006), the government must prove beyond a reasonable doubt both that the accused engaged in certain conduct and that the conduct satisfied at least one of three listed criteria. The latter element is commonly referred to as the "terminal element" of Article 134 and the government must prove that at least one of the article's three clauses has been met: that the accused's conduct was (1) "to the prejudice of good order and discipline," (2) "of a nature to bring discredit upon the armed forces," or (3) a "crime[or] offense[ ] not capital." Article 134. We hold that the Government failed to allege at least one of the three clauses either expressly or by necessary implication and that the charge and specification therefore fail to state an offense under Article 134.

I.

Contrary to his pleas, Appellant [Lance Corporal James N. Fosler, U.S. Marine Corps] was convicted of adultery in violation of Article 134. On September 21, 2009, he was sentenced to a bad-conduct discharge, confinement for thirty days, forfeiture of all pay and allowances, and reduction to the lowest enlisted grade. On February 5, 2010, the convening authority approved the sentence and, with the exception of the bad-conduct discharge, ordered it executed. On October 28, 2010, the United States Navy–Marine Corps Court of Criminal Appeals (CCA) affirmed the findings and the sentence. *United States v. Fosler*, 69 M.J. 669, 678 (N.–M.Ct. Crim. App. 2010). On February 9, 2011, this Court granted review to determine whether the charge and specification leading to Appellant's conviction for adultery in violation of Article 134 stated an offense.

II.

While a drill instructor at the Naval Junior Reserve Officer Training Corps (NJROTC) in Rota, Spain, Appellant admitted to having sexual intercourse on December 26, 2007, with SK, a sixteen-year-old high school student enrolled in NJROTC, the daughter of an active duty Navy servicemember. The evidence demonstrated that other drill instructors and NJROTC students were aware of the sexual relations between Appellant and SK. SK claimed that the intercourse was not consensual.

Appellant was charged with rape and aggravated sexual assault in violation of Article 120, UCMJ, 10 U.S.C. § 920 (2006), and with adultery in violation of Article 134. Appellant was ultimately acquitted of the Article 120 charges. The charge sheet described the Article 134 allegation, the offense of conviction, as follows:

Charge II: VIOLATION OF THE UCMJ, ARTICLE 134

Specification: In that Lance Corporal James N. Fosler, U.S. Marine Corps, Marine Corps Security Force Regiment, on active duty, a married man, did, at or near Naval Station, Rota, Spain, on or about 26 December 2007, . . . wrongfully hav[e] sexual intercourse with [SK], a woman not his wife.

After the end of the Government's case-in-chief, trial defense counsel moved to dismiss the specification both under Rule for Courts–Martial (R.C.M.) 917 (motion for a finding of not guilty due to insufficient evidence), and because the Government "failed to allege [the terminal element] in the charge sheet," and therefore that the charge and specification "fail[ed] to state an offense." As the CCA noted, this second motion should be "considered as a motion to dismiss under R.C.M. 907." *Fosler*, 69 M.J. at 670 n. 1.

The military judge denied both motions. Concerning the motion to dismiss, the military judge stated that "[t]here's no requirement that the government has to either state [which clause of the terminal element is alleged], or state either of them in the [s]pecification." During the findings phase, the military judge instructed the members regarding clauses 1 and 2.

III.

Historically, the express allegation of the terminal element of Article 134 has not been viewed as necessary. The origin of the modern Article 134, the general article, can be traced back to before the founding of the nation—namely, the first American Articles of War in 1775. William Winthrop, *Military Law and Precedents* 720 (2d ed. Government Printing Office 1920) (1895). Two points can be made about jurisprudence under the general article. First, " 'conduct to the prejudice of good order and military discipline' "—and when it was added in 1916, "conduct of a nature to bring discredit upon the armed forces"—"[was] deemed to be involved in every specific military crime," and was therefore available as a lesser included offense (LIO) of the enumerated articles of the Articles of War and later the

MILITARY CRIMES IN GENERAL

UCMJ. *See United States v. Foster,* 40 M.J. 140, 143 (C.M.A. 1994), *overruled in part by United States v. Miller,* 67 M.J. 385, 389 (C.A.A.F. 2009); Winthrop, *supra* at 109. As a consequence, an accused could be convicted under Article 134 as an LIO of nearly any offense charged. As the charged offense was an enumerated article and therefore did not contain the terminal element, its explicit allegation must have been considered unnecessary. The trier of fact was nonetheless required to find that the terminal element had been proven beyond a reasonable doubt to obtain a conviction under Article 134 as an LIO.

Second, the references relied upon by practitioners did not treat the general article's terminal element as a requisite component of the charge and specification.[2] To provide guidance to practitioners, both the *Manual for Courts–Martial (MCM)* and authoritative works such as Colonel Winthrop's treatise included form charges and specifications for the various articles. *See, e.g., Manual for Courts–Martial, United States* app. 6c (1951 ed.); Winthrop, *supra* at 1010–23. This guidance never had the force of law, but was undoubtedly relied upon in everyday practice and generally reflective of the authors' understanding of the law at the time.

With few exceptions, sample specifications provided for the general article did not indicate that the terminal element should be alleged, though the sample charges often suggested specific reference to the general article. . .

This Court previously approved of such practices. . . .

More recent cases have required a greater degree of specificity in charging. The Supreme Court, addressing the relationship between the charged offense and permissible offenses of conviction, explained in *Schmuck v. United States* that the accused's constitutional right to notice "would be placed in jeopardy" if the government were "able to request an instruction on an offense whose elements were not charged in the indictment." 489 U.S. 705, 718 (1989). This concern led the Supreme Court to adopt the elements test as the appropriate method of determining whether an offense is an LIO of the charged offense—and therefore available as an offense of conviction. This test requires that "the indictment contain[ ] the elements of both offenses and thereby gives notice to the defendant that he may be convicted on either charge." *Id.*

In a line of recent cases drawing on *Schmuck,* we have concluded that the historical practice of implying Article 134's terminal element in every enumerated offense was no longer permissible. *See United States v. McMurrin,* 70 M.J. 15, 17 (C.A.A.F. 2011); *United States v. Girouard,* 70 M.J. 5, 9 (C.A.A.F. 2011); *United States v. Jones,* 68 M.J. 465, 468 (C.A.A.F.

---

[2] To understand this point, some background information is helpful. In military justice, a charge consists of two parts: the "charge"—typically, a statement of the article alleged to have been violated—and the "specification"—the more detailed description of the conduct allegedly violative of the article. R.C.M. 307(c)(2),(3).

2010); *Miller*, 67 M.J. at 388–89; *United States v. Medina*, 66 M.J. 21, 24–25 (C.A.A.F. 2008).

The Court's holdings in this line of cases—that an accused's "constitutional rights to notice and to not be convicted of a crime that is not an LIO of the [charged] offense" are violated when an accused is convicted of an Article 134 offense as an LIO of a non-Article 134 charged offense, *see, e.g., Girouard*, 70 M.J. at 10 (citing U.S. Const. amends. V, VI)—call into question the practice of omitting the terminal element from the charge and specification. This is so because not " 'all of the elements' " of the offense of conviction are " 'included in the definition of the offense *of which the defendant is charged.*' " *Id.* (emphasis in original) (quoting *Patterson v. New York*, 432 U.S. 197, 210 (1977)).

In light of this recent case law, we must determine whether the military judge erred by denying Appellant's motion to dismiss for failure to state an offense.

IV.

The Constitution protects against conviction of uncharged offenses through the Fifth and Sixth Amendments. See *Russell v. United States*, 369 U.S. 749, 761 (1962). The rights at issue here include the same rights we addressed in the context of our LIO jurisprudence:

> The rights at issue in this case are constitutional in nature. The Fifth Amendment provides that no person shall be "deprived of life, liberty, or property, without due process of law," U.S. Const. amend. V, and the Sixth Amendment provides that an accused shall "be informed of the nature and cause of the accusation," U.S. Const. amend. VI.

Girouard, 70 M.J. at 10; *see also McMurrin*, 70 M.J. at 18–19 (quoting *Girouard*, 70 M.J. at 10).

Applying these protections, we set aside convictions under Article 134 in the LIO context because the charges and specifications in both cases alleged a violation of an enumerated article and we could not interpret the elements of the enumerated articles to "necessarily include[ ]" the terminal element. *See* Article 79, UCMJ, 10 U.S.C. § 879 (2006); *see, e.g., Jones*, 68 M.J. at 473. . . . none of the enumerated articles we examined contained elements the ordinary understanding of which could be interpreted to mean or necessarily include the concepts of prejudice to "good order and discipline" or "conduct of a nature to bring discredit upon the armed forces," Article 134; *see Girouard*, 70 M.J. at 9.

In the instant case, we are called upon to determine, not whether the terminal element is necessarily included in the elements of the charged offense, but whether it is necessarily implied in the charge and specification. Though the object we must construe is different—elements versus charge and specification—the basic question is the same: using the appropriate interpretive tools, can the relevant statutory or, as here, charging language be interpreted to contain the terminal element such that an Article 134 conviction can be sustained?

The military is a notice pleading jurisdiction. *United States v. Sell*, 11 C.M.R. 202, 206 (C.M.A. 1953). A charge and specification will be found sufficient if they, "first, contain[ ] the elements of the offense charged and fairly inform[ ] a defendant of the charge against which he must defend, and, second, enable[ ] him to plead an acquittal or conviction in bar of future prosecutions for the same offense." *Hamling v. United States*, 418 U.S. 87, 117 (1974); *see also United States v. Resendiz–Ponce*, 549 U.S. 102, 108 (2007) (citations and quotation marks omitted); *United States v. Sutton*, 68 M.J. 455, 455 (C.A.A.F. 2010); *United States v. Crafter*, 64 M.J. 209, 211 (C.A.A.F. 2006); *Sell*, 11 C.M.R. at 206. The rules governing court-martial procedure encompass the notice requirement: "A specification is sufficient if it alleges every element of the charged offense expressly or by necessary implication." R.C.M. 307(c)(3).

The requirement to allege every element expressly or by necessary implication ensures that a defendant understands what he must defend against . . . .

The three clauses of Article 134 constitute "three distinct and separate parts." *United States v. Frantz*, 7 C.M.R. 37, 39 (C.M.A. 1953). Violation of one clause does not necessarily lead to a violation of the other clauses. For example, "disorders and neglects to the prejudice of good order and discipline" is not synonymous with "conduct of a nature to bring discredit upon the armed forces," although some conduct may support conviction under both clauses. . . .

An accused must be given notice as to which clause or clauses he must defend against. As we explained in the context of a guilty plea: "[F]or the purposes of Article 134, UCMJ, it is important for the accused to know whether [the offense in question is] a crime or offense not capital under clause 3, a 'disorder or neglect' under clause 1, conduct proscribed under clause 2, or all three." *Medina*, 66 M.J. at 26. This requirement was based on fair notice. *See id.* Principles of fair notice require the same in contested cases.

Because the terminal element was not expressly alleged, our task is to determine whether the terminal element was necessarily implied. *See* R.C.M. 307(c)(3). To do so, we must interpret the text of the charge and specification. We agree with the court below that *Resendiz–Ponce* does not foreclose the possibility that an element could be implied. *See Fosler*, 69 M.J. at 675. However, in contested cases, when the charge and specification are first challenged at trial, we read the wording more narrowly and will only adopt interpretations that hew closely to the plain text. *Cf. United States v. Watkins*, 21 M.J. 208, 209–10 (C.M.A. 1986).

The Government argues that the terminal element is implied because the specification alleged adultery, the word "wrongfully" was used, and the charge stated "Article 134." These facts do not provide a basis, individually or together, to find that the charge and specification necessarily implied the terminal element.

An allegation of adulterous conduct cannot imply the terminal element. Article 134, if properly charged, would be constitutional as applied to Appellant's adulterous conduct because, as discussed by the Supreme Court in *Levy,* tradition and custom give notice to servicemembers that adulterous conduct can give rise to a violation of the UCMJ. *See* 417 U.S. at 746–47. But this only answers the question of whether adulterous conduct can constitutionally be criminalized under Article 134, not whether the wording of the charge and specification satisfies constitutional requirements. An accused cannot be convicted under Article 134 if the trier of fact determines only that the accused committed adultery; the trier of fact must also determine beyond a reasonable doubt that the terminal element has been satisfied. *See Medina,* 66 M.J. at 27. Because adultery, standing alone, does not constitute an offense under Article 134, the mere allegation that an accused has engaged in adulterous conduct cannot imply the terminal element.

Likewise, the word "wrongfully" cannot of itself imply the terminal element. "Wrongfully" is a word of criminality and, though our case law has been at times unclear, *see United States v. Choate,* 32 M.J. 423, 427 (C.M.A. 1991), words of criminality speak to mens rea and the lack of a defense or justification, not to the elements of an offense . . . .

In a contested case in which Appellant challenged the charge and specification at trial, the inclusion of "Article 134" in the charge does not imply the terminal element. The words "Article 134" do not, by definition, mean prejudicial to "good order and discipline," "of a nature to bring discredit upon the armed forces," or a "crime[or] offense[ ] not capital," and we are unable to construe the words "Article 134" in the charge we now review to embrace the terminal element. . . .

These components of the charge and specification do not imply the terminal element alone or when combined.

V.

The Government also argues that its desired result is compelled by the *MCM* (2008 ed.), pursuant to the President's delegated and Article II powers, and by *Parker v. Levy.*

Congress delegated to the President certain rulemaking authority under Article 36, UCMJ, 10 U.S.C. § 836 (2006), but not everything in the *MCM* represents an exercise of that authority, and the President does not have the authority to decide questions of substantive criminal law. . . . No article of the UCMJ states that the terminal element may be omitted. Even if the President had the authority to do so, he has not set out any Rule for Courts–Martial or Military Rule of Evidence directing that the terminal element need not be alleged expressly or by necessary implication. Some of the *MCM* is merely explanatory or hortatory. The sample specifications and drafters' analysis are included among these categories and do not purport to be binding. *See MCM* pt. I, para. 4, Discussion (2008 ed.) . . . .

* * *

The Government must allege every element expressly or by necessary implication, including the terminal element. The Government did not expressly allege the terminal element in this case. Because Appellant made an R.C.M. 907 motion at trial, we review the language of the charge and specification more narrowly than we might at later stages. *Cf. Watkins,* 21 M.J. at 209–10. In this context, and in light of the changes in Article 134 jurisprudence, we do not adopt the Government's broad reading of the reference in the charge to "Article 134." Absent the historical gloss on the meaning of "Article 134" when that phrase exists in the charge, we are compelled to hold that the charge and specification do not allege the terminal element expressly or by necessary implication. To the extent that prior decisions such as *Mayo* and *Marker* hold to the contrary, they are overruled.

Under principles of stare decisis, we examine "intervening events, reasonable expectations of servicemembers, and the risk of undermining public confidence in the law." *United States v. Boyett,* 42 M.J. 150, 154 (C.A.A.F. 1995). . . . Although the dissenting opinions argue at length for the application of stare decisis, the Supreme Court has explained that "stare decisis cannot possibly be controlling when . . . the decision in question has been proved manifestly erroneous, and its underpinnings eroded, by subsequent decisions of [the Supreme] Court." *United States v. Gaudin,* 515 U.S. 506, 521 (1995).

* * *

Therefore, because an accused must be notified which of the three clauses he must defend against, to survive an R.C.M. 907 motion to dismiss, the terminal element must be set forth in the charge and specification.

VI.

In this case, at the end of the Government's case-in-chief, defense counsel made a motion to dismiss the specification of adultery under Charge II because the Government "failed to allege [the terminal element] in the charge sheet," and therefore "it's a failure to state an offense." This constitutes a motion to dismiss under R.C.M. 907(b)(1)(B), which may be made "at any stage of the proceedings." The military judge denied this motion.

Construing the text of the charge and specification narrowly, as we must based on the posture of the case, they fail to allege the terminal element expressly or by necessary implication. Because allegation of the terminal element is constitutionally required and the Government failed to satisfy that requirement here, the military judge's decision to deny Appellant's motion to dismiss was in error. The remedy for this erroneously denied motion to dismiss is dismissal. *See United States v. Smith*, 39 M.J. 448, 452–53 (C.M.A. 1994).

VII.

Accordingly, the judgment of the United States Navy–Marine Corps Court of Criminal Appeals is reversed. The findings of guilty and the sentence are set aside, and the charge and its specification are dismissed.

ERDMANN and RYAN, JJ., joined.

[Chief Judge Effron's dissenting opinion and Judge Baker's dissenting opinion are omitted.—Eds.]

Problem

The following facts come from *United States v. Gibson*, 39 M.J. 319 (C.M.A. 1994):

. . . Appellant was a midshipman at the United States Naval Academy, and he participated in a "sponsorship" program, in which midshipmen are assigned to local families. The A family sponsored appellant, gave him keys to their home, and treated him as "a member" of their family for the 4 years he attended the Naval Academy. For most of appellant's 4–year relationship with the A family, he was like a brother to Cheri, the older of two daughters. However, during appellant's last year at the Naval Academy, when appellant spent a couple of weekends a month at the A's house, Mrs. A noticed a change in appellant's relationship with her daughter and was worried that the two had become "too close." Mrs. A told appellant she thought Cheri, who was 12 years old at the time and in the 7th grade, had "a crush" on him and asked him not "to lead her on." On one occasion, Mr. A found his daughter sitting on appellant's lap. On another, Mrs. A noticed that appellant and Cheri had been alone together in Cheri's room with the door closed. Mrs. A also was suspicious when she entered the family room late one night and Cheri jumped up from the floor where she had been sitting with appellant.

One day while cleaning Cheri's room, Mrs. A found a letter from Cheri to appellant confirming that the two had an intimate relationship. Mrs. A cried, spoke with Mr. A about the situation, then decided to call appellant, who was at home in Tennessee on leave before graduation. When Mrs. A asked appellant if he had been "intimate" with Cheri, he replied, "Sort of." And when pushed to be more precise, he described their acts as "[t]ouching. Maybe kissing. Maybe fondling or something." Mrs. A instructed appellant to tell his father what he had told her and to call her back.

Based on these facts, Appellant was ultimately convicted of taking indecent liberties with a minor, in violation of Article 134, UCMJ, 10 U.S.C. § 934. He was sentenced to confinement for 1 year, total forfeitures, and dismissal from the naval service. How would you draft the specification for this offense?

The preceding *Fosler* opinion has wide-reaching implications in the military. The Service courts of criminal appeals now must evaluate whether to follow suit by dismissing specifications for listed Article 134 offense if the "terminal element" alleging a violation of good order and discipline or alleging service discrediting conduct is not included. When you read the *United States v. Simmons* opinion below note how the Navy-Marine Corps Court of Criminal Appeals distinguishes the *Fosler* opinion from its superior court, the Court of Appeals for the Armed Forces. As the Navy-Marine Corps Court identifies, Lance Corporal Fosler's defense counsel raised the defective pleading issue at the trial level in a motion to dismiss for failure to state an offense and it was a contested case.

UNITED STATES v. SIMMONS
Navy-Marine Corps Court of Criminal Appeals
2011 WL 4505978 (N.M. Ct. Crim. App. 2011)

BOOKER, Senior Judge:

A military judge sitting as a general court-martial convicted the appellant [Sergeant Matthew W. Simmons, U.S. Marine Corps], pursuant to his pleas, of two offenses involving general orders (specifically, a Department of Defense instruction on uniforms and the Department of Defense Joint Ethics Regulation ["JER"]) and one offense involving the General Article, respectively violations of Articles 92 and 134, Uniform Code of Military Justice, 10 U.S.C. §§ 892 and 934. The convening authority approved only so much of the sentence as extended to confinement for 90 days, a fine of $10,000.00, and a bad-conduct discharge from the United States Marine Corps.

In his initial pleading, the appellant averred that the General Article specification failed to state an offense because it did not allege that his disorder/neglect was prejudicial to good order and discipline or that his conduct was of a nature to bring discredit upon the armed forces. We then specified four additional issues: whether one of the regulations that the appellant violated was issued by competent authority; whether the regulation was punitive; whether the appellant was operating in an official capacity when violating the other general regulation; and whether the military judge correctly calculated the maximum punishment. With the benefit of the parties' briefs on the initial and specified issues, we may now resolve the appellant's case.

Background

The appellant was an active-duty bandsman. He took leave to appear in several commercial pornographic videos that involved sodomy with numerous other men, by his own account being paid $10,000.00 for his performances. Some of the videos included shots of him wearing his Marine dress blue coat with the Marine Corps device, decorations, and rank insignia affixed; others showed him wearing a Marine physical training jacket; and at one point he mentioned that he was a Marine. Out-takes from the videos were used to advertise the videos on a website, www.activeduty.com, and one of those out-takes showed the appellant wearing the blue coat. The appellant's activities came to the attention of his command after a former Marine, an acquaintance, learned of the videos and reported the information to the command.

Discussion

We review a military judge's decision to accept a guilty plea for an abuse of discretion. *E.g., United States v. Eberle,* 44 M.J. 374, 375 (C.A.A.F. 1996). We may find an abuse of discretion only if there is a substantial basis in law or fact for doing so. *United States v. Inabinette,* 66 M.J. 320, 322 (C.A.A.F. 2008). The issues specified reflect our concerns regarding both the legal and the factual basis for several of the pleas.

Order Violations

Our concerns about the legality of the instruction on uniforms led to the first two specified issues. Department of Defense Instruction 1334.01 of 26 October 2005, appended to the record as Appellate Exhibit VII, was issued by the Under Secretary of Defense for Personnel and Readiness, but it does not describe any delegation of authority to that Under Secretary to do so. Because a lawful general regulation may be issued only by "the President or the Secretary of Defense, of Homeland Security, or of a military department, [or by various uniformed officials]," MANUAL FOR COURTS–MARTIAL, UNITED STATES (2008 ed.), Part IV, ¶ 16c(1)(a), and because those orders "which only supply general guidelines or advice for conducting military functions may not be enforceable," *id.* at ¶ 16c(1)(e), we required additional briefing. We are now satisfied that the Instruction clears the necessary hurdles to be considered a "lawful general regulation".

We recognize that any large organization must function through delegations of authority, as it is impossible to have the head of the organization take every single action necessary to the organization's operation. Acting pursuant to statutory authority, specifically section 113 of title 10, United States Code, the Secretary of Defense has delegated areas of his authority to Deputy, Under, and Assistant Secretaries of the Department to ensure that the Department runs smoothly and can discharge its responsibilities. Pertinent to this case, the Secretary of Defense has delegated to the Under Secretary for Personnel and Readiness the authority to regulate in the area of readiness and training. . . . We are satisfied that the Under Secretary was vested with sufficient statutory and regulatory authority to issue, in his own right, this regulation. . . .

We are also satisfied that the regulation is punitive; that is, it was published with a view toward governing conduct of service members rather than simply stating guidelines for performing military functions. . . .

The two order violations alleged both involve the appellant's participation in a commercial video. Due to overlapping language in both the specifications and the respective orders that they invoke, we will discuss these offenses together.

Before beginning our discussion, we note as unresolved a significant factual question, which is what constitutes a "uniform" for purposes of this prosecution. We can tell from the appellant's admissions during the providence colloquy and in the statement of fact, Prosecution Exhibit 1, that the appellant wore *components* of his uniform; the sentencing exhibits also bear this out. When we review a directive, Marine Corps Order P1020.34G of 31 March 2003, provided by the Government in its pleading in response to the specified issues, however, we cannot say with certainty that the terms "uniform" and "uniform items" are interchangeable.

The JER, the regulation around which Specification 1 of Charge I pivots, prohibits the use of one's official capacity for private gain. That regulation does not define "official capacity," although it and regulations and opinions cited by both parties do give examples of what may or may not constitute an "official capacity." The chapter in which the provision cited in the specification appears, fairly read, is aimed at prohibiting the Department of Defense and its employees from becoming too entwined with the operation of commercial enterprises or from giving some commercial enterprises an unfair competitive advantage. *Cf.* 32 C.F.R. § 2635.702(b) and (c) and examples cited. Likewise, the uniform directive prohibits wearing a uniform when to do so would create "an inference of official sponsorship" for a commercial interest. AE VII at ¶ 3.1.2.

Looking first at the colloquy on the JER violation, significantly the appellant never mentions any "official capacity" regarding his appearance in the videos. He does say that he "probably" mentioned that he was a Marine, Record at 73, and that he was wearing part of a uniform when he responded to a question whether he was a Marine. We note, though, that the appellant used a "screen name" for the videos and had stripped his dress blue coat of an aiguillette that identified his unit. He never identified any particular office—Sergeant of the Guard, Drum Major—during the interview. *Cf.* 32 C.F.R. § 2635.702(c)(4) (example of Assistant Attorney General, a public official appointed by the President with the advice and consent of the Senate; *see* 28 U.S.C. § 506). At most, the appellant revealed a status as an active-duty Marine. Just as the appellant's being involved in an accident on liberty with a privately owned vehicle would not create liability on the Marine Corps under the Federal Tort Claims Act, neither does his saying that he was a Marine permit any conclusion that he was acting in an "official capacity" when he appeared in the videos.

We are also not satisfied, on the basis of this record, that the appellant's statements or wear of uniform items may create an inference of service endorsement of the activities depicted. The appellant never wore a complete "uniform," so the general public could never receive "visual evidence of the authority and responsibility vested in the individual by the United States Government." MCO P1020.34G ¶ 1000.3. He did not voice any Marine support for what he was doing or any service views on the propriety or impropriety of his conduct.

We accordingly set aside the guilty findings on Specifications 1 and 3 of Charge I.

General Article Violation

Moving to the Additional Charge and its underlying specification, we agree with the appellant that the specification as alleged failed to state an offense in light of *United States v. Fosler,* 70 M.J. 225 (C.A.A.F. 2011). Our inquiry does not end there, however.

We resolve this assignment adversely to the appellant notwithstanding *Fosler* for two reasons. First, the appellant pleaded guilty to the offenses laid under Article 134, and we note that *Fosler* was a contested case. "Where . . . the specification is not so defective that it 'cannot within reason be construed to charge a crime,' the accused does not challenge the specification at trial, pleads guilty, has a pretrial agreement, satisfactorily completes the providence inquiry, and has suffered no prejudice, the conviction will not be reversed on the basis of defects in the specification." *United States v. Watkins,* 21 M.J. 208, 210 (C.M.A. 1986). Here, the appellant entered into a pretrial agreement that contemplated guilty pleas to the General Article offenses; he received the correct statutory elements and definitions from the military judge; and he satisfactorily completed the providence inquiry.

Even if *Watkins* should for some reason be overruled or severely limited, we note that the military judge, in informing the appellant here of the elements, included the "prejudice" and "discredit" aspects of the two statutory elements of Article 134. The appellant did not object to what is arguably a major change, *see* RULE FOR COURTS–MARTIAL 603(d), MANUAL FOR COURTS–MARTIAL, UNITED STATES (2008 ed.), and thus waived the objection. He did not request repreferral, reinvestigation, rereferral, or the statutory delay afforded between referral and trial. *See also* Art. 35, UCMJ. We are satisfied, then, that the appellant enjoyed what has been described as the "clearly established" right of due process to " 'notice of the specific charge, and a chance to be heard in a trial of the issues raised by that charge.' " *Fosler,* 2011 C.A.A.F. LEXIS 661, at *12–13 (quoting *Cole v. Arkansas,* 333 U.S. 196, 201 (1948)). We emphasize as well that this was a guilty-plea case, and we note that the appellant has only now challenged the legal effect of the specification. "A flawed specification first challenged after trial . . . is viewed with greater tolerance than one which was attacked before findings and sentence." *Watkins,* 21 M.J. at 209.

We therefore affirm the finding of guilty for the Additional Charge and its underlying specification.

Maximum Punishment

* * *

The plea inquiry regarding this offense emphasized that the appellant was guilty not because he was engaged in sodomy, but because he was wearing uniform items during the production of the video. As we have noted, his pleas to wearing the uniform to endorse or advance private interests were improvident; the Department of Defense Instruction at issue, however, does provide that it is likewise a violation to wear the uniform in situations that might reflect discredit upon the armed forces. AE VII at ¶ 3 .1.4. Under these circumstances, then, we look to precedent and find that this offense should be punished as a general neglect or disorder with a maximum punishment of confinement for 4 months and forfeiture of 2/3 pay per month for 4 months. *See United States v. Beaty*, 70 M.J. 39, 46 (C.A.A.F. 2011) and cases cited.

Conclusion

The findings of guilty of specifications 1 and 3 of Charge I and Charge I itself are set aside, and those specifications and that charge are dismissed. The findings of guilty of the Additional Charge and its specification are affirmed. The sentence is set aside, and a rehearing on sentence is authorized; however, no punitive discharge is authorized, nor is any monetary penalty in excess of the equivalent of forfeiture of 2/3 pay per month for 4 months authorized.

Senior Judge CARBERRY and Judge PAYTON–O'BRIEN concur.

Points for Discussion

1. Do you agree with the *Fosler* court's decision requiring the "terminal" element to be included in the charged specification? Was the accused put on notice of the elements of the offenses without the inclusion of the "terminal" element? How?

2. If a trial counsel wants to charge an accused with conduct which is prejudicial to good order and discipline and service discrediting, do both "terminal" elements have to appear in the specification? Can you think of examples of conduct that might be both prejudicial to good order and discipline and service discrediting?

———————

Clause 3 of Article 134 and the Federal Assimilative Crimes Act

While military prosecutors may face difficulties regarding sufficient notice to accused when charging violations of Clauses 1 and 2 of the General Article, Clause 3 of the General Article is less problematic. The *Manual for Courts-Martial* clarifies what falls within prohibited conduct pursuant to Clause 3 as follows:

Article 134

* * *

(4) *Crimes and offenses not capital (clause 3).*

(a) *In general.* . . . the laws which may be applied under clause 3 of Article 134 are divided into two groups: crimes and offenses of unlimited application (crimes which are punishable regardless where they may be committed), and crimes and offenses of local application (crimes which are punishable only if committed in areas of federal jurisdiction).

(b) *Crimes and offenses of unlimited application.*

Certain noncapital crimes and offenses prohibited by the United States Code are made applicable under clause 3 of Article 134 to all persons subject to the code regardless where the wrongful act or omission occurred. Examples include: counterfeiting (18 U.S.C. § 471), and various frauds against the Government not covered by Article 132.

(c) *Crimes and offenses of local application.*

(i) *In general.* A person subject to the code may not be punished under clause 3 of Article 134 for an offense that occurred in a place where the law in question did not apply. . . . Regardless where committed, such an act might be punishable under clauses 1 or 2 of Article 134. There are two types of congressional enactments of local application: specific federal statutes (defining particular crimes), and a general federal statute, the Federal Assimilative Crimes Act (which adopts certain state criminal laws).

(ii) *Federal Assimilative Crimes Act (18 U.S.C. § 13).* The Federal Assimilative Crimes Act is an adoption by Congress of state criminal laws for areas of exclusive or concurrent federal jurisdiction,[2] provided federal criminal law, including the UCMJ, has not defined an applicable offense for the misconduct committed. The Act applies to state laws validly existing at the time of the offense without regard to when these laws were enacted, whether before or after passage of the Act, and whether before or after the acquisition of the land where the offense was committed. For example, if a person committed an act on a military installation in the United States at a certain location over which the United States had either exclusive or concurrent jurisdiction, and it was not an offense specifically defined by federal law (including the UCMJ), that person could be punished for that act by a court-martial if it was a violation of a noncapital offense under the law of the State where the military installation was located. This is possible because the Act adopts the criminal law of the state wherein the military installation is located and applies it as though it were federal law. . . .

MCM, pt. IV, ¶60.a.

---

[2] Both state and federal civil and criminal laws apply in areas of concurrent legislative jurisdiction.

The Federal Assimilative Crimes Act allows military prosecutors to adopt or assimilate state criminal statutes as federal law for offenses that take place in areas concurrent or exclusive jurisdiction. The charge sheet for an accused may allege violations of UCMJ punitive articles, as well as federal and state criminal statutes.

In the case that follows the court grapples with whether an Ohio criminal statute may be properly assimilated to fill a void in the law or whether the existing UCMJ enumerated offense preempts such assimilation.

UNITED STATES v. ROBBINS
Court of Appeals for the Armed Forces
52 M.J. 159 (C.A.A.F. 1999)

GIERKE, Judge:

A military judge sitting as a general court-martial convicted appellant [Airman Gregory L. Robbins, U.S. Air Force], pursuant to his pleas, of assault and battery on his wife on divers occasions and intentional infliction of grievous bodily harm on his wife, in violation of Article 128, Uniform Code of Military Justice, 10 U.S.C. § 928, as well as involuntary manslaughter by terminating the pregnancy of his wife, in violation of § 2903.04 of the Ohio Revised Code, as assimilated into Article 134, UCMJ, 10 U.S.C. 934, by the Federal Assimilative Crimes Act (ACA), 18 U.S.C. § 13. The adjudged and approved sentence provides for a dishonorable discharge, confinement for 8 years, and reduction to the lowest enlisted grade. The Court of Criminal Appeals affirmed the findings and sentence. 48 M.J. 745 (1998).

This Court granted review of the following issue:

WHETHER APPELLANT'S PLEA OF GUILTY TO CHARGE II (RENUMBERED) AND ITS SPECIFICATION IS IMPROVIDENT SINCE THE PREEMPTION DOCTRINE APPLIES TO THIS CHARGE WHICH WAS BROUGHT UNDER THE ASSIMILATIVE CRIMES ACT.

For the reasons set out below, we affirm.

The facts of this case are not disputed. Appellant severely beat his wife with his fists, punching her in the face and body. She was approximately 34 weeks pregnant. Appellant broke his wife's nose and blackened her eye. His punches to her body ruptured her uterus and tore the placenta from the uterine wall. The unborn baby, who was otherwise healthy, was expelled into the mother's abdominal cavity and died before birth.

Appellant now argues that his guilty plea to involuntary manslaughter by the unlawful termination of his wife's pregnancy was improvident because the offense cannot be assimilated into Article 134. Thus, he argues, the offense was not cognizable under the UCMJ. The Government argues that the offense was properly assimilated and that appellant's guilty plea waived any issue of preemption.

We hold that the preemption issue was not waived by appellant's guilty plea. RCM 910(j), Manual for Courts–Martial, United States (1995 ed.), provides that a guilty plea "waives any objection . . . insofar as the objection relates to the factual issue of guilt of the offense(s) to which the plea was made." RCM 905(e) provides that lack of jurisdiction or failure to state an offense are not waived by failure to raise the issue at trial. In this case, the issue relates to subject-matter jurisdiction. If the offense was improperly assimilated, it was not cognizable by a court-martial. Thus, we hold that the preemption issue was not waived by the guilty plea or appellant's failure to raise it at trial.

* * *

The assimilation of state criminal statutes is limited by paragraph 60c(5)(a), Part IV, Manual, *supra,* which provides as follows:

The preemption doctrine prohibits application of Article 134 to conduct covered by Articles 80 through 132. For example, larceny is covered in Article 121, and if an element of that offense is lacking—for example, intent—there can be no larceny or larceny-type offense, either under Article 121 or, because of preemption, under Article 134. Article 134 cannot be used to create a new kind of larceny offense, one without the required intent, where Congress has already set the minimum requirements for such an offense in Article 121.

* * *

In *United States v. McGuinness,* 35 M.J. 149 (1992), this Court held that the preemption doctrine precluded assimilation if two questions are answered in the affirmative:

The primary question is whether Congress intended to limit prosecution for wrongful conduct within a particular area or field to offenses defined in specific articles of the Code; the secondary question is whether the offense charged is composed of a residuum of elements of a specific offense and asserted to be a violation of either Articles 133 or 134, which, because of their sweep, are commonly described as the general articles.

Id. at 151–52, quoting *United States v. Wright,* 5 M.J. 106, 110–11 (C.M.A. 1978).

* * *

In *Lewis v. United States,* 523 U.S. 155 (1998), the Supreme Court laid out the relevant analysis for determining whether assimilation is permissible. It stated:

In our view, the ACA's language and its gap-filling purpose taken together indicate that a court must first ask the question that the ACA's language requires: Is the defendant's "act or omission . . . made punishable by *any* enactment of Congress." 18 U.S.C. § 13(a)(emphasis added). If the answer to this question is "no," that will normally end the matter. The ACA presumably would assimilate the statute. If the answer to the question is "yes," however, the court must ask the further question whether the federal statutes that apply to the "act or omission" preclude application of the state law in question, say, because its application would interfere with the achievement of a federal policy, because the state law would effectively rewrite an offense definition that Congress carefully considered, or because federal statutes reveal an intent to occupy so much of a field as would exclude use of the particular state statute at issue. . . .

* * *

The Act's basic purpose makes it similarly clear that assimilation may not rewrite distinctions among the forms of criminal behavior that Congress intended to create. Hence, ordinarily, there will be no gap for the Act to fill where a set of federal enactments taken together make criminal a single form of wrongful behavior while distinguishing (say, in terms of seriousness) among what amount to different ways of committing the same basic crime.

At the same time, a substantial difference in the kind of wrongful behavior covered (on the one hand by the state statute, on the other, by federal enactments) will ordinarily indicate a gap for a state statute to fill—unless Congress, through the comprehensiveness of its regulation, or through language revealing a conflicting policy, indicates to the contrary in a particular case. The primary question (we repeat) is one of legislative intent: Does applicable federal law indicate an intent to punish conduct such as the defendant's to the exclusion of the particular state statute at issue?

Id. at 164–66 (citations omitted).

In this case, the Ohio statute was assimilated into Article 134 by the ACA. Section 2903.04 of the Ohio Revised Code provides as follows:

(A) No person shall cause the death of another or the unlawful termination of another's pregnancy as a proximate result of the offender's committing or attempting to commit a felony.

* * *

(C) Whoever violates this section is guilty of involuntary manslaughter.

The Ohio legislature enacted the above revision of its involuntary-manslaughter statute with an effective date of September 6, 1996. Appellant assaulted his wife thereby terminating her pregnancy on September 12, 1996.

Before it was amended, § 2903.04(A) provided: "No person shall cause the death of another as a proximate result of the offender's committing or attempting to commit a felony." The term "death of another" had been interpreted by Ohio courts as meaning "the death of another person," and "person" was defined as one "born alive." *State v. Dickinson,* 28 Ohio St.2d 65, 275 N.E.2d 599, 601 (1971). Senate Bill 239 amended § 2901.01 of the Ohio Revised Code to define "person" to include all of the following:

(i) An individual, corporation, business trust, estate, trust, partnership, and association; [and]

(ii) An unborn human who is viable.

In the same bill, § 2903.04 was amended to add the words, "or the unlawful termination of another's pregnancy."

The drafters' analysis of Senate Bill 239 reflects that the House made significant changes to the original Senate Bill, but the language including a viable fetus in the definition of "person" was retained, "so that as a matter of principle, a viable fetus is considered a person in the Criminal Code in the state of Ohio." . . .

* * *

The first House amendment added "causing the unlawful termination of another's pregnancy" to Ohio's homicide statute. This has the effect of making it a homicidal offense to cause the death of a fetus *at any stage of the pregnancy*.

(Emphasis added.)

The Ohio courts have interpreted the statute consistently with the drafters' analysis. *See State v. Coleman,* 124 Ohio App.3d 78, 705 N.E.2d 419 (1997) (statute applicable even if fetus is not viable).

The fact that the Ohio legislature has classified the offense proscribed by § 2903.04 as involuntary manslaughter is not dispositive of the determination whether it can be assimilated. In order to apply the test set forth by the Supreme Court in *Lewis,* this Court must examine the plain language of the Ohio statute. That statute prohibits acts which "cause the death of another *or* the unlawful termination of another's pregnancy." (Emphasis added.) By drafting the "unlawful termination" language in the alternative, the legislature clearly distinguished the offense at issue from the traditional offense of manslaughter.

Congress did not specifically proscribe the killing of a fetus in either the UCMJ or the Federal Criminal Code. Articles 118 and 119 of the UCMJ proscribe murder and manslaughter, both of which are defined in terms of the unlawful killing of "a human being." Congress intended that Articles 118 and 119 be construed "with reference to the common law." . . .

Similarly, the federal murder and manslaughter statutes, 18 U.S.C. §§ 1111 and 1112, define murder and manslaughter as the unlawful killing of "a human being." Although these statutes were intended to "enlarge the common law definition," they still require that an infant be "born alive" to be considered "a human being." The definition was broadened only to the extent that it eliminated the common-law requirement that the child "had existed independently from its mother prior to death." *See United States v. Spencer,* 839 F.2d 1341, 1343 (9th Cir. 1988).

Applying the Supreme Court's *Lewis* analysis, we answer the first question in the negative: Congress did not proscribe the unlawful termination of another's pregnancy in either the UCMJ or the Federal Criminal Code. Under *Lewis*, that negative answer "will normally end the matter."

Applying this Court's analysis in *McGuinness*, we conclude that the offense to which appellant pleaded guilty is not "a residuum of elements of a specific offense," but instead is a separate offense proscribed by the Ohio Revised Code.

The Ohio statute does not conflict with congressional intent to preempt the field. To the contrary, legislation regarding termination of pregnancy is an area traditionally left to the states. *See Roe v. Wade,* 410 U.S. 113 (1973).

The Ohio statute does not enlarge or redefine an offense already proscribed by Congress. Section 2901.01, standing alone, would arguably be a redefinition and enlargement of federal law, because it broadens the definition of "a human being" to include a viable fetus. However, the legislative history reflects that § 2903.04, the provision assimilated in this case, effectively overrides § 2901.01. Section 2903.04 is broader than § 2901.01, because it applies to all fetuses, whereas § 2901.01 applies only to viable fetuses. Rather than redefine "a human being," § 2903.04 creates a new offense. The new offense is distinct from assault-type offenses, where the mother is the victim. It is distinct from homicide under the UCMJ or the Federal Criminal Code, which applies only to a child born alive. As such, § 2903.04 fills a gap in the criminal law and may properly be assimilated.

Since the offense is cognizable by a court-martial, there is no substantial basis to overturn appellant's guilty plea. *See United States v. Prater,* 32 M.J. 433 (C.M.A. 1991). However, to make clear that the offense of which appellant was convicted is not a homicide, we will strike the reference to manslaughter from the specification.

Decision

The specification of Charge II (renumbered) is amended by deleting the words, "commit involuntary manslaughter by" and changing the word "causing" to "cause."

The decision of the United States Air Force Court of Criminal Appeals with respect to the specification as modified, the remaining specifications and charges, and the sentence is affirmed.

[Judge Sullivan's opinion concurring in the result is omitted.–Eds.]

Points for Discussion

1. Subsequent to the *Robbins* opinion, Article 119a, Death or Injury to an Unborn Child and related offenses were added to the UCMJ, to comport with the Unborn Victims of Violence Act of 2004 (Public Law 108-212). Robbins's offense occurred at Wright-Patterson Air Force Base in Ohio. How would the court's opinion in the Robbins case differ if the accused was still charged with violating the Ohio statute?

2. If the Federal Assimilative Crimes Act allows the military to assimilate state criminal statutes for crimes that occur in areas of exclusive or concurrent jurisdiction, does this place the burden on service members to review the local state criminal laws to ensure they are aware of potential offenses? Doesn't this subject service members to more criminal offenses than civilians? *See* Manual for Courts-Martial, pt. IV, para. 60.c.(4)(c)(ii).

12-3. Military Offenses

Failing to Obeying a Lawful General Order—Article 92

Servicemembers who violate or fail to obey a lawful order are subject to prosecution for a violation of Article 92, which provides as follows:

Art. 92. Failure to obey order or regulation

Any person subject to this chapter who—

(1) violates or fails to obey any lawful general order or regulation; (2) having knowledge of any other lawful order issued by a member of the armed forces, which it is his duty to obey, fails to obey the order; or (3) is derelict in the performance of his duties; shall be punished as a court-martial may direct.

10 U.S.C. § 892.

This article contains three different types of order violations. The *Manual for Courts-Martial* provides the elements of each of the first two types of Article 92 order violations as follows:

(1) *Violation of or failure to obey a lawful general order or regulation.*

(a) That there was in effect a certain lawful general order or regulation;

(b) That the accused had a duty to obey it; and(c) That the accused violated or failed to obey the order or regulation.

(2) *Failure to obey other lawful order.*

(a) That a member of the armed forces issued a certain lawful order; (b) That the accused had knowledge of the order; (c) That the accused had a duty to obey the order; and(d) That the accused failed to obey the order.

MCM, pt. IV, ¶16.c.(1)(b).

The U.S. Navy-Marine Corps Court of Criminal Appeals in the previous opinion in *United States v. Simmons*, reviews an Article 92(1) general order violation and in that analysis must determine whether authority to issue the general order or regulation existed and if it was "generally applicable to an armed force which are properly published by the President or the Secretary of Defense, of Homeland Security, or of a military department." MCM, pt. IV,

¶16.c.(1)(a). General orders or regulations may also be issued by a general court-martial convening authority or general or flag officer in a command or a superior commander of either of these, applying to those within the command. Such order or regulation must be punitive in nature and include language indicating that service members who are in violation may be prosecuted. The prosecutor does not need to prove that the accused had knowledge of the general order or regulation because this is a strict liability offense.

The case that follows, *United States v. Leverette*, 9 M.J. 627 (A.C.M.R. 1980), provides an example of how service members may be charged with Article 92(1) general order violations when traveling through other installations and inadvertantly violating the general orders that apply, and ignorance of the order or regulation is not a defense.

UNITED STATES v. LEVERETTE
Army Court of Military Review
9 M.J. 627 (A.C.M.R. 1980)

FULTON, Senior Judge:

In this appeal, the appellant [Private First Class John Leverrette, Jr., U.S. Army] challenges the providency of his plea of guilty to a charge of violating regulations. We must decide whether a soldier on leave visiting an installation to which he is not assigned, who violates general regulations governing the installation, may be subjected to punishment under Article 92(1) of the Uniform Code of Military Justice, 10 U.S.C. s 892(1) (1976), which does not require that actual knowledge of the regulation be proved.

The regulation in question is Headquarters 101st Airborne Division (Air Assault) and Fort Campbell (Kentucky) Regulation 190-7, Military Police: Control of Nongovernment-Owned Weapons, dated 13 January 1975. The regulation provides as follows:

SECTION I. GENERAL

1. PURPOSE. To control nongovernment-owned firearms, handguns, explosive devices, and other weapons at Fort Campbell, Kentucky....

2. SCOPE. This regulation ... applies to all individuals physically on this installation....

3. DEFINITIONS.... ("Handgun" refers to pistols and revolvers; "firearm," to rifles and shotguns)....

SECTION II. REGISTRATION OF NONGOVERNMENT-OWNED FIREARMS AND NONGOVERNMENT-OWNED HANDGUNS

4. REGISTRATION REQUIRED. Except as provided in subparagraphs a and b below, it is unlawful and a criminal offense for any person subject to the UCMJ or any other person to carry or possess any nongovernment-owned firearm or any nongovernment-owned handgun while on the Fort Campbell military reservation unless such item is previously registered

with the Office of the Provost Marshal in accordance with paragraph 22 of this regulation.

a. Personnel newly assigned to family quarters or bachelor quarters shall register . . . (firearms and handguns) within 72 hours after arrival on the military reservation. Such handguns and firearms must be stored in a unit arms room pending registration.

b. Personnel not assigned to Fort Campbell may bring a firearm (see definition in paragraph 3c) onto the Fort Campbell reservation for the explicit purpose of hunting, without prior registration with the Office of the Provost Marshal, provided that the individual can prove that the possession or use of the firearm meets all the following criteria (e. g., as to caliber, type, hunting season, hunting area). . . .

22. REGISTRATION. Registration . . . procedures are as follows:

a. All . . . nongovernment-owned handguns must be registered with the Office of the Provost Marshal prior to bringing them on this installation.

b. Temporary registration may be accomplished by accurately completing DA Form 2496 . . . as indicated in Appendix A and filing the same with either the Provost Marshal's Office, the Weapon's (sic) Registration Section, (or) Gate 4 Military Police. . . .

When the appellant violated this regulation, he was on leave while en route from his former duty station in Korea to a new duty station at Fort Stewart, Georgia. He was visiting relatives or friends near Fort Campbell, where he had been stationed before going to Korea. He brought a privately-owned unregistered .32-caliber pistol (i. e., a handgun) onto the Fort Campbell military reservation. This might have escaped notice had he not used it to rob a barracks drug dealer of his supply of marihuana. Somewhat to the appellant's surprise, the victim reported his loss to the military police.

After the appellant was identified and apprehended, he was attached to a unit at Fort Campbell and charged with violating a lawful general regulation (paragraph 4 of the regulation quoted above) by possessing an unregistered handgun (Charge I); stealing from Private Ricky Furr, by means of force and putting him in fear, a quantity of marihuana (Charge II); and (in the course of the robbery) wrongfully possessing marihuana (Charge III). He pleaded guilty to those charges. In return, the convening authority agreed that, if both a punitive discharge and confinement at hard labor were adjudged, he would suspend any confinement in excess of three months for a period of six months. Appellant's approved sentence includes reduction to the grade of Private E-1, forfeiture of $276.00 pay monthly for five months, confinement at hard labor for five months (the period in excess of three months suspended as agreed), and a bad-conduct discharge from the service.

When appellant entered his guilty plea, the military judge conducted the required hearing. *United States v. Green*, 1 M.J. 453 (C.M.A. 1976); *United States v. Care*, 40 C.M.R. 247 (C.M.A. 1969). In the course of this inquiry, he learned that the appellant was not assigned to any Fort Campbell unit at the time of the offenses. None of the trial participants regarded that as a defense to Charge I. Nevertheless, the appellant now contends that his plea was improvident because, not being assigned to the command, he (a) had no duty to obey the regulation,_and (b) his knowledge of the regulation could not be presumed. We disagree and hold that his plea of guilty was provident.

I

The purpose, scope and terms of the Fort Campbell regulation indicate to us no intended exemption for military persons merely because they happened to be visiting Fort Campbell rather than being stationed there. Nor have we found anything in the Uniform Code of Military Justice, the Manual for Courts-Martial, or in the decided cases that necessarily limits the effect of a commander's orders and regulations to only those persons assigned or attached to his command.[6]

Being on leave may limit the duties one can be required to perform. *See, e. g., United States v. Milldebrandt*, 25 C.M.R. 139 (C.M.A. 1958); Davis, A Treatise on the Military Law of the United States 383 (3d ed. 1915). The member on leave is not, however, exempt from all application of military law. Cf. *United States v. Hooper*, 26 C.M.R. 417 (C.M.A. 1958) (criminal jurisdiction over retired members).

The Manual describes "(g)eneral orders or regulations" below the Secretarial level as those "generally applicable to the command of the officer issuing them throughout the command or a particular subdivision thereof." Manual for Courts-Martial, United States, 1969 (Revised edition), par. 171a. The appellant argues that those words indicate the necessity of a command relationship between the authority issuing general regulations and the persons subject to them. Indeed, some boards of review so construed similar provisions of an earlier Manual. . . . We, however, do not believe that the quoted language requires that interpretation. Instead, we believe that it is intended only to indicate that not all regulations issued by a commander empowered to issue general regulations necessarily qualify as general regulations. Some may be narrower in scope. . . .

Accordingly, we conclude that a command relationship in the organizational sense is not fundamental to the application of a general regulation to an individual member of the service. We hold that the

---

[6] That general orders are not necessarily limited to persons under direct command of the promulgating authority is indicated by former provisions of the Manual which had the effect of establishing a presumption that one subject to the Code knew the content of any regulation or directive of "a territorial, theater, or similar area command (with respect to personnel stationed or having duties within such area)." Manual for Courts-Martial, United States, 1951, par. 154a (4); cf. *United States v. Chunn*, 36 C.M.R. 48 (C.M.A. 1965) (under existing test, base commander was empowered to issue general regulations because of his broad responsibilities, including responsibility for tenant units not under his command).

appellant, who had knowingly entered a military installation, had a duty to obey regulations governing the installation.[8]

II

That the Fort Campbell weapons regulation is of the genus of orders called general regulations has not been disputed. *See* Department of the Army Pamphlet 27-2, Analysis of Contents, Manual for Courts-Martial, United States, 1969, Revised Edition, par. 171a at p. 28-7 (1970). The significance of its classification is that "Article 92(1) contains no requirement that any kind of knowledge be either alleged or proved in a prosecution thereunder for violating or failing to obey a general order or regulation." Manual for Courts-Martial, United States, 1969 (Revised edition), par. 171a.

The second prong of appellant's attack on the providency of his plea of guilty is stated in his brief as follows:

The appellant acknowledges that under the 1969 changes to the Manual for Courts-Martial, the government is relieved of the obligation of proving constructive notice of local general regulations. . . . However, the appellant contends his status, as being assigned to a unit other than the 101st Airborne Division or any other unit on Fort Campbell, makes the presumption of constructive knowledge of the regulation inappropriate in his case.[9]

The question thereby presented is whether appellant's plea of guilty was improvident because the defense of ignorance of the law was available to him. We hold that it was not.

"As a general rule, ignorance or mistake of law, or of properly published regulations or directives of a general nature having the force of law, is not an excuse for the commission of an offense." Manual for Courts-Martial, supra, par. 154a(5); *United States v. International Minerals & Chemical Corp.*, 402 U.S. 558, 563 (1971). . . .

The lawmakers have a wide latitude to declare an offense and to exclude elements of knowledge and diligence from its definition. *Id.* at 228. As to the Uniform Code, Congress and the President have adopted a scheme of strict liability in relation to general orders or regulations while requiring, as to other directives, actual notice as an element of punishable disobedience. *See* Articles 1(5), 90(2), 92(2), Uniform Code of Military Justice, supra. Accordingly, the Manual notes, "except for general orders or regulations, a person cannot be held responsible for a violation of a military regulation or

---

[8] Nor is a command relationship a prerequisite to the effectiveness of orders other than general orders. Articles 1(5), 90(2), 91(2), 92(2), Uniform Code of Military Justice, 10 U.S.C.§801(5), 890(2), 891(2), 892(2) (1976).

[9] We are not blind to the implication stemming from the fact that appellant, as revealed by this record, had been assigned to a unit at Fort Campbell from June 1976 until February 1978 and, therefore, was presumed to know the same regulation during that period. We prefer, however, to base our decision on other grounds.

directive unless he had actual knowledge of the regulation or directive." Manual for Courts-Martial, *supra*, par. 154a (5); *see id.*, pars. 169b, 171b.

In the appellant's situation, we find no denial of due process in holding him to obedience of general regulations governing Fort Campbell regardless of actual notice. He assuredly knew that he was within the territorial or operational area of responsibility of the commander. The existence of the regulation reasonably was to be expected in view of the fact that it was necessitated by Army regulations ... and dealt with a matter notoriously subject to control in the interests of safety and security of the command. Nor was the requirement placed upon the appellant purely passive stemming solely from his presence in the command, as was the case in *Lambert v. California, supra.* Instead, to become subject to the weapon registration requirement, it was necessary that he act affirmatively to enter the post bringing with him the weapon, a potentially dangerous object.

Accordingly, just as we have said that soldiers may sometimes become subject to the general orders or regulations of a command other than their own, so also do we hold that they may in instances such as here be held to obedience of them without regard to actual knowledge. Therefore, the appellant's plea of guilty was not improvident.

III

We deem the remaining assignments of error as similarly nonmeritorious.

* * *

The findings of guilty and the sentence are affirmed.

CLAUSE and FOREMAN, JJ., concur.

"Not all provisions in general orders or regulations can be enforced under Article 92(1). Regulations which only supply general guidelines or advice for conducting military functions may not be enforceable under Article 92(1)." Manual for Court-Martial, pt. IV, para. 16.c.(1)(e). The following case provides an example of this limitation.

UNITED STATES v. GREEN
Army Court of Criminal Appeals
58 M.J. 855 (Army Ct. Crim. App. 2003)

SCHENCK, Judge:

A military judge sitting as a general court-martial convicted appellant [Cadet Jeremy H. Green, United States Army], pursuant to his pleas, of failure to obey a lawful general order by wrongfully possessing drug abuse paraphernalia, failure to obey a lawful order by wrongfully possessing gamma butyrolactone (GBL),1 wrongful possession and use of ketamine,2 and wrongful possession of cocaine, in violation of Articles 92 and 112a, Uniform Code of Military Justice, 10 U.S.C. §§ 892 and 912a [hereinafter UCMJ]. The convening authority approved the adjudged sentence to a dismissal. This case is before the court for review under Article 66, UCMJ, 10 U.S.C. § 866.

We find that appellant's single assignment of error—that the approved sentence is inappropriately severe—has no merit. We find that appellant's single assignment of error—that the approved sentence is inappropriately severe—has no merit. Although not raised as error, we find that appellant's guilty plea to violating a lawful general order (Dep't of Defense Directive 1010.4, Drug and Alcohol Abuse by DoD Personnel (Jan. 11, 1999) [hereinafter DoD Dir. 1010.4]) by wrongfully possessing drug abuse paraphernalia, was improvident because DoD Dir. 1010.4 is not punitive. We will affirm appellant's conviction, however, for the closely-related offense of dereliction of duty, in violation of Article 92(3), UCMJ. . . .

FACTS

At the time of his offenses, appellant was a third-year cadet at the United States Military Academy, West Point, New York. He ranked first in his class of 1,061 based on his Cadet Performance Score (CPS)3 and was assigned as a cadet company first sergeant in a company composed of approximately 130 fellow cadets. As cadet first sergeant, appellant was responsible for enforcement of discipline and accountability. He also worked with the cadet company commander ensuring performance of punishments awarded to cadets and assisting with health and welfare inspections. In general, appellant was expected to lead by example and especially to act as a role model for cadets in his company.

Appellant purchased ketamine in a New York City dance club and he bought GBL by using the Internet. Appellant inhaled ketamine on two occasions. While accompanied by another cadet, appellant snorted ketamine during the drive to a tanning salon in Vails Gate, New York and again on that same day as he returned to West Point. Also on that day, appellant's cadet roommate found a "bullet" (a snorting device) lying on his own bed. His roommate gave the "bullet" to his chain of command, who thereafter conducted a search of appellant's room. The command found a vial of ten micro milliliters of liquid ketamine, two bottles of liquid GBL (seventeen and nineteen milliliters each), and one gram of cocaine in appellant's wall locker. While appellant's room was being searched, appellant telephoned another cadet and warned the cadet to "dump your stuff" because "I'm busted."

Appellant was charged with and pleaded guilty to violating DoD Dir. 1010.4 by "wrongfully possessing drug abuse paraphernalia" for his possession of the "bullet" discovered on his roommate's bed.

LAW

* * *

The President has limited the types of general orders or regulations that may proscribe conduct punishable under Article 92(1), UCMJ. *United States v. Shavrnoch*, 49 M.J. 334, 336 (C.A.A.F. 1998) (citing Manual for Courts-

Martial, United States (1995 ed.) [hereinafter MCM, 1995], Part IV, para. 16c(1)(e)). As our superior court noted over thirty years ago, "[n]o single characteristic of a general order determines whether it applies punitively to members of a command." *United States v. Nardell*, 45 C.M.R. 101, 103 (C.M.A 1972).

To determine whether DoD Dir. 1010.4 falls within the category of a "punitive" order or regulation it must first be examined as a whole, including the purpose statement. 45 C.M.R. at 103–104. This court must determine whether the directive is merely a guideline for conduct or intended to regulate the conduct of individual servicemembers. *Id.* " 'Regulations which only supply general guidelines or advice for conducting military functions may not be enforceable under Article 92(1).' " *Shavrnoch*, 49 M.J. at 336 (quoting MCM, 1995, Part IV, para. 16c(1)(e)).

Second, "direct application of sanctions" for violations of an order or regulation must be "self-evident." *Nardell*, 45 C.M.R. at 103, cited with approval in MCM, 2000, app. A23–5, Analysis of Punitive Articles, at A23–5–16. To be enforceable under Article 92(1), UCMJ, the order or regulation cannot rely on subordinate commanders for implementation to give it effect as a code of conduct. *Id.*; *see also United States v. Scott*, 46 C.M.R. 25, 27 (C.M.A. 1972); *United States v. Hode*, 44 M.J. 816, 818 (A.F. Ct. Crim. App. 1996).

DISCUSSION

Nature of the Regulation

The overall purpose of DoD Dir. 1010.4 is general guidance. It does not seek to regulate the conduct of individual members of a command or to delineate a code of conduct. Specifically, the stated purpose of the directive, as set forth in paragraph 1, is to "update DoD *policies* and responsibilities for drug and alcohol abuse prevention." (emphasis added). This directive tasks various Assistant Secretaries of Defense with promulgating and implementing this general policy.

The direct application of sanctions (or punitive nature) of DoD Dir. 1010.4 is not self-evident. On the contrary, paragraph 2.2 of this directive states that it is "not intended to modify or otherwise affect statutory provisions and those regulations or DoD Directives concerned with determination of misconduct and criminal or civil responsibilities for persons' acts or omissions." Such language is not punitive, does not provide notice regarding possible criminal sanctions for violations, and, by implication, limits the directive's punitive nature.

Further, DoD Dir. 1010.4 expressly delegates implementation. Paragraph 5, "Responsibilities," requires the Under Secretary of Defense for Policy to ensure that the DoD Coordinator for Drug Enforcement Policy and Support "[d]evelop[s] and promulgate[s] policies to ensure the detection and deterrence of drug abuse." Heads of the DoD components are responsible for policy enforcement and program implementation. DoD Dir. 1010.4, at para. 5.4.

During the providence inquiry, the military judge informed appellant that DoD Dir. 1010.4 "prohibits possession of drug abuse paraphernalia." This prohibition supports the directive's general policy to "prevent and eliminate drug and alcohol abuse and dependence from the Department of Defense." DoD Dir. 1010.4, at para. 4. Paragraph 4.8 further provides that it is DoD policy to "[p]rohibit members of the Military Services . . . to possess, sell, or use drug abuse paraphernalia." Considering the "guideposts [described above] and the prescribed purpose of the regulation, we have no choice but to construe paragraph [4.8] thereof as no more than a listing of the drugs and drug-related paraphernalia with which the drug [abuse prevention] program was to be concerned." *Scott*, 46 C.M.R. at 29.

Moreover, "[t]erms in a regulation must be interpreted in light of the regulatory context in which they are found and in view of the purpose of the regulation as a whole." *United States v. Johnston*, 24 M.J. 271, 273 (C.M.A 1987). As this court has stated in the past, "We do not agree that the use of the word 'prohibited' per se is a single characteristic which determines that a general order applies punitively to members of a command." *United States v. Jackson*, 46 C.M.R. 1128, 1129 (A.C.M.R.1973).

We, therefore, hold that DoD Dir. 1010.4 is nonpunitive in nature. It does not unequivocally seek to regulate individual conduct, lacks clear language mandating punitive sanctions, and the "general theme prevalent throughout" is inconsistent with a finding to the contrary. *United States v. Hartgrove*, 44 C.M.R. 621, 623 (A.C.M.R. 1971). *But see United States v. Finsel*, 33 M.J. 739, 742 (A.C.M.R. 1991) (finding a letter regarding use of firearms published under wartime conditions to be punitive, and holding that a specific punitive warning is not required—even in peace time), *aff'd on other grounds*, 36 M.J. 441 (C.M.A. 1993).

We find that the record of trial raises a substantial, unresolved question of law and fact as to the providence of appellant's guilty plea to violating Article 92(1), UCMJ, with respect to Specification 1 of Charge I. See Prater, 32 M.J. at 436. The record indicates "appellant pleaded guilty to a charge involving a legal standard that does not constitute an offense under Article 92(1), thereby undermining his conviction '[a]s a matter of law.' " *Shavrnoch*, 49 M.J. at 339 (quoting United States v. Faircloth, 45 M.J. 172, 174 (C.A.A.F.1996)).

[In an omitted portion of the opinion the court conclude the facts nonetheless supported a conviction of dereliction of duty.]

Point for Discussion

Is it surprising that a cadet who was first in his class would commit the conduct described here? Is dismissal an excessive sentence? For more on courts-martial at the Service Academies, see Michael J. Davidson, *Court-Martialing Cadets*, 36 Cap. U. L. Rev. 635 (2008). The author notes:

COASTAL BOOKSTORE #309
7595 BAYMEADOWS WAY
JACKSONVILLE FL 32256
PHONE: 904-256-1110
FAX: 904-680-7614
WWW.COASTALBOOKSTORE.COM

E   309 002 309-0/4868
HIER: ANN   08/20/13 13:38

MAGGS/MODERN MILITARY JUS
101000 10969809   1 T   206.87

                   Subtotal   206.87
          7.00 SALES TAX   14.41

    Items   1   Total   220.28

T CARD   220.28
Type: UNKNOWN
: ************7029
th Cd: 867113
rm ID: 0002

                   Change Due   0.00

            RETURN POLICY
ST BE IN ORIGINAL CONDITION WHEN
CHASED NO USED BOOK RETURNS PAST
6 NO NEW BOOK RETURNS PAST 8/23
O RETURNS ON INTERSESSION BOOKS
  OTHER MERCHANDISE HAS TWO WEEKS

"Cadets and midshipmen possess a long history of encounters with the military justice system. Indeed, some well-known names in American military history—Custer, Sheridan, Lee—have found themselves facing a court-martial while a cadet." *Id.* at 673.

Failing to Obey other Lawful Order—Articles 90(2), 91(2)

Unlike an Article 92(1) general order violation, Article 92(2), failure to obey other lawful order violations require proof that the accused had knowledge of the order or regulation. As the following case indicates, the order must be directed toward the accused and intended to be an order, not simply guidance. In the *Warren* case, the accused is charged with willfully disobeying Lieutenant Ferriole's order "to settle down and be quiet." While you are reading the case, consider whether this was a legal, specific, clear, mandate, related to a military duty or mission, that was directed at the accused.

UNITED STATES v. WARREN
Court of Military Appeals
13 M.J. 160 (C.M.A. 1982)

PER CURIAM:

As a result of an incident that occurred at Camp Lejeune, North Carolina, on the morning of September 26, 1979, appellant [Private Robert L. Warren, Jr., U.S. Marine Corps] was found guilty by a military judge, sitting as a special court-martial, of disrespect to a superior commissioned officer, willful disobedience of an order from that officer, failure to obey the order of a superior noncommissioned officer, and communicating threats to injure the officer and noncommissioned officer, in violation of Articles 89, 90, 92, and 134 of the Uniform Code of Military Justice, 10 U.S.C. §§ 889, 890, 892, and 934, respectively. The sentence adjudged was a bad-conduct discharge, confinement at hard labor for 3 months, and partial forfeitures for a like period. The findings and sentence were approved by the convening authority and by the officer exercising general court-martial jurisdiction; the United States Navy Court of Military Review affirmed. We granted review of an assigned issue concerning the sufficiency of the evidence to sustain the conviction of willfully disobeying the order of the commissioned officer. 11 M.J. 91.

All of the charges against appellant arose from an unsuccessful effort to get him out of bed and into the field. Sergeant Schnell, his acting platoon sergeant, had attempted to awaken Private Warren—first by words and then by shaking his foot and attempting to pull him from his tent. The platoon commander, Lieutenant Ferriole, had observed these events, which already had resulted in a threat by appellant against Sergeant Schnell. Thereupon, according to the lieutenant

I took Private WARREN over, sat him down by the fire, and started talking to him sir. And, I told him I wanted him to calm down and relax. Take it easy for a minute. And Private WARREN was ranting and raving and babbling on about he was going to get somebody to take care of us all. He was going to get his friend to beat everybody up.

Charge II alleged that appellant had willfully disobeyed an order by Lieutenant Ferriole "to settle down and be quiet." The sanctions for disobedience of an order are grave—indeed, dishonorable discharge and 5 years' confinement for willfully disobeying the order of a superior commissioned officer. Table of Maximum Punishments, para. 127 c, Manual for Court-Martial, United States, 1969 (Revised edition). Thus, it is especially important that a servicemember have adequate notice that words directed to him by an officer are intended as an order, so that he will be well aware that by non-compliance he will subject himself to severe punishment. *Cf.* U.S.Const.Amend. V; *Lambert v. California*, 355 U.S. 225 (1957).

Accordingly, it is well established in military law that

[t]o be classed as an order, a communication must amount to a "positive command." .... The recipient of the order must be placed on notice that the officer who gives the order is bringing his authority to bear to compel compliance. However, "[t]he form in which the command is expressed is immaterial," ... "[i]f the language of a communication lacks specificity of meaning, extrinsic evidence is admissible for the purpose of clarification." *United States v. Mitchell,* [20 C.M.R. 295, 297 (C.M.A. 1955)].

When we apply these principles to the record of trial before us, we conclude that the Government has failed to establish appellant's guilt. In the context in which Lieutenant Ferriole was dealing with appellant—who was emotionally distraught at the time—it is unclear what the officer meant when he "told him I wanted him to calm down and relax. Take it easy for a minute." These words could be construed as an order, but they also might signify that Lieutenant Ferriole, who was the platoon commander, was counseling appellant how better to handle his altercation with Sergeant Schnell. Nowhere else in the record is the ambiguity resolved; indeed, the extrinsic evidence reinforces that ambiguity. Therefore, pursuant to the due process requirement of notice, *Lambert v. California, supra,* we conclude that the Government failed to show that an *order* was given to appellant.

Accordingly, the decision of the United States Navy Court of Military Review is reversed as to Charge II and its specification; and the findings as to that charge are set aside; and the charge is dismissed. However, we are convinced that, under the circumstances of this case, appellant suffered no prejudice as to sentence because of the erroneous findings of guilty. Therefore, the decision below as to the remaining findings and the sentence is affirmed.

Judge COOK concurs in the result.

Dereliction of Duty & Maltreatment of Subordinates

The two cases that follow review the third and final Article 92 offense which is defined in the Manual for Courts-Martial as follows:

(3) *Dereliction in the performance of duties.*

(a) That the accused had certain duties; (b) That the accused knew or reasonably should have known of the duties; and (c) That the accused was (willfully) (through neglect or culpable inefficiency) derelict in the performance of those duties.

MCM, pt. IV, ¶16.c.(1)(b).

A service member may be charged for willful, negligent, or culpably inefficient derelict performance of duties. The Manual for Courts-Martial further explains by stating,

(d) *Ineptitude.* A person is not derelict in the performance of duties if the failure to perform those duties is caused by ineptitude rather than by willfulness, negligence, or culpable inefficiency, and may not be charged under this article, or otherwise punished. For example, a recruit who has tried earnestly during rifle training and throughout record firing is not derelict in the performance of duties if the recruit fails to qualify with the weapon.

MCM, pt. IV, ¶16.c.(1)(b).

The courts in the cases that follow also consider whether the evidence fulfilled the elements of proof for Article 93, Maltreatment of subordinates, for conduct the accused engaged in as a guard at Abu Ghraib prison in Iraq in 2003. Article 93, UCMJ provides as follows:

Art. 93. Cruelty and maltreatment

Any person subject to this chapter who is guilty of cruelty toward, or oppression or maltreatment of, any person subject to his orders shall be punished as a court-martial may direct.

10 U.S.C. § 893.

As the Army Court of Criminal Appeals notes in *United States v. Harman*, 66 M.J. 710 (A.C.C.A. 2008) the government must prove that in the totality of the circumstances, the accused could reasonably have caused physical or mental harm or suffering by his actions and is not required to present evidence that the maltreatment victims actually suffered harm. *Id.* at 717. The court also upholds Specialist Harman's conviction for dereliction of duty, for willfully failing to protect detainees, finding that "she knew or reasonably should have known of her duties to protect the detainees." *Id.* at 716.

UNITED STATES v. HARMAN
Army Court of Criminal Appeals
66 M.J. 710 (Army Ct. Crim. App. 2008)

MAGGS, Judge:

Contrary to her pleas, a panel composed of enlisted and officer members convicted appellant [Specialist Sabrina D. Harman, U.S. Army] of conspiracy to maltreat detainees, dereliction of duty by willfully failing to protect detainees from abuse, and maltreatment of detainees (four specifications), in violation of Articles 81, 92, and 93, Uniform Code of Military Justice, 10 U.S.C. §§ 881, 892, 893 [hereinafter UCMJ]. The panel sentenced appellant to reduction to Private E1, forfeiture of all pay and allowances, confinement for six months, and a bad-conduct discharge. The military judge credited appellant with 51 days towards her sentence of confinement because of illegal pretrial punishment. The convening authority approved only so much of the sentence as provides for reduction to Private E1, confinement for six months, forfeiture of all pay and allowances for six months, and thereafter forfeiture of $1,092.00 per month until the date the discharge is ordered executed, and a bad-conduct discharge. The convening authority also credited appellant with 51 days of confinement credit against the sentence to confinement. In our decretal paragraph, we amend the specification of one charge, but otherwise affirm the approved findings and sentence.

I. Facts

Appellant was a member of the 372nd Military Police Company, a reserve unit headquartered in Maryland. In May 2003, she deployed with the 372nd to Iraq. In August 2003, her unit assumed duties at the Baghdad Central Confinement Facility at Abu Ghraib, Iraq. At Abu Ghraib, appellant served as a guard in a prison structure called "Tier 1" (also known as "the hard site," to distinguish it from tent encampments holding other prisoners).

The charges in this case arise out of three incidents that occurred in Tier 1 during the fall of 2003. Evidence concerning these incidents comes principally from the testimony of the soldiers involved, from witnesses not implicated in the incidents, from photographs and video recordings made during the incidents, from two sworn statements that appellant made to investigators, and from a letter that appellant wrote on 20 October 2003 to her former roommate in the United States.

The Incident of 25 October 2003

The record contains evidence that, on 25 October 2003, several military policemen (MPs) from the 372nd took it upon themselves to "punish" three Iraqi detainees who allegedly had raped a male Iraqi juvenile in the confinement facility. Acting without any claimed or apparent authorization, the persons responsible allegedly screamed at the detainees, ordered them to take off their clothes, and then forced them to crawl and roll down the prison hallway so that their genitals scraped the floor. The soldiers subsequently handcuffed the detainees to each other and posed them in positions to make it appear that they were having homosexual relations. During this time, soldiers took pictures of the detainees. As described below, however, the panel determined that appellant was not guilty of any charges arising out of this incident. We therefore do not consider any of this evidence when assessing the legal and factual sufficiency of the charges.

The Incident of 4 November 2003

On 4 November 2003, a separate incident took place in Tier 1 involving a detainee whom the MPs called "Gilligan." Photographs taken by Staff Sergeant (SSG) IF show the detainee wearing what appears to be a poncho, with his head and face hooded by an empty sandbag. The detainee is standing on a Meals Ready to Eat (MRE) box (i.e., a carton containing a common kind of rations). Wires are attached to his hands. When asked about the detainee, appellant said in a sworn statement to investigators:

> He is nicknamed Gilligan. . . . He was just standing on the MRE box with the sandbag over his head for about an hour. I put the wire on his hands. I do not recall how. I was joking with him and told him if he fell off he would get electrocuted. . . .
>
> . . . .
>
> We were not hurting him. It was not anything that bad.

SSG IF presented similar testimony, although he said that he had put wires on the detainee.

The Incident of 7 November 2003

On 7 November 2003, some detainees in a tent encampment outside Tier 1 participated in a riot. For greater security, soldiers transferred seven of the suspected leaders of the riot onto Tier 1. These detainees were suspected of various serious street crimes, including rape. When the prisoners arrived at Tier 1, they were hooded and handcuffed. Acting without any claim of authority, MPs from the 372nd took it upon themselves to "discipline" these seven detainees. Appellant admitted in her sworn statement that she saw what was taking place, retrieved a digital camera, and then went to join the soldiers.

Shortly after their arrival at the prison, the MPs forced the detainees to sit or lie down on the floor in a pile. While they were on the ground, Sergeant (SGT) JD stomped on their fingers and toes and Corporal (CPL) CG kneeled on the top of the pile. Shortly afterward, SSG IF and CPL CG punched two of the hooded and handcuffed detainees. Appellant witnessed these actions but took no steps to prevent them. On the contrary, Appellant took a picture of CPL CG posing with his armed cocked, ready to punch a hooded detainee. Other soldiers also took photographs and videos throughout the evening.

The MPs subsequently stripped the detainees of their clothes. In her sworn statement, appellant admitted that she used a marker to write "I'm a rapeist (sic)" on the leg of a naked detainee accused of rape. Photographs admitted into evidence show these words starting on or near the detainee's buttocks and running down the back of his thigh.

When the detainees were naked and handcuffed, CPL CG arranged them to form a human pyramid. Appellant witnessed this misconduct and did not report it. Instead, she took a picture of CPL CG and Private First Class (PFC) LE posing with the pyramid of detainees. Appellant then posed for a picture with CPL CG. In the picture, they are smiling and a giving a "thumbs up" symbol with their hands, with appellant leaning over the detainee pyramid. Other forms of misconduct allegedly occurred later in the evening, but the evidence did not implicate appellant.

Appellant did not report the incidents of 4 November or 7 November to her chain of command or to anyone else in authority. In her letter of 20 October 2003 to her former roommate, appellant expressed concern about mistreatment of detainees prior to these three incidents. She wrote: "Again, I thought, okay[,] that's funny, then it hit me, that's a form of molestation. You can't do that. . . . The only reason I want to be there is to get the pictures that prove that the U.S. is not what they think." At no time, however, did appellant turn over any photographs until she came under investigation in January 2004.

II. Issues Arising from the Bill of Particulars

Charge II alleges that appellant committed the offense of dereliction of duty in violation of Article 92. The single specification of this charge asserts that appellant "[w]ho knew, of her duties at or near Baghdad Central Correctional Facility, Abu Ghraib, Iraq, from on or about 20 October 2003 to about 1 December 2003, was derelict in the performance of those duties in that she willfully failed to protect Iraqi detainees from abuse, cruelty and maltreatment, as it was her duty to do." Before trial, appellant moved for a bill of particulars, which the government provided. This bill of particulars, as slightly amended, was subsequently submitted to the panel on both the flyer before trial and the findings worksheet used during deliberations. On the findings worksheet, the bill of particulars reads as follows:

> 1. On or about November 4, 2003, the accused assisted in placing a detainee on a Meals Ready to Eat (MRE) box, sandbag on his head, wires attached to his hands, who was told that if he fell off of the box, he would be electrocuted.
>
> 2. On or about November 4, 2003, the accused placed a wire on the detainee's hand.
>
> 3. On or about November 4, 2003, the accused photographed and witnessed photographs being taken of the detainee standing on the box with wires attached to his hands and did not stop or report this abuse.

4. On or about the night of November 7, 2003, the accused witnessed detainees forced into a pile on the floor with [CPL CG] kneeling on top of said pile and did nothing to stop or report the abuse.

5. On or about the night of November 7, 2003, the accused posed for a photograph with the detainees stripped and placed in a "human pyramid."

6. On or about the night of November 7, 2003, the accused witnessed fellow soldiers taking photographs of detainees while abuse occurred and did nothing to stop or report the abuse.

7. On or about the night of November 7, 2003, the accused witnessed SSG [IF] punch a detainee in the chest and did not stop or report this abuse.

8. Throughout the entire time frame, the accused witnessed other military police soldiers photographing detainees and did nothing to stop or report this abuse.

9. On or about 24–25 October, the accused witnessed other soldiers physically abusing detainees and handcuffing them together while naked and did nothing to stop or report this abuse.

When the panel returned its verdict, the panel announced that it had found appellant guilty of the Specification of Charge II and Charge II, with the exception of the language in paragraphs 1 and 9 of the bill of particulars as quoted above.

The court-martial's procedure in connection with this finding was irregular. Under Rule for Courts–Martial [hereinafter R.C.M.] 918(a), a court-martial makes findings only on specifications and charges. A bill of particulars is not a charge, and it is not a specification or even part of a specification. *See United States v. Rivera*, 62 M.J. 564, 566 (C.G.Ct. Crim. App. 2005). The Discussion to R.C.M. 906(b)(6) explains that a bill of particulars serves "to inform the accused of the nature of the charge with sufficient precision to enable the accused to prepare for trial" and that a bill of particulars "need not be sworn because it is not part of the specification." Accordingly, the military judge should not have required the panel to make findings on the bill of particulars.

In addition, the form of the finding is also irregular. A panel may find an accused guilty of a specification with exceptions. *See* R.C.M. 918(a)(1). But the exceptions must eliminate language that appears in the specification. *See* R.C.M. 918(a)(1) discussion ("One or more words or figures may be excepted from a specification. . . ."). In this case, when the panel found appellant guilty of the Specification of Charge II with exceptions, the exceptions purported to remove language which appeared in the bill of particulars, but not in the specification itself.

In these unusual circumstances, the *Manual for Courts–Martial* offers no clear guidance on the legal effect of the exceptions. To avoid prejudice to the appellant, and with consent given by government counsel at oral argument, we take these three steps:

First, we conclude that the panel intended to find appellant not guilty of any offense arising out of the incident that occurred on 24–25 October 2003 because the panel made an exception for item 9 of the bill of particulars. Apart from item 9 of the bill of particulars, nothing else in the charge sheet addresses the events of this period. Accordingly, in reviewing appellant's finding of guilt, we will not take into account any evidence concerning these dates.

Second, in our decretal paragraph, we will revise the specification to substitute the word and figures "4 November 2003" for "20 October 2003." We take this action because item 9 is the only act listed in the bill of particulars that occurred before 4 November 2003. This action will avoid any possible prejudice to appellant.

Third, in view of the panel's exception for item 1 of the bill of particulars, we conclude that the panel intended to find appellant not guilty of "assisting" in the placement of wires on the hands of the detainee nicknamed "Gilligan" during the incident of 4 November 2003. We do not conclude, however, that the panel intended to acquit appellant of all misconduct that occurred on 4 November 2003. The panel found, in Specification 3 of Charge III, that appellant "at or near Baghdad Central Correctional Facility, Abu Ghraib, Iraq, on or about 6 November 2003, did maltreat a detainee, a person subject to her orders, by placing wires on the detainee's hands while he stood on a Meals Ready to Eat box with this (sic) head covered and then telling him if he fell off the box he would be electrocuted." Thus, we conclude that the panel found that appellant did not provide assistance, but that she did commit the act herself.

III. Factual and Legal Sufficiency of the Evidence

Appellant contends that the evidence is legally and factually insufficient to sustain her conviction. The test for legal sufficiency of the evidence is "whether, considering the evidence in the light most favorable to the prosecution, a reasonable fact finder could have found all of the essential elements beyond a reasonable doubt." *See United States v. Turner*, 25 M.J. 324, 324 (C.M.A. 1987). Further, in resolving legal-sufficiency questions, we are bound to draw every reasonable inference from the evidence of record in favor of the prosecution. *See United States v. Rogers*, 54 M.J. 244, 246 (C.A.A.F. 2000). The test for factual sufficiency is "whether, after weighing the evidence in the record of trial and making allowances for not having personally observed the witnesses, the members of [the appellate court] are themselves convinced of the accused's guilt beyond a reasonable doubt." *Turner*, 25 M.J. at 325.

A. Charge I—Conspiracy

Charge I alleges that appellant committed the offense of conspiracy in violation of Article 81, UCMJ. The single specification asserts that appellant "[d]id, at or near Baghdad Central Correctional Facility, Abu Ghraib, Iraq, on or about 8 November 2003, conspire with Staff Sergeant [IF], Sergeant [JD],

Corporal [CG], Specialist [JS], Specialist [MA] and Private First Class [LE], to commit an offense under the Uniform Code of Military Justice, to wit: maltreatment of subordinates, and in order to effect the object of the conspiracy the said Specialist Harman posed for a 'thumbs up' photograph with said Corporal [CG] behind a pyramid of naked detainees."

* * *

Appellant contends that the evidence did not prove beyond a reasonable doubt that she formed an agreement to commit the maltreatment of subordinates or that she had the specific intent to commit the crime. To support this position, she makes three arguments. First, she asserts that as the most junior enlisted member assigned to perform duties in her part of the prison, she had no choice but to be present when many of the activities characterized as maltreatment occurred. Her passive presence she contends, does not show the existence of a conspiracy. We disagree. As the government argues, while appellant's presence at the prison was mandatory, her misconduct was not. She did not have a duty to appear in a "thumbs up" picture with CPL CG behind the pyramid of naked detainees, to take pictures herself, or to engage in any other concerted misconduct. Her entering into a conspiracy and her participation in the specified overt act were voluntary.

Second, appellant argues that, while she did pose for a "thumbs up" photograph with CPL CG, this photograph does not prove that she shared any common purpose with him to abuse detainees. On the contrary, she asserts, this photo indicates simply that she was posing for a picture as she often did in many of her experiences in Iraq. She contends that the court-martial had no justification for drawing inferences from her act of smiling in the photograph. We disagree. Her smiling face, when seen with the "thumbs up" hand signals, shows approval and encouragement to her co-conspirators as they maltreated the prisoners. An inference that she was joining their purpose is justified.

Third, she contends that the letter that she wrote on 20 October 2003 shows that she did not have the requisite intent. In the letter, as quoted above, she describes abuse in the prison to her roommate in the United States. She says: "The only reason I want to be there is to get the pictures that prove that the U.S. is not what they think." Appellant asserts that this comment demonstrates that she wanted to report criminal wrongdoing and that she would not agree to join a conspiracy. We disagree. Appellant's conscience may have been in one place on 20 October 2003 when she realized that maltreating detainees was wrong, but her intentions and actions were in another when she joined in and encouraged the abuse on 8 November 2003. The circumstances show that she had the intent to commit the offense of conspiracy. We conclude that the evidence was legally and factually sufficient to support her conviction of Charge I and its Specification.

B. Charge II—Dereliction of Duty

We have quoted Charge II, its Specification, and the bill of particular in section II of our opinion above. The charge alleges that appellant committed the offense of dereliction of duty in violation of Article 92. The specification asserts that appellant "[w]ho knew, of her duties at or near Baghdad Central Correctional Facility, Abu Ghraib, Iraq, from on or about 20 October 2003 to about 1 December 2003, was derelict in the performance of those duties in that she willfully failed to protect Iraqi detainees from abuse, cruelty and maltreatment, as it was her duty to do."

* * *

Appellant argues that the evidence is legally and factually insufficient to sustain her conviction for two principal reasons. First, she contends that the evidence does not show that she knew or reasonably should have known of her duties to protect the detainees. She asserts that she was not adequately trained to serve as a prison guard and was not adequately trained in the law of armed conflict. She emphasizes that her company commander testified that her unit was unprepared to perform the mission they were assigned at Abu Ghraib. In addition, given that nudity and handcuffing detainees was common in the prison, she asserts that it was not clear which acts were permissible and which ones were not.

We disagree. Appellant may not have had the ideal training, or even good training, for serving in the prison. Her unit certainly did not behave as a well-trained military police company should. But the facts and reasonable inferences from the facts establish beyond a reasonable doubt that appellant knew that her duties included protecting Iraqi detainees from the kinds of abuse, cruelty, and maltreatment alleged in the specification and in the portions of the bill of particulars of which she was found guilty. On a previous occasion, appellant and another member of her company, SPC MA, removed the handcuffs from a detainee who had been handcuffed for six hours and reported the incident to a non-commissioned officer, an action which resulted in the removal of the responsible MP from duties at the location. In addition, SSG IF testified that prison guards knew that they had a duty to protect and care for the detainees. Finally, in her own letter of 20 October 2003, appellant recognized the wrongfulness of the misconduct. This evidence supports the conclusion that she knew her duties.

Second, appellant argues that she was not derelict in her duties because she was in fact taking steps to expose the abuse, as her letter of 20 October 2003 indicates. She asserts that she was taking photographs to document her company's misconduct, which she was planning to report. We disagree with this argument. Even if we credit what she said in her letter, she was still derelict when she committed the acts detailed in items 2 through 8 of the bill of particulars. She was derelict in her duties when she attached the wires to the hands of the detainee nicknamed "Gilligan" and threatened him with electrocution, as alleged in items 2 and 3 of the bill of particulars. She was also derelict in her duties when she posed in a "thumbs up" photograph as alleged in item 5 of the bill of particulars. She did not take these actions to reveal the wrongdoing of others. In addition, when she witnessed the misconduct of others alleged in items 4, 5, 7, and 8 of the bill of particulars she did nothing to stop it. Although she did take pictures, she did not contact any person in authority to report the misconduct or to turn over the pictures.

C. Charge III—Maltreatment

Charge III accuses appellant of cruelty and maltreatment in violation of Article 93. . . . Our superior court, however, clarified the offense in *United States v. Carson*, 57 M.J. 410, 415 (C.A.A.F. 2002). The parties agree that this case controls.

In *Carson*, the court explained: "The essence of the offense is abuse of authority. Whether conduct constitutes *maltreatment* within the meaning of Article 93, UCMJ, in a particular case requires consideration of the specific facts and circumstances of that case." *Id.* at 415 (emphasis in original). The court in *Carson* recognized that the Military Judges' Benchbook includes "a nonbinding model instruction describing maltreatment as 'unwarranted, harmful, abusive, rough, or other unjustifiable treatment which, under all the circumstances . . . results in mental or physical pain or suffering.'" *See id.* at 413 (quoting Dep't of Army Pam. 27–9, Legal Services: Military Judges' Benchbook, para. 3–17–1 (1 April 2001)). But the court did not agree that the government must prove that the victim actually suffered harm, as the model instruction indicated. The court said:

> We conclude that in a prosecution for maltreatment under Article 93, UCMJ, it is not necessary to prove physical or mental harm or suffering on the part of the victim, although proof of such harm or suffering may be an important aspect of proving that the conduct meets the objective standard. It is only necessary to show, as measured from an objective viewpoint in light of the totality of the circumstances, that the accused's actions reasonably could have caused physical or mental harm or suffering. *Id.* at 415.

Specifications 1 and 2

Specification 1 of Charge III alleges that appellant "at or near Baghdad Central Correctional Facility, Abu Ghraib, Iraq, on or about 8 November 2003 did maltreat several detainees, persons subject to her orders, by taking two or more photographs of the naked detainees in a pyramid of human bodies." Specification 2 alleges that appellant "at or near Baghdad Central Correctional Facility, Abu Ghraib, Iraq, on or about 8 November 2003, did maltreat a detainee, a person subject to her orders, by photographing another guard, Corporal [CG], with one arm cocked back as if he was going to hit the detainee in the neck or back."

Appellant argues that the evidence is legally and factually insufficient to support her conviction of these two specifications because no detainee testified during the findings portion of the trial that he felt maltreated by appellant or that he was even aware that she took photographs of him. We disagree. As explained above, in *Carson*, our superior court specifically held that the government need not prove that the victims of maltreatment actually suffered harm.

In the totality of the circumstances, we conclude that appellant's actions described in Specifications 1 and 2 constitute maltreatment. Taking the photographs reasonably could have caused the detainees mental suffering. No reasonable detainee would want to be abused and, more importantly here, would wish his abusers to record this pointless, humiliating conduct. The detainees, in addition, had no ability to leave or to object or to do anything but what they were told. Appellant abused her authority as a guard in photographing the detainees.

At oral argument, counsel for appellant contended that taking the photographs was trivial in comparison to other misconduct at the prison that has gone uncharged and that may even have been sanctioned by persons in authority. We recognize that context matters. . . .

* * *

Appellant's conduct, however, clearly crossed the line even in its own context, a rough prison in a war zone holding dangerous detainees suspected of serious criminal offenses. Any reasonable observer would agree that taking the photographs of the detainees was abusive. The photographs served no purpose other than to humiliate and degrade.

Specification 3

Specification 3 of Charge III alleges that appellant "at or near Baghdad Central Correctional Facility, Abu Ghraib, Iraq, on or about 6 November 2003, did maltreat a detainee, a person subject to her orders, by placing wires on the detainee's hands while he stood on a Meals Ready to Eat box with this (sic) head covered and then telling him if he fell off the box he would be electrocuted." Appellant contests the legal and factual sufficiency of the evidence on this specification on several grounds.

First, appellant argues that placing wires on a detainee's hands and telling him that he would be electrocuted, when the wires were not, in fact, connected to any electrical outlet, does not constitute maltreatment. We disagree. The evidence shows that the detainee had an empty sandbag over his head as a hood. A reasonable inference is that he was limited in his ability to see whether the wires actually were connected to an electrical outlet. Indeed, the photographs themselves do not show where the wires lead. In addition, the panel could infer, as do we, that appellant would not have told the detainee that he would be electrocuted, and the detainee would not have stood on the box for over an hour, if the threat of electrocution was not credible in the mind of the detainee. This conduct was abusive and constitutes maltreatment under the standards in *Carson*.

Second, appellant asserts that the detainee did not testify and there was no evidence that he was traumatized by these acts in any way. Again, under the standard in *Carson,* we conclude that a reasonable person would feel frightened and threatened. The detainee's actual testimony was not necessary.

Third, appellant argues that the evidence is insufficient because SSG IF testified that he was the one who put the wires on the detainee. This argument, however, ignores appellant's sworn statement in which she admitted that she put the wires on him. We see no conflict. Both soldiers were present, and their own statements show that they each placed the wires on the detainee.

Finally, appellant argues, consistent with her sworn statement, that she believed they were joking when they put the wires on the detainee and that she did not believe he suffered any harm. This argument also has no merit. Under *Carson,* the focus is not on the subjective views of the oppressor or of the victim, but on whether the conduct is objectively abusive. Any reasonable observer would conclude that the conduct was so abusive that it constitutes maltreatment in violation of Article 93.

Specification 4

Specification 4 of Charge III alleges that appellant "at or near Baghdad Central Correctional Facility, Abu Ghraib, Iraq, on or about 8 November 2003 did maltreat a detainee, a person subject to her orders, by writing the word 'rapeist [sic]' on the detainee's leg who was then made to pose naked with other detainees." Appellant admitted in her sworn statement that she wrote the word on the detainee. But she contends that this act does not constitute maltreatment.

Appellant argues that it was not unusual to write words and figures on the bodies of detainees. Testimony established that the MPs at the prison sometimes used markers to write prisoners' cell numbers on their arms. In at least one instance, the MPs also wrote the word "knife" on the hand of a detainee who had been caught with a knife. Appellant further argues that the detainee upon whom she wrote the word was in fact a suspected rapist. She points out that there is no evidence that this detainee knew what was written on him, objected to it, or suffered any harm from it.

We disagree. Again, under *Carson,* it is the objective perspective of a reasonable person, rather than the subjective reaction of the victim, that determines whether maltreatment has occurred. From an objective perspective, appellant's action constituted maltreatment. Staff Sergeant IF testified that guards did not write the names of crimes on detainees. No evidence showed that guards wrote on parts of the body observable only when the detainee was naked. Writing the word on the detainee could serve no purpose other than to humiliate him for the sake of amusement. Specialist JS confirmed this conclusion. He testified that during the incident, appellant was "kind of happy, like it was a joke." For these reasons, we conclude that the evidence was legally and factually sufficient.

IV. Abuse of Discretion in Denying a Challenge for Cause

During individual voir dire, a member of the panel, Command Sergeant Major (CSM) LP, informed the parties that she had been an alternate member for a panel that heard the court-martial of a companion case. . . .

    * * *

Appellant now contends that the military judged erred in denying the challenge for cause of CSM LP. On appeal, both parties have treated the challenge as one for implied bias. They agree on the applicable rules and standard of review. . . .

Appellant argues that the military judge treated CSM LP's knowledge of outcomes in the related cases as essentially inconsequential. She asserts that a member of the public, however, would consider CSM LP's participation in the court martial unfair because she would "carry her knowledge of the outcome of prior cases into the deliberation room" and that there was too great a risk that, despite saying that she could set this knowledge aside, she would not be able to do so. In addition, according to appellant, a member of the public might conclude that CSM LP's senior rank and knowledge would influence other members, resulting in an unfair trial.

. . . We reach the same conclusion here. A member of the public would not believe that a senior non-commissioned officer, like CSM LP, who said she could be objective, would in fact be biased or would serve unfairly merely because she had seen or heard news stories about matters relating to appellant's case.

. . . A member of the public would conclude that CSM LP could be a fair and impartial court member.

VI. Conclusion

For reasons addressed in section II above, we amend the Specification of Charge II as follows:

In that Specialist Sabrina D. Harman, U.S. Army, who knew of her duties at or near Baghdad Central Correctional Facility, Abu Ghraib, Iraq, from on or about 4 November 2003 to about 1 December 2003, was derelict in the performance of those duties in that she willfully failed to protect Iraqi detainees from abuse, cruelty and maltreatment, as it was her duty to do so.

The findings of guilty of the Specification of Charge II and Charge II, as amended, are affirmed. The remaining findings of guilty are affirmed. Reassessing the sentence on the basis of the error noted, the entire record, and applying the principles of *United States v. Sales,* 22 M.J. 305 (C.M.A. 1986), and *United States v. Moffeit,* 63 M.J. 40 (C.A.A.F. 2006), to include the factors identified by Judge Baker in his concurring opinion, we affirm the sentence.

Senior Judge GALLUP and Judge CHIARELLA concur.

UNITED STATES v. HARMAN
Court of Appeals for the Armed Forces
68 M.J. 325 (C.A.A.F. 2010)

Judge STUCKY delivered the opinion of the Court.

Appellant [Specialist Sabrina D. Harman, U.S. Army], an Army reservist assigned as a guard at Abu Ghraib prison in Iraq in 2003, was convicted of various offenses concerning the maltreatment of detainees. We granted review to consider whether the evidence is legally sufficient to sustain the findings of guilty. For the reasons that follow, we find no error and affirm.

I.

Contrary to her pleas, Appellant was convicted at a general court-martial, with officer and enlisted members, of conspiracy to maltreat subordinates; dereliction of duty by failing to protect Iraqi detainees from abuse, cruelty, and maltreatment; and four specifications of maltreatment under Articles 81, 92, and 93, Uniform Code of Military Justice (UCMJ), 10 U.S.C. §§ 881, 892, 893 (2006). Appellant was sentenced to a bad-conduct discharge, confinement for six months, forfeiture of all pay and allowances, and reduction to E-1. The convening authority approved the sentence, with slight modifications to the forfeitures and confinement credits. The United States Army Court of Criminal Appeals (CCA) affirmed. *United States v. Harman*, 66 M.J. 710, 720 (A.Ct. Crim. App. 2008).

Appellant's convictions stem from incidents at Abu Ghraib prison in Iraq where she served as a guard in the fall of 2003. The first incident took place on November 4, 2003. Appellant admitted to investigators that she took a new detainee, who had been placed on a box with a hood over his head, affixed his fingers with wires, and told him he would be electrocuted if he fell off the box. Appellant then photographed the victim who stood on the box for approximately an hour. Appellant admitted it was her idea to attach these wires, though military intelligence officials had not asked her or her colleagues to do so. Appellant thought this was permissible because "[w]e were not hurting him. It was not anything that bad."

On November 7, 2003, more detainees were securely transferred to Appellant's area with handcuffs and sandbags over their heads so they could pose no harm. Other soldiers took it upon themselves to "discipline" the detainees by taking the detainees' clothes off and forcing them into a human pyramid, stepping on their hands and toes, and punching a hooded detainee so hard that he needed medical treatment. Appellant admitted in her sworn statement that she observed what was taking place, retrieved her digital camera, and returned to join the soldiers. Once there, she took numerous pictures, wrote "I'm a rapeist [sic]" on a detainee's naked thigh, and posed in front of the nude pyramid of detainees while smiling and giving a "thumbs up" sign. Appellant's colleagues described their collective mood as "[j]ust laughing and joking." Another servicemember reported the abuse. Later, Appellant told an investigator "I don't think the human pyramid was wrong, nor [my colleague] posing like he was going to hit the prisoner." But she also acknowledged that she was "sure it hurt" to be subject to these measures. Appellant did not report any of these incidents, although she had earlier expressed mixed feelings about mistreatment of detainees.[2] Two soldiers reported some of these incidents, and on January 12, 2004, one of them turned over digital images of the incidents.

II.

This Court reviews questions of legal sufficiency de novo as a matter of law. *United States v. Wilcox,* 66 M.J. 442, 446 (C.A.A.F. 2008). The test for legal sufficiency is " 'whether, after viewing the evidence in the light most favorable to the prosecution, *any* rational trier of fact could have found the essential elements of the crime beyond a reasonable doubt.' " *United States v. Mack,* 65 M.J. 108, 114 (C.A.A.F. 2007) (quoting *Jackson v. Virginia,* 443 U.S. 307, 319 (1979)). We affirm the decision of the lower court.

A. Conspiracy

Appellant argues that her conspiracy conviction was legally insufficient because she had no intent to conspire and because intent cannot be inferred from her "thumbs up" sign. . . .

Appellant's conduct is legally sufficient for a conspiracy conviction because she actively participated in the abuse and encouraged others to do so. As the CCA rightly concluded, Appellant's "smiling face, when seen with the 'thumbs up' hand signals, shows approval and encouragement to her co-conspirators as they maltreated the prisoners. An inference that she was joining their purpose is justified." *Harman,* 66 M.J. at 715. Furthermore, Appellant freely chose to participate in abuse and, in fact, voluntarily left to retrieve her camera so she could return to join and photograph the abuse. Appellant's previous letter to her roommate did not alter the intent manifested during the course of the abuse. Her direct involvement and obvious approbation, combined with her jokes and failure to stop or report the abuse, further support a "reasonable inference[]" of conspiracy "derived from the conduct of the parties themselves." *Mack,* 65 M.J. at 114 (citations omitted).

---

[2] In an October 20, 2003, letter to a former roommate, Appellant claimed she first thought such incidents were "funny then it hit me, that's a form of molestation. You can't do that." She added that "[t]he only reason I want to be there is to get the pictures to prove the U.S. is not what they think. . . . What if that was me in their shoes. . . . Both sides of me think it's wrong."

B. Dereliction of Duty

Appellant was convicted of dereliction of duty for failing to perform her duty to protect Iraqi detainees from abuse, cruelty, and maltreatment, in violation of Article 92, UCMJ. Appellant now argues those convictions were legally insufficient and emphasizes that she was not properly trained. . . .

Appellant's participation goes beyond mere acquiescence or negligent dereliction of duty: she actively and willingly participated in attaching wires to a detainee, writing "rapeist" on a detainee's naked thigh, taking photos, and encouraging others' abuse. Appellant received training in the care, custody and control of detainees as well as in the basic requirements of the Geneva Conventions regarding their treatment. Appellant does not allege that she was unaware of her fundamental duty to care for and protect detainees.[3] Appellant did not require specialized training to know that her actions were wrong, as evidenced by her own admissions as well as her colleagues' decisions to report the abuses. Appellant failed in her duty to protect the detainees, and her conviction was legally sufficient.

C. Maltreatment

Appellant was convicted of four specifications of maltreatment for photographing, placing electrodes on, and writing "rapeist" on detainees, in violation of Article 93, UCMJ. Appellant argues that no detainee suffered harm from her actions since none of them was aware of her photographs or felt pain from the wires. . . . Unlike in *United States v. Smith*, 68 M.J. 316 (C.A.A.F. 2010), Appellant does not assert that the detainees were not subject to her orders. There is "no need to show actual harm, rather 'it is only necessary to show, as measured from an objective viewpoint in light of the totality of the circumstances, that the accused's action reasonably could have caused physical or mental harm or suffering.' " *Id.* at 171–72 (quoting *United States v. Carson*, 57 M.J. 410, 415 (C.A.A.F. 2002)).

In this case, the objective standard of harm is met for all four specifications: as the CCA correctly found, "[n]o reasonable detainee would want to be abused and, more importantly here, would wish his abusers to record this pointless, humiliating conduct." *Harman*, 66 M.J. at 717. At least one detainee was aware he was being photographed at the time of the incidents. It was reasonable for the military judge to find that one detainee would have feared electrocution when guards explicitly told him he would be electrocuted if he fell off the box, irrespective of whether the wires were actually electrified. It is similarly reasonable that the military judge concluded another detainee would suffer from having "rapeist" capriciously

---

[3] Appellant's letter to her roommate, *supra* note 2, shows she appreciated the wrongfulness of her misconduct. The letter also undermines Appellant's simultaneous arguments that she was untrained to recognize maltreatment and that she was really just trying to document and stop abuse.

written on his leg while lying partially naked, hooded, and bound. Appellant's convictions were legally sufficient.

III.

The decision of the United States Army Court of Criminal Appeals is affirmed.

Disrespect, Willful Disobedience, Insubordinate Conduct—Articles 89-91

In addition to Article 92, the UCMJ includes other punitive articles that criminalize failures to obey or violations of lawful orders. Articles 90(2) and 91(2) prohibit willful disobedience of lawful orders of superiors, while Article 89 criminalizes disrespect of superior commissioned officers and Article 91(3) prohibits insubordinate conduct toward warrant officers, petty officers, and warrant officers. The UCMJ provides as follows:

Art. 89. Disrespect toward superior commissioned officer

Any person subject to this chapter who behaves with disrespect toward his superior commissioned officer shall be punished as a court-martial may direct.

10 U.S.C. § 889.

Art. 90. Assaulting or willfully disobeying superior commissioned officer

Any person subject to this chapter who—

(1) strikes his superior commissioned officer or draws or lifts up any weapon or offers any violence against him while he is in the execution of his office; or (2) willfully disobeys a lawful command of his superior commissioned officer; shall be punished, if the offense is committed in time of war, by death or such other punishment as a court-martial may direct, and if the offense is committed at any other time, by such punishment, other than death, as a court-martial may direct.

10 U.S.C. § 890.

Art. 91. Insubordinate conduct toward warrant officer, noncommissioned officer, or petty officer

Any warrant officer or enlisted member who

(1) strikes or assaults a warrant officer, noncommissioned officer, or petty officer, while that officer is in the execution of his office; (2) willfully disobeys the lawful order of a warrant officer, noncommissioned officer, or petty officer; or (3) treats with contempt or is disrespectful in language or deportment toward a warrant officer, noncommissioned officer, or petty officer while that officer is in the execution of his office; shall be punished as a court-martial may direct.

10 U.S.C. § 891.

Pursuant to Article 89, Disrespect toward a superior commissioned officer the subject of the disrespect must be superior in rank or command (if the officer is of another service), need not be present at the time of the conduct, and need not be in the execution of the office. MCM, pt. IV, ¶13.c.(1)(b). The accused must know of the victim's officer status. *Id.* The Manual for Courts-Martial further describes the conduct involved in Article 89 violations as follows:

> (3) Disrespect by words may be conveyed by abusive epithets or epithets or other contemptuous or denunciatory language. Truth is no defense. Disrespect by acts includes neglecting the customary salute, or showing a marked disdain, indifference, insolence, impertinence, undue familiarity, or other rudeness in the presence of the superior officer.

> (4) *Presence.* It is not essential that the disrespectful behavior be in the presence of the superior, but ordinarily one should not be held accountable under this article for what was said or done in a purely private conversation.

Id.

However, for a service member to be found guilty of insubordinate (disrespectful) conduct toward a warrant officer or non-commissioned officer under Article 91(3), the victim of the disrespect must be within sight or hearing of conduct and the victim must be in the execution of his office. *Id.* The victim of either an Article 89 or Article 91 violation may "divest" himself of his status and the protection of these articles based on his own conduct, if his "conduct in relation to the accused under all the circumstances departs substantially from the required standards appropriate to that officer's rank or position under similar circumstances." *Id.* & MCM, pt. IV, ¶14.c.(2)(b).

As is true with the Article 92(2), failure to obey other lawful orders, Article 90, requires that the person giving the order must have the authority to do so and must issue an order that relates to a military duty and is a specific and clear mandate. An Article 90 charge requires willful disobedience. The order cannot be a direction to perform a preexisting duty, or acts already required by law or regulation. *See United States v. Bratcher*, 39 C.M.R. 125 (C.M.A. 1969). In the following case, Technical Sergeant Traxler informs his chain of command that he will not participate in his temporary duty in Operation Desert Shield/Desert Storm in December 1990. He is subsequently given a written order from his commander directing him to "board in conformance with [his temporary duty] orders." The accused even signs acknowledging receipt of the order. While reading the case, consider whether the written order was required and what would have happened if the commander did not provide the written order.

UNITED STATES v. TRAXLER
Court of Military Appeals
39 M.J. 476 (C.M.A. 1994)

WISS, Judge:

Despite his not-guilty pleas, a general court-martial with members convicted Technical Sergeant [Chris E. Traxler, U.S. Air Force] of missing movement of an aircraft through design and willfully disobeying the command of his superior officer to board that same aircraft, in violation of Articles 87 and 90, Uniform Code of Military Justice, 10 U.S.C. §§ 887 and 890, respectively. The members sentenced Traxler to a bad-conduct discharge, confinement for 1 year, reduction to the grade E–5, and a reprimand. The convening authority approved these results, and the Court of Military Review affirmed in an unpublished opinion.

On petition to this Court, we granted review of the first issue raised by appellate defense counsel and specified the second one, stated below as follows:

> WHETHER THE MILITARY JUDGE ERRED BY FAILING TO GRANT THE DEFENSE MOTION TO DISMISS CHARGE II, DISOBEYING A LAWFUL COMMAND TO BOARD AN AIRCRAFT, WHEN THE UNDERLYING OFFENSE OF MISSING MOVEMENT WAS ALSO CHARGED.

* * *

We hold that Traxler properly was convicted both of missing movement through design and willfully disobeying his superior officer's order. We hold further that the two offenses are not multiplicious for findings, *see United States v. Teters,* 37 M.J. 370 (C.M.A. 1993), and that no notion of "ultimate offense" limits the maximum punishment just to that which is provided for missing movement.

I

A

Appellant, among others, received orders to board a certain aircraft for deployment to Europe on a Joint Chiefs of Staff exercise relating to Operation Desert Shield/Desert Storm; deployment was scheduled for December 15, 1990. In response, he told his first sergeant that he would not make the flight. He explained that he had a separation date in July 1991 and would go on terminal leave in April 1991. When the first sergeant retorted that his separation could be delayed, appellant offered additional explanations: He was going to start a business upon separation from the Air Force and, for a variety of reasons, that could not be delayed; also, he had a fear of flying that had resulted from an incident on some earlier military flight.

On December 12, appellant spoke with his commander, Captain Collins, and gave similar reasons why he could not deploy. Collins answered that appellant's duty was to the Air Force and to obeying orders, not to some future civilian business; further, he recommended that appellant see the chief of the mental health clinic for counseling in connection with his fear of flying.

Anticipating that appellant might still balk at his deployment, Collins sought advice from the legal office and drafted a written direct order to board the aircraft. When, on December 15, Collins was called by the flightline supervisor and told that appellant refused to board, Collins went to the flightline with the written order in his pocket.

There, Collins spoke with appellant, and the latter said, "I can't go." When Collins asked why, appellant just said, "I can't go." At this point, Collins took appellant off to the side of the aircraft and told him he was going to read to him a written order and that he wanted appellant to sign its receipt to ensure his understanding of it. The order read: "I hereby give you a direct order to board Aircraft # 63–7790 in conformance with your TDY orders (S.O. TF199 dated 12 Dec 90/31 TAW [Tactical Airlift Wing])." Appellant signed the receipt.

That done, security policemen escorted appellant away from the aircraft. Collins told appellant "that he had up until the time the actual door on the aircraft closed" to change his mind and board. Appellant did not, and so he missed the aircraft's movement.

B

At trial, Collins testified that, after he had referred appellant to the mental health clinic, personnel there reported to Collins that appellant did not have a legitimate fear of flying; had he been told otherwise, Collins indicated that he "would not have" given his order. Collins insisted that, while he had sought advice from the legal office to deal with appellant's refusal, no discussion of punishment of appellant ever arose. Further, he maintained that "punishment was not on [his] mind" when he generated the order. Instead, he testified that the purpose of his order was "to indicate to [appellant] the seriousness of the deployment and that if he actually refused to deploy that he needed to think twice about that thought." He "put the written order together to emphasize the necessity of him to meet a deployment commitment." Collins' "hope was that [appellant] would board the aircraft and depart for Europe."

After entering findings of fact consistent with the foregoing discussion, the military judge announced the following pertinent conclusions as a predicate for denying a defense motion to dismiss the charge of disobeying Captain Collins' order:

B. The duty imposed by the order was not routine in nature but was a specific mandate to perform a particular act at a definite time and place.

C. The accused's violation of the order was a flagrant defiance of military authority in the presence of other military personnel and in the midst of a Joint Chiefs of Staff directed military exercise.

D. Though the accused had a preexisting duty to board the deploying aircraft the order was formulated and issued by Capt. Collins with a view to adding the full authority of his position and rank to ensure the accused's compliance with the directive. It was not formulated for the purpose of enhancing the punitive consequences of a possible violation.

E. Under current applicable decisions by both the Air Force Court of [Military] Review and Court of Military Appeals, the conduct of the accused on or about 15 December 1990 are [sic] properly charged as both violations of Article 87 and Article 90 of the Uniform Code of Military Justice.

After appellant had been convicted of both crimes, counsel and the military judge turned to the question of maximum punishment. Trial counsel indicated that, although the two offenses were separate, the Government would assume the "conservative approach" and "concede multiplicity" for sentencing "since they did in one sense arise out of the same act." Thus, pointing to the maximum punishment for willful disobedience of a superior officer's order, the prosecution urged that appellant's liability extended to a dishonorable discharge, confinement for 5 years, total forfeitures, reduction to E–1, and a fine. *See* para. 14e(2), Part IV, and RCM 1003(b)(3) and (5), Manual for Courts–Martial, United States, 1984.

* * *

... However, since the Government had "conced[ed] multiplicity," he accepted trial counsel's position on the maximum punishment.

II

Appellant argues in this Court that he had a preexisting duty to board the aircraft for deployment and that, accordingly, his disobedience of Captain Collins' order to do what he already had a duty to do cannot be made a separate and more serious crime. In other words, he contends, his "ultimate offense" was failure to deploy, not disobedience of Collins' order, and his punishment therefore is limited to the maximum punishment provided for missing movement by design. *See United States v. Peaches*, 25 M.J. 364 (C.M.A. 1987); *United States v. Bratcher*, 18 U.S.C.MA 125, 39 CMR 125 (1969); *see also United States v. Quarles*, 1 M.J. 231 (C.M.A. 1975).

Appellant's contention is accurate in general concept but is flawed in its imprecision. First, it is not simply the existence of a preexisting duty to do that which was the subject of the order that is material; rather, it is the nature of that preexisting duty. Generally, when the subject of an order from a superior officer amounts merely to performing routine soldierly duties, the order is no more than an admonition to obey the law and, thus, "can have no validity beyond the limit of the ultimate offense committed." *United States v. Bratcher, supra* at 128, 39 CMR at 128; *accord United States v. Peaches, supra* at 366. *Cf. United States v. Pettersen*, 17 M.J. 69, 72 (C.M.A. 1983) ... Here, though, the military judge correctly concluded on the basis of the record that "[t]he duty imposed by" Captain Collins' "order was not routine in nature but was a specific mandate to perform a particular act at a definite time and place." *See United States v. Bratcher, supra* at 128, 39 CMR at 128; para. 14c(2)(d), Part IV.

Second, appellant's contention ignores the materiality of the purpose of the order. "Disobedience of an order which has for its sole object the attainment of some private end, or which is given for the sole purpose of increasing the penalty for an offense which it is expected the accused may commit, is not punishable under" Article 90. Para. 14c(2)(a)(iii). Here, the military judge concluded—again, soundly based on the record—that Captain Collins' order "was not formulated for the purpose of enhancing the punitive consequences of a possible violation."

Rather, as the judge concluded, "the order was formulated and issued by Captain Collins with a view to adding the full authority of his position and rank to ensure the accused's compliance with the directive." *See United States v. Pettersen* and *United States v. Loos,* both *supra.* Captain Collins specifically testified, which is entirely consistent with his objective actions, that his purpose was to emphasize the necessity for appellant to deploy and to bring home to appellant the seriousness of his failure to do so—all in the hope that this would motivate appellant to board the aircraft.

Thus, Captain Collins' order was a "specific mandate" to do "a particular act at a definite time," as opposed to merely notifying appellant that he had a temporary duty scheduled; he delivered the order personally to appellant under circumstances that bore all the indicia of a formal command; and his purpose was to emphasize to appellant the importance of compliance with the earlier directive in the hope that appellant, therefore, would comply. In this posture, the military judge correctly ruled that appellant's willful disobedience of the order was an intentional defiance of the authority of Captain Collins' office and, in that connection, was distinct from his failure to comply with the earlier general directive to deploy. *See para. 14c(2)(f).*

III

* * *

The test for determining whether two offenses are multiplicious is "whether each provision requires proof of an additional fact which the other does not," *Blockburger v. United States,* 284 U.S. 299, 304 (1932). *Accord Schmuck v. United States,* 489 U.S. 705 (1989); *United States v. Teters,* 37 M.J. at 377. Appellant candidly acknowledges, "This analysis would seem to foreclose appellant's argument as to findings multiplicity. . . ." . . . .

* * *

IV

The decision of the United States Air Force Court of Military Review is affirmed.

Chief Judge SULLIVAN and Judges COX, CRAWFORD, and GIERKE concur.

Points for Discussion

1. Technical Sergeant Traxler told his chain of command of his intention not to deploy in violation of his temporary duty orders, why should he be exposed to punishment for both missing movement (Article 87, UCMJ) and failure to obey a lawful order (Article 92(2), UCMJ)? Is that fair?

2. The *Traxler* court holds that a commander can give a personal order to put their full position and rank behind the order to ensure compliance (which is punishable as a separate offense) but the officer cannot do so to enhance punishment. What factors would you consider in making this determination if you were on the appellate court reviewing a commander's order to board a plane when the servicemember already had orders to travel aboard the plane?

12-4. Absence and Duty-Related Offenses

Desertion—Article 85

Absence offenses are frequently charged offenses these offenses under the UCMJ that have no civilian counterpart.

Art. 85. Desertion

(a) Any member of the armed forces who—

(1) without authority goes or remains absent from his unit, organization, or place of duty with intent to remain away therefrom permanently; (2) quits his unit, organization, or place of duty with intent to avoid hazardous duty or to shirk important service; or (3) without being regularly separated from one of the armed forces enlists or accepts an appointment in the same or another one of the armed forces without fully disclosing the fact that he has not been regularly separated, or enters any foreign armed service except when authorized by the United States; is guilty of desertion.

(b) Any commissioned officer of the armed forces who, after tender of his resignation and before notice of its acceptance, quits his post or proper duties without leave and with intent to remain away therefrom permanently is guilty of desertion.

10 U.S.C. § 885.

Essentially, the UCMJ sets forth two common types of desertion: absence with the intent to remain permanently away (Article 85(1)), and quitting an assigned unit with intent to avoid hazardous duty or to shirk important service (Article 85(2)). The remaining offenses: joining another service without a proper discharge offense and quitting officer are not as frequently charged. The *Manual for Courts-Martial* explains that, " 'Hazardous duty' or 'important service' may include service such as duty in a combat or other dangerous area ... [but] services as drill, target practice, maneuvers, and practice marches are not ordinarily 'hazardous duty' or 'important service.' "

The chart below depicts the elements of the offenses and shows aggravating factors when charged and included in the evidence presented beyond a reasonable doubt increases the maximum punishment. Note that many of these offenses require proof of actual knowledge of the hazardous duty, time and place of duty, movement. However, the government may prove actual knowledge by circumstantial evidence. MCM, pt. IV, ¶10.c.(2).

The *Mackey* case which follows reflects that a violation of Article 85(1) Desertion requires proof of intent to permanently remain away from the unit which may be proven by circumstantial evidence. The *Manual for Courts-Martial* describes circumstances "from which an inference may be drawn that the accused intended" to remain permanently away, including a lengthy period of absence and the following:

> that the accused attempted to, or did, dispose of uniforms or other military property; that the accused purchased a ticket for a distant point or was arrested, apprehended, or surrendered a considerable distance from the accused's station; that the accused could have conveniently surrendered to military control but did not; that the accused was dissatisfied with the accused's unit, ship, or with military service; that the accused made remarks indicating an intention to desert; that the accused was under charges or had escaped from confinement at the time of the absence; that the accused made preparations indicative of an intent not to return (for example, financial arrangements); or that the accused enlisted or accepted an appointment in the same or another armed force without disclosing the fact that the accused had not been regularly separated, or entered any foreign armed service without being authorized by the United States.

MCM, pt. IV, ¶9.c.(2)(c).

The *Manual for Courts-Martial* further provides that the following circumstances negate the inference: "previous long and excellent service; that the accused left valuable personal property in the unit or on the ship; or that the accused was under the influence of alcohol or drugs during the absence." *Id.*

[handwritten margin note: Ex. Circumstantial Inferences of Intent to Remain Away]

[handwritten margin note: Ex. Negates Inference of Intent to Remain Away]

UNAUTHORIZED ABSENCES (ARTICLES 85-87, UCMJ)

		Actus Reus	Mens Rea	Aggravating Factors
Desertion (Article 85)	Desertion with intent to remain away permanently	Absence from unit	Intent to remain away permanently	Termination by apprehension; time of war
	Desertion to avoid hazardous or important duty	Quitting unit	Knowledge of hazardous or important duty	Time of war
AWOL (Article 86)	Failure to go	Failure to go to appointed place of duty	Actual knowledge of requirement to be present	From guard to watch
	Going from duty	Leaving appointed place of duty	Actual knowledge of requirement to be present	From guard or watch
	Absence from unit	Being or remaining absent from unit	None (absence must be without authority)	Duration; termination by apprehension; from watch or guard; intent to avoid field exercises
Missing Movement (Article 87)	Missing movement by neglect	Missing movement of unit for significant distance and time	Actual knowledge of movement; or negligence	
	Missing movement by design	Missing movement of unit for significant distance and time	Actual knowledge of movement; or intentionally	

UNITED STATES v. MACKEY

Navy-Marine Corps Court of Military Review

46 C.M.R. 754 (N.M.C.M.R. 1972)

LEHNERT, Judge:

The appellant [Private First Class Donald R. Mackey, U.S. Marine Corps] was tried by general court-martial before a military judge sitting alone on a charge and specification alleging desertion in violation of Article 85, UCMJ. The appellant pleaded not guilty to the charge of desertion, but did plead guilty to the lesser included offense of unauthorized absence for approximately twenty-six months. However, after trial upon the merits, he was found guilty of desertion as charged. The military judge sentenced the appellant to be confined at hard labor for a period of one year and six months, to forfeit all pay and allowances, to be reduced to the grade of private, pay grade E-1, and to be discharged from the service with a dishonorable discharge.

* * *

II

As a second assignment of error the appellant contends that:

"THE EVIDENCE DOES NOT ESTABLISH BEYOND A REASONABLE DOUBT APPELLANT'S INTENT TO REMAIN AWAY PERMANENTLY."

The thrust of appellant's argument is that the inferences to be derived from the evidence that appellant lived at his home of record during his unauthorized absence, that he had retained his summer service uniform, service records, identification card and tags are sufficient to raise a reasonable doubt that the appellant intended to remain away permanently.

The government's case evidenced a period of about 26 months unauthorized absence, an absence which commenced while the appellant was under orders to eventually report to the ground forces in the Western Pacific while some of these forces were engaged in hostilities, and an absence which was terminated by apprehension at a place far removed from his place of duty.

Under the circumstances evidenced in this case, we are of the opinion that the evidence is sufficient to prove beyond reasonable doubt the element of intent away permanently. The assignment of error is denied.

* * *

We agree that the sentence is appropriate although, under the circumstances of this case, we believe that the pretrial confinement of the appellant should be taken into consideration. Since the record does not indicate specifically whether the military judge did so, we will assure consideration by reassessment.

Accordingly, the findings of guilty and only so much of the sentence as provides for confinement at hard labor for 15 months, forfeiture of all pay and allowances, reduction to pay grade E-1, and to be discharged from the service with a dishonorable discharge are affirmed.

Senior Judge TIMBLIN and Judge SELMAN concur.

Absence Without Leave—Article 86

Article 86, Absence without leave, as described in the chart above, occurs when a service member is absent without authority and Article 86 consists of the following three types: (1) failure to go to an appointed place of duty at the time prescribed (also known as failure to repair (FTR)); (2) going from an appointed place of duty; or (3) absenting oneself or remaining absent from an assigned unit, organization, or place of duty at which a person is required to be at a prescribed time. Art. 86, UCMJ, 10 U.S.C. § 885.

Article 86(1) and (2) violations require proof of actual knowledge as to the duty requirements, but actual knowledge need not be proven for Article 86 (3) violations. Article 86(3), Absence without leave (AWOL) charges require proof of absence from the unit. Service members, especially Academy cadets, will plan to return to their unit to ensure their timely arrival, because if they experience an unplanned delay, they may face charges of AWOL upon their later return. If a service member is unable to return, the status of AWOL is not changed because of inability "through sickness, lack of transportation facilities, or other disabilities. But the fact that all or part of a period of unauthorized absence was in a sense enforced or involuntary is a factor in extenuation and should be given due weight when considering the initial disposition of the offense." MCM, pt. IV, ¶10.c.(4)(d). Aggravating factors (which will increase the authorized sentence) for Article 86(3) offenses which if charged require proof, include duration, termination by apprehension, from guard or watch, or with intent to avoid field exercise. *Id.*

Termination or end date for an AWOL charge may sometimes be called into question depending on the circumstances. The following case explains ways in which a servicemembers AWOL status may end.

UNITED STATES v. ROGERS
Army Court of Criminal Appeals
59 M.J. 584 (Army Ct. Crim. App. 2003)

SCHENCK, Judge:

A military judge sitting as a general court-martial found appellant [Private (E-2) Latonya M. Rogers, U.s. Army] guilty, pursuant to her pleas, of desertion, absence without leave (AWOL) (three specifications), larceny (seven specifications), and forgery (eight specifications) in violation of Articles 85, 86, 121, and 123, Uniform Code of Military Justice, 10 U.S.C. §§ 885, 886, 921, and 923 [hereinafter UCMJ]. The military judge sentenced appellant to a dishonorable discharge, confinement for three years, forfeiture of all pay and allowances, a $3,500 fine, and reduction to Private (PVT) E1. Pursuant to a pretrial agreement, the convening authority approved only so much of the sentence as provides for a dishonorable discharge, confinement for twenty months, a $3,500 fine, and reduction to Private E1.

Appellant's case was submitted to this court on its merits for review pursuant to Article 66, UCMJ, 10 U.S.C. § 866. An issue regarding voluntary termination of unauthorized absence merits discussion, but no relief.

FACTS

Appellant pleaded guilty to and was found guilty of three specifications of AWOL from her unit for the following time frames: from on or about 19 June 2001 until on or about 3 July 2001 (when she returned to her company); from on or about 18 October 2001 until on or about 23 October 2001 (when she returned to military control at Fort Hood); and from on or about 31 October 2001 until on or about 4 December 2001 (when she was apprehended in Killeen, Texas, and placed in pretrial confinement). The stipulation of fact, agreed to by all parties and admitted into evidence without objection, states that appellant did not have leave or prior approval for any of these absences.

[handwritten margin note: 3 instances of absence]

During the providence inquiry, appellant told the military judge that she "kept absenting" herself from her unit because she "wanted out of the Army." During her absences, appellant remained in the Fort Hood and Killeen, Texas, area. She also stated, "I was sometimes ... on post." After this disclosure to the military judge, the following colloquy ensued:

> MJ: All right, but were you under the control of your unit when you were on post?
>
> ACC: I went to my unit and I saw like some of my NCOs [noncommissioned officers] and they knew I was AWOL, but they never said anything.
>
> MJ: Mm, huh.
>
> ACC: But I never turned myself [in to] my unit.

LAW AND DISCUSSION

This court reviews a military judge's acceptance of a guilty plea for an abuse of discretion. *United States v. Eberle*, 44 M.J. 374, 375 (C.A.A.F. 1996). We use a *"substantial basis* test for appellate review of the providence of guilty pleas." *United States v. Jordan*, 57 M.J. 236, 238 (C.A.A.F. 2002) (emphasis in original). We will not overturn a guilty plea unless the record of trial shows a substantial basis in law and fact for questioning the guilty plea. *United States v. Prater*, 32 M.J. 433, 436 (C.M.A. 1991). In determining the providence of an appellant's pleas, " 'it is uncontroverted that an appellate court must consider the entire record in a case.' " *United States v. Falk*, 50 M.J. 385, 389 (C.A.A.F. 1999) (quoting *United States v. Johnson*, 42 M.J. 443, 445 (C.A.A.F. 1995)).

"The military judge shall not accept a plea of guilty without making such inquiry of the accused as shall satisfy the military judge that there is a factual basis for the plea." Rule for Courts–Martial [hereinafter R.C.M.] 910(e). The facts disclosed by such inquiry must objectively support the guilty plea. *United States v. Garcia,* 44 M.J. 496, 497–98 (C.A.A.F. 1996). Should the accused set up a matter inconsistent with the plea at any time during the proceeding, the military judge either must resolve the inconsistency or reject the guilty plea. *Id.* at 498; *see also United States v. Davenport,* 9 M.J. 364, 367 (C.M.A. 1980); *United States v. Timmins,* 45 C.M.R. 249, 253 (C.M.A. 1972); UCMJ art. 45(a), 10 U.S.C. § 845(a).

Article 86(3), UCMJ, provides, "Any member of the armed forces who, without authority . . . absents himself [or herself] or remains absent from his [or her] unit, organization, or place of duty at which he [or she] is required to be at the time prescribed; shall be punished as a court-martial may direct." The elements of this AWOL offense are:

(a) That the accused absented himself or herself from his or her unit, organization, or place of duty at which he or she was required to be;

(b) That the absence was without authority from anyone competent to give him or her leave; and

(c) That the absence was for a certain period of time.

Manual for Courts–Martial, United States (2000 ed.) [hereinafter *MCM, 2000*], Part IV, para. 10b(3). Termination by apprehension, as an aggravating factor, must also be proven beyond a reasonable doubt. *Id.*

The *MCM* describes termination of an AWOL through surrender to military authorities, as follows:

A surrender occurs when a person *presents himself* or herself to any military authority, whether or not a member of the same armed force, *notifies that authority* of his or her unauthorized absence status, and *submits or demonstrates a willingness to submit* to military control. Such a surrender terminates the unauthorized absence.

Id. at Part IV, para. 10c(10)(a) (emphasis added).

Courts have also considered various circumstances in which an AWOL service member is considered to have "voluntarily terminated" his or her absence. As early as 1952, our superior court noted that casual presence at a military installation does not, without more, terminate an unauthorized absence. *See United States v. Jackson,* 2 C.M.R. 96, 98 (C.M.A. 1952). The *Jackson* court found that an absentee's presence at his summary court-martial did not terminate his AWOL because the summary court-martial was not aware of the absentee's AWOL status. *Id.* at 192–93, 2 C.M.R. at 98–99. The court remarked that only the exercise of proper military control over an absentee effects an AWOL's termination. *Id.* at 192, 2 C.M.R. at 98; *see also United States v. Raymo,* 1 M.J. 31, 32 (C.M.A. 1975) (finding where an Army officer failed to apprehend an absentee who divulged his status, the officer nonetheless "effectively exercised military control" over the absentee by directing him to the Federal Bureau of Investigation).

In *United States v. Coglin,* 10 M.J. 670, 672–73 (A.C.M.R. 1981), this court described and explained the relevant factors necessary for an absentee to voluntarily terminate an unauthorized absence. We held that PVT Coglin did not voluntarily terminate his absence because he "did not present himself to competent military authorities with the intention of terminating his absence and returning to military duty." *Id.* at 673. Private Coglin went onto a military installation, identified himself, spoke to an E–7 in personnel about a compassionate reassignment, and went to finance to discuss his pay. *Id.* at 671–73. This court found that PVT Coglin was on post for personal reasons and that he did not disclose his AWOL status to the E–7. *Id.* at 671, 673. While PVT Coglin told another NCO, his former squad leader, that he was AWOL, he left post when the NCO threatened to turn him in. *Id.* at 673.

Today, we reaffirm our holding in *Coglin* that an absentee's return to a military installation does not terminate an AWOL if the return involves a casual presence for personal reasons. We conclude that the four-part test described below must be satisfied in order to voluntarily terminate an AWOL. The absentee must do the following:

(1) *present* him or herself with the *intent* to return to military duty. The soldier must accomplish this by an overt act, done in person, and not by telephone or other means;

(2) make this presentment to a military *authority,* that is, someone with authority to apprehend the soldier. Such authorities include, but are not limited to, a commissioned officer, a noncommissioned officer, or a military police officer;

(3) *identify* him or herself to the military authority and *disclose* his or her AWOL *status,* unless the authority is already aware of the soldier's identity and AWOL status; and

(4) *submit* to the actual or constructive *control exercised* over the absentee by the authority to whom he or she has made the necessary disclosure.

We find that appellant did not render her guilty plea to AWOL improvident by stating that she was "sometimes" on post. Appellant did not express an intent to return to military duty. In fact, she "wanted out of the Army." Although the trial judge failed to explain early termination, facts elicited during the providence inquiry indicate that there was no early termination. Specifically, appellant emphasized during the plea inquiry that she never turned herself in to her unit. Appellant's "casual presence" in her unit did not rise to the level of voluntary termination. She did not overtly submit to military control and "no one attempted to exercise any control over the appellant." *Vaughn,* 36 M.J. at 648.

Test to Terminate AWOL

CONCLUSION

If, during a plea inquiry, evidence is adduced indicating the accused's casual presence in the unit area during the AWOL period alleged on the charge sheet, then before accepting the plea the military judge should explain voluntary termination and ensure that no factual basis exists for it. In doing so, the military judge should focus on the requisite factors announced in *Coglin,* and reaffirmed today: presentment with intent to return, presentment to a military authority, identification and disclosure of status, and submission to actual or constructive control.

An accused may properly be found guilty of two or more separate unauthorized absences under one specification, provided that each absence is included within the period alleged in the specification and provided that the accused was not misled. If an accused is found guilty of two or more unauthorized absences under a single specification, the maximum authorized punishment shall not exceed that authorized if the accused had been found guilty as charged in the specification.

In the present case, we find that appellant's comments during the providence inquiry were not inconsistent with her pleas of guilty to AWOL for the periods alleged. Therefore, we will affirm the findings of guilty to Charge II and its Specifications.

We have reviewed the matters personally raised by appellant under *United States v. Grostefon,* 12 M.J. 431 (C.M.A. 1982), and find them to be without merit.

The findings of guilty and sentence are affirmed.

Senior Judge HARVEY and Judge BARTO concur.

APPENDIX

In a contested case involving absence without leave, we suggest use of the following pattern instruction by military judges when the issue of voluntary termination arises:

The evidence has raised the issue of whether the accused voluntarily terminated his unauthorized absence (AWOL) prior to the end-date alleged in (the) Specification ____ of Charge ____. A return to a military (installation) (base) (camp) (post) (facility), without more, does not terminate an AWOL if it involves merely a casual presence based on personal reasons. However, you may find that the accused voluntarily terminated (his)(her) AWOL status if you find the following facts. First, the accused presented (him) (her)self with the intent to return to military duty. The accused must accomplish this by an overt act, done in person, and not by telephone, electronic, or other means. Second, the accused must make this presentment to a military authority, that is, someone with authority to apprehend the soldier. Such authorities include, but are not limited to, a commissioned officer, a noncommissioned officer, or a military police officer. Third, in doing so, the accused must identify (him)(her)self to the military authority and disclose (his)(her) AWOL status, unless the authority is already aware of the accused's identity and AWOL status. Fourth, the accused must submit to the actual or constructive control exercised over (him)(her) by the authority to whom (he)(she) has made the necessary disclosure. The military authority's actions may result in constructive control over the accused and fulfill this requirement, but only if the accused intended to return to military duty and submits to military control.

[If you find that the accused voluntarily terminated (his)(her) absence, but later absented (him) (herself) from his (unit) (place of duty), you may find the accused guilty, by exceptions and substitutions, of two or more separate unauthorized absences under one specification, provided that each absence is included within the overall period alleged in the specification.]

If the issue of voluntary termination is raised by the evidence, the prosecution bears the burden of proof to establish beyond a reasonable doubt that the accused did not voluntarily terminate (his)(her) AWOL. In order to find the accused guilty of AWOL for the entire period alleged in the specification, you must be convinced beyond a reasonable doubt that the accused did not voluntarily terminate his AWOL status prior to the end date indicated in the specification.

* * *

Points for Discussion

1. Do you agree with the court's holding in the *Rogers* case? What if the accused admitted to hiding in the barracks during the period charged in the AWOL specification, do you think that would terminate the AWOL status? The Army Court of Criminal Appeals in *United States v. Estes*, 62 M.J. 544, 555 (Army Ct. Crim. App. 2005) (which is included in Chapter 14-3 of this text), notes that, a "unit is comprised of soldiers, not buildings," and finds that the military judge properly accepted the accused's plea to AWOL for the period charged despite the accused's admission that he was in the barracks during that period.

2. If a service member lies to his squad leader to obtain permission to be absent from the unit, should he still be charged as absent without authority? *See United States v. Duncan*, 60 M.J. 973 (Army Ct. Crim. App. 2005) (holding if an absence is preceded by a false statement or false information provided by the accused the absence is without authority).

Missing Movement

Servicemembers who leave without authority may be also be charged with an Article 87, Missing movement violation. The Manual for Courts-Martial describes the elements of proof as follows:

(1) that the accused was required in the course of duty to move with a ship, aircraft or unit;

(2) that the accused knew of the prospective movement of the ship, aircraft or unit;

(3) That the accused missed the movement of the ship, aircraft or unit; and

(4) that the accused missed the movement through design or neglect.

MCM, pt. IV, ¶11.b.(4).

This offense requires proof that the accused had actual knowledge of the movement (which may be proven by circumstantial evidence) and the movement must be a "move or transfer of a ship, aircraft, or unit involving a substantial distance and period of time." MCM, pt. IV, ¶11.c. "Marches of a short duration with a return to the point of departure, and minor changes in location of ships, aircraft, or units, as when a ship is shifted from one berth to another in the same shipyard or harbor or when a unit is moved from one barracks to another on the same post" do not constitute "movement" for this offense. *Id.* For example, if the unit is scheduled to depart the installation for a twelve-mile road march that would not be a "movement" chargeable under Article 87, Missing movement. *See United States v. Smith*, 2 M.J. 567 (A.C.M.R. 1976).

Depending on the circumstances, a service member may be charged with either missing movement by design (requiring proof of specific intent to miss movement) or due to neglect. Neglect occurs when the service member fails to exercise reasonable care or there is an

> "omission to take such measures as are appropriate under the circumstances to assure presence . . . at the time of a scheduled movement, or doing something without giving attention to its probable consequences in connection with the prospective movement, such as a departure from the vicinity of the prospective movement to such a distance as would make it likely that one could not return in time for the movement." *Id.*

Point for Discussion

If a service member doesn't agree with the reason the unit is deploying (e.g., support in Afghanistan or bombing Libya) and he decides not to move with his unit, should he still be charged with missing movement? If yes, should he be charged with negligently missing movement or missing movement by design?

CHAPTER 13

MORE MILITARY OFFENSES

13-1. Contempt Toward Officials

Whether with justification or not, members of the public sometimes hold politicians in deep disregard, and openly express their disdain for them. Civilians generally need not fear that they will suffer legal repercussions for uttering negative comments about government officials because the First Amendment guarantees civilians great latitude in criticizing public figures. They face no liability for defamatory statements unless the statements are both false and made with actual malice. *See New York Times Co. v. Sullivan*, 376 U.S. 254 (1964).

Officers in the Armed Forces, however, do not have such expansive freedom. They must restrain themselves from making severely disrespectful comments about certain government officers because the UCMJ contains the following provision that has no civilian analogue:

Art. 88. Contempt toward officials

Any commissioned officer who uses contemptuous words against the President, the Vice President, Congress, the Secretary of Defense, the Secretary of a military department, the Secretary of Homeland Security, or the Governor or legislature of any State, Commonwealth, or possession in which he is on duty or present shall be punished as a court-martial may direct.

10 U.S.C. § 888.

Article 88 raises two important issues: (1) What kinds of statements does the Article 88? (2) How is the Article consistent with the First Amendment's protection of freedom of speech? In considering these questions, think also about what policies Article 88 furthers

---

On the issue of what Article 88 prohibits, the MCM explains that the words must be contemptuous and that mere "adverse criticism . . . in the course of a political discussion, even though emphatically expressed, may not be charged as a violation of the article." MCM, pt. IV, ¶12c. Another important point is that "truth or falsity of the statements is immaterial." *Id.* The Manual also says that "expressions of opinion made in a purely private conversation should not ordinarily be charged." *Id.* Further guidance is difficult to find because, remarkably, there have been few reported cases under Article 88 since its adoption in 1950. The following decision involved a prosecution under Article 62 of the Articles of War, the predecessor of Article 88 in the UCMJ. Note that unlike Article 88, Article 62 applied not only to officers, but also to enlisted personnel. *See* Act of June 4, 1920, 41 Stat 759, 801.

SANFORD v. CALLAN
U.S. Court of Appeals for the Fifth Circuit
148 F.2d 376 (5th Cir. 1945)

McCORD, Circuit Judge.

Hugh Callan was convicted by a general court-martial for violations of the 62nd and 96th Articles of War, 10 U.S.C.A. §§ 1534, 1568. He was sentenced to be dishonorably discharged from the service, to forfeit all pay and allowances due or to become due, and to be confined at hard labor for a period of twenty years. The reviewing authority approved the sentence and designated the United States Penitentiary at Atlanta, Georgia, as the place of confinement.

On May 21, 1943, Hugh Callan filed a writ of habeas corpus, and the case was continued, to enable him to secure the evidence of military officers who had been moved to distant assignments since his induction and imprisonment. The trial court on the 14th day of September, 1944, rendered an opinion and entered a judgment sustaining the writ of habeas corpus and discharging the petitioner from custody.

The trial court found that the oath prescribed by the War Department was not administered or taken by petitioner, and that he was not inducted into the Army within the meaning of Section 11 of the Selective Training and Service Act, 50 U.S.C.A. Appendix § 311, and that petitioner was not subject to trial by court-martial, as such court did not have jurisdiction.

Petitioner was convicted of violating the 62nd Article of War in that he used the following disrespectful words against the President of the United States: "The President of the United States is a dirty politician, whose only interest is gaining power as a politician and safeguarding the wealth of the Jews * * * ."

He was also convicted on the further charge of saying within the presence and hearing of enlisted men that: "President Roosevelt and his capitalistic mongers are enslaving the world by their actions in Europe and Asia, by their system of exploiting."

The petitioner was further convicted on the charge of violating the 96th Article of War in that at Camp Blanding, Florida on or about March 14, 1942, he did adhere to the cause of the enemies of the United States, and did advocate their cause by repeatedly stating as the truth that: "He (Private Callan) was opposed to military training in this Army (United States) because they were fighting countries that were right, and that he refused to fight in

Asia, Europe or Africa; that Hitler's plan was one of necessity through moral truth, and that the people of America are vulnerable saps."

He was further convicted on the charge that he did willfully attempt to cause and induce insubordination and refusal of duty among the enlisted men of the 36th Infantry Division, by stating in their presence and hearing that: "The countries we are fighting are in the right; that Japan and Germany were justified in their war against the United States."

He was further convicted on the charge of stating in the presence and hearing of enlisted men that: "Japan and Germany were justified in their war against the United States."

Petitioner does not in his brief or evidence deny the charges and specifications, but only contends that he used respectful language in setting forth his criticisms of the President and of the United States and in expressing his views before enlisted men and officers of the United States Army. Almost his entire argument is to the effect that he did not take the oath prescribed when he was inducted.

A careful reading of the record will disclose that the petitioner possesses a very poor memory. He was unable to remember much of what transpired in sequence when he was examined and inducted into the service, what was said and done and just who was present. He is unable to tell whether he was required to go to a second floor or whether all the transactions incident to his induction were on the first floor. He further explained that he was lost from his group of inductees, that he saw and heard another group take the oath; yet the evidence shows conclusively that only one group at a time would be permitted to enter where the oath was taken, and that they would be required to stand. It is clearly shown that if he had succeeded in passing the guards and entering the room he would have walked into the standing group. Moreover, he testified that he only heard the conclusion of the oath, the words which he heard being, "So help me God." It is shown to a moral certainty that the oath then and there administered to inductees did not contain or conclude with the words, "So help me God" but concluded with the words, "According to the rules and Articles of War."

We are of opinion that when the oath was administered the petitioner was present and such oath was administered to him. However this may be, the petitioner appeared before an officer on the next day and after an interview with that officer, promised that he would fight for his country and make a good soldier. He did not advise that officer that he had not taken the oath. Thereupon he drew and put on a regulation army uniform for enlisted men. He went to Camp Blanding on a train, the fare being paid by the Government. He was fed by the Army. He also drew uniforms or clothing at Camp Blanding and drilled with other enlisted men. He drew pay after he entered the Army.

If we were able to give the weight and credence to the petitioner's evidence that the trial court has given, we nevertheless are of opinion that it would in no wise aid him, since he waived such oath when he voluntarily entered upon the army service. We are led to this conclusion for the reason that petitioner testified that he had no idea of refusing to take the oath, and when asked, "Would you have taken the oath if you had been asked?" he replied "Of course, I comply with the law, I have never violated the law yet." He further testified that, "I admit signing the papers there and it is really not necessary, it is merely a question. I was not in the room at the time this oath was administered, and that is the oath that is involved." He further testified that, 'It is not necessary to go into detail, as I figured the issue involved at that particular time was taking the oath * * * ."

If there can be a doubt that the petitioner did not take the oath it is shown to a moral certainty that he waived such formality and entered upon the service of a soldier and in all respects was inducted into the United States Army. *Hibbs v. Catovolo*, 5 Cir., 145 F.2d 866; *Mayborn v. Heflebower*, 5 Cir., 145 F.2d 864. *Cf. Billings v. Truesdell*, 321 U.S. 542; *Falbo v. United States*, 320 U.S. 549.

Petitioner admits both in his testimony and in his brief that he did use language substantially the same as that charged. His brief bristles with his idea that he should be permitted to denounce the Government and lend aid and comfort to the enemies of the Republic in time of war, and that such conduct is one of his freedoms. The general court-martial clearly had jurisdiction, and the sentence of twenty years did not exceed the punishment authorized by law. Manual for Court-Martial U.S. Army, 1928, p. 188; 50 U.S.C. 33.

It results that the findings, conclusions and judgment of the trial court are erroneous and the judgment is reversed and the cause remanded' with direction that Hugh Callan be forthwith remanded to the custody of Respondent, Joseph W. Sanford, Warden, U.S. Penitentiary, Atlanta, Georgia.

Reversed and remanded, with directions.

Points for Discussion

1. Would Private Callan have violated Article 88 if this case had arisen after adoption of the UCMJ? Change the facts and suppose that Callan were an officer and had said: "The President, like all politicians, carries out the policies favored by his major supporters. He clearly cannot do anything that would alienate Jewish voters." Would this statement violate Article 88?

2. Is Private Callan's sentence of being confined at hard labor for a period of twenty years excessive? Sentences under Article 62 of the Articles of War were severe. *Time* magazine reported in 1925 that Private Paul Crouch had been sentenced to a dishonorable discharge and 40 years at hard labor for saying: "The President may be all right as an individual, but as an institution is a disgrace to the whole God-damned country." *National Affairs: Article 62*, Time, Apr. 20, 1925. The *Manual for Courts-Martial* now sets the maximum penalty for violation of Article 88 as dismissal, forfeiture of all pay and allowances, and confinement for 1 year. MCM, pt. IV, ¶12e.

3. If criticisms are not sufficiently contemptuous to violate article 88, might they still violate article 134, the general article? Consider this historical example.   In September 1924, two serious military aviation accidents occurred. In one, a Navy seaplane disappeared as it attempted to make the first flight to Hawaii from the mainland. In a second, a dirigible accident killed 14 men. Colonel Billy Mitchell, an outspoken military aviation pioneer, severely criticized the military for shortcomings in its aviation programs. He made a well-publicized statement to the press saying "these accidents are the direct result of incompetency, criminal negligence and almost treasonable administration of the national defense by the war and navy departments." James L. Tate, The Army and its Air Corps: Army Policy toward Aviation 1919-1941 (1988). Would these remarks violate Article 88 or Article 134 if made today? Colonel Mitchell was convicted of violating Article 96 in the Articles of War, the predecessor of Article 134. Those interested in seeing a generally accurate dramatization of what happened to Colonel Mitchell, might watch the 1955 film *The Court-Martial of Billy Mitchell* starring Gary Cooper and Elizabeth Montgomery.

Problem

In 1998, Colin Powell, at the time a retired Army general and former Chairman of the Joint Chiefs of Staff, declared that President Bill Clinton was "a disgrace to the Presidency and the Oval Office."   Steven Lee Myers, *Military Warns Soldiers of Failure to Hail Chief*, N.Y. Times, Oct. 21, 1998. General Powell made this criticism based on President Clinton's illicit affair with a young intern and his lying under oath about the affair. Would these comments violate Article 88?

The following case upholds Article 88 against a First Amendment challenge. It was a major decision during the Vietnam Era. The accused was represented by, among others, Eleanor Holmes Norton, who later became the chair of the Equal Opportunities Commission and a Delegate to Congress representing the District of Columbia.

UNITED STATES v. HOWE
Court of Military Appeals
37 C.M.R. 429 (C.M.A. 1967)

KILDAY, Judge:

Petitioner [Second Lieutenant Henry H. Howe, Jr., U. S. Army, Appellant] was arraigned before a general court-martial convened by the Commanding General, United States Army Air Defense Center at Fort Bliss, Texas. He was charged with using contemptuous words against the President of the United States and conduct unbecoming an officer and a gentleman, in violation of Articles 88 and 133, Uniform Code of Military Justice, 10 U.S.C. §§ 888 and 933, respectively. He was also charged, originally, with public use of language disloyal to the United States with design to promote disloyalty and disaffection among the troops and civilian populace, in violation of Article 134, Uniform Code of Military Justice, 10 U.S.C. § 934. As to this last charge, the defense motion to dismiss was sustained by the law officer. He was convicted of the two charges, first above-mentioned, and sentenced to dismissal, total forfeitures, and confinement at hard labor for two years. The convening authority reduced the period of confinement to one year and otherwise approved the sentence. A board of review in the office of the Judge Advocate General of the Army affirmed the findings and sentence.

* * *

The specification under the charge of violation of Article 88, *supra*, reads as follows:

"In that Second Lieutenant Henry H. Howe, Junior, U. S. Army, Headquarters Company, 31st Engineer Battalion, Fort Bliss, Texas, did, in the vicinity of San Jacinto Plaza, El Paso, Texas, on or about 6 November 1965, wrongfully and publicly use contemptuous words against the President of the United States, Lyndon B. Johnson, by carrying and displaying to the public a sign reading as follows, to wit: 'LET'S HAVE MORE THAN A CHOICE BETWEEN PETTY IGNORANT FACISTS IN 1968' and on the other side of the sign the words 'END JOHNSON'S FACIST AGRESSION IN VIET NAM,' or words to that effect."

* * *

The petitioner is a graduate of the University of Colorado where he majored in political science. While a student, he voluntarily participated in the Reserve Officers' Training Corps, and upon graduation he accepted a commission as a second lieutenant in the United States Army Reserve. He was ordered to active duty under that commission and had been on duty approximately twelve months at the time of this occurrence.

* * *

Article 88, Uniform Code of Military Justice, 10 U.S.C. § 888, reads as follows:

"Any commissioned officer who uses contemptuous words against the President, the Vice President, Congress, the Secretary of Defense, the Secretary of a military department, the Secretary of the Treasury, or the Governor or legislature of any State, Territory, Commonwealth, or possession in which he is on duty or present shall be punished as a court-martial may direct."

The petitioner contends that this Article and the charge laid under it violate the Bill of Rights and the First Amendment thereof.

We note that this provision was not new to military law when it was adopted as a part of the Uniform Code of Military Justice. Actually, this provision, and its precursors, are older than the Bill of Rights, older than the Constitution, and older than the Republic itself.

The British Articles of War of 1765, in force at the beginning of our Revolutionary War, provided for the court-martial of any officer or soldier who presumed to use traitorous or disrespectful words against "the Sacred Person of his Majesty, or any of the Royal Family"; and of any officer or soldier who should "behave himself with Contempt or Disrespect towards the General, or other Commander in Chief of Our Forces, or shall speak Words tending to his Hurt or Dishonour."[2]

The Articles of War adopted by the Continental Congress on June 30, 1775, revised the British language to adjust the same to the new concept of "Continental Forces" and made punishable by court-martial the act of any officer or soldier who behaved himself with "contempt or disrespect toward the general or generals, or commanders in chief of the continental forces, or shall speak false words, tending to his or their hurt or dishonor."[3]

The Declaration of Independence, having been signed, the Articles of Confederation and Perpetual Union, having been reported to the Continental Congress, and the confederacy known as "The United States of America," having begun to emerge with the major authority residing in the "United States of America, in Congress assembled," the Continental Congress, on September 20, 1776, adopted new Articles of War making punishable by court-martial the conduct of any officer or soldier who "presume to use traiterous or disrespectful words against the authority of the United States in Congress assembled, or the legislature of any of the United States in which he may be quartered"; and of any officer or soldier, "who shall behave himself with contempt or disrespect towards the general, or other commander-in-chief of the forces of the United States, or shall speak words tending to his hurt or dishonor."[5]

---

[2] The British Articles of War of 1765, section II, provided: "ART. I. Whatsoever Officer or Soldier shall presume to use traiterous or disrespectful Words against the Sacred Person of his Majesty, or any of the Royal Family; if a Commissioned Officer, he shall be cashiered; if a Non-commissioned Officer or Soldier, he shall suffer such Punishment as shall be inflicted upon him by the Sentence of a Court-martial. ART. II. Any Officer or Soldier who shall behave himself with Contempt or Disrespect towards the General, or other Commander in Chief of Our Forces, or shall speak Words tending to his Hurt or Dishonour, shall be punished according to the Nature of his Offence, by the Judgment of a Court-martial. [Winthrop's Military Law and Precedents, 2d ed, 1920 Reprint, at page 932.]

[3] The Articles of War adopted by the Continental Congress on June 30, 1775, contained the following provision: "IV. Any officer or soldier, who shall behave himself with contempt or disrespect towards the general or generals, or commanders in chief of the continental forces, or shall speak false words, tending to his or their hurt or dishonor, shall be punished according to the nature of his offence, by the judgment of a general court-martial." [Winthrop's Military Law and Precedents, 2d ed, 1920 Reprint, at pages 953-954.]

[5] The Articles of War adopted by the Continental Congress on September 20, 1776, contained the following provisions: "Section II. Art. 1. Whatsoever officer or soldier shall presume to use traiterous or disrespectful words against the authority of the

The first session of the First Congress adopted a temporary provision, to remain in effect until the end of the next session of Congress, expressly extending the rules and Articles of War which had been enacted by the United States in Congress assembled. The second session of the First Congress adopted permanent legislation expressly extending those rules and Articles of War.[6]

On December 15, 1791, the President advised the Congress that the required three-fourths of the States had ratified the amendments constituting the Bill of Rights. Thereafter, and on April 10, 1806, the Congress enacted new Articles of War and included therein the following provision:

"ART. 5. Any officer or soldier who shall use contemptuous or disrespectful words against the President of the United States, against the Vice-President thereof, against the Congress of the United States, or against the Chief Magistrate or Legislature of any of the United States, in which he may be quartered, if a commissioned officer, shall be cashiered, or otherwise punished, as a court-martial shall direct; if a noncommissioned officer or soldier, he shall suffer such punishment as shall be inflicted on him by the sentence of a court-martial." [Act of April 10, 1806, 2 Stat 359, 360. Text included in Winthrop's Military Law and Precedents, 2d ed, 1920 Reprint, at page 976.]

With some change in language, the last quoted article of the Articles of War of 1806 was reenacted in the Articles of War adopted by the Congress on June 22, 1874. On August 29, 1916, and again in 1920, substantially the same provision was reenacted by the Congress. It was not changed in 1948 by the Elston Act, which revised the Articles of War after the termination of World War II. And, finally, it was reenacted as Article 88 of the Uniform Code of Military Justice, *supra*. Act of May 5, 1950, 64 Stat 107, 135; Act of August 10, 1956, 70A Stat 36, 67. Now, however, it applies to officers only; that portion of previous Articles relating to "other persons subject to military law" having been deleted.

* * *

In *Schenck v. United States*, 249 U.S. 47 (1919), and . . . also in *Debs v United States*, 249 U.S. 211 (1919), the defendants were charged with con-

---

United States in Congress assembled, or the legislature of any of the United States in which he may be quartered, if a commissioned officer, he shall be cashiered; if a non-commissioned officer or soldier, he shall suffer such punishment as shall be inflicted upon him by the sentence of a court-martial. Art. 2. Any officer or soldier who shall behave himself with contempt or disrespect towards the general, or other commander-in-chief of the forces of the United States, or shall speak words tending to his hurt or dishonor, shall be punished according to the nature of his offence, by the judgment of a court-martial." [Winthrop's Military Law and Precedents, 2d ed, 1920 Reprint, at page 961.]

[6] Act of September 29, 1789, section 4, First Congress, Session I, 1 Stat 95; Act of April 30, 1790, section 13, First Congress, Session II, 1 Stat 119, 121.

spiracy to violate the Espionage Act of June 15, 1917, by causing and attempting to cause insubordination in the military forces and to obstruct the recruiting and enlistment service when the United States was at war with the German Empire. The proof consisted of making speeches, printing and circulating bulletins, and the printing of a newspaper. The Supreme Court, although announcing the "clear and present danger" doctrine (*Schenck*), affirmed those convictions. The proof in *Schenck v. United States, supra,* in which the doctrine was announced and the conviction sustained, was of such a nature as to cause Chief Justice Vinson to observe in *Dennis v United States,* 341 U.S. 494 (1951):

> ". . . The objectionable document denounced conscription and its most inciting sentence was, 'You must do your share to maintain, support and uphold the rights of the people of this country.' 249 U.S. at 51. Fifteen thousand copies were printed and some circulated. This insubstantial gesture toward insubordination in 1917 during war was held to be a clear and present danger of bringing about the evil of military insubordination." [341 U.S. at 504.]

The evil which Article 88 of the Uniform Code, *supra,* seeks to avoid is the impairment of discipline and the promotion of insubordination by an officer of the military service in using contemptuous words toward the Chief of State and the Commander-in-Chief of the Land and Naval Forces of the United States. Under the British Articles of War of 1765, the precursor to Article 88, Uniform Code of Military Justice, *supra,* was included with the offense of sedition under Section II thereof, entitled, "Mutiny." It is similarly separated in the American Articles of War 1776, being grouped with the offenses of sedition and mutiny. Winthrop's Military Law and Precedents, 2d ed, 1920 Reprint, at pages 932 and 961. We need not determine whether a state of war presently exists. We do judicially know that hundreds of thousands of members of our military forces are committed to combat in Vietnam, casualties among our forces are heavy, and thousands are being recruited, or drafted, into our armed forces. That in the present times and circumstances such conduct by an officer constitutes a clear and present danger to discipline within our armed services, under the precedents established by the Supreme Court, seems to require no argument.

The offense denounced by Article 88, *supra,* was an offense in the British forces at the beginning of our Revolutionary War and was readopted by the Continental Congress. It is significant that it was reenacted by the First Congress of which fifteen of the thirty-nine signers of the Constitution were members, including James Madison, the author of the Bill of Rights. *United States v. Culp,* 14 C.M.R. 411 (C.M.A. 1954). It is of even more significance that this provision was readopted by the Ninth Congress in 1806, after the Bill of Rights had been adopted and became a part of the Constitution. This action of Congress constituted a contemporary construction of the Constitution and is entitled to the greatest respect. *United States v Culp, supra.*

That Article 88, *supra*, does not violate the First Amendment is clear. This conclusion is compelled and fortified by the recent action of the Supreme Court in *United States v. Barnett*, 376 U.S. 681, 693 (1964). The reenactment by the First Congress on two occasions of the previously existing Articles adopted by the Continental Congress and the action of Congress in 1806 in reenacting the substantially identical provision, now contained in Article 88, must be regarded as contemporary construction of the constitutional provisions. On no less than six occasions since the enactment of 1806, the Congress has reenacted the provision, with little or no change, as a construction of the Constitution which has been followed since the founding of our government.

* * *

True, petitioner is a reserve officer, rather than a professional officer, but during the time he serves on active duty he is, and must be, controlled by the provisions of military law. In this instance, military restrictions fall upon a reluctant "summer soldier"; but at another time, and differing circumstances, the ancient and wise provisions insuring civilian control of the military will restrict the "man on a white horse."

* * *

Turning to the remaining question of constitutional import, we do not consider Article 88 so vague and uncertain on its face that it violates the due process clause of the Fifth Amendment. It has been said that the constitutional requirement of definiteness is violated by a criminal statute only if that statute fails to give a person of ordinary intelligence fair notice that his contemplated conduct is denounced by the statute. *United States v Harriss*, 347 U.S. 612 (1954). Moreover, the Supreme Court has held that "if the general class of offenses to which the statute is directed is plainly within its terms, the statute will not be struck down as vague, even though marginal cases could be put where doubts might arise. . . . And if this general class of offenses can be made constitutionally definite by a reasonable construction of the statute, this Court is under a duty to give the statute that construction." *Id.*, at page 618. In this regard, "the standard as defined is not a neat, mathematical formulary. Like all verbalizations it is subject to criticism on the score of indefiniteness." *Dennis v United States, supra*, at page 1156. So long as there are ascertainable standards of guilt, that is enough, for impossible standards of specificity are not demanded.

* * *

Whatever the test, Article 88 meets the constitutional norm as to certainty. We need not dwell on its susceptibility of improper application for that possibility has had previous assessment. In the matter of "fair notice," we emphasize that Article 88 is designed to cover the use of "contemptuous" words toward holders of certain offices named therein. "Contemptuous" is used in the ordinary sense as is evidenced by the Manual for Courts-Martial, United States, 1951, paragraph 167. See Webster's Third New International

Dictionary. The proscribed conduct having been made certain and the warnings sufficient, it follows that the language of the Article satisfies the test of definiteness. . . .

* * *

These are the considerations which prompted denial of the accused's petition in the first instance, and require us to deny the petition for reconsideration.

Chief Judge QUINN and Judge FERGUSON concur.

Points for Discussion

1. What is the purpose of Article 88? Is it to maintain uniformity of thought within the military? Is it to keep low-ranking dissident soldiers, like Private Hugh Callan or Second Lieutenant Henry Howe, Jr., from spreading foment among other soldiers of comparable rank? Or is it instead to prevent the military's highest leaders from trying to weaken civilian leadership? *See* Richard W. Aldrich, *Article 88 of the Uniform Code of Military Justice: A Military Muzzle Or Just A Restraint On Military Muscle?*, 33 UCLA L. Rev. 1189 (1986).

2. If there have been few cases since the UCMJ was adopted in 1950, does that mean that the existence of Article 88 has had little effect on service members?

13-2. Conduct Unbecoming of an Officer and Gentleman

Another offense under the UCMJ that has no civilian counterpart is the following:

Art. 133. Conduct unbecoming an officer and gentleman

Any commissioned officer, cadet, or midshipman who is convicted of conduct unbecoming an officer and a gentleman shall be punished as a court-martial may direct.

10 U.S.C. § 933.

What is conduct unbecoming an officer and a gentleman? The Manual for Courts-Martial provides this explanation: "Conduct violative of this article is action or behavior in an official capacity which, in dishonoring or disgracing the person as an officer, seriously compromises the officer's character as a gentleman, or action or behavior in an unofficial or private capacity which, in dishonoring or disgracing the officer personally, seriously compromises the person's standing as an officer." MCM, pt. IV, ¶59c(2). The *Manual for Courts-Martial* further gives these examples: "dishonorable failure to pay a debt; cheating on an exam; opening and reading a letter of another without authority; using insulting or defamatory language to another officer in that officer's presence or about that officer to other military persons; being drunk and disorderly in a public place; public association with known prostitutes;

committing or attempting to commit a crime involving moral turpitude; and failing without good cause to support the officer's family." *Id.* ¶59c(3). A recurring question is whether this article applies to both male and female officers. On this point, the Manual for Courts-Martial declares: "As used in this article, 'gentleman' includes both male and female commissioned officers, cadets, and midshipmen." *Id.* ¶59c(1). The maximum penalty for violation of article 133 is "[d]ismissal, forfeiture of all pay and allowances, and confinement for a period not in excess of that authorized for the most analogous offense for which a punishment is prescribed in this Manual, or, if none is prescribed, for 1 year." *Id.* ¶59e.

Points for Discussion

1. Should conduct unbecoming an officer and a gentleman be a criminal offense? Could the Armed Forces deal with the kind of conduct covered by this article in a manner other than through a court-martial?

2. Must courts defer to the President's view that the word "gentlemen" in article 133 includes females? *See* Gregory E. Maggs, *Judicial Review of the Manual for Courts-Martial*, 160 Mil. L. Rev. 96, 130 (1999) (citing cases holding that the President does not have power to redefine the elements of punitive articles and thus change substantive criminal law). Was it necessary for the President to interpret the word "gentleman" to include females in the Manual for Courts-Martial? Or would it have been sufficient for the President merely to say any conduct that would be unbecoming to an officer and a gentleman is conduct that is prohibited regardless of the sex of person who engages in the conduct?

PARKER v. LEVY
U.S. Supreme Court
417 U.S. 733 (1974)

Mr. Justice REHNQUIST delivered the opinion of the Court.

Appellee Howard Levy, a physician, was a captain in the Army stationed at Fort Jackson, South Carolina. He had entered the Army under the so-called "Berry Plan," under which he agreed to serve for two years in the Armed Forces if permitted first to complete his medical training. From the time he entered on active duty in July 1965 until his trial by court-martial, he was assigned as Chief of the Dermatological Service of the United States Army Hospital at Fort Jackson. On June 2, 1967, appellee was convicted by a general court-martial of violations of Arts. 90, 133, and 134 of the Uniform Code of Military Justice, and sentenced to dismissal from the service, forfeiture of all pay and allowances, and confinement for three years at hard labor.

The facts upon which his conviction rests are virtually undisputed. The evidence admitted at his court-martial trial showed that one of the functions of the hospital to which appellee was assigned was that of training Special

Forces aide men. As Chief of the Dermatological Service, appellee was to conduct a clinic for those aide men. In the late summer of 1966, it came to the attention of the hospital commander that the dermatology training of the students was unsatisfactory. After investigating the program and determining that appellee had totally neglected his duties, the commander called appellee to his office and personally handed him a written order to conduct the training. Appellee read the order, said that he understood it, but declared that he would not obey it because of his medical ethics. Appellee persisted in his refusal to obey the order, and later reviews of the program established that the training was still not being carried out.

During the same period of time, appellee made several public statements to enlisted personnel at the post, of which the following is representative:

"The United States is wrong in being involved in the Viet Nam War. I would refuse to go to Viet Nam if ordered to do so. I don't see why any colored soldier would go to Viet Nam: they should refuse to go to Viet Nam and if sent should refuse to fight because they are discriminated against and denied their freedom in the United States, and they are sacrificed and discriminated against in Viet Nam by being given all the hazardous duty and they are suffering the majority of casualties. If I were a colored soldier I would refuse to go to Viet Nam and if I were a colored soldier and were sent I would refuse to fight. Special Forces personnel are liars and thieves and killers of peasants and murderers of women and children."

Appellee's military superiors originally contemplated nonjudicial proceedings against him under Art. 15 of the Uniform Code of Military Justice, 10 U.S.C. § 815, but later determined that courtmartial proceedings were appropriate. The specification under Art. 90 alleged that appellee willfully disobeyed the hospital commandant's order to establish the training program, in violation of that article, which punishes anyone subject to the Uniform Code of Military Justice who "willfully disobeys a lawful command of his superior commissioned officer." Statements to enlisted personnel were listed as specifications under the charges of violating Arts. 133 and 134 of the Code. Article 133 provides for the punishment of "conduct unbecoming an officer and a gentleman," while Art. 134 proscribes, *inter alia*, "all disorders and neglects to the prejudice of good order and discipline in the armed forces."

The specification under Art. 134 alleged that appellee "did, at Fort Jackson, South Carolina, ... with design to promote disloyalty and disaffection among the troops, publicly utter [certain] statements to divers enlisted personnel at divers times ...." The specification under Art. 133 alleged that appellee did "while in the performance of his duties at the United States Army Hospital ... wrongfully and dishonorably" make statements variously described as intemperate, defamatory, provoking, disloyal, contemptuous, and disrespectful to Special Forces personnel and to enlisted personnel who were patients or under his supervision.

Appellee was convicted by the courtmartial, and his conviction was sustained on his appeals within the military. [Appellee subsequently sought habeas corpus in federal court. The district court denied relief, but the court of appeals reversed.]

I

This Court has long recognized that the military is, by necessity, a specialized society separate from civilian society. We have also recognized that the military has, again by necessity, developed laws and traditions of its own during its long history. The differences between the military and civilian communities result from the fact that "it is the primary business of armies and navies to fight or ready to fight wars should the occasion arise." *United States ex rel. Toth v. Quarles*, 350 U.S. 11, 17. In *In re Grimley*, 137 U.S. 147, 153 (1890), the Court observed: "An army is not a deliberative body. It is the executive arm. Its law is that of obedience. No question can be left open as to the right to command in the officer, or the duty of obedience in the soldier." More recently we noted that "[t]he military constitutes a specialized community governed by a separate discipline from that of the civilian," *Orloff v. Willoughby*, 345 U.S. 83, 94 (1953), and that "the rights of men in the armed forces must perforce be conditioned to meet certain overriding demands of discipline and duty ...." *Burns v. Wilson*, 346 U.S. 137, 140 (1953) (plurality opinion). We have also recognized that a military officer holds a particular position of responsibility and command in the Armed Forces:

> "The President's commission ... recites that "reposing special trust and confidence in the patriotism, valor, fidelity and abilities" of the appointee he is named to the specified rank during the pleasure of the President." *Orloff v. Willoughby, supra*, at 91.

Just as military society has been a society apart from civilian society, so "[m]ilitary law ... is a jurisprudence which exists separate and apart from the law which governs in our federal judicial establishment." *Burns v. Wilson, supra*, at 140. And to maintain the discipline essential to perform its mission effectively, the military has developed what "may not unfitly be called the customary military law" or "general usage of the military service." *Martin v. Mott*, 12 Wheat. 19, 35 (1827). . . .

* * *

An examination of the British antecedents of our military law shows that the military law of Britian had long contained the forebears of Arts. 133 and 134 in remarkably similar language. The Articles of the Earl of Essex (1642) provided that "[a]ll other faults, disorders and offenses, not mentioned in these Articles, shall be punished according to the general customs and laws of war.' One of the British Articles of War of 1765 made punishable 'all Disorders or Neglects ... to the Prejudice of good Order and Military Discipline ...' that were not mentioned in the other articles. Another of those articles provided:

"Whatsoever Commissioned Officer shall be convicted before a General Court-martial, of behaving in a scandalous infamous Manner, such as is unbecoming the Character of an Officer and a Gentleman, shall be discharged from Our Service."

In 1775 the Continental Congress adopted this last article, along with 68 others for the governance of its army. . . .

* * *

From 1806, it remained basically unchanged through numerous congressional re-enactments until it was enacted as Art. 133 of the Uniform Code of Military Justice in 1951.

The British article punishing "all Disorders and Neglects . . ." was also adopted by the Continental Congress in 1775 and re-enacted in 1776. Except for a revision in 1916, which added the clause punishing "all conduct of a nature to bring discredit upon the military service," substantially the same language was preserved throughout the various re-enactments of this article too, until in 1951 it was enacted as Art. 134 of the Uniform Code of Military Justice.

* * *

Decisions of this Court during the last century have recognized that the longstanding customs and usages of the services impart accepted meaning to the seemingly imprecise standards of Arts. 133 and 134. . . .

II

The differences noted by this settled line of authority, first between the military community and the civilian community, and second between military law and civilian law, continue in the present day under the Uniform Code of Military Justice. That Code cannot be equated to a civilian criminal code. It, and the various versions of the Articles of War which have preceded it, regulate aspects of the conduct of members of the military which in the civilian sphere are left unregulated. While a civilian criminal code carves out a relatively small segment of potential conduct and declares it criminal, the Uniform Code of Military Justice essays more varied regulation of a much larger segment of the activities of the more tightly knit military community. In civilian life there is no legal sanction-civil or criminal-for failure to behave as an officer and a gentleman; in the military world, Art. 133 imposes such a sanction on a commissioned officer. The Code likewise imposes other sanctions for conduct that in civilian life is not subject to criminal penalties: disrespect toward superior commissioned officers, Art. 89, 10 U.S.C. § 889; cruelty toward, or oppression or maltreatment of subordinates, Art. 93, 10 U.S.C. § 893; negligent damaging, destruction, or wrongful disposition of military property of the United States, Art. 108, 10 U.S.C. 908; improper hazarding of a vessel, Art. 110, 10 U.S.C. § 910; drunkenness on duty, Art. 112, 10 U.S.C. § 912; and malingering, Art. 115, 10 U.S.C. § 915.

But the other side of the coin is that the penalties provided in the Code vary from death and substantial penal confinement at one extreme to forms of administrative discipline which are below the threshold of what would normally be considered a criminal sanction at the other. Though all of the offenses described in the Code are punishable "as a court-martial may direct," and the accused may demand a trial by court-martial. Art. 15 of the Code also provides for the imposition of nonjudicial "disciplinary punishments" for minor offenses without the intervention of a court-martial. 10 U.S.C. § 815. The punishments imposable under that article are of a limited nature. With respect to officers, punishment may encompass suspension of duty, arrest in quarters for not more than 30 days, restriction for not more than 60 days, and forfeiture of pay for a limited period of time. In the case of enlisted men, such punishment may additionally include, among other things, reduction to the next inferior pay grade, extra fatigue duty, and correctional custody for not more than seven consecutive days. Thus, while legal proceedings actually brought before a court-martial are prosecuted in the name of the Government, and the accused has the right to demand that he be proceeded against in this manner before any sanctions may be imposed upon him, a range of minor sanctions for lesser infractions are often imposed administratively. Forfeiture of pay, reduction in rank, and even dismissal from the service bring to mind the law of labor-management relations as much as the civilian criminal law.

In short, the Uniform Code of Military Justice regulates a far broader range of the conduct of military personnel than a typical state criminal code regulates of the conduct of civilians; but at the same time the enforcement of that Code in the area of minor offenses is often by sanctions which are more akin to administrative or civil sanctions than to civilian criminal ones.

　　* * *

III

Appellee urges that both Art. 133 and Art. 134 (the general article) are "void for vagueness" under the Due Process Clause of the Fifth Amendment and overbroad in violation of the First Amendment. We have recently said of the vagueness doctrine:

> "The doctrine incorporates notions of fair notice or warning. Moreover, it requires legislatures to set reasonably clear guidelines for law enforcement officials and triers of fact in order to prevent 'arbitrary and discriminatory enforcement.' Where a statute's literal scope, unaided by a narrowing state court interpretation, is capable of reaching expression sheltered by the First Amendment, the doctrine demands a greater degree of specificity than in other contexts." *Smith v. Goguen*, 415 U.S. 566, 572-573 (1974).

Each of these articles has been construed by the United States Court of Military Appeals or by other military authorities in such a manner as to at least partially narrow its otherwise broad scope.

The United States Court of Military Appeals has stated that Art. 134 must be judged "not *in vacuo*, but in the context in which the years have placed it," *United States v. Frantz*, 7 C.M.R. 37, 39 (C.M.A. 1953). Article 134 does not make "every irregular, mischievous, or improper act a court-martial offense," *United States v. Sadinsky*, 34 C.M.R. 343, 345 (C.M.A. 1964), but its reach is limited to conduct that is "directly and palpably-as distinguished from indirectly and remotely-prejudicial to good order and discipline." *Ibid*; *United States v. Holiday*, 16 C.M.R. 28, 30 (C.M.A. 1954). It applies only to calls for active opposition to the military policy of the United States, *United States v. Priest*, 45 C.M.R. 338 (C.M.A. 1972), and does not reach all "[d]isagreement with, or objection to, a policy of the Government." *United States v. Harvey*, 42 C.M.R. 141, 146 (C.M.A. 1971).

The Manual for Courts-Martial restates these limitations on the scope of Art. 134. It goes on to say that "[c]ertain disloyal statements by military personnel" may be punishable under Art. 134. "Examples are utterances designed to promote disloyalty or disaffection among troops, as praising the enemy, attacking the war aims of the United States, or denouncing our form of government." Extensive additional interpretative materials are contained in the portions of the Manual devoted to Art. 134, which describe more than sixty illustrative offenses.

The Court of Military Appeals has likewise limited the scope of Art. 133. Quoting from W. Winthrop, Military Law and Precedents (2d ed. 1920), 711-712, that court has stated:

" '. . . To constitute therefore the conduct here denounced, the act which forms the basis of the charge must have a double significance and effect. Though it need not amount to a crime, it must offend so seriously against law, justice, morality or decorum as to expose to disgrace, socially or as a man, the offender, and at the same time must be of such a nature or committed under such circumstances as to bring dishonor or disrepute upon the military profession which he represents.' " *United States v. Howe*, 37 C.M.R. 429, 441-442 (C.M.A. 1967).

The effect of these constructions of Arts. 133 and 134 by the Court of Military Appeals and by other military authorities has been twofold: It has narrowed the very broad reach of the literal language of the articles, and at the same time has supplied considerable specificity by way of examples of the conduct which they cover. It would be idle to pretend that there are not areas within the general confines of the articles' language which have been left vague despite these narrowing constructions. But even though sizable areas of uncertainty as to the coverage of the articles may remain after their official interpretation by authoritative military sources, further content may be supplied even in these areas by less formalized custom and usage. *Dynes v. Hoover*, 20 How. 65 (1857). And there also cannot be the slightest doubt under the military precedents that there is a substantial range of conduct to which both articles clearly apply without vagueness or imprecision. . . .

* * *

We have noted in *Smith v. Goguen*, 415 U.S. 566, 573 (1974), that more precision in drafting may be required because of the vagueness doctrine in the case of regulation of expression. For the reasons which differentiate military society from civilian society, we think Congress is permitted to legislate both with greater breadth and with greater flexibility when prescribing the rules by which the former shall be governed than it is when prescribing rules for the latter. But each of these differentiations relates to how strict a test of vagueness shall be applied in judging a particular criminal statute. None of them suggests that one who has received fair warning of the criminality of his own conduct from the statute in question is nonetheless entitled to attack it because the language would not give similar fair warning with respect to other conduct which might be within its broad and literal ambit. One to whose conduct a statute clearly applies may not successfully challenge it for vagueness.

Because of the factors differentiating military society from civilian society, we hold that the proper standard of review for a vagueness challenge to the articles of the Code is the standard which applies to criminal statutes regulating economic affairs. Clearly, that standard is met here, for as the Court stated in *United States v. National Dairy Products Corp.*, 372 U.S. 29, 32-33 (1963):

> "Void for vagueness simply means that criminal responsibility should not attach where one could not reasonably understand that his contemplated conduct is proscribed. *United States v. Harriss*, 347 U.S. 612, 617 (1954). In determining the sufficiency of the notice a statute must of necessity be examined in the light of the conduct with which a defendant is charged. *Robinson v. United States*, 324 U.S. 282 (1945)."

Since appellee could have had no reasonable doubt that his public statements urging Negro enlisted men not to go to Vietnam if ordered to do so were both "unbecoming an officer and a gentleman," and "to the prejudice of good order and discipline in the armed forces," in violation of the provisions of Art. 133 and Art. 134, respectively, his challenge to them as unconstitutionally vague under the Due Process Clause of the Fifth Amendment must fail.

We likewise reject appellee's contention that Arts. 133 and 134 are facially invalid because of their 'over-breadth.' . . .

* * *

There is a wide range of the conduct of military personnel to which Arts. 133 and 134 may be applied without infringement of the First Amendment. While there may lurk at the fringes of the articles, even in the light of their narrowing construction by the United States Court of Military Appeals, some possibility that conduct which would be ultimately held to be protected by the First Amendment could be included within their prohibition, we deem this insufficient to invalidate either of them at the behest of appellee. His conduct, that of a commissioned officer publicly urging enlisted personnel to refuse to obey orders which might send them into combat, was unprotected under the most expansive notions of the First Amendment. Articles 133 and 134 may constitutionally prohibit that conduct and a sufficiently large number of similar or related types of conduct so as to preclude their invalidation for overbreadth.

* * *

Reversed.

Mr. Justice BLACKMUN, with whom THE CHIEF JUSTICE joins, concurring.

I wholly concur in the Court's opinion. I write only to state what for me is a crucial difference between the majority and dissenting views in this case. My Brother STEWART complains that men of common intelligence must necessarily speculate as to what "conduct unbecoming an officer and a gentleman" or conduct to the "prejudice of good order and discipline in the armed forces" or conduct "of a nature to bring discredit upon the armed forces" really means. He implies that the average soldier or sailor would not reasonably expect, under the general articles, to suffer military reprimand or punishment for engaging in sexual acts with a chicken, or window peeping in a trailer park, or cheating while calling bingo numbers. . . . He argues that "times have surely changed" and that the articles are "so vague and uncertain as to be incomprehensible to the servicemen who are to be governed by them."

These assertions are, of course, no less judicial fantasy than that which the dissent charges the majority of indulging. In actuality, what is at issue here are concepts of "right" and "wrong" and whether the civil law can accommodate, in special circumstances, a system of law which expects more of the individual in the context of a broader variety of relationships than one finds in civilian life.

In my judgment, times have not changed in the area of moral precepts. Fundamental concepts of right and wrong are the same now as they were under the Articles of the Earl of Essex (1642), or the British Articles of War of 1765, or the American Articles of War of 1775, or during the long line of precedents of this and other courts upholding the general articles. And, however unfortunate it may be, it is still necessary to maintain a disciplined and obedient fighting force.

* * *

Mr. Justice DOUGLAS, dissenting.

* * *

I cannot imagine . . . that Congress would think it had the power to authorize the military to curtail the reading list of books, plays, poems, periodicals, papers, and the like which a person in the Armed Services may read. Nor can I believe Congress would assume authority to empower the military to suppress conversations at a bar, ban discussions of public affairs, prevent enlisted men or women or draftees from meeting in discussion groups at times and places and for such periods of time that do not interfere with the performance of military duties.

Congress has taken no such step here. By Art. 133 it has allowed punishment for "conduct unbecoming an officer and a gentleman." In our society where diversities are supposed to flourish it never could be "unbecoming" to express one's views, even on the most controversial public issue.

* * *

The power to draft an army includes, of course, the power to curtail considerably the "liberty" of the people who make it up. But Congress in these articles has not undertaken to cross the forbidden First Amendment line. Making a speech or comment on one of the most important and controversial public issues of the past two decades cannot by any stretch of dictionary meaning be included in "disorders and neglects to the prejudice of good order and discipline in the armed forces." Nor can what Captain Levy said possibly be "conduct of a nature to bring discredit upon the armed forces." He was uttering his own belief-an article of faith that he sincerely held. This was no mere ploy to perform a "subversive" act. Many others who loved their country shared his views. They were not saboteurs. Uttering one's beliefs is sacrosanct under the First Amendment. Punishing the utterances is an "abridgment" of speech in the constitutional sense.

* * *

Mr. Justice STEWART, with whom Mr. Justice DOUGLAS and Mr. Justice BRENNAN join, dissenting.

It is plain that Arts. 133 and 134 are vague on their face; indeed, the opinion of the Court does not seriously contend to the contrary. Men of common intelligence-including judges of both military and civilian courts-must necessarily speculate as to what such terms as "conduct unbecoming an officer and a gentleman" and "conduct of a nature to bring discredit upon the armed forces" really mean. In the past, this Court has held unconstitutional statutes penalizing "misconduct," conduct that was "annoying," "reprehensible," or "prejudicial to the best interests" of a city, and it is significant that military courts have resorted to several of these very terms in describing the sort of acts proscribed by Arts. 133 and 134.

* * *

In short, the general articles are in practice as well as theory 'catch-alls,' designed to allow prosecutions for practically any conduct that may offend the sensibilities of a military commander. Not every prosecution of course, results in a conviction, and the military courts have sometimes overturned convictions when the conduct involved was so marginally related to military discipline as to offend even the loosest interpretations of the General Articles. But these circumstances can hardly be thought to validate the otherwise vague statutes. As the Court said in *United States v. Reese*, 92 U.S. 214, 221: "It would certainly be dangerous if the legislature could set a net large enough to catch all possible offenders, and leave it to the courts to step inside and say who could be rightfully detained, and who should be set at large." At best, the General Articles are just such a net, and suffer from all the vices that our previous decisions condemn.

* * *

The Solicitor General suggests that a certain amount of vagueness in the general articles is necessary in order to maintain high standards of conduct in the military, since it is impossible to predict in advance every offense that might serve to affect morale or discredit the service. It seems to me that this argument was concisely and eloquently rebutted by Judge Aldisert in the Court of Appeals, 478 F.2d 772, 795 (CA 3):

> "[W]hat high standard of conduct is served by convicting an individual of conduct he did not reasonable perceive to be criminal? Is not the essence of high standards in the military, first, knowing one's duty, and secondly, executing it? And, in this regard, would not an even higher standard be served by delineation of the various offenses under Article 134, following by obedience to these standards?"

* * *

Points for Discussion

1. Is the Court correct in saying that the offense of conduct unbecoming an officer and gentleman is sufficiently defined to allow the typical officer to know what constitutes a violation and what does not?   Consider these examples:

a. Following a unit softball game in Germany, an Army first lieutenant accompanied some of his teammates, who were enlisted men, to a house of prostitution operating legally under German law.   While the enlisted men engaged in sexual activity within the house, the lieutenant "did nothing more than look and comment on the physical charms of the hostesses."   Is the lieutenant's conduct a violation of Article 133, UCMJ? *See United States v. Guaglione*, 27 M.J. 268 (C.M.A. 1986).

b. A captain who was a nurse in the Air Force "received an order to submit a urine sample in conjunction with the Air Force's random drug-testing program. After receiving this order, she used a catheter to inject a saline solution into her bladder and provided the saline as a urine sample. Four days later, during an overnight exercise, she explained to an enlisted person what she had done."   The captain was charged with conduct unbecoming for telling the enlisted member what she had done.   Is merely telling the enlisted member what she did an offense under Article 133? *See United States v. Norvell*, 26 M.J. 477 (C.M.A. 1988).

2. Solicitor General Robert H. Bork, in arguing for the government, justified the imprecision of Article 133 by saying: "[A] military officer may carry the responsibilities, literally, of the life and death of the men in his command. It would be not practicable nor wise to codify totally the obligations of officers. The circumstances in which an officer is expected to use his good judgment are too protean to be encapsulated in an exclusive listing." Brief for Appellant, *Parker v. Levy*, 1974 WL 187430, at *36. Even if this is true, does it mean that Congress should have the power to make a vague offense like conduct unbecoming an officer and gentleman a crime? Could Congress make an officer's mere failing to exercise good judgment a crime?

UNITED STATES v. CONLIFFE
Court of Appeals for the Armed Forces
67 M.J. 127 (C.A.A.F. 2009)

Δ Army Cadet

- Guilty plea at Gn Ct M.

- Providence Inquiry

Judge BAKER delivered the opinion of the Court.

Appellant [Mark R. Conliffe, Cadet, U.S. Army] entered guilty pleas before a military judge sitting as a general court-martial at West Point, New York. Following the providence inquiry, the military judge accepted Appellant's pleas and found Appellant guilty of three specifications of housebreaking, five specifications of conduct unbecoming an officer and a gentleman, and "intentionally us[ing] an image recording device for the purpose of videotaping the sexual conduct of [another] without her consent," in violation of Articles 130, 133, and 134, Uniform Code of Military Justice (UCMJ), 10 U.S.C. §§ 930, 933, and 934 (2000), respectively. The adjudged and approved <u>sentence</u> <u>consisted of confinement for eighteen months, forfeiture of all pay and allow-</u> <u>ances for eighteen months, and dismissal from the Army.</u> The United States Army Court of Criminal Appeals affirmed. *United States v. Conliffe*, 65 M.J. 819, 823 (Army Ct. Crim. App. 2007). We granted review of the following issue:

Δ Found guilty
· Housebreaking
· Conduct Unbecoming
· Intentionally videoing sex of another w/o consent

Issue

> WHETHER APPELLANT'S PLEAS OF GUILTY TO THE THREE SPECIFICATIONS OF CHARGE II, HOUSEBREAKING, ARE IMPROVIDENT WHERE THE INTENDED CRIMINAL OFFENSE UPON ENTRY, CONDUCT UNBECOMING AN OFFICER AND GENTLEMAN, IS A PURELY MILITARY OFFENSE.

* * *

Improvident = thoughtless Rash

BACKGROUND

The lower court's opinion provides the facts at issue in this case:

Appellant was a first class cadet (a senior) at the United States Military Academy (the Academy), scheduled for graduation and commissioning as a second lieutenant in May, 2003. . . .

[handwritten margin note: Senior at the military Academy]

[In 2003], appellant twice unlawfully entered the locker room of an Academy women's varsity sports team, concealed his video camera, and secretly filmed undressed women entering and exiting the shower. Similarly, he unlawfully entered the barracks room of one of the female cadets he previously filmed in the locker room, hid the video camera in her barracks room, and secretly filmed her changing clothes. Finally, while on leave at his parents' home in Kentucky, appellant had consensual sexual activity with a civilian woman in his bedroom, but filmed her performing oral sex on him without her knowledge or consent.

[handwritten margin note: Entered the womens locker room 2 times to film girls getting out of the shower]

[handwritten margin note: Entered the female barracks to film a girl.]

[handwritten interlinear note: On leave, filmed a civilian girl giving him oral. ₪ Consent]

* * *

During the providence inquiry concerning the housebreaking offenses, appellant told the military judge that he accomplished his intended goal in each instance by successfully and secretly filming the women undressed or undressing. Each of the three housebreaking specifications [to Charge II] alleged the underlying offense was "utiliz[ing] an imaging device to surreptitiously record the image[s] of [the various victims in the various locations] by hiding a digital video camera in the room, such acts constituting conduct unbecoming an officer and gentleman, therein."

[handwritten margin note: Conduct unbecoming - filming girls ₪ consent]

Conliffe, 65 M.J. at 820–21 (alterations in original).

DISCUSSION

* * *

I. Housebreaking

An accused "who unlawfully enters the building or structure of another with intent to commit a criminal offense therein is guilty of housebreaking." Article 130, UCMJ. It follows that the second element of housebreaking, the element at issue here, "requires a specific intent to enter with the intent to commit [a criminal] offense." *United States v. Peterson*, 47 M.J. 231, 235 (C.A.A.F. 1997). The Manual for Courts–Martial defines a "criminal offense" as "[a]ny act or omission which is punishable by courts-martial, except an act or omission constituting a purely military offense." Manual for Courts–Martial, United States pt. IV, para. 56.c(3) (2002 ed.) (MCM). As such, an act or omission identified as a purely military offense cannot form the basis for the underlying criminal offense required in a housebreaking charge. We must therefore decide whether Appellant pleaded guilty to an act or omission constituting a purely military offense.

[handwritten margin note: (R)]

[handwritten margin note: (I) Whether Ap. plead guilty to an act/omission constituting a purely military offense]

The three specifications of Charge II describe specific acts Appellant engaged in to surreptitiously capture images of women without their knowledge. However, in addition to this descriptive conduct, the specifications link each act directly to Appellant's compromising his status as an officer and a gentleman. The charge sheet describes the surreptitious videotaping as "acts constituting conduct unbecoming an officer and a gentleman."

The military judge made the same link during his plea inquiry. First, the military judge described the elements of housebreaking to Appellant, indicating that Appellant must admit and agree that he unlawfully entered with the intent to surreptitiously record images, "a crime constituting conduct unbecoming an officer and gentleman under Article 133, UCMJ." Second, the military judge explained the two elements necessary to prove conduct unbecoming an officer and a gentleman. Finally, in concluding his inquiry on this charge, the military judge asked Appellan if he believed that his conduct constituted conduct unbecoming an officer and a gentleman. The military judge's focus on Article 133, UCMJ, demonstrates his understanding that Appellant's compromise of his status as an officer and a gentleman, rather than Appellant's act of surreptitious videotaping, formed the underlying offense in the housebreaking charge.

In *United States v. Webb*, this Court held that to satisfy the underlying criminal offense element of housebreaking an accused must possess the "intent to commit the crime stated in the specification." 38 M.J. 62, 68–69 (C.M.A.1993). In this case, the plain language of the specifications, as well as the military judge's colloquy with Appellant, demonstrates that the underlying offense in Appellant's case was the offense of engaging in conduct unbecoming an officer and a gentleman, an Article 133, UCMJ, violation. As a result, the essential inquiry is not whether surreptitious videotaping has a civilian counterpart, and thus is not a "purely military offense," but whether conduct unbecoming an officer and a gentleman is a purely military offense.

II. Purely Military Offense

In light of the military judge's acceptance of Appellant's guilty plea to housebreaking based on the underlying offense of conduct unbecoming an officer and a gentleman, the question becomes whether a violation of Article 133, UCMJ, constitutes a purely military offense for the purposes of Article 130, UCMJ.

> "Any commissioned officer, cadet, or midshipman who is convicted of conduct unbecoming an officer and a gentleman shall be punished as a court-martial may direct." Article 133, UCMJ. The elements of Article 133 are:
>
> (1) That the accused did or omitted to do certain acts; and
>
> (2) That, under the circumstances, these acts or omissions constituted conduct unbecoming an officer and gentleman.

United States v. Boyett, 42 M.J. 150, 152 n. 2 (C.A.A.F. 1995) (quoting MCM pt. IV, para. 59.b.). The focus of Article 133, UCMJ, is the effect of the accused's conduct on his status as an officer, cadet, or midshipman:

> [T]he essence of an Article 133 offense is not whether an accused officer's conduct otherwise amounts to an offense . . . but simply whether the acts meet the standard of conduct unbecoming an officer. . . . [T]he appropriate

[handwritten margin notes: Judge — ① Δ admit to unlawful enter. ② Two element of Conduct Unbecoming. ③ Asked Δ if he believed his Conduct was unbecoming. / Ⅱ Is conduct unbecoming a purely military offense? / Conduct Unbecoming / Judge did not focus on video taping for the housebreaking charge]

The standard: whether act charged is dishonorable or compromising ... Whether it amounts to a crime or not.

CH. 13   MORE MILITARY OFFENSES   513

standard for assessing criminality under Article 133 is whether the conduct or act charged is dishonorable and compromising . . . this notwithstanding whether or not the act otherwise amounts to a crime.

United States v. Giordano, 35 C.M.R. 135, 140 (C.M.A. 1964). A violation of Article 133, UCMJ, necessarily requires proof that the accused is a "commissioned officer, cadet, or midshipman" because the conduct must have disgraced or dishonored the accused in his or her official capacity. *See* Article 133, UCMJ; see also MCM pt. IV, para. 59.c(2); *United States v. Taylor*, 23 M.J. 314, 318 (C.M.A. 1987) ("The test [for Article 133, UCMJ] is whether the conduct has fallen below the standards established for officers."); *United States v. Marsh*, 15 M.J. 252, 253–54 (C.M.A. 1983) (finding that unauthorized absence is a "peculiarly military" offense, or an offense "to which disputed factual issues about the accused's status as a servicemember must be decided by the trier of fact as part of the determination of guilt or innocence and as to which the Government bears the burden of proof beyond reasonable doubt" and which "by its express terms, the statutory prohibition applies only to a member of the armed forces") (quotation marks omitted). It ineluctably follows that Article 133, UCMJ, is a purely military offense when it constitutes the underlying criminal offense for housebreaking. Only a commissioned military officer, cadet, or midshipman can commit the offense and it is only a court-martial that has jurisdiction to prosecute such an offense. *Giordano*, 35 C.M.R. at 140 ("Conduct unbecoming an officer has long been recognized as a military offense. . . ."). Article 133, UCMJ, therefore cannot serve as the underlying criminal offense in a housebreaking charge.

[marginal note: Proof accused is an officer commissioned]

III. Lesser Included Offense of Unlawful Entry

[In an omitted portion of the case, the court affirmed the lesser included offense of unlawful entry for the three specifications under Charge II.—Eds.]

DECISION

The decision of the United States Army Court of Criminal Appeals is reversed with respect to Charge II and the specifications thereunder and the sentence. We affirm only so much of Charge II and its specifications that extend to findings of guilty to the lesser included offense of unlawful entry in violation of Article 134, UCMJ, 10 U.S.C. 934 (2000). The remaining findings are affirmed. However, the record is returned to the Judge Advocate General of the Army for remand to the Court of Criminal Appeals for reassessment of the sentence in light of our action on the findings.

[marginal note: Lesser inc. offense of unlawful entering affirmed.]

[Separate opinions of Judge Erdmann and Judge Ryan are omitted.—Eds.]

[marginal note: Readdress the sent.]

Point for Discussion

Why is conduct unbecoming an officer a "purely military offense"? Should a court determine whether an offense is a purely military offense by conducting a survey of, or making other reference to, state and federal law? Or should it only matter that it is an offense that must be committed by an officer? *See United States v. Contreras*, 69 M.J. 120 (C.A.A.F. 2010) (discussing these issues).

13-3. Adultery

The criminal codes of nearly half of the states still list adultery as a crime, but prosecutors almost never seek to charge any civilians for this offense. *See* Note, *Adultery: A Comparison of Military Law and State Law and The Controversy This Causes Under Our Constitution And Criminal Justice System*, 37 Brandeis L.J. 469, 469-479 & n.4 (1996). The same is not true in the Armed Forces. Adultery is conduct that may violate UCMJ Article 134, the general article. *See* MCM, pt. IV, ¶62a. In the *Manual for Courts-Martial*, the President has defined the elements of adultery as follows:

(1) That the accused wrongfully had sexual intercourse with a certain person;

(2) That, at the time, the accused or the other person was married to someone else; and

(3) That, under the circumstances, the conduct of the accused was to the prejudice of good order and discipline in the armed forces or was of a nature to being discredit upon the armed forces.

Id. ¶62b.

The *Manual for Courts-Martial* further explains that adultery may be prejudicial to good order and discipline when "it has a divisive effect on a unit or organization disciple, moral, or cohesion." It says that adultery would bring discredit on the Armed Forces it would "bring the service into disrepute, make it subject to public ridicule, or lower it in public esteem." *Id.* ¶62c(2). The *Manual for Courts-Martial* further lists a number of factors to consider, including whether the co-actor is a member of the military or the spouse of a member of the military and whether there was a misuse of government time and resources in the facilitation of the offense. *See id.* The maximum punishment for adultery is a dishonorable discharge, forfeiture of all pay and allowances, and confinement for one year.

Points for Discussion

1. How difficult is it for the government to prove the third element of adultery? When would acts of adultery not be prejudicial to good order and discipline or not bring discredit upon the Armed Forces?

2. When a married male servicemember is accused of having non-consensual sex with a woman who is not his wife, the servicemember is sometimes charged with both adultery and rape or aggravated sexual assault. *See, e.g., United States v. Fosler*, 70 M.J. 225 (C.A.A.F. 2011) (included in chapter 12 of this casebook). What is the advantage to the prosecution of pressing both charges? Can adultery be non-consensual?

UNITED STATES v. ORELLANA
Navy-Marine Corps Court of Criminal Appeals
62 M.J. 595 (N.M. Ct. Crim. App. 2005)

DIAZ, Judge:

A military judge, sitting as a general court-martial, convicted the appellant [Angel M. Orellana, Corporal, U.S. Marine Corps], pursuant to his pleas, of conspiracy to commit adultery, false official statement, assault consummated by battery, obstructing justice, and three specifications of adultery, in violation of Articles 81, 107, 128, and 134, Uniform Code of Military Justice, 10 U.S.C. §§ 881, 907, 928, and 934. The military judge sentenced the appellant to confinement for 48 months, reduction to pay grade E–1, and a dishonorable discharge. The convening authority approved the sentence but, in accordance with the terms of the pretrial agreement, suspended all confinement in excess of 18 months and waived automatic forfeitures.

Charges

Sentence
· 48 mo Confine
· Reduc to E1
· Dishon. Disch
& Completely
Affirmed

Δ Arg.

The appellant has raised two assignments of error. He first argues that his conviction for adultery under the first specification of Charge III is unconstitutional based on *Lawrence v. Texas*, 539 U.S. 558 (2003). He next asserts that his plea to making a false official statement was improvident. We have carefully reviewed the record of trial, the appellant's assignments of error, the Government's response, and the appellant's reply. Following that review (and except as noted below), we conclude that the findings and sentence are correct in law and fact and that no error materially prejudicial to the appellant's substantial rights was committed. Arts. 59(a) and 66(c), 10 U.S.C. §§ 859(a) and 866(c), UCMJ. We specifically hold that *Lawrence v. Texas* does not bar the prosecution of adultery under the UCMJ.

Ap Ct.
& Error materially prej. to Ap. rights.

Background

The appellant admitted the following facts during the military judge's providence inquiry:

The appellant was a 23–year–old married Marine noncommissioned officer living aboard Marine Corps Base, Camp Pendleton, California. In October 2000, the appellant approached Ms. "E" (a 19–year–old civilian with no ties to the military) and Ms. E's friend, Ms. "V" (the 14–year–old stepdaughter of a Marine staff noncommissioned officer) near a small exchange on board the base. The appellant introduced himself and eventually befriended the two females.

23 yr old Marine (NCO)

meets 19 yr & 14 yr old girls.

The appellant had sexual intercourse with Ms. E at least five times during the month of October 2000. On each such occasion, the two would rendezvous at the appellant's base quarters while his wife and children were out of town. The appellant admitted that his conduct was service discrediting because "if a civilian person was aware that [he] as a Marine, a noncommissioned officer, was married and [was] having intercourse with [Ms. E] at [his] residence with [his] wife not being home or present, that . . .

Oct 2000
Δ had sex with 19 yr old at his wife's home.

might lower their opinion of the Marine Corps[.]" Record at 39. See also Prosecution Exhibit 1 at 1–2.

Approximately 4 months after his multiple trysts with Ms. E, the appellant invited the 14–year–old Ms. V back to his quarters, where the two had sexual intercourse. The following month (March 2001), he invited Corporal (Cpl) Daniel J. Villanueva to join him on a double date with Ms. E and Ms. V. The appellant and Cpl Villanueva ultimately intended to have sexual intercourse with the two females.

The appellant and Cpl Villanueva picked up the females and drove around before stopping in a parking lot near a local beach. The appellant had sexual intercourse with Ms. E in the back of his car while Cpl Villanueva and Ms. V waited nearby. When the appellant was done, Cpl Villanueva and Ms. V climbed in the car and had sexual intercourse.

In April 2001, the appellant's wife began to suspect his infidelity. In an effort to cover his tracks, the appellant called Ms. V on 21 April 2001, and urged her (if asked) to deny the acts described above. Ms. V's mother taped this conversation.

Cpl Villanueva's wife also suspected her husband's infidelity, and both she and the appellant's wife placed telephone calls to the home of Ms. V and confronted her family. On 24 April 2001, the appellant and his wife began arguing in their quarters over the appellant's infidelity. The appellant's wife struck him in the head. The appellant responded by pushing his wife and punching her on the side of her head with his closed fist. At some point, the police responded to the altercation.

Finally, on 21 May 2001, Naval Criminal Investigative Service Special Agent (SA) Kenneth Proffitt interviewed the appellant regarding his misconduct. SA Proffitt advised the appellant of his Article 31, UCMJ, 10 U.S.C. § 831, rights and then questioned him. During the interview, the appellant denied that he knew Ms. V or that he had ever had sex with her. He also denied going to the beach with Ms. V. SA Proffitt then played the recording of the appellant's telephone conversation with Ms. V, at which point the appellant corrected his false statement.

Adultery

In his first assignment of error, the appellant asserts that his conviction for "private, consensual, heterosexual adultery with an adult [Ms. E]" violates the appellant's constitutional right to privacy. Appellant's Brief at 3. Specifically, he relies on the decision of the U.S. Supreme Court in *Lawrence*, which struck down a Texas statute that criminalized "same sex" sodomy. Finding that the case involved "two adults who, with full and mutual consent from each other, engaged in sexual practices common to a homosexual lifestyle," the Supreme Court concluded that the petitioners in *Lawrence* had a substantive due process right to "engage in their conduct without intervention of the government" because the Texas statute "further[ed] no legitimate state interest which [could] justify its intrusion into the personal and private life of the individual." *Lawrence*, 539 U.S. at 578.

Following *Lawrence*, the Court of Appeals for the Armed Forces (C.A.A.F.) rejected a generalized constitutional attack on the military's sodomy statute (Article 125, UCMJ, 10 U.S.C. § 925). *United States v. Marcum*, 60 M.J. 198 (C.A.A.F. 2004). Instead, C.A.A.F. determined that military courts must apply a contextual, "as-applied" analysis, to determine if a prosecution under Article 125, UCMJ, passes constitutional muster. To that end, a court must consider three questions:

This was a general constitutional attack on military's sodomy statute.

> First, was the conduct that the accused was found guilty of committing of a nature to bring it within the liberty interest identified by the Supreme Court? Second, did the conduct encompass any behavior or factors identified by the Supreme Court as outside the analysis in *Lawrence*? Third, are there additional factors relevant solely in the military environment that affect the nature and reach of the Lawrence liberty interest?

Test from Marcum

Id. at 206–07 (internal citations omitted). *Accord United States v. Stirewalt*, 60 M.J. 297, 304 (C.A.A.F. 2004).

In Lawrence

The appellant contends that *Lawrence* extends a constitutional right of privacy to discreet consensual adultery with an adult "where there is no other legitimate government interest furthered by prosecuting this offense." Appellant's Brief at 5. We conclude that *Lawrence* does not shield the appellant's actions in this case and that the Government had a legitimate interest in prosecuting the appellant for his misconduct.

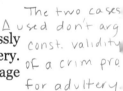

I.

At the outset, we note that neither Lawrence nor Marcum expressly considered the constitutional validity of a criminal prosecution for adultery. The appellant, while acknowledging this fact, nevertheless seizes on language from Justice Scalia's dissenting opinion in *Lawrence*:

The two cases Δ used don't arg const. validity of a crim pro for adultery.

> State laws against bigamy, same-sex marriage, adult incest, prostitution, masturbation, adultery, fornication, bestiality, and obscenity are ... sustainable only in light of *Bowers*'[4] validation of laws based on moral choices. Every single one of these laws is called into question by today's decision; the Court makes no effort to cabin the scope of its decision to exclude them from its holding.

Either way Δ cites the dissent.

Whatever the merit of Justice Scalia's views of the scope of the majority's holding in Lawrence, his opinion remains a dissent and, as such, does not bind us here. In this case, we do not consider a statute intended "to control a personal relationship that, whether or not entitled to formal recognition in

Dissent is not binding

---

[4] *Bowers v. Hardwick*, 478 U.S. 186 (1986). In Bowers, the Court upheld the constitutionality of a Georgia statute making it a criminal offense to engage in sodomy. The Court's decision in Lawrence expressly overruled Bowers.

the law, is within the liberty of persons to choose without being punished as criminals." *Lawrence*, 539 U.S. at 567. What is at issue here is the legitimacy of the appellant's conviction for violating a criminal statute (i.e., adultery) whose primary purpose is to maintain good order and discipline within the service, while secondarily fostering the fundamental social institution of marriage.

We conclude that (*Lawrence* notwithstanding) such a prosecution remains constitutionally viable under Article 134, UCMJ, for it is there that we find sufficient constitutional limits on the Government's ability to prosecute a military accused for adultery.

II.

Adultery is an enumerated offense under Article 134, UCMJ (the "General Article"), which requires proof of the following elements:

(1) That the accused wrongfully had sexual intercourse with a certain person;

(2) That, at the time, the accused or the other person was married to someone else; and

(3) That, under the circumstances, the conduct of the accused was to the prejudice of good order and discipline in the armed forces or was of a nature to bring discredit upon the armed forces.

MANUAL FOR COURTS–MARTIAL, UNITED STATES (2000 ed.), Part IV, ¶ 62b.

Thus, in every case of adultery, military prosecutors must satisfy the "terminal element" required for all prosecutions under clauses (1) or (2) of the General Article as well as prove wrongful sexual intercourse and the existence of a valid marriage.

Prosecutions under clauses (1) and (2) of Article 134, UCMJ, have survived constitutional attacks premised on vagueness or lack of notice that the particular conduct was unlawful. *See Parker v. Levy*, 417 U.S. 733, 755 (1974). As we have previously explained, "[a]t the heart of the Court's reasoning in Parker is its observation that, although the statutory language itself is broad and vague, application of Article 134 has been limited by the President through the Manual for Courts–Martial, by the military appellate courts through case law, and by long established military custom and tradition to behavior that is easily recognized by service members as subject to punitive sanction." *United States v. Peszynski*, 40 M.J. 874, 879 (N.M.C.M.R.1994)(citing *Parker*, 417 U.S. at 752–54).

Because the President has imposed specific limits on the prosecution of such offenses, we agree with the appellant that not every instance of adultery is a criminal offense under military law. Instead, as the 2005 edition of the MCM states, "[t]o constitute an offense under the UCMJ, the adulterous conduct must either be directly prejudicial to good order and discipline or service discrediting." MCM (2005 ed.), Part IV, ¶ 62c(2).   ①

To satisfy the prejudice prong of this terminal element, the offense must have a significant effect on unit or organizational discipline, morale or Ⓡ cohesion, or be "clearly detrimental to the authority or stature of or respect toward a service member." *Id.* On the other hand, "service discrediting" ② conduct is punishable when it "has a tendency . . . to bring the service into disrepute . . . or lower it in public esteem." *Id.*

Moreover, there is no requirement that the Government show actual ⓧ *Actual* damage to the reputation of the military. *Cf. United States v. Hartwig*, 39 *Damage* M.J. 125, 130 (C.M.A. 1994) (holding that in context of Article 133, UCMJ, 10 *Req.* U.S.C. § 933, violation for officer's delivery of sexually lurid letter to child of tender years, prosecution need not prove actual damage to the reputation of the military). Rather, the test is whether the appellant's offense had a "tendency" to bring discredit upon the service. *United States v. Saunders*, 59 M.J. 1, 11 (C.A.A.F. 2003); *Hartwig*, 39 M.J. at 130.

In determining whether an adulterous act is contrary to good order and discipline or service discrediting, the 2005 edition of the MCM counsels *Factors* commanders to consider a list of non-exclusive factors, which include, in relevant part: (1) the military rank, grade or position of the accused and his co-actor; (2) the military status (if any) of the accused's or co-actor's spouse; (3) the impact, if any, of the offense on the ability of the accused or the co-actor to perform their military duties; (4) the misuse, if any, of government time and resources to facilitate the crime; (5) the flagrancy of the act and whether any notoriety ensued; (6) whether the offense was accompanied by other violations of the UCMJ; (7) the negative impact of the conduct on the affected units; and (8) whether the accused or co-actor was legally separated. MCM (2005 ed.), Part IV, ¶ 62c(2)(a)-(i).

After considering the relevant legal principles, we believe that the ⑪ appellant's conduct as alleged in Specification 1 of Charge III satisfies both prongs of the Article 134 terminal element.

      * * *

Conclusion

After thoroughly considering the record of trial and the issues raised and *Sentence* briefed by the appellant, we affirm the findings and the sentence, as approved *Affirmed* by the convening authority. We direct that a supplemental court-martial order be issued to correct the date of the offense under the first specification *& Approved* of Charge III.

Points for Discussion

1. One commentator critical of the *Orellana* decision has written: "[N]ot only did the *Orellana* court not apply *Lawrence* to adultery, but it explicitly based its holding on a rationale based on a moral code. The court emphasized the importance of 'fostering the fundamental social institution of marriage.' . . . . This is precisely the type of rationale the decision in *Lawrence* explicitly rejected." Christopher Scott Maravilla, *The Other Don't Ask, Don't Tell: Adultery Under The Uniform Code Of Military Justice After* Lawrence v. Texas, 37 Cap. U. L. Rev. 659, 674 (2009). Is this an accurate and complete characterization of the decision's rationale?

2. Should military law mirror civilian law on matters of morality such as whether people should be criminally prosecuted for adultery?

13-4. Consensual Sodomy

In *Lawrence v. Texas*, 539 U.S. 558 (2003), the Supreme Court held that a state law making it a crime for two consenting adults to engage in homosexual sodomy was unconstitutional under the due process clause of the Fourteenth Amendment. Despite this conclusion, the UCMJ still contains the following article that criminalizes sodomy, by its terms regardless of whether the sodomy is consensual:

Art. 125. Sodomy

(a) Any person subject to this chapter who engages in unnatural carnal copulation with another person of the same or opposite sex or with an animal is guilty of sodomy. Penetration, however slight, is sufficient to complete the offense.

(b) Any person found guilty of sodomy shall be punished as a court-martial may direct.

10 U.S.C. § 925. The *Manual for Courts-Martial* explains: "It is unnatural carnal copulation for a person to take into that person's mouth or anus the sexual organ of another person or of an animal; or to place that person's sexual organ in the mouth or anus of another person or of an animal; or to have carnal copulation in any opening of the body, except the sexual parts, with another person; or to have carnal copulation with an animal." MCM, pt. IV, ¶51c. The maximum penalty for sodomy with a consenting adult is a dishonorable discharge, forfeiture of all pay and allowances, and confinement for 5 years. *Id.* ¶51e. The maximum penalties for non-consensual sodomy and sodomy with a child are much higher.

The Court of Appeals for the Armed Forces has held, in the following two cases that the principles of *Lawrence v. Texas* are applicable to the Armed Forces, but that military courts must take the unique context of the Armed Forces into account when applying those principles. In reading the case, attempt to identify the exact inquiry the court says should be used in consensual sodomy cases.

UNITED STATES v. MARCUM
U.S. Court of Appeals for the Armed Forces
60 M.J. 198 (C.A.A.F. 2004)

Judge BAKER delivered the opinion of the Court.

Contrary to his pleas, Appellant [Eric P. Marcum, Technical Sergeant, U.S. Air Force] was convicted by officer members of dereliction of duty by providing alcohol to individuals under the age of 21, non-forcible sodomy, forcible sodomy, assault consummated by a battery, indecent assault, and three specifications of committing indecent acts in violation of Articles 92, 125, 128, and 134, Uniform Code of Military Justice [hereinafter UCMJ], 10 U.S.C. §§ 892, 925, 928, and 934 (2000), respectively. Appellant was sentenced to confinement for 10 years, a dishonorable discharge, total forfeitures, and reduction to the lowest enlisted grade. The convening authority reduced the confinement to six years, but otherwise approved the findings and sentence.

The case was reviewed by the Air Force Court of Criminal Appeals, which affirmed the findings and sentence. . . .

* * *

Facts

Appellant, a cryptologic linguist, technical sergeant (E–6), and the supervising noncommissioned officer in a flight of Persian–Farsi speaking intelligence analysts, was stationed at Offutt Air Force Base, Nebraska. His duties included training and supervising airmen newly assigned to the Operations Training Flight.

While off-duty Appellant socialized with airmen from his flight at parties. According to the testimony of multiple members of his unit, airmen "often" spent the night at Appellant's off-base home following these parties. The charges in this case resulted from allegations by some of these subordinate airmen that Appellant engaged in consensual and nonconsensual sexual activity with them.

Among other offenses, Appellant was charged with the forcible sodomy of Senior Airman (SrA) H (E–4). Specifically, Specification 1 of Charge II alleged that Appellant "did, at or near Omaha, Nebraska, between on or about 1 September 1998 and on or about 16 October 1998, commit sodomy with Senior Airman Robert O. H by force and without consent of the said Senior Airman Robert O. H."

With regard to the charged offense, SrA H testified that after a night of drinking with Appellant he stayed at Appellant's apartment and slept on the couch. SrA H further testified that at some point he woke up to find Appellant orally sodomizing him. Although Appellant testified that he "did not perform oral sex on [SrA H] at all," he testified to "kissing [SrA H's] penis twice." When asked "did you, at any time, use any force, coercion, pressure, intimidation or violence?" Appellant responded, "No, sir, I did not and neither did Airman H." Moreover, Appellant testified that the activity that occurred between Appellant and SrA H was "equally participatory."

According to SrA H's testimony, he did not say anything to Appellant at the time of the charged incident, but grabbed the covers, pulled them up over his torso, and turned away from Appellant into the couch. SrA H left the apartment soon after this incident took place. SrA H testified that he didn't protest at the time because he didn't know how Appellant would react. SrA H also testified that Appellant's actions made him scared, angry, and uncomfortable.

According to SrA H, he later confronted Appellant about this incident. He told Appellant, "I just want to make it clear between us that this sort of thing doesn't ever happen again." Nevertheless, SrA H forgave Appellant and continued their friendship. SrA H testified that he considered his relationship with Appellant like that of "a father type son relationship or big brother, little brother type relationship[.]" Subsequent to this incident, SrA H explained how he and Appellant salsa danced together and kissed each other in the "European custom of men." SrA H also told Appellant that he loved him, bought him a t-shirt as a souvenir, and sent numerous e-mails to Appellant expressing his continued friendship.

Appellant and SrA H also provided testimony regarding an incident that occurred prior to the charged offense. SrA H testified that during the incident he woke up in the morning and he was on top of Appellant with his face near Appellant's stomach. Appellant testified, "I was laying on my side, actually almost on top of the couch, with my belly on the couch but turned a little bit like this towards, with my face towards the rest of the living room. Airman H was [on] top of me with, facing me. Airman H was moving his pelvis area against my butt which is what woke me up. He had an erection, he had his arm around me, around the part that was actually touching the couch."

At the time of the charged conduct in question, Appellant and SrA H were both subject to Dep't of the Air Force, Instruction 36–2909 (May 1, 1996). This instruction addresses professional and unprofessional relationships within the Air Force. Dep't of the Air Force, Instruction 36–2909 is subject to criminal sanction through operation of Article 92 (Failure to obey order or regulation). Although this instruction was not admitted into evidence at trial, Appellant admitted during cross-examination that he was "aware of an Air Force policy" and that through his actions he had "broken more than an Air Force policy."

A panel of officers and enlisted members found Appellant "not guilty of forcible sodomy" but guilty of non-forcible sodomy in violation of Article 125. He was convicted on May 21, 2000. The convening authority approved his sentence except for the term of confinement on September 6, 2000.

Subsequent to the trial, action by the convening authority, and the Air Force Court of Criminal Appeals' review in this case, the Supreme Court granted certiorari in *Lawrence v. Texas*, [539 U.S. 558, 578 (2003),] a case

---

Handwritten margin notes (left):

E4 claims to & have said anything to △ just turned away.

Left soon after

E4 confronted △, said never again.
Let it go.

E4 said they'd dance, kiss, say I love you in friendship

Prior incident

E4 Test woke up on top of △

△ test that E4 was humping him, with an arm on him.

△ admitted to breaking policy of unprof. relationships

mixed panel found △ △ guilty of forcible sodomy, but guilty of non-force sodomy.

Convening Auth approved sentence w/o confinement

Handwritten note (bottom):

After the trial & ap the Sup. Ct. granted review of the Lawrence case which challenged const. same sex sodomy challenging the constitutionality of a Texas statute criminalizing same sex sodomy. Lawrence was argued on March 26, 2003, and decided on June 26, 2003. Appellant petitioned this Court for review on September 23, 2002. This Court granted his petition on March 10, 2003. Appellant's supplemental issue regarding the Supreme Court's ruling in Lawrence was granted by this Court on August 29, 2003.

Discussion

A. Article 125 Text

Article 125 states:

(a) Any person subject to this chapter who engages in unnatural carnal copulation with another person of the same or opposite sex or with an animal is guilty of sodomy. Penetration, however slight, is sufficient to complete the offense.

(b) Any person found guilty of sodomy shall be punished as a court-martial may direct.

As we stated in *United States v. Scoby*,

By its terms, Article 125 prohibits every kind of unnatural carnal intercourse, whether accomplished by force or fraud, or with consent. Similarly, the article does not distinguish between an act committed in the privacy of one's home, with no person present other than the sexual partner, and the same act committed in a public place in front of a group of strangers, who fully apprehend in the nature of the act.

5 M.J. 160, 163 (C.M.A. 1978). Thus, Article 125 forbids sodomy whether it is consensual or forcible, heterosexual or homosexual, public or private.

B. Arguments

Appellant challenges his conviction on the ground that *Lawrence* recognized a constitutional liberty interest in sexual intimacy between consenting adults in private. Appellant argues that Article 125 suffers from the same constitutional deficiencies as the Texas statute in *Lawrence* because both statutes criminalize private consensual acts of sodomy between adults. Appellant further contends that in light of the Supreme Court's rejection of *Bowers v. Hardwick*, 478 U.S. 186 (1986), Appellant's conviction violates the Due Process Clause. As a result, Appellant argues that Article 125 is either unconstitutional on its face or unconstitutional as applied to his conduct.

The amici curiae, arguing in support of Appellant's position, assert that Article 125 is unconstitutional on its face. According to the amici, the Supreme Court placed Lawrence within its privacy line of jurisprudence by overruling Bowers and effectively deciding that private, consensual, sexual conduct, including sodomy, is a constitutionally protected liberty interest. *See Lawrence*, 539 U.S. at 577. As with other fundamental rights, the amici contend that a statute purporting to criminalize a fundamental right must be narrowly tailored to accomplish a compelling government interest. The amici argue that Article 125 is not narrowly tailored because it reaches, among other conduct, the private, consensual, off-base, intimate activity of married military persons and their civilian spouses. Arguing in the alternative, quoting *Lawrence*, the amici do not "dispute that the interests in good order and discipline, and in national security, are important. But the importance of those interests is irrelevant, because there is simply no basis to conclude that they are even rationally related to Article 125, let alone sufficiently advanced by that law to justify its onerous burdens on the 'full right' to engage in 'conduct protected by the substantive guarantee of liberty.'" Under both arguments, the amici maintain that the government has no legitimate or compelling military interest in regulating Appellant's private conduct.

The Government argues that *Lawrence* is not applicable in the military environment due to the distinct and separate character of military life from civilian life as recognized by the Supreme Court in *Parker v. Levy*, 417 U.S. 733 (1974). The Government further argues that because the Supreme Court did not expressly state that engaging in homosexual sodomy is a fundamental right, this Court should analyze Article 125 using the rational basis standard of review. Utilizing this standard, the Government contends Article 125 is constitutional because it is rationally related to a legitimate state interest. Specifically, the Government maintains that Article 125 criminalizes conduct that "create[s] an unacceptable risk to the high standards of morale, good order and discipline, and unit cohesion" within the military as recognized by Congress in 10 U.S.C. § 654(a)(15).

* * *

C. The *Lawrence* Decision

The petitioners in *Lawrence* challenged the constitutionality of a Texas statute criminalizing same sex sodomy. *See* 539 U.S. at 562. This statute provided that "[a] person commits an offense if he engages in deviate sexual intercourse with another individual of the same sex." *Id.* at 563 (quoting Texas Penal Code Ann. § 21.061(a) (2003)). The Supreme Court determined at the outset that the statute posed a question of substantive due process: "whether the petitioners were free as adults to engage in the private conduct in the exercise of their liberty under the Due Process Clause of the Fourteenth Amendment to the Constitution." *Id.* at 564. The "pertinent beginning point" for its review, the Supreme Court stated, was *Griswold v. Connecticut*, 381 U.S. 479 (1965). *Id. Griswold* addressed the right to a marital zone of privacy in the context of a Connecticut law proscribing the use of contraception and counseling regarding contraception. *See* 381 U.S. at 482. This liberty interest was subsequently extended outside the marital context in *Eisenstadt v. Baird*, 405 U.S. 438 (1972) (right of individuals, married or unmarried, to have access to contraceptives) and *Carey v. Population Services Int'l*, 431 U.S. 678 (1977) (right to distribute contraception). *See Lawrence*, 539 U.S. at 565–66.

Having framed the question as one of liberty, the Supreme Court indicated that "[t]o say that the issue in *Bowers* was simply the right to engage in certain sexual conduct demeans the claim the individual put forward[.]" *Id.* at 567. The Supreme Court also characterized the statutes in *Bowers* and *Lawrence* as seeking

> to control a personal relationship that, whether or not entitled to formal recognition in the law, is within the liberty of persons to choose without being punished as criminals.
>
> This, as a general rule, should counsel against attempts by the State, or a court, to define the meaning of the relationship or to set its boundaries absent injury to a person or abuse of an institution the law protects.

Id.

Within this framework the Supreme Court overruled *Bowers*: "The rationale of Bowers does not withstand careful analysis. . . . *Bowers* was not correct when it was decided, and it is not correct today. It ought not to remain binding precedent." *Id.* at 577–78.

With respect to the *Lawrence* petitioners, the Court stated:

> The case does involve two adults who, with full and mutual consent from each other, engaged in sexual practices common to a homosexual lifestyle. The petitioners are entitled to respect for their private lives. The State cannot demean their existence or control their destiny by making their private sexual conduct a crime. Their right to liberty under the Due Process Clause gives them the full right to engage in their conduct without intervention of the government. "It is a promise of the Constitution that there is a realm of personal liberty which the government may not enter." The Texas statute furthers no legitimate state interest which can justify its intrusion into the personal and private life of the individual.

Id. at 578 (citing *Planned Parenthood v. Casey*, 505 U.S. 833, 847 (1992)).

While finding the Texas statute unconstitutional, the Supreme Court stated that "[t]he present case does not involve minors. It does not involve persons who might be injured or coerced or who are situated in relationships where consent might not easily be refused. It does not involve public conduct or prostitution." *Id.* The Supreme Court did not expressly state whether or not this text represented an exhaustive or illustrative list of exceptions to the liberty interest identified, whether this text was intended to suggest areas where legislators might affirmatively legislate, or whether this text was intended to do no more than identify areas not addressed by the Court. Nor did the Supreme Court squarely place its analysis within a traditional framework for constitutional review.

(1) Standard of Constitutional Review

The amici, in their primary argument, contend that strict scrutiny should apply to this Court's review of Article 125 because the Article impinges on a fundamental constitutional liberty interest. This follows from the amici's conclusion that "the Supreme Court overruled Bowers . . . , and held the Texas sodomy prohibition unconstitutional because the Due Process Clause of the Fourteenth Amendment protects a fundamental right of adults to make decisions regarding private, consensual sexual conduct, including sodomy." As a result, the amici maintain that Article 125 is unconstitutional because it is not narrowly tailored to achieve a compelling government interest.

In contrast, the Government contends the Supreme Court did not find a fundamental right to engage in homosexual sodomy by overruling *Bowers* because the Supreme Court applied the rational basis standard of review in *Lawrence*. "Rather, by applying a 'rational basis standard of review' to reach their determination that the Texas statute 'furthers no legitimate state interest which can justify its intrusion into the personal and private life of the individual,' the Supreme Court reaffirmed that the right to engage in homosexual sodomy is not a fundamental right."

Although particular sentences within the Supreme Court's opinion may be culled in support of the Government's argument, other sentences may be extracted to support Appellant's argument. On the one hand, the opinion incorporates some of the legal nomenclature typically associated with the rational basis standard of review. For example, as the Government notes, the Supreme Court declared "[t]he Texas statute furthers no legitimate state interest[.]" *See Lawrence*, 539 U.S. at 578. This is the counter-weight applied in the rational basis analysis. Moreover, the Supreme Court did not apply the nomenclature associated with strict scrutiny, i.e., identification of a compelling state interest and narrow tailoring of the statute to accomplish that interest.

On the other hand, the Supreme Court placed Lawrence within its liberty line of cases resting on the *Griswold* foundation. *See id.* at 564–65. These cases treated aspects of liberty and privacy as fundamental rights, thereby, subjecting them to the compelling interest analysis. *See Griswold*, 381 U.S. at 485; *Carey*, 431 U.S. at 686. With regard to the Supreme Court's use of language attributed to the rational basis review, Appellant and the amici argue the Supreme Court is simply stating that the Texas statute does not even accomplish a legitimate interest, let alone a compelling one.

Indeed, in response to the Supreme Court's decision in *Lawrence*, some courts have applied the rational basis standard of review while other courts have applied strict scrutiny. For example, the Court of Appeals of Arizona determined that "the Court applied without explanation the rational basis test, rather than the strict scrutiny review utilized when fundamental rights are impinged, to hold the Texas statute unconstitutional." *Standhardt v. Superior Court of Arizona*, 206 Ariz. 276, 77 P.3d 451, 457 (2003). Whereas the court in *Fields v. Palmdale School District*, 271 F.Supp.2d 1217, 1221 n. 7 (C.D.Cal.2003), concluded, "Many of these fundamental rights, especially those relating to marital activities and family relationships, have been classified by the Supreme Court under a broader 'right to privacy' that is implicit in the Fourteenth Amendment[.]".

The focus by the Government and Appellant on the nature of the Supreme Court's constitutional test in Lawrence is understandable. Utilization of either the rational basis test or strict scrutiny might well prove dispositive of a facial challenge to Article 125. On the one hand, the interests in military readiness, combat effectiveness, or national security arguably would qualify as either rational or compelling governmental interests. On the other hand, it is less certain that Article 125 is narrowly tailored to accomplish these interests.

The Supreme Court did not expressly state which test it used. The Court did place the liberty interest in *Lawrence* within the *Griswold* line of cases. *See Lawrence*, 539 U.S. at 564–65. *Griswold* and *Carey* address fundamental rights. However, the Supreme Court has not determined that all liberty or privacy interests are fundamental rights. In *Lawrence*, the Court did not expressly identify the liberty interest as a fundamental right. Therefore, we will not presume the existence of such a fundamental right in the military environment when the Supreme Court declined in the civilian context to expressly identify such a fundamental right.

What *Lawrence* requires is searching constitutional inquiry. This inquiry may require a court to go beyond a determination as to whether the activity at issue falls within column A—conduct of a nature to bring it within the liberty interest identified in *Lawrence*, or within column B—factors identified by the Supreme Court as outside its *Lawrence* analysis. The Court's analysis reached beyond the immediate facts of the case presented. This is reflected by the Court's decision to rule on the grounds of due process as opposed to equal protection. "Were we to hold the statute invalid under the Equal Protection Clause," the Supreme Court noted, "some might question whether a prohibition would be valid if drawn differently, say, to prohibit the conduct both between same-sex and different-sex participants." 539 U.S. at 575. The Supreme Court also acknowledged "an emerging awareness that liberty gives substantial protection to adult persons in deciding how to conduct their private lives in matters pertaining to sex." *Id.* at 572.

At the same time the Court identified factors, which it did not delimit, that might place conduct outside the *Lawrence* zone of liberty. Thus, the door is held open for lower courts to address the scope and nature of the right identified in *Lawrence*, as well as its limitations, based on contexts and factors the Supreme Court may not have anticipated or chose not to address in *Lawrence*. In our view, this framework argues for contextual, as applied analysis, rather than facial review. This is particularly apparent in the military context.

(2) *Lawrence* in the Military Context

The Supreme Court and this Court have long recognized that "[m]en and women in the Armed Forces do not leave constitutional safeguards and judicial protection behind when they enter military service." *United States v.*

Mitchell, 39 M.J. 131, 135 (C.M.A. 1994) (quoting *Weiss v. United States*, 510 U.S. 163, 194 (1994) (Ginsburg, J., concurring)). "Our citizens in uniform may not be stripped of basic rights simply because they have doffed their civilian clothes." *Goldman v. Weinberger*, 475 U.S. 503, 507 (1986) (citations omitted). As a result, this Court has consistently applied the Bill of Rights to members of the Armed Forces, except in cases where the express terms of the Constitution make such application inapposite. *See United States v. Jacoby*, 29 C.M.R. 244, 246–47 (C.M.A. 1960)("[I]t is apparent that the protections in the Bill of Rights, except those which are expressly or by necessary implication inapplicable, are available to members of our armed forces.").

At the same time, these constitutional rights may apply differently to members of the armed forces than they do to civilians. *See Parker*, 417 U.S. at 743. "The military is, by necessity, a specialized society." Id. Thus, when considering how the First Amendment and Fourth Amendment apply in the military context, this Court has relied on Supreme Court civilian precedent, but has also specifically addressed contextual factors involving military life. *See United States v. Priest*, 45 C.M.R. 338, 344 (C.M.A. 1972) ("[T]he right of free speech in the armed services is not unlimited and must be brought into balance with the paramount consideration of providing an effective fighting force for the defense of our Country."); *see also United States v. McCarthy*, 38 M.J. 398 (C.M.A. 1993) (warrantless entry into military barracks room to effectuate apprehension did not violate Fourth Amendment). In light of the military mission, it is clear that servicemembers, as a general matter, do not share the same autonomy as civilians. *See Parker*, 417 U.S. at 758.

While the Government does not contest the general proposition that the Constitution applies to members of the Armed Forces, it argues that *Lawrence* only applies to civilian conduct. Moreover, with respect to the military, the Government contends that Congress definitively addressed homosexual sodomy by enacting 10 U.S.C. § 654 (2000). According to the Government, pursuant to Congress's Article I authority to make rules and regulations for the Armed Forces, Congress not only prohibited sodomy through Article 125, but with Article 125 as a backdrop, determined in 1993 through 10 U.S.C. § 654 that homosexuality, and, therefore, sodomy was incompatible with military service. In enacting § 654, Congress determined that "[t]he presence in the armed forces of persons who demonstrate a propensity or intent to engage in homosexual acts would create an unacceptable risk to the high standards of morale, good order and discipline, and unit cohesion that are the essence of military capability." 10 U.S.C. § 654(a)(15). Thus, according to the Government, this Court should apply traditional principles of deference to Congress's exercise of its Article I authority and not apply *Lawrence* to the military.

The military landscape, however, is less certain than the Government suggests. The fog of constitutional law settles on separate and shared powers where neither Congress nor the Supreme Court has spoken authoritatively. Congress has indeed exercised its Article I authority to address homosexual sodomy in the Armed Forces, but this occurred prior to the Supreme Court's constitutional decision and analysis in *Lawrence* and at a time when *Bowers* served as the operative constitutional backdrop. Moreover, the Supreme Court did not accept the Government's present characterization of the right as one of homosexual sodomy. The Court stated, "To say that the issue in Bowers was simply the right to engage in certain sexual conduct demeans the claim the individual put forward[.]" *Lawrence*, 539 U.S. at 567. "The State cannot demean their existence or control their destiny by making their private sexual conduct a crime." *Id.* at 578. Nor did the Supreme Court define the liberty interest in Lawrence in a manner that on its face would preclude its application to military members.

Constitutional rights identified by the Supreme Court generally apply to members of the military unless by text or scope they are plainly inapplicable. Therefore, we consider the application of *Lawrence* to Appellant's conduct. However, we conclude that its application must be addressed in context and not through a facial challenge to Article 125. This view is consistent with the principle that facial challenges to criminal statutes are "best when infrequent" and are "especially to be discouraged." *Sabri v. United States*, 541 U.S. 600 (2004). In the military setting, as this case demonstrates, an understanding of military culture and mission cautions against sweeping constitutional pronouncements that may not account for the nuance of military life. This conclusion is also supported by this Court's general practice of addressing constitutional questions on an as applied basis where national security and constitutional rights are both paramount interests. Further, because Article 125 addresses both forcible and non-forcible sodomy, a facial challenge reaches too far. Clearly, the *Lawrence* analysis is not at issue with respect to forcible sodomy.

Thus, this case presents itself to us as a challenge to a discrete criminal conviction based on a discrete set of facts. The question this Court must ask is whether Article 125 is constitutional as applied to Appellant's conduct. This as-applied analysis requires consideration of three questions. First, was the conduct that the accused was found guilty of committing of a nature to bring it within the liberty interest identified by the Supreme Court? Second, did the conduct encompass any behavior or factors identified by the Supreme Court as outside the analysis in *Lawrence*? 539 U.S. at 578. Third, are there additional factors relevant solely in the military environment that affect the nature and reach of the *Lawrence* liberty interest?

D. Is Article 125 Constitutional as Applied to Appellant?

Appellant was charged with dereliction of duty, three specifications of forcible sodomy, three specifications of indecent assault, and two specifications of committing an indecent act. With regard to the charge addressed on appeal, the members found Appellant "not guilty of forcible sodomy, but guilty of non-forcible sodomy." As part of Appellant's contested trial, the following additional facts surrounding his conduct were elicited: The act of sodomy occurred in Appellant's off-base apartment during off-duty hours; no other members of the military were present at the time of the conduct; Appellant was an E–6 and the supervising noncommissioned officer in his flight. His duties included training and supervising airmen. SrA H, an E–4, was one of the airmen Appellant supervised. As a result, SrA H was subordinate to, and directly within, Appellant's chain of command.

The first question we ask is whether Appellant's conduct was of a nature to bring it within the *Lawrence* liberty interest. Namely, did Appellant's conduct involve private, consensual sexual activity between adults? In the present case, the members determined Appellant engaged in non-forcible sodomy. This sodomy occurred off-base in Appellant's apartment and it occurred in private. We will assume without deciding that the jury verdict of non-forcible sodomy in this case satisfies the first question of our as applied analysis.

The second question we ask is whether Appellant's conduct nonetheless encompassed any of the behavior or factors that were identified by the Supreme Court as not involved in *Lawrence*. For instance, did the conduct involve minors? Did it involve public conduct or prostitution? Did it involve persons who might be injured or coerced or who are situated in relationships where consent might not easily be refused? *See id.*

When evaluating whether Appellant's conduct involved persons who might be injured or coerced or who were situated in relationships where consent might not easily be refused, the nuance of military life is significant. An Air Force instruction applicable to Appellant at the time of the offenses included the following proscriptions.

Unduly familiar relationships between members in which one member exercises supervisory or command authority over the other can easily be or become unprofessional. Similarly, as differences in grade increase, even in the absence of a command or supervisory relationship, there may be more risk that the relationship will be, or be perceived to be unprofessional because senior members in military organizations normally exercise authority or some direct or indirect organizational influence over more junior members.

Relationships are unprofessional, whether pursued on or off-duty, when they detract from the authority of superiors or result in, or reasonably create the appearance of, favoritism, misuse of office or position, or the abandonment of organizational goals for personal interests.

Dep't. of the Air Force Instruction, 36–2909 Professional and Unprofessional Relationships, paras. 2.2, 3.1 (May 1, 1996).

For these reasons, the military has consistently regulated relationships between servicemembers based on certain differences in grade in an effort to avoid partiality, preferential treatment, and the improper use of one's rank. *See United States v. McCreight*, 43 M.J. 483, 485 (C.A.A.F. 1996). Indeed, Dep't of the Air Force Instruction 36–2909 is subject to criminal sanction through operation of Article 92, UCMJ. As both the Supreme Court and this Court have recognized elsewhere, "The fundamental necessity for obedience and the consequent necessity for imposition of discipline, may render permissible within the military that which would be constitutionally impermissible outside it." *Parker*, 417 U.S. at 758. While servicemembers clearly retain a liberty interest to engage in certain intimate sexual conduct, "this right must be tempered in a military setting based on the mission of the military, the need for obedience of orders, and civilian supremacy." *United States v. Brown*, 45 M.J. 389, 397 (C.A.A.F. 1996).

In light of Air Force Instructions at the time, Appellant might have been charged with a violation of Article 92 for failure to follow a lawful order. However, the Government chose to proceed under Article 125. Nonetheless, the fact that Appellant's conduct might have violated Article 92 informs our analysis as to whether Appellant's conduct fell within the Lawrence zone of liberty.

As the supervising noncommissioned officer, Appellant was in a position of responsibility and command within his unit with respect to his fellow airmen. He supervised and rated SrA H. Appellant also testified that he knew he should not engage in a sexual relationship with someone he supervised. Under such circumstances, which Appellant acknowledged was prohibited by Air Force policy, SrA H, a subordinate airman within Appellant's chain of command, was a person "who might be coerced" or who was "situated in [a] relationship[] where consent might not easily be refused." *Lawrence*, 539 U.S. at 578. Thus, based on this factor, Appellant's conduct fell outside the liberty interest identified by the Supreme Court. As a result, we need not consider the third step in our *Lawrence* analysis. Nor, given our determination that Appellant's conduct fell outside the liberty interest identified in Lawrence, need we decide what impact, if any, 10 U.S.C. § 654 would have on the constitutionality of Article 125 as applied in other settings.

Appellant's conduct was outside the protected liberty interest recognized in *Lawrence*; it also was contrary to Article 125. As a result, Article 125 is constitutional as applied to Appellant.

* * *

[In a separate part of the opinion, the Court held that Appellant was prejudiced when his trial defense counsel revealed privileged communications during sentencing without Appellant's permission.]

Decision

The decision of the United States Air Force Court of Criminal Appeals is affirmed with respect to the findings, but reversed with respect to the sentence. The sentence is set aside. The record of trial is returned to the Judge Advocate General of the Air Force. A rehearing on sentence is authorized.

CRAWFORD, Chief Judge [dissenting in part and concurring in the result in part]:

* * *

... I agree with the majority's conclusion that Appellant's conviction should not be reversed under *Lawrence v. Texas*.[10] But I disagree with the majority's assumption that Appellant's conduct falls within the protected liberty interest enunciated in Lawrence. There are factual distinctions between the petitioners' offense in Lawrence and Appellant's offense in the case at bar. Because of these significant differences, I would hold that this is not a *Lawrence* case and would reserve for another day the questions of whether and how *Lawrence* applies to the military. The factual differences between Lawrence and Appellant's case are striking. The offense of sodomy with which the petitioners in *Lawrence* were charged occurred in the context of a consensual, adult relationship. The Court noted at the outset of its opinion that at the time of their arrest, the petitioners in *Lawrence* were in Mr. Lawrence's apartment, engaging in a private, consensual sexual act. The Court reiterated this factual context shortly thereafter: "The petitioners were adults at the time of the alleged offense. Their conduct was in private and consensual."[12] At the conclusion of its opinion, the Court once again emphasized the specific factual context of the petitioners' acts:

> The present case does not involve minors. It does not involve persons who might be injured or coerced or who are situated in relationships where consent might not easily be refused. It does not involve public conduct or prostitution. It does not involve whether the government must give formal recognition to any relationship that homosexual persons seek to enter. The case does involve two adults who, with full and mutual consent from each other, engaged in sexual practices common to a homosexual lifestyle.[13]

Indeed, the nature of the petitioners' relationship as described by the Court was central to the Court's conclusion that the State may not curtail the petitioners' " 'intimate and personal choices [which are] central to [their] personal dignity and autonomy.' "[14]

The facts surrounding Appellant's offense are strikingly different. Appellant, a noncommissioned officer, was convicted, in pertinent part, of non-forcible sodomy with Senior Airman H, whom Appellant supervised in his work unit. Appellant was not involved in a romantic relationship with Senior Airman H, as were the petitioners in Lawrence. On the contrary, Appellant's offense occurred after a night of drinking when Senior Airman H "crashed" on Appellant's couch, wearing only boxer shorts and a T-shirt, and

---

[10] 539 U.S. 558.

[12] *Id.* at 564.

[13] *Id.* at 578.

[14] *Id.* at 574 (quoting *Planned Parenthood of Southeastern Pa. v. Casey*, 505 U.S. at 833, 851 (1992)).

awoke to find Appellant performing oral sex on him. Senior Airman H testified that he did not protest Appellant's action for fear of how Appellant would respond. This event followed two other incidents of sexual contact between Appellant and Senior Airman H, which involved touching and dancing, on evenings when Appellant and Senior Airman H had been out drinking and socializing.

Clearly, Appellant's offense occurred in the context of a casual relationship with a subordinate airman who testified that he was too frightened to protest. This is a far cry from the consensual adult relationship, born of intimate and personal choice, which characterized the petitioners' behavior in *Lawrence*. Indeed, Appellant's offense concerned precisely what the Supreme Court stated Lawrence did not concern: an individual, Senior Airman H, who might have been coerced, in a situation where consent might not easily have been refused, given Senior Airman H's subordinate professional position. Senior Airman H himself expressed his fear of rejecting a superior, noncommissioned officer, who was in fact his supervisor at work. This case certainly did not involve "two adults [who acted] with full and mutual consent from each other." In sum, the act for which Appellant was convicted in specification 1 of Charge II was not the kind of mutual and intimate act in the context of which the Supreme Court decided Lawrence.

Points for Discussion

1. Under the "tripartite framework" established by *Marcum*, military courts must address three questions in deciding whether a sodomy prosecution is constitutional:

> First, was the conduct ... of a nature to bring it within the liberty identified by the Supreme Court [in *Lawrence*]? Second, did the conduct encompass any behavior or factors identified by the Supreme Court as outside the analysis in *Lawrence*? Third, are there additional factors relevant solely in the military environment that affect the nature and reach of the *Lawrence* liberty interest?

Marcum, 60 M.J. at 206–07. Findings of guilt where these questions are not thoroughly considered will be reversed. *See United States v. Hartman*, 69 M.J. 467 (C.A.A.F. 2011) (reversing a finding of guilt where the providence inquiry "did not reflect consideration of the Marcum framework").

2. What is *Marcum*'s practical effect on military prosecutions? One commentator writes: "... Article 125 is only mostly dead. ... [C]onsensual sodomy is alive to the extent the charged conduct is prejudicial to good order and discipline. ... [T]he *Lawrence* right to privacy only reaches conduct which is generally not the gravamen of the case. Since only prejudicial sodomy is typically prosecuted, the consensual sodomy prohibition is mostly alive." Major Joel P. Cummings, *Is Article 125, Sodomy a Dead Letter in Light of* Lawrence v. Texas *and the New Article 120*?, Army Lawyer, Jan. 2009, at 1, 28 (2009). How might you rephrase this conclusion in terms of how *Marcum* actually changed the law and court-martial practice?

UNITED STATES v. STIREWALT
U.S. Court of Appeals for the Armed Forces
60 M.J. 297 (C.A.A.F. 2004)

Judge ERDMANN delivered the opinion of the Court.

Health Services Technician Second Class (E–5) Darrell Stirewalt was convicted of a number of offenses involving his female shipmates. Before this Court Stirewalt argues that his prosecution was tainted with unlawful command influence, that the investigating officer had an impermissible conflict of interest and that his conviction for sodomy violated the Fifth Amendment. We affirm the decision of the Coast Guard Court of Criminal Appeals.

* * *

C. Constitutionality of Sodomy Conviction

. . . Stirewalt entered a guilty plea and was convicted of one specification of sodomy under Article 125, UCMJ, 10 U.S.C. § 925 (2000). He now contends that his guilty plea and conviction should be set aside in light of the United States Supreme Court's decision in *Lawrence v. Texas*, 539 U.S. 558 (2003).

The specification that Stirewalt stands convicted under originally alleged that he did, at or near Mobile, Alabama, on or about 8 December 1996, commit sodomy with [LTJG B], by force and without the consent of [LTJG B]. He entered a guilty plea to this specification, with the words by force and without the consent of [LTJG B] excepted and withdrawn. The stipulation of fact underlying his guilty plea indicates that

> [o]n the late evening of 07 December 1996, HS2 Stirewalt and [LTJG B] spoke by phone. Near midnight of that evening, HS2 Stirewalt proceeded to her apartment complex. . . . After knocking on the front door, HS2 Stirewalt was allowed inside by [LTJG B], who at the time of entry, was on the telephone with a fellow Coast Guard officer, LTJG Heidi Rumazza. After entering the apartment, HS2 Stirewalt spoke to Ms. Rumazza for approximately one minute before handing the telephone back to [LTJG B]. [LTJG B] then hung the phone up, sat down on a chair in her living room and began conversing with HS2 Stirewalt. After approximately 20 minutes of conversation, [LTJG B] moved into her bedroom. HS2 Stirewalt followed her into her bedroom. HS2 Stirewalt climbed into bed with [LTJG B] and the two engaged in "sodomy."

We recently concluded in *United States v. Marcum*, 60 M.J. 198 (C.A.A.F. 2004), that constitutional challenges to Article 125 based on the Supreme Court's decision in *Lawrence* must be addressed on an as applied, case-by-case basis. We identified a tripartite framework for addressing *Lawrence* challenges within the military context:

> First, was the conduct that the accused was found guilty of committing of a nature to bring it within the liberty interest identified by the Supreme Court? Second, did the conduct encompass any behavior or factors

identified by the Supreme Court as outside the analysis in Lawrence? 539 U.S. at 578. Third, are there additional factors relevant solely in the military environment that affect the nature and reach of the Lawrence liberty interest?

Marcum, 60 M.J. at 206–07.

In regard to the first two prongs of this tripartite framework, we will assume without deciding that Stirewalt's conduct falls within the liberty interest identified by the Supreme Court and does not encompass behavior or factors outside the Lawrence analysis. Stirewalt's conduct, however, squarely implicates the third prong of the framework. That question asks whether there are additional factors relevant solely in the military environment, not addressed by the Supreme Court, that affect the reach and nature of the *Lawrence* liberty interest in the context presented. *Id.* at 207. It is clear that such factors exist here.

Stirewalt's conduct with [LTJG B] was more than a personal consensual relationship in the privacy of an off-base apartment. At the time of this relationship, [LTJG B] was one of seven officers on the U.S.C.GC SWEETGUM, a cutter with a crew of only 42. The conduct in question occurred between a commissioned department head and her subordinate enlisted crew member:

> Romantic relationships between members are unacceptable when: (1) Members have a supervisor and subordinate relationship ... , or (2) Members are assigned to the same small shore unit (less than 60 members), or (3) Members are assigned to the same cutter .... The nature of operations and personnel interactions on cutters and small shore units makes romantic relationships between members assigned to such units the equivalent of relationships in the chain of command and, therefore, unacceptable. This policy applies regardless of rank, grade, or position.

Coast Guard Personnel Manual, para. 8.H.2.f. (change 26, 1988) (Unacceptable Romantic Relationships).

Coast Guard policy prohibits the following relationships or conduct, regardless of rank, grade, or position of the persons involved .... Romantic relationships outside of marriage between commissioned officers and enlisted personnel. *Id.* at para. 8.H.2.g. (Prohibited Relationships). Interpersonal relationships which raise even a perception of unfairness undermine good leadership and military discipline. *Id.* at para. 8.H.1.c. (Leadership and Military Discipline).

In *Marcum*, we noted that due to concern for military mission accomplishment, "servicemembers, as a general matter, do not share the same autonomy as civilians." *Marcum*, 60 M.J. at 206. We consider Stirewalt's zone of autonomy and liberty interest in light of the established Coast Guard regulations and the clear military interests of discipline and order that they reflect. Based on this analysis, we conclude that Stirewalt's conduct fell outside any protected liberty interest recognized in *Lawrence* and was appropriately regulated as a matter of military discipline under Article 125. The fact that Stirewalt as the subordinate enlisted crew member was charged does not alter the nature of the liberty interest at stake. As a result, Article 125 is constitutional as applied in the present case.

DECISION

The decision of the United States Coast Guard Court of Criminal Appeals is affirmed.

CRAWFORD, Chief Judge (concurring in part and in the result):

I agree with the result in this case but I "would reserve for another day the questions of whether and how *Lawrence* [*v. Texas*, 539 U.S. 558 (2003)] applies to the military."[1] Like *United States v. Marcum*, "the factual differences between Lawrence and Appellant's case are striking" for the reasons mentioned by the majority as well as the circumstances surrounding the charges themselves. "Unlike the petitioners in *Lawrence*, who were both charged with, and convicted of, consensual sodomy without any evidence of force," there was "probable cause that Appellant committed the general offense described in Article 125 with the added element of force,"[3] notwithstanding the reversal of his first conviction. Thus, this is not a case where there was no evidence of force whatsoever. And as the majority notes, this case is one of the exceptions to Lawrence.

If the facts and circumstances of Appellant's case fit into one of the enumerated *Lawrence* exceptions, then it only logically follows that it is not necessary even to assume that the *Lawrence* constitutional analysis applies.

Thus, I concur in part and in the result.

Points for Discussion

1. The third prong of the *Marcum* inquiry asks whether factors unique to the military create exceptions to the applicability of *Lawrence*. One commentator writes based on the *Stirewalt* decision: "This final prong, because of its open-endedness, may cause the most confusion about what conduct is protected within the military context. It is conceivable, albeit unlikely, that virtually all military sodomy convictions with even the slightest military nexus could stand based upon this prong alone." Erik C. Coyne, *Check Your Privacy Rights at the Front Gate: Consensual Sodomy Regulation in Today's Military Following* United States v. Marcum, 35 U. Balt. L. Rev. 239, 255 (2005).

2. The court in *Marcum* believed it was dealing with a situation in which "consent might not easily be refused" given that the person charged with

---

[1] 60 M.J. 198, 212 (C.A.A.F. 2004) (Crawford, C.J. dissenting on Issue I and concurring in the result on Issue III).

[3] *Id.* at 214.

committing sodomy was of superior rank to the other person. Is *Stirewalt* similarly a case in which consent might not easily have been refused?

Problem

The following facts come from *United States v. Powell*, 55 M.J. 633 (A.F. Ct. Crim. App. 2001):

The victim was a high school senior. The appellant was in his final year at the Air Force Academy. They met for the first time on Friday, 6 March 1998, when the appellant, along with other cadets, arrived in Los Angeles, California, to serve as escorts at a charity ball. The appellant and victim were observed getting along well together during activities that day by the sponsors of the ball who paired them together for the event. The next night at the ball, the victim and the appellant danced and interacted socially with other cadets, debutantes, and family members. On Sunday, 8 March, there was a farewell party for the cadets. After the party, the cadets were taken to the airport to return to the Academy. At the airport, the appellant gave the victim a kiss, and they exchanged e-mail addresses and telephone numbers.

The victim testified she was "swept off her feet" by the appellant, and they began e-mailing and calling each other. She said that the appellant injected sex into their conversations and that she responded in kind. However, she told the appellant that she was a virgin and did not want to have sexual intercourse with him. Within a month, the victim agreed to visit the Academy and the appellant sent her an airplane ticket. Other debutantes also planned to visit the Academy during the same time frame.

The victim flew to Colorado Springs, Colorado, on Thursday, 2 April 1998, a day earlier than the other debutantes. The appellant met her at the airport, and they went to the hotel where she and the other debutantes had rented two hotel rooms. After checking-in, the victim and the appellant engaged in kissing, touching, and "oral sex" in her room. The victim said this sexual contact was consensual. The two went out for dinner and then the appellant returned her to the hotel. He went back to the Academy for the evening.

On Friday morning, 3 April, the appellant took the victim to the Academy for a tour. After leaving the Academy, they went to a local park called the Garden of the Gods. While at the park in a cave, they engaged in more consensual kissing, touching, and oral sodomy. The appellant tried to convince her to have sexual intercourse in the cave because it would be "a great place for her first time." She refused and reminded him she was not going to engage in sexual intercourse with him. After getting something to eat and seeing a movie, they returned to the hotel where three of the other debutantes had finally arrived. Later, the appellant left the hotel and went back to the Academy.

On Saturday, 4 April, the victim and the other debutantes attended a parade at the Academy. After the parade, the debutantes and cadets went to a local mall. The victim and appellant rode alone in his car. While returning to the hotel from the mall, the victim performed "oral sex" on the appellant and he fondled her vagina. At the hotel, the appellant informed the victim that he had rented another room at a nearby inn so they could talk later. The appellant and victim moved her luggage to this room. That night, all the cadets and debutantes ate dinner at a local restaurant. After dinner, the appellant and another cadet bought alcoholic beverages to take back to the hotel.

At the hotel, with the appellant's assistance and encouragement, the victim got drunk. She testified that she passed out, had difficulty walking, and felt sick. Witnesses confirmed that her speech was slurred, that she became loud and giggly, and had difficulty walking. The witnesses indicated the appellant was not intoxicated. When the appellant took the victim to the debutantes' other hotel room, one of the cadets became concerned that something sexual might occur because the victim was drunk. The cadet also heard the victim tell the appellant, "Your plan worked, you got me drunk."

Very early on Sunday morning, 5 April, the appellant took the victim to the room he had rented. The victim testified that once there, she passed out on the bed. When she came to, the victim discovered the appellant had removed some of her clothes and was going through her luggage. The next time she woke up, more of her clothes had been removed and the appellant was trying to put a black nightgown on her. The next thing she remembered was the appellant removing the black nightgown and placing a white nightgown on her. When she awoke the next time, the appellant was naked and on top of her. He told her that he wanted to have sex. The victim repeatedly told him no but he pinned her arms with one hand, lifted the nightgown, and penetrated her. After the rape, the victim said whenever she tried to leave the room, the appellant would awaken and insist she return. She called one of the debutantes and tried to signal that she needed help but could not speak freely because the appellant was listening to her. Later that morning, the appellant took the victim to the airport for her return flight to Los Angeles.

Appellant was found guilty of rape, but not guilty of forcible sodomy. Would it have been appropriate to charge appellant with committing consensual sodomy on these facts? Should the Air Force Academy seek to punish cadets for committing consensual conduct of the kind that occurred in this case before the rape? Should the Academy attempt to prevent this kind of conduct before it occurs?

CHAPTER 14

MILITARY DEFENSES

Service members who face trial by court-martial have the opportunity to present affirmative or "special defenses" that deny "wholly or partially, criminal responsibility for those acts."[1] Defenses may be inconsistent and may be raised by evidence presented by the defense, prosecution, or court-martial (military judge or members). R.C.M. 916(a) discussion.

Many military defenses have civilian counterparts such as self-defense, accident, entrapment, inability (physical impossibility, physical inability, inability due to extrinsic factors) and mistake of fact. Partial defenses (which negate the mens rea element of an offense) in the military include those similar to the civilian sector such as voluntary intoxication. Military procedural defenses such as speedy trial (discussed in previous chapters), statute of limitations, former jeopardy, and immunity, also have counterparts in civilian criminal law. This chapter will not review those defenses. Rather, this chapter will discuss defenses that are unique or have a different application in the military.

14-1. Superior Orders

One defense that is specific to the military is the defense of "Obedience to Orders." Essentially, a servicemember who commits an offense in response to a lawful order has a justification for the crime. Rule for Courts-Martial 916(c) and the corresponding rule discussion explain that a "death, injury, or other act caused or done in the proper performance of a legal duty is justified and not unlawful" and that "duty may be imposed by statute, regulation, or order."

The defense of obedience to orders exists when the accused acts, "pursuant to orders unless [he] knew the orders to be unlawful or a person of ordinary sense and understanding would have known the orders to be unlawful." R.C.M. 916(d). Generally, the military judge determines the lawfulness of the

---

[1] Before trial on the merits Defense Counsel must provide notice to Trial Counsel of, "intent to offer the defense of alibi, innocent ingestion, or lack of mental responsibility, or its intent to introduce expert testimony as to the accused's mental condition." R.C.M. 701(b)(4). " 'Alibi' and 'good character' are not special defenses, as they operate to deny that the accused committed one or more of the acts constituting the offense." R.C.M. 916(a) discussion.

order at issue. R.C.M. 916(d) discussion. "An act performed pursuant to an unlawful order is excused unless the accused knew it to be unlawful or a person of ordinary sense and understanding would have known it to be unlawful." *Id.* As the Army Court of Military Review clarifies in the case below, if an accused commits an offense pursuant to an order that appeared legal and he did not know to be illegal, he is entitled to the defense of obedience to orders.

UNITED STATES v. CALLEY
Army Court of Military Review
46 C.M.R. 1131 (Army Ct. Crim. App. 1973)

OPINION AND ACTION ON PETITION FOR NEW TRIAL

ALLEY, Judge:

In much publicized proceedings, appellant [First Lieutenant William L. Calley, Jr., U. S. Army] was convicted by general court-martial of three specifications of premeditated murder and one of assault with intent to commit murder in violation of Articles 118 and 134, Uniform Code of Military Justice, 10 U.S.C. §§ 918 and 934, respectively. He was sentenced to dismissal, forfeiture of all pay and allowances, and confinement at hard labor for life. The convening authority approved dismissal and the forfeitures, but reduced the period of confinement to twenty years. The offenses were committed by First Lieutenant William L. Calley when he was performing as a platoon leader during an airmobile operation in the subhamlet of My Lai (4) in Song My village, Quang Ngai Province, Republic of South Vietnam, on 16 March 1968. Although all charges could have been laid as war crimes, they were prosecuted under the UCMJ. See paragraph 507b, Field Manual 27-10, The Law of Land Warfare (1956).

Appellate defense counsel have presented thirty-one assignments of error and a petition for new trial. For clarity our opinion will consolidate those assignments which warrant discussion under the broad headings of jurisdiction, publicity, command influence, composition of the court-martial, sufficiency of the evidence, discovery and subpoenas, and petition for new trial.

I—JURISDICTION

     * * *

II—PUBLICITY

     * * *

III—COMMAND INFLUENCE

     * * *

IV—COMPOSITION OF THE COURT-MARTIAL

     * * *

V—SUFFICIENCY OF THE EVIDENCE

A. The Evidence. On 16 March 1968 Lieutenant Calley was the 1st platoon leader in C Company, 1st Battalion, 20th Infantry, 11th Light Infantry Brigade, as he had been since he arrived in the Republic of Vietnam in December 1967. The 11th Brigade was assigned to the Americal Division, itself only formally activated in October 1967.

* * *

C Company, appellant's unit, had not experienced much combat prior to 16 March 1968. In its three months of overseas duty, two of which were with Task Force Barker, its operations had consisted of uneventful patrolling, attempted ambushes, providing defense for the fire bases, and providing blocking forces for Task Force missions. The casualties it had sustained were mainly from mines and booby traps. While moving into a blocking position on 25 February 1968 the company became ensnared in a mine field, suffering two killed and thirteen wounded. Appellant was not on this operation, for he had just returned from a three day in-country rest and recuperation leave. On 14 March 1968, a popular sergeant in the second platoon was killed and three others were wounded by a booby trap.

The next day, Captain Medina, commander of C Company, was notified that his company would engage in an upcoming offensive action. . . .

The concept of the operation for C Company was for the 1st and 2nd platoons to sweep rapidly through My Lai (4) and the 3rd platoon to follow. The 3rd platoon would thoroughly search the hamlet and destroy all that could be useful to the enemy. . . .

This was to be the unit's first opportunity to engage decisively the elusive enemy they had been pursuing since their arrival in South Vietnam. The men, as is normal in an untried unit, faced the operation with both anticipation and fear, mindful of the recent casualties taken in less perilous missions.

C Company was transported by helicopter from LZ Dottie about six miles southeast to My Lai (4) in two lifts (Appendix B, Point A). The first lift was completed at approximately 0730 hours; the second lift at 0747 hours. The insertion was preceded by five minutes of preparatory fires of 105 howitzer high explosive rounds and by gunship fire. The insertion, although within 100 meters of the western edge of My Lai (4), was not opposed by hostile fire. In formation with the first and second platoons on line from north to south, the third platoon in reserve and the mortar platoon remaining with the rear to provide support if needed, C Company laid heavy suppressive fires into the subhamlet as the first and second platoons began the assault.

Despite expectations of heavy resistance based upon specific intelligence briefings, C Company moved through My Lai (4) without receiving any fire. The only unit casualty on 16 March 1968 was one self-inflicted wound. No mines or booby traps were detonated. Lead elements of the company had no occasion to call for mortar fires from the weapons platoon; the forward observer with C Company had no occasion to call for any fires from artillery units in direct support. In My Lai (4), the unit encountered only unarmed, unresisting, frightened old men, women, and children, and not the expected elements of the 48th Viet Cong Battalion. The villagers were found in their homes eating breakfast and beginning their morning chores.

The members of C Company reacted to the unexpected absence of opposition in diverse ways. Some continued the mission as if the enemy was in fact being engaged. Most recognized the difference between actual and expected circumstances, so while continuing with the destruction of foodstuffs, livestock, and buildings, reverted to the unit standing operating procedures on collecting and evacuating Vietnamese. Many soldiers took no action at all, but stood passively by while others destroyed My Lai (4). A few, after witnessing inexplicable acts of violence against defenseless villagers, affirmatively refused to harm them.

No single witness at appellant's trial observed all that transpired at My Lai (4). The testimony of the 92 witnesses was shaded by the lapse of time between 16 March 1968 and the commencement of trial in November 1970. Even in the voluminous record, all that happened is not fully revealed. One reason for vagueness and confusion in testimony offered by both sides is that the operation itself was confused, having been planned on the basis of faulty intelligence and conducted with inexperienced troops without adequate command control.

With this caveat as to the evidence, we come to the events which led to charges against appellant. Twenty out of the twenty-seven persons who were members of Lieutenant Calley's understrength platoon on 16 March 1968 testified at his court-martial.

The first platoon arrived on the first lift about 0730 hours. Its initial task was to provide perimeter defense for the insertion of the remainder of the company. After the company was on the ground and organized for assault, the first platoon moved toward My Lai (4) in formation . . . .

    * * *

This formation quickly became disorganized in the subhamlet. Thick vegetation made it difficult for the troops to see who was near, and for the squad leaders and Lieutenant Calley to maintain visual contact with their men and with each other. However, the principal reason why the formation broke down and leaders lost control was the discovery of unresisting, unarmed old men, women and children instead of the expected enemy. The platoon had not been specifically instructed what to do in this event. No civilian collection point had been designated; and the first platoon was supposed to move through the village quickly, not to return to the rear with detainees.

Some villagers were shot by some members of the first platoon when it first entered the subhamlet. Some members collected groups of Vietnamese, without knowing what to do with them, and others stopped to kill livestock. The platoon assault formation became a meandering troop. Lieutenant Calley started out behind his platoon on the western edge of the subhamlet, but emerged at a ditch on the eastern edge before several members of his platoon (Appendix B, Point C; Appendix D). Sergeant Mitchell similarly lost contact with his squad at one time, leaving most of them to search a small cluster of huts and buildings to the southeast of My Lai (4). Sergeant Bacon testified he never saw his platoon leader or even heard from him as he pushed through the subhamlet. Sergeant Cowan lost contact with Lieutenant Calley soon after they entered the village, did not see him inside the village, and came close to him again only as he exited My Lai (4) on the east.

The Vietnamese who were taken in the first platoon's sweep were herded in two general directions, either toward the southern edge of the hamlet near an intersection of trails or easterly in front of the advancing troops.

In the second squad, Sergeant Bacon detailed men to escort a group of men, women and children villagers down a trail (to his right or south) to where he thought the platoon leader would be. Private First Class Doines, a rifleman in Bacon's squad, took ten to fifteen people along a trail running north-south in the middle of the village and left them with Lieutenant Calley. Specialist Four Wood got some people together and sent them toward the right with a guard. Private First Class Kye found about ten old men, women and children in a hootch. They were whisked away to his right by an American soldier. A key witness, Private First Class Conti, stated he encountered Lieutenant Calley on a trail midway through the village. At Lieutenant Calley's direction he rounded up five or six people and put them with a nearby group of thirty to forty, consisting mostly of women and children. At appellant's order he and Private First Class Meadlo, another critical witness, moved these people down the trail and into rice paddies on the southern side of the subhamlet (Appendix B, Point B). Specialist Four Maples searched hootches, gathered some people, and moved them up front as he continued through My Lai (4).

The first squad's contact with the people of My Lai (4) was more significant. Private First Class Meadlo testified that, upon order from Sergeant Mitchell, he collected thirty to forty people near what he remembered as a clearing in the center of the village. Private First Class Dursi recalled that he moved through the village gathering people in a group. He related coming upon PFC Meadlo, who was guarding a group of Vietnamese near some rice paddies next to a trail on the southern side of the village. PFC Dursi later moved his group of fifteen to a ditch on the eastern side. Private First Class Haywood picked up five or six villagers and was told by someone to take the people to Dursi, whom he saw guarding twenty to thirty others on a trail in the south side of the village. A fire team leader in the first squad, Specialist Four Grzesik, stated that he found seven or eight unresisting Vietnamese in a hootch immediately upon entering the village. He left these people with another group of twenty-five farther east in the village, in a small clearing. Specialist Four Boyce rounded up about fifteen people, mostly women and children, and passed them on to someone else. The people assembled in the southern portion of the subhamlet were not the only ones met by the first squad. Specialist Four Hall recalled that thirty to forty people were gathered in front of him, herded easterly through the village, and left at a ditch with Lieutenant Calley, Sergeant Mitchell, and others.

After the first platoon's movement through My Lai (4), which took from ninety minutes to two hours to cover only a third of a mile, the majority of the platoon formed a perimeter defense about 50 to 100 meters east of the ditch on the east side of the subhamlet. The rest of C Company more thoroughly searched and destroyed My Lai (4). The first platoon remained in its defensive position for another two hours or so until after the company had taken a lunch break. C Company then continued its mission with less eventful forays into two other subhamlets of Song My village. At one time later in the afternoon C Company was ordered by the brigade commander to return to My Lai (4) to verify reports of civilian casualties; but after an estimate of twenty-eight killed was radioed in by Captain Medina, that order was countermanded by the division commander.

The fate of villagers gathered by appellant's platoon in the southern portion of My Lai (4) and at the ditch on the subhamlet's eastern boundary was alleged in the following charges:

"CHARGE: Violation of the Uniform Code of Military Justice, Article 118

"Specification 1: In that First Lieutenant William L. Calley, Jr., US Army, 40th Company, The Student Brigade, US Army Infantry School, Fort Benning, Georgia (then a member of Company C, 1st Battalion, 20th Infantry) did, at My Lai 4, Quang Ngai Province, Republic of South Vietnam, on or about 16 March 1968, with premeditation, murder an unknown number, not less than 30, Oriental human beings, males and females of various ages, whose names are unknown, occupants of the village of My Lai 4, by means of shooting them with a rifle.

"Specification 2: In that First Lieutenant William L. Calley, Jr., US Army, 40th Company, The Student Brigade, US Army Infantry School, Fort Benning, Georgia (then a member of Company C, 1st Battalion, 20th Infantry) did, at My Lai 4, Quang Ngai Province, Republic of South Vietnam, on or about 16 March 1968, with premeditation, murder an unknown number of Oriental human beings, not less than seventy, males and females of various ages, whose names are unknown, occupants of the village of My Lai 4, by means of shooting them with a rifle.

"ADDITIONAL CHARGE: Violation of the Uniform Code of Military Justice, Article 118

"Specification 1: In that First Lieutenant William L. Calley, Jr., US Army, Headquarters Company, The Student Brigade, US Army Infantry School, Fort Benning, Georgia (then a member of Company C, 1st Battalion, 20th Infantry) did, at My Lai 4, Quang Ngai Province, Republic of South Vietnam on or about 16 March 1968, with premeditation, murder one Oriental male human being, an occupant of the village of My Lai 4, whose name and age is unknown, by shooting him with a rifle.

"Specification 2: In that First Lieutenant William L. Calley, Jr., US Army, Headquarters Company, The Student Brigade, US Army Infantry School, Fort Benning, Georgia (then a member of Company C, 1st Battalion, 20th Infantry) did, at My Lai 4, Quang Ngai Province, Republic of South Vietnam, on or about 16 March 1968, with premeditation, murder one Oriental human being, an occupant of the village of My Lai 4, approximately two years old, whose name and sex is unknown, by shooting him with a rifle."

Upon motion the military judge ruled that the defense was entitled to a Bill of Particulars.

* * *

As previously described, some of the villagers rooted out of their homes were placed in a group guarded by PFC Paul Meadlo and PFC Dennis Conti. PFC Dursi, who was about fifteen feet from PFC Meadlo watching his own group of Vietnamese, saw Lieutenant Calley come onto the trail and heard him ask Meadlo "if he could take care of that group." A couple of minutes later the appellant returned and, as Dursi remembered, yelled to Meadlo, "Why haven't you wasted them yet? PFC Dursi turned and started to move his group down the trail when he heard M-16 fire from his rear.

PFC Conti recounted that Lieutenant Calley told him and Meadlo "To take care of the people," left, and returned:

"Then he came out and said, 'I thought I told you to take care of them.' Meadlo said, 'We are. We are watching them' and he said 'No, I mean kill them.' "

Conti testified that he saw Lieutenant Calley and Meadlo fire from a distance of ten feet with M-16 rifles on automatic fire into this group of unarmed, unresisting villagers.

Former PFC Meadlo's first appearance as a witness resulted only in his claiming his privilege against self-incrimination. However, he did return to testify at length under a grant of immunity. By the time of trial, he was a civilian. By the time of his testifying, he was presumably satisfied that he was not facing trial himself before a military commission.

Meadlo testified that he was guarding a group of villagers with Conti when Lieutenant Calley approached him and said, "You know what to do with them, Meadlo." He assumed at the time this meant only to continue guarding them. However, appellant returned in ten or fifteen minutes and said, "How come they're not dead?" Meadlo replied, "I didn't know we were supposed to kill them," after which Lieutenant Calley directed, "I want them dead." Meadlo remembered that appellant backed away and began firing into the group before he did the same.

Specialist Four Sledge, a radio operator, remembered moving with appellant to the south side of the village, where they found a group of thirty or forty Vietnamese with Meadlo. After Lieutenant Calley asked the group whether they were Viet Cong, which they naturally disclaimed, Sledge heard him tell Meadlo "to waste them." Sledge was walking away when he heard shooting and screaming from behind him. He glanced back and saw a few people start to fall. He did not see appellant firing.

Appellant, testifying in his own behalf, stated that after he got to the eastern edge of the village he received radio messages from the second platoon leader, who asked him to check out some bunkers in the northeast corner of My Lai (4), and from Captain Medina, who asked what he was doing. He told Captain Medina that he had some bunkers and a small portion of the hamlet to the southeast to check out and that he had a lot of enemy personnel with him. As appellant moved over to Sergeant Mitchell's position to the southeast, he came out of the village and encountered Meadlo with a large group of Vietnamese. Lieutenant Calley recalled he said something to the effect, "Did he know what he was supposed to be doing with those people" and, "To get moving, get on the other side of the ditch." About this time he claimed to have stopped Conti from molesting a female. Instead of continuing to the first squad leader, he returned inside the village to insure that Sergeant Bacon was searching the bunkers and placing his men on perimeter defense. Then, he claims to have received another call from Captain Medina telling him to "waste the Vietnamese and get my people out in line, out in the position they were supposed to be." He yelled to Sergeant Bacon to get moving, and as he passed by Meadlo a second time he told them that if he couldn't move those people to "get rid of them."

There is no doubt that a group of submissive, defenseless Vietnamese, women, children, and old men, being guarded at the trail south of My Lai (4) by PFC Meadlo, were shot down in summary execution either by Meadlo and the appellant or by Meadlo at the order of the appellant. Nor is there doubt that the location of this offense and its occurrence as the first in time of the several charged satisfied the prosecution's responsibility of proof under the specification and Bill of Particulars.

Many of the bodies are depicted in a photograph taken by former Specialist Four Ronald Haeberle near the north-south trail, south of My Lai (4). A great deal of foundation evidence satisfactorily authenticates the photograph as being of the same group of bodies as was the subject of Specification 1 of the Charge and the testimony of Meadlo, Conti, Dursi and Sledge. Although over twenty inert bodies are shown, almost all displaying dreadful wounds, a pathologist-witness could point to only one wound on one body which, in his opinion from viewing the photograph, was certain to have been instantly fatal. Most probably his testimony was the reason for findings amending the charged number of decedents to "not less than one."

2. The Ditch (Appendix B, Point C; Appendix D). Specification 2 of the Charge alleged the premeditated murder of not less than seventy persons.

The court members returned findings of guilty, except the number of victims was reduced to not less than twenty. As outlined by the Bill of Particulars, this offense occurred after the trail incident but before the offenses laid under the Additional Charge.

It is not disputed that during midmorning on 16 March 1968 a large number of unresisting Vietnamese were placed in a ditch on the eastern side of My Lai (4) and summarily executed by American soldiers. We can best begin a recital of the tragic facts and circumstances surrounding this offense by examining the appellant's testimony.

Lieutenant Calley testified that after he passed PFC Meadlo for the second time at the trail, he moved toward Sergeant Mitchell's location in the southeastern part of My Lai (4). He found him near a ditch that ran through that sector. He walked up the ditch until he broke into a clearing. There he discovered some of his men firing upon Vietnamese in another ditch. Lieutenant Calley admitted that he also fired with them and told Meadlo to get his people over the ditch or, if he couldn't move them, to "waste them." He then went north to check out the positions of his men.

Charles Sledge confirmed some of those movements of his platoon leader. However, Sledge remembers important events differently. He heard someone shout that Sergeant Mitchell had some people at a ditch; moved there; saw twenty to thirty Vietnamese women, children, and a few old men; saw Lieutenant Calley and Sergeant Mitchell shove these Vietnamese down into the ditch and fire into them from four or five feet. The victims screamed and fell. A helicopter landed nearby. Lieutenant Calley went to it to talk with the aviator and returned to say to Sledge, "He don't like the way I'm running the show, but I'm the boss here."

Other important witnesses to the mass murder at the ditch were Conti, Hall, Olsen, Dursi, Meadlo, Grzesik and Turner.

After the killings at the trail, Conti went back into the village. Later he exited the east side and heard firing to his front. When he got to its source, Conti found Lieutenant Calley and Sergeant Mitchell firing from six or seven feet into a ditch filled with people who were screaming and trying to crawl up. He described the scene in court:

> "I seen the recoil of the rifles and the muzzle flashes and I looked down, I see a woman try to get up. As she got up I saw Lieutenant Calley fire and hit the side of her head and blow the side of her head off. I left."

Specialist Four Hall collected thirty or forty people, pushed them forward through My Lai (4) to the ditch, left them there, and proceeded to a position in the paddies beyond. He noticed that Sergeant Mitchell, Lieutenant Calley, the platoon's RTO's, and several others stayed behind. Sometime after he got into position Hall heard fully automatic fire behind him coming from the area of the ditch. He saw a helicopter land and appellant converse with its aviator, after which he heard slow, semi-automatic fire from the ditch. Later, when he crossed the ditch on a wooden foot bridge, he saw thirty or forty people in it:

"They were dead. There was blood coming from them. They were just scattered all over the ground in the ditch, some in piles and some scattered out 20, 25 meters perhaps up the ditch. . . . They were very old people, very young children, and mothers. . . . There was blood all over them."

Olsen did not see Lieutenant Calley fire into the villagers, but did see him by the ditch when about two dozen Vietnamese were in it.

"They were—the majority were women and children, some babies. I distinctly remember one middle-aged Vietnamese male dressed in white right at my feet as I crossed. None of the bodies were mangled in any way. There was blood. Some appeared to be dead, others followed me with their eyes as I walked across the ditch."

James Dursi, it will be recalled, moved his group away from the trail when appellant yelled to Meadlo there. He moved his people until he came upon the ditch. He stopped. Lieutenant Calley, and then Meadlo, joined him. Dursi heard Lieutenant Calley tell Meadlo, "We have another job to do" and tell Meadlo and him to put the people into the ditch. He and Meadlo complied. The Vietnamese started to cry and yell. Lieutenant Calley said something like, "Start firing," and fired into the group himself. So did Meadlo, but Dursi refused. Asked why, he testified, "I couldn't go through with it. These little defenseless men, women and kids." After the first of the firing ceased, Lieutenant Calley told Dursi to move across the ditch before he (Dursi) got sick. He did move away from the scenes of blood flowing from chest, arm, and head wounds upon the victims. From the perimeter, to the east, he looked back toward the ditch only once and saw the helicopter land.

Meadlo gave the most graphic and damning evidence. He had wandered back into the village alone after the trail incident. Eventually, he met his fire team leader, Specialist Four Grzesik. They took seven or eight Vietnamese to what he labeled a "ravine," where Lieutenant Calley, Sledge, and Dursi and a few other Americans were located with what he estimated as seventy-five to a hundred Vietnamese. Meadlo remembered also that Lieutenant Calley told him, "We got another job to do, Meadlo," and that the appellant started shoving people into the ravine and shooting them. Meadlo, in contrast to Dursi, followed the directions of his leader and himself fired into the people at the bottom of the "ravine." Meadlo then drifted away from the area but he doesn't remember where.

Specialist Four Grzesik found PFC Meadlo, crying and distraught, sitting on a small dike on the eastern edge of the village. He and Meadlo moved through the village, and came to the ditch, in which Grzesik thought were thirty-five to fifty dead bodies. Lieutenant Calley walked past and ordered Grzesik to take his fire team back into the village and help the following [platoon] in their search. He also remembered that Calley asked him to "finish them off," but he refused.

Specialist Four Turner saw Lieutenant Calley for the first time that day as Turner walked out of the village near the ditch. Meadlo and a few other soldiers were also present. Turner passed within fifteen feet of the area, looked into the ditch and saw a pile of approximately twenty bodies covered with blood. He also saw Lieutenant Calley and Meadlo firing from a distance of five feet into another group of people who were kneeling and squatting in the ditch. Turner recalled he then went north of the ditch about seventy yards, where he joined with Conti at a perimeter position. He remained there for over an hour, watching the ditch. Several more groups of Vietnamese were brought to it, never to get beyond or out of it. In all he thought he observed about ninety or a hundred people brought to the ditch and slaughtered there by Lieutenant Calley and his subordinates.

Other members of the first platoon saw Vietnamese placed into a ditch and appellant and others fire into it. Some members of the third platoon also saw the bloody bodies. Also, the observations of witnesses who were in the supporting helicopters portray a telling, and ghastly, overview of the slaughter at the ditch. Aviators and crew members saw from the air numbers of bodies they variously estimated from about thirty to about one hundred. One aviator, a Lieutenant (then Warrant Officer) Thompson, actually landed near the scene three times. The second time, he spoke with someone, who from the evidence must have been Lieutenant Calley. Thompson succeeded in evacuating a few living Vietnamese despite appellant's deprecations. The evidence from others is certainly persuasive that Lieutenant Calley boasted, "I'm the boss here," after he spoke with an aviator.

There is no dispute as to the fact of killings by and at the instance of appellant at a ditch on the eastern edge of My Lai (4). From appellant's own testimony, and that of his radio operator, it is clear that this second offense preceded those laid under Additional Charge, as was specified in the Bill of Particulars.

That the findings reduced the originally charged number of victims from "not less than seventy" to "not less than twenty" reflects the members' careful adherence to the instructions of the military judge. His instructions permitted findings of guilty only in conformance with the Bill of Particulars, namely, that any deaths found under Specification 2 of the Charge precede those alleged under the Additional Charge. Using the meeting between Lieutenant Calley and the aviator Thompson as a dividing line between the offenses laid under the Charge and those under the Additional Charge, we find the evidence conclusively supports the findings of premeditated murder of not less than twenty human beings.

   3. The Additional Charge. Specification 1 of the Additional Charge alleged the premeditated murder of one male human being and Specification 2, the premeditated murder of one human being approximately two years old. Instructions required that the Government prove these offenses to have occurred in sequence after the mass killing offense at the ditch. The findings

were guilty as charged as to Specification 1 and guilty of assault with intent to commit murder as to Specification 2.

Appellant's conviction of the Additional Charge and its specifications rests squarely on the resolution of conflicts between his testimony and the testimony of Charles Sledge. The members resolved these against appellant, with ample support in the record.

According to Specialist Four Sledge, five or ten minutes after Lieutenant Calley returned from speaking with a helicopter aviator, he and Calley encountered a forty to fifty year old man dressed in white robes as they moved north up the ditch. Appellant repeatedly questioned the man, "Viet Cong adou?" (Are you Viet Cong), to which the man continually replied, "No viec." Suddenly Lieutenant Calley shot the man in the face at point blank range, blowing half his head away. Immediately after this incident Sledge remembered that:

> "Someone hollered, 'there's a child,' You know, running back toward the village. Lieutenant Calley ran back, the little—I don't know if it was a girl or boy—but it was a little baby, and he grabbed it by the arm and threw it into the ditch and fired."

Sledge observed this from a distance of twenty to thirty feet. He recalled that only one shot was fired at the child from a distance of four or five feet. He did not see whether the round struck.

Lieutenant Calley testified that after talking with the aviator, he moved along the platoon's perimeter checking the position of his troops. He did not recall making any statement to Sledge that, "He [the aviator] don't like the way I'm running the show, but I'm the boss here." but did claim that he told Captain Medina over the radio that "a pilot don't like the way things were being done down here." As appellant went northerly along the ditch, a man dressed in white was brought to him for interrogation. He admitted butt-stroking the individual with his M-16, bloodying his face, but denies shooting him. Lieutenant Calley also denied the episode concerning a child that Sledge described.

Appellate defense counsel urge us to discount Sledge's testimony about the Additional Charge because of its apparent inconsistency with testimony from other members of the first platoon. However, after a careful review of the evidence we are convinced that any minor disparities in location and time sequence are capable of resolution. Differences in perception or recollection of physical features in the hamlet, including the ditch, and the passage of time are to be expected. Essentially, the defense contends that Sledge should not be believed and that the appellant's remembrances should be accorded greater weight. Our view of the evidence leads us, as it did the court members, to the opposite conclusion. Appellant's account of the facts and circumstances surrounding the Additional Charge (as well as the other offenses) is riddled with inconsistency and selectivity of recall. He purported to be able to recall all exculpatory material in great detail, but became vague when describing any significant features of the village and its environs and events surrounding the offenses which tended to be incriminating.

The evidence in support of the specifications under the Additional Charge is sufficient in itself to be persuasive beyond reasonable doubt. In addition, this is not a case in which the evidence going to these offenses should be viewed in isolation from the rest of the case. The last two offenses are the conclusion of a course of conduct, consistent with and logically following all the carnage which preceded.

B. Legal Responsibility. Although appellant disputes the assault on the child and killing of the man found under the Additional Charge, his theories of defense at trial and on appeal accept as fact his participation in the killings at the trail and ditch. His testimony differs from others' about the details of his participation, the time spent upon the slayings at the ditch, and the number of the dead. These differences pose no substantial factual issues on appeal.

In an argument of extraordinary scope, appellant asks us to hold that the deaths of the My Lai villagers were not legally requitable in that the villagers had no right to continued life cognizable in our law. The two premises for this view are first, that the history of operations around Pinkville discloses villager sympathy and support for the Viet Cong, so extensive and enduring as to constitute all the villagers as belligerents themselves; and second, that appellant's superiors had determined the belligerent status of the villagers before the operation of 16 March—i.e., as belligerents, the villagers were not entitled to the protections of peaceful civilian status under the Geneva Convention Relative to the Protection of Civilian Persons in Time of War . . . .

This argument is tainted by several fallacies. One is that participation in irregular warfare is done by individuals, although they may organize themselves for the purpose. Slaughtering many for the presumed delicts of a few is not a lawful response to the delicts. We do not know whether the findings specifically included the deaths of infants in arms or children of toddler age, but the fallacy is clear when it is recalled that villagers this young were indiscriminately included in the general carnage. A second fallacy is that the argument is in essence a plea to permit summary execution as a reprisal for irregular villager action favoring the Viet Cong. Reprisal by summary execution of the helpless is forbidden in the laws of land warfare. . . .

Though conceding participation in some killings, the defense abstracts appellant's mental state while he was in My Lai to claim that the evidence was insufficient to support the findings under the original charge.

No claim is made that appellant lacked mental responsibility in the sense of the ordinary sanity tests set out in paragraph 120b, Manual, supra. Insanity as a defense was expressly disavowed at trial and before us, properly so in light of all the evidence.

Granting his own sanity, appellant contends that he was nevertheless not guilty of murder because he did not entertain the requisite mens rea. His specific claims are:

1. He was prompted to kill by provocation such as negated malice and would reduce any offense to manslaughter.

2. Events preceding and during the My Lai operation affected his psychic make-up in a way which deprived him of the capacity to premeditate or to entertain a state of mind of malice.

3. Because he did not bear any individualized ill will toward the villagers, but simply regarded them as enemy in a strict military sense, and because in the context of the operation he was not conscious of any criminal quality to his acts but rather thought that he was properly performing his duty, he is not guilty of unlawful homicide; or at very most is guilty of manslaughter because he was void of malice.

4. His acts were justified because of the orders given to him; or, if the orders and his response do not constitute a complete defense, he is at most guilty of manslaughter.

These claims are inextricably intertwined. To some extent it is necessary that they be taken up individually; however, their aggregate effect may be significant even though the effect of one would not be.

Each claim implies the absence of malice in appellant's mind on 16 March 1968. The defense considers proof of malice to be as indispensable to conviction for murder in violation of Article 118, UCMJ, as it was at common law or under the predecessor Articles of War. See paragraph 179a, Manual for Courts-Martial, United States Army, 1949. The Government, on the other hand, asks us to construe Articles 118 and 119 as being supplanting statutory definitions of murder and manslaughter, so complete in their terms as to express all that is encompassed within the current offenses; and to hold that, by omitting reference to malice, Congress rendered the concept immaterial in military prosecutions.

* * *

Despite omission of the term in Article 118, we are persuaded that the concept of malice retains vitality in the military law of homicide. Malice is still the proper term for describing that state of mind which distinguishes murder from manslaughter. . . .

* * *

We believe the malice essential in murder by intended killing is similar. The requisite malice is not solely established by subjective and personal norms as appellant maintains. . . .

* * *

The instant record discloses no adequate provocation. To be legally adequate, the provocation must be of a quality which would "excite uncontrollable passion in the mind of a reasonable man." . . .

A review of the psychiatric and lay witness testimony persuades us also that appellant was not afflicted with any psychic dysfunction which would preclude his premeditating the killings or harboring malice.

* * *

None of the lay testimony casts doubt on appellant's capacity for a murderous mens rea. Two psychiatrists testified for appellant, one from a hypothetical question and one from personal clinical experience with him. Three testified for the prosecution, all from extensive clinical observation and interviews. The two defense psychiatrists gave some testimony in conclusory terms to the effect that appellant was acting "automatically," that he did not have capacity to premeditate because he was effectively without ability to reflect upon alternative courses of action and choose from them; and that he did not have the capacity to "contrive" the deaths of the villagers. However, both agreed that appellant had capacity to perceive and predict, the two functions essential to the pertinent mens rea. Appellant knew he was armed and what his weapon would do. He had the same knowledge about his subordinates and their arms. He knew that if one aimed his weapon at a villager and fired, the villager would die. Knowing this, he ordered his subordinates to "waste" the villagers at the trail and ditch, to use his own terminology; and fired upon the villagers himself. These bare facts evidence intent to kill, consciously formed and carried out.

What appellant did and said at My Lai even more clearly evidences premeditation as a conscious process. He told Meadlo, concerning the group collected at the trail, "Take care of them," and left to reenter the village. When he returned, his reaction at observing the group alive was surprise and dismay. His then ordering the killing at the trail was not impulsive; it was, we are satisfied, an instance of supervision over a plan he had conceived.

Indicia of appellant's premeditation of the killings at the ditch are abundant. His attitude toward the persons collected there was expressed in his statement to Meadlo, "We have another job to do" and his order to Meadlo and Dursi to shove the persons into the ditch and "start firing." He personally pushed villagers down into the ditch before firing point blank at the group and ordering subordinates to do the same. Villagers were brought to the ditch in batches; and appellant supervised killing them over an extended period of time. Estimates of the period vary from witness to witness. Understandably, appellant's estimate is among the shortest. Close comparison of all testimony leads us to conclude that appellant's supervising and participating in killings at the ditch lasted from forty-five minutes to an hour. He no doubt fired more than one clip into the ditch. He fired into the ditch even after he spoke with Thompson at Thompson's helicopter. It was after that conversation that appellant boasted of "being the boss here." He asked Grzesik to "help finish off" the villagers, and asked Maples, a machine gunner, if he could use his weapon, and ordered Dursi to "start firing" in the ditch. All refused even though appellant was their commissioned superior. (Appellant stated a lack of recollection of these conversations with Grzesik and Maples, but evidence that they occurred was clear and credible.)

These acts and conversations bespeak premeditation. We find not only that the act of killing was consciously conceived, but also that appellant expressed his conception in so many words to Meadlo, Dursi and Grzesik. Prior consideration of the fatal acts is demonstrated most clearly by appellant's compressing the group into a situs most convenient for the killing, namely the bed of the ditch.

The psychiatric theory that appellant acted automatically, without power of choice, explains his conduct not within conscious operations of mind but instead by unconscious impulse activated by a special set of circumstances. It is proposed that appellant came to the My Lai operation affected by anger, anxiety, and also guilt in that he was not present with his platoon during a prior operation in which it sustained casualties; that appellant's capacity for discrimination among concepts and grasping abstractions was of a low order; that his reaction to training, including indoctrination in obedience to orders, was to exhibit conditioned response; and that one of his strong psychic needs was to satisfy and please others. Given this psychic set, the defense argument proceeds, a combination of the orders he purportedly received or thought he received and a confrontation with the Vietnamese he despised and feared touched off an impelling urge to kill of an involuntary nature.

* * *

The remaining defense arguments negating the requisite mens rea may be evaluated by reference to conscious processes of the mind, namely, knowledge and intent; and we need say no more about the automation concept or theories of the unconscious.

That appellant may have regarded his victims impersonally as military enemy to "waste" rather than as objects of individually founded ill will is not inconsistent with the presence of malice. . . .

* * *

Of the several bases for his argument that he committed no murder at My Lai because he was void of mens rea, appellant emphasized most of all that he acted in obedience to orders.

Whether appellant was ever ordered to kill unresisting, unarmed villagers was a contested question of fact. The findings of a court-martial being in the nature of a general verdict, we do not know whether the court found that no such orders were given or, alternatively, concluded that the orders were given but were not exculpatory under the standards given to them in instructions.

Responding to a question during direct examination asking why he gave Meadlo the order, "If he couldn't get rid of them to 'waste them,' " Lieutenant

Calley replied, "Because that was my order. That was the order of the day, sir." The appellant stated he received that order from Captain Medina, "The night before in the company briefings, the platoon leaders' briefing, the following morning before we lifted off, and twice there in the village."

Lieutenant Calley related what he remembered of Captain Medina's remarks to the company at the evening briefing prior to the My Lai (4) operation:

> "He [Medina] started off and he listed the men that we had lost, . . . We were down about 50 percent in strength, and that the only way we would survive in South Vietnam would be to—we'd have to unite, start getting together, start fighting together, and become extremely aggressive and we couldn't afford to take anymore casualties, and that it was the people in the area that we had been operating in that had been taking the casualties on us, and that we would have to start treating them as enemy and you would have to start looking at them as enemy, . . . We were going to start at My Lai (4). And we would have to neutralize My Lai (4) completely and not to let anyone get behind us, and then we would move into My Lai (5) and neutralize it and make sure there was no one left alive in My Lai (5) and so on until we got into the Pinkville area, and we would completely neutralize My Lai (5)—I mean My Lai (1) which is Pinkville. He said it was completely essential that at no time that we lose our momentum of attack because the other two companies that had assaulted the time in there before had let the enemy get behind him or he had passed through enemy, allowing him to get behind him and set up behind him, which would disorganize him when he made his final assault on Pinkville. It would disorganize him, they would lose their momentum of attack, start taking casualties, be more worried about their casualties than their mission, and that was their downfall. So it was our job to go through destroying everyone and everything in there, not letting anyone or anything get behind us and move on into Pinkville, sir."

Appellant further recalled Captain Medina's saying that "the area had been completely covered by PSYWAR operations; that all civilians had left the area and that there was no civilians in the area and anyone there would be considered enemy," and that the unit had "political clearance to destroy and burn everything in the area."

Lieutenant Calley stated that at a platoon leaders' briefing later in the evening Captain Medina reemphasized "that under no circumstances would we let anyone get behind us, nor would we leave anything standing in these villages."

The next morning at LZ Dottie, according to appellant, he was told by Captain Medina "to hang on to some of the Vietnamese in case we encountered a mine field," and "that everybody in that area would be the enemy and everyone there would be destroyed, all enemies would be destroyed."

Lieutenant Calley testified that during his movement through My Lai (4) he received and made several radio transmissions to Captain Medina. When he reached the eastern part of the village, Captain Medina called to ask what he was doing. Appellant continued:

"I told him I had some bunkers up here to check out—that I wanted to check, and that I had that small portion of the hamlet to the southeast, and also there was still a lot of enemy personnel I still had with me. — ... he told me to hurry up and get my people moving and get rid of the people I had there that were detaining me."

Appellant said that after he first encountered PFC Meadlo with a group of people and returned to Sergeant Bacon's location, he received another call from his company commander asking "why I was disobeying his order." His remembrance of Captain Medina's reply to his explanation of what was slowing him down was the specific order, "to waste the Vietnamese and get my people out in line, out in the position they were supposed to be."

On cross examination Lieutenant Calley indicated some confusion as to when he first saw the Vietnamese who were slowing his progress. He also admitted that he didn't describe these people to Captain Medina, except perhaps as Vietnamese or VC, and that he knew these people were slowing him down because "anytime you are moving Vietnamese people, you will be moving slowly." Lieutenant Calley denied knowing if any of the persons detained by his platoon were women and children, and claimed to have discriminated between sexes only when he stopped Dennis Conti from molesting a female.

Captain Medina, who was called as a witness at the request of the court members, gave a different version of his remarks to the company on the eve of the operation:

"The briefing that I conducted for my company was that C Company had been selected to conduct a combat assault operation onto the village of My Lai (4) beginning with LZ time 0730 hours on the morning of the 16th of March, 1968. I gave them the enemy situation, intelligence reports where the 48th VC Battalion was located in the village of My Lai (4). I told them that the VC Battalion was approximately, numbered approximately 250 to 280 men and that we would be outnumbered approximately two to one, and that we could expect a hell of a good fight and that we probably would be engaged. I told them that even though we were outnumbered that we had a double coverage of gunships that were being provided and that the artillery was being placed onto the village and that this would help make up for the difference in ratio between the enemy forces and our company. I told the people that this would give them a chance to engage the 48th VC Battalion, that the 48th VC Battalion was the one that we had been chasing around the Task Force Barker area of operation, and that we would finally get a chance to engage them in combat, and that we would be able to destroy the 48th VC Battalion. . . . The information that I gave also in the briefing to the company was that the 48th VC Battalion was located at the village of My Lai (4), and that the intelligence reports also indicated that the innocent civilians or noncombatants would be gone to market at 0700 hours in the morning. That this was one reason why the artillery preparation was being placed onto the village at 0720 hours with the combat assault LZ time 0730 hours. I did not make any reference to the handling of prisoners."

Captain Medina recalled that someone at the company briefing asked, "Do we kill women and children," and that his reply was, "No, you do not kill women and children. You must use common sense. If they have a weapon and are trying to engage you, then you can shoot back, but you must use common sense." He remembered instructing during the briefing:

> ". . . that Colonel Barker had told me that he had permission from the ARVN's at Quang Ngai to destroy the village of My Lai (4), and I clarified this by saying to destroy the village, by burning the hootches, to kill the livestock, to close the wells and to destroy the food crops."

Captain Medina conceded mentioning to Lieutenant Calley before lift-off "to utilize prisoners to lead the elements through the mine fields." Any congruence between their testimony in regard to communications between them ends here. Although Captain Medina acknowledged that he called the first platoon leader to inform him of the implementation of a contingency plan and so to spread his men out, he denied that Lieutenant Calley ever told him that he had bunkers to check out or that he was having difficulty in handling civilians or that the first platoon had encountered a large number of civilians. Captain Medina further disclaimed that he ever gave an order to the appellant "to move civilians out of the way or get rid of them." He stated he was never informed that the first platoon had gathered women and children and did not know the circumstances under which the inhabitants of My Lai (4) were killed. He came to the pile of bodies at the trial after the killings.

Both appellant and Captain Medina had high stakes in the acceptance of their testimony. Their testimony is not only mutually conflicting, but each conflicts with other witnesses. Of the many witnesses who attended Captain Medina's briefing to C Company on 15 March, no two had precisely the same recollection of his remarks about treatment of noncombatants during the operation, if any were recalled. The only recollection in common is that members of the unit did not expect noncombatant residents of the village to be there the next day. They expected instead to encounter elements of the 48th VC Battalion, their mission being to destroy it. Three defense witnesses interpreted Captain Medina's answer to a question whether women and children were to be considered as enemy as an affirmative directive to kill them. About twenty prosecution and defense witnesses had no recollection of any briefing directive to kill women and children. Whoever are correct, it is important to place Captain Medina's briefing remarks in the context of everyone's anticipation that the insertion of the ground force into My Lai (4) would be resisted by fire from elements of an enemy battalion. Appellant's testimony that during the operation Captain Medina ordered him by radio to kill villagers is not corroborated by the evidence given by third persons. The two radio operators for Captain Medina recalled no orders of that tenor being communicated by him. One had no recollection either way; the other testified positively that no order to kill or waste went over the unit net to Lieutenant Calley. Further, appellant said he ordered the squad leader Sergeant Bacon to search the bunkers which were mentioned in the first purported Medina-Calley radio conversation; and saw and spoke with Sergeant Bacon both before and after the second, telling him at that time where to deploy his squad. Sergeant Bacon, who had previously been called as a defense witness, denied having any contact with or communication from appellant at any of these times.

If the members found that appellant fabricated his claim of obedience to orders, their finding has abundant support in the record. If they found his claim of acting in obedience to orders to be credible, he would nevertheless not automatically be entitled to acquittal. Not every order is exonerating.

The trial judge's instructions under which he submitted the issues raised by evidence of obedience to orders were entirely correct. After fairly summarizing the evidence bearing on the question, he correctly informed the members as a matter of law that any order received by appellant directing him to kill unresisting Vietnamese within his control or within the control of his troops would have been illegal; that summary execution of detainees is forbidden by law. A determination of this sort, being a question of law only, is within the trial judge's province. Article 51(b), UCMJ, 10 U.S.C. § 851(b); paragraph 57b, Manual, supra.

The instructions continued:

"The question does not rest there, however. A determination that an order is illegal does not, of itself, assign criminal responsibility to the person following the order for acts done in compliance with it. Soldiers are taught to follow orders, and special attention is given to obedience of orders on the battlefield. Military effectiveness depends upon obedience to orders. On the other hand, the obedience of a soldier is not the obedience of an automaton. A soldier is a reasoning agent, obliged to respond, not as a machine, but as a person. The law takes these factors into account in assessing criminal responsibility for acts done in compliance with illegal orders.

"The acts of a subordinate done in compliance with an unlawful order given him by his superior are excused and impose no criminal liability upon him unless the superior's order is one which a man of ordinary sense and understanding would, under the circumstances, know to be unlawful, or if the order in question is actually known to the accused to be unlawful."

Judge Kennedy amplified these principles by specifying the burden of proof and the logical sequence for consideration of the questions to be resolved. The members were told that if they found beyond reasonable doubt that appellant actually knew the orders under which he asserted he operated were illegal, the giving of the orders would be no defense; that the final aspect of the obedience question was more objective in nature, namely, that if orders to kill unresisting detainees were given, and if appellant acted in response thereto being unaware that the orders were illegal, he must be acquitted unless the members were satisfied beyond reasonable doubt that a man of ordinary sense and understanding would have known the orders to be unlawful.

* * *

Judge Kennedy's instructions were sound and the members' findings correct. An order of the type appellant says he received is illegal. Its illegality is apparent upon even cursory evaluation by a man of ordinary sense and understanding. . . . The [defense] argument is essentially that obedience to orders is a defense which strikes at mens rea; therefore in logic an obedient subordinate should be acquitted so long as he did not personally know of the order's illegality. Precedent aside, we would not agree with the argument. Heed must be given not only to subjective innocence-through-ignorance in the soldier, but to the consequences for his victims. Also, barbarism tends to invite reprisal to the detriment of our own force or disrepute which interferes with the achievement of war aims, even though the barbaric acts were preceded by orders for their commission. Casting the defense of obedience to orders solely in subjective terms of mens rea would operate practically to abrogate those objective restrainst which are essential to functioning rules of war. The court members, after being given correct standards, properly rejected any defense of obedience to orders.

We find no impediment to the findings that appellant acted with murderous mens rea, including premeditation. The aggregate of all his contentions against the existence of murderous mens rea is no more absolving than a bare claim that he did not suspect he did any wrong act until after the operation, and indeed is not convinced of it yet. This is no excuse in law.

VI—DISCOVERY AND SUBPOENAS

VII—PETITION FOR NEW TRIAL

* * *

Accordingly, the Petition for a New Trial is denied.

VIII—SENTENCE

* * *

These general circumstances, and mitigating factors personal to Lieutenant Calley, were specifically considered by the convening authority who substantially reduced the confinement portion of the sentence to twenty years.

No doubt Lieutenant Calley would never have directed or participated in a mass killing in time of peace. Nevertheless, he committed an atrocity in time of war and it is in the context of war that we judge him. Destructive as war is, war is not an occasion for the unrestrained satisfaction of an individual soldier's proclivity to kill. An officer especially must exert his mind to keep his emotions in check, so that his judgment is not destroyed by fear, hate, or frustration. Probably Lieutenant Calley's judgment, perception, and stability were lesser in quality than the average lieutenant's and these deficiencies are mitigating to some extent. However, the deficiencies did not even approach the point of depriving him of the power of choice. The approved sentence is not too severe a consequence of his choosing to commit mass murder.

The findings and sentence are affirmed.

Senior Judge VINET and Judge CLAUSE concur.

Points for Discussion

1. Which facts in the *Calley* case support the defense of obedience to orders? Do you think Lieutenant Calley had a justification of obedience to orders? Why or why not?

2. Captain Medina, Lieutenant Calley's immediate superior was one of four officers, nine enlisted soldiers, and twelve officers (involved in the cover up) charged; of the twenty-five charged, Lieutenant Calley was the only one convicted, the others were acquitted, such as Captain Medina, or their charges were dismissed. Jeffrey F. Addicott & William A. Hudson, Jr., *Twenty-Five Anniversary of My Lai: Time to Inculcate the Lessons*, 139 Mil. Rev. 153, 160-61 (1993). As the *Calley* court notes, Lieutenant Calley received a sentence from a panel of six officers that included confinement at hard labor for life but the convening authority reduced his sentence to include twenty years confinement at hard labor. Was Calley's sentence of confinement at hard labor for a period of twenty years excessive? Subsequent to the convening authority's action, the Secretary of the Army reduced Lieutenant Calley's sentence to ten years confinement at hard labor and a dismissal, but Lieutenant Calley only served three years under house arrest at Fort Benning, Georgia, and six months at Fort Leavenworth, Kansas, and was released when a federal district judge overturned his case. *Id.* A federal court of appeals reinstated the conviction, but Calley was allowed to remain on parole. *See Calley v. Callaway*, 519 F.2d 184, 190-91 (5th Cir. 1975). President Nixon issued Calley a limited presidential pardon.

14-2. Duress

Unlike some civilian criminal jurisdictions, the defense of necessity (i.e., a defense in which the accused justifies his conduct as the "lesser of two evils" when a situation arises and an accused believes that his actions are necessary to avoid other harm with no alternative that would have caused lesser harm) is not recognized in the military. *See United States v. Banks*, 37 M.J. 700 (A.C.M.R. 1993). *But see United States v. Rockwood*, 52 M.J. 98 (C.A.A.F. 1999). The defense of coercion or duress, however, is recognized in the military. This defense exists if an accused participates in an offense (except killing an innocent person) due to "a reasonable apprehension that [he] or another innocent person would be immediately killed or would immediately suffer serious bodily injury if the accused did not commit the act." R.C.M. 916(h). This reasonable, well-grounded fear of death or serious bodily injury must occur throughout the commission of the offense and the defense does not apply if the accused has a "reasonable opportunity to avoid committing the act without subjecting the accused or another innocent person to the harm threatened . . . ." *Id.* The duress defense only applies while the reasonably grounded fear exists, and an AWOL accused may only have this defense during part of the AWOL period charged. *See United States v. Le,* 59 M.J. 859 (Army Ct. Crim. App. 2004). Also, the duress defense is not acceptable for an accused who disobeys a valid military order to perform a dangerous military duty. *See United States v. Talty,* 17 M.J. 1127 (N.M.C.M.R. 1984).

Points for Discussion

1. If a service member refuses to get his anthrax vaccine, thereby disobeying a lawful order of a superior officer, and claims that he has a well-grounded fear of death or serious bodily injury, does he have a valid assertion of the defense of duress? *See United States v. Washington,* 54 M.J. 936 (A.F. Ct. Crim. App. 2001), *aff'd* 58 M.J. 129 (C.A.A.F. 2003).

2. On August 20, 2003, Army Lieutenant Colonel Allen W. West learned from an intelligence specialist of a plot to ambush his unit and assassinate him at a location north of Baghdad in Iraq. The information implicated Yehiya Kadoori Hamoodi, an Iraqi police officer, who was promptly detained. When Hamoodi refused to offer information, Colonel West fired his weapon near Hamoodi's head to frighten him, an action which prompted the Iraqi to speak. No one was physically hurt, and there was no ambush. Colonel West subsequently was given non-judicial punishment. He retired from the Army and successfully ran for Congress. *See* Deborah Sontag, *How Colonel Risked His Career By Menacing Detainee and Lost,* N.Y. Times, May 27, 2004, at A1. What offense might Colonel West have been charged with? Under what circumstances, if any, might he have a defense of duress?

14-3. Mental Responsibility

The service member facing charges has several opportunities to raise issues regarding his mental health. As discussed in Chapter 7, Pretrial Motions and Interlocutory Appeals, an accused must be mentally competent to stand trial. *See* R.C.M. 909(a) and (b) (capacity to stand trial). Also, the accused's mental health may be a mitigating or extenuating circumstance for the defense to raise during the presentencing phase of the court-martial. *See* R.C.M. 1001(f)(2)(B) (providing that the "court-martial may consider— . . . [e]vidence relating to any mental impairment or deficiency of the accused). The results of a "sanity board" (as described in Chapter 7) may be used by defense counsel to present matters for consideration for both mental competency and mental health issues to be presented during sentencing.

The defense counsel may also use the mental evaluation of the accused to present the affirmative defense that the accused lacked mental responsibility, if at the time of the commission of the criminal act "as a result of a severe mental disease or defect was unable to appreciate the nature and quality or the wrongfulness of the acts." UCMJ Article 50a(a), 10 U.S.C. § 850a(a). *See also* R.C.M. 916(k)(1) & (k)(3)(A) (affirmative defense of lack of mental responsibility); R.C.M. 1203(c)(5) (capacity to understand or cooperate intelligently in appellate proceedings). The accused is presumed responsible and the defense has the burden to establish the accused's lack of mental responsibility by clear and convincing evidence. R.C.M. 916(k)(3)(A). The panel deliberates on findings and if the panel finds the accused guilty of an offense, the panel must then vote to determine whether the defense has been proven by clear and convincing evidence that the accused is not guilty by reason of lack of mental responsibility. *Id.*

Although a mental condition that does not amount to a lack of mental responsibility is not an affirmative defense, *see* R.C.M. 916(k)(2), an accused may be allowed to present evidence of that condition to show that he did not have the requisite state of mind (*mens rea*) element of the offense, *see id.* discussion.

The two cases that follow illustrate how mental health issues may be raised at the appellate level. In evaluating the mental health issues, the court in each case explains the interplay between the lack of capacity to stand trial and the defense of lack of mental responsibility.

UNITED STATES v. ESTES
Army Court of Criminal Appeals
62 M.J. 544 (2005)

SCHENCK, Senior Judge:

A military judge sitting as a special court-martial found appellant Private First Class Jonathan B. Estes, U.S. Army] guilty, pursuant to his pleas, of absence without leave (AWOL) (two specifications), wrongful use of marijuana (three specifications), and wrongful use of cocaine and methylenedioxymethamphetamine (MDMA)[ecstasy] (one specification each), in violation of Articles 86 and 112a, Uniform Code of Military Justice, 10 U.S.C. §§ 886 and 912(a) [hereinafter UCMJ]. The convening authority approved the adjudged sentence to a bad-conduct discharge, confinement for four months, forfeiture of $737.00 pay per month for four months, and reduction to Private E1. This case is before our court for review pursuant to Article 66, UCMJ, 10 U.S.C. § 866.

Appellant asserts his guilty plea was not knowing and voluntary because he had a severe mental disease or defect at the time of his criminal conduct, and his mental disease or defect undermined his trial rendering it fundamentally unfair. Appellant argues that if the military judge inquired about his mental health issues—prompted by remarks appellant made during his unsworn statement—the military judge would have ordered a sanity board. Appellant further claims he did not provide facts sufficient to sustain his plea of guilty to one AWOL specification because appellant did not admit he was absent from his unit, but instead, told the military judge he remained in the barracks during his absence. We find both assignments of error to be without merit.

APPELLANT'S MENTAL DISEASE OR DEFECT
Facts

Appellant pleaded guilty to, and was found guilty of, two AWOL specifications in violation of Article 86, UCMJ, and five drug-use specifications in violation of Article 112a, UCMJ, 10 U.S.C. § 912a, for using marijuana, cocaine, and MDMA on various occasions over a five-month period. Nothing inconsistent with appellant's guilty plea was raised during the providence inquiry.

In his unsworn statement during presentencing, appellant spoke extensively about his spiritual development which started during the summer of 1996. He explained he had found God, recognized himself as a sinner, and knew God would forgive him. Appellant stated he had been reading the Bible and had become wiser. Appellant further stated:

> In fact, it was August the 6th, 1996; I believe that was the day I got saved. And that day, you know, I found God. I know I found God because you know when you find God. You find it in your heart. You feel it. I'm sure you do. And that day, you know, I knew I was going to sin again, and I knew that God would forgive me for my sins. . . .

Thereafter, the military judge did not inquire into or explain to appellant the defense of lack of mental responsibility, nor did he ask appellant if he had discussed the defense with counsel.

Initial Appeal and First Sanity Board

On 30 April 2003, appellant filed a brief with this court claiming in his only assignment of error that his plea to the second AWOL specification was improvident. On 31 October 2003, while awaiting action on this appeal, appellant requested, pursuant to Rule for Courts–Martial [hereinafter R.C.M.] 1203, that our court order an inquiry into both his mental responsibility and mental capacity in accordance with R.C.M. 706.[2] On 10

---

[2] Rule for Courts–Martial 706 authorizes an inquiry to determine: (1) whether a soldier was mentally responsible for his offenses at the time he committed them, and/or (2) whether a soldier has the mental capacity, at trial, to understand the nature of the court-martial proceedings against him and to cooperate intelligently in his own defense. The procedures set forth in R.C.M. 706 apply to inquiries before and during trial, and to inquiries after trial proceedings have ended when a question arises concerning a soldier's mental capacity to understand and cooperate

December 2003, we granted this request and ordered a sanity board to answer specific questions regarding appellant's mental responsibility at the time of his offenses, and his mental capacity to participate and assist in his defense at trial and during the appellate process.

On 23 March 2004, a board consisting of one psychiatrist and two psychologists reported that appellant "appears to be dependent on cannabis at the present time and likely has either a substance induced psychotic disorder or schizoaffective disorder, depressive type." Notwithstanding this diagnosis, the board determined that, at the time of trial, appellant was able to understand the nature of the proceedings and to cooperate intelligently in his defense. It also determined that at the time of his criminal conduct, appellant was able to appreciate the nature and quality or wrongfulness of his conduct. The board further concluded, as a result of his mental condition, appellant was "unable to understand the nature of the appellate proceedings [and] to cooperate intelligently in his pending appeal."

On 4 October 2004, based on the first sanity board's conclusion that appellant could not assist in his appeal because of his severe abuse of illegal drugs, this court stayed appellate proceedings and ordered appellant restored to active duty to receive medical treatment. *See* R.C.M. 1203(c)(5); *see also United States v. Korzeniewski*, 22 C.M.R. 104, 107 (C.M.A. 1956) (holding that a finding of lack of mental capacity tolls proceedings at any stage of the appellate process). We further directed the government to arrange for a new sanity board to examine appellant after completion of his medical treatment to determine his competency to assist in his appeal. We directed that this second board consist of three members, including at least one psychiatrist.

Second Sanity Board

During the months following our October 2004 stay of appellate proceedings, appellant received mental health treatment. He then appeared before a second sanity board which reassessed his condition. On 7 December 2004, the second sanity board, consisting of only one member, a psychiatrist, reported that appellant "suffers from a most serious and severe mental disorder." The board further found, "this disorder does not render him incapable of understanding the nature of the proceedings before him." The board concluded appellant was able to "cooperate appropriately in his appeal" and "understand the nature of the appeal process."

We did not ask the second sanity board for an opinion regarding appellant's competency at the time of trial or responsibility at the time of his offenses; therefore, the board made no express findings on these subjects. But the board made three statements appellant considers relevant to this appeal. First, the board identified "hyper-religiosity of thinking" as one of the manifestations of his illness. Second, the board stated, "Current Psychosocial and Environmental Problems are determined to be of longstanding duration,

---

intelligently in the court-martial appeal process. *See* R.C.M. 909(c); R.C.M. 916(k)(1) discussion; R.C.M. 1203(c)(5).

i.e., months prior to and including his violations under the UCMJ." Third, the board reported that "his thought and substance use disorder came to [override] his appreciation of right and wrong." Although the second sanity board, consisting of only a psychiatrist, did not meet the court-ordered composition requirements, we will still consider its report because the board's composition did fulfill the R.C.M. 706(c)(1) requirements that a sanity board consist of "one or more persons" and "at least one . . . psychiatrist."

Third Sanity Board

Recognizing the second sanity board's composition did not meet the requirements of our October 2004 order, the government requested additional time to convene a three-member board to reevaluate appellant. On 6 January 2005, we granted the government's motion for an extension of time. Thereafter, a third sanity board consisting of the requisite number of members convened and reevaluated appellant in February 2005.

On 28 February 2005, a third sanity board, composed of three psychiatrists and one psychologist, concluded, as did the second sanity board, that appellant suffers from a serious mental disorder, but is competent to assist in his appeal. The third sanity board repeated verbatim the second sanity board's findings that appellant is currently schizophrenic (manifested by "hyper-religiosity of thinking"), suffers from "polysubstance dependence" ("repeated use of . . . cannabis, cocaine and hallucinogens"), and possesses other character traits of "relatively longstanding duration." The third sanity board also found appellant experienced social and environmental problems "of longstanding duration."

Law and Discussion

Appellant now asserts his guilty plea was improvident, i.e., not knowing and voluntary, because "he had a severe mental disease or defect at the time of his criminal conduct that impaired his ability to understand the nature and consequences or wrongfulness of his actions," possibly affording him the defense of lack of mental responsibility. *See* UCMJ art. 45, 10 U.S.C. § 845; R.C.M. 916(k)(1); *United States v. Cortes–Crespo*, 13 M.J. 420, 421 (C.M.A. 1982). Appellant further asserts that, although no one mentioned "appellant's mental disease" at the time of trial, the military judge "had one clue that appellant had severe paranoid schizophrenia: appellant's unsworn statement." Appellate defense counsel cite appellant's religious statements described above, and state they are "consistent with" the second and third sanity boards' conclusions that appellant's disease is manifested by, among other things, his religiosity. We reject this argument.

Whether the Military Judge Erred by Failing to Inquire into Appellant's Mental Responsibility, Discuss the Possibility of the Affirmative Defense, and Satisfy Himself that the Defense Did Not Apply

We review a military judge's acceptance of a guilty plea for an abuse of discretion. . . .

Should an accused set up a matter inconsistent with his plea at any time during the proceeding, "the military judge must either resolve the apparent inconsistency or reject the guilty plea." . . .

The military justice system presumes that all soldiers are sane and competent and, therefore, responsible for their actions. *See* R.C.M. 909(a) and (b) (capacity to stand trial); R.C.M. 916(k)(1) and (k)(3)(A) (affirmative defense of lack of mental responsibility at time of offense); R.C.M. 1203(c)(5) (capacity to understand or cooperate intelligently in appellate proceedings). Although an appellant has the burden of proving lack of mental responsibility for his offenses or lack of mental capacity to stand trial, the standard of proof for each differs. First, the defense bears the burden of proving, by *clear and convincing evidence,* that an accused was unable to appreciate the nature and quality or the wrongfulness of his offenses, *at the time he committed them,* because he suffered from a severe mental disease or defect, i.e., he lacked mental responsibility at the time of his crimes. *See* UCMJ art. 50a(b), 10 U.S.C. § 850a(b); R.C.M. 916(k)(1) and (k)(3)(A).[4] Second, the defense bears the burden of proving, by a *preponderance of the evidence,* that an accused was suffering from a severe mental disease or defect *at trial* which rendered him unable to understand the nature of the proceedings against him or to cooperate intelligently in the defense of his case, i.e., he lacked the mental capacity to participate in his court-martial. *See* R.C.M. 909(e)(2).[5] Third, the defense also bears the burden of proving, by a *preponderance of the evidence,* that an appellant is suffering from a severe mental disease or defect *at the time of his appeal* which renders him unable to understand and to conduct or cooperate intelligently in the appellate proceedings, i.e., he lacks the mental capacity to appeal his convictions. *See* R.C.M. 1203(c)(5).

---

[4] Generally, once the affirmative defenses listed in R.C.M. 916 are raised by the evidence at trial, the government bears the burden of proving beyond a reasonable doubt that the particular defense is not valid or has not been proven in a particular case. However, for the R.C.M. 916(k) affirmative defense of lack of mental responsibility at the time of the offense, there is no shift in burden and the defense bears the burden of proving each element of this defense by clear and convincing evidence.

[5] Unlike the affirmative defense of lack of mental responsibility at the time of the offense, R.C.M. 909 addresses a soldier's mental capacity to stand trial by court-martial. Lack of mental capacity is a procedural defense which prevents or postpones the trial until the accused recovers from his mental disease or defect and can understand and cooperate in his own defense. The defense also bears the burden of proving this procedural defense, but by a preponderance of the evidence.

Our superior court has also recognized certain responsibilities borne by the convening authority, military judge, and the parties. In *United States v. Best,* 61 M.J. 376 (C.A.A.F. 2005), the court stated:

We have emphasized the responsibility of the convening authority and the military judge to order a sanity board when required, as well as the duty of all participants in the process to bring to the attention of the convening authority or military judge any condition or behavior that may reasonably call into question the mental responsibility or competence of an accused. *United States v. Collins,* 60 M.J. 261 (C.A.A.F. 2004).

Id. at 382.

If a question arises regarding the mental responsibility of an accused, R.C.M. 916(k)(3)(B) requires the military judge to either "order [a R.C.M. 706 inquiry into the mental capacity or mental responsibility of the accused,] or satisfy himself that the defense team has fully evaluated the possibility of the affirmative defense." *United States v. Sims,* 33 M.J. 684, 686 (A.C.M.R. 1991).

Appellate defense counsel now assert that, based upon appellant's remarks during his unsworn statement, "the military judge should have inquired of the trial defense counsel whether he had determined if any mental [health] issues existed or if there was a history of mental illness." Furthermore, they contend that after such an inquiry, "a sanity board would surely have been ordered at the time of trial" by the military judge.

We recognize that sometimes remarks made in an unsworn statement should indicate to a military judge that an accused may have a defense of lack of mental responsibility (or insanity) and warrant further inquiry. In *Sims,* for example, we held that the military judge should not have accepted a guilty plea when the accused "explained in an unsworn statement that he had a friend named Corporal Myers that no one else could see or hear," heard voices he did not "have any control over," and was not aware of what he was doing when he took another soldier's money. *Id.* at 685–86.

But we must review the military judge's decision to accept appellant's guilty plea for an abuse of discretion. *See Eberle,* 44 M.J. at 375. Appellant did not raise matters in his unsworn statement concerning his mental state that were inconsistent with his pleas of guilty to AWOL and wrongful use of controlled substances. Having examined appellant's entire unsworn statement, we see nothing that should have indicated to the military judge that appellant might have had a defense based on lack of mental responsibility. Appellant's unsworn statement merely expresses a strong religious sentiment, remorse at having done wrong, and gratitude for forgiveness. We do not conclude that the military judge should have suspected mental illness or a mental responsibility defense based upon these comments. Moreover, the military judge cannot be expected to reject a guilty plea "on the mere possibility of a defense." . . . Therefore, we conclude the military judge did not abuse his discretion by failing to inquire further.

Whether this Court Should Conclude Appellant's Pleas Were Improvident Based on the Sanity Boards' Reports

Unlike the military judge, this court has before it three sanity board reports. In deciding whether appellant's pleas may have been improvident, based on his mental condition either when he committed the offenses or at trial, we may consider these reports even though appellant did not raise the issue of mental responsibility at trial. . . . Furthermore, if appellant's mental condition constituted a "severe mental disease or defect" at the time of the offense that caused him to be "unable to appreciate the nature and quality or the wrongfulness" of his acts, appellant may have had an affirmative defense. R.C.M. 916(k)(1); *see Thompson v. United States,* 60 M.J. 880, 884 (N.M. Ct. Crim. App. 2005).

However, as our superior court has directed, "unless the results of the sanity board give reason to believe that at a rehearing the factfinder would be persuaded to accept the accused's affirmative defense [of a lack of mental responsibility], there is no occasion to order a rehearing." *Massey,* 27 M.J. at 374. The Court of Appeals for the Armed Forces "has made plain that to constitute reversible error, the existence or outcome of a sanity board must have had a substantive effect on the trial." *Best,* 61 M.J. at 382–83. Moreover,

> to prevail on appeal an accused must convince an appellate court that a "different verdict might reasonably result" if the trier of fact had evidence of a lack of mental responsibility that was not available for consideration at trial.

Id. at 383 (quoting *United States v. Breese,* 47 M.J. 5, 6 (C.A.A.F. 1997)). We hold this threshold has not been crossed.

The first sanity board is the only board that specifically addressed the question of whether, at the time of his criminal conduct, appellant was unable to appreciate the nature and quality or wrongfulness of his conduct as a result of his mental disease or defect. The first sanity board is also the only board that specifically addressed the question of whether, at the time of his trial, appellant was unable to understand the nature of the proceeding or unable to cooperate intelligently in his defense as a result of his mental disease and defect. Significantly, the first sanity board answered both of these questions in the negative. These conclusions strongly suggest that if we were to remand this case for a rehearing, the factfinder would not accept appellant's defense of lack of mental responsibility based upon the first sanity board's clinical psychiatric diagnosis of "Cannabis Abuse" at the time of appellant's offenses. *See Thompson,* 60 M.J. at 884 (similarly concluding that although the accused established he was incompetent at the time of appeal, he failed to demonstrate he lacked mental responsibility at the time of his criminal conduct or mental competency at the time of trial).

The second and third sanity board reports do not directly contradict, or report anything inconsistent with, the first board's assessment. The first board found appellant predominantly suffered from "Cannabis Abuse" at the time he committed the charged offenses (December 2001 through May 2002), and with "Cannabis Dependence" at the time the board convened in March 2004. The first sanity board found appellant mentally responsible for his offenses and capable of participating in his court-martial that had occurred twenty months earlier. It was not until December 2004, nine months after the first sanity board's diagnoses and twenty-nine months after appellant's August 2002 court-martial, that the second sanity board found appellant was currently suffering from "Schizophrenia, Paranoid Type" and "Polysubstance Dependence." In February 2005, the third sanity board made the same findings. Although the second and third boards concluded appellant was competent to understand the appellate process and participate in the proceedings, they made no conclusions concerning appellant's mental responsibility at the time of his offenses or his mental capacity at trial, nor did they find appellant's schizophrenia or polysubstance dependence existed at the time of the offenses or at trial.

The third sanity board further found, as did the second, that the only personality disorders appellant exhibited which were "of relatively longstanding duration" were:

> mixed personality traits and ego defense mechanisms . . . an obsessive style of thinking . . . compulsive behavior . . . impulsivity . . . lack of concern . . . [and] behavior [that is] often inflexible [and] perseverative . . . .

Contrary to the defense assertion, we are not persuaded these additional findings equate to a determination that appellant lacked mental responsibility at the time he committed his offenses. Nor are we persuaded that at a rehearing a finder of fact would be convinced these additional findings translate directly into a successful defense of lack of mental responsibility. [6]

---

[6] The first sanity board found appellant exhibited general "Occupational Problems, Problems related to interaction with legal system/crime." The second and third sanity boards elaborated, and found appellant currently suffered from "psychosocial and environmental problems . . . of a longstanding duration, i.e., months prior to and including his violations under [the] UCMJ." Appellate defense counsel assert the statement, that appellant's "thought and substance use disorder came to [override] his appreciation of right and wrong" is tantamount to the second and third boards finding appellant lacked mental responsibility at the time of his offenses. We disagree. Reading this clause in context with the larger paragraph from which it was extracted, the third sanity board appears to be commenting on an unauthorized absence. Although the comment refers to appellant "again departing Fort Bragg," we do not find the comment refers to appellant's second charged AWOL offense. Appellant told the military judge during the providence inquiry he never left Fort Bragg during the period 7 June 2002 through 11 June 2002, his second period of absence. The referenced unauthorized absence may relate to conduct for which appellant was not charged and which occurred during an unknown time.

In this situation, as appellant argues, these reports *may raise the possibility* that a subsequent finder of fact might conclude appellant's mental condition had "an impact on, and perhaps was a major contributing factor to, his criminal conduct." But that is not the standard for ordering a rehearing under *Massey*. As noted above, the standard is whether these sanity board reports "give reason to believe that at a rehearing the factfinder would be persuaded to accept the accused's affirmative defense." *Massey*, 27 M.J. at 374. In view of the specific findings of the first sanity board, that standard has not been met.

Our superior court specifically rejected an alternative lower standard that would allow a rehearing merely "if the sanity inquiry should '*cast doubt upon*' the accused's 'mental responsibility when [he] commit[ed] the offenses.'" *Id.* (quoting *United States v. Massey*, 26 M.J. 671, 673 (A.F.C.M.R.1988)). That is all that has occurred here, and it is not enough. As our superior court's prescribed standard in *Massey* clearly reflects, there is a balance between the policy of giving an accused every possibility to present a defense and the competing policies of efficiency of litigation and finality of judgments.

For the foregoing reasons, we find appellant possessed the requisite mental responsibility and capacity when he committed his offenses, at trial, and during the appellate process. Moreover, appellant said nothing inconsistent during the providence inquiry or in his unsworn statement to render his pleas improvident.

IMPROVIDENT PLEA TO AWOL SPECIFICATION

Facts

Appellant pleaded guilty to, and was found guilty of, unauthorized absence from his unit, to wit: A Company, 51st Signal Battalion (Airborne), Fort Bragg, North Carolina, located at Building H–6308, from on or about Friday, 7 June 2002 until on or about Tuesday, 11 June 2002 (Specification 2 of Charge I), in violation of Article 86, UCMJ. During the providence inquiry, he told the military judge that, during his four-day absence, he slept late in the unit barracks located at Building H–5412, missed several formations, and wandered around post (going to the mess hall and shoppette) without reporting to his unit. The stipulation of fact, agreed to by both parties and admitted into evidence, merely restates the specification without providing any factual description of the offense. Appellant admitted he understood the elements and definitions of the offense as the military judge explained to him, and that, taken together, they accurately described what he did.

At trial, the following colloquy ensued between the military judge and appellant:

MJ: Where were you supposed to be on 7 June?

ACC: Reporting to formations, Your Honor.

MJ: And where did you go?

ACC: I didn't go anywhere, Your Honor. I just—I stayed in my barracks.

MJ: And where was your barracks?

ACC: Hotel–5412, off of Semaphore.

MJ: Is that where the unit is located too, or is that a different location?

ACC: It's—that's the location of where the unit is also, Your Honor.

MJ: Okay. So the 7th of June was a Friday. You just didn't go to work Friday morning?

ACC: I didn't go to work at all, Your Honor.

MJ: The 11th of June was a Tuesday. You went back to work on Tuesday. You just took a long weekend then?

ACC: Yes, Your Honor.

MJ: Where did you go?

ACC: I didn't go anywhere. I just—

[Pause.]

MJ: Stayed in the barracks?

ACC: Yes, Your Honor.

. . . .

MJ: Well, did you stay in your barracks room that entire time? Did you float around post, or what did you do?

ACC: I floated around post a little bit; the chow hall and stuff, maybe the shoppette. But I didn't go anywhere in particular. . . .

. . . .

MJ: So what time was formation on the 7th of June, 0600 or 0630?

ACC: 0630, I believe, Your Honor.

MJ: And you just didn't show up?

ACC: Yes, Your Honor.

MJ: You slept in and just kind of goofed off the rest of the day?

ACC: Yes, Your Honor.

MJ: You did that all weekend, sort of goofed off, stayed around and just didn't do much of anything?

ACC: Yes, Your Honor.

MJ: And Monday was, sort of, the same thing?

ACC: Yes, Your Honor.

MJ: And what time did you go back to work on Tuesday, the 11th?

ACC: I believe I made formation, Your Honor.

MJ: So those 4 days, what were you supposed to be doing? Was the unit off, or were they in [the] field, or what was the unit doing?

ACC: They were busy working. I don't know exactly what they were doing, Your Honor.

MJ: They were busy working and you were busy goofing off?

ACC: Yes, Your Honor.

MJ: Did you understand that you were supposed to be at your place of duty?

ACC: Yes, Your Honor.

. . . .

MJ: Okay. So between the 7th of June and the 11th of June, you were supposed to be in the unit doing something—doing something constructive?

ACC: I could have been doing something constructive at the unit, sir.

MJ: Well, you should have been at formations; at PT formation on the 7th of June?

ACC: Yes, Your Honor.

MJ: And then after PT formation showed up to another formation, at perhaps 0900?

ACC: Yes, Your Honor.

MJ: Some sort of work call formation?

ACC: Yes, Your Honor.

MJ: Then you'd have some sort of duties to do?

ACC: Yes, Your Honor.

MJ: Would you have another formation, perhaps after lunch or, in the afternoon, before you were released?

ACC: In the afternoon, before I was released, Your Honor.

MJ: There would be another formation?

ACC: Yes, Your Honor.

MJ: Did you make any of those formations?

ACC: No, Your honor.

Appellant told the military judge he was not working in any particular position at his unit, but admitted he should have been reporting to formations, did not have permission to stop performing military duties, and purposely avoided working and contacting his chain of command.

Law and Discussion

We again review the military judge's acceptance of appellant's guilty plea for an abuse of discretion, *Eberle,* 44 M.J. at 375, and will not overturn the military judge's acceptance thereof unless the record of trial shows a substantial basis in law and fact for questioning it. . . .

Article 86(3), UCMJ, provides, "Any member of the armed forces who, without authority . . . absents himself or remains absent from his unit, organization, or place of duty at which he is required to be at the time prescribed; shall be punished as a court-martial may direct.". . .

* * *

. . . An "[u]nauthorized absence under Article 86(3) is an instantaneous offense. It is complete at the instant an accused absents himself or herself without authority." *Id.* at Part IV, para. 10c(8). The duration of the absence is not an essential element of the offense but constitutes a matter in aggravation for purposes of determining the authorized maximum punishment. *See id.* at Part IV, paras. 10c(4) and 10c(8).

Appellate defense counsel now assert appellant's guilty plea to AWOL from 7 June 2002 to 11 June 2002 was improvident because appellant did not admit during the plea inquiry that he was "ever absent from his unit." Appellate government counsel agree the plea inquiry does not support the offense of AWOL (in violation of Article 86(3), UCMJ) but urge us to affirm the closely-related offense of failure to go to an appointed place of duty (in violation of Article 86(1), UCMJ). We decline to accept the government concession and find appellant's plea provident to the offense as charged.

We base our decision, in part, upon principles found in *United States v. Vaughn,* 36 M.J. 645 (A.C.M.R. 1992). In *Vaughn,* Private (PVT) Vaughn pleaded guilty to being AWOL from his unit for approximately twenty days. He told the military judge he was supposed to have been at an accountability formation and did not report in order to avoid going to a field exercise. Instead, PVT Vaughn stayed in his barracks room: Our court found that although PVT Vaughn "remained in his room and in the unit area," *id.* at 647, he was AWOL from his unit because his fellow soldiers were "in the field participating in . . . an exercise." *Id.* at 648. Furthermore, we found PVT Vaughn's mere casual presence in the barracks was not inconsistent with his plea of guilty to AWOL for the period charged. *Id.; cf. United States v. LaCaze,* 2 C.M.R. 443, 1952 WL 1755 (A.B.R.1952) (affirming desertion conviction for quitting organization with intent to avoid hazardous duty where soldier absented himself from his unit's forward combat area and remained in his tent near unit rear command post).

Appellate defense counsel argue appellant was not absent from his unit because he remained in the unit barracks.[7] However, the essence of

---

[7] Appellate defense counsel rely upon our sister court's position in *United States v. Skoff,* 1990 CMR LEXIS 1008 (N.M.C.M.R. 2 Oct. 1990) (unpub.). *See United States*

appellant's offense was that he was not present with his fellow soldiers, i.e., his "unit," performing military duties during the work day. During the providence inquiry, appellant admitted he missed all formations on Friday, 7 June 2002, did not go to work all day, and stayed in his barracks room until he returned to duty on Tuesday, 11 June 2002. Appellant admitted his unit was performing military duties without him, and he understood he was supposed to be working with the unit but was busy "goofing off" in the barracks. Although unsure of what his unit was actually doing, appellant stated his unit was working, and he "could have been doing something constructive at the unit" had he not been absent and in the barracks. When the military judge asked appellant whether he intentionally avoided going to the unit to work, appellant answered affirmatively. Appellant stated he purposely missed formations and did not let anyone in his chain of command know he was in his barracks room available to perform any assigned duties.

Appellant's agreement that his barracks building is located "where the unit is also" is of no consequence. Appellant was charged with an unauthorized absence from his unit located at building H–6308, and admitted he remained in the barracks at building H–5412, or elsewhere, from Friday until Tuesday. In all likelihood, these buildings were collocated, and appellant admitted the unit was not in the barracks building. Nevertheless, the building where a unit is normally located may not be the unit's physical location. For example, if a unit is in formation behind the post theater, or conducting training at a confidence course, or participating in a field exercise at a staging area, the unit location will be any of these particular places, not its headquarters.

A unit is comprised of soldiers, not buildings.[9] It is irrelevant that a soldier's barracks room happens to be within the "company area" or under

---

v. Smith, 37 M.J. 583, 586 (N.M.C.M.R.1993) (stating servicemember who remains in barracks that are part of, and controlled by, his assigned unit cannot be absent without authority from that unit). We decline to take our sister court's position that ownership or control of a barracks building is the determining factor in whether a soldier is absent from his unit while remaining in those barracks. *Id.* at 586–87 ("The question is not simply whether an accused, who is charged with absence from his unit, is assigned to a tenant activity or the host installation when he or she remains in the barracks rather than reporting for or remaining on duty. The question is which activity controls the barracks: e.g., what unit or activity assigns personnel to that barracks, posts watches in that barracks, conducts inspections, or has the responsibility for ordering maintenance and repairs.").

[9] In the military context, unit is defined as "a part of a military establishment that has a prescribed organization (as of personnel and materiel)." WEBSTER'S THIRD NEW INTERNATIONAL DICTIONARY OF THE ENGLISH LANGUAGE UNABRIDGED 2500 (1981 ed.). A unit is also "[a]ny military element whose structure is prescribed by competent authority, such as a table of organization and equipment; specifically, part of an organization." Joint Chiefs of Staff, Joint Pub. 1–02, Dep't of Def. Dictionary of Military and Associated Terms, App. A: Abbreviations and Acronyms (12 Apr. 2001) (as amended through 9 June 2004); *see* Army Reg. 310–25, Military Publications: Dictionary of United States Army Terms (Short Title: AD), para. 10 (15

unit control. Under the defense "company area" theory, a soldier required to live in the barracks could remain there, forego engaging in military duties with his fellow soldiers, and yet not be considered absent from his unit. But if the same soldier resided in off-post housing, he would be guilty of an unauthorized absence from his unit by staying at home. We reject this "company area" theory and find the military judge properly accepted appellant's plea of guilty to AWOL for the period charged.

CONCLUSION

We have considered the matters personally asserted by appellant pursuant to *United States v. Grostefon,* 12 M.J. 431 (C.M.A. 1982), and find them to be without merit.

Accordingly, the findings of guilty and the sentence are affirmed.

Judge ZOLPER and Judge WALBURN concur.

Point for Discussion

The court concludes that sanity board reports do not meet the standard for ordering a rehearing unless they "give reason to believe that at a rehearing the fact finder would be persuaded to accept the accused's affirmative defense." The standard was not met in this case. What would be examples of findings that would meet this standard?

UNITED STATES v. AXELSON
Army Court of Criminal Appeals
65 M.J. 501 (Army Ct. Crim. App. 2007)

SCHENCK, Senior Judge:

A military judge sitting as a general court-martial convicted appellant [Major Carl W. Axelson, Jr., U.S. Army], consistent with his pleas, of failure to obey a lawful general regulation and obstruction of justice, both on divers occasions, in violation of Articles 92 and 134, Uniform Code of Military Justice, 10 U.S.C. §§ 892 and 934 [hereinafter UCMJ]. An officer panel sitting as a general court-martial convicted appellant, contrary to his pleas, of attempted premeditated murder,[1] attempted willful disobedience of a superior commissioned officer, willful disobedience of a superior

---

Oct. 1983); Dep't of Army, Field Manual 101–5–1, Operational Terms and Graphics, Ch. 1 (30 Sept. 1997). Units, therefore, are comprised of people, and include soldiers organized into staffs, crews, teams, sections, squads, platoons, etc., that work and train together to accomplish operational missions irrespective of their location.

[1] Appellant pleaded guilty to the lesser-included offense of aggravated assault with a dangerous weapon or other means or force likely to produce death or grievous bodily harm. *See Manual for Courts–Martial, United States* (2000 ed.) [hereinafter *MCM,* 2000], Part IV, para. 43d(2)(b) and 54b(4)(a). All references in this opinion are to the *MCM,* 2000 edition, in effect at the time of appellant's trial, unless otherwise specified.

commissioned officer on divers occasions (two specifications), and obstruction of justice on divers occasions, in violation of Articles 80, 90, and 134, UCMJ, 20 U.S.C. §§ 880, 890, and 934. The convening authority approved the adjudged sentence to a dismissal, confinement for seven years, and forfeiture of all pay and allowances. This case is before our court for review under Article 66(c), UCMJ, 10 U.S.C. § 866(c).

Appellant raises several assignments of error; two—involving his lack of memory—merit discussion but no relief. Specifically, appellant asks our court to set aside the findings of guilty of attempted premeditated murder. First, appellate defense counsel assert relief is warranted because appellant's statements during the plea inquiry and subsequent defense evidence on the merits, including appellant's testimony, raised the defenses of partial mental responsibility and automatism. Furthermore, because the military judge did not explain or discuss these defenses with appellant, appellant's guilty pleas to aggravated assault with a dangerous weapon or other means or force likely to produce death or grievous bodily harm were not "knowing." Second, the defense asserts the military judge erred because he failed to sua sponte instruct the panel regarding the defense of automatism.

We disagree with both assertions of error. In so doing, we hold a military judge's responsibilities regarding affirmative defenses are limited to those listed in Rules for Courts–Martial [hereinafter R.C.M.] 916 ("Defenses") and 920 ("Instructions on Findings"), and to those recognized by this court and our superior courts. These responsibilities apply to guilty plea inquiries *and* to instructions in contested cases. We also hold partial mental responsibility is not a defense to aggravated assault with a dangerous weapon or other means or force likely to produce death or grievous bodily harm. The defense of partial mental responsibility rebuts a specific intent *mens rea* element, such as purposeful, knowing, or premeditated, which this offense lacks under the UCMJ.

I. FACTS

Appellant pleaded guilty to aggravated assault with a dangerous weapon or other means or force likely to produce death or grievous bodily harm, in violation of Article 128, UCMJ, 10 U.S.C. § 928. Following trial on the merits for the greater charged offense, an officer panel convicted appellant of the attempted premeditated murder of his wife by repeatedly striking her about the head, face, and neck with a club (Charge I and its specification).

This charge arose after appellant beat his wife with a club while he and his family were in the hills overlooking Athens, Greece. Although some inconsistencies regarding the facts were presented during trial on the merits, and despite appellant's initial statement to police—that two unknown individuals attacked his wife—it is undisputed that appellant was the attacker. On 6 June 2001, at around 1800, appellant, his wife, and their two infant sons, three-month-old CA and fifteen-month-old JA, drove to the countryside near the Voulas Mountains to take photographs. After appellant stopped the vehicle, his wife went around the vehicle to check on CA, who was in a car seat behind the driver. Appellant took a baton from the driver's door and struck Mrs. Axelson several times. At some point thereafter, bicyclists rode by while Mrs. Axelson lay on the ground beside the vehicle with appellant bent over his wife's body.

Providence Inquiry

During the *Care* inquiry, the military judge accurately explained to appellant the elements of aggravated assault with a dangerous weapon or other means or force likely to produce death or grievous bodily harm, and appellant agreed his conduct satisfied each element. Appellant admitted he beat his wife with a club, with unlawful force or violence, and he used the club as a means or force in a manner likely to produce death or grievous bodily harm. The parties proceeded to discuss the factual predicate supporting this offense without the benefit of a stipulation of fact.

Appellant agreed he did bodily harm to his wife "with a certain weapon or a means or a force by repeatedly striking her about the face, head, and neck with a club," fifteen or sixteen inches long made out of solid wood. The military judge reminded appellant: "[Y]our counsel has indicated that you intend to raise a defense that essentially denies having what the law calls the *mens rea*, the specific intent to either premeditate as to a killing, to intend to kill, or to intend to deliberately or intentionally and purposely inflict grievous bodily harm. Is that correct?" Appellant responded, "Exactly, sir."

After discussing with appellant the meaning of unlawful force or violence and grievous bodily harm, the type of weapon appellant used, how he used it, and the injuries Mrs. Axelson suffered, the military judge engaged appellant in the following colloquy:

MJ: Now, you struck this blow apparently repeatedly, is that right?

ACC: I do not remember that part, sir. I remember once when I realized what was happening.

MJ: Have you heard or seen other reports or indications that there may have been more than one blow?

ACC: Considering I was the only person there, sir, and—yes, sir. I've seen reports.

MJ: You're satisfied then that[,] . . . [h]aving seen those reports, do you believe those are accurate descriptions of what has occurred to her, such that you believe that you did in fact[,] even though you might not personally remember it now, strike her repeatedly?

ACC: Yes, sir.

Subsequently, when describing the obstruction of justice offense (for reporting false information regarding the assault on his wife), appellant stated he parked the vehicle and his wife came around the vehicle to quiet their infant son, CA. Appellant said he walked away, and when he "turned around, [CA] was quiet, and at that time, from what [he] was seeing, [he] believed that [CA] was in danger." He said he believed his wife was holding a pillow over CA's face, and, upon "seeing that," appellant became upset. Appellant then told the military judge, "seeing that and getting upset is the point where [he could not] remember. . . . From after that point, the next thing [he could] recall [was his wife] on the ground and [him] hitting her and the sounds and the noise. And, at that point, [appellant] stopped."

Appellant admitted he read his wife's statement, which described him striking her with the baton/club repeatedly about the head, face, and neck, and believed her statement and report to be truthful. Appellant agreed he and his defense counsel discussed pleading guilty based on reports or statements without completely recollecting the offense. Appellant remembered seeing his wife holding a pillow over CA's head, but his next recollection was seeing his wife "laying on the ground" and "hitting her with the club or baton." The following discussion then ensued:

> MJ: There is a perception. There is a gap. The memory comes back to see her on the ground and he's hitting her, whether it's one of multiple blows, and then stops.
>
> ACC: Just one.
>
> MJ: After she's on the ground.
>
> ACC: Yes, sir.
>
> MJ: So, that's your recollection though?
>
> ACC: That's all I can remember, sir.

At the end of the plea inquiry, appellant again affirmatively acknowledged to the military judge that he understood the elements of the offenses to which he was pleading guilty, the non-applicability of "defense of another," and had no questions regarding these elements. Appellant also expressed satisfaction that each element accurately described his conduct pertaining to each offense, and reaffirmed that "defense of another" did not constitute a legal justification for aggravated assault—even though appellant originally perceived his son to be "in some potential mortal danger."

Trial on the Merits

Following the guilty plea inquiry, both parties presented extensive evidence on the merits regarding the contested offenses to which appellant pleaded not guilty—attempted premeditated murder, attempted willful disobedience of a superior commissioned officer, willful disobedience of a superior commissioned officer on divers occasions (two specifications), and obstruction of justice on divers occasions.

The evidence showed that on the evening of 6 June 2001, appellant drove his wife of one and a half years and their two sons to a scenic, yet secluded, mountainous region to take photos. During the months leading up to the charged offenses, appellant had been engaging in an adulterous affair with "Maria," a Bulgarian national and freelance travel writer.

According to Mrs. Axelson, appellant stopped the vehicle in the shade at one point and told her to check on CA who was in a rear-facing car seat behind appellant. Appellant said he saw "a little red spot" behind the child's ear. Mrs. Axelson went around the vehicle to CA's side, leaned into the vehicle, and checked CA's ears.

She further told the panel:

My husband pinned me down, and at first, he was choking me with his hands, and then eventually with the baton, and then all of a sudden, he stopped. While he was doing that, his facial expression totally deteriorated. It wasn't like him at all. When I looked in his eyes, I could see his toes; that's how much emptiness I saw. It was like he was in a [trance], and like he didn't even recognize me.

Mrs. Axelson described the baton appellant used to attack her as a "black standard edition police nightstick." She also told the panel that while appellant was striking her, he said: " 'You are driving me crazy,' and 'You are ruining my life and I just can't have it anymore.' " When appellant stopped the attack and "snapped out of it," he picked up his wife from the ground outside the vehicle and put her on the front passenger seat floor "curled up in a fetal position."

Appellant then drove with his family between fifteen and thirty minutes to their residence. When they arrived, appellant helped Mrs. Axelson from the vehicle up to their third-floor apartment using the elevator. He brought her inside, removed her clothing, put her in the bathtub, and briefly tended to her wounds. Appellant then went downstairs to get his two sons who were still in the truck. He put them in a playpen when he returned to the apartment. When appellant left to get the boys from the truck, Mrs. Axelson crawled to the telephone, called the U.S. Embassy, and told the receptionist she had "been beaten real badly" and to "send a doctor and the security folks." Initially, she did not remember that her husband was the assailant. Several days after the attack, Mrs. Axelson called the Air Force Office of Special Investigations (AFOSI) and told an agent she was afraid for herself and her two sons because appellant attacked her.

Doctor (Dr.) Trego, who treated Mrs. Axelson during the ambulance ride from a public to a private hospital, testified that due to the assault, Mrs. Axelson lost eleven of her thirty-two teeth, and suffered lacerations, swelling to her lips, and a torn gum line. She also had a bruised and fractured neck, and a crushed trachea (which would require forty pounds of steady force applied for twenty to twenty-five seconds). The victim sustained multiple anterior and posterior cerebral contusions resulting from "a significant degree of force." She also had multiple deep lacerations about the head and face (some down to the bone), resulting from "a significant amount of force" that "literally splits and separates the scalp." Mrs. Axelson also lost approximately four units of blood. Other testimony indicated appellant struck his wife at least eight or nine times with the baton.

In a 10 June 2001 written, sworn statement, appellant initially told investigators, in pertinent part, he stopped his truck to take family photos. He and his older son went for a walk—about 100 yards down the road from, and out of view of, the truck—to get clear photos of Sounio; meanwhile, his wife and younger son stayed near the truck in the shade. Appellant said he and his son immediately returned to the vehicle when he heard what sounded like screams. As he approached the truck, appellant saw one unknown man attacking his wife with a baton, while another was in the truck apparently searching for something. Appellant then got into a scuffle with the man attacking his wife and attempted to take the baton away from him. The man overpowered appellant, pushed him to the ground, and both unknown men fled the scene leaving Mrs. Axelson and the boys terrified and screaming. Appellant then tended to his hysterical wife's injuries. After calling out to some bicyclists for help and deciding what to do next, appellant finally got the whole family into the vehicle and drove home.

During his testimony on the merits, appellant said when he and his family were driving in the mountains on the day of the assault, CA was "crying," his older son, JA, was "whimpering," and he told his wife: "I'm not going anywhere until you quiet [CA] down;" he then "walked away from the truck." When he did not hear CA crying anymore, appellant turned around and he "could see that [his wife] was holding . . . [an] aircraft pillow . . . over [CA's] head." Appellant said that seeing that, and hearing "no noise," made him become "just so scared." He further told the panel he "just [could not] remember what happened next," and "[t]he next memory [he had was of his] wife [on] the ground, and [he] was hitting her with the club, and [he] hit her in the mouth, and [he]'ll never forget the noise . . . and the blood." Later in his testimony, appellant reiterated: "[T]he first thing I remember is the sound, or hitting her in the mouth and the sound and just seeing that blood." Later, when the military judge asked appellant, "[A]re you certain in your own mind then that you at some point had the club in your hand?" appellant responded, "Yes, sir, because I can remember—the first thing, the only thing I can remember at that point is actually going down and hitting her in the mouth . . . with the club."

Doctor (Major) Fey, a mental health clinical psychiatrist, subsequently testified for the defense and stated appellant has suffered from "obsessive/compulsive [disorder (OCD)] . . . for most, . . . if not all[,] of his adult life." Appellant suffered from "generalized anxiety disorder [(GAD)] for a period of [six to seven] months prior to [attacking his wife]." Doctor Fey said appellant was a workaholic who was quiet, withdrawn, controlling, lacked self-esteem, generally did not find pleasure in life, and vomited to relieve stress. Civilian defense counsel then asked Dr. Fey the following questions regarding the defense strategy.

> Q. Well, and, again, to clarify for the court members what we're not raising here. We're not raising . . . an issue of mental responsibility at the time of the act.

A. Right.

Q. In terms of the classic sanity defense.

A. . . . I do not believe he had any mental conditions that would effect his state of mind to be able to premeditate long term.

Q. That would impair—

A. Right. Exactly. . . . [W]hat I'm saying is that there's no psychotic disorder. I don't believe that his obsessive/compulsive personality . . . , his generalized anxiety disorder affected his ability to premeditate from a long-term perspective . . . . [H]is mental state is not a very big issue.

. . .

Q. Was he able to formulate the specific intent to kill at that time?

A. . . . He describes walking away from the car. At this point, he's irritable. Most people would probably be feeling frustrated, perhaps even angry and would recognize that.

. . . .

A. . . . I'm certainly not suggesting that Major Axelson assaulted his wife because his babies were crying; however, I think the jury must consider, considering that Major Axelson has testified that his wife put a pillow on top of the child's head, I think the jury must consider that it . . . could be an impetus to break open, from a metaphoric standpoint, a dam, so he turns around, the child is suddenly not crying. . . . I believe that the jury must consider that this was the impetus and that Major Axelson was in such a state of mind, perhaps rage, that he did not have the capacity to form the intent to kill his wife.

Q. Now, what about this, and I'm going to use the term amnesia, this period of time that he says he has no recollection of what he did?

. . . .

A. . . . I am not a lie detector. It is possible, and the jury must consider that Major Axelson is faking amnesia. Other alternatives are that *he had some medical condition, organic condition, that affected his ability to lay down memories.* I do not believe that that's an issue either. He was not intoxicated. *He did not have any sort of seizure.* He did not have a head injury, et cetera, so I don't believe that there is any reason that he couldn't lay down memories . . . . [Emphasis added.]

. . . .

A. . . . [T]he most important factors that I would consider are, [first,] did his wife have a pillow in front of [CA]'s face[,] because if she did not, I do not believe that there would be such an impetus to bring about an attack of rage like that. . . . The second thing is[,] did he premeditate for longer than just seconds[,] because if he didn't, it comes down to[,] did he premeditate for seconds or did he not have the capacity to premeditate or form intent

. . . . Also, did he lure her up to that hill? Did he lure her out of the car with a rash or was she attending to [CA] to pacify him?

. . . .

A. . . . It's not certain to me why Major Axelson would recall the last hit or part of the assault. That is not clear to me. I think the fear that he was feeling then continued into I would say a state of panic at that point. If you're inclined to believe that Major Axelson is not faking amnesia, at this point, he must have been a very confused individual. His bleeding and battered wife is lying on the ground. He has got a stick in his hand. At this point, I think he was in panic mode.

. . . .

Q. . . . In fact, just within a few hours after his wife was hospitalized, the evidence shows that he was communicating with Maria [by email]. How . . . do you factor that [into] his disorders you described, the obsessive/compulsive disorder, the generalized anxiety disorder?

A: Well, I mean, if you're inclined to believe that he's premeditated and that his plans were to kill his wife, perhaps kill [CA], and establish some kind of life [with] Maria, then one has to interpret those e-mails in that way, but if one is inclined to maybe, whether it's true or not, it doesn't surprise me that an individual[ ] that's generally relying on his relationship with Maria, and again, part is real, part is fantasy. It would not surprise me that that individual would be in contact as a means of dealing with his present problems.

During an Article 39(a), UCMJ, hearing held subsequent to Dr. Fey's testimony, the military judge denied trial counsel's request to release the full R.C.M. 706 sanity board report to the government for use in rebutting appellant's defense.[6] Civilian defense counsel again clarified the defense strategy, stating: "[W]e are putting on a defense to specific intent. It does not shift the burden to the defense . . . ." When the military judge asked, "If in my instructions, I were to limit the characterization of [your defense] to [: 'T]he evidence in this case has raised an issue [of] whether the accused had a character disorder[,'] would that suffice as an instruction in your view?" and "So, you're not seeking mental disease, defect, impairment, condition, deficiency, or behavior disorder?" civilian defense counsel agreed.

---

[6] In response to the military judge's questions, civilian defense counsel agreed the defense was not pursuing a defense of mental disease, defect, impairment, condition, deficiency, or behavior disorder. *See* Military Rule of Evidence [hereinafter Mil. R. Evid.] 302(c) (authorizing release of full sanity board report to rebut defense of lack of mental responsibility); *see also United States v. Benedict,* 27 M.J. 253, 261 (C.M.A. 1988) ("[W]e conclude that a report from a sanity board established pursuant to . . . R.C.M. 706 . . . is not a report of 'opinions or diagnoses . . . kept in the course of a regularly conducted business activity' or that it 'was the regular practice of that business activity to make the . . . report.' *See* Mil.R. Evid. 803(6).") (fourth and fifth alterations in original).

Jury Instructions

Elements

Prior to trial on the merits, the military judge told the jury, with civilian defense counsel's concurrence,[7] that appellant had "entered pleas of guilty" to: (1) "the lesser[-]included offense [of] aggravated assault with a dangerous weapon or a means or force likely to produce death or grievous bodily harm" with respect to attempted premeditated murder (the Specification of Charge I); (2) obstruction of justice (redesignated as Specification 1 of Charge III); and (3) failing to obey a lawful general regulation (the Specification of Additional Charge II) for "wrongfully using his government computer and/or government internet access and/or electronic mail account for viewing, downloading, storing, transferring, sending, and receiving pornography."

The military judge further informed the panel:

I conducted what the law calls a providence inquiry, and I've entered findings of guilty as to the Additional Charge II offense and Specification 1 of Charge III. The government is going to go forward and attempt to prove up the greater offense of attempted premeditated murder in Charge I and its Specification and go forward as [to] all the offenses for which Major Axelson has [pleaded] not guilty, and so those are the issues that are pending before you today, but the defense wanted you to know that he's [pleaded] guilty to that lesser[-]included offense in Charge I as well as to those other two offenses.

The military judge provided the panel (upon its request) with tailored, written instructions regarding the elements of the contested offenses, and told the panel:

---

[7] Since this a mixed-plea case, we must distinguish between facts appellant provided the military judge during the plea inquiry, and those he presented to the members in his testimony on the merits. During the providence inquiry, the military judge correctly explained, and appellant agreed, "that the elements or facts [he was] admitting ... [regarding the] lesser[-]included offense of aggravated assault could be used by the government to assist them in proving up the attempted premeditated murder offense as it was originally charged." *See United States v. Gilchrist*, 61 M.J. 785, 794 (Army Ct. Crim. App.2005) (citing *United States v. Caszatt*, 29 C.M.R. 521, 523 (C.M.A. 1960) (stating guilty plea may "be used to establish facts and elements common to both the greater and lesser offense within the same specification")); *United States v. Ramelb*, 44 M.J. 625, 628–29 (Army Ct. Crim. App.1996) (quoting *United States v. Dorrell*, 18 C.M.R. 424, 425, 1954 WL 2742 (N.B.R.1954) ("It is long-settled judicial policy that while a plea of guilty constitutes a judicial confession of guilt to a particular offense and is considered the strongest proof of guilt under the law, such plea 'admits *only* what has been charged and pleaded to.' ... [I]t may not be used to prove a separate offense.")); *but see United States v. Wahnon*, 1 M.J. 144, 145 (C.M.A. 1975) (stating guilty plea to one charge may not be used as evidence to establish separate charge to which plea of not guilty was entered).

The decision you have now is that the accused is presumed innocent. . . . And, you should also know that as to many of these offenses, and in particular this first offense, the attempted premeditated murder charge, there [are] a number of potential lesser[-]included offenses . . . . You know this much. That the accused [pleaded] guilty to a lesser[-]included offense of aggravated assault with a weapon[ ], means, or force likely to produce death or grievous bodily harm, in violation of Article 128[, UCMJ]. So, that's the bottom level, and that's already been established by his plea of guilty.

In advising the panel on the lesser-included offense of aggravated assault by *intentionally inflicting grievous bodily harm,* the military judge informed the panel:

> Now, as to the second element; that is, that the accused did so by repeatedly striking her about the head, face, and neck with a club, if you find the first element to be proven beyond a reasonable doubt, then the cause of those injuries as described in the second element has been established by the accused's provident plea of guilty to a lesser[-]included offense of aggravated assault with a weapon or a means or force likely to produce death or grievous bodily harm. . . . Additionally, the grievous bodily harm must have been intentionally caused by the accused. . . .

Specific Intent and Premeditation

The military judge told the panel it had to find appellant specifically intended to kill or injure his wife to find him guilty of certain lesser-included offenses other than the aggravated assault (with a dangerous weapon) to which appellant pleaded guilty. He also explained appellant presented evidence regarding his mental health to refute a specific intent *mens rea* element of the charged offense and the lesser-included offenses, and not as proof of a lack-of-mental-responsibility defense. The military judge also told the panel:

> [T]he evidence in this case has raised an issue about whether the accused has a character or personality disorder and the required state of mind with respect to the offenses of attempted premeditated murder, attempted unpremeditated murder, attempted voluntary manslaughter, or aggravated assault by intentionally inflicting grievous bodily harm. You must consider all the relevant facts and circumstances in the evidence before you. One of the elements of these offenses is the requirement of premeditation of the design to kill, and the specific intent to kill [Mrs.] Axelson or the intent to kill her in the heat of sudden passion caused by adequate provocation or the specific intent to inflict grievous bodily harm.
>
> An accused, because of some underlying character or personality disorder, may be mentally incapable of entertaining or formulating the premeditated design to kill, and/or the specific intent to kill a particular named person, here, [Mrs.] Axelson, or the intent to kill her in the heat of

sudden passion caused by adequate provocation or the specific intent to inflict grievous bodily harm upon her. . . .

The burden of proof is upon the government to establish the guilt of the accused by legal and competent evidence beyond a reasonable doubt, [and,] unless, in light of all the evidence, you are satisfied beyond a reasonable doubt that the accused, at the time of the alleged offense for which you find him guilty[,] was mentally capable of entertaining or formulating . . . the specific intent to kill . . . [or] to inflict grievous bodily harm . . ., you must find the accused not guilty of any of those offenses or lesser[-]included offenses in Charge I and its Specification.

Now, this evidence was not offered to demonstrate or refute whether the accused is mentally responsible for his conduct. Lack of mental responsibility; that is, an insanity defense, is not an issue in this case. . . . You may consider evidence of the accused's mental condition before and after the alleged offense and its lesser[-]included offenses . . . , as well as evidence as to the accused's mental condition on the date of the alleged offense. The evidence as to the accused's condition before and after the alleged offense was admitted for the purpose of assisting you to determine the accused's condition on the date of the alleged offense.

II. GUILTY PLEA TO AGGRAVATED ASSAULT

Appellate defense counsel now assert appellant's guilty plea was improvident to aggravated assault with a dangerous weapon or other means or force likely to produce death or grievous bodily harm. The defense argues appellant's statements during the plea inquiry and subsequent defense evidence on the merits, including appellant's testimony, raised the defenses of partial mental responsibility and automatism. Appellant's guilty plea was not "knowing," the defense contends, because the military judge was required to, but did not, explain or discuss these defenses with appellant. We disagree.

* * *

Failure to recall facts pertaining to an offense does not preclude an accused from pleading guilty, nor does it render improvident an accused's guilty plea. *United States v. Moglia,* 3 M.J. 216, 218 (C.M.A. 1977). If an accused "is convinced of his guilt[,] . . . personal awareness is not a prerequisite for a plea of guilty, but, rather, an inquiry must be made to ascertain if an accused is convinced of his own guilt. Such a conviction . . . may be predicated on an accused's assessment of the [g]overnment's evidence against him." *Id.* (internal citations omitted). As long as amnesia does "not preclude him from intelligently cooperating in his defense or taking the stand on his own behalf . . . [and] his amnesic condition [does not] impair his ability to rationally examine and assess the strength of the [g]overnment's evidence against him," an accused may knowingly and voluntarily plead guilty. *United States v. Barreto,* 57 M.J. 127, 130 (C.A.A.F. 2002) (internal citation omitted); *see also United States v. Proctor,* 37 M.J. 330, 336–37 (C.M.A. 1993) (military judge did not err by finding accused mentally competent to stand trial despite accused's delusional psychosis "that God would deliver him from being sentenced"); *United States v. Olvera,* 15 C.M.R. 134, 142 (C.M.A. 1954) (stating amnesiac "still quite competent to assume the witness stand, and to assure the court that he does not remember—and he is certainly able to analyze rationally the probabilities of his having committed the offense"); *Wilson v. United States,* 391 F.2d 460, 463–64 (D.C. Cir. 1968) (setting forth six factors to consider in assessing amnesic defendant's capacity to participate in fair and accurate trial). "When, as here, an accused cannot recall all of the circumstances surrounding his crimes, he may still plead guilty so long as he or she is personally convinced of his guilt and is willing to admit that guilt to the military judge." *United States v. Corralez,* 61 M.J. 737, 741 (A.F. Ct. Crim. App. 2005) (citing *Moglia,* 3 M.J. at 218), *pet. denied,* 63 M.J. 191 (C.A.A.F. 2006).

* * *

Assault with a Dangerous Weapon or Other Means or Force Likely to Produce Death or Grievous Bodily Harm

Aggravated assault with a dangerous weapon or other means or force likely to produce death or grievous bodily harm (as defined in the UCMJ) is an offense that does not include a specific intent *mens rea* element, but includes a physical component. *See* UCMJ art. 128(b)(1); *MCM,* 2000, Part IV, para. 54b(4)(a); *see also United States v. Redding,* 34 C.M.R. 22, 24 (C.M.A. 1963) ("Assault with a dangerous weapon . . . is not a specific intent offense. Rather, it is a general intent crime which may be committed even by a drunken assailant."). The requisite elements are:

(i) That the accused attempted to do, offered to do, or did bodily harm to a certain person;

(ii) That the accused did so with a certain weapon, means, or force;

(iii) That the attempt, offer, or bodily harm was done with unlawful force or violence; and

(iv) That the weapon, means, or force was used in a manner likely to produce death or grievous bodily harm.

MCM, 2000, Part IV, para. 54b(4)(a)(i)-(iv).

Attacking Mens Rea: Partial Mental Responsibility

Rule for Courts–Martial 916 sets forth special or affirmative defenses "which, although not denying that the accused committed the objective acts constituting the offense charged, den[y], wholly or partially, criminal responsibility for those acts." R.C.M. 916(a). These defenses include but are not limited to justification, obedience to orders, self-defense (including defense of others), accident, entrapment, coercion or duress, inability, ignorance or mistake of fact, and lack of mental responsibility. R.C.M. 916(c)-(k). An accused may also raise voluntary intoxication, *see* R.C.M. 916(1)(2), or partial mental responsibility (as discussed below) [10] to refute a specific intent *mens rea* element of an offense.

Rule for Courts–Martial 916(k) distinguishes between the defense of lack of mental responsibility at the time of the offense, *see* R.C.M. 916(k)(1),[11] and

---

[10] Rule for Courts–Martial 916(k)(2) and discussion. "The [UCMJ] has never identified a defense of 'partial mental responsibility.' " *United States v. Mansfield*, 38 M.J. 415, 419 (C.M.A. 1993). But the *MCM*, 1969 (Rev. ed.), para. 120c., stated: "*A mental condition, not amounting to a general lack of mental responsibility* (120b), which produces a lack of mental ability, at the time of the offense, to possess actual knowledge or to entertain a specific intent or a premeditated design to kill, *is a defense to an offense having one of these states of mind as an element*." (Emphasis added.) Thus, partial mental responsibility was recognized as a defense for the first time in the *MCM*, 1969. *See* Dep't of Army, Pam. 27–2, Analysis of Contents, Manual For Courts–Martial, United States 1969, Revised Edition, Chpt. 24 (28 July 1970) and cases cited therein. The *MCM*, 1984 became effective on 1 August 1984. Rule for Courts–Martial 916(k)(2) within the *MCM*, 1984 mirrored the language found in para. 120c. of the *MCM*, 1969. *See* Exec. Order No. 12473, 49 Fed.Reg. 17152 (Apr. 23, 1984). Subsequently, on 14 November 1986, Congress enacted Article 50a, UCMJ, ostensibly dispensing with the defense of partial mental responsibility. *See* National Defense Authorization Act for Fiscal Year 1987, Pub.L. No. 99–661, § 802(a)(1), 100 Stat. 3816, 3905 (codified in 10 U.S.C. § 850a(a)). On 9 March 1987, the President amended R.C.M. 916(k)(2) to reflect the enactment of Article 50a(a), UCMJ, indicating that partial mental responsibility *was not* a defense and prohibiting the admissibility of evidence of a mental condition not amounting to a full lack of mental responsibility "as to whether the accused entertained a state of mind" required for the offense. Exec. Order No. 12586, 52 Fed.Reg. 710 (Mar. 9, 1987); *see also Ellis v. Jacob*, 26 M.J. 90, 91–92 (C.M.A. 1988) (describing the history of this *MCM* change). In 2005, however, R.C.M. 916(k)(2) was modified yet again. *See* Exec. Order No. 13365, 69 Fed.Reg. 71333 (Dec. 3, 2004). Although the rule now states that "[a] mental condition not amounting to a lack of mental responsibility ... is not an affirmative defense," R.C.M. 916(k)(2), the discussion states: "Evidence of a mental condition not amounting to a lack of mental responsibility may be admissible as to whether the accused entertained a state of mind necessary to be proven as an element of the offense." *Id.* at discussion. Despite this R.C.M. 916(k)(2) discussion change— providing for partial mental responsibility (or "impaired mental state") evidence in the military—the United States Supreme Court recently determined that a state does not violate due process by barring mental responsibility defenses other than insanity (the "capacity to tell whether [a criminal act] ... was right or wrong"), and prohibiting evidence to negate "the *mens rea,* or guilty mind," element (i.e., partial mental responsibility defense). *Clark v. Arizona*, 548 U.S. 735 (2006). Consequently, partial mental responsibility remains in military practice a creature of executive enactment, and not a Constitutional requirement.

[11] For the "affirmative defense of lack of mental responsibility at the time of the offense, there is no shift in burden and the defense bears the burden of proving each element of this defense." *Estes*, 62 M.J. at 549 n. 4. Prior to trial on the merits, the defense must notify the government of "its intent to offer the defense of ... lack of mental responsibility," R.C.M. 701(b)(2), and its intent "to introduce expert testimony as to the accused's mental condition." R.C.M. 916(k)(2) discussion.

evidence that amounts to a defense of partial mental responsibility (or "diminished capacity"). *See* R.C.M. 916(k)(2) and discussion. With the former, "the defense bears the burden of proving, by *clear and convincing evidence,* that an accused was unable to appreciate the nature and quality or the wrongfulness of his offenses, *at the time he committed them,* because he suffered from a severe mental disease or defect, i.e., he lacked mental responsibility at the time of his crimes." . . . If, however, the defense presents evidence not amounting to lack of mental responsibility but negating a required *mens rea* element of the offense, i.e., the defense of partial mental responsibility, the defense does not bear the burden of proof. *See Berri,* 33 M.J. at 343 n. 11; *Estes,* 62 M.J. at 549 n. 4; *United States v. Pohlot,* 827 F.2d 889, 897 (3d Cir. 1987).

In appellant's case, R.C.M. 916(k)(2) (2000 ed.), effective at the time of trial, provided that except for the defense of lack of mental responsibility, partial mental responsibility or "[a] mental condition not amounting to a lack of mental responsibility . . . is not a defense, nor is evidence of such a mental condition admissible as to whether the accused entertained a state of mind necessary to be proven as an element of the offense." Despite this R.C.M. provision, in its 1988 *Ellis* opinion our superior court determined: (1) Article 50a(a), UCMJ (and its legislative history) mirrored the federal model and lacked Congressional intent to preclude such evidence; and (2) R.C.M. 916(k)(2) was of questionable Constitutionality. *Ellis,* 26 M.J. at 92–94. On these bases, the *Ellis* Court rejected R.C.M. 916(k)(2)'s ostensible dispensation with anything less than a complete defense of lack of mental responsibility, and held that an accused may present evidence of partial mental responsibility, or evidence of mental disease, defect, or condition to attack required *mens rea* elements of offenses such as premeditation, specific intent, knowledge, or willfulness. *Id.; see also Mansfield,* 38 M.J. at 419 (finding no error where military "judge omitted a phrase [in panel instruction] indicating that appellant need not be insane in order to qualify for the defense of partial mental responsibility"); *Berri,* 33 M.J. at 338 (agreeing with lower court in finding military judge erred by giving instruction that "effectively barred the members from considering the expert evidence on *mens rea*" element); *United States v. Tarver,* 29 M.J. 605, 609 (A.C.M.R. 1989) ("[W]hen the evidence establishes a mental condition which may negate an accused's ability to entertain a required *mens rea* element of an offense, the military judge must, *sua sponte*[,] instruct."); *Pohlot,* 827 F.2d. at 903 (rejecting "government's contention that the Insanity Defense Reform Act[, upon which Article 50a is modeled,] either explicitly or implicitly bars a defendant from introducing evidence of mental abnormality on the issue of *mens rea*"). Therefore, at the time of appellant's trial, the defense of partial mental responsibility—evidence such as relevant psychiatric testimony—negating an intent element was permissible.

Except for the lack of mental responsibility defense discussed previously, "[g]enerally, once the affirmative defenses listed in R.C.M. 916 are raised by the evidence at trial, the government bears the burden of proving beyond a reasonable doubt that the particular defense is not valid or has not been proven in a particular case." *Estes,* 62 M.J. at 549 n. 4. The defense, however, may raise partial mental responsibility to negate a *mens rea* element without bearing the burden required for other affirmative defenses. *See Berri,* 33 M.J. at 343 n. 11 ("As always, the factfinder determines whether *mens rea* has been proven. If admissible evidence suggests that the accused, for whatever reason, including mental abnormality, lacked *mens rea,* the factfinder must weigh it along with any evidence to the contrary."); *Pohlot,* 827 F.2d at 897 ("[U]se of expert testimony [to attack *mens rea*] is entirely distinct from the use of such testimony to relieve a defendant of criminal responsibility based on the insanity defense or one of its variants. . . .").

Contesting Actus Reus: Automatism

Appellant asserts his trial evidence raised the defense of "automatism," which is not a recognized special or affirmative defense listed in R.C.M. 916. Automatism, or the "unconsciousness defense," is viewed in terms of *mens rea* or *actus reus,* and "thus it may be considered as relieving criminal liability either because the [accused] lacks the mental state required for approval of a crime[, e.g., specific intent, willfulness, premeditation, or knowledge], or because the [accused] has not engaged in an act—that is, in a voluntary bodily movement." Eunice A. Eichelberger, Annotation, *Automatism or Unconsciousness as Defense to Criminal Charge,* 27 A.L.R.4th 1067, § 2 (1984) (current through January 2005). A state of automatism renders a person who is capable of action "not conscious of what he is doing[, which is] equated with unconsciousness [or] involuntary action[, and] implies that there must be some attendant disturbance of conscious awareness." Wayne R. LaFave, Criminal Law 406 (3d ed. 2000) (citation omitted).

In asserting "automatism," those charged with an offense may contend they are not liable because they lack the mental state required by the criminal statute. *Id.* at 407. More correctly, an "automaton-defendant" asserts he is not guilty of an offense because his conduct was not a "voluntary bodily movement, and without [such] an act there can be no crime." *Id.* at 407–08 (internal footnote omitted). Voluntary acts do not include: "a reflex or convulsion; a bodily movement during unconsciousness[,] . . . hypnosis or . . . a bodily movement that otherwise is not a product of the effort or determination of the actor, either conscious or habitual." *Id.* at 408 n. 25.

Essentially, in raising this defense, an accused asserts that at the time he committed the offense "he was unconscious or in an automatistic state or was subject to a physical state, such as an epileptic seizure, which ordinarily entails a loss, however temporary, of consciousness." 27 A.L.R.4th 1067, § 1a. Simply because an accused "suffers from amnesia and thus cannot remember the events in question," however, is not enough. LaFave at 407.

"Clinically[,] automatism or unconsciousness has manifested itself in epileptic and postepileptic states, clouded states of consciousness associated with organic brain disease, concussional states following injuries, schizophrenic and acute emotional disturbances, [and] metabolic disorders such as anoxia and hypoglycemia, [or] drug-induced loss of consciousness . . . ." 27 A.L.R.4th 1067, § 2. Therefore, some civilian courts generally recognize the automatism defense brought about by physical conditions such as epilepsy, stroke, or physical or emotional trauma. LaFave at 406. "Mere inability to remember an event, in and of itself, [however,] cannot establish automatism, since relevant inquiry involves the accused's knowledge and control at the time of the conduct, not at the time of trial." *Sellers v. State,* 809 P.2d 676, 686–87 (Okla.Crim.App.1991), *cert. denied,* 502 U.S. 912 (1991); *see also State v. Jenner,* 451 N.W.2d 710, 721 (S.D.1990) (holding defendant's statements, that she did not remember killing her daughter and that she slept through the night while the child died, "were inadequate to require jury instruction[] on" unconsciousness; "[A]mnesia . . . is not a defense to a criminal charge.").

Although "automatic" or involuntary conduct may fall into other defenses acknowledged in the military, as appellate defense counsel concede in their pleadings to this court, military courts have not recognized the defense of automatism.[13] In 1991, our superior court recognized the defense of partial mental responsibility or "element rebuttal," but specifically stated: "What the status of unconsciousness[, i.e., automatism,] might be under the [UCMJ], we do not decide here." *Berri,* 33 M.J. at 341 n. 9, 343. Two years later, our court followed suit and, without recognizing the automatism defense, found an appellant's assertion that "he lacked the required *mens rea* due to automatic and uncontrollable behavior brought on by claustrophobia" to be without merit. *United States v. Campos,* 37 M.J. 894, 901–02 (A.C.M.R. 1993) (agreeing with government assertion that military judge was not persuaded the evidence "negated any intent elements of the offenses").

Discussion

Appellant now asserts his guilty plea to aggravated assault was not "knowing" because the military judge failed to explain or discuss the defenses of partial mental responsibility and automatism. Appellant contends these defenses were raised by his statements during the providence inquiry and

---

[13] Military courts, however, have recognized that when offenses are committed during an epileptic seizure ("fugue" or "automatistic state"), an accused may be afforded a possible defense to criminal liability. . . . An epilepsy defense must be based on

> some substantial evidence . . . tending to show that the accused was in an epileptic seizure when he performed the acts alleged, for a true epileptic seizure dethrones the reason and the condition precludes mental responsibility while it lasts. Not only does the condition deprive the actor of self-control, it also robs him of the power to remember what occurred, and would probably deprive him of the capacity to distinguish right from wrong. The characteristic effect is loss or clouding of the consciousness and automatic behavior, an impairment of all the functions which endow man with the capacity for rational action and choice.

United States v. Burke, 28 C.M.R. 604, 610, 1959 WL 3523 (A.B.R.1959).

during subsequent defense evidence on the merits, including appellant's testimony. We disagree and hold that regardless of appellant's statements and the defense evidence, the military judge had a responsibility to address only defenses recognized in the military justice system and defenses to the offenses to which appellant pleaded guilty.

First, partial mental responsibility was not a defense available to appellant because he pleaded guilty to aggravated assault with a dangerous weapon or other means or force likely to produce death or grievous bodily harm. This general intent offense under the code lacks a specific intent *mens rea* element, such as willfulness or premeditation. Since partial mental responsibility rebuts only a specific intent *mens rea* element, appellant could not have asserted that defense to aggravated assault, and the military judge did not have a responsibility to explain or discuss this defense with appellant. Thus, appellant's ostensible partial mental responsibility or diminished capacity did not render improvident his guilty plea to this type of aggravated assault. . . .

Second, nothing appellant stated during his providence inquiry or on the merits suggested a possible defense to this aggravated assault. The military judge discussed with appellant the concept of "defense of another," and appellant aptly agreed it did not apply under the circumstances. The military judge was under no obligation to explore other potential defenses, i.e., automatism, not raised during the plea inquiry or on the merits. *See Phillippe,* 63 at 310–11 (stating that when "circumstances raise a possible defense, a military judge has a duty to inquire further"). Furthermore, automatism is not a defense listed in R.C.M. 916 or recognized by military law. Appellant did not show how, if at all, his amnesia or failure to remember his misconduct related to, or was part of, a greater physical condition amounting to a recognized defense, i.e., an epileptic seizure or other like "automatistic state." 27 A.L.R.4th 1067, § 1a. On the merits, Dr. Fey testified that appellant exhibited what amounted to character or personality disorders—not any type of seizure at the time of the attack—and stated: "I do not believe [appellant] had any mental conditions that would [have affected] his state of mind to be able to premeditate . . . ." Moreover, although appellant said he could not remember a portion of the attack upon his wife, appellant was "personally convinced of his guilt," *Corralez,* 61 M.J. at 741, able to evaluate the government's evidence against him, and able to "intelligently cooperate[ ] in his defense." *Barreto,* 57 M.J. at 130. Therefore, we find nothing raised by appellant during the plea inquiry or on the merits inconsistent with his guilty plea. Appellant's guilty plea to aggravated assault was "knowing." We now turn to appellant's averments regarding panel instructions.

III. TRIAL ON THE MERITS

Appellate defense counsel now assert the military judge improperly instructed the panel regarding findings. The defense specifically argues that "[t]he military judge . . . instructed the panel that appellant's guilty plea admitted certain elements of the greater offense of attempted premeditated murder. The guilty plea allowed the panel to reject appellant's testimony on its face and conclude that the fact of an intentional act was already established." In attacking the *actus reus* element of appellant's guilty plea to aggravated assault, the defense states in its reply brief: "The issue whether appellant acted voluntarily was more fundamental than his specific intent. . . ." The defense also asserts the military judge erred when he failed to sua sponte instruct the panel regarding the defense of automatism. We disagree with both assertions.

Law

Instructions

* * *

Our superior court has recently held: "A military judge has a sua sponte duty to give certain instructions when reasonably raised by the evidence, even though the instructions are not requested by the parties.". . .

* * *

Prior Guilty Pleas: Informing Members and Use on the Merits

In a case involving a mixed plea,

> in the absence of a specific request made by the accused on the record, members of a court-martial should not be informed of any prior pleas of guilty until after findings on the remaining contested offenses are made. This rule is long-standing and embodied in the [Dep't of Army, Pam. 27–9, Legal Services: Military Judges' Benchbook, para. 2–5–4 (1 Apr. 2001)], R.C.M. 910(g), R.C.M. 913(a) and our decisions in [*United States v. Smith*, 23 M.J. 118 (C.M.A. 1986), *United States v. Rivera*, 23 M.J. 89 (C.M.A. 1986), and *United States v. Davis*, 26 M.J. 445 (C.M.A. 1988)].

United States v. Kaiser, 58 M.J. 146, 149 (C.A.A.F. 2003). If an accused pleads guilty to a lesser-included offense, and the government intends "to prove the greater offense, findings should not be entered until after" trial on the merits, and the military judge should inform the court-martial panel "that if they find the accused not guilty of the greater offense and other contested lesser[-]included offenses, then they must enter a finding of guilty to the lesser[-]included offense to which the accused [pleaded] guilty." *United States v. Baker*, 28 M.J. 900, 901 (A.C.M.R. 1989); R.C.M. 910(g)(2); R.C.M. 913(a); R.C.M. 920(e) discussion.

If the military judge accepts an accused's plea to a lesser-included offense, that guilty plea "may be used to establish 'facts and elements common to both the greater and lesser offense within the same specification.'" *United States v. Grijalva*, 55 M.J. 223, 228 (C.A.A.F. 2001) (quoting *Dorrell*, 18 C.M.R. at 425–26). An accused's plea of guilty fulfills the elements of a lesser offense that can then be used to prove *common* elements of a greater offense to which the accused has pleaded not guilty. *Id.* (holding "military judge did not err by considering appellant's admissions concerning the elements of the lesser-included offense of aggravated assault" in determining appellant was guilty of the greater offense of attempted premeditated murder). The military judge in a judge-alone trial, however, may not use admissions made during the plea inquiry elicited to prove elements contained in the greater offense to which an accused has pleaded not guilty. *Id.* Accordingly, the military judge should inform court-martial members, upon a specific request by an accused on the record, to accept as proven, *common* elements of the greater and lesser-included offenses the accused has admitted by his guilty plea. R.C.M. 920(e) discussion . . . .

* * *

Discussion

The panel convicted appellant of attempting to murder his wife, "with premeditation, *by repeatedly striking [her] about the head, face, and neck with a club.*" (Emphasis added.) Prior to trial on the merits, the military judge properly informed the panel (with appellant's consent) that appellant pleaded guilty to aggravated assault with a dangerous weapon as a lesser-included offense to attempted premeditated murder. He also told the panel the government was going to attempt to prove up the attempted premeditated murder charge. During the merits, the military judge commented to the panel: "So, [aggravated assault with a dangerous weapon is] the bottom level, and that's already been established by [appellant's] plea of guilty."

Before the panel withdrew to deliberate on findings, the military judge instructed the panel in pertinent part:

> In order to find the accused guilty of [attempted premeditated murder], you must be convinced . . . beyond a reasonable doubt first, that . . . the accused did certain acts; that is, *repeatedly strike [his wife] about the head, face [,] and neck with a club* . . . .

(Emphasis added.) The military judge did not specifically describe the elements of the lesser-included offense of aggravated assault with a dangerous weapon or means or force likely to produce death or grievous bodily harm to which appellant pleaded guilty. After explaining the requisite specific intent elements for attempted premeditated murder, and the lesser-included offenses of attempted unpremeditated murder and attempted voluntary manslaughter—and how they differ for each offense—the military judge did cover the elements of aggravated assault by *intentionally inflicting grievous bodily harm.* When instructing on the elements of this lesser-included offense, the military judge told the panel:

> [A]s to the second element; that is, that the accused did so *by repeatedly striking her about the head, face, and neck with a club,* if you find the first element[—describing the injuries—]to be proven beyond a reasonable doubt, then the *cause of those injuries* as described in the second element *has been established by the accused's provident plea of guilty to* a lesser[-

]included offense of *aggravated assault with a weapon or a means or force likely to produce death or grievous bodily harm....*

(Emphasis added.) The military judge also reminded the panel that appellant pleaded "guilty to the next lower lesser[-]included offense of aggravated assault with a weapon, means, or force likely to produce death or grievous bodily harm"—a general intent offense not requiring any specific intent or premeditation.

We find the military judge properly instructed the panel regarding appellant's guilty plea to aggravated assault with a dangerous weapon or means or force likely to produce death or grievous bodily harm as a lesser-included offense of attempted premeditated murder. Nothing in the military judge's instructions regarding appellant's admitted criminal act or *actus reus*, i.e., that he repeatedly struck Mrs. Axelson about the head, face, and neck with a club, was improper. By instructing the panel in this fashion, and based on the particular facts in this case, the panel could properly resolve the issue regarding appellant's specific intent at the time he committed the charged offense.

Appellant testified before the panel during the case on the merits—consistent with his plea inquiry admissions—that he "just [could not] remember what happened next," and "[t]he next memory [he had was of his] wife [on] the ground, and [he] was hitting her with the club, and [he] hit her in the mouth, and [he]'ll never forget the noise . . . and the blood." Later in his testimony, appellant reiterated: "[T]he first thing I remember is the sound, or hitting her in the mouth and the sound and just seeing that blood." Responding to the military judge's question, "[A]re you certain in your own mind then that you at some point had the club in your hand?" appellant responded, "Yes, sir, because I can remember—the first thing, the only thing I can remember at that point is actually going down and hitting her in the mouth . . . with the club."

Doctor Fey testified that appellant exhibited what amounted to character or personality disorders; he suffered from "[OCD] . . . for most . . . of his adult life[,] . . . [and GAD] for a period of [six to seven] months prior to [attacking his wife]." Putting these disorders into perspective for the panel, Dr. Fey stated: "I do not believe [appellant] had any mental conditions that would [have affected] his state of mind to be able to premeditate long term.... [T]here's no psychotic disorder."

Doctor Fey further opined for the panel:

I believe that the jury must consider that [Mrs. Axelson's actions were] the impetus[,] and that Major Axelson was in such a state of mind, perhaps rage, that he did not have the capacity to form the intent to kill his wife.

. . . .

[T]he jury must [also] consider that Major Axelson is faking amnesia. Other alternatives are that he had some medical condition, organic condition, that affected his ability to lay down memories. I do not believe that that's an issue either. He was not intoxicated. He did not have any sort of seizure. He did not have a head injury, et cetera, so I don't believe that there is any reason that he couldn't lay down memories . . . .

With respect to appellant's contention that he remembered only the tail end of the attack, Dr. Fey commented: "It's not certain to me why Major Axelson would recall the last hit or part of the assault."

As for the defense assertion that the military judge erred because he failed to sua sponte instruct the panel regarding the automatism defense, we hold a military judge's responsibilities regarding instructions on affirmative defenses pertain only to those defenses listed in the R.C.M. and recognized in military law. Automatism is not a defense listed in R.C.M. 916 or recognized by military law. Furthermore, a military judge is under no obligation to explore potential defenses not raised on the merits and not requested by the defense at trial. *See Phillippe,* 63 at 310–11 (stating that when "circumstances raise a possible defense, a military judge has a duty to inquire further").

Nevertheless, the evidence presented on the merits did not show appellant had a diagnosed physical condition amounting to a recognized defense under military law, or that appellant's lack of memory (amnesia) related to such a condition. Despite appellant's faulty memory, the record demonstrates appellant believed and admitted he was guilty of committing an aggravated assault with a dangerous weapon upon his wife. He could also evaluate all the evidence against him, and intelligently and meaningfully cooperate in his own defense.

IV. CONCLUSION

We hold a military judge's responsibilities regarding affirmative defenses, in both guilty plea and contested cases, are limited to those listed in R.C.M. 916 and 920, and to those recognized by this court and our superior courts. We also hold partial mental responsibility is not a defense to aggravated assault with a dangerous weapon or other means or force likely to produce death or grievous bodily harm. A partial mental responsibility defense rebuts a specific intent *mens rea* element, which this assault-type offense lacks under the UCMJ.

Moreover, the military judge properly instructed the panel regarding appellant's guilty pleas. In any case, appellant's guilty pleas to the general intent crime of aggravated assault with a dangerous weapon were knowing and voluntary, and therefore, provident. Neither the plea inquiry nor the additional defense evidence on the merits provided any "evidence that appellant's conduct was beyond his control." *Sellers,* 809 P.2d. at 687. No evidence suggested a possible defense of partial mental responsibility or automatism.

Even if automatism was a recognized defense in the military, "the evidence at trial could not have supported the [automatism] defense, [and] the trial court committed no error by [failing] to [sua sponte] instruct." *Id.* In sum,

> [w]hile we cannot characterize the accused's story as inherently improbable in any precise meaning of the term, we cannot avoid the conclusion that—even if accepted in every detail—the accused signally failed to link his amnesia [or lack of memory] to any type of automatism, or to demonstrate that the [brutally] executed [attack on his wife] was related in any way to a "mental defect, disease or derangement" depriving him of legal responsibility.

Olvera, 15 C.M.R. at 140. Appellant has therefore failed in his attempt to convert his "amnesia into an unconsciousness [or automatism] defense." *Jenner,* 451 N.W.2d. at 721 ("[A]mnesia . . . is not a defense to a criminal charge.").

We have considered appellant's remaining assignment of error and find it without merit.

Accordingly, the findings of guilty and the sentence are affirmed.

Judge ZOLPER and Judge WALBURN concur.

Points for Discussion

1. How is raising a defense of automatism different from simply arguing that the government has not proved the *mens rea* element of an offense beyond a reasonable doubt? If the government has not proved the mens rea element, does it matter why the accused lacked the *mens reas* (i.e., because of mental defect or because of something else)?

2. Do you think automatism should be a recognized defense in the military? How would you define it and add it to the Rules for Courts-Martial? What other defenses should be added to the Rules for Courts-Martial

14-4. The Good Soldier Defense

A defense specific to a military accused is the "good soldier" defense. Servicemembers have the opportunity to present a "good soldier" defense reflecting evidence of good military character when that trait is relevant. *See United States v. Wilson,* 28 M.J. 48 (C.M.A. 1989). Military Rule of Evidence 404(a)(1), quoted in the case below, serves as the rule authorizing the admissibility of this evidence. That rule permits the accused to offer evidence of a pertinent character trait that may make it unlikely that he committed the offense charged. *Id.* A general good military character is pertinent if a nexus exists between the criminal circumstances and the military. Courts tend to allow in the accused's evidence of good military character. The defense may present reputation or opinion witnesses but they should meet basic foundational requirements and they must know the accused professionally or socially. *See United States v. Breeding,* 44 M.J. 345 (C.A.A.F. 1996).

As *United States v. Belz*, 20 M.J. 33 (C.M.A. 1985), which follows, reflects "pertinent" and nexis may be loosely interpreted to benefit the accused. In *Belz*, the accused faced drug-related charges and evidence to support the "good soldier" defense should have been admitted as "pertinent."

UNITED STATES v. CLEMONS
Court of Military Appeals
16 M.J. 44 (C.M.A. 1983)

FLETCHER, Judge:

Appellant's [Sergeant Michael W. Clemons, U.S. Army], conviction by court members at a general court-martial* is now before us by way of a grant of review. We are asked to determine whether he was prejudiced by the military judge's failure to admit evidence of his good military character and his character for lawfulness under Mil. R.Evid. 404(a)(1). We hold that the ruling was erroneous, and we are unable to conclude that this error was harmless. Article 59(a), Uniform Code of Military Justice, 10 U.S.C. § 859(a); *see United States v. Hewitt*, 634 F.2d 277 (5th Cir. 1981). Our examination proceeds first to the facts of this case that demonstrate the contested evidence was pertinent to a proper resolution of the charges against appellant.

The findings in this case included conviction of unlawfully entering a barracks room, wrongfully appropriating a television set found therein, and stealing a cassette player. Appellant did not deny entering the unlocked barracks room or taking the television and the cassette player. Rather he asserted that, in order to secure the television and teach the room's occupants a lesson about securing property, it was taken from the room and placed in his office. Also to secure property the cassette player found in a latrine was placed in his office, and later inadvertently placed in his duffle bag following the termination of his duty. During all of these events appellant was on duty as Charge of Quarters the night of February 6 and 7, 1981.

Before defense counsel proceeded to his case-in-chief, trial counsel moved, *in limine*, to prevent introduction of evidence of appellant's general good character. Acknowledging that he intended to introduce evidence of appellant's good military character and character for lawfulness, defense counsel cited as authority for its production Mil. R. Evid. 404(a)(1), which states:

---

* Contrary to his pleas, appellant was found guilty of wrongful appropriation, larceny, and unlawful entry, in violation of Articles 121 and 134, Uniform Code of Military Justice, 10 U.S.C. §§ 921 and 934, respectively. He was sentenced to a bad-conduct discharge, confinement at hard labor for 6 months, forfeiture of $250.00 pay per month for 6 months, and reduction to E-1. The convening authority approved the sentence. [GCMO No. 31, dated October 26, 1981, erroneously reflects findings of Charge II as "Not Guilty of violation of Article 134, UCMJ." The correct finding is: "Not Guilty, but Guilty of a violation of Article 134, UCMJ." (R. 673.)] The Court of Military Review affirmed the approved sentence without opinion.

5 5 5 5 5 5 5 5 5 5 5 5 5 5 5 5 5

Rule 404. *Character Evidence Not Admissible to Prove Conduct; Exceptions; Other Crimes*

(a) *Character evidence generally.* Evidence of a person's character or a trait of a person's character is not admissible for the purpose of proving that the person acted in conformity therewith on a particular occasion, except:

(1) *Character of the accused. Evidence of a pertinent trait of the character of the accused offered by an accused, or by the prosecution to rebut the same.*

(Emphasis in last sentence added.) Nevertheless, the military judge, granting the Government's motion, forbade testimony regarding appellant's good military character and his character for lawfulness, and permitted only evidence of his character for trustworthiness. The military judge stated:

All right. Before I get to that, as to the case you cited [*United States v. Hewitt,* 634 F.2d 277 (5th Cir. 1981), discussed herein], I have read it, and I find that although they do say—state in there that "the character for lawfulness is admissible under the Rule 404," I do not find that that case is binding upon me, and I find that the finding of that appellate court is contrary to what I have been taught and my interpretation of the current rule, Military Rule 404, and in fact contrary to what the law should even be under the Federal Rules of Evidence. And since that is not an appellate court that is senior to this court, I find that although it is interesting and I found it enlightening to read the article, I do not find it binding in any way upon this court, and in fact I find it contrary to what our law is.

The military judge erred both in his misguided view of the applicability of federal precedent, *and* in his substantive rulings regarding Mil. R. Evid. 404(a)(1).

Dealing briefly first with the question of Federal precedent, we note that Mil. R. Evid. 101 states:

Rule 101. *Scope*

(a) *Applicability.* These rules are applicable in courts-martial ... to the extent and with the exceptions stated in rule 1101.

(b) *Secondary sources.* If not otherwise prescribed in this manual or these rules, and insofar as practicable and not inconsistent with or contrary to the Uniform Code of Military Justice or this Manual, courts-martial shall apply:

(1) *First, the rules of evidence generally recognized in the trial of criminal cases in the United States district courts; and*

(2) Second, when not inconsistent with subdivision (b)(1), the rules of evidence at common law.

(Emphasis in (b)(1) added.) The drafters of these rules have stated with respect to section (a) of the above rule:

The decisions of the United States Court of Military Appeals and of the Courts of Military Review must be utilized in interpreting these Rules. *While specific decisions of the Article III courts involving rules which are common both to the Military Rules and the Federal Rules should be considered very persuasive, they are not binding; see Article 36 of the Uniform Code of Military Justice. It should be noted, however, that a significant policy consideration in adopting the Federal Rules of Evidence was to ensure, where possible, common evidentiary law.*

(Emphasis added.) Analysis of the Military Rules of Evidence, Appendix 18, Manual for Courts-Martial, United States, 1969 (Revised edition), Mil. R. Evid. 101(a). . . .

  * * *

There is no inconsistency with military practice in the application of Federal precedent to the interpretation of Mil. R. Evid. 404(a)(1). Thus, we conclude that the military judge's expressed, but unjustified, opinion flies in the face of the scope of the Military Rules of Evidence, and does not pay sufficient deference to the application of Article III Federal court precedent.

It is entirely clear that had this military judge applied Federal precedent, he would have acknowledged clear legal precedent for admission in this case of evidence of appellant's character for lawfulness. *United States v. Hewitt, supra.* . . . *United States v. Angelini,* 678 F.2d 380 (1st Cir. 1982), published subsequent to trial of the instant case, addresses admissibility of evidence of law-abidingness in light of Fed.R.Evid. 404. It concluded that "Rule 404 permits evidence of traits only" and "that evidence of a defendant's character as a law-abiding person is admissible." *Id.* at 382. As *Angelini* states: "Thus, the basic issue is whether the character trait in question would make any fact 'of consequence to the determination' of the case more or less probable than it would be without evidence of the trait. *See* Fed.R.Evid. 401; *United States v. Staggs,* 553 F.2d 1073 (7th Cir. 1977)." *Id.* at 381.

In the instant case, it is clear that the traits of good military character and character for lawfulness each evidenced "a pertinent trait of the character of the accused" in light of the principal theory of the defense case. Mil. R. Evid. 404(a)(1). "The word 'pertinent' is read as synonymous with 'relevant'. *United States v. Staggs,* . . . [*supra* at] 1075; 22 Wright & Graham, *Federal Practice and Procedure: Evidence* § 5236, at 383 (1978)." *United States v. Angelini, supra* at 381. The "Drafters' Analysis" to Mil. R. Evid. 404(a)(1) indicates that "[i]t is the intention of the Committee, however, to allow the defense to introduce evidence of good military character when that specific trait is pertinent." Analysis, *supra,* Mil. R. Evid. 404(a)(1). *United States v. Angelini* and *United States v. Hewitt,* both *supra,* make clear the admissibility of the specific trait of law-abidingness.

In not denying entry into the barracks room or taking the television and cassette player, defense counsel posited the theory that appellant, functioning as Charge of Quarters, was teaching his subordinates a lesson in security and personally securing the property in accordance with military responsibilities. We conclude that, to this end, the excluded evidence was entirely relevant and should have been admitted. Mil. R. Evid. 404(a)(1); *compare United States v. Angelini* with *United States v. Hewitt,* both *supra.* In line with *United States v. Hewitt, supra,* we are unable to say that appellant was not prejudiced. Article 59(a), 10 U.S.C. § 859(a). Accordingly, the decision of the United States Army Court of Military Review is reversed. The findings and sentence are set aside. The record of trial is returned to the Judge Advocate General of the Army. A rehearing may be ordered.

EVERETT, Chief Judge (concurring):

Before the Military Rules of Evidence took effect in 1980, reception of character evidence in trials by court-martial was governed by this provision of the Manual for Courts-Martial:

> To show the probability of his innocence, the accused may introduce evidence of his own good character, including evidence of his military record and standing as shown by authenticated copies of efficiency or fitness reports or otherwise and evidence of his general character as a moral, well-conducted person and law-abiding citizen. However, he may not, for this purpose, introduce evidence as to some specific trait of character unless evidence of that trait would have a reasonable tendency to show that it was unlikely that he committed the offense charged.

Para. 138*f* (2), Manual for Courts-Martial, United States, 1969 (Revised edition). *Accord* para. 138*f* (2), Manual for Courts-Martial, United States, 1951; para. 125*b*, Manual for Courts-Martial, United States Army, 1949. Contrary to the practice that prevailed at one time in most civilian courts, courts-martial could consider not only reputation evidence but also the opinions of the character witnesses based on their contact with the person whose character was in issue. Para. 138*f* (1), Manuals, *supra.*

The willingness of courts-martial to receive evidence of an accused's good character is quite understandable. As we noted in *United States v. Browning,* 5 C.M.R. 27, 29 (C.M.A. 1952), "Wigmore goes so far as to say that evidence of good soldierly character is even stronger than the customary evidence of good general character. Wigmore, Evidence, 3d ed., § 59." Dean Wigmore's rationale was that:

> The soldier is in an environment where all weaknesses or excesses have an opportunity to betray themselves. He is carefully observed by his superiors,—more carefully than falls to the lot of any member of the ordinary civil community; and all his delinquencies and merits are recorded systematically from time to time on his "service record," which follows him throughout his army career and serves as the basis for the terms of his final discharge.

Courts-martial were not unique in admitting evidence of general good character. As Dean Wigmore observed: "Doubtless in practice Courts often are liberal in permitting the defendant to offer his general character." J.

Wigmore, *A Treatise on the Anglo-American System of Evidence in Trials at Common Law* § 59 (3d ed. 1940). A court of appeals recently noted:

> Our own survey convinces us that the actual practice in the states has generally been to permit defendants to establish their character for lawfulness, and that the federal courts have unanimously assumed that to be the practice.

* * *

II

To support the exclusion of the evidence offered by appellant to show that he was a person of law-abiding character, the Government now relies on Mil. R. Evid. 404(a), which prescribes when character evidence is admissible. According to the "Drafters' Analysis, Mil. R. Evid. 404(a)(1), which "allows only evidence of a pertinent trait of character of the accused to be offered in evidence by the defense," makes

> a significant change from paragraph 138*f* of the [1969] Manual which also allows evidence of "general good character" of the accused to be received in order to demonstrate that the accused is less likely to have committed a criminal act. Under the new rule, evidence of general good character is inadmissible because only evidence of a specific trait is acceptable.

Analysis of the Military Rules of Evidence, Appendix 18, 1969 Manual, *supra*, Mil. R. Evid. 404(a)(1). The Government also insists that the reference in Mil. R. Evid. 404(a)(1) to "a pertinent trait of the character of the accused" was intended to impose a more rigorous requirement for reception of character evidence than would have existed if the rule had referred to a "relevant" trait. Otherwise, according to the Government, the Rule would have used the adjective "relevant," which has a meaning explained in Mil. R. Evid. 401.

In *Michelson,* the Supreme Court referred to its holdings that testimony as to a defendant's good character "alone, in some circumstances, may be enough to raise a reasonable doubt of guilt and that in the federal courts a jury in a proper case should be so instructed." 355 U.S. at 476. Many years before, in *Edgington v. United States, supra* 164 U.S. at 367, the Court quoted approvingly the observation of a state supreme court that "[p]roof of . . . [good character] may sometimes be the only mode by which an innocent man can repel the presumption arising from the possession of stolen goods. It is not proof of innocence, although it may be sufficient to raise a doubt of guilt." Our Court has adhered scrupulously to the same view that evidence of an accused's good character may raise a reasonable doubt as to his guilt. *See, e.g., United States v. Browning, supra.* In light of such precedents, it is hard to understand how evidence of a defendant's character as a law-abiding person—or, indeed, his general good character—would not be pertinent in the present case or, indeed, in almost any case that can be imagined. This seems especially true in light of the great weight which for decades has been attributed to character evidence in trials by courts-martial.

In construing Fed.R.Evid. 404(a), from which the corresponding Military Rule was derived, the Court of Appeals held in *United States v. Hewitt,* 634 F.2d 277, 280 (5th Cir. 1981), that evidence of a defendant's "law-abiding" character should not have been excluded. Another Court of Appeals reached a similar conclusion in *United States v. Angelini,* 678 F.2d 380 (1st Cir. 1982). Thus, Federal precedents—which, while not binding, clearly are highly instructive—indicate that in the present case the military judge erred in ruling that appellant could not introduce evidence of his law-abiding character.

Furthermore, if Mil. R. Evid. 404(a) were applied as the Government would urge, a substantial constitutional issue would be raised. Under the guarantees of due process and the sixth amendment, a technical rule of evidence cannot be used to exclude highly material evidence. *Cf. Washington v. Texas,* 388 U.S. 14 (1967) (co-indictee incompetent as defense witness); *Chambers v. Mississippi,* 410 U.S. 284 (1973) (voucher rule and hearsay rule applied to prevent cross-examination of defense witness as to prior statements); *Davis v. Alaska,* 415 U.S. 308 (1974) (cross-examination of prosecution witness prohibited as to his probation for juvenile offense). Since character evidence can itself generate reasonable doubt, its importance cannot be denied. As has already been noted, this is especially true in trials by courts-martial because of the reliability of character evidence under the conditions that prevail in the military community.[6]

In some situations there are strong public policies that favor excluding certain types of relevant evidence. For example, Mil. R. Evid. 412 seeks to protect victims of sex offenses from undergoing at trial the trauma of inquiry into their past sexual history. In *Davis v. Alaska, supra,* the state was seeking to exclude certain otherwise relevant evidence in order to protect its juveniles. However, I can find very little support in public policy for applying Mil. R. Evid. 404(a) in a manner that would prohibit appellant from offering the evidence of his "law-abiding" character. I perceive no risk that the trial would be unduly delayed by the presentation of such evidence or that the court members would be confused. In fact, time was wasted in the present trial while counsel and the judge split hairs as to the difference between evidence of appellant's "trustworthiness," which was admitted, and evidence of "his law-abiding" character, which was excluded.

In line with the Federal precedents, *see e.g., United States v. Hewitt* and *United States v. Angelini,* both *supra,* I concur with the principal opinion that the evidence of appellant's "law-abiding" character should have been admitted. Moreover, the rationale which I have employed leads me to the

---

[6] Moreover, evidence of his good character may be of special importance to a military accused since, due to reassignments or transfers of personnel, separations from the service, and other conditions encountered in the Armed Services, other prospective defense evidence may have become unavailable.

conclusion that Mil. R. Evid. 404(a) should not be interpreted to exclude evidence of an accused's "law-abiding" character in any other trial by court-martial, and that, if it is so construed, it may well be unconstitutional.

In candor, I also must confess that I see very little difference between a person's being of "law-abiding" character and being of "good" character; and I suspect that over the years many witnesses who have testified about a defendant's "good" character really meant to say that he was "law-abiding." To say that the "goodness" of someone's character is a "trait" of his character may involve an unusual construction of the latter term. However, just as the Courts of Appeal in *Hewitt* and *Angelini* stretched "trait" to include "law-abiding" character in order to avoid an unjust—and possibly unconstitutional—result, I would take the same approach with respect to evidence of "general good character." Of course, under my view the scope of the Government's right to present rebuttal evidence would be co-extensive with the scope of the character evidence offered by the accused.

III

The only issue that remains is to determine whether appellant was prejudiced by the exclusion of the evidence about his law-abiding character. In line with the precedents affirming that character evidence can suffice to raise a reasonable doubt, it would seem highly likely that the exclusion of character evidence would be prejudicial unless it was only cumulative. Since the judge allowed evidence of appellant's "trustworthiness" and even permitted some of the defense witnesses to relate specific instances of conduct which tended to support their favorable opinions, I have examined the record of trial to determine whether, in substance, appellant's evidence of his "law-abiding" character was before the court members for their consideration in determining his guilt or innocence. I conclude, however, that the limitations imposed on the defense by the judge's ruling affected appellant's cause adversely. Accordingly, I concur in reversing the decision of the United States Army Court of Military Review.

COOK, Judge (concurring in the result):

I concur that character for lawfulness is a "pertinent trait" within the meaning of Mil. R. Evid. 404(a)(1). *See United States v. Angelini,* 678 F.2d 380 (1st Cir. 1982); *United States v. Hewitt,* 634 F.2d 277 (5th Cir. 1981). In addition, in view of the defense theory that appellant was acting legitimately in his role as a noncommissioned officer, I am persuaded that appellant's military character was "in issue" and "pertinent." However, I agree with Chief Judge EVERETT that decisions of Federal courts construing the Federal Rules of Evidence are highly instructive to, but not binding on, military courts construing the Military Rules of Evidence.

Points for Discussion

1. All three judges agreed that it was error to exclude evidence that Sergeant Clemons was a good soldier, but each wrote a separate opinion. How do the judges' views differ?

2. The good soldier defense, a doctrine designed to aid accused service members, has critics who see it as potentially discriminatory and unfair. One commentator writes:

> Cloaked in the mantle of longstanding court-martial tradition, justified by doctrines of questionable salience, and preserved by judges resistant to the Military Rules of Evidence's limitations on character evidence, the good soldier defense advances the perception that one of the privileges of high rank and long service is immunity from conviction at court-martial. The defense privileges a certain type of accused servicemember--a person of high rank and reputation in the military community--at the expense of the overall fairness of the court-martial system. By permitting the introduction of good military character evidence during the guilt phase of a court-martial, the good soldier defense encourages factfinders to focus on the reputation of accused individuals rather than on their alleged criminal acts. In a system already marked by extraordinary discretion, from a commander's decision about whether and how to bring criminal charges to the separate sentencing phase of trial, the good soldier defense undercuts the military justice system's commitment to an objective trial process by adding an element of subjectivity to the merits phase of a court-martial.

Elizabeth Lutes Hillman, Note, *The "Good Soldier" Defense: Character Evidence and Military Rank at Courts-Martial*, 108 Yale L.J. 87, 88 (1999) (footnote omitted). Which aspects of this criticism do you agree with or disagree with?

UNITED STATES v. BELZ
Court of Military Appeals
20 M.J. 33 (C.M.A. 1985)

COX, Judge:

Appellant [Captain Graham S. F. Belz, U.S. Air Force], was tried by a general court-martial composed of members and a military judge on September 16–21, 1981, at Tyndall Air Force Base, Florida. Contrary to his pleas, he was found guilty of conduct unbecoming an officer by engaging in various drug-related acts, in violation of Article 133, Uniform Code of Military Justice, 10 U.S.C. § 933. He was sentenced to be dismissed from the service, confined at hard labor for 1 year, and forfeit $950.00 pay per month for 1 year. The convening authority approved this sentence except that he reduced the period of confinement and forfeitures to three months. The Court of Military Review affirmed. 14 M.J. 601 (1982).

The issue granted review by this Court is:

WHETHER EVIDENCE OF GOOD MILITARY CHARACTER IS PERTINENT WITHIN THE MEANING OF MIL. R. EVID. 404(a)(1) TO CHARGES OF CONDUCT UNBECOMING AN OFFICER AND A GENTLEMAN.

The trial judge, relying on the decision in *United States v. Cooper*, 11 M.J. 815 (A.F.C.M.R. 1981), ruled that military character was not a pertinent character trait in cases involving drug-abuse offenses. On motion of the prosecution and over objection of defense counsel, he therefore refused to admit on findings defense exhibits A through E, which were Officer Effectiveness Reports purporting to show appellant's proper conduct as a commissioned officer. He later excluded defense exhibits F through J, which were affidavits attesting to appellant's good character as a military officer. *

This Court has held that Mil. R. Evid. 404(a)(1) does not bar admission of military-character evidence where the offense charged under Article 134, UCMJ, 10 U.S.C. § 934, is drug related. *United States v. Kahakauwila*, 19 M.J. 60 (C.M.A. 1984). We have also held that such character-trait evidence is not barred by this evidentiary rule in a drug-offense case if such an offense is charged under Article 92, UCMJ, 10 U.S.C. § 892, or the recently enacted Article 112 *a*, UCMJ, 10 U.S.C. § 912 *a*. *United States v. Vandelinder*, 20 M.J. 41 (C.M.A. 1985). We see no reason why officers charged with drug offenses under Article 133 should be barred from introducing such military character evidence. To the extent that the trial judge proceeded on the erroneous premise rejected in *Vandelinder*, he also erred.

The critical issue in this case and others we have recently decided is whether appellant was prejudiced by exclusion of this evidence. *See United States v. Vandelinder, supra* ; *United States v. Weeks*, 20 M.J. 22 (C.M.A. 1985). Some factors we have considered in resolving this question are the strength of the Government's case, the weakness of the defense's case, the materiality of the evidence, the quality of the military character evidence, and the existence of suitable substitute evidence in the record of trial. *Id.*; *see also United States v. Wilson*, 20 M.J. 31 (C.M.A. 1985); *United States v. Klein*, 20 M.J. 26 (C.M.A. 1985).

Because neither the trial judge nor the Court of Military Review had the benefit of our ruling in *United States v. Vandelinder, supra*, we conclude, consistent with our opinion in *United States v. Weeks, supra*, that it is appropriate for the Court of Military Review to now determine, under these precedents, if appellant was prejudiced by this error.

The decision of the United States Air Force Court of Military Review is set aside. The record of trial is returned to the Judge Advocate General of the Air

---

* All these exhibits were later admitted during the sentencing portion of this court-martial. One affidavit from appellant's brother-in-law, a DEA agent, was admitted during findings to show a demeanor inconsistent with drug use.

Force for remand to that court for findings of fact and conclusions of law on whether appellant was prejudiced by this error.

Chief Judge EVERETT concurs.

Judge FLETCHER did not participate.

Points for Discussion

1. Is the good soldier defense more suited to distinctly military offenses, like conduct unbecoming an officer, than it is to more universal criminal offenses like theft, robbery, or murder?

2. Do you agree with Dean Wigmore (whom Chief Justice Everett quotes in his concurring opinion) that "[t]he soldier is in an environment where all weaknesses or excesses have an opportunity to betray themselves. He is carefully observed by his superiors,—more carefully than falls to the lot of any member of the ordinary civil community; and all his delinquencies and merits are recorded systematically from time to time on his "service record," Wigmore, Evidence, 3d ed., § 59? Does this justify allowing an accused to present a "good soldier" defense? When would a "good soldier" defense not be pertinent?

CHAPTER 15

RELATIONSHIP BETWEEN CIVILIAN COURTS AND MILITARY COURTS

15-1. Court-Martial of Civilians Accompanying an Armed Force in the Field

Wherever there are service members, there are also civilians. Civilian dependents live with service members on many installations. In addition, all of the Armed Services employ thousands of civilians to perform various functions. Civilian employees include secretaries, computer experts, scientists, and so forth. In addition, civilians working for private contractors often provide security, construction, food, and transportation services to military units.

Some of these civilians, unfortunately, commit crimes. When, if ever, may courts-martial try civilians working for or accompanying an Armed Force for their UCMJ offenses? This question raises both statutory and constitutional questions. The applicable statute is Article 2(a)(10), UCMJ, 10 U.S.C. § 802(a)(10). Article 2(a)(10) states that "[i]n time of declared war or a contingency operation, persons serving with or accompanying an armed force in the field" are subject to the UCMJ. A declared war is a war formally declared by Congress under Article I, § 8, of the Constitution. Given that Congress has not declared war since World War II, and is unlikely to do so in the near future, the more important term is "contingency operation." A "contingency operation" is a military operation that

> (A) is designated by the Secretary of Defense as an operation in which members of the armed forces are or may become involved in military actions, operations, or hostilities against an enemy of the United States or against an opposing military force; or (B) results in the call or order to, or retention on, active duty of members of the uniformed services . . . during a war or during a national emergency declared by the President or Congress.

10 U.S.C. § 101(a)(13). The term covers the recent use of force in Afghanistan and Iraq.

The Department of Defense interprets the term "persons serving with or accompanying an armed force in the field" to include civilian employees of the Department of Defense and civilian employees of contractors working for the Department of Defense if they are in the geographic area of active military operations. *See* Memorandum, Secretary of Defense, to Secretaries of the Military Departments, Subject: UCMJ Jurisdiction Over DoD Civilian Employees, DoD Contractor Personnel, and Other Persons Serving with or Accompanying the Armed Forces Overseas During Declared War and in Contingency Operations (10 Mar. 2008). Under this definition, for example, Article 2(a)(10), UCMJ, would cover civilian technicians employed by the Army or by private contractors to maintain complicated weapon systems in Afghanistan or Iraq. But it would not cover State Department contractors in these locations, and it would not reach any contractor at a garrison in the United States.

Whether Article 2(a)(10) is constitutional is a separate issue. As described in Chapter 1 of this book, a plurality of the Supreme Court ruled in *Reid v. Covert*, 354 U.S. 1 (1957) [p. 32], that courts-martial could not try civilian dependents for capital crimes committed on U.S. installations abroad during peacetime. The Supreme Court, however, has not decided whether civilians serving with or accompanying an armed force in the field may be tried by court-martial.

The following case arose in 1970 during the Vietnam conflict. At that time, Article 2(a)(10) applied only "in time of war," and not during what is now called contingency operations. (Article 2(a)(10) was amended to include contingency operations in 2006. *See* Pub.L. 109-364, Div. A, Title V, § 552, 120 Stat. 2217 (Oct. 17, 2006).) It is the most recent case involving contractors to reach the Court of Military Appeals or Court of Appeals for the Armed Forces, and it contains a useful discussion of the constitutional issues at stake.

UNITED STATES v. AVERETTE
U.S. Court of Military Appeals
41 C.M.R. 363 (C.M.A. 1970)

DARDEN, Judge:

Our concern in this case is with the liability for trial by court-martial of a civilian employee of an Army contractor in the Republic of Vietnam. To decide the case we must consider whether the words "in time of war" as used in Article 2(10), Uniform Code of Military Justice, 10 U.S.C. § 802, mean a declared war.

A general court-martial at Long Binh, Vietnam, convicted Raymond G. Averette of conspiracy to commit larceny and attempted larceny of 36,000 United States Government-owned batteries. After earlier appellate review, with some modification of findings, his sentence now stands as confinement at hard labor for one year and a fine of $500.00.

The history of what is now Article 2(10), Code, *supra*, has been developed by Colonel William Winthrop. The British Articles of War in existence at the time of the Revolutionary War contained the precursor, which provided:

"All Suttlers and Retainers to a Camp, and all persons whatsoever serving with Our Armies in the Field, though no inlisted Soldiers, are to be subject to orders, according to the Rules and Discipline of War." [Section XIV, Article XXIII, Winthrop's Military Law and Precedents, 2d ed, 1920 Reprint, page 941.]

The first Articles of War adopted in this country by the Provisional Congress of Massachusetts Bay in April 1775 included a provision nearly identical to the British counterpart. Article XXXII of the American Articles of War, enacted by the Continental Congress in June 1775 had a substantially similar coverage and became Article 23 of Section XIII of the American Articles of War of 1776. The first significant revision of this provision occurred in the Articles of War of 1916, which attempted to expand the exercise of military jurisdiction over civilians to times of peace as well as war in these words:

"All retainers to the camp and all persons accompanying or serving with the armies of the United States without the territorial jurisdiction of the United States, and in time of war all such retainers and persons accompanying or serving with the armies of the United States in the field, both within and without the territorial jurisdiction of the United States, though not otherwise subject to these articles. . . ." [Article 2(d) of the Articles of War of 1916.]

The concept of military jurisdiction over specified classes of civilians in time of peace and war was continued in the enactment of Article 2(10) and (11) of the Uniform Code of Military Justice.

Despite the existence of statutory provisions for the exercise of court-martial jurisdiction over civilians in certain circumstances, the Supreme Court in a series of cases beginning with *Toth v. Quarles*, 350 U.S. 11 (1955), has disapproved the trial by courts-martial of persons not members of the armed forces. *Toth* involved the court-martial of a civilian for an offense committed while he was on active duty. In *Reid v. Covert*, 354 U.S. 1 (1957), the Court held that civilian dependents accompanying the armed forces overseas in time of peace were not triable by court-martial for capital offenses. The Court expanded this holding in *Kinsella v. Singleton*, 361 U.S. 234 (1960), to prohibit military jurisdiction over civilian dependents in time of peace, regardless of whether the offense was capital or noncapital. *Grisham v. Hagan*, 361 U.S. 278 (1960), held civilian employees committing capital offenses not amenable to military jurisdiction; this holding was enlarged to embrace noncapital offenses in *McElroy v. Guagliardo*, decided and reported with *Wilson v. Bohlender*, 361 U.S. 281 (1960). Since all these decisions covered offenses occurring in periods other than a time of declared war, they do not constitute authority that even in time of declared war courts-martial have no jurisdiction to try those who are not members of the armed forces, regardless of the connection between their offenses and the objectives of military discipline. The Supreme Court pointed out in *Reid v. Covert*, *supra*, that the constitutional grants of legislative authority to the Congress, collectively referred to as the war powers, are considerably more extensive than the authority in Article I, section 8, clause 14, of the Constitution to prescribe rules for the government of the armed forces standing alone.

Two cases decided in 1969 are urged upon us as bars to the exercise of court-martial jurisdiction over a civilian. The Fifth Amendment language excepting cases "arising in the land or naval forces" from the requirement for trial by jury was construed in *O'Callahan v. Parker*, 395 U.S. 258 (1969), as a limitation on the authority of Congress to legislate rules for the government of land and naval forces. The factual context of the *O'Callahan* holding involved an accused still on active duty. We find nothing in that opinion that causes us to conclude a civilian accompanying the armed forces in the field in time of a declared war is invulnerable to trial by military courts.

In *Latney v. Ignatius,* 416 F2d 821 (D.C. Cir 1969), the Court of Appeals for the District of Columbia referred to "the spirit of *O'Callahan*, and of the other Supreme Court precedents there reviewed," and concluded that Article 2(10) of the Uniform Code of Military Justice could not be viewed so expansively as to reach a civilian seaman who lived on his ship while waiting for it to turn around in Da Nang, Vietnam, and who was not assimilated to military personnel in terms of living quarters or conditions. Averette, in contrast, was employed every day within Camp Davies, a United States Army installation. He had access to a variety of Army facilities and benefits including the post exchange, the commissary, banking privileges, and other welfare and recreational activities. We should note, though, at this point that the murder for which Latney was tried was not cognizable in a United States District Court while the offenses with which Averette was charged are so cognizable.

Several cases have been cited to us to support a contention that undeclared wars are included within the term "time of war." . . . None of these cases dealt with military jurisdiction over civilians. . . .

In *United States v. Anderson*, 38 C.M.R. 386 (C.M.A. 1968), this Court decided that a two-year statute of limitations for absence without leave had not been tolled because the conflict in Vietnam constitutes a "time of war" within the meaning of Article 43(a), Uniform Code of Military Justice, 10 U.S.C. § 843, which dispenses with the statute of limitations in such circumstances. The three judges rested their reasoning in Anderson on different grounds. The instant case is different from *Anderson* in at least two ways. First, Anderson was a soldier, while Averette was a civilian at the time of his alleged offenses. Second, the statute in question in the present case subjects civilians to courts-martial, while the statute in Anderson affected the statute of limitations for a military offense by a member of the armed forces. Here the constitutionally delicate question of military jurisdiction over civilians recurs.

We conclude that the words "in time of war" mean, for the purposes of Article 2(10), Code, *supra*, a war formally declared by Congress. As a result of the most recent guidance in this area from the Supreme Court we believe that a strict and literal construction of the phrase "in time of war" should be applied. A broader construction of Article 2(10) would open the possibility of civilian prosecutions by military courts whenever military action on a varying scale of intensity occurs.

We do not presume to express an opinion on whether Congress may constitutionally provide for court-martial jurisdiction over civilians in time of a declared war when these civilians are accompanying the armed forces in the field. Our holding is limited-for a civilian to be triable by court-martial in "time of war," Article 2(10) means a war formally declared by Congress. We emphasize our awareness that the fighting in Vietnam qualifies as a war as that word is generally used and understood. By almost any standard of comparison—the number of persons involved, the level of casualties, the ferocity of the combat, the extent of the suffering, and the impact on our nation—the Vietnamese armed conflict is a major military action. But such a recognition should not serve as a shortcut for a formal declaration of war, at least in the sensitive area of subjecting civilians to military jurisdiction.

The decision of the Court of Military Review is reversed. The record of trial is returned to the Judge Advocate General of the Army. The charges are ordered dismissed.

Points for Discussion

1. Would Article 2(a)(10) cover contractors like Averette in a modern conflict like those in Iraq or Afghanistan?

2. In her influential book, Outsourcing War and Peace: Preserving Public Values in a World of Privatized Foreign Affairs (2011), Professor Laura A. Dickinson notes the increasing use of contractors in military operations and argues for greater military disciplinary oversight for contractors. Two of her recommendations are that "Judge Advocates should be given broader authority to train contractors, advise on security-related missions, and oversee contract performance in theater," and that "[m]ilitary commanders should be vested with greater authority to supervise and discipline noncompliant contract personnel." *Id.* at 194. What are some likely advantages and disadvantages of using courts-martial to try civilian contractors?

The first case decided under the revised version of UCMJ Article 2(a)(10) involved a civilian employee of the Army who was also a citizen of Iraq. (Note that review of this case has been sought in the U.S. Court of Appeals for the Armed Forces.)

UNITED STATES v. ALI
Army Court of Criminal Appeals
70 M.J. 514 (Army Ct. Crim. App. 2011)

SIMS, Senior Judge:

A military judge sitting as a general court-martial convicted appellant [Civilian Alaa Mohammad Ali, United States Army], pursuant to his pleas, of making a false official statement, wrongful appropriation, and wrongfully endeavoring to impede an investigation, in violation of Articles 107, 121, and 134 of the Uniform Code of Military Justice, 10 U.S.C. §§ 907, 921, and 934 [hereinafter UCMJ]. The military judge sentenced appellant to five months of confinement. Pursuant to a pretrial agreement, the convening authority approved only so much confinement as appellant had served in pretrial confinement.

PROCEDURAL BACKGROUND

On 22 June 2008, after contesting military jurisdiction, appellant pleaded guilty to three charges in Baghdad, Iraq. After trial, but prior to the convening authority taking action, appellant filed a petition for extraordinary relief with this court, seeking a writ of prohibition on the grounds that his court-martial lacked jurisdiction. Following the denial of his petition by this court, appellant filed a writ-appeal petition with the United States Court of Appeals for the Armed Forces (C.A.A.F.). On the same day that the C.A.A.F. denied appellant's writ petition, the convening authority approved the findings and sentence. Thereafter, appellant's record of trial was forwarded to The Judge Advocate General (TJAG) of the Army for review under Article 69(a), UCMJ, 10 U.S.C. § 869(a).

On 31 March 2010, TJAG forwarded appellant's case to this court pursuant to Article 69(d), UCMJ for review in accordance with Article 66, UCMJ, 10 U.S.C. § 866 and requested that attention be given to the following issues:

A. WHETHER THE COURT–MARTIAL HAD JURISDICTION OVER THE ACCUSED PURSUANT TO ARTICLE 2(A)(10), UNIFORM CODE OF MILITARY JUSTICE;

B. WHETHER THE COURT–MARTIAL HAD SUBJECT[-]MATTER JURISDICTION OVER THE OFFENSES.

When given the opportunity to submit a brief, appellant raised the following assignment of error:

WHETHER THE MILITARY JUDGE ERRED IN RULING THAT THE COURT HAD JURISDICTION TO TRY APPELLANT AND THEREBY VIOLATED THE DUE PROCESS CLAUSE OF THE FIFTH AND SIXTH AMENDMENTS BY REFUSING TO DISMISS THE CHARGES AND SPECIFICATIONS.

FACTS

In 2000, the United States enacted the Military Extraterritorial Jurisdiction Act (MEJA), which created United States federal criminal jurisdiction over persons "employed by the Armed Forces outside the United States." 18 U.S.C. § 3261(a)(1). The MEJA definition of persons "employed by the Armed Forces outside the United States" includes contractors and subcontractors, but not nationals of the host nation in which they are employed. 18 U.S.C. § 3267(1)(a) and (c).

In 2006, Congress amended Article 2(a)(10), UCMJ, 10 U.S.C. § 802(a)(10) which had long authorized UCMJ jurisdiction over "persons serving with or accompanying an armed force in the field" during "time of war." This amendment was effected by replacing the temporal requirement of a "time of war" with "time of declared war or contingency operation."[3]

In January of 2008, appellant, who is an Iraqi-born naturalized citizen of both Canada and Iraq, returned to Iraq from Canada as an employee of the L3 Communications/Titan Corporation (L3/Titan), which was under contract to provide interpreters for the U.S. military in Iraq.[4] Prior to his deployment to Iraq, appellant travelled from Canada to the Continental United States Replacement Center at Fort Benning, Georgia, where he was issued military equipment and provided pre-deployment training. Although no sign-in sheets exist to prove that appellant attended a specific training session in which the applicability of the UCMJ to civilian contractors in Iraq was discussed, there is strong circumstantial evidence that he was present when one of the instructors told the group that contractors were subject to prosecution under the UCMJ, but that the instructor personally did not think that contractors would be prosecuted by the military.

Once in Iraq, appellant was sent to a Combat Outpost (COP) and tasked with providing linguistic support to a squad within the 170th Military Police Company as that unit provided training and advice to Iraqi police units engaged in counter-insurgency operations in and around Hit, Iraq. Although his contract with L3/Titan clearly indicated he would be working in a combat zone, it did not address the applicability of the UCMJ to appellant in that combat zone.

---

[3] Prior to appellant's trial, the Secretary of Defense issued guidance in regard to the implementation of the jurisdictional change. Memorandum from the Sec'y of Def., to Sec'ys of the Military Dep'ts, Chairman of the Joint Chiefs of Staff, Under Sec'ys of Def., Commanders of the Combatant Commands, Subject: UCMJ Jurisdiction Over DoD Civilian Employees, DoD Contractor Personnel, and Other Persons Serving With or Accompanying the Armed Forces Overseas During Declared War and in Contingency Operations (10 Mar. 2008).

[4] Because MEJA specifically exempts citizens of the host nation from federal criminal jurisdiction, it is unlikely that appellant could have been subject to prosecution under that statute due to his status as an Iraqi citizen.

During his deployment, appellant was equipped and dressed similarly to the soldiers he was supporting in that he wore a Kevlar helmet, Interceptor Body Armor, the Army Combat Uniform, and ballistic eyewear. He wore the soldiers' distinctive unit patch and was housed on the COP with other interpreters and the soldiers they supported. Unlike the soldiers he was supporting, however, appellant did not carry a weapon and had the right to refuse to participate in a mission.

Although he was "imbedded" with the unit and generally followed the day-to-day instructions of the unit squad leader, Staff Sergeant (SSG) Butler, his direct supervisor was the L3/Titan site manager, who was located at Al Asad, Iraq. Whenever the squad to which he was attached went out on missions, appellant accompanied that squad and worked alongside the soldiers. As the squad interpreter, he performed a mission-critical function, serving as the direct link between the soldiers and Iraqi police officers being trained. Without his assistance, the squad would not have been able to perform its primary mission. Because enemy insurgents recognized the mission-critical nature of the work of the interpreters, the enemy routinely targeted interpreters in Iraq and had killed more than 300 of them as of the time of appellant's trial.

On 23 February 2008, appellant was involved in a verbal dispute with another interpreter, Mr. Al–U., which turned into a physical altercation resulting in appellant being struck in the back of his head. Appellant promptly reported the assault to a noncommissioned officer who escorted appellant to SSG Butler's room. After receiving the report of the assault, SSG Butler departed the room to go look for Mr. Al–U. Appellant seized this opportunity to take a knife from SSG Butler's military gear, ostensibly for self-defense, and returned to the common room of the building on the COP in which appellant resided. Not long thereafter, Mr. Al–U. entered the common room and initiated another altercation which resulted in appellant using SSG Butler's knife to cut Mr. Al–U. Following the altercation, appellant fled the immediate area, went to the latrines, and hid the knife under the floor boards to prevent the knife from being found by military police. Because there were eyewitnesses to the second altercation, appellant soon admitted to "cutting" Mr. Al–U. After initially claiming to have used a piece of wood, appellant admitted to having used a knife, which he then falsely claimed to have purchased in Canada and brought with him to Iraq.

When L3/Titan officials were informed of the incident, they arranged for appellant to be transferred to the Victory Base Complex (VBC) and to begin supporting a different military unit at that location. On 26 February 2008, the VBC garrison commander restricted appellant to the limits of the VBC. After being restricted, appellant made his way to Al Asad Air Terminal and attempted to depart Iraq. Appellant was apprehended and returned to the VBC, where the garrison commander ordered him into pretrial confinement on the VBC on 29 February 2008. Because appellant could no longer perform his contractual duties while in confinement, L3/Titan terminated his employment on 9 April 2008.

Appellant was originally charged with one specification of aggravated assault with a dangerous weapon. Prior to trial, appellant raised numerous motions to include a motion to dismiss for lack of jurisdiction. After hearing evidence, the military judge denied the jurisdiction motion. On 17 June 2008, appellant was charged with three additional charges related to his actions immediately following the assault. Thereafter, appellant negotiated a pretrial agreement in which the convening authority agreed to dismiss the assault charge and limit confinement to time served if the accused agreed to plead guilty to the three additional charges.

DISCUSSION

Before this court, appellant contends that his court-martial lacked jurisdiction because Congress exceeded the scope of its legislative authority when it amended the UCMJ to extend court-martial jurisdiction to reach civilians during contingency operations and thereby deprived him of the due process protections of the Fifth and Sixth Amendments to the United States Constitution. Appellant argues that a long line of Supreme Court precedent disfavors the exercise of military jurisdiction over civilians and that therefore this court should set aside the findings and sentence in his case.

A. Statutory Analysis

Before addressing appellant's constitutional arguments, we will first evaluate whether appellant and his conduct fit within the statutory jurisdictional framework of the UCMJ. If we find that neither appellant nor his offenses fall within the meaning of the applicable statutory provisions, we need not address his constitutional claims in order to resolve this case.

For court-martial jurisdiction to vest, in all cases there must be jurisdiction over both the offense and the accused. *United States v. Harmon*, 63 M.J. 98, 101 (C.A.A.F. 2006). The issue of jurisdiction is a legal question that this court reviews de novo. *Id.*

In order for there to be court-martial jurisdiction under Article 2(a)(10), UCMJ, three conditions must be met:

1. The offense and trial must occur during either a time of declared war or "a contingency operation;"

2. The person must be "serving with or accompanying an armed force;" and

3. The person must be "in the field."

Because the United States has not been in a state of declared war since World War II, we first must determine whether or not a "contingency operation" existed during the time of the offenses and at the time of trial. In the case at hand, both the offenses and the court-martial occurred during Operation Iraqi Freedom, a military operation that falls squarely within the statutory definition of "contingency operation" as found at 10 U.S.C. § 101(a)(13). Operation Iraqi Freedom is a Secretary of Defense-designated military operation, taking place during a presidentially declared national emergency and which resulted in the call or order to active duty of members of reserve components.

Next, we must determine if appellant was "serving with or accompanying an armed force." The test for making that determination is whether he has "moved with a military operation and whether his presence with the armed force was not merely incidental, but directly connected with, or dependent upon, the activities of the armed force or its personnel." *United States v. Burney*, 21 C.M.R. 98, 110 (C.M.A. 1956). In this case, it is undisputed appellant "moved with a military operation" as he was transported into the theater of operations via military aircraft and was transported by soldiers via military vehicles throughout Iraq as he performed his duties. His presence in Iraq was "not merely incidental" to that of the armed force. Instead, his presence was "directly connected with" and "dependent upon" the activities of the soldiers in the squad to which he was attached. Appellant lived on a combat outpost with them and depended on them for protection and logistical support. He routinely served side-by-side with them as they performed their daily military missions in support of Operation Iraqi Freedom. In fact, as noted by the military judge, appellant was "critical to the mission" in that the squad could not accomplish its mission without him. In short, his presence as an interpreter was essential to the ability of the unit to accomplish its primary mission of training and advising the Iraqi police. Following the altercation with another interpreter on the combat outpost, he continued to accompany the armed force, albeit involuntarily, when he was reassigned to work at the VBC, placed in pretrial confinement on the VBC, and tried on the VBC. Under the totality of the facts of this case, we have no doubt that appellant was "serving with or accompanying an armed force" both at the time of the offenses and at the time of his court-martial.

Lastly, we examine whether appellant was "in the field." At all times relevant to our inquiry, Iraq was specifically designated as a combat zone in which soldiers were authorized hazardous duty pay. Further, all of the offenses in question occurred on a combat outpost in an "area of actual fighting" against enemy insurgent groups. Throughout his deployment, appellant and the troops he supported were under a constant threat of attack by small arms fire, indirect fire, improvised explosive devices, and vehicle-borne explosive devices. Because of his critical role as an interpreter, he was subject to being personally targeted by the enemy. Even after appellant was moved to the VBC for his reassignment, pretrial confinement, and trial, he resided on a military base in central Iraq that was subject to attack by enemy forces.

After a careful consideration of all the salient facts of this case, we have no doubt both appellant and his offenses fall squarely within the jurisdictional language of Article 2(a)(10), UCMJ, as amended. Accordingly, unless Article

2(a)(10), UCMJ, as applied to appellant, is violative of the United States Constitution, military jurisdiction was properly vested in appellant's case.

B. Constitutional Analysis

We must, therefore, examine Article 2(a)(10), UCMJ in light of existing legal and historical precedent to determine whether its application to appellant runs afoul of the Constitution.

The United States Constitution authorizes Congress to "make Rules for the Government and Regulation of the land and naval Forces." Article I, Section 8, Clause 14. Clause 18 of that Article further authorizes Congress to "make all Laws which shall be necessary and proper" to execute the powers vested in the Congress. Article I, Section 8, Clause 18. *Kinsella v. United States ex rel. Singleton*, 361 U.S. 234, 237 (1960); *Reid v. Covert*, 354 U.S. 1, 19 (1957); *Dynes v. Hoover*, 61 U.S. 65 (1857). These two provisions have long been held to constitute a limited authority for Congress to create exceptions, such as trial by courts-martial, to Article III courts. Singleton, 361 U.S. at 237. Because persons subject to trial by courts-martial are not afforded some of the Constitutional rights which are normally recognized in Article III courts, the Supreme Court has cautioned that the authority to convene a court-martial must be limited to "the least possible power adequate to the end proposed." *United States ex rel. Toth v. Quarles*, 350 U.S. 11, 23 (1955) (quoting *Anderson v. Dunn*, 19 U.S. 204 (1821)).

Although the exercise of military jurisdiction over civilians accompanying military forces has long existed in America and actually predates the ratification of the Constitution, it has historically been applied in narrow circumstances in situations where the exercise of such jurisdiction was necessary for the military to maintain good order and discipline on the battlefield. Not surprisingly, the United States Supreme Court has invalidated numerous attempts by Congress and commanders to expand such jurisdiction to include times of peace.

For example, the Supreme Court has twice invalidated the use of military courts to try civilians in times of martial law in geographical locations where there were no ongoing hostilities, the civil administration was not deposed, and the local courts were open.[12] Between 1955 and 1960, the Supreme Court specifically prohibited the use of military courts to try former servicemen who committed offenses on active duty but who "had severed all relationship with the military" at time of trial,[13] to try civilian family members whose only military connection was the fact that they accompanied their service member spouses to overseas locations that were clearly not in a combat zone,[14] and to

[12] *Ex parte Milligan*, 71 U.S. 2, 4 Wall. 2, 18 L.Ed. 281 (1866) (prohibiting the military trial of civilians in Indiana during the Civil War); *Duncan v. Kahanamoku*, 327 U.S. 304 (1946) (prohibiting the military trial of civilians in World War II-era Hawaii).

[13] *United States ex rel. Toth v. Quarles*, 350 U.S. 11 (1955)

[14] *Covert*, 354 U.S. 1, and *Singleton*, 361 U.S. 234.

try civilian employees of the military who commit crimes overseas during times of peace.[15]

Although the instant case, like those previously decided by the Supreme Court, involves a civilian who was subjected to military jurisdiction, it is distinguishable in two very important respects: the appellant in this case committed all of his offenses and was court-martialed (1) during a time of actual hostilities and (2) in a location where actual hostilities were taking place. As noted in *Reid v. Covert*, "the extraordinary circumstances present in an area of actual fighting have been considered sufficient to permit punishment of some civilians in that area by military courts under military rules." *Covert*, 354 U.S. at 33. "In the face of an actively hostile enemy, military commanders necessarily have broad power over persons on the battlefront." *Id.* This recognition by the Supreme Court of the historical use of military courts to try civilians in areas of actual fighting, coupled with the recognition of the broad authority of military commanders on the battlefront would seem to authorize, or at least not prohibit, the exercise of military jurisdiction over appellant by the commander of the United States forces in Iraq.

During the Vietnam conflict, our superior court was faced with a civilian accused who, like appellant, committed his offenses during ongoing hostilities. In *United States v. Averette*, 41 C.M.R. 363 (C.M.A. 1970), the Court of Military Appeals (the predecessor to the Court of Appeals for the Armed Forces) declined to address the constitutional issue and instead strictly interpreted a pre–2006 version of Article 2(a)(10), UCMJ as requiring a declaration of war as a condition precedent to the exercise of court-martial jurisdiction over a civilian contractor serving in Vietnam during that conflict. The majority decided to apply "a strict and literal construction of the phrase 'in time of war'" because to do otherwise "would open the possibility of civilian prosecutions by military courts whenever military action on a varying scale of intensity occurs." *Averette*, 41 C.M.R. at 365. In reaching its holding in *Averette*, the Court of Military Appeals clearly was concerned that the phrase "in time of war" would be sU.S.C.eptible to a broad interpretation which could lead to the exercise of military jurisdiction over civilians in a wide variety of situations in which the military might be engaged in some sort of hostilities short of actual war.

Under the current version of Article 2(a)(10), UCMJ, however, there is no such danger of the broad application of the UCMJ to civilians because Congress has chosen to specifically limit the exercise of military jurisdiction over civilians by requiring either a formal declaration of war by Congress or the existence of a "contingency operation," as that term is narrowly defined by statute. 10 U.S.C. § 101(a)(13) (2000).

---

[15] *Grisham v. Hagan*, 361 U.S. 278 (1960), and *McElroy v. United States ex rel. Guagliardo*, 361 U.S. 281 (1960).

In addition to requiring either a declared war or the existence of a statutorily defined "contingency operation," Article 2(a)(10), UCMJ further limits the reach of military jurisdiction over civilians by requiring that the civilian be "serving with or accompanying an armed force" and that the civilian be "in the field." *See* discussion *supra* at part A. Statutory Analysis. These two requirements, when applied in conjunction with the temporal requirement that either a declared state of war or a contingency operation be in existence, ensure that the exercise of jurisdiction over civilians is "restricted" to the "narrowest jurisdiction deemed absolutely essential to maintaining discipline among troops in active service." *Singleton*, 361 U.S. at 240 (citing *Toth*, 350 U.S. at 22).

In reaching our decision on the constitutionality of Article 2(a)(10), UCMJ, we are mindful of the words of Judge Latimer in *Burney*, wherein he noted that "all grants of jurisdiction to military courts found in the [UCMJ] must be enforced . . . unless we are convinced that they are fundamentally hostile to military due process, or that they have been specifically condemned by the Supreme Court." *Burney*, 21 C.M.R. at 104–05. In this case, we can discern no manner in which the exercise of military jurisdiction over a non-U.S. citizen who knowingly accepted employment supporting U.S. forces in a combat zone during a declared contingency operation would be fundamentally hostile to either military or civilian due process, nor have we found any Supreme Court precedent that specifically precludes the exercise of such jurisdiction.

Accordingly, we find that appellant's court-martial had both personal and subject matter jurisdiction over the appellant. In light of our holding, it follows that the military judge did not err in ruling that the court had jurisdiction over appellant. Additionally, because we find that the exercise of military jurisdiction over appellant was proper, we find no violation of either the Fifth or Sixth Amendment of the United States Constitution by the military judge in his refusal to dismiss the charges and specifications facing appellant.

CONCLUSION

The findings of guilty are affirmed. The court affirms only so much of the sentence as includes 115 days of confinement and orders that appellant be credited with 115 days of confinement credit to be applied against his sentence of confinement.

Senior Judge TOZZI and Judge GALLAGHER concur.

Points for Discussion

1. Would the constitutional issue be more difficult or less difficult if Ali was a U.S. citizen? How important is it that, as a civilian, he is an employee of the U.S. Army and not an employee of a contractor?

2. The court addresses in dicta the Military Extraterritorial Jurisdiction Act of 2000 (MEJA). This Act makes federal civilian criminal laws apply extraterritorially in the case of civilians employed by or accompanying the Armed Forces outside the United States and in the case of service members. The key provision says:

> (a) Whoever engages in conduct outside the United States that would constitute an offense punishable by imprisonment for more than 1 year if the conduct had been engaged in within the special maritime and territorial jurisdiction of the United States
>
> (1) while employed by or accompanying the Armed Forces outside the United States; or
>
> (2) while a member of the Armed Forces subject to chapter 47 of title 10 (the Uniform Code of Military Justice), shall be punished as provided for that offense.

18 U.S.C. § 3261(a). For example, if a federal criminal law would prohibit possessing a certain kind of explosive in the United States, the same law would prohibit a covered civilian employee or contractor or a service member from possessing the explosive in Iraq or Afghanistan. Prosecutions of violations of federal criminal laws, including laws that MEJA causes to apply extraterritorially, occur in the United States in the federal district courts. In the *Ali* case, the court noted that MEJA contains an exception for nationals of the host country, *see id.* § 3261(b), and therefore concluded that MEJA therefore would not have applied to the accused. Another provision prohibits prosecution of service members until they cease to be subject to the UCMJ. *See id.* at 3261(d)(1). If MEJA had existed at the time *Averette* was decided, could Averette have been prosecuted in federal court? If so, what would the charge have been?

15-2. Trial of Service Members in State and Federal Courts

As explained in chapter 1, courts-martial may try members of the military for offenses even if the offenses have no service connection. *See Solorio v. United States*, 483 U.S. 435 (1987). But may state and federal civilian courts also try service members for any offenses over which they have jurisdiction? The constitutional answer to this question is yes. A service member who commits a drug offense, for example, constitutionally might be tried in state court under state anti-drug laws, in federal court for violating the U.S. Criminal Code, or in a court-martial for violating the UCMJ.

In this regard, three important points bear mention. First, the Double Jeopardy Clause of the Fifth Amendment prohibits trying a service member in both a court-martial and a civilian federal court for the same acts. *See Grafton v. United States*, 206 U.S. 333 (1907). But the Double Jeopardy Clause does not prohibit both a state and federal trial. *See United States v. Lanza*, 260 U.S. 377 (1922). The theory is that a state government has separate sovereignty from the federal government and the Double Jeopardy clause only applies to prosecutions by the same sovereign. *See id.* at 385.

Dual prosecutions are not common, but one author has counted 18 published cases in which a service member has been tried in both a state court and a court-martial. *See* Charles L. Pritchard, Jr., *The Pit and the Pendulum: Why the Military Must Change its Policy Regarding Successive State-Military Prosecutions*, Army Lawyer, Nov. 2007, at 1.

Second, despite the existence of other possibilities, in the usual case, service members are tried only by courts-martial. An agreement between the Department of Justice and Department of Defense in fact gives the Department of Defense primary responsibility for discipline in the Armed Forces and requires federal prosecutors to consult with military authorities before bringing a prosecution. *See* Memorandum of Understanding Between the Departments of Justice And Defense Relating to the Investigation and Prosecution of Certain Crimes (August 1984), *reprinted in* MCM, app. 3. Similarly, states usually cede jurisdiction over offenses committed by service members to the military justice system. States, however, could bring prosecutions if they so desired. Notably, the Servicemembers Civil Relief Act, 50 U.S.C. Appx. §§ 501-596, which stays certain kinds of civil actions against service members specifically does not apply to criminal proceedings. *See id.* § 512(a), (b)).

Third, sometimes federal prosecutions are brought against former service members who committed crimes while on active duty but who cannot now be tried by court-martial because they are no longer subject to the UCMJ. The prosecutions may be brought under federal criminal statutes, including those whose jurisdiction is extended by MEJA (discussed in a Point for Discussion following the *Ali* case above). For example, consider the case *United States v. Green*, — F.3d. —, 2011 WL 3568415 (6th Cir.), which the U.S. Court of Appeals for the Sixth Circuit summarized as follows:

> Steven D. Green was convicted and sentenced to life in prison for participating in a sexual assault and multiple murders while stationed in Iraq as an infantryman in the United States Army. Before senior Army officials became aware that Green and three fellow servicemembers were involved in these crimes, Green was discharged due to a personality disorder. When officials discovered Green's involvement in the crimes, his three coconspirators were still on active duty in the Army and thus subject to the Uniform Code of Military Justice. They were tried by courts-martial and each sentenced to between 90 and 110 years imprisonment, which rendered them eligible for parole in ten years. However, the Army had no authority to court-martial Green because he had already been discharged. Thus, civilian prosecutors charged Green under the Military Extraterritorial Jurisdiction Act, which extends federal criminal jurisdiction to persons who commit criminal acts while a member of the Armed Forces but later cease to be subject to military jurisdiction. A federal court jury convicted Green of a number of crimes, including murder and sexual assault, and the district court sentenced him to five consecutive life sentences.

Id. at *1. In an omitted portion of the opinion, the court upheld the constitutionality of the prosecution. *See id.*

The following case, which is the subject of a bestselling book—Joe McGinniss, Fatal Vision (1984)—concerns an initial decision not to try a service member by court-martial followed by a decision to try him in federal court.

UNITED STATES v. MacDONALD
U.S. Supreme Court
456 U.S. 1 (1982)

Chief Justice BURGER delivered the opinion of the Court.

We granted certiorari to decide whether the time between dismissal of military charges and a subsequent indictment on civilian criminal charges should be considered in determining whether the delay in bringing respondent to trial for the murder of his wife and two children violated his rights under the Speedy Trial Clause of the Sixth Amendment.

I

The facts in this case are not in issue; a jury heard and saw all the witnesses and saw the tangible evidence. The only point raised here by petitioner involves a legal issue under the Speedy Trial Clause of the Sixth Amendment. Accordingly, only a brief summary of the facts is called for. In the early morning of February 17, 1970, respondent's pregnant wife and his two daughters, aged 2 and 5, were brutally murdered in their home on the Fort Bragg, N.C., military reservation. At the time, MacDonald, a physician, was a captain in the Army Medical Corps stationed at Fort Bragg. When the military police arrived at the scene following a call from MacDonald, they found the three victims dead and MacDonald unconscious from multiple stab wounds, most of them superficial, but one a life-threatening chest wound which caused a lung to collapse.

At the time and in subsequent interviews, MacDonald told of a bizarre and ritualistic murder. He stated that he was asleep on the couch when he was awakened by his wife's screams. He said he saw a woman with blond hair wearing a floppy hat, white boots, and a short skirt carrying a lighted candle and chanting "acid is groovy; kill the pigs."[1] He claimed that three men

---

[1] A woman generally within this description was apparently seen by the military police as they rushed to answer respondent's call. During the course of this case, considerable suspicion has been focused upon Helena Stoeckley. Stoeckley was 19 at the time and a heavy user of heroin, opium, mescaline, LSD, marihuana, and other drugs; within days after the crime she began telling people that she was involved in the murder or that she at least had accompanied the murderers and watched them commit the crimes. She also wore mourning dress and displayed a funeral wreath on the day of the victims' funeral. The investigation confirmed that she had been seen returning to her apartment at 4:30 on the morning following the killings in the company of men also generally fitting the descriptions given by MacDonald. Stoeckley testified at trial that she had no memory of the night in question because

standing near the couch attacked him, tearing his pajama top, stabbing him, and clubbing him into unconsciousness. When he awoke, he found his wife and two daughters dead. After trying to revive them and covering his wife's body with his pajama top, MacDonald called the military police. He lost consciousness again before the police arrived.

Physical evidence at the scene contradicted MacDonald's account and gave rise to the suspicion that MacDonald himself may have committed the crime.[2] On April 6, 1970, the Army Criminal Investigation Division (CID) advised MacDonald that he was a suspect in the case and confined him to quarters. The Army formally charged MacDonald with the three murders on May 1, 1970. In accordance with Article 32 of the Uniform Code of Military Justice, 10 U.S.C. § 832, the Commanding General of MacDonald's unit appointed an officer to investigate the charges. After hearing a total of 56 witnesses, the investigating officer submitted a report recommending that the charges and specifications against MacDonald be dismissed. The Commanding General dismissed the military charges on October 23, 1970. On December 5, 1970, the Army granted MacDonald's request for an honorable discharge based on hardship.[3]

At the request of the Justice Department, however, the CID continued its investigation. In June 1972, the CID forwarded a 13-volume report to the Justice Department recommending further investigation. Additional reports were submitted during November 1972 and August 1973. Following evaluation of those reports, in August 1974, the Justice Department presented the matter to a grand jury. On January 24, 1975, the grand jury returned an indictment charging MacDonald with the three murders.

Prior to his trial in Federal District Court,[4] MacDonald moved to dismiss the indictment, in part on the grounds that the delay in bringing him to trial violated his Sixth Amendment right to a speedy trial. The District Court denied the motion, but the Court of Appeals allowed an interlocutory appeal

---

she was "stoned" that night. She did, however, admit that at the time of the crime she owned and frequently wore a blond wig and a pair of white boots and that she destroyed them within a few days after the crime because they might connect her with the episode.

[2] Threads from MacDonald's pajama top, supposedly torn in the living room, were found in the master bedroom, some under his wife's body, and in the children's bedroom, but not in the living room. There were 48 puncture holes in the top, yet MacDonald had far fewer wounds. The police were able to identify the bloodstains of each victim, and their location did not support MacDonald's story. Blood matching the type of MacDonald's children was found on MacDonald's glasses and pajama top. Fragments of surgical gloves were found near the bodies of the victims; the gloves from which those fragments came were found under a sink in the house.

[3] MacDonald's discharge barred any further military proceedings against him. *United States ex rel. Toth v. Quarles*, 350 U.S. 11 (1955).

[4] The District Court had jurisdiction because the crimes were committed on military property. 18 U.S.C. §§ 7(3), 1111.

and reversed, holding that the delay between the June 1972 submission of the CID report to the Justice Department and the August 1974 convening of the grand jury violated MacDonald's constitutional right to a speedy trial. *MacDonald v. United States*, 531 F.2d 196 (CA4 1976). We granted certiorari and reversed, holding that a criminal defendant could not appeal the denial of a motion to dismiss on Speedy Trial Clause grounds until after the trial had been completed. *United States v. MacDonald*, 435 U.S. 850 (1978).

MacDonald was then tried and convicted on two counts of second-degree murder and one count of first-degree murder. He was sentenced to three consecutive terms of life imprisonment. On appeal, a divided panel of the Fourth Circuit again held that the indictment violated MacDonald's Sixth Amendment right to a speedy trial and dismissed the indictment. 632 F.2d 258 (1980). The court denied rehearing en banc by an evenly divided vote. 635 F.2d 1115 (1980).

We granted certiorari, 451 U.S. 1016 (1981), and we reverse.

The Sixth Amendment provides that "[i]n all criminal prosecutions, the accused shall enjoy the right to a speedy and public trial. . . ." A literal reading of the Amendment suggests that this right attaches only when a formal criminal charge is instituted and a criminal prosecution begins.

In *United States v. Marion*, 404 U.S. 307, 313 (1971), we held that the Speedy Trial Clause of the Sixth Amendment does not apply to the period before a defendant is indicted, arrested, or otherwise officially accused:

> "On its face, the protection of the Amendment is activated only when a criminal prosecution has begun and extends only to those persons who have been 'accused' in the course of that prosecution. These provisions would seem to afford no protection to those not yet accused, nor would they seem to require the Government to discover, investigate, and accuse any person within any particular period of time. The Amendment would appear to guarantee to a criminal defendant that the Government will move with the dispatch that is appropriate to assure him an early and proper disposition of the charges against him."

In addition to the period after indictment, the period between arrest and indictment must be considered in evaluating a Speedy Trial Clause claim. *Dillingham v. United States*, 423 U.S. 64 (1975). Although delay prior to arrest or indictment may give rise to a due process claim under the Fifth Amendment, *see United States v. Lovasco*, 431 U.S. 783, 788-789 (1977), or to a claim under any applicable statutes of limitations, no Sixth Amendment right to a speedy trial arises until charges are pending.

Similarly, the Speedy Trial Clause has no application after the Government, acting in good faith, formally drops charges. Any undue delay after charges are dismissed, like any delay before charges are filed, must be scrutinized under the Due Process Clause, not the Speedy Trial Clause.

* * *

The Court identified the interests served by the Speedy Trial Clause in United *States v. Marion, supra,* at 320:

"Inordinate delay between arrest, indictment, and trial may impair a defendant's ability to present an effective defense. But the major evils protected against by the speedy trial guarantee exist quite apart from actual or possible prejudice to an accused's defense. To legally arrest and detain, the Government must assert probable cause to believe the arrestee has committed a crime. Arrest is a public act that may seriously interfere with the defendant's liberty, whether he is free on bail or not, and that may disrupt his employment, drain his financial resources, curtail his associations, subject him to public obloquy, and create anxiety in him, his family and his friends."

See also Barker v. Wingo, 407 U.S. 514, 532-533 (1972).

The Sixth Amendment right to a speedy trial is thus not primarily intended to prevent prejudice to the defense caused by passage of time; that interest is protected primarily by the Due Process Clause and by statutes of limitations. The speedy trial guarantee is designed to minimize the possibility of lengthy incarceration prior to trial, to reduce the lesser, but nevertheless substantial, impairment of liberty imposed on an accused while released on bail, and to shorten the disruption of life caused by arrest and the presence of unresolved criminal charges.

Once charges are dismissed, the speedy trial guarantee is no longer applicable. At that point, the formerly accused is, at most, in the same position as any other subject of a criminal investigation. Certainly the knowledge of an ongoing criminal investigation will cause stress, discomfort, and perhaps a certain disruption in normal life. This is true whether or not charges have been filed and then dismissed. This was true in Marion, where the defendants had been subjected to a lengthy investigation which received considerable press attention. But with no charges outstanding, personal liberty is certainly not impaired to the same degree as it is after arrest while charges are pending. After the charges against him have been dismissed, "a citizen suffers no restraints on his liberty and is [no longer] the subject of public accusation: his situation does not compare with that of a defendant who has been arrested and held to answer." *United States v. Marion,* 404 U.S., at 321. Following dismissal of charges, any restraint on liberty, disruption of employment, strain on financial resources, and exposure to public obloquy, stress and anxiety is no greater than it is upon anyone openly subject to a criminal investigation.

III

The Court of Appeals held, in essence, that criminal charges were pending against MacDonald during the entire period between his military arrest and his later indictment on civilian charges. We disagree. In this case, the homicide charges initiated by the Army were terminated less than a year after the crimes were committed; after that, there was no criminal prosecution pending on which MacDonald could have been tried until the grand jury, in January 1975, returned the indictment on which he was tried and convicted. During the intervening period, MacDonald was not under arrest, not in custody, and not subject to any "criminal prosecution." Inevitably, there were undesirable consequences flowing from the initial accusation by the Army and the continuing investigation after the Army charges were dismissed. Indeed, even had there been no charges lodged by the Army, the ongoing comprehensive investigation would have subjected MacDonald to stress and other adverse consequences. However, once the charges instituted by the Army were dismissed, MacDonald was legally and constitutionally in the same posture as though no charges had been made. He was free to go about his affairs, to practice his profession, and to continue with his life.

There is nothing to suggest that the Justice Department acted in bad faith in not securing an indictment until January 1975. After the Army dismissed its charges, it continued its investigation at the request of the Justice Department; the Army's initial 13-volume report was not submitted to the Justice Department until June 1972, and supplemental reports were filed as late as August 1973. Within a year, the Justice Department completed its review of the massive evidence thus accumulated and submitted the evidence to a grand jury. The grand jury returned the indictment five months later.

Plainly the indictment of an accused-perhaps even more so the indictment of a physician-for the heinous and brutal murder of his pregnant wife and two small children is not a matter to be hastily arrived at either by the prosecution authorities or by a grand jury. The devastating consequences to an accused person from the very fact of such an indictment is a matter which responsible prosecutors must weigh carefully. The care obviously given the matter by the Justice Department is certainly not any indication of bad faith or deliberate delay.

The Court of Appeals acknowledged, and MacDonald concedes, that the delay between the civilian indictment and trial was caused primarily by MacDonald's own legal manuevers and, in any event, was not sufficient to violate the Speedy Trial Clause. Accordingly, the judgment of the Court of Appeals is reversed, and the case is remanded for further proceedings consistent with this opinion.

Reversed and remanded.

   * * *

Justice MARSHALL, with whom Justice BRENNAN and Justice BLACKMUN join, dissenting.

   * * *

... After his honorable discharge, MacDonald moved to California and resumed the practice of medicine. In 1971, the CID again interviewed him. From January 1972 to January 1974, he repeatedly requested the

Government to complete its investigation, and offered to submit to further interviews. The Justice Department declined to question him or to advise him when the investigation would terminate. In January 1974, the Department wrote that "this case is under active investigation and will remain under consideration for the foreseeable future." There was no further correspondence.

The Government did not present the case to a civilian grand jury until August 1974. MacDonald waived his right to remain silent and testified before the grand jury for a total of more than five days. Numerous other witnesses testified, the bodies of the victims were exhumed, and the FBI reinvestigated certain aspects of the crime. An indictment was returned on January 24, 1975. The indictment charged MacDonald with three counts of first-degree murder.

The Government offered no legitimate reason-not even docket congestion-for the delay between the submission of the June 1972 report and the presentation to the grand jury in August 1974. The Court of Appeals explained:

> "The leisurely pace from June 1972 until the indictment was returned in January 1975 appears to have been primarily for the government's convenience. The Assistant United States Attorney for the Eastern District of North Carolina, who is familiar with the case, expressed an even harsher assessment of the delay. He told the magistrate at the bail hearing that the tangible evidence had been known to the government since the initial investigation in 1970 but that it had not been fully analyzed by the F.B.I. until the latter part of 1974. He explained that the F.B.I. analysis was tardy 'because of government bureaucracy.' "

The FBI's failure to complete its analysis until 1974 is the only Government justification for the delay that the District Court mentioned in its initial decision denying MacDonald's motion to dismiss on speedy trial grounds. In its post-trial decision, the District Court again denied the motion, but stated its belief that "the case could have been put before the grand jury at a much earlier date than it was." 485 F. Supp. 1087, 1089 (E.D.N.C. 1979).

II

The majority's analysis is simple: the Speedy Trial Clause offers absolutely no protection to a criminal defendant during the period that a charge is not technically pending. But simplicity has its price. The price, in this case, is disrespect for the language of the Clause, important precedents of this Court, and speedy trial policies.

"In all criminal prosecutions," the Sixth Amendment recites, "the accused shall enjoy the right to a speedy and public trial." On its face, the Sixth Amendment would seem to apply to one who has been publicly accused, has obtained dismissal of those charges, and has then been charged once again with the same crime by the same sovereign. Nothing in the language suggests that a defendant must be continuously under indictment in order to obtain the benefits of the speedy trial right. Rather, a natural reading of the language is that the Speedy Trial Clause continues to protect one who has been accused of a crime until the government has completed its attempts to try him for that crime.

* * *

Points for Discussion

1. If service members can be tried in federal district courts, is there any need for courts-martial? Is it ethical for the government to select a different forum to try an accused after ruling out one forum?

2. One author critical of speedy trial decisions like *MacDonald* comments:

> "In the civilian world, the government lacks the power to affect a defendant's life and livelihood, short of an indictment or imposition of pretrial restraint, which, in turn, would trigger the citizen's Sixth Amendment speedy trial rights. In the military, the government—as represented by the commander—may impose numerous adverse administrative actions on the member based, at best, only on suspicion, and without preferring charges."

Thomas G. Becker, *Games Lawyers Play: Pre-Preferral Delay, Due Process, and the Myth Of Speedy Trial in the Military Justice System*, 45 A.F. L. Rev. 1, 8 (1998). Could the *MacDonald* case be cited as a possible example?

15-3. Status of Forces Agreements in Foreign Countries

The United States stations service members in many foreign countries. What happens if these service members commit crimes? Can foreign governments arrest them, try them, and upon a finding of guilty punish them? The answers to these questions are found in more than 100 "status of forces agreements" (SOFAs) into which the United States and foreign nations have entered. *See* R. Chuck Mason, *Status of Forces Agreement (SOFA): What Is It, and How Has It Been Utilized?*, Congressional Research Service Report RL34531 (Jan. 5, 2011). Some of these SOFAs are found in treaties, while others are found in less formal agreements like base leases, while still others are composed of a combination of treaties and less formal agreements.

The following excerpt comes from the SOFA between the United States and the Republic of Korea. It contains provision similar to those found in SOFAs between the United States and other nations.

––––––––––––

Agreement under Article IV of the Mutual Defense Treaty Between the United States of America and the Republic of Korea, Regarding Facilities and Areas and the Status of United States Armed Forces in the Republic of Korea

T.I.A.S. No. 6127, 17 U.S.T. 1677 (Feb. 9, 1967), as amended, State Dept. No. 01-56, 2001 WL 681233 (Jan. 18, 2001)

* * *

ARTICLE XXII

Criminal Jurisdiction

1. Subject to the provisions of this Article,

(a) the military authorities of the United States shall have the right to exercise within the Republic of Korea all criminal and disciplinary jurisdiction conferred on them by the law of the United States over members of the United States armed forces or civilian component, and their dependents;

(b) the authorities of the Republic of Korea shall have jurisdiction over the members of the United States armed forces or civilian component, and their dependents, with respect to offenses committed within the territory of the Republic of Korea and punishable by the law of the Republic of Korea.

2. (a) The military authorities of the United States shall have the right to exercise exclusive jurisdiction over members of the United States armed forces or civilian component, and their dependents, with respect to offenses, including offenses relating to its security, punishable by the law of the United States, but not by the law of the Republic of Korea.

(b) The authorities of the Republic of Korea shall have the right to exercise exclusive jurisdiction over members of the United States armed forces or civilian component, and their dependents, with respect to offenses, including offenses relating to the security of the Republic of Korea, punishable by its law but not by the law of the United States.

(c) For the purpose of this paragraph and of paragraph 3 of this Article, a security offense against a State shall include:

(i) treason against the State;

(ii) sabotage, espionage or violation of any law relating to official secrets of that State, or secrets relating to the national defense of that State.

3. In cases where the right to exercise jurisdiction is concurrent the following rules shall apply:

(a) The military authorities of the United States shall have the primary right to exercise jurisdiction over members of the United States armed forces or civilian component, and their dependents, in relation to:

(i) offenses solely against the property or security of the United States, or offenses solely against the person or property of another member of the United States armed forces or civilian component or of a dependent;

(ii) offenses arising out of any act or omission done in the performance of official duty.

(b) In the case of any other offense, the authorities of the Republic of Korea shall have the primary right to exercise jurisdiction.

* * *

5. (a) The military authorities of the United States and the authorities of the Republic of Korea shall assist each other in the arrest of members of the United States armed forces, the civilian component, or their dependents in the territory of the Republic of Korea and in handing them over to the authority which is to have custody in accordance with the following provisions.

(b) The authorities of the Republic of Korea shall notify promptly the military authorities of the United States of the arrest of any member of the United States armed forces, or civilian component, or a dependent. The military authorities of the United States shall promptly notify the authorities of the Republic of Korea of the arrest of a member of the United States armed forces, the civilian component, or a dependent in any case in which the Republic of Korea has the primary right to exercise jurisdiction.

* * *

6. (a) The military authorities of the United States and the authorities of the Republic of Korea shall assist each other in the carrying out of all necessary investigations into offenses, and in the collection and production of evidence, including the seizure and, in proper cases, the handing over of objects connected with an offense. The handing over of such objects may, however, be made subject to their return within the time specified by the authority delivering them.

* * *

7. (a) A death sentence shall not be carried out in the Republic of Korea by the military authorities of the United States if the legislation of the Republic of Korea does not provide for such punishment in a similar case.

* * *

9. Whenever a member of the United States armed forces or civilian component or a dependent is prosecuted under the jurisdiction of the Republic of Korea he shall be entitled:

(a) to a prompt and speedy trial;

(b) to be informed, in advance of trial, of the specific charge or charges made against him;

(c) to be confronted with the witnesses against him;

(d) to have compulsory process for obtaining witnesses in his favor, if they are within the jurisdiction of the Republic of Korea;

(e) to have legal representation of his own choice for his defense or to have free or assisted legal representation under the conditions prevailing for the time being in the Republic of Korea;

(f) if he considers it necessary, to have the services of a competent interpreter; and

(g) to communicate with a representative of the Government of the United States and to have such a representative present at his trial.

* * *

Points for Discussion

1. In *United States v. Simmons*, 2009 WL 6835721 (Army Ct. Crim. App. 2009), an unreported decision that is not controlling precedent, there was a delay in prosecution of a soldier accused of raping his wife, a foreign national, in Korea. Trial counsel tried to justify the delay by explaining to the military judge that "under the Status of Forces Agreement between the United States and the Republic of Korea, the Republic of Korea had primary jurisdiction over the case" and that the United States therefore had to seek a waiver before beginning the prosecution. Did trial counsel correctly interpret the SOFA? Would the result be different if the accused had been charged with raping someone other than his wife?

2. Why would the United States want primary jurisdiction over certain kinds of cases? Are there any countries in which the United States should not allow local authorities to prosecute service members at all?

The following case considers whether a service member has the right to challenge the government's compliance with a SOFA.

UNITED STATES v. MURPHY
U.S. Court of Appeals for the Armed Forces
50 M.J. 4 (C.A.A.F. 1998)

Chief Judge COX delivered the opinion of the Court.

Appellant, Sergeant (SGT) James T. Murphy, stands convicted of three specifications of premeditated murder, in violation of Article 118, Uniform Code of Military Justice, 10 U.S.C. § 918, and single specifications of larceny, bigamy, and false swearing, in violation of Articles 121 and 134, UCMJ, 10 U.S.C. §§ 921 and 934, respectively. He was sentenced by a general court-martial to death. The Court of Military Review (now the Court of Criminal Appeals) affirmed his convictions and sentence to death. 36 M.J. 1137 (1993). His appeal is mandated by Article 67(a)(1), UCMJ, 10 U.S.C. § 867(a)(1)(1994).

Appellant has raised numerous issues in his appeal, many of which are classic appellate issues relating to the trial, the jurisdiction of the court-martial, evidentiary rulings, discovery questions, and the like. However, interspersed among these are numerous collateral attacks on his conviction, primarily based upon his claims of ineffective assistance of counsel. See APPENDIX for a complete list of the issues raised by appellant.

Upon careful consideration of appellant's claims, we agree that he received ineffective assistance of counsel as to his sentencing case. Accordingly, we set aside the decision of the Court of Military Review and return the record to the Judge Advocate General of the Army for further action consistent with the decretal paragraph of this opinion.

Unlike the practice in the United States Courts of Appeals and District Courts, neither the UCMJ nor the Manual for Courts–Martial, United States, 1984, provides procedures for collateral, post-conviction attacks on guilty verdicts. *See* 28 U.S.C. § 2255, et seq. Nevertheless, we have relied upon a variety of procedures to ensure that a military accused's rights are fully protected. *See, e.g., United States v. Henry*, 42 M.J 231, 238 (1995) (remanded to Court of Criminal Appeals for consideration of affi.davits of respective parties); *United States v. DuBay*, 17 U.S.C.MA 147, 37 CMR 411 (1967) (evidentiary hearing). In this case, we have elected to consider not only the record of trial, but also numerous affidavits filed subsequent to the trial in order to determine if appellant has shown good cause for relief to be granted. Arts. 67 and 59(a), UCMJ, 10 U.S.C. §§ 867 and 859(a), respectively. In so doing, we have carefully considered all of the issues raised by appellant before the Court. However, we will discuss only two general areas of concern: one of these, in personam jurisdiction of the court-martial to try him, by its very nature must be resolved at the threshold; the other, in our view, is dispositive of his appeal.

First, we will consider whether there was jurisdiction, under principles of international law, to try appellant in Germany, by United States General Court–Martial, for the murder of his former wife and former stepson, who were German citizens and were not his "dependents" at the time of the homicide. Second, we will consider whether appellant is entitled to a new trial on the ground that he did not receive effective assistance of counsel.

THE FACTS

Petra Murphy, a citizen and resident of Germany, had been married to appellant. She had a 5-year-old son, Tim, before she married appellant, and she had a second son, James, Jr., by appellant. During the months prior to the murders, she and appellant had an ongoing, acrimonious divorce proceeding pending in the German courts. In June 1987, appellant married Beate, another German citizen, although he had not yet divorced Petra. In July 1987, appellant visited North Carolina, where he obtained a divorce from Petra on the grounds of a 1–year separation. In August 1987, appellant received military orders requiring him to transfer to Redstone Arsenal, Alabama.

Sometime between August 16, when Petra was last seen alive by a fellow church member, and August 20, when appellant left Germany, appellant went to Petra's apartment. There, according to his confessions, he killed her by smashing in her head with a hammer. He also admitted that he killed Tim and James, Jr.

The bodies were discovered on August 23, when Petra's pastor, Chief Warrant Officer Two Smith, tried to ascertain why she had missed several church activities. Smith went to her apartment, where he encountered an unusual odor. He reported his findings to the German police. They investigated and discovered the bodies of the three victims.

This discovery precipitated an investigation by both the German authorities and the U.S. Army Criminal Investigation Command (CID). On August 27, 1987, appellant gave the first of several confessions to the authorities. Ultimately, he gave a written statement to the CID, in which he admitted that he had killed his former wife and the two children.

Appellant was taken into custody at Redstone Arsenal and was returned to Germany, where he was placed in pretrial confinement by the U.S. Army in the Mannheim Confinement Facility, Germany. While there, he also confessed his guilt to two fellow inmates, and he made incriminating statements to Sergeant First Class James Marek.

THE JURISDICTIONAL QUESTIONS

The Constitution of Germany prohibits imposition of the death penalty. From that vantage point, appellant now asserts that he was "100 percent" in favor of having the German Government exercise jurisdiction over the offenses in question. His basic premise is that primary jurisdiction over the homicides of his former wife and her son was with the German Government, and that the German Government would have exercised jurisdiction over this case had the German authorities realized they had primary jurisdiction. *See* Art. VII.3, North Atlantic Treaty Organization Status of Forces Agreement (NATO SOFA), 4 UST 1800, as applicable to Germany effective July 1, 1963, 14 UST 531. More specifically, his attack is three-fold.

First, he asserts that, by operation of certain laws and regulations, he was denied effective assistance of counsel in presenting his views to the German authorities. Specifically, he claims that his detailed defense counsel were prohibited by law, the Logan Act, 18 U.S.C. § 953 (1982), and by military regulation, U.S. Army Europe Regulation 550–56, from actively representing him in the negotiations with the local German prosecutors concerning the question of jurisdiction.

Second, he contends that the German prosecutors were acting under a false belief that the United States had primary jurisdiction over the case under the existing NATO SOFA, and he argues that American authorities had either mistakenly or purposely informed the German prosecutor that all of the victims in the case were "dependents" within the meaning of the treaty when, in fact, they were not. If this is the case, argues appellant, jurisdiction over him was acquired in contravention of a treaty, the NATO SOFA. Relying on the distinctions made by the Supreme Court in two landmark cases, *Ker v. Illinois*, 119 U.S. 436 (1886), and *United States v. Rauscher*, 119 U.S. 407 (1886), appellant argues that, if he is correct, then the United States was without jurisdiction to try him.

Third, appellant argues that he was clearly prejudiced. In this regard, appellant contends that a letter from the German Minister of Justice to the Attorney General of the United States clearly shows that German authorities would have exercised jurisdiction if they had not been mistaken about the true facts.

Government counsel counter these arguments in several ways. They assert that: (a) appellant has no standing to raise the issue; (b) appellant waived any claim for relief because he did not object to the trial prior to completion of the court-martial; and (c) in any event, to the extent that any claim for relief must be based upon Government misconduct, the United States was free of any wrongdoing here.

We resolve all of these claims against appellant. We agree with the Army Court of Military Review that appellant has no standing to object to the process. RCM 201(d)(3), Manual, supra, as amended, provides:

Where an act or omission is subject to trial by court-martial and by one or more civil tribunals, foreign or domestic, the determination which nation, state, or agency will exercise jurisdiction is a matter for the nations, states, and agencies concerned, and is not a right of the suspect or accused.

This provision is based upon principles of sovereignty long recognized by the Supreme Court. *See Ponzi v. Fessenden*, 258 U.S. 254, 260 (1922), which states:

One accused of crime has a right to a full and fair trial according to the law of the government whose sovereignty he is alleged to have offended, but he has no more than that. . . . He may not complain if one sovereignty waives its strict right to exclusive custody of him for vindication of its laws in order that the other may also subject him to conviction of crime against it.

See also Wilson v. Girard, 354 U.S. 524 (1957).

Assuming, however, that appellant has standing to complain about the exercise of jurisdiction over him by the U.S. Army, he nevertheless loses. The Supreme Court in *Solorio v. United States*, 483 U.S. 435 (1987), held that the test for whether a military court-martial has jurisdiction to try an accused is the military status of the accused. *But cf. Loving v. United States*, 517 U.S. 748, 774 (1996) (Stevens, J., concurring); *compare with Relford v. Commandant, U.S. Disciplinary Barracks, Ft. Leavenworth*, 401 U.S. 355, 365 (1971) (query whether appellant satisfies all twelve factors to defeat jurisdiction in military court-martial).

It is uncontested that, at all times pertinent to this case, appellant was a member of the U.S. Army and subject to the jurisdiction of the court-martial. Art. 2, UCMJ, 10 U.S.C. § 802. Furthermore, he was taken into custody in the United States and was never released to the custody and control of Germany. Accordingly, even if the conduct of United States military authorities in Germany misled German authorities into a decision not to seek the return of appellant to the custody of Germany for prosecution, appellant was, nevertheless, lawfully subject to the jurisdiction of the court-martial. In *personam* jurisdiction over him existed because of his status as a soldier in the Army, not as a result of his person being turned over to the United States by a foreign government pursuant to an extradition treaty. Therefore, his reliance on *United States v. Rauscher* is misplaced.

We need not decide whether the Logan Act or the U.S. Army Europe Regulation can indeed prevent a defense counsel from communicating with German prosecutors. Nor do we resolve the issue by holding that appellant waived his right to contest jurisdiction. That merely raises other questions as to the competence of his attorneys, which we discuss next.

* * *

[The remainder of the case is omitted.]

Points for Discussion

1. Usually American service members prefer to be tried by a court-martial under the UCMJ, rather than to be tried in a foreign court. Why is that? Why is SGT Murphy's case different? Can you think of other situations in which service members might wish to be tried in foreign courts?

2. If United States military authorities did in fact mislead German authorities, what is the appropriate response if SGT Murphy cannot raise the violation in his case? How should the Attorney General respond to the German Minister of Justice's letter asserting that Germany would have exercised jurisdiction?

15-4. Courts of Inquiry

A court of inquiry is a special form of military court "vested with the power to investigate the nature of a transaction or accusation of an officer ...." Black's Law Dictionary (9th ed. 2009). Courts of inquiry find facts, draw conclusions, and sometimes make recommendations to commanders. But courts of inquiry do not impose criminal penalties or other sanctions. Indeed, they often investigate matters that are not crimes at all.

A prominent historical example of a court of inquiry concerns an event that occurred during the closing days of the Civil War. According to an able article by then-Lieutenant Colonel Marc L. Warren, *Relief and Review: The Case of Major General G. K. Warren*, Army Lawyer, May 1996, at 36, the following events occurred: On 1 April 1865, Major General Phillip Sheridan relieved Major General Gouverneur K. Warren of his command of the Fifth

Army Corps. General Sheridan concluded that General Warren had not moved sufficiently aggressively and rapidly against the enemy and that he had failed to inspire his troops. This action effectively ended the military career of General Warren, who had until that time served with great distinction.[1] Afterwards, General Warren repeatedly petitioned superiors, including the successive Presidents of the United States to convene a Board of Inquiry to investigate whether General Sheridan had been justified in his action. Fourteen years later, in 1879, President Rutherford B. Hayes, acceded to the request. After three years of investigation and deliberation, the Board of Inquiry finally determined that General Sheridan's decision to relieve General Warren was improper under the circumstances. Sadly, General Warren never received this news because he died several months before the Board of Inquiry reached its conclusion. Why would a formal court of inquiry be important in a matter like this?

In modern times, a court of inquiry might be used by the Navy to determine important questions such as what caused a collision of ships. The following excerpt from a much longer report provides an example:

---

13 Apr 01

From: Vice Admiral John B. Nathman, U.S. Navy Rear Admiral Paul F. Sullivan, U.S. Navy Rear Admiral David M. Stone, U.S. Navy Rear Admiral Isamu Ozawa, JMSDF

To: Commander in Chief, U.S. Pacific Fleet

Subj: COURT OF INQUIRY INTO THE CIRCUMSTANCES SURROUNDING THE COLLISION BETWEEN USS GREENEVILLE (SSN 772) AND JAPANESE M/V EHIME MARU THAT OCCURRED OFF THE COAST OF OAHU, HAWAII ON 9 FEBRUARY 2001

* * *

PRELIMINARY STATEMENT

1. On 9 February 2001, at 1343 local time, the USS GREENEVILLE (SSN 772) and the Japanese Motor Vessel (M/V) EHIME MARU collided in waters nine

---

[1] General Warren was known as the "Hero of Little Roundtop" based on his actions at Gettysburg. A glimpse of General Warren's military demeanor may be gleaned from an exchange between him and General Gordon G. Meade during the Wilderness campaign. General Meade told General Warren to "cooperate" with General Sedgwick. Warren responded:

> You are the commander of this Army and can give orders and I'll obey them, or you can put Sedgwick in command and he can give the orders and I will obey them, or you can put me in command and I will give the orders and Sedgwick will obey them, but I'll be Goddamned if I'll cooperate with Sedgwick or anyone else.

Warren, *supra*, at 36 (quoting other sources).

miles south of Oahu, Hawaii. Within minutes of the collision, the M/V EHIME MARU was lost, along with nine of her embarked complement.

* * *

3. On 17 February 2001, Commander in Chief, U.S. Pacific Fleet, appointed this Court of Inquiry to conduct additional factfinding and analysis. Specifically, the Court of Inquiry was directed to accomplish the following:

a. To inquire into all of the facts and circumstances connected with the collision, resulting deaths and injuries to the Japanese passengers and crew of the Japanese M/V EHIME MARU, the damages resulting therefrom, and any fault, neglect, or responsibility for the incident;

b. To examine the operational policies and practices of Commander, Submarine Force, U.S. Pacific Fleet's implementation of the Distinguished Visitor Embarkation (DVE) Program;

c. To examine the propriety of the assigned location for USS GREENEVILLE's operations on 9 February; and d. To examine and make findings as to whether Captain Robert L. Brandhuber, Chief of Staff, Submarine Force, U.S. Pacific Fleet, as senior officer onboard USS GREENEVILLE on 9 February, was in a position to intervene and prevent the chain of events leading to the collision.

4. The Convening Authority named the following individuals as parties to the Court of Inquiry:

a. Commander Scott D. Waddle, U.S. Navy, Commanding Officer, USS GREENEVILLE;

b. Lieutenant Commander Gerald K. Pfeifer, U.S. Navy, Executive Officer, USS GREENEVILLE;

c. Lieutenant (Junior Grade) Michael J. Coen, U.S. Navy, USS GREENEVILLE, Officer of the Deck at the time of collision.

5. At the invitation of the Convening Authority, Rear Admiral Isamu Ozawa of the Japan Maritime Self-Defense Force participated as an advisor and non-voting member of the Court.   Authority for Rear Admiral Ozawa's appointment was based primarily upon Section 0211.h of reference (a), which specifically permits participation of entities with an interest in the subject under inquiry. The Court welcomed and benefited from Rear Admiral Ozawa's active involvement throughout the investigative process. While participating in the Court's deliberations, Rear Admiral Ozawa did not vote on the findings of fact, opinions, and recommendations. Only that evidence introduced in open court and available to all parties was considered in the Court's deliberations.

* * *

FINDINGS OF FACT

I. The Collision Introduction

* * *

5. EHIME MARU was a vessel owned by the Ehime Prefecture, Japan, and used by the Prefecture's Uwajima Marine Products High School. The ship operated under Japanese registry, number 135174. (Exhibits 54, 60).

6. Constructed and launched in 1996, EHIME MARU was a "moving classroom" for high school students preparing for employment in the marine products industry. The ship's specific objectives were to develop student's experience at sea and to provide hands-on training as to:

    a. Long-line tuna fishing;

    b. Maritime navigation, instrumentation, and operation;

    c. Marine engines; and d. Oceanographic observation and research of marine life resources. (Exhibit 54).

7. EHIME MARU was approximately 190 feet in length, with a total tonnage of 500 tons. The ship had a white hull and superstructure, a blue line around the hull, a band of black at the top of its stack, and a whirlpool-like logo in red and blue amidships. The top of the Bridge was approximately 24 feet above the waterline. EHIME MARU's highest point, the center radar mast, stood approximately 48 feet above the water. (Exhibits 10, 53, 54).

* * *

12. EHIME MARU was underway at approximately 1200. The ship's complement consisted of 35 people: 20 crew, 2 instructors, and 13 students. Exhibit 53).

* * *

37. GREENEVILLE's sole mission on 9 February was to conduct a public affairs "distinguished visitor" (DV) embark for 16 civilian guests. (Testimony of CDR Waddle, page 1693, 1700; RADM Konetzni, page 759-61; RADM Griffiths, page 89, 226; CAPT Brandhuber, page 818; LCDR Werner, page 1510; Exhibit 32). (For information on SUBPAC's DV Embarkation Program, and additional details regarding GREENEVILLE's DV embark of 9 February, see section III, infra).

* * *

56. Throughout the morning, civilian guests toured the submarine in small groups, under the supervision of assigned escorts. The guests viewed officer and enlisted quarters, the Torpedo Room, Sonar Room, and the Control Room. While in the Control Room, guests were allowed to take the planes, under the direct supervision of the Planesman. While in the Sonar Room, sonar recordings of whale sounds were played for the guests. (Testimony of LCDR Meador, page 1297-98; LT Pritchett, page 1356-57; MM1 Harris, page 1251; Exhibits 64, 65).

* * *

221. At approximately 13:42:25, GREENEVILLE commenced [an] emergency surface.

a. This involved forcing 4500 psi high-pressure air into the submarine's forward and aft main ballast tanks for a period of 10 seconds.

b. This large volume of air forced water out of the ballast tanks, quickly creating a condition of positive buoyancy, thereby forcing the ship to the surface.

c. Submarines maintain this capability in case of casualty.

d. Once initiated, surfacing of the ship was unavoidable. (Testimony of RADM Griffiths, page 153-55, 213-17; MMC Streyle, page 1241; Exhibit 39, 40).

* * *

223. The CO performed the emergency surfacing maneuver to demonstrate to the civilian guests the capability of a submarine to ascend in the event of a casualty. He was also mindful of a training value and benefit to the crew. The CO had confidence in his submarine that the EMBT Blow System would operate as designed. (Testimony of CDR Waddle, page 1687-91, 1702-04).

224. As GREENEVILLE was coming to the surface, the CO used the 1MC to inform the guests of what was happening to the submarine. (Testimony of LT Mahoney, page 1386; LT Pritchett, page 1363; STS1 Reyes, page 1200; FT1 Seacrest, page 1581).

225. GREENEVILLE surfaced underneath EHIME MARU at approximately 13:43:15. (Exhibit 4).

226. When the collision occurred, the GREENEVILLE crew felt a shudder and two loud thumps. (Testimony of LCDR Meador, page 1300; LT Mahoney, page 1386; MMCM Coffman, page 1333; ETCS Smith, page 1291; ET1 Thomas, page 1083; STS1 McGiboney, page 1429; FT1 Seacrest, page 1581; Exhibit 75).

227. GREENEVILLE impacted EHIME MARU just aft of the submarine's sail on the port side. The submarine's rudder then sliced through EHIME MARU from starboard to port. (Testimony of RADM Griffiths, page 147).

228. EHIME MARU immediately began to sink. (Testimony of LCDR Meador, page 1300; Exhibit 53).

* * *

II. The Search and Rescue (SAR) Operation

Onboard M/V EHIME MARU

229. At the moment of collision, Captain Ohnishi felt a lifting of the stern of the ship, accompanied by two violent banging sounds. EHIME MARU came to a halt. (Exhibit 53).

230. The collision resulted in an immediate loss of power onboard EHIME MARU. (Exhibit 53).

231. A crewmember reported to Captain Ohnishi that there was a surfaced submarine on the aft port side. When Captain Ohnishi looked to see the submarine, he noted EHIME MARU's aft portholes being abnormally close to the surface of the ocean. (Exhibit 53).

232. Captain Ohnishi told crewmembers to gather everyone at the assigned mustering station, the deck area aft of the Bridge. EHIME MARU's Communications Chief went to switch on the EPIRB. (Exhibit 53).

233. Captain Ohnishi went to the chart room to retrieve documents, and noticed people already at the muster station. The Captain then proceeded to the mustering area to conduct a head count, but water was already washing over the deck. The Captain and others in the deck area were swept into the sea. (Exhibit 53).

234. EHIME MARU's life rafts were automatically deployed and surfaced. The survivors climbed, and assisted others, into the life rafts. From a total complement of 35, 26 individuals entered the life rafts. (Exhibit 53).

235. EHIME MARU sank in less than 10 minutes. (Exhibit 53).

236. Survivors from EHIME MARU noted considerable amounts of flotsam in the water. They called and searched for any additional survivors who might still be in the sea. No other person was ever sighted. (Exhibit 53).

Onboard USS GREENEVILLE

237. After hearing the loud noises and experiencing the shudder made by the collision, the CO stated, "what the hell was that?" (Exhibit 1, enclosures 4 & 15; Exhibits 64, 65).

238. The CO raised the Number 2 periscope. The XO raised the Number 1 periscope. Both saw a fishing vessel aft of GREENEVILLE. The CO indicated to the Control Room that the submarine had hit a ship. He asked that the guests proceed to the Crew's Mess. (Exhibit 1, enclosure (2); Exhibits 64, 65, 75).

    * * *

OPINIONS

I. The Collision

    * * *

9. A principal cause of the collision was an artificial urgency created by the CO in the Control Room to complete all afternoon DV events and return to Pearl Harbor as close to schedule as possible. (FF 78-85, 89, 92, 101, 103, 110, 132, 136, 138, 144, 145, 157-160, 162-166, 176, 194, 196, 197, 199, 202-206, 208).

10. A principal cause of the collision was the CO's disregard of standard submarine operating procedures and his own Standing Orders. (FF 125, 129,

132, 138, 140-142, 145, 150, 157, 158, 161-163, 166, 171, 172, 179-182, 194, 196, 197, 199, 202-204, 208).

11. A principal cause of the collision was the failure of the ship's contact management team to work together and pass information to each other about the surface contact picture. (FF 45, 49, 50, 63-67, 74, 76, 77, 92-94, 101, 110, 129, 132, 138, 140-145, 149, 150, 157-160, 162-164, 166, 171, 172, 176, 194, 199, 202, 203, 206, 208, 217).

12. While managing 3 surface contacts was well within GREENEVILLE's capability, the artificial urgency in the Control Room on 9 February caused the contact management team to miss or fail to identify important contact information that would have made it clear contact S-13 was close. (FF 45, 49, 50, 63-67, 72, 74, 76, 77, 92-94, 101, 110, 129, 132, 138, 140-145, 149, 150, 157-160, 162-164, 166, 171, 172, 176, 194, 199, 202, 203, 206, 208, 217).

* * *

14. The artificial urgency created by the CO caused him to deviate from NWP guidance and his own Standing Orders when performing TMA, the ascent to periscope depth, and his visual search at periscope depth. (FF 125, 129, 132, 138, 140-142, 145, 150, 157, 158, 161-163, 166, 171, 172, 179-182, 194, 196, 197, 199, 202-204, 208).

* * *

24. Had the CO conducted a proper search in accordance with NWP 3-13.10 guidance and his own Standing Order 6, he would have detected EHIME MARU. (FF 179-182, 194, 196, 197, 199, 202, 203, 208).

* * *

29. GREENEVILLE's command climate and the presence of civilian guests onboard affected the performance of watchstanders, and thereby indirectly contributed to the collision. (FF 16, 57, 58, 77, 82, 85, 95, 101, 102, 110, 111, 132, 150, 151, 157-160, 162-164, 166, 176, 177, 194, 199, 202, 203, 216, 217, 220, 224, 363, 364, 366, 416, 429, 430).

* * *

31. The crew held a false sense of security and confidence in their own professional skills. They believed they were better than they really were, and lost the ability to critically assess themselves. (FF 16, 18, 19, 21, 23, 27-29, 32, 33, 41, 63, 64, 66, 67, 72, 76, 77, 89, 92-94, 132, 138, 140-144, 150, 152, 157-160, 162-164, 166, 176, 194, 202, 203, 208, 215-217).

* * *

36. The large number of civilians in the Control Room created a physical barrier between watchstanders and equipment displays that hindered the normal flow of contact information among members of GREENEVILLE's contact management team. (FF 95, 177, 363, 364).

* * *

39. The CO was inappropriately disposed to entertain his civilian guests rather than safely demonstrate GREENEVILLE's operational capabilities. For example:

a. His unauthorized excursion to test depth to obtain deep seawater samples as mementos and driving the ship at flank speed needlessly exposed civilians to classified information.

b. Breaking "rig for dive" to obtain mementos inappropriately placed entertainment before safety of own ship.

c. Permitting the use of the Sonar Working Tape Recorder to play whale sounds for civilians took an important piece of equipment off-line.

d. Autographing pictures for his guests after lunch contributed to the delay of afternoon ship maneuvers. All these actions denote an inappropriate informality regarding shipboard operations on 9 February. (FF 16, 30, 37, 47, 55-58, 82, 102, 111, 151, 184, 194, 203, 220, 223, 224, 324, 326, 327, 346, 356, 357, 363, 364, 366).

* * *

RECOMMENDATIONS

I. The Collision

1. That the Commander in Chief, U.S. Pacific Fleet, take GREENEVILLE's CO, CDR Scott D. Waddle, to Admiral's Mast to answer for his actions on 9 February.* While mindful of the serious and painful consequences of his failures that day, the Court recommends against court-martial due to the absence of any criminal intent or deliberate misconduct on his part. While his actions were negligent and careless and represented a serious departure from the high standards expected of officers in command, they were not so egregious as to warrant trial by court-martial. In reaching its recommendation, the Court also considered CDR Waddle's 20 years of dedicated and faithful service to the Navy and country.

2. That the new Commanding Officer of USS GREENEVILLE take the FTOW, FT1(SS) Patrick T. Seacrest, to Captain's Mast to answer for his actions on 9 February. In addition, that Petty Officer Seacrest be made to requalify before standing another underway watch as FTOW.

3. That the new Commanding Officer of USS GREENEVILLE admonish the XO, LCDR Gerald K. Pfeifer, for his lack of oversight of the enlisted watchbill and failure to ensure only qualified personnel were permitted to stand watch.

4. That the new Commanding Officer of USS GREENEVILLE admonish the OOD, LT(jg) Michael J. Coen, for his lack of foresight and attention to detail in standing his watch.

---

* Nonjudicial punishment may be based on the record of a court of inquiry. See MCM, pt. V, ¶4.d.—Eds.

5. That the new Commanding Officer of USS GREENEVILLE admonish the COB, MMCM(SS) Douglas Coffman, for his lack of forceful backup of the chain of command, lack of oversight of the enlisted watchbill, and failure to ensure only qualified personnel were permitted to stand watch.

6. That the new Commanding Officer of USS GREENEVILLE admonish the Sonar Supervisor, STS1(SS) Edward McGiboney, for poor watchstanding and backup of the contact management team and failure to ensure only qualified personnel were permitted to stand watch in Sonar. In addition, that Petty Officer McGiboney be made to requalify before standing another underway watch as Sonar Supervisor.

* * *

Points for Discussion

1. What factors may have made it important to conduct a formal court of inquiry following this incident? Note the detail of the citations indicating the rigor of the proceedings and report. Could the Navy simply have proceeded to conduct criminal investigations instead?

2. The United States subsequently paid $13 million to families of the victims of the accident and paid $11.47 million for the destroyed vessel, cargo, and other costs. Cmdr. Scott D. Waddle was given a letter of reprimand, and he retired from the Navy. *See* Howard French, *Japanese Accept U.S. Offer in Ship Accident*, N.Y. Times, Nov. 14, 2001, at A15. Was justice done in this case? Bad luck followed the ship. In early 2002, not long after the court of inquiry completed its investigation, the *USS Greenville* was involved in another incident. The vessel struck the *USS Ogden* off the coast of Oman causing a fuel leak. *See Accident-Prone Sub Bumps U.S. Warship*, N.Y. Times, Jan. 28, 2002, at A10.

CHAPTER 16

TRIAL OF ENEMY COMBATANTS BY MILITARY COMMISSION

16-1. Introduction and Historical Overview

A military commission is a form of military tribunal which the United States and other nations have used throughout history to try persons accused of war crimes or of violations of martial law.[1] Military commissions resemble courts-martial, but historically they have had less formal procedures. During the Civil War, thousands of military commissions tried offenses. The most prominent case was the trial of the Lincoln conspirators. In the years immediately following World War II, the Allied nations used military commissions to try hundreds of German and Japanese service members and civilians for war crimes.[2]

---

[1] Parts of this chapter are adapted from Gregory E. Maggs, Terrorism and the Law: Cases and Materials (2d ed. 2010).

[2] The principal post-World War II military tribunals included the following:

(1) The International Military Tribunal, Nuremberg. In October 1945, an international military tribunal composed of judges from the United States, Great Britain, France, and the Soviet Union tried 24 leading Nazi figures and six organizations for war crimes and for crimes against humanity.

(2) The Nuremberg Military Tribunals. In addition to the International Military Tribunal, the United States also used military commissions in Nuremberg to try 12 separate cases involving 182 defendants, most of whom were high ranking German officers.

(3) The Dachau Trials. From 1945 to 1948, U.S. Army military tribunals also tried 1672 persons in a total of 489 cases. The accused included concentration camp guards, civilians who had killed allied airmen after they were shot down or crashed, and German soldiers accused of committing various war crimes. These trials took place at the former Dachau Concentration Camp.

(4) Other Military Trials of German Defendants. In addition to the more famous trials, the United States, Britain, France, the Soviet Union, the Netherlands, Norway, Canada, and Greece also used military tribunals to try thousands of other minor German war criminals.

(5) The International Military Tribunal for the Far East (also known as the Tokyo War Crimes Tribunal). A military tribunal with judges from the United States, the Soviet Union, the United Kingdom, France, the Netherlands, the Republic of China, Australia, New Zealand, Canada, India, and the Philippines tried 28 high-level Japanese defendants for war crimes.

In November 2001, shortly after the 9/11 attacks, President George W. Bush ordered the Armed Forces to use military commissions to try suspected al-Qaida terrorists and others for war crimes. *See* Military Order of November 13, 2001, 66 Fed. Reg. 57833 (Nov. 13, 2001). In promulgating this order, the President relied on his constitutional power as the Commander in Chief, *see* U.S. Const. art II, § 2, cl. 1; on the authority granted to him by Congress to use military force against the persons responsible for the 9/11 attacks, Authorization to Use Military Force (AUMF), Pub. L. No. 107-40, 115 Stat. 224 (Sept. 18, 2001), and on a few general provisions in the Uniform Code of Military Justice which recognize military commissions as a form of military tribunal, *see* 10 U.S.C. §§ 821, 836.

Following years of litigation over the authority of the President's order— and with only a handful of prosecutions brought or pending—Congress decided to provide express support to the President's effort to use military commissions to try suspected terrorists. Congress first passed the Military Commissions Act of 2006, Pub. L. No. 109-366, 120 Stat. 2600 [hereinafter MCA 2006], which created a complete military justice system for military commissions, a system that is comparable in complexity to the court-martial system established by the UCMJ. Congress subsequently amended the Military Commissions Act of 2006 with the Military Commissions Act of 2009, Pub. L. No. 111-84, § 948b(a), 123 Stat. 2190 [hereinafter MCA 2009]. This new legislation clarified many details and provided additional protections to the accused. Despite this extensive legislation, efforts to use military commissions have remained controversial and have proceeded very slowly. Military commissions, however, still bear study because they ultimately may be used to try the men accused of plotting the 9/11 attacks and other prominent terrorists.

Points for Discussion

1. What arguments might be made for trying suspected al-Qaida terrorists in military tribunals rather than trying them in federal civilian courts (as various al-Qaida terrorists have already been tried)? Does prosecuting terrorism cases in federal court raise unacceptable security risks? Is the federal court system too slow? Do the federal courts lack expertise in terrorism matters? Would the accused have "excessive" rights and procedural protections in federal court? Note that President Bush said in his order directing the use of military commissions "that it is not practicable to apply in military commissions under this order the principles of law and the rules of evidence generally recognized in the trial of criminal cases in the

---

(6) Other Military Trials of Japanese Defendants. The United States, Australia, Britain, and China also tried hundreds of lesser Japanese war criminals by military commission in Japan, China, the Phillippines, and various Pacific islands. For instance, in *Johnson v. Eisentrager,* 339 U.S. 763 (1950), the Supreme Court considered the case of Germans whom a United States military commission had convicted of violating the terms of Germany's surrender.

United States district courts." Why might military commissions be superior in this regard?

What arguments might be made against the use of military commissions? Are military tribunals inherently unfair to the accused if they do not follow ordinary court procedures? Do military judges and officers lack sufficient experience with terrorism to handle the cases? Are the procedures to be used by military commission untested and thus subject to slow and costly appellate challenges?

2. Khalid Sheik Mohammed is suspected, based on his own confessions and other evidence, of being the mastermind behind the 9/11 attacks that killed nearly 3000 people. Although Mohammed has been in military custody since 2003, as of 2011 he had not yet faced trial. In 2008, charges against Mohammed and four other 9/11 conspirators were referred to a military commission at the U.S. naval base located at Guantanamo Bay, Cuba. But in 2009, the Attorney General announced that Mohammed and the others would be tried in federal court instead of a military commission. The charges before military commissions were then withdrawn. Congress responded by blocking funds for prosecuting Mohammad in federal court. In 2011, the Attorney General announced that Mohammad would be tried by military commission after all. *See* Charlie Savage & Benjamin Weiser, *In a Reversal, Military Trials For 9/11 Cases*, N.Y. Times, Apr. 5, 2011, at A1. Senator Charles E. Schumer (D-N.Y.), who opposed trial in federal court, praised the decision to return the trial to military commissions. He is quoted as saying: "While not unexpected, this is the final nail in the coffin of that wrong-headed idea [i.e., trial in federal court]. I have always said that the perpetrators of this horrible crime should get the ultimate penalty, and I believe this proposal by the administration can make that happen." *Id.* Should the choice of forum for trying someone take so long? Should the forum really make much difference if the ultimate goal is justice?

The two leading cases on military commissions during the World War II-era were *Ex parte Quirin*, 317 U.S. 1 (1942), and *Application of Yamashita*, 327 U.S. 1 (1946). In *Quirin*, the Supreme Court addressed three issues: whether the President has authority to use military commissions to try enemy combatants for war crimes; which offenses are triable by military commission; and whether trials by military commission must afford the accused all of the guarantees of the Fifth and Sixth Amendments. In *Yamashita*, the Court provided additional guidance on the nature of offenses triable by military commission and the procedures that military commissions must follow. Although subsequent developments have cast doubt on much of what the Supreme Court said in *Quirin* and *Yamashita*, the cases remain influential legal landmarks. As you will see, they are cited in the materials included throughout this chapter.

EX PARTE QUIRIN
U.S. Supreme Court
317 U.S. 1 (1942)

Mr. Chief Justice STONE delivered the opinion of the Court.

These cases are brought here by petitioners' several applications for leave to file petitions for habeas corpus in this Court, and by their petitions for certiorari to review orders of the District Court for the District of Columbia, which denied their applications for leave to file petitions for habeas corpus in that court.

The question for decision is whether the detention of petitioners by respondent for trial by Military Commission, appointed by Order of the President of July 2, 1942, on charges preferred against them purporting to set out their violations of the law of war and of the Articles of War, is in conformity to the laws and Constitution of the United States.

* * *

The following facts appear from the petitions or are stipulated. Except as noted they are undisputed.

All the petitioners were born in Germany; all have lived in the United States. All returned to Germany between 1933 and 1941. All except petitioner Haupt are admittedly citizens of the German Reich, with which the United States is at war. Haupt came to this country with his parents when he was five years old; it is contended that he became a citizen of the United States by virtue of the naturalization of his parents during his minority and that he has not since lost his citizenship. The Government, however, takes the position that on attaining his majority he elected to maintain German allegiance and citizenship or in any case that he has by his conduct renounced or abandoned his United States citizenship. . . . For reasons presently to be stated we do not find it necessary to resolve these contentions.

After the declaration of war between the United States and the German Reich, petitioners received training at a sabotage school near Berlin, Germany, where they were instructed in the use of explosives and in methods of secret writing. Thereafter petitioners, with a German citizen, Dasch, proceeded from Germany to a seaport in Occupied France, where petitioners Burger, Heinck and Quirin, together with Dasch, boarded a German submarine which proceeded across the Atlantic to Amagansett Beach on Long Island, New York. The four were there landed from the submarine in the hours of darkness, on or about June 13, 1942, carrying with them a supply of explosives, fuses and incendiary and timing devices. While landing they wore German Marine Infantry uniforms or parts of uniforms. Immediately after landing they buried their uniforms and the other articles mentioned and proceeded in civilian dress to New York City.

The remaining four petitioners at the same French port boarded another German submarine, which carried them across the Atlantic to Ponte Vedra

Beach, Florida. On or about June 17, 1942, they came ashore during the hours of darkness wearing caps of the German Marine Infantry and carrying with them a supply of explosives, fuses, and incendiary and timing devices. They immediately buried their caps and the other articles mentioned and proceeded in civilian dress to Jacksonville, Florida, and thence to various points in the United States. All were taken into custody in New York or Chicago by agents of the Federal Bureau of Investigation. All had received instructions in Germany from an officer of the German High Command to destroy war industries and war facilities in the United States, for which they or their relatives in Germany were to receive salary payments from the German Government. They also had been paid by the German Government during their course of training at the sabotage school and had received substantial sums in United States currency, which were in their possession when arrested. The currency had been handed to them by an officer of the German High Command, who had instructed them to wear their German uniforms while landing in the United States.

The President, as President and Commander in Chief of the Army and Navy, by Order of July 2, 1942, appointed a Military Commission and directed it to try petitioners for offenses against the law of war and the Articles of War, and prescribed regulations for the procedure on the trial and for review of the record of the trial and of any judgment or sentence of the Commission. On the same day, by Proclamation, the President declared that "all persons who are subjects, citizens or residents of any nation at war with the United States or who give obedience to or act under the direction of any such nation, and who during time of war enter or attempt to enter the United States * * * through coastal or boundary defenses, and are charged with committing or attempting or preparing to commit sabotage, espionage, hostile or warlike acts, or violations of the law of war, shall be subject to the law of war and to the jurisdiction of military tribunals."

The Proclamation also stated in terms that all such persons were denied access to the courts.

Pursuant to direction of the Attorney General, the Federal Bureau of Investigation surrendered custody of petitioners to respondent, Provost Marshal of the Military District of Washington, who was directed by the Secretary of War to receive and keep them in custody, and who thereafter held petitioners for trial before the Commission.

On July 3, 1942, the Judge Advocate General's Department of the Army prepared and lodged with the Commission the following charges against petitioners, supported by specifications:

1. Violation of the law of war.

2. Violation of Article 81 of the Articles of War, defining the offense of relieving or attempting to relieve, or corresponding with or giving intelligence to, the enemy.

3. Violation of Article 82, defining the offense of spying.

4. Conspiracy to commit the offenses alleged in charges 1, 2 and 3.

The Commission met on July 8, 1942, and proceeded with the trial, which continued in progress while the causes were pending in this Court. On July 27th, before petitioners' applications to the District Court, all the evidence for the prosecution and the defense had been taken by the Commission and the case had been closed except for arguments of counsel. It is conceded that ever since petitioners' arrest the state and federal courts in Florida, New York, and the District of Columbia, and in the states in which each of the petitioners was arrested or detained, have been open and functioning normally.

* * *

Petitioners' main contention is that the President is without any statutory or constitutional authority to order the petitioners to be tried by military tribunal for offenses with which they are charged; that in consequence they are entitled to be tried in the civil courts with the safeguards, including trial by jury, which the Fifth and Sixth Amendments guarantee to all persons charged in such courts with criminal offenses. In any case it is urged that the President's Order, in prescribing the procedure of the Commission and the method for review of its findings and sentence, and the proceedings of the Commission under the Order, conflict with Articles of War adopted by Congress—particularly Articles 38, 43, 46, 50 1/2 and 70—and are illegal and void.

* * *

The Constitution confers on the President the "executive Power," Art II, § 1, cl. 1, and imposes on him the duty to "take Care that the Laws be faithfully executed." Art. II, § 3. It makes him the Commander in Chief of the Army and Navy, Art. II, §2, cl. 1, and empowers him to appoint and commission officers of the United States. Art. II, § 3, cl. 1.

The Constitution thus invests the President as Commander in Chief with the power to wage war which Congress has declared, and to carry into effect all laws passed by Congress for the conduct of war and for the government and regulation of the Armed Forces, and all laws defining and punishing offences against the law of nations, including those which pertain to the conduct of war.

By the Articles of War, 10 U.S.C. §§ 1471-1593, Congress has provided rules for the government of the Army. It has provided for the trial and punishment, by courts martial, of violations of the Articles by members of the armed forces and by specified classes of persons associated or serving with the Army. Arts. 1, 2. But the Articles also recognize the "military commission" appointed by military command as an appropriate tribunal for the trial and punishment of offenses against the law of war not ordinarily tried by court martial. See Arts. 12, 15. Articles 38 and 46 authorize the President, with certain limitations, to prescribe the procedure for military commissions. Articles 81 and 82 authorize trial, either by court martial or military commission, of those charged with relieving, harboring or corresponding with the enemy and those charged with spying. And Article 15 declares that "the provisions of these articles conferring jurisdiction upon courts-martial shall not be construed as depriving military commissions * * * or other military tribunals of concurrent jurisdiction in respect of offenders or offenses that by statute or by the law of war may be triable by such military commissions * * * or other military tribunals." Article 2 includes among those persons subject to military law the personnel of our own military establishment. But this, as Article 12 provides, does not exclude from that class "any other person who by the law of war is subject to trial by military tribunals" and who under Article 12 may be tried by court martial or under Article 15 by military commission.

* * *

From the very beginning of its history this Court has recognized and applied the law of war as including that part of the law of nations which prescribes, for the conduct of war, the status, rights and duties of enemy nations as well as of enemy individuals. By the Articles of War, and especially Article 15, Congress has explicitly provided, so far as it may constitutionally do so, that military tribunals shall have jurisdiction to try offenders or offenses against the law of war in appropriate cases. Congress, in addition to making rules for the government of our Armed Forces, has thus exercised its authority to define and punish offenses against the law of nations by sanctioning, within constitutional limitations, the jurisdiction of military commissions to try persons for offenses which, according to the rules and precepts of the law of nations, and more particularly the law of war, are cognizable by such tribunals. And the President, as Commander in Chief, by his Proclamation in time of war his invoked that law. By his Order creating the present Commission he has undertaken to exercise the authority conferred upon him by Congress, and also such authority as the Constitution itself gives the Commander in Chief, to direct the performance of those functions which may constitutionally be performed by the military arm of the nation in time of war.

An important incident to the conduct of war is the adoption of measures by the military command not only to repel and defeat the enemy, but to seize and subject to disciplinary measures those enemies who in their attempt to thwart or impede our military effort have violated the law of war. It is unnecessary for present purposes to determine to what extent the President as Commander in Chief has constitutional power to create military commissions without the support of Congressional legislation. For here Congress has authorized trial of offenses against the law of war before such commissions. We are concerned only with the question whether it is within the constitutional power of the national government to place petitioners upon trial before a military commission for the offenses with which they are charged. We must therefore first inquire whether any of the acts charged is an offense against the law of war cognizable before a military tribunal, and if so whether the Constitution prohibits the trial. We may assume that there are acts regarded in other countries, or by some writers on international law, as offenses against the law of war which would not be triable by military tribunal here, either because they are not recognized by our courts as violations of the law of war or because they are of that class of offenses constitutionally triable only by a jury. It was upon such grounds that the Court denied the right to proceed by military tribunal in Ex parte Milligan, supra. But as we shall show, these petitioners were charged with an offense against the law of war which the Constitution does not require to be tried by jury.

It is no objection that Congress in providing for the trial of such offenses has not itself undertaken to codify that branch of international law or to mark its precise boundaries, or to enumerate or define by statute all the acts which that law condemns. . . .

By universal agreement and practice the law of war draws a distinction between the armed forces and the peaceful populations of belligerent nations and also between those who are lawful and unlawful combatants. Lawful combatants are subject to capture and detention as prisoners of war by opposing military forces. Unlawful combatants are likewise subject to capture and detention, but in addition they are subject to trial and punishment by military tribunals for acts which render their belligerency unlawful. The spy who secretly and without uniform passes the military lines of a belligerent in time of war, seeking to gather military information and communicate it to the enemy, or an enemy combatant who without uniform comes secretly through the lines for the purpose of waging war by destruction of life or property, are familiar examples of belligerents who are generally deemed not to be entitled to the status of prisoners of war, but to be offenders against the law of war subject to trial and punishment by military tribunals. *See* Winthrop, Military Law, 2d Ed., pp. 1196-1197, 1219-1221; Instructions for the Government of Armies of the United States in the Field, approved by the President, General Order No. 100, April 24, 1863, sections IV and V. Such was the practice of our own military authorities before the adoption of the Constitution,[9] and during the Mexican and Civil Wars.[10]

---

[9] On September 29, 1780, Major John Andre, Adjutant-General to the British Army, was tried by a "Board of General Officers" appointed by General Washington, on a charge that he had come within the lines for an interview with General Benedict Arnold and had been captured while in disguise and travelling under an assumed name. The Board found that the facts charged were true, and that when captured Major Andre had in his possession papers containing intelligence, for the enemy, and reported their conclusion that "Major Andre * * * ought to be considered as a Spy from the enemy, and that agreeably to the law and usage of nations * * * he ought to suffer death." Major Andre was hanged on October 2, 1780. Proceedings of a Board of General Officers Respecting Major John Andre, Sept. 29, 1780, printed at Philadelphia in 1780.

[10] During the Mexican War military commissions were created in a large number of instances for the trial of various offenses. See General Orders cited in 2 Winthrop, Military Law (2d Ed. 1896) p. 1298, note 1.

* * *

Our Government, by thus defining lawful belligerents entitled to be treated as prisoners of war, has recognized that there is a class of unlawful belligerents not entitled to that privilege, including those who though combatants do not wear "fixed and distinctive emblems." And by Article 15 of the Articles of War Congress has made provision for their trial and punishment by military commission, according to "the law of war."

By a long course of practical administrative construction by its military authorities, our Government has likewise recognized that those who during time of war pass surreptitiously from enemy territory into our own, discarding their uniforms upon entry, for the commission of hostile acts involving destruction of life or property, have the status of unlawful combatants punishable as such by military commission. This precept of the law of war has been so recognized in practice both here and abroad, and has so generally been accepted as valid by authorities on international law[12] that we think it must be regarded as a rule or principle of the law of war recognized by this Government by its enactment of the Fifteenth Article of War.

Specification 1 of the First charge is sufficient to charge all the petitioners with the offense of unlawful belligerency, trial of which is within the jurisdiction of the Commission, and the admitted facts affirmatively show that the charge is not merely colorable or without foundation.

Specification 1 states that petitioners "being enemies of the United States and acting for * * * the German Reich, a belligerent enemy nation, secretly and covertly passed, in civilian dress, contrary to the law of war, through the

---

During the Civil War the military commission was extensively used for the trial of offenses against the law of war. Among the more significant cases for present purposes are the following:

* * *

On January 17, 1865, Robert C. Kennedy, a Captain of the Confederate Army, who was shown to have attempted, while in disguise, to set fire to the City of New York, and to have been seen in disguise in various parts of New York State, was convicted on charges of acting as a spy and violation of the law of war "in undertaking to carry on irregular and unlawful warfare." He was sentenced to be hanged, and the sentence was confirmed by the reviewing authority. Dept. of the East, G.O. No. 24, March 20, 1865.

* * *

... For other cases of violations of the law of war punished by military commissions during the Civil War see 2 Winthrop, Military Laws and Precedents (2d ed. 1896) 1310-11.

[12] [Citations omitted.] ... These authorities are unanimous in stating that a soldier in uniform who commits the acts mentioned would be entitled to treatment as a prisoner of war; it is the absence of uniform that renders the offender liable to trial for violation of the laws of war.

military and naval lines and defenses of the United States * * * and went behind such lines, contrary to the law of war, in civilian dress * * * for the purpose of committing * * * hostile acts, and, in particular, to destroy certain war industries, war utilities and war materials within the United States."

This specification so plainly alleges violation of the law of war as to require but brief discussion of petitioners' contentions. As we have seen, entry upon our territory in time of war by enemy belligerents, including those acting under the direction of the armed forces of the enemy, for the purpose of destroying property used or useful in prosecuting the war, is a hostile and war-like act. It subjects those who participate in it without uniform to the punishment prescribed by the law of war for unlawful belligerents. It is without significance that petitioners were not alleged to have borne conventional weapons or that their proposed hostile acts did not necessarily contemplate collision with the Armed Forces of the United States. Paragraphs 351 and 352 of the Rules of Land Warfare, already referred to, plainly contemplate that the hostile acts and purposes for which unlawful belligerents may be punished are not limited to assaults on the Armed Forces of the United States. Modern warfare is directed at the destruction of enemy war supplies and the implements of their production and transportation quite as much as at the armed forces. Every consideration which makes the unlawful belligerent punishable is equally applicable whether his objective is the one or the other. The law of war cannot rightly treat those agents of enemy armies who enter our territory, armed with explosives intended for the destruction of war industries and supplies, as any the less belligerent enemies than are agent similarly entering for the purpose of destroying fortified places or our Armed Forces. By passing our boundaries for such purposes without uniform or other emblem signifying their belligerent status, or by discarding that means of identification after entry, such enemies become unlawful belligerents subject to trial and punishment.

* * *

But petitioners insist that even if the offenses with which they are charged are offenses against the law of war, their trial is subject to the requirement of the Fifth Amendment that no person shall be held to answer for a capital or otherwise infamous crime unless on a presentment or indictment of a grand jury, and that such trials by Article III, § 2, and the Sixth Amendment must be by jury in a civil court. . . .

Presentment by a grand jury and trial by a jury of the vicinage where the crime was committed were at the time of the adoption of the Constitution familiar parts of the machinery for criminal trials in the civil courts. But they were procedures unknown to military tribunals, which are not courts in the sense of the Judiciary Article, *Ex parte Vallandigham*, 1 Wall. 243; *In re Vidal*, 179 U.S. 126; *cf. Williams v. United States*, 289 U.S. 553, and which in the natural course of events are usually called upon to function under conditions precluding resort to such procedures. As this Court has often recognized, it was not the purpose or effect of § 2 of Article III, read in the light of the common law, to enlarge the then existing right to a jury trial. The object was to preserve unimpaired trial by jury in all those cases in which it had been recognized by the common law and in all cases of a like nature as they might arise in the future, *District of Columbia v. Colts*, 282 U.S. 63, but not to bring within the sweep of the guaranty those cases in which it was then well understood that a jury trial could not be demanded as of right.

The Fifth and Sixth Amendments, while guaranteeing the continuance of certain incidents of trial by jury which Article III, § 2 had left unmentioned, did not enlarge the right to jury trial as it had been established by that Article. *Callan v. Wilson*, 127 U.S. 540, 549. Hence petty offenses triable at common law without a jury may be tried without a jury in the federal courts, notwithstanding Article III, § 2, and the Fifth and Sixth Amendments. *Schick v. United States*, 195 U.S. 65; *District of Columbia v. Clawans*, 300 U.S. 617. Trial by jury of criminal contempts may constitutionally be dispensed with in the federal courts in those cases in which they could be tried without a jury at common law. *Ex parte Terry*, 128 U.S. 289, 302, 304 . . . . Similarly, an action for debt to enforce a penalty inflicted by Congress is not subject to the constitutional restrictions upon criminal prosecutions. *United States v. Zucker*, 161 U.S. 475 . . . .

All these are instances of offenses committed against the United States, for which a penalty is imposed, but they are not deemed to be within Article III, § 2 or the provisions of the Fifth and Sixth Amendments relating to "crimes" and "criminal prosecutions." In the light of this long-continued and consistent interpretation we must concluded that § 2 of Article III and the Fifth and Sixth Amendments cannot be taken to have extended the right to demand a jury to trials by military commission, or to have required that offenses against the law of war not triable by jury at common law be tried only in the civil courts.

The fact that "cases arising in the land or naval forces" are excepted from the operation of the Amendments does not militate against this conclusion. Such cases are expressly excepted from the Fifth Amendment, and are deemed excepted by implication from the Sixth. *Ex parte Milligan, supra,* 4 Wall. 123, 138, 139. It is argued that the exception, which excludes from the Amendment cases arising in the armed forces, has also by implication extended its guaranty to all other cases; that since petitioners, not being members of the Armed Forces of the United States, are not within the exception, the Amendment operates to give to them the right to a jury trial. But we think this argument misconceives both the scope of the Amendment and the purpose of the exception.

We may assume, without deciding, that a trial prosecuted before a military commission created by military authority is not one "arising in the land * * * forces," when the accused is not a member of or associated with those forces. But even so, the exception cannot be taken to affect those trials before military commissions which are neither within the exception nor within the provisions of Article III, § 2, whose guaranty the Amendments did not enlarge. No exception is necessary to exclude from the operation of these provisions cases never deemed to be within their terms. An express exception from Article III, § 2, and from the Fifth and Sixth Amendments, of trials of petty offenses and of criminal contempts has not been found necessary in order to preserve the traditional practice of trying those offenses without a jury. It is no more so in order to continue the practice of trying, before military tribunals without a jury, offenses committed by enemy belligerents against the law of war.

* * *

We cannot say that Congress in preparing the Fifth and Sixth Amendments intended to extend trial by jury to the cases of alien or citizen offenders against the law of war otherwise triable by military commission, while withholding it from members of our own armed forces charged with infractions of the Articles of War punishable by death. It is equally inadmissible to construe the Amendments—whose primary purpose was to continue unimpaired presentment by grand jury and trial by petit jury in all those cases in which they had been customary—as either abolishing all trials by military tribunals, save those of the personnel of our own armed forces, or what in effect comes to the same thing, as imposing on all such tribunals the necessity of proceeding against unlawful enemy belligerents only on presentment and trial by jury. We conclude that the Fifth and Sixth Amendments did not restrict whatever authority was conferred by the Constitution to try offenses against the law of war by military commission, and that petitioners, charged with such an offense not required to be tried by jury at common law, were lawfully placed on trial by the Commission without a jury.

* * *

Accordingly, we conclude that Charge I, on which petitioners were detained for trial by the Military Commission, alleged an offense which the President is authorized to order tried by military commission; that his Order convening the Commission was a lawful order and that the Commission was lawfully constituted; that the petitioners were held in lawful custody and did not show cause for their discharge. It follows that the orders of the District Court should be affirmed, and that leave to file petitions for habeas corpus in this Court should be denied.

Mr. Justice MURPHY took no part in the consideration or decision of these cases.

Points for Discussion

1. The fourth specification charged the accused with conspiracy to commit violations of the law of war. In *Hamdan v. Rumsfeld*, 548 U.S. 557 (2006), a plurality of the Supreme Court concluded that conspiracy to commit violations of the law of war is not itself a violation of the law of war and that therefore such a conspiracy cannot not be tried by a military commission (at least not absent addition Congressional authorization). Justice Stevens, writing for himself and four other justices, reasoned that *Quirin* was not contrary precedent: "That the defendants in *Quirin* were charged with conspiracy is not persuasive, since the Court declined to address whether the offense actually qualified as a violation of the law of war—let alone one triable by military commission." *Id.* at 605 (Stevens, J.). Why might the charge of conspiracy be especially important in any prosecution arising out of the 9/11 attacks? In response to this conclusion, Congress in the Military Commissions Act of 2006 specifically made conspiracy a crime that is triable by military commission. *See* 10 U.S.C. § 950t(29).

2. Justice Scalia wrote of the *Quirin* decision: "The case was not this Court's finest hour. The Court upheld the commission and denied relief in a brief per curiam issued the day after oral argument concluded . . . ; a week later the Government carried out the commission's death sentence upon six saboteurs, including Haupt. The Court eventually explained its reasoning in a written opinion issued several months later." *Hamdi v. Rumsfeld*, 542 U.S. 507, 569 (2004) (Scalia, J., dissenting). Why might the military commission and the Court have seen a need for great speed in handling the matter? How does the speed compare with the use of military commissions after 9/11?

APPLICATION OF YAMASHITA
U.S. Supreme Court
327 U.S. 1 (1946)

Mr. Chief Justice STONE delivered the opinion of the Court.

* * *

From the petitions and supporting papers it appears that prior to September 3, 1945, petitioner was the Commanding General of the Fourteenth Army Group of the Imperial Japanese Army in the Philippine Islands. On that date he surrendered to and became a prisoner of war of the United States Army Forces in Baguio, Philippine Islands. On September 25th, by order of respondent, Lieutenant General Wilhelm D. Styer, Commanding General of the United States Army Forces, Western Pacific, which command embraces the Philippine Islands, petitioner was served with a charge prepared by the Judge Advocate General's Department of the Army, purporting to charge petitioner with a violation of the law of war. On October 8, 1945, petitioner, after pleading not guilty to the charge, was held for trial before a military commission of five Army officers appointed by order of General Styer. The order appointed six Army officers, all lawyers, as defense counsel. Throughout the proceedings which followed, including those before this Court, defense counsel have demonstrated their professional skill and resourcefulness and their proper zeal for the defense with which they were charged.

On the same date a bill of particulars was filed by the prosecution, and the commission heard a motion made in petitioner's behalf to dismiss the charge on the ground that it failed to state a violation of the law of war. On October 29th the commission was reconvened, a supplemental bill of particulars was filed, and the motion to dismiss was denied. The trial then proceeded until its conclusion on December 7, 1945, the commission hearing two hundred and eighty-six witnesses, who gave over three thousand pages of testimony. On that date petitioner was found guilty of the offense as charged and sentenced to death by hanging.

The petitions for habeas corpus set up that the detention of petitioner for the purpose of the trial was unlawful for reasons which are now urged as showing that the military commission was without lawful authority or jurisdiction to place petitioner on trial, as follows:

* * *

(b) that the charge preferred against petitioner fails to charge him with a violation of the law of war; * * * The Court's discussion of another issue, namely, the legality of the procedures used, appears in Chapter 19 at page 276 below.—Ed.

* * *

In *Ex parte Quirin*, 317 U.S. 1, we had occasion to consider at length the sources and nature of the authority to create military commissions for the trial of enemy combatants for offenses against the law of war. We there pointed out that Congress, in the exercise of the power conferred upon it by Article I, § 8, Cl. 10 of the Constitution to "define and punish * * * Offenses against the Law of Nations * * *," of which the law of war is a part, had by the Articles of War (10 U.S.C. §§ 1471-1593) recognized the "military commission" appointed by military command, as it had previously existed in United States Army practice, as an appropriate tribunal for the trial and punishment of offenses against the law of war. Article 15 declares that "the provisions of these articles conferring jurisdiction upon courts-martial shall not be construed as depriving military commissions * * * or other military tribunals of concurrent jurisdiction in respect of offenders of offenses that by statute or by the law of war may be triable by such military commissions * * * or other military tribunals." See a similar provision of the Espionage Act of 1917, 50 U.S.C. § 38. Article 2 includes among those persons subject to the Articles of War the personnel of our own military establishment. But this, as Article 12 indicates, does not exclude from the class of persons subject to trial by military commissions "any other person who by the law of war is subject to trial by military tribunals," and who, under Article 12, may be tried by court martial, or under Article 15 by military commission.

We further pointed out that Congress, by sanctioning trial of enemy combatants for violations of the law of war by military commission, had not attempted to codify the law of war or to mark its precise boundaries. Instead, by Article 15 it had incorporated, by reference, as within the preexisting jurisdiction of military commissions created by appropriate military command, all offenses which are defined as such by the law of war, and which may constitutionally be included within that jurisdiction. It thus adopted the system of military common law applied by military tribunals so far as it should be recognized and deemed applicable by the courts, and as further defined and supplemented by the Hague Convention, to which the United States and the Axis powers were parties.

We also emphasized in *Ex parte Quirin*, as we do here, that on application for habeas corpus we are not concerned with the guilt or innocence of the petitioners. We consider here only the lawful power of the commission to try the petitioner for the offense charged. In the present cases it must be recognized throughout that the military tribunals which Congress has sanctioned by the Articles of War are not courts whose rulings and judgments are made subject to review by this Court. See *Ex parte Vallandigham*, 1 Wall. 243; *In re Vidal*, 179 U.S. 126; *cf. Ex parte Quirin, supra*, 317 U.S. 39. They are tribunals whose determinations are reviewable by the military authorities either as provided in the military orders constituting such tribunals or as provided by the Articles of War. Congress conferred on the courts no power to review their determinations save only as it has granted judicial power "to grant writs of habeas corpus for the purpose of an inquiry into the cause of the restraint of liberty." 28 U.S.C. §§ 451, 452. The courts may inquire whether the detention complained of is within the authority of those detaining the petitioner. If the military tribunals have lawful authority to hear, decide and condemn, their action is not subject to judicial review merely because they have made a wrong decision on disputed facts. Correction of their errors of decision is not for the courts but for the military authorities which are alone authorized to review their decisions.

Finally, we held in *Ex parte Quirin, supra*, 317 U.S. 24, 25, as we hold now, that Congress by sanctioning trials of enemy aliens by military commission for offenses against the law of war had recognized the right of the accused to make a defense. It has not foreclosed their right to contend that the Constitution or laws of the United States withhold authority to proceed with the trial. It has not withdrawn, and the Executive branch of the government could not, unless there was suspension of the writ, withdraw from the courts the duty and power to make such inquiry into the authority of the commission as may be made by habeas corpus.

* * *

The Charge.   Neither Congressional action nor the military orders constituting the commission authorized it to place petitioner on trial unless the charge preferred against him is of a violation of the law of war. The charge, so far as now relevant, is that petitioner, between October 9, 1944 and September 2, 1945, in the Philippine Islands, "while commander of armed forces of Japan at war with the United States of America and its allies, unlawfully disregarded and failed to discharge his duty as commander to control the operations of the members of his command, permitting them to commit brutal atrocities and other high crimes against people of the United

States and of its allies and dependencies, particularly the Philippines; and he * * * thereby violated the laws of war."

Bills of particulars, filed by the prosecution by order of the commission, allege a series of acts, one hundred and twenty-three in number, committed by members of the forces under petitioner's command, during the period mentioned. The first item specifies the execution of a "a deliberate plan and purpose to massacre and exterminate a large part of the civilian population of Batangas Province, and to devastate and destroy public, private and religious property therein, as a result of which more than 25,000 men, women and children, all unarmed noncombatant civilians, were brutally mistreated and killed, without cause or trial, and entire settlements were devastated and destroyed wantonly and without military necessity." Other items specify acts of violence, cruelty and homicide inflicted upon the civilian population and prisoners of war, acts of wholesale pillage and the wanton destruction of religious monuments.

It is not denied that such acts directed against the civilian population of an occupied country and against prisoners of war are recognized in international law as violations of the law of war. Articles 4, 28, 46, and 47, Annex to Fourth Hague Convention, 1907, 36 Stat. 2277, 2296, 2303, 2306, 2307. But it is urged that the charge does not allege that petitioner has either committed or directed the commission of such acts, and consequently that no violation is charged as against him. But this overlooks the fact that the gist of the charge is an unlawful breach of duty by petitioner as an army commander to control the operations of the members of his command by "permitting them to commit" the extensive and widespread atrocities specified. The question then is whether the law of war imposes on an army commander a duty to take such appropriate measures as are within his power to control the troops under his command for the prevention of the specified acts which are violations of the law of war and which are likely to attend the occupation of hostile territory by an uncontrolled soldiery, and whether he may be charged with personal responsibility for his failure to take such measures when violations result. That this was the precise issue to be tried was made clear by the statement of the prosecution at the opening of the trial.

It is evident that the conduct of military operations by troops whose excesses are unrestrained by the orders or efforts of their commander would almost certainly result in violations which it is the purpose of the law of war to prevent. Its purpose to protect civilian populations and prisoners of war from brutality would largely be defeated if the commander of an invading army could with impunity neglect to take reasonable measures for their protection. Hence the law of war presupposes that its violation is to be avoided through the control of the operations of war by commanders who are to some extent responsible for their subordinates.

This is recognized by the Annex to Fourth Hague Convention of 1907, respecting the laws and customs of war on land. Article I lays down as a condition which an armed force must fulfill in order to be accorded the rights of lawful belligerents, that it must be "commanded by a person responsible for his subordinates." 36 Stat. 2295. Similarly Article 19 of the Tenth Hague Convention, relating to bombardment by naval vessels, provides that commanders in chief of the belligerent vessels "must see that the above Articles are properly carried out." 36 Stat. 2389. And Article 26 of the Geneva Red Cross Convention of 1929, 47 Stat. 2074, 2092, for the amelioration of the condition of the wounded and sick in armies in the field, makes it "the duty of the commanders-in-chief of the belligerent armies to provide for the details of execution of the foregoing articles (of the convention), as well as for unforeseen cases." And, finally, Article 43 of the Annex of the Fourth Hague Convention, 36 Stat. 2306, requires that the commander of a force occupying enemy territory, as was petitioner, "shall take all the measures in his power to restore, and ensure, as far as possible, public order and safety, while respecting, unless absolutely prevented, the laws in force in the country."

These provisions plainly imposed on petitioner, who at the time specified was military governor of the Philippines, as well as commander of the Japanese forces, an affirmative duty to take such measures as were within his power and appropriate in the circumstances to protect prisoners of war and the civilian population. This duty of a commanding officer has heretofore been recognized, and its breach penalized by our own military tribunals.[3] A like principle has been applied so as to impose liability on the United States in international arbitrations. Case of Jenaud, 3 Moore, International Arbitrations, 3000; Case of "The Zafiro," 5 Hackworth, Digest of International Law, 707.

Congress, in the exercise of its constitutional power to define and punish offenses against the law of nations, of which the law of war is a part, has recognized the "military commission" appointed by military command, as it had previously existed in United States army practice, as an appropriate tribunal for the trial and punishment of offenses against the law of war. Espionage Act 1917, tit. 1,§ 7, 50 U.S.C. § 38; Articles of War, arts. 2, 12, 15, 10 U.S.C §§ 1473, 1483, 1486; U.S.C. Const. art. 1, § 8, cl. 10.

We do not make the laws of war but we respect them so far as they do not conflict with the commands of Congress or the Constitution. There is no contention that the present charge, thus read, is without the support of evidence, or that the commission held petitioner responsible for failing to take measures which were beyond his control or inappropriate for a commanding officer to take in the circumstances.[4] We do not here appraise

---

[3] Failure of an officer to take measures to prevent murder of an inhabitant of an occupied country committed in his presence. Gen. Orders No. 221, Hq.Div. of the Philippines, August 17, 1901. And in Gen. Orders No. 264, Hq. Div. of the Philippines, September 9, 1901, it was held that an officer could not be found guilty for failure to prevent a murder unless it appeared that the accused had "the power to prevent" it.

[4] In its findings the commission took account of the difficulties "faced by the accused, with respect not only to the swift and overpowering advance of American forces, but

the evidence on which petitioner was convicted. We do not consider what measures, if any, petitioner took to prevent the commission, by the troops under his command, of the plain violations of the law of war detailed in the bill of particulars, or whether such measures as he may have taken were appropriate and sufficient to discharge the duty imposed upon him. These are questions within the peculiar competence of the military officers composing the commission and were for it to decide. *See Smith v. Whitney*, 116 U.S. 167, 178. It is plain that the charge on which petitioner was tried charged him with a breach of his duty to control the operations of the members of his command, by permitting them to commit the specified atrocities. This was enough to require the commission to hear evidence tending to establish the culpable failure of petitioner to perform the duty imposed on him by the law of war and to pass upon its sufficiency to establish guilt.

Obviously charges of violations of the law of war triable before a military tribunal need not be stated with the precision of a common law indictment. But we conclude that the allegations of the charge, tested by any reasonable standard, adequately allege a violation of the law of war and that the commission had authority to try and decide the issue which it raised.

* * *

Petitioner [Yamashita] further urges that by virtue of Article 63 of the Geneva Convention of 1929, 47 Stat. 2052, he is entitled to the benefits afforded by the 25th and 38th Articles of War to members of our own forces.* Article 63 provides: "Sentence may be pronounced against a prisoner of war only by the same courts and according to the same procedure as in the case of persons belonging to the armed forces of the detaining Power." Since petitioner is a prisoner of war, and as the 25th and 38th Articles of War apply to the trial of any person in our own armed forces, it is said that Article 63 requires them to be applied in the trial of petitioner. But we think examination of Article 63 in its setting in the Convention plainly shows that it refers to sentence "pronounced against a prisoner of war" for an offense

---

also to errors of his predecessors, weakness in organization, equipment, supply * * *, training, communication, discipline and morale of his troops," and "the tactical situation, the character, training and capacity of staff officers and subordinate commanders, as well as the traits of character of his troops." It nonetheless found that petitioner had not taken such measures to control his troops as were "required by the circumstances." We do not weigh the evidence. We merely hold that the charge sufficiently states a violation against the law of war, and that the commission, upon the facts found, could properly find petitioner guilty of such a violation.

* The Articles of War governed ordinary courts-martial used for trying U.S. soldiers. Article 25 of the Articles of War restricted the use of depositions as evidence against the accused in capital cases. Article 38 authorized the President to promulgate rules of evidence and procedure for courts-martial but required these rules to be consistent with the Articles of War.–Ed.

committed while a prisoner of war, and not for a violation of the law of war committed while a combatant.

Article 63 of the Convention appears in part 3, entitled "Judicial Suits," of Chapter 3, "Penalties Applicable to Prisoners of War," of Section V, "Prisoners' Relations with the Authorities," one of the sections of Title III, "Captivity." All taken together relate only to the conduct and control of prisoners of war while in captivity as such. Chapter 1 of Section V, Article 42, deals with complaints of prisoners of war because of the conditions of captivity. Chapter 2, Articles 43 and 44, relates to those of their number chosen by prisoners of war to represent them.

Chapter 3 of Section V, Articles 45 through 67, is entitled "Penalties Applicable to Prisoners of War." Part 1 of that chapter, Articles 45 through 53, indicates what acts of prisoners of war, committed while prisoners, shall be considered offenses, and defines to some extent the punishment which the detaining power may impose on account of such offenses.[8]

Punishment is of two kinds—"disciplinary" and "judicial," the latter being the more severe. Article 52 requires that leniency be exercised in deciding whether an offense requires disciplinary or judicial punishment. Part 2 of Chapter 3 is entitled "Disciplinary Punishments," and further defines the extent of such punishment, and the mode in which it may be imposed. Part 3, entitled "Judicial Suits," in which Article 63 is found, describes the procedure by which "judicial" punishment may be imposed. The three parts of Chapter 3, taken together, are thus a comprehensive description of the substantive offenses which prisoners of war may commit during their imprisonment, of

---

[8] Part 1 of Chapter 3, "General Provisions," provides in Articles 45 and 46 that prisoners of war are subject to the regulations in force in the armies of the detaining power, that punishments other than those provided "for the same acts for soldiers of the national armies" may not be imposed on prisoners of war, and that "collective punishment for individual acts" is forbidden. Article 47 provides that "Acts constituting an offense against discipline, and particularly attempted escape, shall be verified immediately; for all prisoners of war, commissioned or not, preventive arrest shall be reduced to the absolute minimum. Judicial proceedings against prisoners of war shall be conducted as rapidly as the circumstances permit * * *. In all cases, the duration of preventive imprisonment shall be deducted from the disciplinary or the judicial punishment inflicted." Article 48 provides that prisoners of war, after having suffered "the judicial of disciplinary punishment which has been imposed on them" are not to be treated differently from other prisoners, but provides that "prisoners punished as a result of attempted escape may be subjected to special surveillance." Article 49 recites that prisoners "given disciplinary punishment may not be deprived of the prerogatives attached to their rank." Articles 50 and 51 deal with escaped prisoners who have been retaken or prisoners who have attempted to escape. Article 52 provides: "Belligerents shall see that the competent authorities exercise the greatest leniency in deciding the question of whether an infraction committed by a prisoner of war should be punished more than once because of the same act or the same count."

the penalties which may be imposed on account of such offenses, and of the procedure by which guilt may be adjudged and sentence pronounced.

We think it clear, from the context of these recited provisions, that part 3, and Article 63 which it contains, apply only to judicial proceedings directed against a prisoner of war for offenses committed while a prisoner of war. Section V gives no indication that this part was designed to deal with offenses other than those referred to in parts 1 and 2 of chapter 3.

* * *

It thus appears that the order convening the commission was a lawful order, that the commission was lawfully constituted, that petitioner was charged with violation of the law of war, and that the commission had authority to proceed with the trial, and in doing so did not violate any military, statutory or constitutional command. We have considered, but find it unnecessary to discuss other contentions which we find to be without merit. We therefore conclude that the detention of petitioner for trial and his detention upon his conviction, subject to the prescribed review by the military authorities were lawful, and that the petition for certiorari, and leave to file in this Court petitions for writs of habeas corpus and prohibition should be, and they are

Denied.

Mr. Justice JACKSON took no part in the consideration or decision of these cases.

Mr. Justice MURPHY, dissenting.

* * *

The Court, in my judgment, demonstrates conclusively that the military commission was lawfully created in this instance and that petitioner could not object to its power to try him for a recognized war crime. Without pausing here to discuss the third and fourth issues, however, I find it impossible to agree that the charge against the petitioner stated a recognized violation of the laws of war.

It is important, in the first place, to appreciate the background of events preceding this trial. From October 9, 1944, to September 2, 1945, the petitioner was the Commanding General of the 14th Army Group of the Imperial Japanese Army, with headquarters in the Philippines. The reconquest of the Philippines by the armed forces of the United States began approximately at the time when the petitioner assumed this command. Combined with a great and decisive sea battle, an invasion was made on the island of Leyte on October 20, 1944. "In the six days of the great naval action the Japanese position in the Philippines had become extremely critical. Most of the serviceable elements of the Japanese Navy had become committed to the battle with disastrous results. The strike had miscarried, and General MacArthur's land wedge was firmly implanted in the vulnerable flank of the enemy * * *. There were 260,000 Japanese troops scattered over the

Philippines but most of them might as well have been on the other side of the world so far as the enemy's ability to shift them to meet the American thrusts was concerned. If General MacArthur succeeded in establishing himself in the Visayas where he could stage, exploit, and spread under cover of overwhelming naval and air superiority, nothing could prevent him from overrunning the Philippines." Biennial Report of the Chief of Staff of the United States Army, July 1, 1943, to June 30, 1945, to the Secretary of War, p. 74.

By the end of 1944 the island of Leyte was largely in American hands. And on January 9, 1945, the island of Luzon was invaded. "Yamashita's inability to cope with General MacArthur's swift moves, his desired reaction to the deception measures, the guerrillas, and General Kenney's aircraft combined to place the Japanese in an impossible situation. The enemy was forced into a piecemeal commitment of his troops." *Ibid.*, p. 78. It was at this time and place that most of the alleged atrocities took place. Organized resistance around Manila ceased on February 23. Repeated land and air assaults pulverized the enemy and within a few months there was little left of petitioner's command except a few remnants which had gathered for a last stand among the precipitous mountains.

As the military commission here noted, "The Defense established the difficulties faced by the Accused with respect not only to the swift and overpowering advance of American forces, but also to the errors of his predecessors, weaknesses in organization, equipment, supply with especial reference to food and gasoline, training, communication, discipline and morale of his troops. It was alleged that the sudden assignment of Naval and Air Forces to his tactical command presented almost insurmountable difficulties. This situation was followed, the Defense contended, by failure to obey his orders to withdraw troops from Manila, and the subsequent massacre of unarmed civilians, particularly by Naval forces. Prior to the Luzon Campaign, Naval forces had reported to a separate ministry in the Japanese Government and Naval Commanders may not have been receptive or experienced in this instance with respect to a joint land operation under a single commander who was designated from the Army Service."

The day of final reckoning for the enemy arrived in August, 1945. On September 3, the petitioner surrendered to the United States Army at Baguio, Luzon. He immediately became a prisoner of war and was interned in prison in conformity with the rules of international law. On September 25, approximately three weeks after surrendering, he was served with the charge in issue in this case. Upon service of the charge he was removed from the status of a prisoner of war and placed in confinement as an accused war criminal. Arraignment followed on October 8 before a military commission specially appointed for the case. Petitioner pleaded not guilty. He was also served on that day with a bill of particulars alleging 64 crimes by troops under his command. A supplemental bill alleging 59 more crimes by his troops was filed on October 29, the same day that the trial began. No continuance was allowed for preparation of a defense as to the supplemental bill.   The trial continued uninterrupted until December 5, 1945.   On December 7 petitioner was found guilty as charged and was sentenced to be hanged.

The petitioner was accused of having "unlawfully disregarded and failed to discharge his duty as commander to control the operations of the members of his command, permitting them to commit brutal atrocities and other high crimes." The bills of particular further alleged that specific acts of atrocity were committed by "members of the armed forces of Japan under the command of the accused."   Nowhere was it alleged that the petitioner personally committed any of the atrocities, or that he ordered their commission, or that he had any knowledge of the commission thereof by members of his command.

The findings of the military commission bear out this absence of any direct personal charge against the petitioner.   The commission merely found that atrocities and other high crimes "have been committed by members of the Japanese armed forces under your command * * * that they were not sporadic in nature but in many cases were methodically supervised by Japanese officers and noncommissioned officers * * * that during the period in question you failed to provide effective control of your troops as was required by the circumstances."

In other words, read against the background of military events in the Philippines subsequent to October 9, 1944, these charges amount to this: "We, the victorious American forces, have done everything possible to destroy and disorganize your lines of communication, your effective control of your personnel, your ability to wage war. In those respects we have succeeded. We have defeated and crushed your forces.   And now we charge and condemn you for having been inefficient in maintaining control of your troops during the period when we were so effectively besieging and eliminating your forces and blocking your ability to maintain effective control. Many terrible atrocities were committed by your disorganized troops.   Because these atrocities were so widespread we will not bother to charge or prove that you committed, ordered or condoned any of them. We will assume that they must have resulted from your inefficiency and negligence as a commander.   In short, we charge you with the crime of inefficiency in controlling your troops. We will judge the discharge of your duties by the disorganization which we ourselves created in large part.   Our standards of judgment are whatever we wish to make them."

Nothing in all history or in international law, at least as far as I am aware, justifies such a charge against a fallen commander of a defeated force. To use the very inefficiency and disorganization created by the victorious forces as the primary basis for condemning officers of the defeated armies bears no resemblance to justice or to military reality.

    * * *

The only conclusion I can draw is that the charge made against the petitioner is clearly without precedent in international law or in the annals of recorded military history. This is not to say that enemy commanders may escape punishment for clear and unlawful failures to prevent atrocities. But that punishment should be based upon charges fairly drawn in light of established rules of international law and recognized concepts of justice.

But the charge in this case, as previously noted, was speedily drawn and filed but three weeks after the petitioner surrendered. The trial proceeded with great dispatch without allowing the defense time to prepare an adequate case. Petitioner's rights under the due process clause of the Fifth Amendment were grossly and openly violated without any justification. All of this was done without any thorough investigation and prosecution of those immediately responsible for the atrocities, out of which might have come some proof or indication of personal culpability on petitioner's part. Instead the loose charge was made that great numbers of atrocities had been committed and that petitioner was the commanding officer; hence he must have been guilty of disregard of duty. Under that charge the commission was free to establish whatever standard of duty on petitioner's part that it desired. By this flexible method a victorious nation may convict and execute any or all leaders of a vanquished foe, depending upon the prevailing degree of vengeance and the absence of any objective judicial review.

At a time like this when emotions are understandably high it is difficult to adopt a dispassionate attitude toward a case of this nature. Yet now is precisely the time when that attitude is most essential. While peoples in other lands may not share our beliefs as to due process and the dignity of the individual, we are not free to give effect to our emotions in reckless disregard of the rights of others. We live under the Constitution, which is the embodiment of all the high hopes and aspirations of the new world. And it is applicable in both war and peace. We must act accordingly. Indeed, an uncurbed spirt of revenge and retribution, masked in formal legal procedure for purposes of dealing with a fallen enemy commander, can do more lasting harm than all of the atrocities giving rise to that spirit. The people's faith in the fairness and objectiveness of the law can be seriously undercut by that spirit. The fires of nationalism can be further kindled. And the hearts of all mankind can be embittered and filled with hatred, leaving forlorn and impoverished the noble ideal of malice toward none and charity to all. These are the reasons that lead me to dissent in these terms.

Mr. Justice RUTLEDGE, dissenting.

Not with ease does one find his views at odds with the Court's in a matter of this character and gravity. Only the most deeply felt convictions could force one to differ. That reason alone leads me to do so now, against strong considerations for withholding dissent.

More is at stake than General Yamashita's fate. There could be no possible sympathy for him if he is guilty of the atrocities for which his death is sought. But there can be and should be justice administered according to law. In this stage of war's aftermath it is too early for Lincoln's great spirit, best lighted in the Second Inaugural, to have wide hold for the treatment of foes. It is not too early, it is never too early, for the nation steadfastly to follow its great constitutional traditions, none older or more universally protective against unbridled power than due process of law in the trial and punishment of men, that is, of all men, whether citizens, aliens, alien enemies or enemy belligerents. It can become too late.

* * *

It is not in our tradition for anyone to be charged with crime which is defined after his conduct, alleged to be criminal, has taken place; or in language not sufficient to inform him of the nature of the offense or to enable him to make defense. Mass guilt we do not impute to individuals, perhaps in any case but certainly in none where the person is not charged or shown actively to have participated in or knowingly to have failed in taking action to prevent the wrongs done by others, having both the duty and the power to do so.

* * *

Mr. Justice MURPHY joins in this opinion.

Points for Discussion

1. What specific reasons did the Court give for concluding that failing to control the operations of subordinates under an officer's command is a violation of the laws of war? How did the Court respond to Justice Rutledge's assertions that the offense was defined after it was committed and that the definition is too vague? The issue of what crime can be tried by military commission remains important today. The final case in this chapter, *United States v. Hamdan*, 2011 WL 2923945 (U.S. Ct. Mil. Comm. Rev.), concerns the question of whether a military commission may try an accused for the crime of providing military aid to terrorists.

2. The Court in *Yamashita* concluded that Article 63 of the Geneva Convention of 1929 did not require the military commission to follow the procedures used in courts-martial when trying a prisoner of war for offenses committed before the prisoner was captured. The Supreme Court in *Hamdan v. Rumsfeld*, 548 U.S. 557 (2006), included in the next section of this chapter, held that the Third Geneva Convention of 1949, which replaced the Geneva Convention of 1929, effected a change in the law on this point. The Court in *Hamdan* explained:

"At least partially in response to subsequent criticism of General Yamashita's trial, ... the Third Geneva Convention of 1949 extended prisoner-of-war protections to individuals tried for crimes committed before their capture. *See* 3 Int'l Comm. of Red Cross, Commentary: Geneva Convention Relative to the Treatment of Prisoners of War 413 (J. Pictet gen. ed. 1960) (explaining that Article 85, which extends the Convention's protections to "[p]risoners of war prosecuted under the laws of the Detaining Power for acts committed prior to capture," was adopted in response to judicial interpretations of the 1929 Geneva Convention, including this Court's decision in *Yamashita*)."

548 U.S. at 619. This interpretation of the Third Geneva Convention was controversial. Congress reacted by including the following provision in the MCA 2006 (as amended by the MCA 2009): "No alien unprivileged enemy belligerent subject to trial by military commission under this chapter may invoke the Geneva Conventions as a basis for a private right of action." 10 U.S.C. § 948b(e). How would a court or military commission now respond to an accused's contention that the military commission procedures differ from court-martial procedures? Why would Congress want to preclude the accused from relying on the Geneva Conventions?

16-2. Constitutional and other Limitations

As explained previously, after the attacks of 9/11, President George W. Bush ordered the establishment of military commissions to try terrorists suspected of war crimes. One of the first detainees to face trial by military commission was Salim Ahmed Hamdan. At the time of the decision, Congress had not yet enacted the MCA 2006 and MCA 2009. Accordingly, the military commission would have followed procedures promulgated by the Department of Defense under the authority of the President's order. Hamdan contended that some of these administratively promulgated procedures were unlawful. The Supreme Court agreed with Hamdan on several points, as indicated in the excerpt of his case below.

The Court's decision is complicated and admittedly difficult to follow. The Court's reasoning might be summarized (or perhaps re-characterized) as resting on three syllogisms:

(1) The major premise of the first syllogism was that [absent contrary Congressional authorization] the President only has authority to establish military commissions in accordance with the laws of war (as the Court had previously concluded). The minor premise of this syllogism was that the Geneva Conventions of 1949 are part of the laws of war. Therefore, the Court reasoned, military commissions are authorized only if they are constituted in accordance with the requirements of the Geneva Conventions.

(2) The major premise of the second syllogism was that "Common Article 3" of the Geneva Conventions sets forth rules that apply to conflicts "not of an international character." The minor premise here was that the war between the United States and al Qaeda does not have an international character because it is not a war between two separate nations (al Qaeda being a terrorist organization, rather than a state). The Court concluded, therefore, that Common Article 3 of the Geneva Conventions applies to the conflict between the United States and al Qaeda.

(3) The major premise of the third syllogism was that Common Article 3, by its terms, permits the trial of detainees only by a "regularly constituted court." The minor premise was that the military commissions were not regularly constituted because their rules violated article 36(b) of the UCMJ [because they were not "uniform" with the rules for courts-martial]. . . . The Court, therefore decided that the military commissions violated Common Article 3 of the Geneva Conventions and were unauthorized.

Gregory E. Maggs, *Foreword to the Symposium on the New Face of Armed Conflict: Enemy Combatants after Hamdan v. Rumsfeld*, 75 Geo. Wash. L. Rev. 971, 980-981 (2007) (footnotes omitted). The Court also rejected the argument that the rights granted by the Geneva Conventions are not judicially enforceable. *See id.* In reading the case, attempt to find these aspects of the Court's reasoning.

As described in the following section of this chapter, the MCA 2006 and MCA 2009 undo various parts of the Supreme Court's decision. But the decision nonetheless provides a framework for assessing the constitutional and other limitations of military commissions in the future.

HAMDAN v. RUMSFELD
U.S. Supreme Court
548 U.S. 557 (2006)

Justice STEVENS announced the judgment of the Court and delivered the opinion of the Court with respect to Parts I through IV, Parts VI through VI-D-iii, Part VI-D-v, and Part VII, and an opinion with respect to Parts V and VI-D-iv, in which Justice SOUTER, Justice GINSBURG, and Justice BREYER join.

Petitioner Salim Ahmed Hamdan, a Yemeni national, is in custody at an American prison in Guantanamo Bay, Cuba. In November 2001, during hostilities between the United States and the Taliban (which then governed Afghanistan), Hamdan was captured by militia forces and turned over to the U.S. military. In June 2002, he was transported to Guantanamo Bay. Over a year later, the President deemed him eligible for trial by military commission for then-unspecified crimes. After another year had passed, Hamdan was charged with one count of conspiracy "to commit . . . offenses triable by military commission." App. to Pet. for Cert. 65a.

Hamdan filed petitions for writs of habeas corpus and mandamus to challenge the Executive Branch's intended means of prosecuting this charge. He concedes that a court-martial constituted in accordance with the Uniform Code of Military Justice (UCMJ), 10 U.S.C. § 801 et seq. (2000 ed. and Supp. III), would have authority to try him. His objection is that the military commission the President has convened lacks such authority, for two principal reasons: First, neither congressional Act nor the common law of war supports trial by this commission for the crime of conspiracy—an offense that, Hamdan says, is not a violation of the law of war. Second, Hamdan contends, the procedures that the President has adopted to try him violate the most basic tenets of military and international law, including the principle that a defendant must be permitted to see and hear the evidence against him.

The District Court granted Hamdan's request for a writ of habeas corpus. 344 F. Supp.2d 152 (DC 2004). The Court of Appeals for the District of Columbia Circuit reversed. 415 F.3d 33 (2005). Recognizing, as we did over a half-century ago, that trial by military commission is an extraordinary measure raising important questions about the balance of powers in our constitutional structure, *Ex parte Quirin*, 317 U.S. 1, 19 (1942), we granted certiorari. . . .

* * *

I.

On September 11, 2001, agents of the al Qaeda terrorist organization hijacked commercial airplanes and attacked the World Trade Center in New York City and the national headquarters of the Department of Defense in Arlington, Virginia. Americans will never forget the devastation wrought by these acts. Nearly 3,000 civilians were killed.

Congress responded by adopting a Joint Resolution authorizing the President to "use all necessary and appropriate force against those nations, organizations, or persons he determines planned, authorized, committed, or aided the terrorist attacks ... in order to prevent any future acts of international terrorism against the United States by such nations, organizations or persons." Authorization for Use of Military Force (AUMF), 115 Stat. 224, note following 50 U.S.C. § 1541 (2000 ed., Supp. III). Acting pursuant to the AUMF, and having determined that the Taliban regime had supported al Qaeda, the President ordered the Armed Forces of the United States to invade Afghanistan. In the ensuing hostilities, hundreds of individuals, Hamdan among them, were captured and eventually detained at Guantanamo Bay.

On November 13, 2001, while the United States was still engaged in active combat with the Taliban, the President issued a comprehensive military order intended to govern the "Detention, Treatment, and Trial of Certain Non-Citizens in the War Against Terrorism," 66 Fed. Reg. 57833 (hereinafter November 13 Order or Order). Those subject to the November 13 Order include any noncitizen for whom the President determines "there is reason to believe" that he or she (1) "is or was" a member of al Qaeda or (2) has engaged or participated in terrorist activities aimed at or harmful to the United States. *Id.*, at 57834. Any such individual "shall, when tried, be tried by military commission for any and all offenses triable by military commission that such individual is alleged to have committed, and may be punished in accordance with the penalties provided under applicable law, including imprisonment or death." *Ibid.* The November 13 Order vested in the Secretary of Defense the power to appoint military commissions to try individuals subject to the Order, but that power has since been delegated to

John D. Altenberg, Jr., a retired Army major general and longtime military lawyer who has been designated "Appointing Authority for Military Commissions."

On July 3, 2003, the President announced his determination that Hamdan and five other detainees at Guantanamo Bay were subject to the November 13 Order and thus triable by military commission. In December 2003, military counsel was appointed to represent Hamdan. Two months later, counsel filed demands for charges and for a speedy trial pursuant to Article 10 of the UCMJ, 10 U.S.C. § 810. On February 23, 2004, the legal adviser to the Appointing Authority denied the applications, ruling that Hamdan was not entitled to any of the protections of the UCMJ. Not until July 13, 2004, after Hamdan had commenced this action in the United States District Court for the Western District of Washington, did the Government finally charge him with the offense for which, a year earlier, he had been deemed eligible for trial by military commission.

The charging document, which is unsigned, contains 13 numbered paragraphs. The first two paragraphs recite the asserted bases for the military commission's jurisdiction—namely, the November 13 Order and the President's July 3, 2003, declaration that Hamdan is eligible for trial by military commission. The next nine paragraphs, collectively entitled "General Allegations," describe al Qaeda's activities from its inception in 1989 through 2001 and identify Osama bin Laden as the group's leader. Hamdan is not mentioned in these paragraphs.

Only the final two paragraphs, entitled "Charge: Conspiracy," contain allegations against Hamdan. Paragraph 12 charges that "from on or about February 1996 to on or about November 24, 2001," Hamdan "willfully and knowingly joined an enterprise of persons who shared a common criminal purpose and conspired and agreed with [named members of al Qaeda] to commit the following offenses triable by military commission: attacking civilians; attacking civilian objects; murder by an unprivileged belligerent; and terrorism." App. to Pet. for Cert. 65a. There is no allegation that Hamdan had any command responsibilities, played a leadership role, or participated in the planning of any activity.

Paragraph 13 lists four "overt acts" that Hamdan is alleged to have committed sometime between 1996 and November 2001 in furtherance of the "enterprise and conspiracy": (1) he acted as Osama bin Laden's "bodyguard and personal driver," "believ[ing]" all the while that bin Laden "and his associates were involved in" terrorist acts prior to and including the attacks of September 11, 2001; (2) he arranged for transportation of, and actually transported, weapons used by al Qaeda members and by bin Laden's bodyguards (Hamdan among them); (3) he "drove or accompanied [O]sama bin Laden to various al Qaida-sponsored training camps, press conferences, or lectures," at which bin Laden encouraged attacks against Americans; and (4) he received weapons training at al Qaeda-sponsored camps. *Id.*, at 65a-67a.

After this formal charge was filed, the United States District Court for the Western District of Washington transferred Hamdan's habeas and mandamus petitions to the United States District Court for the District of Columbia. Meanwhile, a Combatant Status Review Tribunal (CSRT) convened pursuant to a military order issued on July 7, 2004, decided that Hamdan's continued detention at Guantanamo Bay was warranted because he was an "enemy combatant."1 1. An "enemy combatant" is defined by the military order as "an individual who was part of or supporting Taliban or al Qaeda forces, or associated forces that are engaged in hostilities against the United States or its coalition partners." Memorandum from Deputy Secretary of Defense Paul Wolfowitz re: Order Establishing Combatant Status Review Tribunal § a (Jul. 7, 2004) .... Separately, proceedings before the military commission commenced.

* * *

IV

The military commission, a tribunal neither mentioned in the Constitution nor created by statute, was born of military necessity. *See* W. Winthrop, Military Law and Precedents 831 (rev. 2d ed. 1920) (hereinafter Winthrop). Though foreshadowed in some respects by earlier tribunals like the Board of General Officers that General Washington convened to try British Major John Andre for spying during the Revolutionary War, the commission "as such" was inaugurated in 1847. *Id.*, at 832; G. Davis, A Treatise on the Military Law of the United States 308 (2d ed. 1909) (hereinafter Davis). As commander of occupied Mexican territory, and having available to him no other tribunal, General Winfield Scott that year ordered the establishment of both " 'military commissions' " to try ordinary crimes committed in the occupied territory and a "council of war" to try offenses against the law of war. Winthrop 832 (emphases in original).

When the exigencies of war next gave rise to a need for use of military commissions, during the Civil War, the dual system favored by General Scott was not adopted. Instead, a single tribunal often took jurisdiction over ordinary crimes, war crimes, and breaches of military orders alike. As further discussed below, each aspect of that seemingly broad jurisdiction was in fact supported by a separate military exigency. Generally, though, the need for military commissions during this period—as during the Mexican War—was driven largely by the then very limited jurisdiction of courts-martial: "The *occasion* for the military commission arises principally from the fact that the jurisdiction of the court-martial proper, in our law, is restricted by statute almost exclusively to members of the military force and to certain specific offences defined in a written code." *Id.*, at 831 (emphasis in original).

Exigency alone, of course, will not justify the establishment and use of penal tribunals not contemplated by Article I, § 8 and Article III, § 1 of the Constitution unless some other part of that document authorizes a response to the felt need. See *Ex parte Milligan*, 4 Wall. 2, 121 (1866) ("Certainly no part of the judicial power of the country was conferred on [military commissions]"); *Ex parte Vallandigham*, 1 Wall. 243, 251 (1864); see also *Quirin*, 317 U.S., at 25 ("Congress and the President, like the courts, possess no power not derived from the Constitution"). And that authority, if it exists, can derive only from the powers granted jointly to the President and Congress in time of war. *See id.*, at 26-29; *In re Yamashita*, 327 U.S. 1, 11 (1946).

The Constitution makes the President the "Commander in Chief" of the Armed Forces, Art. II, § 2, cl. 1, but vests in Congress the powers to "declare War . . . and make Rules concerning Captures on Land and Water," Art. I, § 8, cl. 11, to "raise and support Armies," *id.*, cl. 12, to "define and punish . . . Offences against the Law of Nations," *id.*, cl. 10, and "To make Rules for the Government and Regulation of the land and naval Forces," *id.*, cl. 14. The interplay between these powers was described by Chief Justice Chase in the seminal case of *Ex parte Milligan*:

> "The power to make the necessary laws is in Congress; the power to execute in the President. Both powers imply many subordinate and auxiliary powers. Each includes all authorities essential to its due exercise. But neither can the President, in war more than in peace, intrude upon the proper authority of Congress, nor Congress upon the proper authority of the President . . . . Congress cannot direct the conduct of campaigns, nor can the President, or any commander under him, without the sanction of Congress, institute tribunals for the trial and punishment of offences, either of soldiers or civilians, unless in cases of a controlling necessity, which justifies what it compels, or at least insures acts of indemnity from the justice of the legislature." 4 Wall., at 139-140.

Whether Chief Justice Chase was correct in suggesting that the President may constitutionally convene military commissions "without the sanction of Congress" in cases of "controlling necessity" is a question this Court has not answered definitively, and need not answer today. For we held in *Quirin* that Congress had, through Article of War 15, sanctioned the use of military commissions in such circumstances. 317 U.S., at 28 ("By the Articles of War, and especially Article 15, Congress has explicitly provided, so far as it may constitutionally do so, that military tribunals shall have jurisdiction to try offenders or offenses against the law of war in appropriate cases"). Article 21 of the UCMJ, the language of which is substantially identical to the old Article 15 and was preserved by Congress after World War II,[22] reads as follows:

> "Jurisdiction of courts-martial not exclusive.
>
> "The provisions of this code conferring jurisdiction upon courts-martial shall not be construed as depriving military commissions, provost

---

[22] Article 15 was first adopted as part of the Articles of War in 1916. *See* Act of Aug. 29, 1916, ch. 418, § 3, Art. 15, 39 Stat. 652. When the Articles of War were codified and re-enacted as the UCMJ in 1950, Congress determined to retain Article 15 because it had been "construed by the Supreme Court (*Ex Parte Quirin*, 317 U.S. 1 (1942))." S.Rep. No. 486, 81st Cong., 1st Sess., 13 (1949).

courts, or other military tribunals of concurrent jurisdiction in respect of offenders or offenses that by statute or by the law of war may be tried by such military commissions, provost courts, or other military tribunals." 64 Stat. 115.

We have no occasion to revisit *Quirin*'s controversial characterization of Article of War 15 as congressional authorization for military commissions. Cf. Brief for Legal Scholars and Historians as Amici Curiae 12-15. Contrary to the Government's assertion, however, even *Quirin* did not view the authorization as a sweeping mandate for the President to "invoke military commissions when he deems them necessary." Brief for Respondents 17. Rather, the *Quirin* Court recognized that Congress had simply preserved what power, under the Constitution and the common law of war, the President had had before 1916 to convene military commissions—with the express condition that the President and those under his command comply with the law of war. See 317 U.S., at 28-29.[23] That much is evidenced by the Court's inquiry, following its conclusion that Congress had authorized military commissions, into whether the law of war had indeed been complied with in that case. *See ibid.*

The Government would have us dispense with the inquiry that the Quirin Court undertook and find in either the AUMF or the DTA specific, overriding authorization for the very commission that has been convened to try Hamdan. Neither of these congressional Acts, however, expands the President's authority to convene military commissions. First, while we assume that the AUMF activated the President's war powers, *see Hamdi v. Rumsfeld,* 542 U.S. 507, (2004) (plurality opinion), and that those powers include the authority to convene military commissions in appropriate circumstances, see *id.,* at 518; *Quirin,* 317 U.S., at 28-29; *see also Yamashita,* 327 U.S., at 11, there is nothing in the text or legislative history of the AUMF even hinting that Congress intended to expand or alter the authorization set forth in Article 21 of the UCMJ. *Cf. Yerger,* 8 Wall., at 105 ("Repeals by implication are not favored").

Likewise, the DTA cannot be read to authorize this commission. Although the DTA, unlike either Article 21 or the AUMF, was enacted after the President had convened Hamdan's commission, it contains no language authorizing that tribunal or any other at Guantanamo Bay. The DTA obviously "recognize[s]" the existence of the Guantanamo Bay commissions in the weakest sense, Brief for Respondents 15, because it references some of the military orders governing them and creates limited judicial review of their "final decision[s]," DTA § 1005(e)(3), 119 Stat. 2743. But the statute also pointedly reserves judgment on whether "the Constitution and laws of the United States are applicable" in reviewing such decisions and whether, if they

---

[23] Whether or not the President has independent power, absent congressional authorization, to convene military commissions, he may not disregard limitations that Congress has, in proper exercise of its own war powers, placed on his powers. *See Youngstown Sheet & Tube Co. v. Sawyer,* 343 U.S. 579, 637 (1952) (Jackson, J., concurring). The Government does not argue otherwise.

are, the "standards and procedures" used to try Hamdan and other detainees actually violate the "Constitution and laws." *Ibid.*

Together, the UCMJ, the AUMF, and the DTA at most acknowledge a general Presidential authority to convene military commissions in circumstances where justified under the "Constitution and laws," including the law of war. Absent a more specific congressional authorization, the task of this Court is, as it was in *Quirin*, to decide whether Hamdan's military commission is so justified. It is to that inquiry we now turn.

* * *

VI

Whether or not the Government has charged Hamdan with an offense against the law of war cognizable by military commission, the commission lacks power to proceed. The UCMJ conditions the President's use of military commissions on compliance not only with the American common law of war, but also with the rest of the UCMJ itself, insofar as applicable, and with the "rules and precepts of the law of nations," [*Ex Parte Quirin*, 317 U.S. 1, 28 (1942)]— including, inter alia, the four Geneva Conventions signed in 1949. *See* [*Application of Yamashita*, 327 U.S. 1, 20-21, 23-24 (1946)]. The procedures that the Government has decreed will govern Hamdan's trial by commission violate these laws.

A

The commission's procedures are set forth in Commission Order No. 1, which was amended most recently on August 31, 2005—after Hamdan's trial had already begun. Every commission established pursuant to Commission Order No. 1 must have a presiding officer and at least three other members, all of whom must be commissioned officers. § 4(A)(1). The presiding officer's job is to rule on questions of law and other evidentiary and interlocutory issues; the other members make findings and, if applicable, sentencing decisions. § 4(A)(5). The accused is entitled to appointed military counsel and may hire civilian counsel at his own expense so long as such counsel is a U.S. citizen with security clearance "at the level SECRET or higher." §§ 4(C)(2)-(3).

The accused also is entitled to a copy of the charge(s) against him, both in English and his own language (if different), to a presumption of innocence, and to certain other rights typically afforded criminal defendants in civilian courts and courts-martial. See §§ 5(A)-(P). These rights are subject, however, to one glaring condition: The accused and his civilian counsel may be excluded from, and precluded from ever learning what evidence was presented during, any part of the proceeding that either the Appointing Authority or the presiding officer decides to "close." Grounds for such closure "include the protection of information classified or classifiable . . .; information protected by law or rule from unauthorized disclosure; the physical safety of participants in Commission proceedings, including prospective witnesses; intelligence and law enforcement sources, methods, or activities; and other national security interests." § 6(B)(3). Appointed military defense counsel must be privy to these closed sessions, but may, at the presiding officer's discretion, be forbidden to reveal to his or her client what took place therein. *Ibid.*

Another striking feature of the rules governing Hamdan's commission is that they permit the admission of any evidence that, in the opinion of the presiding officer, "would have probative value to a reasonable person." § 6(D)(1). Under this test, not only is testimonial hearsay and evidence obtained through coercion fully admissible, but neither live testimony nor witnesses' written statements need be sworn. *See* §§ 6(D)(2)(b), (3). Moreover, the accused and his civilian counsel may be denied access to evidence in the form of "protected information" (which includes classified information as well as "information protected by law or rule from unauthorized disclosure" and "information concerning other national security interests," §§ 6(B)(3), 6(D)(5)(a)(v)), so long as the presiding officer concludes that the evidence is "probative" under § 6(D)(1) and that its admission without the accused's knowledge would not "result in the denial of a full and fair trial." § 6(D)(5)(b).[43]

Once all the evidence is in, the commission members (not including the presiding officer) must vote on the accused's guilt. A two-thirds vote will suffice for both a verdict of guilty and for imposition of any sentence not including death (the imposition of which requires a unanimous vote). § 6(F). Any appeal is taken to a three-member review panel composed of military officers and designated by the Secretary of Defense, only one member of which need have experience as a judge. § 6(H)(4). The review panel is directed to "disregard any variance from procedures specified in this Order or elsewhere that would not materially have affected the outcome of the trial before the Commission." *Ibid.* Once the panel makes its recommendation to the Secretary of Defense, the Secretary can either remand for further proceedings or forward the record to the President with his recommendation as to final disposition. § 6(H)(5). The President then, unless he has delegated the task to the Secretary, makes the "final decision." § 6(H)(6). He may change the commission's findings or sentence only in a manner favorable to the accused. *Ibid.*

---

[43] As the District Court observed, this section apparently permits reception of testimony from a confidential informant in circumstances where "Hamdan will not be permitted to hear the testimony, see the witness's face, or learn his name. If the government has information developed by interrogation of witnesses in Afghanistan or elsewhere, it can offer such evidence in transcript form, or even as summaries of transcripts." 344 F. Supp. 2d 152, 168 (D.D.C. 2004). Finally, a presiding officer's determination that evidence "would not have probative value to a reasonable person" may be overridden by a majority of the other commission members. § 6(D)(1).

B

Hamdan raises both general and particular objections to the procedures set forth in Commission Order No. 1. His general objection is that the procedures' admitted deviation from those governing courts-martial itself renders the commission illegal. Chief among his particular objections are that he may, under the Commission Order, be convicted based on evidence he has not seen or heard, and that any evidence admitted against him need not comply with the admissibility or relevance rules typically applicable in criminal trials and court-martial proceedings.

The Government objects to our consideration of any procedural challenge at this stage on the grounds that (1) the abstention doctrine espoused in [*Schlesinger v. Councilman*, 420 U.S. 738 (1975)], precludes pre-enforcement review of procedural rules, (2) Hamdan will be able to raise any such challenge following a "final decision" under the DTA, and (3) "there is . . . no basis to presume, before the trial has even commenced, that the trial will not be conducted in good faith and according to law." Brief for Respondents 45-46, nn. 20-21. The first of these contentions was disposed of in Part III, supra, and neither of the latter two is sound.

First, because Hamdan apparently is not subject to the death penalty (at least as matters now stand) and may receive a sentence shorter than 10 years' imprisonment, he has no automatic right to review of the commission's "final decision" before a federal court under the DTA. See § 1005(e)(3), 119 Stat. 2743. Second, contrary to the Government's assertion, there is a "basis to presume" that the procedures employed during Hamdan's trial will violate the law: The procedures are described with particularity in Commission Order No. 1, and implementation of some of them has already occurred. One of Hamdan's complaints is that he will be, and indeed already has been, excluded from his own trial. See Reply Brief for Petitioner 12; App. to Pet. for Cert. 45a. Under these circumstances, review of the procedures in advance of a "final decision"—the timing of which is left entirely to the discretion of the President under the DTA—is appropriate. We turn, then, to consider the merits of Hamdan's procedural challenge.

C

In part because the difference between military commissions and courts-martial originally was a difference of jurisdiction alone, and in part to protect against abuse and ensure evenhandedness under the pressures of war, the procedures governing trials by military commission historically have been the same as those governing courts-martial. *See, e.g.*, 1 The War of the Rebellion 248 (2d series 1894) (General Order 1 issued during the Civil War required military commissions to "be constituted in a similar manner and their proceedings be conducted according to the same general rules as courts-martial in order to prevent abuses which might otherwise arise"). Accounts of commentators from Winthrop through General Crowder—who drafted Article of War 15 and whose views have been deemed "authoritative" by this Court,

[*Madsen v. Kinsella*, 343 U.S. 341, 353 (1952)]—confirm as much.   As recently as the Korean and Vietnam wars, during which use of military commissions was contemplated but never made, the principle of procedural parity was espoused as a background assumption. *See* Paust, *Antiterrorism Military Commissions: Courting Illegality*, 23 Mich. J. Int'l L. 1, 3-5 (2001-2002).

There is a glaring historical exception to this general rule. The procedures and evidentiary rules used to try General Yamashita near the end of World War II deviated in significant respects from those then governing courts-martial. See 327 U.S. 1. The force of that precedent, however, has been seriously undermined by post-World War II developments.

* * *

At least partially in response to subsequent criticism of General Yamashita's trial, the UCMJ's codification of the Articles of War after World War II expanded the category of persons subject thereto to include defendants in Yamashita's (and Hamdan's) position, and the Third Geneva Convention of 1949 extended prisoner-of-war protections to individuals tried for crimes committed before their capture. *See* 3 Int'l Comm. of Red Cross, Commentary: Geneva Convention Relative to the Treatment of Prisoners of War 413 (1960) (hereinafter GCIII Commentary) (explaining that Article 85, which extends the Convention's protections to "[p]risoners of war prosecuted under the laws of the Detaining Power for acts committed prior to capture," was adopted in response to judicial interpretations of the 1929 Convention, including this Court's decision in *Yamashita*). The most notorious exception to the principle of uniformity, then, has been stripped of its precedential value.

The uniformity principle is not an inflexible one; it does not preclude all departures from the procedures dictated for use by courts-martial. But any departure must be tailored to the exigency that necessitates it. See Winthrop 835, n. 81. That understanding is reflected in Article 36 of the UCMJ, which provides:

> "(a) The procedure, including modes of proof, in cases before courts-martial, courts of inquiry, military commissions, and other military tribunals may be prescribed by the President by regulations which shall, so far as he considers practicable, apply the principles of law and the rules of evidence generally recognized in the trial of criminal cases in the United States district courts, but which may not be contrary to or inconsistent with this chapter.

> "(b) All rules and regulations made under this article shall be uniform insofar as practicable and shall be reported to Congress." 70A Stat. 50.

Article 36 places two restrictions on the President's power to promulgate rules of procedure for courts-martial and military commissions alike. First, no procedural rule he adopts may be "contrary to or inconsistent with" the UCMJ—however practical it may seem. Second, the rules adopted must be "uniform insofar as practicable." That is, the rules applied to military commissions must be the same as those applied to courts-martial unless such uniformity proves impracticable.

Hamdan argues that Commission Order No. 1 violates both of these restrictions; he maintains that the procedures described in the Commission Order are inconsistent with the UCMJ and that the Government has offered no explanation for their deviation from the procedures governing courts-martial, which are set forth in the Manual for Courts-Martial, United States (2005 ed.) (Manual for Courts-Martial). Among the inconsistencies Hamdan identifies is that between § 6 of the Commission Order, which permits exclusion of the accused from proceedings and denial of his access to evidence in certain circumstances, and the UCMJ's requirement that "[a]ll . . . proceedings" other than votes and deliberations by courts-martial "shall be made a part of the record and shall be in the presence of the accused." 10 U.S.C. § 839(c) (Supp. 2006). Hamdan also observes that the Commission Order dispenses with virtually all evidentiary rules applicable in courts-martial.

The Government has three responses. First, it argues, only 9 of the UCMJ's 158 Articles—the ones that expressly mention "military commissions"49 49. Aside from Articles 21 and 36, discussed at length in the text, the other seven Articles that expressly reference military commissions are: (1) 28 (requiring appointment of reporters and interpreters); (2) 47 (making it a crime to refuse to appear or testify "before a court-martial, military commission, court of inquiry, or any other military court or board"); (3) 48 (allowing a "court-martial, provost court, or military commission" to punish a person for contempt); (4) 49(d) (permitting admission into evidence of a "duly authenticated deposition taken upon reasonable notice to the other parties" only if "admissible under the rules of evidence" and only if the witness is otherwise unavailable); (5) 50 (permitting admission into evidence of records of courts of inquiry "if otherwise admissible under the rules of evidence," and if certain other requirements are met); (6) 104 (providing that a person accused of aiding the enemy may be sentenced to death or other punishment by military commission or court-martial); and (7) 106 (mandating the death penalty for spies convicted before military commission or court-martial). —actually apply to commissions, and Commission Order No. 1 sets forth no procedure that is "contrary to or inconsistent with" those 9 provisions. Second, the Government contends, military commissions would be of no use if the President were hamstrung by those provisions of the UCMJ that govern courts-martial. Finally, the President's determination that "the danger to the safety of the United States and the nature of international terrorism" renders it impracticable "to apply in military commissions . . . the principles of law and rules of evidence generally recognized in the trial of criminal cases in the United States district courts," November 13 Order § 1(f), is, in the Government's view, explanation enough for any deviation from court-martial procedures. See Brief for Respondents 43-47, and n. 22.

Hamdan has the better of this argument. Without reaching the question whether any provision of Commission Order No. 1 is strictly "contrary to or inconsistent with" other provisions of the UCMJ, we conclude that the "practicability" determination the President has made is insufficient to justify variances from the procedures governing courts-martial. Subsection (b) of Article 36 was added after World War II, and requires a different showing of impracticability from the one required by subsection (a). Subsection (a) requires that the rules the President promulgates for courts-martial, provost courts, and military commissions alike conform to those that govern procedures in Article III courts, "so far as *he considers* practicable." 10 U.S.C. § 836(a) (emphasis added). Subsection (b), by contrast, demands that the rules applied in courts-martial, provost courts, and military commissions— whether or not they conform with the Federal Rules of Evidence—be "uniform *insofar as practicable.*" § 836(b) (emphasis added). Under the latter provision, then, the rules set forth in the Manual for Courts-Martial must apply to military commissions unless impracticable.

The President here has determined, pursuant to subsection (a), that it is impracticable to apply the rules and principles of law that govern "the trial of criminal cases in the United States district courts," § 836(a), to Hamdan's commission. We assume that complete deference is owed that determination. The President has not, however, made a similar official determination that it is impracticable to apply the rules for courts-martial. And even if subsection (b)'s requirements may be satisfied without such an official determination, the requirements of that subsection are not satisfied here.

Nothing in the record before us demonstrates that it would be impracticable to apply court-martial rules in this case. There is no suggestion, for example, of any logistical difficulty in securing properly sworn and authenticated evidence or in applying the usual principles of relevance and admissibility. Assuming arguendo that the reasons articulated in the President's Article 36(a) determination ought to be considered in evaluating the impracticability of applying court-martial rules, the only reason offered in support of that determination is the danger posed by international terrorism. Without for one moment underestimating that danger, it is not evident to us why it should require, in the case of Hamdan's trial, any variance from the rules that govern courts-martial.

* * *

Under the circumstances, then, the rules applicable in courts-martial must apply. Since it is undisputed that Commission Order No. 1 deviates in many significant respects from those rules, it necessarily violates Article 36(b).

The Government's objection that requiring compliance with the court-martial rules imposes an undue burden both ignores the plain meaning of Article 36(b) and misunderstands the purpose and the history of military commissions. The military commission was not born of a desire to dispense a more summary form of justice than is afforded by courts-martial; it developed, rather, as a tribunal of necessity to be employed when courts-martial lacked jurisdiction over either the accused or the subject matter. *See* Winthrop 831. Exigency lent the commission its legitimacy, but did not further justify the wholesale jettisoning of procedural protections. That history explains why the military commission's procedures typically have been the ones used by courts-martial. That the jurisdiction of the two tribunals today may sometimes overlap, see Madsen, 343 U.S., at 354, does not detract from the force of this history; Article 21 did not transform the military commission from a tribunal of true exigency into a more convenient adjudicatory tool. Article 36, confirming as much, strikes a careful balance between uniform procedure and the need to accommodate exigencies that may sometimes arise in a theater of war. That Article not having been complied with here, the rules specified for Hamdan's trial are illegal.

D

The procedures adopted to try Hamdan also violate the Geneva Conventions. The Court of Appeals dismissed Hamdan's Geneva Convention challenge on three independent grounds: (1) the Geneva Conventions are not judicially enforceable; (2) Hamdan in any event is not entitled to their protections; and (3) even if he is entitled to their protections, Councilman abstention is appropriate. Judge Williams, concurring, rejected the second ground but agreed with the majority respecting the first and the last. As we explained in Part III, supra, the abstention rule applied in Councilman, 420 U.S. 738, is not applicable here. And for the reasons that follow, we hold that neither of the other grounds the Court of Appeals gave for its decision is persuasive.

i

The Court of Appeals relied on *Johnson v. Eisentrager*, 339 U.S. 763, (1950), to hold that Hamdan could not invoke the Geneva Conventions to challenge the Government's plan to prosecute him in accordance with Commission Order No. 1. Eisentrager involved a challenge by 21 German nationals to their 1945 convictions for war crimes by a military tribunal convened in Nanking, China, and to their subsequent imprisonment in occupied Germany. The petitioners argued, inter alia, that the 1929 Geneva Convention rendered illegal some of the procedures employed during their trials, which they said deviated impermissibly from the procedures used by courts-martial to try American soldiers. See *id.*, at 789. We rejected that claim on the merits because the petitioners (unlike Hamdan here) had failed to identify any prejudicial disparity "between the Commission that tried [them] and those that would try an offending soldier of the American forces of like rank," and in any event could claim no protection, under the 1929 Convention, during trials for crimes that occurred before their confinement as prisoners of war. *Id.*, at 790.

Buried in a footnote of the opinion, however, is this curious statement suggesting that the Court lacked power even to consider the merits of the Geneva Convention argument:

> "We are not holding that these prisoners have no right which the military authorities are bound to respect. The United States, by the Geneva Convention of July 27, 1929, 47 Stat.2021, concluded with forty-six other countries, including the German Reich, an agreement upon the treatment to be accorded captives. These prisoners claim to be and are entitled to its protection. It is, however, the obvious scheme of the Agreement that responsibility for observance and enforcement of these rights is upon political and military authorities. Rights of alien enemies are vindicated under it only through protests and intervention of protecting powers as the rights of our citizens against foreign governments are vindicated only by Presidential intervention." *Id.*, at 789, n. 14.

The Court of Appeals, on the strength of this footnote, held that "the 1949 Geneva Convention does not confer upon Hamdan a right to enforce its provisions in court." 415 F.3d, at 40.

Whatever else might be said about the *Eisentrager* footnote, it does not control this case. We may assume that "the obvious scheme" of the 1949 Conventions is identical in all relevant respects to that of the 1929 Convention,[57] and even that that scheme would, absent some other provision of law, preclude Hamdan's invocation of the Convention's provisions as an independent source of law binding the Government's actions and furnishing petitioner with any enforceable right. For, regardless of the nature of the rights conferred on Hamdan, cf. United States v. RaU.S.C.her, 119 U.S. 407 (1886), they are, as the Government does not dispute, part of the law of war. *See Hamdi*, 542 U.S., at 520-521 (plurality opinion). And compliance with the law of war is the condition upon which the authority set forth in Article 21 is granted.

ii

For the Court of Appeals, acknowledgment of that condition was no bar to *Hamdan*'s trial by commission. As an alternative to its holding that Hamdan could not invoke the Geneva Conventions at all, the Court of Appeals concluded that the Conventions did not in any event apply to the armed conflict during which Hamdan was captured. The court accepted the Executive's assertions that Hamdan was captured in connection with the United States' war with al Qaeda and that that war is distinct from the war with the Taliban in Afghanistan. It further reasoned that the war with al

---

[57] *But see*, e.g., 4 Int'l Comm. of Red Cross, Commentary: Geneva Convention Relative to the Protection of Civilian Persons in Time of War 21 (1958) (hereinafter GCIV Commentary) (the 1949 Geneva Conventions were written "first and foremost to protect individuals, and not to serve State interests"); GCIII Commentary 91 ("It was not . . . until the Conventions of 1949 . . . that the existence of 'rights' conferred in prisoners of war was affirmed").

Qaeda evades the reach of the Geneva Conventions. *See* 415 F.3d, at 41-42. We, like Judge Williams, disagree with the latter conclusion.

The conflict with al Qaeda is not, according to the Government, a conflict to which the full protections afforded detainees under the 1949 Geneva Conventions apply because Article 2 of those Conventions (which appears in all four Conventions) renders the full protections applicable only to "all cases of declared war or of any other armed conflict which may arise between two or more of the High Contracting Parties." 6 U.S. T., at 3318. Since Hamdan was captured and detained incident to the conflict with al Qaeda and not the conflict with the Taliban, and since al Qaeda, unlike Afghanistan, is not a "High Contracting Party"—i.e., a signatory of the Conventions, the protections of those Conventions are not, it is argued, applicable to Hamdan.[60]

We need not decide the merits of this argument because there is at least one provision of the Geneva Conventions that applies here even if the relevant conflict is not one between signatories.[61]

The Court of Appeals thought, and the Government asserts, that Common Article 3 does not apply to Hamdan because the conflict with al Qaeda, being " 'international in scope,' " does not qualify as a " 'conflict not of an international character.' " 415 F.3d, at 41. That reasoning is erroneous. The term "conflict not of an international character" is used here in contradistinction to a conflict between nations. So much is demonstrated by the "fundamental logic [of] the Convention's provisions on its application." *Id.*, at 44 (Williams, J., concurring). Common Article 2 provides that "the present Convention shall apply to all cases of declared war or of any other armed conflict which may arise between two or more of the High Contracting Parties." 6 U.S. T., at 3318 (Art. 2, ¶ 1). High Contracting Parties (signatories) also must abide by all terms of the Conventions vis-à-vis one another even if one party to the conflict is a nonsignatory "Power," and must so abide vis-à-vis the nonsignatory if "the latter accepts and applies" those terms. *Ibid.* (Art. 2, ¶ 3). Common Article 3, by contrast, affords some minimal protection, falling short of full protection under the Conventions, to individuals

---

[60] The President has stated that the conflict with the Taliban is a conflict to which the Geneva Conventions apply. See White House Memorandum, Humane Treatment of Taliban and al Qaeda Detainees 2 (Feb. 7, 2002) . . . .

[61] Hamdan observes that Article 5 of the Third Geneva Convention requires that if there be "any doubt" whether he is entitled to prisoner-of-war protections, he must be afforded those protections until his status is determined by a "competent tribunal." 6 U.S. T., at 3324. See also Headquarters Depts. of Army, Navy, Air Force, and Marine Corps, Army Regulation 190-8, Enemy Prisoners of War, Retained Personnel, Civilian Internees and Other Detainees (1997), App. 116. Because we hold that Hamdan may not, in any event, be tried by the military commission the President has convened pursuant to the November 13 Order and Commission Order No. 1, the question whether his potential status as a prisoner of war independently renders illegal his trial by military commission may be reserved.

associated with neither a signatory nor even a nonsignatory "Power" who are involved in a conflict "in the territory of" a signatory. The latter kind of conflict is distinguishable from the conflict described in Common Article 2 chiefly because it does not involve a clash between nations (whether signatories or not). In context, then, the phrase "not of an international character" bears its literal meaning. See, e.g., J. Bentham, Introduction to the Principles of Morals and Legislation 6, 296 (J. Burns & H. Hart eds. 1970) (using the term "international law" as a "new though not inexpressive appellation" meaning "betwixt nation and nation"; defining "international" to include "mutual transactions between sovereigns as such"); Commentary on the Additional Protocols to the Geneva Conventions of 12 August 1949, p. 1351 (1987) ("[A] non-international armed conflict is distinct from an international armed conflict because of the legal status of the entities opposing each other").

    * * *

iii

Common Article 3, then, is applicable here and, as indicated above, requires that Hamdan be tried by a "regularly constituted court affording all the judicial guarantees which are recognized as indispensable by civilized peoples." 6 U. S. T., at 3320 (Art. 3, ¶ 1(d)). While the term "regularly constituted court" is not specifically defined in either Common Article 3 or its accompanying commentary, other sources disclose its core meaning. The commentary accompanying a provision of the Fourth Geneva Convention, for example, defines " 'regularly constituted' " tribunals to include "ordinary military courts" and "definitely exclud[e] all special tribunals." GCIV Commentary 340 (defining the term "properly constituted" in Article 66, which the commentary treats as identical to "regularly constituted"); see also Yamashita, 327 U.S., at 44 (Rutledge, J., dissenting) (describing military commission as a court "specially constituted for a particular trial"). And one of the Red Cross' own treatises defines "regularly constituted court" as used in Common Article 3 to mean "established and organized in accordance with the laws and procedures already in force in a country." Int'l Comm. of Red Cross, 1 Customary International Humanitarian Law 355 (2005); see also GCIV Commentary 340 (observing that "ordinary military courts" will "be set up in accordance with the recognized principles governing the administration of justice").

The Government offers only a cursory defense of Hamdan's military commission in light of Common Article 3. *See* Brief for Respondents 49-50. As Justice KENNEDY explains, that defense fails because "[t]he regular military courts in our system are the courts-martial established by congressional statutes." Post, at 2803 (opinion concurring in part). At a minimum, a military commission "can be 'regularly constituted' by the standards of our military justice system only if some practical need explains deviations from court-martial practice." Post, at 2804. As we have explained, see Part VI-C, supra, no such need has been demonstrated here.

iv*

Inextricably intertwined with the question of regular constitution is the evaluation of the procedures governing the tribunal and whether they afford "all the judicial guarantees which are recognized as indispensable by civilized peoples." 6 U.S. T., at 3320 (Art. 3, ¶ 1(d)). Like the phrase "regularly constituted court," this phrase is not defined in the text of the Geneva Conventions. But it must be understood to incorporate at least the barest of those trial protections that have been recognized by customary international law. Many of these are described in Article 75 of Protocol I to the Geneva Conventions of 1949, adopted in 1977 (Protocol I). Although the United States declined to ratify Protocol I, its objections were not to Article 75 thereof. Indeed, it appears that the Government "regard[s] the provisions of Article 75 as an articulation of safeguards to which all persons in the hands of an enemy are entitled." Taft, *The Law of Armed Conflict After 9/11: Some Salient Features*, 28 Yale J. Int'l L. 319, 322 (2003). Among the rights set forth in Article 75 is the "right to be tried in [one's] presence." Protocol I, Art. 75(4)(e).

* * *

[In an omitted portion of the case, the plurality also concluded that a military commission could not try the offense of conspiracy to commit war crimes because such a conspiracy was not itself recognized as a war crime. Also omitted for brevity are a number of separate opinions. Justice Breyer filed a concurring opinion in which Justices Kennedy, Souter and Ginsburg joined. Justice Kennedy concurred in part and filed an opinion in which Justices Souter, Ginsburg and Breyer joined in part. Justice Scalia filed dissenting opinion in which Justices Thomas and Alito joined. Justice Thomas filed a dissenting opinion in which Justice Scalia joined and Justice Alito joined in part. Justice Alito filed dissenting opinion in which Justices Scalia and Thomas joined in part. Chief Justice Roberts did not participate.]

Points for Discussion

1. If the Supreme Court showed deference to military commissions in *Quirin* and *Yamashita*, it did not do so in *Hamdan*. What might account for the difference? Was the military commission to be used in *Hamdan* likely to be less fair than the military commissions used in *Quirin* and *Yamashita*? Or was the Supreme Court in 2006 just less willing to defer to the executive in general, and military in particular, than the Court was in the 1940s?

2. Did the Court leave open the possibility that Congress could address the shortcomings in the military commission system established by the President?

---

* Part VI-D-iv of Justice Stevens's opinion is a plurality opinion. It received only four votes and therefore does not represent the opinion of the Court.—Eds.

16-3. The Military Commissions Acts of 2006 and 2009

In response to the *Hamdan* decision, Congress in a bipartisan vote just months later enacted the MCA 2006. This legislation systematically addressed each part of the Court's reasoning.

In part V of the *Hamdan* majority opinion, the Court concluded that the President did not have any specific statutory authorization to use military commissions (and as a result the Court concluded that the laws of war limited the President). Congress responded to this holding by giving the President specific authority: "The President is authorized to establish military commissions under this chapter for offenses triable by military commission as provided in this chapter." 10 U.S.C. § 948b(b).

In part VI.C., the Court concluded that UCMJ article 36(b), 10 U.S.C. § 836(b), required the procedural and evidentiary rules for military commissions to be "uniform insofar as practicable" with the rules for courts-martial. Congress responded to this holding by revising article 36(b) to say: "All rules and regulations made under this article shall be uniform insofar as practicable, except insofar as applicable to military commissions . . . ." 10 U.S.C. § 836(b).[1]

In part VI.D. the Court upheld Hamdan's contention that the procedures would violate his rights under the Geneva Convention. Congress responded to this conclusion by providing: "No alien unprivileged enemy belligerent subject to trial by military commission under this chapter may invoke the Geneva Conventions as a basis for a private right of action." 10 U.S.C. § 948b(e).

In addition, as noted in a Point for Discussion following the *Quirin* case, a plurality of the Supreme Court concluded that a conspiracy to commit violations of the law of war is not itself a violation of the law of war and that it therefore such a conspiracy cannot be tried by a military commission absent addition Congressional authorization. In response to this conclusion, Congress in the Military Commissions Act of 2006 specifically made conspiracy a crime that is triable by military commission. *See* 10 U.S.C. § 950t(29).

---

[1] Students using this book may see the Court's reasoning on this point to rest on a fundamental misunderstanding of the Uniform Code of Military Justice. The requirement of uniformity, as explained in Chapter 1, was to make procedures of military tribunals uniform across the services: the Army, Navy, Marine Corps, Air Force, and Coast Guard. It was not to make all different kinds of tribunals—general courts-martial, boards of inquiry, etc.—uniform in their procedures. Such an effort would be impossible. Justice Thomas noted this point in his dissent. *See Hamdan*, 548 U.S. at 712 n.17 (Thomas, J., dissenting) ("Article 36(b)'s uniformity requirement pertains to uniformity between the three branches of the Armed Forces, and no more.").

Points for Discussion

1. Do these changes suggest that Congress felt that the Supreme Court had incorrectly decided *Hamdan*? Or might they merely indicate that statutory changes were necessary to make cases like *Hamdan* come out a different way?

2. Is it likely that the Supreme Court will agree that this legislation corrected the problems of using military commissions?

The MCA 2006 and MCA 2009 set up a complete criminal justice system centered on the use of military commissions, just as the Uniform Code of Military Justice sets up a complete criminal justice system centered on the use of courts-martial. And as it takes a whole textbook to explain the UCMJ, it would likewise require a complete volume to describe the current statutory scheme. Such an effort is beyond the scope of this book.

Three key points, however, deserve attention. The first concerns the personal jurisdiction of the military commissions. According to 10 U.S.C. § 948c, "Any *alien unprivileged enemy belligerent* is subject to trial by military commission as set forth in this chapter" (emphasis added). An alien is a person who is not a U.S. citizen. The terms privileged belligerents and unprivileged enemy belligerents are defined as follows:

> (6) Privileged belligerent.—The term "privileged belligerent" means an individual belonging to one of the eight categories enumerated in Article 4 of the Geneva Convention Relative to the Treatment of Prisoners of War.

> (7) Unprivileged enemy belligerent.—The term "unprivileged enemy belligerent" means an individual (other than a privileged belligerent) who—

>> (A) has engaged in hostilities against the United States or its coalition partners;

>> (B) has purposefully and materially supported hostilities against the United States or its coalition partners; or

>> (C) was a part of al Qaeda at the time of the alleged offense under this chapter.

Id. §§ 948c(6) & (7). Article 4 of the Geneva Convention includes both members of a regular armed force and, among others, combatants who meet these criteria:

> (a) that of being commanded by a person responsible for his subordinates;

> (b) that of having a fixed distinctive sign recognizable at a distance;

> (c) that of carrying arms openly;

> (d) that of conducting their operations in accordance with the laws and customs of war.

Geneva Convention Relative to the Treatment of Prisoners of War, art. 4.A.(2), Aug. 12, 1949, 6 U.S.T. 3316, 75 U.N.T.S. 135. This definition would cover regular Iraqi forces whom the United States battled in 2003, but it presumably would not cover al-Qaida or Taliban fighters.

The second point is the MCA 2006 and MCA 2009 define the offenses triable by military commission. These offenses include:

(1) Murder of protected persons
(2) Attacking civilians
(3) Attacking civilian objects
(4) Attacking protected property
(5) Pillaging
(6) Denying quarter
(7) Taking hostages
(8) Employing poison or similar weapons
(9) Using protected persons as a shield
(10) Using protected property as a shield
(11) Torture
(12) Cruel or inhuman treatment
(13) Intentionally causing serious bodily injury
(14) Mutilating or maiming
(15) Murder in violation of the law of war
(16) Destruction of property in violation of the law of war
(17) Using treachery or perfidy
(18) Improperly using a flag of truce
(19) Improperly using a distinctive emblem
(20) Intentionally mistreating a dead body
(21) Rape
(22) Sexual assault or abuse
(23) Hijacking or hazarding a vessel or aircraft
(24) Terrorism
(25) Providing material support for terrorism
(26) Wrongfully aiding the enemy
(27) Spying
(28) Attempts
(29) Conspiracy
(30) Solicitation
(31) Contempt
(32) Perjury and obstruction of justice

10 U.S.C. § 950t(1)-(32). Many of these offenses are traditional war crimes, but some of them are not. It remains unclear after *Hamdan* whether Congress can give a military commission the power to try an offense that is not a war crime.

Third, the MCA 2006 and MCA 2009 start with the presumption that the rules of evidence will be the same as those applicable to courts-martial, but provide that the Secretary of Defense can make exceptions (subject to important limitations protecting the fundamental rights of the accused). 10 U.S.C. § 949a.

Although the United States has detained many aliens since 2001, only a few have been tried. The following case concerns an alien detained at Guantanamo, and who could be tried by military commission, but who has not been charged.

AL-BIHANI v. OBAMA
U.S. Court of Appeals for the District of Columbia Circuit
590 F.3d 866 (D.C. Cir. 2010)

BROWN, Circuit Judge:

Ghaleb Nassar Al-Bihani appeals the denial of his petition for a writ of habeas corpus and seeks reversal or remand. He claims his detention is unauthorized by statute and the procedures of his habeas proceeding were constitutionally infirm. We reject these claims and affirm the denial of his petition.

I

Al-Bihani, a Yemeni citizen, has been held at the U.S. naval base detention facility in Guantanamo Bay, Cuba since 2002. He came to Guantanamo by a circuitous route. It began in Saudi Arabia in the first half of 2001 when a local sheikh issued a religious challenge to Al-Bihani. In response, Al-Bihani traveled through Pakistan to Afghanistan eager to defend the Taliban's Islamic state against the Northern Alliance. Along the way, he stayed at what the government alleges were Al Qaeda-affiliated guesthouses; Al-Bihani only concedes they were affiliated with the Taliban. During this transit period, he may also have received instruction at two Al Qaeda terrorist training camps, though Al-Bihani disputes this. What he does not dispute is that he eventually accompanied and served a paramilitary group allied with the Taliban, known as the 55th Arab Brigade, which included Al Qaeda members within its command structure and which fought on the front lines against the Northern Alliance. He worked as the brigade's cook and carried a brigade-issued weapon, but never fired it in combat. Combat, however-in the form of bombing by the U.S.-led Coalition that invaded Afghanistan in response to the attacks of September 11, 2001-forced the 55th to retreat from the front lines in October 2001. At the end of this protracted retreat, Al-Bihani and the rest of the brigade surrendered, under orders, to Northern Alliance forces, and they kept him in custody until his handover to U.S. Coalition forces in early 2002. The U.S. military sent Al-Bihani to Guantanamo for detention and interrogation.

After the Supreme Court held in *Rasul v. Bush*, 542 U.S. 466, 483-84 (2004), that the statutory habeas jurisdiction of federal courts extended to Guantanamo Bay, Al-Bihani filed a habeas petition with the U.S. District Court for the District of Columbia, challenging his detention under 28 U.S.C.

§ 2241(a). The district court stayed the petition until the Supreme Court in *Boumediene v. Bush*, 553 U.S. 723 (2008), held that the section of the Military Commissions Act of 2006 (2006 MCA), Pub.L. No. 109-366, 120 Stat. 2600 (codified in part at 28 U.S.C. § 2241 & note), that withdrew jurisdiction from the courts to entertain habeas petitions filed by Guantanamo detainees was an unconstitutional suspension of the writ. 128 S.Ct. at 2274. Boumediene held that detainees were entitled to proceed with habeas challenges under procedures crafted to account for the special circumstances of wartime detention. *Id.* at 2276.

Soon after the Boumediene decision, the district court, acting with admirable dispatch, revived Al-Bihani's petition and convened counsel to discuss the process to be used. The district court finalized the procedure in a published case management order. *See Al Bihani v. Bush* (CMO), 588 F. Supp.2d 19 (D.D.C. 2008) (case management order). The order established that the government had the burden of proving the legality of Al-Bihani's detention by a preponderance of the evidence; it obligated the government to explain the legal basis for Al-Bihani's detention, to share all documents used in its factual return, and to turn over any exculpatory evidence found in preparation of its case. To Al-Bihani, the order afforded the opportunity to file a traverse and supplements to the traverse rebutting the government's factual return, to introduce new evidence, and to move for discovery upon a showing of good cause and the absence of undue burden on the government. The order reserved the district court's discretion, when appropriate, to adopt a rebuttable presumption in favor of the accuracy of the government's evidence and to admit relevant and material hearsay, the credibility and weight of which the opposing party could challenge. The order also scheduled status conferences to clarify any discovery and evidentiary issues with the government's factual return and to identify issues of law and fact prior to the habeas hearing where such issues would be contested. *See id.* at 20-21.

After the parties filed their cases in accordance with the case management order and the district court held a day and a half of hearings, the district court denied Al-Bihani's petition. Adopting a definition that allowed the government to detain anyone "who was part of or supporting Taliban or al Qaeda forces, or associated forces that are engaged in hostilities against the United States or its coalition partners," the district court found Al-Bihani's actions met the standard. *See Al Bihani v. Obama* (Mem.Op.), 594 F.Supp.2d 35, 38, 40 (D.D.C.2009) (memorandum opinion). It cited as sufficiently credible the evidence-primarily drawn from Al-Bihani's own admissions during interrogation-that Al-Bihani stayed at Al Qaeda-affiliated guesthouses and that he served in and retreated with the 55th Arab Brigade. See *id.* at 39-40. The district court declined to rely on evidence drawn from admissions-later recanted by Al-Bihani-that he attended Al Qaeda training camps on his way to the front lines. See *id.* at 39.

* * *

II

Al-Bihani's many arguments present this court with two overarching questions regarding the detainees at the Guantanamo Bay naval base. The first concerns whom the President can lawfully detain pursuant to statutes passed by Congress. The second asks what procedure is due to detainees challenging their detention in habeas corpus proceedings. The Supreme Court has provided scant guidance on these questions, consciously leaving the contours of the substantive and procedural law of detention open for lower courts to shape in a common law fashion. See *Hamdi v. Rumsfeld*, 542 U.S. 507, 522 n. 1 (2004) (plurality opinion of O'Connor, J.) ("The permissible bounds of the [enemy combatant] category will be defined by the lower courts as subsequent cases are presented to them."); *Boumediene*, 128 S. Ct. at 2276 ("We make no attempt to anticipate all of the evidentiary and access-to-counsel issues ... and the other remaining questions [that] are within the expertise and competence of the District Court to address in the first instance."). In this decision, we aim to narrow the legal uncertainty that clouds military detention.

A

Al-Bihani challenges the statutory legitimacy of his detention by advancing a number of arguments based upon the international laws of war. He first argues that relying on "support," or even "substantial support" of Al Qaeda or the Taliban as an independent basis for detention violates international law. As a result, such a standard should not be read into the ambiguous provisions of the Authorization for Use of Military Force (AUMF), Pub.L. No. 107-40, § 2(a), 115 Stat. 224, 224 (2001) (reprinted at 50 U.S.C. § 1541 note), the Act empowering the President to respond to the attacks of September 11, 2001. Al-Bihani interprets international law to mean anyone not belonging to an official state military is a civilian, and civilians, he says, must commit a direct hostile act, such as firing a weapon in combat, before they can be lawfully detained. Because Al-Bihani did not commit such an act, he reasons his detention is unlawful. Next, he argues the members of the 55th Arab Brigade were not subject to attack or detention by U.S. Coalition forces under the laws of co-belligerency because the 55th, although allied with the Taliban against the Northern Alliance, did not have the required opportunity to declare its neutrality in the fight against the United States. His third argument is that the conflict in which he was detained, an international war between the United States and Taliban-controlled Afghanistan, officially ended when the Taliban lost control of the Afghan government. Thus, absent a determination of future dangerousness, he must be released. See Geneva Convention Relative to the Treatment of Prisoners of War (Third Geneva Convention) art. 118, Aug. 12, 1949, 6 U.S.T. 3316, 75 U.N.T.S. 135. Lastly, Al-Bihani posits a type of "clean hands" theory by which any authority the government has to detain him is undermined by its failure to accord him the prisoner-of-war status to which he believes he is entitled by international law.

Before considering these arguments in detail, we note that all of them rely heavily on the premise that the war powers granted by the AUMF and other statutes are limited by the international laws of war. This premise is mistaken. There is no indication in the AUMF, the Detainee Treatment Act of 2005, Pub.L. No. 109-148, div. A, tit. X, 119 Stat. 2739, 2741-43, or the MCA of 2006 or 2009, that Congress intended the international laws of war to act as extra-textual limiting principles for the President's war powers under the AUMF. The international laws of war as a whole have not been implemented domestically by Congress and are therefore not a source of authority for U.S. courts. *See* Restatement (Third) of Foreign Relations Law of The United States § 111(3)-(4) (1987). Even assuming Congress had at some earlier point implemented the laws of war as domestic law through appropriate legislation, Congress had the power to authorize the President in the AUMF and other later statutes to exceed those bounds. See *id.* § 115(1)(a). Further weakening their relevance to this case, the international laws of war are not a fixed code. Their dictates and application to actual events are by nature contestable and flu*id.* See *id.* § 102 cmts. b & c (stating there is "no precise formula" to identify a practice as custom and that "[i]t is often difficult to determine when [a custom's] transformation into law has taken place"). Therefore, while the international laws of war are helpful to courts when identifying the general set of war powers to which the AUMF speaks, see Hamdi, 542 U.S. at 520, their lack of controlling legal force and firm definition render their use both inapposite and inadvisable when courts seek to determine the limits of the President's war powers. Therefore, putting aside that we find Al-Bihani's reading of international law to be unpersuasive, we have no occasion here to quibble over the intricate application of vague treaty provisions and amorphous customary principles. The sources we look to for resolution of Al-Bihani's case are the sources courts always look to: the text of relevant statutes and controlling domestic caselaw.

Under those sources, Al-Bihani is lawfully detained whether the definition of a detainable person is, as the district court articulated it, "an individual who was part of or supporting Taliban or al Qaeda forces, or associated forces that are engaged in hostilities against the United States or its coalition partners," or the modified definition offered by the government that requires that an individual "substantially support" enemy forces. The statutes authorizing the use of force and detention not only grant the government the power to craft a workable legal standard to identify individuals it can detain, but also cabin the application of these definitions. The AUMF authorizes the President to "use all necessary and appropriate force against those nations, organizations, or persons he determines planned, authorized, committed, or aided the terrorist attacks that occurred on September 11, 2001, or harbored such organizations or persons." AUMF § 2(a). The Supreme Court in Hamdi ruled that "necessary and appropriate force" includes the power to detain combatants subject to such force. 542 U.S. at 519. Congress, in the 2006 MCA, provided guidance on the class of persons subject to detention under the AUMF by defining "unlawful enemy combatants" who can be tried by military commission. 2006 MCA sec. 3, § 948a(1). The 2006 MCA authorized the trial of an individual who "engaged in hostilities or who has purposefully and materially supported hostilities against the United States or its co-belligerents who is not a lawful enemy combatant (including a person who is part of the Taliban, al Qaeda, or associated forces)." *Id.* § 948a(1)(A)(i). In 2009, Congress enacted a new version of the MCA with a new definition that authorized the trial of "unprivileged enemy belligerents," a class of persons that includes those who "purposefully and materially supported hostilities against the United States or its coalition partners." Military Commissions Act of 2009 (2009 MCA) sec. 1802, §§ 948a(7), 948b(a), 948c, Pub.L. No. 111-84, tit. XVIII, 123 Stat. 2190, 2575-76. The provisions of the 2006 and 2009 MCAs are illuminating in this case because the government's detention authority logically covers a category of persons no narrower than is covered by its military commission authority. Detention authority in fact sweeps wider, also extending at least to traditional P.O.W.s, see *id.* § 948a(6), and arguably to other categories of persons. But for this case, it is enough to recognize that any person subject to a military commission trial is also subject to detention, and that category of persons includes those who are part of forces associated with Al Qaeda or the Taliban or those who purposefully and materially support such forces in hostilities against U.S. Coalition partners.

In light of these provisions of the 2006 and 2009 MCAs, the facts that were both found by the district court and offered by Al-Bihani in his traverse place Al-Bihani within the "part of" and "support" prongs of the relevant statutory definition. The district court found Al Qaeda members participated in the command structure of the 55th Arab Brigade, see Mem. Op. at 40, making the brigade an Al Qaeda-affiliated outfit, and it is unquestioned that the 55th fought alongside the Taliban while the Taliban was harboring Al Qaeda. Al-Bihani's evidence confirmed these points, establishing that the 55th "supported the Taliban against the Northern Alliance," a Coalition partner, and that the 55th was "aided, or even, at times, commanded, by al-Qaeda members." Brief for Petitioner-Appellant at 33. Al-Bihani's connections with the 55th therefore render him detainable. His acknowledged actions-accompanying the brigade on the battlefield, carrying a brigade-issued weapon, cooking for the unit, and retreating and surrendering under brigade orders-strongly suggest, in the absence of an official membership card, that he was part of the 55th. Even assuming, as he argues, that he was a civilian "contractor" rendering services, see *id.* at 32, those services render Al-Bihani detainable under the "purposefully and materially supported" language of both versions of the MCA. That language constitutes a standard whose outer bounds are not readily identifiable. But wherever the outer bounds may lie, they clearly include traditional food operations essential to a fighting force and the carrying of arms. Viewed in full, the facts show Al-Bihani was part of and supported a group-prior to and after September 11-that was affiliated with Al Qaeda and Taliban forces and engaged in hostilities against a U.S. Coalition partner. Al-Bihani, therefore, falls squarely within the scope of the President's statutory detention powers.

The government can also draw statutory authority to detain Al-Bihani directly from the language of the AUMF. The AUMF authorizes force against those who "harbored . . . organizations or persons" the President determines "planned, authorized, committed, or aided the terrorist attacks of September 11, 2001." AUMF § 2(a). It is not in dispute that Al Qaeda is the organization responsible for September 11 or that it was harbored by the Taliban in Afghanistan. It is also not in dispute that the 55th Arab Brigade defended the Taliban against the Northern Alliance's efforts to oust the regime from power. Drawing from these facts, it cannot be disputed that the actual and foreseeable result of the 55th's defense of the Taliban was the maintenance of Al Qaeda's safe haven in Afghanistan. This result places the 55th within the AUMF's wide ambit as an organization that harbored Al Qaeda, making it subject to U.S. military force and its members and supporters-including Al-Bihani-eligible for detention.

Al-Bihani disagrees with this conclusion, arguing that the 55th Arab Brigade was not lawfully subject to attack and detention. He points to the international laws of co-belligerency to demonstrate that the brigade should have been allowed the opportunity to remain neutral upon notice of a conflict between the United States and the Taliban. We reiterate that international law, including the customary rules of co-belligerency, do not limit the President's detention power in this instance. But even if Al-Bihani's argument were relevant to his detention and putting aside all the questions that applying such elaborate rules to this situation would raise, the laws of co-belligerency affording notice of war and the choice to remain neutral have only applied to nation states. See 2 L. Oppenheim, International Law: A Treatise § 74 (1906). The 55th clearly was not a state, but rather an irregular fighting force present within the borders of Afghanistan at the sanction of the Taliban. Any attempt to apply the rules of co-belligerency to such a force would be folly, akin to this court ascribing powers of national sovereignty to a local chapter of the Freemasons.

While we think the facts of this case show Al-Bihani was both part of and substantially supported enemy forces, we realize the picture may be less clear in other cases where facts may indicate only support, only membership, or neither. We have no occasion here to explore the outer bounds of what constitutes sufficient support or indicia of membership to meet the detention standard. We merely recognize that both prongs are valid criteria that are independently sufficient to satisfy the standard.

With the government's detention authority established as an initial matter, we turn to the argument that Al-Bihani must now be released according to longstanding law of war principles because the conflict with the Taliban has allegedly ended. See Hamdi, 542 U.S. at 521. Al-Bihani offers the court a choice of numerous event dates-the day Afghans established a post-Taliban interim authority, the day the United States recognized that authority, the day Hamid Karzai was elected President-to mark the official end of the conflict. No matter which is chosen, each would dictate the release of Al-Bihani if we follow his reasoning. His argument fails on factual and practical grounds. First, it is not clear if Al-Bihani was captured in the conflict with the Taliban or with Al Qaeda; he does not argue that the conflict with Al Qaeda is over. Second, there are currently 34,800 U.S. troops and a total of 71,030 Coalition troops in Afghanistan, see N. Atl. Treaty Org. [NATO], International Security Assistance Force and Afghan National Army Strength & Laydown, at 2, Oct. 22, 2009, available at http:// www. nato. int/ ISAF/ docu/ epub/ pdf/ isaf__ placemat. pdf, with tens of thousands more to be added soon. The principle Al-Bihani espouses—were it accurate—would make each successful campaign of a long war but a Pyrrhic prelude to defeat. The initial success of the United States and its Coalition partners in ousting the Taliban from the seat of government and establishing a young democracy would trigger an obligation to release Taliban fighters captured in earlier clashes. Thus, the victors would be commanded to constantly refresh the ranks of the fledgling democracy's most likely saboteurs.

In response to this commonsense observation, Al-Bihani contends the current hostilities are a different conflict, one against the Taliban reconstituted in a non-governmental form, and the government must prove that Al-Bihani would join this insurgency in order to continue to hold him. But even the laws of war upon which he relies do not draw such fine distinctions. The Geneva Conventions require release and repatriation only at the "cessation of active hostilities." Third Geneva Convention art. 118. That the Conventions use the term "active hostilities" instead of the terms "conflict" or "state of war" found elsewhere in the document is significant. It serves to distinguish the physical violence of war from the official beginning and end of a conflict, because fighting does not necessarily track formal timelines. See *id*. art. 2 (provisions apply "even if the state of war is not recognized"), art. 118 (discussing the possibility of the cessation of active hostilities even in the absence of an agreement to cease hostilities). The Conventions, in short, codify what common sense tells us must be true: release is only required when the fighting stops.

Even so, we do not rest our resolution of this issue on international law or mere common sense. The determination of when hostilities have ceased is a political decision, and we defer to the Executive's opinion on the matter, at least in the absence of an authoritative congressional declaration purporting to terminate the war. See Ludecke v. Watkins, 335 U.S. 160, 168-70 & n. 13 (1948) ("[T]ermination [of a state of war] is a political act."). Al-Bihani urges the court to ignore Ludecke's controlling precedent because the President in that case had pronounced that a war was ongoing, whereas in this case the President has made no such pronouncement. We reject Al-Bihani's entreaty. A clear statement requirement is at odds with the wide deference the judiciary is obliged to give to the democratic branches with regard to questions concerning national security. In the absence of a determination by the political branches that hostilities in Afghanistan have ceased, Al-Bihani's continued detention is justified.

Al-Bihani also argues he should be released because the government's failure to accord him P.O.W. status violated international law and undermined its otherwise lawful authority to detain him. Even assuming Al-Bihani is entitled to P.O.W. status, we find no controlling authority for this "clean hands" theory in statute or in caselaw. The AUMF, DTA, and MCA of 2006 and 2009 do not hinge the government's detention authority on proper identification of P.O.W.s or compliance with international law in general. In fact, the MCA of 2006, in a provision not altered by the MCA of 2009, explicitly precludes detainees from claiming the Geneva conventions-which include criteria to determine who is entitled to P.O.W. status-as a source of rights. *See* 2006 MCA sec. 5(a). And the citation Al-Bihani gives to support his theory is not controlling. The section of Justice Souter's separate opinion in Hamdi in which he discusses a clean hands theory was part of his dissent in that case. See 542 U.S. at 553 (Souter, J., concurring in part, dissenting in part, and concurring in the judgment) ("For me, it suffices that the Government has failed to justify [detention] in the absence of . . . a showing that the detention conforms to the laws of war. . . . [T]his disposition does not command a majority of the Court."). Moreover, Justice Souter's opinion fails to identify any other controlling authority that establishes or discusses this theory in any way. This leaves no foundation for Al-Bihani's clean hands argument, and it fails to persuade.

* * *

III

Al-Bihani's detention is authorized by statute and there was no constitutional defect in the district court's habeas procedure that would have affected the outcome of the proceeding. For these reasons, the order of the district court denying Al-Bihani's petition for a writ of habeas corpus is

Affirmed.

Points for Discussion

1. The court notes that "for this case, it is enough to recognize that any person subject to a military commission trial is also subject to detention." Is that true even if the person is never charged? Is there a time limit for bringing trials?

2. At the time of this decision, Al-Bihani had been in captivity for approximately nine years. How much longer will he have to remain a prisoner if the United States can hold him for the duration of the conflict in Afghanistan?

16-4. The Court of Military Commission Review

The MCA 2006 and MCA 2009 establish an appellate review system. Decisions of the military commissions are reviewed by a new court called the "U.S. Court of Military Commission Review." 10 U.S.C. § 950f. The U.S. Court of Military Commission Review's decisions in turn are reviewed by the U.S. Court of Appeals for the D.C. Circuit and by the U.S. Supreme Court. *See* 10 U.S.C. § 950g. Persons eligible to serve as judges on the Court of Military Commission Review include "persons who are appellate military judges" assigned to the court by the Secretary of Defense and "additional judges" appointed by the President with the advice and consent of the Senate. 10 U.S.C. § 950f(b).[1]

The following decision concerns the appeal of Salim Ahmed Hamdan, who was tried by a military commission under the MCA 2006 and MCA 2009 after the Supreme Court's decision in *Hamdan v. Rumsfeld*, 548 U.S. 557 (2006).

UNITED STATES v. HAMDAN
Court of Military Commission Review
801 F. Supp. 2d 1247 (C.M.C.R. 2011)

BEFORE THE COURT EN BANC BRAND, CONN, HOFFMAN, SIMS, GALLAGHER, PERLAK, ORR, Appellate Military Judges.

Appellant [Salim Ahmed Hamdan] was convicted, contrary to his pleas, of five specifications of providing material support for terrorism, in violation of the Military Commissions Act of 2006, 10 U.S.C. § 950v(b)(25), at a military commission convened at U.S. Naval Station, Guantanamo Bay, Cuba. The military commission sentenced him to 66 months confinement, and the convening authority approved the findings and sentence. . . .

I. STATEMENT OF FACTS

The record establishes and the military commission found that appellant joined and became a member of al Qaeda, a well-established terrorist organization, with the knowledge that al Qaeda has engaged in and engages in terrorism. He had the intent to join in al Qaeda's purposes, and he subsequently took actions to further al Qaeda's goals and purposes.

As early as 1989, Usama bin Laden associated with al Qaeda's Shura Counsel, especially the leader of the Egyptian Islamic Jihad Movement, Dr. Ayman al-Zawahiri, and Omar Abdel Rahman, the Blind Shaykh. Rahman was "the joint spiritual leader of the two leading terrorist organizations in Egypt, the Islamic Jihad and Al–Gama'at al-Islamiyya." Al Qaeda, a military organization, has been involved in various violent activities directed against U.S. civilian and military personnel since at least 1991. "In December 1991, Islamic militants launched a failed bomb attack at a hotel in Aden, Yemen targeting 100 U.S. soldiers who were staying there en route to peacekeeping

---

[1] One of the co-authors of this book, former Appellant Military Judge Lisa Schenck, has served as a judge on the U.S. Court of Military Commission Review.

duties in nearby Somalia." The 1991 Aden bombing, which killed two tourists, was "in response to a 'fatwah,' or religious edict, issued on behalf of [al-Qaeda] in late 1991—which condemned the presence of U.S. military peacekeepers as an attempt to colonize the Muslim world."

In late 1992, bin Laden led meetings of terrorists at al Qaeda guesthouses in Khartoum, Sudan. Al Banshiri, al Qaeda's chief military commander, told al Qaeda members that al Qaeda hoped the United States would become involved in the civil war in Somalia so "that we make a big war with them." Bin Laden announced to 30–40 al Qaeda members in late 1993 that "the American army now they came to the Horn of Africa, and we have to stop the head of the snake ... the snake is America, and we have to stop them. We have to cut the head and stop them." In 1993, al Qaeda's leaders sent al Qaeda Shura Council member Mohammed Atef (a.k.a. Abu Hafs al Masri) to Somalia to organize and train for an attack upon U.S. forces. In October 1993, Somali militiamen used rocket-propelled grenades to shoot down two U.S. Blackhawk helicopters over Mogadishu. Eighteen U.S. military personnel and numerous militiamen were killed in the ensuing street battle. Shortly thereafter, Abu Hafs spoke with al Qaeda members in the Sudan and stated, "everything happening in Somalia, it's our responsibility ... the al Qaeda group, our group."

In January 1996, Rahman was convicted in U.S. federal court of conspiracy for inspiring the February 1993 bombing of the World Trade Center. *United States v. Rahman*, 189 F.3d 88, 103 (2d Cir .1999). In early 1996, Mohammed bin Attash, a close associate of bin Laden, convinced appellant that he should go from his home in Yemen to Tajikistan for Jihad. Bin Attash gave appellant a false passport and an airline ticket to fly from Yemen to Pakistan. Appellant stayed in guest houses in Pakistan, and then he went to Afghanistan. Once in Afghanistan, appellant spent 30–40 days at Al Farouq, an al Qaeda training camp. While there, appellant received training on a variety of weapons, including AK–47s, machine guns, pistols, and rockets. After training, appellant became a driver for an al Qaeda guest house where he ferried people and supplies between Al Farouq and the guest houses. Shortly thereafter, appellant was introduced to bin Laden, gained his trust, and became a primary driver for him. Appellant was trained on convoy techniques and standard operating procedures to engage in if one of bin Laden's compounds came under attack. In addition to serving as bin Laden's driver, appellant also served as his bodyguard. All bodyguards and drivers were armed.

During this period as bin Laden's personal driver and bodyguard, appellant pledged bayat, or "unquestioned allegiance" to bin Laden. The bayat extended to bin Laden's campaign to conduct jihad against Jews and crusaders and to liberate the Arabian Peninsula from infidels; however, appellant reserved the right to withdraw his bayat if bin Laden undertook a mission with which he did not agree. The record does not reveal any instance where appellant exercised this prerogative and refused to support an al Qaeda mission or declined to obey bin Laden's orders.

Appellant, on numerous occasions, delivered requests for logistical support, including weapons and ammunition, to al Qaeda's logistical officer and subsequently delivered the military supplies to the Panjshir Valley. Appellant also delivered bin Laden's orders for military supplies. Appellant repeatedly attended anti-Western lectures given by bin Laden. This began with his own training at an al Qaeda training camp and continued throughout his association with bin Laden, including driving him to training camps and other meetings.

In August 1996, bin Laden issued a video which included a "declaration of war" against the Americans who were occupying land in the Arabian Peninsula (1996 Jihad Declaration). Bin Laden's 1996 Jihad Declaration encouraged the killing of American soldiers in the Arabian Peninsula, and he called upon Muslims everywhere to carry out operations to expel Americans and non-Muslims from the Arabian Peninsula by use of "explosions and jihad" stating:

My Muslim Brothers of The World: Your brothers in Palestine and in the land of the two Holy Places are calling upon your help and asking you to take part in the fighting against the enemy—your enemy and their enemy—the Americans and the Israelis. They are asking you to do whatever you can, with one['s] own means and ability, to expel the enemy, humiliated and defeated, out of the sanctities of Islam.

In February 1998, bin Laden held a press conference in Afghanistan and announced the founding of the "World Islamic Front Against Jews and Crusaders." "Bin Laden and his colleagues signed a joint fatwah requiring all Muslims able to do so to kill Americans—whether civilian or military— anywhere they can be found and to 'plunder their money.'" Bin Laden issued a declaration called "The Nuclear Bomb of Islam" which included the statement, "it is the duty of Muslims to prepare as much force as possible to terrorize the enemies of God." On August 7, 1998, al Qaeda operatives detonated truck bombs outside the American Embassies in Nairobi, Kenya and Dar es Salaam, Tanzania, killing 257 people, including 12 Americans, and wounding thousands more. Before the bombings of the U.S. Embassies in Nairobi and Tanzania in 1998, appellant knew that a terrorist attack outside of Afghanistan targeting Americans was going to take place. Bin Laden did not know how the U.S. would react, so bin Laden left his compound in Kandahar the day after the attacks and went to Kabul for 10 days. In 1998, appellant drove bin Laden to a press conference related to the 1998 East African Embassy bombings. While there, appellant met al-Zawahiri. On August 20, 1998, the United States retaliated, sending tomahawk missiles and striking "terrorist training camps in Afghanistan and a suspected chemical weapons laboratory in Khartoum, Sudan." Shaykh Omar Abdel Rahman responded from inside his American jail cell by urging new recruits to join the cause and issuing a new fatwah, saying, "Oh, Muslims everywhere!

Cut the transportation of their countries, tear it apart, destroy their economy, burn their companies, eliminate their interests, sink their ships, shoot down their planes, kill them on the sea, air, or land. Kill them when you find them, take them and encircle them . . . ."

In October 2000, al Qaeda operatives exploded a bomb alongside the USS COLE, "killing 17 American sailors, wounding 39 others, and causing nearly $250 million in damage. The COLE operation came at the direction and urging of Usama bin Laden, Abu Hafs Al Masri, and other senior [al-Qaeda] leaders." At the time of the USS COLE bombing, appellant was in Yemen. He believed that due to his close association with bin Laden, he might be apprehended, so he made arrangements to return to Afghanistan. Appellant knew that the scope of bin Laden and al Qaeda's operations included terrorist attacks targeting Americans outside of Afghanistan.

Appellant drove bin Laden in a convoy in August 2001 to a large gathering with 150–200 attendees, mostly Egyptian Islamic Jihad members and al Qaeda members. After the dinner, al-Zawahiri and bin Laden announced that the Egyptian Islamic Jihad and al Qaeda were merged. Subsequently, appellant drove bin Laden to meetings with al-Zawahiri and drove in convoys with both bin Laden and al-Zawahiri.

Al Qaeda's actions achieved worldwide infamy when, on September 11, 2001, 19 men recruited by al Qaeda hijacked four commercial airliners on the east coast of the United States and crashed one into the Pentagon in Washington D.C. and two into the World Trade Center towers in New York. The fourth aircraft crashed in Pennsylvania after the passengers attacked the hijackers.

Seven to ten days before September 11, 2001, bin Laden told appellant they were evacuating the compound because an operation was about to take place. Two days prior to the operation, appellant took bin Laden to Kabul, where they stayed until just after the 9/11 attack. The day after the attack, at dinner, bin Laden confirmed that he was responsible for the 9/11 operation. Subsequently, appellant drove bin Laden to Lahore, a military camp with numerous tunnels and structures for hiding. After a week hiding there with bin Laden, appellant continued to transport bin Laden around Afghanistan, changing locations every few days to help bin Laden escape retaliation by the United States. Shortly after 9/11, appellant drove bin Laden and al-Zawahiri to a camp outside of Kabul where bin Laden made a video talking about Jews, Americans, and jihad.

Congress passed the Authorization for Use of Military Force resolution (AUMF) one week after the September 11, 2001 terrorist attacks. Pub.L. No. 107-40, 115 Stat. 224 (2001). The AUMF authorizes the President to "use all necessary and appropriate force against those nations, organizations, or persons he determines planned, authorized, committed, or aided the terrorist attacks." *Id.* The President ordered the armed forces to Afghanistan "to subdue al Qaeda and quell the Taliban regime that was known to support it." *Hamdi v. Rumsfeld*, 542 U.S. 507, 510 (2004). Subsequently, United States and allied armed forces engaged in military operations in Afghanistan where appellant was seized on November 24, 2001.

II. CHARGE AND SPECIFICATIONS WITH GUILTY FINDINGS

Appellant was convicted of two types of providing material support for terrorism. First, he provided material support for carrying out an act of terrorism. Second, he provided material support to an international terrorist organization. See 2007 M.M.C., Part IV, ¶¶ 6(25)bA and 6(25)bB. The five specifications of which he was convicted begin with identical language:

In that Hamdan, a person subject to trial by military commission as an alien unlawful enemy combatant, did, in Afghanistan and other countries, from in or about February l996 to on or about November 24, 2001, in context of or associated with an armed conflict—

The specifications continue with individualized allegations as follows:

Specification 2: [Hamdan] with knowledge that al Qaeda has engaged in or engages in terrorism, did provide material support or resources, to wit: personnel, himself, to al Qaeda, an international terrorist organization engaged in hostilities against the United States, with the intent to provide such material support and resources to al Qaeda, by becoming a member of the organization and performing at least one of the following:

a. Received training at an al Qaeda training camp;

b. Served as a driver for Usama bin Laden transporting him to various locations in Afghanistan;

c. Served as Usama bin Laden's armed bodyguard at various locations throughout Afghanistan;

d. Transported weapons or weapons systems or other supplies for the purpose of delivering or attempting to deliver said weapons or weapons systems to Taliban or al Qaeda members and associates.

Specification 5: [Hamdan did] provide material support and resources to wit: service or transportation by serving as a driver for Usama bin Laden by transporting him to various locations in Afghanistan knowing that by providing said service or transportation he was directly facilitating communication and planning used for an act of terrorism.

Specification 6: [Hamdan did] with knowledge that al Qaeda, an international terrorist organization engaged in hostilities against the United States, had engaged in or engages in terrorism, intentionally provide material support or resources to al Qaeda, to wit: service or transportation to Usama bin Laden by transporting him to various areas in Afghanistan knowing that by providing said service or transportation he was directly facilitating communication and planning used for acts of terrorism.

Specification 7: [Hamdan did] provide material support and resources to wit: service as an armed body guard for Usama bin Laden, knowing that by providing said service as an armed bodyguard he was protecting the leader of al Qaeda and facilitating communication and planning used for acts of terrorism.

Specification 8: [Hamdan did] with knowledge that al Qaeda, an international terrorist organization has engaged in hostilities against the United States, had engaged in or engages in terrorism, intentionally provide material support or resources, to al Qaeda, to wit: service as an armed body guard for Usama bin Laden by knowing that by providing said service as an armed body guard for Usama bin Laden he was protecting the leader of al Qaeda and facilitating communication and planning used for acts of terrorism.

* * *

IV. ISSUES

Appellant urges this court to vacate the findings and sentence of the military commission for three reasons. First, he contends the military commission, established pursuant to Congress's Article I power to "define and punish . . . Offenses against the Law of Nations," lacked subject matter jurisdiction over the offense of providing material support for terrorism, because it is not a violation of the international law of war. Second, he argues his conviction for that offense is the result of an ex post facto prosecution prohibited by both the U.S. Constitution and international law, because 10 U.S.C. § 950v(b)(25) was signed into law on October 17, 2006, several years after the alleged conduct in the charges occurred. Third, he claims that the 2006 M.C.A. violates the Constitution by making aliens, but not citizens, subject to trial by military commission. Our Court also granted appellant's motion to be heard on two issues relating to appellant's second argument, and appellant continued to maintain that his prosecution was barred because the offenses were ex post facto.

* * *

VII. PROVIDING MATERIAL SUPPORT FOR TERRORISM AS A LAW OF WAR OFFENSE

[Following nearly 60 pages of reasoning (omitted here for brevity) the court reached the following conclusions:]

When the Supreme Court in [*Ex parte Quirin*, 317 U.S. 1 (1942)] analyzed whether the military commission had jurisdiction to adjudicate the cases of the Nazi saboteurs, the Court examined the charged offenses, noting the Congress incorporated by reference through the 15th Article of War, "as within the jurisdiction of military commissions, all offenses which are defined as such by the law of war." 317 U.S. at 30 (internal citation omitted). "Congress had the choice of crystallizing . . . every offense against the law of war, or of adopting the system of common law applied by military tribunals so far as it should be recognized and deemed applicable by the courts. It chose the latter course." *Id.*

In the instant case, Congress exercised authority derived from the Constitution to define and punish offenses against the law of nations by codifying an existing law of war violation into a clear and comprehensively defined offense of providing material support to terrorism. The President, through the Secretary of Defense, further defined the procedures for military commissions in the M.M.C. in a manner that is similar to the Manual for Courts–Martial (MCM). Congress's stated purpose for the 2006 M.C.A. was to "codify offenses that have traditionally been triable by military commissions." In this case, we find, in defining and punishing providing material support for terrorism in the 2006 M.C.A., that is precisely what Congress has done. Congress did not create a new offense, providing material support for terrorism was an existing law of war offense since at least 1996.

For purposes of compliance with the Define and Punish Clause of the Constitution, the standard of review for whether an offense as codified by Congress violates the law of war is not clearly established by applicable precedents. However, we find that the evidence supporting the 2006 M.C.A. offense of providing material support for terrorism as a pre-existing law of war offense far exceeds even the "substantial showing" standard advanced in [*Hamdan v. Rumsfeld*, 548 U.S. 557 (2006)] that "the Government must make a substantial showing that the crime for which it seeks to try a defendant by military commission is acknowledged to be an offense against the law of war."

When appellant's charged offenses began in 1996, the underlying wrongful conduct of providing material support for terrorism, as now defined under the 2006 M.C.A., was a cognizable offense under the law of war. Crimes equivalent to providing material support for terrorism had been recognized in various United Nations Security Council Resolutions, regional conventions, and the domestic criminal codes, among other authorities. Military commission trials in the 19th and 20th centuries involved violations of the law of war similar to wrongfully providing material support to terrorism. Many of these offenses violated the laws and customs of war because they engaged in an unlawful belligerency, used an illegal means of warfare, or targeted protected persons. Additionally, the conduct of providing assistance to others with knowledge that those they assist, have, or intend to violate the laws and customs of war has long been tried as a law of war offense.

In light of our holding that providing material support for terrorism is a codification of a pre-existing law-of-war violation, we conclude that the Ex Post Facto Clause of the Constitution was not violated by appellant's conviction for providing material support to terrorism under the M.C.A. of 2006.

VIII. EQUAL PROTECTION

The military commission judge ruled that the 2006 M.C.A. properly established jurisdiction over appellant and his offenses, notwithstanding its jurisdictional limitation to aliens. On appeal, appellant disputes the military commission judge's ruling by asserting that he possesses a "fundamental right" to equality in criminal proceedings arising from a constitutional entitlement to identical trial forum and procedural treatment to that enjoyed by U.S. citizens. . . .

    * * *

Appellant argues that discriminatory language of the M.C.A. statute is subject to strict scrutiny because it infringes on his "fundamental rights" to due process. Appellant contends that the alienage distinction was designed to "prevent the disfavored and disenfranchised group from using the political process to protect itself" and that "[l]egislation such as the M.C.A. aimed solely at the politically powerless attracts strict scrutiny." Appellant cites to cases including *Clark v. Jeter*, 486 U.S. 456, 461 (1988), *Plyler v. Doe*, 457 U.S. 202, 216–17 (1982), Douglas v. California, 372 U.S. 353, 358 (1963), and *Griffin v. Illinois*, 351 U.S. 12, 15–17, (1956), to make his point that such a fundamental right as equality in criminal proceedings is subject to strict scrutiny. Appellant's Brief 26–30.

Appellant's cited authority is not persuasive and is readily distinguishable. None of the cases he cites involve competing national interests, all of the cases were tried in Article III courts, all of the cases involved the application of the Fourteenth Amendment, and only one case, Plyler, involves an alien party. Nothing in those precedents suggests that the Supreme Court intended courts to apply heightened scrutiny in cases involving disparate treatment by the federal government of nonresident alien enemy combatants captured abroad.

On the contrary, precedent clearly mandates that deference be given to congressional classifications based on alienage where foreign policy interests are strongly implicated. In *United States v. Lopez–Florez*, 63 F.3d 1468 (9th Cir. 1995), appellants challenged their conviction under the Hostage Taking Act, 18 U.S.C. § 1203, claiming that it violated the Equal Protection Clause of the Fifth Amendment by "impermissibly classifying offenders and victims on the basis of alienage." *Id.* at 1470. The court held that Congress's plenary control over immigration legislation and the accompanying low level of judicial review "dictate a similarly low level of review here, where foreign policy interests are strongly implicated." *Id.* at 1474. In fact, the 11th Circuit expressly held that "congressional classifications based on alienage are subject to rational basis review." In additional to congressional authority, the President traditionally has had broad authority in matters relating to enemy aliens. In 1950, the Supreme Court stated:

> Executive power over enemy aliens, undelayed and unhampered by litigation, has been deemed, throughout our history, essential to war-time security. This is in keeping with the practices of the most enlightened of nations and has resulted in treatment of alien enemies more considerate than that which has prevailed among any of our enemies and some of our allies. [The Alien and Sedition Act of 1789] was enacted or suffered to continue by men who helped found the Republic and formulate the Bill of

Rights, and although it obviously denies enemy aliens the constitutional immunities of citizens, it seems not then to have been supposed that a nation's obligations to its foes could ever be put on a parity with those to its defenders.

Eisentrager, 339 U.S. at 774–75. We find, therefore, that the strong foreign policy implications associated with the war on terror, coupled with the recognition of the President's power over enemy aliens in times of war and Congress's power to enact legislation pertaining to aliens and its war powers, dictate the M.C.A.'s alienage distinction be reviewed under the deferential rational basis standard. See pages 15–22, supra. (discussing authority of Congress and the Executive in the areas of war powers and foreign affairs).

* * *

Rational basis analysis requires a two-step inquiry: (1) whether there is a legitimate government purpose identifiable, regardless of actual motives; and (2) whether a rational basis exists to believe that the legislation would further that purpose. *United States v. Ferreira*, 275 F.3d 1020, 1026 (11th Cir. 2001) (citing *Joel v. City of Orlando*, 232 F.3d 1353, 1357 (11th Cir. 2000)).

Appellant argues that the M.C.A.'s legislative history suggests that Congress intended to create a discriminatory regime of lesser criminal procedures meant to punish aliens. The M.C.A.'s legislative history recognizes that persons tried under the M.C.A. may be captured on the battlefield under conditions where widely-used police investigative procedures cannot be applied. Appellant's assertions that Congress engaged in pernicious discrimination against aliens is not persuasive and wholly irrelevant so long as there is a "conceivably rational basis, [regardless of] whether that basis was actually considered by the legislative body." *Ferreira*, 275 F.3d at 1026 (noting that "the actual motives of the enacting governmental body are entirely irrelevant").

The first prong of the inquiry, whether a legitimate government interest exists, is easily satisfied as Congress enacted the M.C.A. to create a forum and a process by which to bring to justice foreign unlawful combatants whose purpose is to terrorize American citizens. There can be no more legitimate purpose of a government than to protect its citizens from its enemies. The second prong of the test, whether there is a rational basis to believe that the legislation will further the legitimate purpose, is met as Congress and the President have rightly determined that the treatment of foreign detainees captured on the battlefield in a foreign land has foreign policy implications, for which they are responsible. The legislation distinguishes between alien unlawful enemy combatants and the rest of the world and has a rational connection to its purpose.

Reviewing the military commission judge's ruling de novo, we agree that the Fifth Amendment's equal protection component is not applicable to AUECs, who are tried at Guantanamo, Cuba, under the M.C.A. Nevertheless, after performing a functional analysis under *Boumediene*, we conclude that

Congress established reasonable procedures in the M.C.A. for protecting the rights of AUECs and preserving national security. The M.C.A. provides due process, which is similar to the procedural protections received by defendants in U.S. District Courts, by accused U.S. military personnel at courts-martial, and by accused persons tried before international tribunals under the sponsorship of the United Nations.

Appellant was represented throughout his trial by counsel and received a full and fair trial. He was found not guilty of the majority of the charges. He was sentenced to serve only a few months of confinement after his trial, and has been returned to Yemen. We decline to find that appellant, as an unlawful enemy alien combatant, is entitled to more due process under the Fifth Amendment than he received.

We find, therefore, that Congress had a rational basis for the disparate treatment of aliens in the M.C.A. and that such disparate treatment does not violate the equal protection component of the Fifth Amendment.

X. CONCLUSION

Appellant's assigned errors and legal arguments are without merit. Pursuant to the 2006 M.C.A., these proceedings, the findings, and appellant's sentence are the product of lawful, Congressionally-created processes, "affording all the judicial guarantees of all civilized peoples." *See supra* n. 8.

The findings and approved sentence are correct in law and fact and no error materially prejudicial to the substantial rights of the Appellant occurred. 2009 M.C.A. §§ 950a(a) and 950f(d). Accordingly, the findings and sentence are affirmed.

Points for Discussion

1. This case presents fundamental challenges to the MCA 2006 and MCA 2009. What would happen to the military commission system if a court were to conclude that Congress cannot define war crimes, that the ex post facto clause barred application of crimes only fully defined after 2006, or that military commissions cannot discriminate against aliens? This decision has been appealed to the U.S. Court of Appeals for the D.C. Circuit.

2. Hamdan's trial under the President's Military Order started in 2004, and it was halted by the District Court. His sentence was announced by the military commission on August 7, 2008. Is filing a habeas petition while one's client is in pretrial confinement in the client's best interest? If this decision stands, did the Supreme Court's 2006 decision in *Hamdan* actually help Salim Hamdan?

INDEX

References in the following index entries are to Chapter and Section numbers.